access literatur

ACCESS LITERATURE

An Introduction to Fiction, Poetry, and Drama

Barbara Barnard
Nassau Community College, State University of New York

David Winn
Hunter College, City University of New York

THOMSON

WADSWORTH

United States • Australia • Brazil • Canada
Mexico • Singapore • Spain • United Kingdom

Access Literature:
An Introduction to Fiction, Poetry, and Drama
Barbara Barnard/David F. Winn

Publisher: *Michael Rosenberg*
Acquisitions Editor: *Aron Keesbury*
Development Editor: *Laurie Runion*
Editorial Assistant: *Cheryl Forman*
Technology Project Manager: *Joe Gallagher*
Senior Marketing Manager: *Mary Jo Southern*
Marketing Assistant: *Dawn Giovanniello*
Associate MarCom Manager: *Patrick Rooney*
Associate Project Manager, Editorial Production:
  Karen Stocz

Production Assistant: *Jennifer Kostka*
Senior Print Buyer:
  Mary Beth Hennebury
Permissions Editor: *Sue Howard*
Photo Manager: *Sheri Blaney*
Text Designer: *Garry Harman*
Cover Designer: *Yvo Riezebos Design*
Compositor: *GGS Book Services,*
  Atlantic Highlands
Printer: *Malloy Incorporated*

Cover Photos: *L to R: Front* ©: Hemera; Hemera;
Franz-Marc Frei/Corbis: V&A Amages: Alamy;
DPA/Landov; *Back* ©: Popperfoto/Alamy;
Hemera; Hemera; Jean Gaamy/Magnum; Mark
Sims/Index Stock Imagery; *Spine* ©: William
Manning/Corbis

Thomson Higher Education
25 Thomson Place
Boston, MA 02210-1202
USA

For more information about our products,
contact us at:
Thomson Learning Academic Resource
Center 1-800-423-0563

For permission to use material from this
text or product, submit a request online at
http://www.thomsonrights.com
Any additional questions about permissions
can be submitted by e-mail to
thomsonrights@thomson.com

ISBN 0-1550-6966-7

BRIEF CONTENTS

CONTENTS

FYI:
Why I Wrote
"The Yellow
Wallpaper" 186

From Page to
Screen:
Physical and Social
Setting 208

Pop Culture: What is Metafiction? The Surreal and Outlandish Meditations of Mel Brooks and The Simpsons 466

CHAPTER **15** **Imagery and Symbolism** 629

FYI:
Poetry: The
Heartbeat Knows No
Borders 664

CHAPTER **Figures Of Speech** 667

FYI:
Poets Laureate—The
People's Poets 694

CHAPTER **Sound, Rhythm and Meter** 697

Pop Culture:
Nü Metal, Nü Standard 724

FYI:
William Blake—Visual Artist and Verbal Artist 744

CHAPTER **19** **Fixed Forms** 773

Pop Culture:
Dee Dee and the Slam
Dance Sonnet **802**

**Pop Culture:
Open-Form Film:
Tarantino Chops up
Chronology 850**

CHAPTER **21** **Myth and Poetry** 853

FYI:
The Myth of Icarus,
Imagined by Poet and
Painter **886**

CHAPTER **22** **Cutting Edges: Protest and
Performance Poetry** 895

**Pop Culture:
Music without
Music—Artists Cross
from Music to Spoken
Word 932**

CHAPTER **23** **A Bookshelf of Poetry** 935

CHAPTER **The Lives of Poets** 997

CHAPTER **34** **Access to Lit Crit: Pathways to Interpretation** 1479

PREFACE

Why Another Literature Anthology?

Access Literature is a compact, three-genre literature textbook designed for the Introduction to Literature, Writing About Literature, or Literature for Composition course. It covers fiction, poetry, and drama, and introduces students to the elements of literature they need to understand in order to analyze and write critically about literary texts. *Access Literature* provides students with a grounding in the traditional canon that is a vital part of our literary heritage, while at the same time presenting the diverse voices that are an essential part of our cultural record and an exciting force in contemporary literature.

What makes *Access Literature* different from other introduction to literature texts is the inclusion of images from everyday culture in order to show students how much they already know about literary concepts such as irony, point of view, and symbolism, for example. Students already savvy to the importance of setting in other media (even if only intuitively), will more easily understand how setting functions in a work of literature when presented with a photo of a bookstore pretending to be a comfortable study, and when the workings of that artifice are made clear. Students already familiar with plot will appreciate that even the television commercials use plot in ways similar to literature. Movie posters, tattoos, urban street murals, computer icons—all are visual texts our students interpret with ease every day. In *Access Literature*, we have found visual gateways into discussion of more difficult literary concepts as well. The way a student understands irony as presented visually in a movie poster, for example, becomes a gateway to understanding irony in literary texts.

Each chapter begins with visual images related to the students' everyday world, followed by a brief commentary explaining how the images reflect the concepts being taught in that chapter. For example, Chapter 6 (covering point of view in fiction) begins with screen shots from popular video and computer games. The commentary explains how the perspective of a narrator in a work of fiction resembles the perspective of the video game player's persona in the narrative of an interactive electronic game. Thus the student's familiar activity of choosing a character to "be" in a video game becomes a gateway to understanding what we mean by first person narration or third person limited omniscient narration in fiction.

A Student-Centered Approach

We believe that helping students learn to read, think, and write well is one means by which we empower them to go out and become engaged, to take an active part in their world. Quite often we find that students present themselves for college instruction with little background in or understanding of literature in a formal sense, but with a hunger for storytelling and a love of the rhythms of music. These existing interests, with the right approach, can be translated into an understanding of complex narratives, poems, and works of drama. A student who realizes—through our real-world and pop culture examples and visuals—that her interest in and knowledge of movies and music is also transferable to an interest in short stories or plays is well on her way to being able to participate in the kind of literary discourse we would like our students to be capable of.

Flexibility for Instructors

We are concerned not only about individual students and how they learn, but also about individual instructors and the need for flexibility compatible with different teaching styles and various ways of organizing the course syllabus. *Access Literature* offers a progressive balance of traditional texts and diverse voices—a variety of selections to ensure that our book is flexible enough to be adapted to different teaching styles and emphases. Chapters as well as reading selections can be taught in any order, and we have included a thematic table of contents in the instructor's manual for those who would prefer to organize the syllabus thematically. The thematic listing is also useful for generating essay topics.

Features of Access Literature

Chapter Openers from Everyday Culture that Engage Students

Chapter openers begin with visual images drawn from a wide range of familiar places, from TV commercials to graffiti, from NASCAR to the World Wrestling Federation. *Access Literature* welcomes students into literary discourse by helping them realize that the elements of literature they discuss in the classroom simply reflect concepts and ideas that we encounter in our daily lives. In other words, literature itself is simply a reflection of human experience, and everyday culture is the access point from which students can begin to understand literature:

- In Chapter 1, movie posters serve to visually represent elements such as setting, characterization, and irony.
- Computer icons help to explain metaphor and symbolism in Chapter 8.

- In Chapter 20, advertisements help illustrate open form in poetry.
- Protest and performance poetry are introduced in Chapter 22 using graffiti.
- In Chapter 26, WWF scenarios provide an illustration of conflict and climax in the discussion of plot and form in drama.

Literature and Its Access Points

Access Literature offers instructors and students a full array of readings, and information on the authors who bring this literature to life.

- **The Readings**—We have sought a rich diversity of works to represent characters and voices from various socioeconomic backgrounds as well as diverse racial and cultural experiences. Our students increasingly need a sense that literature's interests and themes are cross-cultural, that our world community is growing closer, that there is more and more cultural cross-fertilization. We believe that it is important for this to be represented accurately not only to students at urban and remarkably international campuses like our own, but also at campuses where the student population may not yet be as diverse.
- **The "Bookshelf" Chapters**—In addition to the carefully-selected readings used to illustrate literary concepts in each element's chapter, there are also collections of additional readings in fiction (Chapter 12), poetry (Chapter 23), and drama (Chapter 31).
- **Author Pictures and Biographical Information**—Author photos and their bios help students realize that these works of literature were written by real people with real lives. In the poetry unit, biographical notes on 59 poets are collected in a separate chapter.
- **In-depth Author Profile Chapters**—Profile chapters of Flannery O'Connor in fiction, Langston Hughes in poetry, and David Ives in drama lead off each unit. In choosing these three authors, we liked the mix of a contemporary writer, a modern poet and an avant-garde playwright. We feel the thematic balance is optimum here too: O'Connor raises profound moral questions, Hughes brings to the fore the importance of racial history and progress in American society, and David Ives' irreverent, cutting-edge comedies never fail to delight students. These profile chapters not only give students a close look at the three writers' lives and work but also serve to introduce students to discourse in each genre.
- **"Talking Lit" Readings**—At the end of most chapters, we have included reading selections that include excerpts from critical articles, interviews, reviews, and other materials that help illuminate the literary texts in each chapter.

Closer Looks at Literature

In addition to the chapters one would expect in a literature text, we have also included chapters designed to offers students a different view of literature:

- **Chapters on Myth**—Within each genre unit, we have included a chapter on myth: Myth and Fiction (Chapter 9), Myth and Poetry (Chapter 21), and Myth and Drama (Chapter 29). We have found that students respond well to a discovery of cross-cultural mythic patterns in literature. The study of mythic patterns— as defined by Carl Jung and later elucidated by Joseph Campbell—leads students to extraordinary recognitions having to do with universal human experience as well as the specifically American experience.

- **Cutting Edge Chapters**—Each genre unit also contains a Cutting Edges chapter that examines works that are avant-garde, provocative, and grassroots: Chapter 11, "Metafiction and Avant-Pop," Chapter 22, "Protest and Performance Poetry," and Chapter 30, "Grassroots Theater."

Assignments that Engage and Teach

- **Your Turn—Talking and Writing about Lit**—Following the works of literature, students will find study questions, writing topics, and DIY (Do It Yourself) creative writing exercises. We find that many students who are difficult to engage respond well when asked to try out the craft of fiction, poetry, or playwriting themselves. Our DIY topics are easy to spot; each is accompanied by an oval DIY icon.

- **"Questions to Ask About"**—Each genre profile chapter, introducing that genre, includes a list of "Questions to Ask About" the works in that genre. These boxes can serve as essay prompts, study guides for exams, or advice to help students when they are exploring reading selections.

Student Essays

Student essays on fiction, poetry, and drama topics appear within the genre units as well as in the writing and research chapters at the back of the book. We have included a total of twelve student pieces that serve not only to model a range of rhetorical modes, but also to demonstrate to students that they can produce literary commentary, that theirs are also voices offering interesting interpretation and discussion of the works of literature we read together.

Sidebars That Speak Students' Language

In our own classes, we find ourselves using frequent examples from film, popular culture, and common culture in order to explain literary concepts to students. This led us to the idea of including such materials in the book in sidebars and boxes and giving the book a contemporary, magazine-like design that students will find more appealing. Three types of sidebars appear in the book:

- **From Page to Screen Boxes**—As most instructors have learned, references to films are a reliable way to connect with what students already know about plot, characterization, setting, symbolism, metaphor, etc. We have included "Page to Screen" boxes throughout *Access Literature* to help your students realize how much they already know about plot, characterization, setting, symbolism, etc., through their enjoyment and discussion of movies.

- **Pop Culture Boxes**—The material in the Pop Culture boxes draws attention to the similarities between discussion of a work of literature and discussion of music, a comic book, video game, or film, using textual and visual images and examples that make the connection vivid.

- **FYI Boxes**—These informative boxes may contain (for example) further biographical information on the writer, on trends in literature, historical information, interviews, or visual material that relates to one or more of the readings in the chapter.

Critical Thinking, Research, and Theory

Although we have provided a chapter at the back of the text on "Talking and Writing About Lit" (Chapter 32), the teaching of critical thinking skills and writing strategies is not confined to that chapter alone but is present everywhere in the book. Instruction in literary analysis is woven into the chapter material across the span of these pages. This encourages students to think about generating ideas for essays and approaches to organizing them. Perhaps most crucially, it can also be a way to help them learn critical thinking skills in the context of, for instance, explaining characterization in a story, or comparing two poems, or demonstrating how Shakespeare uses dramatic irony in a scene. We believe we should be helping our students learn to think independently at every step, just as a parent who teaches a child to ride a bicycle runs alongside for a time but hopes to be able before long to step out of the way and watch the child ride upright unassisted.

Knowing that students at this stage of their development as writers and thinkers still need a guiding hand, our chapter "Talking and Writing About Lit" guides students through the writing process as it also models effective rhetorical modes for literary analysis. It contains student essays in each genre as well as one on fiction and film. The student writers are analyzing and explicating works that appear in the text.

Also in Unit Four of the text is "Sources for Researching Lit" (Chapter 33), which includes instruction in how to find reliable sources (including electronic sources), write the research paper, format in-text citations, and create the Works Cited list (MLA style guidelines are modeled for students). This chapter also contains a student research paper that was written by our son Jake Winn—a college student—whose critical thinking skills frequently surpass our own.

Lastly, Unit Four contains "Access to Lit Crit: Whose Interpretation Is It?" In this chapter various critical approaches to interpretation are explained and modeled through analysis (from the perspective of each of the schools of critical theory) of Eudora Welty's "A Worn Path." A wonderful film production of "A Worn Path" (directed by Bruce R. Schwarz) is available from Wadsworth, for those who would like to combine literary criticism with film criticism.

At the back of the text, we have also included a very usable Glossary of Literary Terms. The words defined there appear in bold type in chapter discussions, and we have provided an index of terms so that students are also referred to the pages in text where these concepts are explained and used in the context of literary analysis.

Ancillaries

The ancillary program for *Access Literature* includes an instructor's manual and DVDs and videos from the Wadsworth Original Film Series in Literature.

The instructor's manual for *Access Literature* includes:

• Suggestions for using each of the chapter features
• Thematic Table of Contents
• Sample Syllabii
• An introduction to using Lit21
• Brief discussions of the "Your Turn" questions, three suggestions for writing projects, and a suggestion for a group activity
• "A Way Into" section for each poem that offers instructors a starting point for discussing each poem
• Suggestions for using the "Talking Lit" selections

In addition, five of the reading selections in *Access Literature* are available on VHS or DVD for any instructor adopting *Access Literature*, including Alice Walker's "Everyday Use," John Updike's "A&P," Langston Hughes' "Salvation," Eudora Welty's "A Worn Path," and Raymond Carver's "Cathedral."

In these pages, we seek to help you, the instructor, establish a conversation with your students in a way that both informs and delights them. We hope, then, that our text is informative, democratic, and inspiring.

Acknowledgments

We would like to thank our extraordinary son, Jake Winn, himself a writer, who has been our pop culture consultant and film expert (and self-proclaimed "television scientist") throughout the project, and who drafted the text for the Pop

Culture and Page to Screen boxes throughout the book (and some of the chapter openers as well). We couldn't have done it without you, Jake! We would also like to thank our extraordinary editors Aron Keesbury, Acquisitions Editor, and Laurie Runion, Developmental Editor. Their creativity, sense of design, and knowledge of literature (and just plain fire-in-the-belly determination to get this project finished) shaped the book innumerable ways. And Barbara wishes to thank her colleagues and dear friends Amy King, Michael Steinman, and Elizabeth Wood for their unflagging support and encouragement. Thanks also to Jessie Swigger for her work on chapters 33 and 34, and the instructor's manual; to Tony Perriello for his help with chapter opening material; Christi Conti for her help in checking the author birth/death dates; and Marita Sermolins and Cheryl Forman for their editorial support. And thank you to our production and marketing team: Karen Stocz, Project Manager; Mary Jo Southern, Marketing Manager; Sheri Blaney, Photo Manager; Sharon Donahue, Photo Researcher; Garry Harmon, Designer; Sue Howard, Permission Researcher; and our copyeditors.

And special thanks also for the many helpful suggestions we received from our reviewers, who helped shape this project:

Elizabeth Abele, *Nassau Community College*

Carmela Arnoldt, *Glendale Community College*

Abby Bardi, *Prince George Community College*

Mary Bayer, *Grand Rapids Community College*

Janet Beck, *Appalachian State University*

Linda Belau, *University of Texas—Pan Am*

Jose Blanco, *Miami Dade College*

Ed Cameraon, *University of Texas—Pan Am*

Jennifer Cole Neville, *Wentworth Intitute of Technology*

Ronald Dotterer, *Salisbury State Univeristy*

Rudra Vilias Dundzila, *Truman College*

Tony D'Souza, *Shasta College*

Walter Eggers, *University of New Hampshire*

Carol Farber, *Nassau Community College*

Julie Fleenor, *William Rainey Harper College*

Muriel Fuqua, *Daytona Beach Community College*

Diana Gatz, *St. Petersburg College*

Phyllis Gilbert, *MiraCosta College*

David Howell, *Appalachian State University*

Andrea Kaston Tange, *Eastern Michigan University*

Elizabeth Kleinfeld, *Red Rocks Community College*

Stand Kozikowski, *Bryant College*

Dennis Kriewald, *Laredo Community College*

Donald Kummings, *University of Wisconsin—Parkside*

Leon Lewis, *Appalachian State University*

Deborah Meats, *Pittsburgh State University*

Joanna Mink, *Minnesota State University*

Melinda Morton, *Appalachian State University*

Charmaine Mosby, *Western Kentucky University*

Emil Mucchetti, *Texas A&M University—Kingsville*

Steven Ryan, *Austin Peay State University*

Derek Royal, *University of Texas—Commerce*

Jennifer Sheeler, *Longwood University*
Julie Shigekuni, *University of New Mexico*
David Sudol, *Arizona State University*
Tony Trigilio, *Columbia College Chicago*

Barbara Williamson, *Spokane Falls Community College*
Laura Mandell Zaidman, *University of South Carolina Sumter*
Tom Zaniello, *Northern Kentucky University*

INTRODUCTION
for Students—Getting Literature

Whose Lit Is It Anyway?

If you thumb through this book, you will see an array of visual images, from movie posters to fine art, from computer icons to subway graffiti, from video game screen shots to famous authors. We hope our book looks interesting to you from the first time you open its cover. In creating works of literature, fiction writers, poets, and playwrights (whose works you will encounter here) are hoping to embody human experience—life itself—within their stories and lyrics. Literature is not the dry and dusty stuff you dread; it is instead like life itself—full of sights, sounds, smells, powerful and quirky characters, blood, death, joy, shock, disappointment and hope.

You may read from many sources of information on a daily basis (the newspaper, a biography of a recent political figure, a recipe book, your biology textbook). Unlike these more strictly informational types of writing, literature is **imaginative writing**. Fiction writers, poets, and playwrights strive in each of these imaginative **genres** (types of writing) to convey not simply information or factual knowledge, but also emotional knowledge, and often even what we call wisdom, or vision. Imaginative writing attempts to reflect the whole of human experience, in all of its various dimensions. The study of literature is an invitation to come along and explore the territory each writer guides us through, and to make discoveries there. Each author's territory is filled with sights and sounds, and vivacious or mysterious characters greet us at every turn. It is a journey of the head and of the heart. Fiction writer Eudora Welty says it this way:

> Both reading and writing are experiences—lifelong—in the course of which we who encounter words used in certain ways are persuaded by them to be brought mind and heart within the presence, the power, of the imagination. This we find to be above all the power to reveal, with nothing barred. (*The Eye of the Story*, 134)

The three **genres** of imaginative writing which we will be studying, then, are fiction, poetry, and drama. Although **fiction** includes short, medium length, and long forms (the short story, the novella, and the novel), we will focus on the short story. Reading shorter fictions allows for greater cultural breadth in our discussion, and it helps illustrate a broad range of fictional techniques and styles. We will also study **poetry**, and you will find that the craft of writing poems has been equally varied. We will read long and short poems, lyric and narrative poems, poems in fixed forms and poems in open form. And we will study **drama** by reading plays which illustrate the general elements of the craft of playwriting. We will explore the work of William Shakespeare, still considered the greatest dramatist in the English language, and works by modern and contemporary playwrights as well.

It is important to study these forms of imaginative writing which we call literature, then, because of what sets them apart from more reportorial and informational forms of writing. But there are also things which the study of literature has in common with the study of other forms of written expression. Reading fiction, poetry and drama in a context where you are encouraged to think, interpret, discuss, compare ideas, and do your own writing about what you discover will also help you sharpen your analytical skills. Much attention is given today to the importance of developing critical thinking skills, and the study of literature offers an excellent opportunity to do just that. At the same time, you will be sampling stories, poems, and plays that most readers find pleasurable to discover and discuss.

A third reason to value the study of literature is that it provides a window on other cultures, perspectives, ways of life, even other historical periods. All writers are storytellers. Reading the stories told by voices from many cultural backgrounds not only helps us to broaden our understanding and appreciation of our differences and unique attributes, it also helps us to discover how very much we have in common. Among people of every cultural heritage represented in American society, stories are told and remembered. And in every culture in our global community storytellers are at work creating many forms of literature. Human beings need these ways of exploring their experience and trying to explain their environment and their lives to themselves. People who succeed especially well at this task often seem like spokespersons for an entire culture or group or historical period. Examples might be: the African-American dramatist August Wilson, whose cycle of plays about the Black experience of American society spans many decades; William Shakespeare, similarly, for Elizabethan England (and, truly, for all of us); and Chinua Achebe, whose fictions explore tradition and change in post-colonial Africa. In addition to these more familiar examples, new or often over-looked voices will be heard here as well: Bi Shumin, who makes real the experience of contemporary mainland Chinese characters; Junot Diaz, who makes vivid the experience of Latino Americans recently arrived from the Caribbean; and Anna Castillo, the Chicago-born poet of Toltec/Aztec ancestry, who depicts her people's experience, both ancient and modern. Despite the variety of cultural and geographical landscapes represented here, there is nonetheless a common project that all of these imaginative writers are engaged in. Truly, it is the territory of the human heart that they are all exploring first and foremost.

No one needs to be taught to enjoy stories and lyrics and dramas: the desire for them is clearly universal and instinctive. These creative forms existed in one way or another even before written language, and certainly long before Johann Gutenberg's printing press (ca. 1437) began to make the printed word more widely available in the Western world (the Chinese, incidentally, used movable type as early as 970). No, we don't need to be taught the enjoyment of literature or the desire for a story. But we can learn, through study and discussion, how to understand more fully what we are reading. Sharpening one's skills of analysis can help to accomplish this.

Learning to **analyze** and discuss literature simply means learning to ask incisive questions. **Analysis** may sound to some students like a thing to be dreaded; it's a word that, for some, conjures up a notion of a process that is sterile, bloodless, or elitist. Literature, though, is anything but that; it is full of life and noise and action; it is vivacious; it is rowdy with sights and sounds, smells, unforgettable characters. Literary analysis is simply a matter of taking the story (or poem or play) apart, down to its nuts and bolts, to see what makes it run. Analysis is also exploration and discovery, a journey through each writer's territory, gathering there what meanings, ideas, and insights the writer has worked to reveal to us.

The questions we ask, the discussion we have about a short story or play, are much like the discussions of films, comic books, video game narratives, and even the stories that are the underpinnings of WWF scenarios and rap artists' raps. It's all storytelling.

Furthermore, what we call the "elements" of literature—plot, character, setting, symbolism, metaphor, theme, rhyme, rhythm, conflict, myth, to mention a few—are all present in the everyday world around us. This may sound like a radical statement, but in a sense it's also stating the obvious. In the chapters that follow, you may recognize many things that you already know (the "aha!" factor). These recognitions will hopefully be followed by an assurance and confidence about discussing literature (the "I get it; I already know this stuff" effect). The suggestion of irony in a movie poster or trailer (like that for *Hell Boy*) will translate into confidence in recognizing irony in stories, poems, and plays. The "aha!" that computer icons are actually symbols for things in the real world as well as cyber-metaphors about them will morph into the knowledgeable discussion of symbolism in a Nathaniel Hawthorne story or metaphor in a poem by Langston Hughes.

Even movie posters use elements of literature to entice the

viewer into the story. This is true because both literature and the movies are reflections of real life. Whereas literature is often misunderstood as the musty remains of people long dead, the fact is that the same **elements**—plot, character, setting, and point of view—we use to interpret films reveal themselves in literature as well.

In the poster for *Bruce Almighty*, the **plot** (sequence of events) is largely revealed through the picture, in which Jim Carrey uses the world as a yo-yo; the tag line is "In Bruce We Trust?" The complete workings of the plot are not revealed, but visual clues give us a hint about the content of the movie. The heavenly clouds and the tag line suggest that Jim Carrey's character, Bruce, is somehow standing in for God. The image of the world as a yo-yo and our common knowledge of Jim Carrey's film roles tell us that this plot will be comedic.

The poster for the 1980s classic *The Breakfast Club* uses **characterization** (a vivid depiction of characters) to appeal to viewers. The plot of the film is built around the interaction of five high school **caricatures** (the jock, the prom queen, the misfit, the nerd, and the freak) within a small space, where they are forced to interact.

The *Pirates of the Caribbean* poster reveals a dramatic **setting** (place where the action takes place) from that film—the looming pirate ship, the sun blazing like an explosion behind it, the jagged cliffs, and the mysterious port city in the distance. In *Crouching Tiger, Hidden Dragon*, although there are strong secondary characters, we are very much in the **point of view** of (looking from the perspective of) the main characters, played by Michelle Yeoh and Chow Yun Fat. In other words, it is their perspective on events that matters most to us. Looking at movie posters in this way makes us aware that the elements we discover and discuss in literary works are the same ones we are also familiar with in **pop culture** (including movies) and in everyday life.

Active Reading

The excitement and variety of life itself is mirrored in the excitement and variety of literature. Stories, poems, and plays are full of surprising characters, startling lines, and unexpected adventures. Reading can also be a window into other cultures and other time periods. Poet Donald Hall writes (in *The Contemporary Essay*):

> We read to become more human. When we read *Gilgamesh*—the oldest surviving narrative, a Babylonian epic from 2000 B.C.—we connect with other human beings. We raise a glass across four thousand years of time and drink with our ancestors the old wine of friendship, courage, loss, and the will to survive. (7)

Donald Hall says he practices **active reading**—in other words, reading that is not passive. He suggests that our critical thinking abilities need to be at work while reading and, surprisingly, so should our lips and tongues and sense of hearing. According to Hall, "A century ago, even sixty years ago, silent reading was noisier to the mental ear because people were used to hearing books read aloud" (8). He explains that "as they read alone, [readers] decided in what tone or with what feeling they would enunciate each word." "Mental mimickry," says Hall, "makes for *active* reading" (8).

Another helpful thing to keep in mind is that we adjust our reading strategy to fit the work at hand. While we might read a short story or play only once before class discussion, we typically need to read a poem more than once. The use of language in poetry is more compact, and usually the poet has invested a great deal of meaning (often multiple meanings) in each line. Of course, when you are brainstorming ideas for writing an essay, it will help to reread the works you're writing about (see "Talking and Writing About Lit" in Chapter 32). When we reread, we make new discoveries, and new possibilities for meaning are revealed. But don't leave out the pure pleasure of the story, poem, or play. Let yourself enjoy the reading before you try to analyze it.

It's good to have a dictionary with you when you're reading (whether it's a hardback college edition on your desk or a paperback dictionary you toss in your book bag). When you look up unfamiliar words and find out what they mean, you make those words your own. This is how we build our vocabularies and increase our mastery of language. Word power! It's hard to be an active reader unless you know the meaning of the words. As Donald Hall says, "We cannot supply the tone of a word unless we understand its meaning" (8). It's also good to use a dictionary or encyclopedia to follow up on references to unfamiliar historical persons or events, place names, or concepts.

Learn to read closely. Learning to read carefully and critically is useful to us in everyday life. If we know how to be good critical readers of the daily newspaper, political campaign literature, and other forms of writing we encounter daily, we'll be more well-informed citizens. This means asking questions of the text, rather than passively assuming or accepting its meaning. For help with "questioning" literary texts, refer to the lists of study questions at the end of Chapter 2, "Questions to Ask about Fiction," Chapter 13, "Questions to Ask about Poetry," and Chapter 24, "Questions to Ask about Drama." In his trademark assertive style, Donald Hall recommends that the reader "Put the author on the witness stand and make him tell not only the truth but the whole truth" (9).

Annotating and Arguing with the Text—Be More Than Marginal

The best way to read closely and actively is to own the book and to make notes for yourself directly on the pages. This helps you to generate ideas and think critically while reading. We suggest you highlight or underline key passages and make notes in your margins. If the book is borrowed, you might take notes on a separate piece of paper, listing the passages to remember where they are. When possible, photocopy pages or whole chapters of a library book from which you will quote or paraphrase ideas. If you photocopy them, then you can make notes on them, underline key passages, and even "argue" with the author in the margins. Your instructor may require you to submit photocopies (or printouts from the Internet) of any materials you use outside of your textbook.

As you read through a work a second time, underline the passages that you feel are important. Note ideas that come to mind about characters, plot, setting, or other elements of the work in the margins. Ask questions of the text in the margins, whether it is simply placing a question mark next to a puzzling passage or writing an abbreviated question to be considered later. Keep track of "evidence" that might be needed when writing about the work—especially quotations that could be pulled out later to illustrate key points and develop an argument for your inter- pretation of the piece. You may want to use marks similar to the ones we've used in the following pages to comment on Grace Paley's story, Victor Hernández Cruz's poem, and the scene from William Shakespeare's *Othello*. Or, you may find it more effective to develop a different shorthand, one that fits your own way of thinking.

Grace Paley (b.1922)

Samuel (1968)

Third person voice

P.O.V omniscient

PLOT is chronological, but see jump ahead in time at the end.

SETTING— physical & social

Some boys are very tough. They're afraid of nothing. They are the ones who climb a wall and take a bow at the top. Not only are they brave on the roof, but they make a lot of noise in the darkest part of the cellar where even the super hates to go. They also jiggle and hop on the platform between the locked doors of the subway cars.

Four boys are jiggling on the swaying platform. Their names are Alfred, Calvin, Samuel, and Tom. The men and the women in the cars on either side watch them. They don't like them to jiggle or jump but don't want to interfere. Of course some of the men in the cars were once brave boys like these. One of them had ridden the tail of a speeding truck from New York to Rockaway Beach without getting off, without his sore fingers losing hold. Nothing happened to him then or later. He had made a compact with other boys who preferred to watch: Starting at Eighth Avenue and Fifteenth Street, he would get to some specified place, maybe Twenty-third and the river, by hopping the tops of the moving trucks. This was hard to do when one truck turned a corner in the wrong direction and the nearest truck was a couple of feet too high. He made three or four starts before succeeding. He had gotten this idea from a film at school called *The Romance of Logging*. He had finished high school, married a good friend, was in a responsible job and going to night school.

men's view

These two men and others looked at the four boys jumping and jiggling on the platform and thought, It must be fun to ride that way, especially now the weather is nice and we're out of the tunnel and way high over the Bronx. Then they thought, These kids do seem to be acting sort of stupid. They *are* little. Then they thought of some of the brave things they had done when they were boys and jiggling didn't seem so risky.

women's view

The ladies in the car became very angry when they looked at the four boys. Most of them brought their brows together and hoped the boys could see

collective & individual views

men's view

their extreme <u>disapproval.</u> One of the ladies wanted to get up and say, Be careful you dumb kids, get off that platform or I'll call a cop. But three of the boys were Negroes and the fourth was something else she couldn't tell for sure. She was afraid they'd be fresh and laugh at her and embarrass her. She wasn't afraid they'd hit her, but she was <u>afraid of embarrassment.</u> <u>Another lady thought,</u> Their mothers never know where they are. <u>It wasn't true in this particular case.</u> <u>Their mothers all knew that they had gone to see the</u> <u>missile exhibit on Fourteenth Street.</u>

biased view of one "lady," and another

omniscient narrator sets the record straight

5

Out on the platform, whenever the train accelerated, the boys would raise their hands and point them up to the sky to act like rockets going off, then they rat-tat-tatted the shatterproof glass pane like machine guns, although no machine guns had been exhibited.

For some reason known only to the motorman, the train began a sudden slowdown. <u>The lady who</u> <u>was afraid of embarrassment</u> saw the boys jerk forward and backward and grab the swinging guard chains. <u>She had her own boy at home.</u> She stood up with determination and went to the door. She slid it open and said, "<u>You boys will be hurt.</u> You'll be killed. I'm going to call the conductor if you don't just go into the next car and sit down and be quiet."

foreshadowing

foreshadowing

<u>Two of the boys</u> said, "Yes'm," and acted as though they were about to go. Two of them blinked their eyes a couple of times and pressed their lips together. The train resumed its speed. The door slid shut, parting the lady and the boys. She leaned against the side door because she had to get off at the next stop.

The boys opened their eyes wide at each other and laughed. The lady blushed. The boys looked at her and laughed harder. They began to pound each other's back. Samuel laughed the hardest and pounded Alfred's back until Alfred coughed and the tears came. Alfred held tight to the chain hook. Samuel pounded him even harder when he saw the tears. He said, "Why you bawling? You a baby, huh?" and laughed. One of the men <u>whose boyhood had</u> <u>been more watchful than brave</u> became angry. He stood up straight and looked at the boys for a couple of seconds. Then he walked in a citizenly way to the end of the car, where he pulled the emergency cord.

irony

Almost at once, with a (terrible) hiss, the pressure of air abandoned the brakes and the wheels were caught and held.

word choice

People standing in the most secure places fell forward, then backward. Samuel had let go of his hold on the chain so he could pound Tom as well as Alfred. All the passengers in the cars (whipped) back and forth, but he (pitched) only forward and fell head first to be crushed and killed between the cars.

10 The train had stopped (hard), halfway into the station, and the conductor called at once for the trainmen who knew about this kind of death and how to take the body from the wheels and brakes. There was silence except for passengers from other cars who asked, What happened! What happened! (The ladies) waited around wondering if he might be an only child. (The men) recalled other afternoons with very bad endings. (The little boys) stayed close to each other, leaning and touching shoulders and arms and legs.

collective views

When the policeman knocked at the door and told her about it, Samuel's mother began to scream. She screamed all day and moaned all night, though the doctors tried to quiet her with pills.

Oh, oh, she hopelessly cried. She did not know how she could ever find another boy like that one. However, she was a young woman and <u>she became pregnant</u>. Then for a few months she was hopeful. <u>The child born to her was a boy.</u> They brought him to be seen and nursed. She smiled. But immediately she saw that this baby wasn't Samuel. <u>She and her husband together have had other children, but never again will a boy exactly like Samuel be known.</u>

Explore point-of-view strategy
What does Paley gain by using omniscient view? Does this P.O.V. choice serve the writer well?

PLOT
Leaps ahead in time

Themes
Every life unique, irreplaceable. Irony—"citizenly" man caused death, or was it Samuel's own fault? Can we lay blame? Who's responsible?
No single "moral lesson" here. This poses questions instead. Undermines romantic notions of youthful adventure.

Victor Hernández Cruz (b. 1949)

Today Is a Day of Great Joy (1968)

• Speaker = Poet
• Celebrates the power of
 poetry—a powerful public
 role (from Puerto Rico)

when they stop poems   *metaphors!*
in the mail & clap
their hands & dance to   *poems = music*
them
when women become pregnant   5
by the side of poems   *poems can impregnate you; make you*
the strongest sounds making *pregnant w/ images, ideas.*
the river go along

                             a force that drives rivers

it is a great day

as poems fall down to   10

movie crowds in restaurants *poems as food*
in bars

when poems start to   *battering rams*
knock down walls to
choke politicians   *stranglers*   15
when poems scream &
begin to break the air

that is the time of
true poets that is
the time of greatness   20

a true poet aiming   *a poet as archer or gunman,*
poems & watching things   *shooting things down*
fall to the ground

it is a great day.   *closure, certainty*

William Shakespeare (1564–1616)

Othello (1604?)

From Act I, Scene 3, lines 183–260

DESDEMONA.   (continued)
How to respect you; you are the lord of duty,
I am hitherto your daughter. But here's my husband,
And so much duty as my mother showed   185
To you, preferring you before her father,
So much I challenge that I may profess
Due to the Moor my lord.

Desdemona's strength——she braves her father's and society's disapproval to marry Othello.

BRABANTIO.   God be with you! I have done.
Please it your Grace, on to the state affairs.
I had rather to adopt a child than get° it.   190
Come hither, Moor.
I here do give thee that with all my heart
Which, but thou hast already, with all my heart
I would keep from thee. For your sake, jewel,
I am glad at soul I have no other child,   195
For thy escape would teach me tyranny,
To hang clogs on them. I have done, my lord.

Alternates between blank verse, rhymed and metered verse, and prose

DUKE.   Let me speak like yourself, and lay a **sentence**°

maxim

Which, as a grise° or step, may help these lovers
Into your favor.   200
When remedies are past, the griefs are ended
By seeing the worst, which late on hopes depended.
To mourn a mischief that is past and gone
Is the next way to draw new mischief on.
What cannot be preserved when fortune takes,
Patient her injury a mockery makes.
The robbed that smiles steals something from the thief.
He robs himself that spends a bootless grief.

Don't weary yourself crying over spilt milk.

BRABANTIO.   So let the Turk of Cyprus us beguile,
We lose it not so long as we can smile.   210
He bears the sentence well that nothing bears

---

190. get: beget   **198. sentence:** proverbial saying   **199. grise:** degree

But the free comfort which from thence he hears.
But he bears both the sentence and the sorrow
That, to pay grief, must of poor patience borrow.
These sentences, to sugar or to gall,
Being strong on both sides, are equivocal.   215
But words are words. I never yet did hear
That the bruisèd heart was piercèd through the ear.
I humbly beseech you, proceed to the affairs of state.

DUKE.   The Turk with a most mightly preparation
  makes for Cyprus. Othello, the fortitude of the place
  is best known to you, and though we have there a
  substitute° of most allowed sufficiency, yet opinion,
  a sovereign mistress of effects, throws a more safer
  voice on you. You must therefore be content to
  slubber° the gloss of your new fortunes with this
  more stubborn and boisterous expedition.   225

OTHELLO.   The tyrant custom, most grave Senators,
  Hath made the flinty and steel couch of war
  My thrice-driven bed of down. I do agnize°
  A natural and prompt alacrity
  I find in hardness,° and do undertake
  These present wars against the Ottomites.
  Most humbly therefore bending to your state,
  I crave fit disposition for my wife,
  Due reference of place and exhibition,°
  With such accommodation and besort°   235
  As levels with her breeding.

DUKE.   If you please,
  Be 't at her father's.

BRABANTIO.   I'll not have it so.

OTHELLO.   Nor I.

DESDEMONA.   Nor I. I would not there reside,
  To put my father in impatient thoughts
  By being in his eye. Most gracious Duke,
  To my unfolding lend your prosperous° ear,   240
  And let me find a charter in your voice
  To assist my simpleness.

DUKE.   What would you, Desdemona?

Note—Rhymed couplets in iambic pentameter

But, this is what happens to Othello

Prose

Theme of Judgment
In this scene, good "judgment" and reason prevail—but by the end of Act I, we are left with only Iago's scheming presence on stage.

Look up:
Ottomites
Cyprus
equivocal
bereft

---

222. **substitute:** deputy commander   224. **Slubber:** tarnish
228. **agnize:** confess   230. **hardness:** hardship   234. **exhibition:**
allowance   235. **besort:** attendants   241. **prosperous:** favorable

DESDEMONA. That I did love the Moor to live with him, 245
My downright violence and <u>storm of fortunes</u>
May <u>trumpet to the world</u>. My heart's subdued
Even to the very quality° of my lord.
I saw Othello's visage in his mind,
And to his honors and his valiant parts°   250
Did I my soul and fortunes consecrate.
So that, dear lords, if I be left behind,
<u>A moth of peace</u>, and he go to the war,
The rites for which I love him are ⟨bereft⟩ me,
And I a heavy interim shall support   255
By his dear absence. Let me go with him.
OTHELLO.   Let her have your voices.
Vouch with me, Heaven, I therefore beg it not
To please the palate of my appetite,
Nor to comly with heat—the young affects

Desdemona decides she joins Othello's way of life.

figurative language

Desdemona's strength of character

They have not yet consummated their marriage, but that is not his reason for wanting her to go with him.

---

248. quality: profession   **250. parts:** qualities

Talking Lit

Annie Dillard and Victor Hernández Cruz write about the difficulties and the pleasures of creating literary works.

Annie Dillard from *The Writing Life*

It takes years to write a book—between two and ten years. Less is so rare as to be statistically insignificant. One American writer has written a dozen major books over six decades. He wrote one of those books, a perfect novel, in three months. He speaks of it, still, with awe, almost whispering. Who wants to offend the spirit that hands out such books?

Faulkner wrote *As I Lay Dying* in six weeks; he claimed he knocked it off in his spare time from a twelve-hour-a-day job performing manual labor. There are other examples from other continents and centuries, just as albinos, assassins, saints, big people, and little people show up from time to time in large populations. Out of a human population on earth of four and a half billion, perhaps twenty people can write a book in a year. Some people lift cars, too. Some people enter week-long sled-dog races, go over Niagara Falls in barrels, fly planes through the Arc de Triomphe. Some people feel no pain in childbirth. Some people eat cars. There is no call to take human extremes as norms.

Writing a book, full time, takes between two and ten years. The long poem, John Berryman said, takes between five and ten years. Thomas Mann was a prodigy of production. Working full time, he wrote a page a day. That is 365 pages a year, for he did write every day—a good-sized book a year. At a page a day, he was one of the most prolific writers who ever lived. Flaubert wrote steadily, with only the usual, appalling, strains. For twenty-five years he finished a big book every five to seven years. My guess is that full-time writers average a book every five years: seventy-three usable pages a year, or a usable fifth of a page a day. The years that biographers and other nonfiction writers spend amassing and mastering materials are well matched by the years novelists and short-story writers spend fabricating solid worlds that answer to immaterial truths. On plenty of days the writer can write three or four pages, and on plenty of other days he concludes he must throw them away.

Octavio Paz cites the example of "Saint-Pol-Roux, who used to hang the inscription 'The poet is working' from his door while he slept."

The notion that one can write better during one season of the year than another Samuel Johnson labeled, "Imagination operating upon luxury." Another luxury for an idle imagination is the writer's own feeling about the work. There is neither a proportional relationship, nor an inverse one, between a writer's estimation of a work in progress and its actual quality. The feeling that the work is magnificent, and the feeling that it is abominable, are both mosquitoes to be repelled, ignored, or killed, but not indulged.

The reason to perfect a piece of prose as it progresses—to secure each sentence before building on it—is that original writing fashions a form. It unrolls out into nothingness. It grows cell to cell, bole to bough to twig to leaf; any careful word may suggest a route, may begin a strand of metaphor or event out of which much, or all, will develop. Perfecting the work inch by inch, writing from the first word toward the last, displays the courage and fear this method induces. The strain, like Giacometti's penciled search for precision and honesty, enlivens the work and impels it toward its truest end. A pile of decent work behind him, no matter how small, fuels the writer's hope, too; his pride emboldens and impels him. One Washington writer—Charlie Butts—so prizes momentum, and so fears self-consciousness, that he writes fiction in a rush of his own devising. He leaves his house on distracting errands, hurries in the door, and without taking off his coat, sits at a typewriter and retypes in a blur of speed all of the story he has written to date. Impetus propels him to add another sentence or two before he notices he is writing and seizes up. Then he leaves the house and repeats the process; he runs in the door and retypes the entire story, hoping to squeeze out another sentence the way some car engines turn over after the ignition is off, or the way Warner Bros.' Wile E. Coyote continues running for several yards beyond the edge of a cliff, until he notices.

Victor Hernández Cruz, "Mountains in the North: Hispanic Writing in the U.S.A."

The earth is migration, everything is moving, changing interchanging, appearing, disappearing. National languages melt, sail into each other; languages are made of fragments, like bodies are made of fragments of something in the something. Who'd want to stand still, go to the edges where you see clear the horizon, explore the shape of the coast? Are poets not the antennas of the race? Then tune into the chatter, the murmur that arises from the collection. Add and subtract, submit it to your mathematics. Take and give. Enlarge, diminish. The Romans ate everything up and now we dance Latin to African music, so we don't exactly fall into the things through the words. Columbus thought he came to the land of India and he even mistook Cuba for Japan. Language is clarification of the inner, of the part that does not rot. Moving through a terrain, languages would sound out gradation scale—Italian, Spanish, Portuguese—and so move through the whole planet making a tapestry. Old geography lingers in the language of the conquistadores: names of rivers and fruits. Our Spanish—which has Latin and Italian—has Taino, Siboney, Chichimeca. It has sounds coming out of it that amaze it and over the years it has been spiced, making it a rich instrument full of our history, our adventures, our desires, ourselves. The Caribbean is a place of great convergence; it mixes and uniforms diversities; it is a march of rhythm and style.

Those of us who have ventured off into writing should be in awe of the possibilities inherent in our tradition. Writing is behind the scenes; it is not like music and dance which engulf the masses. Poetry gets to the people in the form of lyrics within a bolero or a salsa tune. It is a valid form of expression, for it contains image and story line; it places old proverbs at the entrance of our contemporary ears. Poetry also lives in the oral tradition known as declamation. There is a warehouse of poems from the Spanish which are memorized and bellowed from the various corners of balconies and colors. The moon is in the tongue between the cheeks, the troubadours move between ceiba trees and plazas, their poetry full of the battles of love, romance, lost love, what to do within the pain of departure. Conversation, spontaneous chitchat constantly interchanging, is a poetry that arises all around us; it is poetry in flight, it is the magic of words bouncing off the pueblos, off the trees into the vines, it comes through the floor like an anaconda, it darts like lizards, it soars like garzas: this language of the Caribbean, this criollo incarnation. Full of passion and opinions, this is the language of our parents. We are the sons and daughters of campesinos, fishermen, farmers who cultivated café and tobacco, cutters of cane whose eyes contain the memory of ardent green vistas out of wooden windows within the hottest tropicality. They have pictures of the ocean tongues and the vibrant hugging of the coast upon a sofa within their retinas. They were spiritual mediums and santeros who worshiped natural forces tapped since time immemorial by African and indigenous societies.

As the children of these immigrants, we are at the center of a world debate; we can speak of the shift from agriculture to industry to technology and the toll it has taken upon the human equilibrium. Let us look at it with clear eyes in our trajectory from one language (Spanish) to another (English). What have we lost or gained? Claro, there is the beautiful lyricism, rhyming and blending of that great romance language, exemplified even in the reading of books on mechanical operations in which the words are still sonorous despite the subject. Is there an inner flower which passions its fragrance despite its being clothed in English words? I believe that this is happening in much U.S. Hispanic literature; the syntax of the

English is being changed. This can be seen very prominently within the work of Alurista, a Chicano poet. In his recent work, the subject is the language itself: it is not that he merely plays with the language as some Anglo language experimenters do, for his poetry still contains social meanings directed towards personal and political change and awareness. We also find in the prose work of Rudolfo Anaya a natural Spanish pastoral style resounding through his English, a very relaxed, unharsh sentence. In both the English and the Spanish the poets and writers uphold a sensibility of Hispanitude.

We battle the sterility of Anglo culture, of television clichés; we labor at being ourselves in a land of weirdos, electric freaks who sit mesmerized in front of screens and buttons, only stopping to eat the farthest reaches of junk or to jerk off about some personal need to be understood, barking about having the freedom to do whatever nauseous things their lifestyles call for. You know that a pastime of the North American middle class now is to go out to fields and dress up in military fatigues and play war, shoot the commies or, better yet, shoot third-world guerrillas—shoot real guerrillas—and after that get back in the pickup and go down to Burger King and eat whatever that is. Meanwhile, the ozone layer is disappearing and, what's that song sung by Richie Havens, "Here Comes the Sun"? Then they have that thing where they eat until they almost explode and then stick their fingers down their throat and vomit, solely to start the process again. It's an image culture: what you see is all there is. Jane Fonda in *Barbarella* was offering body; now that she has gained consciousness she is offering more body and even better build.

Did Richard Rodriguez fall down hard? Well there are those who jump quickly to attack him because he seemed to say the opposite of what was being fought for. Of course we must strive for an English that is standard and universal, a language that can be understood by as many people as possible, but why lose the Spanish in the process? We should change the English and give it spice, Hispanic mobility, all this can be done within the framework of understanding, whether the reader is Anglo or Latino.

U.S. Hispanics have not blended into Northern Americana because our roots stay fresh. Due to the close proximity of the Americas, rushes of tropical electricity keep coming up to inform the work and transform the North American literary landscape. The location and atmosphere of stories and poetry have been taken to places that until now North American authors were only able to write about from the position of tourists. The literature is full of border towns, farm workers, the lives of salsa musicians blowing through northern cities. The racial and cultural mixing of our cultures keeps us jumping through a huge spectrum of styles and philosophies. In terms of history, we can walk the planet with our genes, imagine ourselves in the Sevilla of the Arabs holding court with ibn 'Arabi and al-Ghazálí, quickly switch over to the halls of Tenochtitlán, then once again wake up in our contemporary reality dancing Yoruba choreography in some club in Manhattan near a subway train. You can change the content and mix into the infinite. Worlds exist simultaneously, flashes of scenarios, linguistic stereo; they conflict, they debate, Spanish and English constantly breaking into each other like ocean waves. Your head scatters with adverbs over the horizon.

FROM PAGE TO SCREEN

OXFORD WORLD'S CLASSIC

JAMES FENIMORE COOPER
THE LAST OF THE MOHICAN

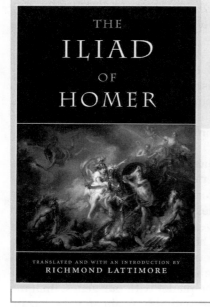

THE
ILIAD
OF
HOMER

TRANSLATED AND WITH AN INTRODUCTION BY
RICHMOND LATTIMORE

Many people assume that literature is remote from our experience—old, outdated, past its prime. What we sometimes forget is that the writers featured in books like this one have set the stage for many modern entertainers and filmmakers.

It's not much of a stretch to think of William Blake—a poet writing around the turn of the nineteenth century with a radical perspective on religion—as an earlier incarnation of shock rocker Marilyn Manson, or Edgar Allen Poe—who was writing psychological thrillers in the 1800s—as his day's M. Night Shamaylan, the writer/director of the movies *The Sixth Sense* and *Signs*. We now recognize the last generation's musicians as poets, people like Bob Dylan and Jim Morrison. Today's poets—artists like 50-Cent or Avril Levign—can count themselves in the same family. Whereas we might use a day off to go see the latest blockbuster film at our local theater, our predecessors used their spare time to

All art forms borrow from each other for the purpose of enrichment. Architects can draw from ancient and colonial styles to arrive at their contemporary geometries—structures which improve human living. Musicians are constantly blending and mixing the rhythms of the earth; Caribbean music is like

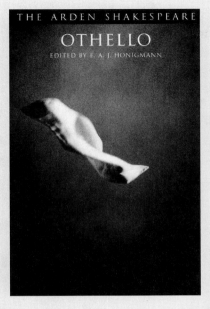

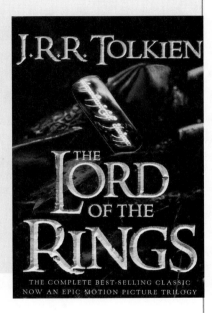

catch the latest Greek tragedy or take in a Shakespeare performance.

Throughout this text you'll encounter boxes like this which will help bridge the gap between eras. Sometimes the connections are obvious. Today's artists often visit yesterday's by adapting, covering, or paying homage to earlier works. Some artists, including Quentin Tarantino and Sean "P. Diddy" Combs, have based their artistic careers on modern-izing past films and music. Some of the most recent block-buster movies have been adapted from existing works of modern literature and have become works that stand alone as separate from their first incarnation. One notable example is the recent adaptation of *The Lord of the Rings* from books into film. And Tolkien's original works have their origins in still older texts. The tales are drawn largely from classic mythological ideas of good and evil, epic battles, fantastic creatures, and heroes with special powers. The idea of small hobbits tak-ing on big tasks is something we can also see in the biblical stories of Samson and of David's facing Goliath. The epic battles are also similar to those in the Greek epic *The Iliad*, which has recently been adapted in the feature film *Troy*.

Andalucía and the Ivory Coast. In New York's Latin-Jazz fusion in the forties and fifties there are cuts where Tito Puente jams with Charlie Parker; this is like a toning of temperaments, or adjusting reality to get the most out of it. It seems to be the center of the musician to translate, rearrange, to give personal flavor to a variety of rhythms and melodies.

PART 1

Fiction

The works of fiction that follow in Part 1 are examples of modern and contemporary short stories. The urge to tell a story, though, is ancient and instinctive. Storytelling has existed in every culture on earth since before the dawn of written language. We tell stories to each other to remember great deeds, to commemorate important rites of passage, to memorialize collective experiences of a people, to teach the young their heritage, and to describe personal and cultural identity. We also share our stories in our day-to-day lives. We tell about our experiences during morning rush hour, or who we met in the grocery store, or what we did over the weekend. The desire to tell—and to hear—a story is universal. Is there any place on earth where the child being put to bed at night doesn't say to an adult or older sibling, "Please, tell me a story"?

PROFILE OF A FICTION WRITER
FLANNERY O'CONNOR
(1925–1964)

A man with the image of Jesus tattooed on his back, a Bible salesman who steals the wooden leg of a woman with a Ph.D., a family on vacation shot dead by a sociopathic killer who calls himself The Misfit—this is the world inhabited by Flannery O'Connor's characters. It may sound frightening or grotesque, but it is also often hilarious, and it is always brim full of human frailties, human variety, and rather startling doses of truth. Born in 1925 in Savannah, Georgia, O'Connor was the only child of Roman Catholic parents in the largely Protestant South. While Flannery O'Connor's native region (and setting for her fiction) may be the American South, her characters' hearts—and their often tainted, thwarted, or misunderstood aspirations—are those of people everywhere.

Religion and Violence in O'Connor's Fiction

Flannery O'Connor was a devout and observant Catholic all of her life, but she had a great intellectual curiosity and enjoyed learning from people of other religious faiths and other worldviews. Some misunderstand O'Connor's work as parochial or narrow, but you have only to read her letters and short stories to find a cutting and humorous wit which questions every aspect of our human nature. Sadly, one territory of

Flannery as editor of her college magazine *The Corinthian*. She also served on the yearbook and newspapers staffs at Georgia State College for Women

human experience that was well-known to her was death. When she was thirteen, her father was diagnosed with disseminated lupus, an incurable, degenerative disease in which the immune system attacks the body's own substances. An unusual aspect of her life journey is that O'Connor had the rather rare experience of living many years faced with her own (possibly imminent) death. After learning that she herself was suffering from the same disease that had killed her father, O'Connor returned to Georgia to live on her mother's farm in Milledgeville. By the time she died of lupus at the age of thirty-nine, she was accustomed to thinking about the cruelties of death, and she had reconciled herself to the knowledge that her own life would be short. Even at the end, however, her letters and the testimony of her family and friends reveal her lively, curious, and ferociously brave worldview.

Hers was a tragically short life, yet Flannery O'Connor managed to pack a good bit of experience into it. Shortly after her father's death in 1941, she received her B.A. from Georgia State College for Women in Milledgeville. Then she earned a fellowship to the University of Iowa Writers Workshop, where she received her M.F.A. degree in fiction writing in 1947. O'Connor published two novels, *Wise Blood* (1951) and *The Violent Bear It Away* (1960), but she was best known for her short stories, collected in *A Good Man Is Hard to Find* (1955) and *Everything That Rises Must Converge* (1965, published posthumously). Her essays were collected posthumously in a volume entitled *Mystery and Manners* in 1969. Also published after her death, *The Complete Stories of Flannery O'Connor* (1971) won the National Book Award. In 1979 her friends and literary executors Sally and Robert Fitzgerald published *The Habit of Being: Selected Letters of Flannery O'Connor*.

Some readers have had difficulty reconciling the violence and deviance depicted in O'Connor's fiction with her deeply religious worldview. Referring to some Catholic readers who criticized her fiction, she said, "They read a little corruption as total corruption. The writer has to make the corruption believable before he can make the grace meaningful" (*The Habit of Being*, 516). Moments of grace abound in O'Connor's stories, along with moments when grace (or self-enlightenment or epiphany or redemption) are available to a character who may or may not perceive the opportunity. Despite his criminal nature and the evil act he has just committed, The Misfit himself recognizes, in "A Good Man Is Hard to Find," that such a moment had happened for the grandmother. "'She would have been a good woman,' The Misfit says, 'if it had been somebody there to shoot her every minute of her life.'"

Great Fiction/Large Doses of Humor, Wisdom, Irony

O'Connor's fiction has a way of looking human frailty and even depravity straight in the face. However, balancing these sometimes shocking scenes are this writer's sense of humor and her affection for her characters, even when she mocks them. Hers is a tragicomic view of the world that makes possible a shock and then possibly a smile at the role reversal that takes place for Joy/Hulga and Manley Pointer at the end of "Good Country People." It also makes possible a degree of sympathy with the tattooed antihero O. E. Parker (in "Parker's Back") when the extraordinary measures he takes for winning the love and respect of his devout new bride ironically have the opposite effect.

Some say that if fiction is to be successful, the writer must show the universal through the particular—to show what is true for all of us through the authentic details of a few well-drawn characters. Flannery O'Connor possessed this skill in abundance, and though her stories are filled with characters that many refer to as "Southern grotesques," these characters are busy revealing to us what William Faulkner (in his 1950 Nobel acceptance speech) called "the problems of the human heart in conflict with itself." Nothing could be more universal than that.

The Writer's Voice and the Reader's Response

Maybe it seems too obvious to say, but writers are very fond of words! Words to a writer are like paint to the painter. The writer arranges words consciously and carefully, with an appreciation for their sounds as well as for the nuances of their meanings. This passion for words grows out of oral storytelling for some, but for many writers, it grows out of a love of reading. This idea that reading can inform and stimulate writing is important to the study of literature generally and to the study of fiction particularly. When reading a work of fiction, you should be willing to ask questions of the story, which often helps generate ideas for discussion or writing. As we move through our exploration of fiction, interesting questions about the stories will come more and more readily to your mind. Many interesting essay topics and ideas come about in just this way.

As you read through one or more of Flannery O'Connor's stories here, the habit of "questioning the text" might become more and more automatic for you, and possible answers to those questions may pop into your mind too. O'Connor's story "Good Country People," for instance, might be approached by a number of different paths. How has O'Connor deliberately written the narrative so that we know how the principal characters feel and what they are thinking? From whose perspective is the story told: Joy/Hulga's and/or Mrs. Hopewell's? Does the narrative perspective change during the course of the story? How does O'Connor's careful choice of words when describing Manley Pointer give us a highly visual sense of what he looks like? And then there's irony. This story contains many ironies—the first of which is the title itself (though we don't know that the first time we read it). A good deal happens toward the end of the story that is not at all what we expect to happen, and that is called **situational irony**. Another way to talk about situational irony in the story is to look at the instances in which there is a discrepancy between appearance and reality. That is, things appear to be one way on the surface, but when what's under the surface is revealed to us, it is quite different than what we'd first thought. In other words, things are not what they appear to be. We might think about this kind of irony in terms of Manley Pointer's behavior and worldview, for instance. As you can tell, we're avoiding the temptation to give away the ending. If you haven't read the story yet, you might be rather surprised by what happens.

The Elements of Fiction

The **elements of fiction** are the techniques, strategies, and methods (plot, characterization, setting, point of view, etc.) used by the writers in a particular genre (in this case, fiction). The elements also include those concepts (irony, theme, symbol, etc.) that help readers grasp the writer's craft and help readers discuss the meanings that arise from a given work of fiction. The creation of a short story involves a great deal of effort; ordinarily, the writer has labored long to invest his or her story with meaning, usually revising, rewriting, and fine-tuning its effects. Readers then respond variously to the story. Usually, most of its readers can agree on a good many things about a story; however, there are also always nuances of difference between readers' interpretations of characters, events, and endings. Most writers are pleased to know that multiple interpretations of their works are possible. In fact, it is the more complex and more successful works of fiction that are most likely to evoke different responses from different readers.

As you begin to read the stories written by Flannery O'Connor, you will notice references and details that suggest that the stories are set several decades earlier than the present time (remember that Flannery O'Connor died in 1964). You can assume most of her stories are taking place in the middle of the twentieth century. You will also notice the use of dialect in her stories. You might say that her characters speak with a Southern accent, which reveals to us the region of the country in which the stories are set. Also remember that, as pointed out earlier, O'Connor felt the fiction writer needs to show the bad side of human nature in order to illuminate moments of "grace" or possibilities for goodness. African American writer Alice Walker has something to say below, in her "Talking Lit" selection, about O'Connor's quite disturbing but honest depiction of racial prejudice.

Flannery O'Connor

Good Country People (1955)

Besides the neutral expression that she wore when she was alone, Mrs. Freeman had two others, forward and reverse, that she used for all her human dealings. Her forward expression was steady and driving like the advance of a heavy truck. Her eyes never swerved to left or right but turned as the story turned as if they followed a yellow line down the center of it. She seldom used the other expression because it was not often necessary for her to retract a statement, but when she did, her face came to a complete stop, there was an almost imperceptible movement of her black eyes, during which they seemed to be receding, and then the observer would see that Mrs. Freeman, though she might stand there as real as

several grain sacks thrown on top of each other, was no longer there in spirit. As for getting anything across to her when this was the case, Mrs. Hopewell had given it up. She might talk her head off. Mrs. Freeman could never be brought to admit herself wrong on any point. She would stand there and if she could be brought to say anything, it was something like, "Well, I wouldn't of said it was and I wouldn't of said it wasn't," or letting her gaze range over the top kitchen shelf where there was an assortment of dusty bottles, she might remark, "I see you ain't ate many of them figs you put up last summer."

They carried on their most important business in the kitchen at breakfast. Every morning Mrs. Hopewell got up at seven o'clock and lit her gas heater and Joy's. Joy was her daughter, a large blonde girl who had an artificial leg. Mrs. Hopewell thought of her as a child though she was thirty-two years old and highly educated. Joy would get up while her mother was eating and lumber into the bathroom and slam the door, and before long, Mrs. Freeman would arrive at the back door. Joy would hear her mother call, "Come on in," and then they would talk for a while in low voices that were indistinguishable in the bathroom. By the time Joy came in, they had usually finished the weather report and were on one or the other of Mrs. Freeman's daughters, Glynese or Carramae, Joy called them Glycerin and Caramel. Glynese, a redhead, was eighteen and had many admirers; Carramae, a blonde, was only fifteen but already married and pregnant. She could not keep anything on her stomach. Every morning Mrs. Freeman told Mrs. Hopewell how many times she had vomited since the last report.

Mrs. Hopewell liked to tell people that Glynese and Carramae were two of the finest girls she knew and that Mrs. Freeman was a *lady* and that she was never ashamed to take her anywhere or introduce her to anybody they might meet. Then she would tell how she had happened to hire the Freemans in the first place and how they were a godsend to her and how she had had them four years. The reason for her keeping them so long was that they were not trash. They were good country people. She had telephoned the man whose name they had given as a reference and he had told her that Mr. Freeman was a good farmer but that his wife was the nosiest woman ever to walk the earth. "She's got to be into everything," the man said. "If she don't get there before the dust settles, you can bet she's dead, that's all. She'll want to know all your business. I can stand him real good," he had said, "but me nor my wife neither could

have stood that woman one more minute on this place." That had put Mrs. Hopewell off for a few days.

She had hired them in the end because there were no other applicants but she had made up her mind beforehand exactly how she would handle the woman. Since she was the type who had to be into everything, then, Mrs. Hopewell had decided, she would not only let her be into everything, she would *see to it* that she was into everything— she would give her the responsibility of everything, she would put her in charge. Mrs. Hopewell had no bad qualities of her own but she was able to use other people's in such a constructive way that she never felt the lack. She had hired the Freemans and she had kept them four years.

Nothing is perfect. This was one of 5 Mrs. Hopewell's favorite sayings. Another was: that is life! And still another, the most important, was: well, other people have their opinions too. She would make these statements, usually at the table, in a tone of gentle insistence as if no one held them but her, and the large hulking Joy, whose constant outrage had obliterated every expression from her face, would stare just a little to the side of her, her eyes icy blue, with the look of someone who has achieved blindness by an act of will and means to keep it.

When Mrs. Hopewell said to Mrs. Freeman that life was like that, Mrs. Freeman would say, "I always said so myself." Nothing had been arrived at by anyone that had not first been arrived at by her. She was quicker than Mr. Freeman. When Mrs. Hopewell said to her after they had been on the place a while, "You know, you're the wheel behind the wheel," and winked, Mrs. Freeman had said, "I know it. I've always been quick. It's some that are quicker than others."

"Everybody is different," Mrs. Hopewell said.

"Yes, most people is," Mrs. Freeman said.

"It takes all kinds to make the world."

10   "I always said it did myself."

The girl was used to this kind of dialogue for breakfast and more of it for dinner; sometimes they had it for supper too. When they had no guest they ate in the kitchen because that was easier. Mrs. Freeman always managed to arrive at some point during the meal and to watch them finish it. She would stand in the doorway if it were summer but in the winter she would stand with one elbow on top of the refrigerator and look down on them, or she would stand by the gas heater, lifting the back of her skirt slightly. Occasionally she would stand against the wall and roll her head from side to side. At no time was she in any hurry to leave. All this was very trying on Mrs. Hopewell but she was a woman of great patience. She realized that nothing is perfect and that in the Freemans she had good country people and that if, in this day and age, you get good country people, you had better hang onto them.

She had had plenty of experience with trash. Before the Freemans she had averaged one tenant family a year. The wives of these farmers were not the kind you would want to be around you for very long. Mrs. Hopewell, who had divorced her husband long ago, needed someone to walk over the fields with her; and when Joy had to be impressed for these services, her remarks were usually so ugly and her face so glum that Mrs. Hopewell would say, "If you can't come pleasantly, I don't want you at all," to which the girl, standing square and rigid-shouldered with her neck thrust slightly forward, would reply, "If you want me, here I am—LIKE I AM."

Mrs. Hopewell excused this attitude because of the leg (which had been shot off in a hunting accident when Joy was ten). It was hard for Mrs. Hopewell to realize that her child was thirty-two now and that for more than twenty years she had had only one leg. She thought of her still as a child because it tore her heart to think instead of the poor stout girl in her thirties who had never danced a step or had any *normal* good times. Her name was really Joy but as soon as she was twenty-one and away from home, she had had it legally changed. Mrs. Hopewell was certain that she had thought and thought until she had hit upon the ugliest name in any language. Then she had gone and had the beautiful name, Joy, changed without telling her mother until after she had done it. Her legal name was Hulga.

When Mrs. Hopewell thought the name, Hulga, she thought of the broad blank hull of a battleship. She would not use it. She continued to call her Joy to which the girl responded but in a purely mechanical way.

15   Hulga had learned to tolerate Mrs. Freeman who saved her from taking walks with her mother. Even Glynese and Carramae were useful when they occupied attention that might otherwise have been directed at her. At first she had thought she could not stand Mrs. Freeman for she had found that it was not possible to be rude to her. Mrs. Freeman would take on strange resentments and for days together she would be sullen but the source of her displeasure was always obscure; a direct attack, a positive leer, blatant ugliness to her face—these never touched her. And without warning one day, she began calling her Hulga.

She did not call her that in front of Mrs. Hopewell who would have been incensed but when she and the girl happened to be out of the house together, she would say something and add the name Hulga to the end of it, and the big spectacled Joy-Hulga would scowl and redden as if her privacy had been intruded upon. She considered the name her personal affair. She had arrived at it first purely on the basis of its ugly sound and then the full genius of its fitness had struck her. She had a vision of the name working like the ugly sweating Vulcan who stayed in the furnace and to whom, presumably, the goddess had to come when called. She saw it as the name of her highest creative act. One of her major triumphs was that her mother had not been able to turn her dust into Joy, but the greater one was that she had been able to turn it herself into Hulga. However, Mrs. Freeman's relish for using the name only irritated her. It was as if Mrs. Freeman's beady steel-pointed eyes had penetrated far enough behind her face to reach some secret fact. Something about her seemed to fascinate Mrs. Freeman and then one day Hulga realized that it was the artificial leg. Mrs. Freeman had a special fondness for the details of secret infections, hidden deformities, assaults upon children. Of diseases, she preferred the lingering or incurable. Hulga had heard Mrs. Hopewell give her the details of the hunting accident, how the leg had been literally blasted off, how she had never lost consciousness. Mrs. Freeman could listen to it any time as if it had happened an hour ago.

When Hulga stumped into the kitchen in the morning (she could walk without making the awful noise but she made it—Mrs. Hopewell was certain—because it was ugly-sounding), she glanced at them and did not speak. Mrs. Hopewell would be in her red kimono with her hair tied around her head in rags. She would be sitting at the table, finishing her breakfast and Mrs. Freeman would be hanging by her elbow outward from the refrigerator, looking down at the table. Hulga always put her eggs on the stove to boil and then stood over them with her arms folded, and Mrs. Hopewell would look at her—a kind of indirect gaze divided between her and Mrs. Freeman—and would think that if she would only keep

herself up a little, she wouldn't be so bad looking. There was nothing wrong with her face that a pleasant expression wouldn't help. Mrs. Hopewell said that people who looked on the bright side of things would be beautiful even if they were not.

Whenever she looked at Joy this way, she could not help but feel that it would have been better if the child had not taken the Ph.D. It had certainly not brought her out any and now that she had it, there was no more excuse for her to go to school again. Mrs. Hopewell thought it was nice for girls to go to school to have a good time but Joy had "gone through." Anyhow, she would not have been strong enough to go again. The doctors had told Mrs. Hopewell that with the best of care, Joy might see forty-five. She had a weak heart. Joy had made it plain that if it had not been for this condition, she would be far from these red hills and good country people. She would be in a university lecturing to people who knew what she was talking about. And Mrs. Hopewell could very well picture her there, looking like a scarecrow and lecturing to more of the same. Here she went about all day in a six-year-old skirt and a yellow sweat shirt with a faded cowboy on a horse embossed on it. She thought this was funny; Mrs. Hopewell thought it was idiotic and showed simply that she was still a child. She was brilliant but she didn't have a grain of sense. It seemed to Mrs. Hopewell that every year she grew less like other people and more like herself—bloated, rude, and squint-eyed. And she said such strange things! To her own mother she had said—without warning, without excuse, standing up in the middle of a meal with her face purple and her mouth half full—"Woman! do you ever look inside? Do you ever look inside and see what you are *not*? God!" she had cried sinking down again and staring at her plate, "Malebranche was right: we are not our own light. We are not our own light!" Mrs. Hopewell had no idea to this day what brought that on. She had only made the remark, hoping Joy would take it in, that a smile never hurt anyone.

The girl had taken the Ph.D. in philosophy and this left Mrs. Hopewell at a complete loss. You could say, "My daughter is a nurse," or "My daughter is a schoolteacher," or even, "My daughter is a chemical engineer." You could not say, "My daughter is a philosopher." That was something that had ended with the Greeks and Romans. All day Joy sat on her neck in a deep chair, reading. Sometimes she went for walks but she didn't like dogs or cats or birds or flowers or nature or nice young men. She looked at nice young men as if she could smell their stupidity.

20 One day Mrs. Hopewell had picked up one of the books the girl had just put down and opening it at random, she read, "Science, on the other hand, has to assert its soberness and seriousness afresh and declare that it is concerned solely with what-is. Nothing—how can it be for science anything but a horror and a phantasm? If science is right, then one thing stands firm: science wishes to know nothing of nothing. Such is after all the strictly scientific approach to Nothing. We know it by wishing to know nothing of Nothing." These words had been underlined with a blue pencil and they worked on Mrs. Hopewell like some evil incantation in gibberish. She shut the book quickly and went out of the room as if she were having a chill.

This morning when the girl came in, Mrs. Freeman was on Carramae. "She thrown up four times after supper," she said, "and was up twict in the night after three o'clock. Yesterday she didn't do nothing but ramble in the bureau drawer. All she did. Stand up there and see what she could run up on."

"She's got to eat," Mrs. Hopewell muttered, sipping her coffee, while she watched Joy's back at the stove. She was wondering what the child had said to the Bible salesman. She could not imagine what kind of a conversation she could possibly have had with him.

He was a tall gaunt hatless youth who had called yesterday to sell them a Bible. He had appeared at the door, carrying a large black suitcase that weighted him so heavily on one side that he had to brace himself against the door facing. He seemed on the point of collapse but he said in a cheerful voice, "Good morning, Mrs. Cedars!" and set the suitcase down on the mat. He was not a bad-looking young man though he had on a bright blue suit and yellow socks that were not pulled up far enough. He had prominent face bones and a streak of sticky-looking brown hair falling across his forehead.

"I'm Mrs. Hopewell," she said.

"Oh!" he said, pretending to look puz- 25 zled but with his eyes sparkling, "I saw it said 'The Cedars' on the mailbox so I thought you was Mrs. Cedars!" and he burst out in a pleasant laugh. He picked up the satchel and under cover of a pant, he fell forward into her hall. It was rather as if the suitcase had moved first, jerking him after it. "Mrs. Hopewell!" he said and grabbed her hand. "I hope you are well!" and he laughed again and then all at once his face sobered completely. He paused and gave her a straight earnest look and said, "Lady, I've come to speak of serious things."

"Well, come in," she muttered, none too pleased because her dinner was almost ready. He came into the parlor and sat down on the edge of a straight chair and put the suitcase between his feet and glanced around the room as if he were sizing her up by it. Her silver gleamed on the two sideboards; she decided he had never been in a room as elegant as this.

"Mrs. Hopewell," he began, using her name in a way that sounded almost intimate, "I know you believe in Chrustian service."

"Well yes," she murmured.

"I know," he said and paused, looking very wise with his head cocked on one side, "that you're a good woman. Friends have told me."

30 Mrs. Hopewell never liked to be taken for a fool. "What are you selling?" she asked.

"Bibles," the young man said and his eye raced around the room before he added, "I see you have no family Bible in your parlor, I see that is the one lack you got!"

Mrs. Hopewell could not say, "My daughter is an atheist and won't let me keep the Bible in the parlor." She said, stiffening slightly, "I keep my Bible by my bedside." This was not the truth. It was in the attic somewhere.

"Lady," he said, "the word of God ought to be in the parlor."

"Well, I think that's a matter of taste," she began. "I think . . ."

35 "Lady," he said, "for a Chrustian, the word of God ought to be in every room in the house besides in his heart. I know you're a Chrustian because I can see it in every line of your face."

She stood up and said, "Well, young man, I don't want to buy a Bible and I smell my dinner burning."

He didn't get up. He began to twist his hands and looking down at them, he said softly, "Well lady, I'll tell you the truth—not many people want to buy one nowadays and besides, I know I'm real simple. I don't know how to say a thing but to say it. I'm just a country boy." He glanced up into her unfriendly face. "People like you don't like to fool with country people like me!"

"Why!" she cried, "good country people are the salt of the earth! Besides, we all have different ways of doing, it takes all kinds to make the world go 'round. That's life!"

"You said a mouthful," he said.

40 "Why, I think there aren't enough good country people in the world!" she said,

stirred. "I think that's what's wrong with it!"

His face had brightened. "I didn't inraduce myself," he said. "I'm Manley Pointer from out in the country around Willohobie, not even from a place, just from near a place."

"You wait a minute," she said. "I have to see about my dinner." She went out to the kitchen and found Joy standing near the door where she had been listening.

"Get rid of the salt of the earth," she said, "and let's eat."

Mrs. Hopewell gave her a pained look and turned the heat down under the vegetables. "I can't be rude to anybody," she murmured and went back into the parlor.

45 He had opened the suitcase and was sitting with a Bible on each knee.

"You might as well put those up," she told him. "I don't want one."

"I appreciate your honesty," he said. "You don't see any more real honest people unless you go way out in the country."

"I know," she said, "real genuine folks!" Through the crack in the door she heard a groan.

"I guess a lot of boys come telling you they're working their way through college," he said, "but I'm not going to tell you that. Somehow," he said, "I don't want to go to college. I want to devote my life to Chrustian service. See," he said, lowering his voice, "I got this heart condition. I may not live long. When you know it's something wrong with you and you may not live long, well then, lady . . ." He paused, with his mouth open, and stared at her.

50 He and Joy had the same condition! She knew that her eyes were filling with tears but she collected herself quickly and murmured, "Won't you stay for dinner? We'd love to have you!" and was sorry the instant she heard herself say it.

"Yes mam," he said in an abashed voice, "I would sher love to do that!"

Joy had given him one look on being introduced to him and then throughout the meal had not glanced at him again. He had addressed several remarks to her, which she had pretended not to hear. Mrs. Hopewell could not understand deliberate rudeness, although she lived with it, and she felt she had always to overflow with hospitality to make up for Joy's lack of courtesy. She urged him to talk about himself and he did. He said he was the seventh child of twelve and that his father had been crushed under a tree when he himself was eight year old. He had been crushed very badly, in fact, almost cut in two and was practically not recognizable. His mother had got along the best she could by hard working and she had always seen that her children went to Sunday School and that they read the Bible every evening. He was now nineteen year old and he had been selling Bibles for four months. In that time he had sold seventy-seven Bibles and had the promise of two more sales. He wanted to become a missionary because he thought that was the way you could do most for people. "He who losest his life shall find it," he said simply and he was so sincere, so genuine and earnest that Mrs. Hopewell would not for the world have smiled. He prevented his peas from sliding onto the table by blocking them with a piece of bread which he later cleaned his plate with. She could see Joy observing sidewise how he handled his knife and fork and she saw too that every few minutes, the boy would dart a keen appraising glance at the girl as if he were trying to attract her attention.

After dinner Joy cleared the dishes off the table and disappeared and Mrs. Hopewell was left to talk with him. He told her again about his childhood and his father's accident and about various things that had happened to him. Every five minutes or so she would stifle a yawn. He sat for two hours until finally she told him she must go because she had an appointment in town. He packed his Bibles and thanked her and prepared to leave, but in the doorway he stopped and wrung her hand and said that not on any of his trips had he met a lady as nice as her and he asked if he could come again. She had said she would always be happy to see him.

Joy had been standing in the road, apparently looking at something in the distance, when he came down the steps toward her, bent to the side with his heavy valise. He stopped where she was standing and confronted her directly. Mrs. Hopewell could not hear what he said but she trembled to think what Joy would say to him. She could see that after a minute Joy said something and that then the boy began to speak again, making an excited gesture with his free hand. After a minute Joy said something else at which the boy began to speak once more. Then to her amazement, Mrs. Hopewell saw the two of them walk off together, toward the gate. Joy had walked all the way to the gate with him and Mrs. Hopewell could not imagine what they had said to each other, and she had not yet dared to ask.

Mrs. Freeman was insisting upon her attention. She had moved from the refrigerator to the heater so that Mrs. Hopewell had to turn and face her in order to seem to be listening. "Glynese gone out with Harvey Hill again last night," she said. "She had this sty."

"Hill," Mrs. Hopewell said absently, "is that the one who works in the garage?"

"Nome, he's the one that goes to chiropracter school," Mrs. Freeman said. "She had this sty. Been had it two days. So she says when he brought her in the other night he says, 'Lemme get rid of that sty for you,' and she says, 'How?' and he says, 'You just lay yourself down acrost the seat of that car and I'll show you.' So she done it and he popped her neck. Kept on a-popping it several times until she made him quit. This morning," Mrs. Freeman said, "she ain't got no sty. She ain't got no traces of a sty."

"I never heard of that before," Mrs. Hopewell said.

"He ast her to marry him before the Ordinary," Mrs. Freeman went on, "and she told him she wasn't going to be married in no *office*."

60 "Well, Glynese is a fine girl," Mrs. Hopewell said. "Glynese and Carramae are both fine girls."

"Carramae said when her and Lyman was married Lyman said it sure felt sacred to him. She said he said he wouldn't take five hundred dollars for being married by a preacher."

"How much would he take?" the girl asked from the stove.

"He said he wouldn't take five hundred dollars," Mrs. Freeman repeated.

"Well we all have work to do," Mrs. Hopewell said.

65 "Lyman said it just felt more sacred to him," Mrs. Freeman said. "The doctor wants Carramae to eat prunes. Says instead of medicine. Says them cramps is coming from pressure. You know where I think it is?"

"She'll be better in a few weeks," Mrs. Hopewell said.

"In the tube," Mrs. Freeman said. "Else she wouldn't be as sick as she is."

Hulga had cracked her two eggs into a saucer and was bringing them to the table along with a cup of coffee that she had filled too full. She sat down carefully and began to eat, meaning to keep Mrs. Freeman there by questions if for any reason she showed an inclination to leave. She could perceive her mother's eye on her. The first round-about question would be about the Bible salesman and she did not wish to bring it on. "How did he pop her neck?" she asked.

Mrs. Freeman went into a description of how he had popped her neck. She said he owned a '55 Mercury but that Glynese said she would rather marry a man with only a '36 Plymouth who would be married by a preacher. The girl asked what if he had a '32 Plymouth and Mrs. Freeman said what Glynese had said was a '36 Plymouth.

70 Mrs. Hopewell said there were not many girls with Glynese's common sense. She said what she admired in those girls was their common sense. She said that reminded her that they had had a nice visitor yesterday, a young man selling Bibles. "Lord," she said, "he bored me to death but he was so sincere and genuine I couldn't be rude to him. He was just good country people, you know," she said, "—just the salt of the earth."

"I seen him walk up," Mrs. Freeman said, "and then later—I seen him walk off," and Hulga could feel the slight shift in her voice, the slight insinuation, that he had not walked off alone, had he? Her face remained expressionless but the color rose into her neck and she seemed to swallow it down with the next spoonful of egg. Mrs. Freeman was looking at her as if they had a secret together.

"Well, it takes all kinds of people to make the world go 'round," Mrs. Hopewell said. "It's very good we aren't all alike."

"Some people are more alike than others," Mrs. Freeman said.

Hulga got up and stumped, with about twice the noise that was necessary, into her room and locked the door. She was to meet the Bible salesman at ten o'clock at the gate. She had thought about it half the night. She had started thinking of it as a great joke and then she had begun to see profound implications in it. She had lain in bed imagining dialogues for them that were insane on the surface but that reached below to depths that no Bible salesman would be aware of. Their conversation yesterday had been of this kind.

75 He had stopped in front of her and had simply stood there. His face was bony and sweaty and bright, with a little pointed nose in the center of it, and his look was different from what it had been at the dinner table. He

was gazing at her with open curiosity, with fascination, like a child watching a new fantastic animal at the zoo, and he was breathing as if he had run a great distance to reach her. His gaze seemed somehow familiar but she could not think where she had been regarded with it before. For almost a minute he didn't say anything. Then on what seemed an insuck of breath, he whispered, "You ever ate a chicken that was two days old?"

The girl looked at him stonily. He might have just put this question up for consideration at the meeting of a philosophical association. "Yes," she presently replied as if she had considered it from all angles.

"It must have been mighty small!" he said triumphantly and shook all over with little nervous giggles, getting very red in the face, and subsiding finally into his gaze of complete admiration, while the girl's expression remained exactly the same.

"How old are you?" he asked softly.

She waited some time before she answered. Then in a flat voice she said, "Seventeen."

80 His smiles came in succession like waves breaking on the surface of a little lake. "I see you got a wooden leg," he said. "I think you're brave. I think you're real sweet."

The girl stood blank and solid and silent.

"Walk to the gate with me," he said. "You're a brave sweet little thing and I liked you the minute I seen you walk in the door."

Hulga began to move forward.

"What's your name?" he asked, smiling down on the top of her head.

85 "Hulga," she said.

"Hulga," he murmured, "Hulga. Hulga. I never heard of anybody name Hulga before. You're shy, aren't you, Hulga?" he asked.

She nodded, watching his large red hand on the handle of the giant valise.

"I like girls that wear glasses," he said. "I think a lot. I'm not like these people that

a serious thought don't ever enter their heads. It's because I may die."

"I may die too," she said suddenly and looked up at him. His eyes were very small and brown, glittering feverishly.

"Listen," he said, "don't you think 90 some people was meant to meet on account of what all they got in common and all? Like they both think serious thoughts and all?" He shifted the valise to his other hand so that the hand nearest her was free. He caught hold of her elbow and shook it a little. "I don't work on Saturday," he said. "I like to walk in the woods and see what Mother Nature is wearing. O'er the hills and far away. Pic-nics and things. Couldn't we go on a pic-nic tomorrow? Say yes, Hulga," he said and gave her a dying look as if he felt his insides about to drop out of him. He had even seemed to sway slightly toward her.

During the night she had imagined that she seduced him. She imagined that the two of them walked on the place until they came to the storage barn beyond the two back fields and there, she imagined, that things came to such a pass that she very easily seduced him and that then, of course, she had to reckon with his remorse. True genius can get an idea across even to an inferior mind. She imagined that she took his remorse in hand and changed it into a deeper understanding of life. She took all his shame away and turned it into something useful.

She set off for the gate at exactly ten o'clock, escaping without drawing Mrs. Hopewell's attention. She didn't take anything to eat, forgetting that food is usually taken on a picnic. She wore a pair of slacks and a dirty white shirt, and as an afterthought, she had put some Vapex on the collar of it since she did not own any perfume. When she reached the gate no one was there.

She looked up and down the empty highway and had the furious feeling that she had been tricked, that he had only meant to make her walk to the gate after the idea of him. Then suddenly he stood up, very tall, from behind a bush on the opposite embankment. Smiling, he lifted his hat which was new and wide-brimmed. He had not worn it yesterday and she wondered if he had bought it for the occasion. It was toast-colored with a red and white band around it and was slightly too large for him. He stepped from behind the bush still carrying the black valise. He had on the same suit and the same yellow socks sucked down in his shoes from walking. He crossed the highway and said, "I knew you'd come!"

The girl wondered acidly how he had known this. She pointed to the valise and asked, "Why did you bring your Bibles?"

95 He took her elbow, smiling down on her as if he could not stop. "You can never tell when you'll need the word of God, Hulga," he said. She had a moment in which she doubted that this was actually happening and then they began to climb the embankment. They went down into the pasture toward the woods. The boy walked lightly by her side, bouncing on his toes. The valise did not seem to be heavy today; he even swung it. They crossed half the pasture without saying anything and then, putting his hand easily on the small of her back, he asked softly, "Where does your wooden leg join on?"

She turned an ugly red and glared at him and for an instant the boy looked abashed. "I didn't mean you no harm," he said. "I only meant you're so brave and all. I guess God takes care of you."

"No," she said, looking forward and walking fast, "I don't even believe in God."

At this he stopped and whistled. "No!" he exclaimed as if he were too astonished to say anything else.

She walked on and in a second he was bouncing at her side, fanning with his hat. "That's very unusual for a girl," he

remarked, watching her out of the corner of his eye. When they reached the edge of the wood, he put his hand on her back again and drew her against him without a word and kissed her heavily.

The kiss, which had more pressure 100 than feeling behind it, produced that extra surge of adrenaline in the girl that enables one to carry a packed trunk out of a burning house, but in her, the power went at once to the brain. Even before he released her, her mind, clear and detached and ironic anyway, was regarding him from a great distance, with amusement but with pity. She had never been kissed before and she was pleased to discover that it was an unexceptional experience and all a matter of the mind's control. Some people might enjoy drain water if they were told it was vodka. When the boy, looking expectant but uncertain, pushed her gently away, she turned and walked on, saying nothing as if such business, for her, were common enough.

He came along panting at her side, trying to help her when he saw a root that she might trip over. He caught and held back the long swaying blades of thorn vine until she had passed beyond them. She led the way and he came breathing heavily behind her. Then they came out on a sunlit hillside, sloping softly into another one a little smaller. Beyond, they could see the rusted top of the old barn where the extra hay was stored.

The hill was sprinkled with small pink weeds. "Then you ain't saved?" he asked suddenly, stopping.

The girl smiled. It was the first time she had smiled at him at all. "In my economy," she said, "I'm saved and you are damned but I told you I didn't believe in God."

Nothing seemed to destroy the boy's look of admiration. He gazed at her now as if the fantastic animal at the zoo had put its paw through the bars and given him a loving poke. She thought he looked as if he wanted to kiss her again and she walked on before he had the chance.

105   "Ain't there somewheres we can sit down sometime?" he murmured, his voice softening toward the end of the sentence.

    "In that barn," she said.

    They made for it rapidly as if it might slide away like a train. It was a large two-story barn, cool and dark inside. The boy pointed up the ladder that led into the loft and said, "It's too bad we can't go up there."

    "Why can't we?" she asked.

    "Yer leg," he said reverently.

110   The girl gave him a contemptuous look and putting both hands on the ladder, she climbed it while he stood below, apparently awestruck. She pulled herself expertly through the opening and then looked down at him and said, "Well, come on if you're coming," and he began to climb the ladder, awkwardly bringing the suitcase with him.

    "We won't need the Bible," she observed.

    "You never can tell," he said, panting. After he had got into the loft, he was a few seconds catching his breath. She had sat down in a pile of straw. A wide sheath of sunlight, filled with dust particles, slanted over her. She lay back against a bale, her face turned away, looking out the front opening of the barn where hay was thrown from a wagon into the loft. The two pink-speckled hillsides lay back against a dark ridge of woods. The sky was cloudless and cold blue. The boy dropped down by her side and put one arm under her and the other over her and began methodically kissing her face, making little noises like a fish. He did not remove his hat but it was pushed far enough back not to interfere. When her glasses got in his way, he took them off of her and slipped them into his pocket.

    The girl at first did not return any of the kisses but presently she began to and after she had put several on his cheek, she reached his lips and remained there, kissing him again and again as if she were trying to draw all the breath out of him. His breath was clear and sweet like a child's and the kisses were sticky like a child's. He mumbled about loving her and about knowing when he first seen her that he loved her, but the mumbling was like the sleepy fretting of a child being put to sleep by his mother. Her mind, throughout this, never stopped or lost itself for a second to her feelings. "You ain't said you loved me none," he whispered finally, pulling back from her. "You got to say that."

    She looked away from him off into the hollow sky and then down at a black ridge and then down farther into what appeared to be two green swelling lakes. She didn't realize he had taken her glasses but this landscape could not seem exceptional to her for she seldom paid any close attention to her surroundings.

    "You got to say it," he repeated. "You 115 got to say you love me."

    She was always careful how she committed herself. "In a sense," she began, "if you use the word loosely, you might say that. But it's not a word I use. I don't have illusions. I'm one of those people who see *through* to nothing."

    The boy was frowning. "You got to say it. I said it and you got to say it," he said.

    The girl looked at him almost tenderly. "You poor baby," she murmured. "It's just as well you don't understand," and she pulled him by the neck, face-down, against her. "We are all damned," she said, "but some of us have taken off our blindfolds and see that there's nothing to see. It's a kind of salvation."

    The boy's astonished eyes looked blankly through the ends of her hair. "Okay," he almost whined, "but do you love me or don'tcher?"

    "Yes," she said and added, "in a sense. 120 But I must tell you something. There mustn't be anything dishonest between us." She lifted his head and looked him in the eye. "I am thirty years old," she said. "I have a number of degrees."

The boy's look was irritated but dogged. "I don't care," he said. "I don't care a thing about what all you done. I just want to know if you love me or don'tcher?" and he caught her to him and wildly planted her face with kisses until she said, "Yes, yes."

"Okay then," he said, letting her go. "Prove it."

She smiled, looking dreamily out on the shifty landscape. She had seduced him without even making up her mind to try. "How?" she asked, feeling that he should be delayed a little.

He leaned over and put his lips to her ear. "Show me where your wooden leg joins on," he whispered.

125 The girl uttered a sharp little cry and her face instantly drained of color. The obscenity of the suggestion was not what shocked her. As a child she had sometimes been subject to feelings of shame but education had removed the last traces of that as a good surgeon scrapes for cancer; she would no more have felt it over what he was asking than she would have believed in his Bible. But she was as sensitive about the artificial leg as a peacock about his tail. No one ever touched it but her. She took care of it as someone else would his soul, in private and almost with her own eyes turned away. "No," she said.

"I known it," he muttered, sitting up. "You're just playing me for a sucker."

"Oh no no!" she cried. "It joins on at the knee. Only at the knee. Why do you want to see it?"

The boy gave her a long penetrating look. "Because," he said, "it's what makes you different. You ain't like anybody else."

She sat staring at him. There was nothing about her face or her round freezing-blue eyes to indicate that this had moved her; but she felt as if her heart had stopped and left her mind to pump her blood. She decided that for the first time in her life she was face to face with real innocence. This boy, with an instinct that came from beyond wisdom, had touched the truth about her. When after a minute, she said in a hoarse high voice, "All right," it was like surrendering to him completely. It was like losing her own life and finding it again, miraculously, in his.

Very gently he began to roll the slack 130 leg up. The artificial limb, in a white sock and brown flat shoe, was bound in a heavy material like canvas and ended in an ugly jointure where it was attached to the stump. The boy's face and his voice were entirely reverent as he uncovered it and said, "Now show me how to take it off and on."

She took it off for him and put it back on again and then he took it off himself, handling it as tenderly as if it were a real one. "See!" he said with a delighted child's face. "Now I can do it myself!"

"Put it back on," she said. She was thinking that she would run away with him and that every night he would take the leg off and every morning put it back on again. "Put it back on," she said.

"Not yet," he murmured, setting it on its foot out of her reach. "Leave it off for a while. You got me instead."

She gave a little cry of alarm but he pushed her down and began to kiss her again. Without the leg she felt entirely dependent on him. Her brain seemed to have stopped thinking altogether and to be about some other function that it was not very good at. Different expressions raced back and forth over her face. Every now and then the boy, his eyes like two steel spikes, would glance behind him where the leg stood. Finally she pushed him off and said, "Put it back on me now."

"Wait," he said. He leaned the other 135 way and pulled the valise toward him and opened it. It had a pale blue spotted lining and there were only two Bibles in it. He took one of these out and opened the cover of it. It was hollow and contained a pocket flask of whiskey, a pack of cards, and a small blue box with printing on it. He laid these out in front of her one at a time in an evenly-spaced row, like one presenting offerings at the shrine of a goddess. He put the blue box in her hand. THIS PRODUCT TO BE USED ONLY FOR THE PREVENTION OF DISEASE, she read, and dropped it. The boy was unscrewing the top of the flask. He stopped and pointed, with a smile, to the deck of cards. It was not an ordinary deck but one with an obscene picture on the back of each card. "Take a swig," he said, offering her the bottle first. He held it in front of her, but like one mesmerized, she did not move.

Her voice when she spoke had an almost pleading sound. "Aren't you," she murmured, "aren't you just good country people?"

The boy cocked his head. He looked as if he were just beginning to understand that she might be trying to insult him. "Yeah," he said, curling his lip slightly, "but it ain't held me back none. I'm as good as you any day in the week."

"Give me my leg," she said.

He pushed it farther away with his foot. "Come on now, let's begin to have us a good time," he said coaxingly. "We ain't got to know one another good yet."

140 "Give me my leg!" she screamed and tried to lunge for it but he pushed her down easily.

"What's the matter with you all of a sudden?" he asked, frowning as he screwed the top on the flask and put it quickly back inside the Bible. "You just a while ago said you didn't believe in nothing. I thought you was some girl!"

Her face was almost purple. "You're a Christian!" she hissed. "You're a fine Christian! You're just like them all—say one

thing and do another. You're a perfect Christian, you're . . ."

The boy's mouth was set angrily. "I hope you don't think," he said in a lofty indignant tone, "that I believe in that crap! I may sell Bibles but I know which end is up and I wasn't born yesterday and I know where I'm going!"

"Give me my leg!" she screeched. He jumped up so quickly that she barely saw him sweep the cards and the blue box into the Bible and throw the Bible into the valise. She saw him grab the leg and then she saw it for an instant slanted forlornly across the inside of the suitcase with a Bible at either side of its opposite ends. He slammed the lid shut and snatched up the valise and swung it down the hole and then stepped through himself.

When all of him had passed but his 145 head, he turned and regarded her with a look that no longer had any admiration in it. "I've gotten a lot of interesting things," he said. "One time I got a woman's glass eye this way. And you needn't to think you'll catch me because Pointer ain't really my name. I use a different name at every house I call at and don't stay nowhere long. And I'll tell you another thing, Hulga," he said, using the name as if he didn't think much of it, "you ain't so smart. I been believing in nothing ever since I was born!" and then the toast-colored hat disappeared down the hole and the girl was left, sitting on the straw in the dusty sunlight. When she turned her churning face toward the opening, she saw his blue figure struggling successfully over the green speckled lake.

Mrs. Hopewell and Mrs. Freeman, who were in the back pasture, digging up onions, saw him emerge a little later from the woods and head across the meadow toward the highway. "Why, that looks like that nice dull young man that tried to sell me a Bible yesterday," Mrs. Hopewell said, squinting. "He must have been selling them to the Negroes back in there. He was so simple," she said, "but I guess the world would be better off if we were all that simple."

Mrs. Freeman's gaze drove forward and just touched him before he disappeared under the hill. Then she returned her attention to the evil-smelling onion shoot she was lifting from the ground. "Some can't be that simple," she said. "I know I never could."

····•▶ *Your* **Turn**
Talking and Writing about Lit

1. In "Good Country People," why does Joy/Hulga have two names? How does this device assist O'Connor in conveying characterization of the daughter?

2. Explain the irony of the story's title. What other examples of irony can you identify in the story?

3. Write an essay exploring the similarities and contrasts between Manley Pointer in "Good Country People" and Arnold Friend in "Where Are You Going, Where Have You Been?" by Joyce Carol Oates (Chapter 12).

4. **DIY** Editors can often have an interesting and positive influence on a book or piece of writing. This is true of the book you hold in your hands now (*Access Literature*), and it's also true of some of Flannery O'Connor's stories. The ending (the last two paragraphs) of "Good Country People" was actually added at the suggestion of her editor Robert Giroux. Originally, O'Connor had written a very different ending. Reread the existing ending, and then write a new ending for the story yourself, an ending that would put a different spin on the story's meaning.

A Good Man Is Hard to Find (1955)

The grandmother didn't want to go to Florida. She wanted to visit some of her connections in east Tennessee and she was seizing at every chance to change Bailey's mind. Bailey was the son she lived with, her only boy. He was sitting on the edge of his chair at the table, bent over the orange sports section of the *Journal*. "Now look here, Bailey," she said, "see here, read this," and she stood with one hand on her thin hip and the other rattling the newspaper at his bald head. "Here this fellow that calls himself The Misfit is aloose from the Federal Pen and headed toward Florida and you read here what it says he did to these people. Just you read it. I wouldn't take my children in any direction with a criminal like that aloose in it. I couldn't answer to my conscience if I did."

Bailey didn't look up from his reading so she wheeled around then and faced the children's mother, a young woman in slacks, whose face was as broad and innocent as a cabbage and was tied around with a green head-kerchief that had two points on the top like rabbit's ears. She was sitting on the sofa, feeding the baby his apricots out of a jar. "The children have been to Florida before," the old lady said. "You all ought to take them somewhere else for a change so they would see different parts of the world and be broad. They never have been to east Tennessee."

The children's mother didn't seem to hear her but the eight-year-old boy, John Wesley, a stocky child with glasses, said, "If you don't want to go to Florida, why dontcha stay at home?" He and the little girl, June Star, were reading the funny papers on the floor.

"She wouldn't stay at home to be queen for a day," June Star said without raising her yellow head.

5   "Yes and what would you do if this fellow, The Misfit, caught you?" the grandmother said.

"I'd smack his face," John Wesley said.

"She wouldn't stay at home for a million bucks," June Star said. "Afraid she'd miss something. She has to go everywhere we go."

"All right, Miss," the grandmother said. "Just remember that the next time you want me to curl your hair."

June Star said her hair was naturally curly.

10   The next morning the grandmother was the first one in the car, ready to go. She had her big black valise that looked like the head of a hippopotamus in one corner, and underneath it she was hiding a basket with Pitty Sing, the cat, in it. She didn't intend for the cat to be left alone in the house for three days because he would miss her too much and she was afraid he might brush against one of the gas burners and accidentally asphyxiate himself. Her son, Bailey, didn't like to arrive at a motel with a cat.

She sat in the middle of the back seat with John Wesley and June Star on either side

of her. Bailey and the children's mother and the baby sat in front and they left Atlanta at eight forty-five with the mileage on the car at 55890. The grandmother wrote this down because she thought it would be interesting to say how many miles they had been when they got back. It took them twenty minutes to reach the outskirts of the city.

The old lady settled herself comfortably, removing her white cotton gloves and putting them up with her purse on the shelf in front of the back window. The children's mother still had on slacks and still had her hair tied up in a green kerchief, but the grandmother had on a navy blue straw sailor hat with a bunch of white violets on the brim and a navy blue dress with a small white dot in the print. Her collars and cuffs were white organdy trimmed with lace and at her neckline she had pinned a purple spray of cloth violets containing a sachet. In case of an accident, anyone seeing her dead on the highway would know at once that she was a lady.

She said she thought it was going to be a good day for driving, neither too hot nor too cold, and she cautioned Bailey that the speed limit was fifty-five miles an hour and that the patrolmen hid themselves behind billboards and small clumps of trees and sped out after you before you had a chance to slow down. She pointed out interesting details of the scenery: Stone Mountain; the blue granite that in some places came up to both sides of the highway; the brilliant red clay banks slightly streaked with purple; and the various crops that made rows of green lace-work on the ground. The trees were full of silver-white sunlight and the meanest of them sparkled. The children were reading comic magazines and their mother had gone back to sleep.

"Let's go through Georgia fast so we won't have to look at it much," John Wesley said.

"If I were a little boy," said the grand- 15 mother, "I wouldn't talk about my native state that way. Tennessee has the mountains and Georgia has the hills."

"Tennessee is just a hillbilly dumping ground," John Wesley said, "and Georgia is a lousy state too."

"You said it," June Star said.

"In my time," said the grandmother, folding her thin veined fingers, "children were more respectful of their native states and their parents and everything else. People did right then. Oh look at the cute little pickaninny!" she said and pointed to a Negro child standing in the door of a shack. "Wouldn't that make a picture, now?" she asked and they all turned and looked at the little Negro out of the back window. He waved.

"He didn't have any britches on," June Star said.

20 "He probably didn't have any," the grandmother explained. "Little niggers in the country don't have things like we do. If I could paint, I'd paint that picture," she said.

The children exchanged comic books.

The grandmother offered to hold the baby and the children's mother passed him over the front seat to her. She set him on her knee and bounced him and told him about the things they were passing. She rolled her eyes and screwed up her mouth and stuck her leathery thin face into his smooth bland one. Occasionally he gave her a faraway smile. They passed a large cotton field with five or six graves fenced in the middle of it, like a small island. "Look at the graveyard!" the grandmother said, pointing it out. "That was the old family burying ground. That belonged to the plantation."

"Where's the plantation?" John Wesley asked.

"Gone With the Wind," said the grandmother. "Ha. Ha."

25 When the children finished all the comic books they had brought, they opened the lunch and ate it. The grandmother ate a peanut butter sandwich and an olive and would not let the children throw the box and the paper napkins out the window. When there was nothing else to do they played a game by choosing a cloud and making the other two guess what shape it suggested. John Wesley took one the shape of a cow and June Star guessed a cow and John Wesley said, no, an automobile, and June Star said he didn't play fair, and they began to slap each other over the grandmother.

The grandmother said she would tell them a story if they would keep quiet. When she told a story, she rolled her eyes and waved her head and was very dramatic. She said once when she was a maiden lady she had been courted by a Mr. Edgar Atkins Teagarden from Jasper, Georgia. She said he was a very good-looking man and a gentleman and that he brought her a watermelon every Saturday afternoon with his initials cut in it, E. A. T. Well, one Saturday, she said, Mr. Teagarden brought the watermelon and there was nobody at home and he left it on the front porch and returned in his buggy to Jasper, but she never got the watermelon, she said, because a nigger boy ate it when he saw the initials, E. A. T.! This story tickled John Wesley's funny bone and he giggled and giggled but June Star didn't think it was any good. She said she wouldn't marry a man that just brought her a watermelon on Saturday. The grandmother said she would have done well to marry Mr. Teagarden because he was a gentleman and had bought Coca-Cola stock when it first came out and that he had died only a few years ago, a very wealthy man.

They stopped at The Tower for barbecued sandwiches. The Tower was a part stucco and part wood filling station and dance hall set in a clearing outside of Timothy. A fat man named Red Sammy Butts ran it and there were signs stuck here and there on the building and for miles up and down the highway saying, TRY RED SAMMY'S FAMOUS BARBEQUE. NONE LIKE FAMOUS RED SAMMY'S! RED SAM! THE FAT BOY WITH THE HAPPY LAUGH! A VETERAN! RED SAMMY'S YOUR MAN!

Red Sammy was lying on the bare ground outside The Tower with his head under a truck while a gray monkey about a foot high, chained to a small chinaberry tree, chattered nearby. The monkey sprang back into the tree and got on the highest limb as soon as he saw the children jump out of the car and run toward him.

Inside, The Tower was a long dark room with a counter at one end and tables at the other and dancing space in the middle. They all sat down at a board table next to the nickelodeon and Red Sam's wife, a tall burnt-brown woman with hair and eyes lighter than her skin, came and took their order. The children's mother put a dime in the machine and played "The Tennessee Waltz," and the grandmother said that tune always made her want to dance. She asked Bailey if he would like to dance but he only glared at her. He didn't have a naturally sunny disposition like she did and trips made him nervous. The grandmother's brown eyes were very bright. She swayed her head from side to side and pretended she was dancing in her chair. June Star said play something she could tap to so the children's mother put in another dime and played a fast number and June Star stepped out onto the dance floor and did her tap routine.

30 "Ain't she cute?" Red Sam's wife said, leaning over the counter. "Would you like to come be my little girl?"

"No I certainly wouldn't," June Star said. "I wouldn't live in a broken-down place like this for a million bucks!" and she ran back to the table.

"Ain't she cute?" the woman repeated, stretching her mouth politely.

"Aren't you ashamed?" hissed the grandmother.

Red Sam came in and told his wife to quit lounging on the counter and hurry up with these people's order. His khaki trousers reached just to his hip bones and his stomach hung over them like a sack of meal swaying under his shirt. He came over and sat down at a table nearby and let out a combination sigh and yodel. "You can't win," he said. "You can't win," and he wiped his sweating red face off with a gray handkerchief. "These days you don't know who to trust," he said. "Ain't that the truth?"

"People are certainly not nice like they 35 used to be," said the grandmother.

"Two fellers come in here last week," Red Sammy said, "driving a Chrysler. It was a old beat-up car but it was a good one and these boys looked all right to me. Said they worked at the mill and you know I let them fellers charge the gas they bought? Now why did I do that?"

"Because you're a good man!" the grandmother said at once.

"Yes'm, I suppose so," Red Sam said as if he were struck with this answer.

His wife brought the orders, carrying the five plates all at once without a tray, two in each hand and one balanced on her arm. "It isn't a soul in this green world of God's that you can trust," she said. "And I don't count nobody out of that, not nobody," she repeated, looking at Red Sammy.

"Did you read about that criminal, 40 The Misfit, that's escaped?" asked the grandmother.

"I wouldn't be a bit surprised if he didn't attact this place right here," said the woman. "If he hears about it being here, I wouldn't be none surprised to see him. If he hears it's two cent in the cash register, I wouldn't be atall surprised if he . . ."

"That'll do," Red Sam said. "Go bring these people their Co'-Colas," and the woman went off to get the rest of the order.

"A good man is hard to find," Red Sammy said. "Everything is getting terrible. I remember the day you could go off and leave your screen door unlatched. Not no more."

He and the grandmother discussed better times. The old lady said that in her opinion Europe was entirely to blame for the way things were now. She said the way Europe acted you would think we were made of money and Red Sam said it was no use talking about it, she was exactly right. The children ran outside into the white sunlight and looked at the monkey in the lacy chinaberry tree. He was busy catching fleas on himself and biting each one carefully between his teeth as if it were a delicacy.

45 They drove off again into the hot afternoon. The grandmother took cat naps and woke up every few minutes with her own snoring. Outside of Toombsboro she woke up and recalled an old plantation that she had visited in this neighborhood once when she was a young lady. She said the house had six white columns across the front and that there was an avenue of oaks leading up to it and two little wooden trellis arbors on either side in front where you sat down with your suitor after a stroll in the garden. She recalled exactly which road to turn off to get to it. She knew that Bailey would not be willing to lose any time looking at an old house, but the more she talked about it, the more she wanted to see it once again and find out if the little twin arbors were still standing. "There was a secret panel in this house," she said craftily, not telling the truth but wishing that she were, "and the story went that all the family silver was hidden in it when Sherman came through but it was never found . . ."

"Hey!" John Wesley said. "Let's go see it! We'll find it! We'll poke all the woodwork and find it! Who lives there? Where do you turn off at? Hey Pop, can't we turn off there?"

"We never have seen a house with a secret panel!" June Star shrieked. "Let's go to the house with the secret panel! Hey Pop, can't we go see the house with the secret panel!"

"It's not far from here, I know," the grandmother said. "It wouldn't take over twenty minutes."

Bailey was looking straight ahead. His jaw was as rigid as a horseshoe. "No," he said.

50 The children began to yell and scream that they wanted to see the house with the secret panel. John Wesley kicked the back of the front seat and June Star hung over her mother's shoulder and whined desperately into her ear that they never had any fun even on their vacation, that they could never do what THEY wanted to do. The baby began to scream and John Wesley kicked the back of the seat so hard that his father could feel the blows in his kidney.

"All right!" he shouted and drew the car to a stop at the side of the road. "Will you all shut up? Will you all just shut up for one second? If you don't shut up, we won't go anywhere."

"It would be very educational for them," the grandmother murmured.

"All right," Bailey said, "but get this: this is the only time we're going to stop for anything like this. This is the one and only time."

"The dirt road that you have to turn down is about a mile back," the grandmother directed. "I marked it when we passed."

"A dirt road," Bailey groaned. 55

After they had turned around and were headed toward the dirt road, the grandmother recalled other points about the house, the beautiful glass over the front doorway and the candle-lamp in the hall. John Wesley said that the secret panel was probably in the fireplace.

"You can't go inside this house," Bailey said. "You don't know who lives there."

"While you all talk to the people in front, I'll run around behind and get in a window," John Wesley suggested.

"We'll all stay in the car," his mother said.

60 They turned onto the dirt road and the car raced roughly along in a swirl of pink dust. The grandmother recalled the times when there were no paved roads and thirty miles was a day's journey. The dirt road was hilly and there were sudden washes in it and sharp curves on dangerous embankments. All at once they would be on a hill, looking down over the blue tops of trees for miles around, then the next minute, they would be in a red depression with the dust-coated trees looking down on them.

"This place had better turn up in a minute," Bailey said, "or I'm going to turn around."

The road looked as if no one had traveled on it for months.

"It's not much farther," the grandmother said and just as she said it, a horrible thought came to her. The thought was so embarrassing that she turned red in the face and her eyes dilated and her feet jumped up, upsetting her valise in the corner. The instant the valise moved, the newspaper top she had over the basket under it rose with a snarl and Pitty Sing, the cat, sprang onto Bailey's shoulder.

The children were thrown to the floor and their mother, clutching the baby, was thrown out the door onto the ground; the old lady was thrown into the front seat. The car turned over once and landed right-side-up in a gulch off the side of the road. Bailey remained in the driver's seat with the cat—gray-striped with a broad white face and an orange nose—clinging to his neck like a caterpillar.

65 As soon as the children saw they could move their arms and legs, they scrambled out of the car, shouting, "We've had an ACCIDENT!" The grandmother was curled up under the dashboard, hoping she was injured so that Bailey's wrath would not come down on her all at once. The horrible thought she had had before the accident was that the house she had remembered so vividly was not in Georgia but in Tennessee.

Bailey removed the cat from his neck with both hands and flung it out the window against the side of a pine tree. Then he got out of the car and started looking for the children's mother. She was sitting against the side of the red gutted ditch, holding the screaming baby, but she only had a cut down her face and a broken shoulder. "We've had an ACCIDENT!" the children screamed in a frenzy of delight.

"But nobody's killed," June Star said with disappointment as the grandmother limped out of the car, her hat still pinned to her head but the broken front brim standing up at a jaunty angle and the violet spray hanging off the side. They all sat down in the ditch, except the children, to recover from the shock. They were all shaking.

"Maybe a car will come along," said the children's mother hoarsely.

"I believe I have injured an organ," said the grandmother, pressing her side, but no one answered her. Bailey's teeth were clattering. He had on a yellow sport shirt with bright blue parrots designed in it and his face was as yellow as the shirt. The grandmother decided that she would not mention that the house was in Tennessee.

70 The road was about ten feet above and they could see only the tops of the trees on the other side of it. Behind the ditch they were sitting in there were more woods, tall and dark and deep. In a few minutes they saw a car some distance away on top of a hill, coming slowly as if the occupants were watching them. The grandmother stood up and waved both arms dramatically to attract their attention. The car continued to come

on slowly, disappeared around a bend and appeared again, moving even slower, on top of the hill they had gone over. It was a big black battered hearse-like automobile. There were three men in it.

It came to a stop just over them and for some minutes, the driver looked down with a steady expressionless gaze to where they were sitting, and didn't speak. Then he turned his head and muttered something to the other two and they got out. One was a fat boy in black trousers and a red sweat shirt with a silver stallion embossed on the front of it. He moved around on the right side of them and stood staring, his mouth partly open in a kind of loose grin. The other had on khaki pants and a blue striped coat and a gray hat pulled down very low, hiding most of his face. He came around slowly on the left side. Neither spoke.

The driver got out of the car and stood by the side of it, looking down at them. He was an older man than the other two. His hair was just beginning to gray and he wore silver-rimmed spectacles that gave him a scholarly look. He had a long creased face and didn't have on any shirt or undershirt. He had on blue jeans that were too tight for him and was holding a black hat and a gun. The two boys also had guns.

"We've had an ACCIDENT!" the children screamed.

The grandmother had the peculiar feeling that the bespectacled man was someone she knew. His face was as familiar to her as if she had known him all her life but she could not recall who he was. He moved away from the car and began to come down the embankment, placing his feet carefully so that he wouldn't slip. He had on tan and white shoes and no socks, and his ankles were red and thin. "Good afternoon," he said. "I see you all had you a little spill."

75 "We turned over twice!" said the grandmother.

"Oncet," he corrected. "We seen it happen. Try their car and see will it run, Hiram," he said quietly to the boy with the gray hat.

"What you got that gun for?" John Wesley asked. "Whatcha gonna do with that gun?"

"Lady," the man said to the children's mother, "would you mind calling them children to sit down by you? Children make me nervous. I want all you all to sit down right together there where you're at."

"What are you telling US what to do for?" June Star asked.

Behind them the line of woods gaped 80 like a dark open mouth. "Come here," said their mother.

"Look here now," Bailey began suddenly, "we're in a predicament! We're in . . ."

The grandmother shrieked. She scrambled to her feet and stood staring. "You're The Misfit!" she said. "I recognized you at once!"

"Yes'm," the man said, smiling slightly as if he were pleased in spite of himself to be known, "but it would have been better for all of you, lady, if you hadn't of reckernized me."

Bailey turned his head sharply and said something to his mother that shocked even the children. The old lady began to cry and The Misfit reddened.

"Lady," he said, "don't you get upset. 85 Sometimes a man says things he don't mean. I don't reckon he meant to talk to you thataway."

"You wouldn't shoot a lady, would you?" the grandmother said and removed a clean handkerchief from her cuff and began to slap at her eyes with it.

The Misfit pointed the toe of his shoe into the ground and made a little hole and then covered it up again. "I would hate to have to," he said.

"Listen," the grandmother almost screamed, "I know you're a good man. You don't look a bit like you have common blood. I know you must come from nice people!"

"Yes mam," he said, "finest people in the world." When he smiled he showed a row of strong white teeth. "God never made a finer woman than my mother and my daddy's heart was pure gold," he said. The boy with the red sweat shirt had come around behind them and was standing with his gun at his hip. The Misfit squatted down on the ground. "Watch them children, Bobby Lee," he said. "You know they make me nervous." He looked at the six of them huddled together in front of him and he seemed to be embarrassed as if he couldn't think of anything to say. "Ain't a cloud in the sky," he remarked, looking up at it. "Don't see no sun but don't see no cloud neither."

90 "Yes, it's a beautiful day," said the grandmother. "Listen," she said, "you shouldn't call yourself The Misfit because I know you're a good man at heart. I can just look at you and tell."

"Hush!" Bailey yelled. "Hush! Everybody shut up and let me handle this!" He was squatting in the position of a runner about to sprint forward but he didn't move.

"I pre-chate that, lady," The Misfit said and drew a little circle in the ground with the butt of his gun.

"It'll take a half a hour to fix this here car," Hiram called, looking over the raised hood of it.

"Well, first you and Bobby Lee get him and that little boy to step over yonder with you," The Misfit said, pointing to Bailey and John Wesley. "The boys want to ast you something," he said to Bailey. "Would you mind stepping back in them woods there with them?"

95 "Listen," Bailey began, "we're in a terrible predicament! Nobody realizes what this is," and his voice cracked. His eyes were as blue and intense as the parrots in his shirt and he remained perfectly still.

The grandmother reached up to adjust her hat brim as if she were going to the woods with him but it came off in her hand. She stood staring at it and after a second she let it fall on the ground. Hiram pulled Bailey up by the arm as if he were assisting an old man. John Wesley caught hold of his father's hand and Bobby Lee followed. They went off toward the woods and just as they reached the dark edge, Bailey turned and supporting himself against a gray naked pine trunk, he shouted, "I'll be back in a minute, Mamma, wait on me!"

"Come back this instant!" his mother shrilled but they all disappeared into the woods.

"Bailey Boy!" the grandmother called in a tragic voice but she found she was looking at The Misfit squatting on the ground in front of her. "I just know you're a good man," she said desperately. "You're not a bit common!"

"Nome, I ain't a good man," The Misfit said after a second as if he had considered her statement carefully, "but I ain't the worst in the world neither. My daddy said I was a different breed of dog from my brothers and sisters. 'You know,' Daddy said, 'it's some that can live their whole life out without asking about it and it's others has to know why it is, and this boy is one of the latters. He's going to be into everything!'" He put on his black hat and looked up suddenly and then away deep into the woods as if he were embarrassed again. "I'm sorry I don't have on a shirt before you ladies," he said, hunching his shoulders slightly. "We buried our clothes that we had on when we escaped and we're just making do until we can get better. We borrowed these from some folks we met," he explained.

"That's perfectly all right," the grandmother said. "Maybe Bailey has an extra shirt in his suitcase." 100

"I'll look and see terrectly," The Misfit said.

"Where are they taking him?" the children's mother screamed.

"Daddy was a card himself," The Misfit said. "You couldn't put anything over on him. He never got in trouble with the Authorities though. Just had the knack of handling them."

"You could be honest too if you'd only try," said the grandmother. "Think how wonderful it would be to settle down and live a comfortable life and not have to think about somebody chasing you all the time."

105   The Misfit kept scratching in the ground with the butt of his gun as if he were thinking about it. "Yes'm, somebody is always after you," he murmured.

The grandmother noticed how thin his shoulder blades were just behind his hat because she was standing up looking down on him. "Do you ever pray?" she asked.

He shook his head. All she saw was the black hat wiggle between his shoulder blades. "Nome," he said.

There was a pistol shot from the woods, followed closely by another. Then silence. The old lady's head jerked around. She could hear the wind move through the tree tops like a long satisfied insuck of breath. "Bailey Boy!" she called.

"I was a gospel singer for a while," The Misfit said. "I been most everything. Been in the arm service, both land and sea, at home and abroad, been twict married, been an undertaker, been with the railroads, plowed Mother Earth, been in a tornado, seen a man burnt alive oncet," and looked up at the children's mother and the little girl who were sitting close together, their faces white and their eyes glassy; "I even seen a woman flogged," he said.

110   "Pray, pray," the grandmother began, "pray, pray . . ."

"I never was a bad boy that I remember of," The Misfit said in an almost dreamy voice, "but somewheres along the line I done something wrong and got sent to the penitentiary. I was buried alive," and he looked up and held her attention to him by a steady stare.

"That's when you should have started to pray," she said. "What did you do to get sent to the penitentiary that first time?"

"Turn to the right, it was a wall," The Misfit said, looking up again at the cloudless sky. "Turn to the left, it was a wall. Look up it was a ceiling, look down it was a floor. I forget what I done, lady. I set there and set there, trying to remember what it was I done and I ain't recalled it to this day. Oncet in a while, I would think it was coming to me, but it never come."

"Maybe they put you in by mistake," the old lady said vaguely.

"Nome," he said. "It wasn't no mis-   115 take. They had the papers on me."

"You must have stolen something," she said.

The Misfit sneered slightly. "Nobody had nothing I wanted," he said. "It was a head-doctor at the penitentiary said what I had done was kill my daddy but I known that for a lie. My daddy died in nineteen ought nineteen of the epidemic flu and I never had a thing to do with it. He was buried in the Mount Hopewell Baptist churchyard and you can go there and see for yourself."

"If you would pray," the old lady said, "Jesus would help you."

"That's right," The Misfit said.

"Well then, why don't you pray?" she   120 asked trembling with delight suddenly.

"I don't want no hep," he said. "I'm doing all right by myself."

Bobby Lee and Hiram came ambling back from the woods. Bobby Lee was dragging a yellow shirt with bright blue parrots in it.

"Thow me that shirt, Bobby Lee," The Misfit said. The shirt came flying at him and landed on his shoulder and he put it on. The grandmother couldn't name what the shirt reminded her of. "No, lady," The Misfit said while he was buttoning it up, "I found out the crime don't matter. You can do one thing or you can do another, kill a man or take a tire off his car, because sooner or later you're going to forget what it was you done and just be punished for it."

The children's mother had begun to make heaving noises as if she couldn't get her breath. "Lady," he asked, "would you and that little girl like to step off yonder with Bobby Lee and Hiram and join your husband?"

125 "Yes, thank you," the mother said faintly. Her left arm dangled helplessly and she was holding the baby, who had gone to sleep, in the other. "Hep that lady up, Hiram," The Misfit said as she struggled to climb out of the ditch, "and Bobby Lee, you hold onto that little girl's hand."

"I don't want to hold hands with him," June Star said. "He reminds me of a pig."

The fat boy blushed and laughed and caught her by the arm and pulled her off into the woods after Hiram and her mother.

Alone with The Misfit, the grandmother found that she had lost her voice. There was not a cloud in the sky nor any sun. There was nothing around her but woods. She wanted to tell him that he must pray. She opened and closed her mouth several times before anything came out. Finally she found herself saying, "Jesus, Jesus," meaning, Jesus will help you, but the way she was saying it, it sounded as if she might be cursing.

"Yes'm," The Misfit said as if he agreed. "Jesus thown everything off balance. It was the same case with Him as with

me except He hadn't committed any crime and they could prove I had committed one because they had the papers on me. Of course," he said, "they never shown me my papers. That's why I sign myself now. I said long ago, you get you a signature and sign everything you do and keep a copy of it. Then you'll know what you done and you can hold up the crime to the punishment and see do they match and in the end you'll have something to prove you ain't been treated right. I call myself The Misfit," he said, "because I can't make what all I done wrong fit what all I gone through in punishment."

There was a piercing scream from the 130 woods, followed closely by a pistol report. "Does it seem right to you, lady, that one is punished a heap and another ain't punished at all?"

"Jesus!" the old lady cried. "You've got good blood! I know you wouldn't shoot a lady! I know you come from nice people! Pray! Jesus, you ought not to shoot a lady. I'll give you all the money I've got!"

"Lady," The Misfit said, looking beyond her far into the woods, "there never was a body that give the undertaker a tip."

There were two more pistol reports and the grandmother raised her head like a parched old turkey hen crying for water and called, "Bailey Boy, Bailey Boy!" as if her heart would break.

"Jesus was the only One that ever raised the dead." The Misfit continued, "and He shouldn't have done it. He thrown everything off balance. If He did what He said, then it's nothing for you to do but throw away everything and follow Him, and if He didn't, then it's nothing for you to do but enjoy the few minutes you got left the best way you can—by killing somebody or burning down his house or doing some other meanness to him. No pleasure but meanness," he said and his voice had become almost a snarl.

135   "Maybe He didn't raise the dead," the old lady mumbled, not knowing what she was saying and feeling so dizzy that she sank down in the ditch with her legs twisted under her.

    "I wasn't there so I can't say He didn't," The Misfit said. "I wisht I had of been there," he said, hitting the ground with his fist. "It ain't right I wasn't there because if I had of been there I would of known. Listen lady," he said in a high voice, "if I had of been there I would of known and I wouldn't be like I am now." His voice seemed about to crack and the grandmother's head cleared for an instant. She saw the man's face twisted close to her own as if he were going to cry and she murmured, "Why you're one of my babies. You're one of my own children!" She reached out and touched him on the shoulder. The Misfit sprang back as if a snake had bitten him and shot her three times through the chest. Then he put his gun down on the ground and took off his glasses and began to clean them.

    Hiram and Bobby Lee returned from the woods and stood over the ditch, looking down at the grandmother who half sat and half lay in a puddle of blood with her legs crossed under her like a child's and her face smiling up at the cloudless sky.

    Without his glasses, The Misfit's eyes were red-rimmed and pale and defenseless-looking. "Take her off and throw her where you thrown the others," he said, picking up the cat that was rubbing itself against his leg.

    "She was a talker, wasn't she?" Bobby Lee said, sliding down the ditch with a yodel.

    "She would of been a good woman," 140 The Misfit said, "if it had been somebody there to shoot her every minute of her life."

    "Some fun!" Bobby Lee said.

    "Shut up, Bobby Lee," The Misfit said. "It's no real pleasure in life."

·····▶ *Your* **Turn**

Thinking and Writing about Lit

1. In O'Connor's "A Good Man Is Hard to Find," what purpose does the stop at Red Sammy's have in terms of advancing the plot of the story?

2. Some readers complain that there are no likable characters in "A Good Man Is Hard to Find." Do you think that is a problem, or do you think it is a deliberate part of O'Connor's plan?

3. **DIY** What would happen if you changed one of the characters in the story to be "the good man (or woman)" that is hard to find? Which character would you alter to be a "good" character with whom many readers could identify? How would this change in characterization affect the meaning of the story?

Parker's Back (1965)

Parker's wife was sitting on the front porch floor, snapping beans. Parker was sitting on the step, some distance away, watching her sullenly. She was plain, plain. The skin on her face was thin and drawn as tight as the skin on an onion and her eyes were gray and sharp like the points of two icepicks. Parker understood why he had married her—he couldn't have got her any other way—but he couldn't understand why he stayed with her now. She was pregnant and pregnant women were not his favorite kind. Nevertheless, he stayed as if she had him conjured. He was puzzled and ashamed of himself.

The house they rented sat alone save for a single tall pecan tree on a high embankment overlooking a highway. At intervals a car would shoot past below and his wife's eyes would swerve suspiciously after the sound of it and then come back to rest on the newspaper full of beans in her lap. One of the things she did not approve of was automobiles. In addition to her other bad qualities, she was forever sniffing up sin. She did not smoke or dip, drink whiskey, use bad language or paint her face, and God knew some paint would have improved it, Parker thought. Her being against color, it was the more remarkable she had married him. Sometimes he supposed that she had married him because she meant to save him. At other times he had a suspicion that she actually liked everything she said she didn't. He could account for her one way or another; it was himself he could not understand.

She turned her head in his direction and said, "It's no reason you can't work for a man. It don't have to be a woman."

"Aw shut your mouth for a change," Parker muttered.

If he had been certain she was jealous 5 of the woman he worked for he would have been pleased but more likely she was concerned with the sin that would result if he and the woman took a liking to each other. He had told her that the woman was a hefty young blonde; in fact she was nearly seventy years old and too dried up to have an interest in anything except getting as much work out of him as she could. Not that an old woman didn't sometimes get an interest in a young man, particularly if he was as attractive as Parker felt he was, but this old woman looked at him the same way she looked at her old tractor—as if she had to put up with it because it was all she had. The tractor had broken down the second day Parker was on it and she had set him at once to cutting bushes, saying out of the side of her mouth to the nigger, "Everything he touches, he breaks." She also asked him to wear his shirt when he worked; Parker had removed it even though the day was not sultry; he put it back on reluctantly.

This ugly woman Parker married was his first wife. He had had other women but he had planned never to get himself tied up legally. He had first seen her one morning when his truck broke down on the highway. He had managed to pull it off the road into a neatly swept yard on which sat a peeling two-room house. He got out and opened the hood of the truck and began to study the motor. Parker had an extra sense that told him when there was a woman nearby watching him. After he had leaned over the motor a few minutes, his neck began to prickle. He cast his eye over the empty yard and porch of the house. A woman he could not see was either nearby beyond a clump of honeysuckle or in the house, watching him out the window.

Suddenly Parker began to jump up and down and fling his hand about as if he had mashed it in the machinery. He doubled over and held his hand close to his chest. "God dammit!" he hollered, "Jesus Christ in hell! Jesus God Almighty damm! God dammit to hell!" he went on, flinging out the same few oaths over and over as loud as he could.

Without warning a terrible bristly claw slammed the side of his face and he fell backwards on the hood of the truck. "You don't talk no filth here!" a voice close to him shrilled.

Parker's vision was so blurred that for an instant he thought he had been attacked by some creature from above, a giant hawk-eyed angel wielding a hoary weapon. As his sight cleared, he saw before him a tall raw-boned girl with a broom.

10 "I hurt my hand," he said. "I HURT my hand." He was so incensed that he forgot that he hadn't hurt his hand. "My hand may be broke," he growled although his voice was still unsteady.

"Lemme see it," the girl demanded.

Parker stuck out his hand and she came closer and looked at it. There was no mark on the palm and she took the hand and turned it over. Her own hand was dry and hot and rough and Parker felt himself jolted back to life by her touch. He looked more closely at her. I don't want nothing to do with this one, he thought.

The girl's sharp eyes peered at the back of the stubby reddish hand she held. There emblazoned in red and blue was a tattooed eagle perched on a cannon. Parker's sleeve was rolled to the elbow. Above the eagle a serpent was coiled about a shield and in the spaces between the eagle and the serpent there were hearts, some with arrows through them. Above the serpent there was a spread hand of cards. Every space on the skin of Parker's arm, from wrist to elbow, was covered in some loud design. The girl

gazed at this with an almost stupefied smile of shock, as if she had accidentally grasped a poisonous snake; she dropped the hand.

"I got most of my other ones in foreign parts," Parker said. "These here I mostly got in the United States. I got my first one when I was only fifteen year old."

"Don't tell me," the girl said, "I don't 15 like it. I ain't got any use for it."

"You ought to see the ones you can't see," Parker said and winked.

Two circles of red appeared like apples on the girl's cheeks and softened her appearance. Parker was intrigued. He did not for a minute think that she didn't like the tattoos. He had never yet met a woman who was not attracted to them.

Parker was fourteen when he saw a man in a fair, tattooed from head to foot. Except for his loins which were girded with a panther hide, the man's skin was patterned in what seemed from Parker's distance—he was near the back of the tent, standing on a bench—a single intricate design of brilliant color. The man, who was small and sturdy, moved about on the platform, flexing his muscles so that the arabesque of men and beasts and flowers on his skin appeared to have a subtle motion of its own. Parker was filled with emotion, lifted up as some people are when the flag passes. He was a boy whose mouth habitually hung open. He was heavy and earnest, as ordinary as a loaf of bread. When the show was over, he had remained standing on the bench, staring where the tattooed man had been, until the tent was almost empty.

Parker had never before felt the least motion of wonder in himself. Until he saw the man at the fair, it did not enter his head that there was anything out of the ordinary about the fact that he existed. Even then it did not enter his head, but a peculiar unease settled in him. It was as if a blind boy had been turned so gently in a different direction that he did not know his destination had been changed.

20   He had his first tattoo some time after— the eagle perched on the cannon. It was done by a local artist. It hurt very little, just enough to make it appear to Parker to be worth doing. This was peculiar too for before he had thought that only what did not hurt was worth doing. The next year he quit school because he was sixteen and could. He went to the trade school for a while, then he quit the trade school and worked for six months in a garage. The only reason he worked at all was to pay for more tattoos. His mother worked in a laundry and could support him, but she would not pay for any tattoo except her name on a heart, which he had put on, grumbling. However, her name was Betty Jean and nobody had to know it was his mother. He found out that the tattoos were attractive to the kind of girls he liked but who had never liked him before. He began to drink beer and get in fights. His mother wept over what was becoming of him. One night she dragged him off to a revival with her, not telling him where they were going. When he saw the big lighted church, he jerked out of her grasp and ran. The next day he lied about his age and joined the navy.

Parker was large for the tight sailor's pants but the silly white cap, sitting low on his forehead, made his face by contrast look thoughtful and almost intense. After a month or two in the navy, his mouth ceased to hang open. His features hardened into the features of a man. He stayed in the navy five years and seemed a natural part of the gray mechanical ship, except for his eyes, which were the same pale slate-color as the ocean and reflected the immense spaces around him as if they were a microcosm of the mysterious sea. In port Parker wandered about comparing the run-down places he was in to Birmingham, Alabama. Everywhere he went he picked up more tattoos.

He had stopped having lifeless ones like anchors and crossed rifles. He had a tiger and a panther on each shoulder, a cobra coiled about a torch on his chest, hawks on his thighs, Elizabeth II and Philip over where his stomach and liver were respectively. He did not care much what the subject was so long as it was colorful; on his abdomen he had a few obscenities but only because that seemed the proper place for them. Parker would be satisfied with each tattoo about a month, then something about it that had attracted him would wear off. Whenever a decent-sized mirror was available, he would get in front of it and study his overall look. The effect was not of one intricate arabesque of colors but of something haphazard and botched. A huge dissatisfaction would come over him and he would go off and find another tattooist and have another space filled up. The front of Parker was almost completely covered but there were no tattoos on his back. He had no desire for one anywhere he could not readily see it himself. As the space on the front of him for tattoos decreased, his dissatisfaction grew and became general.

After one of his furloughs, he didn't go back to the navy but remained away without official leave, drunk, in a rooming house in a city he did not know. His dissatisfaction, from being chronic and latent, had suddenly become acute and raged in him. It was as if the panther and the lion and the serpents and the eagles and the hawks had penetrated his skin and lived inside him in a raging warfare. The navy caught up with him, put him in the brig for nine months and then gave him a dishonorable discharge.

After that Parker decided that country air was the only kind fit to breathe. He rented the shack on the embankment and bought the old truck and took various jobs which he kept as long as it suited him. At the time he met his future wife, he was buying apples by the bushel and selling them for the same price by the pound to isolated homesteaders on back country roads.

25 "All that there," the woman said, pointing to his arm, "is no better than what a fool Indian would do. It's a heap of vanity." She seemed to have found the word she wanted. "Vanity of vanities," she said.

Well what the hell do I care what she thinks of it? Parker asked himself, but he was plainly bewildered. "I reckon you like one of these better than another anyway," he said, dallying until he thought of something that would impress her. He thrust the arm back at her. "Which you like best?"

"None of them," she said, "but the chicken is not as bad as the rest."

"What chicken?" Parker almost yelled.

She pointed to the eagle.

30 "That's an eagle," Parker said. "What fool would waste their time having a chicken put on themselves?"

"What fool would have any of it?" the girl said and turned away. She went slowly back to the house and left him there to get going. Parker remained for almost five minutes, looking agape at the dark door she had entered.

The next day he returned with a bushel of apples. He was not one to be outdone by anything that looked like her. He liked women with meat on them, so you didn't feel their muscles, much less their old bones. When he arrived, she was sitting on the top step and the yard was full of children, all as thin and poor as herself; Parker remembered it was Saturday. He hated to be making up to a woman when there were children around, but it was fortunate he had brought the bushel of apples off the truck. As the children approached him to see what he carried, he gave each child an apple and told it to get lost; in that way he cleared out the whole crowd.

The girl did nothing to acknowledge his presence. He might have been a stray pig or goat that had wandered into the yard and she too tired to take up the broom and send it off. He set the bushel of apples down next to her on the step. He sat down on a lower step.

"Hep yourself," he said, nodding at the basket; then he lapsed into silence.

She took an apple quickly as if the bas- 35 ket might disappear if she didn't make haste. Hungry people made Parker nervous. He had always had plenty to eat himself. He grew very uncomfortable. He reasoned he had nothing to say so why should he say it? He could not think now why he had come or why he didn't go before he wasted another bushel of apples on the crowd of children. He supposed they were her brothers and sisters.

She chewed the apple slowly but with a kind of relish of concentration, bent slightly but looking out ahead. The view from the porch stretched off across a long incline studded with iron weed and across the highway to a vast vista of hills and one small mountain. Long views depressed Parker. You look out into space like that and you begin to feel as if someone were after you, the navy or the government or religion.

"Who them children belong to, you?" he said at length.

"I ain't married yet," she said. "They belong to momma." She said it as if it were only a matter of time before she would be married.

Who in God's name would marry her? Parker thought.

A large barefooted woman with a wide 40 gap-toothed face appeared in the door behind Parker. She had apparently been there for several minutes.

"Good evening," Parker said.

The woman crossed the porch and picked up what was left of the bushel of apples. "We thank you," she said and returned with it into the house.

"That your old woman?" Parker muttered.

The girl nodded. Parker knew a lot of sharp things he could have said like "You got my sympathy," but he was gloomily silent. He just sat there, looking at the view. He thought he must be coming down with something.

45 "If I pick up some peaches tomorrow I'll bring you some," he said.

"I'll be much obliged to you," the girl said.

Parker had no intention of taking any basket of peaches back there but the next day he found himself doing it. He and the girl had almost nothing to say to each other. One thing he did say was, "I ain't got any tattoo on my back."

"What you got on it?" the girl said.

"My shirt," Parker said. "Haw."

50 "Haw, haw," the girl said politely.

Parker thought he was losing his mind. He could not believe for a minute that he was attracted to a woman like this. She showed not the least interest in anything but what he brought until he appeared the third time with two cantaloups. "What's your name?" she asked.

"O. E. Parker," he said.

"What does the O. E. stand for?"

"You can just call me O. E.," Parker said. "Or Parker. Don't nobody call me by my name."

55 "What's it stand for?" she persisted.

"Never mind," Parker said. "What's yours?"

"I'll tell you when you tell me what them letters are the short of," she said. There was just a hint of flirtatiousness in her tone and it went rapidly to Parker's head. He had never revealed the name to any man or woman, only to the files of the navy and the government, and it was on his baptismal record which he got at the age of a month; his mother was a Methodist. When the name leaked out of the navy files, Parker narrowly missed killing the man who used it.

"You'll go blab it around," he said.

"I'll swear I'll never tell nobody," she said. "On God's holy word I swear it."

Parker sat for a few minutes in silence. 60 Then he reached for the girl's neck, drew her ear close to his mouth and revealed the name in low voice.

"Obadiah," she whispered. Her face slowly brightened as if the name came as a sign to her. "Obadiah," she said.

The name still stank in Parker's estimation.

"Obadiah Elihue," she said in a reverent voice.

"If you call me that aloud, I'll bust your head open," Parker said. "What's yours?"

"Sarah Ruth Cates," she said. 65

"Glad to meet you, Sarah Ruth," Parker said.

Sarah Ruth's father was a Straight Gospel preacher but he was away, spreading it in Florida. Her mother did not seem to mind his attention to the girl so long as he brought a basket of something with him when he came. As for Sarah Ruth herself, it was plain to Parker after he had visited three times that she was crazy about him. She liked him even though she insisted that pictures on the skin were vanity of vanities and even after hearing him curse, and even after she had asked him if he was saved and he had replied that he didn't see it was anything in particular to save him from. After that, inspired, Parker had said, "I'd be saved enough if you was to kiss me."

She scowled. "That ain't being saved," she said.

Not long after that she agreed to take a ride in his truck. Parker parked it on a deserted road and suggested to her that they lie down together in the back of it.

"Not until after we're married," she 70 said—just like that.

"Oh that ain't necessary," Parker said and as he reached for her, she thrust him away with such force that the door of the truck came off and he found himself flat on his back on the ground. He made up his mind then and there to have nothing further to do with her.

They were married in the County Ordinary's office because Sarah Ruth thought churches were idolatrous. Parker had no opinion about that one way or the other. The Ordinary's office was lined with cardboard file boxes and record books with dusty yellow slips of paper hanging on out of them. The Ordinary was an old woman with red hair who had held office for forty years and looked as dusty as her books. She married them from behind the iron-grill of a stand-up desk and when she finished, she said with a flourish, "Three dollars and fifty cents and till death do you part!" and yanked some forms out of a machine.

Marriage did not change Sarah Ruth a jot and it made Parker gloomier than ever. Every morning he decided he had had enough and would not return that night; every night he returned. Whenever Parker couldn't stand the way he felt, he would have another tattoo, but the only surface left on him now was his back. To see a tattoo on his own back he would have to get two mirrors and stand between them in just the correct position and this seemed to Parker a good way to make an idiot of himself. Sarah Ruth who, if she had had better sense, could have enjoyed a tattoo on his back, would not even look at the ones he had elsewhere. When he attempted to point out especial details of them, she would shut her eyes tight and turn her back as well. Except in total darkness, she preferred Parker dressed and with his sleeves rolled down.

"At the judgement seat of God, Jesus is going to say to you, 'What you been doing all your life besides have pictures drawn all over you?'" she said.

75 "You don't fool me none," Parker said, "you're just afraid that hefty girl I work for'll like me so much she'll say, 'Come on, Mr. Parker, let's you and me . . .'"

"You're tempting sin," she said, "and at the judgement seat of God you'll have to answer for that too. You ought to go back to selling the fruits of the earth."

Parker did nothing much when he was at home but listen to what the judgement seat of God would be like for him if he didn't change his ways. When he could, he broke in with tales of the hefty girl he worked for. "'Mr. Parker,'" he said she said, "'I hired you for your brains.'" (She had added, "So why don't you use them?")

"And you should have seen her face the first time she saw me without my shirt," he said. "'Mr. Parker,' she said, 'you're a walking panner-rammer!'" This had, in fact, been her remark but it had been delivered out of one side of her mouth.

Dissatisfaction began to grow so great in Parker that there was no containing it outside of a tattoo. It had to be his back. There was no help for it. A dim half-formed inspiration began to work in his mind. He visualized having a tattoo put there that Sarah Ruth would not be able to resist—a religious subject. He thought of an open book with HOLY BIBLE tattooed under it and an actual verse printed on the page. This seemed just the thing for a while; then he began to hear her say, "Ain't I already got a real Bible? What you think I want to read the same verse over and over for when I can read it all?" He needed something better even than the Bible! He thought about it so much that he began to lose sleep. He was already losing flesh—Sarah Ruth just threw food in the pot and let it boil. Not knowing for certain why he continued to stay with a woman who was both ugly and pregnant and no cook made him generally nervous and irritable, and he developed a little tic in the side of his face.

80 Once or twice he found himself turning around abruptly as if someone were trailing him. He had had a granddaddy who had ended in the state mental hospital, although not until he was seventy-five, but

as urgent as it might be for him to get a tattoo, it was just as urgent that he get exactly the right one to bring Sarah Ruth to heel. As he continued to worry over it, his eyes took on a hollow preoccupied expression. The old woman he worked for told him that if he couldn't keep his mind on what he was doing, she knew where she could find a fourteen-year-old colored boy who could. Parker was too preoccupied even to be offended. At any time previous, he would have left her then and there, saying drily, "Well, you go ahead on and get him then."

Two or three mornings later he was baling hay with the old woman's sorry baler and her broken down tractor in a large field, cleared save for one enormous old tree standing in the middle of it. The old woman was the kind who would not cut down a large old tree because it was a large old tree. She had pointed it out to Parker as if he didn't have eyes and told him to be careful not to hit it as the machine picked up hay near it. Parker began at the outside of the field and made circles inward toward it. He had to get off the tractor every now and then and untangle the baling cord or kick a rock out of the way. The old woman had told him to carry the rocks to the edge of the field, which he did when she was there watching. When he thought he could make it, he ran over them. As he circled the field his mind was on a suitable design for his back. The sun, the size of a golf ball, began to switch regularly from in front to behind him, but he appeared to see it both places as if he had eyes in the back of his head. All at once he saw the tree reaching out to grasp him. A ferocious thud propelled him into the air, and he heard himself yelling in an unbelievably loud voice, "GOD ABOVE!"

He landed on his back while the tractor crashed upside down into the tree and burst into flame. The first thing Parker saw were his shoes, quickly being eaten by the fire; one was caught under the tractor, the other was some distance away, burning by itself. He was not in them. He could feel the hot breath of the burning tree on his face. He scrambled backwards, still sitting, his eyes cavernous, and if he had known how to cross himself he would have done it.

His truck was on a dirt road at the edge of the field. He moved toward it, still sitting, still backwards, but faster and faster; halfway to it he got up and began a kind of forward-bent run from which he collapsed on his knees twice. His legs felt like two old rusted rain gutters. He reached the truck finally and took off in it, zigzagging up the road. He drove past his house on the embankment and straight for the city, fifty miles distant.

Parker did not allow himself to think on the way to the city. He only knew that there had been a great change in his life, a leap forward into a worse unknown, and that there was nothing he could do about it. It was for all intents accomplished.

The artist had two large cluttered rooms over a chiropodist's office on a back street. Parker, still barefooted, burst silently in on him at a little after three in the afternoon. The artist, who was about Parker's own age—twenty-eight—but thin and bald, was behind a small drawing table, tracing a design in green ink. He looked up with an annoyed glance and did not seem to recognize Parker in the hollow-eyed creature before him.

"Let me see the book you got with all the pictures of God in it," Parker said breathlessly. "The religious one."

The artist continued to look at him with his intellectual, superior state. "I don't put tattoos on drunks," he said.

"You know me!" Parker cried indignantly. "I'm O. E. Parker! You done work for me before and I always paid!"

The artist looked at him another moment as if he were not altogether sure. "You've fallen off some," he said. "You must have been in jail."

"Married," Parker said.

"Oh," said the artist. With the aid of mirrors the artist had tattooed on the top of his head a miniature owl, perfect in every detail. It was about the size of a half-dollar and served him as a show piece. There were cheaper artists in town but Parker had never wanted anything but the best. The artist went over to a cabinet at the back of the room and began to look over some art books. "Who are you interested in?" he said, "saints, angels, Christs or what?"

"God," Parker said.

"Father, Son or Spirit?"

"Just God," Parker said impatiently. "Christ. I don't care. Just so it's God."

95 The artist returned with a book. He moved some papers off another table and put the book down on it and told Parker to sit down and see what he liked. "The up-t-date ones are in the back," he said.

Parker sat down with the book and wet his thumb. He began to go through it, beginning at the back where the up-to-date pictures were. Some of them he recognized— The Good Shepherd, Forbid Them Not, The Smiling Jesus, Jesus the Physician's Friend, but he kept turning rapidly backwards and the pictures became less and less reassuring. One showed a gaunt green dead face streaked with blood. One was yellow with sagging purple eyes. Parker's heart began to beat faster and faster until it appeared to be roaring inside him like a great generator. He flipped the pages quickly, feeling that when he reached the one ordained, a sign would come. He continued to flip through until he had almost reached the front of the book. On one of the pages a pair of eyes glanced at him swiftly. Parker sped on, then stopped. His heart too appeared to cut off; there was absolute silence. It said as plainly as if silence were a language itself, GO BACK.

Parker returned to the picture—the haloed head of a flat stern Byzantine Christ with all-demanding eyes. He sat there

trembling; his heart began slowly to beat again as if it were being brought to life by a subtle power.

"You found what you want?" the artist asked.

Parker's throat was too dry to speak. He got up and thrust the book at the artist, opened at the picture.

"That'll cost you plenty," the artist said. 100 "You don't want all those little blocks though, just the outline and some better features."

"Just like it is," Parker said, "just like it is or nothing."

"It's your funeral," the artist said, "but I don't do that kind of work for nothing."

"How much?" Parker asked.

"It'll take maybe two days work."

"How much?" Parker said. 105

"On time or cash?" the artist asked. Parker's other jobs had been on time, but he had paid.

"Ten down and ten for every day it takes," the artist said.

Parker drew ten dollar bills out of his wallet; he had three left in.

"You come back in the morning," the artist said, putting the money in his own pocket. "First I'll have to trace out of the book."

"No no!" Parker said. "Trace it now 110 or gimme my money back," and his eyes blared as if he were ready for a fight.

The artist agreed. Any one stupid enough to want a Christ on his back, he reasoned, would be just as likely as not to change his mind the next minute, but once the work was begun he could hardly do so.

While he worked on the tracing, he told Parker to go wash his back at the sink with the special soap he used there. Parker did it and returned to pace back and forth across the room, nervously flexing his shoulders. He wanted to go look at the picture again but at the same time he did not want to. The artist got up finally and had

Parker lie down on the table. He swabbed his back with ethyl chloride and then began to outline the head on it with his iodine pencil. Another hour passed before he took up his electric instrument. Parker felt no particular pain. In Japan he had had a tattoo of the Buddha done on his upper arm with ivory needles; in Burma, a little brown root of a man had made a peacock on each of his knees using thin pointed sticks, two feet long; amateurs had worked on him with pins and soot. Parker was usually so relaxed and easy under the hand of the artist that he often went to sleep, but this time he remained awake, every muscle taut.

At midnight the artist said he was ready to quit. He propped one mirror, four feet square, on a table by the wall and took a smaller mirror off the lavatory wall and put it in Parker's hands. Parker stood with his back to the one on the table and moved the other until he saw a flashing burst of color reflected from his back. It was almost completely covered with little red and blue and ivory and saffron squares; from them he made out the lineaments of the face—a mouth, the beginning of heavy brows, a straight nose, but the face was empty; the eyes had not yet been put in. The impression for the moment was almost as if the artist had tricked him and done the Physician's Friend.

"It don't have eyes," Parker cried out.

115 "That'll come," the artist said, "in due time. We have another day to go on it yet."

Parker spent the night on a cot at the Haven of Light Christian Mission. He found these the best places to stay in the city because they were free and included a meal of sorts. He got the last available cot and because he was still barefooted, he accepted a pair of secondhand shoes which, in his confusion, he put on to go to bed; he was still shocked from all that had happened to him. All night he lay awake in the long dormitory of cots with lumpy figures on them. The only light was from a phosphorescent cross glowing at the end of the room. The tree reached out to grasp him again, then burst into flame; the shoe burned quietly by itself; the eyes in the book said to him distinctly GO BACK and at the same time did not utter a sound. He wished that he were not in this city, not in this Haven of Light Mission, not in a bed by himself. He longed miserably for Sarah Ruth. Her sharp tongue and icepick eyes were the only comfort he could bring to mind. He decided he was losing it. Her eyes appeared soft and dilatory compared with the eyes in the book, for even though he could not summon up the exact look of those eyes, he could still feel their penetration. He felt as though, under their gaze, he was as transparent as the wing of a fly.

The tattooist had told him not to come until ten in the morning, but when he arrived at that hour, Parker was sitting in the dark hallway on the floor, waiting for him. He had decided upon getting up that, once the tattoo was on him, he would not look at it, that all his sensations of the day and night before were those of a crazy man and that he would return to doing things according to his own sound judgement.

The artist began where he left off. "One thing I want to know," he said presently as he worked over Parker's back, "why do you want this on you? Have you gone and got religion? Are you saved?" he asked in a mocking voice.

Parker's throat felt salty and dry. "Naw," he said, "I ain't got no use for none of that. A man can't save his self from whatever it is he don't deserve none of my sympathy." These words seemed to leave his mouth like wraiths and to evaporate at once as if he had never uttered them.

"Then why . . ."   120

"I married this woman that's saved," Parker said. "I never should have done it. I ought to leave her. She's done gone and got pregnant."

"That's too bad," the artist said. "Then it's her making you have this tattoo."

"Naw," Parker said, "she don't know nothing about it. It's a surprise for her."

"You think she'll like it and lay off you a while?"

125 "She can't hep herself," Parker said. "She can't say she don't like the looks of God." He decided he had told the artist enough of his business. Artists were all right in their place but he didn't like them poking their noses into the affairs of regular people. "I didn't get no sleep last night," he said. "I think I'll get some now."

That closed the mouth of the artist but it did not bring him any sleep. He lay there, imagining how Sarah Ruth would be struck speechless by the face on his back and every now and then this would be interrupted by a vision of the tree of fire and his empty shoe burning beneath it.

The artist worked steadily until nearly four o'clock, not stopping to have lunch, hardly pausing with the electric instrument except to wipe the dripping dye off Parker's back as he went along. Finally he finished. "You can get up and look at it now," he said.

Parker sat up but he remained on the edge of the table.

The artist was pleased with his work and wanted Parker to look at it at once. Instead Parker continued to sit on the edge of the table, bent forward slightly but with a vacant look. "What ails you?" the artist said. "Go look at it."

130 "Ain't nothing ail me," Parker said in a sudden belligerent voice. "That tattoo ain't going nowhere. It'll be there when I get there." He reached for his shirt and began gingerly to put it on.

The artist took him roughly by the arm and propelled him between the two mirrors. "Now *look*," he said, angry at having his work ignored.

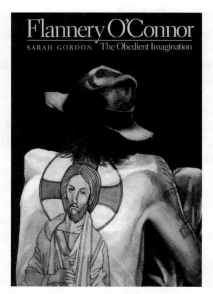

An artist's idea of what Parker's tattoo might look like. From the book cover of Sarah Gordon's *The Obedient Imagination*.

Parker looked, turned white and moved away. The eyes in the reflected face continued to look at him—still, straight, all-demanding, enclosed in silence.

"It was your idea, remember," the artist said. "I would have advised something else."

Parker said nothing. He put on his shirt and went out the door while the artist shouted, "I'll expect all of my money!"

Parker headed toward a package shop 135 on the corner. He bought a pint of whiskey and took it into a nearby alley and drank it all in five minutes. Then he moved on to a pool hall nearby which he frequented when he came to the city. It was a well-lighted barnlike place with a bar up one side and gambling machines on the other and pool tables in the back. As soon as Parker entered, a large man in a red and black checkered shirt hailed him by slapping him on the back and yelling, "Yeyyyyyy boy! O. E. Parker!"

Parker was not yet ready to be struck on the back. "Lay off," he said, "I got a fresh tattoo there."

"What you got this time?" the man asked and then yelled to a few at the machines. "O. E.'s got him another tattoo."

"Nothing special this time," Parker said and slunk over to a machine that was not being used.

"Come on," the big man said, "let's have a look at O. E.'s tattoo," and while Parker squirmed in their hands, they pulled up his shirt. Parker felt all the hands drop away instantly and his shirt fell again like a veil over the face. There was a silence in the pool room which seemed to Parker to grow from the circle around him until it extended to the foundations under the building and upward through the beams in the roof.

140   Finally someone said, "Christ!" Then they all broke into noise at once. Parker turned around, an uncertain grin on his face.

"Leave it to O. E.!" the man in the checkered shirt said. "That boy's a real card!"

"Maybe he's gone and got religion," someone yelled.

"Not on your life," Parker said.

"O. E.'s got religion and is witnessing for Jesus, ain't you, O. E.?" a little man with a piece of cigar in his mouth said wryly. "An o-riginal way to do it if I ever saw one."

145   "Leave it to Parker to think of a new one!" the fat man said.

"Yyeeeeeeyyyyyyy boy!" someone yelled and they all began to whistle and curse in compliment until Parker said, "Aaa shut up."

"What'd you do it for?" somebody asked.

"For laughs," Parker said. "What's it to you?"

"Why ain't you laughing then?" somebody yelled. Parker lunged into the midst of them and like a whirlwind on a summer's day there began a fight that raged amid overturned tables and swinging fists until two of them grabbed him and ran to the door with him and threw him out. Then a calm descended on the pool hall as nerve shattering as if the long barnlike room were the ship from which Jonah had been cast into the sea.

Parker sat for a long time on the 150 ground in the alley behind the pool hall, examining his soul. He saw it as a spider web of facts and lies that was not at all important to him but which appeared to be necessary in spite of his opinion. The eyes that were now forever on his back were eyes to be obeyed. He was as certain of it as he had ever been of anything. Throughout his life, grumbling and sometimes cursing, often afraid, once in rapture, Parker had obeyed whatever instinct of this kind had come to him—in rapture when his spirit had lifted at the sight of the tattooed man at the fair, afraid when he had joined the navy, grumbling when he had married Sarah Ruth.

The thought of her brought him slowly to his feet. She would know what he had to do. She would clear up the rest of it, and she would at least be pleased. It seemed to him that, all along, that was what he wanted, to please her. His truck was still parked in front of the building where the artist had his place, but it was not far away. He got in it and drove out of the city and into the country night. His head was almost clear of liquor and he observed that his dissatisfaction was gone, but he felt not quite like himself. It was as if he were himself but a stranger to himself, driving into a new country though everything he saw was familiar to him, even at night.

He arrived finally at the house on the embankment, pulled the truck under the pecan tree and got out. He made as much noise as possible to assert that he was still in charge here, that his leaving her for a night without word meant nothing except it was the way he did things. He slammed the car door, stamped up the two steps and across the porch and rattled the door knob. It did not respond to his touch. "Sarah Ruth!" he yelled, "let me in."

There was no lock on the door and she had evidently placed the back of a chair against the knob. He began to beat on the door and rattle the knob at the same time.

He heard the bed springs screak and bent down and put his head to the keyhole, but it was stopped up with paper. "Let me in!" he hollered, bamming on the door again. "What you got me locked out for?"

155   A sharp voice close to the door said, "Who's there?"

"Me," Parker said, "O. E."

He waited a moment.

"Me," he said impatiently, "O. E."

Still no sound from inside.

160   He tried once more. "O. E.," he said, bamming the door two or three more times. "O. E. Parker. You know me."

There was a silence. Then the voice said slowly, "I don't know no O. E."

"Quit fooling," Parker pleaded. "You ain't got any business doing me this way. It's me, old O. E., I'm back. You ain't afraid of me."

"Who's there?" the same unfeeling voice said.

Parker turned his head as if he expected someone behind him to give him the answer. The sky had lightened slightly and there were two or three streaks of yellow floating above the horizon. Then as he stood there, a tree of light burst over the skyline.

165   Parker fell back against the door as if he had been pinned there by a lance.

"Who's there?" the voice from inside said and there was a quality about it now that seemed final. The knob rattled and the voice said peremptorily, "Who's there, I ast you?"

Parker bent down and put his mouth near the stuffed keyhole. "Obadiah," he whispered and all at once he felt the light pouring through him, turning his spider web soul into a perfect arabesque of colors, a garden of trees and birds and beasts.

"Obadiah Elihue!" he whispered.

The door opened and he stumbled in. Sarah Ruth loomed there, hands on her hips. She began at once, "That was no hefty blonde woman you was working for and you'll have to pay her every penny on her tractor you busted up. She don't keep insurance on it. She came here and her and me had us a long talk and I . . ."

Trembling, Parker set about lighting   170
the kerosene lamp.

"What's the matter with you, wasting that kerosene this near day light?" she demanded. "I ain't got to look at you."

A yellow glow enveloped them. Parker put the match down and began to unbutton his shirt.

"And you ain't going to have none of me this near morning," she said.

"Shut your mouth," he said quietly. "Look at this and then I don't want to hear no more out of you." He removed the shirt and turned his back to her.

"Another picture," Sarah Ruth   175
growled. "I might have known you was off after putting some more trash on yourself."

Parker's knees went hollow under him. He wheeled around and cried, "Look at it! Don't just say that! *Look* at it!"

"I done looked," she said.

"Don't you know who it is?" he cried in anguish.

"No, who is it?" Sarah Ruth said. "It ain't anybody I know."

"It's him," Parker said.   180

"Him who?"

"God!" Parker cried.

"God? God don't look like that!"

"What do you know how he looks?" Parker moaned. "You ain't seen him."

"He don't *look*," Sarah Ruth said. "He's   185
a spirit. No man shall see his face."

"Aw listen," Parker groaned, "this is just a picture of him."

"Idolatry!" Sarah Ruth screamed. "Idolatry! Enflaming yourself, with idols under every green tree! I can put up with lies and vanity but I don't want no idolator in this house!" and she grabbed up the broom and began to thrash him across the shoulders with it.

Parker was too stunned to resist. He sat there and let her beat him until she had nearly knocked him senseless and large welts had formed on the face of the tattooed Christ. Then he staggered up and made for the door.

She stamped the broom two or three times on the floor and went to the window and shook it out to get the taint of him off it. Still gripping it, she looked toward the pecan tree and her eyes hardened still more. There he was—who called himself Obadiah Elihue— leaning against the tree, crying like a baby.

·····▶ *Your* Turn
Thinking and Writing about Lit

1. A student of ours named Arzu Ket wrote an essay entitled "Tattoo Parlors and Epiphanies in 'Parker's Back.'" What moments in the story do you think qualify as epiphanies (sudden revelations or realizations that may be formative for a character)? Is the ending an epiphany too?

2. Describe the ways in which irony operates in the scene where Parker's wife views the tattoo of Jesus. Why does she react the way she does?

3. **DIY** Write a story about a friend of yours who has tattoos. How do the tattoos she (or he) has chosen connect to personal experience or aspects of identity for that person? Try to convey the way your friend feels about the tattoos while you depict her or him as a fictional character.

Talking Lit

Below are selections written by literary critics, friends, and admirers of Flannery O'Connor and by Flannery O'Connor herself.

Alice Walker, Excerpt from "Beyond the Peacock: The Reconstruction of Flannery O'Connor" from the book. *In Search of Our Mothers' Gardens: Womanist Prose*

I discovered O'Connor when I was in college in the North and took a course in Sourthern writers and the South . . .

She was for me the first great modern writer from the South, and was, in any case, the only one I had read who wrote such sly, demythifying sentences about white women as: "The woman would be more or less pretty—yellow hair, far ankles, muddy-colored eyes."

Her white male characters do not fare any better—all of them misfits, thieves, deformed madman, idiot children, illiterates, and murderers, and her black characters, male and female, appear equally shallow, demented, and absurd. That she retained a certain distance (only, however, in her later, mature work) from the inner workings of her black characters seems to me all to her credit, since, by deliberately limiting her treatment of them to cover their observable demeanor and actions, she leaves them free, in the reader's imagination, to inhabit another landscape, another life, than the one she creates for them. This is a kind of grace many writers do not have when dealing with representatives of an oppressed people within a story, and their insistence on knowing everything, on being God, in fact, has burdened us with more stereotypes than we can ever hope to shed . . .

But essential O'Connor is not about race at all, which is why it is so refreshing, coming, as it does, out of such a racial culture. If it can be said to be "about" anything, then it is "about" prophets and prophecy, "about" revelations, and "about" the impact of supernatural grace on human beings who don't have a chance of spiritual growth without it.

Sally Fitzgerald, from the Introduction to *The Habit of Being: Selected Letters of Flannery O'Connor*

Among the papers in the Flannery O'Connor Memorial Room of the library of her college, Georgia College, in Milledgeville, I came across a tiny, scrappy notebook, about three inches by four, kept by Flannery when she was twelve. It was scrappy in both senses of the word. On the first page a warning to snoopers—"I know some folks that don't mind thier own bisnis"—called me to order and reminded me that it would be well to walk gingerly through her correspondence, bearing in mind what she herself would have objected to as a breach of privacy, particularly the privacy of her friends. No great loss, for there was something here of much greater interest. Reading through her letters, I felt her living presence in them. Their tone, their content, and even the number and range of those she corresponded with, revealed the vivid life in her, and much of the quality of a personality often badly guessed at.

Katherine Anne Porter wrote to Flannery's friends, the Gossetts, after they had taken her to lunch with Flannery and her mother at the farm, "I am always astonished at Flannery's pictures which show nothing of her grace. She was very slender with beautiful, smooth feet and ankles; she had a fine, clear, rosy skin and beautiful eyes. I could wish I had some record of her as she appeared to me . . ."

Most of her friends wish the same thing, both literally and figuratively. But she was not photogenic in maturity, or at least the camera was often as unjust as what was written about her. I have come to think that the true likeness of Flannery O'Connor will be painted by herself, a self-portrait in words, to be found in her letters. Read in sequence—from the beginning in 1948, when she wrote asking Elizabeth McKee to become her literary agent, through to the last note of 1964 on her bedside table, waiting to be posted—her letters sketch the lineaments, add the chiaroscuro of depth and space and the color of life itself. There she stands, to me, a phoenix risen from her own words: calm, slow, funny, courteous, both modest and very sure of herself, intense, sharply penetrating, devout but never pietistic, downright, occasionally fierce, and honest in a way that restores honor to the word. Perhaps because I remember her as smiling and laughing often when she was a part of our family in the Connecticut woods, her self-portrait wears, for me at least, a smile I recall very clearly. The mindless camera records on Flannery's face the ravages of ill health; her letters wipe them all away, not in a cosmetic sense, but by means of something that lay within and imparted the fine clarity and youthfulness Katherine Anne Porter perceived. And her offhand way of speaking of her physical ordeal, when she did, tells more about her gallantry than any encomium could make real.

Letters were always important to her. When she lived with us, she took a daily walk to the mailbox, half a mile away at the bottom of our ridge. One thing it always contained was a letter from Regina O'Connor, who wrote to her, and to whom she wrote, every single day. This daily exchange of news and talk between them ought to be mentioned, just to keep the record straight, since none of those letters will appear in the collection. Flannery shared news items from Milledgeville with us, and we came to feel that we knew all her kin well, long before we met them. Her strong family feeling was manifest even then.

On the subject of Mrs. O'Connor herself, I can report a remark that Flannery made to me the last time I talked to her. She told me that she had fully come to terms with her confinement, and with the physical danger in which she lived; that she had, in fact, only one great fear—that her mother would die before she did. "I don't know," she said, "what I would do without her." The letters themselves are full of Mrs. O'Connor: she is quoted, referred to, relished and admired, joked with and about, altogether clearly loved.

What else, though, do the letters tell us of the storyteller herself? The overriding impression is of a *joie de vivre*, rooted in her talent and the possibilities of her work, which she correctly saw as compensating her fully for any deprivations she had to accept, and as offering her a scope for living that most of us never dream of encompassing. From this sensibility grew a wonderful appreciation of the world's details: the vagaries of human personality; the rich flow of the language she heard around her; the beauty of Andalusia, the family farm outside Milledgeville where the O'Connors went to live after Flannery fell ill, and of the birds, homely or regal, with which she peopled it; the hospitality she and her mother offered to friends and strangers alike; good food, always a pleasure to her; talk, books, and letters. These letters reveal her to have been anything but reclusive by inclination: to have been, on the contrary, notably gregarious. She enjoyed company and sought it, sending warm invitations to her old and new friends to come to Andalusia. Once her inviolable three-hour morning stint of writing was done, she looked for, and throve on, companionship. When people couldn't come, she wrote to them, and looked forward to hearing from them in return. She participated in the lives of her friends, interested herself in their work, their children, their health, and their adventures. Anything but dour, she never ceased to be amused, even in extremis. In a letter after her return from the hospital and surgery, in 1964, she wrote: "One of my nurses was a dead ringer for Mrs. Turpin. Her Claud was named Otis. She told all the time about what a good nurse she was. Her favorite grammatical construction was 'it were.' She said she treated everybody alike whether it were a person with money or a black nigger. She told me all about the low life in Wilkinson County. I seldom know in any given circumstances whether the Lord is giving me a reward or a punishment. She didn't know she was funny and it was agony to laugh and I reckon she increased my pain about 100%."

The world of the absurd delighted her. She regaled us with Hadacol advertisements; birth announcements of infants with names that had to be read to be believed; such news items as the attendance of Roy Rogers' horse at a church service in California, or the award of first prize in an amateur contest to a crimped and beribboned seven-year-old singing "A Good Man Is Hard to Find"; and the wonderful mugs of a gospel quartet promised as a Coming Attraction somewhere. All these things filled her with glee, and gleefully she passed them on. She could write fine country talk, of course, and often did, to amuse her friends and herself. The next letter, however, might set forth in strong clear style a literary or theological insight that shed light in every direction.

Flannery O'Connor, "A Reasonable Use of the Unreasonable" from *Mystery and Manners*

Mary Flannery O'Connor (sitting center) with fellow student writers, 1945.

Last fall* I received a letter from a student who said she would be "graciously appreciative" if I would tell her "just what enlightenment" I expected her to get from each of my stories. I suspect she had a paper to write. I wrote her back to forget about the enlightenment and just try to enjoy them. I knew that was the most unsatisfactory answer I could have given because, of course, she didn't want to enjoy them, she just wanted to figure them out.

In most English classes the short story has become a kind of literary specimen to be dissected. Every time a story of mine appears in a Freshman anthology, I have a vision of it, with its little organs laid open, like a frog in a bottle.

I realize that a certain amount of this what-is-the-significance has to go on, but I think something has gone wrong in the process when, for so many students, the story becomes simply a problem to be solved, something which you evaporate to get Instant Enlightenment.

A story really isn't any good unless it successfully resists paraphrase, unless it hangs on and expands in the mind. Properly, you analyze to enjoy, but it's equally true that to analyze with any discrimination, you have to have enjoyed already, and I think that the best reason to hear a story read is that it should stimulate that primary enjoyment.

I don't have any pretensions to being an Aeschylus or Sophocles and providing you in this story with a cathartic experience out of your mythic background, though this story I'm going to read certainly calls up a good deal of the South's mythic background, and it should elicit from you a degree of pity and terror, even though its way of being serious is a comic one. I do think, though, that like the Greeks you should know what is going to happen in this story so that any element of suspense in it will be transferred from its surface to its interior.

I would be most happy if you had already read it, happier still if you knew it well, but since experience has taught me to keep my expectations along these lines modest, I'll tell you that this is the story of a family of six which, on its way driving to Florida, gets wiped out by an escaped convict who calls himself The

---

* **Last fall:** I.e., in 1962. These remarks were made by Flannery O'Connor at Hollins College, Virginia, to introduce a reading of her story, "A Good Man Is Hard to Find," on October 14, 1963.

Misfit. The family is made up of the Grandmother and her son, Bailey, and his children, John Wesley and June Star and the baby, and there is also the cat and the children's mother. The cat is named Pitty Sing, and the Grandmother is taking him with them, hidden in a basket.

Now I think it behooves me to try to establish with you the basis on which reason operates in this story. Much of my fiction takes its character form a reasonable use of the unreasonable, though the reasonableness of my use of it may not always be apparent. The assumptions that underlie this use of it, however, are those of the central Christian mysteries. These are assumptions to which a large part of the modern audience takes exception. About this I can only say that there are perhaps other ways than my own in which this story could be read, but none other by which it could have been written. Belief, in my own case anyway, is the engine that makes perception operate.

The heroine of this story, the Grandmother, is in the most significant position life offers the Christian. She is facing death. And to all appearances she, like the rest of us, is not too well prepared for it. She would like to see the event postponed. Indefinitely.

I've talked to a number of teachers who use this story in class and who tell their students that the Grandmother is evil, that in fact, she's a witch, even down to the cat. One of these teachers told me that his students, and particularly his Southern students, resisted this interpretation with a certain bemused vigor, and he didn't understand why. I had to tell him that they resisted it because they all had grandmothers or great-aunts just like her at home, and they knew, from personal experience, that the old lady lacked comprehension, but that she had a good heart. The Southerner is usually tolerant of those weaknesses that proceed from innocence, and he knows that a taste for self-preservation can be readily combined with the missionary spirit.

This same teacher was telling his students that morally The Misfit was several cuts above the Grandmother. He had a really sentimental attachment to The Misfit. But then a prophet gone wrong is almost always more interesting than your grandmother, and you have to let people take their pleasures where they find them.

It is true that the old lady is a hypocritical old soul; her wits are no match for The Misfit's, nor is her capacity for grace equal to his; yet I think the unprejudiced reader will feel that the Grandmother has a special kind of triumph in this story which instinctively we do not allow to someone altogether bad.

I often ask myself what makes a story work, and what makes it hold up as a story, and I have decided that it is probably some action, some gesture of a character that is unlike any other in the story, one which indicates where the real heart of the story lies. This would have to be an action or a gesture which was both totally right and totally unexpected; it would have to be one that was both in character and beyond character; it would have to suggest both the world and eternity. The action or gesture I'm talking about would have to be on the anagogical level, that is, the level which has to do with the Divine life and our participation in it. It would be a gesture that transcended any neat allegory that might have been intended or any pat moral categories a reader could make. It would be a gesture which somehow made contact with mystery.

There is a point in this story where such a gesture occurs. The Grandmother is at last alone, facing The Misfit. Her head clears for an instant and she realizes, even in her limited way, that she is responsible for the man before her and joined to him by ties of kinship which have their roots deep in the mystery she has been merely prattling about so far. And at this point, she does the right thing, she makes the right gesture.

I find that students are often puzzled by what she says and does here, but I think myself that if I took out this gesture and what she says with it, I would have no story. What was left would not be worth your attention. Our age not only does not have a very sharp eye for the almost imperceptible intrusions of grace, it no longer has much feeling for the nature of the violences which precede and follow them. The devil's greatest wile, Baudelaire has said, is to convince us that he does not exist.

I suppose the reasons for the use of so much violence in modern fiction will differ with each writer who uses it, but in my own stories I have found that violence is strangely capable of returning my characters to reality and preparing them to accept their moment of grace. Their heads are so hard that almost nothing else will do the work. This idea, that reality is something to which we must be returned at considerable cost, is one which is seldom understood by the casual reader, but it is one which is implicit in the Christian view of the world.

I don't want to equate The Misfit with the devil. I prefer to think that, however unlikely this may seem, the old lady's gesture, like the mustard-seed, will grow to be a great crow-filled tree in The Misfit's heart, and will be enough of a pain to him there to turn him into the prophet he was meant to become. But that's another story.

This story has been called grotesque, but I prefer to call it literal. A good story is literal in the same sense that a child's drawing is literal. When a child draws, he doesn't intend to distort but to set down exactly what he sees, and as his gaze is direct, he sees the lines that create motion. Now the lines of motion that interest the writer are usually invisible. They are lines of spiritual motion. And in this story you should be on the lookout for such things as the action of grace in the Grandmother's soul, and not for the dead bodies.

We hear many complaints about the prevalence of violence in modern fiction, and it is always assumed that this violence is a bad thing and meant to be an end in itself. With the serious writer, violence is never an end in itself. It is the extreme situation that best reveals what we are essentially, and I believe these are times when writers are more interested in what we are essentially than in the tenor of our daily lives.

John Gardner, "Aesthetic Law and Artistic Mystery" from *The Art of Fiction*

Art depends heavily on feeling, intuition, taste. It is feeling, not some rule, that tells the abstract painter to put his yellow here and there, not there, and may later tell him that it should have been brown or purple or pea-green. It's feeling that makes the composer break surprisingly from his key, feeling that gives the writer the rhythms of his sentences, the pattern of rise and fall in his episodes, the proportions

"I don't enjoy looking at these old pictures either, but it doesn't hurt my reputation for people to think I'm a lover of fine arts."

Flannery's original caption to her original cartoon: "I don't enjoy looking at these old pictures either, but it doesn't hurt my reputation for people to think I'm a lover of fine arts." While O'Connor was a student at Georgia State College for Women she was known for her humorous cartoons made from linoleum cuts. Her block print cartoons were published in the yearbook, the *Spectrum*; the newspaper, the *Colonnade*; and the literary magazine, the *Corinthian*. One yearbook describes her cartoons as "the bright spot of our existence."

of alternating elements, so that dialogue goes on only so long before a shift to description or narrative summary or some physical action. The great writer has an instinct for these things. He has, like a great comedian, an infallible sense of timing. And his instinct touches every thread of his fabric, even the murkiest fringes of symbolic structure. He knows when and where to think up and spring surprises, those startling leaps of the imagination that characterize all of the very greatest writing.

Obviously this is not to imply that cool intellect is useless to the writer. What Fancy sends, the writer must order by Judgment. He must think out completely, as coolly as any critic, what his fiction means, or is trying to mean. He must complete his equations, think out the subtlest implications of what he's said, get at the truth not just of his characters and action but also of his fiction's form, remembering that neatness can be carried too far, so that the work begins to seem fussy and overwrought, anal compulsive, unspontaneous, and remembering that, on the other hand, mess is no adequate alternative. He must think as cleanly as a mathematician, but he must also know by intuition when to sacrifice precision for some higher good, how to simplify, take short cuts, keep the foreground up there in front and the background back.

The first and last important rule for the creative writer, then, is that though there may be rules (formulas) for ordinary, easily publishable fiction—imitation fiction—there are no rules for real fiction, any more than there are rules for serious visual art or musical composition. There are techniques—hundreds of them—that, like carpenter's tricks, can be studied and taught; there are moral and aesthetic considerations every serious writer must sooner or later brood on a little, whether or not he broods in a highly systematic way; there are common mistakes—infelicities, clodpole ways of doing things—that show up repeatedly in unsuccessful fiction and can be shown for what they are by analysis of how they undermine the fiction's intended effects; there are, in short, a great many things every serious writer needs to think about; but there are no rules. Name one, and instantly some literary artist will offer us some new work that breaks the rule yet persuades us. Invention, after all, is art's main business, and one of the great joys of every artist comes with making the outrageous acceptable, as when the painter makes sharply clashing colors harmonious or a writer in the super-realistic tradition introduces—convincingly—a ghost.

Three Letters about "Parker's Back" from *The Habit of Being: Selected Letters of Flannery O'Connor*

To "A."

17 July 64

I agree with all you got to say about this ["Parker's Back"] and enclose a better barroom scene. You sound like Caroline to the teeth. I sent it to her same time as I sent it to you and got a telegram back saying some mechanical details would follow but she thought it unique, that I had succeeded in dramatizing a heresy. Well not in those terms did I set out but only thinking that the spirit moveth where it listeth. I found out about tattooing from a book I found in the Marboro list called *Memoirs of a Tattooist*. The old man that wrote it took tattooing as a high art and a great profession. No nonsense. Picture of his wife in it—very demure Victorian lady in off-shoulder gown. Everything you can see except her face & hands is tattooed. Looks like fabric. HE DID IT.

It's the other story that was published but this one ["Judgement Day"] is so different I aim to sell it again. I'll send that when I get up the steam to copy it. I can sit up at the typewriter about an hour at a time and I reckon I put in two and a half hours a day but you can't do much that way.

I'm cheered you got that raise. The Republican convention wasn't much. I look forward to the Democratic as they are better at the corn.

There's a right interesting review of Richard Hughes' *Fox in the Attic* by Walker Percy in the summer 64 *Sewanee*. Hate to subject you to this writing (hand) (mine). It's almost as bad as yours.

To Maryat Lee

21 July 64

I seemed to be doing all right and then I got another spell [of kidney infection] and tomorrow I'm going to the Baldwin County to spend the day and have a blood transfusion as the hemoglobin has dropped to below eight again. I'll take *The Tin Drum* along.

The racial front appears to have switched momentarily to Harlem. Are you anticipating? Do you ride the subways at night by yourself? NY sounds to me like a lousy place to live now.

I'm still puttering on my story ["Parker's Back"] that I thought I'd finished but not long at a time. I go across the room & I'm exhausted.

To "A."

25 July 64

No Caroline didn't mean the tattoos [in "Parker's Back"] were the heresy. Sarah Ruth was the heretic—the notion that you can worship in pure spirit. Caroline gave me a lot of advice about the story but most of it I'm ignoring. She thinks every story must be built according to the pattern of the Roman arch and she would enlarge the beginning and the end, but I'm letting it lay. I did well to write it at all. I had another transfusion Wednesday but it don't seem to have done much good.

We can worry about the interpitations of "Revelation" but not its fortunes. I had a letter from the O. Henry prize people & it got first.

Student Essay

Read Anita Shoup's interesting essay "Fine Manners in the Face of Death: Shirley Jackson's 'The Lottery' and Flannery O'Connor's 'A Good Man Is Hard to Find'" in Chapter 32. Of these two stories, student author Anita writes: "The authors seem to agree that when an individual or individuals are operating outside the bounds of reasonable behavior, most people will continue to play by the rules, and this will place them at a distinct disadvantage."

Q U E S T I O N S

TO ASK ABOUT FICTION

Many concepts mentioned below have not yet been explained in this book. You will find useful discussions of them in the coming chapters, and you may find yourself looking back at this list of "questions to ask about fiction" as you study and write about the short stories to come. We suggest putting a sticky-note or a paper clip on this page so you can come back to it again and again.

1. Whose voice is speaking? Can you identify who is narrating the story? Is the narrator omniscient (or all knowing)? Is it told from the perspective of just one character? Is it a first-person voice ("I") or a third-person voice ("she," "he," "they")? Is the story told from the perspective of a participant in the story or of an observer?

2. What is the nature of the voice? Is it casual and conversational, speaking to us in everyday language? Is it a more formal or distant voice? What is the level of diction the writer has chosen to use (formal, informal, mixed)? Is the level of diction the same in the dialogue and in the narrative? Does the diction vary from character to character in the dialogue

or in first-person narration? Does the writer use a dialect of English along with, or instead of, standard English?

3. What kind of plot strategy has the fiction writer chosen to use? Do events in the story begin at the beginning, or does the story begin smack in the middle of things? Does the writer employ flashbacks or foreshadowing (scenes from the past, hints of the future)? What is the central conflict (or source of tension) in the story? What other kinds of conflicts can you identify?

4. Has the writer used setting to help reveal the central characters in the story? Does setting play a role in revealing themes? What aspects of setting are important in this particular work (interior or exterior physical settings, social setting, historical time and place, climate, or seasons)?

5. Who is the central character? Might there be two main characters, or does this story have a single central character? What kinds of conflict (or tensions or problems) help reveal character here? Are there external conflicts (between characters, between a character and his or her environment)? Are there internal conflicts (within the main character or characters)?

6. What is the tone of the story (this is often thought of as atmosphere or mood, but it also involves the *author's attitude toward the subject at hand*)? Is irony an aspect of characterization or theme here? Are there any symbolic objects, characters, or events (which seem to represent larger meanings, in addition to their literal significance in the story)?

7. Does the writer make use of figurative language (metaphor, simile, personification, etc.) to convey ideas and emotions? Figures of speech are not meant literally, but they add spice and sensory detail to the storytelling. Does the story's title relate to its theme?

8. Is this a realistic story, or does the writer also use some nonrealistic or fantastic details? How do these nonrealistic elements work across the span of the story, and how do they enhance the story's meaning or themes? Does the story make use of any mythic patterns (like the hero's quest, kidnapping and rescue, initiation, or coming-of-age)?

Drivers wanted.

1 800 DRIVE VW

PLOT

Even commercials use plot. The
Volkswagen commercial represented by these storyboards is a mini-narrative, a story with characters, setting, drama, and plot. The viewer first sees the main character and the setting, a long shot of a red Volkswagen in an urban neighborhood [board 1]. The viewer is then introduced to the other characters: the driver, who cares enough about his car to wipe an invisible spot off the dashboard, and his passenger [board 2]. The characters don't speak throughout the commercial, and don't have to in order for the plot to unfold. The driver and his passenger are then seen looking at something [board 3]. From their perspective, the viewer then sees a chair that has apparently been put out with the trash by its owner [board 4]. The next shot shows the two companions from the front, still silently driving, but now with the chair in the backseat [board 5]. We then see them [board 6] continue to cruise along in silence, with the chair, and the viewer seems to think all is okay until they look at each other, puzzled and silently communicating to each other that something is wrong [boards 6, 7]. A medium shot of the car follows, with the driver looking to his left where he and his companion had dumped the chair, back on the sidewalk with the trash, apparently smelling too bad to be kept [boards 8, 9].

This commercial's plot follows a beginning-middle-end pattern, and dramatic conflict exists between the two people and the smell of the chair. The exposition occurs in the first two boards, when we are introduced to the characters. The rising action occurs in the third, fourth, fifth, and sixth boards, when they spot, and then obtain, the chair, and continue along, silent and content. The climax occurs in the seventh board when they discover that something's wrong. The falling action occurs in the eighth board, when the characters resolve their problem by removing the offending passenger. Finally, resolution is confirmed in the ninth board, where the two companions drive the car away from the chair, all three free of its odor.

Have you ever walked into the middle of a conversation? You didn't know what your friends were talking about, but you were immediately caught up in what they were saying? The story of "Killings" opens at the funeral of Frank, with his older brother, Steve, saying, "I should kill him." We have absolutely no idea who he means or why, but we certainly feel curious—and so we read on, turning the pages of André Dubus's story (which appears later in this chapter) to see what happens. Dubus's plot unfolds at the pace he, the writer, has chosen, and the scenes, characters, and events are revealed in an order that serves his purposes in terms of what he wants the story to focus on. In the making of fiction, **plot** is "the author's deliberate selection and arrangement of incidents in a story." More than one hundred years ago, French writer Guy de Maupassant expressed it this way:

> A writer would find it impossible to describe everything in life, because he would need at least a volume a day to list the multitude of unimportant incidents filling up our hours.
>
> Some selectivity is required—which is the first blow to the "entire truth" theory [of realistic literature]. (from the Preface to *Pierre and Jean*, 1888)

In other words, writers choose which details and incidents will be depicted (either from experience or from imagination or, as is most often the case, a combination of both). Writers also arrange these incidents in a way that helps illuminate what they want to show.

Beginning-Middle-End
or Middle-Beginning-End

De Maupassant also explains (in his "Talking Lit" piece at the end of this chapter) that writers don't necessarily arrange events **chronologically**, but, of course, they can choose to do so if they wish. A story arranged chronologically is one that follows the clock (or the calendar); it has a beginning, a middle, and an end, in that order. An example of this is Guy de Maupassant's own story "The Necklace," which you will read later in this chapter. This story begins at the beginning, providing the reader with background information about the main characters, the Loisels, and introducing the overall problem of Mathilde Loisel's discomfort with her status in life. This problem is developed and illuminated throughout the middle of the story, using scenes before, during, and after a ball the Loisels attend to "show forth" (as writer Eudora Welty says) the characters' situation. The story then comes to an ending—a somewhat surprising one.

Some stories do not begin at the beginning of the action, of course. André Dubus's story "Killings," for example, begins **in medias res**, a term borrowed from Latin which means "in the middle of things." The opening scene takes place at

Frank's funeral (which is in the middle of the story), and it isn't until later that we find out why, how, and by whom he was killed (the beginning of the story) and what the resolution of the characters' problems might be, if any (the ending).

Sources of Conflict

Another useful concept to discuss in connection with plot is tension or **conflict**. Many critics and writers feel that conflict is an essential element of fiction and drama. This does not imply that there must be a physical conflict (a fight or a war) in a piece of fiction but that there needs to be some source of tension. Two other terms are useful here. The central character may be called the **protagonist**, and the force opposing that central character may be called the **antagonist**. In previous discussions of literature, you may have encountered a list like the one below to help define the types of conflict that arise in literature:

- The character in conflict with another character
- The character in conflict with the environment (physical or social context)
- The character in conflict with herself or himself

The first two items above are types of **external conflict**, and the last is called **internal conflict** (or inner conflict). As you can see, the conflict does not have to be in the form of a "fight" or power struggle with another character, but each of these types of conflict pits a protagonist against an opposing force of some sort.

Many critics and writers consider the last, the conflict within a character, to be the most important in fiction. We could use "The Necklace" to illustrate this view. We can find in de Maupassant's story examples of the two types of external conflict. Tension is created here by the disparity between what Madame Loisel and Monsieur Loisel want (a character versus another character). She wants "dainty dinners," "shining silverware," and "delicious dishes served on marvelous plates." When he "uncovered the soup tureen and declared with an enchanted air, 'Ah, the good *pot-au-feu*! I don't know anything better than that,'" he is expressing his satisfaction with his life as it is, not feeling the need for "shining silverware" to enjoy his *pot-au-feu* (soup). So we have a tension between what he wants and what she wants, which is the sort of character–character conflict that doesn't require a fight for us to recognize the tension. Second, we see that Madame Loisel is in conflict with her environment. Because she was born into a lower-class family, her social status dictates a certain role for her in late nineteenth-century French society. However, she is in conflict with those expectations that she "know her place" and "stay in her place." She is thus in tension with the social environment of her community and society. This is a form of external conflict as well (a character versus his or her environment). In some stories, on the other hand, the character is in conflict with the physical environment—for instance, a natural force like a storm.

Critics and writers agree, though, that the internal conflict (a character versus herself or himself) is often most fundamental to the tensions revealed in a story. For example, the tension which exists inside Madame Loisel is a result of the discrepancy between the status she is allotted in life (because of her birth circumstances, her limited access to education, and her marriage to a clerk) and the status she desires to have. Some readers will find her motives justifiable ("she has the right to be ambitious"); others will find them shallow ("it's just material greed"); and still others will not blame her but will look for explanations in her social context, which places such a high value on material possessions and appearances. It's not hard to see how this story's themes might relate to our own time as well, to the kinds of social pressure many of us cope with—the pressure to drive a certain kind of car, to live in a "good" neighborhood, or to wear particular brands of clothing.

The Conventional Resolution Versus the Open-Ended Story

We pointed out above that "The Necklace" has a chronological story line, and it is an example of a **conventional plot** in another sense as well. You may previously have discussed plot in terms of the rising and falling of the action in a traditional story, and often a triangle- or a parabola-shaped diagram is used to illustrate the shape of the traditional plot structure.

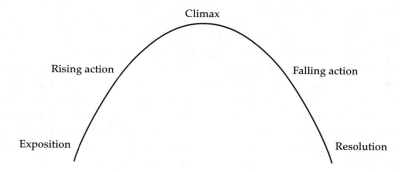

The diagram illustrates (on the left side of the shape) the **rising action** (or developing problem), the **climax** of the action (at the top of the shape), and the **falling action** (on the right side, descending), also called the **dénouement**, which in French means "untying of the knot." The problems of the characters are "unknotted," then, on the down slope, and the story proceeds toward its **resolution**. "Resolution" does not necessarily require a happy ending, by the way, as the resolution (or closure to the story) may be that the main character dies (or some other "negative" ending). The term resolution has more to do, then, with our sense of an outcome being known, rather than with the necessity of a particular or a "happy" outcome.

Some readers may feel inclined to say, "Wait, that's not the way it always is in real life; in real life, we don't always have a resolution to a problem." This is true, of course, and in the late nineteenth century one writer recognized this quite clearly. His name was Anton Chekhov (1860–1904), and he is frequently thought of as "the father of the modern short story" for two particular innovations that he made in the short story form. Some of his stories are **slice-of-life** stories, or stories which present a portrait or snapshot of a character in a situation but are not strongly plotted and may not have a beginning, middle, and end. Second, and most important, most of his stories are **open-ended** stories; that is, no clear resolution is provided to the reader at the end. The characters may be in the midst of a process (a tentative or partial resolution) or they may simply be left in the throes of their problems without even a tentative resolution evident. The diagram of an open-ended story might look somewhat like this:

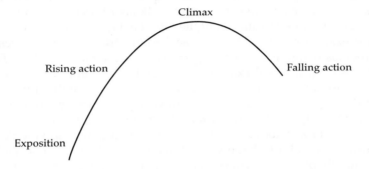

The character Matt Fowler, at the end of André Dubus's "Killings," has not experienced a resolution to his problem. Now he dreams of leaves falling on two graves, not just one, and he certainly doesn't seem to be resting easy. In Chekhov's story "The Lady with the Pet Dog" (which you will read in Chapter 10), Anna and Gurov are left in the midst of their affair and in the midst of their problem, with no solution in sight. Chekhov would say (along with those readers who may have protested the notion of "resolution" earlier) that this is true to life, since our problems aren't always solved by the end of the day, or by the end of the story.

Looking Back and Looking Ahead— Flashback and Foreshadowing

Two other useful terms for discussing plot are flashback and foreshadowing. In "Killings," André Dubus uses **flashbacks** when he shifts back in time to depict scenes from Frank and Mary Ann's relationship and from Richard Strout's earlier life. Dubus uses **foreshadowing** whenever he gives us a hint or clue regarding what is to come. In the first scene (at the funeral), when Matt's son, Steve, says, "I should kill him," even though the reader doesn't yet know about whom he's talking or why, the ominous, emotionally charged statement is a foreshadowing of what is to come.

How we Talk About Literature

In addition to our recognition throughout this book of the connections between literature and real life (literature attempts at every turn to depict real life), we will also be practicing ways in which to talk about literature. In the discussion above, when we wanted to talk about the different types of conflict in fiction, we used specific examples from "The Necklace" to illustrate the three types of conflict. In the previous paragraph, when we wanted to say something about flashback and foreshadowing, we used examples from Dubus's "Killings" to show what we meant. Likewise, in your discussions of works of literature (both in class discussion and in the papers you will be asked to write), you will be looking into the story (or poem or play) itself to find examples of what you mean.

We talked above about chronological and nonchronological plots and about flashbacks and foreshadowing. When you read Amy Tan's "Half and Half" (later in this chapter), you will encounter another interesting plot strategy often used in fiction: the use of more than one time period, as in "Killings," but for a different purpose. In "Half and Half," we begin in the present time with an older narrator who looks back on past experiences. At the center of Tan's story is a particular scene from the past (in this case, the death of the main character's younger brother, Bing) which helps illuminate the present. Writers sometimes call this plot strategy a "frame" story because the present scenes frame or surround the narration of a past event or events. You might also think of the concept of a picture within a picture. There are infinite possibilities for how a plot can be structured, and we have illustrated only a few basic concepts here to help open up the discussion.

Readings

Guy de Maupassant (1850–1893)

Guy de Maupassant was born near Dieppe, France. Early in his life, de Maupassant was influenced by the great French novelist Gustave Flaubert, who was a friend of the parents of the young de Maupassant. As a young man, de Maupassant fought in the Franco-Prussian war (1870–1871). During the ten-year period following the war, he was Flaubert's apprentice in the art of fiction writing. He also worked with novelist Emile Zola. During his brief life, de Maupassant produced an impressive body of work: nearly three hundred short stories, six novels, several plays, volumes of poetry, essays, articles, and travel books. His novels include *A Life* (1883), *Handsome Friend* (1885), and *Pierre and Jean* (1888). His short stories are available in his collected works. De Maupassant died of syphilis in 1893.

The Necklace (1884)

Translated by Marjorie Laurie

She was one of those pretty and charming girls who are sometimes, as if by a mistake of destiny, born in a family of clerks. She had no dowry, no expectations, no means of being known, understood, loved, wedded by any rich and distinguished man; and she let herself be married to a little clerk at the Ministry of Public Instructions.

She dressed plainly because she could not dress well, but she was as unhappy as though she had really fallen from her proper station, since with women there is neither caste nor rank: and beauty, grace, and charm act instead of family and birth. Natural fineness, instinct for what is elegant, suppleness of wit, are the sole hierarchy, and make from women of the people the equals of the very greatest ladies.

She suffered ceaselessly, feeling herself born for all the delicacies and all the luxuries. She suffered from the poverty of her dwelling, from the wretched look of the walls, from the worn-out chairs, from the ugliness of the curtains. All those things, of which another woman of her rank would never even have been conscious, tortured her and made her angry. The sight of the little Breton peasant, who did her humble housework, aroused in her regrets which were despairing, and distracted dreams. She thought of the silent antechambers hung with Oriental tapestry, lit by tall bronze candelabra, and of the two great footmen in knee breeches who sleep in the big armchairs, made drowsy by the heavy warmth of the hot-air stove. She thought of the long *salons* fitted up with ancient silk, of the delicate furniture carrying priceless curiosities, and of the coquettish perfumed boudoirs made for talks at five o'clock with intimate friends, with men famous and sought after, whom all women envy and whose attention they all desire.

When she sat down to dinner, before the round table covered with a tablecloth three days old, opposite her husband, who uncovered the soup tureen and declared with an enchanted air, "Ah, the good *pot-au-feu*! I don't know anything better than that," she thought of dainty dinners, of shining silverware, of tapestry which peopled the walls with ancient personages and with strange birds flying in the midst of a fairy forest; and she thought of delicious dishes served on marvelous plates, and of the whispered gallantries which you listen to with a sphinxlike smile, while you are eating the pink flesh of a trout or the wings of a quail.

5   She had no dresses, no jewels, nothing. And she loved nothing but that; she felt made for that. She would so have liked to please, to be envied, to be charming, to be sought after.

She had a friend, a former schoolmate at the convent, who was rich, and whom she did not like to go and see any more, because she suffered so much when she came back.

But one evening, her husband returned home with a triumphant air, and holding a large envelope in his hand.

"There," said he. "Here is something for you."

She tore the paper sharply, and drew out a printed card which bore these words:

10   "The Minister of Public Instruction and Mme. Georges Ramponneau request the honor of M. and Mme. Loisel's company at the palace of the Ministry on Monday evening, January eighteenth."

Instead of being delighted, as her husband hoped, she threw the invitation on the table with disdain, murmuring:

"What do you want me to do with that?"

"But, my dear, I thought you would be glad. You never go out, and this is such a fine opportunity. I had awful trouble to get it. Everyone wants to go; it is very select, and they are not giving many invitations to clerks. The whole official world will be there."

She looked at him with an irritated glance, and said, impatiently:

15   "And what do you want me to put on my back?"

He had not thought of that; he stammered:

"Why, the dress you go to the theater in. It looks very well, to me."

He stopped, distracted, seeing his wife was crying. Two great tears descended slowly from the corners of her eyes toward the corners of her mouth. He stuttered:

"What's the matter? What's the matter?"

But, by violent effort, she had con- 20 quered her grief, and she replied, with a calm voice, while she wiped her wet cheeks:

"Nothing. Only I have no dress and therefore I can't go to this ball. Give your card to some colleague whose wife is better equipped than I."

He was in despair. He resumed:

"Come, let us see, Mathilde. How much would it cost, a suitable dress, which you could use on other occasions. Something very simple?"

She reflected several seconds, making her calculations and wondering also what sum she could ask without drawing on herself an immediate refusal and a frightened exclamation from the economical clerk.

Finally, she replied, hesitatingly: 25

"I don't know exactly, but I think I could manage it with four hundred francs."

He had grown a little pale, because he was laying aside just that amount to buy a gun and treat himself to a little shooting next summer on the plain of Nanterre, with several friends who went to shoot larks down there, of a Sunday.

But he said:

"All right. I will give you four hundred francs. And try to have a pretty dress."

The day of the ball drew near, and 30 Mme. Loisel seemed sad, uneasy, anxious. Her dress was ready, however. Her husband said to her one evening:

"What is the matter? Come, you've been so queer these last three days."

And she answered:

"It annoys me not to have a single jewel, not a single stone, nothing to put on.

I shall look like distress. I should almost rather not go at all."

He resumed:

35 "You might wear natural flowers. It's very stylish at this time of the year. For ten francs you can get two or three magnificent roses."

She was not convinced.

"No; there's nothing more humiliating than to look poor among other women who are rich."

But her husband cried:

"How stupid you are! Go look up your friend Mme. Forestier, and ask her to lend you some jewels. You're quite thick enough with her to do that."

40 She uttered a cry of joy:

"It's true. I never thought of it."

The next day she went to her friend and told of her distress.

Mme. Forestier went to a wardrobe with a glass door, took out a large jewelbox, brought it back, opened it, and said to Mme. Loisel:

"Choose, choose, my dear."

45 She saw first of all some bracelets, then a pearl necklace, then a Venetian cross, gold and precious stones of admirable workmanship. She tried on the ornaments before the glass, hesitated, could not make up her mind to part with them, to give them back. She kept asking:

"Haven't you any more?"

"Why, yes. Look. I don't know what you like."

All of a sudden she discovered, in a black satin box, a superb necklace of diamonds, and her heart began to beat with an immoderate desire. Her hands trembled as she took it. She fastened it around her throat, outside her high necked dress, and remained lost in ecstasy at the sight of herself.

Then she asked, hesitating, filled with anguish:

"Can you lend me that, only that?"   50

"Why, yes, certainly."

She sprang upon the neck of her friend, kissed her passionately, then fled with her treasure.

The day of the ball arrived. Mme. Loisel made a great success. She was prettier than them all, elegant, gracious, smiling, and crazy with joy. All the men looked at her, asked her name, endeavored to be introduced. All the attachés of the Cabinet wanted to waltz with her. She was remarked by the minister himself.

She danced with intoxication, with passion, made drunk by pleasure, forgetting all, in the triumph of her beauty, in the glory of her success, in a sort of cloud of happiness composed of all this homage, of all this admiration, of all these awakened desires, and of that sense of complete victory which is so sweet to a woman's heart.

She went away about four o'clock in   55 the morning. Her husband had been sleeping since midnight, in a little deserted anteroom, with three other gentlemen whose wives were having a good time. He threw over her shoulders the wraps which he had brought, modest wraps of common life, whose poverty contrasted with the elegance of the ball dress. She felt this, and wanted to escape so as not to be remarked by the other women, who were enveloping themselves in costly furs.

Loisel held her back.

"Wait a bit. You will catch cold outside. I will go and call a cab."

But she did not listen to him, and rapidly descended the stairs. When they were in the street they did not find a carriage; and they began to look for one, shouting after the cabmen whom they saw passing by at a distance.

They went down toward the Seine, in despair, shivering with cold. At last they found on the quay one of those ancient noctambulant coupés[1] which, exactly as if they were ashamed to show their misery during the day, are never seen round Paris until after nightfall.

60 It took them to their door in the Rue des Martyrs, and once more, sadly, they climbed up homeward. All was ended, for her. And as to him, he reflected that he must be at the Ministry at ten o'clock.

She removed the wraps which covered her shoulders before the glass, so as once more to see herself in all her glory. But suddenly she uttered a cry. She no longer had the necklace around her neck!

Her husband, already half undressed, demanded:

"What is the matter with you?"

She turned madly toward him:

65 "I have—I have—I've lost Mme. Forestier's necklace."

He stood up, distracted.

"What!—how?—impossible!"

And they looked in the folds of her dress, in the folds of her cloak, in her pockets, everywhere. They did not find it.

He asked:

70 "You're sure you had it on when you left the ball?"

"Yes, I felt it in the vestibule of the palace."

"But if you had lost it in the street we should have heard it fall. It must be in the cab."

"Yes. Probably. Did you take his number?"

"No. And you, didn't you notice it?"

75 "No."

They looked, thunderstruck, at one another. At last Loisel put on his clothes.

"I shall go back on foot," said he, "over the whole route which we have taken to see if I can find it."

---

[1]**coupés:** An enclosed four-wheeled carriage.

And he went out. She sat waiting on a chair in her ball dress, without strength to go to bed, overwhelmed, without fire, without a thought.

Her husband came back about seven o'clock. He had found nothing.

80 He went to Police Headquarters, to the newspaper offices, to offer a reward; he went to the cab companies—everywhere, in fact, whither he was urged by the least suspicion of hope.

She waited all day, in the same condition of mad fear before this terrible calamity.

Loisel returned at night with a hollow, pale face; he had discovered nothing.

"You must write to your friend," said he, "that you have broken the clasp of her necklace and that you are having it mended. That will give us time to turn round."

She wrote at his dictation.

85 At the end of a week they had lost all hope.

And Loisel, who had aged five years, declared:

"We must consider how to replace that ornament."

The next day they took the box which had contained it, and they went to the jeweler whose name was found within. He consulted his books.

"It was not I, madame, who sold that necklace; I must simply have furnished the case."

90 Then they went from jeweler to jeweler, searching for a necklace like the other, consulting their memories, sick both of them with chagrin and anguish.

They found, in a shop at the Palais Royal, a string of diamonds which seemed to them exactly like the one they looked for. It was worth forty thousand francs. They could have it for thirty-six.

So they begged the jeweler not to sell it for three days yet. And they made a bargain that he should buy it back for thirty-four thousand francs, in case they found the other one before the end of February.

Loisel possessed eighteen thousand francs which his father had left him. He would borrow the rest.

He did borrow, asking a thousand francs of one, five hundred of another, five louis here, three louis there. He gave notes, took up ruinous obligations, dealt with usurers and all the race of lenders. He compromised all the rest of his life, risked his signature without even knowing if he could meet it; and, frightened by the pains yet to come, by the black misery which was about to fall upon him, by the prospect of all the physical privation and of all the moral tortures which he was to suffer, he went to get the new necklace, putting down upon the merchant's counter thirty-six thousand francs.

95   When Mme. Loisel took back the necklace, Mme. Forestier said to her, with a chilly manner:

"You should have returned it sooner; I might have needed it."

She did not open the case, as her friend had so much feared. If she had detected the substitution, what would she have thought, what would she have said? Would she not have taken Mme. Loisel for a thief?

Mme. Loisel now knew the horrible existence of the needy. She took her part, moreover, all of a sudden, with heroism. That dreadful debt must be paid. She would pay it. They dismissed their servant; they changed their lodgings; they rented a garret under the roof.

She came to know what heavy housework meant and the odious cares of the kitchen. She washed the dishes, using her rosy nails on the greasy pots and pans. She washed the dirty linen, the shirts, and the dishcloths, which she dried upon a line; she carried the slops down to the street every morning, and carried up the water, stopping for breath at every landing. And, dressed like a woman of the people, she went to the fruiterer, the grocer, the butcher, her basket on her arm, bargaining, insulted, defending her miserable money sou by sou.

Each month they had to meet some 100 notes, renew others, obtain more time.

Her husband worked in the evening making a fair copy of some tradesman's accounts, and late at night he often copied manuscript for five sous a page.

And this life lasted for ten years.

At the end of ten years, they had paid everything, everything, with the rates of usury, and the accumulations of the compound interest.

Mme. Loisel looked old now. She had become the woman of impoverished households—strong and hard and rough. With frowsy hair, skirts askew, and red hands, she talked loud while washing the floor with great swishes of water. But sometimes, when her husband was at the office, she sat down near the window, and she thought of that gay evening of long ago, of that ball where she had been so beautiful and so fêted.

What would have happened if she had 105 not lost that necklace? Who knows? Who knows? How life is strange and changeful! How little a thing is needed for us to be lost or to be saved!

But, one Sunday, having gone to take a walk in the Champs Elysées to refresh herself from the labor of the week, she suddenly perceived a woman who was leading a child. It was Mme. Forestier, still young, still beautiful, still charming.

Mme. Loisel felt moved. Was she going to speak to her? Yes, certainly. And now that she had paid, she was going to tell her all about it. Why not?

She went up.

"Good-day, Jeanne."

The other, astonished to be familiarly 110 addressed by this plain goodwife, did not recognize her at all, and stammered.

"But—madam!—I do not know—you must be mistaken."

"No. I am Mathilde Loisel."

Her friend uttered a cry.

"Oh, my poor Mathilde! How you are changed!"

115 "Yes, I have had days hard enough, since I have seen you, days wretched enough—and that because of you!"

"Of me! How so?"

"Do you remember that diamond necklace which you lent me to wear at the ministerial ball?"

"Yes. Well?"

"Well, I lost it."

120 "What do you mean? You brought it back."

"I brought you back another just like it. And for this we have been ten years paying. You can understand that it was not easy for us, who had nothing. At last it is ended, and I am very glad."

Mme. Forestier had stopped.

"You say that you bought a necklace of diamonds to replace mine?"

"Yes. You never noticed it, then! They were very like."

And she smiled with a joy which was 125 proud and naïve at once.

Mme. Forestier, strongly moved, took her two hands.

"Oh, my poor Mathilde! Why, my necklace was paste. It was worth at most five hundred francs!"

····▶ *Your* **Turn**

Talking and Writing about Lit

1. What types of conflict become evident in "The Necklace"? Are there external conflicts? Are there internal conflicts?

2. Do you think that Madame Loisel is a victim of fate, or do you feel she is to blame for her difficulties?

3. **DIY** Some readers have pointed out an additional dimension to de Maupassant's surprise ending. If the necklace Madame Loisel borrowed was paste (an imitation) but the one the Loisels replaced it with was real, does her wealthy friend owe her some money? Write a page of dialogue that might follow Madame Forestier's last line, "Oh, my poor Mathilde! Why, my necklace was paste. It was worth at most five hundred francs!"

André Dubus (1936–1999)

André Dubus was born and raised in Lake Charles, Louisiana, and became an officer in the U.S. Marine Corps at the age of twenty-two. After five years in the military, he returned to civilian life and to academia. He earned his M.F.A. degree in creative writing at the University of Iowa in 1966 and then began his career of writing and college teaching. Dubus published eight highly admired collections of short fiction, including *Collected Stories* (1988), *Dancing After Hours* (1996), and *Meditations from a Movable Chair* (1998). The last collection grew out of his experience of becoming a paraplegic after being struck by a car as he attempted to help a stalled motorist on the highway. Dubus died of a heart attack in 1999. His story "Killings," below, was made into the award-winning film *In the Bedroom*, starring Sissy Spacek, Tom Wilkinson, and Marisa Tomei.

Killings (1979)

On the August morning when Matt Fowler buried his youngest son, Frank, who had lived for twenty-one years, eight months, and four days, Matt's older son, Steve, turned to him as the family left the grave and walked between their friends, and said: "I should kill him." He was twenty-eight, his brown hair starting to thin in front where he used to have a cowlick. He bit his lower lip, wiped his eyes, then said it again. Ruth's arm, linked with Matt's, tightened; he looked at her. Beneath her eyes there was swelling from the three days she had suffered. At the limousine Matt stopped and looked back at the grave, the casket, and the Congregationalist minister who he thought had probably had a difficult job with the eulogy though he hadn't seemed to, and the old funeral director who was saying something to the six young pallbearers. The grave was on a hill and overlooked the Merrimack, which he could not see from where he stood; he looked at the opposite bank, at the apple orchard with its symmetrically planted trees going up a hill.

Next day Steve drove with his wife back to Baltimore where he managed the branch office of a bank, and Cathleen, the middle child, drove with her husband back to Syracuse. They had left the grandchildren with friends. A month after the funeral Matt played poker at Willis Trottier's because Ruth, who knew this was the second time he had been invited, told him to go, he couldn't sit home with her for the rest of her life; she was all right. After the game Willis went outside to tell everyone good night and, when the others had driven away, he walked with Matt to his car. Willis was a short, silver-haired man who had opened a diner after World War II, his trade then mostly very early breakfast, which he cooked, and then lunch for the men who worked at the leather and shoe factories. He now owned a large restaurant.

"He walks the Goddamn streets," Matt said.

"I know. He was in my place last night, at the bar. With a girl."

"I don't see him. I'm in the store all 5 the time. Ruth sees him. She sees him too much. She was at Sunnyhurst today getting cigarettes and aspirin, and there he was. She can't even go out for cigarettes and aspirin. It's killing her."

"Come back in for a drink."

Matt looked at his watch. Ruth would be asleep. He walked with Willis back into the house, pausing at the steps to look at the star-lit sky. It was a cool summer night; he thought vaguely of the Red Sox, did not even know if they were at home tonight; since it happened he had not been able to think about any of the small pleasures he believed he had earned, as he had earned also what was shattered now forever: the quietly harried and quietly pleas-urable days of fatherhood. They went inside. Willis's wife, Martha, had gone to bed hours ago, in the rear of the large house which was rigged with burglar and fire alarms. They went downstairs to the game room; the tele-vision set suspended from the ceiling, the pool table, the poker table with beer cans, cards, chips, filled ashtrays, and the six chairs where Matt and his friends had sat, the friends picking up the old banter as though he had only been away on vacation; but he could see the affection and courtesy in their eyes. Willis went behind the bar and mixed them each a Scotch and soda; he stayed behind the bar and looked at Matt sitting on the stool.

"How often have you thought about it?" Willis said.

"Every day since he got out. I didn't think about bail. I thought I wouldn't have to worry about him for years. She sees him all the time. It makes her cry."

10 "He was in my place a long time last night. He'll be back."

"Maybe he won't."

"The band. He likes the band."

"What's he doing now?"

"He's tending bar up to Hampton Beach. For a friend. Ever notice even the worst bastard always has friends? He couldn't get work in town. It's just tourists and kids up to Hampton. Nobody knows him. If they do, they don't care. They drink what he mixes."

"Nobody tells me about him." 15

"I hate him, Matt. My boys went to school with him. He was the same then. Know what he'll do? Five at the most. Remember that woman about seven years ago? Shot her husband and dropped him off the bridge in the Merrimack with a hundred-pound sack of cement and said all the way through it that nobody helped her. Know where she is now? She's in Lawrence now, a secretary. And who-ever helped her, where the hell is he?"

"I've got a .38 I've had for years, I take it to the store now. I tell Ruth it's for the night deposits. I tell her things have changed; we got junkies here now too. Lots of people without jobs. She knows though."

"What does she know?"

"She knows I started carrying it after the first time she saw him in town. She knows it's in case I see him, and there's some kind of a situation—"

He stopped, looked at Willis, and fin- 20 ished his drink. Willis mixed him another.

"What kind of situation?"

"Where he did something to me. Where I could get away with it."

"How does Ruth feel about that?"

"She doesn't know."

"You said she does, she's got it figured 25 out."

He thought of her that afternoon: When she went into Sunnyhurst, Strout was wait-ing at the counter while the clerk bagged the things he had bought; she turned down an aisle and looked at soup cans until he left.

"Ruth would shoot him herself, if she thought she could hit him."

"You got a permit?"

"No."

"I do. You could get a year for that." 30

"Maybe I'll get one. Or maybe I won't. Maybe I'll just stop bringing it to the store."

***

Richard Strout was twenty-six years old, a high school athlete, football scholarship to the University of Massachusetts where he lasted for almost two semesters before quitting in advance of the final grades that would have forced him not to return. People then said: Dickie can do the work; he just doesn't want to. He came home and did construction work for his father but refused his father's offer to learn the business; his two older brothers had learned it, so that Strout and Sons trucks going about town, and signs on construction sites, now slashed wounds into Matt Fowler's life. Then Richard married a young girl and became a bartender, his salary and tips augmented and perhaps sometimes matched by his father, who also posted his bond. So his friends, his enemies (he had those: fist fights or, more often, boys and then young men who had not fought him when they thought they should have), and those who simply knew him by face and name, had a series of images of him which they recalled when they heard of the killing: the high school running back, the young drunk in bars, the oblivious hard-hatted young man eating lunch at a counter, the bartender who could perhaps be called courteous but not more than that: as he tended bar, his dark eyes and dark, wide-jawed face appeared less sullen, near blank.

One night he beat Frank. Frank was living at home and waiting for September, for graduate school in economics, and working as a lifeguard at Salisbury Beach, where he met Mary Ann Strout, in her first month of separation. She spent most days at the beach with her two sons. Before ten o'clock one night Frank came home; he had driven to the hospital first, and he walked into the living room with stitches over his right eye and both lips bright and swollen.

"I'm all right," he said, when Matt and Ruth stood up, and Matt turned off the television, letting Ruth get to him first: the tall, muscled but slender suntanned boy. Frank tried to smile at them but couldn't because of his lips.

"It was her husband, wasn't it?" Ruth said.

"Ex," Frank said. "He dropped in."

Matt gently held Frank's jaw and turned his face to the light, looked at the stitches, the blood under the white of the eye, the bruised flesh.

"Press charges," Matt said.

"No."

"What's to stop him from doing it again? Did you hit him at all? Enough so he won't want to next time?"

"I don't think I touched him."

"So what are you going to do?"

"Take karate," Frank said, and tried again to smile.

"That's not the problem," Ruth said.

"You know you like her," Frank said.

"I like a lot of people. What about the boys? Did they see it?"

"They were asleep."

"Did you leave her alone with him?"

"He left first. She was yelling at him. I believe she had a skillet in her hand."

"Oh for God's sake," Ruth said.

Matt had been dealing with that too: at the dinner table on evenings when Frank wasn't home, was eating with Mary Ann; or, on the other nights—and Frank was with her every night—he talked with Ruth while they watched television, or lay in bed with the windows open and he smelled the night air and imagined, with both pride and muted sorrow, Frank in Mary Ann's arms. Ruth didn't like it because Mary Ann was in the process of divorce, because she had two children, because she was four years older than Frank, and finally—she told this in bed, where she had during all of their marriage told him of her deepest feelings: of love, of passion, of fears about one of the children, of pain Matt had caused her or she had caused him—she was against it because of what she had heard; that the marriage had gone bad early, and for most of it Richard and Mary Ann had both played around.

"That can't be true," Matt said. "Strout wouldn't have stood for it."

"Maybe he loves her."

"He's too hot-tempered. He couldn't have taken that."

55 But Matt knew Strout had taken it, for he had heard the stories too. He wondered who had told them to Ruth; and he felt vaguely annoyed and isolated; living with her for thirty-one years and still not knowing what she talked about with her friends. On these summer nights he did not so much argue with her as try to comfort her, but finally there was no difference between the two: she had concrete objections, which he tried to overcome. And in his attempt to do this, he neglected his own objections, which were the same as hers, so that as he spoke to her he felt as disembodied as he sometimes did in the store when he helped a man choose a blouse or dress or piece of costume jewelry for his wife.

"The divorce doesn't mean anything," he said. "She was young and maybe she liked his looks and then after a while she realized she was living with a bastard. I see it as a positive thing."

"She's not divorced yet."

"It's the same thing. Massachusetts has crazy laws, that's all. Her age is no problem. What's it matter when she was born? And that other business: even if it's true, which it probably isn't, it's got nothing to do with Frank, and it's in the past. And the kids are no problem. She's been married six years; she ought to have kids. Frank likes them. He plays with them. And he's not going to marry her anyway, so it's not a problem of money."

"Then what's he doing with her?"

60 "She probably loves him, Ruth. Girls always have. Why can't we just leave it at that?"

"He got home at six o'clock Tuesday morning."

"I didn't know you knew. I've already talked to him about it."

Which he had: since he believed almost nothing he told Ruth, he went to Frank with what he believed. The night before, he had followed Frank to the car after dinner.

"You wouldn't make much of a burglar," he said.

"How's that?" 65

Matt was looking up at him; Frank was six feet tall, an inch and a half taller than Matt, who had been proud when Frank at seventeen outgrew him; he had only felt uncomfortable when he had to reprimand or caution him. He touched Frank's bicep, thought of the young taut passionate body, believed he could sense the desire, and again he felt the pride and sorrow and envy too, not knowing whether he was envious of Frank or Mary Ann.

"When you came in yesterday morning, I woke up. One of these mornings your mother will. And I'm the one who'll have to talk to her. She won't interfere with you. Okay? I know it means—" But he stopped, thinking: I know it means getting up and leaving that suntanned girl and going sleepy to the car, I know—

"Okay," Frank said, and touched Matt's shoulder and got into the car.

There had been other talks, but the only long one was their first one: a night driving to Fenway Park, Matt having ordered the tickets so they could talk, and knowing when Frank said yes, he would go, that he knew the talk was coming too. It took them forty minutes to get to Boston, and they talked about Mary Ann until they joined the city traffic along the Charles River, blue in the late sun. Frank told him all the things that Matt would later pretend to believe when he told them to Ruth.

"It seems like a lot for a young guy to 70 take on," Matt finally said.

"Sometimes it is. But she's worth it."

"Are you thinking about getting married?"

"We haven't talked about it. She can't for over a year. I've got school."

"I *do* like her," Matt said.

75 He did. Some evenings, when the long summer sun was still low in the sky, Frank brought her home; they came into the house smelling of suntan lotion and the sea, and Matt gave them gin and tonics and started the charcoal in the backyard, and looked at Mary Ann in the lawn chair; long and very light brown hair (Matt thinking that twenty years ago she would have dyed it blonde), and the long brown legs he loved to look at; her face was pretty; she had probably never in her adult life gone unnoticed into a public place. It was in her wide brown eyes that she looked older than Frank; after a few drinks Matt thought what he saw in her eyes was something erotic, testament to the rumors about her; but he knew it wasn't that, or all that; she had, very young, been through a sort of pain that his children, and he and Ruth, had been spared. In the moments of his recognizing that pain, he wanted to tenderly touch her hair, wanted with some gesture to give her solace and hope. And he would glance at Frank, and hope they would love each other, hope Frank would soothe that pain in her heart, take it from her eyes; and her divorce, her age, and her children did not matter at all. On the first two evenings she did not bring her boys, and then Ruth asked her to bring them the next time. In bed that night Ruth said, "She hasn't brought them because she's embarrassed. She shouldn't feel embarrassed."

Richard Strout shot Frank in front of the boys. They were sitting on the living room floor watching television, Frank sitting on the couch, and Mary Ann just returning from the kitchen with a tray of sandwiches. Strout came in the front door and shot Frank twice in the chest and once in the face with a 9 mm. automatic. Then he looked at the boys and Mary Ann, and went home to wait for the police.

It seemed to Matt that from the time Mary Ann called weeping to tell him until now, a Saturday night in September, sitting in the car with Willis, parked beside Strout's car, waiting for the bar to close, that he had not so much moved through his life as wandered through it, his spirits like a dazed body bumping into furniture and corners. He had always been a fearful father: when his children were young, at the start of each summer he thought of them drowning in a pond or the sea, and he was relieved when he came home in the evenings and they were there; usually that relief was his only acknowledgment of his fear, which he never spoke of, and which he controlled within his heart. As he had when they were very young and all of them in turn, Cathleen too, were drawn to the high oak in the backyard, and had to climb it. Smiling, he watched them, imagining the fall: and he was poised to catch the small body before it hit the earth. Or his legs were poised; his hands were in his pockets or his arms were folded and, for the child looking down, he appeared relaxed and confident while his heart beat with the two words he wanted to call out but did not: *Don't fall.* In winter he was less afraid: he made sure the ice would hold him before they skated, and he brought or sent them to places where they could sled without ending in the street. So he and his children had survived their childhood, and he only worried about them when he knew they were driving a long distance, and then he lost Frank in a way no father expected to lose his son, and he felt that all the fears he had borne while they were growing up, and all the grief he had been afraid of, had backed up like a huge wave and struck him on the beach and swept him out to sea. Each day he felt the same and when he was able to forget how he felt, when he was able to force himself not to feel that way, the eyes of his clerks and customers defeated him. He wished those eyes were oblivious, even cold; he felt he was withering in their tenderness. And beneath his listless wandering, every day in his soul he shot Richard Strout in the face; while Ruth, going about town on errands, kept seeing him. And at nights in bed she would hold Matt and cry, or sometimes she was silent and Matt would touch her tightening arm, her clenched fist.

As his own right fist was now, squeezing the butt of the revolver, the last of the drinkers having left the bar, talking to each other, going to their separate cars which were in the lot in front of the bar, out of Matt's vision. He heard their voices, their cars, and then the ocean again, across the street. The tide was in and sometimes it smacked the sea wall. Through the windshield he looked at the dark red side wall of the bar, and then to his left, past Willis, at Strout's car, and through its windows he could see the now-emptied parking lot, the road, the sea wall. He could smell the sea.

The front door of the bar opened and closed again and Willis looked at Matt then at the corner of the building; when Strout came around it alone Matt got out of the car, giving up the hope he had kept all night (and for the past week) that Strout would come out with friends, and Willis would simply drive away; thinking: *All right then. All right*; and he went around the front of Willis's car, and at Strout's he stopped and aimed over the hood at Strout's blue shirt ten feet away. Willis was aiming too, crouched on Matt's left, his elbow resting on the hood.

80 "Mr. Fowler," Strout said. He looked at each of them, and at the guns. "Mr. Trottier."

Then Matt, watching the parking lot and the road, walked quickly between the car and the building and stood behind Strout. He took one leather glove from his pocket and put it on his left hand.

"Don't talk. Unlock the front and back and get in."

Strout unlocked the front door, reached in and unlocked the back, then got in, and Matt slid into the back seat, closed the door with his gloved hand, and touched Strout's head once with the muzzle.

"It's cocked. Drive to your house."

When Strout looked over his shoulder 85 to back the car, Matt aimed at his temple and did not look at his eyes.

"Drive slowly," he said. "Don't try to get stopped."

They drove across the empty front lot and onto the road, Willis's headlights shining into the car; then back through town, the sea wall on the left hiding the beach, though far out Matt could see the ocean; he uncocked the revolver; on the right were the places, most with their neon signs off, that did so much business in summer: the lounges and cafés and pizza houses, the street itself empty of traffic, the way he and Willis had known it would be when they decided to take Strout at the bar rather than knock on his door at two o'clock one morning and risk that one insomniac neighbor. Matt had not told Willis he was afraid he could not be alone with Strout for very long, smell his smells, feel the presence of his flesh, hear his voice, and then shoot him. They left the beach town and then were on the high bridge over the channel: to the left the smacking curling white at the breakwater and beyond that the dark sea and the full moon, and down to his right the small fishing boats bobbing at anchor in the cove. When they left the bridge, the sea was blocked by abandoned beach cottages, and Matt's left hand was sweating in the glove. Out here in the dark in the car he believed Ruth knew. Willis had come to his house at eleven and asked if he wanted a nightcap; Matt went to the bedroom for his wallet, put the gloves in one trouser pocket and the .38 in the other and went back to the living room, his hand in his pocket covering the bulge of the cool cylinder pressed against his fingers, the butt against his palm. When Ruth said good night she looked at his face, and he felt she could see in his eyes the gun, and the night he was going to. But he knew he couldn't trust what he saw. Willis's wife had taken her sleeping pill, which gave her eight hours—the reason, Willis had told Matt, he had the alarms installed, for nights when he was late at the restaurant—and when it was all done and Willis got home he would leave ice and a trace of Scotch and soda in two glasses in the game room and tell Martha in the morning that he had left the restaurant early and brought Matt home for a drink.

"He was making it with my wife." Strout's voice was careful, not pleading.

Matt pressed the muzzle against Strout's head, pressed it harder than he wanted to, feeling through the gun Strout's head flinching and moving forward; then he lowered the gun to his lap.

90   "Don't talk," he said.

Strout did not speak again. They turned west, drove past the Dairy Queen closed until spring, and the two lobster restaurants that faced each other and were crowded all summer and were now also closed, onto the short bridge crossing the tidal stream, and over the engine Matt could hear through his open window the water rushing inland under the bridge; looking to his left he saw its swift moonlit current going back into the marsh which, leaving the bridge, they entered: the salt marsh stretching out on both sides, the grass tall in patches but mostly low and leaning earthward as though wind-blown, a large dark rock sitting as though it rested on nothing but itself, and shallow pools reflecting the bright moon.

Beyond the marsh they drove through woods, Matt thinking now of the hole he and Willis had dug last Sunday afternoon after telling their wives they were going to Fenway Park. They listened to the game on a transistor radio, but heard none of it as they dug into the soft earth on the knoll they had chosen because elms and maples sheltered it. Already some leaves had fallen. When the hole was deep enough they covered it and the piled earth with dead branches, then cleaned their shoes and pants and went to a restaurant farther up in New Hampshire where they ate sandwiches and drank beer and watched the rest of the game on television. Looking at the back of Strout's head he thought of Frank's grave; he had not been back to it; but he would go before winter, and its second burial of snow.

He thought of Frank sitting on the couch and perhaps talking to the children as they watched television, imagined him feeling young and strong, still warmed from the sun at the beach, and feeling loved, hearing Mary Ann moving about in the kitchen, hearing her walking into the living room; maybe he looked up at her and maybe she said something, looking at him over the tray of sandwiches, smiling at him, saying something the way women do when they offer food as a gift, then the front door opening and this son of a bitch coming in and Frank seeing that he meant the gun in his hand, this son of a bitch and his gun the last person and thing Frank saw on earth.

When they drove into town the streets were nearly empty: a few slow cars, a policeman walking his beat past the darkened fronts of stores. Strout and Matt both glanced at him as they drove by. They were on the main street, and all the stoplights were blinking yellow. Willis and Matt had talked about that too; the lights changed at midnight, so there would be no place Strout had to stop and where he might try to run.

Strout turned down the block where he lived and Willis's headlights were no longer with Matt in the back seat. They had planned that too, had decided it was best for just the one car to go to the house, and again Matt had said nothing about his fear of being alone with Strout, especially in his house: a duplex, dark as all the houses on the street were, the street itself lit at the corner of each block. As Strout turned into the driveway Matt thought of the one insomniac neighbor, thought of some man or woman sitting alone in the dark living room, watching the all-night channel from Boston. When Strout stopped the car near the front of the house, Matt said: "Drive it to the back."

95   He touched Strout's head with the muzzle.

"You wouldn't have it cocked, would you? For when I put on the brakes."

Matt cocked it, and said: "It is now."

Strout waited a moment; then he eased the car forward, the engine doing little more than idling, and as they approached the garage he gently braked. Matt opened the door, then took off the glove and put it in his pocket. He stepped out and shut the door with his hip and said: "All right."

Strout looked at the gun, then got out, and Matt followed him across the grass, and as Strout unlocked the door Matt looked quickly at the row of small backyards on either side, and scattered tall trees, some evergreens, others not, and he thought of the red and yellow leaves on the trees over the hole, saw them falling soon, probably in two weeks, dropping slowly, covering. Strout stepped into the kitchen.

100   "Turn on the light."

Strout reached to the wall switch, and in the light Matt looked at his wide back, the dark blue shirt, the white belt, the red plaid pants.

"Where's your suitcase?"

"My suitcase?"

"Where is it?"

"In the bedroom closet."   105

"That's where we're going then. When we get to a door you stop and turn on the light."

They crossed the kitchen, Matt glancing at the sink and stove and refrigerator: no dishes in the sink or even the dish rack beside it, no grease splashings on the stove, the refrigerator door clean and white. He did not want to look at any more but he looked quickly at all he could see: in the living room magazines and newspapers in a wicker basket, clean ashtrays, a record player, the records shelved next to it, then down the hall where, near the bedroom door, hung a color photograph of Mary Ann and the two boys sitting on a lawn—there was no house in the picture—Mary Ann smiling at the camera or Strout or whoever held the camera, smiling as she had on Matt's lawn this summer while he waited for the charcoal and they all talked and he looked at her brown legs and at Frank touching her arm, her shoulder, her hair; he moved down the hall with her smile in his mind, wondering: was that when they were both playing around and she was smiling like that at him and they were happy, even sometimes, making it worth it? He recalled her eyes, the pain in them, and he was conscious of the circles of love he was touching with the hand that held the revolver so tightly now as Strout stopped at the door at the end of the hall.

"There's no wall switch."

"Where's the light?"

"By the bed."   110

"Let's go."

Matt stayed a pace behind, then Strout leaned over and the room was lighted: the bed, a double one, was neatly made; the ashtray on the bedside table clean, the bureau top dustless, and no photographs; probably so the girl—who *was* she?—would not have to see Mary Ann in the bedroom she believed was theirs. But because Matt was a father and a husband, though never an ex-husband, he knew (and did not want to know) that this bedroom had never been theirs alone. Strout turned around; Matt looked at his lips, his wide jaw, and thought of Frank's doomed and fearful eyes looking up from the couch.

"Where's Mr. Trottier?"

"He's waiting. Pack clothes for warm weather."

115 "What's going on?"

"You're jumping bail."

"Mr. Fowler—"

He pointed the cocked revolver at Strout's face. The barrel trembled but not much, not as much as he had expected. Strout went to the closet and got the suitcase from the floor and opened it on the bed. As he went to the bureau, he said: "He was making it with my wife. I'd go pick up my kids and he'd be there. Sometimes he spent the night. My boys told me."

He did not look at Matt as he spoke. He opened the top drawer and Matt stepped closer so he could see Strout's hands: underwear and socks, the socks rolled, the underwear folded and stacked. He took them back to the bed, arranged them neatly in the suitcase, then from the closet he was taking shirts and trousers and a jacket; he laid them on the bed and Matt followed him to the bathroom and watched from the door while he packed those things a person accumulated and that became part of him so that at times in the store Matt felt he was selling more than clothes.

120 "I wanted to try to get together with her again." He was bent over the suitcase. "I couldn't even talk to her. He was always with her. I'm going to jail for it; if I ever get out I'll be an old man. Isn't that enough?"

"You're not going to jail."

Strout closed the suitcase and faced Matt, looking at the gun. Matt went to his

rear, so Strout was between him and the lighted hall; then using his handkerchief he turned off the lamp and said: "Let's go."

They went down the hall, Matt looking again at the photograph, and through the living room and kitchen, Matt turning off the lights and talking, frightened that he was talking, that he was telling this lie he had not planned: "It's the trial. We can't go through that, my wife and me. So you're leaving. We've got you a ticket, and a job. A friend of Mr. Trottier's. Out west. My wife keeps seeing you. We can't have that anymore."

Matt turned out the kitchen light and put the handkerchief in his pocket, and they went down the two brick steps and across the lawn. Strout put the suitcase on the floor of the back seat, then got into the front seat and Matt got in the back and put on his glove and shut the door.

"They'll catch me. They'll check pas- 125 senger lists."

"We didn't use your name."

"They'll figure that out too. You think I wouldn't have done it myself if it was that easy?"

He backed into the street, Matt looking down the gun barrel but not at the profiled face beyond it.

"You were alone," Matt said. "We've got it worked out."

"There's no planes this time of night, 130 Mr. Fowler."

"Go back through town. Then north on 125."

They came to the corner and turned, and now Willis's headlights were in the car with Matt.

"Why north, Mr. Fowler?"

"Somebody's going to keep you for a while. They'll take you to the airport." He uncocked the hammer and lowered the revolver to his lap and said wearily: "No more talking."

135   As they drove back through town, Matt's body sagged, going limp with his spirit and its new and false bond with Strout, the hope his lie had given Strout. He had grown up in this town whose streets had become places of apprehension and pain for Ruth as she drove and walked, doing what she had to do; and for him too, if only in his mind as he worked and chatted six days a week in his store; he wondered now if his lie would have worked, if sending Strout away would have been enough; but then he knew that just thinking of Strout in Montana or whatever place lay at the end of the lie he had told, thinking of him walking the streets there, loving a girl there (who *was* she?) would be enough to slowly rot the rest of his days. And Ruth's. Again he was certain that she knew, that she was waiting for him.

   They were in New Hampshire now, on the narrow highway, passing the shopping center at the state line, and then houses and small stores and sandwich shops. There were few cars on the road. After ten minutes he raised his trembling hand, touched Strout's neck with the gun, and said: "Turn in up here. At the dirt road."

   Strout flicked on the indicator and slowed.

   "Mr. Fowler?"

   "They're waiting here."

140   Strout turned very slowly, easing his neck away from the gun. In the moonlight the road was light brown, lighter and yellowed where the headlights shone; weeds and a few trees grew on either side of it, and ahead of them were the woods.

   "There's nothing back here, Mr. Fowler."

   "It's for your car. You don't think we'd leave it at the airport, do you?"

   He watched Strout's large, big-knuckled hands tighten on the wheel, saw Frank's face that night: not the stitches and bruised eye and swollen lips, but his own hand gently touching Frank's jaw, turning his wounds to the light. They rounded a bend in the road and were out of sight of the highway: tall trees all around them now, hiding the moon. When they reached the abandoned gravel pit on the left, the bare flat earth and steep pale embankment behind it, and the black crowns of trees at its top, Matt said: "Stop here."

   Strout stopped but did not turn off the engine. Matt pressed the gun hard against his neck, and he straightened in the seat and looked in the rearview mirror, Matt's eyes meeting his in the glass for an instant before looking at the hair at the end of the gun barrel.

   "Turn it off."   145

   Strout did, then held the wheel with two hands, and looked in the mirror.

   "I'll do twenty years, Mr. Fowler; at least. I'll be forty-six years old."

   "That's nine years younger than I am," Matt said, and got out and took off the glove and kicked the door shut. He aimed at Strout's ear and pulled back the hammer. Willis's headlights were off and Matt heard him walking on the soft thin layer of dust, the hard earth beneath it. Strout opened the door, sat for a moment in the interior light, then stepped out onto the road. Now his face was pleading. Matt did not look at his eyes, but he could see it in the lips.

   "Just get the suitcase. They're right up the road."

   Willis was beside him now, to his left. 150 Strout looked at both guns. Then he opened the back door, leaned in, and with a jerk brought the suitcase out. He was turning to face them when Matt said: "Just walk up the road. Just ahead."

   Strout turned to walk, the suitcase in his right hand, and Matt and Willis followed; as Strout cleared the front of his car he dropped the suitcase and, ducking, took one step that was the beginning of a sprint to his right. The gun kicked in Matt's hand, and the explosion of the shot surrounded him, isolated him in a nimbus of sound that cut him off from all his time, all his history, isolated him standing absolutely still on the dirt road with the gun in his hand, looking down at Richard Strout squirming on his belly, kicking one leg behind him, pushing himself forward, toward the woods. Then Matt went to him and shot him once in the back of the head.

Driving south to Boston, wearing both gloves now, staying in the middle lane and looking often in the rearview mirror at Willis's headlights, he relived the suitcase dropping, the quick dip and turn of Strout's back, and the kick of the gun, the sound of the shot. When he walked to Strout, he still existed within the first shot, still trembled and breathed with it. The second shot and the burial seemed to be happening to someone else, someone he was watching. He and Willis each held an arm and pulled Strout face-down off the road and into the woods, his bouncing sliding belt white under the trees where it was so dark that when they stopped at the top of the knoll, panting and sweating, Matt could not see where Strout's blue shirt ended and the earth began. They pulled off the branches then dragged Strout to the edge of the hole and went behind him and lifted his legs and pushed him in. They stood still for a moment. The woods were quiet save for their breathing, and Matt remembered hearing the movements of birds and small animals after the first shot. Or maybe he had not heard them. Willis went down to the road. Matt could see him clearly out on the tan dirt, could see the glint of Strout's car and, beyond the road, the gravel pit. Willis came back up the knoll with the suitcase. He dropped it in the hole and took off his gloves and they went down to his car for the spades. They worked quietly. Sometimes they paused to listen to the woods. When they were finished Willis turned on his flashlight and they covered the earth with leaves and branches and then went down to the spot in front of the car, and while Matt held the light Willis crouched and sprinkled dust on the blood, backing up till he reached the grass and leaves, then he used leaves until they had worked up to the grave again. They did not stop. They walked around the grave and through the woods, using the light on the ground, looking up through the trees to where they ended at the lake. Neither of them spoke above the sounds of their heavy and clumsy strides through low brush and over fallen branches. Then they reached it: wide and dark, lapping softly at the bank, pine needles smooth under Matt's feet, moonlight on the lake, a small island near its middle, with black, tall evergreens. He took out the gun and threw for the island: taking two steps back on the pine needles, striding with the throw and going to one knee as he followed through, looking up to see the dark shapeless object arcing downward, splashing.

They left Strout's car in Boston, in front of an apartment building on Commonwealth Avenue. When they got back to town Willis drove slowly over the bridge and Matt threw the keys into the Merrimack. The sky was turning light. Willis let him out a block from his house, and walking home he listened for sounds from the houses he passed. They were quiet. A light was on in his living room. He turned it off and undressed in there, and went softly toward the bedroom; in the hall he smelled the smoke, and he stood in the bedroom doorway and looked at the orange of her cigarette in the dark. The curtains were closed. He went to the closet and put his shoes on the floor and felt for a hanger.

"Did you do it?" she said.

He went down the hall to the bathroom and in the dark he washed his hands and face. Then he went to her, lay on his back, and pulled the sheet up to his throat.

"Are you all right?" she said.

155

"I think so."

Now she touched him, lying on her side, her hand on his belly, his thigh.

"Tell me," she said.

160 He started from the beginning, in the parking lot at the bar; but soon with his eyes closed and Ruth petting him, he spoke of Strout's house: the order, the woman presence, the picture on the wall.

"The way she was smiling," he said.

"What about it?"

"I don't know. Did you ever see Strout's girl? When you saw him in town?"

"No."

165 "I wonder who she was."

Then he thought: *not was: is. Sleeping now she is his girl.* He opened his eyes, then closed them again. There was more light beyond the curtains. With Ruth now he left Strout's house and told again his lie to Strout, gave him again that hope that Strout must have for a while believed, else he would have to believe only the gun pointed at him for the last two hours of his life. And with Ruth he saw again the dropping suitcase, the darting move to the right: and he told of the first shot, feeling her hand on him but his heart isolated still, beating on the road still in that explosion like thunder. He told her the rest, but the words had no images for him, he did not see himself doing what the words said he had done; he only saw himself on that road.

"We can't tell the other kids," she said. "It'll hurt them, thinking he got away. But we mustn't."

"No."

She was holding him, wanting him, and he wished he could make love with her but he could not. He saw Frank and Mary Ann making love in her bed, their eyes closed, their bodies brown and smelling of the sea; the other girl was faceless, bodiless, but he felt her sleeping now; and he saw Frank and Strout, their faces alive; he saw red and yellow leaves falling on the earth, then snow; falling and freezing and falling; and holding Ruth, his cheek touching her breast, he shuddered with a sob that he kept silent in his heart.

····•▶ *Your* **Turn**
Talking and Writing about Lit

1. Why does Dubus begin "Killings" with the funeral? What effect does it have on the reader not to know at the outset who has been killed or how?

2. Analyze the plot of "Killings," noting the ways in which it is not chronological (note examples of flashback and foreshadowing). What has the author gained by arranging events in this order?

3. Does Matt Fowler feel satisfied by his revenge at the end of the story? How do you know? Cite "evidence" from the story—in the form of quotations and specific details—to support your view.

4. **DIY** "Killings" is written in the third-person point of view, but all of the action is seen from the perspective of the father, Matt Fowler, and we also have access to Matt's thoughts and feelings throughout the story. Rewrite two pages of the story from the point of view of a different character (Richard Strout, Frank, Ruth, or Mary Ann).

Amy Tan (b. 1952)

Amy Tan was born in Oakland, California, to parents who had recently emigrated from mainland China. After her father's death, Tan and her mother lived for a time in Switzerland. She returned to the United States to finish her education and received her M.A. in linguistics from San Jose State University. In 1984, a journey with her mother to visit China was a formative experience for Amy Tan as a writer. After attending the Squaw Valley Writers Conference, where her work received encouragement and recognition, she published *The Joy Luck Club* (1989), which was not only a critical success, but also became a best-seller and was made into a movie. Tan's second book was *The Kitchen God's Wife* (1991). Both works of fiction are story cycles, comprising interlocking stories and recurring characters.

Half and Half (1989)

As proof of her faith, my mother used to carry a small leatherette Bible when she went to the First Chinese Baptist Church every Sunday. But later, after my mother lost her faith in God, that leatherette Bible wound up wedged under a too-short table leg, a way for her to correct the imbalances of life. It's been there for over twenty years.

My mother pretends that Bible isn't there. Whenever anyone asks her what it's doing there, she says, a little too loudly, "Oh, this? I forgot." But I know she sees it. My mother is not the best housekeeper in the world, and after all these years that Bible is still clean white.

Tonight I'm watching my mother sweep under the same kitchen table, something she does every night after dinner. She gently pokes her broom around the table leg propped up by the Bible. I watch her, sweep after sweep, waiting for the right moment to tell her about Ted and me, that we're getting divorced. When I tell her, I know she's going to say, "This cannot be."

And when I say that it is certainly true, that our marriage is over, I know what else she will say: "Then you must save it."

And even though I know it's hope-less—there's absolutely nothing left to save—I'm afraid if I tell her that, she'll still persuade me to try.

I think it's ironic that my mother wants me to fight the divorce. Seventeen years ago she was chagrined when I started dating Ted. My older sisters had dated only Chinese boys from church before getting married.

Ted and I met in a politics of ecology class when he leaned over and offered to pay me two dollars for the last week's notes. I refused the money and accepted a cup of coffee instead. This was during my second semester at UC Berkeley, where I had enrolled as a liberal arts major and later changed to fine arts. Ted was in his third year in pre-med, his choice, he told me, ever since he dissected a fetal pig in the sixth grade.

I have to admit that what I initially found attractive in Ted were precisely the things that made him different from my brothers and the Chinese boys I had dated: his brashness; the assuredness in which he asked for things and expected to get them; his opinionated manner; his angular face and lanky body; the thickness of his arms; the fact that his parents immigrated from Tarrytown, New York, not Tientsin, China.

My mother must have noticed these same differences after Ted picked me up one evening at my parents' house. When I returned home, my mother was still up, watching television.

10 "He is American," warned my mother, as if I had been too blind to notice. "A *waigoren*."[1]

"I'm American too," I said. "And it's not as if I'm going to marry him or something."

Mrs. Jordan also had a few words to say. Ted had casually invited me to a family picnic, the annual clan reunion held by the polo fields in Golden Gate Park. Although we had dated only a few times in the last month—and certainly had never slept together, since both of us lived at home—Ted introduced me to all his relatives as his girlfriend, which, until then, I didn't know I was.

Later, when Ted and his father went off to play volleyball with the others, his mother took my hand, and we started walking along the grass, away from the crowd. She squeezed my palm warmly but never seemed to look at me.

"I'm so glad to meet you *finally*," Mrs. Jordan said. I wanted to tell her I wasn't really Ted's girlfriend, but she went on. "I think it's nice that you and Ted are having such a lot of fun together. So I hope you won't misunderstand what I have to say."

And then she spoke quietly about 15 Ted's future, his need to concentrate on his medical studies, why it would be years before he could even think about marriage. She assured me she had nothing whatsoever against minorities; she and her husband, who owned a chain of office-supply stores, personally knew many fine people who were Oriental, Spanish, and even black. But Ted was going to be in one of those professions where he would be judged by a different standard, by patients and other doctors who might not be as understanding as the Jordans were. She said it was so unfortunate the way the rest of the world was, how unpopular the Vietnam War was.

"Mrs. Jordan, I am not Vietnamese," I said softly, even though I was on the verge of shouting. "And I have no intention of marrying your son."

When Ted drove me home that day, I told him I couldn't see him anymore. When he asked me why, I shrugged. When he pressed me, I told him what his mother had said, verbatim, without comment.

"And you're just going to sit there! Let my mother decide what's right?" he shouted, as if I were a co-conspirator who had turned traitor. I was touched that Ted was so upset.

"What should we do?" I asked, and I had a pained feeling I thought was the beginning of love.

In those early months, we clung to 20 each other with a rather silly desperation, because, in spite of anything my mother or Mrs. Jordan could say, there was nothing that really prevented us from seeing one another. With imagined tragedy hovering over us, we became inseparable, two halves creating the whole: yin and yang. I was

---

[1]**waigoren:** any person who is a foreigner or, more specifically, any person who is not Chinese.

victim to his hero. I was always in danger and he was always rescuing me. I would fall and he would lift me up. It was exhilarating and draining. The emotional effect of saving and being saved was addicting to both of us. And that, as much as anything we ever did in bed, was how we made love to each other: conjoined where my weaknesses needed protection.

"What should we do?" I continued to ask him. And within a year of our first meeting we were living together. The month before Ted started medical school at UCSF we were married in the Episcopal church, and Mrs. Jordan sat in the front pew, crying as was expected of the groom's mother. When Ted finished his residency in dermatology, we bought a run-down three-story Victorian with a large garden in Ashbury Heights. Ted helped me set up a studio downstairs so I could take in work as a freelance production assistant for graphic artists.

Over the years, Ted decided where we went on vacation. He decided what new furniture we should buy. He decided we should wait until we moved into a better neighborhood before having children. We used to discuss some of these matters, but we both knew the question would boil down to my saying, "Ted, you decide." After a while, there were no more discussions. Ted simply decided. And I never thought of objecting. I preferred to ignore the world around me, obsessing only over what was in front of me: my T-square, my X-acto knife, my blue pencil.

But last year Ted's feelings about what he called "decision and responsibility" changed. A new patient had come to him asking what she could do about the spidery veins on her cheeks. And when he told her he could suck the red veins out and make her beautiful again, she believed him. But instead, he accidentally sucked a nerve out, and the left side of her smile fell down and she sued him.

After he lost the malpractice lawsuit—his first, and a big shock to him I now realize—he started pushing me to make decisions. Did I think we should buy an American car or a Japanese car? Should we change from whole-life to term insurance? What did I think about that candidate who supported the contras? What about a family?

I thought about things, the pros and 25 the cons. But in the end I would be so confused, because I never believed there was ever any one right answer, yet there were many wrong ones. So whenever I said, "You decide," or "I don't care," or "Either way is fine with me," Ted would say in his impatient voice, "No, *you* decide. You can't have it both ways, none of the responsibility, none of the blame."

I could feel things changing between us. A protective veil had been lifted and Ted now started pushing me about everything. He asked me to decide on the most trivial matters, as if he were baiting me. Italian food or Thai. One appetizer or two. Which appetizer. Credit card or cash. Visa or MasterCard.

Last month, when he was leaving for a two-day dermatology course in Los Angeles, he asked if I wanted to come along and then quickly, before I could say anything, he added, "Never mind, I'd rather go alone."

"More time to study," I agreed.

"No, because you can never make up your mind about anything," he said.

And I protested, "But it's only with 30 things that aren't important."

"Nothing is important to you, then," he said in a tone of disgust.

"Ted, if you want me to go, I'll go."

And it was as if something snapped in him. "How the hell did we ever get married? Did you just say 'I do' because the minister said 'repeat after me'? What would you have done with your life if I had never married you? Did it ever occur to you?"

This was such a big leap in logic, between what I said and what he said, that I thought we were like two people standing apart on separate mountain peaks, recklessly leaning forward to throw stones at one another, unaware of the dangerous chasm that separated us.

35   But now I realize Ted knew what he was saying all along. He wanted to show me the rift. Because later that evening he called from Los Angeles and said he wanted a divorce.

Ever since Ted's been gone, I've been thinking, Even if I had expected it, even if I had known what I was going to do with my life, it still would have knocked the wind out of me.

When something that violent hits you, you can't help but lose your balance and fall. And after you pick yourself up, you realize you can't trust anybody to save you—not your husband, not your mother, not God. So what can you do to stop yourself from tilting and falling all over again?

My mother believed in God's will for many years. It was as if she had turned on a celestial faucet and goodness kept pouring out. She said it was faith that kept all these good things coming our way, only I thought she said "fate," because she couldn't pronounce that "th" sound in "faith."

And later, I discovered that maybe it was fate all along, that faith was just an illusion that somehow you're in control. I found out the most *I* could have was hope, and with that I was not denying any possibility, good or bad. I was just saying, If there is a choice, dear God or whatever you are, here's where the odds should be placed.

40   I remember the day I started thinking this, it was such a revelation to me. It was the day my mother lost her faith in God. She found that things of unquestioned certainty could never be trusted again.

We had gone to the beach, to a secluded spot south of the city near Devil's Slide. My father had read in *Sunset* magazine that this was a good place to catch ocean perch. And although my father was not a fisherman but a pharmacist's assistant who had once been a doctor in China, he believed in his *nengkan*, his ability to do anything he put his mind to. My mother believed she had *nengkan* to cook anything my father had a mind to catch. It was this belief in their *nengkan* that had brought my parents to America. It had enabled them to have seven children and buy a house in the Sunset district with very little money. It had given them the confidence to believe their luck would never run out, that God was on their side, that the house gods had only benevolent things to report and our ancestors were pleased, that lifetime warranties meant our lucky streak would never break, that all the elements were in balance, the right amount of wind and water.

So there we were, the nine of us: my father, my mother, my two sisters, four brothers, and myself, so confident as we walked along our first beach. We marched in single file across the cool gray sand, from oldest to youngest. I was in the middle, fourteen years old. We would have made quite a sight, if anyone else had been watching, nine pairs of bare feet trudging, nine pairs of shoes in hand, nine black-haired heads turned toward the water to watch the waves tumbling in.

The wind was whipping the cotton trousers around my legs and I looked for some place where the sand wouldn't kick into my eyes. I saw we were standing in the hollow of a cove. It was like a giant bowl, cracked in half, the other half washed out to sea. My mother walked toward the right, where the beach was clean, and we all followed. On this side, the wall of the cove curved around and protected the beach from both the rough surf and the wind. And along this wall, in its shadow, was a reef ledge that started at the edge of the beach and continued out past the cove where the waters became rough. It seemed as though a person could walk out to sea on this reef, although it looked very rocky and slippery. On the other side of the cove, the wall was more jagged, eaten away by the water. It was pitted with crevices, so when the waves crashed against the wall, the water spewed out of these holes like white gulleys.

Thinking back, I remember that this beach cove was a terrible place, full of wet shadows that chilled us and invisible specks that flew into our eyes and made it hard for us to see the dangers. We were all blind with the newness of this experience: a Chinese family trying to act like a typical American family at the beach.

45   My mother spread out an old striped bedspread, which flapped in the wind until nine pairs of shoes weighed it down. My father assembled his long bamboo fishing pole, a pole he had made with his own two hands, remembering its design from his childhood in China. And we children sat huddled shoulder to shoulder on the blanket, reaching into the grocery sack full of bologna sandwiches, which we hungrily ate salted with sand from our fingers.

Then my father stood up and admired his fishing pole, its grace, its strength. Satisfied, he picked up his shoes and walked to the edge of the beach and then onto the reef to the point just before it was wet. My two older sisters, Janice and Ruth, jumped up from the blanket and slapped their thighs to get the sand off. Then they slapped each other's backs and raced off down the beach shrieking. I was about to get up and chase them, but my mother nodded toward my four brothers and reminded me: "*Dangsying tamende shenti,*" which means "Take care of them," or literally, "Watch out for their

bodies." These bodies were the anchors of my life: Matthew, Mark, Luke, and Bing. I fell back onto the sand, groaning as my throat grew tight, as I made the same lament: "Why?" Why did *I* have to care for them?

And she gave me the same answer: "*Yiding.*"[2]

I must. Because they were my brothers. My sisters had once taken care of me. How else could I learn responsibility? How else could I appreciate what my parents had done for me?

Matthew, Mark, and Luke were twelve, ten, and nine, old enough to keep themselves loudly amused. They had already buried Luke in a shallow grave of sand so that only his head stuck out. Now they were starting to pat together the outlines of a sand-castle wall on top of him.

But Bing was only four, easily excitable 50 and easily bored and irritable. He didn't want to play with the other brothers because they had pushed him off to the side, admonishing him, "No, Bing, you'll just wreck it."

So Bing wandered down the beach, walking stiffly like an ousted emperor, picking up shards of rock and chunks of driftwood and flinging them with all his might into the surf. I trailed behind, imagining tidal waves and wondering what I would do if one appeared. I called to Bing every now and then, "Don't go too close to the water. You'll get your feet wet." And I thought how much I seemed like my mother, always worried beyond reason inside, but at the same time talking about the danger as if it were less than it really was. The worry surrounded me, like the wall of the cove, and it made me feel everything had been considered and was now safe.

My mother had a superstition, in fact, that children were predisposed to certain dangers on certain days, all depending on

---

[2]**Yiding:** must.

their Chinese birthdate. It was explained in a little Chinese book called *The Twenty-Six Malignant Gates*. There, on each page, was an illustration of some terrible danger that awaited young innocent children. In the corners was a description written in Chinese, and since I couldn't read the characters, I could only see what the picture meant.

The same little boy appeared in each picture: climbing a broken tree limb, standing by a falling gate, slipping in a wooden tub, being carried away by a snapping dog, fleeing from a bolt of lightning. And in each of these pictures stood a man who looked as if he were wearing a lizard costume. He had a big crease in his forehead, or maybe it was actually that he had two round horns. In one picture, the lizard man was standing on a curved bridge, laughing as he watched the little boy falling forward over the bridge rail, his slippered feet already in the air.

It would have been enough to think that even one of these dangers could befall a child. And even though the birthdates corresponded to only one danger, my mother worried about them all. This was because she couldn't figure out how the Chinese dates, based on the lunar calendar, translated into American dates. So by taking them all into account, she had absolute faith she could prevent every one of them.

55 The sun had shifted and moved over the other side of the cove wall. Everything had settled into place. My mother was busy keeping sand from blowing onto the blanket, then shaking sand out of shoes, and tacking corners of blankets back down again with the now clean shoes. My father was still standing at the end of the reef, patiently casting out, waiting for *nengkan* to manifest itself as a fish. I could see small figures farther down on the beach, and I could tell they were my sisters by their two dark heads and yellow pants. My brothers' shrieks were mixed with those of seagulls. Bing had found an empty soda bottle and was using this to dig sand next to the dark cove wall. And I sat on the sand, just where the shadows ended and the sunny part began.

Bing was pounding the soda bottle against the rock, so I called to him, "Don't dig so hard. You'll bust a hole in the wall and fall all the way to China." And I laughed when he looked at me as though he thought what I said was true. He stood up and started walking toward the water. He put one foot tentatively on the reef and I warned him, "Bing."

"I'm gonna see Daddy," he protested.

"Stay close to the wall, then, away from the water," I said. "Stay away from the mean fish."

And I watched as he inched his way along the reef, his back hugging the bumpy cove wall. I still see him, so clearly that I almost feel I can make him stay there forever.

I see him standing by the wall, safe, calling to 60 my father, who looks over his shoulder toward Bing. How glad I am that my father is going to watch him for a while! Bing starts to walk over and then something tugs on my father's line and he's reeling as fast as he can.

Shouts erupt. Someone has thrown sand in Luke's face and he's jumped out of his sand grave and thrown himself on top of Mark, thrashing and kicking. My mother shouts for me to stop them. And right after I pull Luke off Mark, I look up and see Bing walking alone to the edge of the reef. In the confusion of the fight nobody notices. I am the only one who sees what Bing is doing.

Bing walks one, two, three steps. His little body is moving so quickly, as if he spotted something wonderful by the water's edge. And I think, *He's going to fall in*. I'm expecting it. And just as I think this, his feet are already in the air, in a moment of balance, before he splashes into the sea and disappears without leaving so much as a ripple in the water.

I sank to my knees watching that spot where he disappeared, not moving, not saying anything. I couldn't make sense of it. I was thinking, Should I run to the water and try to pull him out? Should I shout to my father? Can I rise on my legs just enough? Can I take it all back and forbid Bing from joining my father on the ledge?

And then my sisters were back, and one of them said, "Where's Bing?" There was silence for a few seconds and then shouts and sand flying as everyone rushed past me toward the water's edge. I stood there unable to move as my sisters looked by the cove wall, as my brothers scrambled to see what lay behind pieces of driftwood. My mother and father were trying to part the waves with their hands.

65   We were there for many hours. I remember the search boats and the sunset when dusk came. I had never seen a sunset like that: a bright orange flame touching the water's edge and then fanning out, warming the sea. When it became dark, the boats turned their yellow orbs on and bounced up and down on the dark shiny water.

As I look back, it seems unnatural to think about the colors of the sunset and boats at a time like that. But we all had strange thoughts. My father was calculating minutes, estimating the temperature of the water, readjusting his estimate of when Bing fell. My sisters were calling, "Bing! Bing!" as if he were hiding in some bushes high above the beach cliffs. My brothers sat in the car, quietly reading comic books. And when the boats turned off their yellow orbs, my mother went for a swim. She had never swum a stroke in her life, but her faith in her own *nengkan* convinced her that what these Americans couldn't do, she could. She could find Bing.

And when the rescue people finally pulled her out of the water, she still had her *nengkan* intact. Her hair, her clothes, they were all heavy with the cold water, but she stood quietly, calm and regal as a mermaid queen who had just arrived out of the sea. The police called off the search, put us all in our car, and sent us home to grieve.

I had expected to be beaten to death, by my father, by my mother, by my sisters and brothers. I knew it was my fault. I hadn't watched him closely enough, and yet I saw him. But as we sat in the dark living room, I heard them, one by one whispering their regrets.

"I was selfish to want to go fishing," said my father.

"We shouldn't have gone for a walk," 70 said Janice, while Ruth blew her nose yet another time.

"Why'd you have to throw sand in my face?" moaned Luke. "Why'd you have to make me start a fight?"

And my mother quietly admitted to me, "I told you to stop their fight. I told you to take your eyes off him."

If I had had any time at all to feel a sense of relief, it would have quickly evaporated, because my mother also said, "So now I am telling you, we must go and find him, quickly, tomorrow morning." And everybody's eyes looked down. But I saw it as my punishment: to go out with my mother, back to the beach, to help her find Bing's body.

Nothing prepared me for what my mother did the next day. When I woke up, it was still dark and she was already dressed. On the kitchen table was a thermos, a teacup, the white leatherette Bible, and the car keys.

"Is Daddy ready?" I asked.   75

"Daddy's not coming," she said.

"Then how will we get there? Who will drive us?"

She picked up the keys and I followed her out the door to the car. I wondered the whole time as we drove to the beach how she had learned to drive overnight. She used no map. She drove smoothly ahead, turning down Geary, then the Great Highway, signaling at all the right times, getting on the Coast Highway and easily winding the car around the sharp curves that often led inexperienced drivers off and over the cliffs.

When we arrived at the beach, she walked immediately down the dirt path and over to the end of the reef ledge, where I had seen Bing disappear. She held in her hand the white Bible. And looking out over the water, she called to God, her small voice carried up by the gulls to heaven. It began with "Dear God" and ended with "Amen," and in between she spoke in Chinese.

80 "I have always believed in your blessings," she praised God in that same tone she used for exaggerated Chinese compliments. "We knew they would come. We did not question them. Your decisions were our decisions. You rewarded us for our faith.

"In return we have always tried to show our deepest respect. We went to your house. We brought you money. We sang your songs. You gave us more blessings. And now we have misplaced one of them. We were careless. This is true. We had so many good things, we couldn't keep them in our mind all the time.

"So maybe you hid him from us to teach us a lesson, to be more careful with your gifts in the future. I have learned this. I have put it in my memory. And now I have come to take Bing back."

I listened quietly as my mother said these words, horrified. And I began to cry when she added, "Forgive us for his bad manners. My daughter, this one standing here, will be sure to teach him better lessons of obedience before he visits you again."

After her prayer, her faith was so great that she saw him, three times, waving to her from just beyond the first wave. *"Nale!"*— There! And she would stand straight as a sentinel, until three times her eyesight failed her and Bing turned into a dark spot of churning seaweed.

My mother did not let her chin fall 85 down. She walked back to the beach and put the Bible down. She picked up the thermos and teacup and walked to the water's edge. Then she told me that the night before she had reached back into her life, back when she was a girl in China, and this is what she had found.

"I remember a boy who lost his hand in a firecracker accident," she said. "I saw the shreds of this boy's arm, his tears, and then I heard his mother's claim that he would grow back another hand, better than the last. This mother said she would pay back an ancestral debt ten times over. She would use a water treatment to soothe the wrath of Chu Jung, the three-eyed god of fire. And true enough, the next week this boy was riding a bicycle, both hands steering a straight course past my astonished eyes!"

And then my mother became very quiet. She spoke again in a thoughtful, respectful manner.

"An ancestor of ours once stole water from a sacred well. Now the water is trying to steal back. We must sweeten the temper of the Coiling Dragon who lives in the sea. And then we must make him loosen his coils from Bing by giving him another treasure he can hide."

My mother poured out tea sweetened with sugar into the teacup, and threw this into the sea. And then she opened her fist. In her palm was a ring of watery blue sapphire, a gift from her mother, who had died many years before. This ring, she told me, drew coveting stares from women and made them inattentive to the children they guarded so jealously. This would make the Coiling Dragon forgetful of Bing. She threw the ring into the water

90   But even with this, Bing did not appear right away. For an hour or so, all we saw was seaweed drifting by. And then I saw her clasp her hands to her chest, and she said in a wondrous voice, "See, it's because we were watching the wrong direction." And I too saw Bing trudging wearily at the far end of the beach, his shoes hanging in his hand, his dark head bent over in exhaustion. I could feel what my mother felt. The hunger in our hearts was instantly filled. And then the two of us, before we could even get to our feet, saw him light a cigarette, grow tall, and become a stranger.

"Ma, let's go," I said as softly as possible.

"He's there," she said firmly. She pointed to the jagged wall across the water. "I see him. He is in a cave, sitting on a little step above the water. He is hungry and a little cold, but he has learned now not to complain too much."

And then she stood up and started walking across the sandy beach as though it were a solid paved path, and I was trying to follow behind, struggling and stumbling in the soft mounds. She marched up the steep path to where the car was parked, and she wasn't even breathing hard as she pulled a large inner tube from the trunk. To this lifesaver, she tied the fishing line from my father's bamboo pole. She walked back and threw the tube into the sea, holding onto the pole.

"This will go where Bing is. I will bring him back," she said fiercely. I had never heard so much *nengkan* in my mother's voice.

95   The tube followed her mind. It drifted out, toward the other side of the cove where it was caught by stronger waves. The line became taut and she strained to hold on

tight. But the line snapped and then spiraled into the water.

We both climbed toward the end of the reef to watch. The tube had now reached the other side of the cove. A big wave smashed it into the wall. The bloated tube leapt up and then it was sucked in, under the wall and into a cavern. It popped out. Over and over again, it disappeared, emerged, glistening black, faithfully reporting it had seen Bing and was going back to try to pluck him from the cave. Over and over again, it dove and popped back up again, empty but still hopeful. And then, after a dozen or so times, it was sucked into the dark recess, and when it came out, it was torn and lifeless.

At that moment, and not until that moment, did she give up. My mother had a look on her face that I'll never forget. It was one of complete despair and horror, for losing Bing, for being so foolish as to think she could use faith to change fate. And it made me angry—so blindingly angry—that everything had failed us.

I know now that I had never expected to find Bing, just as I know now I will never find a way to save my marriage. My mother tells me, though, that I should still try.

"What's the point?" I say. "There's no hope. There's no reason to keep trying."

"Because you must," she says. "This is   100 not hope. Not reason. This is your fate. This is your life, what you must do."

"So what can I do?"

And my mother says, "You must think for yourself, what you must do. If someone tells you, then you are not trying." And then she walks out of the kitchen to let me think about this.

I think about Bing, how I knew he was in danger, how I let it happen. I think about my marriage, how I had seen the signs, really I had. But I just let it happen. And I think now that fate is shaped half by expectation, half by inattention. But somehow, when you lose something you love, faith takes over. You have to pay attention to what you lost. You have to undo the expectation.

My mother, she still pays attention to it. That Bible under the table, I know she sees it. I remember seeing her write in it before she wedged it under.

I lift the table and slide the Bible out. I put the Bible on the table, flipping quickly through the pages, because I know it's there. On the page before the New Testament begins, there's a section called "Deaths," and that's where she wrote "Bing Hsu" lightly, in erasable pencil. 105

·····▶ *Your* Turn
Talking and Writing about Lit

1. Amy Tan's "Half and Half" contains a story within the story. Why has Tan arranged events in this way? How does this arrangement help illuminate the themes in the story?

2. Is "Half and Half" an open-ended story, or does it have resolution?

3. **DIY** In two or three pages, rewrite the crisis scene in which Bing is lost. In your version Bing is recovered after all, but you will need to decide how his family finds him and under what circumstances.

William Faulkner (1897–1962)

All of William Faulkner's major works are set in a mythical county called Yoknapatawpha, which is actually based on his home county in Mississippi. Faulkner also spent some time away from home in Hollywood where he wrote screenplays to support his family. He was born in New Albany, Mississippi, and moved at the age of five to Oxford, Mississippi, his home for the remainder of his life. Faulkner is universally admired as one of the best American novelists of the twentieth century. He won the Nobel Prize in Literature in 1952 for his antiracist novel *Intruder in the Dust*. Among Faulkner's most admired novels are *The Sound and the Fury* (1929), *As I Lay Dying* (1930), *Light in August* (1932), and *Absalom, Absalom!* (1936).

A Rose for Emily (1930)

I

When Miss Emily Grierson died, our whole town went to her funeral: the men through a sort of respectful affection for a fallen monument, the women mostly out of curiosity to see the inside of her house, which no one save an old manservant—a combined gardener and cook—had seen in at least ten years.

It was a big, squarish frame house that had once been white, decorated with cupolas and spires and scrolled balconies in the heavily lightsome style of the seventies, set on what had once been our most select street. But garages and cotton gins had encroached and obliterated even the august names of that neighborhood; only Miss Emily's house was left, lifting its stubborn and coquettish decay above the cotton wagons and the gasoline pumps—an eyesore among eyesores. And now Miss Emily had gone to join the representatives of those august names where they lay in the cedar-bemused cemetery among the ranked and anonymous graves of Union and Confederate soldiers who fell at the battle of Jefferson.

Alive, Miss Emily had been a tradition, a duty, and a care; a sort of hereditary obligation upon the town, dating from that day in 1894 when Colonel Sartoris, the mayor—he who fathered the edict that no Negro woman should appear on the streets without an apron—remitted her taxes, the dispensation dating from the death of her father on into perpetuity. Not that Miss Emily would have accepted charity. Colonel Sartoris invented an involved tale to the effect that Miss Emily's father had loaned money to the town, which the town, as a matter of business, preferred this way of repaying. Only a man of Colonel Sartoris' generation and thought could have invented it, and only a woman could have believed it.

When the next generation, with its more modern ideas, became mayors and aldermen, this arrangement created some little dissatisfaction. On the first of the year they mailed her a tax notice. February came, and there was no reply. They wrote her a formal letter, asking her to call at the sheriff's office at her convenience. A week later the mayor wrote her himself, offering to call or to send his car for her, and received in reply a note on paper of an archaic shape, in a thin, flowing calligraphy in faded ink, to the effect that she no longer went out at all. The tax notice was also enclosed, without comment.

They called a special meeting of the Board of Aldermen. A deputation waited upon her, knocked at the door through which no visitor had passed since she ceased giving china-painting lessons eight or ten years earlier. They were admitted by the old Negro into a dim hall from which a stairway mounted into still more shadow. It smelled of dust and disuse—a close, dank smell. The Negro led them into the parlor. It was furnished in heavy, leather-covered furniture. When the Negro opened the blinds of one window, they could see that the leather was cracked; and when they sat down, a faint dust rose sluggishly about their thighs, spinning with slow motes in the single sun-ray. On a tarnished gilt easel before the fireplace stood a crayon portrait of Miss Emily's father.

They rose when she entered—a small, fat woman in black, with a thin gold chain descending to her waist and vanishing into her belt, leaning on an ebony cane with a tarnished gold head. Her skeleton was small and spare; perhaps that was why what would have been merely plumpness in another was obesity in her. She looked bloated, like a body long submerged in motionless water, and of that pallid hue. Her eyes, lost in the fatty ridges of her face, looked like two small pieces of coal pressed into a lump of dough as they moved from one face to another while the visitors stated their errand.

She did not ask them to sit. She just stood in the door and listened quietly until the spokesman came to a stumbling halt. Then they could hear the invisible watch ticking at the end of the gold chain.

Her voice was dry and cold. "I have no taxes in Jefferson. Colonel Sartoris explained it to me. Perhaps one of you can gain access to the city records and satisfy yourselves."

"But we have. We are the city authorities, Miss Emily. Didn't you get a notice from the sheriff, signed by him?"

10 "I received a paper, yes," Miss Emily said. "Perhaps he considers himself the sheriff . . . I have no taxes in Jefferson."

"But there is nothing on the books to show that, you see. We must go by the—"

"See Colonel Sartoris. I have no taxes in Jefferson."

"But, Miss Emily—"

"See Colonel Sartoris." (Colonel Sartoris had been dead almost ten years.) "I have no taxes in Jefferson. Tobe!" The Negro appeared. "Show these gentlemen out."

II

15 So she vanquished them, horse and foot, just as she had vanquished their fathers thirty years before about the smell. That was two years after her father's death and a short time after her sweetheart—the one we believed would marry her—had deserted her. After her father's death she went out very little; after her sweetheart went away, people hardly saw her at all. A few of the ladies had the temerity to call, but were not received, and the only sign of life about the place was the Negro man—a young man then—going in and out with a market basket.

"Just as if a man—any man—could keep a kitchen properly," the ladies said; so they were not surprised when the smell developed. It was another link between the gross, teeming world and the high and mighty Griersons.

A neighbor, a woman, complained to the mayor, Judge Stevens, eighty years old.

"But what will you have me do about it, madam?" he said.

"Why, send her word to stop it," the woman said. "Isn't there a law?"

"I'm sure that won't be necessary," 20 Judge Stevens said. "It's probably just a snake or a rat that nigger of hers killed in the yard. I'll speak to him about it."

The next day he received two more complaints, one from a man who came in diffident deprecation. "We really must do something about it, Judge. I'd be the last one in the world to bother Miss Emily, but we've got to do something." That night the Board of Aldermen met—three graybeards and one younger man, a member of the rising generation.

"It's simple enough," he said. "Send her word to have her place cleaned up. Give her a certain time to do it in, and if she don't . . ."

"Dammit, sir," Judge Stevens said, "will you accuse a lady to her face of smelling bad?"

So the next night, after midnight, four men crossed Miss Emily's lawn and slunk about the house like burglars, sniffing along the base of the brickwork and at the cellar openings while one of them performed a regular sowing motion with his hand out of a sack slung from his shoulder. They broke open the cellar door and sprinkled lime there, and in all the outbuildings. As they recrossed the lawn, a window that had been dark was lighted and Miss Emily sat in it, the light behind her, and her upright torso motionless as that of an idol. They crept quietly across the lawn and into the shadow of the locusts that lined the street. After a week or two the smell went away.

25   That was when people had begun to feel really sorry for her. People in our town, remembering how old lady Wyatt, her great-aunt, had gone completely crazy at last, believed that the Griersons held themselves a little too high for what they really were. None of the young men were quite good enough for Miss Emily and such. We had long thought of them as a tableau, Miss Emily a slender figure in white in the background, her father a spraddled silhouette in the foreground, his back to her and clutching a horsewhip, the two of them framed by the back-flung front door. So when she got to be thirty and was still single, we were not pleased exactly, but vindicated; even with insanity in the family she wouldn't have turned down all of her chances if they had really materialized.

When her father died, it got about that the house was all that was left to her; and in a way, people were glad. At last they could pity Miss Emily. Being left alone, and a pauper, she had become humanized. Now she too would know the old thrill and the old despair of a penny more or less.

The day after his death all the ladies prepared to call at the house and offer condolence and aid, as is our custom. Miss Emily met them at the door, dressed as usual and with no trace of grief on her face. She told them that her father was not dead. She did that for three days, with the ministers calling on her, and the doctors, trying to persuade her to let them dispose of the body. Just as they were about to resort to law and force, she broke down, and they buried her father quickly.

We did not say she was crazy then. We believed she had to do that. We remembered all the young men her father had driven away, and we knew that with nothing left, she would have to cling to that which had robbed her, as people will.

III

She was sick for a long time. When we saw her again, her hair was cut short, making her look like a girl, with a vague resemblance to those angels in colored church windows—sort of tragic and serene.

The town had just let the contracts for 30 paving the sidewalks, and in the summer after her father's death they began the work. The construction company came with niggers and mules and machinery, and a foreman named Homer Barron, a Yankee—a big, dark, ready man, with a big voice and eyes lighter than his face. The little boys would follow in groups to hear him cuss the niggers, and the niggers singing in time to the rise and fall of picks. Pretty soon he knew everybody in town. Whenever you heard a lot of laughing anywhere about the square, Homer Barron would be in the center of the group. Presently we began to see him and Miss Emily on Sunday afternoons driving in the yellow-wheeled buggy and the matched team of bays from the livery stable.

At first we were glad that Miss Emily would have an interest, because the ladies all said, "Of course a Grierson would not think seriously of a Northerner, a day laborer." But there were still others, older people, who said that even grief could not cause a real lady to forget *noblesse oblige*—without calling it *noblesse oblige*. They just said, "Poor Emily. Her kinsfolk should come to her." She had some kin in Alabama; but years ago her father had fallen out with them over the estate of old lady Wyatt, the crazy woman, and there was no communication between the two families. They had not even been represented at the funeral.

And as soon as the old people said, "Poor Emily," the whispering began. "Do you suppose it's really so?" they said to one another. "Of course it is. What else could . . ." This behind their hands; rustling of craned silk and satin behind jalousies closed upon the sun of Sunday afternoon as the thin, swift clop-clop-clop of the matched team passed: "Poor Emily."

She carried her head high enough— even when we believed that she was fallen. It was as if she demanded more than ever the recognition of her dignity as the last Grierson; as if it had wanted that touch of earthiness to reaffirm her imperviousness. Like when she bought the rat poison, the arsenic. That was over a year after they had begun to say "Poor Emily," and while the two female cousins were visiting her.

"I want some poison," she said to the druggist. She was over thirty then, still a slight woman, though thinner than usual, with cold, haughty black eyes in a face the flesh of which was strained across the temples and about the eyesockets as you imagine a lighthouse-keeper's face ought to look. "I want some poison," she said.

35 "Yes, Miss Emily. What kind? For rats and such? I'd recom—"

"I want the best you have. I don't care what kind."

The druggist named several. "They'll kill anything up to an elephant. But what you want is—"

"Arsenic," Miss Emily said. "Is that a good one?"

"Is . . . arsenic? Yes, ma'am. But what you want—"

40 "I want arsenic."

The druggist looked down at her. She looked back at him, erect, her face like a strained flag. "Why, of course," the druggist said. "If that's what you want. But the law requires you to tell what you are going to use it for."

Miss Emily just stared at him, her head tilted back in order to look him eye for eye, until he looked away and went and got the arsenic and wrapped it up. The Negro delivery boy brought her the package; the druggist didn't come back. When she opened the package at home there was written on the box, under the skull and bones: "For rats."

IV

So the next day we all said, "She will kill herself"; and we said it would be the best thing. When she had first begun to be seen with Homer Barron, we had said, "She will marry him." Then we said, "She will persuade him yet," because Homer himself had remarked—he liked men, and it was known that he drank with the younger men in the Elks' Club—that he was not a marrying man. Later we said, "Poor Emily," behind the jalousies as they passed on Sunday afternoon in the glittering buggy, Miss Emily with her head high and Homer Barron with his hat cocked and a cigar in his teeth, reins and whip in a yellow glove.

Then some of the ladies began to say that it was a disgrace to the town and a bad example to the young people. The men did not want to interfere, but at last the ladies forced the Baptist minister—Miss Emily's people were Episcopal—to call upon her. He would never divulge what happened during that interview, but he refused to go back again. The next Sunday they again drove about the streets, and the following day the minister's wife wrote to Miss Emily's relations in Alabama.

So she had blood-kin under her roof 45 again and we sat back to watch developments. At first nothing happened. Then we were sure that they were to be married. We learned that Miss Emily had been to the jeweler's and ordered a man's toilet set in silver, with the letters H. B. on each piece. Two days later we learned that she had bought a complete outfit of men's clothing, including a nightshirt, and we said, "They are married." We were really glad. We were glad because the two female cousins were even more Grierson than Miss Emily had ever been.

So we were not surprised when Homer Barron—the streets had been finished some time since—was gone. We were a little disappointed that there was not a public blowing-off, but we believed that he had gone on to prepare for Miss Emily's coming, or to give her a chance to get rid of the cousins. (By that time it was a cabal, and we were all Miss Emily's allies to help circumvent the cousins.) Sure enough, after another week they departed. And, as we had expected all along, within three days Homer Barron was back in town. A neighbor saw the Negro man admit him at the kitchen door at dusk one evening.

And that was the last we saw of Homer Barron. And of Miss Emily for some time. The Negro man went in and out with the market basket, but the front door remained closed. Now and then we would see her at a window for a moment, as the men did that night when they sprinkled the lime, but for almost six months she did not appear on the streets. Then we knew that this was to be expected too; as if that quality of her father which had thwarted her woman's life so many times had been too virulent and too furious to die.

When we next saw Miss Emily, she had grown fat and her hair was turning gray. During the next few years it grew grayer and grayer until it attained an even pepper-and-salt iron-gray, when it ceased turning. Up to the day of her death at seventy-four it was still that vigorous iron-gray, like the hair of an active man.

From that time on her front door remained closed, save for a period of six or seven years, when she was about forty, during which she gave lessons in china-painting. She fitted up a studio in one of the downstairs rooms, where the daughters and granddaughters of Colonel Sartoris' contemporaries were sent to her with the same regularity and in the same spirit that they were sent to church on Sundays with a twenty-five-cent piece for the collection plate. Meanwhile her taxes had been remitted.

Then the newer generation became the 50 backbone and the spirit of the town, and the painting pupils grew up and fell away and did not send their children to her with boxes of color and tedious brushes and pictures cut from the ladies' magazines. The front door closed upon the last one and remained closed for good. When the town got free postal delivery, Miss Emily alone refused to let them fasten the metal numbers above her door and attach a mailbox to it. She would not listen to them.

Daily, monthly, yearly we watched the Negro grow grayer and more stooped, going in and out with the market basket. Each December we sent her a tax notice, which would be returned by the post office a week later, unclaimed. Now and then we would see her in one of the downstairs windows—she had evidently shut up the top floor of the house—like the carven torso of an idol in a niche, looking or not looking at us, we could never tell which. Thus she passed from generation to generation—dear, inescapable, impervious, tranquil, and perverse.

And so she died. Fell ill in the house filled with dust and shadows, with only a doddering Negro man to wait on her. We did not even know she was sick; we had long since given up trying to get any information from the Negro. He talked to no one, probably not even to her, for his voice had grown harsh and rusty, as if from disuse.

She died in one of the downstairs rooms, in a heavy walnut bed with a curtain, her gray head propped on a pillow yellow and moldy with age and lack of sunlight.

V

The Negro met the first of the ladies at the front door and let them in, with their hushed, sibilant voices and their quick, curious glances, and then he disappeared. He walked right through the house and out the back and was not seen again.

55   The two female cousins came at once. They held the funeral on the second day, with the town coming to look at Miss Emily beneath a mass of bought flowers, with the crayon face of her father musing profoundly above the bier and the ladies sibilant and macabre; and the very old men—some in their brushed Confederate uniforms—on the porch and the lawn, talking of Miss Emily as if she had been a contemporary of theirs, believing that they had danced with her and courted her perhaps, confusing time with its mathematical progression, as the old do, to whom all the past is not a diminishing road but, instead, a huge meadow which no winter ever quite touches, divided from them now by the narrow bottle-neck of the most recent decade of years.

Already we knew that there was one room in that region above stairs which no one had seen in forty years, and which would have to be forced. They waited until Miss Emily was decently in the ground before they opened it.

The violence of breaking down the door seemed to fill this room with pervading dust. A thin, acrid pall as of the tomb seemed to lie everywhere upon this room decked and furnished as for a bridal: upon the valance curtains of faded rose color, upon the rose-shaded lights, upon the dressing table, upon the delicate array of crystal and the man's toilet things backed with tarnished silver, silver so tarnished that the monogram was obscured. Among them lay a collar and tie, as if they had just been removed, which, lifted, left upon the surface a pale crescent in the dust. Upon a chair hung the suit, carefully folded; beneath it the two mute shoes and the discarded socks.

The man himself lay in the bed.

For a long while we just stood there, looking down at the profound and fleshless grin. The body had apparently once lain in the attitude of an embrace, but now the long sleep that outlasts love, that conquers even the grimace of love, had cuckolded him. What was left of him, rotted beneath what was left of the nightshirt, had become inextricable from the bed in which he lay; and upon him and upon the pillow beside him lay that even coating of the patient and biding dust.

Then we noticed that in the second pil- 60 low was the indentation of a head. One of us lifted something from it, and leaning forward, that faint and invisible dust dry and acrid in the nostrils, we saw a long strand of iron-gray hair.

• • • • •▶ *Your* **Turn**
    Talking and Writing about Lit

    1. Discuss the use of flashbacks and foreshadowing in Faulkner's "A Rose for Emily."

2. In "A Rose for Emily," Faulkner uses an unusual point-of-view strategy—writing in the "we" voice, the first-person plural. In a sense, the story is told from the collective point of view of the townspeople. Write an essay of two or three pages arguing why this is a good point-of-view strategy, or, alternatively, that a different perspective would be better (for example, what would the story be like if told in the first-person ("I") voice of Emily herself or of Homer Barron?

3. (DIY) This is a story that moves around in time and is not presented chronologically. Create a time line for Faulkner's story that *is* arranged chronologically and that cites a paragraph from the story in which each time frame is depicted. For instance, you will begin with Emily's youth, which is represented rather visually in paragraph 25. The last item on your time line will be the discovery of the upstairs room and the iron-gray hair on the pillow in paragraph 60.

Talking Lit

In the following selections, a writer from the mid-nineteenth century and a writer from the mid-twentieth century discuss the deliberate use of plotting in fiction and the importance of inner conflict.

Guy De Maupassant, from the Preface to *Pierre and Jean*
Translated by Mallay Charters

[The serious writer's] goal is not to tell us a story, to entertain or to move us, but to make us think and to make us understand the deep and hidden meaning of events. By virtue of having seen and meditated, he views the universe, objects, facts, and human beings in a certain way which is personal, the result of combining his observations and reflections. It is this personal view of the world that he tries to communicate to us by reproducing it in fiction. To move us, as he has been moved himself by the spectacle of life, he must reproduce it before our eyes with a scrupulous accuracy. He should compose his work so adroitly, and with such dissimulation and apparent simplicity, that it is impossible to uncover its plan or to perceive his intentions.

Instead of fabricating an adventure and spinning it out in a way that keeps it interesting until the end, the writer will pick up his characters at a certain point of their existence and carry them, by natural transitions, to the following period. He will show how minds are modified under the influence of environmental circumstances, and how sentiments and passions are developed. In this fashion, he will show our loves, our hates, our struggles in all kinds of social conditions; and how social interests, financial interests, political interests, and personal interests all compete with each other.

The writer's cleverness with his plot will thus consist not in the use of sentiment or charm, in an engaging beginning or an emotional catastrophe, but in the adroit grouping of small constant facts from which the reader will grasp a definitive sense of the work. . . . [The author] should know how to eliminate, among the minute and innumerable daily occurrences, all those which are useless to him. He must emphasize those which would have escaped the notice of less clear-sighted observers, which give the story its effect and value as fiction. . . .

A writer would find it impossible to describe everything in life, because he would need at least a volume a day to list the multitude of unimportant incidents filling up our hours.

Some selectivity is required—which is the first blow to the "entire truth" theory [of realistic literature].

Life, moreover, is composed of the most unpredictable, disparate, and contradictory elements. It is brutal, inconsequential, and disconnected, full of inexplicable, illogical, catastrophes.

This is why the writer, having selected a theme, will take from this chaotic life, encumbered with hazards and trivialities, only the details useful to his subject and omit all the others.

One example out of a thousand: The number of people in the world who die every day in accidents is considerable. But can we drop a roof tile on a main character's head, or throw him under the wheels of a car, in the middle of a narrative, under the pretext that it is necessary to have an accident?

Life can leave everything the same as it was. Or it can speed up some events and drag out others. Literature, on the other hand, presents cleverly orchestrated events and concealed transitions, essential incidents high-lighted by the writer's skill alone. In giving every detail its exact degree of shading in accordance with its importance, the author produces the profound impression of the particular truth he wishes to point out.

To make things seem real on the page consists in giving the complete *illusion* of reality, following the logical order of facts, and not servilely transcribing the pell-mell succession of chronological events in life.

I conclude from this analysis that writers who call themselves realists should more accurately call themselves illusionists.

How childish, moreover, to believe in an absolute reality, since we each carry a personal one in our thoughts and in our senses. Our eyes, our ears, our sense of smell and taste create as many truths as there are individuals. Our minds, diversely impressed by the reception of the senses' information, comprehend, analyze, and judge as if each of us belonged to a separate race.

Thus each of us makes, individually, a personal illusion of the world. It may be a poetic, sentimental, joyful, melancholy, sordid, or dismal one, according to our nature. The writer's goal is to reproduce this illusion of life faithfully, using all the literary techniques at his disposal.

William Faulkner, Nobel Prize Acceptance Speech

I feel that this award was not made to me as a man, but to my work—a life's work in the agony and sweat of the human spirit, not for glory and least of all for profit, but to create out of the materials of the human spirit something which did not exist before. So this award is only mine in trust. It will not be difficult to find a dedication for the money part of it commensurate with the purpose and significance of its origin. But I would like to do the same with the acclaim too, by using this moment as a pinnacle from which I might be listened to by the young men and women already dedicated to the same anguish and travail, among whom is already that one who will some day stand here where I am standing.

Our tragedy today is a general and universal physical fear so long sustained by now that we can even bear it. There are no longer problems of the spirit. There is only the question: When will I be blown up? Because of this, the young man or woman writing today has forgotten the problems of the human heart in conflict with itself which alone can make good writing because only that is worth writing about, worth the agony and the sweat.

He must learn them again. He must teach himself that the basest of all things is to be afraid; and, teaching himself that, forget it forever, leaving no room in his workshop for anything but the old verities and truths of the heart, the old universal truths lacking which any story is ephemeral and doomed—love and honor and pity and pride and compassion and sacrifice. Until he does so, he labors under a curse. He writes not of love but of lust, of defeats in which nobody loses anything of value, of victories without hope and, worst of all, without pity or compassion. His griefs grieve on no universal bones, leaving no scars. He writes not of the heart but of the glands.

Until he relearns these things, he will write as though he stood among and watched the end of man. I decline to accept the end of man. It is easy enough to say that man is immortal simply because he will endure: that when the last ding-dong of doom has clanged and faded from the last worthless rock hanging tideless in the last red and dying evening, that even then there will still be one more sound: that of his puny inexhaustible voice, still talking. I refuse to accept this. I believe that man will not merely endure: he will prevail. He is immortal, not because he alone among creatures has an inexhaustible voice, but because he has a soul, a spirit capable of compassion and sacrifice and endurance. The poet's, the writer's, duty is to write about these things. It is his privilege to help man endure by lifting his heart, by reminding him of the courage and honor and hope and pride and compassion and pity and sacrifice which have been the glory of his past. The poet's voice need not merely be the record of man, it can be one of the props, the pillars to help him endure and prevail.

FROM PAGE TO SCREEN

The Song Remains the Same

Many of the successful plot formulas created in the early days of film came from writers who were later recognized as great literary figures. Humphrey Bogart's portrayal of hard-boiled detective Philip Marlowe in *The Big Sleep* was adapted for the screen (from the pages of Raymond

William Faulkner wrote the scre[...] adaptation for Raymond Chand[...] detective novel *The Big Sleep*, wh[...] became the screenplay for the m[...] *The Big Sleep* (1946) with Humph[...] Bogart and Lauren Bacall. See William Faulkner's stories in thi[...] chapter and Chapter 12.

F. Scott Fitzgerald worked on the screen adaptation for *Gone with the Wind*, which became the screenplay for the movie *Gone with the Wind* (1939). See Fitzgerald's story "Babylon Revisited" in Chapter 5.

Chandler's detective novels) by celebrated author William Faulkner. F. Scott Fitzgerald worked on the screen adaptation for *Gone with the Wind*, one of the most recognizable romantic dramas ever, based on the 1936 novel written by Margaret Mitchell. Dorothy Parker set a generic plot bar herself with *A Star Is Born*. The very recognizable plot follows a girl who leaves her small hometown to become an actress in Hollywood. Much like the movie *Gia*, starring Angelina Jolie, or any number of other dashed-dreams tales, substance abuse enters the picture and the girl's career spirals downward to nothingness. Hollywood has offered us similar fare with happier endings in films like *Coyote Ugly* starring Piper Perabo, Mariah Carey's *Glitter*, and, more recently, *Honey* with Jessica Alba.

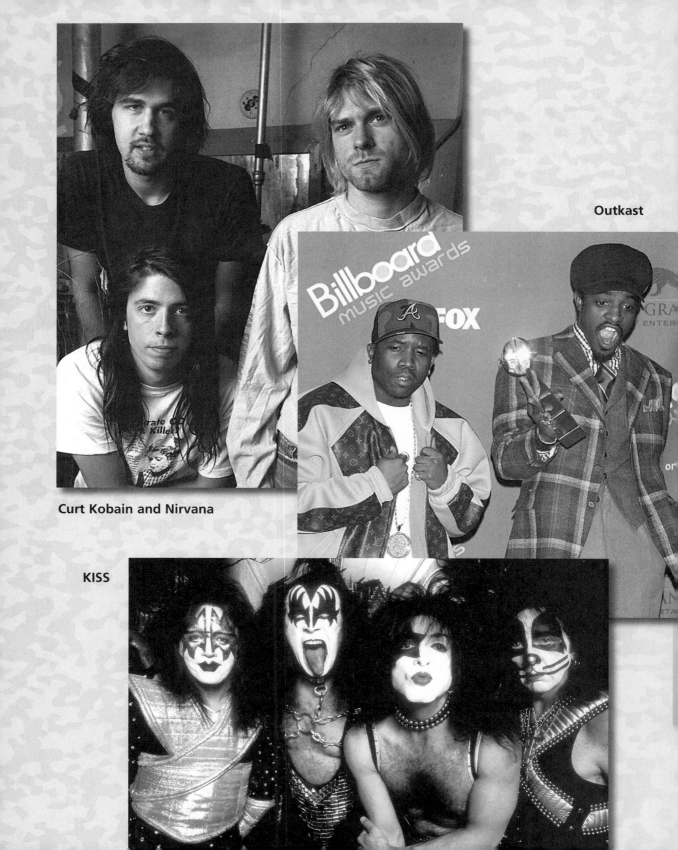

Outkast

Curt Kobain and Nirvana

KISS

CHARACTERIZATION

Avril Lavigne

Even musical artists use characterization. Although fictional characters don't have to be good or even likeable, they are usually depicted as people whose actions we can understand because of our own life experiences. Major record labels aim for the same kind of recognition when establishing an image for a musical artist.

A musician's image is almost as important to some listeners as the music. Often a band's image will promote its attitude and musical style so that consumers have an idea of what they sound like even before hearing them. Even though what makes them distinct is their music, we often identify them through the characters presented in their promotional materials.

Sometimes the goal of an author's character or a musical act's image is to be fantastic enough to be interesting but flawed enough to seem human. While reading about the characters Bartleby (in "Bartleby the Scrivener") and Sonny (in "Sonny's Blues") in this chapter, some readers may find similarities to the 1990s down-and-out Grunge scene that spawned the popular band Nirvana.

Members of Outkast were successful in promoting themselves as characters to an audience on their double album *SpeakerBoxxx/The Love Below*. Outkast's music has been hailed as an eccentric combination of modern and classic rap with a variety of other musical influences. The style they project displays this image: Andre 3000 (right) often dresses in an eccentric way, while Big Boi sports the classic look popular in the Hip-Hop movement since the early 1980s.

How would you describe your best friend to someone who had never met him or her? The fiction writer faces a similar task in depicting fictional characters. Eudora Welty wrote (in *The Eye of the Story*) that "writing fiction . . . comes out of life and has the object of showing it," which is especially true in the writer's creation of characters. The teacher of fiction writing often reminds students to "show, don't tell," and it is this rule of thumb that Welty also has in mind. In saying this, writers acknowledge that if too much of the storytelling remains indirect ("telling" *about* a character instead of depicting that character directly), the reader will not be engaged in the story or find it to be true to life. If the story, however, contains sufficient direct depiction of characters (with "showing" scenes so that we get to know them through dialogue and action), then the reader's own senses will be engaged, and the reader will feel caught up in the dream that fiction creates on the page (as novelist John Gardner used to say). The effect is that something similar to the dream or "movie" created in the mind of the writer is playing also in the mind of the reader (taking into account readers' different experiences, ideas, and responses).

Major or Minor, Round or Flat

A number of methods of characterization are available to the writer to reveal characters effectively in fiction. In a realistic story, the fiction writer would use most or all of these methods to depict well-rounded characters. A character is said to be a **round** character when he or she is more fully developed. The central characters in the story, the **major characters**, need to be more completely known to the reader. We need to get a sense of their personality, motivations, habits of speech, gestures, behavior, and often even habits of thought. On the other hand, characters depicted less completely are often referred to as **flat** characters because we do not have the fully fleshed-out understanding of them that we do of the major characters. These characters, who are more peripheral to the story, could be called **minor characters**.

To depict major (or central) characters, then, the fiction writer uses various methods. (Please note that as we move through our discussion of the various methods of characterization used by fiction writers, we will be citing specific quotations and examples from works of fiction, just as you will be doing as you write about literature yourself. When you use a quotation, make sure the source of that quotation is provided.)

Methods of Characterization

Telling, or **exposition**, is the indirect method of characterization. Through exposition we may learn about the characters' situations or personal histories in a way that helps deepen our understanding of their more directly depicted actions in the present. In paragraph 53 of James Baldwin's "Sonny's Blues," Baldwin provides exposition to fill the reader in on what happened while Sonny was away in prison and how his brother (who is also the narrator of the story) felt about his return:

> Then I kept in constant touch with him and I sent him whatever I could and I went to meet him when he came back to New York. When I saw him many things I thought I had forgotten came flooding back to me. This was because I had begun, finally, to wonder about Sonny, about the life that Sonny lived inside.

These three sentences serve to summarize and "collapse" the passage of several years and bring us forward to a period of time that Baldwin wants to depict more directly and completely. We are then launched into a fully rendered **scene** in which we get to know the characters through various methods, including **dialogue**— that is, words spoken aloud. In fiction, dialogue is usually enclosed in quotation marks. Here is a particularly revealing passage of dialogue from a later scene in "Sonny's Blues." In this scene, Baldwin wants to show the immediate conflict between the two brothers, but he is also showing their personalities and motivations on a deeper level at the same time. The scene also serves to help illustrate one of the important themes of the story. Sonny has just told his older brother (who teaches high school mathematics and is the narrator of the story) what he wants to do with his life—he wants to be a jazz musician.

> "Well, Sonny," I said, gently, "you know people can't always do exactly what they *want* to do—"
> "*No*, I don't know that," said Sonny, surprising me. "I think people *ought* to do what they want to do, what else are they alive for?" (paragraphs 140–142)

The following passage uses other direct methods of characterization as well. It includes **actions** and **behavior** as well as **physical descriptions** of characters.

> . . . He stopped in front of me, leaning against the stove, arms loosely folded. "Look, brother. I don't want to stay in Harlem no more, I really don't." He was very earnest. He looked at me, then over toward the kitchen window. There was something in his eyes I'd never seen before, some thoughtfulness, some worry all his own. He rubbed the muscle of one arm. "It's time I was getting out of here." (paragraph 153)

All of these direct methods of characterization appeal to our senses (which are sight, sound, touch, taste, and smell). The writer knows that if he or she can succeed in appealing to our senses, the scene will be more vivid; and if the writer has done the work well, as Baldwin has here, the reader will feel that the characters are true to life. Another direct method of characterization is to reveal the character through his or her own **thoughts**, which is happening here as we listen to Baldwin's narrator:

> The seven years' difference in our ages lay between us like a chasm: I wondered if these years would ever operate between us as a bridge. I was remembering, and it made it hard to catch my breath, that I had been there when he was born; and I had heard the first words he had ever spoken. When he started to walk, he walked from our mother straight to me. I caught him just before he fell when he took the first steps he ever took in this world. (paragraph 58)

When Sonny's brother reveals such information in his thoughts, the passage provides characterization both of the person described (his brother Sonny) and of the narrator himself. Here we learn about Sonny's first steps, but, more important, we learn how his brother, the narrator of the story, *feels* about that memory. This passage, in other words, helps characterize the narrator as someone who cares deeply about his younger brother, in spite of the many differences between them.

The two brothers in "Sonny's Blues" might also be said to be **foil characters** to one another. That is, the sense of their personalities is heightened, or illuminated, by the contrasts between them. The intensity of Sonny's worldview and his longings and troubles is all the more heightened when balanced against the contrasting stability and sensibleness of his math teacher brother's routine and stable life.

Dynamic and Static Characters

An interesting question to ask about Baldwin's story is: Who is the main character? Is it Sonny, or is it the narrator? What reasons can you give for your choice? Is it possible to have two main characters in a short story?

Another interesting question to ask about characters in fiction has to do with whether those characters change as a consequence of the experiences they encounter in the story. It is said that a character who changes is **dynamic** and a character who does not change is **static**. In "Sonny's Blues," both Sonny and the narrator are dynamic characters (unlike Isabel, the narrator's wife, who is static). For this reason, some readers will want to assert that they are both main characters. Others may feel that Sonny's brother is the main character because he is the narrator, and it is the change taking place in him (especially his increased understanding of Sonny's worldview) that we have the greatest access to and that is the central focus of the story. Still others may choose to argue that Sonny is the main character and that the narrator, although he is changed as a result of these events, is mainly there to observe and report on the life of Sonny. These are good questions to ask about Herman Melville's "Bartleby the Scrivener"—another story you'll read in this chapter—in which the narrator, the lawyer, is clearly a dynamic character, and Bartleby is usually regarded as a static character (even though he is one of the major characters in the story).

Character and Theme

Bharati Mukherjee's story "A Father" is an interesting study in how the themes of a story can be embodied in its characters. The three family members— Mr. Bhowmick, Mrs. Bhowmick, and Babli—help convey ideas about generational conflict and, most important to Mukherjee, about immigration and identity. The three major characters depict varying degrees of comfort or discomfort with their first culture and with their new culture. The village women in Ranchi (who are minor characters) want no part of the Americanization represented to them by the Bhowmicks. Mr. Bhowmick, however, feels himself pulled in two ways about his life in Detroit. On the one hand, he wants to think of himself as a modern man; on the other, he is the family member most resistant to assimilating the ways of a new culture.

Mr. Bhowmick is the character who wishes to retain what he feels is valuable in his first culture (his statue of Kali-Mata and his belief in the significance of sneezes represent this). Mrs. Bhowmick has a more unreserved acceptance of American ways—until the last scene, that is. Babli is the character who represents the most complete acceptance of American culture, or what she interprets to be American culture. She is not, however, the main character; it is from Mr. Bhowmick's perspective that the story is narrated, and it is his thoughts and feelings that we have access to throughout the story.

Bharati Mukherjee is, by the way, a female writer widely admired for her ability to tell a story convincingly from either a male or female point of view. Mukherjee's work is also distinctive for its treatment of the immigrant experience, which she says she sees as "a set of fluid identities to be celebrated" (see the Introduction to her book *Darkness*, which appears in the "Talking Lit" section of this chapter).

Readings

James Baldwin (1924–1987)

James Baldwin, the son of a Pentecostal minister, was born in Harlem. His two early novels, which established him as a major American voice in fiction, are *Go Tell It on the Mountain* (1953, roughly based on his religious awakening and his brief service at the age of fourteen as a Pentecostal minister) and *Giovanni's Room* (1956, dealing with the difficulties of being a black homosexual living in a largely white, heterosexual society). To escape the pall of racism in the United States, Baldwin lived much of his adult life abroad, especially in France. He was also a dramatist, essayist, and memorist. Other books by Baldwin are *The Big Sea* (1940), *Notes of a Native Son* (1955), *Nobody Knows My Name* (1961), *Another Country* (1962), *The Fire Next Time* (1963), and *Going to Meet the Man* (1965).

Sonny's Blues (1957)

I read about it in the paper, in the subway, on my way to work. I read it, and I couldn't believe it, and I read it again. Then perhaps I just stared at it, at the newsprint spelling out his name, spelling out the story. I stared at it in the swinging lights of the subway car, and in the faces and bodies of the people, and in my own face, trapped in the darkness which roared outside.

It was not to be believed and I kept telling myself that, as I walked from the subway station to the high school. And at the same time I couldn't doubt it. I was scared, scared for Sonny. He became real to me again. A great block of ice got settled in my belly and kept melting there slowly all day long, while I taught my classes algebra. It was a special kind of ice. It kept melting, sending trickles of ice water all up and down my veins, but it never got less. Sometimes it hardened and seemed to expand until I felt my guts were going to come spilling out or that I was going to choke or scream. This would always be at a moment when I was remembering some specific thing Sonny had once said or done.

When he was about as old as the boys in my classes his face had been bright and open, there was a lot of copper in it; and he'd had wonderfully direct brown eyes, and great gentleness and privacy. I wondered what he looked like now. He had been picked up, the evening before, in a raid on an apartment downtown, for peddling and using heroin.

I couldn't believe it: but what I mean by that is that I couldn't find any room for it anywhere inside me. I had kept it outside me for a long time. I hadn't wanted to know. I had had suspicions, but I didn't name them, I kept putting them away. I told myself that Sonny was wild, but he wasn't crazy. And he'd always been a good boy, he hadn't ever turned hard or evil or disrespectful, the way kids can, so quick, so quick, especially in Harlem. I didn't want to believe that I'd ever see my brother going down, coming to nothing, all that light in his face gone out, in the condition I'd already seen so many others. Yet it had happened and here I was, talking about algebra to a lot of boys who might, every one of them for all I knew, be popping off needles every time they went to the head. Maybe it did more for them than algebra could.

I was sure that the first time Sonny had ever had horse, he couldn't have been much older than these boys were now. These boys, now, were living as we'd been living then, they were growing up with a rush and their heads bumped abruptly against the low ceiling of their actual possibilities. They were filled with rage. All they really knew were two darknesses, the darkness of their lives, which was now closing in on them, and the darkness of the movies, which had blinded them to that other darkness, and in which they now, vindictively, dreamed, at once more together than they were at any other time, and more alone.

When the last bell rang, the last class ended, I let out my breath. It seemed I'd been holding it for all that time. My clothes were wet—I may have looked as though I'd been sitting in a steam bath, all dressed up, all afternoon. I sat alone in the classroom a long time. I listened to the boys outside, downstairs, shouting and cursing and laughing. Their laughter struck me for perhaps the first time. It was not the joyous laughter which—God knows why—one

5

associates with children. It was mocking and insular, its intent to denigrate. It was disenchanted, and in this, also, lay the authority of their curses. Perhaps I was listening to them because I was thinking about my brother and in them I heard my brother. And myself.

One boy was whistling a tune, at once very complicated and very simple, it seemed to be pouring out of him as though he were a bird, and it sounded very cool and moving through all that harsh, bright air, only just holding its own through all those other sounds.

I stood up and walked over to the window and looked down into the courtyard. It was the beginning of the spring and the sap was rising in the boys. A teacher passed through them every now and again, quickly, as though he or she couldn't wait to get out of that courtyard, to get those boys out of their sight and off their minds. I started collecting my stuff. I thought I'd better get home and talk to Isabel.

The courtyard was almost deserted by the time I got downstairs. I saw this boy standing in the shadow of a doorway, looking just like Sonny. I almost called his name. Then I saw that it wasn't Sonny, but somebody we used to know, a boy from around our block. He'd been Sonny's friend. He'd never been mine, having been too young for me, and, anyway, I'd never liked him. And now, even though he was a grown-up man, he still hung around that block, still spent hours on the street corners, was always high and raggy. I used to run into him from time to time and he'd often work around to asking me for a quarter or fifty cents. He always had some real good excuse, too, and I always gave it to him, I don't know why.

10   But now, abruptly, I hated him. I couldn't stand the way he looked at me, partly like a dog, partly like a cunning child. I wanted to ask him what the hell he was doing in the school courtyard.

He sort of shuffled over to me, and he said, "I see you got the papers. So you already know about it."

"You mean about Sonny? Yes, I already know about it. How come they didn't get you?"

He grinned. It made him repulsive and it also brought to mind what he'd looked like as a kid. "I wasn't there. I stay away from them people."

"Good for you." I offered him a cigarette and I watched him through the smoke. "You come all the way down here just to tell me about Sonny?"

"That's right." He was sort of shaking 15 his head and his eyes looked strange, as though they were about to cross. The bright sun deadened his damp dark brown skin and it made his eyes look yellow and showed up the dirt in his kinked hair. He smelled funky. I moved a little away from him and I said, "Well, thanks. But I already know about it and I got to get home."

"I'll walk you a little ways," he said. We started walking. There were a couple of kids still loitering in the courtyard and one of them said goodnight to me and looked strangely at the boy beside me.

"What're you going to do?" he asked me. "I mean, about Sonny?"

"Look. I haven't seen Sonny for over a year. I'm not sure I'm going to do anything. Anyway, what the hell *can* I do?"

"That's right," he said quickly, "ain't nothing you can do. Can't much help old Sonny no more, I guess."

It was what I was thinking and so it 20 seemed to me he had no right to say it.

"I'm surprised at Sonny, though," he went on—he had a funny way of talking, he looked straight ahead as though he were talking to himself—"I thought Sonny was a smart boy, I thought he was too smart to get hung."

"I guess he thought so too," I said sharply, "and that's how he got hung. And how about you? You're pretty goddamn smart, I bet."

Then he looked directly at me, just for a minute. "I ain't smart," he said. "If I was smart, I'd have reached for a pistol a long time ago."

"Look. Don't tell *me* your sad story, if it was up to me, I'd give you one." Then I felt guilty—guilty, probably, for never having supposed that the poor bastard *had* a story of his own, much less a sad one, and I asked, quickly, "What's going to happen to him now?"

25 He didn't answer this. He was off by himself some place. "Funny thing," he said, and from his tone we might have been discussing the quickest way to get to Brooklyn, "when I saw the papers this morning, the first thing I asked myself was if I had anything to do with it. I felt sort of responsible."

I began to listen more carefully. The subway station was on the corner, just before us, and I stopped. He stopped, too. We were in front of a bar and he ducked slightly, peering in, but whoever he was looking for didn't seem to be there. The juke box was blasting away with something black and bouncy and I half watched the barmaid as she danced her way from the juke box to her place behind the bar. And I watched her face as she laughingly responded to something someone said to her, still keeping time to the music. When she smiled one saw the little girl, one sensed the doomed, still-struggling woman beneath the battered face of the semi-whore.

"I never *give* Sonny nothing," the boy said finally, "but a long time ago I come to

school high and Sonny asked me how it felt." He paused, I couldn't bear to watch him, I watched the barmaid, and I listened to the music which seemed to be causing the pavement to shake. "I told him it felt great." The music stopped, the barmaid paused and watched the juke box until the music began again. "It did."

All this was carrying me some place I didn't want to go. I certainly didn't want to know how it felt. It filled everything, the people, the houses, the music, the dark, quicksilver barmaid, with menace; and this menace was their reality.

"What's going to happen to him now?" I asked again.

"They'll send him away some place 30 and they'll try to cure him." He shook his head. "Maybe he'll even think he's kicked the habit. Then they'll let him loose"—he gestured, throwing his cigarette into the gutter. "That's all."

"What do you mean, that's *all*?"

But I knew what he meant.

"I *mean*, that's *all*." He turned his head and looked at me, pulling down the corners of his mouth. "Don't you know what I mean?" he asked, softly.

"How the hell *would* I know what you mean?" I almost whispered it, I don't know why.

"That's right," he said to the air, "how 35 would *he* know what I mean?" He turned toward me again, patient and calm, and yet I somehow felt him shaking, shaking as though he were going to fall apart. I felt that ice in my guts again, the dread I'd felt all afternoon; and again I watched the barmaid, moving about the bar, washing glasses, and singing. "Listen. They'll let him out and then it'll just start all over again. That's what I mean."

"You mean—they'll let him out. And then he'll just start working his way back in again. You mean he'll never kick the habit. Is that what you mean?"

"That's right," he said, cheerfully. *"You see what I mean."*

"Tell me," I said at last, "why does he want to die? He must want to die, he's killing himself, why does he want to die?"

He looked at me in surprise. He licked his lips. "He don't want to die. He wants to live. Don't nobody want to die, ever."

40 Then I wanted to ask him—too many things. He could not have answered, or if he had, I could not have borne the answers. I started walking. "Well, I guess it's none of my business."

"It's going to be rough on old Sonny," he said. We reached the subway station. "This is your station?" he asked. I nodded. I took one step down. "Damn!" he said, suddenly. I looked up at him. He grinned again. "Damn it if I didn't leave all my money home. You ain't got a dollar on you, have you? Just for a couple of days, is all."

All at once something inside gave and threatened to come pouring out of me. I didn't hate him any more. I felt that in another moment I'd start crying like a child.

"Sure," I said. "Don't sweat." I looked in my wallet and didn't have a dollar, I only had a five. "Here," I said. "That hold you?"

He didn't look at it—he didn't want to look at it. A terrible closed look came over his face, as though he were keeping the number on the bill a secret from him and me. "Thanks," he said, and now he was dying to see me go. "Don't worry about Sonny. Maybe I'll write him or something."

45 "Sure," I said. "You do that. So long."

"Be seeing you," he said. I went on down the steps.

And I didn't write Sonny or send him anything for a long time. When I finally did, it was just after my little girl died, he wrote me back a letter which made me feel like a bastard.

Here's what he said:

Dear brother,

You don't know how much I needed to 50 hear from you. I wanted to write you many a time but I dug how much I must have hurt you and so I didn't write. But now I feel like a man who's been trying to climb up out of some deep, real deep and funky hole and just saw the sun up there, outside. I got to get outside.

I can't tell you much about how I got here. I mean I don't know how to tell you. I guess I was afraid of something or I was trying to escape from something and you know I have never been very strong in the head (smile). I'm glad Mama and Daddy are dead and can't see what's happened to their son and I swear if I'd known what I was doing I would never have hurt you so, you and a lot of other fine people who were nice to me and who believed in me.

I don't want you to think it had anything to do with me being a musician. It's more than that. Or maybe less than that. I can't get anything straight in my head down here and I try not to think about what's going to happen to me when I get outside again. Sometime I think I'm going to flip and *never* get outside and sometime I think I'll come straight back. I tell you one thing, though, I'd rather blow my brains out than go through this again. But that's what they all say, so they tell me. If I tell you when I'm coming to New York and if you could meet me, I sure would appreciate it. Give my love to Isabel and the kids and I was sure sorry to hear about little Gracie. I wish I could be like Mama and say the Lord's will be done, but I don't know it seems to me that trouble is the one thing that never does get stopped and I don't know what good it does to blame it on the Lord. But maybe it does some good if you believe it.

Your brother,
Sonny

55   Then I kept in constant touch with him and I sent him whatever I could and I went to meet him when he came back to New York. When I saw him many things I thought I had forgotten came flooding back to me. This was because I had begun, finally, to wonder about Sonny, about the life that Sonny lived inside. This life, whatever it was, had made him older and thinner and it had deepened the distant stillness in which he had always moved. He looked very unlike my baby brother. Yet, when he smiled, when we shook hands, the baby brother I'd never known looked out from the depths of his private life, like an animal waiting to be coaxed into the light.

    "How you been keeping?" he asked me.

    "All right. And you?"

    "Just fine." He was smiling all over his face. "It's good to see you again."

    "It's good to see you."

60   The seven years' difference in our ages lay between us like a chasm: I wondered if these years would ever operate between us as a bridge. I was remembering, and it made it hard to catch my breath, that I had been there when he was born; and I had heard the first words he had ever spoken. When he started to walk, he walked from our mother straight to me. I caught him just before he fell when he took the first steps he ever took in this world.

    "How's Isabel?"

    "Just fine. She's dying to see you."

    "And the boys?"

    "They're fine, too. They're anxious to see their uncle."

65   "Oh, come on. You know they don't remember me."

    "Are you kidding? Of course they remember you."

    He grinned again. We got into a taxi. We had a lot to say to each other, far too much to know how to begin.

    As the taxi began to move, I asked, "You still want to go to India?"

    He laughed. "You still remember that. Hell, no. This place is Indian enough for me."

    "It used to belong to them," I said. 70

    And he laughed again. "They damn sure knew what they were doing when they got rid of it."

    Years ago, when he was around fourteen, he'd been all hipped on the idea of going to India. He read books about people sitting on rocks, naked, in all kinds of weather, but mostly bad, naturally, and walking barefoot through hot coals and arriving at wisdom. I used to say that it sounded to me as though they were getting away from wisdom as fast as they could. I think he sort of looked down on me for that.

    "Do you mind," he asked, "if we have the driver drive alongside the park? On the west side—I haven't seen the city in so long."

    "Of course not," I said. I was afraid that I might sound as though I were humoring him, but I hoped he wouldn't take it that way.

    So we drove along, between the green 75 of the park and the stony, lifeless elegance of hotels and apartment buildings, toward the vivid, killing streets of our childhood. These streets hadn't changed, though housing projects jutted up out of them now like rocks in the middle of a boiling sea. Most of the houses in which we had grown up had vanished, as had the stores from which we had stolen, the basements in which we had first tried sex, the rooftops from which we had hurled tin cans and bricks. But houses exactly like the houses of our past yet dominated the landscape, boys exactly like the boys we once had been found themselves smothering in these houses, came down into the streets for light and air and found themselves encircled by disaster. Some escaped the trap, most didn't. Those who got out always left something of themselves behind, as some animals amputate a leg and leave it in the trap. It might be said, perhaps, that I had escaped, after all, I was a school teacher; or that Sonny had, he hadn't lived in Harlem for years. Yet, as the cab moved uptown through streets which seemed, with a rush, to darken with dark people, and as I covertly studied Sonny's face, it came to me that what we both were seeking through our separate cab windows was that part of ourselves which had been left behind. It's always at the hour of trouble and confrontation that the missing member aches.

We hit 110th Street and started rolling up Lenox Avenue. And I'd known this avenue all my life, but it seemed to me again, as it had seemed on the day I'd first heard about Sonny's trouble, filled with a hidden menace which was its very breath of life.

"We almost there," said Sonny.

"Almost." We were both too nervous to say anything more.

We live in a housing project. It hasn't been up long. A few days after it was up it seemed uninhabitably new, now, of course, it's already rundown. It looks like a parody of the good, clean, faceless life—God knows the people who live in it do their best to make it a parody. The beat-looking grass lying around isn't enough to make their lives green, the hedges will never hold out the streets, and they know it. The big windows fool no one, they aren't big enough to make space out of no space. They don't bother with the windows, they watch the TV screen instead. The playground is most popular with the children who don't play at jacks, or skip rope, or roller skate, or swing, and they can be found in it after dark. We moved in partly because it's not too far from where I teach, and partly for the kids; but it's really just like the houses in which Sonny and I grew up. The same things happen, they'll have the same things to remember. The moment Sonny and I started into

the house I had the feeling that I was simply bringing him back into the danger he had almost died trying to escape.

Sonny has never been talkative. So I don't know why I was sure he'd be dying to talk to me when supper was over the first night. Everything went fine, the oldest boy remembered him, and the youngest boy liked him, and Sonny had remembered to bring something for each of them; and Isabel, who is really much nicer than I am, more open and giving, had gone to a lot of trouble about dinner and was genuinely glad to see him. And she's always been able to tease Sonny in a way that I haven't. It was nice to see her face so vivid again and to hear her laugh and watch her make Sonny laugh. She wasn't, or, anyway, she didn't seem to be, at all uneasy or embarrassed. She chatted as though there were no subject which had to be avoided and she got Sonny past his first, faint stiffness. And thank God she was there, for I was filled with that icy dread again. Everything I did seemed awkward to me, and everything I said sounded freighted with hidden meaning. I was trying to remember everything I'd heard about dope addiction and I couldn't help watching Sonny for signs. I wasn't doing it out of malice. I was trying to find out something about my brother. I was dying to hear him tell me he was safe.

"Safe!" my father grunted, whenever Mama suggested trying to move to a neighborhood which might be safer for children. "Safe, hell! Ain't no place safe for kids, nor nobody."

He always went on like this, but he wasn't, ever, really as bad as he sounded, not even on weekends, when he got drunk. As a matter of fact, he was always on the lookout for "something a little better," but he died before he found it. He died suddenly, during a drunken weekend in the middle of the war, when Sonny was fifteen.

He and Sonny hadn't ever got on too well. And this was partly because Sonny was the apple of his father's eye. It was because he loved Sonny so much and was frightened for him, that he was always fighting with him. It doesn't do any good to fight with Sonny. Sonny just moves back, inside himself, where he can't be reached. But the principal reason that they never hit it off is that they were so much alike. Daddy was big and rough and loud-talking, just the opposite of Sonny, but they both had—that same privacy.

Mama tried to tell me something about this, just after Daddy died. I was home on leave from the army.

This was the last time I ever saw my mother alive. Just the same, this picture gets all mixed up in my mind with pictures I had of her when she was younger. The way I always see her is the way she used to be on a Sunday afternoon, say, when the old folks were talking after the big Sunday dinner. I always see her wearing pale blue. She'd be sitting on the sofa. And my father would be sitting in the easy chair, not far from her. And the living room would be full of church folks and relatives. There they sit, in chairs all around the living room, and the night is creeping up outside, but nobody knows it yet. You can see the darkness growing against the windowpanes and you hear the street noises every now and again, or maybe the jangling beat of a tambourine from one of the churches close by, but it's real quiet in the room. For a moment nobody's talking, but every face looks darkening, like the sky outside. And my mother rocks a little from the waist, and my father's eyes are closed. Everyone is looking at something a child can't see. For a minute they've forgotten the children. Maybe a kid is lying on the rug, half asleep. Maybe somebody's got a kid in his lap and is absent-mindedly stroking the kid's head. Maybe there's a kid, quiet and big-eyed, curled up in a big chair in the corner. The silence, the darkness coming, and the darkness in the faces frightens the child obscurely. He hopes that the hand which strokes his forehead will never stop—will never die. He hopes that there will never come a time when the old folks won't be sitting around the living room, talking about where they've come from, and what they've seen, and what's happened to them and their kinfolk.

But something deep and watchful in the child knows that this is bound to end, is already ending. In a moment someone will get up and turn on the light. Then the old folks will remember the children and they won't talk any more that day. And when light fills the room, the child is filled with darkness. He knows that every time this happens he's moved just a little closer to that darkness outside. The darkness outside is what the old folks have been talking about. It's what they've come from. It's what they endure. The child knows that they won't talk any more because if he knows too much about what's happened to *them*, he'll know too much too soon, about what's going to happen to *him*. 85

The last time I talked to my mother, I remember I was restless. I wanted to get out and see Isabel. We weren't married then and we had a lot to straighten out between us.

There Mama sat, in black, by the window. She was humming an old church song, *Lord, you brought me from a long ways off*. Sonny was out somewhere. Mama kept watching the streets.

"I don't know," she said, "if I'll ever see you again, after you go off from here. But I hope you'll remember the things I tried to teach you."

"Don't talk like that," I said, and smiled. "You'll be here a long time yet."

She smiled, too, but she said nothing. She was quiet for a long time. And I said, 90

"Mama, don't you worry about nothing. I'll be writing all the time, and you be getting the checks. . . ."

"I want to talk to you about your brother," she said, suddenly. "If anything happens to me he ain't going to have nobody to look out for him."

"Mama," I said, "ain't nothing going to happen to you *or* Sonny. Sonny's all right. He's a good boy and he's got good sense."

"It ain't a question of his being a good boy," Mama said, "nor of his having good sense. It ain't only the bad ones, nor yet the dumb ones that gets sucked under." She stopped, looking at me. "Your Daddy once had a brother," she said, and she smiled in a way that made me feel she was in pain. "You didn't never know that, did you?"

"No," I said, "I never knew that," and I watched her face.

95 "Oh, yes," she said, "your Daddy had a brother." She looked out of the window again. "I know you never saw your Daddy cry. But *I* did—many a time, through all these years."

I asked her, "What happened to his brother? How come nobody's ever talked about him?"

This was the first time I ever saw my mother look old.

"His brother got killed," she said, "when he was just a little younger than you are now. I knew him. He was a fine boy. He was maybe a little full of the devil, but he didn't mean nobody no harm."

Then she stopped and the room was silent, exactly as it had sometimes been on those Sunday afternoons. Mama kept looking out into the streets.

100 "He used to have a job in the mill," she said, "and, like all young folks, he just liked to perform on Saturday nights. Saturday nights, him and your father would drift around to different places, go to dances and things like that, or just sit around with people they knew, and your father's brother would sing, he had a fine voice, and play along with himself on his guitar. Well, this particular Saturday night, him and your father was coming home from some place, and they were both a little drunk and there was a moon that night, it was bright like day. Your father's brother was feeling kind of good, and he was whistling to himself, and he had his guitar slung over his shoulder. They was coming down a hill and beneath them was a road that turned off from the highway. Well, your father's brother, being always kind of frisky, decided to run down this hill, and he did, with that guitar banging and clanging behind him, and he ran across the road, and he was making water behind a tree. And your father was sort of amused at him and he was still coming down the hill, kind of slow. Then he heard a car motor and that same minute his brother stepped from behind the tree, into the road, in the moonlight. And he started to cross the road. And your father started to run down the hill, he says he don't know why. This car was full of white men. They was all drunk, and when they seen your father's brother they let out a great whoop and holler and they aimed the car straight at him. They was having fun, they just wanted to scare him, the way they do sometimes, you know. But they was drunk. And I guess the boy, being drunk, too, and scared, kind of lost his head. By the time he jumped it was too late. Your father says he heard his brother scream when the car rolled over him, and he heard the wood of that guitar when it give, and he heard them strings go flying, and he heard them white men shouting, and the car kept on a-going and it ain't stopped till this day. And, time your father got down the hill, his brother weren't nothing but blood and pulp."

Tears were gleaming on my mother's face. There wasn't anything I could say.

"He never mentioned it," she said, "because I never let him mention it before you children. Your Daddy was like a crazy man that night and for many a night thereafter. He says he never in his life seen anything as dark as that road after the lights of that car had gone away. Weren't nothing, weren't nobody on that road, just your Daddy and his brother and that busted guitar. Oh, yes. Your Daddy never did really get right again. Till the day he died he weren't sure but that every white man he saw was the man that killed his brother."

She stopped and took out her handkerchief and dried her eyes and looked at me.

"I ain't telling you all this," she said, "to make you scared or bitter or to make you hate nobody. I'm telling you this because you got a brother. And the world ain't changed."

105   I guess I didn't want to believe this. I guess she saw this in my face. She turned away from me, toward the window again, searching those streets.

"But I praise my Redeemer," she said at last, "that He called your Daddy home before me. I ain't saying it to throw no flowers at myself, but, I declare, it keeps me from feeling too cast down to know I helped your father get safely through this world. Your father always acted like he was the roughest, strongest man on earth. And everybody took him to be like that. But if he hadn't had *me* there—to see his tears!"

She was crying again. Still, I couldn't move. I said, "Lord, Lord, Mama, I didn't know it was like that."

"Oh, honey," she said, "there's a lot that you don't know. But you are going to find it out." She stood up from the window and came over to me. "You got to hold on to your brother," she said, "and don't let him fall, no matter what it looks like is happening to him and no matter how evil you gets with him. You going to be evil with him

many a time. But don't you forget what I told you, you hear?"

"I won't forget," I said. "Don't you worry, I won't forget. I won't let nothing happen to Sonny."

My mother smiled as though she were 110 amused at something she saw in my face. Then, "You may not be able to stop nothing from happening. But you got to let him know you's *there*."

Two days later I was married, and then I was gone. And I had a lot of things on my mind and I pretty well forgot my promise to Mama until I got shipped home on a special furlough for her funeral.

And, after the funeral, with just Sonny and me alone in the empty kitchen, I tried to find out something about him.

"What do you want to do?" I asked him.

"I'm going to be a musician," he said.

For he had graduated, in the time I had 115 been away, from dancing to the juke box to finding out who was playing what, and what they were doing with it, and he had bought himself a set of drums.

"You mean, you want to be a drummer?" I somehow had the feeling that being a drummer might be all right for other people but not for my brother Sonny.

"I don't think," he said, looking at me very gravely, "that I'll ever be a good drummer. But I think I can play a piano."

I frowned. I'd never played the role of the older brother quite so seriously before, had scarcely ever, in fact, *asked* Sonny a damn thing. I sensed myself in the presence of something I didn't really know how to handle, didn't understand. So I made my frown a little deeper as I asked: "What kind of musician do you want to be?"

He grinned. "How many kinds do you think there are?"

"Be *serious*," I said.   120

He laughed, throwing his head back, and then looked at me. "I *am* serious."

"Well, then, for Christ's sake, stop kidding around and answer a serious question. I mean, do you want to be a concert pianist, you want to play classical music and all that, or—or what?" Long before I finished he was laughing again. "For Christ's *sake*, Sonny!"

He sobered, but with difficulty. "I'm sorry. But you sound so—*scared!*" and he was off again.

"Well, you may think it's funny now, baby, but it's not going to be so funny when you have to make your living at it, let me tell you *that*. " I was furious because I knew he was laughing at me and I didn't know why.

125 "No," he said, very sober now, and afraid, perhaps, that he'd hurt me, "I don't want to be a classical pianist. That isn't what interests me. I mean"—he paused, looking hard at me, as though his eyes would help me to understand, and then gestured helplessly, as though perhaps his hand would help—"I mean, I'll have a lot of studying to do, and I'll have to study *everything*, but, I mean, I want to play *with*—jazz musicians." He stopped. "I want to play jazz," he said.

Well, the word had never before sounded as heavy, as real, as it sounded that afternoon in Sonny's mouth. I just looked at him and I was probably frowning a real frown by this time. I simply couldn't see why on earth he'd want to spend his time hanging around nightclubs, clowning around on bandstands, while people pushed each other around a dance floor. It seemed— beneath him, somehow. I had never thought about it before, had never been forced to, but I suppose I had always put jazz musicians in a class with what Daddy called "good-time people."

"Are you *serious*?"

"Hell, *yes*, I'm serious."

He looked more helpless than ever, and annoyed, and deeply hurt.

I suggested, helpfully: "You mean— 130 like Louis Armstrong?"

His face closed as though I'd struck him. "No. I'm not talking about none of that old-time, down home crap."

"Well, look, Sonny, I'm sorry, don't get mad. I just don't altogether get it, that's all. Name somebody—you know, a jazz musician you admire."

"Bird."

"Who?"

"Bird! Charlie Parker! Don't they teach 135 you nothing in the goddamn army?"

I lit a cigarette. I was surprised and then a little amused to discover that I was trembling. "I've been out of touch," I said. "You'll have to be patient with me. Now. Who's this Parker character?"

"He's just one of the greatest jazz musicians alive," said Sonny, sullenly, his hands in his pockets, his back to me. "Maybe *the* greatest," he added, bitterly, "that's probably why *you* never heard of him."

"All right," I said, "I'm ignorant. I'm sorry. I'll go out and buy all the cat's records right away, all right?"

"It don't," said Sonny, with dignity, "make any difference to me. I don't care what you listen to. Don't do me no favors."

I was beginning to realize that I'd 140 never seen him so upset before. With another part of my mind I was thinking that this would probably turn out to be one of those things kids go through and that I shouldn't make it seem important by pushing it too hard. Still, I didn't think it would do any harm to ask: "Doesn't all this take a lot of time? Can you make a living at it?"

He turned back to me and half leaned, half sat, on the kitchen table. "Everything takes time," he said, "and—well, yes, sure, I can make a living at it. But what I don't seem to be able to make you understand is that it's the only thing I want to do."

"Well, Sonny," I said, gently, "you know people can't always do exactly what they *want* to do—"

"*No*, I don't know that," said Sonny, surprising me. "I think people *ought* to do what they want to do, what else are they alive for?"

"You getting to be a big boy," I said desperately, "it's time you started thinking about your future."

145 "I'm thinking about my future," said Sonny, grimly. "I think about it all the time."

I gave up. I decided, if he didn't change his mind, that we could always talk about it later. "In the meantime," I said, "you got to finish school." We had already decided that he'd have to move in with Isabel and her folks. I knew this wasn't the ideal arrangement because Isabel's folks are inclined to be dicty and they hadn't especially wanted Isabel to marry me. But I didn't know what else to do. "And we have to get you fixed up at Isabel's."

There was a long silence. He moved from the kitchen table to the window. "That's a terrible idea. You know it yourself."

"Do you have a *better* idea?"

He just walked up and down the kitchen for a minute. He was as tall as I was. He had started to shave. I suddenly had the feeling that I didn't know him at all.

150 He stopped at the kitchen table and picked up my cigarettes. Looking at me with a kind of mocking, amused defiance, he put one between his lips. "You mind?"

"You smoking already?"

He lit the cigarette and nodded, watching me through the smoke. "I just wanted to see if I'd have the courage to smoke in front of you." He grinned and blew a great cloud of smoke to the ceiling. "It was easy." He looked at my face. "Come on, now. I bet you was smoking at my age, tell the truth."

I didn't say anything but the truth was on my face, and he laughed. But now there was something very strained in his laugh. "Sure. And I bet that ain't all you was doing."

He was frightening me a little. "Cut the crap," I said. "We already decided that you was going to go and live at Isabel's. Now what's got into you all of a sudden?"

"*You* decided it," he pointed out. "I 155 didn't decide nothing." He stopped in front of me, leaning against the stove, arms loosely folded. "Look, brother. I don't want to stay in Harlem no more, I really don't." He was very earnest. He looked at me, then over toward the kitchen window. There was something in his eyes I'd never seen before, some thoughtfulness, some worry all his own. He rubbed the muscle of one arm. "It's time I was getting out of here."

"Where do you want to *go*, Sonny?"

"I want to join the army. Or the navy, I don't care. If I say I'm old enough, they'll believe me."

Then I got mad. It was because I was so scared. "You must be crazy. You god-damn fool, what the hell do you want to go and join the *army* for?"

"I just told you. To get out of Harlem."

"Sonny, you haven't even finished 160 *school*. And if you really want to be a musician, how do you expect to study if you're in the *army*?"

He looked at me, trapped, and in anguish. "There's ways. I might be able to work out some kind of deal. Anyway, I'll have the G.I. Bill when I come out."

"*If* you come out." We stared at each other. "Sonny, please. Be reasonable. I know the setup is far from perfect. But we got to do the best we can."

"I ain't learning nothing in school," he said. "Even when I go." He turned away from me and opened the window and threw his cigarette out into the narrow alley. I watched his back. "At least, I ain't learning nothing you'd want me to learn." He slammed the window so hard I thought the glass would fly out, and turned back to me. "And I'm sick of the stink of these garbage cans!"

"Sonny," I said, "I know how you feel. But if you don't finish school now, you're going to be sorry later that you didn't." I grabbed him by the shoulders. "And you only got another year. It ain't so bad. And I'll come back and I swear I'll help you do *whatever* you want to do. Just try to put up with it till I come back. Will you please do that? For me?"

165   He didn't answer and he wouldn't look at me.

"Sonny. You hear me?"

He pulled away. "I hear you. But you never hear anything *I* say."

I didn't know what to say to that. He looked out of the window and then back at me. "OK," he said, and sighed. "I'll try."

Then I said, trying to cheer him up a little, "They got a piano at Isabel's. You can practice on it."

170   And as a matter of fact, it did cheer him up for a minute. "That's right," he said to himself. "I forgot that." His face relaxed a little. But the worry, the thoughtfulness, played on it still, the way shadows play on a face which is staring into the fire.

But I thought I'd never hear the end of that piano. At first, Isabel would write me, saying how nice it was that Sonny was so serious about his music and how, as soon as he came in from school, or wherever he had been when he was supposed to be at school, he went straight to that piano and stayed there until suppertime. And, after supper, he went back to that piano and stayed there until everybody went to bed. He was at the piano all day Saturday and all day Sunday. Then he bought a record player and started playing records. He'd play one record over and over again, all day long sometimes, and

he'd improvise along with it on the piano. Or he'd play one section of the record, one chord, one change, one progression, then he'd do it on the piano. Then back to the record. Then back to the piano.

Well, I really don't know how they stood it. Isabel finally confessed that it wasn't like living with a person at all, it was like living with sound. And the sound didn't make any sense to her, didn't make any sense to any of them—naturally. They began, in a way, to be afflicted by this presence that was living in their home. It was as though Sonny were some sort of god, or monster. He moved in an atmosphere which wasn't like theirs at all. They fed him and he ate, he washed himself, he walked in and out of their door; he certainly wasn't nasty or unpleasant or rude, Sonny isn't any of those things; but it was as though he were all wrapped up in some cloud, some fire, some vision all his own; and there wasn't any way to reach him.

At the same time, he wasn't really a man yet, he was still a child, and they had to watch out for him in all kinds of ways. They certainly couldn't throw him out. Neither did they dare to make a great scene about that piano because even they dimly sensed, as I sensed, from so many thousands of miles away, that Sonny was at that piano playing for his life.

But he hadn't been going to school. One day a letter came from the school board and Isabel's mother got it—there had, apparently, been other letters but Sonny had torn them up. This day, when Sonny came in, Isabel's mother showed him the letter and asked where he'd been spending his time. And she finally got it out of him that he'd been down in Greenwich Village, with musicians and other characters, in a white girl's apartment. And this scared her and she started to scream at him and what came up, once she began—though she denies it to this day—was what sacrifices they were making to give Sonny a decent home and how little he appreciated it.

175   Sonny didn't play the piano that day. By evening, Isabel's mother had calmed down but then there was the old man to deal with, and Isabel herself. Isabel says she did her best to be calm but she broke down and started crying. She says she just watched Sonny's face. She could tell, by watching him, what was happening with him. And what was happening was that they penetrated his cloud, they had reached him. Even if their fingers had been a thousand times more gentle than human fingers ever are, he could hardly help feeling that they had stripped him naked and were spitting on that nakedness. For he also had to see that his presence, that music, which was life or death to him, had been torture for them and that they had endured it, not at all for his sake, but only for mine. And Sonny couldn't take that. He can take it a little better today than he could then but he's still not very good at it and, frankly, I don't know anybody who is.

The silence of the next few days must have been louder than the sound of all the music ever played since time began. One morning, before she went to work, Isabel was in his room for something and she suddenly realized that all of his records were gone. And she knew for certain that he was gone. And he was. He went as far as the navy would carry him. He finally sent me a postcard from some place in Greece and that was the first I knew that Sonny was still alive. I didn't see him any more until we were both back in New York and the war had long been over.

He was a man by then, of course, but I wasn't willing to see it. He came by the house from time to time, but we fought almost every time we met. I didn't like the way he carried himself, loose and dreamlike

all the time, and I didn't like his friends, and his music seemed to be merely an excuse for the life he led. It sounded just that weird and disordered.

Then we had a fight, a pretty awful fight, and I didn't see him for months. By and by I looked him up, where he was living, in a furnished room in the Village, and I tried to make it up. But there were lots of people in the room and Sonny just lay on his bed, and he wouldn't come downstairs with me, and he treated these other people as though they were his family and I weren't. So I got mad and then he got mad, and then I told him that he might just as well be dead as live the way he was living. Then he stood up and he told me not to worry about him any more in life, that he *was* dead as far as I was concerned. Then he pushed me to the door and the other people looked on as though nothing were happening, and he slammed the door behind me. I stood in the hallway, staring at the door. I heard somebody laugh in the room and then the tears came to my eyes. I started down the steps, whistling to keep from crying, I kept whistling to myself, *You going to need me, baby, one of these cold, rainy days.*

I read about Sonny's trouble in the spring. Little Grace died in the fall. She was a beautiful little girl. But she only lived a little over two years. She died of polio and she suffered. She had a slight fever for a couple of days, but it didn't seem like anything and we just kept her in bed. And we would certainly have called the doctor, but the fever dropped, she seemed to be all right. So we thought it had just been a cold. Then, one day, she was up, playing, Isabel was in the kitchen fixing lunch for the two boys when they'd come in from school, and she heard Grace fall down in the living room. When you have a lot of children you don't always start running when one of them falls, unless they start screaming or something. And, this time, Grace was quiet. Yet, Isabel says that when she heard that *thump* and then that silence, something happened in her to make her afraid. And she ran to the living room and there was little Grace on the floor, all twisted up, and the reason she hadn't screamed was that she couldn't get her breath. And when she did scream, it was the worst sound, Isabel says, that she'd ever heard in all her life, and she still hears it sometimes in her dreams. Isabel will sometimes wake me up with a low, moaning, strangled sound and I have to be quick to awaken her and hold her to me and where Isabel is weeping against me seems a mortal wound.

180   I think I may have written Sonny the very day that little Grace was buried. I was sitting in the living room in the dark, by myself, and I suddenly thought of Sonny. My trouble made his real.

One Saturday afternoon, when Sonny had been living with us, or, anyway, been in our house, for nearly two weeks, I found myself wandering aimlessly about the living room, drinking from a can of beer, and trying to work up the courage to search Sonny's room. He was out, he was usually out whenever I was home, and Isabel had taken the children to see their grandparents. Suddenly I was standing still in front of the living room window, watching Seventh Avenue. The idea of searching Sonny's room made me still. I scarcely dared to admit to myself what I'd be searching for. I didn't know what I'd do if I found it. Or if I didn't.

On the sidewalk across from me, near the entrance to a barbecue joint, some people were holding an old-fashioned revival meeting. The barbecue cook, wearing a dirty white apron, his conked hair reddish and metallic in the pale sun, and a cigarette between his lips, stood in the doorway, watching them. Kids and older people

paused in their errands and stood there, along with some older men and a couple of very tough-looking women who watched everything that happened on the avenue, as though they owned it, or were maybe owned by it. Well, they were watching this, too. The revival was being carried on by three sisters in black, and a brother. All they had were their voices and their Bibles and a tambourine. The brother was testifying and while he testified two of the sisters stood together, seeming to say, amen, and the third sister walked around with the tambourine outstretched and a couple of people dropped coins into it. Then the brother's testimony ended and the sister who had been taking up the collection dumped the coins into her palm and transferred them to the pocket of her long black robe. Then she raised both hands, striking the tambourine against the air, and then against one hand, and she started to sing. And the two other sisters and the brother joined in.

It was strange, suddenly, to watch, though I had been seeing these street meetings all my life. So, of course, had everybody else down there. Yet, they paused and watched and listened and I stood still at the window. *"Tis the old ship of Zion,"* they sang, and the sister with the tambourine kept a steady, jangling beat, *"it has rescued many a thousand!"* Not a soul under the sound of their voices was hearing this song for the first time, not one of them had been rescued. Nor had they seen much in the way of rescue work being done around them. Neither did they especially believe in the holiness of the three sisters and the brother, they knew too much about them, knew where they lived, and how. The woman with the tambourine, whose voice dominated the air, whose face was bright with joy, was divided by very little from the woman who stood watching her, a cigarette between her heavy, chapped lips, her hair a cuckoo's nest, her face scarred and swollen from many beatings, and her black eyes glittering like coal. Perhaps they both knew this, which was why, when, as rarely, they addressed each other, they addressed each other as Sister. As the singing filled the air the watching, listening faces underwent a change, the eyes focusing on something within; the music seemed to soothe a poison out of them; and time seemed, nearly, to fall away from the sullen, belligerent, battered faces, as though they were fleeing back to their first condition, while dreaming of their last. The barbecue cook half shook his head and smiled, and dropped his cigarette and disappeared into his joint. A man fumbled in his pockets for change and stood holding it in his hand impatiently, as though he had just remembered a pressing appointment further up the avenue. He looked furious. Then I saw Sonny, standing on the edge of the crowd. He was carrying a wide, flat notebook with a green cover, and it made him look, from where I was standing, almost like a schoolboy. The coppery sun brought out the copper in his skin, he was very faintly smiling, standing very still. Then the singing stopped, the tambourine turned into a collection plate again. The furious man dropped in his coins and vanished, so did a couple of the women, and Sonny dropped some change in the plate, looking directly at the woman with a little smile. He started across the avenue, toward the house. He has a slow, loping walk, something like the way Harlem hipsters walk, only he's imposed on this his own half-beat. I had never really noticed it before.

I stayed at the window, both relieved and apprehensive. As Sonny disappeared from my sight, they began singing again. And they were still singing when his key turned in the lock.

185 "Hey," he said.

"Hey, yourself. You want some beer?"

"No. Well, maybe." But he came up to the window and stood beside me, looking out. "What a warm voice," he said.

They were singing *If I could only hear my mother pray again!*

"Yes," I said, "and she can sure beat that tambourine."

"But what a terrible song," he said, 190 and laughed. He dropped his notebook on the sofa and disappeared into the kitchen. "Where's Isabel and the kids?"

"I think they went to see their grandparents. You hungry?"

"No." He came back into the living room with his can of beer. "You want to come some place with me tonight?"

I sensed, I don't know how, that I couldn't possibly say no. "Sure. Where?"

He sat down on the sofa and picked up his notebook and started leafing through it. "I'm going to sit in with some fellows in a joint in the Village."

"You mean, you're going to play, 195 tonight?"

"That's right." He took a swallow of his beer and moved back to the window. He gave me a sidelong look. "If you can stand it."

"I'll try," I said.

He smiled to himself and we both watched as the meeting across the way broke up. The three sisters and the brother, heads bowed, were singing *God be with you till we meet again*. The faces around them were very quiet. Then the song ended. The small crowd dispersed. We watched the three women and the lone man walk slowly up the avenue.

"When she was singing before," said Sonny, abruptly, "her voice reminded me for a minute of what heroin feels like sometimes—when it's in your veins. It makes you feel sort of warm and cool at the same time. And distant. And—and sure." He sipped his beer, very deliberately not looking at me. I watched his face. "It makes you feel—in control. Sometimes you've got to have that feeling."

200   "Do you?" I sat down slowly in the easy chair.

"Sometimes." He went to the sofa and picked up his notebook again. "Some people do."

"In order," I asked, "to play?" And my voice was very ugly, full of contempt and anger.

"Well"—he looked at me with great, troubled eyes, as though, in fact, he hoped his eyes would tell me things he could never otherwise say—"they *think* so. And *if* they think so—!"

"And what do *you* think?" I asked.

205   He sat on the sofa and put his can of beer on the floor. "I don't know," he said, and I couldn't be sure if he were answering my question or pursuing his thoughts. His face didn't tell me. "It's not so much to *play*. It's to *stand* it, to be able to make it at all. On any level." He frowned and smiled: "In order to keep from shaking to pieces."

"But these friends of yours," I said, "they seem to shake themselves to pieces pretty goddamn fast."

"Maybe." He played with the notebook. And something told me that I should curb my tongue, that Sonny was doing his best to talk, that I should listen. "But of course you only know the ones that've gone to pieces. Some don't—or at least they haven't *yet* and that's just about all *any* of us can say." He paused. "And then there are some who just live, really, in hell, and they know it and they see what's happening and they go right on. I don't know." He sighed, dropped the notebook, folded his arms. "Some guys, you can tell from the way they play, they on something *all* the time. And you can see that, well, it makes something real for them. But of course," he picked up his beer from the floor and sipped it and put the can down again, "they *want* to, too,

you've got to see that. Even some of them that say they don't—*some*, not all."

"And what about you?" I asked—I couldn't help it. "What about you? Do *you* want to?"

He stood up and walked to the window and remained silent for a long time. Then he sighed. "Me," he said. Then: "While I was downstairs before, on my way here, listening to that woman sing, it struck me all of a sudden how much suffering she must have had to go through—to sing like that. It's *repulsive* to think you have to suffer that much."

I said: "But there's no way not to 210 suffer—is there, Sonny?"

"I believe not," he said and smiled, "but that's never stopped anyone from trying." He looked at me. "Has it?" I realized, with this mocking look, that there stood between us, forever, beyond the power of time or forgiveness, the fact that I had held silence—so long!—when he had needed human speech to help him. He turned back to the window. "No, there's no way not to suffer. But you try all kinds of ways to keep from drowning in it, to keep on top of it, and to make it seem—well, like *you*. Like you did something, all right, and now you're suffering for it. You know?" I said nothing. "Well you know," he said, impatiently, "why *do* people suffer? Maybe it's better to do something to give it a reason, *any* reason."

"But we just agreed," I said, "that there's no way not to suffer. Isn't it better, then, just to—take it?"

"But nobody just takes it," Sonny cried, "that's what I'm telling you! *Everybody* tries not to. You're just hung up on the *way* some people try—it's not *your* way!"

The hair on my face began to itch, my face felt wet. "That's not true," I said, "that's not true. I don't give a damn what other people do, I don't even care how they suffer.

I just care how *you* suffer." And he looked at me. "Please believe me," I said, "I don't want to see you—die—trying not to suffer."

215   "I won't," he said, flatly, "die trying not to suffer. At least, not any faster than anybody else."

"But there's no need," I said, trying to laugh, "is there? in killing yourself."

I wanted to say more, but I couldn't. I wanted to talk about will power and how life could be—well, beautiful. I wanted to say that it was all within; but was it? or, rather, wasn't that exactly the trouble? And I wanted to promise that I would never fail him again. But it would all have sounded—empty words and lies.

So I made the promise to myself and prayed that I would keep it.

"It's terrible sometimes, inside," he said, "that's what's the trouble. You walk these streets, black and funky and cold, and there's not really a living ass to talk to, and there's nothing shaking, and there's no way of getting it out—that storm inside. You can't talk it and you can't make love with it, and when you finally try to get with it and play it, you realize *nobody's* listening. So *you've* got to listen. You got to find a way to listen."

220   And then he walked away from the window and sat on the sofa again, as though all the wind had suddenly been knocked out of him. "Sometimes you'll do *anything* to play, even cut your mother's throat." He laughed and looked at me. "Or your brother's." Then he sobered. "Or your own." Then: "Don't worry. I'm all right now and I think I'll *be* all right. But I can't forget—where I've been. I don't mean just the physical place I've been, I mean where I've *been*. And *what* I've been."

"What have you been, Sonny?" I asked.

He smiled—but sat sideways on the sofa, his elbow resting on the back, his fingers playing with his mouth and chin, not looking at me. "I've been something I didn't recognize, didn't know I could be. Didn't know anybody could be." He stopped, looking inward, looking helplessly young, looking old. "I'm not talking about it now because I feel *guilty* or anything like that—maybe it would be better if I did, I don't know. Anyway, I can't really talk about it. Not to you, not to anybody," and now he turned and faced me. "Sometimes, you know, and it was actually when I was most *out* of the world, I felt that I was in it, that I was *with* it, really, and I could play or I didn't really have to *play*, it just came out of me, it was there. And I don't know how I played, thinking about it now, but I know I did awful things, those times, sometimes, to people. Or it wasn't that I *did* anything to them—it was that they weren't real." He picked up the beer can; it was empty; he rolled it between his palms: "And other times—well, I needed a fix, I needed to find a place to lean, I needed to clear a space to *listen*—and I couldn't find it, and I—went crazy, I did terrible things to *me*, I was terrible *for* me." He began pressing the beer can between his hands, I watched the metal begin to give. It glittered, as he played with it, like a knife, and I was afraid he would cut himself, but I said nothing. "Oh well. I can never tell you. I was all by myself at the bottom of something, stinking and sweating and crying and shaking, and I smelled it, you know? *my* stink, and I thought I'd die if I couldn't get away from it and yet, all the same, I knew that everything I was doing was just locking me in with it. And I didn't know," he paused, still flattening the beer can, "I didn't know, I *still* don't know, something kept telling me that maybe it was good to smell your own stink, but I didn't think that *that* was what I'd been trying to do—and—who can stand it?" and he abruptly dropped the ruined beer can, looking at me with a small, still smile, and then rose, walking to the window as though it were the lodestone rock. I watched his face, he watched the avenue. "I couldn't tell you when Mama died—but the reason I wanted to leave Harlem so bad was to get away from drugs. And then, when I ran away, that's what I was running from—really. When I came back, nothing had changed, I hadn't changed, I was just—older." And he stopped, drumming with his fingers on the windowpane. The sun had vanished, soon darkness would fall. I watched his face. "It can come again," he said, almost as though speaking to himself. Then he turned to me. "It can come again," he repeated. "I just want you to know that."

"All right," I said, at last. "So it can come again. All right."

He smiled, but the smile was sorrowful. "I had to try to tell you," he said.

225 "Yes," I said. "I understand that."

"You're my brother," he said, looking straight at me, and not smiling at all.

"Yes," I repeated, "yes. I understand that."

He turned back to the window, looking out. "All that hatred down there," he said, "all that hatred and misery and love. It's a wonder it doesn't blow the avenue apart."

We went to the only nightclub on a short, dark street, downtown. We squeezed through the narrow, chattering, jam-packed bar to the entrance of the big room, where the bandstand was. And we stood there for a moment, for the lights were very dim in this room and we couldn't see. Then, "Hello, boy," said a voice and an enormous black man, much older than Sonny or myself, erupted out of all that atmospheric lighting and put an arm around Sonny's shoulder. "I been sitting right here," he said, "waiting for you."

He had a big voice, too, and heads in 230 the darkness turned toward us.

Sonny grinned and pulled a little away, and said, "Creole, this is my brother. I told you about him."

Creole shook my hand. "I'm glad to meet you, son," he said, and it was clear that he was glad to meet me *there*, for Sonny's sake. And he smiled, "You got a real musician in *your* family," and he took his arm from Sonny's shoulder and slapped him, lightly, affectionately, with the back of his hand.

"Well. Now I've heard it all," said a voice behind us. This was another musician, and a friend of Sonny's, a coal-black, cheerful-looking man, built close to the ground. He immediately began confiding to me, at the top of his lungs, the most terrible things about Sonny, his teeth gleaming like a lighthouse and his laugh coming up out of him like the beginning of an earthquake. And it turned out that everyone at the bar knew Sonny, or almost everyone; some were musicians, working there, or nearby, or not working, some were simply hangers-on, and some were there to hear Sonny play. I was introduced to all of them and they were all very polite to me. Yet, it was clear that, for them, I was only Sonny's brother. Here, I was in Sonny's world. Or, rather: his kingdom. Here, it was not even a question that his veins bore royal blood.

They were going to play soon and Creole installed me, by myself, at a table in a dark corner. Then I watched them, Creole, and the little black man, and Sonny, and the others, while they horsed around, standing just below the bandstand. The light from the bandstand spilled just a little short of them and, watching them laughing and gesturing and moving about, I had the feeling that they, nevertheless, were being most careful not to step into that circle of light too suddenly: that if they moved into the light too suddenly, without thinking, they would perish in flame. Then, while I watched, one of them, the small, black man, moved into the light and crossed the bandstand and started fooling around with his drums. Then—being funny and being, also, extremely ceremonious—Creole took Sonny by the arm and led him to the piano. A woman's voice called Sonny's name and a few hands started clapping. And Sonny, also being funny and being ceremonious, and so touched, I think, that he could have cried, but neither hiding it nor showing it, riding it like a man, grinned, and put both hands to his heart and bowed from the waist.

235   Creole then went to the bass fiddle and a lean, very bright-skinned brown man jumped up on the bandstand and picked up his horn. So there they were, and the atmosphere on the bandstand and in the room began to change and tighten. Someone stepped up to the microphone and announced them. Then there were all kinds of murmurs. Some people at the bar shushed others. The waitress ran around, frantically getting in the last orders, guys and chicks got closer to each other, and the lights on the bandstand, on the quartet, turned to a kind of indigo. Then they all looked different there. Creole looked about him for the last time, as though he were making certain that all his chickens were in the coop, and then he—jumped and struck the fiddle. And there they were.

        All I know about music is that not many people ever really hear it. And even then, on the rare occasions when something opens within, and the music enters, what we mainly hear, or hear corroborated, are personal, private, vanishing evocations. But the man who creates the music is hearing something else, is dealing with the roar rising from the void and imposing order on it as it hits the air. What is evoked in him, then, is of another order, more terrible because it has

no words, and triumphant, too, for that same reason. And his triumph, when he triumphs, is ours. I just watched Sonny's face. His face was troubled, he was working hard, but he wasn't with it. And I had the feeling that, in a way, everyone on the bandstand was waiting for him, both waiting for him and pushing him along. But as I began to watch Creole, I realized that it was Creole who held them all back. He had them on a short rein. Up there, keeping the beat with his whole body, wailing on the fiddle, with his eyes half closed, he was listening to everything, but he was listening to Sonny. He was having a dialogue with Sonny. He wanted Sonny to leave the shoreline and strike out for the deep water. He was Sonny's witness that deep water and drowning were not the same thing—he had been there, and he knew. And he wanted Sonny to know. He was waiting for Sonny to do the things on the keys which would let Creole know that Sonny was in the water.

        And, while Creole listened, Sonny moved, deep within, exactly like someone in torment. I had never before thought of how awful the relationship must be between the musician and his instrument. He has to fill it, this instrument, with the breath of life, his own. He has to make it do what he wants it to do. And a piano is just a piano. It's made out of so much wood and wires and little hammers and big ones, and ivory. While there's only so much you can do with it, the only way to find this out is to try; to try and make it do everything.

        And Sonny hadn't been near a piano for over a year. And he wasn't on much better terms with his life, not the life that stretched before him now. He and the piano stammered, started one way, got scared, stopped; started another way, panicked, marked time, started again; then seemed to have found a direction, panicked again, got stuck. And the face I saw on Sonny I'd never seen before.

Everything had been burned out of it, and, at the same time, things usually hidden were being burned in, by the fire and fury of the battle which was occurring in him up there.

Yet, watching Creole's face as they neared the end of the first set, I had the feeling that something had happened, something I hadn't heard. Then they finished, there was scattered applause, and then, without an instant's warning, Creole started into something else, it was almost sardonic, it was *Am I Blue*. And, as though he commanded, Sonny began to play. Something began to happen. And Creole let out the reins. The dry, low, black man said something awful on the drums, Creole answered, and the drums talked back. Then the horn insisted, sweet and high, slightly detached perhaps, and Creole listened, commenting now and then, dry, and driving, beautiful and calm and old. Then they all came together again, and Sonny was part of the family again. I could tell this from his face. He seemed to have found, right there beneath his fingers, a damn brand-new piano. It seemed that he couldn't get over it. Then, for awhile, just being happy with Sonny, they seemed to be agreeing with him that brand-new pianos certainly were a gas.

240   Then Creole stepped forward to remind them that what they were playing was the blues. He hit something in all of them, he hit something in me, myself, and the music tightened and deepened, apprehension began to beat the air. Creole began to tell us what the blues were all about. They were not about anything very new. He and his boys up there were keeping it new, at the risk of ruin, destruction, madness, and death, in order to find new ways to make us listen. For, while the tale of how we suffer, and how we are delighted, and how we may triumph is never new, it always must be heard. There isn't any other tale to tell, it's the only light we've got in all this darkness.

And this tale, according to that face, that body, those strong hands on those strings, has another aspect in every country, and a new depth in every generation. Listen, Creole seemed to be saying, listen. Now these are Sonny's blues. He made the little black man on the drums know it, and the bright, brown man on the horn. Creole wasn't trying any longer to get Sonny in the water. He was wishing him Godspeed. Then he stepped back, very slowly, filling the air with the immense suggestion that Sonny speak for himself.

Then they all gathered around Sonny and Sonny played. Every now and again one of them seemed to say, amen. Sonny's fingers filled the air with life, his life. But that life contained so many others. And Sonny went all the way back, he really began with the spare, flat statement of the opening phrase of the song. Then he began to make it his. It was very beautiful because it wasn't hurried and it was no longer a lament. I seemed to hear with what burning he had made it his, with what burning we had yet to make it ours, how we could cease lamenting. Freedom lurked around us and I understood, at last, that he could help us to be free if we would listen, that he would never be free until we did. Yet, there was no battle in his face now. I heard what he had gone through, and would continue to go through until he came to rest in earth. He had made it his: that long line, of which we knew only Mama and Daddy. And he was giving it back, as everything must be given back, so that, passing through death, it can live forever. I saw my mother's face again, and felt, for the first time, how the stones of the road she had walked on must have bruised her feet. I saw the moonlit road where my father's brother died. And it brought something else back to me, and carried me past it. I saw my little girl again and felt Isabel's tears again, and I felt my own tears begin to rise. And I was yet aware that this was only a moment, that the world waited outside, as hungry as a tiger, and that trouble stretched above us, longer than the sky.

Then it was over. Creole and Sonny let out their breath, both soaking wet, and grinning. There was a lot of applause and some of it was real. In the dark, the girl came by and I asked her to take drinks to the bandstand. There was a long pause, while they talked up there in the indigo light and after awhile I saw the girl put a Scotch and milk on top of the piano for Sonny. He didn't seem to notice it, but just before they started playing again, he sipped from it and looked toward me, and nodded. Then he put it back on top of the piano. For me, then, as they began to play again, it glowed and shook above my brother's head like the very cup of trembling.

····•► *Your* **Turn**
Talking and Writing about Lit

1. Who is the main character in "Sonny's Blues"? How do we know this?

2. How does Baldwin use figurative language to enhance the reader's understanding of the characters' emotional experiences?

3. What effect does it have that the story is narrated from the perspective of Sonny's brother? How would the story be different if it were told from Sonny's own point of view?

4. **DIY** Do you have a sibling (or cousin or other family member) who is quite different from you? Write a scene of dialogue in which the two of you discuss a subject about which you have very different views.

Herman Melville (1819–1891)

Herman Melville was born in New York City, the son of a merchant from New England who died while Melville was a child. As a young man, Melville worked at many jobs, including clerk, farmhand, teacher, and cabin boy on a whaling ship. He experienced shipwreck in the South Seas, and when he returned to New York, he wrote several novels based on his adventures, among them *Typee* (1846) and *Omoo* (1847). These were fairly successful, but his real masterpiece, the novel *Moby Dick* (1851), was not understood or appreciated during his lifetime. Like *Moby Dick*, Melville's novel *Billy Budd* (published posthumously in 1924) did not receive critical acclaim until long after his death. As his work became less popular, Melville had to take a job as a customs inspector in New York in order to support his family.

Bartleby, the Scrivener (1853)

A STORY OF WALL STREET

I am a rather elderly man. The nature of my avocations, for the last thirty years, has brought me into more than ordinary contact with what would seem an interesting and somewhat singular set of men, of whom, as yet, nothing, that I know of, has ever been written—I mean, the law-copyists, or scriveners. I have known very many of them, professionally and privately, and, if I pleased, could relate divers histories, at which good-natured gentlemen might smile, and sentimental souls might weep. But I waive the biographies of all other scriveners, for a few passages in the life of Bartleby, who was a scrivener, the strangest I ever saw, or heard of. While, of other law-copyists, I might write the complete life, of Bartleby nothing of that sort can be done. I believe that no materials exist, for a full and satisfactory biography of this man. It is an irreparable loss to literature. Bartleby was one of those beings of whom nothing is ascertainable, except from the original sources, and, in his case, those are very small. What my own astonished eyes saw of Bartleby, *that* is all I know of him, except, indeed, one vague report, which will appear in the sequel.

Ere introducing the scrivener, as he first appeared to me, it is fit I make some mention of myself, my *employés*, my business, my chambers, and general surroundings, because some such description is indispensable to an adequate understanding of the chief character about to be presented. Imprimis:[1] I am a man who, from his youth upwards, has been filled with a profound conviction that the easiest way of life is the best. Hence, though I belong to a profession proverbially energetic and nervous, even to turbulence at times, yet nothing of that sort have I ever suffered to invade my peace. I am one of those unambitious lawyers who never address a jury, or in any way draw down public applause; but, in the cool tranquillity of a snug retreat, do a snug business among rich men's bonds, and mortgages, and title-deeds. All who know me, consider me an eminently *safe* man. The late John Jacob Astor,[2] a personage little given to poetic enthusiasm, had no hesitation in pronouncing my first grand point to be prudence; my next, method. I do not speak it in vanity, but simply record the fact, that I was not unemployed in my profession by the late John Jacob Astor; a name which, I admit, I love to repeat; for it hath a rounded and orbicular sound to it, and rings like unto bullion. I will freely add, that I was not insensible to the late John Jacob Astor's good opinion.

Sometime prior to the period at which this little history begins, my avocations had been largely increased. The good old office, now extinct in the State of New York, of a Master in Chancery, had been conferred upon me. It was not a very arduous office, but very pleasantly remunerative. I seldom lose my temper; much more seldom indulge in dangerous indignation at wrongs and outrages; but I must be permitted to be rash here and declare, that I consider the sudden and violent abrogation of the office of Master in Chancery, by the new Constitution, as a—— premature act; inasmuch as I had counted upon a life-lease of the profits, whereas I only received those of a few short years. But this is by the way.

---

[1]**Imprimis:** In the first place.

[2]**John Jacob Astor** (1763–1848): An enormously wealthy American capitalist.

My chambers were up stairs, at No.— Wall Street. At one end, they looked upon the white wall of the interior of a spacious skylight shaft, penetrating the building from top to bottom.

5   This view might have been considered rather tame than otherwise, deficient in what landscape painters call "life." But, if so, the view from the other end of my chambers offered, at least, a contrast, if nothing more. In that direction, my windows commanded an unobstructed view of a lofty brick wall, black by age and everlasting shade; which wall required no spyglass to bring out its lurking beauties, but, for the benefit of all near-sighted spectators, was pushed up to within ten feet of my window-panes. Owing to the great height of the surrounding buildings, and my chambers being on the second floor, the interval between this wall and mine not a little resembled a huge square cistern.

At the period just preceding the advent of Bartleby, I had two persons as copyists in my employment, and a promising lad as an office-boy. First, Turkey; second, Nippers; third, Ginger Nut. These may seem names, the like of which are not usually found in the Directory. In truth, they were nicknames, mutually conferred upon each other by my three clerks, and were deemed expressive of their respective persons or characters. Turkey was a short, pursy Englishman, of about my own age— that is, somewhere not far from sixty. In the morning, one might say, his face was of a fine florid hue, but after twelve o'clock, meridian—his dinner hour—it blazed like a grate full of Christmas coals; and continued blazing—but, as it were, with a gradual wane—till six o'clock, P.M., or thereabouts; after which, I saw no more of the proprietor of the face, which, gaining its meridian with the sun, seemed to set with it, to rise, culminate, and decline the following day, with the like regularity and undiminished glory.

There are many singular coincidences I have known in the course of my life, not the least among which was the fact, that, exactly when Turkey displayed his fullest beams from his red and radiant countenance, just then, too, at the critical moment, began the daily period when I considered his business capacities as seriously disturbed for the remainder of the twenty-four hours. Not that he was absolutely idle, or averse to business then; far from it. The difficulty was, he was apt to be altogether too energetic. There was a strange, inflamed, flurried, flighty recklessness of activity about him. He would be incautious in dipping his pen into his inkstand. All his blots upon my documents were dropped there after twelve o'clock, meridian. Indeed, not only would he be reckless, and sadly given to making blots in the afternoon, but, some days, he went further, and was rather noisy. At such times, too, his face flamed with augmented blazonry, as if cannel coal had been heaped on anthracite. He made an unpleasant racket with his chair; spilled his sand-box; in mending his pens, impatiently split them all to pieces, and threw them on the floor in a sudden passion; stood up, and leaned over his table, boxing his papers about in a most indecorous manner, very sad to behold in an elderly man like him. Nevertheless, as he was in many ways a most valuable person to me, and all the time before twelve o'clock, meridian, was the quickest, steadiest creature, too, accomplishing a great deal of work in a style not easily to be matched—for these reasons, I was willing to overlook his eccentricities, though, indeed, occasionally, I remonstrated with him. I did this very gently, however, because, though the civilest, nay, the blandest and most reverential of men in the morning, yet, in the afternoon, he was disposed, upon provocation, to be slightly rash with his tongue—in fact, insolent. Now, valuing his morning services as

I did, and resolved not to lose them—yet, at the same time, made uncomfortable by his inflamed ways after twelve o'clock—and being a man of peace, unwilling by my admonitions to call forth unseemly retorts from him, I took upon me, one Saturday noon (he was always worse on Saturdays) to hint to him, very kindly, that, perhaps, now that he was growing old, it might be well to abridge his labors; in short, he need not come to my chambers after twelve o'clock, but, dinner over, had best go home to his lodgings, and rest himself till tea-time. But no; he insisted upon his afternoon devotions. His countenance became intolerably fervid, as he oratorically assured me—gesticulating with a long ruler at the other end of the room—that if his services in the morning were useful, how indispensable, then, in the afternoon?

"With submission, sir," said Turkey, on this occasion, "I consider myself your right-hand man. In the morning I but marshal and deploy my columns; but in the afternoon I put myself at their head, and gallantly charge the foe, thus"—and he made a violent thrust with the ruler.

"But the blots, Turkey," intimated I.

"True; but, with submission, sir, behold these hairs! I am getting old. Surely, sir, a blot or two of a warm afternoon is not to be severely urged against gray hairs. Old age—even if it blot the page—is honorable. With submission, sir, we *both* are getting old."

10   This appeal to my fellow-feeling was hardly to be resisted. At all events, I saw that go he would not. So, I made up my mind to let him stay, resolving, nevertheless, to see to it that, during the afternoon, he had to do with my less important papers.

Nippers, the second on my list, was a whiskered, sallow, and, upon the whole, rather piratical-looking young man, of about five-and-twenty. I always deemed him the victim of two evil powers—ambition and indigestion. The ambition was evinced by a certain impatience of the duties of a mere copyist, an unwarrantable usurpation of strictly professional affairs such as the original drawing up of legal documents. The indigestion seemed betokened in an occasional nervous testiness and grinning irritability, causing the teeth to audibly grind together over mistakes committed in copying; unnecessary maledictions, hissed, rather than spoken in the heat of business; and especially by a continual discontent with the height of the table where he worked. Though of a very ingenious mechanical turn, Nippers could never get this table to suit him. He put chips under it, blocks of various sorts, bits of pasteboard, and at last went so far as to attempt an exquisite adjustment, by final pieces of folded blotting-paper. But no invention would answer. If, for the sake of easing his back, he brought the table-lid at a sharp angle well up towards his chin, and wrote there like a man using the steep roof of a Dutch house for his desk, then he declared that it stopped the circulation in his arms. If now he lowered the table to his waistbands, and stooped over it in writing, then there was a sore aching in his back. In short, the truth of the matter was, Nippers knew not what he wanted. Or, if he wanted anything, it was to be rid of a scrivener's table altogether. Among the manifestations of his diseased ambition was a fondness he had for receiving visits from certain ambiguous-looking fellows in seedy coats, whom he called his clients. Indeed, I was aware that not only was he, at times, considerable of a ward-politician, but he occasionally did a little business at the justices' courts, and was not unknown on the steps of the Tombs.[3] I have good reason to believe, however, that one individual who called upon him at my

---

[3]**The Tombs:** A jail in New York City.

chambers, and who, with a grand air, he insisted was his client, was no other than a dun, and the alleged title-deed, a bill. But, with all his failings, and the annoyances he caused me, Nippers, like his compatriot Turkey, was a very useful man to me; wrote a neat, swift hand; and, when he chose, was not deficient in a gentlemanly sort of deportment. Added to this, he always dressed in a gentlemanly sort of way; and so, incidentally, reflected credit upon my chambers. Whereas, with respect to Turkey, I had much ado to keep him from being a reproach to me. His clothes were apt to look oily, and smell of eating-houses. He wore his pantaloons very loose and baggy in summer. His coats were execrable, his hat not to be handled. But while the hat was a thing of indifference to me, inasmuch as his natural civility and deference, as a dependent Englishman, always led him to doff it the moment he entered the room, yet his coat was another matter. Concerning his coats, I reasoned with him; but with no effect. The truth was, I suppose, that a man with so small an income could not afford to sport such a lustrous face and a lustrous coat at one and the same time. As Nippers once observed, Turkey's money went chiefly for red ink. One winter day, I presented Turkey with a highly respectable-looking coat of my own—a padded gray coat, of a most comfortable warmth, and which buttoned straight up from the knee to the neck. I thought Turkey would appreciate the favor, and abate his rashness and obstreperousness of afternoons. But no; I verily believe that buttoning himself up in so downy and blanket-like a coat had a pernicious effect upon him—upon the same principle that too much oats are bad for horses. In fact, precisely as a rash, restive horse is said to feel his oats, so Turkey felt his coat. It made him insolent. He was a man whom prosperity harmed.

Though concerning the self-indulgent habits of Turkey, I had my own private surmises, yet, touching Nippers, I was well persuaded, that whatever might be his faults in other respects, he was, at least, a temperate young man. But indeed, nature herself seemed to have been his vintner, and, at his birth, charged him so thoroughly with an irritable, brandy-like disposition, that all subsequent potations were needless. When I consider how, amid the stillness of my chambers, Nippers would sometimes impatiently rise from his seat, and stooping over his table, spread his arms wide apart, seize the whole desk, and move it, and jerk it, with a grim, grinding motion on the floor, as if the table were a perverse voluntary agent, intent on thwarting and vexing him, I plainly perceive that, for Nippers, brandy-and-water were altogether superfluous.

It was fortunate for me that, owing to its peculiar cause—indigestion—the irritability and consequent nervousness of Nippers were mainly observable in the morning, while in the afternoon he was comparatively mild. So that, Turkey's paroxysms only coming on about twelve o'clock, I never had to do with their eccentricities at one time. Their fits relieved each other, like guards. When Nippers' was on, Turkey's was off; and *vice versa*. This was a good natural arrangement, under the circumstances.

Ginger Nut, the third on my list, was a lad, some twelve years old. His father was a carman, ambitious of seeing his son on the bench instead of a cart, before he died. So he sent him to my office, as student at law, errand-boy, cleaner, and sweeper, at the rate of one dollar a week. He had a little desk to himself, but he did not use it much. Upon inspection, the drawer exhibited a great array of the shells of various sorts of nuts. Indeed, to this quick-witted youth, the whole noble science of the law was contained in a nutshell. Not the least among the employments of Ginger Nut, as well as one which he discharged with the most alacrity, was his duty as cake and apple purveyor for Turkey and Nippers. Copying lawpapers being proverbially a dry, husky sort of business, my two scriveners were fain to moisten their mouths very often with Spitzenbergs, to be had at the numerous stalls nigh the Custom House and Post Office. Also, they sent Ginger Nut very frequently for that peculiar cake—small, flat, round, and very spicy—after which he had been named by them. Of a cold morning, when business was but dull, Turkey would gobble up scores of these cakes, as if they were mere wafers—indeed, they sell them at the rate of six or eight for a penny—the scrape of his pen blending with the crunching of the crisp particles in his mouth. Of all the fiery afternoon blunders and flurried rashness of Turkey, was his once moistening a ginger-cake between his lips, and clapping it on to a mortgage, for a seal. I came within an ace of dismissing him then. But he mollified me by making an oriental bow, and saying—

15 "With submission, sir, it was generous of me to find you in stationery on my own account."

Now my original business—that of a conveyancer and title hunter, and drawer-up of recondite documents of all sorts—was considerably increased by receiving the Master's office. There was now great work for scriveners. Not only must I push the clerks already with me, but I must have additional help.

In answer to my advertisement, a motionless young man one morning stood upon my office threshold, the door being open, for it was summer. I can see that figure now—pallidly neat, pitiably respectable, incurably forlorn! It was Bartleby.

After a few words touching his qualifications, I engaged him, glad to have among my corps of copyists a man of so singularly sedate an aspect, which I thought might operate beneficially upon the flighty temper of Turkey, and the fiery one of Nippers.

I should have stated before that ground-glass folding-doors divided my premises into two parts, one of which was occupied by my scriveners, the other by myself. According to my humor, I threw open these doors, or closed them. I resolved to assign Bartleby a corner by the folding-doors, but on my side of them, so as to have this quiet man within easy call, in case any trifling thing was to be done. I placed his desk close up to a small side-window in that part of the room, a window which originally had afforded a lateral view of certain grimy brickyards and bricks, but which, owing to subsequent erections, commanded at present no view at all, though it gave some light. Within three feet of the panes was a wall, and the light came down from far above, between two lofty buildings, as from a very small opening in a dome. Still further to a satisfactory arrangement, I procured a high green folding screen, which might entirely isolate Bartleby from my sight, though not remove him from my voice. And thus, in a manner, privacy and society were conjoined.

20 At first, Bartleby did an extraordinary quantity of writing. As if long famishing for something to copy, he seemed to gorge himself on my documents. There was no pause for digestion. He ran a day and night line, copying by sunlight and by candle-light. I should have been quite delighted with his application, had he been cheerfully industrious. But he wrote on silently, palely, mechanically.

It is, of course, an indispensable part of a scrivener's business to verify the accuracy of his copy, word by word. Where there are two or more scriveners in an office, they assist each other in this examination, one reading from the copy, the other holding the original. It is a very dull, wearisome, and lethargic affair. I can readily imagine that, to some sanguine temperaments, it would be altogether intolerable. For example, I cannot credit that the mettlesome poet, Byron, would have contentedly sat down with Bartleby to examine a law document of, say five hundred pages, closely written in a crimpy hand.

Now and then, in the haste of business, it had been my habit to assist in comparing some brief document myself, calling Turkey or Nippers for this purpose. One object I had, in placing Bartleby so handy to me behind the screen, was, to avail myself of his services on such trivial occasions. It was on the third day, I think, of his being with me, and before any necessity had arisen for having his own writing examined, that, being much hurried to complete a small affair I had in hand, I abruptly called to Bartleby. In my haste and natural expectancy of instant compliance, I sat with my head bent over the original on my desk, and my right hand sideways, and somewhat nervously extended with the copy, so that, immediately upon emerging from his retreat, Bartleby might snatch it and proceed to business without the least delay.

In this very attitude did I sit when I called to him, rapidly stating what it was I wanted him to do—namely, to examine a small paper with me. Imagine my surprise, nay, my consternation, when, without moving from his privacy, Bartleby, in a singularly mild, firm voice, replied, "I would prefer not to."

I sat awhile in perfect silence, rallying my stunned faculties. Immediately it occurred to me that my ears had deceived me, or Bartleby had entirely misunderstood my meaning. I repeated my request in the clearest tone I could assume; but in quite as clear a one came the previous reply, "I would prefer not to."

25 "Prefer not to," echoed I, rising in high excitement, and crossing the room with a stride. "What do you mean? Are you moon-struck? I want you to help me compare this sheet here—take it," and I thrust it towards him.

"I would prefer not to," said he.

I looked at him steadfastly. His face was leanly composed; his gray eye dimly calm. Not a wrinkle of agitation rippled him. Had there been the least uneasiness, anger, impatience, or impertinence in his manner; in other words, had there been anything ordinarily human about him, doubtless I should have violently dismissed him from the premises. But as it was, I should have as soon thought of turning my pale plaster-of-paris bust of Cicero out of doors. I stood gazing at him awhile, as he went on with his own writing, and then reseated myself at my desk. This is very strange, thought I. What had one best do? But my business hurried me. I concluded to forget the matter for the present, reserving it for my future leisure. So, calling Nippers from the other room, the paper was speedily examined.

A few days after this, Bartleby concluded four lengthy documents, being quadruplicates of a week's testimony taken before me in my High Court of Chancery. It became necessary to examine them. It was an important suit, and great accuracy was imperative. Having all things arranged, I called Turkey, Nippers, and Ginger Nut, from the next room, meaning to place the four copies in the hands of my four clerks, while I should read from the original. Accordingly, Turkey, Nippers, and Ginger Nut had taken their seats in a row, each with his document in hand, when I called to Bartleby to join this interesting group.

"Bartleby! quick, I am waiting."

I heard a slow scrape of his chair legs 30 on the uncarpeted floor, and soon he appeared standing at the entrance of his hermitage.

"What is wanted?" said he, mildly.

"The copies, the copies," said I, hurriedly. "We are going to examine them. There"—and I held towards him the fourth quadruplicate.

"I would prefer not to," he said, and gently disappeared behind the screen.

For a few moments I was turned into a pillar of salt, standing at the head of my seated column of clerks. Recovering myself, I advanced towards the screen, and demanded the reason for such extraordinary conduct.

35 "*Why* do you refuse?"

"I would prefer not to."

With any other man I should have flown outright into a dreadful passion, scorned all further words, and thrust him ignominiously from my presence. But there was something about Bartleby that not only strangely disarmed me, but, in a wonderful manner, touched and disconcerted me. I began to reason with him.

"These are your own copies we are about to examine. It is labor saving to you, because one examination will answer for your four papers. It is common usage. Every copyist is bound to help examine his copy. Is it not so? Will you not speak? Answer!"

"I prefer not to," he replied in a flutelike tone. It seemed to me that, while I had been addressing him, he carefully revolved every statement that I made; fully comprehended the meaning; could not gainsay the irresistible conclusion; but, at the same time, some paramount consideration prevailed with him to reply as he did.

40 "You are decided, then, not to comply with my request—a request made according to common usage and common sense?"

He briefly gave me to understand, that on that point my judgment was sound. Yes: his decision was irreversible.

It is not seldom the case that, when a man is browbeaten in some unprecedented and violently unreasonable way, he begins to stagger in his own plainest faith. He begins, as it were, vaguely to surmise that, wonderful as it may be, all the justice and all the reason is on the other side. Accordingly, if any disinterested persons are present, he turns to them for some reinforcement for his own faltering mind.

"Turkey," said I, "what do you think of this? Am I not right?"

"With submission, sir," said Turkey, in his blandest tone, "I think that you are."

"Nippers," said I, "what do *you* think 45 of it?"

"I think I should kick him out of the office."

(The reader of nice perceptions will have perceived that, it being morning, Turkey's answer is couched in polite and tranquil terms, but Nippers replies in illtempered ones. Or, to repeat a previous sentence, Nippers' ugly mood was on duty, and Turkey's off.)

"Ginger Nut," said I, willing to enlist the smallest suffrage in my behalf, "what do *you* think of it?"

"I think, sir, he's a little *luny*," replied Ginger Nut, with a grin.

"You hear what they say," said I, turn- 50 ing towards the screen, "come forth and do your duty."

But he vouchsafed no reply. I pondered a moment in sore perplexity. But once more business hurried me. I determined again to postpone the consideration of this dilemma to my future leisure. With a little trouble we made out to examine the papers without Bartleby, though at every page or two Turkey deferentially dropped his opinion that this proceeding was quite out of the common; while Nippers, twitching in his chair with a dyspeptic nervousness, ground out, between his set teeth, occasional hissing maledictions against the stubborn oaf behind the screen. And for his (Nippers') part, this was the first and the last time he would do another man's business without pay.

Meanwhile Bartleby sat in his hermitage, oblivious to everything but his own peculiar business there.

Some days passed, the scrivener being employed upon another lengthy work. His late remarkable conduct led me to regard his ways narrowly. I observed that he never went to dinner; indeed, that he never went anywhere. As yet I had never, of my personal knowledge, known him to be outside of my office. He was a perpetual sentry in the corner. At about eleven o'clock though, in the morning, I noticed that Ginger Nut would advance toward the opening in Bartleby's screen, as if silently beckoned thither by a gesture invisible to me where I sat. The boy would then leave the office, jingling a few pence, and reappear with a handful of ginger-nuts, which he delivered in the hermitage, receiving two of the cakes for his trouble.

He lives, then, on ginger-nuts, thought I; never eats a dinner, properly speaking; he must be a vegetarian, then, but no; he never eats even vegetables, he eats nothing but ginger-nuts. My mind then ran on in reveries concerning the probable effects upon the human constitution of living entirely on ginger-nuts. Ginger-nuts are so called, because they contain ginger as one of their peculiar constituents, and the final flavoring one. Now, what was ginger? A hot, spicy thing. Was Bartleby hot and spicy? Not at all. Ginger, then, had no effect upon Bartleby. Probably he preferred it should have none.

55   Nothing so aggravates an earnest person as a passive resistance. If the individual so resisted be of a not inhumane temper, and the resisting one perfectly harmless in his passivity, then, in the better moods of the former, he will endeavor charitably to construe to his imagination what proves impossible to be solved by his judgment. Even so, for the most part, I regarded Bartleby and his ways. Poor fellow! thought I, he means no mischief; it is plain he intends no insolence; his aspect sufficiently evinces that his eccentricities are involuntary. He is useful to me. I can get along with him. If I turn him away, the chances are he will fall in with some less indulgent employer, and then he will be rudely treated, and perhaps driven forth miserably to starve. Yes. Here I can cheaply purchase a delicious self-approval. To befriend Bartleby; to humor him in his strange wilfulness, will cost me little or nothing, while I lay up in my soul what will eventually prove a sweet morsel for my conscience. But this mood was not invariable with me. The passiveness of Bartleby sometimes irritated me. I felt strangely goaded on to encounter him in new opposition—to elicit some angry spark from him answerable to my own. But, indeed, I might as well have essayed to strike fire with my knuckles against a bit of Windsor soap. But one afternoon the evil impulse in me mastered me, and the following little scene ensued:

"Bartleby," said I, "when those papers are all copied, I will compare them with you."

"I would prefer not to."

"How? Surely you do not mean to persist in that mulish vagary?"

No answer.

I threw open the folding-doors nearby, 60 and turning upon Turkey and Nippers, exclaimed:

"Bartleby a second time says, he won't examine his papers. What do you think of it, Turkey?"

It was afternoon, be it remembered. Turkey sat glowing like a brass boiler; his bald head steaming; his hands reeling among his blotted papers.

"Think of it?" roared Turkey, "I think I'll just step behind his screen, and black his eyes for him!"

So saying, Turkey rose to his feet and threw his arms into a pugilistic position. He was hurrying away to make good his promise, when I detained him, alarmed at the effect of incautiously rousing Turkey's combativeness after dinner.

65 "Sit down, Turkey," said I, "and hear what Nippers has to say. What do you think of it, Nippers? Would I not be justified in immediately dismissing Bartleby?"

"Excuse me, that is for you to decide, sir. I think his conduct quite unusual, and, indeed, unjust, as regards Turkey and myself. But it may only be a passing whim."

"Ah," exclaimed I, "you have strangely changed your mind, then—you speak very gently of him now."

"All beer," cried Turkey; "gentleness is effects of beer—Nippers and I dined together to-day. You see how gentle *I* am, sir. Shall I go and black his eyes?"

"You refer to Bartleby, I suppose. No, not to-day, Turkey," I replied; "pray, put up your fists."

70 I closed the doors, and again advanced towards Bartleby. I felt additional incentives tempting me to my fate. I burned to be rebelled against again. I remembered that Bartleby never left the office.

"Bartleby," said I, "Ginger Nut is away; just step around to the Post Office, won't you?" (it was but a three minutes' walk) "and see if there is anything for me."

"I would prefer not to."

"You *will* not?"

"I *prefer* not."

75 I staggered to my desk, and sat there in a deep study. My blind inveteracy returned. Was there any other thing in which I could procure myself to be ignominiously repulsed by this lean, penniless wight?—my hired clerk? What added thing is there, perfectly reasonable, that he will be sure to refuse to do?

"Bartleby!"

No answer.

"Bartleby," in a louder tone.

No answer.

"Bartleby," I roared. 80

Like a very ghost, agreeably to the laws of magical invocation, at the third summons, he appeared at the entrance of his hermitage.

"Go to the next room, and tell Nippers to come to me."

"I prefer not to," he respectfully and slowly said, and mildly disappeared.

"Very good, Bartleby," said I, in a quiet sort of serenely-severe self-possessed tone, intimating the unalterable purpose of some terrible retribution very close at hand. At the moment I half intended something of the kind. But upon the whole, as it was drawing towards my dinner-hour, I thought it best to put on my hat and walk home for the day, suffering much from perplexity and distress of mind.

Shall I acknowledge it? The conclusion 85 of this whole business was, that it soon became a fixed fact of my chambers, that a pale young scrivener, by the name of Bartleby, had a desk there; that he copied for me at the usual rate of four cents a folio (one hundred words); but he was permanently exempt from examining the work done by him, that duty being transferred to Turkey and Nippers, one of compliment, doubtless, to their superior acuteness; moreover, said Bartleby was never, on any account, to be dispatched on the most trivial errand of any sort; and that even if entreated to take upon him such a matter, it was generally understood that he would "prefer not to"—in other words, that he would refuse point-blank.

As days passed on, I became considerably reconciled to Bartleby. His steadiness, his freedom from all dissipation, his incessant industry (except when he chose to throw himself into a standing revery behind his screen), his great stillness, his unalterableness of demeanor under all circumstances, made him a valuable acquisition. One prime thing was this—*he was always there*—first in the morning, continually through the day, and the last at night. I had a singular confidence in his honesty. I felt my most precious papers perfectly safe in his hands. Sometimes, to be sure, I could not, for the very soul of me, avoid falling into sudden spasmodic passions with him. For it was exceeding difficult to bear in mind all the time those strange peculiarities, privileges, and unheard-of exemptions, forming the tacit stipulations on Bartleby's part under which he remained in my office. Now and then, in the eagerness of dispatching pressing business, I would inadvertently summon Bartleby, in a short, rapid tone, to put his finger, say, on the incipient tie of a bit of red tape with which I was about compressing some papers. Of course, from behind the screen the usual answer, "I prefer not to," was sure to come; and then, how could a human creature, with the common infirmities of our nature, refrain from bitterly exclaiming upon such perverseness—such unreasonableness? However, every added repulse of this sort which I received only tended to lessen the probability of my repeating the inadvertence.

Here it must be said, that, according to the custom of most legal gentlemen occupying chambers in densely populated law buildings, there were several keys to my door. One was kept by a woman residing in the attic, which person weekly scrubbed and daily swept and dusted my apartments. Another was kept by Turkey for convenience sake. The third I sometimes carried in my own pocket. The fourth I knew not who had.

Now, one Sunday morning I happened to go to Trinity Church, to hear a celebrated preacher, and finding myself rather early on the ground I thought I would walk round to my chambers for a while. Luckily I had my key with me; but upon applying it to the lock, I found it resisted by something inserted from the inside. Quite surprised, I called out; when to my consternation a key was turned from within; and thrusting his lean visage at me, and holding the door ajar, the apparition of Bartleby appeared, in his shirt-sleeves, and otherwise in a strangely tattered *dshabille,* saying quietly that he was sorry, but he was deeply engaged just then, and—preferred not admitting me at present. In a brief word or two, he moreover added, that perhaps I had better walk round the block two or three times, and by that time he would probably have concluded his affairs.

Now, the utterly unsurmised appearance of Bartleby, tenanting my law-chambers of a Sunday morning, with his cadaverously gentlemanly *nonchalance,* yet withal firm and self-possessed, had such a strange effect upon me, that incontinently I slunk away from my own door, and did as desired. But not without sundry twinges of impotent rebellion against the mild effrontery of this unaccountable scrivener. Indeed, it was his wonderful mildness chiefly, which not only disarmed me, but unmanned me, as it were. For I consider that one, for the time, is sort of unmanned when he tranquilly permits his hired clerk to dictate to him, and order him away from his own premises. Furthermore, I was full of uneasiness as to what Bartleby could possibly be doing in my office in his shirt-sleeves, and in an otherwise dismantled condition of a Sunday morning. Was anything amiss going on? Nay, that was out of the question. It was not to be thought of for a moment that Bartleby was an immoral person. But what could he be doing there?—copying? Nay again, whatever might be his eccentricities, Bartleby was an eminently decorous person. He would be the last man to sit down to his desk in any state approaching to nudity. Besides, it was Sunday; and there was something about Bartleby that forbade the supposition that he would by any secular occupation violate the proprieties of the day.

90   Nevertheless, my mind was not pacified; and full of a restless curiosity, at last I returned to the door. Without hindrance I inserted my key, opened it, and entered. Bartleby was not to be seen. I looked round anxiously, peeped behind his screen; but it was very plain that he was gone. Upon more closely examining the place, I surmised that for an indefinite period Bartleby must have ate, dressed, and slept in my office, and that too without plate, mirror, or bed. The cushioned seat of a rickety old sofa in one corner bore the faint impress of a lean, reclining form. Rolled away under his desk, I found a blanket; under the empty grate, a blacking box and brush; on a chair, a tin basin, with soap and a ragged towel; in a newspaper a few crumbs of ginger-nuts and a morsel of cheese. Yes, thought I, it is evident enough that Bartleby has been making his home here, keeping bachelor's hall all by himself. Immediately then the thought came sweeping across me, what miserable friendlessness and loneliness are here revealed! His poverty is great; but his solitude, how horrible! Think of it. Of a Sunday, Wall Street is deserted as Petra;[4] and every night of every day it is an emptiness. This building, too, which of week-days hums with industry and life, at nightfall echoes with sheer vacancy, and all through Sunday is forlorn. And here Bartleby makes his home; sole spectator of a solitude which he has seen all populous—a sort of innocent and transformed Marius brooding among the ruins of Carthage?[5]

---

[4]**Petra:** An ancient Arabian city abandoned for many centuries.
[5]**Marius . . . of Carthage:** Gaius Marius (157–86 B.C.): Exiled Roman general who sought refuge in Carthage, a city destroyed by the Romans.

For the first time in my life a feeling of overpowering stinging melancholy seized me. Before, I had never experienced aught but a not unpleasing sadness. The bond of a common humanity now drew me irresistibly to gloom. A fraternal melancholy! For both I and Bartleby were sons of Adam. I remembered the bright silks and sparkling faces I had seen that day, in gala trim, swan-like sailing down the Mississippi of Broadway; and I contrasted them with the pallid copyist, and thought to myself, Ah, happiness courts the light, so we deem the world is gay; but misery hides aloof, so we deem that misery there is none. These sad fancyings—chimeras, doubtless, of a sick and silly brain—led on to other and more special thoughts, concerning the eccentricities of Bartleby. Presentiments of strange discoveries hovered round me. The scrivener's pale form appeared to me laid out, among uncaring strangers, in its shivering winding-sheet.

Suddenly I was attracted by Bartleby's closed desk, the key in open sight left in the lock.

I mean no mischief, seek the gratification of no heartless curiosity, thought I; besides, the desk is mine, and its contents, too, so I will make bold to look within. Everything was methodically arranged, the papers smoothly placed. The pigeon-holes were deep, and removing the files of documents, I groped into their recesses. Presently I felt something there, and dragged it out. It was an old bandanna handkerchief, heavy and knotted. I opened it, and saw it was a saving's bank.

I now recalled all the quiet mysteries which I had noted in the man. I remembered that he never spoke but to answer; that, though at intervals he had considerable time to himself, yet I had never seen him reading— no, not even a newspaper; that for long periods he would stand looking out, at his pale window behind the screen, upon the dead brick wall; I was quite sure he never visited any refectory or eating-house; while his pale face clearly indicated that he never drank beer like Turkey; or tea and coffee even, like other men; that he never went anywhere in particular that I could learn; never went out for a walk, unless, indeed, that was the case at present; that he had declined telling who he was, or whence he came, or whether he had any relatives in the world; that though so thin and pale, he never complained of ill-health. And more than all, I remembered a certain unconscious air of pallid—how shall I call it?—of pallid haughtiness, say, or rather an austere reserve about him, which had positively awed me into my tame compliance with his eccentricities, when I had feared to ask him to do the slightest incidental thing for me, even though I might know, from his long-continued motionlessness, that behind his screen he must be standing in one of those dead-wall reveries of his.

95   Revolving all these things, and coupling them with the recently discovered fact, that he made my office his constant abiding place and home, and not forgetful of his morbid moodiness; revolving all these things, a prudential feeling began to steal over me. My first emotions had been those of pure melancholy and sincerest pity; but just in proportion as the forlornness of Bartleby grew and grew to my imagination, did that same melancholy merge into fear, that pity into repulsion. So true it is, and so terrible, too, that up to a certain point the thought or sight of misery enlists our best affections; but, in certain special cases, beyond that point it does not. They err who would assert that invariably this is owing to the inherent selfishness of the human heart. It rather proceeds from a certain hopelessness of remedying excessive and organic ill. To a sensitive being, pity is not seldom pain.

And when at last it is perceived that such pity cannot lead to effectual succor, common sense bids the soul be rid of it. What I saw that morning persuaded me that the scrivener was the victim of innate and incurable disorder. I might give alms to his body; but his body did not pain him; it was his soul that suffered, and his soul I could not reach.

I did not accomplish the purpose of going to Trinity Church that morning. Somehow, the things I had seen disqualified me for the time from church-going. I walked homeward, thinking what I would do with Bartleby. Finally, I resolved upon this—I would put certain calm questions to him the next morning, touching his history, etc., and if he declined to answer them openly and unreservedly (and I supposed he would prefer not), then to give him a twenty dollar bill over and above whatever I might owe him, and tell him his services were no longer required; but that if in any other way I could assist him, I would be happy to do so, especially if he desired to return to his native place, wherever that might be, I would willingly help to defray the expenses. Moreover, if, after reaching home, he found himself at any time in want of aid, a letter from him would be sure of a reply.

The next morning came.

"Bartleby," said I, gently calling to him behind his screen.

No reply.

"Bartleby," said I, in a still gentler tone, 100 "come here; I am not going to ask you to do anything you would prefer not to do—I simply wish to speak to you."

Upon this he noiselessly slid into view.

"Will you tell me, Bartleby, where you were born?"

"I would prefer not to."

"Will you tell me *anything* about yourself?"

"I would prefer not to."   105

"But what reasonable objection can you have to speak to me? I feel friendly towards you."

He did not look at me while I spoke, but kept his glance fixed upon my bust of Cicero, which, as I then sat, was directly behind me, some six inches above my head.

"What is your answer, Bartleby?" said I, after waiting a considerable time for a reply, during which his countenance remained immovable, only there was the faintest conceivable tremor of the white attenuated mouth.

"At present I prefer to give no answer," he said, and retired into his hermitage.

110   It was rather weak in me I confess, but his manner, on this occasion, nettled me. Not only did there seem to lurk in it a certain calm disdain, but his perverseness seemed ungrateful, considering the undeniable good usage and indulgence he had received from me.

Again I sat ruminating what I should do. Mortified as I was at his behavior, and resolved as I had been to dismiss him when I entered my office, nevertheless I strangely felt something superstitious knocking at my heart, and forbidding me to carry out my purpose, and denouncing me for a villain if I dared to breathe one bitter word against this forlornest of mankind. At last, familiarly drawing my chair behind his screen, I sat down and said: "Bartleby, never mind, then, about revealing your history; but let me entreat you, as a friend, to comply as far as may be with the usages of this office. Say now, you will help to examine papers tomorrow or next day: in short, say now, that in a day or two you will begin to be a little reasonable:—say so, Bartleby."

"At present I would prefer not to be a little reasonable," was his mildly cadaverous reply.

Just then the folding-doors opened, and Nippers approached. He seemed suffering from an unusually bad night's rest, induced by severer indigestion than common. He overheard those final words of Bartleby.

"*Prefer not*, eh?" gritted Nippers—"I'd *prefer* him, if I were you, sir," addressing me—"I'd *prefer* him; I'd give him preferences, the stubborn mule! What is it, sir, pray, that he *prefers* not to do now?"

Bartleby moved not a limb.   115

"Mr. Nippers," said I, "I'd prefer that you would withdraw for the present."

Somehow, of late, I had got into the way of involuntarily using this word "prefer" upon all sorts of not exactly suitable occasions. And I trembled to think that my contact with the scrivener had already and seriously affected me in a mental way. And what further and deeper aberration might it not yet produce? This apprehension had not been without efficacy in determining me to summary measures.

As Nippers, looking very sour and sulky, was departing, Turkey blandly and deferentially approached.

"With submission, sir," said he, "yesterday I was thinking about Bartleby here, and I think that if he would but prefer to take a quart of good ale every day, it would do much towards mending him, and enabling him to assist in examining his papers."

"So you have got the word, too," said   120 I, slightly excited.

"With submission, what word, sir?" asked Turkey, respectfully crowding himself into the contracted space behind the screen, and by so doing, making me jostle the scrivener. "What word, sir?"

"I would prefer to be left alone here," said Bartleby, as if offended at being mobbed in his privacy.

"*That's* the word, Turkey," said I—"*that's* it."

"Oh, *prefer*? oh yes—queer word. I never use it myself. But, sir, as I was saying, if he would but prefer—"

125   "Turkey," interrupted I, "you will please withdraw."

"Oh certainly, sir, if you prefer that I should."

As he opened the folding-door to retire, Nippers at his desk caught a glimpse of me, and asked whether I would prefer to have a certain paper copied on blue paper or white. He did not in the least roguishly accent the word "prefer." It was plain that it involuntarily rolled from his tongue. I thought to myself, surely I must get rid of a demented man, who already has in some degree turned the tongues, if not the heads of myself and clerks. But I thought it prudent not to break the dismission at once.

The next day I noticed that Bartleby did nothing but stand at his window in his dead-wall revery. Upon asking him why he did not write, he said that he had decided upon doing no more writing.

"Why, how now? what next?" exclaimed I, "do no more writing?"

130   "No more."

"And what is the reason?"

"Do you not see the reason for yourself?" he indifferently replied.

I looked steadfastly at him, and perceived that his eyes looked dull and glazed. Instantly it occurred to me, that his unexampled diligence in copying by his dim window for the first few weeks of his stay with me might have temporarily impaired his vision.

I was touched. I said something in condolence with him. I hinted that of course he did wisely in abstaining from writing for a while; and urged him to embrace that opportunity of taking wholesome exercise in the open air. This, however, he did not do. A few days after this, my other clerks being absent, and being in a great hurry to dispatch certain letters by the mail, I thought that, having nothing else earthly to do, Bartleby would surely be less inflexible than usual, and carry these letters to the Post Office. But he blankly declined. So, much to my inconvenience, I went myself.

Still added days went by. Whether 135 Bartleby's eyes improved or not, I could not say. To all appearance, I thought they did. But when I asked him if they did, he vouchsafed no answer. At all events, he would do no copying. At last, in reply to my urgings, he informed me that he had permanently given up copying.

"What!" exclaimed I; "suppose your eyes should get entirely well—better than ever before—would you not copy then?"

"I have given up copying," he answered, and slid aside.

He remained as ever, a fixture in my chamber. Nay—if that were possible—he became still more of a fixture than before. What was to be done? He would do nothing in the office; why should he stay there? In plain fact, he had now become a millstone to me, not only useless as a necklace, but afflictive to bear. Yet I was sorry for him. I speak less than truth when I say that, on his own account, he occasioned me uneasiness. If he would but have named a single relative or friend, I would instantly have written, and urged their taking the poor fellow away to some convenient retreat. But he seemed alone, absolutely alone in the universe. A bit of wreck in the mid-Atlantic. At length, necessities connected with my business tyrannized over all other considerations. Decently as I could, I told Bartleby that in six days' time he must unconditionally leave the office. I warned him to take measures, in the interval, for procuring some other abode. I offered to assist him in this endeavor, if he himself would but take the first step towards a removal. "And when you finally quit me, Bartleby," added I, "I shall see that you go not away entirely unprovided. Six days from this hour, remember."

At the expiration of that period, I peeped behind the screen, and lo! Bartleby was there.

140 I buttoned up my coat, balanced myself; advanced slowly towards him, touched his shoulder, and said, "The time has come; you must quit this place; I am sorry for you; here is money; but you must go."

"I would prefer not," he replied, with his back still towards me.

"You *must*."

He remained silent.

Now I had an unbounded confidence in this man's common honesty. He had frequently restored to me sixpences and shillings carelessly dropped upon the floor, for I am apt to be very reckless in such shirt-button affairs. The proceeding, then, which followed will not be deemed extraordinary.

145 "Bartleby," said I, "I owe you twelve dollars on account; here are thirty-two, the odd twenty are yours—Will you take it?" and I handed the bills towards him.

But he made no motion.

"I will leave them here, then," putting them under a weight on the table. Then taking my hat and cane and going to the door, I tranquilly turned and added—"After you have removed your things from these offices, Bartleby, you will of course lock the door—since every one is now gone for the day but you—and if you please, slip your key underneath the mat, so that I may have it in the morning. I shall not see you again; so good-bye to you. If, hereafter, in your new place of abode, I can be of any service to you, do not fail to advise me by letter. Good-bye, Bartleby, and fare you well."

But he answered not a word; like the last column of some ruined temple, he remained standing mute and solitary in the middle of the otherwise deserted room.

As I walked home in a pensive mood, my vanity got the better of my pity. I could not but highly plume myself on my masterly management in getting rid of Bartleby. Masterly I call it, and such it must appear to any dispassionate thinker. The beauty of my procedure seemed to consist in its perfect quietness. There was no vulgar bullying, no bravado of any sort, no choleric hectoring, and striding to and fro across the apartment, jerking out vehement commands for Bartleby to bundle himself off with his beggarly traps. Nothing of the kind. Without loudly bidding Bartleby depart—as an inferior genius might have done—I *assumed* the ground that depart he must; and upon that assumption built all I had to say. The more I thought over my procedure, the more I was charmed with it. Nevertheless, next morning, upon awakening, I had my doubts—I had somehow slept off the fumes of vanity. One of the coolest and wisest hours a man has, is just after he awakes in the morning. My procedure seemed as sagacious as ever—but only in theory. How it would prove in practice—there was the rub. It was truly a beautiful thought to have assumed Bartleby's departure; but, after all, that assumption was simply my own, and none of Bartleby's. The great point was, not whether I had assumed that he would quit me, but whether he would prefer to do so. He was more a man of preferences than assumptions.

150 After breakfast, I walked down town, arguing the probabilities *pro* and *con*. One moment I thought it would prove a miserable failure, and Bartleby would be found all alive at my office as usual; the next moment it seemed certain that I should find his chair empty. And so I kept veering about. At the corner of Broadway and Canal Street, I saw quite an excited group of people standing in earnest conversation.

"I'll take odds he doesn't," said a voice as I passed.

"Doesn't go?—done!" said I, "put up your money."

I was instinctively putting my hand in my pocket to produce my own, when I remembered that this was an election day. The words I had overheard bore no reference to Bartleby, but to the success or non-success of some candidate for the mayoralty. In my intent frame of mind, I had, as it were, imagined that all Broadway shared in my excitement, and were debating the same question with me. I passed on, very thankful that the uproar of the street screened my momentary absent-mindedness.

As I had intended, I was earlier than usual at my office door. I stood listening for a moment. All was still. He must be gone. I tried the knob. The door was locked. Yes, my procedure had worked to a charm; he indeed must be vanished. Yet a certain melancholy mixed with this: I was almost sorry for my brilliant success. I was fumbling under the door mat for the key, which Bartleby was to have left there for me, when accidentally my knee knocked against a panel, producing a summoning sound, and in response a voice came to me from within—"Not yet; I am occupied."

155

It was Bartleby.

I was thunderstruck. For an instant I stood like the man who, pipe in mouth, was killed one cloudless afternoon long ago in Virginia, by summer lightning; at his own warm open window he was killed, and remained leaning out there upon the dreamy afternoon, till some one touched him, when he fell.

"Not gone!" I murmured at last. But again obeying that wondrous ascendancy which the inscrutable scrivener had over me, and from which ascendancy, for all my chafing, I could not completely escape, I slowly went down stairs and out into the street, and while walking round the block, considered what I should next do in this unheard-of perplexity. Turn the man out by an actual thrusting I could not; to drive him

away by calling him hard names would not do; calling in the police was an unpleasant idea; and yet, permit him to enjoy his cadaverous triumph over me—this, too, I could not think of. What was to be done? or, if nothing could be done, was there anything further that I could *assume* in the matter? Yes, as before I had prospectively assumed that Bartleby would depart, so now I might retrospectively assume that departed he was. In the legitimate carrying out of this assumption, I might enter my office in a great hurry, and pretending not to see Bartleby at all, walk straight against him as if he were air. Such a proceeding would in a singular degree have the appearance of a home-thrust. It was hardly possible that Bartleby could withstand such an application of the doctrine of assumptions. But upon second thoughts the success of the plan seemed rather dubious. I resolved to argue the matter over with him again.

"Bartleby," said I, entering the office, with a quietly severe expression, "I am seriously displeased. I am pained, Bartleby. I had thought better of you. I had imagined you of such a gentlemanly organization, that in any delicate dilemma a slight hint would suffice—in short, an assumption. But it appears I am deceived. Why," I added, unaffectedly starting, "you have not even touched that money yet," pointing to it, just where I had left it the evening previous.

He answered nothing.

"Will you, or will you not, quit me?" I now demanded in a sudden passion, advancing close to him.

"I would prefer *not* to quit you," he replied, gently emphasizing the *not*.

"What earthly right have you to stay here? Do you pay any rent? Do you pay my taxes? Or is this property yours?"

He answered nothing.

"Are you ready to go on and write now? Are your eyes recovered? Could you

160

copy a small paper for me this morning? or help examine a few lines? or step round to the Post Office? In a word, will you do anything at all, to give a coloring to your refusal to depart the premises?"

165   He silently retired into his hermitage.

I was now in such a state of nervous resentment that I thought it but prudent to check myself at present from further demonstrations. Bartleby and I were alone. I remembered the tragedy of the unfortunate Adams and the still more unfortunate Colt[6] in the solitary office of the latter; and how poor Colt, being dreadfully incensed by Adams, and imprudently permitting himself to get wildly excited, was at unawares hurried into his fatal act—an act which certainly no man could possibly deplore more than the actor himself. Often it had occurred to me in my ponderings upon the subject that had that altercation taken place in the public street, or at a private residence, it would not have terminated as it did. It was the circumstance of being alone in a solitary office, up stairs, of a building entirely unhallowed by humanizing domestic associations—an uncarpeted office, doubtless, of a dusty haggard sort of appearance—this it must have been, which greatly helped to enhance the irritable desperation of the hapless Colt.

But when this old Adam of resentment rose in me and tempted me concerning Bartleby, I grappled him and threw him. How? Why, simply by recalling the divine injunction: "A new commandment give I unto you, that ye love one another." Yes, this it was that saved me. Aside from higher considerations, charity often operates as a vastly wise and prudent principle—a great

safeguard to its possessor. Men have committed murder for jealousy's sake, and anger's sake, and hatred's sake, and selfishness' sake, and spiritual pride's sake; but no man, that ever I heard of, ever committed a diabolical murder for sweet charity's sake. Mere self-interest, then, if no better motive can be enlisted, should, especially with high-tempered men, prompt all beings to charity and philanthropy. At any rate, upon the occasion in question, I strove to drown my exasperated feelings towards the scrivener by benevolently construing his conduct. Poor fellow, poor fellow! thought I, he don't mean anything; and besides, he has seen hard times, and ought to be indulged.

I endeavored, also, immediately to occupy myself, and at the same time to comfort my despondency. I tried to fancy, that in the course of the morning, at such time as might prove agreeable to him, Bartleby, of his own free accord, would emerge from his hermitage and take up some decided line of march in the direction of the door. But no. Half-past twelve o'clock came; Turkey began to glow in the face, overturn his inkstand, and become generally obstreperous; Nippers abated down into quietude and courtesy; Ginger Nut munched his noon apple; and Bartleby remained standing at his window in one of his profoundest dead-wall reveries. Will it be credited? Ought I to acknowledge it? That afternoon I left the office without saying one further word to him.

Some days now passed, during which, at leisure intervals I looked a little into "Edwards on the Will," and "Priesty on Necessity."[7] Under the circumstances, those books induced a salutary feeling. Gradually I slid into the persuasion that these troubles

---

[6]**John C. Colt:** Brother of the gun maker. Killed Samuel Adams during a quarrel in 1842, leading to a sensational court case. Colt committed suicide just before he was to be hanged.

[7]**Jonathan Edwards,** Freedom of the Will (1754), Joseph Priestley, Doctrine of Philosophical Necessity (1777): Both argued that human beings do not have free will.

of mine, touching the scrivener, had been all predestined from eternity, and Bartleby was billeted upon me for some mysterious purpose of an all-wise Providence, which it was not for a mere mortal like me to fathom. Yes, Bartleby, stay there behind your screen, thought I; I shall persecute you no more; you are harmless and noiseless as any of these old chairs; in short, I never feel so private as when I know you are here. At last I see it, I feel it; I penetrate to the predestined purpose of my life. I am content. Others may have loftier parts to enact; but my mission in this world, Bartleby, is to furnish you with office-room for such period as you may see fit to remain.

170   I believe that this wise and blessed frame of mind would have continued with me, had it not been for the unsolicited and uncharitable remarks obtruded upon me by my professional friends who visited the rooms. But thus it often is, that the constant friction of illiberal minds wears out at last the best resolves of the more generous. Though to be sure, when I reflected upon it, it was not strange that people entering my office should be struck by the peculiar aspect of the unaccountable Bartleby, and so be tempted to throw out some sinister observations concerning him. Sometimes an attorney, having business with me, and calling at my office, and finding no one but the scrivener there, would undertake to obtain some sort of precise information from him touching my whereabouts; but without heeding his idle talk, Bartleby would remain standing immovable in the middle of the room. So after contemplating him in that position for a time, the attorney would depart, no wiser than he came.

Also, when a reference was going on, and the room full of lawyers and witnesses, and business was driving fast, some deeply-occupied legal gentleman present, seeing Bartleby wholly unemployed, would request him to run round to his (the legal gentleman's) office and fetch some papers for him. Thereupon, Bartleby would tranquilly decline, and yet remain idle as before. Then the lawyer would give a great stare, and turn to me. And what could I say? At last I was made aware that all through the circle of my professional acquaintance, a whisper of wonder was running round, having reference to the strange creature I kept at my office. This worried me very much. And as the idea came upon me of his possibly turning out a long-lived man, and keeping occupying my chambers, and denying my authority; and perplexing my visitors; and scandalizing my professional reputation; and casting a general gloom over the premises; keeping soul and body together to the last upon his savings (for doubtless he spent but half a dime a day), and in the end perhaps outlive me, and claim possession of my office by right of his perpetual occupancy: as all these dark anticipations crowded upon me more and more, and my friends continually intruded their relentless remarks upon the apparition in my room; a great change was wrought in me. I resolved to gather all my faculties together, and forever rid me of this intolerable incubus.

Ere revolving any complicated project, however, adapted to this end, I first simply suggested to Bartleby the propriety of his permanent departure. In a calm and serious tone, I commended the idea to his careful and mature consideration. But, having taken three days to meditate upon it, he apprised me, that his original determination remained the same; in short, that he still preferred to abide with me.

What shall I do? I now said to myself, buttoning up my coat to the last button. What shall I do? what ought I to do? what does conscience say I *should* do with this man, or, rather, ghost. Rid myself of him, I must; go, he shall. But how? You will not thrust him, the poor, pale, passive mortal— you will not thrust such a helpless creature out of your door? you will not dishonor yourself by such cruelty? No, I will not, I cannot do that. Rather would I let him live and die here, and then mason up his remains in the wall. What, then, will you do? For all your coaxing, he will not budge. Bribes he leaves under your own paperweight on your table; in short, it is quite plain that he prefers to cling to you.

Then something severe, something unusual must be done. What! surely you will not have him collared by a constable, and commit his innocent pallor to the common jail? And upon what ground could you procure such a thing to be done?—a vagrant, is he? What! he a vagrant, a wanderer, who refuses to budge? It is because he will *not* be a vagrant, then, that you seek to count him *as* a vagrant. That is too absurd. No visible means of support; there I have him. Wrong again; for indubitably he *does* support himself, and that is the only unanswerable proof that any man can show of his possessing the means so to do. No more, then. Since he will not quit me, I must quit him. I will change my offices; I will move elsewhere, and give him fair notice, that if I find him on my new premises I will then proceed against him as a common trespasser.

175 Acting accordingly, next day I thus addressed him: "I find these chambers too far from the City Hall; the air is unwholesome. In a word, I propose to remove my offices next week, and shall no longer require your services. I tell you this now, in order that you may seek another place."

He made no reply, and nothing more was said.

On the appointed day I engaged carts and men, proceeded to my chambers, and having but little furniture, everything was removed in a few hours. Throughout, the scrivener remained standing behind the screen, which I directed to be removed the last thing. It was withdrawn; and, being folded up like a huge folio, left him the motionless occupant of a naked room. I stood in the entry watching him a moment, while something from within me upbraided me.

I re-entered, with my hand in my pocket—and—and my heart in my mouth.

"Good-bye, Bartleby; I am going—good-bye, and God some way bless you; and take that," slipping something in his hand. But it dropped upon the floor, and then—strange to say—I tore myself from him whom I had so longed to be rid of.

Established in my new quarters, for a 180 day or two I kept the door locked, and started at every footfall in the passages. When I returned to my rooms, after any little absence, I would pause at the threshold for an instant, and attentively listen, ere applying my key. But these fears were needless. Bartleby never came nigh me.

I thought all was going well, when a perturbed-looking stranger visited me, inquiring whether I was the person who had recently occupied rooms at No.—Wall Street.

Full of forebodings, I replied that I was.

"Then, sir," said the stranger, who proved a lawyer, "you are responsible for the man you left there. He refuses to do any copying; he refuses to do anything; he says he prefers not to; and he refuses to quit the premises."

"I am very sorry, sir," said I, with assumed tranquillity, but an inward tremor, "but, really, the man you allude to is nothing to me—he is no relation or apprentice of mine, that you should hold me responsible for him."

"In mercy's name, who is he?" 185

"I certainly cannot inform you. I know nothing about him. Formerly I employed him as a copyist; but he has done nothing for me now for some time past."

"I shall settle him, then—good morning, sir."

Several days passed, and I heard nothing more; and, though I often felt a charitable prompting to call at the place and see poor

Bartleby, yet a certain squeamishness, of I know not what, withheld me.

All is over with him, by this time, thought I, at last, when, through another week, no further intelligence reached me. But, coming to my room the day after, I found several persons waiting at my door in a high state of nervous excitement.

190 "That's the man—here he comes," cried the foremost one, whom I recognized as the lawyer who had previously called upon me alone.

"You must take him away, sir, at once," cried a portly person among them, advancing upon me, and whom I knew to be the landlord of No.—Wall Street. "These gentlemen, my tenants, cannot stand it any longer; Mr. B———," pointing to the lawyer, "has turned him out of his room, and he now persists in haunting the building generally, sitting upon the banisters of the stairs by day, and sleeping in the entry by night. Everybody is concerned; clients are leaving the offices; some fears are entertained of a mob; something you must do, and that without delay."

Aghast at this torrent, I fell back before it, and would fain have locked myself in my new quarters. In vain I persisted that Bartleby was nothing to me—no more than to any one else. In vain—I was the last person known to have anything to do with him, and they held me to the terrible account. Fearful, then, of being exposed in the papers (as one person present obscurely threatened), I considered the matter, and, at length, said, that if the lawyer would give me a confidential interview with the scrivener, in his (the lawyer's) own room, I would, that afternoon, strive my best to rid them of the nuisance they complained of.

Going up stairs to my old haunt, there was Bartleby silently sitting upon the banister at the landing.

"What are you doing here, Bartleby?" said I.

"Sitting upon the banister," he mildly 195 replied.

I motioned him into the lawyer's room, who then left us.

"Bartleby," said I, "are you aware that you are the cause of great tribulation to me, by persisting in occupying the entry after being dismissed from the office?"

No answer.

"Now one of two things must take place. Either you must do something, or something must be done to you. Now what sort of business would you like to engage in? Would you like to re-engage in copying for some one?"

"No; I would prefer not to make any 200 change."

"Would you like a clerkship in a dry-goods store?"

"There is too much confinement about that. No, I would not like a clerkship; but I am not particular."

"Too much confinement," I cried, "why, you keep yourself confined all the time!"

"I would prefer not to take a clerkship," he rejoined, as if to settle that little item at once.

"How would a bar-tender's business 205 suit you? There is no trying of the eye-sight in that."

"I would not like it at all; though, as I said before, I am not particular."

His unwonted wordiness inspirited me. I returned to the charge.

"Well, then, would you like to travel through the country collecting bills for the merchants? That would improve your health."

"No, I would prefer to be doing something else."

"How, then, would going as a com- 210 panion to Europe, to entertain some young gentleman with your conversation—how would that suit you?"

"Not at all. It does not strike me that there is anything definite about that. I like to be stationary. But I am not particular."

"Stationary you shall be, then," I cried, now losing all patience, and, for the first time in all my exasperating connection with him, fairly flying into a passion. "If you do not go away from these premises before night, I shall feel bound—indeed, I *am* bound—to—to quit the premises myself!" I rather absurdly concluded, knowing not with what possible threat to try to frighten his immobility into compliance. Despairing of all further efforts, I was precipitately leaving him, when a final thought occurred to me—one which had not been wholly unindulged before.

"Bartleby," said I, in the kindest tone I could assume under such exciting circumstances, "will you go home with me now— not to my office, but my dwelling—and remain there till we can conclude upon some convenient arrangement for you at our leisure? Come, let us start now, right away."

"No: at present I would prefer not to make any change at all."

215   I answered nothing; but, effectually dodging every one by the suddenness and rapidity of my flight, rushed from the building, ran up Wall Street towards Broadway, and, jumping into the first omnibus, was soon removed from pursuit. As soon as tranquillity returned, I distinctly perceived that I had now done all that I possibly could, both in respect to the demands of the landlord and his tenants, and with regard to my own desire and sense of duty, to benefit Bartleby, and shield him from rude persecution. I now strove to be entirely care-free and quiescent; and my conscience justified me in the attempt; though, indeed, it was not so successful as I could have wished. So fearful was I of being again hunted out by the incensed landlord and his exasperated tenants, that, surrendering my business to Nippers, for a few days, I drove about the upper part of the town and through the suburbs, in my rockaway; crossed over to Jersey City and Hoboken, and paid fugitive visits to Manhattanville and Astoria. In fact, I almost lived in my rockaway for the time.

When again I entered my office, lo, a note from the landlord lay upon the desk. I opened it with trembling hands. It informed me that the writer had sent to the police, and had Bartleby removed to the Tombs as a vagrant. Moreover, since I knew more about him than anyone else, he wished me to appear at that place, and make a suitable statement of the facts. These tidings had a conflicting effect upon me. At first I was indignant; but, at last, almost approved. The landlord's energetic, summary disposition, had led him to adopt a procedure which I do not think I would have decided upon myself; and yet, as a last resort, under such peculiar circumstances, it seemed the only plan.

As I afterwards learned, the poor scrivener, when told that he must be conducted to the Tombs, offered not the slightest obstacle, but, in his pale, unmoving way, silently acquiesced.

Some of the compassionate and curious by-standers joined the party; and headed by one of the constables arm-in-arm with Bartleby, the silent procession filed its way through all the noise, and heat, and joy of the roaring thoroughfares at noon.

The same day I received the note, I went to the Tombs, or, to speak more properly, the Halls of Justice. Seeking the right officer, I stated the purpose of my call, and was informed that the individual I described was, indeed, within. I then assured the functionary that Bartleby was a perfectly honest man, and greatly to be compassionated, however unaccountably eccentric. I narrated all I knew, and closed by suggesting the idea of letting him remain in as indulgent confinement as possible, till something less harsh might be done— though indeed, I hardly knew what. At all events, if nothing else could be decided upon, the almshouse must receive him. I then begged to have an interview.

220 Being under no disgraceful charge, and quite serene and harmless in all his ways, they had permitted him freely to wander about the prison, and, especially, in the inclosed grass-platted yards thereof. And so I found him there, standing all alone in the quietest of the yards, his face towards a high wall, while all around, from the narrow slits of the jail windows, I thought I saw peering out upon him the eyes of murderers and thieves.

"Bartleby!"

"I know you," he said, without looking round— "and I want nothing to say to you."

"It was not I that brought you here, Bartleby," said I, keenly pained at his implied suspicion. "And to you, this should not be so vile a place. Nothing reproachful attaches to you by being here. And see, it is not so sad a place as one might think. Look, there is the sky, and here is the grass."

"I know where I am," he replied, but would say nothing more, and so I left him.

225 As I entered the corridor again, a broad meat-like man, in an apron, accosted me, and, jerking his thumb over his shoulder, said—"Is that your friend?"

"Yes."

"Does he want to starve? If he does, let him live on the prison fare, that's all."

"Who are you?" asked I, not knowing what to make of such an unofficially speaking person in such a place.

"I am the grub-man. Such gentlemen as have friends here, hire me to provide them with something good to eat."

230 "Is this so?" said I, turning to the turnkey.

He said it was.

"Well, then," said I, slipping some silver into the grub-man's hands (for so they called him), "I want you to give particular attention to my friend there; let him have the best dinner you can get. And you must be as polite to him as possible."

"Introduce me, will you?" said the grub-man, looking at me with an expression which seemed to say he was all impatience for an opportunity to give a specimen of his breeding.

Thinking it would prove of benefit to the scrivener, I acquiesced; and, asking the grub-man his name, went up with him to Bartleby.

"Bartleby, this is a friend; you will find   235 him very useful to you."

"Your sarvant, sir, your sarvant," said the grub-man, making a low salutation behind his apron. "Hope you find it pleasant here, sir; nice grounds—cool apartments— hope you'll stay with us some time—try to make it agreeable. What will you have for dinner to-day?"

"I prefer not to dine to-day," said Bartleby, turning away. "It would disagree with me; I am unused to dinners." So saying, he slowly moved to the other side of the inclosure, and took up a position fronting the deadwall.

"How's this?" said the grub-man, addressing me with a stare of astonishment. "He's odd, ain't he?"

"I think he is a little deranged," said I, sadly.

"Deranged? deranged is it? Well, now,   240 upon my word, I thought that friend of yourn was a gentleman forger; they are always pale and genteel-like, them forgers. I can't help pity 'em—can't help it, sir. Did you know Monroe Edwards?" he added, touchingly, and paused. Then, laying his hand piteously on my shoulder, sighed, "he died of consumption at Sing-Sing. So you weren't acquainted with Monroe?"

"No, I was never socially acquainted with any forgers. But I cannot stop longer. Look to my friend yonder. You will not lose by it. I will see you again."

Some few days after this, I again obtained admission to the Tombs, and went through the corridors in quest of Bartleby; but without finding him.

"I saw him coming from his cell not long ago," said a turnkey, "may be he's gone to loiter in the yards."

So I went in that direction.

245   "Are you looking for the silent man?" said another turnkey, passing me. "Yonder he lies—sleeping in the yard there. 'Tis not twenty minutes since I saw him lie down."

The yard was entirely quiet. It was not accessible to the common prisoners. The surrounding walls, of amazing thickness, kept off all sounds behind them. The Egyptian character of the masonry weighed upon me with its gloom. But a soft imprisoned turf grew under foot. The heart of the eternal pyramids, it seemed, wherein, by some strange magic, through the clefts, grass-seed, dropped by birds, had sprung.

Strangely huddled at the base of the wall, his knees drawn up, and lying on his side, his head touching the cold stones, I saw the wasted Bartleby. But nothing stirred. I paused; then went close up to him; stooped over, and saw that his dim eyes were open; otherwise he seemed profoundly sleeping. Something prompted me to touch him. I felt his hand, when a tingling shiver ran up my arm and down my spine to my feet.

The round face of the grub-man peered upon me now. "His dinner is ready. Won't he dine to-day, either? Or does he live without dining?"

"Lives without dining," said I, and closed the eyes.

250   "Eh!—He's asleep, ain't he?"

"With kings and counselors,"[8] murmured I.

---

[8]**"With kings and counselors":** From Job 3:13–14, "then had I been at rest,/With kings and counselors of the earth,/which built desolate places for themselves."

There would seem little need for proceeding further in this history. Imagination will readily supply the meagre recital of poor Bartleby's interment. But, ere parting with the reader, let me say, that if this little narrative has sufficiently interested him, to awaken curiosity as to who Bartleby was, and what manner of life he led prior to the present narrator's making his acquaintance, I can only reply, that in such curiosity I fully share, but am wholly unable to gratify it. Yet here I hardly know whether I should divulge one little item of rumor, which came to my ear a few months after the scrivener's decease. Upon what basis it rested, I could never ascertain; and hence, how true it is I cannot now tell. But, inasmuch as this vague report has not been without a certain suggestive interest to me, however sad, it may prove the same with some others; and so I will briefly mention it. The report was this: that Bartleby had been a subordinate clerk in the Dead Letter Office at Washington, from which he had been suddenly removed by a change in the administration. When I think over this rumor, hardly can I express the emotions which seize me. Dead letters! does it not sound like dead men? Conceive a man by nature and misfortune prone to a pallid hopelessness, can any business seem more fitted to heighten it than that of continually handling these dead letters, and assorting them for the flames? For by the cart-load they are annually burned. Sometimes from out the folded paper the pale clerk takes a ring—the finger it was meant for, perhaps, moulders in the grave; a bank-note sent in swiftest charity—he whom it would relieve, nor eats nor hungers any more; pardon for those who died despairing; hope for those who died unhoping; good tidings for those who died stifled by unrelieved calamities. On errands of life, these letters speed to death.

Ah, Bartleby! Ah, humanity!

•••••▶ *Your* **Turn**
Talking and Writing about Lit

1. Who is the main character in "Bartleby the Scrivener"? What reasons would we have for arguing that the lawyer is the main character? What reasons would there be to argue that Bartleby is the main character?

2. Why does Melville spend so much time at the outset of the story making us aware of the lawyer's relationships with his employees and his attitudes toward them?

3. What would you identify as the main themes of the story? Does this story have resolution, or is it open ended?

4. **DIY** The fiction writer Charles Baxter says that one of his favorite ways to develop a story is to imagine a situation and then throw in a character who totally does not belong there. Write a scene in which two siblings (or coworkers or friends) are chatting in familiar surroundings. Suddenly, in walks someone who is breathtakingly out of place. Who is that person? What does he or she look like? What do they say? What happens next?

Bharati Mukherjee (b. 1940)

Bharati Mukherjee was born in Calcutta, India, and grew up in India and England. She studied creative writing at the University of Iowa, where she met and married American writer Clark Blaise in 1963. The couple lived in Canada for ten years, then returned to the United States, where Mukherjee became a U.S. citizen. She and her husband have traveled to India together and collaborated on two nonfiction books about their impressions of Indian culture. Since returning to the United States, she has taught at several colleges and universities. She and Blaise now live in the Berkeley area, and Mukherjee teaches at the University of California, Berkeley. Her short story collections are *Darkness* (1985) and *The Middleman and Other Stories* (1988). Her novels include *Jasmine* (1989), *The Holder of the World* (1994), and *Leave It to Me* (1997).

A Father (1985)

One Wednesday morning in mid-May Mr. Bhowmick woke up as he usually did at 5:43 a.m., checked his Rolex against the alarm clock's digital readout, punched down the alarm (set for 5:45), then nudged his wife awake. She worked as a claims investigator for an insurance company that had an office in a nearby shopping mall. She didn't really have to leave the house until

8:30, but she liked to get up early and cook him a big breakfast. Mr. Bhowmick had to drive a long way to work. He was a naturally dutiful, cautious man, and he set the alarm clock early enough to accommodate a margin for accidents.

While his wife, in a pink nylon negligee she had paid for with her own MasterCard card, made him a new version of French toast from a clipping ("Eggs-cellent Recipes!") Scotchtaped to the inside of a kitchen cupboard, Mr. Bhowmick brushed his teeth. He brushed, he gurgled with the loud, hawking noises that he and his brother had been taught as children to make in order to flush clean not merely teeth but also tongue and palate.

After that he showered, then, back in the bedroom again, he recited prayers in Sanskrit to Kali, the patron goddess of his family, the goddess of wrath and vengeance. In the pokey flat of his childhood in Ranchi, Bihar, his mother had given over a whole bedroom to her collection of gods and goddesses. Mr. Bhowmick couldn't be that extravagant in Detroit. His daughter, twenty-six and an electrical engineer, slept in the other of the two bedrooms in his apartment. But he had done his best. He had taken Woodworking I and II at a nearby recreation center and built a grotto for the goddess. Kali-Mata was eight inches tall, made of metal and painted a glistening black so that the metal glowed like the oiled, black skin of a peasant woman. And though Kali-Mata was totally nude except for a tiny gilt crown and a garland strung together from sinner's chopped off heads, she looked warm, cozy, *pleased*, in her makeshift wooden shrine in Detroit. Mr. Bhowmick had gathered quite a crowd of admiring, fellow woodworkers in those final weeks of decoration.

"Hurry it up with the prayers," his wife shouted from the kitchen. She was an agnostic, a believer in ambition, not grace. She frequently complained that his prayers had gotten so long that soon he wouldn't have time to go to work, play duplicate bridge with the Ghosals, or play the tabla in the Bengali Association's one Sunday per month musical soirees. Lately she'd begun to drain him in a wholly new way. He wasn't praying, she nagged; he was shutting her out of his life. There'd be no peace in the house until she hid Kali-Mata in a suitcase.

She nagged, and he threatened to beat 5 her with his shoe as his father had threatened his mother: it was the thrust and volley of marriage. There was no question of actually taking off a shoe and applying it to his wife's body. She was bigger than he was. And, secretly, he admired her for having the nerve, the agnosticism, which as a college boy in backward Bihar he too had claimed.

"I have time," he shot at her. He was still wrapped in a damp terry towel.

"You have time for everything but domestic life."

It was the fault of the shopping mall that his wife had started to buy pop psychology paperbacks. These paperbacks preached that for couples who could sit down and talk about their "relationship," life would be sweet again. His engineer daughter was on his wife's side. She accused him of holding things in.

"Face it, Dad," she said. "You have an affect deficit."

But surely everyone had feelings they 10 didn't want to talk about or talk over. He definitely did not want to blurt out anything about the sick-in-the-guts sensations that came over him most mornings and that he couldn't bubble down with Alka-Seltzer or smother with Gas-X. The women in his family were smarter than him. They were cheerful, outgoing, more American somehow.

How could he tell these bright, mocking women that in the 5:43 a.m. darkness, he sensed invisible presences: gods and snakes frolicked in the master bedroom, little white sparks of cosmic static crackled up the legs of his pajamas. Something was out there in the dark, something that could invent accidents and coincidences to remind mortals that even in Detroit they were no more than mortal. His wife would label this paranoia and dismiss it. Paranoia, premonition: whatever it was, it had begun to undermine his composure.

Take this morning. Mr. Bhowmick had woken up from a pleasant dream about a man taking a Club Med vacation, and the postdream satisfaction had lasted through the shower, but when he'd come back to the shrine in the bedroom, he'd noticed all at once how scarlet and saucy was the tongue that Kali-Mata stuck out at the world. Surely he had not lavished such alarming detail, such admonitory colors on that flap of flesh.

Watch out, ambulatory sinners. Be careful out there, the goddess warned him, and not with the affection of Sergeant Esterhaus, either.

"French toast must be eaten hot-hot," his wife nagged. "Otherwise they'll taste like rubber."

15 Mr. Bhowmick laid the trousers of a two-trouser suit he had bought on sale that winter against his favorite tweed jacket. The navy stripes in the trousers and the small, navy tweed flecks in the jacket looked quite good together. So what if the Chief Engineer had already started wearing summer cottons?

"I am coming, I am coming," he shouted back. "You want me to eat hot-hot, you start the frying only when I am sitting down. You didn't learn anything from Mother in Ranchi?"

"Mother cooked French toast from fancy recipes? I mean French Sandwich Toast with complicated filling?"

He came into the room to give her his testiest look. "You don't know the meaning of complicated cookery. And mother had to get the coal fire of the *chula* going first."

His daughter was already at the table. "Why don't you break down and buy her a microwave oven? That's what I mean about sitting down and talking things out." She had finished her orange juice. She took a plastic measure of Slim-Fast out of its can and poured the powder into a glass of skim milk. "It's ridiculous."

Babli was not the child he would have 20 chosen as his only heir. She was brighter certainly than the sons and daughters of the other Bengalis he knew in Detroit, and she had been the only female student in most of her classes at Georgia Tech, but as she sat there in her beige linen business suit, her thick chin dropping into a polka-dotted cravat, he regretted again that she was not the child of his dreams. Babli would be able to help him out moneywise if something happened to him, something so bad that even his pension plans and his insurance policies and his money market schemes wouldn't be enough. But Babli could never comfort him. She wasn't womanly or tender the way that unmarried girls had been in the wistful days of his adolescence. She could sing Hindi film songs, mimicking exactly the high, artificial voice of Lata Mungeshkar, and she had taken two years of dance lessons at Sona Devi's Dance Academy in Southfield, but these accomplishments didn't add up to real femininity. Not the kind that had given him palpitations in Ranchi.

Mr. Bhowmick did his best with his wife's French toast. In spite of its filling of marshmallows, apricot jam and maple syrup, it tasted rubbery. He drank two cups of Darjeeling tea, said, "Well, I'm off," and took off.

All might have gone well if Mr. Bhowmick hadn't fussed longer than usual about putting his briefcase and his trenchcoat in the backseat. He got in behind the wheel of his Oldsmobile, fixed his seatbelt and was just about to turn the key in the ignition when his neighbor, Al Stazniak, who was starting up his Buick Skylark, sneezed. A sneeze at the start of a journey brings bad luck. Al Stazniak's sneeze was fierce, made up of five short bursts, too loud to be ignored.

Be careful out there! Mr. Bhowmick could see the goddess's scarlet little tongue tip wagging at him.

He was a modern man, an intelligent man. Otherwise he couldn't have had the options in life that he did have. He couldn't have given up a good job with perks in Bombay and found a better job with General Motors in Detroit. But Mr. Bhowmick was also a prudent enough man to know that some abiding truth lies bunkered within each wanton Hindu superstition. A sneeze was more than a sneeze. The heedless are carried off in ambulances. He had choices to make. He could ignore the sneeze, and so challenge the world unseen by men. Perhaps Al Stazniak had hayfever. For a sneeze to be a potent omen, surely it had to be unprovoked and terrifying, a thunderclap cleaving the summer skies. Or he could admit the smallness of mortals, undo the fate of the universe by starting over, and go back inside the apartment, sit for a second on the sofa, then re-start his trip.

25   Al Stazniak rolled down his window. "Everything okay?"

Mr. Bhowmick nodded shyly. They weren't really friends in the way neighbors can sometimes be. They talked as they parked or pulled out of their adjacent parking stalls. For all Mr. Bhowmick knew, Al Stazniak had no legs. He had never seen the man out of his Skylark.

He let the Buick back out first. Everything was okay, yes, please. All the same he undid his seatbelt. Compromise, adaptability, call it what you will. A dozen times a day he made these small trade-offs between new-world reasonableness and old-world beliefs.

While he was sitting in his parked car, his wife's ride came by. For fifty dollars a month, she was picked up and dropped off by a hard up, newly divorced woman who worked at a florist's shop in the same mall. His wife came out the front door in brown K-Mart pants and a burgundy windbreaker. She waved to him, then slipped into the passenger seat of the florist's rusty Japanese car.

He was a metallurgist. He knew about rust and ways of preventing it, secret ways, thus far unknown to the Japanese.

Babli's fiery red Mitsubishi was still in 30 the lot. She wouldn't leave for work for another eight minutes. He didn't want her to know he'd been undone by a sneeze. Babli wasn't tolerant of superstitions. She played New Wave music in her tapedeck. If asked about Hinduism, all she'd ever said to her American friends was that "it's neat." Mr. Bhowmick had heard her on the phone years before. The cosmos balanced on the head of a snake was like a beachball balanced on the snout of a circus seal. "This Hindu myth stuff," he'd heard her say, "is like a series of super graphics."

He'd forgiven her. He could probably forgive her anything. It was her way of surviving high school in a city that was both native to her, and alien.

There was no question of going back where he'd come from. He hated Ranchi. Ranchi was no place for dreamers. All through his teenage years, Mr. Bhowmick had dreamed of success abroad. What form that success would take he had left vague. Success had meant to him escape from the constant plotting and bitterness that wore out India's middle class.

Babli should have come out of the apartment and driven off to work by now. Mr. Bhowmick decided to take a risk, to dash inside and pretend he'd left his brief-case on the coffee table.

When he entered the living room, he noticed Babli's spring coat and large vinyl pocketbook on the sofa. She was probably sorting through the junk jewelry on her dresser to give her business suit a lift. She read hints about dressing in women's magazines and applied them to her person with seriousness. If his luck held, he could sit on the sofa, say a quick prayer and get back to the car without her catching on.

35   It surprised him that she didn't shout out from her bedroom, "Who's there?" What if he had been a rapist?

Then he heard Babli in the bathroom. He heard unlady-like squawking noises. She was throwing up. A squawk, a spitting, then the horrible gurgle of a waterfall.

A revelation came to Mr. Bhowmick. A woman vomiting in the privacy of the bathroom could mean many things. She was coming down with the flu. She was nervous about a meeting. But Mr. Bhowmick knew at once that his daughter, his untender, unloving daughter whom he couldn't love and hadn't tried to love, was not, in the larger world of Detroit, unloved. Sinners are everywhere, even in the bosom of an upright, unambitious family like the Bhowmicks. It was the goddess sticking out her tongue at him.

The father sat heavily on the sofa, shrinking from contact with her coat and pocketbook. His brisk, bright engineer daughter was pregnant. Someone had taken time to make love to her. Someone had thought her tender, feminine. Someone even now was perhaps mooning over her. The idea excited him. It was go grotesque and wondrous. At twenty-six Babli had found the man of her dreams; whereas at twenty-six Mr. Bhowmick had given up on truth, beauty and poetry and exchanged them for two years at Carnegie Tech.

Mr. Bhowmick's tweed-jacketed body sagged against the sofa cushions. Babli would abort, of course. He knew his Babli. It was the only possible option if she didn't want to bring shame to the Bhowmick family. All the same, he could see a chubby baby boy on the rug, crawling to his granddaddy. Shame like that was easier to hide in Ranchi. There was always a barren womb sanctified by marriage that could claim sudden fructifying by the goddess Parvati. Babli would do what she wanted. She was headstrong and independent and he was afraid of her.

Babli staggered out of the bathroom. 40 Damp stains ruined her linen suit. It was the first time he had seen his daughter look ridiculous, quite unprofessional. She didn't come into the living room to investigate the noise he'd made. He glimpsed her shoeless stockinged feet flip-flop on collapsed arches down the hall to her bedroom.

"Are you all right?" Mr. Bhowmick asked, standing in the hall. "Do you need Sinutab?"

She wheeled around. "What're you doing here?"

He was the one who should be angry. "I'm feeling poorly too," he said. "I'm taking the day off."

"I feel fine," Babli said.

Within fifteen minutes Babli had 45 changed her clothes and left. Mr. Bhowmick had the apartment to himself all day. All day for praising or cursing the life that had brought him along with its other surprises an illegitimate grandchild.

It was his wife that he blamed. Coming to America to live had been his wife's idea. After the wedding, the young Bhowmicks had spent two years in Pittsburgh on his student visa, then gone back home to Ranchi for nine years. Nine crushing years. Then the job in Bombay had come through. All during those nine years his wife had screamed and wept. She was a woman of wild, progressive ideas—she'd called them her "American" ideas—and she'd been martyred by her neighbors for them. American *memsahib. Markin mem, Markin mem.* In bazaars the beggar boys had trailed her and hooted. She'd done provocative things. She'd hired a *chamar* woman who by caste rules was forbidden to cook for higher caste families, especially for widowed mothers of decent men. This had caused a blowup in the neighborhood. She'd made other, lesser errors. While other wives shopped and cooked every day, his wife had cooked the whole week's menu on weekends.

"What's the point of having a refrigerator, then?" She'd been scornful of the Ranchi women.

His mother, an old-fashioned widow, had accused her of trying to kill her by poisoning. "You are in such a hurry? You want to get rid of me quick-quick so you can go back to the States?"

Family life had been turbulent.

50 He had kept aloof, inwardly siding with his mother. He did not love his wife now, and he had not loved her then. In any case, he had not defended her. He felt some affection, and he felt guilty for having shunned her during those unhappy years. But he had thought of it then as revenge. He had wanted to marry a beautiful woman. Not being a young man of means, only a young man with prospects, he had had no right to yearn for pure beauty. He cursed his fate and after a while, settled for a barrister's daughter, a plain girl with a wide, flat plank of a body and myopic eyes. The barrister had sweetened the deal by throwing in an all-expenses-paid two years' study at Carnegie Tech to which Mr. Bhowmick had been admitted. Those two years had changed his wife from pliant girl to ambitious woman. She wanted America, nothing less.

It was his wife who had forced him to apply for permanent resident status in the U.S. even though he had a good job in Ranchi as a government engineer. The putting together of documents for the immigrant visa had been a long and humbling process. He had had to explain to a chilly clerk in the Embassy that, like most Indians of his generation, he had no birth certificate. He had to swear out affidavits, suffer through police checks, bribe orderlies whose job it was to move his dossier from desk to desk. The decision, the clerk had advised him, would take months, maybe years. He hadn't dared hope that merit might be rewarded. Merit could collapse under bad luck. It was for grace that he prayed.

While the immigration papers were being processed, he had found the job in Bombay. So he'd moved his mother in with his younger brother's family, and left his hometown for good. Life in Bombay had been lighthearted, almost fulfilling. His wife had thrown herself into charity work with the same energy that had offended the Ranchi women. He was happy to be in a big city at last. Bombay was the Rio de Janeiro of the East; he'd read that in a travel brochure. He drove out to Nariman Point at least once a week to admire the necklace of municipal lights, toss coconut shells into the dark ocean, drink beer at the Oberoi-Sheraton where overseas Indian girls in designer jeans beckoned him in sly ways. His nights were full. He played duplicate bridge, went to the movies, took his wife to Bingo nights at his club. In Detroit he was a lonelier man.

Then the green card had come through. For him, for his wife, and for the daughter who had been born to them in Bombay. He sold what he could sell, and put in his brother's informal trust what he couldn't to save on taxes. Then he had left for America, and one more start.

All through the week, Mr. Bhowmick watched his daughter. He kept furtive notes on how many times she rushed to the bathroom and made hawking, wrenching noises, how many times she stayed late at the office, calling her mother to say she'd be taking in a movie and pizza afterwards with friends.

55 He had to tell her that he knew. And he probably didn't have much time. She shouldn't be on Slim-Fast in her condition. He had to talk things over with her. But what would he say to her? What position could he take? He had to choose between public shame for the family, and murder.

For three more weeks he watched her and kept his silence. Babli wore shifts to the office instead of business suits, and he liked her better in those garments. Perhaps she was dressing for her young man, not from necessity. Her skin was pale and blotchy by turn. At breakfast her fingers looked stiff, and she had trouble with silverware.

Two Saturdays running, he lost badly at duplicate bridge. His wife scolded him. He had made silly mistakes. When was Babli meeting this man? Where? He must be American; Mr. Bhowmick prayed only that he was white. He pictured his grandson crawling to him, and the grandson was always fat and brown and buttery-skinned, like the infant Krishna. An American son-in-law was a terrifying notion. Why was she not mentioning men, at least, preparing the way for the major announcement? He listened sharply for men's names, rehearsed little lines like, "Hello, Bob, I'm Babli's old man," with a cracked little laugh. Bob, Jack, Jimmy, Tom. But no names surfaced. When she went out for pizza and a movie it was with the familiar set of Indian girls and their strange, unpopular, American friends, all without men. Mr. Bhowmick tried to be reasonable. Maybe she had already gotten married and was keeping it secret. "Well, Bob, you and Babli sure had Mrs. Bhowmick and me going there, heh-heh," he mumbled one

night with the Sahas and Ghosals, over cards. "Pardon?" asked Pronob Saha. Mr. Bhowmick dropped two tricks, and his wife glared. "Such stupid blunders," she fumed on the drive back. A new truth was dawning; there would be no marriage for Babli. Her young man probably was not so young and not so available. He must be already married. She must have yielded to passion or been raped in the office. His wife seemed to have noticed nothing. Was he a murderer, or a conspirator? He kept his secret from his wife; his daughter kept her decision to herself.

Nights, Mr. Bhowmick pretended to sleep, but as soon as his wife began her snoring—not real snores so much as loud, gaspy gulpings for breath—he turned on his side and prayed to Kali-Mata.

In July, when Babli's belly had begun to push up against the waistless dresses she'd bought herself, Mr. Bhowmick came out of the shower one weekday morning and found the two women screaming at each other. His wife had a rolling pin in one hand. His daughter held up a *National Geographic* as a shield for her head. The crazy look that had been in his wife's eyes when she'd shooed away beggar kids was in her eyes again.

"Stop it!" His own boldness over- 60 whelmed him. "Shut up! Babli's pregnant, so what? It's your fault, you made us come to the States."

Girls like Babli were caught between rules, that's the point he wished to make. They were too smart, too impulsive for a backward place like Ranchi, but not tough nor smart enough for sex-crazy places like Detroit.

"My fault?" his wife cried. "I told her to do hanky-panky with boys? I told her to shame us like this?"

She got in one blow with the rolling pin. The second glanced off Babli's shoulder and fell on his arms which he had stuck out for his grandson's sake.

"I'm calling the police," Babli shouted. She was out of the rolling pin's range. "This is brutality. You can't do this to me."

65 "Shut up! Shut your mouth, foolish woman." He wrenched the weapon from his wife's fist. He made a show of taking off his shoe to beat his wife on the face.

"What do you know? You don't know anything." She let herself down slowly on a dining chair. Her hair, curled overnight, stood in wild whorls around her head. "Nothing."

"And you do!" He laughed. He remembered her tormentors, and laughed again. He had begun to enjoy himself. Now *he* was the one with the crazy, progressive ideas.

"Your daughter is pregnant, yes," she said, "any fool knows that. But ask her the name of the father. Go, ask."

He stared at his daughter who gazed straight ahead, eyes burning with hate, jaw clenched with fury.

"Babli?" 70

"Who needs a man?" she hissed. "The father of my baby is a bottle and a syringe. Men louse up your lives. I just want a baby. Oh, don't worry—he's a certified fit donor. No diseases, college graduate, above average, and he made the easiest twenty-five dollars of his life—"

"Like animals," his wife said. For the first time he heard horror in her voice. His daughter grinned at him. He saw her tongue, thick and red, squirming behind her row of perfect teeth.

"Yes, yes, yes," she screamed, "like livestock. Just like animals. You should be happy—that's what marriage is all about, isn't it? Matching bloodlines, matching horoscopes, matching castes, matching, matching, matching . . ." and it was difficult to know if she was laughing or singing, or mocking and like a madwoman.

Mr. Bhowmick lifted the rolling pin high above his head and brought it down hard on the dome of Babli's stomach. In the end, it was his wife who called the police.

····•▶ *Your* **Turn**
Talking and Writing about Lit

1. What is Mr. Bhowmick's attitude toward assimilation in "A Father"? How does Mrs. Bhowmick feel about American culture? How does Babli view assimilation?

2. How does Mukherjee make us aware of Mr. Bhowmick's desire to be a modern man? How does she make us aware of his desire to hold onto traditions from his first culture?

3. **DIY** Some readers are displeased by, or disturbed by, the last scene in "A Father." Leave aside the fact that Mukherjee probably intended to shake us up a bit in the last scene (to get us to think about things), and write a new ending for the story.

Charlotte Perkins Gilman (1860–1935)

Born into a prominent and educated family, Gilman was nonetheless raised in poverty and provided with only four years of formal education after her father, Frederick Beecher Perkins, left his wife and children to fend for themselves. As an adult, Charlotte married artist Walter Stetson. After the birth of their daughter in 1885, Charlotte fell into a depression and was placed under the care of the famous "nerve doctor" of the time, S. Weir Mitchell. He prescribed complete isolation and forced feeding, and he forbade her to do any writing or reading. In a speech delivered to the Radcliffe student body around the same time, Dr. Mitchell said, "I no more want [women] to be preachers, lawyers, or platform orators, than I want men to be seamstresses or nurses of children." He believed that women should be permitted only to learn child care and domestic skills, their brains being unsuited to higher education. Out of this experience grew the story "The Yellow Wallpaper," first published in May 1892 in *The New England Magazine*. Later (in 1900), Gilman married her cousin, George Houghton Gilman, and this was evidently a much happier match for her. Two important books by Charlotte Perkins Gilman are *Women and Economics* (1898) and *Herland* (1915).

The Yellow Wallpaper (1892)

It is very seldom that mere ordinary people like John and myself secure ancestral halls for the summer.

A colonial mansion, a hereditary estate, I would say a haunted house and reach the height of romantic felicity—but that would be asking too much of fate!

Still I will proudly declare that there is something queer about it.

Else, why should it be let so cheaply? And why have stood so long untenanted?

5 John laughs at me, of course, but one expects that in marriage.

John is practical in the extreme. He has no patience with faith, an intense horror of superstition, and he scoffs openly at any talk of things not to be felt and seen and put down in figures.

John is a physician, and *perhaps*— (I would not say it to a living soul, of course, but this is dead paper and a great relief to my mind)—*perhaps* that is one reason I do not get well faster.

You see, he does not believe I am sick! And what can one do?

If a physician of high standing, and 10 one's own husband, assures friends and relatives that there is really nothing the matter with one but temporary nervous depression—a slight hysterical tendency— what is one to do?

My brother is also a physician, and also of high standing, and he says the same thing.

So I take phosphates or phosphites— whichever it is, and tonics, and journeys, and air, and exercise, and am absolutely forbidden to "work" until I am well again.

Personally, I disagree with their ideas.

Personally, I believe that congenial work, with excitement and change, would do me good.

15   But what is one to do?

I did write for a while in spite of them; but it *does* exhaust me a good deal—having to be so sly about it, or else meet with heavy opposition.

I sometimes fancy that in my condition if I had less opposition and more society and stimulus—but John says the very worst thing I can do is to think about my condition, and I confess it always makes me feel bad.

So I will let it alone and talk about the house.

The most beautiful place! It is quite alone, standing well back from the road, quite three miles from the village. It makes me think of English places that you read about, for there are hedges and walls and gates that lock, and lots of separate little houses for the gardeners and people.

20   There is a *delicious* garden! I never saw such a garden—large and shady, full of box-bordered paths, and lined with long grape-covered arbors with seats under them.

There were greenhouses, too, but they are all broken now.

There was some legal trouble, I believe, something about the heirs and co-heirs; anyhow, the place has been empty for years.

That spoils my ghostliness, I am afraid, but I don't care—there is something strange about the house—I can feel it.

I even said so to John one moonlight evening, but he said what I felt was a *draught*, and shut the window.

25   I get unreasonably angry with John sometimes. I'm sure I never used to be so sensitive. I think it is due to this nervous condition.

But John says if I feel so, I shall neglect proper self-control; so I take pains to control myself—before him, at least, and that makes me very tired.

I don't like our room a bit. I wanted one downstairs that opened on the piazza and had roses all over the window, and such pretty old-fashioned chintz hangings! but John would not hear of it.

He said there was only one window and not room for two beds, and no near room for him if he took another.

He is very careful and loving, and hardly lets me stir without special direction.

I have a schedule prescription for each 30 hour in the day; he takes all care from me, and so I feel basely ungrateful not to value it more.

He said we came here solely on my account, that I was to have perfect rest and all the air I could get. "Your exercise depends on your strength, my dear," said he, "and your food somewhat on your appetite; but air you can absorb all the time." So we took the nursery at the top of the house.

It is a big, airy room, the whole floor nearly, with windows that look all ways, and air and sunshine galore. It was nursery first and then playroom and gymnasium, I should judge; for the windows are barred for little children, and there are rings and things in the walls.

The paint and paper look as if a boys' school had used it. It is stripped off—the paper—in great patches all around the head of my bed, about as far as I can reach, and in a great place on the other side of the room low down. I never saw a worse paper in my life.

One of those sprawling flamboyant patterns committing every artistic sin.

It is dull enough to confuse the eye in 35 following, pronounced enough to constantly irritate and provoke study, and when you follow the lame uncertain curves for a little distance they suddenly commit suicide—plunge off at outrageous angles, destroy themselves in unheard of contradictions.

The color is repellant, almost revolting; a smouldering unclean yellow, strangely faded by the slow-turning sunlight.

It is a dull yet lurid orange in some places, a sickly sulphur tint in others.

No wonder the children hated it! I should hate it myself if I had to live in this room long.

There comes John, and I must put this away,—he hates to have me write a word.

40 We have been here two weeks, and I haven't felt like writing before, since that first day.

I am sitting by the window now, up in this atrocious nursery, and there is nothing to hinder my writing as much as I please, save lack of strength.

John is away all day, and even some nights when his cases are serious.

I am glad my case is not serious!

But these nervous troubles are dreadfully depressing.

45 John does not know how much I really suffer. He knows there is no *reason* to suffer, and that satisfies him.

Of course it is only nervousness. It does weigh on me so not to do my duty in any way!

I meant to be such a help to John, such a real rest and comfort, and here I am a comparative burden already!

Nobody would believe what an effort it is to do what little I am able,—to dress and entertain, and order things.

It is fortunate Mary is so good with the baby. Such a dear baby!

50 And yet I *cannot* be with him, it makes me so nervous.

I suppose John never was nervous in his life. He laughs at me so about this wallpaper!

At first he meant to repaper the room, but afterward he said that I was letting it get the better of me, and that nothing was worse for a nervous patient than to give way to such fancies.

He said that after the wallpaper was changed it would be the heavy bedstead, and then the barred windows, and then that gate at the head of the stairs, and so on.

"You know the place is doing you good," he said, "and really, dear, I don't care to renovate the house just for a three months' rental."

"Then do let us go downstairs," I said, 55 "there are such pretty rooms there."

Then he took me in his arms and called me a blessed little goose, and said he would go down cellar, if I wished, and have it whitewashed into the bargain.

But he is right enough about the beds and windows and things.

It is an airy and comfortable room as anyone need wish, and, of course, I would not be so silly as to make him uncomfortable just for a whim.

I'm really getting quite fond of the big room, all but that horrid paper.

Out of one window I can see the gar- 60 den, those mysterious deep-shaded arbors, the riotous old-fashioned flowers, and bushes and gnarly trees.

Out of another I get a lovely view of the bay and a little private wharf belonging to the estate. There is a beautiful shaded lane that runs down there from the house. I always fancy I see people walking in these numerous paths and arbors, but John has cautioned me not to give way to fancy in the least. He says that with my imaginative power and habit of story-making, a nervous weakness like mine is sure to lead to all manner of excited fancies, and that I ought to use my will and good sense to check the tendency. So I try.

I think sometimes that if I were only well enough to write a little it would relieve the press of ideas and rest me.

But I find I get pretty tired when I try.

It is so discouraging not to have any advice and companionship about my work. When I get really well, John says we will ask

Cousin Henry and Julia down for a long visit; but he says he would as soon put fireworks in my pillow-case as to let me have those stimulating people about now.

65   I wish I could get well faster.

But I must not think about that. This paper looks to me as if it *knew* what a vicious influence it had!

There is a recurrent spot where the pattern lolls like a broken neck and two bulbous eyes stare at you upside down.

I get positively angry with the impertinence of it and the everlastingness. Up and down and sideways they crawl, and those absurd, unblinking eyes are everywhere. There is one place where two breadths didn't match, and the eyes go all up and down the line, one a little higher than the other.

I never saw so much expression in an inanimate thing before, and we all know how much expression they have! I used to lie awake as a child and get more entertainment and terror out of blank walls and plain furniture than most children could find in a toy-store.

70   I remember what a kindly wink the knobs of our big, old bureau used to have, and there was one chair that always seemed like a strong friend.

I used to feel that if any of the other things looked too fierce I could always hop into that chair and be safe.

The furniture in this room is no worse than inharmonious, however, for we had to bring it all from downstairs. I suppose when this was used as a playroom they had to take the nursery things out, and no wonder! I never saw such ravages as the children have made here.

The wallpaper, as I said before, is torn off in spots, and it sticketh closer than a brother—they must have had perseverance as well as hatred.

Then the floor is scratched and gouged and splintered, the plaster itself is dug out

here and there, and this great heavy bed, which is all we found in the room, looks as if it had been through the wars.

But I don't mind it a bit—only the paper.   75

There comes John's sister. Such a dear girl as she is, and so careful of me! I must not let her find me writing.

She is a perfect and enthusiastic housekeeper, and hopes for no better profession. I verily believe she thinks it is the writing which made me sick!

But I can write when she is out, and see her a long way off from these windows.

There is one that commands the road, a lovely shaded winding road, and one that just looks off over the country. A lovely country, too, full of great elms and velvet meadows.

This wallpaper has a kind of sub-   80 pattern in a different shade, a particularly irritating one, for you can only see it in certain lights, and not clearly then.

But in the places where it isn't faded and where the sun is just so—I can see a strange, provoking, formless sort of figure, that seems to skulk about behind that silly and conspicuous front design.

There's sister on the stairs!

Well, the Fourth of July is over! The people are all gone and I am tired out. John thought it might do me good to see a little company, so we just had mother and Nellie and the children down for a week.

Of course I didn't do a thing. Jennie sees to everything now.

But it tired me all the same.   85

John says if I don't pick up faster he shall send me to Weir Mitchell[1] in the fall.

---

[1]**Dr. S. Weir Mitchell** (1829–1914) was an eminent Philadelphia neurologist who advocated "rest cures" for nervous disorders. He was the author of *Diseases of the Nervous System, Especially of Women* (1881).

But I don't want to go there at all. I had a friend who was in his hands once, and she says he is just like John and my brother, only more so!

Besides, it is such an undertaking to go so far.

I don't feel as if it was worthwhile to turn my hand over for anything, and I'm getting dreadfully fretful and querulous.

90 I cry at nothing, and cry most of the time.

Of course I don't when John is here, or anybody else, but when I am alone.

And I am alone a good deal just now. John is kept in town very often by serious cases, and Jennie is good and lets me alone when I want her to.

So I walk a little in the garden or down that lovely lane, sit on the porch under the roses, and lie down up here a good deal.

I'm getting really fond of the room in spite of the wallpaper. Perhaps *because* of the wallpaper.

95 It dwells in my mind so!

I lie here on this great immovable bed— it is nailed down, I believe—and follow that pattern about by the hour. It is as good as gymnastics, I assure you. I start, we'll say, at the bottom, down in the corner over there where it has not been touched, and I determine for the thousandth time that I *will* follow that pointless pattern to some sort of a conclusion.

I know a little of the principle of design, and I know this thing was not arranged on any laws of radiation, or alternation, or repetition, or symmetry, or anything else that I ever heard of.

It is repeated, of course, by the breadths, but not otherwise.

Looked at in one way each breadth stands alone, the bloated curves and flourishes—a kind of "debased Romanesque" with *delirium tremens*—go waddling up and down in isolated columns of fatuity.

But, on the other hand, they connect 100 diagonally, and the sprawling outlines run off in great slanting waves of optic horror, like a lot of wallowing seaweeds in full chase.

The whole thing goes horizontally, too, at least it seems so, and I exhaust myself in trying to distinguish the order of its going in that direction.

They have used a horizontal breadth for a frieze, and that adds wonderfully to the confusion.

There is one end of the room where it is almost intact, and there, when the crosslights fade and the low sun shines directly upon it, I can almost fancy radiation after all,—the interminable grotesques seem to form around a common centre and rush off in headlong plunges of equal distraction.

It makes me tired to follow it. I will take a nap I guess.

I don't know why I should write this. 105
I don't want to.
I don't feel able.

And I know John would think it absurd. But I *must* say what I feel and think in some way—it is such a relief!

But the effort is getting to be greater than the relief.

Half the time now I am awfully lazy, 110 and lie down ever so much.

John says I mustn't lose my strength, and has me take cod liver oil and lots of tonics and things, to say nothing of ale and wine and rare meat.

Dear John! He loves me very dearly, and hates to have me sick. I tried to have a real earnest reasonable talk with him the other day, and tell him how I wish he would let me go and make a visit to Cousin Henry and Julia.

But he said I wasn't able to go, nor able to stand it after I got there; and I did not make out a very good case for myself, for I was crying before I had finished.

It is getting to be a great effort for me to think straight. Just this nervous weakness I suppose.

115 And dear John gathered me up in his arms, and just carried me upstairs and laid me on the bed, and sat by me and read to me till it tired my head.

He said I was his darling and his comfort and all he had, and that I must take care of myself for his sake, and keep well.

He says no one but myself can help me out of it, that I must use my will and self-control and not let any silly fancies run away with me.

There's one comfort, the baby is well and happy, and does not have to occupy this nursery with the horrid wallpaper.

If we had not used it, that blessed child would have! What a fortunate escape! Why, I wouldn't have a child of mine, an impressionable little thing, live in such a room for worlds.

120 I never thought of it before, but it is lucky that John kept me here after all, I can stand it so much easier than a baby, you see.

Of course I never mention it to them any more—I am too wise, but I keep watch of it all the same.

There are things in the wallpaper that nobody knows but me, or ever will.

Behind that outside pattern the dim shapes get clearer every day.

It is always the same shape, only very numerous.

125 And it is like a woman stooping down and creeping about behind that pattern. I don't like it a bit. I wonder—I begin to think—I wish John would take me away from here!

It is so hard to talk with John about my case, because he is so wise, and because he loves me so.

But I tried it last night.

It was moonlight. The moon shines in all around just as the sun does.

I hate to see it sometimes, it creeps so slowly, and always comes in by one window or another.

130 John was asleep and I hated to waken him, so I kept still and watched the moonlight on that undulating wallpaper till I felt creepy.

The faint figure behind seemed to shake the pattern, just as if she wanted to get out.

I got up softly and went to feel and see if the paper *did* move, and when I came back John was awake.

"What is it, little girl?" he said. "Don't go walking about like that—you'll get cold."

I thought it was a good time to talk, so I told him that I really was not gaining here, and that I wished he would take me away.

135 "Why, darling!" said he, "our lease will be up in three weeks, and I can't see how to leave before.

"The repairs are not done at home, and I cannot possibly leave town just now. Of course if you were in any danger, I could and would, but you really are better, dear, whether you can see it or not. I am a doctor, dear, and I know. You are gaining flesh and color, your appetite is better, I feel really much easier about you."

"I don't weigh a bit more," said I, "nor as much; and my appetite may be better in the evening when you are here but it is worse in the morning when you are away!"

"Bless her little heart!" said he with a big hug, "she shall be as sick as she pleases! But now let's improve the shining hours by going to sleep, and talk about it in the morning!"

"And you won't go away?" I asked gloomily.

140 "Why, how can I, dear? It is only three weeks more and then we will take a nice little trip of a few days while Jennie is getting the house ready. Really dear you are better!"

"Better in body perhaps—" I began, and stopped short, for he sat up straight and looked at me with such a stern, reproachful look that I could not say another word.

"My darling," said he, "I beg you, for my sake and for our child's sake, as well as for your own, that you will never for one instant let that idea enter your mind! There is nothing so dangerous, so fascinating, to a temperament like yours. It is a false and foolish fancy. Can you trust me as a physician when I tell you so?"

So of course I said no more on that score, and we went to sleep before long. He thought I was asleep first, but I wasn't, and lay there for hours trying to decide whether that front pattern and the back pattern really did move together or separately.

On a pattern like this, by daylight, there is a lack of sequence, a defiance of law, that is a constant irritant to a normal mind.

145 The color is hideous enough, and unreliable enough, and infuriating enough, but the pattern is torturing.

You think you have mastered it, but just as you get well underway in following, it turns back-somersault and there you are. It slaps you in the face, knocks you down, and tramples upon you. It is like a bad dream.

The outside pattern is a florid arabesque, reminding one of a fungus. If you can imagine a toadstool in joints, an interminable string of toadstools, budding and sprouting in endless convolutions— why, that is something like it.

That is, sometimes!

There is one marked peculiarity about this paper, a thing nobody seems to notice but myself, and that is that it changes as the light changes.

150 When the sun shoots in through the east window—I always watch for that first long, straight ray—it changes so quickly that I never can quite believe it.

That is why I watch it always.

By moonlight—the moon shines in all night when there is a moon—I wouldn't know it was the same paper.

At night in any kind of light, in twilight, candlelight, lamplight, and worst of all by moonlight, it becomes bars! The outside pattern I mean, and the woman behind it is as plain as can be.

I didn't realize for a long time what the thing was that showed behind, that dim sub-pattern, but now I am quite sure it is a woman.

By daylight she is subdued, quiet. I 155 fancy it is the pattern that keeps her so still. It is so puzzling. It keeps me quiet by the hour.

I lie down ever so much now. John says it is good for me, and to sleep all I can.

Indeed he started the habit by making me lie down for an hour after each meal.

It is a very bad habit I am convinced, for you see I don't sleep.

And that cultivates deceit, for I don't tell them I'm awake—O, no!

The fact is I am getting a little afraid 160 of John.

He seems very queer sometimes, and even Jennie has an inexplicable look.

It strikes me occasionally, just as a scientific hypothesis,—that perhaps it is the paper!

I have watched John when he did not know I was looking, and come into the room suddenly on the most innocent excuses, and I've caught him several times *looking at the paper!* And Jennie too. I caught Jennie with her hand on it once.

She didn't know I was in the room, and when I asked her in a quiet, a very quiet voice, with the most restrained manner possible, what she was doing with the paper— she turned around as if she had been caught stealing, and looked quite angry—asked me why I should frighten her so!

165   Then she said that the paper stained everything it touched, that she had found yellow smooches on all my clothes and John's, and she wished we would be more careful!

Did not that sound innocent? But I know she was studying that pattern, and I am determined that nobody shall find it out but myself!

Life is very much more exciting now than it used to be. You see I have something more to expect, to look forward to, to watch. I really do eat better, and am more quiet than I was.

John is so pleased to see me improve! He laughed a little the other day, and said I seemed to be flourishing in spite of my wallpaper.

I turned it off with a laugh. I had no intention of telling him it was *because* of the wallpaper—he would make fun of me. He might even want to take me away.

170   I don't want to leave now until I have found it out. There is a week more, and I think that will be enough.

I'm feeling ever so much better! I don't sleep much at night, for it is so interesting to watch developments; but I sleep a good deal in the daytime.

In the daytime it is tiresome and perplexing.

There are always new shoots on the fungus, and new shades of yellow all over it. I cannot keep count of them, though I have tried conscientiously.

It is the strangest yellow, that wallpaper! It makes me think of all the yellow things I ever saw—not beautiful ones like buttercups, but old foul, bad yellow things.

175   But there is something else about that paper—the smell! I noticed it the moment we came into the room, but with so much air and sun it was not bad. Now we have had a week of fog and rain, and whether the windows are open or not, the smell is here.

It creeps all over the house.

I find it hovering in the dining-room, skulking in the parlor, hiding in the hall, lying in wait for me on the stairs.

It gets into my hair.

Even when I go to ride, if I turn my head suddenly and surprise it—there is that smell!

Such a peculiar odor, too! I have spent   180 hours in trying to analyze it, to find what it smelled like.

It is not bad—at first, and very gentle, but quite the subtlest, most enduring odor I ever met.

In this damp weather it is awful, I wake up in the night and find it hanging over me.

It used to disturb me at first. I thought seriously of burning the house—to reach the smell.

But now I am used to it. The only thing I can think of that it is like is the *color* of the paper! A yellow smell.

There is a very funny mark on this   185 wall, low down, near the mopboard. A streak that runs round the room. It goes behind every piece of furniture, except the bed, a long, straight, even *smooch*, as if it had been rubbed over and over.

I wonder how it was done and who did it, and what they did it for. Round and round and round—round and round and round—it makes me dizzy!

I really have discovered something at last.

Through watching so much at night, when it changes so, I have finally found out.

The front pattern *does* move—and no wonder! The woman behind shakes it!

Sometimes I think there are a great   190 many women behind, and sometimes only one, and she crawls around fast, and her crawling shakes it all over.

Then in the very bright spots she keeps still, and in the very shady spots she just takes hold of the bars and shakes them hard.

And she is all the time trying to climb through. But nobody could climb through that pattern—it strangles so; I think that is why it has so many heads.

They get through, and then the pattern strangles them off and turns them upside down, and makes their eyes white!

If those heads were covered or taken off it would not be half so bad.

195 I think that woman gets out in the daytime!

And I'll tell you why—privately—I've seen her!

I can see her out of every one of my windows!

It is the same woman, I know, for she is always creeping, and most women do not creep by daylight.

I see her in that long shaded lane, creeping up and down. I see her in those dark grape arbors, creeping all around the garden.

200 I see her on that long road under the trees, creeping along, and when a carriage comes she hides under the blackberry vines.

I don't blame her a bit. It must be very humiliating to be caught creeping by daylight!

I always lock the door when I creep by daylight. I can't do it at night, for I know John would suspect something at once.

And John is so queer now, that I don't want to irritate him. I wish he would take another room! Besides, I don't want anybody to get that woman out at night but myself.

I often wonder if I could see her out of all the windows at once.

205 But, turn as fast as I can, I can only see out of one at one time.

And though I always see her, she *may* be able to creep faster than I can turn!

I have watched her sometimes away off in the open country, creeping as fast as a cloud shadow in a high wind.

If only that top pattern could be gotten off from the under one! I mean to try it, little by little.

I have found out another funny thing, but I shan't tell it this time! It does not do to trust people too much.

There are only two more days to get 210 this paper off, and I believe John is beginning to notice. I don't like the look in his eyes.

And I heard him ask Jennie a lot of professional questions, about me. She had a very good report to give.

She said I slept a good deal in the daytime.

John knows I don't sleep very well at night, for all I'm so quiet!

He asked me all sorts of questions too, and pretended to be very loving and kind.

As if I couldn't see through him! 215

Still, I don't wonder he acts so, sleeping under this paper for three months.

It only interests me, but I feel sure John and Jennie are secretly affected by it.

Hurrah! This is the last day, but it is enough. John to stay in town over night, and won't be out until this evening.

Jennie wanted to sleep with me—the sly thing! But I told her I should undoubtedly rest better for a night all alone.

That was clever, for really I wasn't 220 alone a bit! As soon as it was moonlight and that poor thing began to crawl and shake the pattern, I got up and ran to help her.

I pulled and she shook, I shook and she pulled, and before morning we had peeled off yards of that paper.

A strip about as high as my head and half around the room.

And then when the sun came and that awful pattern began to laugh at me, I declared I would finish it to-day!

We go away to-morrow, and they are moving all my furniture down again to leave things as they were before.

225 Jennie looked at the wall in amazement, but I told her merrily that I did it out of pure spite at the vicious thing.

She laughed and said she wouldn't mind doing it herself, but I must not get tired.

How she betrayed herself that time!

But I am here, and no person touches this paper but me,—not *alive!*

She tried to get me out of the room—it was too patent! But I said it was so quiet and empty and clean now that I believed I would lie down again and sleep all I could, and not to wake me even for dinner—I would call when I woke.

230 So now she is gone, and the servants are gone, and the things are gone, and there is nothing left but that great bedstead nailed down, with the canvas mattress we found on it.

We shall sleep downstairs to-night, and take the boat home to-morrow.

I quite enjoy the room, now it is bare again.

How those children did tear about here! This bedstead is fairly gnawed!

235 But I must get to work.

I have locked the door and thrown the key down into the front path.

I don't want to go out, and I don't want to have anybody come in, till John comes.

I want to astonish him.

I've got a rope up here that even Jennie did not find. If that woman does get out, and tries to get away, I can tie her!

240 But I forgot I could not reach far without anything to stand on!

This bed will *not* move!

I tried to lift and push it until I was lame, and then I got so angry I bit off a little piece at one corner—but it hurt my teeth.

Then I peeled off all the paper I could reach standing on the floor. It sticks horribly and the pattern just enjoys it! All those strangled heads and bulbous eyes and waddling fungus growths just shriek with derision!

I am getting angry enough to do something desperate. To jump out of the window would be admirable exercise, but the bars are too strong even to try.

Besides I wouldn't do it. Of course not. 245 I know well enough that a step like that is improper and might be misconstrued.

I don't like to *look* out of the windows even—there are so many of those creeping women, and they creep so fast.

I wonder if they all come out of that wallpaper as I did?

But I am securely fastened now by my well-hidden rope—you don't get *me* out in the road there!

I suppose I shall have to get back behind the pattern when it comes night, and that is hard!

It is so pleasant to be out in this great 250 room and creep around as I please!

I don't want to go outside. I won't, even if Jennie asks me to.

For outside you have to creep on the ground, and everything is green instead of yellow.

But here I can creep smoothly on the floor, and my shoulder just fits in that long smooch around the wall, so I cannot lose my way.

Why, there's John at the door!

It is no use, young man, you can't 255 open it!

How he does call and pound!

Now he's crying for an axe.

It would be a shame to break down that beautiful door!

"John dear!" said I in the gentlest voice, "the key is down by the front steps, under a plantain leaf!"

That silenced him for a few moments. 260

Then he said—very quietly indeed, "Open the door, my darling!"

"I can't," said I. "The key is down by the front door under a plantain leaf!"

And then I said it again, several times, very gently and slowly, and said it so often that he had to go and see, and he got it of course, and came in. He stopped short by the door.

"What is the matter?" he cried. "For God's sake, what are you doing!"

I kept on creeping just the same, but I 265 looked at him over my shoulder.

"I've got out at last," said I, "in spite of you and Jane. And I've pulled off most of the paper, so you can't put me back!"

Now why should that man have fainted? But he did, and right across my path by the wall, so that I had to creep over him every time!

••••••▶ *Your* **Turn**
Talking and Writing about Lit

1. In "The Yellow Wallpaper," Gilman uses the first-person voice (the "I" narrator) in order to put us in the perspective of the woman who is confined to her room. Do you think this is a good choice? What would be the effect if another character were telling the story instead (her husband, for example)?

2. What do you think is the most important method of characterization in Gilman's story? Which character do we come to know the best?

3. **DIY** Gilman has chosen to tell the story in chronological order. What would be the effect if she had begun in medias res (in the middle of things, as in Dubus's "Killings" in Chapter 3) and then flashed back to the beginning of the action? Rewrite the story using a plot sequence like Dubus's. You might title your rewrite "The Yellow Wallpaper Retold" in order to acknowledge that you are writing a takeoff on Gilman's well-known story.

Talking Lit

In this introduction to her short story collection *Darkness*, Mukherjee discusses immigration as "a set of fluid identities to be celebrated."

Bharati Mukherjee, From the Introduction to *Darkness*, 1985

Most of these stories were written in a three-month burst of energy in the spring of 1984, in Atlanta, Georgia, while I was writer-in-residence at Emory University. "The World According to Hsü," "Isolated Incidents," "Courtly Vision" and "Hindus" were written a little earlier, in Montreal and Toronto.

That energy interests me now.

For a writer, energy is aggression; urgency colliding with confidence. Suddenly, everything is possible. Excluded worlds are opened, secretive characters reveal themselves. The writing-self is somehow united with the universe.

Until Atlanta—and it could have been anywhere in America—I had thought of myself, in spite of a white husband and two assimilated sons, as an expatriate. In my fiction, and in my Canadian experience, "immigrants" were lost souls, put upon and pathetic. Expatriates, on the other hand, knew all too well who and what they were, and what foul fate had befallen them. Like V. S. Naipaul, in whom I imagined a model, I tried to explore state-of-the-art expatriation. Like Naipaul, I used a mordant and self-protective irony in describing my characters' pain. Irony promised both detachment from, and superiority over, those well-bred post-colonials much like myself, adrift in the new world, wondering if they would ever belong.

If you have to wonder, if you keep looking for signs, if you wait—surrendering little bits of a reluctant self every year, clutching the souvenirs of an ever-retreating past—you'll never belong, anywhere.

In the years that I spent in Canada—1966 to 1980—I discovered that the country is hostile to its citizens who had been born in hot, moist continents like Asia; that the country proudly boasts of its opposition to the whole concept of cultural assimilation. In the Indian immigrant community I saw a family of shared grievances. The purely "Canadian" stories in this collection were difficult to write and even more painful to live through. They are uneasy stories about expatriation.

The transformation as writer, and as resident of the new world, occurred with the act of immigration to the United States. Suddenly I was no longer aggrieved, except as a habit of mind. I had moved from being a "visible minority," against whom the nation had officially incited its less-visible citizens to react, to being just another immigrant. If I may put it in its harshest terms, it would be this: in Canada, I was frequently taken for a prostitute or shoplifter, frequently assumed to be a domestic, praised by astonished auditors that I didn't have a "sing-song" accent. The society itself, or important elements in that society, routinely made crippling assumptions about me, and about my "kind." In the United States, however, I see *myself* in those same outcasts; I see myself in an article on a Trinidad-Indian hooker; I see myself in the successful executive who slides Hindi film music in his tape deck as he drives into Manhattan; I see myself in the shady accountant who's trying to marry off his loose-living daughter; in professors, domestics, high school students, illegal busboys in ethnic restaurants. It's possible—with sharp ears and the right equipment—to hear America singing even in the seams of the dominant culture. In fact, it may be the best listening post for the next generation of Whitmans. For me, it is a movement away from the aloofness of expatriation, to the exuberance of immigration.

I have joined imaginative forces with an anonymous, driven, underclass of semi-assimilated Indians with sentimental attachments to a distant homeland but no real desire for permanent return. I see my "immigrant" story replicated in a dozen American cities, and instead of seeing my Indianness as a fragile identity to be preserved against obliteration (or worse, a "visible" disfigurement to be hidden),

Why I Wrote "The Yellow Wallpaper"

By Charlotte Perkins Gilman

Many and many a reader has asked me that. When the story first came out, in the *New England Magazine* about 1891, a Boston physician made protest in *The Transcript*. Such a story ought not to be written, he said; it was enough to drive anyone mad to read it.

Another physician, in Kansas I think, wrote to say that it was the best description of incipient insanity he had ever seen, and—begging my pardon—had I been there?

Now the story of the story is this: For many years I suffered from a severe and continuous nervous breakdown tending to melancholia—and beyond. During about the third year of this trouble I went, in devout faith and some faint stir of hope, to a noted specialist in nervous diseases, the best known in the country. This wise man put me to bed and applied the rest-cure, to which a still-good physique responded so promptly that he concluded there was nothing much the matter with me, and sent me home with solemn advice to "live as domestic a

I see it now as a set of fluid identities to be celebrated. I see myself as an American writer in the tradition of other American writers whose parents or grandparents had passed through Ellis Island. Indianness is now a metaphor, a particular way of partially comprehending the world. Though the characters in these stories are, or were, "Indian," I see most of these as stories of broken identities and discarded languages, and the will to bond oneself to a new community, against the ever-present fear of failure and betrayal. The book I dream of updating is no longer *A Passage to India*—it's *Call It Sleep*.

Bernard Malamud, to whom this book is dedicated, is a man I have known for over twenty years as a close friend, but Bernard Malamud the writer is a man I have known only for these past two years, after I learned to read his stories as part of the same celebration.

life as far as possible," to "have but two hours' intellectual life a day," and "never to touch pen, brush, or pencil again" as long as I lived. This was in 1887.

I went home and obeyed those directions for some three months, and came so near the borderline of utter mental ruin that I could see over.

Then, using the remnants of intelligence that remained, and helped by a wise friend, I cast the noted specialist's advice to the winds and went to work again—work, the normal life of every human being; work, in which is joy and growth and service, without which one is a pauper and a parasite— ultimately recovering some measure of power.

Being naturally moved to rejoicing by this narrow escape, I wrote "The Yellow Wallpaper," with its embellishments and additions, to carry out the ideal (I never had hallucinations or objections to my mural decorations) and sent a copy to the physician who so nearly drove me mad. He never acknowledged it.

The little book is valued by alienists and as a good specimen of one kind of literature. It has, to my knowledge, saved one woman from a similar fate—so terrifying her family that they let her out into normal activity and she recovered.

But the best result is this. Many years later I was told that the great specialist had admitted to friends that he had altered his treatment of neurasthenia since reading "The Yellow Wallpaper."

It was not intended to drive people crazy, but to save people from being driven crazy, and it worked.

SETTING

Even bookstores use Setting.

More reminiscent of a comfortable study than a retail chain, the seating areas at some Barnes and Noble bookstores feature overstuffed chairs, coffee tables, and reading lamps to encourage shoppers to browse and lounge. And if that doesn't draw customers in, the café is just past the fiction aisle. At some stores, the café features sandwiches, salads, and fancy coffee so that browsers don't have to leave the store when they're hungry or craving a cappuccino. This physical setting provides book buyers with a sense of place that is appropriate to the products sold in the store. A stocked kitchen and a warm, inviting sitting area allows the book browser to grab a cup of coffee and cozy up to a plush easy chair for some quiet reading time. The customers remain in the store for longer periods of time, and more time with the books increases the odds that they will buy one. And even if customers don't buy a book, they may have bought a coffee to browse with.

As is true in fiction, the bookstore's story is served by creating a setting appropriate to the theme—the appreciation of good books and a good cup of java.

Have you ever opened up a book you wanted to read or sat down to watch a movie and felt drawn into the setting of the story? Maybe the story or novel or film opened in a pyramid, a tomb, a haunted house, or at a beach party, and that setting was described or depicted so vividly that you could imagine being there right from the start. If you've ever experienced this, then you understand the importance of setting.

Physical Setting—A Sense of Place

Certainly one of the most familiar ways in which **setting** plays an important role in fiction is in giving the characters a place to be and making that place vivid to the reader. In Albert Camus' "The Guest," which you'll read in this chapter, the setting comes to life as a background and context for the characters' actions.

> On the blackboard the four rivers of France, drawn with four different colored chalks, had been flowing toward their estuaries for the past three days. Snow had suddenly fallen in mid-October after eight months of drought without the transition of rain, and the twenty pupils, more or less, who lived in the villages scattered over the plateau had stopped coming. With fair weather they would return. (paragraph 2)

This passage introduces us to the **interior setting** of the classroom, as well as the **exterior setting** of the plateau and its scattered villages. Weather is also a factor in the story, and descriptions of the climate help convey the harsh landscape in which these characters live in Algeria (a largely Muslim country on the north coast of Africa that was a French colony for 100 years).

Time and Setting

Historical setting also plays a role in "The Guest." The war the characters refer to in the story is the French-Algerian war, which began in 1954 and ended in 1962 when Algeria won its independence from French rule (Camus first published the story in 1957). The main character in "The Guest," Daru (a French schoolteacher serving the local population in a remote Arab village), will be affected personally and profoundly by the brewing conflict. Thus, both **place** and **time** are crucial aspects of setting here. Camus skillfully uses precise sensory details to bring this setting to life for the reader: "The snow was melting faster and faster and the sun was drinking up the puddles at once, rapidly cleaning the plateau, which gradually dried and vibrated like the air itself. When they resumed walking, the ground rang under their feet" (paragraph 103).

Setting and Theme

In "The Guest," the starkness of the Algerian plateau where the story is set reflects the tough ethical choices the characters must make during the course of the story. In Eudora Welty's "A Worn Path" (also in this chapter), the exterior setting helps Welty reveal the character of the grandmother (Phoenix) as she overcomes obstacles in the natural setting. Through effective descriptions of Phoenix's stamina in coping with and overcoming both natural and man-made obstacles, the strength of her character is made known to us. The setting in which her character is revealed is made vivid to the reader from the first sentence of the story: "It was December—a bright frozen day in the early morning." The next sentences sketch for us her situation:

> Far out in the country there was an old Negro woman with her head tied in a red rag, coming along a path through the pinewoods. Her name was Phoenix Jackson. She was very old and small and she walked slowly in the dark pine shadows, moving a little from side to side in her steps, with the balanced heaviness and lightness of a pendulum in a grandfather clock. She carried a thin, small cane made from an umbrella, and with this she kept tapping the frozen earth in front of her. (paragraph 1)

Like the obstacles Odysseus (aka the Roman Ulysses) overcomes in the Greek poet Homer's *Odyssey* (written down ca. 900–850 B.C.E.), Phoenix overcomes a series of obstacles, showing her strength of character, during her journey: the hills she must climb, the thorny bushes, the log spanning the creek, the barbed-wire fence, the buzzard, the field of dead corn, the scarecrow, the big black dog and the white hunter, and the tower of steps to the doctor's office. Upon reaching the pinnacle of the doctor's office, she has reached her goal; now she must make her way back home to her grandson, as Odysseus made his long journey back to Penelope.

Past, Present, and Future Time

Historical time is an important part of the setting of Camus' "The Guest," but time can be important in a story's setting in other ways. In the fourth story in this chapter, F. Scott Fitzgerald's "Babylon Revisited," the dilemma of the central character, Charlie Wales, is defined by the interplay of past, present, and future, and Charlie seems to live in several time frames at once as he struggles to make sense of his life in the present. This could also be said of Sherman Alexie's narrator in "The Only Traffic Signal on the Reservation Doesn't Flash Red Anymore," our third reading. The way in which the narrator contemplates the relationship of events in the past to events in the present time is an important aspect of setting and a useful vehicle for theme. Through the similarity of past and present, both the narrator and the reader recognize the repetition of the troubles (alcoholism, joblessness, poverty) of past generations in the present generation. Happily, the story ends with the main characters intending to set their feet on a different path. The fact that they are drinking Pepsi instead of beer suggests that they may have the capacity to make a change for the better.

Social Setting

In addition to the various aspects of place and time in fiction, the **social setting** can be an important part of the context in which the characters operate and from which themes arise. In Sherman Alexie's story, the narrator, Victor, relates with refreshing humor and candor the experience of his reservation community. In Alexie's fiction, the community often seems like a character itself, encompassing the lives of the individual members of his Spokane/Coeur D'Alene reservation in Washington state: "Adrian and I sat on the porch and watched the reservation. Nothing happened. From our chairs made rockers by unsteady legs, we could see that the only traffic signal on the reservation had stopped working" (paragraph 11). The preceding sentence functions both literally and symbolically, as we learn that the youth of the reservation are operating with too few constraints and too few opportunities for change: "It's hard to be optimistic on the reservation. When a glass sits on a table here, people don't wonder if it's half filled or half empty. They just hope it's good beer" (paragraph 72). The time setting shifts to one year later, and Adrian and Victor are still sitting on the porch watching the reservation. Adrian says, "'Shit, that damn traffic signal is still broken. Look.'" And the narrator observes, "Adrian pointed down the road and he was right. But what's the point of fixing it in a place where the STOP signs are just suggestions?" (paragraphs 106–107). Hope and the possibility for change are present, however, in a small detail that has shifted in the last scene with Victor and Adrian on the porch:

> A year later, Adrian and I sat on the same porch in the same chairs. We'd done things in between, like ate and slept and read the newspaper. It was another hot summer. Then again summer is supposed to be hot.
> "I'm thirsty," Adrian said. "Give me a beer."
> "How many times do I have to tell you? We don't drink anymore."
> "Shit," Adrian said. "I keep forgetting. Give me a goddamn Pepsi." (paragraphs 81–84)

It may seem like a small detail, but in the social setting in which Victor and Adrian live, it looms large, as they watch sixteen-year-old Julius Windmaker—last year's star basketball player on the reservation—stagger down the road, drunk at 2:00 in the afternoon.

While the social setting in Alexie's story is used to help reveal common experiences among characters in a community, the social and physical settings in Fitzgerald's "Babylon Revisited" often help illuminate *differences* in social status and lifestyle. Fitzgerald's skillful use of descriptive detail brings every one of his scenes to life in sharp relief. The early scene in the Ritz Bar and the encounter with Lorraine and Duncan show him in settings that remind us (and him) of his former dissolute life. The scene of judgment in his sister-in-law Marion's house in Paris shows us a strikingly different social setting, one in which Charlie struggles to demonstrate that he is respectable and sober enough to win custody of his daughter, Honoria. The colliding of Charlie's two worlds when the drunken Lorraine and Duncan arrive at Marion's house causes a crisis for Charlie's plans for his and Honoria's future. The contrasting social and physical environments depicted in the story help Fitzgerald show us the poignant situation of a man caught between past and present, between a life of extravagance and waste on the one hand and potential for change and happiness on the other. The story is open ended, and each reader is left to decide for himself or herself what might be the outcome for Charlie Wales.

Readings

Albert Camus (1913–1960)

Albert Camus, of French heritage, was born in Mondovi, Algeria, and died in an automobile accident near Paris. He is known as one of the most prominent of the French existentialist writers. Camus' works of fiction are his novels *The Stranger* (1942), *The Plague* (1940), and *The Fall* (1956) and his collection of short fiction, *Exile and the Kingdom* (1957). Camus also published numerous essays and plays. He often wrote—as in his story "The Guest"—about the relationship between France and her Muslim former colony Algeria, and he referred to himself as an "Algerian Frenchman."

The Guest (1957)

Translated by Justin O'Brien

The schoolmaster was watching the two men climb toward him. One was on horseback, the other on foot. They had not yet tackled the abrupt rise leading to the schoolhouse built on the hillside. They were toiling onward, making slow progress in the snow, among the stones, on the vast expanse of the high, deserted plateau. From time to time the horse stumbled. Without hearing anything yet, he could see the breath issuing from the horse's nostrils. One of the men, at least, knew the region. They were following the trail although it had disappeared days ago under a layer of dirty white snow. The schoolmaster calculated that it would take them half an hour to get onto the hill. It was cold; he went back into the school to get a sweater.

He crossed the empty, frigid class-room. On the blackboard the four rivers of France, drawn with four different colored chalks, had been flowing toward their estu-aries for the past three days. Snow had sud-denly fallen in mid-October after eight months of drought without the transition of rain, and the twenty pupils, more or less, who lived in the villages scattered over the plateau had stopped coming. With fair weather they would return. Daru now heated only the single room that was his lodging, adjoining the classroom and giving also onto the plateau to the east. Like the class windows, his window looked to the south too. On that side the school was a few kilometers from the point where the plateau began to slope toward the south. In clear weather could be seen the purple mass of the mountain range where the gap opened onto the desert.

Somewhat warmed, Daru returned to the window from which he had first seen the two men. They were no longer visible. Hence they must have tackled the rise. The sky was not so dark, for the snow had stopped falling during the night. The morn-ing had opened with a dirty light which had scarcely become brighter as the ceiling of clouds lifted. At two in the afternoon it seemed as if the day were merely beginning. But still this was better than those three days when the thick snow was falling amidst unbroken darkness with little gusts of wind that rattled the double door of the class-room. Then Daru had spent long hours in his room, leaving it only to go to the shed and feed the chickens or get some coal. Fortunately the delivery truck from Tadjid, the nearest village to the north, had brought his supplies two days before the blizzard. It would return in forty-eight hours.

Besides, he had enough to resist a siege, for the little room was cluttered with bags of wheat that the administration left as a stock to distribute to those of his pupils whose families had suffered from the drought. Actually they had all been victims because they were all poor. Every day Daru would distribute a ration to the children. They had missed it, he knew, during these bad days. Possibly one of the fathers or big brothers would come this afternoon and he could supply them with grain. It was just a matter of carrying them over to the next har-vest. Now shiploads of wheat were arriving from France and the worst was over. But it would be hard to forget that poverty, that army of ragged ghosts wandering in the sunlight, the plateaus burned to a cinder month after month, the earth shriveled up little by little, literally scorched, every stone bursting into dust under one's foot. The sheep had died then by thousands and even a few men, here and there, sometimes with-out anyone's knowing.

In contrast with such poverty, he who 5 lived almost like a monk in his remote schoolhouse, nonetheless satisfied with the little he had and with the rough life, had felt like a lord with his white-washed walls, his narrow couch, his unpainted shelves, his well, and his weekly provision of water and food. And suddenly this snow, without warning, without the foretaste of rain. This is the way the region was, cruel to live in, even without men—who didn't help mat-ters either. But Daru had been born here. Everywhere else, he felt exiled.

He stepped out onto the terrace in front of the schoolhouse. The two men were now halfway up the slope. He recognized the horseman as Balducci, the old gendarme he had known for a long time. Balducci was holding on the end of a rope an Arab who was walking behind him with hands bound and head lowered. The gendarme waved a greeting to which Daru did not reply, lost as he was in contemplation of the Arab dressed in a faded blue jellaba, his feet in sandals but covered with socks of heavy raw wool, his head surmounted by a narrow, short *chèche*. They were approaching. Balducci was holding back his horse in order not to hurt the Arab, and the group was advancing slowly.

Within earshot, Balducci shouted: "One hour to do the three kilometers from El Ameur!" Daru did not answer. Short and square in his thick sweater, he watched them climb. Not once had the Arab raised his head. "Hello," said Daru when they got up onto the terrace. "Come in and warm up." Balducci painfully got down from his horse without letting go the rope. From under his bristling mustache he smiled at the schoolmaster. His little dark eyes, deep-set under a tanned forehead, and his mouth surrounded with wrinkles made him look attentive and studious. Daru took the bridle, led the horse to the shed, and came back to the two men, who were now waiting for him in the school. He led them into his room. "I am going to heat up the classroom," he said. "We'll be more comfortable there." When he entered the room again, Balducci was on the couch. He had undone the rope tying him to the Arab, who had squatted near the stove. His hands still bound, the *chèche* pushed back on his head, he was looking toward the window. At first Daru noticed only his huge lips, fat, smooth, almost Negroid; yet his nose was straight, his eyes were dark and full of fever. The *chèche* revealed an obstinate forehead and, under the weathered skin now rather discolored by the cold, the whole face had a restless and rebellious look that struck Daru when the Arab, turning his face toward him, looked him straight in the eyes. "Go into the other room," said the schoolmaster, "and I'll make you some mint tea." "Thanks," Balducci said. "What a chore! How I long for retirement." And addressing his prisoner in Arabic: "Come on, you." The Arab got up and, slowly, holding his bound wrists in front of him, went into the classroom.

With the tea, Daru brought a chair. But Balducci was already enthroned on the nearest pupil's desk and the Arab had squatted against the teacher's platform facing the stove, which stood between the desk and the window. When he held out the glass of tea to the prisoner, Daru hesitated at the sight of his bound hands. "He might perhaps be untied." "Sure," said Balducci. "That was for the trip." He started to get to his feet. But Daru, setting the glass on the floor, had knelt beside the Arab. Without saying anything, the Arab watched him with his feverish eyes. Once his hands were free, he rubbed his swollen wrists against each other, took the glass of tea, and sucked up the burning liquid in swift little sips.

"Good," said Daru. "And where are you headed?"

Balducci withdrew his mustache from the tea. "Here, son." 10

"Odd pupils! And you're spending the night?"

"No. I'm going back to El Ameur. And you will deliver this fellow to Tinguit. He is expected at police headquarters."

Balducci was looking at Daru with a friendly little smile.

"What's this story?" asked the schoolmaster. "Are you pulling my leg?"

"No, son. Those are the orders." 15

"The orders? I'm not ..." Daru hesitated, not wanting to hurt the old Corsican. "I mean, that's not my job."

"What! What's the meaning of that? In wartime people do all kinds of jobs."

"Then I'll wait for the declaration of war!"

Balducci nodded.

"O.K. But the orders exist and they 20 concern you too. Things are brewing, it appears. There is talk of a forthcoming revolt. We are mobilized, in a way."

Daru still had his obstinate look.

"Listen, son," Balducci said. "I like you and you must understand. There's only a dozen of us at El Ameur to patrol throughout the whole territory of a small department and I must get back in a hurry. I was told to hand this guy over to you and return without delay. He couldn't be kept there. His village was beginning to stir; they wanted to take him back. You must take him to Tinguit tomorrow before the day is over. Twenty kilometers shouldn't faze a husky fellow like you. After that, all will be over. You'll come back to your pupils and your comfortable life."

Behind the wall the horse could be heard snorting and pawing the earth. Daru was looking out the window. Decidedly, the weather was clearing and the light was increasing over the snowy plateau. When all the snow was melted, the sun would take over again and once more would burn the fields of stone. For days, still, the unchanging sky would shed its dry light on the solitary expanse where nothing had any connection with man.

"After all," he said, turning around toward Balducci, "what did he do?" And, before the gendarme had opened his mouth, he asked: "Does he speak French?"

25 "No, not a word. We had been looking for him for a month, but they were hiding him. He killed his cousin."

"Is he against us?"

"I don't think so. But you can never be sure."

"Why did he kill?"

"A family squabble, I think. One owed the other grain, it seems. It's not at all clear. In short, he killed his cousin with a billhook. You know, like a sheep, *kreezk!*"

30 Balducci made the gesture of drawing a blade across his throat and the Arab, his attention attracted, watched him with a sort of anxiety. Daru felt a sudden wrath against the man, against all men with their rotten spite, their tireless hates, their blood lust.

But the kettle was singing on the stove. He served Balducci more tea, hesitated, then served the Arab again, who, a second time, drank avidly. His raised arms made the jellaba fall open and the schoolmaster saw his thin, muscular chest.

"Thanks, kid," Balducci said. "And now, I'm off."

He got up and went toward the Arab, taking a small rope from his pocket.

"What are you doing?" Daru asked dryly.

Balducci, disconcerted, showed him 35 the rope.

"Don't bother."

The old gendarme hesitated. "It's up to you. Of course, you are armed?"

"I have my shotgun."

"Where?"

"In the trunk." 40

"You ought to have it near your bed."

"Why? I have nothing to fear."

"You're crazy, son. If there's an uprising, no one is safe, we're all in the same boat."

"I'll defend myself. I'll have time to see them coming."

Balducci began to laugh, then sud- 45 denly the mustache covered the white teeth.

"You'll have time? O.K. That's just what I was saying. You have always been a little cracked. That's why I like you, my son was like that."

At the same time he took out his revolver and put it on the desk.

"Keep it; I don't need two weapons from here to El Ameur."

The revolver shone against the black paint of the table. When the gendarme turned toward him, the schoolmaster caught the smell of leather and horseflesh.

50 "Listen, Balducci," Daru said suddenly, "every bit of this disgusts me, and first of all your fellow here. But I won't hand him over. Fight, yes, if I have to. But not that."

The old gendarme stood in front of him and looked at him severely.

"You're being a fool," he said slowly. "I don't like it either. You don't get used to putting a rope on a man even after years of it, and you're even ashamed—yes, ashamed. But you can't let them have their way."

"I won't hand him over," Daru said again.

"It's an order, son, and I repeat it."

55 "That's right. Repeat to them what I've said to you: I won't hand him over."

Balducci made a visible effort to reflect. He looked at the Arab and at Daru. At last he decided.

"No, I won't tell them anything. If you want to drop us, go ahead; I'll not denounce you. I have an order to deliver the prisoner and I'm doing so. And now you'll just sign this paper for me."

"There's no need. I'll not deny that you left him with me."

"Don't be mean with me. I know you'll tell the truth. You're from hereabouts and you are a man. But you must sign, that's the rule."

60 Daru opened his drawer, took out a little square bottle of purple ink, the red wooden penholder with the "sergeant-major" pen he used for making models of penmanship, and signed. The gendarme carefully folded the paper and put it into his wallet. Then he moved toward the door.

"I'll see you off," Daru said.

"No," said Balducci. "There's no use being polite. You insulted me."

He looked at the Arab, motionless in the same spot, sniffed peevishly, and turned away toward the door. "Good-by, son," he said. The door shut behind him. Balducci appeared suddenly outside the window and then disappeared. His footsteps were muffled by the snow. The horse stirred on the other side of the wall and several chickens fluttered in fright. A moment later Balducci reappeared outside the window leading the horse by the bridle. He walked toward the little rise without turning around and disappeared from sight with the horse following him. A big stone could be heard bouncing down. Daru walked back toward the prisoner, who, without stirring, never took his eyes off him. "Wait," the schoolmaster said in Arabic and went toward the bedroom. As he was going through the door, he had a second thought, went to the desk, took the revolver, and stuck it in his pocket. Then, without looking back, he went into his room.

For some time he lay on his couch watching the sky gradually close over, listening to the silence. It was this silence that had seemed painful to him during the first days here, after the war. He had requested a post in the little town at the base of the foothills separating the upper plateaus from the desert. There, rocky walls, green and black to the north, pink and lavender to the south, marked the frontier of eternal summer. He had been named to a post farther north, on the plateau itself. In the beginning, the solitude and the silence had been hard for him on these wastelands peopled only by stones. Occasionally, furrows suggested cultivation, but they had been dug to uncover a certain kind of stone good for building. The only plowing here was to harvest rocks. Elsewhere a thin layer of soil accumulated in the hollows would be scraped out to enrich paltry village gardens. This is the way it was: bare rock covered three quarters of the region. Towns sprang up, flourished, then disappeared; men came by, loved one another or fought bitterly, then died. No one in this desert, neither he nor his guest, mattered. And yet, outside this desert neither of them, Daru knew, could have really lived.

65   When he got up, no noise came from the classroom. He was amazed at the unmixed joy he derived from the mere thought that the Arab might have fled and that he would be alone with no decision to make. But the prisoner was there. He had merely stretched out between the stove and the desk. With eyes open, he was staring at the ceiling. In that position, his thick lips were particularly noticeable, giving him a pouting look. "Come," said Daru. The Arab got up and followed him. In the bedroom, the schoolmaster pointed to a chair near the table under the window. The Arab sat down without taking his eyes off Daru.

"Are you hungry?"

"Yes," the prisoner said.

Daru set the table for two. He took flour and oil, shaped a cake in a frying-pan, and lighted the little stove that functioned on bottled gas. While the cake was cooking, he went out to the shed to get cheese, eggs, dates, and condensed milk. When the cake was done he set it on the window sill to cool, heated some condensed milk diluted with water, and beat up the eggs into an omelette. In one of his motions he knocked against the revolver stuck in his right pocket. He set the bowl down, went into the classroom, and put the revolver in his desk drawer. When he came back to the room, night was falling. He put on the light and served the Arab. "Eat," he said. The Arab took a piece of the cake, lifted it eagerly to his mouth, and stopped short.

"And you?" he asked.

70   "After you. I'll eat too."

The thick lips opened slightly. The Arab hesitated, then bit into the cake determinedly.

The meal over, the Arab looked at the schoolmaster. "Are you the judge?"

"No, I'm simply keeping you until tomorrow."

"Why do you eat with me?"

"I'm hungry."   75

The Arab fell silent. Daru got up and went out. He brought back a folding bed from the shed, set it up between the table and the stove, perpendicular to his own bed. From a large suitcase which, upright in a corner, served as a shelf for papers, he took two blankets and arranged them on the camp bed. Then he stopped, felt useless, and sat down on his bed. There was nothing more to do or to get ready. He had to look at this man. He looked at him, therefore, trying to imagine his face bursting with rage. He couldn't do so. He could see nothing but the dark yet shining eyes and the animal mouth.

"Why did you kill him?" he asked in a voice whose hostile tone surprised him.

The Arab looked away.

"He ran away. I ran after him."

He raised his eyes to Daru again and   80
they were full of a sort of woeful interrogation. "Now what will they do to me?"

"Are you afraid?"

He stiffened, turning his eyes away.

"Are you sorry?"

The Arab stared at him openmouthed. Obviously he did not understand. Daru's annoyance was growing. At the same time he felt awkward and self-conscious with his big body wedged between the two beds.

"Lie down there," he said impatiently.   85
"That's your bed."

The Arab didn't move. He called to Daru:

"Tell me!"

The schoolmaster looked at him.

"Is the gendarme coming back tomorrow?"

"I don't know."   90

"Are you coming with us?"

"I don't know. Why?"

The prisoner got up and stretched out on top of the blankets, his feet toward the window. The light from the electric bulb shone straight into his eyes and he closed them at once.

"Why?" Daru repeated, standing beside the bed.

95   The Arab opened his eyes under the blinding light and looked at him, trying not to blink.

"Come with us," he said.

In the middle of the night, Daru was still not asleep. He had gone to bed after undressing completely; he generally slept naked. But when he suddenly realized that he had nothing on, he hesitated. He felt vulnerable and the temptation came to him to put his clothes back on. Then he shrugged his shoulders; after all, he wasn't a child and, if need be, he could break his adversary in two. From his bed he could observe him, lying on his back, still motionless with his eyes closed under the harsh light. When Daru turned out the light, the darkness seemed to coagulate all of a sudden. Little by little, the night came back to life in the window where the starless sky was stirring gently. The schoolmaster soon made out the body lying at his feet. The Arab still did not move, but his eyes seemed open. A faint wind was prowling around the schoolhouse. Perhaps it would drive away the clouds and the sun would reappear.

During the night the wind increased. The hens fluttered a little and then were silent. The Arab turned over on his side with his back to Daru, who thought he heard him moan. Then he listened for his guest's breathing, become heavier and more regular. He listened to that breath so close to him and mused without being able to go to sleep. In this room where he had been sleeping alone for a year, this presence bothered him. But it bothered him also by imposing on him a sort of brotherhood he knew well but refused to accept in the present circumstances. Men who share the same rooms, soldiers or prisoners, develop a strange alliance as if, having cast off their armor with their clothing, they fraternized every evening, over and above their differences, in the ancient community of dream and fatigue. But Daru shook himself; he didn't like such musings, and it was essential to sleep.

A little later, however, when the Arab stirred slightly, the schoolmaster was still not asleep. When the prisoner made a second move, he stiffened, on the alert. The Arab was lifting himself slowly on his arms with almost the motion of a sleepwalker. Seated upright in bed, he waited motionless without turning his head toward Daru, as if he were listening attentively. Daru did not stir; it had just occurred to him that the revolver was still in the drawer of his desk. It was better to act at once. Yet he continued to observe the prisoner, who, with the same slithery motion, put his feet on the ground, waited again, then began to stand up slowly. Daru was about to call out to him when the Arab began to walk, in a quite natural but extraordinarily silent way. He was heading toward the door at the end of the room that opened into the shed. He lifted the latch with precaution and went out, pushing the door behind him but without shutting it. Daru had not stirred. "He is running away," he merely thought. "Good riddance!" Yet he listened attentively. The hens were not fluttering; the guest must be on the plateau. A faint sound of water reached him, and he didn't know what it was until the Arab again stood framed in the doorway, closed the door carefully, and came back to bed without a sound. Then Daru turned his back on him and fell asleep. Still later he seemed, from the depths of his sleep, to hear furtive steps around the schoolhouse. "I'm dreaming! I'm dreaming!" he repeated to himself. And he went on sleeping.

100   When he awoke, the sky was clear; the loose window let in a cold, pure air. The Arab was asleep, hunched up under the blankets now, his mouth open, utterly relaxed. But when Daru shook him, he started dreadfully, staring at Daru with wild eyes as if he had never seen him and such a frightened expression that the schoolmaster stepped back. "Don't be afraid. It's me. You must eat." The Arab nodded his head and said yes. Calm had returned to his face, but his expression was vacant and listless.

The coffee was ready. They drank it seated together on the folding bed as they munched their pieces of the cake. Then Daru led the Arab under the shed and showed him the faucet where he washed. He went back into the room, folded the blankets and the bed, made his own bed and put the room in order. Then he went through the classroom and out onto the terrace. The sun was already rising in the blue sky; a soft, bright light was bathing the deserted plateau. On the ridge the snow was melting in spots. The stones were about to reappear. Crouched on the edge of the plateau, the schoolmaster looked at the deserted expanse. He thought of Balducci. He had hurt him, for he had sent him off in a way as if he didn't want to be associated with him. He could still hear the gendarme's farewell and, without knowing why, he felt strangely empty and vulnerable. At that moment, from the other side of the schoolhouse, the prisoner coughed. Daru listened to him almost despite himself and then, furious, threw a pebble that whistled through the air before sinking into the snow. That man's stupid crime revolted him, but to hand him over was contrary to honor. Merely thinking of it made him smart with humiliation. And he cursed at one and the same time his own people who had sent him this Arab and the Arab too who had dared to kill and not managed to get away. Daru got up, walked in a circle on the terrace, waited motionless, and then went back into the schoolhouse.

The Arab, leaning over the cement floor of the shed, was washing his teeth with two fingers. Daru looked at him and said: "Come." He went back into the room ahead of the prisoner. He slipped a hunting-jacket on over his sweater and put on walking-shoes. Standing, he waited until the Arab had put on his *chèche* and sandals. They went into the classroom and the school-master pointed to the exit, saying: "Go ahead." The fellow didn't budge. "I'm coming," said Daru. The Arab went out. Daru went back into the room and made a package of pieces of rusk, dates, and sugar. In the classroom, before going out, he hesitated a second in front of his desk, then crossed the threshold and locked the door. "That's the way," he said. He started toward the east, followed by the prisoner. But, a short distance from the schoolhouse, he thought he heard a slight sound behind them. He retraced his steps and examined the surroundings of the house; there was no one there. The Arab watched him without seeming to understand. "Come on," said Daru.

They walked for an hour and rested beside a sharp peak of limestone. The snow was melting faster and faster and the sun was drinking up the puddles at once, rapidly cleaning the plateau, which gradually dried and vibrated like the air itself. When they resumed walking, the ground rang under their feet. From time to time a bird rent the space in front of them with a joyful cry. Daru breathed in deeply the fresh morning light. He felt a sort of rapture before the vast familiar expanse, now almost entirely yellow under its dome of blue sky. They walked an hour more, descending toward the south. They reached a level height made up of crumbly rocks. From there on, the plateau sloped down, eastward, toward a low plain where there were a few spindly trees and, to the south, toward outcroppings of rock that gave the landscape a chaotic look.

Daru surveyed the two directions. There was nothing but the sky on the horizon. Not a man could be seen. He turned toward the Arab, who was looking at him blankly. Daru held out the package to him. "Take it," he said. "There are dates, bread, and sugar. You can hold out for two days. Here are a thousand francs too." The Arab took the package and the money but kept his full hands at chest level as if he didn't know what to do with what was being given him. "Now look," the schoolmaster said as he pointed in the direction of the east, "there's the way to Tinguit. You have a two-hour walk. At Tinguit you'll find the administration and the police. They are expecting you." The Arab looked toward the east, still holding the package and the money against his chest. Daru took his elbow and turned him rather roughly toward the south. At the foot of the height on which they stood could be seen a faint path. "That's the trail across the plateau. In a day's walk from here you'll find pasturelands and the first nomads. They'll take you in and shelter you according to their law." The Arab had now turned toward Daru and a sort of panic was visible in his expression. "Listen," he said. Daru shook his head: "No, be quiet. Now I'm leaving you." He turned his back on him, took two long steps in the direction of the school, looked hesitantly at the motionless Arab, and started off again. For a few minutes he heard nothing but his own step resounding on the cold ground and did not turn his head. A moment later, however, he turned around. The Arab was still there on the edge of the hill, his arms hanging now, and he was looking at the schoolmaster. Daru felt something rise in his throat. But he swore with impatience, waved vaguely, and started off again. He had already gone some distance when he again stopped and looked. There was no longer anyone on the hill.

Daru hesitated. The sun was now 105 rather high in the sky and was beginning to beat down on his head. The schoolmaster retraced his steps, at first somewhat uncertainly, then with decision. When he reached the little hill, he was bathed in sweat. He climbed it as fast as he could and stopped, out of breath, at the top. The rock-fields to the south stood out sharply against the blue sky, but on the plain to the east a steamy heat was already rising. And in that slight haze, Daru, with heavy heart, made out the Arab walking slowly on the road to prison.

A little later, standing before the window of the classroom, the schoolmaster was watching the clear light bathing the whole surface of the plateau, but he hardly saw it. Behind him on the blackboard, among the winding French rivers, sprawled the clumsily chalked-up words he had just read: "You handed over our brother. You will pay for this." Daru looked at the sky, the plateau, and, beyond, the invisible lands stretching all the way to the sea. In this vast landscape he had loved so much, he was alone.

······▶ *Your* Turn
Talking and Writing about Lit

1. Analyze Camus' use of plot in "The Guest." How has he arranged the order of scenes in the story to create suspense?

2. In what ways do Daru and Balducci serve as foil characters to one another? How is the contrast between these characters' worldviews instrumental in revealing the writer's themes?

3. Explain the various ways in which setting is used in the story to reveal important themes.

4. DIY Reread the passages in which Camus describes the plateau and the schoolhouse. Write a two-paragraph description of a place that is familiar to you, but use descriptive detail to make the place seem sinister or spooky.

Eudora Welty (1909–2001)

Eudora Welty was born in Jackson, Mississippi. She left her hometown temporarily to acquire her B.A. at the University of Wisconsin and then spent a year studying advertising at Columbia University Graduate School of Business. She returned afterward to Jackson where she spent the remainder of her life. Welty worked for a time as a journalist before settling into her remarkable career as a fiction writer. One of the foremost American short story writers of the twentieth century, she produced many story collections, including *A Curtain of Green* (1941), *The Wide Net* (1943), *Delta Wedding* (1946), and *The Golden Apples* (1949). Her novel *The Optimist's Daughter* was awarded the Pulitzer Prize in 1972. She also produced two works of nonfiction—*The Eye of the Story* (1977) and *One Writer's Beginnings* (1984)—which have been much cherished by those of us who love her stories and admire her mastery of the craft of fiction.

A Worn Path (1941)

It was December—a bright frozen day in the early morning. Far out in the country there was an old Negro woman with her head tied in a red rag, coming along a path through the pinewoods. Her name was Phoenix Jackson. She was very old and small and she walked slowly in the dark pine shadows, moving a little from side to side in her steps, with the balanced heaviness and lightness of a pendulum in a grandfather clock. She carried a thin, small cane made from an umbrella, and with this she kept tapping the frozen earth in front of her. This made a grave and persistent noise in the still air, that seemed meditative like the chirping of a solitary little bird.

She wore a dark striped dress reaching down to her shoe tops, and an equally long apron of bleached sugar sacks, with a full pocket: all neat and tidy, but every time she took a step she might have fallen over her shoelaces, which dragged from her unlaced shoes. She looked straight ahead. Her eyes were blue with age. Her skin had a pattern all its own of numberless branching wrinkles and as though a whole little tree stood in the middle of her forehead, but a golden color ran underneath, and the two knobs of her cheeks were illumined by a yellow burning under the dark. Under the red rag her hair came down on her neck in the frailest of ringlets, still black, and with an odor like copper.

Now and then there was a quivering in the thicket. Old Phoenix said, "Out of my way, all you foxes, owls, beetles, jack rabbits, coons and wild animals! . . . Keep out from under these feet, little bobwhites. . . . Keep the big wild hogs out of my path. Don't let none of those come running my direction. I got a long way." Under her small black-freckled hand her cane, limber as a buggy whip, would switch at the brush as if to rouse up any hiding things.

On she went. The woods were deep and still. The sun made the pine needles almost too bright to look at, up where the wind rocked. The cones dropped as light as feathers. Down in the hollow was the mourning dove—it was not too late for him.

5   The path ran up a hill. "Seem like there is chains about my feet, time I get this far," she said, in the voice of argument old people keep to use with themselves. "Something always take a hold of me on this hill—pleads I should stay."

After she got to the top she turned and gave a full, severe look behind her where she had come. "Up through pines," she said at length. "Now down through oaks."

Her eyes opened their widest, and she started down gently. But before she got to the bottom of the hill a bush caught her dress.

Her fingers were busy and intent, but her skirts were full and long, so that before she could pull them free in one place they were caught in another. It was not possible to allow the dress to tear. "I in the thorny bush," she said. "Thorns, you doing your appointed work. Never want to let folks pass, no sir. Old eyes thought you was a pretty little *green* bush."

Finally, trembling all over, she stood free, and after a moment dared to stoop for her cane.

"Sun so high!" she cried, leaning back 10 and looking, while the thick tears went over her eyes. "The time getting all gone here."

At the foot of this hill was a place where a log was laid across the creek.

"Now comes the trial," said Phoenix.

Putting her right foot out, she mounted the log and shut her eyes. Lifting her skirt, leveling her cane fiercely before her, like a festival figure in some parade, she began to march across. Then she opened her eyes and she was safe on the other side.

"I wasn't as old as I thought," she said.

But she sat down to rest. She spread her 15 skirts on the bank around her and folded her hands over her knees. Up above her was a tree in a pearly cloud of mistletoe. She did not dare to close her eyes, and when a little boy brought her a plate with a slice of marble-cake on it she spoke to him. "That would be acceptable," she said. But when she went to take it there was just her own hand in the air.

So she left that tree, and had to go through a barbed-wire fence. There she had to creep and crawl, spreading her knees and stretching her fingers like a baby trying to climb the steps. But she talked loudly to herself: she could not let her dress be torn now, so late in the day, and she could not pay for having her arm or her leg sawed off if she got caught fast where she was.

At last she was safe through the fence and risen up out in the clearing. Big dead trees, like black men with one arm, were standing in the purple stalks of the withered cotton field. There sat a buzzard.

"Who you watching?"

In the furrow she made her way along.

"Glad this not the season for bulls," 20 she said, looking sideways, "and the good Lord made his snakes to curl up and sleep in the winter. A pleasure I don't see no two-headed snake coming around that tree, where it come once. It took a while to get by him, back in the summer."

She passed through the old cotton and went into a field of dead corn. It whispered and shook and was taller than her head. "Through the maze now," she said, for there was no path.

Then there was something tall, black, and skinny there, moving before her.

At first she took it for a man. It could have been a man dancing in the field. But she stood still and listened, and it did not make a sound. It was as silent as a ghost.

"Ghost," she said sharply, "who be you the ghost of? For I have heard of nary death close by."

25   But there was no answer—only the ragged dancing in the wind.

She shut her eyes, reached out her hand, and touched a sleeve. She found a coat and inside that an emptiness, cold as ice.

"You scarecrow," she said. Her face lighted. "I ought to be shut up for good," she said with laughter. "My senses is gone. I too old. I the oldest people I ever know. Dance, old scarecrow," she said, "while I dancing with you."

She kicked her foot over the furrow, and with mouth drawn down, shook her head once or twice in a little strutting way. Some husks blew down and whirled in streamers about her skirts.

Then she went on, parting her way from side to side with the cane, through the whispering field. At last she came to the end, to a wagon track where the silver grass blew between the red ruts. The quail were walking around like pullets, seeming all dainty and unseen.

30   "Walk pretty," she said. "This the easy place. This the easy going."

She followed the track, swaying through the quiet bare fields, through the little strings of trees silver in their dead leaves, past cabins silver from weather, with the doors and windows boarded shut, all like old women under a spell sitting there. "I walking in their sleep," she said, nodding her head vigorously.

In a ravine she went where a spring was silently flowing through a hollow log. Old Phoenix bent and drank. "Sweet-gum makes the water sweet," she said, and drank more. "Nobody know who made this well, for it was here when I was born."

The track crossed a swampy part where the moss hung as white as lace from every limb. "Sleep on, alligators, and blow your bubbles." Then the track went into the road.

Deep, deep the road went down between the high green-colored banks. Overhead the live-oaks met, and it was as dark as a cave.

A black dog with a lolling tongue came   35 up out of the weeds by the ditch. She was meditating, and not ready, and when he came at her she only hit him a little with her cane. Over she went in the ditch, like a little puff of milkweed.

Down there, her senses drifted away. A dream visited her, and she reached her hand up, but nothing reached down and gave her a pull. So she lay there and presently went to talking. "Old woman," she said to herself, "that black dog come up out of the weeds to stall you off, and now there he sitting on his fine tail, smiling at you."

A white man finally came along and found her—a hunter, a young man, with his dog on a chain.

"Well, Granny!" he laughed. "What are you doing there?"

"Lying on my back like a June-bug waiting to be turned over, mister," she said, reaching up her hand.

He lifted her up, gave her a swing in   40 the air, and set her down. "Anything broken, Granny?"

"No sir, them old dead weeds is springy enough," said Phoenix, when she had got her breath. "I thank you for your trouble."

"Where do you live, Granny?" he asked, while the two dogs were growling at each other.

"Away back yonder, sir, behind the ridge. You can't even see it from here."

"On your way home?"

45   "No sir, I going to town."

"Why, that's too far! That's as far as I walk when I come out myself, and I get something for my trouble." He patted the stuffed bag he carried, and there hung down a little closed claw. It was one of the bob-whites, with its beak hooked bitterly to show it was dead. "Now you go on home, Granny!"

"I bound to go to town, mister," said Phoenix. "The time come around."

He gave another laugh, filling the whole landscape. "I know you old colored people! Wouldn't miss going to town to see Santa Claus!"

But something held old Phoenix very still. The deep lines in her face went into a fierce and different radiation. Without warning, she had seen with her own eyes a flashing nickel fall out of the man's pocket onto the ground.

50   "How old are you, Granny?" he was saying.

"There is no telling, mister," she said, "no telling."

Then she gave a little cry and clapped her hands and said, "Git on away from here, dog! Look! Look at that dog!" She laughed as if in admiration. "He ain't scared of nobody. He a big black dog." She whispered, "Sic him!"

"Watch me get rid of that cur," said the man. "Sic him, Pete! Sic him!"

Phoenix heard the dogs fighting, and heard the man running and throwing sticks. She even heard a gunshot. But she was slowly bending forward by that time, further and further forward, the lid stretched down over her eyes, as if she were doing this in her sleep. Her chin was lowered almost to her knees. The yellow palm of her hand came out from the fold of her apron. Her fingers slid down and along the ground under the piece of money with the grace and care they would have in lifting an egg from under a setting hen. Then she slowly straightened up, she stood erect, and the nickel was in her apron pocket. A bird flew by. Her lips moved. "God watching me the whole time. I come to stealing."

The man came back, and his own dog 55 panted about them. "Well, I scared him off that time," he said, and then he laughed and lifted his gun and pointed it at Phoenix.

She stood straight and faced him.

"Doesn't the gun scare you?" he said, still pointing it.

"No, sir, I seen plenty go off closer by, in my day, and for less than what I done," she said, holding utterly still.

He smiled, and shouldered the gun. "Well, Granny," he said, "you must be a hundred years old, and scared of nothing. I'd give you a dime if I had any money with me. But you take my advice and stay home, and nothing will happen to you."

"I bound to go on my way, mister," 60 said Phoenix. She inclined her head in the red rag. Then they went in different directions, but she could hear the gun shooting again and again over the hill.

She walked on. The shadows hung from the oak trees to the road like curtains. Then she smelled wood-smoke, and smelled the river, and she saw a steeple and the cabins on their steep steps. Dozens of little black children whirled around her. There ahead was Natchez shining. Bells were ringing. She walked on.

In the paved city it was Christmas time. There were red and green electric lights strung and crisscrossed everywhere, and all turned on in the daytime. Old Phoenix would have been lost if she had not distrusted her eyesight and depended on her feet to know where to take her.

She paused quietly on the sidewalk where people were passing by. A lady came along in the crowd, carrying an armful of red-, green-, and silver-wrapped presents;

she gave off perfume like the red roses in hot summer, and Phoenix stopped her.

"Please, missy, will you lace up my shoe?" She held up her foot.

65 "What do you want, Grandma?"

"See my shoe," said Phoenix. "Do all right for out in the country, but wouldn't look right to go in a big building."

"Stand still then, Grandma," said the lady. She put her packages down on the sidewalk beside her and laced and tied both shoes tightly.

"Can't lace 'em with a cane," said Phoenix. "Thank you, missy. I doesn't mind asking a nice lady to tie up my shoe, when I gets out on the street."

Moving slowly and from side to side, she went into the big building, and into a tower of steps, where she walked up and around and around until her feet knew to stop.

70 She entered a door, and there she saw nailed up on the wall the document that had been stamped with the gold seal and framed in the gold frame, which matched the dream that was hung up in her head.

"Here I be," she said. There was a fixed and ceremonial stiffness over her body.

"A charity case, I suppose," said an attendant who sat at the desk before her.

But Phoenix only looked above her head. There was sweat on her face, the wrinkles in her skin shone like a bright net.

"Speak up, Grandma," the woman said. "What's your name? We must have your history, you know. Have you been here before? What seems to be the trouble with you?"

75 Old Phoenix only gave a twitch to her face as if a fly were bothering her.

"Are you deaf?" cried the attendant.

But then the nurse came in.

"Oh, that's just old Aunt Phoenix," she said. "She doesn't come for herself—she has a little grandson. She makes these trips just as regular as clockwork. She lives away back off the Old Natchez Trace." She bent down. "Well, Aunt Phoenix, why don't you just take a seat? We won't keep you standing after your long trip." She pointed.

The old woman sat down, bolt upright in the chair.

"Now, how is the boy?" asked the 80 nurse.

Old Phoenix did not speak.

"I said, how is the boy?"

But Phoenix only waited and stared straight ahead, her face very solemn and withdrawn into rigidity.

"Is his throat any better?" asked the nurse. "Aunt Phoenix, don't you hear me? Is your grandson's throat any better since the last time you came for the medicine?"

With her hands on her knees, the old 85 woman waited, silent, erect and motionless, just as if she were in armor.

"You mustn't take up our time this way, Aunt Phoenix," the nurse said. "Tell us quickly about your grandson, and get it over. He isn't dead, is he?"

At last there came a flicker and then a flame of comprehension across her face, and she spoke.

"My grandson. It was my memory had left me. There I sat and forgot why I made my long trip."

"Forgot?" The nurse frowned. "After you came so far?"

Then Phoenix was like an old woman 90 begging a dignified forgiveness for waking up frightened in the night. "I never did go to school, I was too old at the Surrender," she said in a soft voice. "I'm an old woman without an education. It was my memory fail me. My little grandson, he is just the same, and I forgot it in the coming."

"Throat never heals, does it?" said the nurse, speaking in a loud, sure voice to old Phoenix. By now she had a card with something written on it, a little list. "Yes.

Swallowed lye. When was it?—January— two, three years ago—"

Phoenix spoke unasked now. "No, missy, he not dead, he just the same. Every little while his throat began to close up again, and he not able to swallow. He not get his breath. He not able to help himself. So the time come around, and I go on another trip for the soothing medicine."

"All right. The doctor said as long as you came to get it, you could have it," said the nurse. "But it's an obstinate case."

"My little grandson, he sit up there in the house all wrapped up, waiting by himself," Phoenix went on. "We is the only two left in the world. He suffer and it don't seem to put him back at all. He got a sweet look. He going to last. He wear a little patch quilt and peep out holding his mouth open like a little bird. I remembers so plain now. I not going to forget him again, no, the whole enduring time. I could tell him from all the others in creation."

95   "All right." The nurse was trying to hush her now. She brought her a bottle of medicine. "Charity," she said, making a check mark in a book.

Old Phoenix held the bottle close to her eyes, and then carefully put it into her pocket.

"I thank you," she said.

"It's Christmas time, Grandma," said the attendant. "Could I give you a few pennies out of my purse?"

"Five pennies is a nickel," said Phoenix stiffly.

"Here's a nickel," said the attendant.   100

Phoenix rose carefully and held out her hand. She received the nickel and then fished the other nickel out of her pocket and laid it beside the new one. She stared at her palm closely, with her head on one side.

Then she gave a tap with her cane on the floor.

"This is what come to me to do," she said. "I going to the store and buy my child a little windmill they sells, made out of paper. He going to find it hard to believe there such a thing in the world. I'll march myself back where he waiting, holding it straight up in this hand."

She lifted her free hand, gave a little nod, turned around, and walked out of the doctor's office. Then her slow step began on the stairs, going down.

⸱⸱⸱⸱⸱➤ *Your* **Turn**
Talking and Writing about Lit

1. How is the character of Phoenix Jackson revealed through the use of setting in the story?

2. Why has the author chosen to have the story take place in winter? How does this choice of season serve Welty's purposes in terms of what she wants to show in the story?

3. **DIY** Write a two-page account of a "journey quest" of your own. This might be the story of a "mock quest" or humorous "quest" to the shopping mall to get an item of clothing for a Saturday night party, or it might be a serious quest with a great deal at stake. Your account may be factual or fictional, or a mix of the two.

FROM PAGE TO SCREEN

Physical and Social Setting

The obstacles in the physical landscape are many for Phoenix Jackson in "A Worn Path." Here we see her about to cross the creek on a fallen tree, but she also overcomes thorn bushes, dogs, a scarecrow, a hunter who points his gun at her, and, at the end, the steep stairs to the doctor's office.

Phoenix at the start of her journey from the Wadsworth production of "A Worn Path."

Sherman Alexie (b. 1966)

Sherman Alexie, a Native American from the Spokane/Coeur d'Alene tribe, was born and raised on the Spokane Reservation in Wellpinit, Washington. Alexie has published several books of poetry, including the award-winning *The Business of Fancydancing* (1992). He has also published two novels, *Reservation Blues* (1995) and *Indian Killer* (1996), both of which have received prizes and awards. Alexie's short story collection *The Lone Ranger and Tonto Fistfight in Heaven* (1993) has been produced as the film *Smoke Signals* (1998), which won two awards at the prestigious Sundance Film Festival. Alexie wrote the screenplay for *Smoke Signals* himself. During his school years, Alexie overcame serious learning disabilities and physical difficulties resulting from fetal alcohol syndrome caused by his parents' alcoholism. His love of language and reading helped him triumph over his disabilities to become one of our most prominent contemporary American writers.

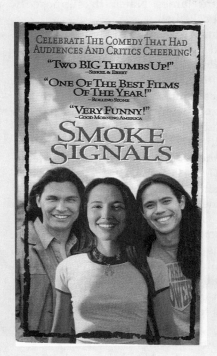

In *Smoke Signals*, the obstacles are more social than physical. That is, the dramatic tensions of the story hinge on the interaction between characters within a social context, and Alexie builds the viewer's understanding that we are watching more than just the lives of the individual characters; we are watching a film that attempts to depict for everyone a sense of the reservation's social realities and a sense of the reservation community's position within the social context of America as a whole. At the same time, as the video cover here shows, friendship and fun are not overlooked.

Smoke Signals is a Miramax film based on Sherman Alexie's short story collection *The Lone Ranger and Tonto Fistfight in Heaven;* screenplay by Sherman Alexie. *Smoke Signals* won two awards at the prestigious Sundance Film Festival.

The Only Traffic Signal on the Reservation Doesn't Flash Red Anymore (1993)

"**G**o ahead," Adrian said. "Pull the trigger."

I held a pistol to my temple. I was sober but wished I was drunk enough to pull the trigger.

"Go for it," Adrian said. "You chicken-shit."

While I still held that pistol to my temple, I used my other hand to flip Adrian off. Then I made a fist with my third hand to gather a little bit of courage or stupidity, and wiped sweat from my forehead with my fourth hand.

"Here," Adrian said. "Give me the damn thing." 5

Adrian took the pistol, put the barrel in his mouth, smiled around the metal, and pulled the trigger. Then he cussed wildly, laughed, and spit out the BB.

"Are you dead yet?" I asked.

"Nope," he said. "Not yet. Give me another beer."

"Hey, we don't drink no more, remember? How about a Diet Pepsi?"

"That's right, enit? I forgot. Give me a Pepsi." 10

Adrian and I sat on the porch and watched the reservation. Nothing happened. From our chairs made rockers by unsteady legs, we could see that the only traffic signal on the reservation had stopped working.

"Hey, Victor," Adrian asked. "Now when did that thing quit flashing?"

"Don't know," I said.

It was summer. Hot. But we kept our shirts on to hide our beer bellies and chicken-pox scars. At least, I wanted to hide my beer belly. I was a former basketball star fallen out of shape. It's always kind of sad when that happens. There's nothing more unattractive than a vain man, and that goes double for an Indian man.

15 "So," Adrian asked. "What you want to do today?"

"Don't know."

We watched a group of Indian boys walk by. I'd like to think there were ten of them. But there were actually only four or five. They were skinny, darkened by sun, their hair long and wild. None of them looked like they had showered for a week.

Their smell made me jealous.

They were off to cause trouble somewhere, I'm sure. Little warriors looking for honor in some twentieth-century vandalism. Throw a few rocks through windows, kick a dog, slash a tire. Run like hell when the tribal cops drove slowly by the scene of the crime.

20 "Hey," Adrian asked. "Isn't that the Windmaker boy?"

"Yeah," I said and watched Adrian lean forward to study Julius Windmaker, the best basketball player on the reservation, even though he was only fifteen years old.

"He looks good," Adrian said.

"Yeah, he must not be drinking."

"Yet."

25 "Yeah, yet."

Julius Windmaker was the latest in a long line of reservation basketball heroes, going all the way back to Aristotle Polatkin, who was shooting jumpshots exactly one year before James Naismith supposedly invented basketball.

I'd only seen Julius play a few times, but he had that gift, that grace, those fingers like a goddamn medicine man. One time, when the tribal school traveled to Spokane to play this white high school team, Julius scored sixty-seven points and the Indians won by forty.

"I didn't know they'd be riding horses," I heard the coach of the white team say when I was leaving.

I mean, Julius was an artist, moody. A couple times he walked right off the court during the middle of a game because there wasn't enough competition. That's how he was. Julius could throw a crazy pass, surprise us all, and send it out of bounds. But nobody called it a turnover because we all knew that one of his teammates should've been there to catch the pass. We loved him.

"Hey, Julius," Adrian yelled from the 30 porch. "You ain't shit."

Julius and his friends laughed, flipped us off, and shook their tail feathers a little as they kept walking down the road. They all knew Julius was the best ballplayer on the reservation these days, maybe the best ever, and they knew Adrian was just confirming that fact.

It was easier for Adrian to tease Julius because he never really played basketball. He was more detached about the whole thing. But I used to be quite a ballplayer. Maybe not as good as some, certainly not as good as Julius, but I still felt that ache in my bones, that need to be better than everyone else. It's that need to be the best, that feeling of immortality, that drives a ballplayer. And when it disappears, for whatever reason, that ballplayer is never the same person, on or off the court.

I know when I lost it, that edge. During my senior year in high school we made it to the state finals. I'd been playing like crazy, hitting everything. It was like throwing rocks into the ocean from a little rowboat. I couldn't miss. Then, right before the championship game, we had our pregame meeting in the first-aid room of the college where the tournament was held every year.

It took a while for our coach to show up so we spent the time looking at these first-aid manuals. These books had all kinds of horrible injuries. Hands and feet smashed flat in printing presses, torn apart by lawn-mowers, burned and dismembered. Faces that had gone through windshields, dragged over gravel, split open by garden tools. The stuff was disgusting, but we kept looking, flipping through photograph after photograph, trading books, until we all wanted to throw up.

35   While I looked at those close-ups of death and destruction, I lost it. I think every-body in that room, everybody on the team, lost that feeling of immortality. We went out and lost the championship game by twenty points. I missed every shot I took. I missed everything.

"So," I asked Adrian. "You think Julius will make it all the way?"

"Maybe, maybe."

There's a definite history of reserva-tion heroes who never finish high school, who never finish basketball seasons. Hell, there's been one or two guys who played just a few minutes of one game, just enough to show what they could have been. And there's the famous case of Silas Sirius, who made one move and scored one basket in his entire basketball career. People still talk about it.

"Hey," I asked Adrian. "Remember Silas Sirius?"

40   "Hell," Adrian said. "Do I remember? I was there when he grabbed that defensive rebound, took a step, and flew the length of the court, did a full spin in midair, and then dunked that fucking ball. And I don't mean

it looked like he flew, or it was so beautiful it was almost like he flew. I mean, he flew, period."

I laughed, slapped my legs, and knew that I believed Adrian's story more as it sounded less true.

"Shit," he continued. "And he didn't grow no wings. He just kicked his legs a lit-tle. Held that ball like a baby in his hand. And he was smiling. Really. Smiling when he flew. Smiling when he dunked it, smiling when he walked off the court and never came back. Hell, he was still smiling ten years after that."

I laughed some more, quit for a sec-ond, then laughed a little longer because it was the right thing to do.

"Yeah," I said. "Silas was a ballplayer."

"Real ballplayer," Adrian agreed.   45

In the outside world, a person can be a hero one second and a nobody the next. Think about it. Do white people remember the names of those guys who dove into that icy river to rescue passengers from that plane wreck a few years back? Hell, white people don't even remember the names of the dogs who save entire families from burning up in house fires by barking. And, to be honest, I don't remember none of those names either, but a reservation hero is remembered. A reservation hero is a hero forever. In fact, their status grows over the years as the stories are told and retold.

"Yeah," Adrian said. "It's too bad that damn diabetes got him. Silas was always talking about a comeback."

"Too bad, too bad."

We both leaned further back into our chairs. Silence. We watched the grass grow, the rivers flow, the winds blow.

"Damn," Adrian asked. "When did   50 that fucking traffic signal quit working?"

"Don't know."

"Shit, they better fix it. Might cause an accident."

We both looked at each other, looked at the traffic signal, knew that about only one

car an hour passed by, and laughed our
asses off. Laughed so hard that when we
tried to rearrange ourselves, Adrian ended
up with my ass and I ended up with his.
That looked so funny that we laughed them
off again and it took us most of an hour to
get them back right again.

Then we heard glass breaking in the
distance.

55 "Sounds like beer bottles," Adrian
said.

"Yeah, Coors Light, I think."

"Bottled 1988."

We started to laugh, but a tribal cop
drove by and cruised down the road where
Julius and his friends had walked earlier.

"Think they'll catch them?" I asked
Adrian.

60 "Always do."

After a few minutes, the tribal cop
drove by again, with Julius in the backseat
and his friends running behind.

"Hey," Adrian asked. "What did he do?"

"Threw a brick through a BIA pickup's
windshield," one of the Indian boys yelled
back.

"Told you it sounded like a pickup
window," I said.

65 "Yeah, yeah, a 1982 Chevy."

"With red paint."

"No, blue."

We laughed for just a second. Then
Adrian sighed long and deep. He rubbed his
head, ran his fingers through his hair,
scratched his scalp hard.

"I think Julius is going to go bad," he
said.

70 "No way," I said. "He's just horsing
around."

"Maybe, maybe."

It's hard to be optimistic on the reservation. When a glass sits on a table here,
people don't wonder if it's half filled or half
empty. They just hope it's good beer. Still,
Indians have a way of surviving. But it's

almost like Indians can easily survive the
big stuff. Mass murder, loss of language and
land rights. It's the small things that hurt the
most. The white waitress who wouldn't take
an order, Tonto, the Washington Redskins.

And, just like everybody else, Indians
need heroes to help them learn how to survive. But what happens when our heroes
don't even know how to pay their bills?

"Shit, Adrian," I said. "He's just a kid."

"Ain't no children on a reservation." 75

"Yeah, yeah, I've heard that before.
Well," I said. "I guess that Julius is pretty
good in school, too."

"And?"

"And he wants to maybe go to college."

"Really?"

"Really," I said and laughed. And I 80
laughed because half of me was happy and
half of me wasn't sure what else to do.

A year later, Adrian and I sat on the
same porch in the same chairs. We'd done
things in between, like ate and slept and read
the newspaper. It was another hot summer.
Then again, summer is supposed to be hot.

"I'm thirsty," Adrian said. "Give me a
beer."

"How many times do I have to tell
you? We don't drink anymore."

"Shit," Adrian said. "I keep forgetting.
Give me a goddamn Pepsi."

"That's a whole case for you today 85
already."

"Yeah, yeah, fuck these substitute
addictions."

We sat there for a few minutes, hours,
and then Julius Windmaker staggered down
the road.

"Oh, look at that," Adrian said. "Not
even two in the afternoon and he's drunk as
a skunk."

"Don't he have a game tonight?"

"Yeah, he does." 90

"Well, I hope he sobers up in time."

"Me, too."

I'd only played one game drunk and it was in an all-Indian basketball tournament after I got out of high school. I'd been drinking that night before and woke up feeling kind of sick, so I got drunk again. Then I went out and played a game. I felt disconnected the whole time. Nothing seemed to fit right. Even my shoes, which had fit perfectly before, felt too big for my feet. I couldn't even see the basketball or basket clearly. They were more like ideas. I mean, I knew where they were generally supposed to be, so I guessed at where I should be. Somehow or another, I scored ten points.

"He's been drinking quite a bit, enit?" Adrian asked.

95   "Yeah, I hear he's even been drinking Sterno."

"Shit, that'll kill his brain quicker than shit."

Adrian and I left the porch that night and went to the tribal school to watch Julius play. He still looked good in his uniform, although he was a little puffy around the edges. But he just wasn't the ballplayer we remembered or expected. He missed shots, traveled, threw dumb passes that we all knew were dumb passes. By the fourth quarter, Julius sat at the end of the bench, hanging his head, and the crowd filed out, all talking about which of the younger players looked good. We talked about some kid named Lucy in the third grade who already had a nice move or two.

Everybody told their favorite Julius Windbreaker stories, too. Times like that, on a reservation, a basketball game felt like a funeral and wake all rolled up together.

Back at home, on the porch, Adrian and I sat wrapped in shawls because the evening was kind of cold.

100   "It's too bad, too bad," I said. "I thought Julius might be the one to make it all the way."

"I told you he wouldn't. I told you so."

"Yeah, yeah. Don't rub it in."

We sat there in silence and remembered all of our heroes, ballplayers from seven generations, all the way back. It hurts to lose any of them because Indians kind of see ballplayers as saviors. I mean, if basketball would have been around, I'm sure Jesus Christ would've been the best point guard in Nazareth. Probably the best player in the entire world. And in the beyond. I just can't explain how much losing Julius Windmaker hurt us all.

"Well," Adrian asked. "What do you want to do tomorrow?"

"Don't know."   105

"Shit, that damn traffic signal is still broken. Look."

Adrian pointed down the road and he was right. But what's the point of fixing it in a place where the STOP signs are just suggestions?

"What time is it?" Adrian asked.

"I don't know. Ten, I think."

"Let's go somewhere."   110

"Where?"

"I don't know, Spokane, anywhere. Let's just go."

"Okay," I said, and we both walked inside the house, shut the door, and locked it tight. No. We left it open just a little bit in case some crazy Indian needed a place to sleep. And in the morning we found crazy Julius passed out on the living room carpet.

"Hey, you bum," Adrian yelled. "Get off my floor."

"This is my house, Adrian," I said.   115

"That's right. I forgot. Hey, you bum, get your ass off Victor's floor."

Julius groaned and farted but he didn't wake up. It really didn't bother Adrian that Julius was on the floor, so he threw an old blanket on top of him. Adrian and I grabbed our morning coffee and went back out to sit on the porch. We had both just about finished our cups when a group of Indian kids walked by, all holding basketballs of various shapes and conditions.

"Hey, look," Adrian said. "Ain't that the Lucy girl?"

I saw that it was, a little brown girl with scarred knees, wearing her daddy's shirt.

120 "Yeah, that's her," I said.

"I heard she's so good that she plays for the sixth grade boys team."

"Really? She's only in the third grade herself, isn't she?"

"Yeah, yeah, she's a little warrior."

Adrian and I watched those Indian children walk down the road, walking toward another basketball game.

"God, I hope she makes it all the way," 125 I said.

"Yeah, yeah," Adrian said, stared into the bottom of his cup, and then threw it across the yard. And we both watched it with all of our eyes, while the sun rose straight up above us and settled down behind the house, watched the cup revolve, revolve, until it came down whole to the ground.

····· ▶ *Your* **Turn**
Talking and Writing about Lit

1. The social and physical settings in "The Only Traffic Signal on the Reservation Doesn't Flash Red Anymore" are carefully described to reveal several themes. The story also operates in two time periods. Why is it important that the story is set in two different time periods?

2. Despite its rather serious themes, this is a story which makes unusual use of humor and hyperbole (the use of overstatement or exaggeration—sometimes for comic effects). Illustrate the use of humorous exaggeration in Alexie's story.

3. **DIY** In the second question above, we have referred to Alexie's use of humor and hyperbole. Write a scene of your own in which you retell an incident that happened to you or to a friend, using wild exaggeration to achieve a humorous effect. Your exaggerated details may be humorous or they may be spooky.

F. Scott Fitzgerald (1896–1940)

F. Scott Fitzgerald was born in St. Paul, Minnesota. Fitzgerald attended Princeton University but did not graduate; instead, he joined the army in 1917. When he returned to civilian life, he began to enjoy success as a writer, publishing *This Side of Paradise* (1920) and then *The Great Gatsby* (1925), his greatest novel. Later came the novels *Tender Is the Night* (1934) and *The Last Tycoon* (1940), which was published posthumously after Fitzgerald died of a heart attack. Fitzgerald also published nearly 160 short stories.

Babylon[1] Revisited (1931)

I

And where's Mr. Campbell?" Charlie asked.

"Gone to Switzerland. Mr. Campbell's a pretty sick man, Mr. Wales."

"I'm sorry to hear that. And George Hardt?" Charlie inquired.

"Back in America, gone to work."

5 "And where is the Snow Bird?"

"He was in here last week. Anyway, his friend, Mr. Schaeffer, is in Paris."

Two familiar names from the long list of a year and a half ago. Charlie scribbled an address in his notebook and tore out the page.

"If you see Mr. Schaeffer, give him this," he said. "It's my brother-in-law's address. I haven't settled on a hotel yet."

He was not really disappointed to find Paris was so empty. But the stillness in the Ritz bar[2] was strange and portentous. It was not an American bar any more—he felt polite in it, and not as if he owned it. It had gone back into France. He felt the stillness from the moment he got out of the taxi and saw the doorman, usually in a frenzy of activity at this hour, gossiping with a *chasseur*[3] by the servants' entrance.

10 Passing through the corridor, he heard only a single, bored voice in the once-clamorous women's room. When he turned into the bar he traveled the twenty feet of green carpet with his eyes fixed straight ahead by old habit; and then, with his foot firmly on the rail, he turned and surveyed the room, encountering only a single pair of eyes that fluttered up from a newspaper in the corner. Charlie asked for the head barman, Paul, who in the latter days of the bull market[4] had come to work in his own custom-built car—disembarking, however, with due nicety at the nearest corner. But Paul was at his country house today and Alix giving him information.

"No, no more," Charlie said, "I'm going slow these days."

Alix congratulated him: "You were going pretty strong a couple of years ago."

"I'll stick to it all right," Charlie assured him. "I've stuck to it for over a year and a half now."

"How do you find conditions in America?" 15

"I haven't been to America for months. I'm in business in Prague, representing a couple of concerns there. They don't know about me down there."

Alix smiled.

"Remember the night of George Hardt's bachelor dinner here?" said Charlie. "By the way, what's become of Claude Fessenden?"

Alix lowered his voice confidentially: "He's in Paris, but he doesn't come here any more. Paul doesn't allow it. He ran up a bill of thirty thousand francs, charging all his drinks and his lunches, and usually his dinner, for more than a year. And when Paul finally told him he had to pay, he gave him a bad check."

Alix shook his head sadly.

"I don't understand it, such a dandy 20 fellow. Now he's all bloated up—" He made a plump apple of his hands.

---

[1]**Babylon:** This ancient city is a symbol of orgiastic decadence.
[2]**Ritz Bar:** Hangout for wealthy and glamorous Americans.
[3]*chasseur*: Hotel servant who runs various errands (French).

[4]**bull market:** The period of prosperity for players of the stock market that immediately preceded the crash of 1929, which was the beginning of the Great Depression.

Charlie watched a group of strident queens installing themselves in a corner.

"Nothing affects them," he thought. "Stocks rise and fall, people loaf or work, but they go on forever." The place oppressed him. He called for the dice and shook with Alix for the drink.

"Here for long, Mr. Wales?"

"I'm here for four or five days to see my little girl."

25　"Oh-h! You have a little girl?"

Outside, the fire-red, gas-blue, ghost-green signs shone smokily through the tranquil rain. It was late afternoon and the streets were in movement; the *bistros*[5] gleamed. At the corner of the Boulevard des Capucines he took a taxi. The Place de la Concorde moved by in pink majesty; they crossed the logical Seine, and Charlie felt the sudden provincial quality of the Left Bank.[6]

Charlie directed his taxi to the Avenue de l'Opéra, which was out of his way. But he wanted to see the blue hour spread over the magnificent façade, and imagine that the cab horns, playing endlessly the first few bars of *Le Plus que Lent*, were the trumpets of the Second Empire.[7] They were closing the iron grill in front of Brentano's Book-store, and people were already at dinner behind the trim little bourgeois hedge of Duval's. He had never eaten at a really cheap restaurant in Paris. Five-course dinner, four francs fifty, eighteen cents, wine included. For some odd reason he wished that he had.

As they rolled on to the Left Bank and he felt its sudden provincialism, he thought, "I spoiled this city for myself. I didn't realize it, but the days came along one after another, and then two years were gone, and everything was gone, and I was gone."

He was thirty-five, and good to look at. The Irish mobility of his face was sobered by a deep wrinkle between his eyes. As he rang his brother-in-law's bell in the Rue Palatine, the wrinkle deepened till it pulled down his brows; he felt a cramping sensation in his belly. From behind the maid who opened the door darted a lovely little girl of nine who shrieked "Daddy!" and flew up, struggling like a fish, into his arms. She pulled his head around by one ear and set her cheek against his.

"My old pie," he said.　　　　　　30

"Oh, daddy, daddy, daddy, daddy, dads, dads, dads!"

She drew him into the salon, where the family waited, a boy and a girl his daughter's age, his sister-in-law and her husband. He greeted Marion with his voice pitched carefully to avoid either feigned enthusiasm or dislike, but her response was more frankly tepid, though she minimized her expression of unalterable distrust by directing her regard toward his child. The two men clasped hands in a friendly way and Lincoln Peters rested his for a moment on Charlie's shoulder.

The room was warm and comfortably American. The three children moved intimately about, playing through the yellow oblongs that led to other rooms; the cheer of six o'clock spoke in the eager smacks of the fire and the sounds of French activity in the kitchen. But Charlie did not relax; his heart sat up rigidly in his body and he drew confidence from his daughter, who from time to time came close to him, holding in her arms the doll he had brought.

"Really extremely well," he declared in answer to Lincoln's question. "There's a lot

---

[5] ***bistros:*** Small cafés.

[6] **Left Bank:** South side of the Seine River; site of the student quarter and in recent tradition the Bohemian part of Paris.

[7] **Second Empire:** I.e., that of Louis Napoleon of France (1852–70), a period of bourgeois ostentation, which seemed, in retrospect, glamorous. "*Le Plus que Lent*": slower than slow (French); refers to the parodistic piano composition (*Le Plus que Lente*) by Claude Debussy (1882–1918).

of business there that isn't moving at all, but we're doing even better than ever. In fact, damn well. I'm bringing my sister over from America next month to keep house for me. My income last year was bigger than it was when I had money. You see, the Czechs—"

His boasting was for a specific purpose; but after a moment, seeing a faint restiveness in Lincoln's eye, he changed the subject:

"Those are fine children of yours, well brought up, good manners."

"We think Honoria's a great little girl too."

Marion Peters came back from the kitchen. She was a tall woman with worried eyes, who had once possessed a fresh American loveliness. Charlie had never been sensitive to it and was always surprised when people spoke of how pretty she had been. From the first there had been an instinctive antipathy between them.

"Well, how do you find Honoria?" she asked.

"Wonderful. I was astonished how much she's grown in ten months. All the children are looking well."

"We haven't had a doctor for a year. How do you like being back in Paris?"

"It seems very funny to see so few Americans around."

"I'm delighted," Marion said vehemently. "Now at least you can go into a store without their assuming you're a millionaire. We've suffered like everybody, but on the whole it's a good deal pleasanter."

"But it was nice while it lasted," Charlie said. "We were a sort of royalty, almost infallible, with a sort of magic around us. In the bar this afternoon"—he stumbled, seeing his mistake—"there wasn't a man I knew."

She looked at him keenly. "I should think you'd have had enough of bars."

"I only stayed a minute. I take one drink every afternoon, and no more."

"Don't you want a cocktail before dinner?" Lincoln asked.

"I take only one drink every afternoon, and I've had that."

"I hope you keep to it," said Marion.

Her dislike was evident in the coldness with which she spoke, but Charlie only smiled; he had larger plans. Her very aggressiveness gave him an advantage, and he knew enough to wait. He wanted them to initiate the discussion of what they knew had brought him to Paris.

At dinner he couldn't decide whether Honoria was most like him or her mother. Fortunate if she didn't combine the traits of both that had brought them to disaster. A great wave of protectiveness went over him. He thought he knew what to do for her. He believed in character; he wanted to jump back a whole generation and trust in character again as the eternally valuable element. Everything else wore out.

He left soon after dinner, but not to go home. He was curious to see Paris by night with clearer and more judicious eyes than those of other days. He bought a *strapontin* for the Casino and watched Josephine Baker[8] go through her chocolate arabesques.

After an hour he left and strolled toward Montmartre, up the Rue Pigalle into the Place Blanche. The rain had stopped and there were a few people in evening clothes disembarking from taxis in front of cabarets, and *cocottes*[9] prowling singly or in pairs, and many Negroes. He passed a lighted door from which issued music, and stopped with the sense of familiarity; it was Bricktop's, where he had parted with so many hours and so much money. A few doors farther on he found

---

[8]**Josephine Baker:** A celebrated black dancer of the epoch. "*Strapontin*": a bracket seat in the aisle, cheaper than regular seats.
[9]***cocottes:*** Prostitutes who flourish on the Boulevard Clichy between Pigalle and Place Blanche. Montmartre is a district in northern Paris.

another ancient rendezvous and incautiously put his head inside. Immediately an eager orchestra burst into sound, a pair of professional dancers leaped to their feet and a maître d'hôtel swooped toward him, crying, "Crowd just arriving, sir!" But he withdrew quickly.

"You have to be damn drunk," he thought.

55 Zelli's was closed, the bleak and sinister cheap hotels surrounding it were dark; up in the Rue Blanche there was more light and a local, colloquial French crowd. The Poet's Cave had disappeared, but the two great mouths of the Café of Heaven and the Café of Hell still yawned—even devoured, as he watched, the meager contents of a tourist bus—a German, a Japanese, and an American couple who glanced at him with frightened eyes.

So much for the effort and ingenuity of Montmartre. All the catering to vice and waste was on an utterly childish scale, and he suddenly realized the meaning of the word "dissipate"—to dissipate into thin air; to make nothing out of something. In the little hours of the night every move from place to place was an enormous human jump, an increase of paying for the privilege of slower and slower motion.

He remembered thousand-franc notes given to an orchestra for playing a single number, hundred-franc notes tossed to a doorman for calling a cab.

But it hadn't been given for nothing.

It had been given, even the most wildly squandered sum, as an offering to destiny that he might not remember the things most worth remembering, the things that now he would always remember—his child taken from his control, his wife escaped to a grave in Vermont.

60 In the glare of a *brasserie*[1] a woman spoke to him. He bought her some eggs and coffee, and then, eluding her encouraging stare, gave her a twenty-franc note and took a taxi to his hotel.

II

He woke upon a fine fall day—football weather. The depression of yesterday was gone and he liked the people on the streets. At noon he sat opposite Honoria at Le Grand Vatel, the only restaurant he could think of not reminiscent of champagne dinners and long luncheons that began at two and ended in a blurred and vague twilight.

"Now, how about vegetables? Oughtn't you to have some vegetables?"

"Well, yes."

"Here's *épinards* and *chou-fleur* and carrots and *haricots*."[2]

"I'd like *chou-fleur*."   65

"Wouldn't you like to have two vegetables?"

"I usually only have one at lunch."

The waiter was pretending to be inordinately fond of children. "*Qu'elle est mignonne la petite! Elle parle exactement comme une Française.*"[3]

"How about dessert? Shall we wait and see?"

The waiter disappeared. Honoria 70 looked at her father expectantly.

"What are we going to do?"

"First, we're going to that toy store in the Rue Saint-Honoré and buy you anything you like. And then we're going to the vaudeville at the Empire."

She hesitated. "I like it about the vaudeville, but not the toy store."

"Why not?"

"Well, you brought me this doll." She 75 had it with her. "And I've got lots of things. And we're not rich any more, are we?"

----

[1]*brasserie:* Small restaurant (French) that also serves drinks.

[2]*haricots:* Beans (French). "*Épinards*": spinach (French). "*Chou-fleur*": cauliflower (French).
[3]*"Qu'elle est . . . comme une Française:* What a darling little girl! She speaks exactly like a French girl (French).

"We never were. But today you are to have anything you want."

"All right," she agreed resignedly.

When there had been her mother and a French nurse he had been inclined to be strict; now he extended himself, reached out for a new tolerance; he must be both parents to her and not shut any of her out of communication.

"I want to get to know you," he said gravely. "First let me introduce myself. My name is Charles J. Wales, of Prague."

80 "Oh, daddy!" her voice cracked with laughter.

"And who are you, please?" he persisted, and she accepted a rôle immediately: "Honoria Wales, Rue Palatine, Paris."

"Married or single?"

"No, not married. Single."

He indicated the doll. "But I see you have a child, madame."

85 Unwilling to disinherit it, she took it to her heart and thought quickly: "Yes, I've been married, but I'm not married now. My husband is dead."

He went on quickly, "And the child's name?"

"Simone. That's after my best friend at school."

"I'm very pleased that you're doing so well at school."

"I'm third this month," she boasted. "Elsie"—that was her cousin—"is only about eighteenth, and Richard is about at the bottom."

90 "You like Richard and Elsie, don't you?"

"Oh, yes. I like Richard quite well and I like her all right."

Cautiously and casually he asked: "And Aunt Marion and Uncle Lincoln— which do you like best?"

"Oh, Uncle Lincoln, I guess."

He was increasingly aware of her presence. As they came in, a murmur of " . . . adorable" followed them, and now the people at the next table bent all their silences upon her, staring as if she were something no more conscious than a flower.

"Why don't I live with you?" she 95 asked suddenly. "Because mamma's dead?"

"You must stay here and learn more French. It would have been hard for daddy to take care of you so well."

"I don't really need much taking care of any more. I do everything for myself."

Going out of the restaurant, a man and a woman unexpectedly hailed him.

"Well, the old Wales!"

"Hello there, Lorraine. . . . Dunc." 100

Sudden ghosts out of the past: Duncan Schaeffer, a friend from college.

Lorraine Quarrles, a lovely, pale blonde of thirty; one of a crowd who had helped them make months into days in the lavish times of three years ago.

"My husband couldn't come this year," she said, in answer to his question. "We're poor as hell. So he gave me two hundred a month and told me I could do my worst on that. . . . This your little girl?"

"What about coming back and sitting down?" Duncan asked.

"Can't do it." He was glad for an 105 excuse. As always, he felt Lorraine's passionate, provocative attraction, but his own rhythm was different now.

"Well, how about dinner?" she asked.

"I'm not free. Give me your address and let me call you."

"Charlie, I believe you're sober," she said judicially. "I honestly believe he's sober, Dunc. Pinch him and see if he's sober."

Charlie indicated Honoria with his head. They both laughed.

"What's your address?" said Duncan 110 skeptically.

He hesitated, unwilling to give the name of his hotel.

"I'm not settled yet. I'd better call you. We're going to see the vaudeville at the Empire."

"There! That's what I want to do," Lorraine said. "I want to see some clowns and acrobats and jugglers. That's just what we'll do, Dunc."

"We've got to do an errand first," said Charlie. "Perhaps we'll see you there."

115 "All right, you snot. . . . Good-by, beautiful little girl."

"Good-by."

Honoria bobbed politely.

Somehow, an unwelcome encounter. They liked him because he was functioning, because he was serious; they wanted to see him, because he was stronger than they were now, because they wanted to draw a certain sustenance from his strength.

At the Empire, Honoria proudly refused to sit upon her father's folded coat. She was already an individual with a code of her own, and Charlie was more and more absorbed by the desire of putting a little of himself into her before she crystallized utterly. It was hopeless to try to know her in so short a time.

120 Between the acts they came upon Duncan and Lorraine in the lobby where the band was playing.

"Have a drink?"

"All right, but not up at the bar. We'll take a table."

"The perfect father."

Listening abstractedly to Lorraine, Charlie watched Honoria's eyes leave their table, and he followed them wistfully about the room, wondering what they saw. He met her glance and she smiled.

125 "I liked that lemonade," she said.

What had she said? What had he expected? Going home in a taxi afterward, he pulled her over until her head rested against his chest.

"Darling, do you ever think about your mother?"

"Yes, sometimes," she answered vaguely.

"I don't want you to forget her. Have you got a picture of her?"

"Yes, I think so. Anyhow, Aunt Marion 130 has. Why don't you want me to forget her?"

"She loved you very much."

"I loved her too."

They were silent for a moment.

"Daddy, I want to come and live with you," she said suddenly.

His heart leaped; he had wanted it to 135 come like this.

"Aren't you perfectly happy?"

"Yes, but I love you better than anybody. And you love me better than anybody, don't you, now that mummy's dead?"

"Of course I do. But you won't always like me best, honey. You'll grow up and meet somebody your own age and go marry him and forget you ever had a daddy."

"Yes, that's true," she agreed tranquilly.

He didn't go in. He was coming back at 140 nine o'clock and he wanted to keep himself fresh and new for the thing he must say then.

"When you're safe inside, just show yourself in that window."

"All right. Good-by, dads, dads, dads, dads."

He waited in the dark street until she appeared, all warm and glowing, in the window above and kissed her fingers out into the night.

III

They were waiting. Marion sat behind the coffee service in a dignified black dinner dress that just faintly suggested mourning. Lincoln was walking up and down with the animation of one who had already been talking. They were as anxious as he was to get into the question. He opened it almost immediately:

"I suppose you know what I want to 145 see you about—why I really came to Paris."

Marion played with the black stars on her necklace and frowned.

"I'm awfully anxious to have a home," he continued. "And I'm awfully anxious to have Honoria in it. I appreciate your taking in Honoria for her mother's sake, but things have changed now"—he hesitated and then continued more forcibly—"changed radically with me, and I want to ask you to reconsider the matter. It would be silly for me to deny that about three years ago I was acting badly—"

Marion looked up at him with hard eyes.

"—but all that's over. As I told you, I haven't had more than a drink a day for over a year, and I take that drink deliberately, so that the idea of alcohol won't get too big in my imagination. You see the idea?"

150 "No," said Marion succinctly.

"It's a sort of stunt I set myself. It keeps the matter in proportion."

"I get you," said Lincoln. "You don't want to admit it's got any attraction for you."

"Something like that. Sometimes I forget and don't take it. But I try to take it. Anyhow, I couldn't afford to drink in my position. The people I represent are more than satisfied with what I've done, and I'm bringing my sister over from Burlington to keep house for me, and I want awfully to have Honoria too. You know that even when her mother and I weren't getting along well we never let anything that happened touch Honoria. I know she's fond of me and I know I'm able to take care of her and—well, there you are. How do you feel about it?"

He knew that now he would have to take a beating. It would last an hour or two hours, and it would be difficult, but if he modulated his inevitable resentment to the chastened attitude of the reformed sinner, he might win his point in the end.

155 Keep your temper, he told himself. You don't want to be justified. You want Honoria.

Lincoln spoke first: "We've been talking it over ever since we got your letter last month. We're happy to have Honoria here. She's a dear little thing, and we're glad to be able to help her, but of course that isn't the question—"

Marion interrupted suddenly. "How long are you going to stay sober, Charlie?" she asked.

"Permanently, I hope."

"How can anybody count on that?"

"You know I never did drink heavily 160 until I gave up business and came over here with nothing to do. Then Helen and I began to run around with—"

"Please leave Helen out of it. I can't bear to hear you talk about her like that."

He stared at her grimly; he had never been certain how fond of each other the sisters were in life.

"My drinking only lasted about a year and a half—from the time we came over until I—collapsed."

"It was time enough."

"It was time enough," he agreed. 165

"My duty is entirely to Helen," she said. "I try to think what she would have wanted me to do. Frankly, from the night you did that terrible thing you haven't really existed for me. I can't help that. She was my sister."

"Yes."

"When she was dying she asked me to look out for Honoria. If you hadn't been in a sanitarium then, it might have helped matters."

He had no answer.

"I'll never in my life be able to forget 170 the morning when Helen knocked at my door, soaked to the skin and shivering, and said you'd locked her out."

Charlie gripped the sides of the chair. This was more difficult than he expected; he wanted to launch out into a long expostulation and explanation, but he only said: "The night I locked her out—" and she interrupted, "I don't feel up to going over that again."

After a moment's silence Lincoln said: "We're getting off the subject. You want Marion to set aside her legal guardianship and give you Honoria. I think the main point for her is whether she has confidence in you or not."

"I don't blame Marion," Charlie said slowly, "but I think she can have entire confidence in me. I had a good record up to three years ago. Of course, it's within human possibilities I might go wrong any time. But if we wait much longer I'll lose Honoria's childhood and my chance for a home." He shook his head, "I'll simply lose her, don't you see?"

"Yes, I see," said Lincoln.

175 "Why didn't you think of all this before?" Marion asked.

"I suppose I did, from time to time, but Helen and I were getting along badly. When I consented to the guardianship, I was flat on my back in a sanitarium and the market had cleaned me out. I knew I'd acted badly, and I thought if it would bring any peace to Helen, I'd agree to anything. But now it's different. I'm functioning, I'm behaving damn well, so far as—"

"Please don't swear at me," Marion said.

He looked at her, startled. With each remark the force of her dislike became more and more apparent. She had built up all her fear of life into one wall and faced it toward him. This trivial reproof was possibly the result of some trouble with the cook several hours before. Charlie became increasingly alarmed at leaving Honoria in this atmosphere of hostility against himself; sooner or later it would come out, in a word here, a shake of the head there, and some of that distrust would be irrevocably implanted in Honoria. But he pulled his temper down out of his face and shut it up inside him; he had

won a point, for Lincoln realized the absurdity of Marion's remark and asked her lightly since when she had objected to the word "damn."

"Another thing," Charlie said: "I'm able to give her certain advantages now. I'm going to take a French governess to Prague with me. I've got a lease on a new apartment—"

He stopped, realizing that he was blundering. They couldn't be expected to accept with equanimity the fact that his income was again twice as large as their own.

"I suppose you can give her more luxuries than we can," said Marion. "When you were throwing away money we were living along watching every ten francs. . . . I suppose you'll start doing it again."

"Oh, no," he said. "I've learned. I worked hard for ten years, you know—until I got lucky in the market, like so many people. Terribly lucky. It won't happen again."

There was a long silence. All of them felt their nerves straining, and for the first time in a year Charlie wanted a drink. He was sure now that Lincoln Peters wanted him to have his child.

Marion shuddered suddenly; part of her saw that Charlie's feet were planted on the earth now, and her own maternal feeling recognized the naturalness of his desire; but she had lived for a long time with a prejudice—a prejudice founded on a curious disbelief in her sister's happiness, and which, in the shock of one terrible night, had turned to hatred for him. It had all happened at a point in her life where the discouragement of ill health and adverse circumstances made it necessary for her to believe in tangible villainy and a tangible villain.

"I can't help what I think!" she cried out suddenly. "How much you were responsible for Helen's death, I don't know. It's something you'll have to square with your own conscience."

180

185

An electric current of agony surged through him; for a moment he was almost on his feet, an unuttered sound echoing in his throat. He hung on to himself for a moment, another moment.

"Hold on there," said Lincoln uncomfortably. "I never thought you were responsible for that."

"Helen died of heart trouble," Charlie said dully.

"Yes, heart trouble." Marion spoke as if the phrase had another meaning for her.

190　Then, in the flatness that followed her outburst, she saw him plainly and she knew he had somehow arrived at control over the situation. Glancing at her husband, she found no help from him, and as abruptly as if it were a matter of no importance, she threw up the sponge.

"Do what you like!" she cried, springing up from her chair. "She's your child. I'm not the person to stand in your way. I think if it were my child I'd rather see her—" She managed to check herself. "You two decide it. I can't stand this. I'm sick. I'm going to bed."

She hurried from the room; after a moment Lincoln said:

"This has been a hard day for her. You know how strongly she feels—" His voice was almost apologetic: "When a woman gets an idea in her head."

"Of course."

195　"It's going to be all right. I think she sees now that you—can provide for the child, and so we can't very well stand in your way or Honoria's way."

"Thank you, Lincoln."

"I'd better go along and see how she is."

"I'm going."

He was still trembling when he reached the street, but a walk down the Rue Bonaparte to the *quais*[4] set him up, and as he crossed the Seine, fresh and new by the *quai* lamps, he felt exultant. But back in his room he couldn't sleep. The image of Helen haunted him. Helen whom he had loved so until they had senselessly begun to abuse each other's love, tear it into shreds. On that terrible February night that Marion remembered so vividly, a slow quarrel had gone on for hours. There was a scene at the Florida, and then he attempted to take her home, and then she kissed young Webb at a table; after that there was what she had hysterically said. When he arrived home alone he turned the key in the lock in wild anger. How could he know she would arrive an hour later alone, that there would be a snowstorm in which she wandered about in slippers, too confused to find a taxi? Then the aftermath, her escaping pneumonia by a miracle, and all the attendant horror. They were "reconciled," but that was the beginning of the end, and Marion, who had seen with her own eyes and who imagined it to be one of many scenes from her sister's martyrdom, never forgot.

Going over it again brought Helen 200 nearer, and in the white, soft light that steals upon half sleep near morning he found himself talking to her again. She said that he was perfectly right about Honoria and that she wanted Honoria to be with him. She said she was glad he was being good and doing better. She said a lot of other things— very friendly things—but she was in a swing in a white dress, and swinging faster and faster all the time, so that at the end he could not hear clearly all that she said.

IV

He woke up feeling happy. The door of the world was open again. He made plans, vistas, futures for Honoria and himself, but suddenly he grew sad, remembering all the plans he and Helen had made. She had not

---

[4]***quais:*** Paved riverbanks (French).

planned to die. The present was the thing—work to do and someone to love. But not to love too much, for he knew the injury that a father can do to a daughter or a mother to a son by attaching them too closely: afterward, out in the world, the child would seek in the marriage partner the same blind tenderness and, failing probably to find it, turn against love and life.

It was another bright, crisp day. He called Lincoln Peters at the bank where he worked and asked if he could count on taking Honoria when he left for Prague. Lincoln agreed that there was no reason for delay. One thing—the legal guardianship. Marion wanted to retain that a while longer. She was upset by the whole matter, and it would oil things if she felt that the situation was still in her control for another year. Charlie agreed, wanting only the tangible, visible child.

Then the question of a governess. Charles sat in a gloomy agency and talked to a cross Béarnaise and to a buxom Breton peasant, neither of whom he could have endured. There were others whom he would see tomorrow.

He lunched with Lincoln Peters at Griffons, trying to keep down his exultation.

205   "There's nothing quite like your own child," Lincoln said. "But you understand how Marion feels too."

"She's forgotten how hard I worked for seven years there," Charlie said. "She just remembers one night."

"There's another thing," Lincoln hesitated. "While you and Helen were tearing around Europe throwing money away, we were just getting along. I didn't touch any of the prosperity because I never got ahead enough to carry anything but my insurance. I think Marion felt there was some kind of injustice in it—you not even working toward the end, and getting richer and richer."

"It went just as quick as it came," said Charlie.

"Yes, a lot of it stayed in the hands of *chasseurs* and saxophone players and maîtres d'hôtel—well, the big party's over now. I just said that to explain Marion's feeling about those crazy years. If you drop in about six o'clock tonight before Marion's too tired, we'll settle the details on the spot."

Back at his hotel, Charlie found a *pneumatique*[5] that had been redirected from the Ritz bar where Charlie had left his address for the purpose of finding a certain man.   210

DEAR CHARLIE: You were so strange when we saw you the other day that I wondered if I did something to offend you. If so, I'm not conscious of it. In fact, I have thought about you too much for the last year, and it's always been in the back of my mind that I might see you if I came over here. We *did* have such good times that crazy spring, like the night you and I stole the butcher's tricycle, and the time we tried to call on the president and you had the old derby rim and the wire cane. Everybody seems so old lately, but I don't feel old a bit. Couldn't we get together some time today for old time's sake? I've got a vile hang-over for the moment, but will be feeling better this afternoon and will look for you about five in the sweatshop at the Ritz.

Always devotedly,
Lorraine

His first feeling was one of awe that he had actually, in his mature years, stolen a tricycle and pedaled Lorraine all over the Étoile between the small hours and dawn. In retrospect it was a nightmare. Locking out Helen didn't fit in with any other act of his life, but the tricycle incident did—it was one of many. How many weeks or months of

---

[5]***pneumatique:*** Message delivered speedily by special Parisian system (French).

dissipation to arrive at that condition of utter irresponsibility?

He tried to picture how Lorraine had appeared to him then—very attractive; Helen was unhappy about it, though she said nothing. Yesterday, in the restaurant, Lorraine had seemed trite, blurred, worn away. He emphatically did not want to see her, and he was glad Alix had not given away his hotel address. It was a relief to think, instead, of Honoria, to think of Sundays spent with her and of saying good morning to her and of knowing she was there in his house at night, drawing her breath in the darkness.

At five he took a taxi and bought presents for all the Peters—a piquant cloth doll, a box of Roman soldiers, flowers for Marion, big linen handkerchiefs for Lincoln.

215 He saw, when he arrived in the apartment, that Marion had accepted the inevitable. She greeted him now as though he were a recalcitrant member of the family, rather than a menacing outsider. Honoria had been told she was going; Charlie was glad to see that her tact made her conceal her excessive happiness. Only on his lap did she whisper her delight and the question "When?" before she slipped away with the other children.

He and Marion were alone for a minute in the room, and on an impulse he spoke out boldly:

"Family quarrels are bitter things. They don't go according to any rules. They're not like aches or wounds; they're more like splits in the skin that won't heal because there's not enough material. I wish you and I could be on better terms."

"Some things are hard to forget," she answered. "It's a question of confidence." There was no answer to this and presently she asked, "When do you propose to take her?"

"As soon as I can get a governess. I hoped the day after tomorrow."

"That's impossible. I've got to get her 220 things in shape. Not before Saturday."

He yielded. Coming back into the room, Lincoln offered him a drink.

"I'll take my daily whisky," he said.

It was warm here, it was a home, people together by a fire. The children felt very safe and important; the mother and father were serious, watchful. They had things to do for the children more important than his visit here. A spoonful of medicine was, after all, more important than the strained relations between Marion and himself. They were not dull people, but they were very much in the grip of life and circumstances. He wondered if he couldn't do something to get Lincoln out of his rut at the bank.

A long peal at the door-bell; the *bonne à tout faire*[6] passed through and went down the corridor. The door opened upon another long ring, and then voices, and the three in the salon looked up expectantly; Richard moved to bring the corridor within his range of vision, and Marion rose. Then the maid came back along the corridor, closely followed by the voices, which developed under the light into Duncan Schaeffer and Lorraine Quarrles.

They were gay, they were hilarious, they 225 were roaring with laughter. For a moment Charlie was astounded; unable to understand how they ferreted out the Peters' address.

"Ah-h-h!" Duncan wagged his finger roguishly at Charlie. "Ah-h-h!"

They both slid down another cascade of laughter. Anxious and at a loss, Charlie shook hands with them quickly and presented them to Lincoln and Marion. Marion nodded, scarcely speaking. She had drawn back a step toward the fire; her little girl stood beside her, and Marion put an arm about her shoulder.

---

[6]***bonne à tout faire:*** Maid of all work (French).

With growing annoyance at the intru- sion, Charlie waited for them to explain themselves. After some concentration Duncan said:

"We came to invite you out to dinner. Lorraine and I insist that all this shishi, cagy business 'bout your address got to stop."

230 Charlie came closer to them, as if to force them backward down the corridor.

"Sorry, but I can't. Tell me where you'll be and I'll phone you in half an hour."

This made no impression. Lorraine sat down suddenly on the side of a chair, and focusing her eyes on Richard, cried, "Oh, what a nice little boy! Come here, little boy." Richard glanced at his mother, but did not move. With a perceptible shrug of her shoul- ders, Lorraine turned back to Charlie:

"Come and dine. Sure your cousins won' mine. See you so sel'om. Or solemn."

"I can't," said Charlie sharply. "You two have dinner and I'll phone you."

235 Her voice became suddenly unpleas- ant. "All right, we'll go. But I remember once when you hammered on my door at four A.M. I was enough of a good sport to give you a drink. Come on, Dunc."

Still in slow motion, with blurred, angry faces, with uncertain feet, they retired along the corridor.

"Good night," Charlie said.

"Good night!" responded Lorraine emphatically.

When he went back into the salon Marion had not moved, only now her son was standing in the circle of her other arm. Lincoln was still swinging Honoria back and forth like a pendulum from side to side.

240 "What an outrage!" Charlie broke out. "What an absolute outrage!"

Neither of them answered. Charlie dropped into an armchair, picked up his drink, set it down again and said:

"People I haven't seen for two years having the colossal nerve—"

He broke off. Marion had made the sound "Oh!" in one swift, furious breath, turned her body from him with a jerk and left the room.

Lincoln set down Honoria carefully.

"You children go in and start your 245 soup," he said, and when they obeyed, he said to Charlie:

"Marion's not well and she can't stand shocks. That kind of people make her really physically sick."

"I didn't tell them to come here. They wormed your name out of somebody. They deliberately—"

"Well, it's too bad. It doesn't help mat- ters. Excuse me a minute."

Left alone, Charlie sat tense in his chair. In the next room he could hear the children eating, talking in monosyllables, already oblivious to the scene between their elders. He heard a murmur of conversation from a farther room and then the ticking bell of a telephone receiver picked up, and in a panic he moved to the other side of the room and out of earshot.

In a minute Lincoln came back. "Look 250 here, Charlie. I think we'd better call off din- ner for tonight. Marion's in bad shape."

"Is she angry with me?"

"Sort of," he said, almost roughly. "She's not strong and—"

"You mean she's changed her mind about Honoria?"

"She's pretty bitter right now. I don't know. You phone me at the bank tomorrow."

"I wish you'd explain to her I never 255 dreamed these people would come here. I'm just as sore as you are."

"I couldn't explain anything to her now."

Charlie got up. He took his coat and hat and started down the corridor. Then he opened the door of the dining room and said in a strange voice, "Good night, children."

Honoria rose and ran around the table to hug him.

"Good night, sweetheart," he said vaguely, and then trying to make his voice more tender, trying to conciliate something, "Good night, dear children."

V

260 Charlie went directly to the Ritz bar with the furious idea of finding Lorraine and Duncan, but they were not there, and he realized that in any case there was nothing he could do. He had not touched his drink at the Peters', and now he ordered a whisky-and-soda. Paul came over to say hello.

"It's a great change," he said sadly. "We do about half the business we did. So many fellows I hear about back in the States lost everything, maybe not in the first crash, but then in the second. Your friend George Hardt lost every cent, I hear. Are you back in the States?"

"No, I'm in business in Prague."

"I heard that you lost a lot in the crash."

"I did," and he added grimly, "but I lost everything I wanted in the boom."

265   "Selling short."

"Something like that."

Again the memory of those days swept over him like a nightmare—the people they had met travelling; then people who couldn't add a row of figures or speak a coherent sentence. The little man Helen had consented to dance with at the ship's party, who had insulted her ten feet from the table; the women and girls carried screaming with drink or drugs out of public places—

—The men who locked their wives out in the snow, because the snow of twenty-nine wasn't real snow. If you didn't want it to be snow, you just paid some money.

He went to the phone and called the Peters' apartment; Lincoln answered.

"I called up because this thing is on my 270 mind. Has Marion said anything definite?"

"Marion's sick," Lincoln answered shortly. "I know this thing isn't altogether your fault, but I can't have her go to pieces about it. I'm afraid we'll have to let it slide for six months; I can't take the chance of working her up to this state again."

"I see."

"I'm sorry, Charlie."

He went back to his table. His whisky glass was empty, but he shook his head when Alix looked at it questioningly. There wasn't much he could do now except send Honoria some things; he would send her a lot of things tomorrow. He thought rather angrily that this was just money—he had given so many people money. . . .

"No, no more," he said to another 275 waiter. "What do I owe you?"

He would come back some day; they couldn't make him pay forever. But he wanted his child, and nothing was much good now, beside that fact. He wasn't young any more, with a lot of nice thoughts and dreams to have by himself. He was absolutely sure Helen wouldn't have wanted him to be so alone.

• • • • •▶ *Your* **Turn**

Talking and Writing about Lit

1. How would you explain the relationship between past, present, and future in the life of Charlie Wales, as depicted in the story? What purpose do the characters Duncan Schaeffer and Lorraine Quarrles serve?

2. Analyze Fitzgerald's use of narrative point of view in the story. Does the voice of the story remain in a single character's perspective, or does the perspective shift at any point?

3. **DIY** Did you ever try to change a habit of your own? Write a brief account of that experience which takes place in two time periods: in the past before you changed the habit and in the present after you changed the habit.

Talking Lit

In this excerpt from her book of essays on fiction, Eudora Welty gives other examples of colliding social worlds in short stories and also discusses the intersection of plot and setting in terms of the character's "situation."

Eudora Welty, "Looking at Short Stories" from *The Eye of the Story*

Looking at short stories as readers and writers together should be a companionable thing. And why not? Stories in their bardic and fairy-tale beginnings were *told*, the listeners—and judgers—all in a circle.

E. M. Forster, in *Aspects of the Novel*, described the great age of the narrative:

> Neanderthal man listened to stories, if one may judge by the shape of his skull. The primitive audience was an audience of shock-heads, gaping around the camp-fire, fatigued with contending against the mammoth or woolly-rhinoceros, and only kept awake by suspense. What would happen next? The novelist droned on, and as soon as the audience guessed what happened next, they either fell asleep or killed him.

That suspense is still with us, but it seems to me that now it exists as something shared. Reader and writer make it a double experience. It is part of the great thing in which they share most—pleasure. And it is certainly part of the strong natural curiosity which readers feel to varying degree and which writers feel to the most compelling degree as to how any one story ever gets told. The only way a writer can satisfy his own curiosity is to write it. And how different this already makes it from telling it! Suspense, pleasure, curiosity, all are bound up in the making of the written story.

Forster went on to distinguish between what Neanderthal man told, the narrative thread, and what the written story has made into an art, the plot. "The king died and then the queen died" is the narrative thread; "The king died and then the queen died of grief" is a plot. We have all come from asking What next? to asking Why? The word which, of course, opened up everything, or as much of everything as the writer is able to handle.

To take a story:

Jack Potter, the town marshal of Yellow Sky, has gone to San Anton' and got married and is bringing his bride back in a Pullman as a dazzling surprise for his hometown. And while the train is on its way, back in Yellow Sky Scratchy Wilson gets drunk and turns loose with both hands. Everybody runs to cover: he has come to shoot up the town. "And his boots had red tops with gilded imprints, of the kind beloved in winter by little sledding boys on the hillsides of New England . . . The only sounds were his terrible invitations . . . He comfortably fusilladed the windows of his most intimate friend. The man was playing with the town; it was a toy for him." The train comes in, Scratchy and the marshal are face to face, and Potter says, "I ain't got a gun on me, Scratchy," and takes only a minute to make up his mind to be shot on his wedding day. "If you ain't got a gun, why ain't you got a gun?" "I ain't got a gun because I've just come from San Anton' with my wife. I'm married." "Married? Married? . . . Is this the lady?" "Yes; this is the lady." "'Well,' said Wilson at last, slowly, I s'pose it's all off now.' He was not a student of chivalry; it was merely that in the presence of this condition he was a simple child of the earlier plains." He picked up his starboard revolver, and, placing both weapons in their holsters, he went away.

Two predicaments meet here, in Stephen Crane's "The Bride Comes to Yellow Sky." You might say they are magnetized toward each other—and collide. One is vanquished with neatness and absurdity; as he goes away, Scratchy's "feet made funnel-shaped tracks in the heavy sand." Here are the plainest equivalents of comedy, two situations in a construction simple as a seesaw, and not without a seesaw's kind of pleasure in reading; like Scratchy Wilson, Crane is playing with us here.

In Katherine Mansfield's "Miss Brill," there is only one character and a single situation; Miss Brill's action consists nearly altogether in sitting down—she goes out to sit in the park, returns to sit on her bed. There is no collision. Rather, the forces meeting in the public gardens have, at the story's end, passed through each other and come out at the other side; there has been not a collision, but a change—something more significant. This is because, although there is one small situation going on, a large, complex one is implied. Life itself corresponds to the part of Scratchy Wilson, so to speak. Not violent life, merely life in a park on Sunday afternoon in Paris. All that it usually does for Miss Brill is promenade, yet, life being life, it does finally threaten. How much more deadly to such a lady than a flourished pistol is a remark overheard about herself. Reality comes to leer at her from a pleasant place, and she has not come prepared to bear it. And so she, who in her innocence could spare even pity for this world—pity, the spectator's emotion—is defeated. A word is spoken and the blow falls and Miss Brill retires, ridiculously easy to mow down, as the man with the pistols was easy to stare down in "Yellow Sky" for comedy's sake. But Miss Brill was from the first defenseless and on the losing side; her defeat is the deeper for it and one feels sure it is for always. So this story, instead of being a simple situation, is an impression of a situation, and tells more for being so.

Looking at these two stories by way of their plots in skeleton, we can't help but notice something; their plots are not unlike. "The Bride Comes to Yellow Sky" is its more unpretentious form, "Miss Brill" shows an interesting variation. It is a plot with two sides, or two halves, or two opposites, or two states of mind or feeling side by side; even one such in repeat would be a form of this. The plot is, of course, life *versus* death, which includes nearly every story in the world.

It could be said equally well that most stories (and novels too) have plots of the errand of search. An idea this pervasive simply pervades life, and the generality that could include in one quick list "The Bear," "The Jolly Corner," "The Short Happy Life of Francis Macomber" and "Araby" doesn't tell us really anything.

And so, plainly, we must distinguish plots not by their skeletons but by their full bodies; for they are embodiments, little worlds. Here is another: let us try to distinguish it as if it were literally a little world, and spinning closely now into our vision.

Now, the first thing we notice about this story is that we can't really see its solid outlines—it seems bathed in something of its own. It is wrapped in an atmosphere. This is what makes it shine, perhaps, as well as what obscures, at first glance, its plain real shape.

We are bearing in mind that the atmosphere in a story may be not the least of its glories, and also the fact that it may give a first impression that will prove contrary to what lies under it. Some action stories fling off the brightest clouds of obscuring and dazzling light, like ours here. Penetrate that atmosphere and the object may show quite dark within, for all its clouds of speed, those primary colors of red and yellow and blue. It looks like one of Ernest Hemingway's stories, and it is.

A story behaves, it goes through motions—that's part of it. Some stories leave a train of light behind them, meteor-like, so that much later than they strike our eyes we may see their meaning like an aftereffect. And Faulkner's seem not meteors but comets; they have a course of their own that brings them around more than once; they reappear in their own time in the sense that they reiterate their meaning and show a whole further story over and beyond their single significance.

If we have thought of Hemingway's stories as being bare and solid as billiard balls, so scrupulously cleaned of adjectives, of every unneeded word, as they are, of being plain throughout as a verb is plain, we may come to think twice about it, from our stargazer distance. The atmosphere that cloaks D. H. Lawrence's stories is of sensation, which is pure but thick cover, a cloak of self-illuminating air, but the atmosphere that surrounds Hemingway's is just as thick and to some readers less illuminating. Action can indeed be inscrutable, more so than sensation can. It can be just as voluptuous, too, just as vaporous, and, as I am able to see it, much more desperately concealing.

In one of Hemingway's early stories, "Indian Camp," Nick goes with his father, a doctor, to see a sick Indian woman. She is suffering in labor and the doctor operates on her without an anaesthetic. In the bunk above her head, her husband lies with a sore foot. After the operation is over and the child successfully born, the husband is found to have slit his throat because he had not been able to bear his wife's suffering. Nick asks, "Is dying hard, Daddy?" "No, I think it's pretty easy," his father says.

Is this still a red and blue world? I see it as dark as night. Not that it is obscure; rather, it's opaque. Action can be radiant, but in this writer who has action to burn, it is not. The stories are opaque by reason of his intention, which is to moralize. We are to be taught by Hemingway, who is instructive by method, that the world is dangerous and full of fear, and that there is a way we had better be. There is nothing for it but, with bravery, to observe the ritual. And so action can step in front of reality just as surely and with more agility than even sentimentality can. Our belligerent planet Mars has an unknown and unrevealed heart.

Nevertheless, this is not where we stop seeing. For what comes of this, his method? In a painting by Goya, who himself used light, action and morality dramatically, of course, the bullring and the great turbulent wall of spectators are cut in diagonal halves by a great shadow of afternoon (unless you see it as the dark sliced away by the clear, golden light): half the action revealed and half hidden in dense, clotting shade. It's like this in Hemingway's plots. And it seems to be the halving that increases the story.

One power of his, his famous use of dialogue, derives as well from the fact that something is broken in two; language slips, meets a barrier, a shadow is inserted between the speakers. It is an obscuring and at the same time a revealing way to write dialogue, and only great skill can manage it—and make us aware at the same time that communication of a limited kind is now going on as best it can.

As we now see Hemingway's story, not transparent, not radiant, but lit from outside the story, from a moral source, we see that light's true nature: it is a spotlight. And his stories are all taking place as entirely in the present as plays we watch being acted on the stage. Pasts and futures are among the things his characters have not. Outside this light, they are nothing.

Clearly, the fact that stories have plots in common is of no more account than that many people have blue eyes. Plots are, indeed, what the story writer sees with, and so do we as we read. The plot is the Why. Why? is asked and replied to at various depths; the fishes in the sea are bigger the deeper we go. To learn that character is a more awe-inspiring fish and (in a short story, though not, I think, in a novel) one some degrees deeper down than situation, we have only to read Chekhov. What constitutes the reality of his characters is what they reveal to us. And the possibility that they may indeed reveal everything is what makes fictional characters differ so greatly from us in real life; yet isn't it strange that they don't really *seem* to differ? This is one clue to the extraordinary magnitude of character in fiction. Characters in the plot connect us with the vastness of our secret life, which is endlessly explorable. This is their role. What happens to them is what they have been put here to show.

In his story "The Darling," the darling's first husband, the theatre manager, dies suddenly *because* of the darling's sweet passivity; this is the causality of fiction. In everyday or real life he might have held on to his health for years. But under Chekhov's hand he is living and dying in dependence on, and in revelation of, Olenka's character. He can only last a page and a half. Only by force of the story's circumstance is he here at all; Olenka took him up to begin with because he lived next door.

> Olenka listened to Kukin with silent gravity, and sometimes tears came into her eyes. In the end his misfortunes touched her; she grew to love him. He was a small thin man, with a yellow face; as he talked his mouth worked on one side, and there

was always an expression of despair on his face; yet he aroused a deep and genuine affection in her. She was always fond of someone, and could not exist without loving. In earlier days she had loved her papa, who now sat in a darkened room, breathing with difficulty; she had loved her aunt, who used to come every other year from Bryansk; and before that, when she was at school, she had loved her French master. She was a gentle, soft-hearted, compassionate girl, with mild, tender eyes and very good health. At the sight of her full rosy cheeks, her soft white neck with a little dark mole on it, and the kind, naïve smile, which came into her face when she listened to anything pleasant, men thought, "Yes, not half bad," and smiled too, while lady-visitors could not refrain from seizing her hand in the middle of a conversation, exclaiming in a gush of delight, "You darling!"

Kukin proposes and they are married.

And when he had a closer view of her neck and her plump, fine shoulders, he threw up his hand and said "You darling!" . . . And what Kukin said about the theatre and the actors she repeated. Like him she despised the public for their ignorance and indifference to art; she took part in the rehearsals, she corrected the actors, she kept an eye on the behavior of the musicians, and when there was an unfavorable notice in the local paper, she shed tears, and then went to the editor's office to set things right . . .

And when Kukin dies, Olenka's cry of heartbreak is this: "Vanitchka, my precious, my darling! Why did I ever meet you! Why did I know you and love you! Your poor broken-hearted Olenka is all alone without you!"

With variations the pattern is repeated, and we are made to feel it as plot, aware of its clear open stress, the variations all springing from Chekhov's boundless and minute perception of character. The timber-merchant, another neighbor, is the one who walks home from the funeral with Olenka. The outcome follows tenderly, is only natural. After three days, he calls. "He did not stay long, only about ten minutes, and he did not say much, but when he left, Olenka loved him—loved him so much that she lay awake all night in a perfect fever."

Olenka and Pustovalov get along very well together when they are married.

"Timber gets dearer every year; the price rises twenty per cent," she would say to her customers and friends . . . "And the freight!" she would add, covering her checks with her hands in horror, "the freight!" . . . It seemed to her that she had been in the timber trade for ages and ages; and that the most important and necessary thing in life was timber; and there was something intimate and touching to her in the very sound of words such as "post," "beam," "pole," "batten," "lath," "plank," and the like.

Even in her dreams Olenka is in the timber business, dreaming of "perfect mountains of planks and boards," and cries out in her sleep, so that Pustovalov says to her tenderly, "Olenka, what's the matter, darling? Cross yourself!" But the timber merchant inevitably goes out in the timber yard one day without his cap on; he catches cold and dies, to leave Olenka a widow once more. "I've nobody, now you've left me, my darling," she sobs after the funeral. "How can I live without you?"

And the timber merchant is succeeded by a veterinary surgeon—who gets transferred to Siberia. But the plot is not repetition—it is direction. The love which Olenka bears to whatever is nearest her reaches its final and, we discover, its truest mold in maternalism: for there it is most naturally innocent of anything but form-less, thoughtless, blameless *embracing*; the true innocence is in never perceiving. Only mother love could endure in a pursuit of such blind regard, caring so little for the reality of either life involved so long as love wraps them together, Chekhov tells us—unpretentiously, as he tells everything, and with the simplest of conclud-ing episodes. Olenka's character is seen purely then for what it is: limpid reflection, mindless and purposeless regard, love that falls like the sun and rain on all alike, vacant when there is nothing to reflect.

We know this because, before her final chance to love, Olenka is shown to us truly alone:

> [She] got thinner and plainer; and when people met her in the street they did not look at her as they used to, and did not smile to her; evidently her best years were over and left behind, and now a new sort of life had begun for her, which did not bear thinking about . . . And what was worst of all, she had no opinions of any sort. She saw the objects about her and understood what she saw, but could not form any opinions about them, and did not know what to talk about. And how awful it is not to have any opin-ions! She wanted a love that would absorb her whole being, her whole soul and reason —that would give her ideas and an object in life, and would warm her old blood.

The answer is Sasha, the ten-year-old son of the veterinary surgeon, an unex-pected blessing from Siberia—a schoolchild. The veterinarian has another wife now, but this no longer matters. "Olenka, with arms akimbo, walked about the yard giving directions. Her face was beaming, and she was brisk and alert, as though she had waked from a long sleep . . . " "An island is a piece of land entirely surrounded by water," Sasha reads aloud. "'An island is a piece of land,' she repeated, and this was the first opinion to which she gave utterance with positive conviction, after so many years of silence and dearth of ideas." She would follow Sasha halfway to school, until he told her to go back. She would go to bed think-ing blissfully of Sasha, "who lay sound asleep in the next room, sometimes crying out in his sleep, 'I'll give it to you! Get away! Shut up!'"

The darling herself *is* the story; all else is sacrificed to her; deaths and depar-tures are perfunctory and to be expected. The last words of the story are the child's and a protest, but they are delivered in sleep, as indeed protest to the darlings of this world will always be—out of inward and silent rebellion alone, as this master makes plain.

It is when the plot, whatever it is, is nearest to becoming the same thing on the outside as it is deep inside, that it is purest. When it is identifiable in every motion and progression of its own with the motions and progressions of the story's feel-ing and its intensity, then this is plot put to its highest use.

C H A P T E R **6**

POINT OF VIEW

Even video games use point of view.
Video games—surely the most interactive form of storytelling yet devised—invite the player to interact with other characters in the story, but they also often invite the player to *be* a character in the story and to view the story from that particular character's perspective. ID Software's lucrative "first person shooter" games popularized this kind of video game story seen from the first person view. Looking through the eyes of the main character, you "walked" through the corridors looking for Nazi soldiers, demons, or other evil-doers. These games accomplished a degree of submersion that had'nt existed before in the more two-dimensional games. The effect of first-person narration in fiction is similar. We become closer to our main character (perhaps even imagining ourselves in his or her shoes) when that character talks directly to us in the "I" voice.

Many of the recent popular games, such as the Resident Evil series, and the Onimusha Trilogy use a perspective like the third-person limited omniscient strategy in fiction (further defined in the chapter). We remain largely with one character throughout the game, controlling only their actions and seeing what relates to them. We are concerned with our main character's actions and exercise control over them, but we do not control the thoughts or movements of other characters.

Other games, like Sim City, Roller Coaster Tycoon, and the Real Time Strategy war games such as Warcraft and Starcraft, are like third person fully omniscient narratives. That is, the gamer exercises total control over the environment, building entire worlds, controlling the actions of those worlds' inhabitants, and having access to the movement and thought of each individual character. If Charles Dickens were alive today, he would likely be a Sim City kind of guy.

Sitting alone or with a friend to play an interactive video game, often the first thing you do is choose which character you will "be" in the story. When a writer gets an idea for a story, he or she will also begin imagining the events of the story from a particular perspective. The story might be told by an individual character who is part of the action or by a character who is merely an observer. Or, instead, the story might be told from a perspective completely outside the minds of the characters, looking at the action as if through the lens of a camera, from a distance. The term **point of view**, then, when used in a literary discussion, means the perspective—the viewpoint—from which the story is told.

Choose Your Character and Start the Game

Once we know that the writer thinks consciously about point-of-view choices, and once we understand the possibilities of point of view available, then we are better able to discuss how the writer's choice of perspective plays a part in revealing character, theme, and every aspect of the story.

Point-of-view choice can be seen as another way in which the writer deliberately selects and arranges material in the story (as we noted in the chapter on plot), offering it through the chosen narrative perspective. Because of this, in some cases, the story's contents may give the appearance of being chosen by the point-of-view character through whose eyes we are viewing events. For instance, Bonaparte, Frank O'Connor's narrator in "Guests of the Nation" (in this chapter), focuses in detail on the comradely card games between the prisoners and the hostages, and also on the heated discussions of religion. However, this too is accomplished deliberately by O'Connor, the writer. As is true of our video game players in the chapter opener, the writer is like a puppeteer who "pulls the strings" of the point-of-view character and all other characters as well in order to reveal what he wishes to show to the reader. Having Bonaparte narrate the story serves O'Connor well in a number of ways. Bonaparte is a participant in the sociable card games, but, because he does not fiercely take sides during the religious discussions, he is a reliable and cool-headed narrator of the events.

Point of View and Theme

The detailed scenes depicting the card games and religious arguments are not just there because they are what Bonaparte might see. They are there because they are part of the writer's deliberate selection and arrangement of events to illuminate what he chooses to show in the story. The religious arguments focus the story on ethical and moral questions from the very beginning, and the card games help show the way in which Hawkins and Belcher become, for a time, "guests of the nation" instead of hostages. You can see, then, how choosing a certain point of view helps the writer reveal themes (meanings and ideas) in the story. When we talk about the story, discussing the point of view is one of the many pathways to follow to discover meaning in a work of fiction.

Types of Narrative Point of View

Narrators usually speak either in the **third-person voice** ("he," "she," or "they") or in the **first-person voice** (the "I" or, less frequently, the "we" voice). It is often said that a story cannot be told in the **second-person voice** ("you"), and certainly this is a choice which writers rarely make, though it has occasionally been used successfully. In addition, writers sometimes shift point of view within a single story, if it suits their purposes. An example would be found in Ralph Ellison's "Flying Home," which you'll read in this chapter. We might call this strategy a **mixed point of view**. A chart listing the types of narrative point of view appears at the end of this discussion.

Third-Person Voices

There are three basic types of third-person narrators: **objective, limited omniscient**, and **fully omniscient**. We might define these three types of third-person narration in terms of degrees of limitation and degrees of access—that is, by how much access the narrator has to the internal thoughts and feelings of the characters. The most limited third-person narrator is the **objective narrator**. If the writer uses this angle of sight, or point of view, the narrator does not have access to any internal thoughts or feelings of the characters. The objective narrator acts like the eye of a camera (the camera alone, without any voice-over to accompany the photographs or film). The objective narrator is limited to making external observations about the characters—physical descriptions, movement and behavior, and dialogue. It may also convey detailed descriptions of the setting. The objective narrator does not at any time, however, enter into the thoughts of a character. The objective point of view is rarely used, but the classic example of it is Shirley Jackson's "The Lottery" (see Chapter 8), in which an eerie atmosphere is created by the matter-of-fact narration of a shocking incident, related by an objective narrator who can give us only external indications of what human emotions are at play.

> The people had done it so many times that they only half listened to the directions; most of them were quiet, wetting their lips, not looking around. Then Mr. Summers raised one hand high and said, "Adams." . . . Mr. Adams reached into the black box and took out a folded paper. He held it firmly by one corner as he turned and went hastily back to his place in the crowd, where he stood a little apart from his family, not looking down at his hand. (paragraph 20)

The external observations of this narrator—for example, "wetting their lips, not looking around"—might give us clues that the characters are nervous, and we might also learn about the state of their minds through their own spoken remarks (dialogue), but we are not given access to what they are thinking.

The second type of third-person narration is called limited omniscient. When this narrative strategy is used, the story is told through internal access to the mind of one character. This strategy is called "limited" because it is deliberately limited to the perspective of a single character. To the reader, this perspective can often feel very much like the use of the first-person narration because we have access to the thoughts and feelings of a character through whose eyes we see the story's events and through whose interpretive views we come to know the other characters in the story. Ralph Ellison's story "Flying Home" opens this way:

> When Todd came to, he saw two faces suspended above him in a sun so hot and blinding that he could not tell if they were black or white. He stirred, feeling a pain that burned as though his whole body had been laid open to the sun which glared into his eyes. (paragraph 1)

This third-person voice is located within the intensely felt thoughts of the character Todd. He does not know where he is, and we are located within his perspective (*limited* to it) so that we do not know where he is either, until he discovers it. This suits Ellison's purpose well here because he wants the events of the story to lead the reader to an understanding of what such experiences are like for his main character. Likewise, in André Dubus's "Killings" (in Chapter 3), Bharati Mukherjee's "A Father" (in Chapter 4), and Ernest Hemingway's "Soldier's Home" (in this chapter), we have access to the thoughts and feelings of only one character. All of the story's events and all of the other characters are viewed through the "filter" of that character's perspective and opinions. The limited omniscient voice does employ a slightly greater distance between character and reader than the first-person voice, but the same kind of internal information can be made known to the reader with either.

The third type of third-person narration is the **omniscient** (or **fully omniscient**) voice. This narrative voice, which has the greatest access to both internal and external information, is often called the God-like narrator, the seemingly "all knowing" voice of much nineteenth-century fiction. By using this perspective, the storytelling voice can shift around among time periods within the story, revealing events that have taken place in the past, or will take place in the future (Isabel Allende does both in "The Judge's Wife" in this chapter as does Grace Paley in "Samuel" in Chapter 1).

The omniscient narrator can also provide awareness of events which are occurring in different locations at the same time. The fully omniscient narrator also has access to internal thoughts and feelings (unlike the objective narrator) and can, in fact, enter the minds of any number of characters, or even provide the reader with an understanding of a "community voice" or "group consciousness" (as in Paley's "Samuel," Chapter 1). The fully omniscient narrator can also reveal the details of past, present, or future events. This capability always remains under the control of the writer, however. The fully omniscient voice has the ability to reveal who committed a murder five years ago, but if it serves the purposes of the story better to withhold that information, then, of course, the writer may choose not to reveal it or to reveal it at a carefully chosen moment in the story. The writer is at all times in control of what is revealed and also when it is revealed (again, selection and arrangement). One function of plotting, in the hands of the writer, is to exercise wisely that power to decide what to reveal and when. Allende's omniscient narrator in "The Judge's Wife" has the ability to go inside the thoughts of Juana the Forlorn, for instance, but this does not mean the story must do so. Keeping the story largely in the alternating perspectives of Doña Casilda and Nicolas Vidal suits Allende's purposes better, given what she wants to reveal.

Distinctions between the three classic categories of third-person narrators (objective, limited omniscient, and fully omniscient) are not always clear cut. For instance, Allende's story may, on a first reading, appear to be in the third-person limited omniscient point of view, with access to the minds of both main characters: Nicolas Vidal and Doña Casilda. On closer examination, however, most readers will decide that the story would be more accurately described as fully omniscient. We do receive information about past events and future events which doesn't seem to come from the perspective of Nicolas or Casilda, and the narrative even relates Judge Hidalgo's activities and thoughts (when he is alone in his office during Juana's confinement, in paragraph 13), thoughts and activities of which neither Casilda nor Vidal would be aware.

First-Person Voices

Writers and critics categorize first-person narrators in various ways: first-person singular, the perspective of a major or minor character, or first-person plural. The most common type of first-person voice is the **first-person singular** narrator (the "I" voice). Bonaparte, the narrator of O'Connor's "Guests of the Nation," is such a narrator. His is a reasoned and compassionate voice that holds our trust from the beginning to the end of the story, right up through his intensely felt final sentences: ". . . and I was somehow very small and very lost and lonely like a child astray in the snow. And anything that happened to me afterwards, I never felt the same about again."

Looking at categories of first-person narration in terms of major or minor characters can sometimes be useful too. O'Connor's narrator Bonaparte speaks, of course, from the **perspective of a major character**. A story can also be narrated from the **perspective of a minor character**, and although this is a less common strategy, it can be quite effective. Such narrators, who are not at the center of the action, are often called "observer narrators" or "peripheral narrators."

The use of a **first-person plural** narrator is rare. The most well-known example of this strategy is to be found in William Faulkner's "A Rose for Emily" (in Chapter 3). In it, the "we" voice represents the voice of the townspeople, or we might simply say, the voice of the town.

> So the next day we all said, "She will kill herself"; and we said it would be the best thing. When she had first begun to be seen with Homer Barron, we had said, "She will marry him." Then we said, "She will persuade him yet." (paragraph 43)

Mixed Voices

Ralph Ellison's "Flying Home" is useful for illustrating another point-of-view strategy because it does not remain in the third-person voice throughout. In "Flying
Home," Ellison makes use of a mixed point-of-view strategy, shifting from the third-
person voice to the first person, and back, in order to achieve the desired effects. His
sections in the first person are flashbacks to childhood incidents which help explain
the present feelings of the main character, Todd, an African American U. S. Air Force
pilot during World War II who, during a training exercise, crashes into a field in rural
Georgia. His injuries are so painful and disorienting that he is in an almost halluci-
natory state of mind during much of the story, nearly believing himself to be in a past
time. The childhood incidents relived by the character Todd (in the first-person
voice) are connected to his love of flying and his early fascination with airplanes.
They are also sometimes connected to early experiences of racism, which is likewise
an aspect of his experience in the present time of the story.

> It was as though an endless series of hangars had been shaken ajar in the air-base of
> his memory and from each, like a young wasp emerging from its cell, arose the
> memory of a plane.
>   The first time I ever saw a plane I was very small and planes were new in the
> world. I was only four-and-a-half and the only plane that I had ever seen was a
> model suspended from the ceiling of the automobile exhibit at the State Fair. But I
> did not know that it was only a model. (from paragraphs 145–46)

If you look closely at the above excerpt, you will see that Ellison has shifted
from the third-person limited omniscient point of view to the first-person point of
view (from "he" to "I"). This helps accomplish his purpose of increasing the immediacy and poignancy of the childhood memories which Todd relives as he lies
injured on the field. This mixing of point-of-view strategies within a single work is
not actually new, however; Russian author Leo Tolstoy made frequent use of it in
the nineteenth century.

Even this way of describing the flexibility of point-of-view choices (as
"mixed") may not be sufficiently flexible, however, because it is each writer, within
the intentions of each work of fiction, who decides, paragraph by paragraph, line by
line, what to reveal and when, how much to reveal, and how much detail to provide.
If the writer uses a fully omniscient narrator, will it be the (typically) nineteenth-
century **editorializing omniscient** narrator of which Tolstoy was a master, a narrator who offers God-like judgments upon the action and the characters? Or will it be
a more modern, carefully **neutral omniscient** narrator, one who allows the reader to
make up his or her own mind about how to judge the characters? Contemporary
readers usually have a reduced tolerance for a didactic ("editorializing") narrator,
unless it is in the form of a parody of that self-important, sermonizing voice. Or—
and this is a very important "or"—unless it is a beloved writer of an earlier period
whose vision is treasured, sermonizing or not. An American example would be
Nathaniel Hawthorne. For instance, in the last paragraph of his story "The
Birthmark" (Chapter 8), Hawthorne's narrator says, somewhat didactically,

> Alas! it was too true! The fatal hand had grappled with the mystery of life, and was the bond by which an angelic spirit kept itself in union with a mortal frame. . . . Thus ever does the gross fatality of earth exult in its invariable triumph over the immortal essence which in this dim sphere of half development, demands the completeness of a higher state. (paragraph 90)

That is a bit of a lecture, to say the least. Hawthorne's editorializing narrator then goes on to say what the fictional character should have done that he didn't do:

> Yet, had Aylmer reached a profounder wisdom, he need not thus have flung away the happiness which would have woven his mortal life of the selfsame texture with the celestial. The momentary circumstance was too strong for him; he failed to look beyond the shadowy scope of time, and, living once for all in eternity, to find the perfect future in the present. (paragraph 90)

Here, the narrator exclaims that the character Aylmer made a terrible mistake by throwing away his beautiful, though human, wife Giorgiana in pursuit of an unnatural ideal of perfection. Dissecting the characters' motives or passing judgment on what they should have done but didn't is, then, an activity more common in nineteenth-century fiction. Most contemporary writers would leave it up to the reader to interpret such things rather than tell us what to think.

A point-of-view issue which we have discussed in this chapter, but have left until Chapter 7, is reliability. A narrator can be reliable or he or she can be naive or unreliable, with any degree of trustworthiness or untrustworthiness in between. Some issues discussed in Chapter 7, then, could also be viewed as further subtleties of point of view—voice, style, diction, tone, reliability, and irony.

POINT OF VIEW STRATEGIES

Third-Person Voices	I. Objective (no internal access to thoughts and feelings)
	2. Limited omniscient (internal access to 1 or 2 characters)
	3. Fully omniscient ("all-knowing")
Second-Person Voice	Possible, but rarely used
First-Person Voices	1. Major character 1. Singular ("I")
	or
	2. Minor character 2. Plural ("we")
Mixed Voices	Any combination of the above if the writer chooses to shift between two different point-of-view strategies

Readings

Frank O'Connor (1903–1966)

Frank O'Connor was the pen name of Michael Francis O'Donovan, who was born in Cork, Ireland. His parents were so poor that he was able to attend the Christian Brothers School only through the fourth grade. He briefly served with the Irish Republican Army during the Irish uprising of 1918–1921, and his story "Guests of the Nation" reflects that experience. When "Guests of the Nation," O'Connor's first publication, appeared in the *Atlantic Monthly*, he was twenty-eight years old. His first collection of short stories, titled after the successful short story, appeared the same year, 1931. From then on, O'Connor was able to make a living from his writing. Although his family had been unable to afford him an education in his youth, he educated himself through voracious reading and study.

During the 1950s he lived in the United States, taught at Harvard and Northwestern universities, and published two important works of literary criticism: *The Mirror in the Roadway* (1956) and *The Lonely Voice* (1963). O'Connor wrote in several literary genres, but his best achievement was in the short story. He published nearly fifty books during his lifetime, and various editions of his collected works are available.

Guests of the Nation (1931/1954)

I

At dusk the big Englishman, Belcher, would shift his long legs out of the ashes and say "Well, chums, what about it?" and Noble or me would say "All right, chum" (for we had picked up some of their curious expressions), and the little Englishman, Hawkins, would light the lamp and bring out the cards. Sometimes Jeremiah Donovan would come up and supervise the game and get excited over Hawkins's cards, which he always played badly, and shout at him as if he was one of our own "Ah, you divil, you, why didn't you play the tray?"

But ordinarily Jeremiah was a sober and contented poor devil like the big Englishman, Belcher, and was looked up to only because he was a fair hand at documents, though he was slow enough even with them. He wore a small cloth hat and big gaiters over his long pants, and you seldom saw him with his hands out of his pockets. He reddened when you talked to him, tilting from toe to heel and back, and looking down all the time at his big farmer's feet. Noble and me used to make fun of his broad accent, because we were from the town.

I couldn't at the time see the point of me and Noble guarding Belcher and Hawkins at all, for it was my belief that you could have planted that pair down anywhere from this to Claregalway and they'd have taken root there like a native weed. I never in my short experience seen two men to take to the country as they did.

They were handed on to us by the Second Battalion when the search for them became too hot, and Noble and myself, being young, took over with a natural feeling of responsibility, but Hawkins made us look like fools when he showed that he knew the country better than we did.

5   "You're the bloke they calls Bonaparte," he says to me. "Mary Brigid O'Connell told me to ask you what you done with the pair of her brother's socks you borrowed."

For it seemed, as they explained it, that the Second used to have little evenings, and some of the girls of the neighborhood turned in, and, seeing they were such decent chaps, our fellows couldn't leave the two Englishmen out of them. Hawkins learned to dance "The Walls of Limerick," "The Siege of Ennis," and "The Waves of Tory" as well as any of them, though, naturally, he couldn't return the compliment, because our lads at that time did not dance foreign dances on principle.

So whatever privileges Belcher and Hawkins had with the Second they just naturally took with us, and after the first day or two we gave up all pretense of keeping a close eye on them. Not that they could have got far, for they had accents you could cut with a knife and wore khaki tunics and overcoats with civilian pants and boots. But it's my belief that they never had any idea of escaping and were quite content to be where they were.

It was a treat to see how Belcher got off with the old woman of the house where we were staying. She was a great warrant to scold, and cranky even with us, but before ever she had a chance of giving our guests, as I may call them, a lick of her tongue, Belcher had made her his friend for life. She was breaking sticks, and Belcher, who hadn't been more than ten minutes in the house, jumped up from his seat and went over to her.

"Allow me, madam," he says, smiling his queer little smile, "please allow me"; and he takes the bloody hatchet. She was struck too paralytic to speak and after that, Belcher would be at her heels, carrying a bucket, a basket, or a load of turf, as the case might be. As Noble said, he got into looking before she leapt, and hot water, or any little thing she wanted, Belcher would have it ready for her. For such a huge man (and though I am five foot ten myself I had to look up at him) he had an uncommon shortness or should I say lack? of speech. It took us some time to get used to him, walking in and out, like a ghost, without a word. Especially because Hawkins talked enough for a platoon, it was strange to hear big Belcher with his toes in the ashes come out with a solitary "Excuse me, chum" or "That's right, chum." His one and only passion was cards, and I will say for him that he was a good card-player. He could have fleeced myself and Noble, but whatever we lost to him Hawkins lost to us, and Hawkins played with the money Belcher gave him.

Hawkins lost to us because he had too   10
much old gab, and we probably lost to Belcher for the same reason. Hawkins and Noble would spit at one another about religion into the early hours of the morning, and Hawkins worried the soul out of Noble, whose brother was a priest, with a string of questions that would puzzle a cardinal. To make it worse even in treating of holy subjects, Hawkins had a deplorable tongue. I never in all my career met a man who could mix such a variety of cursing and bad language into an argument. He was a terrible

man, and a fright to argue. He never did a stroke of work, and when he had no one else to talk to, he got stuck in the old woman.

He met his match in her, for one day when he tried to get her to complain profanely of the drought, she gave him a great come-down by blaming it entirely on Jupiter Pluvius (a deity neither Hawkins nor I have ever heard of, though Noble said that among the pagans it was believed that he had something to do with the rain). Another day he was swearing at the capitalists for starting the German war when the old lady laid down her iron, puckered up her little crab's mouth, and said: "Mr. Hawkins, you can say what you like about the war, and think you'll deceive me because I'm only a simple poor countrywoman, but I know what started the war. It was the Italian Count that stole the heathen divinity out of the temple in Japan. Believe me, Mr. Hawkins, nothing but sorrow and want can follow the people that disturb the hidden powers."

A queer old girl, all right.

II

We had our tea one evening, and Hawkins lit the lamp and we all sat into cards. Jeremiah Donovan came in too, and sat down and watched us for a while, and it suddenly struck me that he had no great love for the two Englishmen. It came as a great surprise to me, because I hadn't noticed anything about him before.

Late in the evening a really terrible argument blew up between Hawkins and Noble, about capitalists and priests and love of your country.

15   "The capitalists," says Hawkins with an angry gulp, "pays the priests to tell you about the next world so as you won't notice what the bastards are up to in this."

"Nonsense, man!" says Noble, losing his temper. "Before ever a capitalist was thought of, people believed in the next world."

Hawkins stood up as though he was preaching a sermon.

"Oh, they did, did they?" he says with a sneer. "They believed all the things you believe, isn't that what you mean? And you believe that God created Adam, and Adam created Shem, and Shem created Jehoshophat. You believe all that silly old fairytale about Eve and Eden and the apple. Well, listen to me, chum. If you're entitled to hold a silly belief—like that, I'm entitled to hold my silly belief which is that the first thing your God created was a bleeding capitalist, with morality and Rolls-Royce complete. Am I right, chum?" he says to Belcher.

"You're right, chum," says Belcher with his amused smile, and got up from the table to stretch his long legs into the fire and stroke his moustache. So, seeing that Jeremiah Donovan was going, and that there was no knowing when the argument about religion would be over, I went out with him. We strolled down to the village together, and then he stopped and started blushing and mumbling and saying I ought to be behind, keeping guard on the prisoners. I didn't like the tone he took with me, and anyway I was bored with life in the cottage, so I replied by asking him what the hell we wanted guarding them at all for. I told him I'd talked it over with Noble, and that we'd both rather be out with a fighting column.

"What use are those fellows to us?" 20 says I.

He looked at me in surprise and said: "I thought you knew we were keeping them as hostages."

"Hostages?" I said.

"The enemy have prisoners belonging to us," he says, "and now they're talking of shooting them. If they shoot our prisoners, we'll shoot theirs."

"Shoot them?" I said.

25 "What else did you think we were keeping them for?" he says.

"Wasn't it very unforeseen of you not to warn Noble and myself of that in the beginning?" I said.

"How was it?" says he. "You might have known it."

"We couldn't know it, Jeremiah Donovan," says I. "How could we when they were on our hands so long?"

"The enemy have our prisoners as long and longer," says he.

30 "That's not the same thing at all," says I.

"What difference is there?" says he.

I couldn't tell him, because I knew he wouldn't understand. If it was only an old dog that was going to the vet's, you'd try and not get too fond of him, but Jeremiah Donovan wasn't a man that would ever be in danger of that.

"And when is this thing going to be decided?" says I.

"We might hear tonight," he says. "Or tomorrow or the next day at latest. So if it's only hanging round here that's a trouble to you, you'll be free soon enough."

35 It wasn't the hanging round that was a trouble to me at all by this time. I had worse things to worry about. When I got back to the cottage the argument was still on. Hawkins was holding forth in his best style, maintaining that there was no next world, and Noble was maintaining that there was; but I could see that Hawkins had had the best of it.

"Do you know what, chum?" he was saying with a saucy smile. "I think you're just as big a bleeding unbeliever as I am. You say you believe in the next world, and you know just as much about the next world as I do, which is sweet damn-all. What's heaven? You don't know. Where's heaven? You don't know. You know sweet damn-all! I ask you again, do they wear wings?"

"Very well, then," says Noble, "they do. Is that enough for you? They do wear wings."

"Where do they get them, then? Who makes them? Have they a factory for wings? Have they a sort of store where you hands in your chit and takes your bleeding wings?"

"You're an impossible man to argue with," says Noble. "Now, listen to me—" And they were off again.

40 It was long after midnight when we locked up and went to bed. As I blew out the candle I told Noble what Jeremiah Donovan was after telling me. Noble took it very quietly. When we'd been in bed about an hour he asked me did I think we ought to tell the Englishmen. I didn't think we should, because it was more than likely that the English wouldn't shoot our men, and even if they did, the brigade officers, who were always up and down with the Second Battalion and knew the Englishmen well, wouldn't be likely to want them plugged. "I think so too," says Noble. "It would be great cruelty to put the wind up them now."

"It was very unforeseen of Jeremiah Donovan anyhow," says I.

It was next morning that we found it so hard to face Belcher and Hawkins. We went about the house all day scarcely saying a word. Belcher didn't seem to notice; he was stretched into the ashes as usual, with his usual look of waiting in quietness for something unforeseen to happen, but Hawkins noticed and put it down to Noble's being beaten in the argument of the night before.

"Why can't you take a discussion in the proper spirit?" he says severely. "You and your Adam and Eve! I'm a Communist, that's what I am. Communist or anarchist, it all comes to much the same thing." And for hours he went round the house, muttering when the fit took him. "Adam and Eve! Adam and Eve! Nothing better to do with their time than picking bleeding apples!"

III

I don't know how we got through that day, but I was very glad when it was over, the tea things were cleared away, and Belcher said in his peaceable way: "Well, chums, what about it?" We sat round the table and Hawkins took out the cards, and just then I heard Jeremiah Donovan's footstep on the path and a dark presentiment crossed my mind. I rose from the table and caught him before he reached the door.

45   "What do you want?" I asked.

"I want those two soldier friends of yours," he says, getting red.

"Is that the way, Jeremiah Donovan?" I asked.

"That's the way. There were four of our lads shot this morning, one of them a boy of sixteen."

"That's bad," I said.

50   At that moment Noble followed me out, and the three of us walked down the path together, talking in whispers. Feeney, the local intelligence officer, was standing by the gate.

"What are you going to do about it?" I asked Jeremiah Donovan.

"I want you and Noble to get them out; tell them they're being shifted again; that'll be the quietest way."

"Leave me out of that," says Noble under his breath.

Jeremiah Donovan looks at him hard.

55   "All right," he says. "You and Feeney get a few tools from the shed and dig a hole by the far end of the bog. Bonaparte and myself will be after you. Don't let anyone see you with the tools. I wouldn't like it to go beyond ourselves."

We saw Feeney and Noble go round to the shed and went in ourselves. I left Jeremiah Donovan to do the explanations. He told them that he had orders to send them back to the Second Battalion. Hawkins let out a mouthful of curses, and you could see that though Belcher didn't say anything, he was a bit upset too. The old woman was for having them stay in spite of us, and she didn't stop advising them until Jeremiah Donovan lost his temper and turned on her. He had a nasty temper, I noticed. It was pitch-dark in the cottage by this time, but no one thought of lighting the lamp, and in the darkness the two Englishmen fetched their topcoats and said good-bye to the old woman.

"Just as a man makes a home of a bleeding place, some bastard at headquarters thinks you're too cushy and shunts you off," says Hawkins, shaking her hand.

"A thousand thanks, madam," says Belcher. "A thousand thanks for everything"—as though he'd made it up.

We went round to the back of the house and down towards the bog. It was only then that Jeremiah Donovan told them. He was shaking with excitement.

"There were four of our fellows shot in 60 Cork this morning and now you're to be shot as a reprisal."

"What are you talking about?" snaps Hawkins. "It's bad enough being mucked about as we are without having to put up with your funny jokes."

"It isn't a joke," says Donovan. "I'm sorry, Hawkins, but it's true," and begins on the usual rigmarole about duty and how unpleasant it is.

I never noticed that people who talk a lot about duty find it much of a trouble to them.

"Oh, cut it out!" says Hawkins.

"Ask Bonaparte," says Donovan, see- 65 ing that Hawkins isn't taking him seriously. "Isn't it true, Bonaparte?"

"It is," I say, and Hawkins stops.

"Ah, for Christ's sake, chum!"

"I mean it, chum," I say.

"You don't sound as if you mean it."

70 "If he doesn't mean it, I do," says Donovan, working himself up.

"What have you against me, Jeremiah Donovan?"

"I never said I had anything against you. But why did your people take out four of our prisoners and shoot them in cold blood?"

He took Hawkins by the arm and dragged him on, but it was impossible to make him understand that we were in earnest. I had the Smith and Wesson in my pocket and I kept fingering it and wondering what I'd do if they put up a fight for it or ran, and wishing to God they'd do one or the other. I knew if they did run for it, that I'd never fire on them. Hawkins wanted to know was Noble in it, and when we said yes, he asked us why Noble wanted to plug him. Why did any of us want to plug him? What had he done to us? Weren't we all chums? Didn't we understand him and didn't he understand us? Did we imagine for an instant that he'd shoot us for all the so-and-so officers in the so-and-so British Army?

By this time we'd reached the bog, and I was so sick I couldn't even answer him. We walked along the edge of it in the darkness, and every now and then Hawkins would call a halt and begin all over again, as if he was wound up, about our being chums, and I knew that nothing but the sight of the grave would convince him that we had to do it. And all the time I was hoping that something would happen; that they'd run for it or that Noble would take over the responsibility from me. I had the feeling that it was worse on Noble than on me.

IV

75 At last we saw the lantern in the distance and made towards it. Noble was carrying it, and Feeney was standing somewhere in the darkness behind him, and the picture of them so still and silent in the bogland brought it home to me that we were in earnest, and banished the last bit of hope I had.

Belcher, on recognizing Noble, said: "Hallo, chum," in his quiet way, but Hawkins flew at him at once, and the argument began all over again, only this time Noble had nothing to say for himself and stood with his head down, holding the lantern between his legs.

It was Jeremiah Donovan who did the answering. For the twentieth time, as though it was haunting his mind, Hawkins asked if anybody thought he'd shoot Noble.

"Yes, you would," says Jeremiah Donovan.

"No, I wouldn't, damn you!"

"You would, because you'd know 80 you'd be shot for not doing it."

"I wouldn't, not if I was to be shot twenty times over. I wouldn't shoot a pal. And Belcher wouldn't—isn't that right, Belcher?"

"That's right, chum," Belcher said, but more by way of answering the question than of joining in the argument. Belcher sounded as though whatever unforeseen thing he'd always been waiting for had come at last.

"Anyway, who says Noble would be shot if I wasn't? What do you think I'd do if I was in his place, out in the middle of a blasted bog?"

"What would you do?" asks Donovan.

"I'd go with him wherever he was 85 going, of course. Share my last bob with him and stick by him through thick and thin. No one can ever say of me that I let down a pal."

"We had enough of this," says Jeremiah Donovan, cocking his revolver. "Is there any message you want to send?"

"No, there isn't."

"Do you want to say your prayers?"

Hawkins came out with a cold-blooded remark that even shocked me and turned on Noble again.

90 "Listen to me, Noble," he says. "You and me are chums. You can't come over to my side, so I'll come over to your side. That show you I mean what I say? Give me a rifle and I'll go along with you and the other lads."

Nobody answered him. We knew that was no way out.

"Hear what I'm saying?" he says. "I'm through with it. I'm a deserter or anything else you like. I don't believe in your stuff, but it's no worse than mine. That satisfy you?"

Noble raised his head, but Donovan began to speak and he lowered it again without replying.

"For the last time, have you any messages to send?" says Donovan in a cool, excited sort of voice.

95 "Shut up, Donovan! You don't understand me, but these lads do. They're not the sort to make a pal and kill a pal. They're not the tools of any capitalist."

I alone of the crowd saw Donovan raise his Webley to the back of Hawkins's neck, and as he did so I shut my eyes and tried to pray. Hawkins had begun to say something else when Donovan fired, and as I opened my eyes at the bang, I saw Hawkins stagger at the knees and lie out flat at Noble's feet, slowly and as quiet as a kid falling asleep, with the lantern-light on his lean legs and bright farmer's boots. We all stood very still, watching him settle out in the last agony.

Then Belcher took out a handkerchief and began to tie it about his own eyes (in our excitement we'd forgotten to do the same for Hawkins), and, seeing it wasn't big enough, turned and asked for the loan of mine. I gave it to him and he knotted the two together and pointed with his foot at Hawkins.

"He's not quite dead," he says. "Better give him another."

Sure enough, Hawkins's left knee is beginning to rise. I bend down and put my gun to his head; then, recollecting myself, I get up again. Belcher understands what's in my mind.

"Give him his first," he says. "I don't 100 mind. Poor bastard, we don't know what's happening to him now."

I knelt and fired. By this time I didn't seem to know what I was doing. Belcher, who was fumbling a bit awkwardly with the handkerchiefs, came out with a laugh as he heard the shot. It was the first time I heard him laugh and it sent a shudder down my back; it sounded so unnatural.

"Poor bugger!" he said quietly. "And last night he was so curious about it all. It's very queer, chums, I always think. Now he knows as much about it as they'll ever let him know, and last night he was all in the dark."

Donovan helped him to tie the handkerchiefs about his eyes. "Thanks, chum," he said. Donovan asked if there were any messages he wanted sent.

"No, chum," he says, "not for me. If any of you would like to write to Hawkins's mother, you'll find a letter from her in his pocket. He and his mother were great chums. But my missus left me eight years ago. Went away with another fellow and took the kid with her. I like the feeling of a home, as you may have noticed, but I couldn't start again after that."

It was an extraordinary thing, but in 105 those few minutes Belcher said more than in all the weeks before. It was just as if the sound of the shot had started a flood of talk in him and he could go on the whole night like that, quite happily, talking about himself. We stood round like fools now that he couldn't see us any longer. Donovan looked at Noble, and Noble shook his head. Then Donovan raised his Webley, and at that moment Belcher gives his queer laugh again. He may have thought we were talking about him, or perhaps he noticed the same thing I'd noticed and couldn't understand it.

"Excuse me, chums," he says. "I feel I'm talking the hell of a lot, and so silly, about my being so handy about a house and things like that. But this thing came on me suddenly. You'll forgive me, I'm sure."

"You don't want to say a prayer?" asks Donovan.

"No, chum," he says. "I don't think it would help. I'm ready, and you boys want to get it over."

"You understand that we're only doing our duty?" says Donovan.

110   Belcher's head was raised like a blind man's, so that you could only see his chin and the tip of his nose in the lantern-light.

"I never could make out what duty was myself," he said. "I think you're all good lads, if that's what you mean. I'm not complaining."

Noble, just as if he couldn't bear any more of it, raised his fist at Donovan, and in a flash Donovan raised his gun and fired. The big man went over like a sack of meal, and this time there was no need of a second shot.

I don't remember much about the burying, but that it was worse than all the rest because we had to carry them to the grave. It was all mad lonely with nothing but a patch of lantern-light between ourselves and the dark, and birds hooting and screeching all round, disturbed by the guns. Noble went through Hawkins's belongings to find the letter from his mother, and then joined his hands together. He did the same with Belcher. Then, when we'd filled the grave, we separated from Jeremiah Donovan and

Feeney and took our tools back to the shed. All the way we didn't speak a word. The kitchen was dark and cold as we'd left it, and the old woman was sitting over the hearth, saying her beads. We walked past her into the room, and Noble struck a match to light the lamp. She rose quietly and came to the doorway with all her cantankerousness gone.

"What did ye do with them?" she asked in a whisper, and Noble started so that the match went out in his hand.

"What's that?" he asked without turn-   115 ing around.

"I heard ye," she said.

"What did you hear?" asked Noble.

"I heard ye. Do ye think I didn't hear ye, putting the spade back in the houseen?"

Noble struck another match and this time the lamp lit for him.

"Was that what ye did to them?" she   120 asked.

Then, by God, in the very doorway, she fell on her knees and began praying, and after looking at her for a minute or two Noble did the same by the fireplace. I pushed my way out past her and left them at it. I stood at the door, watching the stars and listening to the shrieking of the birds dying out over the bogs. It is so strange what you feel at times like that that you can't describe it. Noble says he saw everything ten times the size, as though there were nothing in the whole world but that little patch of bog with the two Englishmen stiffening into it, but with me it was as if the patch of bog where the Englishmen were was a million miles away, and even Noble and the old woman, mumbling behind me, and the birds and the bloody stars were all far away, and I was somehow very small and very lost and lonely like a child astray in the snow. And anything that happened to me afterwards, I never felt the same about again.

····▶ *Your* **Turn**
Talking and Writing about Lit

1. Why does O'Connor choose to tell the story from the point of view of Bonaparte? What would be the effect if the events were narrated from Jeremiah Donovan's perspective? How might the story's meaning change?

2. Why does the writer choose to begin "Guests of the Nation" with a game of cards?

3. What is the significance of the title "Guests of the Nation"?

4. **DIY** Rewrite either the first three or the last three pages of "Guests of the Nation" from the point of view of Jeremiah Donovan, Hawkins, Belcher, or Noble.

Isabel Allende (b. 1942)

Isabel Allende, who is from Chile, was born in Peru, the daughter of a Chilean diplomat. Her father disappeared mysteriously when she was a young girl. In 1973 her father's first cousin, Salvador Allende, was assassinated during his term as president of Chile. To escape the political oppression which was most likely the cause of these two deaths, Allende moved to Venezuela in 1975. There she worked as a journalist and teacher and began to write her first novel, *House of Spirits* (1985). The English translation launched her terrifically successful international career, and she is now one of the most highly respected contemporary Latin American women writers. She has published three other novels, *Of Love and Shadows* (1987), *Eva Luna* (1988), and *The Infinite Plan* (1993), as well as a collection of short stories, *The Stories of Eva Luna* (1991).

The Judge's Wife (1989)

Translated by Nick Caistor

Nicolas Vidal always knew he would lose his head over a woman. So it was foretold on the day of his birth, and later confirmed by the Turkish woman in the corner shop the one time he allowed her to read his fortune in the coffee grounds. Little did he imagine though that it would be on account of Casilda, Judge Hidalgo's wife. It was on her wedding day that he first glimpsed her. He was not impressed, preferring his women dark-haired and brazen. This ethereal slip of a girl in her wedding gown, eyes filled with wonder, and fingers obviously unskilled in the art of rousing a man to pleasure, seemed to him almost ugly. Mindful of his destiny, he had always been wary of any emotional contact with women, hardening his heart and restricting himself to the briefest of encounters whenever the demands of manhood needed satisfying. Casilda, however, appeared so insubstantial, so distant, that he cast aside all precaution and, when the fateful moment arrived, forgot the prediction that usually weighed in all his decisions. From the roof of the bank, where he was crouching with two of his men, Nicolas Vidal peered down at this young lady from the capital. She had a dozen equally pale and dainty relatives with her, who spent the whole of the ceremony fanning themselves with an air of utter bewilderment, then departed straight away, never to return. Along with everyone else in the town, Vidal was convinced the young bride would not withstand the climate, and that within a few months the old women would be dressing her up again, this time for her funeral. Even if she did survive the heat and the dust that filtered in through every pore to lodge itself in the soul, she would be bound to succumb to the fussy habits of her confirmed bachelor of a husband. Judge Hidalgo was twice her age, and had slept alone for so many years he didn't have the slightest notion of how to go about pleasing a woman. The severity and stubbornness with which he executed the law even at the expense of justice had made him feared throughout the province. He refused to apply any common sense in the exercise of his profession, and was equally harsh in his condemnation of the theft of a chicken as of a premeditated murder. He dressed formally in black, and, despite the all-pervading dust in this godforsaken town, his boots always shone with beeswax. A man such as he was never meant to be a husband, and yet not only did the gloomy wedding-day prophecies remain unfulfilled, but Casilda emerged happy and smiling from three pregnancies in rapid succession. Every Sunday at noon she would go to mass with her husband, cool

and collected beneath her Spanish mantilla, seemingly untouched by our pitiless summer, as wan and frail-looking as on the day of her arrival: a perfect example of delicacy and refinement. Her loudest words were a soft-spoken greeting; her most expressive gesture was a graceful nod of the head. She was such an airy, diaphanous creature that a moment's carelessness might mean she disappeared altogether. So slight an impression did she make that the changes noticeable in the Judge were all the more remarkable. Though outwardly he remained the same— he still dressed as black as a crow and was as stiff-necked and brusque as ever—his judgments in court altered dramatically. To general amazement, he found the youngster who robbed the Turkish shopkeeper innocent, on the grounds that she had been selling him short for years, and the money he had taken could therefore be seen as compensation. He also refused to punish an adulterous wife, arguing that since her husband himself kept a mistress he did not have the moral authority to demand fidelity. Word in the town had it that the Judge was transformed the minute he crossed the threshold at home: that he flung off his gloomy apparel, rollicked with his children, chuckled as he sat Casilda on his lap. Though no one ever succeeded in confirming these rumors, his wife got the credit for his newfound kindness, and her reputation grew accordingly. None of this was of the slightest interest to Nicolas Vidal, who as a wanted man was sure there would be no mercy shown him the day he was brought in chains before the Judge. He paid no heed to the talk about Doña Casilda, and the rare occasions he glimpsed her from afar only confirmed his first impression of her as a lifeless ghost.

Born thirty years earlier in a windowless room in the town's only brothel, Vidal was the son of Juana the Forlorn and an unknown father. The world had no place for him. His mother knew it, and so tried to wrench him from her womb with sprigs of parsley, candle butts, douches of ashes, and other violent purgatives, but the child clung to life. Once, years later, Juana was looking at her mysterious son and realized that, while all her infallible methods of aborting might have failed to dislodge him, they had none the less tempered his soul to the hardness of iron. As soon as he came into the world, he was lifted in the air by the midwife who examined him by the light of an oil lamp. She saw he had four nipples.

"Poor creature: he'll lose his head over a woman," she predicted, drawing on her wealth of experience.

Her words rested on the boy like a deformity. Perhaps a woman's love would have made his existence less wretched. To atone for all her attempts to kill him before birth, his mother chose him a beautiful first name, and an imposing family name picked at random. But the lofty name of Nicolas Vidal was no protection against the fateful cast of his destiny. His face was scarred from knife fights before he reached his teens, so it came as no surprise to decent folk that he ended up a bandit. By the age of twenty, he had become the leader of a band of desperadoes. The habit of violence toughened his sinews. The solitude he was condemned to for fear of falling prey to a woman lent his face a doleful expression. As soon as they saw him, everyone in the town knew from his eyes, clouded by tears he would never allow to fall, that he was the son of Juana the Forlorn. Whenever there was an outcry after a crime had been committed in the region, the police set out with dogs to track him down, but after scouring the hills invariably returned empty-handed. In all honesty they preferred it that way, because they could never have fought him. His gang gained such a fearsome reputation that the surrounding villages and estates paid to keep them away. This money would have been plenty for his men, but Nicolas Vidal kept them constantly on horseback in a whirlwind of death and destruction so they would not lose their taste for battle. Nobody dared take them on. More than once, Judge Hidalgo had asked the government to send troops to reinforce the police, but after several useless forays the soldiers returned to their barracks and Nicolas Vidal's gang to their exploits. On one occasion only did Vidal come close to falling into the hands of justice, and then he was saved by his hardened heart.

Weary of seeing the laws flouted, 5 Judge Hidalgo resolved to forget his scruples and set a trap for the outlaw. He realized that to defend justice he was committing an injustice, but chose the lesser of two evils. The only bait he could find was Juana the Forlorn, as she was Vidal's sole known relative. He had her dragged from the brothel where by now, since no clients were willing to pay for her exhausted charms, she scrubbed floors and cleaned out the lavatories. He put her in a specially made cage which was set up in the middle of the Plaza de Armas, with only a jug of water to meet her needs.

"As soon as the water's finished, she'll start to squawk. Then her son will come running, and I'll be waiting for him with the soldiers," Judge Hidalgo said.

News of this torture, unheard of since the days of slavery, reached Nicolas Vidal's ears shortly before his mother drank the last of the water. His men watched as he received the report in silence, without so much as a flicker of emotion on his blank lone wolf's face, or a pause in the sharpening of his dagger blade on a leather strap. Though for many years he had had no contact with Juana, and retained few happy childhood memories, this was a question of honor. No man can accept such an insult, his gang reasoned as they got guns and horses ready to rush into the ambush and, if need be, lay down their lives. Their chief showed no sign of being in a hurry. As the hours went by tension mounted in the camp. The perspiring, impatient men stared at each other, not daring to speak. Fretful, they caressed the butts of their revolvers and their horses' manes, or busied themselves coiling their lassos. Night fell. Nicolas Vidal was the only one in the camp who slept. At dawn, opinions were divided. Some of the men reckoned he was even more heartless than they had ever imagined, while others maintained their leader was planning a spectacular ruse to free his mother. The one thing that never crossed any of their minds was that his courage might have failed him, for he had always proved he had more than enough to spare. By noon, they could bear the suspense no longer, and went to ask him what he planned to do.

"I'm not going to fall into his trap like an idiot," he said.

"What about your mother?"

10   "We'll see who's got more balls, the Judge or me," Nicolas Vidal coolly replied.

By the third day, Juana the Forlorn's cries for water had ceased. She lay curled on the cage floor, with wildly staring eyes and swollen lips, moaning softly whenever she regained consciousness, and the rest of the time dreaming she was in hell. Four armed guards stood watch to make sure nobody brought her water. Her groans penetrated the entire town, filtering through closed shutters or being carried by the wind through the cracks in doors. They got stuck in corners, where dogs worried at them, and passed them on in their howls to the newly born, so that whoever heard them was driven to distraction. The Judge couldn't prevent a steady stream of people filing through the square to show their sympathy

for the old woman, and was powerless to stop the prostitutes going on a sympathy strike just as the miners' fortnight holiday was beginning. That Saturday, the streets were thronged with lusty workmen desperate to unload their savings, who now found nothing in town apart from the spectacle of the cage and this universal wailing carried mouth to mouth down from the river to the coast road. The priest headed a group of Catholic ladies to plead with Judge Hidalgo for Christian mercy and to beg him to spare the poor old innocent woman such a frightful death, but the man of the law bolted his door and refused to listen to them. It was then they decided to turn to Doña Casilda.

The Judge's wife received them in her shady living room. She listened to their pleas looking, as always, bashfully down at the floor. Her husband had not been home for three days, having locked himself in his office to wait for Nicolas Vidal to fall into his trap. Without so much as glancing out of the window, she was aware of what was going on, for Juana's long-drawn-out agony had forced its way even into the vast rooms of her residence. Doña Casilda waited until her visitors had left, dressed her children in their Sunday best, tied a black ribbon round their arms as a token of mourning, then strode out with them in the direction of the square. She carried a food hamper and a bottle of fresh water for Juana the Forlorn. When the guards spotted her turning the corner, they realized what she was up to, but they had strict orders, and barred her way with their rifles. When, watched now by a small crowd, she persisted, they grabbed her by the arms. Her children began to cry.

Judge Hidalgo sat in his office overlooking the square. He was the only person in the town who had not stuffed wax in his ears, because his mind was intent on the ambush and he was straining to catch the sound of horses' hoofs, the signal for action. For three long days and nights he put up with Juana's groans and the insults of the townspeople gathered outside the courtroom, but when he heard his own children start to wail he knew he had reached the bounds of his endurance. Vanquished, he walked out of the office with his three days' beard, his eyes bloodshot from keeping watch, and the weight of a thousand years on his back. He crossed the street, turned into the square and came face to face with his wife. They gazed at each other sadly. In seven years, this was the first time she had gone against him, and she had chosen to do so in front of the whole town. Easing the hamper and the bottle from Casilda's grasp, Judge Hidalgo himself opened the cage to release the prisoner.

"Didn't I tell you he wouldn't have the balls?" laughed Nicolas Vidal when the news reached him.

15   His laughter turned sour the next day, when he heard that Juana the Forlorn had hanged herself from the chandelier in the brothel where she had spent her life, overwhelmed by the shame of her only son leaving her to fester in a cage in the middle of the Plaza de Armas.

"That Judge's hour has come," said Vidal.

He planned to take the Judge by surprise, put him to a horrible death, then dump him in the accursed cage for all to see. The Turkish shopkeeper sent him word that the Hidalgo family had left that same night for a seaside resort to rid themselves of the bitter taste of defeat.

The Judge learned he was being pursued when he stopped to rest at a wayside inn. There was little protection for him there until an army patrol could arrive, but he had a few hours' start, and his motor car could outrun the gang's horses. He calculated he could make it to the next town and summon help there. He ordered his wife and children

into the car, put his foot down on the accelerator, and sped off along the road. He ought to have arrived with time to spare, but it had been ordained that Nicolas Vidal was that day to meet the woman who would lead him to his doom.

Overburdened by the sleepless nights, the townspeople's hostility, the blow to his pride, and the stress of this race to save his family, Judge Hidalgo's heart gave a massive jolt, then split like a pomegranate. The car ran out of control, turned several somersaults and finally came to a halt in the ditch. It took Doña Casilda some minutes to work out what had happened. Her husband's advancing years had often led her to think what it would be like to be left a widow, yet she had never imagined he would leave her at the mercy of his enemies. She wasted little time dwelling on her situation, knowing she must act at once to get her children to safety. When she gazed around her, she almost burst into tears. There was no sign of life in the vast plain baked by a scorching sun, only barren cliffs beneath an unbounded sky bleached colorless by the fierce light. A second look revealed the dark shadow of a passage or cave on a distant slope, so she ran towards it with two children in her arms and the third clutching her skirts.

One by one she carried her children up 20 the cliff. The cave was a natural one, typical of many in the region. She peered inside to be certain it wasn't the den of some wild animal, sat her children against its back wall, then, dry-eyed, kissed them good-bye.

"The troops will come to find you a few hours from now. Until then, don't for any reason whatsoever come out of here, even if you hear me screaming—do you understand?"

Their mother gave one final glance at the terrified children clinging to each other, then clambered back down to the road. She reached the car, closed her husband's eyes, smoothed back her hair and settled down to wait. She had no idea how many men were in Nicolas Vidal's gang, but prayed there were a lot of them so it would take them all the more time to have their way with her. She gathered strength pondering on how long it would take her to die if she determined to do it as slowly as possible. She willed herself to be desirable, luscious, to create more work for them and thus gain time for her children.

Casilda did not have long to wait. She soon saw a cloud of dust on the horizon and heard the gallop of horses' hoofs. She clenched her teeth. Then, to her astonishment, she saw there was only one rider, who stopped a few yards from her, gun at the ready. By the scar on his face she recognized Nicolas Vidal, who had set out all alone in pursuit of Judge Hidalgo, as this was a private matter between the two men. The Judge's wife understood she was going to have to endure something far worse than a lingering death.

A quick glance at her husband was enough to convince Vidal that the Judge was safely out of his reach in the peaceful sleep of death. But there was his wife, a shimmering presence in the plain's glare. He leapt from his horse and strode over to her. She did not flinch or lower her gaze, and to his amazement he realized that for the first time in his life another person was facing him without fear. For several seconds that stretched to eternity, they sized each other up, trying to gauge the other's strength, and their own powers of resistance. It gradually dawned on both of them that they were up against a formidable opponent. He lowered his gun. She smiled.

Casilda won each moment of the ensuing hours. To all the wiles of seduction known since the beginning of time she added new ones born of necessity to bring this man to the heights of rapture. Not only did she work on his body like an artist, stimulating his every fiber to pleasure, but she brought all the delicacy of her spirit into play on her side. Both knew their lives were at stake, and this added a new and terrifying dimension to their meeting. Nicolas Vidal had fled from love since birth, and knew nothing of intimacy, tenderness, secret laughter, the riot of the senses, the joy of shared passion. Each minute brought the detachment of troops and the noose that much nearer, but he gladly accepted this in return for her prodigious gifts. Casilda was a passive, demure, timid woman who had been married to an austere old man in front of whom she had never even dared appear naked. Not once during that unforgettable afternoon did she forget that her aim was to win time for her children, and yet at some point, marvelling at her own possibilities, she gave herself completely, and felt something akin to gratitude towards him. That was why, when she heard the soldiers in the distance, she begged him to flee to the hills. Instead, Nicolas Vidal chose to fold her in a last embrace, thus fulfilling the prophecy that had sealed his fate from the start.

•••••➤*Your* Turn
Talking and Writing about Lit

1. What is Allende's point-of-view strategy in "The Judge's Wife"? How does this choice of narrative point of view serve her purposes thematically?

2. Who is the main character—Doña Casilda or Nicholas Vidal? Why?

3. Analyze the use of irony in Allende's story.

4. **DIY** Rewrite the first three pages of the story or the last three pages of the story from Juana the Forlorn's point of view.

Ernest Hemingway (1899–1961)

Ernest Hemingway was born in Oak Park, Illinois. During World War I, he was seriously wounded while serving with the Italian army at the Austrian front. After his recovery, he worked abroad as a newspaper correspondent, and while in Europe, he developed friendships with some prominent writers of the time, among them Gertrude Stein and Ezra Pound, who encouraged him to develop his own writing style. Hemingway is also known for his enjoyment of the outdoors and his pursuit of such sports as hunting (including big-game hunting), fishing, and bullfighting. Hemingway's most highly acclaimed novels are *The Sun Also Rises* (1926), *A Farewell to Arms* (1929), *For Whom the Bell Tolls* (1940), and *The Old Man and the Sea* (1952). His best-known stories appear in *In Our Time* (1925) and *Men without Women* (1927). Hemingway was awarded the Nobel Prize in 1954. In 1961, when his popularity was on the wane and he learned he had cancer, Hemingway committed suicide.

Soldier's Home (1925)

Krebs went to the war from a Methodist college in Kansas. There is a picture which shows him among his fraternity brothers, all of them wearing exactly the same height and style collar. He enlisted in the Marines in 1917 and did not return to the United States until the second division returned from the Rhine in the summer of 1919.

There is a picture which shows him on the Rhine with two German girls and another corporal. Krebs and the corporal look too big for their uniforms. The German girls are not beautiful. The Rhine does not show in the picture.

By the time Krebs returned to his home town in Oklahoma the greeting of heroes was over. He came back much too late. The men from the town who had been drafted had all been welcomed elaborately on their return. There had been a great deal of hysteria. Now the reaction had set in. People seemed to think it was rather ridiculous for Krebs to be getting back so late, years after the war was over.

At first Krebs, who had been at Belleau Wood, Soissons, the Champagne, St. Mihiel, and in the Argonne* did not want to talk about the war at all. Later he felt the need to talk but no one wanted to hear about it. His

---

*Belleau Wood . . . Argonne: Sites of battles in World War I in which American troops were instrumental in pushing back the Germans.

town had heard too many atrocity stories to be thrilled by actualities. Krebs found that to be listened to at all he had to lie, and after he had done this twice he, too, had a reaction against the war and against talking about it. A distaste for everything that had happened to him in the war set in because of the lies he had told. All of the times that had been able to make him feel cool and clear inside himself when he thought of them; the times so long back when he had done the one thing, the only thing for a man to do, easily and naturally, when he might have done something else, now lost their cool, valuable quality and then were lost themselves.

5   His lies were quite unimportant lies and consisted in attributing to himself things other men had seen, done, or heard of, and stating as facts certain apocryphal incidents familiar to all soldiers. Even his lies were not sensational at the pool room. His acquaintances, who had heard detailed accounts of German women found chained to machine guns in the Argonne forest and who could not comprehend, or were barred by their patriotism from interest in, any German machine gunners who were not chained, were not thrilled by his stories.

Krebs acquired the nausea in regard to experience that is the result of untruth or exaggeration, and when he occasionally met another man who had really been a soldier and they talked a few minutes in the dressing room at a dance he fell into the easy pose of the old soldier among other soldiers: that he had been badly, sickeningly frightened all the time. In this way he lost everything.

During this time, it was late summer, he was sleeping late in bed, getting up to walk down town to the library to get a book, eating lunch at home, reading on the front porch until he became bored, and then walking down through the town to spend the hottest hours of the day in the cool dark of the pool room. He loved to play pool.

In the evening he practiced on his clarinet, strolled down town, read, and went to bed. He was still a hero to his two young sisters. His mother would have given him breakfast in bed if he had wanted it. She often came in when he was in bed and asked him to tell her about the war, but her attention always wandered. His father was noncommittal.

Before Krebs went away to the war he had never been allowed to drive the family motor car. His father was in the real estate business and always wanted the car to be at his command when he required it to take clients out into the country to show them a piece of farm property. The car always stood outside the First National Bank building where his father had an office on the second floor. Now, after the war, it was still the same car.

Nothing was changed in the town 10 except that the young girls had grown up. But they lived in such a complicated world of already defined alliances and shifting feuds that Krebs did not feel the energy or the courage to break into it. He liked to look at them, though. There were so many good-looking young girls. Most of them had their hair cut short. When he went away only little girls wore their hair like that or girls that were fast. They all wore sweaters and shirt waists with round Dutch collars. It was a pattern. He liked to look at them from the front porch as they walked on the other side of the street. He liked to watch them walking under the shade of the trees. He liked the round Dutch collars above their sweaters. He liked their silk stockings and flat shoes. He liked their bobbed hair and the way they walked.

When he was in town their appeal to him was not very strong. He did not like them when he saw them in the Greek's ice cream parlor. He did not want them themselves really. They were too complicated.

There was something else. Vaguely he wanted a girl but he did not want to have to work to get her. He would have liked to have a girl but he did not want to have to spend a long time getting her. He did not want to get into the intrigue and the politics. He did not want to have to do any courting. He did not want to tell any more lies. It wasn't worth it.

He did not want any consequences. He did not want any consequences ever again. He wanted to live along without consequences. Besides he did not really need a girl. The army had taught him that. It was all right to pose as though you had to have a girl. Nearly everybody did that. But it wasn't true. You did not need a girl. That was the funny thing. First a fellow boasted how girls mean nothing to him, that he never thought of them, that they could not touch him. Then a fellow boasted that he could not get along without girls, that he had to have them all the time, that he could not go to sleep without them.

That was all a lie. It was all a lie both ways. You did not need a girl unless you thought about them. He learned that in the army. Then sooner or later you always got one. When you were really ripe for a girl you always got one. You did not have to think about it. Sooner or later it would come. He had learned that in the army.

Now he would have liked a girl if she had come to him and not wanted to talk. But here at home it was all too complicated. He knew he could never get through it all again. It was not worth the trouble. That was the thing about French girls and German girls. There was not all this talking. You couldn't talk much and you did not need to talk. It was simple and you were friends. He thought about France and then he began to think about Germany. On the whole he had liked Germany better. He did not want to

leave Germany. He did not want to come home. Still, he had come home. He sat on the front porch.

He liked the girls that were walking 15 along the other side of the street. He liked the look of them much better than the French girls or the German girls. But the world they were in was not the world he was in. He would like to have one of them. But it was not worth it. They were such a nice pattern. He liked the pattern. It was exciting. But he would not go through all the talking. He did not want one badly enough. He liked to look at them all, though. It was not worth it. Not now when things were getting good again.

He sat there on the porch reading a book on the war. It was a history and he was reading about all the engagements he had been in. It was the most interesting reading he had ever done. He wished there were more maps. He looked forward with a good feeling to reading all the really good histories when they would come out with good detail maps. Now he was really learning about the war. He had been a good soldier. That made a difference.

One morning after he had been home about a month his mother came into his bedroom and sat on the bed. She smoothed her apron.

"I had a talk with your father last night, Harold," she said, "and he is willing for you to take the car out in the evenings."

"Yeah?" said Krebs, who was not fully awake. "Take the car out? Yeah?"

"Yes. Your father has felt for some time 20 that you should be able to take the car out in the evenings whenever you wished but we only talked it over last night."

"I'll bet you made him," Krebs said.

"No. It was your father's suggestion that we talk the matter over."

"Yeah. I'll bet you made him," Krebs sat up in bed.

"Will you come down to breakfast, Harold?" his mother said.

25 "As soon as I get my clothes on," Krebs said.

His mother went out of the room and he could hear her frying something downstairs while he washed, shaved, and dressed to go down into the dining-room for breakfast. While he was eating breakfast his sister brought in the mail.

"Well, Hare," she said. "You old sleepyhead. What do you ever get up for?"

Krebs looked at her. He liked her. She was his best sister.

"Have you got the paper?" he asked.

30 She handed him the Kansas City *Star* and he shucked off its brown wrapper and opened it to the sporting page. He folded the *Star* open and propped it against the water pitcher with his cereal dish to steady it, so he could read while he ate.

"Harold," his mother stood in the kitchen doorway, "Harold, please don't muss up the paper. Your father can't read his *Star* if it's been mussed."

"I won't muss it," Krebs said.

His sister sat down at the table and watched him while he read.

"We're playing indoor over at school this afternoon," she said. "I'm going to pitch."

35 "Good," said Krebs. "How's the old wing?"

"I can pitch better than lots of the boys. I tell them all you taught me. The other girls aren't much good."

"Yeah?" said Krebs.

"I tell them all you're my beau. Aren't you my beau, Hare?"

"You bet."

40 "Couldn't your brother really be your beau just because he's your brother?"

"I don't know."

"Sure you know. Couldn't you be my beau, Hare, if I was old enough and if you wanted to?"

"Sure. You're my girl now."

"Am I really your girl?"

"Sure." 45

"Do you love me?"

"Uh, huh."

"Will you love me always?"

"Sure."

"Will you come over and watch me 50 play indoor?"

"Maybe."

"Aw, Hare, you don't love me. If you loved me, you'd want to come over and watch me play indoor."

Krebs's mother came into the dining-room from the kitchen. She carried a plate with two fried eggs and some crisp bacon on it and a plate of buckwheat cakes.

"You run along, Helen," she said. "I want to talk to Harold."

She put the eggs and bacon down in 55 front of him and brought in a jug of maple syrup for the buckwheat cakes. Then she sat down across the table from Krebs.

"I wish you'd put down the paper a minute, Harold," she said.

Krebs took down the paper and folded it.

"Have you decided what you are going to do yet, Harold?" his mother said, taking off her glasses.

"No," said Krebs.

"Don't you think it's about time?" His 60 mother did not say this in a mean way. She seemed worried.

"I hadn't thought about it," Krebs said.

"God has some work for everyone to do," his mother said. "There can be no idle hands in His Kingdom."

"I'm not in His Kingdom," Krebs said.

"We are all of us in His Kingdom."

Krebs felt embarrassed and resentful 65 as always.

"I've worried about you so much, Harold," his mother went on. "I know the temptations you must have been exposed to. I know how weak men are. I know what your own dear grandfather, my own father, told us about the Civil War and I have prayed for you. I pray for you all day long, Harold."

Krebs looked at the bacon fat hardening on his plate.

"Your father is worried, too," his mother went on. "He thinks you have lost your ambition, that you haven't got a definite aim in life. Charley Simmons, who is just your age, has a good job and is going to be married. The boys are all settling down; they're all determined to get somewhere; you can see that boys like Charley Simmons are on their way to being really a credit to the community."

Krebs said nothing.

70 "Don't look that way, Harold," his mother said. "You know we love you and I want to tell you for your own good how matters stand. Your father does not want to hamper your freedom. He thinks you should be allowed to drive the car. If you want to take some of the nice girls out riding with you, we are only too pleased. We want you to enjoy yourself. But you are going to have to settle down to work, Harold. Your father doesn't care what you start in at. All work is honorable as he says. But you've got to make a start at something. He asked me to speak to you this morning and then you can stop in and see him at his office."

"Is that all?" Krebs said.

"Yes. Don't you love your mother, dear boy?"

"No," Krebs said.

His mother looked at him across the table. Her eyes were shiny. She started crying.

75 "I don't love anybody," Krebs said.

It wasn't any good. He couldn't tell her, he couldn't make her see it. It was silly to have said it. He had only hurt her. He went over and took hold of her arm. She was crying with her head in her hands.

"I didn't mean it," he said. "I was just angry at something. I didn't mean I didn't love you."

His mother went on crying. Krebs put his arm on her shoulder.

"Can't you believe me, mother?"

His mother shook her head.   80

"Please, please, mother. Please believe me."

"All right," his mother said chokily. She looked up at him. "I believe you, Harold."

Krebs kissed her hair. She put her face up to him.

"I'm your mother," she said. "I held you next to my heart when you were a tiny baby."

Krebs felt sick and vaguely nauseated.   85

"I know, Mummy," he said. "I'll try and be a good boy for you."

"Would you kneel and pray with me, Harold?" his mother asked.

They knelt down beside the dining-room table and Krebs's mother prayed.

"Now, you pray, Harold," she said.

"I can't," Krebs said.   90

"Try, Harold."

"I can't."

"Do you want me to pray for you?"

"Yes."

So his mother prayed for him and then 95 they stood up and Krebs kissed his mother and went out of the house. He had tried so to keep his life from being complicated. Still, none of it had touched him. He had felt sorry for his mother and she had made him lie. He would go to Kansas City and get a job and she would feel all right about it. There would be one more scene maybe before he got away. He would not go down to his father's office. He would miss that one. He wanted his life to go smoothly. It had just gotten going that way. Well, that was all over now, anyway. He would go over to the schoolyard and watch Helen play indoor baseball.

·····▶ *Your* Turn
Talking and Writing about Lit

1. Hemingway is known for his spare, economical, and direct writing style; yet, in "Soldier's Home," he deliberately employs an uncharacteristically repetitive and circular style (for example, see paragraphs 10–15). Why do you think he wrote in this style when imagining the story from Krebs's third-person limited omniscient view?

2. Sometimes, on the other hand, much is said by saying nothing. What does it mean when, in paragraph 67, Krebs "looked at the bacon fat hardening on his plate" and remained silent?

3. Why do you think Hemingway begins the story with two photographs? What does he gain by "showing" us these two different pictures of Krebs?

4. **DIY** Write an additional brief scene for this story in which Krebs tries to talk to one of the girls from the town. Imagine what she would say to him and what he would answer. Write this as if it follows right after Hemingway's own ending in paragraph 95, and imagine it takes place as Krebs is watching Helen play indoor baseball. Then write your own final ending for the story. Does Krebs go to Kansas City in your ending? Do we know what becomes of him, or is your version also open ended?

Ralph Ellison (1914–1994)

Most people in the know agree that Ralph Ellison's novel *Invisible Man* (1952) is one of the masterpieces of American fiction. Not only does it portray the African American experience, it is also a coming-of-age novel which illuminates universal themes about growing up, feeling like an outsider, and finding our identity. *Invisible Man* won the National Book Award in 1953. Ellison was born in Oklahoma City, Oklahoma, in 1914, and he began his college-level study at Tuskegee Institute in 1933. Later, he moved to New York City, where he met Langston Hughes and Richard Wright, both of whom encouraged his work. He also published a collection of his essays, *Shadow and Act* (1964), and was a professor of contemporary literature and culture at New York University. His novel *Juneteenth*, begun in 1954 and left in manuscript form when he died in 1994, was published posthumously (that is, after his death) in 1999.

Flying Home (1944)

When Todd came to, he saw two faces suspended above him in a sun so hot and blinding that he could not tell if they were black or white. He stirred, feeling a pain that burned as though his whole body had been laid open to the sun which glared into his eyes. For a moment an old fear of being touched by white hands seized him. Then the very sharpness of the pain began slowly to clear his head. Sounds came to him dimly. He done come to. Who are they? he thought Naw he ain't, I coulda sworn he was white. Then he heard clearly:

"You hurt bad?"

Something within him uncoiled. It was a Negro sound.

"He's still out," he heard.

5 "Give 'im time. . . . Say, son, you hurt bad?"

Was he? There was that awful pain. He lay rigid, hearing their breathing and trying to weave a meaning between them and his being stretched painfully upon the ground. He watched them warily, his mind traveling back over a painful distance. Jagged scenes, swiftly unfolding as in a movie trailer, reeled through his mind, and he saw himself piloting a tailspinning plane and landing and landing and falling from the cockpit and trying to stand. Then, as in a great silence, he remembered the sound of crunching bone, and now, looking up into the anxious faces of an old Negro man and a boy from where he lay in the same field, the memory sickened him and he wanted to remember no more.

"How you feel, son?"

Todd hesitated, as though to answer would be to admit an inacceptable weakness. Then, "It's my ankle," he said.

"Which one?"

"The left." 10

With a sense of remoteness he watched the old man bend and remove his boot, feeling the pressure ease.

"That any better?"

"A lot. Thank you."

He had the sensation of discussing someone else, that his concern was with some far more important thing, which for some reason escaped him.

"You done broke it bad," the old man 15 said. "We have to get you to a doctor."

He felt that he had been thrown into a tailspin. He looked at his watch; how long had he been here? He knew there was but one important thing in the world, to get the plane back to the field before his officers were displeased.

"Help me up," he said. "Into the ship."

"But it's broke too bad. . . ."

"Give me your arm!"

"But, son . . ." 20

Clutching the old man's arm he pulled himself up, keeping his left leg clear, thinking, "I'd never make him understand," as the leather-smooth face came parallel with his own.

"Now, let's see."

He pushed the old man back, hearing a bird's insistent shrill. He swayed giddily. Blackness washed over him, like infinity.

"You best sit down."

"No, I'm O.K." 25

"But, son. You jus' gonna make it worse. . . ."

It was a fact that everything in him cried out to deny, even against the flaming pain in his ankle. He would have to try again.

"You mess with that ankle they have to cut your foot off," he heard.

Holding his breath, he started up again. It pained so badly that he had to bite his lips to keep from crying out and he allowed them to help him down with a pang of despair.

30   "It's best you take it easy. We gon' git you a doctor."

Of all the luck, he thought. Of all the rotten luck, now I have done it. The fumes of high-octane gasoline clung in the heat, taunting him.

"We kin ride him into town on old Ned," the boy said.

Ned? He turned, seeing the boy point toward an ox team browsing where the buried blade of a plow marked the end of a furrow. Thoughts of himself riding an ox through the town, past streets full of white faces, down the concrete runways of the airfield made swift images of humiliation in his mind. With a pang he remembered his girl's last letter. "Todd," she had written, "I don't need the papers to tell me you had the intelligence to fly. And I have always known you to be as brave as anyone else. The papers annoy me. Don't you be contented to prove over and over again that you're brave or skillful just because you're black, Todd. I think they keep beating that dead horse because they don't want to say why you boys are not yet fighting. I'm really disappointed, Todd. Anyone with brains can learn to fly, but then what? What about using it, and who will you use it for? I wish, dear, you'd write about this. I sometimes think they're playing a trick on us. It's very humiliating. . . ." He wiped cold sweat from his face, thinking. What does she know of humiliation? She's never been down South. Now the humiliation would come. When you must have them judge you, knowing that they never accept your mistakes as your own, but hold it against your whole race— that was humiliation. Yes, and humiliation was when you could never be simply yourself, when you were always a part of this old black ignorant man. Sure, he's all right. Nice

and kind and helpful. But he's not you. Well, there's one humiliation I can spare myself.

"No," he said, "I have orders not to leave the ship. . . ."

"Aw," the old man said. Then turning to   35 the boy, "Teddy, then you better hustle down to Mister Graves and get him to come. . . ."

"No, wait!" he protested before he was fully aware. Graves might be white. "Just have him get word to the field, please. They'll take care of the rest."

He saw the boy leave, running.

"How far does he have to go?"

"Might' nigh a mile."

He rested back, looking at the dusty   40 face of his watch. But now they know something has happened, he thought. In the ship there was a perfectly good radio, but it was useless. The old fellow would never operate it. That buzzard knocked me back a hundred years, he thought. Irony danced within him like the gnats circling the old man's head. With all I've learned I'm dependent upon this "peasant's" sense of time and space. His leg throbbed. In the plane, instead of time being measured by the rhythms of pain and a kid's legs, the instruments would have told him at a glance. Twisting upon his elbows he saw where dust had powdered the plane's fuselage, feeling the lump form in his throat that was always there when he thought of flight. It's crouched there, he thought, like the abandoned shell of a locust. I'm naked without it. Not a machine, a suit of clothes you wear. And with a sudden embarrassment and wonder he whispered, "It's the only dignity I have. . . ."

He saw the old man watching, his torn overalls clinging limply to him in the heat. He felt a sharp need to tell the old man what he felt. But that would be meaningless. If I tried to explain why I need to fly back, he'd think I was simply afraid of white officers. But it's more than fear . . . a sense of anguish clung to him like the veil of sweat that hugged his face. He watched the old man, hearing him humming snatches of a tune as he admired the plane. He felt a furtive sense of resentment. Such old men often came to the field to watch the pilots with childish eyes. At first it had made him proud; they had been a meaningful part of a new experience. But soon he realized they did not understand his accomplishments and they came to shame and embarrass him, like the distasteful praise of an idiot. A part of the meaning of flying had gone then, and he had not been able to regain it. If I were a prizefighter I would be more human, he thought. Not a monkey doing tricks, but a man. They were pleased simply that he was a Negro who could fly, and that was not enough. He felt cut off from them by age, by understanding, by sensibility, by technology and by his need to measure himself against the mirror of other men's appreciation. Somehow he felt betrayed, as he had when as a child he grew to discover that his father was dead. Now for him any real appreciation lay with his white officers; and with them he could never be sure. Between ignorant black men and condescending whites, his course of flight seemed mapped by the nature of things away from all needed and natural landmarks. Under some sealed orders, couched in ever more technical and mysterious terms, his path curved swiftly away from both the shame the old man symbolized and the cloudy terrain of white men's regard. Flying blind, he knew but one point of landing and there he would receive his wings. After that the enemy would appreciate his skill and he would assume his deepest meaning, he thought sadly, neither from those who condescended nor from those who praised without understanding, but from the enemy who would recognize his manhood and skill in terms of hate. . . .

He sighed, seeing the oxen making queer, prehistoric shadows against the dry brown earth.

"You just take it easy, son," the old man soothed. "That boy won't take long. Crazy as he is about airplanes."

"I can wait," he said.

"What kinda airplane you call this 45 here'n?"

"An Advanced Trainer," he said, seeing the old man smile. His fingers were like gnarled dark wood against the metal as he touched the low-slung wing.

"'Bout how fast can she fly?"

"Over two hundred an hour."

"Lawd! That's so fast I bet it don't seem like you moving!"

Holding himself rigid, Todd opened 50 his flying suit. The shade had gone and he lay in a ball of fire.

"You mind if I take a look inside? I was always curious to see. . . ."

"Help yourself. Just don't touch anything."

He heard him climb upon the metal wing, grunting. Now the questions would start. Well, so you don't have to think to answer. . . .

He saw the old man looking over into the cockpit, his eyes bright as a child's.

"You must have to know a lot to work 55 all these here things."

He was silent, seeing him step down and kneel beside him.

"Son, how come you want to fly way up there in the air?"

Because it's the most meaningful act in the world . . . because it makes me less like you, he thought.

But he said: "Because I like it, I guess. It's as good a way to fight and die as I know."

"Yeah? I guess you right," the old man 60 said. "But how long you think before they gonna let you all fight?"

He tensed. This was the question all Negroes asked, put with the same timid hopefulness and longing that always opened a greater void within him than that he had felt beneath the plane the first time he had flown. He felt light-headed. It came to him suddenly that there was something sinister about the conversation, that he was flying unwillingly into unsafe and uncharted regions. If he could only be insulting and tell this old man who was trying to help him to shut up!

"I bet you one thing. . . ."

"Yes?"

"That you was plenty scared coming down."

65   He did not answer. Like a dog on a trail the old man seemed to smell out his fears and he felt anger bubble within him.

"You sho' scared me. When I seen you coming down in that thing with it a-rollin' and a-jumpin' like a pitchin' hoss, I thought sho' you was a goner. I almost had me a stroke!"

He saw the old man grinning, "Ever'thin's been happening round here this morning, come to think of it."

"Like what?" he asked.

"Well, first thing I know, here come two white fellers looking for Mister Rudolph, that's Mister Graves's cousin. That got me worked up right away. . . ."

70   "Why?"

"Why? 'Cause he done broke outta the crazy house, that's why. He liable to kill somebody," he said. "They oughta have him by now though. Then here you come. First I think it's one of them white boys. Then doggone if you don't fall outta there. Lawd, I'd done heard about you boys but I haven't never seen one o' you-all. Cain't tell you how it felt to see somebody what look like me in a airplane!"

The old man talked on, the sound streaming around Todd's thoughts like air flowing over the fuselage of a flying plane. You were a fool, he thought, remembering how before the spin the sun had blazed bright against the billboard signs beyond the town, and how a boy's blue kite had bloomed beneath him, tugging gently in the wind like a strange, odd-shaped flower. He had once flown such kites himself and tried to find the boy at the end of the invisible cord. But he had been flying too high and too fast. He had climbed steeply away in exultation. Too steeply, he thought. And one of the first rules you learn is that if the angle of thrust is too steep the plane goes into a spin. And then, instead of pulling out of it and going into a dive you let a buzzard panic you. A lousy buzzard!

"Son, what made all that blood on the glass?"

"A buzzard," he said, remembering how the blood and feathers had sprayed back against the hatch. It had been as though he had flown into a storm of blood and blackness.

"Well, I declare! They's lots of 'em 75 around here. They after dead things. Don't eat nothing what's alive."

"A little bit more and he would have made a meal out of me," Todd said grimly.

"They bad luck all right. Teddy's got a name for 'em, calls 'em jimcrows," the old man laughed.

"It's a damned good name."

"They the damnedest birds. Once I seen a hoss all stretched out like he was sick, you know. So I hollers, 'Gid up from there, suh!' Just to make sho! An' doggone, son, if I don't see two ole jimcrows come flying right up outa that hoss's insides! Yessuh! The sun was shinin' on 'em and they couldn't a been no greasier if they'd been eating barbecue."

Todd thought he would vomit, his 80 stomach quivered.

"You made that up," he said.

"Nawsuh! Saw him just like I see you."

"Well, I'm glad it was you."

"You see lots a funny things down here, son."

85 "No, I'll let you see them," he said.

"By the way, the white folks round here don't like to see you boys up there in the sky. They ever bother you?"

"No."

"Well, they'd like to."

"Someone always wants to bother someone else," Todd said. "How do you know?"

90 "I just know."

"Well," he said defensively, "no one has bothered us."

Blood pounded in his ears as he looked away into space. He tensed, seeing a black spot in the sky, and strained to confirm what he could not clearly see.

"What does that look like to you?" he asked excitedly.

"Just another bad luck, son."

95 Then he saw the movement of wings with disappointment. It was gliding smoothly down, wings outspread, tail feathers gripping the air, down swiftly—gone behind the green screen of trees. It was like a bird he had imagined there, only the sloping branches of the pines remained, sharp against the pale stretch of sky. He lay barely breathing and stared at the point where it had disappeared, caught in a spell of loathing and admiration. Why did they make them so disgusting and yet teach them to fly so well? It's like when I was up in heaven, he heard, starting.

The old man was chuckling, rubbing his stubbed chin.

"What did you say?"

"Sho', I died and went to heaven . . . maybe by time I tell you about it they be done come after you."

"I hope so," he said wearily.

100 "You boys ever sit around and swap lies?"

"Not often. Is this going to be one?"

"Well, I ain't so sho', on account of it took place when I was dead."

The old man paused, "That wasn't no lie 'bout the buzzards, though."

"All right," he said.

"Sho' you want to hear 'bout heaven?" 105

"Please," he answered, resting his head upon his arm.

"Well, I went to heaven and right away started to sproutin' me some wings. Six good ones, they was. Just like them the white angels had. I couldn't hardly believe it. I was so glad that I went off on some clouds by myself and tried 'em out. You know, 'cause I didn't want to make a fool outta myself the first thing. . . ."

It's an old tale, Todd thought. Told me years ago. Had forgotten. But at least it will keep him from talking about buzzards.

He closed his eyes, listening.

". . . First thing I done was to git up on 110 a low cloud and jump off. And doggone, boy, if them wings didn't work! First I tried the right; then I tried the left; then I tried 'em both together. Then Lawd, I started to move on out among the folks. I let 'em see me. . . ."

He saw the old man gesturing flight with his arms, his face full of mock pride as he indicated an imaginary crowd, thinking, It'll be in the newspapers, as he heard, ". . . so I went and found me some colored angels—somehow I didn't believe I was an angel till I seen a real black one, ha, yes! Then I was sho'—but they tole me I better come down 'cause us colored folks had to wear a special kin' a harness when we flew. That was how come they wasn't flyin'. Oh yes, an' you had to be extra strong for a black man even, to fly with one of them harnesses. . . . "

This is a new turn, Todd thought, what's he driving at?

"So I said to myself, I ain't gonna be bothered with no harness! Oh naw! 'Cause if

God let you sprout wings you oughta have sense enough not to let nobody make you wear something what gits in the way of flyin'. So I starts to flyin'. Heck, son," he chuckled, his eyes twinkling, "you know I had to let eve'ybody know that old Jefferson could fly good as anybody else. And I could too, fly smooth as a bird! I could even loop-the-loop—only I had to make sho' to keep my long white robe down roun' my ankles. . . ."

Todd felt uneasy. He wanted to laugh at the joke, but his body refused, as of an independent will. He felt as he had as a child when after he had chewed a sugar-coated pill which his mother had given him, she had laughed at his efforts to remove the terrible taste.

115 ". . . Well," he heard, "I was doing all right 'til I got to speeding. Found out I could fan up a right strong breeze, I could fly so fast. I could do all kin'sa stunts too. I started flying up to the stars and divin' down and zooming roun' the moon. Man, I like to scare the devil outa some ole white angels. I was raisin' hell. Not that I meant any harm, son. But I was just feeling good. It was so good to know I was free at last. I accidentally knocked the tips offa some stars and they tell me I caused a storm and a coupla lynchings down here in Macon County—though I swear I believe them boys what said that was making up lies on me. . . ."

He's mocking me, Todd thought angrily. He thinks it's a joke. Grinning down at me. . . . His throat was dry. He looked at his watch; why the hell didn't they come? Since they had to, why? One day I was flying down one of them heavenly streets. You got yourself into it, Todd thought. Like Jonah in the whale.

"Justa throwin' feathers in everybody's face. An 'ole Saint Peter called me in. Said, 'Jefferson, tell me two things, what you doin' flyin' without a harness; an' how come you flyin' so fast?' So I tole him I was flyin' without a harness 'cause it got in my way, but I couldn'ta been flyin' so fast, 'cause I wasn't usin' but one wing. Saint Peter said, 'You wasn't flyin' with but one wing?' 'Yessuh,' I says, scared-like. So he says, 'Well, since you got sucha extra fine pair of wings you can leave off yo' harness awhile. But from now on none of that there one-wing flyin', 'cause you gittin' up too damn much speed!'"

And with one mouth full of bad teeth you're making too damned much talk, thought Todd. Why don't I send him after the boy? His body ached from the hard ground and seeking to shift his position he twisted his ankle and hated himself for crying out.

"It gittin' worse?"

"I . . . I twisted it," he groaned. 120

"Try not to think about it, son. That's what I do."

He bit his lip, fighting pain with counter-pain as the voice resumed its rhythmical droning. Jefferson seemed caught in his own creation.

". . . After all that trouble I just floated roun' heaven in slow motion. But I forgot, like colored folks will do, and got to flyin' with one wing again. This time I was restin' my old broken arm and got to flyin' fast enough to shame the devil. I was comin' so fast, Lawd, I got myself called befo' ole Saint Peter again. He said, 'Jeff, didn't I warn you 'bout that speedin'?' 'Yessuh,' I says, 'but it was an accident.' He looked at me sad-like and shook his head and I knowed I was gone. He said, 'Jeff, you and that speedin' is a danger to the heavenly community. If I was to let you keep on flyin', heaven wouldn't be nothin' but uproar. Jeff, you got to go!' Son, I argued and pleaded with that old white man, but it didn't do a bit of good. They rushed me straight to them pearly gates and gimme a parachute and a map of the state of Alabama. . . ."

Todd heard him laughing so that he could hardly speak, making a screen between them upon which his humiliation glowed like fire.

125 "Maybe you'd better stop awhile," he said, his voice unreal.

"Ain't much more," Jefferson laughed. "When they gimme the parachute ole Saint Peter ask me if I wanted to say a few words before I went. I felt so bad I couldn't hardly look at him, specially with all them white angels standin' around. Then somebody laughed and made me mad. So I tole him, 'Well, you done took my wings. And you puttin' me out. You got charge of things so's I can't do nothin' about it. But you got to admit just this: While I was up here I was the flyinest sonofabitch what ever hit heaven!'"

At the burst of laughter Todd felt such an intense humiliation that only great violence would wash it away. The laughter which shook the old man like a boiling purge set up vibrations of guilt within him which not even the intricate machinery of the plane would have been adequate to transform and he heard himself screaming, "Why do you laugh at me this way?"

He hated himself at that moment, but he had lost control. He saw Jefferson's mouth fall open, "What—?"

"Answer me!"

130 His blood pounded as though it would surely burst his temples and he tried to reach the old man and fell, screaming, "Can I help it because they won't let us actually fly? Maybe we are a bunch of buzzards feeding on a dead horse, but we can hope to be eagles, can't we? Can't we?"

He fell back, exhausted, his ankle pounding. The saliva was like straw in his mouth. If he had the strength he would strangle this old man. This grinning, gray-headed clown who made him feel as he felt when watched by the white officers at the field. And yet this old man had neither power, prestige, rank nor technique. Nothing that could rid him of this terrible feeling. He watched him, seeing his face struggle to express a turmoil of feeling.

"What you mean, son? What you talking 'bout . . . ?"

"Go away. Go tell your tales to the white folks."

"But I didn't mean nothing like that . . . . I . . . I wasn't tryin' to hurt your feelings. . . ."

"Please. Get the hell away from me!" 135

"But I didn't, son. I didn't mean all them things a-tall."

Todd shook as with a chill, searching Jefferson's face for a trace of the mockery he had seen there. But now the face was somber and tired and old. He was confused. He could not be sure that there had ever been laughter there, that Jefferson had ever really laughed in his whole life. He saw Jefferson reach out to touch him and shrank away, wondering if anything except the pain, now causing his vision to waver, was real. Perhaps he had imagined it all.

"Don't let it get you down, son," the voice said pensively.

He heard Jefferson sigh wearily, as though he felt more than he could say. His anger ebbed, leaving only the pain.

"I'm sorry," he mumbled. 140

"You just wore out with pain, was all. . . ."

He saw him through a blur, smiling. And for a second he felt the embarrassed silence of understanding flutter between them.

"What you was doin' flyin' over this section, son? Wasn't you scared they might shoot you for a cow?"

Todd tensed. Was he being laughed at again? But before he could decide, the pain shook him and a part of him was lying calmly behind the screen of pain that had fallen between them, recalling the first time he had ever seen a plane. It was as though an endless series of hangars had been shaken ajar in the air-base of his memory and from each, like a young wasp emerging from its cell, arose the memory of a plane.

145   The first time I ever saw a plane I was very small and planes were new in the world. I was four-and-a-half and the only plane that I had ever seen was a model suspended from the ceiling of the automobile exhibit at the State Fair. But I did not know that it was only a model. I did not know how large a real plane was, nor how expensive. To me it was a fascinating toy, complete in itself, which my mother said could only be owned by rich little white boys. I stood rigid with admiration, my head straining backwards as I watched the gray little plane describing arcs above the gleaming tops of the automobiles. And I vowed that, rich or poor, someday I would own such a toy. My mother had to drag me out of the exhibit and not even the merry-go-round, the Ferris wheel, or the racing horses could hold my attention for the rest of the Fair. I was too busy imitating the tiny drone of the plane with my lips, and imitating with my hands the motion, swift and circling, that it made in flight.

After that I no longer used the pieces of lumber that lay about our back yard to construct wagons and autos . . . now it was used for airplanes. I built biplanes, using pieces of board for wings, a small box for the fuselage, another piece of wood for the rudder. The trip to the Fair had brought something new into my small world. I asked my mother repeatedly when the Fair would come back again. I'd lie in the grass and watch the sky, and each fighting bird became a soaring plane. I would have been good a year just to have seen a plane again. I became a nuisance to everyone with my questions about airplanes. But planes were new to the old folks, too, and there was little that they could tell me. Only my uncle knew some of the answers. And better still, he could carve propellers from pieces of wood that would whirl rapidly in the wind, wobbling noisily upon oiled nails.

I wanted a plane more than I'd wanted anything; more than I wanted the red wagon with rubber tires, more than the train that ran on a track with its train of cars. I asked my mother over and over again:

"Mamma?"

"What do you want, boy?" she'd say.

"Mamma, will you get mad if I ask   150 you?" I'd say.

"What do you want now? I ain't got time to be answering a lot of fool questions. What you want?"

"Mamma, when you gonna get me one . . . ?" I'd ask.

"Get you one what?" she'd say.

"You know, Mamma; what I been asking you. . . ."

"Boy," she'd say, "if you don't want a   155 spanking you better come on an' tell me what you talking about so I can get on with my work."

"Aw, Mamma, you know. . . ."

"What I just tell you?" she'd say.

"I mean when you gonna buy me a airplane."

"AIRPLANE! Boy, is you crazy? How many times I have to tell you to stop that foolishness. I done told you them things cost too much. I bet I'm gon' wham the living daylight out of you if you don't quit worrying me 'bout them things!"

But this did not stop me, and a few   160 days later I'd try all over again.

Then one day a strange thing happened. It was spring and for some reason I had been hot and irritable all morning. It was a beautiful spring. I could feel it as I played barefoot in the backyard. Blossoms hung from the thorny black locust trees like clusters of fragrant white grapes. Butterflies flickered in the sunlight above the short new dew-wet grass. I had gone in the house for bread and butter and coming out I heard a steady unfamiliar drone. It was unlike anything I had ever heard before. I tried to place the sound. It was no use. It was a sensation like that I had when searching for my father's watch, heard ticking unseen in a room. It made me feel as though I had forgotten to perform some task that my mother had ordered . . . then I located it, overhead. In the sky, flying quite low and about a hundred yards off was a plane! It came so slowly that it seemed barely to move. My mouth hung wide; my bread and butter fell into the dirt. I wanted to jump up and down and cheer. And when the idea struck I trembled with excitement: "Some little white boy's plane's done flew away and all I got to do is stretch out my hands and it'll be mine!" It was a little plane like that at the Fair, flying no higher than the eaves of our roof. Seeing it come steadily forward I felt the world grow warm with promise. I opened the screen and climbed over it and clung there, waiting. I would catch the plane as it came over and swing down fast and run into the house before anyone could see me. Then no one could come to claim the plane. It droned nearer. Then when it hung like a silver cross in the blue directly above me I stretched out my hand and grabbed. It was like sticking my finger through a soap bubble. The plane flew on, as though I had simply blown my breath after it. I grabbed again, frantically, trying to catch the tail. My fingers clutched the air and disappointment surged tight and hard in my throat. Giving one last desperate grasp, I strained forward. My fingers ripped against the screen. I was falling. The ground burst hard against me. I drummed the earth with my heels and when my breath returned, I lay there bawling.

My mother rushed through the door.

"What's the matter, chile! What on earth is wrong with you?"

"It's gone! It's gone!"

"What gone?"　165

"The airplane. . . ."

"Airplane?"

"Yessum, jus' like the one at the Fair. . . . I . . . I tried to stop it an' it kep' right on going. . . ."

"When, boy?"

"Just now," I cried, through my tears.　170

"Where it go, boy, what way?"

"Yonder, there. . . ."

She scanned the sky, her arms akimbo and her checkered apron flapping in the wind as I pointed to the fading plane. Finally she looked down at me, slowly shaking her head.

"It's gone! It's gone!" I cried.

"Boy, is you a fool?" she said. "Don't　175 you see that there's a real airplane 'stead of one of them toy ones?"

"Real . . . ?" I forgot to cry. "Real?"

"Yass, real. Don't you know that thing you reaching for is bigger'n a auto? You here trying to reach for it and I bet it's flying 'bout two hundred miles higher'n this roof." She was disgusted with me. "You come on in this house before somebody else sees what a fool you done turned out to be. You must think these here lil ole arms of you'n is mighty long. . . ."

I was carried into the house and undressed for bed and the doctor was called. I cried bitterly, as much from the disappointment of finding the plane so far beyond my reach as from the pain.

When the doctor came I heard my mother telling him about the plane and asking if anything was wrong with my mind. He explained that I had had a fever for several hours. But I was kept in bed for a week and I constantly saw the plane in my sleep, flying just beyond my fingertips, sailing so slowly that it seemed barely to move. And each time I'd reach out to grab it I'd miss and through each dream I'd hear my grandma warning:

> Young man, young man
> Yo' arms too short
> To box with God. . . .

180 "Hey, son!"

At first he did not know where he was and looked at the old man pointing, with blurred eyes.

"Ain't that one of you-all's airplanes coming after you?"

As his vision cleared he saw a small black shape above a distant field, soaring through waves of heat. But he could not be sure and with the pain he feared that somehow a horrible recurring fantasy of being split in twain by the whirling blades of a propeller had come true.

"You think he sees us?" he heard.

185 "See? I hope so."

"He's coming like a bat outa hell!"

Straining, he heard the faint sound of a motor and hoped it would soon be over.

"How you feeling?"

"Like a nightmare," he said.

190 "Hey, he's done curved back the other way!"

"Maybe he saw us," he said. "Maybe he's gone to send out the ambulance and ground crew." And, he thought with despair, maybe he didn't even see us.

"Where did you send the boy?"

"Down to Mister Graves," Jefferson said. "Man what owns this land."

"Do you think he phoned?"

195 Jefferson looked at him quickly.

"Aw sho'. Dabney Graves is got a bad name on accounta them killings but he'll call though. . . ."

"What killings?"

"Them five fellers . . . ain't you heard?" he asked with surprise.

"No."

"Everybody knows 'bout Dabney 200 Graves, especially the colored. He done killed enough of us."

Todd had the sensation of being caught in a white neighborhood after dark.

"What did they do?" he asked.

"Thought they was men," Jefferson said. "An' some he owed money, like he do me. . . ."

"But why do you stay here?"

"You black, son." 205

"I know, but . . ."

"You have to come by the white folks, too."

He turned away from Jefferson's eyes, at once consoled and accused. And I'll have to come by them soon, he thought with despair. Closing his eyes, he heard Jefferson's voice as the sun burned bloodred upon his lips.

"I got nowhere to go," Jefferson said, "an' they'd come after me if I did. But Dabney Graves is a funny fellow. He's all the time making jokes. He can be mean as hell, then he's liable to turn right around and back the colored against the white folks. I seen him do it. But me, I hates him for that more'n anything else. 'Cause just as soon as he gits tired helping a man he don't care what happens to him. He just leaves him stone cold. And then the other white folks is double hard on anybody he done helped. For him it's just a joke. He don't give a hilla beans for nobody—but hisself. . . ."

Todd listened to the thread of detach- 210 ment in the old man's voice. It was as though he held his words arm's length before him to avoid their destructive meaning.

"He'd just as soon do you a favor and then turn right around and have you strung up. Me, I stays outa his way 'cause down here that's what you gotta do."

If my ankle would only ease for a while, he thought. The closer I spin toward the earth the blacker I become, flashed through his mind. Sweat ran into his eyes and he was sure that he would never see the plane if his head continued whirling. He tried to see Jefferson, what it was that Jefferson held in his hand? It was a little black man, another Jefferson! A little black Jefferson that shook with fits of belly-laughter while the other Jefferson looked on with detachment. Then Jefferson looked up from the thing in his hand and turned to speak, but Todd was far away, searching the sky for a plane in a hot dry land on a day and age he had long forgotten. He was going mysteriously with his mother through empty streets where black faces peered from behind drawn shades and someone was rapping at a window and he was looking back to see a hand and a frightened face frantically beckoning from a cracked door and his mother was looking down the empty perspective of the street and shaking her head and hurrying him along and at first it was only a flash he saw and a motor was droning as through the sun-glare he saw it gleaming silver as it circled and he was seeing a burst like a puff of white smoke and hearing his mother yell, Come along, boy, I got no time for them fool airplanes, I got no time, and he saw it a second time, the plane flying high, and the burst appeared suddenly and fell slowly, billowing out and sparkling like fireworks and he was watching and being hurried along as the air filled with a flurry of white pinwheeling cards that caught in the wind and scattered over the rooftops and into the gutters and a woman was running and snatching a card and reading it and screaming and he darted into the shower, grabbing as in winter he grabbed for snowflakes and bounding away at his mother's, Come on here, boy! Come on, I

say! and he was watching as she took the card away, seeing her face grow puzzled and turning taut as her voice quavered, "Niggers Stay From the Polls," and died to a moan of terror as he saw the eyeless sockets of a white hood staring at him from the card and above he saw the plane spiraling gracefully, agleam in the sun like a fiery sword. And seeing it soar he was caught, transfixed between a terrible horror and a horrible fascination.

The sun was not so high now, and Jefferson was calling and gradually he saw three figures moving across the curving roll of the field.

"Look like some doctors, all dressed in white," said Jefferson.

They're coming at last, Todd thought. 215 And he felt such a release of tension within him that he thought he would faint. But no sooner did he close his eyes than he was seized and he was struggling with three white men who were forcing his arms into some kind of coat. It was too much for him, his arms were pinned to his sides and as the pain blazed in his eyes, he realized that it was a straitjacket. What filthy joke was this?

"That oughta hold him, Mister Graves," he heard.

His total energies seemed focused in his eyes as he searched their faces. That was Graves; the other two wore hospital uniforms. He was poised between two poles of fear and hate as he heard the one called Graves saying, "He looks kinda purty in that there suit, boys. I'm glad you dropped by."

"This boy ain't crazy, Mister Graves," one of the others said. "He needs a doctor, not us. Don't see how you led us way out here anyway. It might be a joke to you, but your cousin Rudolph liable to kill somebody. White folks or niggers, don't make no difference. . . ."

Todd saw the man turn red with anger. Graves looked down upon him, chuckling.

220 "This nigguh belongs in a straitjacket, too, boys. I knowed that the minit Jeff's kid said something 'bout a nigguh flyer. You all know you cain't let the nigguh git up that high without his going crazy. The nigguh brain ain't built right for high altitudes. . . ."

Todd watched the drawling red face, feeling that all the unnamed horror and obscenities that he had ever imagined stood materialized before him.

"Let's git outta here," one of the attendants said.

Todd saw the other reach toward him, realizing for the first time that he lay upon a stretcher as he yelled.

"Don't put your hands on me!"

225 They drew back, surprised.

"What's that you say, nigguh?" asked Graves.

He did not answer and thought that Graves's foot was aimed at his head. It landed on his chest and he could hardly breathe. He coughed helplessly, seeing Graves's lips stretch taut over his yellow teeth, and tried to shift his head. It was as though a half-dead fly was dragging slowly across his face and a bomb seemed to burst within him. Blasts of hot, hysterical laughter tore from his chest, causing his eyes to pop and he felt that the veins in his neck would surely burst. And then a part of him stood behind it all, watching the surprise in Graves's red face and his own hysteria. He thought he would never stop, he would laugh himself to death. It rang in his ears like Jefferson's laughter and he looked for him, centering his eyes desperately upon his face, as though somehow he had become his sole salvation in an insane world of outrage and humiliation. It brought a certain relief. He was suddenly aware that although his body was still contorted it was an echo that no longer rang in his ears. He heard Jefferson's voice with gratitude.

"Mister Graves, the Army done tole him not to leave his airplane."

"Nigguh, Army or no, you gittin' off my land! That airplane can stay 'cause it was paid for by taxpayers' money. But you gittin' off. An' dead or alive, it don't make no difference to me."

Todd was beyond it now, lost in a 230 world of anguish.

"Jeff," Graves said, "you and Teddy come and grab holt. I want you to take this here black eagle over to that nigguh airfield and leave him."

Jefferson and the boy approached him silently. He looked away, realizing and doubting at once that only they could release him from his overpowering sense of isolation.

They bent for the stretcher. One of the attendants moved toward Teddy.

"Think you can manage it, boy?"

"I think I can, suh," Teddy said. 235

"Well, you better go behind then, and let yo' pa go ahead so's to keep that leg elevated."

He saw the white men walking ahead of Jefferson and the boy carried him along in silence. Then they were pausing and he felt a hand wiping his face; then he was moving again. And it was as though he had been lifted out of his isolation, back into the world of men. A new current of communication flowed between the man and boy and himself. They moved him gently. Far away he heard a mockingbird liquidly calling. He raised his eyes, seeing a buzzard poised unmoving in space. For a moment the whole afternoon seemed suspended and he waited for the horror to seize him again. Then like a song within his head he heard the boy's soft humming and saw the dark bird glide into the sun and glow like a bird of flaming gold.

····▶ *Your* **Turn**
Talking and Writing about Lit

1. What does Ellison accomplish by using the unusual point-of-view strategy in "Flying Home"? What is accomplished in terms of characterization by shifting between the third-person limited omniscient view and the first-person view of Todd?

2. How do Ellison's choices regarding narrative point of view help illuminate the themes in the story?

3. What are the sources of conflict in the story? Are these conflicts resolved in the end? Do you interpret the story's final image as a hopeful one, or is the ending ambiguous?

4. **DIY** Think of an activity of yours that means a great deal to you and that you became interested in at an early age (such as sports, reading, cooking, spending time with a parent or sibling). Write a scene in which you are engaged in that activity in the present; then write a flashback to the moment you first felt the spark of interest in that activity (if you can't remember the exact moment, you can imagine it—try your hand at writing fiction!).

POP CULTURE

Point of View in Press and Politics

Both ends of the political spectrum often accuse the media of being slanted to the opposite camp. The left complains about a corporate-run media which favors a right-wing pro-business position; the right, on the other hand, complains about a liberal media run by bleeding hearts and artists. Both sides are well represented by different media organs, which presents almost comically different perspectives on the same events.

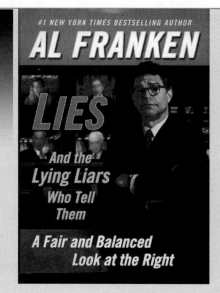

Al Franken's *LIES and the Lying Liars Who Tell Them: A Fair and Balanced Look at the Right*

Talking Lit

Author and critic Michael Steinman wrote an introduction to the work of Frank O'Connor and to the story "Guests of the Nation."

Michael Steinman, from *A Frank O'Connor Reader*

Simultaneously a story of war's inhumanity and the friendships it destroys, "Guests of the Nation" moves inexorably from harmony to desolation. Although O'Connor said modestly it was only an imitation of an Isaac Babel story in *The Red Cavalry*, its singularity came from his experiences during the Troubles: "One day, when I was sitting on my bed in an Irish internment camp . . . I overheard a group of country boys talking about two English soldiers whom they had held as hostages and who soon got to know the countryside better than their guards. It was obvious from the conversation that the two English boys had won the affection and understanding of our own fellows, though it wasn't the understanding of soldiers who find they have much in common, but

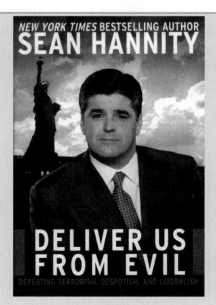

Sean Hannity's *Deliver Us from Evil: Defeating Terrorism, Despotism, and Liberalism*

Two media outlets can report on the same story and use entirely different word choices in their descriptions, thus putting a "spin" on the story. Sean Hannity, an acknowledged conservative, of the *Hannity and Colmes* debate show on Fox News, described an audio clip of Senator Ted Kennedy speaking as "Ted Kennedy Ramblings." David M. Halbfinger, of the *New York Times*, described the same event as "a master [whipping] up a storm," speaking highly of Ted Kennedy as a master orator.

In literature, as in the media, how the story is told depends on who is telling it—from whose perspective we're viewing the issues (or the action).

the understanding of two conflicting ways of life which must either fight or be friends" ("Interior Voices," 10).

A first reading will leave one shaken by the cold cruelty of those who profess devotion to "duty," "principle," and ideology, ignoring human beings; deeper readings reveal that every detail is resonant from "foreign dances" and card games among "chums" to arguments about capitalism and life after death, Belcher's last comments about home and family. Appropriately, John Hildebidle has described it as a story of family, although its members are related to one another by circumstances and affection rather than blood (180). Bonaparte's famous last sentence, "And anything that happened to me afterwards, I never felt the same about again," echoes Gogol's "The Overcoat" and is *the* introduction to any O'Connor short story—a transfiguring experience for its characters and the reader.

This 1954 version departs stylistically from the first text, written "with the mind of a young poet . . . in a fever, weeping, laughing, singing the dialogue to myself" ("Voices," 201–2); the revision gains clarity from two decades of experience. Had O'Connor written no more after March 1930, we would still remember him for this story.

Student Essay

Dominic Pignataro became interested in how two authors who had experiences in very different wars were able to tell their stories using different point-of-view strategies. In his essay, Pignataro compares Hemingway's story, included in this chapter, and Tim O'Brien's story, which appears in Chapter 11.

Dominic Pignataro
Prof. Barbara Barnard
English 102-JE

Two Authors, Two Ways to Tell a War Story:
Point of View in "How to Tell a True War Story"
and "Soldier's Home"

Tim O'Brien's and Ernest Hemingway's accounts of war and war's aftermath ring true particularly because both of these writers served in the military (and in combat situations) themselves. Their life experience brings authenticity to their fictional accounts of the Vietnam war and World War I. O'Brien, who was drafted into the army, served as a combat infantryman during the Vietnam war, and Hemingway volunteered as an ambulance driver during World War I (although he was actually fighting with a combat unit when he was wounded at the front). Although both authors drew on personal experiences of war and its aftermath in the telling of their stories, there is also a striking difference between the two, and that is their use of point-of-view strategies. "Soldier's Home" is told in the third-person limited omniscient point of view, whereas O'Brien's story is written in the first-person voice. One factor that may have contributed to the two authors' different decisions about point of view is the different time periods in which the stories were written.

Because Hemingway stays very carefully inside the limited omniscient perspective of Krebs, we the readers are often forced to assess and interpret details and events—and especially Krebs's own thoughts and feelings that we are privy to—that the story does not interpret for us. Two examples would be when we are told that Krebs "felt embarrassed and resentful" (paragraph 65) and he also "felt sick

Pignataro 2

and vaguely nauseated" (paragraph 85) about being home and about the small town life that he'd thought he left behind when he headed for the war in the first place. Hemingway leaves it up to the reader to determine who or what Krebs has these feelings toward; these feelings could be directed against the people of the town, toward the town itself, or they could even represent what the war has done to change him or his true feelings about the town and his own life.

O'Brien's use of first-person narration is in some ways similar to Hemingway's use of limited omniscient narration, but in many ways it's different. O'Brien gives the reader a detailed description of the narrator's feelings, emotions, and opinions, which keeps the reader out of the dark, giving us a fuller understanding of the main character's motives and thoughts. O'Brien takes the reader directly into the story and into the war; he makes us feel like we are there:

> Twenty years later, I can still see the sunlight on Lemon's face. I can see him turning, looking back at Rat Kiley, then he laughed and took that curious half step from shade into sunlight, his face suddenly brown and shining, and when his foot touched down, in that instant, he must've thought it was the sunlight that was killing him. It was not the sunlight. It was a rigged 105 round. (paragraph 105)

This writer gives direct detail and he tells the story like he is talking directly to the reader, which is the complete opposite of how Hemingway tells his story. Hemingway beats around the bush, you might say, and he gives vague descriptions that don't always make the reader feel involved in the story. On the whole, I feel that the point-of-view strategy used by O'Brien was more effective. I was

Pignataro 3

drawn into the story by his personal, conversational tone, his complete and vivid descriptions, his frank (and sometimes graphic) representations of what war really is. O'Brien covers what happens during a war and after the war, whereas Hemingway is more concerned with the aftermath of war for just one character.

These differences are, to this reader, the most important points. However, one similarity is important to mention. One thing their use of third-person limited omniscient narration and first-person narration have in common is that both use a wealth of information about the inner experience of war through the emotional journey of a central character. A limitation in both stories might be this intense focus on only one character's view of the war. As we read both stories, we tend to agree with that main character's views, and this may limit the reader's experience of the stories. That said, the most interesting thing to me about these limited perspectives was that these perceptions were written by two men who had actually served in wars themselves, and so the stories always had a ring of truth to them. These two writers from different time periods both showed us how to tell a true war story. They gave a deeper meaning to the aftermath of war and what it can do to an individual and to all people of the world whom it affects as a whole.

All-American Slam®

Three scrambled eggs with Cheddar cheese. Plus hash browns or grits, two bacon strips, two sausage links and bread.

Grand Slam Slugger®

Two buttermilk pancakes, two eggs*, two bacon strips and two sausage links, plus hash browns or grits or choice of bread. Served with a small glass of juice and coffee.

French Toast Slam®

Two thick slices of our Fabulous French Toast with two eggs*, two bacon strips and two sausage links.

Lumberjack Slam®

Three buttermilk pancakes, a slice of grilled honey ham, two bacon strips, two sausage links and two eggs* plus hash browns or grits and choice of bread.

Original Grand Slam®

Buttermilk pancakes, eggs*, bacon and sausage. Two of each!

Two-Egg* Breakfast

Two eggs* served ... strips and two sausage ... browns or grits and bread.

Meat Lover's Skillet

Diced ham, bacon and sausage over seasoned country-fried potatoes. Topped with shredded Cheddar cheese and two eggs*. Served with choice of bread.

Moons Over My Hammy®

Ham and scrambled egg sandwich with Swiss and American cheese on grilled sourdough. Served with choice of hash browns or grits.

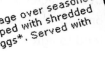

Breakfast Sampler

... good tastes! Two eggs any ..., two bacon strips, two pork sausage links, two ham strips, hash browns and two fluffy buttermilk pancakes

Rooty Tooty Fresh and Fruity®

It's two delicious! Two eggs, two bacon strips, two pork sausage links and two buttermilk pancakes crowned with your choice of fruit topping and whipped topping

- Blueberry
- Strawberry
- Cinnamon-Apple

International Passport Breakfast

The best of all worlds! Two eggs, two bacon strips, two sausage links and your choice of two same-style pancakes

- Swedish

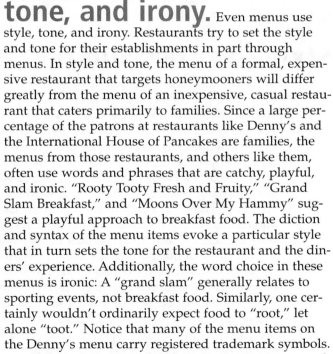

STYLE, TONE OF VOICE, AND IRONY

Even menus use style, tone, and irony. Even menus use style, tone, and irony. Restaurants try to set the style and tone for their establishments in part through menus. In style and tone, the menu of a formal, expensive restaurant that targets honeymooners will differ greatly from the menu of an inexpensive, casual restaurant that caters primarily to families. Since a large percentage of the patrons at restaurants like Denny's and the International House of Pancakes are families, the menus from those restaurants, and others like them, often use words and phrases that are catchy, playful, and ironic. "Rooty Tooty Fresh and Fruity," "Grand Slam Breakfast," and "Moons Over My Hammy" suggest a playful approach to breakfast food. The diction and syntax of the menu items evoke a particular style that in turn sets the tone for the restaurant and the diners' experience. Additionally, the word choice in these menus is ironic: A "grand slam" generally relates to sporting events, not breakfast food. Similarly, one certainly wouldn't ordinarily expect food to "root," let alone "toot." Notice that many of the menu items on the Denny's menu carry registered trademark symbols.

Like most companies, these restaurants use words to sell their products and their corporate image. Given that fact, do you suppose the narrators of the menus are reliable? See the explanation of "Reliability and Unreliability" below.

When telling about a sad experience, we choose different words to describe it than we'd choose when telling of a happy (or scary or weird) experience. And we automatically use a different tone of voice in a job interview than we use when talking to our friends. Authors also vary their use of style and tone depending on what they wish to convey.

He had been a good soldier. That made a difference.
(Ernest Hemingway, "Soldier's Home," paragraph 16)

He did not want any consequences. He did not want any consequences ever again. He wanted to live along without consequences.
(Ernest Hemingway, "Soldier's Home," paragraph 12)

Krebs acquired the nausea in regard to experience that is the result of untruth or exaggeration, and when he occasionally met another man who had really been a soldier and they talked a few minutes in the dressing room at a dance he fell into the easy pose of the old soldier among other soldiers: that he had been badly, sickeningly frightened all the time.
(Ernest Hemingway, "Soldier's Home," paragraph 6)

Below we will examine Hemingway's reasons for these stylistic shifts.

Style—Syntax, Diction, and Dialect

Style in fiction has to do with the writer's use of language in a distinctive way. We often say that a certain writer has a particular style. For instance, Ernest Hemingway's style is often said to be terse and direct, as in the first example above. It should be pointed out, however, that writers are often versatile and may choose to use language in a different way in one story (or novel) than in another. For example, while terse, compact sentences predominate in a typical Hemingway short story, in his story "Soldier's Home" (Chapter 6), he has sometimes used winding, repetitive, slow-moving sentences. This is intentional on Hemingway's part because "Soldier's Home" is a very internal story, focused throughout on the inner thoughts and feelings of one returning soldier, Krebs. The character is almost immobilized by the experience of war and returning home from war. The winding, circular style of the narrative in this particular Hemingway story reflects Krebs's state of mind, as in the second and third examples above. The use of sentence structure as an element of style, as has just been described, can be referred to as **syntax**.

Another aspect of style is **diction** or word choice. Diction is often categorized as being informal (relaxed, colloquial words; even slang could be included), middle (the way we usually speak in the classroom, for example), or formal (very sophisticated language, including vocabulary not readily understood by most people). When you read "How I Met My Husband," you'll see how Alice Munro uses a mix of middle diction and informal diction in the voice of the story. She does not make use of formal diction, as it would not be in keeping with her narrator's character. Sometimes the use of informal diction in the narrator Edie's voice might also be said to be in **dialect**, as the author makes use of a regional flavor in the language. For example, the narrator says of another character, "I bet she never put down fruit in her life" (paragraph 14)—the use of "put down" is in keeping with the character's region and class. She means that the character Loretta Bird never did any home canning (preserving) of fruit. On the other hand, when Edie says in the first paragraph, "We saw it come over the treetops, all red and silver, the first close-up plane I ever saw," this is an example of the use of informal diction to characterize the young narrator, but it is not necessarily a use of dialect. Note the lively use of dialect and informal language in Junot Díaz's "Fiesta, 1980":

> Mami looked really nice that day. The United States had finally put some meat on her; she was no longer the same flaca who had arrived here three years before. She had cut her hair short and was wearing tons of cheap-ass jewelry which on her didn't look too lousy. She smelled like herself, like the wind through a tree. (paragraph 3)

About the style and singularity of each writer's voice, Eudora Welty wrote, "For the source of the short story is usually lyrical. And all writers speak from and speak to, emotions eternally the same in all of us: love, pity, terror do not show favorites or leave any of us out" (Welty, *The Eye of the Story*, 108).

Tone and Voice

Tone in fiction refers to the author's attitude toward the subject. Munro's sentence about "the first close-up plane I ever saw" in the previous paragraph is spoken in the voice of Edie, our young narrator, and the tone is one of childlike wonderment; we are put in touch with the young girl's enjoyment of this first direct experience with an airplane: "We saw it come over the treetops, all red and silver." This tone is conveyed largely through word choice. If, on the other hand, the airplane were described in more formal language and if it were compared to the appearance of a buzzard circling, the tone might be one of menace rather than wonder. In that case, the use of imagery (picturing the plane as a buzzard) would also help convey tone. Tone is an important aspect of **narrative voice** in fiction. In contrast to the childlike voice of Munro's young narrator, this chapter also contains a story, "Carnal Knowledge," by T. Coraghessan Boyle, a writer who is known for his use of the satirical or ironic tone of voice—more on that below.

Three Types of Irony

Sometimes the tone of a story (or a passage within a story) conveys **irony**. Three basic types of irony can be found in fiction: verbal irony, situational irony, and dramatic irony. **Verbal irony** (also called sarcasm) occurs when there is a discrepancy between what the voice says and what it means; sometimes, the narrator or speaker means the opposite of what he or she has said. If the weather is gloomy, dark, and dripping and a character exclaims, "Well, it certainly is a bright, sunny day today, isn't it!" then we recognize the use of verbal irony. There is no mistaking the ironic "spin" the speaker gives to this statement.

A second type of irony, and the one found most often in fiction, is **situational irony**. We know we are in the presence of situational irony when we recognize a discrepancy between appearance and reality or when a situation in which what happens is not what we expect to happen. In Boyle's "Carnal Knowledge," there is often a discrepancy between what appears to be true and what is actually the case. For example, the character Alena appears to be the defender of animals, but she is the one who waves the "grisly banner," displaying the dead bodies of animals (paragraph 47). Also, at various times in the story, what happens is not what we expect to happen. For example, in the end of the story, the characters' apparent liberation of the Thanksgiving turkeys turns out to be quite the opposite of what they'd intended when the "freed" turkeys meet their death on the nearby highway—this is heavily ironic. Boyle's story contains many such ironic moments, but we might even say that the character of Alena herself is ironic, and the relationship between Alena and the narrator is also ironic. The story's ironic view of the characters and their activities is, in fact, so pervasively mocking that we might also say that the story is an example of **satire**, inasmuch as Boyle exposes the characters' excesses, hypocrisies, faults, and foibles (as does all good satire). Because he does this in a mocking tone, we are aware that it is intentional.

A third type of irony in fiction, known as **dramatic irony**, occurs when the reader (or the audience in a play or film) knows more than a character or characters know. At the end of Flannery O'Connor's "Good Country People" (Chapter 2), Mrs. Hopewell looks out across the field, sees Manley Pointer in the distance, and says, "'Why, that looks like that nice dull young man that tried to sell me a Bible yesterday'" and "'He was so simple . . . but I guess the world would be better off if we were all that simple.'" This is a moment of dramatic irony because the reader knows that Manley Pointer is not at all the simple young man that Mrs. Hopewell believes him to be; he is, in fact, quite the opposite. We also recognize dramatic irony at the end of Raymond Carver's "Cathedral" (which you'll read in this chapter). The narrator (the husband) might not be able to articulate it, but the reader knows that in a sense the blind man "sees" more clearly than the narrator, a "sighted" man, does. This is ironic because it's a reversal and it's not what we expect, but it's also dramatic irony because the reader knows more than the narrator does about what is happening in that last scene.

Reliability and Unreliability

Another aspect of narrative, which is often related to issues of style, tone, and voice, is **reliability** or **unreliability**. When a narrator is depicted—especially in the first-person voice—in the immediacy of a situation, feeling his or her way through an experience and uncertain about what is to happen next, the writer may be employing a **naïve** or **unreliable narrator**. This narrative strategy is often useful in **coming-of-age stories**, also called **initiation stories**, which depict a single experience or experiences (and often a turning point or a revelation) in the life of a young character. For instance, in Alice Munro's "How I Met My Husband," the young Edie can be said to be a naïve and, at times, unreliable narrator. During her first visit to the pilot, Chris Watters, Edie suddenly recalls her responsibilities: "Now I remembered the children and I was scared again, in case one of them had waked up and called me and I wasn't there" (paragraph 75). She leaves abruptly: "I tore off across the fairgrounds, scared I'd see the car heading home from town. My sense of time was mixed up, I didn't know how long I'd been out of the house" (paragraph 79). And, indeed, the reader does not know either, since our information is coming, at this point, from the naïve perspective of the younger Edie. This device is frequently effective in drawing the reader into the character's experience, encouraging readers to experience events from the perspective of the naïve or unreliable narrator. It should also be noted here that Munro's narrative strategy in "How I Met My Husband" is a complex one; at times, we also view events from the more mature perspective of the older Edie looking back on past experience.

The naïve voice or child's voice may be the most common sort of unreliable narrator, but narrators may be unreliable for other reasons as well. In Ralph Ellison's "Flying Home" (Chapter 6), we view events through both the first-person and third-person perspective of Todd, and he can be unreliable at times, simply because he is in severe pain from his injuries. He may at times be hallucinating, and he is certainly sometimes dreaming. Viewing events from the point of view of the injured pilot draws readers into his experience. We are confused along with him when, in the opening scene of the story, he looks up and cannot discern whether the people hovering over him are black or white: because he doesn't know, we the readers don't know either.

The above examples are examples of what we might call "innocent" unreliable narrators. Fiction writers also sometimes use an unreliable narrator, one who is simply untrustworthy. In such a story, we may be drawn into the narrator's view of things at the outset, but eventually we realize that the writer has deliberately created a narrator who cannot be trusted. In Raymond Carver's "Cathedral" (in this chapter), we discover we cannot trust the narrator's perceptions about blind people, about race, about ordinary everyday courtesies. A related device used by Carver in this particular story is the foil character. The narrator's wife often perceives things in a strikingly different light than her husband. In a sense, her more generous, more sensible view is a reality check which exposes the narrator's prejudices and shortsightedness to the reader. In the next chapter, we will consider the somewhat related issues of fantasy, hyperbole, and ambiguity, along with the chapter's primary topics of metaphor, image, and symbol.

Readings

Alice Munro (b. 1931)

Alice Munro grew up on a farm in rural Ontario, Canada. After two years at the University of Western Ontario, she married and moved to British Columbia. Munro began to write fiction early in her life, but her career progressed slowly at first, as she remarried and then raised three children. She published her first collection of short fiction, *Dance of the Happy Shades*, in 1968. Munro has since published many short story collections, including *Lives of Girls and Women* (1971), *Something I've Been Meaning to Tell You* (1974), *The Beggar Maid: Stories of Flo and Rose* (1979), *The Moons of Jupiter* (1982), *The Progress of Love* (1986), and *Friend of My Youth* (1990). She has won three Governor General's Awards in Canada for her fiction.

How I Met My Husband (1974)

We heard the plane come over at noon, roaring through the radio news, and we were sure it was going to hit the house, so we all ran out into the yard. We saw it come over the treetops, all red and silver, the first close-up plane I ever saw. Mrs. Peebles screamed.

"Crash landing," their little boy said. Joey was his name.

"It's okay," said Dr. Peebles. "He knows what he's doing." Dr. Peebles was only an animal doctor, but had a calming way of talking, like any doctor.

This was my first job—working for Dr. and Mrs. Peebles, who had bought an old house out on the Fifth Line, about five miles out of town. It was just when the trend was starting of town people buying up old farms, not to work them but to live on them.

5   We watched the plane land across the road, where the fairgrounds used to be. It did make a good landing field, nice and level for the old race track, and the barns and display sheds torn down now for scrap lumber so there was nothing in the way. Even the old grandstand bays had burned.

"All right," said Mrs. Peebles, snappy as she always was when she got over her nerves. "Let's go back in the house. Let's not stand here gawking like a set of farmers."

She didn't say that to hurt my feelings. It never occurred to her.

I was just setting the dessert down when Loretta Bird arrived, out of breath, at the screen door.

"I thought it was going to crash into the house and kill youse all!"

She lived on the next place and the Peebleses thought she was a country-woman, they didn't know the difference. She and her husband didn't farm, he worked on the roads and had a bad name for drinking. They had seven children and couldn't get credit at the HiWay Grocery. The Peebleses made her welcome, not knowing any better, as I say, and offered her dessert.

Dessert was never anything to write home about, at their place. A dish of Jell-O or sliced bananas or fruit out of a tin. "Have a house without a pie, be ashamed until you die," my mother used to say, but Mrs. Peebles operated differently.

Loretta Bird saw me getting the can of peaches.

"Oh, never mind," she said. "I haven't got the right kind of a stomach to trust what comes out of those tins, I can only eat home canning."

I could have slapped her. I bet she never put down fruit in her life.

15   "I know what he's landed here for," she said. "He's got permission to use the fairgrounds and take people up for rides. It costs a dollar. It's the same fellow who was over at Palmerston last week and was up the lakeshore before that. I wouldn't go up, if you paid me."

"I'd jump at the chance," Dr. Peebles said. "I'd like to see this neighborhood from the air."

Mrs. Peebles said she would just as soon see it from the ground. Joey said he wanted to go and Heather did, too. Joey was nine and Heather was seven.

"Would you, Edie?" Heather said.

I said I didn't know. I was scared, but I never admitted that, especially in front of children I was taking care of.

20   "People are going to be coming out here in their cars raising dust and trampling your property, if I was you I would complain," Loretta said. She hooked her legs around the chair rung and I knew we were in for a lengthy visit. After Dr. Peebles went back to his office or out on his next call and Mrs. Peebles went for her nap, she would hang around me while I was trying to do the dishes. She would pass remarks about the Peebleses in their own house.

"She wouldn't find time to lay down in the middle of the day, if she had seven kids like I got."

She asked me did they fight and did they keep things in the dresser drawer not to have babies with. She said it was a sin if they did. I pretended I didn't know what she was talking about.

I was fifteen and away from home for the first time. My parents had made the effort and sent me to high school for a year, but I didn't like it. I was shy of strangers and the work was hard, they didn't make it nice for you or explain the way they do now. At the end of the year the averages were published in the paper, and mine came out at the very bottom, 37 percent. My father said that's enough and I didn't blame him. The last thing I wanted, anyway, was to go on and end up teaching school. It happened the very day the paper came out with my disgrace in it, Dr. Peebles was staying at our place for dinner, having just helped one of our cows have twins, and he said I looked smart to him and his wife was looking for a girl to help. He said she felt tied down, with the two children, out in the country. I guess she would, my mother said, being polite, though I could tell from her face she was wondering what on earth it would be like to have only two children and no barn work, and then to be complaining.

When I went home I would describe to them the work I had to do, and it made everybody laugh. Mrs. Peebles had an automatic washer and dryer, the first I ever saw. I have had those in my own home for such a long time now it's hard to remember how much of a miracle it was to me, not having to struggle with the wringer and hang up and haul down. Let alone not having to heat water. Then there was practically no baking. Mrs. Peebles said she couldn't make pie crust, the most amazing thing I ever heard a woman admit. I could, of course, and I could make light biscuits and a white cake and dark cake, but they didn't want it, she said they watched their figures. The only thing I didn't like about working there, in fact, was feeling half hungry a lot of the time. I used to bring back a box of doughnuts made out at home, and hide them under my bed. The children found out, and I didn't mind sharing, but I thought I better bind them to secrecy.

25   The day after the plane landed Mrs. Peebles put both children in the car and

drove over to Chesley, to get their hair cut. There was a good woman then at Chesley for doing hair. She got hers done at the same place, Mrs. Peebles did, and that meant they would be gone a good while. She had to pick a day Dr. Peebles wasn't going out into the country, she didn't have her own car. Cars were still in short supply then, after the war.

I loved being left in the house alone, to do my work at leisure. The kitchen was all white and bright yellow, with fluorescent lights. That was before they ever thought of making the appliances all different colors and doing the cupboards like dark old wood and hiding the lighting. I loved light. I loved the double sink. So would anybody new-come from washing dishes in a dishpan with a rag-plugged hole on an oilcloth-covered table by light of a coal-oil lamp. I kept everything shining.

The bathroom too. I had a bath in there once a week. They wouldn't have minded if I took one oftener, but to me it seemed like asking too much, or maybe risking making it less wonderful. The basin and the tub and the toilet were all pink, and there were glass doors with flamingoes painted on them, to shut off the tub. The light had a rosy cast and the mat sank under your feet like snow, except that it was warm. The mirror was three-way. With the mirror all steamed up and the air like a perfume cloud, from things I was allowed to use, I stood up on the side of the tub and admired myself naked, from three directions. Sometimes I thought about the way we lived out at home and the way we lived here and how one way was so hard to imagine when you were living the other way. But I thought it was still a lot easier, living the way we lived at home, to picture something like this, the painted flamingoes and the warmth and the soft mat, than it was anybody knowing only things like this to picture how it was the other way. And why was that?

I was through my jobs in no time, and had the vegetables peeled for supper and sitting in cold water besides. Then I went into Mrs. Peebles' bedroom. I had been in there plenty of times, cleaning, and I always took a good look in her closet, at the clothes she had hanging there. I wouldn't have looked in her drawers, but a closet is open to anybody. That's a lie. I would have looked in drawers, but I would have felt worse doing it and been more scared she could tell.

Some clothes in her closet she wore all the time, I was quite familiar with them. Others she never put on, they were pushed to the back. I was disappointed to see no wedding dress. But there was one long dress I could just see the skirt of, and I was hungering to see the rest. Now I took note of where it hung and lifted it out. It was satin, a lovely weight on my arm, light bluish-green in color, almost silvery. It had a fitted, pointed waist and a full skirt and an off-the-shoulder fold hiding the little sleeves.

Next thing was easy. I got out of my own things and slipped it on. I was slimmer at fifteen than anybody would believe who knows me now and the fit was beautiful. I didn't, of course, have a strapless bra on, which was what it needed, I just had to slide my straps down my arms under the material. Then I tried pinning up my hair, to get the effect. One thing led to another. I put on rouge and lipstick and eyebrow pencil from her dresser. The heat of the day and the weight of the satin and all the excitement made me thirsty, and I went out to the kitchen, got-up as I was, to get a glass of ginger ale with ice cubes from the refrigerator. The Peebleses drank ginger ale, or fruit drinks, all day, like water, and I was getting so I did too. Also there was no limit on ice cubes, which I was so fond of I would even put them in a glass of milk.

I turned from putting the ice tray back and saw a man watching me through the screen. It was the luckiest thing in the world I didn't spill the ginger ale down the front of me then and there.

"I never meant to scare you. I knocked but you were getting the ice out, you didn't hear me."

I couldn't see what he looked like, he was dark the way somebody is pressed up against a screen door with the bright daylight behind them. I only knew he wasn't from around here.

"I'm from the plane over there. My name is Chris Watters and what I was wondering was if I could use that pump."

35 There was a pump in the yard. That was the way the people used to get their water. Now I noticed he was carrying a pail.

"You're welcome," I said. "I can get it from the tap and save you pumping." I guess I wanted him to know we had piped water, didn't pump ourselves.

"I don't mind the exercise." He didn't move, though, and finally he said, "Were you going to a dance?"

Seeing a stranger there had made me entirely forget how I was dressed.

"Or is that the way ladies around here generally get dressed up in the afternoon?"

40 I didn't know how to joke back then. I was too embarrassed.

"You live here? Are you the lady of the house?"

"I'm the hired girl."

Some people change when they find that out, their whole way of looking at you and speaking to you changes, but his didn't.

"Well, I just wanted to tell you you look very nice. I was so surprised when I looked in the door and saw you. Just because you looked so nice and beautiful."

45 I wasn't even old enough then to realize how out of the common it is, for a man to say something like that to a woman, or somebody he is treating like a woman. For a man to say a word like *beautiful*. I wasn't old

enough to realize or to say anything back, or in fact to do anything but wish he would go away. Not that I didn't like him, but just that it upset me so, having him look at me, and me trying to think of something to say.

He must have understood. He said good-bye, and thanked me, and went and started filling his pail from the pump. I stood behind the Venetian blinds in the dining room, watching him. When he had gone, I went into the bedroom and took the dress off and put it back in the same place. I dressed in my own clothes and took my hair down and washed my face, wiping it on Kleenex, which I threw in the wastebasket.

The Peebleses asked me what kind of man he was. Young, middle-aged, short, tall? I couldn't say.

"Good-looking?" Dr. Peebles teased me.

I couldn't think a thing but that he would be coming to get his water again, he would be talking to Dr. or Mrs. Peebles, making friends with them, and he would mention seeing me that first afternoon, dressed up. Why not mention it? He would think it was funny. And no idea of the trouble it would get me into.

50 After supper the Peebleses drove into town to go to a movie. She wanted to go somewhere with her hair fresh done. I sat in my bright kitchen wondering what to do, knowing I would never sleep. Mrs. Peebles might not fire me, when she found out, but it would give her a different feeling about me altogether. This was the first place I ever worked but I really had picked up things about the way people feel when you are working for them. They like to think you aren't curious. Not just that you aren't dishonest, that isn't enough. They like to feel you don't notice things, that you don't think or wonder about anything but what they liked to eat and how they liked things ironed, and so on. I don't mean they weren't

kind to me, because they were. They had me eat my meals with them (to tell the truth I expected to, I didn't know there were families who don't) and sometimes they took me along in the car. But all the same.

I went up and checked on the children being asleep and then I went out. I had to do it. I crossed the road and went in the old fairgrounds gate. The plane looked unnatural sitting there, and shining with the moon. Off at the far side of the fairgrounds, where the bush was taking over, I saw his tent.

He was sitting outside it smoking a cigarette. He saw me coming.

"Hello, were you looking for a plane ride? I don't start taking people up till tomorrow." Then he looked again and said, "Oh, it's you. I didn't know you without your long dress on."

My heart was knocking away, my tongue was dried up. I had to say something. But I couldn't. My throat was closed and I was like a deaf-and-dumb.

55 "Did you want to ride? Sit down. Have a cigarette."

I couldn't even shake my head to say no, so he gave me one.

"Put it in your mouth or I can't light it. It's a good thing I'm used to shy ladies."

I did. It wasn't the first time I had smoked a cigarette, actually. My girl friend out home, Muriel Lowe, used to steal them from her brother.

"Look at your hand shaking. Did you just want to have a chat, or what?"

60 In one burst I said, "I wisht you wouldn't say anything about that dress."

"What dress? Oh, the long dress."

"It's Mrs. Peebles'."

"Whose? Oh, the lady you work for? Is that it? She wasn't home so you got dressed up in her dress, eh? You got dressed up and played queen. I don't blame you. You're not smoking the cigarette right. Don't just puff. Draw it in. Did anybody ever show you how

to inhale? Are you scared I'll tell on you? Is that it?"

I was so ashamed at having to ask him to connive this way I couldn't nod. I just looked at him and he saw *yes*.

"Well I won't. I won't in the slightest 65 way mention it or embarrass you. I give you my word of honor."

Then he changed the subject, to help me out, seeing I couldn't even thank him.

"What do you think of this sign?"

It was a board sign lying practically at my feet.

SEE THE WORLD FROM THE SKY. ADULTS $1.00, CHILDREN 50¢. QUALIFIED PILOT.

"My old sign was getting pretty 70 beat up, I thought I'd make a new one. That's what I've been doing with my time today."

The lettering wasn't all that handsome, I thought. I could have done a better one in half an hour.

"I'm not an expert at sign making."

"It's very good," I said.

"I don't need it for publicity, word of mouth is usually enough. I turned away two carloads tonight. I felt like taking it easy. I didn't tell them ladies were dropping in to visit me."

Now I remembered the children and I 75 was scared again, in case one of them had waked up and called me and I wasn't there.

"Do you have to go so soon?"

I remembered some manners. "Thank you for the cigarette."

"Don't forget. You have my word of honor."

I tore off across the fairgrounds, scared I'd see the car heading home from town. My sense of time was mixed up, I didn't know how long I'd been out of the house. But it was all right, it wasn't late, the children were asleep. I got in bed myself and lay thinking what a lucky end to the day, after all, and among things to be grateful for

I could be grateful Loretta Bird hadn't been the one who caught me.

80   The yard and borders didn't get trampled, it wasn't as bad as that. All the same it seemed very public, around the house. The sign was on the fairgrounds gate. People came mostly after supper but a good many in the afternoon, too. The Bird children all came without fifty cents between them and hung on the gate. We got used to the excitement of the plane coming in and taking off, it wasn't excitement anymore. I never went over, after that one time, but would see him when he came to get his water. I would be out on the steps doing sitting-down work, like preparing vegetables, if I could.

"Why don't you come over? I'll take you up in my plane."

"I'm saving my money," I said, because I couldn't think of anything else.

"For what? For getting married?"

I shook my head.

85   "I'll take you up for free if you come sometime when it's slack. I thought you would come, and have another cigarette."

I made a face to hush him, because you never could tell when the children would be sneaking around the porch, or Mrs. Peebles herself listening in the house. Sometimes she came out and had a conversation with him. He told her things he hadn't bothered to tell me. But then I hadn't thought to ask. He told her he had been in the war, that was where he learned to fly a plane, and now he couldn't settle down to ordinary life, this was what he liked. She said she couldn't imagine anybody liking such a thing. Though sometimes, she said, she was almost bored enough to try anything herself, she wasn't brought up to living in the country. It's all my husband's idea, she said. This was news to me.

"Maybe you ought to give flying lessons," she said.

"Would you take them?"

She just laughed.

90   Sunday was a busy flying day in spite of it being preached against from two pulpits. We were all sitting out watching. Joey and Heather were over on the fence with the Bird kids. Their father had said they could go, after their mother saying all week they couldn't.

A car came down the road past the parked cars and pulled up right in the drive. It was Loretta Bird who got out, all importance, and on the driver's side another woman got out, more sedately. She was wearing sunglasses.

"This is a lady looking for the man that flies the plane," Loretta Bird said. "I heard her inquire in the hotel coffee shop where I was having a Coke and I brought her out."

"I'm sorry to bother you," the lady said. "I'm Alice Kelling, Mr. Watters' fiancée."

This Alice Kelling had on a pair of brown and white checked slacks and a yellow top. Her bust looked to me rather low and bumpy. She had a worried face. Her hair had had a permanent, but had grown out, and she wore a yellow band to keep it off her face. Nothing in the least pretty or even young-looking about her. But you could tell from how she talked she was from the city, or educated, or both.

95   Dr. Peebles stood up and introduced himself and his wife and me and asked her to be seated.

"He's up in the air right now, but you're welcome to sit and wait. He gets his water here and he hasn't been yet. He'll probably take his break about five."

"That is him, then?" said Alice Kelling, wrinkling and straining at the sky.

"He's not in the habit of running out on you, taking a different name?" Dr. Peebles laughed. He was the one, not his wife, to offer iced tea. Then she sent me into the kitchen to fix it. She smiled. She was wearing sunglasses too.

"He never mentioned his fiancée," she said.

100 I loved fixing iced tea with lots of ice and slices of lemon in tall glasses. I ought to have mentioned before, Dr. Peebles was an abstainer, at least around the house, or I wouldn't have been allowed to take the place. I had to fix a glass for Loretta Bird too, though it galled me, and when I went out she had settled in my lawn chair, leaving me the steps.

"I knew you was a nurse when I first heard you in that coffee shop."

"How would you know a thing like that?"

"I get my hunches about people. Was that how you met him, nursing?"

"Chris? Well yes. Yes, it was."

105 "Oh, were you overseas?" said Mrs. Peebles.

"No, it was before he went overseas. I nursed him when he was stationed at Centralia and had a ruptured appendix. We got engaged and then he went overseas. My, this is refreshing, after a long drive."

"He'll be glad to see you," Dr. Peebles said. "It's a rackety kind of life, isn't it, not staying one place long enough to really make friends."

"Youse've had a long engagement," Loretta Bird said.

Alice Kelling passed that over. "I was going to get a room at the hotel, but when I was offered directions I came on out. Do you think I could phone them?"

110 "No need," Dr. Peebles said. "You're five miles away from him if you stay at the hotel. Here, you're right across the road. Stay with us. We've got rooms on rooms, look at this big house."

Asking people to stay, just like that, is certainly a country thing, and maybe seemed natural to him now, but not to Mrs. Peebles, from the way she said, oh yes, we have plenty of room. Or to Alice Kelling, who kept protesting, but let herself be worn down. I got the feeling it was a temptation to her, to be that close. I was trying for a look at her ring. Her nails were painted red, her fingers were freckled and wrinkled. It was a tiny stone. Muriel Lowe's cousin had one twice as big.

Chris came to get his water, late in the afternoon just as Dr. Peebles had predicted. He must have recognized the car from a way off. He came smiling.

"Here I am chasing after you to see what you're up to," called Alice Kelling. She got up and went to meet him and they kissed, just touched, in front of us.

"You're going to spend a lot on gas that way," Chris said.

Dr. Peebles invited Chris to stay for 115 supper, since he had already put up the sign that said: NO MORE RIDES TILL 7 P.M. Mrs. Peebles wanted it served in the yard, in spite of the bugs. One thing strange to anybody from the country is this eating outside. I had made a potato salad earlier and she had made a jellied salad, that was one thing she could do, so it was just a matter of getting those out, and some sliced meat and cucumbers and fresh leaf lettuce. Loretta Bird hung around for some time saying, "Oh, well, I guess I better get home to those yappers," and, "It's so nice just sitting here, I sure hate to get up," but nobody invited her, I was relieved to see, and finally she had to go.

That night after rides were finished Alice Kelling and Chris went off somewhere in her car. I lay awake till they got back. When I saw the car lights sweep my ceiling I got up to look down on them through the slats of my blind. I don't know what I thought I was going to see. Muriel Lowe and I used to sleep on her front veranda and watch her sister and her sister's boy friend saying good night. Afterward we couldn't get to sleep, for longing for somebody to kiss us and rub up against us and we would talk about suppose you were out in a boat with a boy and he wouldn't bring you in to shore unless you did it, or what if somebody got you trapped in a barn, you would have to, wouldn't you, it wouldn't be your fault. Muriel said her two girl cousins used to try with a toilet paper roll that one of them was a boy. We wouldn't do anything like that; just lay and wondered.

All that happened was that Chris got out of the car on one side and she got out on the other and they walked off separately—him toward the fairgrounds and her toward the house. I got back in bed and imagined about me coming home with him, not like that.

Next morning Alice Kelling got up late and I fixed a grapefruit for her the way I had learned and Mrs. Peebles sat down with her to visit and have another cup of coffee. Mrs. Peebles seemed pleased enough now, having company. Alice Kelling said she guessed she better get used to putting in a day just watching Chris take off and come down, and Mrs. Peebles said she didn't know if she should suggest it because Alice Kelling was the one with the car, but the lake was only twenty-five miles away and what a good day for a picnic.

Alice Kelling took her up on the idea and by eleven o'clock they were in the car, with Joey and Heather and a sandwich lunch I had made. The only thing was that Chris hadn't come down, and she wanted to tell him where they were going.

120   "Edie'll go over and tell him," Mrs. Peebles said. "There's no problem."

Alice Kelling wrinkled her face and agreed.

"Be sure and tell him we'll be back by five!"

I didn't see that he would be concerned about knowing this right away, and I thought of him eating whatever he ate over there, alone, cooking on his camp stove, so I got to work and mixed up a crumb cake and

baked it, in between the other work I had to do; then, when it was a bit cooled, wrapped it in a tea towel. I didn't do anything to myself but take off my apron and comb my hair. I would like to have put some makeup on, but I was too afraid it would remind him of the way he first saw me, and that would humiliate me all over again.

He had come and put another sign on the gate: NO RIDES THIS P.M. APOLOGIES. I worried that he wasn't feeling well. No sign of him outside and the tent flap was down. I knocked on the pole.

"Come in," he said, in a voice that   125 would just as soon have said *Stay out*.

I lifted the flap.

"Oh, it's you. I'm sorry. I didn't know it was you."

He had been just sitting on the side of the bed, smoking. Why not at least sit and smoke in the fresh air?

"I brought a cake and hope you're not sick," I said.

"Why would I be sick? Oh—that sign.   130 That's all right. I'm just tired of talking to people. I don't mean you. Have a seat." He pinned back the tent flap. "Get some fresh air in here."

I sat on the edge of the bed, there was no place else. It was one of those fold-up cots, really: I remembered and gave him his fiancée's message.

He ate some of the cake. "Good."

"Put the rest away for when you're hungry later."

"I'll tell you a secret. I won't be around here much longer."

"Are you getting married?"   135

"Ha ha. What time did you say they'd be back?"

"Five o'clock."

"Well, by that time, this place will have seen the last of me. A plane can get further than a car." He unwrapped the cake and ate another piece of it, absentmindedly.

"Now you'll be thirsty."

140 "There's some water in the pail."

"It won't be very cold. I could bring some fresh. I could bring some ice from the refrigerator."

"No," he said. "I don't want you to go. I want a nice long time of saying good-bye to you."

He put the cake away carefully and sat beside me and started those little kisses, so soft, I can't ever let myself think about them, such kindness in his face and lovely kisses, all over my eyelids and neck and ears, all over, then me kissing back as well as I could (I had only kissed a boy on a dare before, and kissed my own arms for practice) and we lay back on the cot and pressed together, just gently, and he did some other things, not bad things or not in a bad way. It was lovely in the tent, that smell of grass and hot tent cloth with the sun beating down on it, and he said, "I wouldn't do you any harm for the world." Once, when he had rolled on top of me and we were sort of rocking together on the cot, he said softly, "Oh, no," and freed himself and jumped up and got the water pail. He splashed some of it on his neck and face, and the little bit left, on me lying there.

"That's to cool us off, miss."

145 When we said good-bye I wasn't at all sad, because he held my face and said, "I'm going to write you a letter. I'll tell you where I am and maybe you can come and see me. Would you like that? Okay then. You wait." I was really glad I think to get away from him, it was like he was piling presents on me I couldn't get the pleasure of till I considered them alone.

No consternation at first about the plane being gone. They thought he had taken somebody up, and I didn't enlighten them. Dr. Peebles had phoned he had to go to the country, so there was just us having supper, and then Loretta Bird thrusting her head in the door and saying, "I see he's took off."

"What?" said Alice Kelling, and pushed back her chair.

"The kids come and told me this afternoon he was taking down his tent. Did he think he'd run through all the business there was round here? He didn't take off without letting you know, did he?"

"He'll send me word," Alice Kelling said. "He'll probably phone tonight. He's terribly restless, since the war."

"Edie, he didn't mention to you, did 150 he?" Mrs. Peebles said. "When you took over the message?"

"Yes," I said. So far so true.

"Well why didn't you say?" All of them were looking at me. "Did he say where he was going?"

"He said he might try Bayfield," I said. What made me tell such a lie? I didn't intend it.

"Bayfield, how far is that?" said Alice Kelling.

Mrs. Peebles said, "Thirty, thirty-five 155 miles."

"That's not far. Oh, well, that's really not far at all. It's on the lake, isn't it?"

You'd think I'd be ashamed of myself, setting her on the wrong track. I did it to give him more time, whatever time he needed. I lied for him, and also, I have to admit, for me. Women should stick together and not do things like that. I see that now, but didn't then. I never thought of myself as being in any way like her, or coming to the same troubles, ever.

She hadn't taken her eyes off me. I thought she suspected my lie.

"When did he mention this to you?"

"Earlier." 160

"When you were over at the plane?"

"Yes."

"You must've stayed and had a chat." She smiled at me, not a nice smile. "You must've stayed and had a little visit with him."

"I took a cake," I said, thinking that telling some truth would spare me telling the rest.

165 "We didn't have a cake," said Mrs. Peebles rather sharply.

"I baked one."

Alice Kelling said, "That was very friendly of you."

"Did you get permission," said Loretta Bird. "You never know what these girls'll do next," she said. "It's not they mean harm so much, as they're ignorant."

"The cake is neither here nor there," Mrs. Peebles broke in. "Edie, I wasn't aware you knew Chris that well."

170 I didn't know what to say.

"I'm not surprised," Alice Kelling said in a high voice. "I knew by the look of her as soon as I saw her. We get them at the hospital all the time." She looked hard at me with her stretched smile. "Having their babies. We have to put them in a special ward because of their diseases. Little country tramps. Fourteen and fifteen years old. You should see the babies they have, too."

"There was a bad woman here in town had a baby that pus was running out of its eyes," Loretta Bird put in.

"Wait a minute," said Mrs. Peebles. "What is this talk? Edie. What about you and Mr. Watters? Were you intimate with him?"

"Yes," I said. I was thinking of us lying on the cot and kissing, wasn't that intimate? And I would never deny it.

175 They were all one minute quiet, even Loretta Bird.

"Well," said Mrs. Peebles. "I am surprised. I think I need a cigarette. This is the first of any such tendencies I've seen in her," she said, speaking to Alice Kelling, but Alice Kelling was looking at me.

"Loose little bitch." Tears ran down her face. "Loose little bitch, aren't you? I

knew as soon as I saw you. Men despise girls like you. He just made use of you and went off, you know that, don't you? Girls like you are just nothing, they're just public conveniences, just filthy little rags!"

"Oh, now," said Mrs. Peebles.

"Filthy," Alice Kelling sobbed. "Filthy 180 little rags!"

"Don't get yourself upset," Loretta Bird said. She was swollen up with pleasure at being in on this scene. "Men are all the same."

"Edie, I'm very surprised," Mrs. Peebles said. "I thought your parents were so strict. You don't want to have a baby, do you?"

I'm still ashamed of what happened next. I lost control, just like a six-year-old, I started howling. "You don't get a baby from just doing that!"

"You see. Some of them are that ignorant," Loretta Bird said.

But Mrs. Peebles jumped up and caught my arms and shook me.

"Calm down. Don't get hysterical. 185 Calm down. Stop crying. Listen to me. Listen. I'm wondering, if you know what being intimate means. Now tell me. What did you think it meant?"

"Kissing," I howled.

She let go. "Oh, Edie. Stop it. Don't be silly. It's all right. It's all a misunderstanding. Being intimate means a lot more than that. Oh, I *wondered*."

"She's trying to cover up, now," said Alice Kelling. "Yes. She's not so stupid. She sees she got herself in trouble."

"I believe her," Mrs. Peebles said. "This is an awful scene."

"Well there is one way to find out," 190 said Alice Kelling, getting up. "After all, I am a nurse."

Mrs. Peebles drew a breath and said, "No. No. Go to your room, Edie. And stop that noise. This is too disgusting."

I heard the car start in a little while. I tried to stop crying, pulling back each wave as it started over me. Finally I succeeded, and lay heaving on the bed.

Mrs. Peebles came and stood in the doorway.

"She's gone," she said. "That Bird woman too. Of course, you know you should never have gone near that man and that is the cause of all this trouble. I have a headache. As soon as you can, go and wash your face in cold water and get at the dishes and we will not say any more about this."

195 Nor we didn't. I didn't figure out till years later the extent of what I had been saved from. Mrs. Peebles was not very friendly to me afterward, but she was fair. Not very friendly is the wrong way of describing what she was. She had never been very friendly. It was just that now she had to see me all the time and it got on her nerves, a little.

As for me, I put it all out of my mind like a bad dream and concentrated on waiting for my letter. The mail came every day except Sunday, between one-thirty and two in the afternoon, a good time for me because Mrs. Peebles was always having her nap. I would get the kitchen all cleaned and then go up to the mailbox and sit in the grass, waiting. I was perfectly happy, waiting, I forgot all about Alice Kelling and her misery and awful talk and Mrs. Peebles and her chilliness and the embarrassment of whether she had told Dr. Peebles and the face of Loretta Bird, getting her fill of other people's troubles. I was always smiling when the mailman got there, and continued smiling even after he gave me the mail and I saw today wasn't the day. The mailman was a Carmichael. I knew by his face because there are a lot of Carmichaels living out by us and so many of them have a sort of sticking-out top lip. So I asked his name (he

was a young man, shy, but good-humored, anybody could ask him anything) and then I said, "I knew by your face!" He was pleased by that and always glad to see me and got a little less shy. "You've got the smile I've been waiting on all day!" he used to holler out the car window.

It never crossed my mind for a long time a letter might not come. I believed in it coming just like I believed the sun would rise in the morning. I just put off my hope from day to day, and there was the goldenrod out around the mailbox and the children gone back to school, and the leaves turning, and I was wearing a sweater when I went to wait. One day walking back with the hydro bill stuck in my hand, that was all, looking across at the fairgrounds with the full-blown milkweed and dark teasels, so much like fall, it just struck me: *No letter was ever going to come.* It was an impossible idea to get used to. No, not impossible. If I thought about Chris's face when he said he was going to write to me, it was impossible, but if I forgot that and thought about the actual tin mailbox, empty, it was plain and true. I kept on going to meet the mail, but my heart was heavy now like a lump of lead. I only smiled because I thought of the mailman counting on it, and he didn't have an easy life, with the winter driving ahead.

Till it came to me one day there were women doing this with their lives, all over. There were women just waiting and waiting by mailboxes for one letter or another. I imagined me making this journey day after day and year after year, and my hair starting to go gray, and I thought, I was never made to go on like that. So I stopped meeting the mail. If there were women all through life waiting, and women busy and not waiting, I knew which I had to be. Even though there might be things the second kind of women have to pass up and never know about, it still is better.

I was surprised when the mailman phoned the Peebleses' place in the evening and asked for me. He said he missed me. He asked if I would like to go to Goderich, where some well-known movie was on, I forget now what. So I said yes, and I went out with him for two years and he asked me to marry him, and we were engaged a year more while I got my things together, and then we did marry. He always tells the children the story of how I went after him by sitting by the mailbox every day, and naturally I laugh and let him, because I like for people to think what pleases them and makes them happy.

····▶ *Your* Turn
Talking and Writing about Lit

1. Who is the narrator in Alice Munro's "How I Met My Husband"?

2. How does Edie's use of language (diction) characterize her?

3. Is Edie a reliable narrator or a naïve narrator? How does this use of narrative strategy serve the writer's purposes, given what she wants to show in the story?

4. **DIY**   In paragraphs 30–65, Chris Watters inadvertently surprises Edie when she's dressed up in Mrs. Peebles's fancy gown, and his tone is amused and understanding. Write a scene in which Alice Kelling surprises her instead. How will the tone of the dialogue (on both sides of the conversation) need to be changed?

Junot Díaz (b. 1968)

Junot Díaz was born in Santo Domingo, Dominican Republic. His fiction began to attract enthusiastic attention with the 1996 publication of his short story collection *Drown* (from which "Fiesta, 1980" is taken). He received his B.A. from Rutgers University and his M.F.A. in creative writing from Cornell University. Díaz received a Guggenheim Fellowship and numerous other awards, and his short stories have appeared in the *New Yorker*, *Story, Paris Review, Best American Short Stories* (1996, 1997, 1998, and 2000), *Pushcart Prize XXII*, and *African Voices*. Díaz is an associate professor in the program in writing at the Massachusetts Institute of Technology.

Fiesta, 1980 (1996)

Mami's youngest sister—my tía Yrma—finally made it to the United States that year. She and tío Miguel got themselves an apartment in the Bronx, off the Grand Concourse and everybody decided that we should have a party. Actually, my pops decided, but everybody—meaning Mami, tía Yrma, tío Miguel and their neighbors— thought it a dope idea. On the afternoon of the party Papi came back from work around six. Right on time. We were all dressed by then, which was a smart move on our part. If Papi had walked in and caught us lounging around in our underwear, he would have kicked our asses something serious.

He didn't say nothing to nobody, not even my moms. He just pushed past her, held up his hand when she tried to talk to him and headed right into the shower. Rafa gave me the look and I gave it back to him; we both knew Papi had been with that Puerto Rican woman he was seeing and wanted to wash off the evidence quick.

Mami looked really nice that day. The United States had finally put some meat on her; she was no longer the same flaca who had arrived here three years before. She had cut her hair short and was wearing tons of cheap-ass jewelry which on her didn't look too lousy. She smelled like herself, like the wind through a tree. She always waited until the last possible minute to put on her perfume because she said it was a waste to spray it on early and then have to spray it on again once you got to the party.

We—meaning me, my brother, my little sister and Mami—waited for Papi to finish his shower. Mami seemed anxious, in her usual dispassionate way. Her hands adjusted the buckle of her belt over and over again. That morning, when she had gotten us up for school, Mami told us that she wanted to have a good time at the party. I want to dance, she said, but now, with the sun sliding out of the sky like spit off a wall, she seemed ready just to get this over with.

5 Rafa didn't much want to go to no party either, and me, I never wanted to go anywhere with my family. There was a baseball game in the parking lot outside and we could hear our friends, yelling, Hey, and, Cabrón, to one another. We heard the pop of a ball as it sailed over the cars, the clatter of an aluminum bat dropping to the concrete.

Not that me or Rafa loved baseball; we just liked playing with the local kids, thrashing them at anything they were doing. By the sounds of the shouting, we both knew the game was close, either of us could have made a difference. Rafa frowned and when I frowned back, he put up his fist. Don't you mirror me, he said.

Don't you mirror me, I said.

He punched me—I would have hit him back but Papi marched into the living room with his towel around his waist, looking a lot smaller than he did when he was dressed. He had a few strands of hair around his nipples and a surly closed-mouth expression, like maybe he'd scalded his tongue or something.

Have they eaten? he asked Mami.

She nodded. I made you something.

You didn't let him eat, did you?   10

Ay, Dios mío, she said, letting her arms fall to her side.

Ay, Dios mío, is right, Papi said.

I was never supposed to eat before our car trips, but earlier, when she had put out our dinner of rice, beans and sweet platanos, guess who had been the first one to clean his plate? You couldn't blame Mami really, she had been busy—cooking, getting ready, dressing my sister Madai. I should have reminded her not to feed me but I wasn't that sort of son.

Papi turned to me. Coño, muchacho, why did you eat?

Rafa had already started inching away   15
from me. I'd once told him I considered him a low-down chickenshit for moving out of the way every time Papi was going to smack me.

Collateral damage, Rafa had said. Ever heard of it?

No.

Look it up.

Chickenshit or not, I didn't dare glance at him. Papi was old-fashioned; he expected your undivided attention when you were getting your ass whupped. You couldn't look him in the eye either—that wasn't allowed. Better to stare at his belly button, which was perfectly round and immaculate. Papi pulled me to my feet by my ear.

20   If you throw up—

I won't, I cried, tears in my eyes, more out of reflex than pain.

Ya, Ramón, ya. It's not his fault, Mami said.

They've known about this party forever. How did they think we were going to get there? Fly?

He finally let go of my ear and I sat back down. Madai was too scared to open her eyes. Being around Papi all her life had turned her into a major-league wuss. Anytime Papi raised his voice her lip would start trembling, like some specialized tuning fork. Rafa pretended that he had knuckles to crack and when I shoved him, he gave me a *Don't start* look. But even that little bit of recognition made me feel better.

25   I was the one who was always in trouble with my dad. It was like my God-given duty to piss him off, to do everything the way he hated. Our fights didn't bother me too much. I still wanted him to love me, something that never seemed strange or contradictory until years later, when he was out of our lives.

By the time my ear stopped stinging Papi was dressed and Mami was crossing each one of us, solemnly, like we were heading off to war. We said, in turn, Bendición, Mami, and she poked us in our five cardinal spots while saying, Que Dios te bendiga.

This was how all our trips began, the words that followed me every time I left the house.

None of us spoke until we were inside Papi's Volkswagen van. Brand-new, lime-green and bought to impress. Oh, we were impressed, but me, every time I was in that VW and Papi went above twenty miles an hour, I vomited. I'd never had trouble with

cars before—that van was like my curse. Mami suspected it was the upholstery. In her mind, American things—appliances, mouthwash, funny-looking upholstery—all seemed to have an intrinsic badness about them. Papi was careful about taking me anywhere in the VW, but when he had to, I rode up front in Mami's usual seat so I could throw up out a window.

¿Cómo te sientes? Mami asked over my shoulder when Papi pulled onto the turnpike. She had her hand on the base of my neck. One thing about Mami, her palms never sweated.

I'm OK, I said, keeping my eyes straight   30 ahead. I definitely didn't want to trade glances with Papi. He had this one look, furious and sharp, that always left me feeling bruised.

Toma. Mami handed me four mentas. She had thrown three out her window at the beginning of our trip, an offering to Eshú; the rest were for me.

I took one and sucked it slowly, my tongue knocking it up against my teeth. We passed Newark Airport without any incident. If Madai had been awake she would have cried because the planes flew so close to the cars.

How's he feeling? Papi asked.

Fine, I said. I glanced back at Rafa and he pretended like he didn't see me. That was the way he was, at school and at home. When I was in trouble, he didn't know me. Madai was solidly asleep, but even with her face all wrinkled up and drooling she looked cute, her hair all separated into twists.

I turned around and concentrated on   35 the candy. Papi even started to joke that we might not have to scrub the van out tonight. He was beginning to loosen up, not checking his watch too much. Maybe he was thinking about that Puerto Rican woman or maybe he was just happy that we were all together. I could never tell. At the toll, he was feeling positive enough to actually get out of the van and search around under the basket for dropped coins. It was something he had once done to amuse Madai, but now it was habit. Cars behind us honked their horns and I slid down in my seat. Rafa didn't care; he grinned back at the other cars and waved. His actual job was to make sure no cops were coming. Mami shook Madai awake and as soon as she saw Papi stooping for a couple of quarters she let out this screech of delight that almost took off the top of my head.

That was the end of the good times. Just outside the Washington Bridge, I started feeling woozy. The smell of the upholstery got all up inside my head and I found myself with a mouthful of saliva. Mami's hand tensed on my shoulder and when I caught Papi's eye, he was like, No way. Don't do it.

The first time I got sick in the van Papi was taking me to the library. Rafa was with us and he couldn't believe I threw up. I was famous for my steel-lined stomach. A third-world childhood could give you that. Papi was worried enough that just as quick as Rafa could drop off the books we were on our way home. Mami fixed me one of her honey-and-onion concoctions and that made my stomach feel better. A week later we tried the library again and on this go-around I couldn't get the window open in time. When Papi got me home, he went and cleaned out the van himself, an expression of askho on his face. This was a big deal, since Papi almost never cleaned anything himself. He came back inside and found me sitting on the couch feeling like hell.

It's the car, he said to Mami. It's making him sick.

This time the damage was pretty minimal, nothing Papi couldn't wash off the door with a blast of the hose. He was pissed, though; he jammed his finger into my cheek, a nice solid thrust. That was the way he was with his punishments: imaginative. Earlier that year I'd written an essay in school called "My Father the Torturer," but the teacher made me write a new one. She thought I was kidding.

We drove the rest of the way to the Bronx in silence. We only stopped once, so I could brush my teeth. Mami had brought along my toothbrush and a tube of toothpaste and while every car known to man sped by us she stood outside with me so I wouldn't feel alone. 40

Tío Miguel was about seven feet tall and had his hair combed up and out, into a demi-fro. He gave me and Rafa big spleen-crushing hugs and then kissed Mami and finally ended up with Madai on his shoulder. The last time I'd seen Tío was at the airport, his first day in the United States. I remembered how he hadn't seemed all that troubled to be in another country.

He looked down at me. Carajo, Yunior, you look horrible!

He threw up, my brother explained.

I pushed Rafa. Thanks a lot, ass-face.

Hey, he said. Tío asked. 45

Tío clapped a bricklayer's hand on my shoulder. Everybody gets sick sometimes, he said. You should have seen me on the plane over here. Dios mío! He rolled his Asian-looking eyes for emphasis. I thought we were all going to die.

Everybody could tell he was lying. I smiled like he was making me feel better.

Do you want me to get you a drink? Tío asked. We got beer and rum.

Miguel, Mami said. He's young.

Young? Back in Santo Domingo, he'd 50 be getting laid by now.

Mami thinned her lips, which took some doing.

Well, it's true, Tío said.

So, Mami, I said. When do I get to go visit the D.R.?

That's enough, Yunior.

55   It's the only pussy you'll ever get, Rafa said to me in English.

Not counting your girlfriend, of course.

Rafa smiled. He had to give me that one.

Papi came in from parking the van. He and Miguel gave each other the sort of handshakes that would have turned my fingers into Wonder bread.

Coño, compa'i, ¿cómo va todo? they said to each other.

60   Tía came out then, with an apron on and maybe the longest Lee Press-On Nails I've ever seen in my life. There was this one guru motherfucker in the *Guinness Book of World Records* who had longer nails, but I tell you, it was close. She gave everybody kisses, told me and Rafa how guapo we were—Rafa, of course, believed her—told Madai how bella she was, but when she got to Papi, she froze a little, like maybe she'd seen a wasp on the tip of his nose, but then kissed him all the same.

Mami told us to join the other kids in the living room. Tío said, Wait a minute, I want to show you the apartment. I was glad Tía said, Hold on, because from what I'd seen so far, the place had been furnished in Contemporary Dominican Tacky. The less I saw, the better. I mean, I liked plastic sofa covers but damn, Tío and Tía had taken it to another level. They had a disco ball hanging in the living room and the type of stucco ceilings that looked like stalactite heaven. The sofas all had golden tassels dangling from their edges. Tía came out of the kitchen with some people I didn't know and by the time she got done introducing everybody, only Papi and Mami were given the guided tour of the four-room third-floor apartment. Me and Rafa joined the kids in the living room. They'd already started eating. We were hungry, one of the girls explained, a pastelito in hand. The boy was about three years younger than me but the girl who'd spoken, Leti, was my age. She and another girl were on the sofa together and they were cute as hell.

Leti introduced them: the boy was her brother Wilquins and the other girl was her neighbor Mari. Leti had some serious tetas and I could tell that my brother was going to gun for her. His taste in girls was predictable. He sat down right between Leti and Mari and by the way they were smiling at him I knew he'd do fine. Neither of the girls gave me more than a cursory one-two, which didn't bother me. Sure, I liked girls but I was always too terrified to speak to them unless we were arguing or I was calling them stupidos, which was one of my favorite words that year. I turned to Wilquins and asked him what there was to do around here. Mari, who had the lowest voice I'd ever heard, said, He can't speak.

What does that mean?

He's mute.

I looked at Wilquins incredulously. He   65 smiled and nodded, as if he'd won a prize or something.

Does he understand? I asked.

Of course he understands, Rafa said. He's not dumb.

I could tell Rafa had said that just to score points with the girls. Both of them nodded. Low-voice Mari said, He's the best student in his grade.

I thought, Not bad for a mute. I sat next to Wilquins. After about two seconds of TV Wilquins whipped out a bag of dominos and motioned to me. Did I want to play? Sure. Me and him played Rafa and Leti and we whupped their collective asses twice, which put Rafa in a real bad mood. He looked at me like maybe he wanted to take a swing, just one to make him feel better. Leti kept whispering into Rafa's ear, telling him it was OK.

70   In the kitchen I could hear my parents slipping into their usual modes. Papi's voice was loud and argumentative; you didn't have to be anywhere near him to catch his drift. And Mami, you had to put cups to your ears to hear hers. I went into the kitchen a few times—once so the tíos could show off how much bullshit I'd been able to cram in my head the last few years; another time for a bucket-sized cup of soda. Mami and Tía were frying tostones and the last of the pastelitos. She appeared happier now and the way her hands worked on our dinner you would think she had a life somewhere else making rare and precious things. She nudged Tía every now and then, shit they must have been doing all their lives. As soon as Mami saw me though, she gave me the eye. Don't stay long, that eye said. Don't piss your old man off.

Papi was too busy arguing about Elvis to notice me. Then somebody mentioned María Montez and Papi barked, María Montez? Let me tell *you* about María Montez, compa'i.

Maybe I was used to him. His voice—louder than most adults'—didn't bother me none, though the other kids shifted uneasily in their seats. Wilquins was about to raise the volume on the TV, but Rafa said, I wouldn't do that. Muteboy had balls, though. He did it anyway and then sat down. Wilquins's pop came into the living room a second later, a bottle of Presidente in hand. That dude must have had Spider-senses or something. Did you raise that? he asked Wilquins and Wilquins nodded.

Is this your house? his pops asked. He looked ready to beat Wilquins silly but he lowered the volume instead.

See, Rafa said. You nearly got your *ass kicked*.

75 I met the Puerto Rican woman right after Papi had gotten the van. He was taking me on short trips, trying to cure me of my vomiting. It wasn't really working but I looked forward to our trips, even though at the end of each one I'd be sick. These were the only times me and Papi did anything together. When we were alone he treated me much better, like maybe I was his son or something.

Before each drive Mami would cross me.

Bendición, Mami, I'd say.

She'd kiss my forehead. Que Dios te bendiga. And then she would give me a handful of mentas because she wanted me to be OK. Mami didn't think these excursions would cure anything, but the one time she had brought it up to Papi he had told her to shut up, what did she know about anything anyway?

Me and Papi didn't talk much. We just drove around our neighborhood. Occasionally he'd ask, How is it?

And I'd nod, no matter how I felt.   80

One day I was sick outside of Perth Amboy. Instead of taking me home he went the other way on Industrial Avenue, stopping a few minutes later in front of a light blue house I didn't recognize. It reminded me of the Easter eggs we colored at school, the ones we threw out the bus windows at other cars.

The Puerto Rican woman was there and she helped me clean up. She had dry papery hands and when she rubbed the towel on my chest, she did it hard, like I was a bumper she was waxing. She was very thin and had a cloud of brown hair rising above her narrow face and the sharpest blackest eyes you've ever seen.

He's cute, she said to Papi.

Not when he's throwing up, Papi said.

What's your name? she asked me. Are 85 you Rafa?

I shook my head.

Then it's Yunior, right?

I nodded.

You're the smart one, she said, suddenly happy with herself. Maybe you want to see my books?

90   They weren't hers. I recognized them as ones my father must have left in her house. Papi was a voracious reader, couldn't even go cheating without a paperback in his pocket.

Why don't you go watch TV? Papi suggested. He was looking at her like she was the last piece of chicken on earth.

We got plenty of channels, she said. Use the remote if you want.

The two of them went upstairs and I was too scared of what was happening to poke around. I just sat there, ashamed, expecting something big and fiery to crash down on our heads. I watched a whole hour of the news before Papi came downstairs and said, Let's go.

About two hours later the women laid out the food and like always nobody but the kids thanked them. It must be some Dominican tradition or something. There was everything I liked—chicharrones, fried chicken, tostones, sancocho, rice, fried cheese, yuca, avocado, potato salad, a meteor-sized hunk of pernil, even a tossed salad which I could do without—but when I joined the other kids around the serving table, Papi said, Oh no you don't, and took the paper plate out of my hand. His fingers weren't gentle.

95   What's wrong now? Tía asked, handing me another plate.

He ain't eating, Papi said. Mami pretended to help Rafa with the pernil.

Why can't he eat?

Because I said so.

The adults who didn't know us made like they hadn't heard a thing and Tío just smiled sheepishly and told everybody to go ahead and eat. All the kids—about ten of them now—trooped back into the living room with their plates a-heaping and all the adults ducked into the kitchen and the dining room, where the radio was playing loud-ass bachatas. I was the only one without a plate. Papi stopped me before I could get away from him. Her kept his voice nice and low so nobody else could hear him.

If you eat anything, I'm going to beat 100 you. ¿Entiendes?

I nodded.

And if your brother gives you any food, I'll beat him too. Right here in front of everybody. ¿Entiendes?

I nodded again. I wanted to kill him and he must have sensed it because he gave my head a little shove.

All the kids watched me come in and sit down in front of the TV.

What's wrong with your dad? Leti 105 asked.

He's a dick, I said.

Rafa shook his head. Don't say that shit in front of people.

Easy for you to be nice when you're eating, I said.

Hey, if I was a pukey little baby, I wouldn't get no food either.

I almost said something back but I con- 110 centrated on the TV. I wasn't going to start it. No fucking way. So I watched Bruce Lee beat Chuck Norris into the floor of the Colosseum and tried to pretend that there was no food anywhere in the house. It was Tía who finally saved me. She came into the living room and said, Since you ain't eating, Yunior, you can at least help me get some ice.

I didn't want to, but she mistook my reluctance for something else.

I already asked your father.

She held my hand while we walked; Tía didn't have any kids but I could tell she wanted them. She was the sort of relative who always remembered your birthday but who you only went to visit because you had to. We didn't get past the first-floor landing before she opened her pocketbook and handed me the first of three pastelitos she had smuggled out of the apartment.

Go ahead, she said. And as soon as you get inside make sure you brush your teeth.

115   Thanks a lot, Tía, I said.

Those pastelitos didn't stand a chance.

She sat next to me on the stairs and smoked her cigarette. All the way down on the first floor and we could still hear the music and the adults and the television. Tía looked a ton like Mami; the two of them were both short and light-skinned. Tía smiled a lot and that was what set them apart the most.

How is it at home, Yunior?

What do you mean?

120   How's it going in the apartment? Are you kids OK?

I knew an interrogation when I heard one, no matter how sugar-coated it was. I didn't say anything. Don't get me wrong, I loved my tía, but something told me to keep my mouth shut. Maybe it was family loyalty, maybe I just wanted to protect Mami or I was afraid that Papi would find out—it could have been anything really.

Is your mom all right?

I shrugged.

Have there been lots of fights?

125   None, I said. Too many shrugs would have been just as bad as an answer. Papi's at work too much.

Work, Tía said, like it was somebody's name she didn't like.

Me and Rafa, we didn't talk much about the Puerto Rican woman. When we ate dinner at her house, the few times Papi had taken us over there, we still acted like nothing was out of the ordinary. Pass the ketchup, man. No sweat, bro. The affair was like a hole in our living room floor, one we'd gotten so used to circumnavigating that we sometimes forgot it was there.

By midnight all the adults were crazy dancing. I was sitting outside Tía's bedroom—where Madai was sleeping—trying not to attract attention. Rafa had me guarding the door; he and Leti were in there too, with some of the other kids, getting busy no doubt. Wilquins had gone across the hall to bed so I had me and the roaches to mess around with.

Whenever I peered into the main room I saw about twenty moms and dads dancing and drinking beers. Every now and then somebody yelled, ¡Quisqueya! And then everybody else would yell and stomp their feet. From what I could see my parents seemed to be enjoying themselves.

Mami and Tía spent a lot of time side 130 by side, whispering, and I kept expecting something to come of this, a brawl maybe. I'd never once been out with my family when it hadn't turned to shit. We weren't even theatrical or straight crazy like other families. We fought like sixth-graders, without any real dignity. I guess the whole night I'd been waiting for a blowup, something between Papi and Mami. This was how I always figured Papi would be exposed, out in public, where everybody would know.

You're a cheater!

But everything was calmer than usual. And Mami didn't look like she was about to say anything to Papi. The two of them danced every now and then but they never lasted more than a song before Mami joined Tía again in whatever conversation they were having.

I tried to imagine Mami before Papi. Maybe I was tired, or just sad, thinking about the way my family was. Maybe I already knew how it would all end up in a few years, Mami without Papi, and that was why I did it. Picturing her alone wasn't easy. It seemed like Papi had always been with her, even when we were waiting in Santo Domingo for him to send for us.

The only photograph our family had of Mami as a young woman, before she married Papi, was the one that somebody took of her at an election party that I found one day while rummaging for money to go to the arcade. Mami had it tucked into her immigration papers. In the photo, she's surrounded by laughing cousins I will never meet, who are all shiny from dancing, whose clothes are rumpled and loose. You can tell it's night and hot and that the mosquitos have been biting. She sits straight and even in a crowd she stands out, smiling quietly like maybe she's the one everybody's celebrating. You can't see her hands but I imagined they're knotting a straw or a bit of thread. This was the woman my father met a year later on the Malecón, the woman Mami thought she'd always be.

135   Mami must have caught me studying her because she stopped what she was doing and gave me a smile, maybe her first one of the night. Suddenly I wanted to go over and hug her, for no other reason than I loved her, but there were about eleven fat jiggling bodies between us. So I sat down on the tiled floor and waited.

I must have fallen asleep because the next thing I knew Rafa was kicking me and saying, Let's go. He looked like he'd been hitting those girls off; he was all smiles. I got to my feet in time to kiss Tía and Tío goodbye. Mami was holding the serving dish she had brought with her.

Where's Papi? I asked.

He's downstairs, bringing the van around. Mami leaned down to kiss me.

You were good today, she said.

140   And then Papi burst in and told us to get the hell downstairs before some pendejo cop gave him a ticket. More kisses, more handshakes and then we were gone.

I don't remember being out of sorts after I met the Puerto Rican woman, but I must have been because Mami only asked me questions when she thought something was wrong in my life. It took her about ten passes but finally she cornered me one afternoon when we were alone in the apartment. Our upstairs neighbors were beating the crap out of their kids, and me and her had been listening to it all afternoon. She put her hand on mine and said, Is everything OK, Yunior? Have you been fighting with your brother?

Me and Rafa had already talked. We'd been in the basement, where our parents couldn't hear us. He told me that yeah, he knew about her.

Papi's taken me there twice now, he said.

Why didn't you tell me? I asked.

What the hell was I going to say? *Hey,* 145 *Yunior, guess what happened yesterday? I met Papi's sucia!*

I didn't say anything to Mami either. She watched me, very very closely. Later I would think, maybe if I had told her, she would have confronted him, would have done something, but who can know these things? I said I'd been having trouble in school and like that everything was back to normal between us. She put her hand on my shoulder and squeezed and that was that.

We were on the turnpike, just past Exit 11, when I started feeling it again. I sat up from leaning against Rafa. His fingers smelled and he'd gone to sleep almost as soon as he got into the van. Madai was out too but at least she wasn't snoring.

In the darkness, I saw that Papi had a hand on Mami's knee and that the two of them were quiet and still. They weren't slumped back or anything; they were both wide awake, bolted into their seats. I couldn't see either of their faces and no matter how hard I tried I could not imagine their expres- sions. Neither of them moved. Every now and then the van was filled with the bright rush of somebody else's headlights. Finally I said, Mami, and they both looked back, already knowing what was happening.

•••••▶ *Your* **Turn**
Talking and Writing about Lit

1. Reread the first three paragraphs of "Fiesta, 1980." List five or more words that show how Díaz's use of style and tone establish the narrator Yunior's character and depict the social setting in which he lives.

2. In addition to using dialect in the story, Díaz uses Spanish words and phrases where his characters would authentically use them. What does his use of dialect—including "Spanglish"—accomplish in the story?

3. **DIY** In a brief scene, create a dialogue between yourself and a family member. Try to use words and phrases that help to characterize distinctive characters and a distinctive social setting.

T. Coraghessan Boyle (b. 1948)

FESTIVAL OF BOOKS **T. Coraghessan Boyle**

T. Coraghessan Boyle is the author of sixteen books of fiction, including, most recently, *After the Plague* (2001), *Drop City* (2003), and *The Inner Circle* (2004). His books have also been published in German, French, Italian, Dutch, Portuguese, Spanish, Russian, Hebrew, Korean, Japanese, Danish, Swedish, Lithuanian, Latvian, Polish, Hungarian, and Bulgarian! His stories have appeared in most of the major American magazines, including the *New Yorker, Harper's, Esquire, Atlantic Monthly, Playboy, Paris Review, GQ, Antaeus,* and *Granta,* and he has received many literary awards. Boyle teaches in the English Department at the University of Southern California. "Carnal Knowledge" appeared in Boyle's short story collection *Without a Hero and Other Stories* (1994).

Carnal Knowledge (1994)

I'd never really thought much about meat. It was there in the supermarket in a plastic wrapper; it came between slices of bread with mayo and mus- tard and a dill pickle on the side; it sputtered and smoked on the grill till somebody flipped it over, and then it appeared on the plate, between the baked potato and the julienne carrots, neatly cross-hatched and floating in a puddle of red juice. Beef, mutton, pork, venison, dripping burgers, and greasy ribs—it was all the same to me, food, the body's fuel, something to savor a moment on the tongue before the digestive system went to work on it. Which is not to say I was totally unconscious of the deeper implications. Every once in a while I'd eat at home, a quartered chicken, a package of Shake 'n Bake, Stove Top stuffing, and frozen peas, and as I hacked away at the stippled yellow skin and pink flesh of the sanitized bird I'd wonder at the darkish bits of organ clinging to the ribs—what was that, liver? kidney?—but in the end it didn't make me any less fond of Kentucky Fried or Chicken McNuggets. I saw those ads in the magazines, too, the ones that showed the veal calves penned up in their own waste, their limbs atrophied and their veins so pumped full of antibiotics they couldn't control their bowels, but when I took a date to Anna Maria's, I could never resist the veal scallopini.

And then I met Alena Jorgensen.

It was a year ago, two weeks before Thanksgiving—I remember the date because it was my birthday, my thirtieth, and I'd called in sick and gone to the beach to warm my face, read a book, and feel a little sorry for myself. The Santa Anas were blowing and it was clear all the way to Catalina, but there was an edge to the air, a scent of winter hanging over Utah, and as far as I could see in either direction I had the beach pretty much to myself. I found a sheltered spot in a tumble of boulders, spread a blanket, and settled down to attack the pastrami on rye I'd brought along for nourishment. Then I turned to my book—a comfortingly apocalyptic tract about the demise of the planet—and let the sun warm me as I read about the denuding of the rain forest, the poisoning of the atmosphere, and the swift silent eradication of species. Gulls coasted by overhead. I saw the distant glint of jetliners.

I must have dozed, my head thrown back, the book spread open in my lap, because the next thing I remember, a strange dog was hovering over me and the sun had dipped behind the rocks. The dog was big, wild-haired, with one staring blue eye, and it just looked at me, ears slightly cocked, as if it expected a Milk-Bone or something. I was startled— not that I don't like dogs, but here was this woolly thing poking its snout in my face—and I guess that I must have made some sort of defensive gesture, because the dog staggered back a step and froze. Even in the confusion of the moment I could see that there was something wrong with this dog, an unsteadiness, a gimp, a wobble to its legs. I felt a mixture of pity and revulsion—had it been hit by a car, was that it?—when all at once I became aware of a wetness on the breast of my windbreaker, and an unmistakable odor rose to my nostrils: I'd been pissed on.

Pissed on. As I lay there unsuspecting, 5 enjoying the sun, the beach, the solitude, this stupid beast had lifted its leg and used me as a pissoir—and now it was poised there on the edge of the blanket as if it expected a reward. A sudden rage seized me. I came up off the blanket with a curse, and it was only then that a dim apprehension seemed to seep into the dog's other eye, the brown one, and it lurched back and fell on its face, just out of reach. And then it lurched and fell again, bobbing and weaving across the sand like a seal out of water. I was on my feet now, murderous, glad to see that the thing was hobbled—it would simplify the task of running it down and beating it to death.

"Alf!" a voice called, and as the dog floundered in the sand, I turned and saw Alena Jorgensen poised on the boulder behind me. I don't want to make too much of the moment, don't want to mythologize it or clutter the scene with allusions to Aphrodite rising from the waves or accepting the golden apple from Paris, but she was a pretty impressive sight. Bare-legged, fluid, as tall and uncompromising as her Nordic ancestors, and dressed in a Gore-Tex bikini and hooded sweatshirt unzipped to the waist, she blew me away, in any event. Piss-spattered and stupefied, I could only gape up at her.

"You bad boy," she said, scolding, "you get out of there." She glanced from the dog to me and back again. "Oh, you bad boy, what have you done?" she demanded, and I was ready to admit to anything, but it was the dog she was addressing, and the dog flopped over in the sand as if it had been shot. Alena skipped lightly down from the rock, and in the next moment, before I could protest, she was rubbing at the stain on my windbreaker with the wadded-up hem of her sweatshirt.

I tried to stop her—"It's all right," I said, "it's nothing," as if dogs routinely pissed on my wardrobe—but she wouldn't hear of it.

"No," she said, rubbing, her hair flying in my face, the naked skin of her thigh pressing unconsciously to my own, "no, this is terrible, I'm so embarrassed—Alf, you bad boy—I'll clean it for you, I will, it's the least—oh, look at that, it's stained right through to your T-shirt—"

10   I could smell her, the mousse she used in her hair, a lilac soap or perfume, the salt-sweet odor of her sweat—she'd been jogging, that was it. I murmured something about taking it to the cleaner's myself.

She stopped rubbing and straightened up. She was my height, maybe even a fraction taller, and her eyes were ever so slightly mismatched, like the dog's: a deep earnest blue in the right iris, shading to sea-green and turquoise in the left. We were so close

we might have been dancing. "Tell you what," she said, and her face lit with a smile, "since you're so nice about the whole thing, and most people wouldn't be, even if they knew what poor Alf has been through, why don't you let me wash it for you—and the T-shirt too?"

I was a little disconcerted at this point—I was the one who'd been pissed on, after all—but my anger was gone. I felt weightless, adrift, like a piece of fluff floating on the breeze. "Listen," I said, and for the moment I couldn't look her in the eye, "I don't want to put you to any trouble . . ."

"I'm ten minutes up the beach, and I've got a washer and dryer. Come on, it's no trouble at all. Or do you have plans? I mean, I could just pay for the cleaner's if you want . . ."

I was between relationships—the person I'd been seeing off and on for the past year wouldn't even return my calls—and my plans consisted of taking a solitary late-afternoon movie as a birthday treat, then heading over to my mother's for dinner and the cake with the candles. My Aunt Irene would be there, and so would my grandmother. They would exclaim over how big I was and how handsome and then they would begin to contrast my present self with my previous, more diminutive incarnations, and finally work themselves up to a spate of reminiscence that would continue unabated till my mother drove them home. And then, if I was lucky, I'd go out to a singles bar and make the acquaintance of a divorced computer programmer in her mid-thirties with three kids and bad breath.

I shrugged. "Plans? No, not really. I   15 mean, nothing in particular."

Alena was housesitting a one-room bungalow that rose stumplike from the sand, no more than fifty feet from the tide line. There were trees in the yard behind it and the place was sandwiched between glass fortresses with crenellated decks, whipping flags, and great hulking concrete pylons. Sitting on the couch inside, you could feel the dull reverberation of each wave hitting the shore, a slow steady pulse that forever defined the place for me. Alena gave me a faded UC Davis sweatshirt that nearly fit, sprayed a stain remover on my T-shirt and windbreaker, and in a single fluid motion flipped down the lid of the washer and extracted two beers from the refrigerator beside it.

There was an awkward moment as she settled into the chair opposite me and we concentrated on our beers. I didn't know what to say. I was disoriented, giddy, still struggling to grasp what had happened. Fifteen minutes earlier I'd been dozing on the beach, alone on my birthday and feeling sorry for myself, and now I was ensconced in a cozy beach house, in the presence of Alena Jorgensen and her naked spill of leg, drinking a beer. "So what do you do?" she said, setting her beer down on the coffee table.

I was grateful for the question, too grateful maybe. I described to her at length how dull my job was, nearly ten years with the same agency, writing ad copy, my brain gone numb with disuse. I was somewhere in the middle of a blow-by-blow account of our current campaign for a Ghanian vodka distilled from calabash husks when she said, "I know what you mean," and told me she'd dropped out of veterinary school herself. "After I saw what they did to the animals. I mean, can you see neutering a dog just for our convenience, just because it's easier for us if they don't have a sex life?" Her voice grew hot. "It's the same old story, species fascism at its worst."

Alf was lying at my feet, grunting softly and looking up mournfully out of his staring blue eye, as blameless a creature as ever lived. I made a small noise of agreement and then focused on Alf. "And your dog," I said, "he's arthritic? Or is it hip dysplasia or what?" I was pleased with myself for the question—aside from "tapeworm," "hip dysplasia" was the only veterinary term I could dredge up from the memory bank, and I could see that Alf's problems ran deeper than worms.

Alena looked angry suddenly. "Don't I 20 wish," she said. She paused to draw a bitter breath. "There's nothing wrong with Alf that wasn't inflicted on him. They tortured him, maimed him, mutilated him."

"Tortured him?" I echoed, feeling the indignation rise in me—this beautiful girl, this innocent beast. "Who?"

Alena leaned forward and there was real hate in her eyes. She mentioned a prominent shoe company—spat out the name, actually. It was an ordinary name, a familiar one, and it hung in the air between us, suddenly sinister. Alf had been part of an experiment to market booties for dogs—suede, cordovan, patent leather, the works. The dogs were made to pace a treadmill in their booties, to assess wear; Alf was part of the control group.

"Control group?" I could feel the hackles rising on the back of my neck.

"They used eighty-grit sandpaper on the treads, to accelerate the process." Alena shot a glance out the window to where the surf pounded the shore; she bit her lip. "Alf was one of the dogs without booties."

I was stunned. I wanted to get up and 25 comfort her, but I might as well have been grafted to the chair. "I don't believe it," I said. "How could anybody—"

"Believe it," she said. She studied me a moment, then set down her beer and crossed the room to dig through a cardboard box in the corner. If I was moved by the emotion she'd called up, I was moved even more by the sight of her bending over the box in her Gore-Tex bikini; I clung to the edge of the chair as if it were a plunging roller coaster. A moment later she dropped a dozen file folders in my lap. The uppermost bore the name of the shoe company, and it was crammed with news clippings, several pages of a diary relating to plant operations and workers' shifts at the Grand Rapids facility, and a floor plan of the laboratories. The folders beneath it were inscribed with the names of cosmetics firms, biomedical research centers, furriers, tanners, meat-packers. Alena perched on the edge of the coffee table and watched as I shuffled through them.

"You know the Draize test?"

I gave her a blank look.

"They inject chemicals into rabbits' eyes to see how much it'll take before they go blind. The rabbits are in cages, thousands of them, and they take a needle and jab it into their eyes—and you know why, you know in the name of what great humanitarian cause this is going on, even as we speak?"

30 I didn't know. The surf pounded at my feet. I glanced at Alf and then back into her angry eyes.

"Mascara, that's what. Mascara. They torture countless thousands of rabbits so women can look like sluts."

I thought the characterization a bit harsh, but when I studied her pale lashes and tight lipstickless mouth, I saw that she meant it. At any rate, the notion set her off, and she launched into a two-hour lecture, gesturing with her flawless hands, quoting figures, digging through her files for the odd photo of legless mice or morphine-addicted gerbils. She told me how she'd rescued Alf herself, raiding the laboratory with six other members of the Animal Liberation Front, the militant group in honor of which Alf had been named. At first, she'd been content to write letters and carry placards,

but now, with the lives of so many animals at stake, she'd turned to more direct action: harassment, vandalism, sabotage. She described how she'd spiked trees with Earth-First!ers in Oregon, cut miles of barbed-wire fence on cattle ranches in Nevada, destroyed records in biomedical research labs up and down the coast and insinuated herself between the hunters and the bighorn sheep in the mountains of Arizona. I could only nod and exclaim, smile ruefully and whistle in a low "holy cow!" sort of way. Finally, she paused to level her unsettling eyes on me. "You know what Isaac Bashevis Singer said?"

We were on our third beer. The sun was gone. I didn't have a clue.

Alena leaned forward. "'Every day is Auschwitz for the animals.'"

I looked down into the amber aperture 35 of my beer bottle and nodded my head sadly. The dryer had stopped an hour and a half ago. I wondered if she'd go out to dinner with me, and what she could eat if she did. "Uh, I was wondering," I said, "if . . . if you might want to go out for something to eat—"

Alf chose that moment to heave himself up from the floor and urinate on the wall behind me. My dinner proposal hung in the balance as Alena shot up off the edge of the table to scold him and then gently usher him out the door. "Poor Alf," she sighed, turning back to me with a shrug. "But listen, I'm sorry if I talked your head off—I didn't mean to, but it's rare to find somebody on your own wavelength."

She smiled. *On your own wavelength:* the words illuminated me, excited me, sent up a tremor I could feel all the way down in the deepest nodes of my reproductive tract. "So how about dinner?" I persisted. Restaurants were running through my head—would it have to be veggie? Could there be even a whiff of grilled flesh on the air? Curdled goat's milk and tabbouleh, tofu, lentil soup, sprouts: *Every day is Auschwitz for the animals.* "No place with meat, of course."

She just looked at me.

"I mean, I don't eat meat myself," I lied, "or actually, not anymore"—since the pastrami sandwich, that is—"but I don't really know any place that . . ." I trailed off lamely.

40   "I'm a Vegan," she said.

After two hours of blind bunnies, butchered calves and mutilated pups, I couldn't resist the joke. "I'm from Venus myself."

She laughed, but I could see she didn't find it all that funny. Vegans didn't eat meat or fish, she explained, or milk or cheese or eggs, and they didn't wear wool or leather—or fur, of course.

"Of course," I said. We were both standing there, hovering over the coffee table. I was beginning to feel a little foolish.

"Why don't we just eat here," she said.

45   The deep throb of the ocean seemed to settle in my bones as we lay there in bed that night, Alena and I, and I learned all about the fluency of her limbs and the sweetness of her vegetable tongue. Alf sprawled on the floor beneath us, wheezing and groaning in his sleep, and I blessed him for his incontinence and his doggy stupidity. Something was happening to me—I could feel it in the way the boards shifted under me, feel it with each beat of the surf—and I was ready to go along with it. In the morning, I called in sick again.

Alena was watching me from bed as I dialed the office and described how the flu had migrated from my head to my gut and beyond, and there was a look in her eye that told me I would spend the rest of the day right there beside her, peeling grapes and dropping them one by one between her parted and expectant lips. I was wrong. Half an hour later, after a breakfast of brewer's yeast and what appeared to be some sort of bark marinated in yogurt, I found myself marching up and down the sidewalk in front of a fur emporium in Beverly Hills, waving a placard that read HOW DOES IT FEEL TO WEAR A CORPSE? in letters that dripped like blood.

It was a shock. I'd seen protest marches on TV, antiwar rallies and civil rights demonstrations and all that, but I'd never warmed my heels on the pavement or chanted slogans or felt the naked stick in my hand. There were maybe forty of us in all, mostly women, and we waved our placards at passing cars and blocked traffic on the sidewalk. One woman had smeared her face and hands with cold cream steeped in red dye, and Alena had found a ratty mink stole somewhere—the kind that features whole animals sewed together, snout to tail, their miniature limbs dangling—and she'd taken a can of crimson spray paint to their muzzles so that they looked freshly killed. She brandished this grisly banner on a stick high above her head, whooping like a savage and chanting, "Fur is death, fur is death," over and over again till it became a mantra for the crowd. The day was unseasonably warm, the Jaguars glinted in the sun and the palms nodded in the breeze, and no one, but for a single tight-lipped salesman glowering from behind the store's immaculate windows, paid the slightest bit of attention to us.

I marched out there on the street, feeling exposed and conspicuous, but marching nonetheless—for Alena's sake and for the sake of the foxes and martens and all the rest, and for my own sake too: with each step I took I could feel my consciousness expanding like a balloon, the breath of saintliness seeping steadily into me. Up to this point I'd worn suede and leather like anybody else, ankle boots and Air Jordans, a bombardier jacket I'd had since high school. If I'd drawn the line with fur, it was only because I'd never had any use for it. If I lived in the Yukon—and sometimes, drowsing through a meeting at work, I found myself fantasizing about it—I would have worn fur, no compunction, no second thoughts.

But not anymore. Now I was the protestor, a placard waver, now I was fighting for the right of every last weasel and lynx to grow old and die gracefully, now I was Alena Jorgensen's lover and a force to be reckoned with. Of course, my feet hurt and I was running sweat and praying that no one from work would drive by and see me there on the sidewalk with my crazy cohorts and denunciatory sign.

50 We marched for hours, back and forth, till I thought we'd wear a groove in the pavement. We chanted and jeered and nobody so much as looked at us twice. We could have been Hare Krishnas, bums, antiabortionists, or lepers, what did it matter? To the rest of the world, to the uninitiated masses to whose sorry number I'd belonged just twenty-four hours earlier, we were invisible. I was hungry, tired, discouraged. Alena was ignoring me. Even the woman in red-face was slowing down, her chant a hoarse whisper that was sucked up and obliterated in the roar of traffic. And then, as the afternoon faded toward rush hour, a wizened silvery old woman who might have been an aging star or a star's mother or even the first dimly remembered wife of a studio exec got out of a long white car at the curb and strode fearlessly toward us. Despite the heat—it must have been eighty degrees at this point—she was wearing an ankle-length silver fox coat, a bristling shouldery wafting mass of peltry that must have decimated every burrow on the tundra. It was the moment we'd been waiting for.

A cry went up, shrill and ululating, and we converged on the lone old woman like a Cheyenne war party scouring the plains. The man beside me went down on all fours and howled like a dog. Alena slashed the air with her limp mink, and the blood sang in my ears. "Murderer!" I screamed, getting into it. "Torturer! Nazi!" The strings in my neck were tight. I didn't know what I was saying. The crowd gibbered. The placards danced. I was so close to the old woman I could smell her—her perfume, a whiff of mothballs from the coat—and it intoxicated me, maddened me, and I stepped in front of her to block her path with all the seething militant bulk of my one hundred eighty-five pounds of sinew and muscle.

I never saw the chauffeur. Alena told me afterward that he was a former kickboxing champion who'd been banned from the sport for excessive brutality. The first blow seemed to drop down from above, a shell lobbed from deep within enemy territory; the others came at me like a windmill churning in a storm. Someone screamed. I remember focusing on the flawless rigid pleats of the chauffeur's trousers, and then things got a bit hazy.

I woke to the dull thump of the surf slamming at the shore and the touch of Alena's lips on my own. I felt as if I'd been broken on the wheel, dismantled, and put back together again. "Lie still," she said, and her tongue moved against my swollen cheek. Stricken, I could only drag my head across the pillow and gaze into the depths of her particolored eyes. "You're one of us now," she whispered.

Next morning I didn't even bother to call in sick.

By the end of the week I'd recovered 55 enough to crave meat, for which I felt deeply ashamed, and to wear out a pair of vinyl huaraches on the picket line. Together, and with various coalitions of antivivisectionists, militant Vegans, and cat lovers, Alena and I tramped a hundred miles of sidewalk, spray-painted inflammatory slogans across the windows of supermarkets and burger stands, denounced tanners, furriers, poulterers, and sausage makers, and somehow found time to break up a cockfight in Pacoima. It was exhilarating, heady, dangerous. If I'd been disconnected in the past, I was plugged in now. I felt righteous—for the first time in my life I had a cause—and I had Alena, Alena above all. She fascinated me, fixated me, made me feel like a tomcat leaping in and out of second-story windows, oblivious to the free-fall and the picket fence below. There was her beauty, of course, a triumph of evolution and the happy interchange of genes going all the way back to the cavemen, but it was more than that—it was her commitment to animals, to the righting of wrongs, to morality that made her irresistible. Was it love? The term is something I've always had difficulty with, but I suppose it was. Sure it was. Love, pure and simple. I had it, it had me.

"You know what?" Alena said one night as she stood over the miniature stove, searing tofu in oil and garlic. We'd spent the afternoon demonstrating out front of a tortilla factory that used rendered animal fat as a congealing agent, after which we'd been chased three blocks by an overweight assistant manager at Von's who objected to Alena's spray-painting MEAT IS DEATH over the specials in the front window. I was giddy with the adolescent joy of it. I sank into the couch with a beer and watched Alf limp across the floor to fling himself down and lick at a suspicious spot on the floor. The surf boomed like thunder.

"What?" I said.

"Thanksgiving's coming."

I let it ride a moment, wondering if I should invite Alena to my mother's for the big basted bird stuffed with canned oysters and buttered bread crumbs, and then realized it probably wouldn't be such a great idea. I said nothing.

She glanced over her shoulder. "The animals don't have a whole lot to be thankful for, that's for sure. It's just an excuse for the meat industry to butcher a couple million turkeys, is all it is." She paused; hot safflower oil popped in the pan. "I think it's time for a little road trip," she said. "Can we take your car?"

"Sure, but where are we going?"

She gave me her Gioconda smile. "To liberate some turkeys."

In the morning I called my boss to tell him I had pancreatic cancer and wouldn't be in for a while, then we threw some things in the car, helped Alf scrabble into the back seat, and headed up Route 5 for the San Joaquin Valley. We drove for three hours through a fog so dense the windows might as well have been packed with cotton. Alena was secretive, but I could see she was excited. I knew only that we were on our way to rendezvous with a certain "Rolfe," a longtime friend of hers and a big name in the world of ecotage and animal rights, after which we would commit some desperate and illegal act, for which the turkeys would be eternally grateful.

There was a truck stalled in front of the sign for our exit at Calpurnia Springs, and I had to brake hard and jerk the wheel around twice to keep the tires on the pavement. Alena came up out of her seat and Alf slammed into the armrest like a sack of meal, but we made it. A few minutes later we were gliding through the ghostly vacancy of the town itself, lights drifting past in a nimbus of fog, glowing pink, yellow, and white, and then there was only the blacktop road and the pale void that engulfed it. We'd gone ten miles or so when Alena instructed me to slow down and began to study the right-hand shoulder with a keen, unwavering eye.

65   The earth breathed in and out. I squinted hard into the soft drifting glow of the headlights. "There, there!" she cried and I swung the wheel to the right, and suddenly we were lurching along a pitted dirt road that rose up from the blacktop like a goat path worn into the side of a mountain. Five minutes later Alf sat up in the back seat and began to whine, and then a crude unpainted shack began to detach itself from the vagueness around us.

    Rolfe met us on the porch. He was tall and leathery, in his fifties, I guessed, with a shock of hair and rutted features that brought Samuel Beckett to mind. He was wearing gumboots and jeans and a faded lumberjack shirt that looked as if it had been washed a hundred times. Alf took a quick pee against the side of the house, then fumbled up the steps to roll over and fawn at his feet.

    "Rolfe!" Alena called, and there was too much animation in her voice, too much familiarity, for my taste. She took the steps in a bound and threw herself in his arms. I watched them kiss, and it wasn't a fatherly-daughterly sort of kiss, not at all. It was a kiss with some meaning behind it, and I didn't like it. Rolfe, I thought: What kind of name is that?

    "Rolfe," Alena gasped, still a little breathless from bouncing up the steps like a cheerleader, "I'd like you to meet Jim."

    That was my signal. I ascended the porch steps and held out my hand. Rolfe gave me a look out of the hooded depths of his eyes and then took my hand in a hard calloused grip, the grip of the wood splitter, the fence mender, the liberator of hothouse turkeys and laboratory mice. "A pleasure," he said, and his voice rasped like sandpaper.

70   There was a fire going inside, and Alena and I sat before it and warmed our hands while Alf whined and sniffed and Rolfe served Red Zinger tea in Japanese cups the size of thimbles. Alena hadn't stopped chattering since we stepped through the door, and Rolfe came right back at her in his woodsy rasp, the two of them exchanging names and news and gossip as if they were talking in code. I studied the reproductions of teal and widgeon that hung from the peeling walls, noted the case of Heinz vegetarian beans in the corner and the half-gallon of Jack Daniel's on the mantel. Finally, after the third cup of tea, Alena settled back in her chair—a huge old Salvation Army sort of thing with a soiled antimacassar—and said, "So what's the plan?"

    Rolfe gave me another look, a quick predatory darting of the eyes, as if he weren't sure I could be trusted, and then turned back to Alena. "Hedda Gabler's Range-Fed Turkey Ranch," he said. "And no, I don't find the name cute, not at all." He looked at me now, a long steady assay. "They grind up the heads for cat food, and the neck, the organs, and the rest, that they wrap up in paper and stuff back in the body cavity like it was a war atrocity or something. Whatever did a turkey go and do to us to deserve a fate like that?"

    The question was rhetorical, even if it seemed to have been aimed at me, and I made no response other than to compose my face in a look that wedded grief, outrage, and resolve. I was thinking of all the turkeys I'd sent to their doom, of the plucked wishbones, the pope's noses,* and the crisp browned skin I used to relish as a kid. It brought a lump to my throat, and something more: I realized I was hungry.

    "Ben Franklin wanted to make them our national symbol," Alena chimed in, "did you know that? But the meat eaters won out."

---

pope's noses: Slang for the fleshy tail sections of turkeys and other poultry.

"Fifty thousand birds," Rolfe said, glancing at Alena and bringing his incendiary gaze back to rest on me. "I have information they're going to start slaughtering them tomorrow, for the fresh-not-frozen market."

75 "Yuppie poultry," Alena's voice was drenched in disgust.

For a moment, no one spoke. I became aware of the crackling of the fire. The fog pressed at the windows. It was getting dark.

"You can see the place from the highway," Rolfe said finally, "but the only access is through Calpurnia Springs. It's about twenty miles—twenty-two point three, to be exact."

Alena's eyes were bright. She was gazing on Rolfe as if he'd just dropped down from heaven. I felt something heave in my stomach.

"We strike tonight."

80 Rolfe insisted that we take my car— "Everybody around here knows my pickup, and I can't take any chances on a little operation like this"—but we did mask the plates, front and back, with an inch-thick smear of mud. We blackened our faces like commandos and collected our tools from the shed out back—tin snips, a crowbar, and two five-gallon cans of gasoline. "Gasoline?" I said, trying the heft of the can. Rolfe gave me a craggy look. "To create a diversion," he said. Alf, for obvious reasons, stayed behind in the shack.

If the fog had been thick in daylight, it was impenetrable now, the sky collapsed upon the earth. It took hold of the headlights and threw them back at me till my eyes began to water from the effort of keeping the car on the road. But for the ruts and bumps we might have been floating in space. Alena sat up front between Rolfe and me, curiously silent. Rolfe didn't have much to say either, save for the occasional grunted command: "Hang a right here"; "Hard left"; "Easy, easy." I thought about meat and jail and the heroic proportions to which I was about to swell in Alena's eyes and what I intended to do to her when we finally got to bed. It was 2:00 A.M. by the dashboard clock.

"Okay," Rolfe said, and his voice came at me so suddenly it startled me, "pull over here—and kill the lights."

We stepped out into the hush of night and eased the doors shut behind us. I couldn't see a thing, but I could hear the not-so-distant hiss of traffic on the highway, and another sound, too, muffled and indistinct, the gentle unconscious suspiration of thousands upon thousands of my fellow creatures. And I could smell them, a seething rancid odor of feces and feathers and naked scaly feet that crawled down my throat and burned my nostrils. "Whew," I said in a whisper, "I can smell them."

Rolfe and Alena were vague presences at my side. Rolfe flipped open the trunk and in the next moment I felt the heft of a crowbar and a pair of tin snips in my hand. "Listen, you, Jim," Rolfe whispered, taking me by the wrist in his iron grip and leading me half-a-dozen steps forward. "Feel this?"

I felt a grid of wire, which he promptly 85 cut: *snip, snip, snip.*

"This is their enclosure—they're out there in the day, scratching around in the dirt. You get lost, you follow this wire. Now, you're going to take a section out of this side, Alena's got the west side and I've got the south. Once that's done I signal with the flashlight and we bust open the doors to the turkey houses—they're these big low white buildings, you'll see them when you get close—and flush the birds out. Don't worry about me or Alena. Just worry about getting as many birds out as you can."

I was worried. Worried about everything, from some half-crazed farmer with a shotgun or AK-47 or whatever they carried these days, to losing Alena in the fog, to the turkeys themselves: How big were they? Were they violent? They had claws and beaks, didn't they? And how were they going to feel about me bursting into their bedroom in the middle of the night?

"And when the gas cans go up, you hightail it back to the car, got it?"

I could hear the turkeys tossing in their sleep. A truck shifted gears out on the highway. "I think so," I whispered.

90 "And one more thing—be sure to leave the keys in the ignition."

This gave me pause. "But—"

"The getaway." Alena was so close I could feel her breath on my ear. "I mean, we don't want to be fumbling around for the keys when all hell is breaking loose out there, do we?"

I eased open the door and reinserted the keys in the ignition, even though the automatic buzzer warned me against it. "Okay," I murmured, but they were already gone, soaked up in the shadows and the mist. At this point my heart was hammering so loudly I could barely hear the rustling of the turkeys—this is crazy, I told myself, it's hurtful and wrong, not to mention illegal. Spray-painting slogans was one thing, but this was something else altogether. I thought of the turkey farmer asleep in his bed, an entrepreneur working to make America strong, a man with a wife and kids and a mortgage . . . but then I thought of all those innocent turkeys consigned to death, and finally I thought of Alena, long-legged and loving, and the way she came to me out of the darkness of the bathroom and the boom of the surf. I took the tin snips to the wire.

I must have been at it half an hour, forty-five minutes, gradually working my way toward the big white sheds that had begun to emerge from the gloom up ahead, when I saw Rolfe's flashlight blinking off to my left. This was my signal to head to the nearest shed, snap off the padlock with my crowbar, fling open the doors, and herd a bunch of cranky suspicious gobblers out into the night. It was now or never. I looked twice round me and then broke for the near shed in an awkward crouching gait. The turkeys must have sensed that something was up—from behind the long white windowless wall there arose a watchful gabbling, a soughing of feathers that fanned up like a breeze in the treetops. *Hold on, you toms and hens*, I thought, *freedom is at hand*. A jerk of the wrist, and the padlock fell to the ground. Blood pounded in my ears, I took hold of the sliding door and jerked it open with a great dull booming reverberation— and suddenly, there they were, turkeys, thousands upon thousands of them, cloaked in white feathers under a string of dim yellow bulbs. The light glinted in their reptilian eyes. Somewhere a dog began to bark.

I steeled myself and sprang through 95 the door with a shout, whirling the crowbar over my head, "All right!" I boomed, and the echo gave it back to me a hundred times over, "this is it! Turkeys, on your feet!" Nothing. No response. But for the whisper of rustling feathers and the alertly cocked heads, they might have been sculptures, throw pillows, they might as well have been dead and butchered and served up with yams and onions and all the trimmings. The barking of the dog went up a notch. I thought I heard voices.

The turkeys crouched on the concrete floor, wave upon wave of them, stupid and immovable; they perched in the rafters, on shelves and platforms, huddled in wooden stalls. Desperate, I rushed into the front rank of them, swinging my crowbar, stamping my feet, and howling like the wishbone plucker I once was. That did it. There was a shriek from the nearest bird and the others took it up till an unholy racket filled the place, and now they were moving, tumbling down from their perches, flapping their wings in a storm of dried excrement and pecked-over grain, pouring across the concrete floor till it vanished beneath them. Encouraged, I screamed again—"Yeeee-ha-ha-ha-ha!"—and beat at the aluminum walls with the crowbar as the turkeys shot through the doorway and out into the night.

It was then that the black mouth of the doorway erupted with light and the *ka-boom!* of the gas cans sent a tremor through the earth. *Run!* a voice screamed in my head, and the adrenaline kicked in and all of a sudden I was scrambling for the door in a hurricane of turkeys. They were everywhere, flapping their wings, gobbling and screeching, loosing their bowels in panic. Something hit the back of my legs and all at once I was down amongst them, on the floor, in the dirt and feathers and wet turkey shit. I was a roadbed, a turkey expressway. Their claws dug at my back, my shoulders, the crown of my head. Panicked now, choking on feathers and dust and worse, I fought to my feet as the big screeching birds launched themselves round me, and staggered out into the barnyard. "There! Who's that there?" a voice roared, and I was off and running.

What can I say? I vaulted turkeys, kicked them aside like so many footballs, slashed and tore at them as they sailed through the air. I ran till my lungs felt as if they were burning right through my chest, disoriented, bewildered, terrified of the shotgun blast I was sure would cut me down at any moment. Behind me the fire raged and lit the fog till it glowed blood-red and hellish. But where was the fence? And where the car?

I got control of my feet then and stood stock-still in a flurry of turkeys, squinting into the wall of fog. Was that it? Was that the car over there? At that moment I heard an engine start up somewhere behind me—a familiar engine with a familiar coughing gurgle in the throat of the carburetor—and then the lights blinked on briefly three hundred yards away. I heard the engine race and listened, helpless, as the car roared off in the opposite direction. I stood there a moment longer, forlorn and forsaken, and then I ran blindly off into the night, putting the fire and the shouts and the barking and the incessant mindless squawking of the turkeys as far behind me as I could.

When dawn finally broke, it was only just 100 perceptibly, so thick was the fog. I'd made my way to a blacktop road—which road and where it led I didn't know—and sat crouched and shivering in a clump of weed just off the shoulder. Alena wouldn't desert me, I was sure of that—she loved me, as I loved her; needed me, as I needed her—and I was sure she'd be cruising along the back roads looking for me. My pride was wounded, of course, and if I never laid eyes on Rolfe again I felt I wouldn't be missing much, but at least I hadn't been drilled full of shot, savaged by farm dogs, or pecked to death by irate turkeys. I was sore all over, my shin throbbed where I'd slammed into something substantial while vaulting through the night, there were feathers in my hair, and my face and arms were a mosaic of cuts and scratches and long trailing fissures of dirt. I'd been sitting there for what seemed like hours, cursing Rolfe, developing suspicions about Alena and unflattering theories about environmentalists in general, when finally I heard the familiar slurp and roar of my Chevy Citation cutting through the mist ahead of me.

Rolfe was driving, his face impassive. I flung myself into the road like a tattered beggar, waving my arms over my head and giving vent to my joy, and he very nearly ran me down. Alena was out of the car before it stopped, wrapping me up in her arms, and then she was bundling me into the rear seat with Alf and we were on our way back to the hideaway. "What happened?" she cried, as if she couldn't have guessed. "Where were you? We waited as long as we could."

I was feeling sulky, betrayed, feeling as if I was owed a whole lot more than a perfunctory hug and a string of insipid questions. Still, as I told my tale I began to warm to it—they'd got away in the car with the heater going, and I'd stayed behind to fight the turkeys, the farmers, and the elements, too, and if that wasn't heroic, I'd like to know what was. I looked into Alena's admiring eyes and pictured Rolfe's shack, a nip or two from the bottle of Jack Daniel's, maybe a peanut-butter-and-tofu sandwich, and then the bed, with Alena in it. Rolfe said nothing.

Back at Rolfe's, I took a shower and scrubbed the turkey droppings from my pores, then helped myself to the bourbon. It was ten in the morning and the house was dark—if the world had ever been without fog, there was no sign of it here. When Rolfe stepped out on the porch to fetch an armload of firewood, I pulled Alena down into my lap. "Hey," she murmured, "I thought you were an invalid."

She was wearing a pair of too-tight jeans and an oversize sweater with nothing underneath it. I slipped my hand inside the sweater and found something to hold on to. "Invalid?" I said, nuzzling at her sleeve. "Hell, I'm a turkey liberator, an ecoguerrilla, a friend of the animals and the environment, too."

She laughed, but she pushed herself up and crossed the room to stare out the occluded window. "Listen, Jim," she said, "what we did last night was great, really great, but it's just the beginning." Alf looked up at her expectantly. I heard Rolfe fumbling around on the porch, the thump of wood on wood. She turned around to face me now. "What I mean is, Rolfe wants me to go up to Wyoming for a little bit, just outside of Yellowstone—"

Me? Rolfe wants me? There was no invitation in that, no plurality, no acknowledgment of all we'd done and meant to each other. "For what?" I said. "What do you mean?"

"There's this grizzly—a pair of them, actually—and they've been raiding places outside the park. One of them made off with the mayor's Doberman the other night and the people are up in arms. We—I mean Rolfe and me and some other people from the old Bolt Weevils in Minnesota?—we're going to go up there and make sure the Park Service—or the local yahoos—don't eliminate them. The bears, I mean."

My tone was corrosive. "You and Rolfe?"

"There's nothing between us, if that's what you're thinking. This has to do with animals, that's all."

"Like us?"

She shook her head slowly. "Not like us, no. We're the plague on this planet, don't you know that?"

Suddenly I was angry. Seething. Here I'd crouched in the bushes all night, covered in turkey crap, and now I was part of a plague. I was on my feet. "No, I don't know that."

She gave me a look that let me know it didn't matter, that she was already gone, that her agenda, at least for the moment, didn't include me and there was no use arguing about it. "Look," she said, her voice dropping as Rolfe slammed back through the door with a load of wood, "I'll see you in

L.A. in a month or so, okay?" She gave me an apologetic smile. "Water the plants for me?"

An hour later I was on the road again. I'd helped Rolfe stack the wood beside the fireplace, allowed Alena to brush my lips with a good-bye kiss, and then stood there on the porch while Rolfe locked up, lifted Alf into the bed of his pickup, and rumbled down the rutted dirt road with Alena at his side. I watched till their brake lights dissolved in the drifting gray mist, then fired up the Citation and lurched down the road behind them. *A month or so:* I felt hollow inside. I pictured her with Rolfe, eating yogurt and wheat germ, stopping at motels, wrestling grizzlies, and spiking trees. The hollowness opened up, cored me out till I felt as if I'd been plucked and gutted and served up on a platter myself.

115 I found my way back through Calpurnia Springs without incident—there were no roadblocks, no flashing lights and grim-looking troopers searching trunks and back seats for a tallish thirty-year-old ecoterrorist with turkey tracks down his back— but after I turned onto the highway for Los Angeles, I had a shock. Ten miles up the road my nightmare materialized out of the gloom: red lights everywhere, signal flares and police cars lined up on the shoulder. I was on the very edge of panicking, a beat away from cutting across the median and giving them a run for it, when I saw the truck jackknifed up ahead. I slowed to forty, thirty, and then hit the brakes again. In a moment I was stalled in a line of cars and there was something all over the road, ghostly and white in the fog. At first I thought it must have been flung from the truck, rolls of toilet paper or crates of soap powder ruptured on the pavement. It was neither. As I inched closer, the tires creeping now, the pulse of the lights in my face,

I saw that the road was coated in feathers, turkey feathers. A storm of them. A blizzard. And more: there was flesh there too, slick and greasy, a red pulp ground into the surface of the road, thrown up like slush from the tires of the car ahead of me, ground beneath the massive wheels of the truck. Turkeys. Turkeys everywhere.

The car crept forward. I flicked on the windshield wipers, hit the washer button, and for a moment a scrim of diluted blood obscured the windows and the hollowness opened up inside of me till I thought it would suck me inside out. Behind me, someone was leaning on his horn. A trooper loomed up out of the gloom, waving me on with the dead yellow eye of his flashlight. I thought of Alena and felt sick. All there was between us had come to this, expectations gone sour, a smear on the road. I wanted to get out and shoot myself, turn myself in, close my eyes, and wake up in jail, in a hair shirt, in a straitjacket, anything. It went on. Time passed. Nothing moved. And then, miraculously, a vision began to emerge from behind the smeared glass and the gray belly of the fog, lights glowing golden in the waste. I saw the sign, Gas/Food/Lodging, and my hand was on the blinker.

It took me a moment, picturing the place, the generic tile, the false cheer of the lights, the odor of charred flesh hanging heavy on the air, Big Mac, three-piece dark meat, carne asada, cheeseburger. The engine coughed. The lights glowed. I didn't think of Alena then, didn't think of Rolfe or grizzlies or the doomed bleating flocks and herds, or of the blind bunnies and cancerous mice—I thought only of the cavern opening inside me and how to fill it. "Meat," and I spoke the word aloud, talking to calm myself as if I'd awakened from a bad dream, "it's only meat."

·····▶ *Your* **Turn**
Talking and Writing about Lit

1. Boyle's "Carnal Knowledge" is the kind of story whose meaning increases on a second reading. After reading Boyle's story once for pleasure, look back over it. How many passages do you notice that seem suddenly ironic, and even funnier, on a second reading?

2. Remember that the word *tone* (as a literary term) refers to the author's attitude toward the subject. How would you describe the tone of Boyle's narrative? What words or passages can you cite as examples of tone?

3. **DIY** In the beginning of paragraph 45, Boyle's narrator describes the sound of the surf from Alena's bedroom as "The deep throb of the ocean," but in the beginning of paragraph 53, he calls the same sound "the dull thump of the surf slamming at the shore." Clearly, something has happened to change his perception of his surroundings. Write a scene in which your narrator is excited about something at the outset (a blind date, a concert, a first day of class), but then his or her attitude changes as the experience turns out quite differently than expected.

Raymond Carver (1939–1988)

Carver's parents were itinerant workers, originally from Arkansas, and he grew up moving up and down the West Coast while his father acquired and lost various jobs. He spent a significant portion of his childhood in an Oregon logging town. Carver, who also wrote poetry, published numerous collections of short fiction. Among them are *Will You Please Be Quiet, Please?* (1976), *What We Talk About When We Talk about Love* (1981), and *Cathedral* (1983). He has received many awards for his fiction and poetry, including NEA grants, a Guggenheim Fellowship, the Mildred and Harold Strauss Living Award, the Brandeis Citation in fiction, and *Poetry* magazine's Levinson Prize. Carver was elected to the American Academy and Institute of Arts and Letters and was awarded a Doctorate of Letters from Hartford University. His work has been published in more than twenty languages. Carver taught at Syracuse University and other campuses, and he lived, until his death in 1988, in Port Angeles, Washington, with his second wife, the poet Tess Gallagher.

Cathedral (1983)

This blind man, an old friend of my wife's, he was on his way to spend the night. His wife had died. So he was visiting the dead wife's relatives in Connecticut. He called my wife from his in-laws'. Arrangements were made. He would come by train, a five-hour trip, and my wife would meet him at the station. She hadn't seen him since she worked for him one summer in Seattle ten years ago. But she and the blind man had kept in touch. They made tapes and mailed them back and forth. I wasn't enthusiastic about his visit. He was no one I knew. And his being blind bothered me. My idea of blindness came from the movies. In the movies, the blind moved slowly and never laughed. Sometimes they were led by seeing-eye dogs. A blind man in my house was not something I looked forward to.

That summer in Seattle she had needed a job. She didn't have any money. The man she was going to marry at the end of the summer was in officers' training school. He didn't have any money, either. But she was in love with the guy, and he was in love with her, etc. She'd seen something in the paper: HELP WANTED—*Reading to Blind Man*, and a telephone number. She phoned and went over, was hired on the spot. She'd worked with this blind man all summer. She read stuff to him, case studies, reports, that sort of thing. She helped him organize his little office in the county social-service department. They'd become good friends, my wife and the blind man. How do I know these things? She told me. And she told me something else. On her last day in the office, the blind man asked if he could touch her face. She agreed to this. She told me he touched his fingers to every part of her face, her nose—even her neck! She never forgot it. She even tried to write a poem about it. She was always trying to write a poem. She wrote a poem or two every year, usually after something really important had happened to her.

When we first started going out together, she showed me the poem. In the poem, she recalled his fingers and the way they had moved around over her face. In the poem, she talked about what she had felt at the time, about what went through her mind when the blind man touched her nose and lips. I can remember I didn't think much of the poem. Of course, I didn't tell her that. Maybe I just don't understand poetry. I admit it's not the first thing I reach for when I pick up something to read.

Anyway, this man who'd first enjoyed her favors, the officer-to-be, he'd been her childhood sweetheart. So okay. I'm saying that at the end of the summer she let the blind man run his hands over her face, said goodbye to him, married her childhood etc., who was now a commissioned officer, and she moved away from Seattle. But they'd kept in touch, she and the blind man. She made the first contact after a year or so. She called him up one night from an Air Force base in Alabama. She wanted to talk. They talked. He asked her to send him a tape and tell him about her life. She did this. She sent the tape. On the tape, she told the blind man about her husband and about their life together in the military. She told the blind man she loved her husband but she didn't like it where they lived and she didn't like it that he was a part of the military-industrial thing. She told the blind man she'd written a poem and he was in it. She told him that she was writing a poem about what it was like to be an Air Force officer's wife. The poem wasn't finished yet. She was still writing it.

The blind man made a tape. He sent her the tape. She made a tape. This went on for years. My wife's officer was posted to one base and then another. She sent tapes from Moody AFB, McGuire, McConnell, and finally Travis, near Sacramento, where one night she got to feeling lonely and cut off from people she kept losing in that moving-around life. She got to feeling she couldn't go it another step. She went in and swallowed all the pills and capsules in the medicine chest and washed them down with a bottle of gin. Then she got into a hot bath and passed out.

5   But instead of dying, she got sick. She threw up. Her officer—why should he have a name? he was the childhood sweetheart, and what more does he want?—came home from somewhere, found her, and called the ambulance. In time, she put it all on a tape and sent the tape to the blind man. Over the years, she put all kinds of stuff on tapes and sent the tapes off lickety-split. Next to writing a poem every year, I think it was her chief means of recreation. On one tape, she told the blind man she'd decided to live away from her officer for a time. On another tape, she told him about her divorce. She and I began going out, and of course she told her blind man about it. She told him everything, or so it seemed to me. Once she asked me if I'd like to hear the latest tape from the blind man. This was a year ago. I was on the tape, she said. So I said okay, I'd listen to it. I got us drinks and we settled down in the living room. We made ready to listen. First she inserted the tape into the player and adjusted a couple of dials. Then she pushed a lever. The tape squeaked and someone began to talk in this loud voice. She lowered the volume. After a few minutes of harmless chitchat, I heard my own name in the mouth of this stranger, this blind man I didn't even know! And then this: "From all you've said about him, I can only conclude—" But we were interrupted,

a knock at the door, something, and we didn't ever get back to the tape. Maybe it was just as well. I'd heard all I wanted to.

Now this same blind man was coming to sleep in my house.

"Maybe I could take him bowling," I said to my wife. She was at the draining board doing scalloped potatoes. She put down the knife she was using and turned around.

"If you love me," she said, "you can do this for me. If you don't love me, okay. But if you had a friend, any friend, and the friend came to visit, I'd make him feel comfortable." She wiped her hands with the dish towel.

"I don't have any blind friends," I said.

"You don't have *any* friends," she said. 10 "Period. Besides," she said, "goddamn it, his wife's just died! Don't you understand that? The man's lost his wife!"

I didn't answer. She'd told me a little about the blind man's wife. Her name was Beulah. Beulah! That's a name for a colored woman.

"Was his wife a Negro?" I asked.

"Are you crazy?" my wife said. "Have you just flipped or something?" She picked up a potato. I saw it hit the floor, then roll under the stove. "What's wrong with you?" she said. "Are you drunk?"

"I'm just asking," I said.

Right then my wife filled me in with 15 more detail than I cared to know. I made a drink and sat at the kitchen table to listen. Pieces of the story began to fall into place.

Beulah had gone to work for the blind man the summer after my wife had stopped working for him. Pretty soon Beulah and the blind man had themselves a church wedding. It was a little wedding—who'd want to go to such a wedding in the first place?—just the two of them, plus the minister and the minister's wife. But it was a church wedding just the same. It was what Beulah had wanted, he'd said. But even then Beulah must have been carrying the cancer in her glands. After they had been inseparable for eight years—my wife's word, *inseparable*—Beulah's health went into a rapid decline. She died in a Seattle hospital room, the blind man sitting beside the bed and holding on to her hand. They'd married, lived and worked together, slept together—had sex, sure—and then the blind man had to bury her. All this without his having ever seen what the goddamned woman looked like. It was beyond my understanding. Hearing this, I felt sorry for the blind man for a little bit. And then I found myself thinking what a pitiful life this woman must have led. Imagine a woman who could never see herself as she was seen in the eyes of her loved one. A woman who could go on day after day and never receive the smallest compliment from her beloved. A woman whose husband could never read the expression on her face, be it misery or something better. Someone who could wear makeup or not—what difference to him? She could, if she wanted, wear green eye-shadow around one eye, a straight pin in her nostril, yellow slacks and purple shoes, no matter. And then to slip off into death, the blind man's hand on her hand, his blind eyes streaming tears—I'm imagining now—her last thought maybe this: that he never even knew what she looked like, and she on an express to the grave. Robert was left with a small insurance policy and half of a twenty-peso Mexican coin. The other half of the coin went into the box with her. Pathetic.

So when the time rolled around, my wife went to the depot to pick him up. With nothing to do but wait—sure, I blamed him for that—I was having a drink and watching the TV when I heard the car pull into the drive. I got up from the sofa with my drink and went to the window to have a look.

I saw my wife laughing as she parked the car. I saw her get out of the car and shut the door. She was still wearing a smile. Just amazing. She went around to the other side of the car to where the blind man was already starting to get out. This blind man, feature this, he was wearing a full beard! A beard on a blind man! Too much, I say. The blind man reached into the back seat and dragged out a suitcase. My wife took his arm, shut the car door, and, talking all the way, moved him down the drive and then up the steps to the front porch. I turned off the TV. I finished my drink, rinsed the glass, dried my hands. Then I went to the door.

My wife said, "I want you to meet Robert. Robert, this is my husband. I've told you all about him." She was beaming. She had this blind man by his coat sleeve.

The blind man let go of his suitcase 20 and up came his hand.

I took it. He squeezed hard, held my hand, and then he let it go.

"I feel like we've already met," he boomed.

"Likewise," I said. I didn't know what else to say. Then I said, "Welcome. I've heard a lot about you." We began to move then, a little group, from the porch into the living room, my wife guiding him by the arm. The blind man was carrying his suitcase in his other hand. My wife said things like, "To your left here, Robert. That's right. Now watch it, there's a chair. That's it. Sit down right here. This is the sofa. We just bought this sofa two weeks ago."

I started to say something about the old sofa. I'd liked that old sofa. But I didn't say anything. Then I wanted to say something else, small-talk, about the scenic ride along the Hudson. How going *to* New York, you should sit on the right-hand side of the train, and coming *from* New York, the left-hand side.

"Did you have a good train ride?" I 25 said. "Which side of the train did you sit on, by the way?"

"What a question, which side!" my wife said. "What's it matter which side?" she said.

"I just asked," I said.

"Right side," the blind man said. "I hadn't been on a train in nearly forty years. Not since I was a kid. With my folks. That's been a long time. I'd nearly forgotten the sensation. I have winter in my beard now," he said. "So I've been told, anyway. Do I look distinguished, my dear?" the blind man said to my wife.

"You look distinguished, Robert," she said. "Robert," she said. "Robert, it's just so good to see you."

30   My wife finally took her eyes off the blind man and looked at me. I had the feeling she didn't like what she saw. I shrugged.

I've never met, or personally known, anyone who was blind. This blind man was late forties, a heavy-set, balding man with stooped shoulders, as if he carried a great weight there. He wore brown slacks, brown shoes, a light-brown shirt, a tie, a sports coat. Spiffy. He also had this full beard. But he didn't use a cane and he didn't wear dark glasses. I'd always thought dark glasses were a must for the blind. Fact was, I wished he had a pair. At first glance, his eyes looked like anyone else's eyes. But if you looked close, there was something different about them. Too much white in the iris, for one thing, and the pupils seemed to move around in the sockets without his knowing it or being able to stop it. Creepy. As I stared at his face, I saw the left pupil turn in toward his nose while the other made an effort to keep in one place. But it was only an effort, for that eye was on the roam without his knowing it or wanting it to be.

I said, "Let me get you a drink. What's your pleasure? We have a little of everything. It's one of our pastimes."

"Bub, I'm a Scotch man myself," he said fast enough in this big voice.

"Right," I said. Bub! "Sure you are. I knew it."

He let his fingers touch his suitcase, 35 which was sitting alongside the sofa. He was taking his bearings. I didn't blame him for that.

"I'll move that up to your room," my wife said.

"No, that's fine," the blind man said loudly. "It can go up when I go up."

"A little water with the Scotch?" I said.

"Very little," he said.

"I knew it," I said.   40

He said, "Just a tad. The Irish actor, Barry Fitzgerald? I'm like that fellow. When I drink water, Fitzgerald said, I drink water. When I drink whiskey, I drink whiskey." My wife laughed. The blind man brought his hand up under his beard. He lifted his beard slowly and let it drop.

I did the drinks, three big glasses of Scotch with a splash of water in each. Then we made ourselves comfortable and talked about Robert's travels. First the long flight from the West Coast to Connecticut, we covered that. Then from Connecticut up here by train. We had another drink concerning that leg of the trip.

I remembered having read somewhere that the blind didn't smoke because, as speculation had it, they couldn't see the smoke they exhaled. I thought I knew that much and that much only about blind people. But this blind man smoked his cigarette down to the nubbin and then lit another one. This blind man filled his ashtray and my wife emptied it.

When we sat down at the table for dinner, we had another drink. My wife heaped Robert's plate with cube steak, scalloped potatoes, green beans. I buttered him up two slices of bread. I said, "Here's bread and butter for you." I swallowed some of my drink. "Now let us pray," I said, and the blind man lowered his head. My wife looked at me, her mouth agape. "Pray the phone won't ring and the food doesn't get cold," I said.

45   We dug in. We ate everything there was to eat on the table. We ate like there was no tomorrow. We didn't talk. We ate. We scarfed. We grazed that table. We were into serious eating. The blind man had right away located his foods, he knew just where everything was on his plate. I watched with admiration as he used his knife and fork on the meat. He'd cut two pieces of meat, fork the meat into his mouth, and then go all out for the scalloped potatoes, the beans next, and then he'd tear off a hunk of buttered bread and eat that. He'd follow this up with a big drink of milk. It didn't seem to bother him to use his fingers once in a while, either.

We finished everything, including half a strawberry pie. For a few moments, we sat as if stunned. Sweat beaded on our faces. Finally, we got up from the table and left the dirty plates. We didn't look back. We took ourselves into the living room and sank into our places again. Robert and my wife sat on the sofa. I took the big chair. We had us two or three more drinks while they talked about the major things that had come to pass for them in the past ten years. For the most part, I just listened. Now and then I joined in. I didn't want him to think I'd left the room, and I didn't want her to think I was feeling left out. They talked of things that had happened to them—to them!—these past ten years. I waited in vain to hear my name on my wife's sweet lips: "And then my dear husband came into my life"— something like that. But I heard nothing of the sort. More talk of Robert. Robert had done a little of everything, it seemed, a regular blind jack-of-all-trades. But most recently he and his wife had had an Amway distributorship, from which, I gathered, they'd earned their living, such as it was. The blind man was also a ham radio operator.

He talked in his loud voice about conversations he'd had with fellow operators in Guam, in the Philippines, in Alaska, and even in Tahiti. He said he'd have a lot of friends there if he ever wanted to go visit those places. From time to time, he'd turn his blind face toward me, put his hand under his beard, ask me something. How long had I been in my present position? (Three years.) Did I like my work? (I didn't.) Was I going to stay with it? (What were the options?) Finally, when I thought he was beginning to run down, I got up and turned on the TV.

My wife looked at me with irritation. She was heading toward a boil. Then she looked at the blind man and said, "Robert, do you have a TV?"

The blind man said, "My dear, I have two TVs. I have a color set and a black-and-white thing, an old relic. It's funny, but if I turn the TV on, and I'm always turning it on, I turn on the color set. It's funny, don't you think?"

I didn't know what to say to that. I had absolutely nothing to say to that. No opinion. So I watched the news program and tried to listen to what the announcer was saying.

"This is a color TV," the blind man   50 said. "Don't ask me how, but I can tell."

"We traded up a while ago," I said.

The blind man had another taste of his drink. He lifted his beard, sniffed it, and let it fall. He leaned forward on the sofa. He positioned his ashtray on the coffee table, then put the lighter to his cigarette. He leaned back on the sofa and crossed his legs at the ankles.

My wife covered her mouth, and then she yawned. She stretched. She said, "I think I'll go upstairs and put on my robe. I think I'll change into something else. Robert, you make yourself comfortable," she said.

"I'm comfortable," the blind man said.

55   "I want you to feel comfortable in this house," she said.

    "I am comfortable," the blind man said.

After she'd left the room, he and I listened to the weather report and then to the sports roundup. By that time, she'd been gone so long I didn't know if she was going to come back. I thought she might have gone to bed. I wished she'd come back downstairs. I didn't want to be left alone with a blind man. I asked him if he wanted another drink, and he said sure. Then I asked if he wanted to smoke some dope with me. I said I'd just rolled a number. I hadn't, but I planned to do so in about two shakes.

    "I'll try some with you," he said.

    "Damn right," I said. "That's the stuff."

60   I got our drinks and sat down on the sofa with him. Then I rolled us two fat numbers. I lit one and passed it. I brought it to his fingers. He took it and inhaled.

    "Hold it as long as you can," I said. I could tell he didn't know the first thing.

    My wife came back downstairs wearing her pink robe and her pink slippers.

    "What do I smell?" she said.

    "We thought we'd have us some cannabis," I said.

65   My wife gave me a savage look. Then she looked at the blind man and said, "Robert, I didn't know you smoked."

    He said, "I do now, my dear. There's a first time for everything. But I don't feel anything yet."

    "This stuff is pretty mellow," I said. "This stuff is mild. It's dope you can reason with," I said. "It doesn't mess you up."

    "Not much it doesn't, bub," he said, and laughed.

    My wife sat on the sofa between the blind man and me. I passed her the number. She took it and toked and then passed it back to me. "Which way is this going?" she said. Then she said, "I shouldn't be smoking this. I can hardly keep my eyes open as it is. That dinner did me in. I shouldn't have eaten so much."

    "It was the strawberry pie," the blind 70 man said. "That's what did it," he said, and he laughed his big laugh. Then he shook his head.

    "There's more strawberry pie," I said.

    "Do you want some more, Robert?" my wife said.

    "Maybe in a little while," he said.

    We gave our attention to the TV. My wife yawned again. She said, "Your bed is made up when you feel like going to bed, Robert. I know you must have had a long day. When you're ready to go to bed, say so." She pulled his arm. "Robert?"

    He came to and said, "I've had a real 75 nice time. This beats tapes, doesn't it?"

    I said, "Coming at you," and I put the number between his fingers. He inhaled, held the smoke, and then let it go. It was like he'd been doing it since he was nine years old.

    "Thanks, bub," he said. "But I think this is all for me. I think I'm beginning to feel it," he said. He held the burning roach out for my wife.

    "Same here," she said. "Ditto. Me, too." She took the roach and passed it to me. "I may just sit here for a while between you two guys with my eyes closed. But don't let me bother you, okay? Either one of you. If it bothers you, say so. Otherwise, I may just sit here with my eyes closed until you're ready to go to bed," she said. "Your bed's made up, Robert, when you're ready. It's right next to our room at the top of the stairs. We'll show you up when you're ready. You wake me up now, you guys, if I fall asleep." She said that and then she closed her eyes and went to sleep.

    The news program ended. I got up and changed the channel. I sat back down on the sofa. I wished my wife hadn't pooped out. Her head lay across the back of the sofa, her mouth open. She'd turned so that her robe had slipped away from her legs, exposing a juicy thigh. I reached to draw her robe back over her, and it was then that I glanced at the blind man. What the hell! I flipped the robe open again.

80 "You say when you want some strawberry pie," I said.

"I will," he said.

I said, "Are you tired? Do you want me to take you up to your bed? Are you ready to hit the hay?"

"Not yet," he said. "No, I'll stay up with you, bub. If that's all right. I'll stay up until you're ready to turn in. We haven't had a chance to talk. Know what I mean? I feel like me and her monopolized the evening." He lifted his beard and he let it fall. He picked up his cigarettes and his lighter.

"That's all right," I said. Then I said, "I'm glad for the company."

85 And I guess I was. Every night I smoked dope and stayed up as long as I could before I fell asleep. My wife and I hardly ever went to bed at the same time. When I did go to sleep, I had these dreams. Sometimes I'd wake up from one of them, my heart going crazy.

Something about the church and the Middle Ages was on the TV. Not your run-of-the-mill TV fare. I wanted to watch something else. I turned to the other channels. But there was nothing on them, either. So I turned back to the first channel and apologized.

"Bub, it's all right," the blind man said. "It's fine with me. Whatever you want to watch is okay. I'm always learning something. Learning never ends. It won't hurt me to learn something tonight. I got ears," he said.

We didn't say anything for a time. He was leaning forward with his head turned at me, his right ear aimed in the direction of the set.

Very disconcerting. Now and then his eyelids drooped and then they snapped open again. Now and then he put his fingers into his beard and tugged, like he was thinking about something he was hearing on the television.

On the screen, a group of men wearing cowls was being set upon and tormented by men dressed in skeleton costumes and men dressed as devils. The men dressed as devils wore devil masks, horns, and long tails. This pageant was part of a procession. The Englishman who was narrating the thing said it took place in Spain once a year. I tried to explain to the blind man what was happening.

"Skeletons," he said. "I know about 90 skeletons," he said, and he nodded.

The TV showed this one cathedral. Then there was a long, slow look at another one. Finally, the picture switched to the famous one in Paris, with its flying buttresses and its spires reaching up to the clouds. The camera pulled away to show the whole of the cathedral rising above the skyline.

There were times when the Englishman who was telling the thing would shut up, would simply let the camera move around over the cathedrals. Or else the camera would tour the countryside, men in fields walking behind oxen. I waited as long as I could. Then I felt I had to say something. I said, "They're showing the outside of this cathedral now. Gargoyles. Little statues carved to look like monsters. Now I guess they're in Italy. Yeah, they're in Italy. There's paintings on the walls of this one church."

"Are those fresco paintings, bub?" he asked, and he sipped from his drink.

I reached for my glass. But it was empty. I tried to remember what I could remember. "You're asking me are those frescoes?" I said. "That's a good question. I don't know."

The camera moved to a cathedral out- 95 side Lisbon. The differences in the Portuguese cathedral compared with the French and Italian were not that great. But they were there. Mostly the interior stuff. Then something occurred to me, and I said, "Something has occurred to me. Do you have any idea what a cathedral is? What they look like, that is? Do you follow me? If somebody says cathedral to you, do you have any notion what they're talking about? Do you know the difference between that and a Baptist church, say?"

He let the smoke dribble from his mouth. "I know they took hundreds of workers fifty or a hundred years to build," he said. "I just heard the man say that, of course. I know generations of the same families worked on a cathedral. I heard him say that, too. The men who began their life's work on them, they never lived to see the completion of their work. In that wise, bub, they're no different from the rest of us, right?" He laughed. Then his eyelids drooped again. His head nodded. He seemed to be snoozing. Maybe he was imagining himself in Portugal. The TV was showing another cathedral now. This one was in Germany. The Englishman's voice droned on. "Cathedrals," the blind man said. He sat up and rolled his head back and forth. "If you want the truth, bub, that's about all I know. What I just said. What I heard him say. But maybe you could describe one to me? I wish you'd do it. I'd like that. If you want to know, I really don't have a good idea."

I stared hard at the shot of the cathedral on the TV. How could I even begin to describe it? But say my life depended on it. Say my life was being threatened by an insane guy who said I had to do it or else.

I stared some more at the cathedral before the picture flipped off into the countryside. There was no use. I turned to the blind man and said, "To begin with, they're very tall." I was looking around the room for clues. "They reach way up. Up and up. Toward the sky. They're so big, some of them, they have to have these supports. To help hold them up, so to speak. These supports are called buttresses. They remind me of viaducts, for some reason. But maybe you don't know viaducts, either? Sometimes the cathedrals have devils and such carved into the front. Sometimes lords and ladies. Don't ask me why this is," I said.

He was nodding. The whole upper part of his body seemed to be moving back and forth.

"I'm not doing so good, am I?" I said.   100

He stopped nodding and leaned forward on the edge of the sofa. As he listened to me, he was running his fingers through his beard. I wasn't getting through to him, I could see that. But he waited for me to go on just the same. He nodded, like he was trying to encourage me. I tried to think what else to say. "They're really big," I said. "They're massive. They're built of stone. Marble, too, sometimes. In those olden days, when they built cathedrals, men wanted to be close to God. In those olden days, God was an important part of everyone's life. You could tell this from their cathedral-building. I'm sorry," I said, "but it looks like that's the best I can do for you. I'm just no good at it."

"That's all right, bub," the blind man said. "Hey, listen. I hope you don't mind my asking you. Can I ask you something? Let me ask you a simple question, yes or no. I'm just curious and there's no offense. You're my host. But let me ask if you are in any way religious? You don't mind my asking?"

I shook my head. He couldn't see that, though. A wink is the same as a nod to a blind man. "I guess I don't believe in it. In anything. Sometimes it's hard. You know what I'm saying?"

"Sure, I do," he said.

"Right," I said.   105

The Englishman was still holding forth. My wife sighed in her sleep. She drew a long breath and went on with her sleeping.

"You'll have to forgive me," I said. "But I can't tell you what a cathedral looks like. It just isn't in me to do it. I can't do any more than I've done."

The blind man sat very still, his head down, as he listened to me.

I said, "The truth is, cathedrals don't mean anything special to me. Nothing. Cathedrals. They're something to look at on late-night TV. That's all they are."

110 It was then that the blind man cleared his throat. He brought something up. He took a handkerchief from his back pocket. Then he said, "I get it, bub. It's okay. It happens. Don't worry about it," he said. "Hey, listen to me. Will you do me a favor? I got an idea. Why don't you find us some heavy paper? And a pen. We'll do something. We'll draw one together. Get us a pen and some heavy paper. Go on, bub, get the stuff," he said.

So I went upstairs. My legs felt like they didn't have any strength in them. They felt like they did after I'd done some running. In my wife's room, I looked around. I found some ballpoints in a little basket on her table. And then I tried to think where to look for the kind of paper he was talking about.

Downstairs, in the kitchen, I found a shopping bag with onion skins in the bottom of the bag. I emptied the bag and shook it. I brought it into the living room and sat down with it near his legs. I moved some things, smoothed the wrinkles from the bag, spread it out on the coffee table.

The blind man got down from the sofa and sat next to me on the carpet.

He ran his fingers over the paper. He went up and down the sides of the paper. The edges, even the edges. He fingered the corners.

115 "All right," he said. "All right, let's do her."

He found my hand, the hand with the pen. He closed his hand over my hand. "Go ahead, bub, draw," he said. "Draw. You'll see. I'll follow along with you. It'll be okay. Just begin now like I'm telling you. You'll see. Draw," the blind man said.

So I began. First I drew a box that looked like a house. It could have been the house I lived in. Then I put a roof on it. At either end of the roof, I drew spires. Crazy.

"Swell," he said. "Terrific. You're doing fine," he said. "Never thought anything like this could happen in your lifetime, did you, bub? Well, it's a strange life, we all know that. Go on now. Keep it up."

I put in windows with arches. I drew flying buttresses. I hung great doors. I couldn't stop. The TV station went off the air. I put down the pen and closed and opened my fingers. The blind man felt around over the paper. He moved the tips of his fingers over the paper, all over what I had drawn, and he nodded.

"Doing fine," the blind man said.   120

I took up the pen again, and he found my hand. I kept at it. I'm no artist. But I kept drawing just the same.

My wife opened up her eyes and gazed at us. She sat up on the sofa, her robe hanging open. She said, "What are you doing? Tell me, I want to know."

I didn't answer her.

The blind man said, "We're drawing a cathedral. Me and him are working on it. Press hard," he said to me. "That's right. That's good," he said. "Sure. You got it, bub. I can tell. You didn't think you could. But you can, can't you? You're cooking with gas now. You know what I'm saying? We're going to really have us something here in a minute. How's the old arm?" he said. "Put some people in there now. What's a cathedral without people?"

My wife said, "What's going on? Robert,   125 what are you doing? What's going on?"

"It's all right," he said to her. "Close your eyes now," the blind man said to me.

I did it. I closed them just like he said.

"Are they closed?" he said. "Don't fudge."

"They're closed," I said.

130 "Keep them that way," he said. He said, "Don't stop now. Draw."

So we kept on with it. His fingers rode my fingers as my hand went over the paper. It was like nothing else in my life up to now.

Then he said, "I think that's it. I think you got it," he said. "Take a look. What do you think?"

But I had my eyes closed. I thought I'd keep them that way for a little longer. I thought it was something I ought to do.

"Well?" he said. "Are you looking?"

My eyes were still closed. I was in my house. I knew that. But I didn't feel like I was inside anything. 135

"It's really something," I said.

·····➤ *Your* **Turn**
Talking and Writing about Lit

1. Explain why it is ironic that the blind man helps the narrator draw a cathedral in the end of Carver's story "Cathedral"?

2. Carver's narrator in "Cathedral" can be called an unreliable narrator, inasmuch as we often do not trust his perceptions of other people and events. Cite three examples of his "unreliability."

3. **DIY** Writers often create stories in which the narrator is someone quite different than themselves. They write stories from the points of view of narrators of a different gender, different cultural background, or different personal experiences. Write a brief scene from the point of view of an unreliable narrator. This character who narrates the story may be someone radically different than yourself, and your task is to imagine what things look like from inside a mind quite different from your own, someone whose perceptions are, for some reason (you choose the reason), out of sync with reality as you know it.

Talking Lit

Novelist Sue Miller writes about why it's important to understand that a character in a work of fiction doesn't necessarily represent the author.

Sue Miller, "Virtual Reality: The Perils of Seeking a Novelist's Facts in Her Fiction"

Before my last, recent book tour, I made myself memorize a quotation from an interview with John Cheever that began, "It seems to me that any confusion between autobiography and fiction debases fiction." Thus girded, armored, I hoped to silence forever the questioner who sits there in the third row waiting to ask, "How much of your work is autobiographical?"

I'd go on, quoting away: "The role autobiography plays in fiction is like that of reality to a dream. As you dream your ship, you perhaps know the boat, but you're going towards a coast that is quite strange; you're wearing strange clothes, the language being spoken around you is a language you don't understand, but the woman on the left is your wife."

Take that!

Only it didn't work. What I got back, in one form or another, was: "O.K., sure. But really, how much?" What's more, a friend who came to one of the readings told me that I'd been unkind, that I'd seemed contemptuous of someone who was, after all, simply and genuinely curious. Which made me wonder: Why did it bother me so much, that recurring question? Far more than the question about my work habits or the one about whether I use a computer or not.

Here's what I think: It bothers me because I sense in it a kind of potential diminishment—yes, debasing—of the work I do. What the questioner seems to be somehow suggesting is that my writing is possibly no more than the stringing together of episodes lifted directly from my life, or from the lives of fascinating characters I have known.

Every writer has met the guy at the party who says he, too, has always wanted to write a novel, if only he had the time, because he's got such a great story to tell. And it seems to me that it's that same guy asking the question at the reading. Maybe this is why the question rises so often: because the guy really wants to know how to do it, how to make fiction from the interesting or painful or shocking things that have happened to him.

There's a way in which readers are encouraged in this by writers who embrace the cult of experience, the notion that the writer needs to have lived a certain *kind* of bold, engaged life, right out there on the edge of . . . well, something or other, in order to have anything worthwhile to write about. What's worthwhile? Well, war, for instance. Adventure on the high seas, or the highways, or the river. The gutter life in Paris, the drug life in New York. No wonder anyone who has even marginally partaken of any of these feels justified in thinking he must have a book in him. Somewhere.

But if experience were all, we *would* all have a book. As Flannery O'Connor said, anyone who's survived infancy has enough material for countless stories. The fact is, you can make a story of anything, anything at all. What's hard—and what's interesting—about a story is not so much the *thing* that's in it, but what's made of that thing. And then, of course, the making itself. But there is no necessary life to have lived or scene to have witnessed. No experiential sine qua non. As Henry James said of the material of fiction, "Why . . . adventure, more than . . . matrimony, or celibacy, or parturition, or cholera?"

Women, more than men, seem always to have known this, perhaps because they have until relatively recently written out of constrained lives, limited worlds: for the most part, in fact, the worlds of matrimony and celibacy and parturition. They had to learn to notice everything; to make much from little. Too little, it has seemed to

FROM PAGE TO SCREEN

Moment "of" Epiphany

Epiphany (ĭ-pĭf´-nē) *n.*, *pl.*–**nies**. . . . **3.a.** A sudden manifestation of the essence of meaning of something. **b.** A comprehension or perception of reality by means of sudden intuitive realization.

Screen shot from the Wadsworth production of *Cathedral*, with James Eckhouse as the husband, Allyce Beasley as the wife and Mark Rolston as Robert

some critics. No writer of the domestic, female or male, could please the likes of Tom Wolfe, for instance. When I read his prescriptions for contemporary fiction, I remember Cheever bemoaning the size of his own gift in comparison with Bellow's, regretting his homely material, wishing for the sweep of Augie March or Henderson.

So *is* the life's shape the shape of the fiction then? *Is* it all autobiographical? Is that what Cheever was suffering from? Do I write as I do because I've lived and worked primarily with children and families? Is it true that we have no choice but to echo what's happened to us and to those we know? Do we writers need to shed our bathrobes, get dressed at last and shuffle blinking out of our studies into the bright light of day, find jobs as laborers or insurance executives or physicians or models or pimps in order to have something wilder, something more exciting, something more relevant to contemporary life to write about?

Surely not. Surely the writer's job is to make relevant the world she wishes to write about. How? By writing well and carefully and powerfully. By using humor, as Cheever did; or violence, as O'Connor did; or rue, as Chekhov did, to make the territory of her imagination compelling and somehow universal. And that holds true whether the territory of the imagination is close to the literal truth of her life or far from it.

Sometimes the distance *is* minimal, minimal enough for the fiction to cause lifelong hard feelings: the use of a fictional alter ego, for example, or of changes so

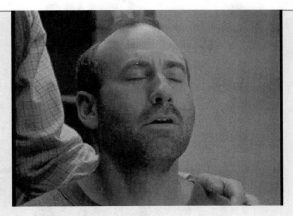

A moment of epiphany

The adjacent definition is from the *American Heritage College Dictionary* (3rd edition). The other numbered definitions (1 and 2) that appear before this one (though are not printed here) are religious in nature, and this helps illustrate the fact that the word "epiphany" is one that is "borrowed" from religious language. In religious discussion, epiphany might refer specifically to a religious revelation. In the discussion of literature, the word refers to a moment of sudden revelation, illumination, or realization. This revelation doesn't necessarily have any relation to religious experience (though it could). A good example occurs in the final scene of Raymond Carver's short story "Cathedral," when the blind man, Robert, is drawing the cathedral with the narrator (the husband). The culmination of this moment of epiphany is in the very ending of the film, when the narrator has a look of joy and discovery on his face, so different from his earlier cynicism and sarcasm. Through the blind man, he has discovered a new way of seeing.

slight that they seem like a kind of cruel joke. Sometimes, especially with what is called domestic fiction—fiction practiced in one way or another by Updike, Munro, Roth, Carver, Ford, McDermott—family or friends can end up feeling misused, abused. There are certainly writers who seem nearly deliberately provocative in this way: the burning-bridges school of art.

For the true writer, though, however close the events may be to his life, there is some distance, some remove, that allows for the shaping of the work. The shaping, after all, is what it's all about. Every reader can sense the difference between a writer who embodies meaning through the events he describes and the writer who seems simply mired in those events. It is that struggle for meaning that lets the writer escape the tyranny of what really happened and begin to dream his fictional dream.

As to what happens in the dream, in the story, well, we all have the *kinds* of event we prefer, but surely this is a matter of preference, not worth. You find in the story of a quest for a white whale the embodiment of the human struggle for control, for wholeness? Fine. For me everyday life in the hands of a fine writer seems similarly charged with meaning. When I write, I want to bring a sense of that charge, that meaning, to what may fairly be called the domestic. O.K.?

So, come on, really, how much is autobiographical?

All of it. None.

E-Mail

Doc.01

Trash

C H A P T E R

METAPHOR, IMAGE AND SYMBOL

Even computers use image and symbol.

On most computers today, images and symbols are evident the moment you log on. Commonly called "icons," these images and symbols are prevalent in nearly every operating system, and each one symbolizes a particular function or series of functions. Tiny arrows, numbers, letters, printers, question marks, bullets, magnifying glasses—the computer brings the user face-to-face with hundreds of icons each and every time the computer is powered on.

Icons, like the tiny trash can icon, for example, are metaphors and symbols for real processes. The button with the small picture of the trash can on it symbolizes the process of removing a file from its current folder or program and placing it in a recycle bin (another symbol) or deleting it from the computer altogether. The statement "Press this button if you want to delete this file" would serve the same purpose as the tiny picture of the trash can, but not quite so economically.

Emoticons are computer icons that distill textual expression of any one of a number of emotions into one tiny picture that, when typed by the computer user, conveys a representation of that user's emotion. To use emoticons is to use imagery—that is, using language that appeals to the senses.

Have you ever found yourself searching for that perfect phrase to describe an emotional moment or experience (falling in love, having an accident, the pain of losing a loved one, or the joy of recognizing an old friend)? We search our word-memory banks for just the right comparison: "It was like . . . it was like . . . it was like. . . ."

"I knew he wouldn't dawdle, but he didn't return soon, and when he hadn't returned later either my heart began to flutter like a fish on a hook." Author Bi Shumin writes this from the point of view of a character, a mother worried about her son. The mother character's heart is not literally a fish, as we know, but the way she feels, her emotions at that moment, are best conveyed by likening her heart to a fish fluttering on a hook. This conveys the feeling of fighting or trembling, but it also conveys the emotional experience, so important for the fiction writer to depict.

Figures of Speech

Although this chapter will discuss the use of metaphor, imagery, and symbolism in greater depth, readers have already encountered many examples of these literary elements in the stories we've already discussed. For instance, James Baldwin's "Sonny's Blues" (Chapter 4) is rich in **figurative language** (figures of speech not meant to be taken literally). When Baldwin's narrator feels ice water in his veins, it is not literally ice water, but instead the phrase represents the dread and fear he feels. When he says of the children that "their heads bumped abruptly against the low ceiling of their actual possibilities," we know that he is not referring to a literal ceiling but a figurative one.

Alice Walker, in "Everyday Use," has her narrator, Mrs. Johnson, use figurative language to describe her older daughter, Dee, during her high school years:

> She used to read to us without pity; forcing words, lies, other folks' habits, whole lives upon us two, sitting trapped and ignorant underneath her voice. She washed us in a river of make-believe, burned us with a lot of knowledge we didn't necessarily need to know. Pressed us to her with the serious way she read, to shove us away at just the moment, like dimwits, we seemed about to understand. (paragraph 11)

Alice Walker doesn't mean that Mrs. Johnson and her other daughter, Maggie, were literally trapped beneath Dee's voice, nor were they literally burned with knowledge; but illustrating the experience with these metaphors makes the experience more vivid to the reader. A **metaphor** is an implied comparison of two *dis*similar things. The comparison being implied in the first instance here is that Dee's voice was so dominating that it was as if her voice sat on top of them. This implied comparison has emotional and visual aspects to it that a more abstract or general statement could not capture. If the writer had said "her voice was dominating," it would not have the same emotional power as the figurative language used by Walker. A **simile** is a closely related figure of speech which makes a direct comparison of two things, using the words "like" or "as" or other words of direct comparison. If the above idea were expressed as a simile, it might read, "listening to her read was like being trapped underneath her voice." A simile is used to describe the character of Hakim's arrogance: "He just stood there grinning, looking down on me like somebody inspecting a Model A car." He may look at Mrs. Johnson as if she were behind the times, but the story reveals that, contrary to appearances, Mrs. Johnson knows far more about life than Dee or Hakim do. We can also call this moment ironic because there is a discrepancy between appearance and reality (irony is discussed in Chapter 7).

Imagery

Walker's story (in this chapter) also uses **imagery** (sensory detail, using language that appeals to the senses) to achieve its effects. Near the end of "Everyday Use," when the narrator looks at her younger daughter, Maggie, and realizes she should give the coveted quilts to her instead of Dee, she uses sensory detail (rather than abstractions) to convey the way the moment feels: "When I looked at her like that something hit me in the top of my head and ran down to the soles of my feet." This kind of description is infused with feeling, and it is the sensory details that make it so emotionally powerful. Nathaniel Hawthorne also uses imagery to turn up the emotional heat in "The Birthmark" (in this chapter). When you read this story, you will note the contrast between the image that represents how many people who knew Georgiana had felt about her birthmark before she met Aylmer ("Georgiana's lovers were wont to say that some fairy at her birth hour had laid her tiny hand upon the infant's cheek") and the sensory details that represent the way Aylmer feels about the mark (he "was so startled with the intense glow of the birthmark upon the whiteness of her cheek that he could not restrain a strong convulsive shudder"). The sensory details in the two descriptions give us an emotional reaction to the characters being depicted.

Symbolism

Georgiana's birthmark in the shape of a human hand is also a **symbol**. The birthmark represents Georgiana's (and everyone's) mortality, her humanness, her connection to the earthbound rather than the celestial. But it also represents her life force, her connection to nature, and her heart (in the spiritual sense). Aylmer has spent his life developing his "head" (his intellect), with mixed results; but he has neglected his "heart," which is one reason he makes the mistake of trying to remove the heart from his wife. Without one's heart (or without one's humanity), the story shows, life cannot be maintained.

The birthmark is an example of a **contextual symbol** or **literary symbol**. The birthmark has this bundle of meanings within this particular work of literature, although in other contexts, it might have a different meaning. A **universal symbol** or a **conventional symbol** would, on the other hand, be one that is recognized by most people within a culture to have a certain meaning wherever it appears (universally). Examples of conventional or universal symbols might be a wedding ring, a Star of David, or a Christian cross. As with "The Birthmark," the principal symbol in Shumin's "Broken Transformers" (in this chapter) appears in the title. The Transformers, in additional to being literal objects in the story, have multiple possibilities for interpretation, as do all good symbols. The broken Transformers may represent the way in which relationships are transformed by important experiences and the ways in which the mother and the son both change individually in the course of the story, but they also represent the way Chinese culture is being transformed by Western influences. At the same time, the Transformers operate as literal objects in the story, the toys broken by the son and his friend, Fatty. Incidentally, when you read "Broken Transformers," be sure to notice also that it is full of startlingly fresh imagery and figures of speech, which help convey meaning and emotion in the story. When the mother says, "It is a cat's responsibility to teach her kitten how to catch mice" (paragraph 81), this is a figurative way to refer to her responsibility to help her son learn how to navigate in the world.

In Alice Walker's "Everyday Use," there are a number of symbolic objects—for example, the churn top and dasher, the butter dish, the quilts (all of which represent Dee and Maggie's authentic heritage). Events can also be symbolic. In Shirley Jackson's "The Lottery" (in this chapter), the behavior of the townspeople leading up to and surrounding the horrific ending is symbolic of the kind of scapegoating we see in real life when people exclude, stigmatize, or victimize others for "reasons" that are invalid, or even bizarre, to sensible people.

Readings

Alice Walker (b. 1944)

Alice Walker was born in Eatonton, Georgia, to parents who worked as sharecroppers and dairy farmers. Her mother also worked as a domestic employee in order to piece together a living for the family. Later, Walker published a collection of essays entitled *In Search of Our Mothers' Gardens* (1984), a tribute to black women of her mother's generation and earlier generations who passed on the will to survive, to succeed, and to create. A versatile writer, Walker has published essays, poetry, and short fiction as well as novels. Her best-known novel is *The Color Purple* (1982), which won both a Pulitzer Prize and the National Book Award.

Everyday Use (1973)

For your grandmama

I will wait for her in the yard that Maggie and I made so clean and wavy yesterday afternoon. A yard like this is more comfortable than most people know. It is not just a yard. It is like an extended living room. When the hard clay is swept clean as a floor and the fine sand around the edges lined with tiny, irregular grooves, anyone can come and sit and look up into the elm tree and wait for the breezes that never come inside the house.

Maggie will be nervous until after her sister goes: she will stand hopelessly in corners, homely and ashamed of the burn scars down her arms and legs, eying her sister with a mixture of envy and awe. She thinks her sister has held life always in the palm of one hand, that "no" is a word the world never learned to say to her.

You've no doubt seen those TV shows where the child who has "made it" is confronted, as a surprise, by her own mother and father, tottering in weakly from backstage. (A pleasant surprise, of course: What would they do if parent and child came on the show only to curse out and insult each other?) On TV mother and child embrace and smile into each other's faces. Sometimes the mother and father weep, the child wraps them in her arms and leans across the table to tell how she would not have made it without their help. I have seen these programs.

Sometimes I dream a dream in which Dee and I are suddenly brought together on a TV program of this sort. Out of a dark and soft-seated limousine I am ushered into a bright room filled with many people. There I meet a smiling, gray, sporty man like Johnny Carson who shakes my hand and tells me what a fine girl I have. Then we are on the stage and Dee is embracing me with tears in her eyes. She pins on my dress a large orchid, even though she had told me once that she thinks orchids are tacky flowers.

In real life I am a large, big-boned 5 woman with rough, man-working hands. In the winter I wear flannel nightgowns to bed and overalls during the day. I can kill and clean a hog as mercilessly as a man. My fat keeps me hot in zero weather. I can work outside all day, breaking ice to get water for washing; I can eat pork liver cooked over the open fire minutes after it comes steaming from the hog. One winter I knocked a bull calf straight in the brain between the eyes with a sledge hammer and had the meat hung up to chill before nightfall. But of course all this does not show on television. I am the way my daughter would want me to be: a hundred pounds lighter, my skin like an uncooked barley pancake. My hair glistens in the hot bright lights. Johnny Carson has much to do to keep up with my quick and witty tongue.

But that is a mistake. I know even before I wake up. Who ever knew a Johnson with a quick tongue? Who can even imagine me looking a strange white man in the eye? It seems to me I have talked to them always with one foot raised in flight, with my head turned in whichever way is farthest from them. Dee, though. She would always look anyone in the eye. Hesitation was no part of her nature.

"How do I look, Mama?" Maggie says, showing just enough of her thin body enveloped in pink skirt and red blouse for me to know she's there, almost hidden by the door.

"Come out into the yard," I say.

Have you ever seen a lame animal, perhaps a dog run over by some careless person rich enough to own a car, sidle up to someone who is ignorant enough to be kind to him? That is the way my Maggie walks. She has been like this, chin on chest, eyes on ground, feet in shuffle, ever since the fire that burned the other house to the ground.

10   Dee is lighter than Maggie, with nicer hair and a fuller figure. She's a woman now, though sometimes I forget. How long ago was it that the other house burned? Ten, twelve years? Sometimes I can still hear the flames and feel Maggie's arms sticking to me, her hair smoking and her dress falling off her in little black papery flakes. Her eyes seemed stretched open, blazed open by the flames reflected in them. And Dee. I see her standing off under the sweet gum tree she used to dig gum out of; a look of concentration on her face as she watched the last dingy gray board of the house fall in toward the red-hot brick chimney. Why don't you do a dance around the ashes? I'd wanted to ask her. She had hated the house that much.

I used to think she hated Maggie, too. But that was before we raised the money, the church and me, to send her to Augusta to school. She used to read to us without pity; forcing words, lies, other folks' habits,

whole lives upon us two, sitting trapped and ignorant underneath her voice. She washed us in a river of make-believe, burned us with a lot of knowledge we didn't necessarily need to know. Pressed us to her with the serious way she read, to shove us away at just the moment, like dimwits, we seemed about to understand.

Dee wanted nice things. A yellow organdy dress to wear to her graduation from high school; black pumps to match a green suit she'd made from an old suit somebody gave me. She was determined to stare down any disaster in her efforts. Her eyelids would not flicker for minutes at a time. Often I fought off the temptation to shake her. At sixteen she had a style of her own: and knew what style was.

I never had an education myself. After second grade the school was closed down. Don't ask me why: in 1927 colored asked fewer questions than they do now. Sometimes Maggie reads to me. She stumbles along goodnaturedly but can't see well. She knows she is not bright. Like good looks and money, quickness passed her by. She will marry John Thomas (who has mossy teeth in an earnest face) and then I'll be free to sit here and I guess just sing church songs to myself. Although I never was a good singer. Never could carry a tune. I was always better at a man's job. I used to love to milk till I was hooked in the side in '49. Cows are soothing and slow and don't bother you, unless you try to milk them the wrong way.

I have deliberately turned my back on the house. It is three rooms, just like the one that burned, except the roof is tin; they don't make shingle roofs any more. There are no real windows, just some holes cut in the sides, like the portholes in a ship, but not round and not square, with rawhide holding the shutters up on the outside. This house is in a pasture, too, like the other one. No doubt when Dee sees it she will want to tear it down. She wrote me once that no matter where we "choose" to live, she will manage to come see us. But she will never bring her friends. Maggie and I thought about this and Maggie asked me, "Mama, when did Dee ever *have* any friends?"

15   She had a few. Furtive boys in pink shirts hanging about on washday after school. Nervous girls who never laughed. Impressed with her, they worshipped the well-turned phrase, the cute shape, the scalding humor that erupted like bubbles in lye. She read to them.

When she was courting Jimmy T she didn't have much time to pay to us, but turned all her faultfinding power on him. He *flew* to marry a cheap city girl from a family of ignorant flashy people. She hardly had time to recompose herself.

When she comes I will meet—but there they are!

Maggie attempts to make a dash for the house, in her shuffling way, but I stay her with my hand. "Come back here," I say. And she stops and tries to dig a well in the sand with her toe.

It is hard to see them clearly through the strong sun. But even the first glimpse of leg out of the car tells me it is Dee. Her feet were always neat-looking, as if God himself had shaped them with a certain style. From the other side of the car comes a short, stocky man. Hair is all over his head a foot long and hanging from his chin like a kinky mule tail. I hear Maggie suck in her breath. "Uhnnnh," is what it sounds like. Like when you see the wriggling end of a snake just in front of your foot on the road. "Uhnnnh."

20   Dee next. A dress down to the ground, in this hot weather. A dress so loud it hurts my eyes. There are yellows and oranges enough to throw back the light of the sun. I feel my whole face warming from the heat waves it throws out. Earrings gold, too, and hanging down to her shoulders. Bracelets dangling and making noises when she moves her arm up to shake the folds of the dress out of her armpits. The dress is loose and flows, and as she walks closer, I like it. I hear Maggie go "Uhnnnh" again. It is her sister's hair. It stands straight up like the wool on a sheep. It is black as night and around the edges are two long pigtails that rope about like small lizards disappearing behind her ears.

"Wa-su-zo-Tean-o!" she says, coming on in that gliding way the dress makes her move. The short stocky fellow with the hair to his navel is all grinning and he follows up with "Asalamalakim, my mother and sister!" He moves to hug Maggie but she falls back, right up against the back of my chair. I feel her trembling there and when I look up I see the perspiration falling off her chin.

"Don't get up," says Dee. Since I am stout it takes something of a push. You can see me trying to move a second or two before I make it. She turns, showing white heels through her sandals, and goes back to the car. Out she peeks next with a Polaroid. She stoops down quickly and lines up picture after picture of me sitting there in front of the house with Maggie cowering behind me. She never takes a shot without making sure the house is included. When a cow comes nibbling around the edge of the yard she snaps it and me and Maggie *and* the house. Then she puts the Polaroid in the back seat of the car, and comes up and kisses me on the forehead.

Meanwhile Asalamalakim is going through motions with Maggie's hand. Maggie's hand is as limp as a fish, and probably as cold, despite the sweat, and she keeps trying to pull it back. It looks like Asalamalakim wants to shake hands but wants to do it fancy. Or maybe he don't know how people shake hands. Anyhow, he soon gives up on Maggie.

"Well," I say. "Dee."

25 "No, Mama," she says. "Not 'Dee,' Wangero Leewanika Kemanjo!"

"What happened to 'Dee'?" I wanted to know.

"She's dead," Wangero said. "I couldn't bear it any longer, being named after the people who oppress me."

"You know as well as me you was named after your aunt Dicie," I said. Dicie is my sister. She named Dee. We called her "Big Dee" after Dee was born.

"But who was *she* named after?" asked Wangero.

30 "I guess after Grandma Dee," I said.

"And who was she named after?" asked Wangero.

"Her mother," I said, and saw Wangero was getting tired. "That's about as far back as I can trace it," I said. Though, in fact, I probably could have carried it back beyond the Civil War through the branches.

"Well," said Asalamalakim, "there you are."

"Uhnnnh," I heard Maggie say.

35 "There I was not," I said, "before 'Dicie' cropped up in our family, so why should I try to trace it that far back?"

He just stood there grinning, looking down on me like somebody inspecting a Model A car. Every once in a while he and Wangero sent eye signals over my head.

"How do you pronounce this name?" I asked.

"You don't have to call me by it if you don't want to," said Wangero.

"Why shouldn't I?" I asked. "If that's what you want us to call you, we'll call you."

40 "I know it might sound awkward at first," said Wangero.

"I'll get used to it," I said. "Ream it out again."

Well, soon we got the name out of the way. Asalamalakim had a name twice as long and three times as hard. After I tripped over it two or three times he told me to just call him Hakim-a-barber. I wanted to ask him was he a barber, but I didn't really think he was, so I didn't ask.

"You must belong to those beef-cattle peoples down the road," I said. They said "Asalamalakim" when they met you, too, but they didn't shake hands. Always too busy: feeding the cattle, fixing the fences, putting up salt-lick shelters, throwing down hay. When the white folks poisoned some of the herd the men stayed up all night with rifles in their hands. I walked a mile and a half just to see the sight.

Hakim-a-barber said, "I accept some of their doctrines, but farming and raising cattle is not my style." (They didn't tell me, and I didn't ask, whether Wangero [Dee] had really gone and married him.)

45 We sat down to eat and right away he said he didn't eat collards and pork was unclean. Wangero, though, went on through the chitlins and corn bread, the greens and everything else. She talked a blue streak over the sweet potatoes. Everything delighted her. Even the fact that we still used the benches her daddy made for the table when we couldn't afford to buy chairs.

"Oh, Mama!" she cried. Then turned to Hakim-a-barber. "I never knew how lovely these benches are. You can feel the rump prints," she said, running her hands underneath her and along the bench. Then she gave a sigh and her hand closed over Grandma Dee's butter dish. "That's it!" she said. "I knew there was something I wanted to ask you if I could have." She jumped up from the table and went over in the corner where the churn stood, the milk in it clabber by now. She looked at the churn and looked at it.

"This churn top is what I need," she said. "Didn't Uncle Buddy whittle it out of a tree you all used to have?"

"Yes," I said.

"Uh huh," she said happily. "And I want the dasher, too."

50 "Uncle Buddy whittle that, too?" asked the barber.

Dee (Wangero) looked up at me.

"Aunt Dee's first husband whittled the dash," said Maggie so low you almost couldn't hear her. "His name was Henry, but they called him Stash."

"Maggie's brain is like an elephant's," Wangero said, laughing. "I can use the churn top as a centerpiece for the alcove table," she said, sliding a plate over the churn, "and I'll think of something artistic to do with the dasher."

When she finished wrapping the dasher the handle stuck out. I took it for a moment in my hands. You didn't even have to look close to see where hands pushing the dasher up and down to make butter had left a kind of sink in the wood. In fact, there were a lot of small sinks; you could see where thumbs and fingers had sunk into the wood. It was beautiful light yellow wood, from a tree that grew in the yard where Big Dee and Stash had lived.

55 After dinner Dee (Wangero) went to the trunk at the foot of my bed and started rifling through it. Maggie hung back in the kitchen over the dishpan. Out came Wangero with two quilts. They had been pieced by Grandma Dee and then Big Dee and me had hung them on the quilt frames on the front porch and quilted them. One was in the Lone Star pattern. The other was Walk Around the Mountain. In both of them were scraps of dresses Grandma Dee had worn fifty and more years ago. Bits and pieces of Grandpa Jarrell's Paisley shirts. And one teeny faded blue piece, about the size of a penny matchbox, that was from

Great Grandpa Ezra's uniform that he wore in the Civil War.

"Mama," Wangero said sweet as a bird. "Can I have these old quilts?"

I heard something fall in the kitchen, and a minute later the kitchen door slammed.

"Why don't you take one or two of the others?" I asked. "These old things was just done by me and Big Dee from some tops your grandma pieced before she died."

"No," said Wangero. "I don't want those. They are stitched around the borders by machine."

"That'll make them last better," I said.   60

"That's not the point," said Wangero. "These are all pieces of dresses Grandma used to wear. She did all this stitching by hand. Imagine!" She held the quilts securely in her arms, stroking them.

"Some of the pieces, like those lavender ones, come from old clothes her mother handed down to her," I said, moving up to touch the quilts. Dee (Wangero) moved back just enough so that I couldn't reach the quilts. They already belonged to her.

"Imagine!" she breathed again, clutching them closely to her bosom.

"The truth is," I said, "I promised to give them quilts to Maggie, for when she marries John Thomas."

She gasped like a bee had stung her.   65

"Maggie can't appreciate these quilts!" she said. "She'd probably be backward enough to put them to everyday use."

"I reckon she would," I said. "God knows I been saving 'em for long enough with nobody using 'em. I hope she will!" I didn't want to bring up how I had offered Dee (Wangero) a quilt when she went away to college. Then she had told me they were old-fashioned, out of style.

"But they're *priceless!*" she was saying now, furiously; for she has a temper. "Maggie would put them on the bed and in five years they'd be in rags. Less than that!"

"She can always make some more," I said. "Maggie knows how to quilt."

70   Dee (Wangero) looked at me with hatred. "You just will not understand. The point is these quilts, *these* quilts!"

"Well," I said, stumped. "What would *you* do with them?"

"Hang them," she said. As if that was the only thing you *could* do with quilts.

Maggie by now was standing in the door. I could almost hear the sound her feet made as they scraped over each other.

"She can have them, Mama," she said, like somebody used to never winning anything, or having anything reserved for her.

"I can 'member Grandma Dee without the quilts."

I looked at her hard. She had filled her 75 bottom lip with checkerberry snuff and it gave her face a kind of dopey, hangdog look. It was Grandma Dee and Big Dee who taught her how to quilt herself. She stood there with her scarred hands hidden in the folds of her skirt. She looked at her sister with something like fear but she wasn't mad at her. This was Maggie's portion. This was the way she knew God to work.

When I looked at her like that something hit me in the top of my head and ran down to the soles of my feet. Just like when I'm in church and the spirit of God touches

FROM PAGE TO SCREEN

Symbolism in "Everyday Use"

From the very first scene in "Everyday Use," the differences between Dee/Wangero and Maggie are striking. Maggie is clearly close to her mother and her community. Dee, who has not seen her mother or sister for six long years, gets out of the car and takes a photograph of

Maggie and Mrs. Johnson from the Wadsworth production of "Everyday Use."

me and I get happy and shout. I did something I never had done before: hugged Maggie to me, then dragged her on into the room, snatched the quilts out of Miss Wangero's hands and dumped them into Maggie's lap. Maggie just sat there on my bed with her mouth open.

"Take one or two of the others," I said to Dee.

But she turned without a word and went out to Hakim-a-barber.

"You just don't understand," she said, as Maggie and I came out to the car.

80 "What don't I understand?" I wanted to know.

"Your heritage," she said. And then she turned to Maggie, kissed her, and said, "You ought to try to make something of yourself, too, Maggie. It's really a new day for us. But from the way you and Mama still live you'd never know it."

She put on some sunglasses that hid everything above the tip of her nose and her chin.

Maggie smiled; maybe at the sunglasses. But a real smile, not scared. After we watched the car dust settle I asked Maggie to bring me a dip of snuff. And then the two of us sat there just enjoying, until it was time to go in the house and go to bed.

A stunned and indignant Mrs. Johnson as Dee tries to take the best quilts for herself.

them from a distance before she even greets them properly.

Once we get into the heart of the story, we see that Alice Walker has used many symbolic objects to develop her themes. The churn top and dasher, the benches with the rump prints, the butter dish, and, of course, the quilts, are all objects that represent family and cultural heritage. Dee demands the most precious quilts—pieced together by her female forebears—which she wants to hang on her wall in her apartment in Chicago, as decorations. Her accusation that Maggie would only put the quilts to "everyday use" helps her mother, Mrs. Johnson, experience a moment of epiphany. She takes the quilts away from Dee and bestows them on her younger daughter, Maggie, who lives her heritage every day and understands it better than the arrogant Dee who is estranged from her own culture.

·····▶*Your* Turn

Talking and Writing about Lit

1. Discuss several symbolic objects, characters, or occurrences in "Everyday Use." What do they represent?

2. Who is the main character in the story? Why? Is there any character who changes during the course of the story?

3. Explain how the use of humor and irony enrich the story.

4. **DIY** In "Everyday Use," Mrs. Johnson knows more than Dee and Hakim because of her greater experience of the past and of life in general and because of her authentic understanding of her heritage. Write a scene in which the situation is reversed. In your scene, a person of your parents' generation profoundly misunderstands something which the young character or characters in your scene understand perfectly well. You may want to aim for two levels of awareness in your scene, as Walker has done in "Everyday Use." That is, we see what's going on on the surface of a scene (in dialogue—what the characters say to each other), but we also have access to the narrator's thoughts (as we do to Mrs. Johnson's), and the narrator knows more than the other characters do. In your scene, the person more knowledgeable will be the young character (your narrator), and he or she will make comments in the narration that make this clear to the reader.

Nathaniel Hawthorne (1804–1864)

Nathaniel Hawthorne was born in Salem, Massachusetts, and was a descendent of a Puritan judge who had participated in the Salem witch trials of 1692. This connection caused Hawthorne a good deal of soul searching, and his exploration of related issues (such as scapegoating and how society judges individuals who are different) emerges in his fiction. Hawthorne's most important novel, *The Scarlet Letter* (1850), in widely regarded as a masterpiece of American literature. Another well-known novel of Hawthorne's is *The Blithedale Romance* (1852). His short stories are collected in the two volumes of *Twice-Told Tales* (1837 and 1842) and in *Mosses from an Old Manse* (1846).

The Birthmark (1843)

In the latter part of the last century there lived a man of science, an eminent proficient in every branch of natural philosophy, who not long before our story opens had made experience of a spiritual affinity more attractive than any chemical one. He had left his laboratory to the care of an assistant, cleared his fine countenance from the furnace smoke, washed the stain of acids from his fingers, and persuaded a beautiful woman to become his wife. In those days when the comparatively recent discovery of electricity and other kindred mysteries of Nature seemed to open paths into the region of miracle, it was not unusual for the love of science to rival the love of woman in its depth and absorbing energy. The higher intellect, the imagination, the spirit, and even the heart might all find their congenial ailment in pursuits which, as some of their ardent votaries believed, would ascend from one step of powerful intelligence to another, until the philosopher should lay his hand on the secret of creative force and perhaps make new worlds for himself. We know not whether Aylmer possessed this degree of faith in man's ultimate control over Nature. He had devoted himself, however, too unreservedly to scientific studies ever to be weaned from them by any second passion. His love for his young wife might prove the stronger of the two; but it could only be by intertwining itself with his love of science, and uniting the strength of the latter to his own.

Such a union accordingly took place, and was attended with truly remarkable consequences and a deeply impressive moral. One day, very soon after their marriage, Aylmer sat gazing at his wife with a trouble in his countenance that grew stronger until he spoke.

"Georgiana," said he, "has it never occurred to you that the mark upon your cheek might be removed?"

"No, indeed," said she, smiling; but perceiving the seriousness of his manner, she blushed deeply. "To tell you the truth it has been so often called a charm that I was simple enough to imagine it might be so."

5   "Ah, upon another face perhaps it might," replied her husband; "but never on yours. No, dearest Georgiana, you came so nearly perfect from the hand of Nature that this slightest possible defect, which we hesitate whether to term a defect or a beauty, shocks me, as being the visible mark of earthly imperfection."

"Shocks you, my husband!" cried Georgiana, deeply hurt; at first reddening with momentary anger, but then bursting into tears. "Then why did you take me from my mother's side? You cannot love what shocks you!"

To explain this conversation it must be mentioned that in the center of Georgiana's left cheek there was a singular mark, deeply interwoven, as it were, with the texture and substance of her face. In the usual state of her complexion—a healthy though delicate bloom—the mark wore a tint of deeper crimson, which imperfectly defined its shape amid the surrounding rosiness. When she blushed it gradually became more indistinct, and finally vanished amid the triumphant rush of blood that bathed the whole cheek with its brilliant glow. But if any shifting motion caused her to turn pale, there was the mark again, a crimson stain upon the snow, in what Aylmer sometimes deemed an almost fearful distinctness. Its shape bore not a little similarity to the human hand, though of the smallest pygmy size. Georgiana's lovers were wont to say that some fairy at her birth hour had laid her tiny hand upon the infant's cheek, and left this impress there in token of the magic endowments that were to give her such sway over all hearts. Many a desperate swain would have risked life for the privilege of pressing his lips to the mysterious hand. It must not be concealed, however, that the impression wrought by this fairy sign manual varied exceedingly, according to the difference of temperament in the beholders. Some fastidious persons—but they were exclusively of her own sex—affirmed that the bloody hand, as they chose to call it, quite destroyed the effect of Georgiana's beauty, and rendered her countenance even hideous. But it would be as reasonable to say that one of those small blue stains which sometimes occur in the purest statuary marble would convert the Eve of Powers to a monster. Masculine observers, if the birthmark did not heighten their admiration, contented themselves with wishing it away, that the world might possess one living specimen of ideal loveliness without the semblance of a flaw. After his marriage,—for he thought little or nothing of the matter before,—Aylmer discovered that this was the case with himself.

Had she been less beautiful,—if Envy's self could have found aught else to sneer at,—he might have felt his affection heightened by the prettiness of this mimic hand, now vaguely portrayed, now lost, now stealing forth again and glimmering to and fro with every pulse of emotion that throbbed within her heart; but seeing her otherwise so perfect, he found this one defect grow more and more intolerable with every moment of their united lives. It was the fatal flaw of humanity which Nature, in one shape or another, stamps ineffaceably on all her productions, either to imply that they are temporary and finite, or that their perfection must be wrought by toil and pain. The crimson hand expressed the ineludible gripe* in which mortality clutches the highest and purest of earthly mold, degrading them into kindred with the lowest, and even with the very brutes, like whom their visible frames return to dust. In this manner, selecting it as the symbol of his wife's liability to sin, sorrow, decay, and death, Aylmer's somber imagination was not long in rendering the birthmark a frightful object, causing him more trouble and horror than ever Georgiana's beauty, whether of soul or sense, had given him delight.

------

*gripe: Grip.

At all the seasons which should have been their happiest, he invariably and without intending it, nay, in spite of a purpose to the contrary, reverted to this one disastrous topic. Trifling as it at first appeared, it so connected itself with innumerable trains of thought and modes of feeling that it became the central point of all. With the morning twilight Aylmer opened his eyes upon his wife's face and recognized the symbol of imperfection; and when they sat together at the evening hearth his eyes wandered stealthily to her cheek, and beheld, flickering with the blaze of the wood fire, the spectral hand that wrote mortality where he would fain have worshiped. Georgiana soon learned to shudder at his gaze. It needed but a glance with the peculiar expression that his face often wore to change the roses of her cheek into a deathlike paleness, amid which the crimson hand was brought strongly out, like a bas-relief of ruby on the whitest marble.

Late one night when the lights were 10 growing dim, so as hardly to betray the stain on the poor wife's cheek, she herself, for the first time, voluntarily took up the subject.

"Do you remember, my dear Aylmer," said she, with a feeble attempt at a smile, "have you any recollection of a dream last night about this odious hand?"

"None! none whatever!" replied Aylmer, starting; but then he added, in a dry, cold tone, affected for the sake of concealing the real depth of his emotion, "I might well dream of it; for before I fell asleep it had taken a pretty firm hold of my fancy."

"And you did dream of it?" continued Georgiana hastily, for she dreaded lest a gush of tears should interrupt what she had to say. "A terrible dream! I wonder that you can forget it. Is it possible to forget this one expression?—'It is in her heart now; we must have it out!' Reflect, my husband; for by all means I would have you recall that dream."

The mind is in a sad state when Sleep, the all-involving, cannot confine her specters within the dim region of her sway, but suffers them to break forth, affrighting this actual life with secrets that perchance belong to a deeper one. Aylmer now remembered his dream. He had fancied himself with his servant Aminadab, attempting an operation for the removal of the birthmark; but the deeper went the knife, the deeper sank the hand, until at length its tiny grasp appeared to have caught hold of Georgiana's heart; whence, however, her husband was inexorably resolved to cut or wrench it away.

15   When the dream had shaped itself perfectly in his memory, Aylmer sat in his wife's presence with a guilty feeling. Truth often finds its way to the mind close muffled in robes of sleep, and then speaks with uncompromising directness of matters in regard to which we practice an unconscious self-deception during our waking moments. Until now he had not been aware of the tyrannizing influence acquired by one idea over his mind, and of the lengths which he might find in his heart to go for the sake of giving himself peace.

"Aylmer," resumed Georgiana solemnly, "I know not what may be the cost to both of us to rid me of this fatal birthmark. Perhaps its removal may cause cureless deformity; or it may be the stain goes as deep as life itself. Again: do we know that there is a possibility, on any terms, of unclasping the firm grip of this little hand which was laid upon me before I came into the world?"

"Dearest Georgiana, I have spent much thought upon the subject," hastily interrupted Aylmer. "I am convinced of the perfect practicability of its removal."

"If there be the remotest possibility of it," continued Georgiana, "let the attempt be made at whatever risk. Danger is nothing to me; for life, while this hateful mark makes me the object of your horror and disgust,— life is a burden which I would fling down with joy. Either remove this dreadful hand, or take my wretched life! You have deep science. All the world bears witness of it. You have achieved great wonders. Cannot you remove this little, little mark, which I cover with the tips of two small fingers? Is this beyond your power, for the sake of your own peace, and to save your poor wife from madness?"

"Noblest, dearest, tenderest wife," cried Aylmer rapturously, "doubt not my power. I have already given this matter the deepest thought—thought which might almost have enlightened me to create a being less perfect than yourself. Georgiana, you have led me deeper than ever into the heart of science. I feel myself fully competent to render this dear cheek as faultless as its fellow; and then, most beloved, what will be my triumph when I shall have corrected what Nature left imperfect in her fairest work! Even Pygmalion, when his sculptured woman assumed life, felt not greater ecstasy than mine will be."

"It is resolved, then," said Georgiana, 20 faintly smiling. "And, Aylmer, spare me not, though you should find the birthmark take refuge in my heart at last."

Her husband tenderly kissed her cheek—her right cheek—not that which bore the impress of the crimson hand.

The next day Aylmer apprised his wife of a plan that he had formed whereby he might have opportunity for the intense thought and constant watchfulness which the proposed operation would require; while Georgiana, likewise, would enjoy the perfect repose essential to its success. They were to seclude themselves in the extensive apartments occupied by Aylmer as a laboratory, and where, during his toilsome youth, he had made discoveries in the elemental powers of

Nature that had roused the admiration of all the learned societies in Europe. Seated calmly in this laboratory, the pale philosopher had investigated the secrets of the highest cloud region and of the profoundest mines; he had satisfied himself of the causes that kindled and kept alive the fires of the volcano; and had explained the mystery of fountains, and how it is that they gush forth, some so bright and pure, and others with such rich medicinal virtues, from the dark bosom of the earth. Here, too, at an earlier period, he had studied the wonders of the human frame, and attempted to fathom the very process by which Nature assimilates all her precious influences from earth and air, and from the spiritual world, to create and foster man, her masterpiece. The latter pursuit, however, Aylmer had long laid aside in unwilling recognition of the truth—against which all seekers sooner or later stumble—that our great creative Mother, while she amuses us with apparently working in the broadest sunshine, is yet severely careful to keep her own secrets, and, in spite of her pretended openness, shows us nothing but results. She permits us, indeed, to mar, but seldom to mend, and, like a jealous patentee, on no account to make. Now, however, Aylmer resumed these half-forgotten investigations,—not, of course, with such hopes or wishes as first suggested them, but because they involved much physiological truth and lay in the path of his proposed scheme for the treatment of Georgiana.

As he led her over the threshold of the laboratory, Georgiana was cold and tremulous. Aylmer looked cheerfully into her face, with intent to reassure her, but was so startled with the intense glow of the birthmark upon the whiteness of her cheek that he could not restrain a strong convulsive shudder. His wife fainted.

"Aminadab! Aminadab!" shouted Aylmer, stamping violently on the floor.

Forthwith there issued from an inner 25 apartment a man of low stature, but bulky frame, with shaggy hair hanging about his visage, which was grimed with the vapors of the furnace. This personage had been Aylmer's underworker during his whole scientific career, and was admirably fitted for that office by his great mechanical readiness, and the skill with which, while incapable of comprehending a single principle, he executed all the details of his master's experiments. With his vast strength, his shaggy hair, his smoky aspect, and the indescribable earthiness that encrusted him, he seemed to represent man's physical nature; while Aylmer's slender figure, and pale, intellectual face, were no less apt a type of the spiritual element.

"Throw open the door of the boudoir, Aminadab," said Aylmer, "and burn a pastille."

"Yes, master," answered Aminadab, looking intently at the lifeless form of Georgiana; and then he muttered to himself, "If she were my wife, I'd never part with that birthmark."

When Georgiana recovered consciousness she found herself breathing an atmosphere of penetrating fragrance, the gentle potency of which had recalled her from her deathlike faintness. The scene around her looked like enchantment. Aylmer had converted those smoky, dingy, somber rooms, where he had spent his brightest years in recondite pursuits, into a series of beautiful apartments not unfit to be the secluded abode of a lovely woman. The walls were hung with gorgeous curtains, which imparted the combination of grandeur and grace that no other species of adornment can achieve; and as they fell from the ceiling to the floor, their rich and ponderous folds, concealing all angles and straight lines, appeared to shut in the scene from infinite space. For aught Georgiana knew, it might be a pavilion among the clouds. And Aylmer, excluding the sunshine, which would have interfered with his chemical processes, had supplied its place with perfumed lamps, emitting flames of various hue, but all uniting in a soft, empurpled radiance. He now knelt by his wife's side, watching her earnestly, but without alarm; for he was confident in his science, and felt that he could draw a magic circle round her within which no evil might intrude.

"Where am I? Ah, I remember," said Georgiana faintly; and she placed her hand over her cheek to hide the terrible mark from her husband's eyes.

30 "Fear not, dearest!" exclaimed he. "Do not shrink from me! Believe me, Georgiana, I even rejoice in this single imperfection, since it will be such a rapture to remove it."

"Oh, spare me!" sadly replied his wife. "Pray do not look at it again. I never can forget that convulsive shudder."

In order to soothe Georgiana, and, as it were, to release her mind from the burden of actual things, Aylmer now put in practice some of the light and playful secrets which science had taught him among its profounder lore. Airy figures, absolutely bodiless ideas, and forms of unsubstantial beauty came and danced before her, imprinting their momentary footsteps on beams of light. Though she had some indistinct idea of the method of these optical phenomena, still the illusion was almost perfect enough to warrant the belief that her husband possessed sway over the spiritual world. Then again, when she felt a wish to look forth from her seclusion, immediately, as if her thoughts were answered, the procession of external existence flitted across a screen. The scenery and the figures of actual life were perfectly represented, but with that bewitching, yet indescribable difference which always makes a picture, an image, or a shadow so much more attractive than the original. When wearied of this, Aylmer bade her cast her eyes upon a vessel containing a quantity of earth. She did so, with little interest at first; but was soon startled to perceive the germ of a plant shooting upward from the soil. Then came the slender stalk; the leaves gradually unfolded themselves; and amid them was a perfect and lovely flower.

"It is magical!" cried Georgiana. "I dare not touch it."

"Nay, pluck it," answered Aylmer: "pluck it, and inhale its brief perfume while you may. The flower will wither in a few moments and leave nothing save its brown seed vessels; but thence may be perpetuated a race as ephemeral as itself."

But Georgiana had no sooner touched 35 the flower than the whole plant suffered a blight, its leaves turning coal-black as if by the agency of fire.

"There was too powerful a stimulus," said Aylmer thoughtfully.

To make up for this abortive experiment, he proposed to take her portrait by a scientific process of his own invention. It was to be effected by rays of light striking upon a polished plate of metal. Georgiana assented; but, on looking at the result, was affrighted to find the features of the portrait blurred and indefinable; while the minute figure of a hand appeared where the cheek should have been. Aylmer snatched the metallic plate and threw it into a jar of corrosive acid.

Soon, however, he forgot these mortifying failures. In the intervals of study and chemical experiment he came to her flushed and exhausted, but seemed invigorated by her presence, and spoke in glowing language of the resources of his art. He gave a history of the long dynasty of the alchemists, who spent so many ages in quest of the universal solvent by which the golden principle might be elicited from all things vile and base. Aylmer appeared to believe that, by the plainest scientific logic, it was altogether within the limits of possibility to discover this long-sought medium; "but," he added, "a philosopher who should go deep enough to acquire the power would attain too lofty a wisdom to stoop to the exercise of it." Not less singular were his opinions in regard to the elixir vitae. He more than intimated that it was at his option to concoct a liquid that should prolong life for years, perhaps interminably; but that it would produce a discord in Nature which all the world, and chiefly the quaffer of the immortal nostrum, would find cause to curse.

"Aylmer, are you in earnest?" asked Georgiana, looking at him with amazement and fear. "It is terrible to possess such power, or even to dream of possessing it."

40 "Oh, do not tremble, my love," said her husband. "I would not wrong either you or myself by working such inharmonious effects upon our lives; but I would have you consider how trifling, in comparison, is the skill requisite to remove this little hand."

At the mention of the birthmark, Georgiana, as usual, shrank as if a red-hot iron had touched her cheek.

Again Aylmer applied himself to his labors. She could hear his voice in the distant furnace-room giving directions to Aminadab, whose harsh, uncouth, misshapen tones were audible in response, more like the grunt or growl of a brute than human speech. After hours of absence, Aylmer reappeared and proposed that she should now examine his cabinet of chemical products and natural treasures of the earth. Among the former he showed her a small vial, in which, he remarked, was contained a gentle yet most powerful fragrance, capable of impregnating all the breezes that blow across a kingdom. They were of inestimable value, the contents of that little vial; and, as he said so, he threw some of the perfume into the air and filled the room with piercing and invigorating delight.

"And what is this?" asked Georgiana, pointing to a small crystal globe containing a gold-colored liquid. "It is so beautiful to the eye that I could imagine it the elixir of life."

"In one sense it is," replied Aylmer; "or rather, the elixir of immortality. It is the most precious poison that ever was concocted in this world. By its aid I could apportion the lifetime of any mortal at whom you might point your finger. The strength of the dose would determine whether he were to linger out years, or drop dead in the midst of a breath. No king on his guarded throne could keep his life if I, in my private station, should deem that the welfare of millions justified me in depriving him of it."

"Why do you keep such a terrific 45 drug?" inquired Georgiana in horror.

"Do not mistrust me, dearest," said her husband, smiling; "its virtuous potency is yet greater than its harmful one. But see! here is a powerful cosmetic. With a few drops of this in a vase of water, freckles may be washed away as easily as the hands are cleansed. A stronger infusion would take the blood out of the cheek, and leave the rosiest beauty a pale ghost."

"Is it with this lotion that you intend to bathe my cheek?" asked Georgiana, anxiously.

"Oh, no," hastily replied her husband; "this is merely superficial. Your case demands a remedy that shall go deeper."

In his interviews with Georgiana, Aylmer generally made minute inquiries as to her sensations and whether the confinement of the rooms and the temperature of the atmosphere agreed with her. These questions had such a particular drift that Georgiana began to conjecture that she was already subjected to certain physical influences, either breathed in with the fragrant air or taken with her food. She fancied likewise, but it might be altogether fancy, that there was a stirring up of her system—a strange, indefinite sensation creeping through her veins, and tingling, half painfully, half pleasurably, at her heart. Still, whenever she dared to look into the mirror, there she beheld herself pale as a white rose and with the crimson birthmark stamped upon her cheek. Not even Aylmer now hated it so much as she.

50   To dispel the tedium of the hours which her husband found it necessary to devote to the processes of combination and analysis, Georgiana turned over the volumes of his scientific library. In many dark old tomes she met with chapters full of romance and poetry. They were the works of the philosophers of the middle ages, such as Albertus Magnus, Cornelius Agrippa, Paracelsus, and the famous friar who created the prophetic Brazen Head. All these antique naturalists stood in advance of their centuries, yet were imbued with some of their credulity, and therefore were believed, and perhaps imagined themselves to have acquired from the investigation of Nature a power above Nature, and from physics a sway over the spiritual world. Hardly less curious and imaginative were the early volumes of the Transactions of the Royal Society, in which the members, knowing little of the limits of natural possibility, were continually recording wonders or proposing methods whereby wonders might be wrought.

But to Georgiana the most engrossing volume was a large folio from her husband's own hand, in which he had recorded every experiment of his scientific career, its original aim, the methods adopted for its development, and its final success or failure, with the circumstances to which either event was attributable. The book, in truth, was both the history and emblem of his ardent, ambitious, imaginative, yet practical and laborious life. He handled physical details as if there were nothing beyond them; yet spiritualized them all, and redeemed himself from materialism by his strong and eager aspiration towards the infinite. In his grasp the veriest clod of earth assumed a soul. Georgiana, as she read, reverenced Aylmer and loved him more profoundly than ever, but with a less entire dependence on his judgment than heretofore. Much as he had accomplished, she could not but observe that his most splendid successes were almost invariably failures, if compared with the ideal at which he aimed. His brightest diamonds were the merest pebbles, and felt to be so by himself, in comparison with the inestimable gems which lay hidden beyond his reach. The volume, rich with achievements that had won renown for its author, was yet as melancholy a record as ever mortal hand had penned. It was the sad confession and continual exemplification of the shortcomings of the composite man, the spirit burdened with clay and working in matter, and of the despair that assails the higher nature of finding itself so miserably thwarted by the earthly part. Perhaps every man of genius in whatever sphere might recognize the image of his own experience in Aylmer's journal.

So deeply did these reflections affect Georgiana that she laid her face upon the open volume and burst into tears. In this situation she was found by her husband.

"It is dangerous to read in a sorcerer's books," said he with a smile, though his countenance was uneasy and displeased. "Georgiana, there are pages in that volume which I can scarcely glance over and keep my senses. Take heed lest it prove as detrimental to you."

"It has made me worship you more than ever," said she.

"Ah, wait for this one success," 55 rejoined he, "then worship me if you will. I shall deem myself hardly unworthy of it. But come, I have sought you for the luxury of your voice. Sing to me, dearest."

So she poured out the liquid music of her voice to quench the thirst of his spirit. He then took his leave with a boyish exuberance of gaiety, assuring her that her seclusion would endure but a little longer, and that the result was already certain. Scarcely had he departed when Georgiana felt irresistibly impelled to follow him. She had forgotten to inform Aylmer of a symptom which for two or three hours past had begun to excite her attention. It was a sensation in the fatal birthmark, not painful, but which induced a restlessness throughout her system. Hastening after her husband, she intruded for the first time into the laboratory.

The first thing that struck her eye was the furnace, that hot and feverish worker, with the intense glow of its fire, which by the quantities of soot clustered above it seemed to have been burning for ages. There was a distilling apparatus in full operation. Around the room were retorts, tubes, cylinders, crucibles, and other apparatus of chemical research. An electrical machine stood ready for immediate use. The atmosphere felt oppressively close, and was tainted with gaseous odors which had been tormented forth by the process of science. The severe and homely simplicity of the apartment, with its naked walls and brick pavement, looked strange, accustomed as Georgiana had become to the fantastic elegance of her boudoir. But what chiefly, indeed almost solely, drew her attention, was the aspect of Aylmer himself.

He was pale as death, anxious and absorbed, and hung over the furnace as if it depended upon his utmost watchfulness whether the liquid which it was distilling should be the draught of immortal happiness or misery. How different from the sanguine and joyous mien that he had assumed for Georgiana's encouragement!

"Carefully now, Aminadab; carefully, thou human machine; carefully, thou man of clay!" muttered Aylmer, more to himself than his assistant. "Now, if there be a thought too much or too little, it is all over."

"Ho! ho!" mumbled Aminadab. 60 "Look, master! look!"

Aylmer raised his eyes hastily, and at first reddened, then grew paler than ever, on beholding Georgiana. He rushed towards her and seized her arm with a gripe that left the print of his fingers upon it.

"Why do you come hither? Have you no trust in your husband?" cried he impetuously. "Would you throw the blight of that fatal birthmark over my labors? It is not well done. Go, prying woman, go!"

"Nay, Aylmer," said Georgiana with the firmness of which she possessed no stinted endowment, "it is not you that have a right to complain. You mistrust your wife; you have concealed the anxiety with which you watch the development of this experiment. Think not so unworthily of me, my husband. Tell me all the risk we run, and fear not that I shall shrink; for my share in it is far less than your own."

"No, no, Georgiana!" said Aylmer impatiently; "it must not be."

"I submit," replied she calmly. "And, 65 Aylmer, I shall quaff whatever draught you bring me; but it will be on the same principle that would induce me to take a dose of poison if offered by your hand."

"My noble wife," said Aylmer, deeply moved, "I knew not the height and depth of your nature until now. Nothing shall be concealed. Know, then, that this crimson hand, superficial as it seems, has clutched its grasp into your being with a strength of which I had no previous conception. I have already administered agents powerful enough to do aught except to change your entire physical system. Only one thing remains to be tried. If that fails us we are ruined."

"Why did you hesitate to tell me this?" asked she.

"Because, Georgiana," said Aylmer in a low voice, "there is danger."

"Danger? There is but one danger—that this horrible stigma shall be left upon my cheek!" cried Georgiana. "Remove it, remove it, whatever be the cost, or we shall both go mad!"

70 "Heaven knows your words are too true," said Aylmer sadly. "And now, dearest, return to your boudoir. In a little while all will be tested."

He conducted her back and took leave of her with a solemn tenderness which spoke far more than his words how much was now at stake. After his departure Georgiana became rapt in musings. She considered the character of Aylmer, and did it completer justice than at any previous moment. Her heart exulted, while it trembled, at his honorable love—so pure and lofty that it would accept nothing less than perfection nor miserably make itself contented with an earthlier nature than he had dreamed of. She felt how much more precious was such a sentiment than that meaner kind which would have borne with the imperfection for her sake, and have been guilty of treason to holy love by degrading its perfect idea to the level of the actual; and with her whole spirit she prayed that, for a single moment, she might satisfy his highest and deepest conception. Longer than one moment she well knew it could not be; for his spirit was ever on the march, ever ascending, and each instant required something that was beyond the scope of the instant before.

The sound of her husband's footsteps aroused her. He bore a crystal goblet containing a liquor colorless as water, but bright enough to be the draught of immortality. Aylmer was pale; but it seemed rather the consequence of a highly wrought state of mind and tension of spirit than of fear or doubt.

"The concoction of the draught has been perfect," said he, in answer to Georgiana's look. "Unless all my science have deceived me, it cannot fail."

"Save on your account, my dearest Aylmer," observed his wife, "I might wish to put off this birthmark of mortality by relinquishing mortality itself in preference to any other mode. Life is but a sad possession to those who have attained precisely the degree of moral advancement at which I stand. Were I weaker and blinder it might be happiness. Were I stronger, it might be endured hopefully. But, being what I find myself, methinks I am of all mortals the most fit to die."

"You are fit for heaven without tasting 75 death!" replied her husband. "But why do we speak of dying? The draught cannot fail. Behold its effect upon this plant."

On the window seat there stood a geranium diseased with yellow blotches, which had overspread all its leaves. Aylmer poured a small quantity of the liquid upon the soil in which it grew. In a little time, when the roots of the plant had taken up the moisture, the unsightly blotches began to be extinguished in a living verdure.

"There needed no proof," said Georgiana quietly. "Give me the goblet. I joyfully stake all upon your word."

"Drink, then, thou lofty creature!" exclaimed Aylmer, with fervid admiration. "There is no taint of imperfection on thy spirit. Thy sensible frame, too, shall soon be all perfect."

She quaffed the liquid and returned the goblet to his hand.

"It is grateful," said she, with a placid 80 smile. "Methinks it is like water from a heavenly fountain; for it contains I know not what of unobtrusive fragrance and deliciousness. It allays a feverish thirst that had parched me for many days. Now, dearest, let me sleep. My earthly senses are closing over my spirit like the leaves around the heart of a rose at sunset."

She spoke the last words with a gentle reluctance, as if it required almost more energy than she could command to pronounce the faint and lingering syllables. Scarcely had they loitered through her lips ere she was lost in slumber. Aylmer sat by her side, watching her aspect with the emotions proper to a man the whole value of whose existence was involved in the process now to be tested. Mingled with this mood, however, was the philosophic investigation characteristic of the man of science. Not the minutest symptom escaped him. A heightened flush of the cheek, a slight irregularity of breath, a quiver of the eyelid, a hardly perceptible tremor through the frame,—such were the details which, as the moments passed, he wrote down in his folio volume. Intense thought had set its stamp upon every previous page of that volume, but the thoughts of years were all concentrated upon the last.

While thus employed, he failed not to gaze often at the fatal hand, and not without a shudder. Yet once, by a strange and unaccountable impulse, he pressed it with his lips. His spirit recoiled, however, in the very act; and Georgiana, out of the midst of her deep sleep, moved uneasily and murmured as if in remonstrance. Again Aylmer resumed his watch. Nor was it without avail. The crimson hand, which at first had been strongly visible upon the marble paleness of Georgiana's cheek, now grew more faintly outlined. She remained not less pale than ever; but the birthmark, with every breath that came and went, lost somewhat of its former distinctness. Its presence had been awful; its departure was more awful still. Watch the stain of the rainbow fading out of the sky, and you will know how that mysterious symbol passed away.

"By Heaven! it is well-nigh gone!" said Aylmer to himself, in almost irrepressible ecstasy. "I can scarcely trace it now. Success! success! And now it is like the faintest rose color. The lightest flush of blood across her cheek would overcome it. But she is so pale!"

He drew aside the window curtain and suffered the light of natural day to fall into the room and rest upon her cheek. At the same time he heard a gross, hoarse chuckle, which he had long known as his servant Aminadab's expression of delight.

"Ah, clod! ah, earthly mass!" cried 85 Aylmer, laughing in a sort of frenzy, "you have served me well! Matter and spirit— earth and heaven—have both done their part in this! Laugh, thing of the senses! You have earned the right to laugh."

These exclamations broke Georgiana's sleep. She slowly unclosed her eyes and gazed into the mirror which her husband had arranged for that purpose. A faint smile flitted over her lips when she recognized how barely perceptible was now that crimson hand which had once blazed forth with such disastrous brilliancy as to scare away all their happiness. But then her eyes sought Aylmer's face with a trouble and anxiety that he could by no means account for.

"My poor Aylmer!" murmured she.

"Poor? Nay, richest, happiest, most favored!" exclaimed he. "My peerless bride, it is successful! You are perfect!"

"My poor Aylmer," she repeated, with a more than human tenderness, "you have aimed loftily; you have done nobly. Do not repent that with so high and pure a feeling, you have rejected the best the earth could offer. Aylmer, dearest Aylmer, I am dying!"

Alas! it was too true! The fatal hand 90 had grappled with the mystery of life, and was the bond by which an angelic spirit kept itself in union with a mortal frame. As the last crimson tint of the birthmark—that sole token of human imperfection—faded from her cheek, the parting breath of the now perfect woman passed into the atmosphere, and her soul, lingering a moment near her husband, took its heavenward flight. Then a hoarse, chuckling laugh was heard again! Thus ever does the gross fatality of earth exult in its invariable triumph over the immortal essence which, in this dim sphere of half development, demands the completeness of a higher state. Yet, had Aylmer reached a profounder wisdom, he need not thus have flung away the happiness which would have woven his mortal life of the self-same texture with the celestial. The momentary circumstance was too strong for him; he failed to look beyond the shadowy scope of time, and, living once for all in eternity, to find the perfect future in the present.

·····▶ *Your* Turn
Talking and Writing about Lit

1. Could the characters themselves in "The Birthmark" be seen as symbolic? What might the main characters represent?

2. "The Birthmark" is written in the third-person omniscient point of view; in addition, it is an example of the editorializing omniscient narrator. That is, the omniscient narrative voice is not necessarily neutral but, instead, sometimes offers judgments regarding the characters' actions and even the theme of the story. Can you find examples of the editorializing omniscient voice in the story?

3. This is a story in which the importance of setting is multifaceted. Explain how Hawthorne uses the historical context as well as the physical setting to reveal the story's characters and themes.

4. In what ways has Hawthorne used foreshadowing to prepare the reader for the story's ending?

5. **DIY** Have you ever known a person who was determined to change a partner in a relationship? Write two pages of dialogue between two characters (of any gender/s) in which one of them reveals to the other a trait of the partner's that he or she doesn't like and is determined to change. What is the other partner's reaction? The outcome is up to you, the writer—you are in control!

Bi Shumin (b. 1952)

Bi Shumin was born in Shandong, China. In her adult life, she served in the army, worked as a practicing physician for twenty years, and became a professional writer. Her works include *Kunlun Mountains, A Red Carpet*, and *Flying Northward*. Two subjects frequently dealt with in her fiction are army life and the impact of Western cultural influences on contemporary life in mainland China.

Broken Transformers (1992)

Translated by Shi Junbao

"Mum, let's go. I don't want a Transformer," said my ten-year-old son.

We were standing in a newly opened department store. As mother of a low-income family I was used to steering my son firmly away from toy counters; but this store had taken me by surprise; its manager had shrewdly filled the entrance hall with brightly colored playthings instead of the usual dull array of cosmetics.

I stood in the doorway, debating whether or not to leave. There had been a sign outside saying the store sold wool, and I desperately needed to knit myself a new hat and scarf. Still, wool could be bought elsewhere.

I gripped my son's hand and drew him towards me intending to make up some excuse to get him out of the store, and thus out of temptation's way. Ten was an age, after all, at which innocence gradually begins to give way to questioning, and I didn't want him to become conscious too early of the power of money and thus of our limited supply. At the same time I hated the thought of his disappointment at not being able to have the toy he so adored. I felt like covering his eyes with my palm!

5 The last thing I expected him to say was, "Mum, let's leave. I don't want a Transformer." I was at a loss to know how to express my gratitude.

I hated the monstrous cartoon family which had my son glued to the TV set every Saturday and Sunday night; not only did it prevent me watching the news, but it had so captured the imagination of thousands of children that the toy replicas now pouring into the stores were sucking money from parents like locusts devouring crops.

If we hadn't been in the crowded store I would have bent down and kissed his smooth brow, now covered with beads of salty sweet sweat. But it immediately became clear to me that my sense of relief was premature, for his feet were as though rooted to the spot. His neck twisted towards the counter and he stared, through long dark eyelashes, at the colorful range of robots which stared back at him in disdain.

My heart bled as I looked admiringly at his lithe young neck which, like the branch of a willow tree, seemed able to twist back endlessly without incurring discomfort. Was it only a matter of a hat and a scarf?

A perfect example of the trend towards "late marriage and late birth" characteristic of the time, I had now passed the age of forty while my son was only ten. I had been through all the turmoil and confusion, whereas his was still to come. My troubles tended to be physical, like the fact that the first northern winter winds had nearly frozen my head off and, worse, I had discovered I was beginning to lose my hair which was, moreover, turning grey. This was not only thoroughly unattractive, but meant I was even less well insulated than before. I considered myself pretty good with my hands; as well as lathing machine parts I could also knit and sew. For some time now I had been planning to knit myself a really good hat and scarf and had even told my husband about it. He had, as a gesture towards financing the project, stubbed out his cigarette. I knew he wouldn't give up permanently, of that I had been convinced from the very first day I met him, no matter what other money-saving hobbies he might dispense with. We also saved by eating less meat at dinner, concentrating our chopsticks on vegetables and hoping our son wouldn't notice the decline.

10   Despite the fact that since the boy's birth cold winds tended to cause a painful throbbing in my head, I could still do without a hat; my old square scarf would suffice, though no doubt I would look odd, like a solemn Arab woman or Mother Hen from the children's cartoon series. But so what? As long as my son could get his beloved robot.

I glanced at the Transformers. They were so expensive that the price of a hat and scarf would be enough to cover maybe the leg of one of the larger models.

And what would my husband say? He had always maintained that spoiled the child and warned me that ours was just an ordinary "blue-collar family" which shouldn't aspire to the same heights of those better-off.

But was it to be the case that no "blue-collar" worker should ever own a Transformer?

I had enough money with me for one of the smallest models available, and knew I could make up a story about the hat and scarf which would satisfy my husband and indicate that I didn't need them.

15   It was at this point, just as I had made up my mind to buy it, that my son suddenly turned towards the exit, saying resolutely, "Mum, let's go. The paper says Transformers are only foreign kids' cast-offs. They move them into China to get our money."

He tugged my hand with his little damp one and glanced back at the toys as though taking a last look at a corpse. Then he quickened his short legs and made for the door as if fearful the Transformers might otherwise snatch him back.

He sounded like an adult, the logic of his argument certainly exceeded anything I might have come up with and it occurred to me that in comparison with our boy, who was, moreover, a model student at school, my husband and I were selfish.

Spurred by this revelation I strode back to the counter and, without giving a second's thought as to who profited by my action, whether foreigners or Hong Kong Chinese, I impulsively took possession of the smallest Transformer money could buy. Suddenly I no longer cared about the pains I would get in my head and neck. This purchase was a token of appreciation for my son's understanding and an expression of our mutual love.

That evening he skipped dinner in order to play with his robot. He put a black toy pistol into its hand and the creature, with a twist and a turn, obligingly turned into an exquisite streamlined bomber. The thermo-colored American trademark turned from red to blue and back to red in his warm little hands.

"Convertible Transformer fights for 20 justice and freedom with an iron will . . ." he sang sweetly. It was the theme song from the TV series.

Although my husband had grumbled, I felt the purchase had been a wise one. True, Transformers were expensive, but the moments of happiness they gave were priceless. In the event of my son growing up to be an important public figure, I didn't want to have to read in his autobiography: I liked toys when I was little but my family was too poor to afford them, so I could only watch the other children playing with theirs. . . .

Of course he might also simply turn out to be a blue-collar worker; either way I was loath to leave him with any regrets about his childhood. Children are, after all, easy to satisfy: the smallest Transformer intoxicates them.

"Don't neglect your homework now," I cautioned in an unusually serious, perhaps overcompensatory, tone of voice. He earnestly promised not to.

Over the next few days I carried out spot checks on his homework and was satisfied to find that he had lost none of his willpower; he allowed himself to play with his toy only after finishing his work.

25 Winter finally arrived with a vengeance.

My husband prolonged his prohibition on cigarettes, and though I tried to reassure him that my old scarf was perfectly adequate, his response was gloomy. "You should have a pair of warm boots," he said.

I gave him a grateful smile and made a face indicating that it was indeed cold down there.

One evening I suddenly found my son playing with a different Transformer; this one was yellow, and much larger and fiercer than his own.

"What's this?" I asked, almost severely. All the guidebooks on "parenting" warned us not to ignore any new tangents a child went off on.

30 "Transformer Giant," he answered calmly, as though discussing a close relative.

Thanks to the protracted TV series, I was equipped with basic knowledge of the Transformer family and I knew that the Giant was one of the principal characters.

Be that as it may, its name was not important to me—its owner was. Without softening my voice I demanded to know whose it was. His reply was matter-of-fact. "One of my classmates," he said, without registering my suspicion. "Almost everybody has one and they're all different, so we trade to play."

Although I felt a slight twinge of guilt about my tone of voice, I couldn't guarantee I wouldn't react in the same way in the future. Dishonesty was above all others the thing I feared most in children and I was constantly on the lookout for it.

The kids were clever. They traded like primitive tribes. It was new phenomenon, and I wasn't sure whether to oppose or support it. "Giant or not," I said to my elated son, "don't let it ruin your school work, and be careful with other people's toys."

He nodded his assent. I could always 35 rely on him to listen.

Somebody was tapping at the door.

My son ran over and hospitably pulled it wide open. But the visitor slowly closed it again as if he wished to remain outside. Presently a round head hesitantly pushed its way through the crack. It was my son's classmate, one who seemed to go by the name of Fatty and who regularly dropped by to get my son to help him with his homework. Only this time Fatty hadn't come for help. He neither entered nor retreated but remained hovering on the threshold facing my son and glancing up at me with a miserable expression on his face. Finally he stammered out in embarrassment, "I'm so sorry . . . I broke your toy. . . ."

The blood drained from my son's cheeks. I had never seen such an agonized look pass across his face. He took the dismantled toy from Fatty, held it before his eyes and blew on it softly, as though it were a wounded pigeon.

After the initial shock had subsided, my son looked at me to rescue him. For one bitter moment the sacrificed hat and scarf flashed across my mind, but there was nothing we could do except face it. Trying to avoid my son's eye, I said, "It's up to you. It's your toy, what do you think we should do?"

Perhaps inhibited by my presence, he 40 remained silent. I therefore discreetly moved into the inner room and listened intently. I could hear Fatty wheezing in the silence and longed to put an end to his misery by running out and saying, "Fatty, you may leave now." But the verdict, whatever it was, had to come from my son.

"How did you smash it?" I heard him ask, with anger in his voice.

"I just . . . then, flop . . ." Fatty must have been gesticulating. An exasperated gurgle appeared to be my son's stifled response.

What was I to do? Maybe I should go out and intervene. Transformers cost money, but magnanimity is something that no amount of money can buy; and although I believed my son had absorbed the moral principles I had instilled in him over the years, I nevertheless recognized that to him a small Transformer was the equivalent of a color TV set or a deluxe camera to an adult. The prolonged silence was agony, for him and for Fatty as well as for me.

Finally he spoke. He seemed to have covered a great deal of mental ground and his voice, though weak, was none the less clear: "Don't worry . . ."

45 Fatty grasped the opportunity and fled, as though afraid that my son might otherwise change his mind.

I heaved a long sigh of relief, as if I too had just returned from a long journey. Emerging, I kissed my son's sweaty forehead.

"It's dead," he said as his eyes filled with tears.

"I'll try and glue it together," I said comfortingly, though with little hope of success.

I duly went flat out to fix it, drawing on all my resources of skill and ingenuity. After spending a great deal more time and effort on it than I would have spent knitting a hat, it finally became recognizable again as a toy. But though it looked all right, it was too delicate to touch and it could no longer change shapes.

50 My son, meanwhile, devoted himself to the Giant. A Transformer should change shape, he said, otherwise it was just a trinket. So saying, he deftly changed the shape of the toy he had in his hand. One has to admire the Americans. Who else would come up with the idea of turning the belly of a fighter into a robot's head and then proceed to create a machine that executes the transition so flawlessly?

A good toy attracts both children and grown-ups, but no sooner had I begun to move closer to watch him play than I heard an ominous crash and saw the toy collapse in pieces.

What had happened? We looked at each other in horror.

Unfortunately, though we could hardly believe it, the truth was all too painfully clear: he had broken the Giant.

For a while my son tried to fix it, but only ended up with more pieces than he had started with. Realizing the situation was hopeless, he gathered the pieces together, wrapped them in a sheet of paper and prepared to leave the house.

"Where are you going?" I asked, still in 55 a state of shock.

"To return the toy and apologize," he said, looking calm and prepared.

"Is it Fatty's?" I asked, with a glimmer of hope.

"No." He then mentioned a name.

Hers! My heart plunged, then leapt into my throat.

The only impression I had ever been 60 able to gain of this girl was that she was like a delicate flower and had a very arrogant mother. The family was well heeled—my husband would call them "wealthy"—and it was entirely natural that they should have bought such a large and ferocious-looking toy for their daughter.

"You're going . . . like this?" I stammered.

"Should I take something with me?" he asked, confused.

I looked at his limpid eyes and refrained from further comment.

"OK, mum, I'm off." He disappeared out the door.

65 "Come home soon," I called after him apprehensively.

I knew he wouldn't dawdle, but he didn't return soon, and when he hadn't returned later either my heart began to flutter like fish on a hook.

I should have warned him that people were all different, that he might not be pardoned, even though he himself had forgiven a similar accident. I should have prepared him better for the possibility of an unpleasant scene, otherwise he might cry.

On the other hand things might turn out OK. His classmate might have asked him hospitably to stay a little, while her mother peeled him an orange, which my son would naturally push back politely. He is a lovable boy. They would surely forgive him in the same manner in which we had forgiven little Fatty.

The more I thought about it the more I convinced myself that that could be the only possible outcome. Moreover I congratulated myself now on not having filled his heart with my own cynical suspicions.

70 But as time passed, no matter how I tried to reassure myself, I grew increasingly concerned.

At last he returned, his footstep so light that, deep in thought as I was, I didn't even notice he was there until he was standing right in front of me.

One look at him was enough to convince me that he had undergone a profound inner trauma. I could also tell that he had been crying and that he had already dried his tears in the cold wind so that I wouldn't notice. A child often reveals more when he is hiding something.

I did not have the heart to get him to go into details; it would have been too painful.

"Mum, they want us . . . to compensate . . ." he said finally, as large, cold teardrops rolled down his cheeks and on to my hand.

I now had to deal not only with a bro- 75 ken toy but with a broken heart.

"It's only natural," I said, wiping away his tears, "that they'd want to be compensated for their loss."

"Then let me go and find Fatty and ask him to compensate me for mine. All he said was 'I'm sorry.' Will that do?" he asked, jumping up to leave.

"Don't go!" I pulled him back. He struggled wildly, suddenly seeming to have acquired the strength of a calf.

"Why, mum? Tell me!" he demanded, lifting his head.

I didn't know how to respond. Some- 80 times principles are all very well and, like beautiful clothes can be very attractive, but they are not the stuff from which clothes are actually made.

I had to give him an answer. It is a cat's responsibility to teach her kitten how to catch mice. I had to provide my son with an explanation, no matter how impractical it might be.

"The words 'I'm sorry' mean you are being courteous. Their value ought not to be counted in terms of money."

He nodded quietly. I probably sounded like one of his teachers, so he forced himself to listen.

"You forgave Fatty when he broke your Transformer," I continued, patiently trying to explain things in terms he would understand. "He was relieved. That was a nice thing to do."

"But, mum, I haven't been forgiven for 85 a similar mistake!" he protested. His sense of shame seemed to override my reasoned arguments.

"Well, son, there are many ways of solving a problem. Problems are like Transformers; they can either be a robot, a plane or a car . . . Understand?"

"Yeah." He nodded reluctantly. I knew he was unconvinced, and just wanted to placate me.

I let go of his hand, exhausted.

He relaxed and stood aside.

90 The large broken toy was going to involve a hideous amount of money, and though we hadn't yet reached the stage where we needed to go to the pawn shop—which our street didn't have anyway—we were still pretty broke.

Sitting on the bad news, we waited for my husband to come home. My son looked at me pitifully. Was he hoping I would not tell him about the incident at all, or hoping I would do it quickly?

I dreaded the prospect, but knew it had to be done, and despite my inclination to postpone the reckoning I knew it would be better in the long run to get it over and done with immediately.

On hearing the news, my husband managed temporarily to retain his composure.

"Tell me," he said calmly, "how did you come to break the thing?" He couldn't bring himself to give it a name.

95 "I just twisted it, and 'flop,' it broke . . ." stammered my son, looking at me appealingly for support. I'd seen it happen, certainly, but I couldn't have said how.

But describing how it broke was in any event unimportant. The consequence was that our son would never again be able to play with such a costly toy.

My husband's eyebrows locked and the ferocity of his expression sent my son scurrying behind me for protection. Suddenly he exploded.

"Tell me," he said, his voice rising in a crescendo, "did you break it on purpose or deliberately?"

I frankly couldn't see what the difference was between "on purpose" and "deliberately," but didn't dare interfere.

100 "I did it . . . on purpose. No, dad, I did it deliberately . . ." Desperately searching for whichever seemed the less incriminating, he lurched from one to the other, shrinking beneath his father's glare.

"You little wretch! A whole month's salary won't pay for this thing, yet you think you can go around lording it like the master of some grand mansion. I'll give you a hiding you'll never forget."

With that he raised his arm, and as it came crashing down I lifted my own to intercept the blow. A blinding pain instantly spread from my side down to my fingers. He was a strong man, a laborer, and it was fortunate I had blocked him.

For a few moments my son was stunned, then he let out a sharp cry, as if it had been he who had been hit.

"You've got a nerve to blubber like that!" shouted my husband, breathing heavily. "That damn thing your mother bought you already cost her her wool hat, and now that! That's our fuel and cabbage for the whole winter gone!" Then he turned to me and added, "It's your fault for spoiling him."

I let him rant. As long as he didn't 105 resort to violence again I could cope. My son had never been beaten before.

That winter, on one particularly freezing day when the sun seemed to be emanating blasts of cold air instead of warmth, I arrived home to find that the stove was barely alight. My son was waiting for me, his face burning red and his eyes glittering like stars reflected in a pool. I was afraid he had a fever.

"Close your eyes, mum," he said. That sweet tone of his voice reassured me that he was not ill.

I closed my eyes quietly. I thought he must have a little surprise for me: a perfect exam paper perhaps, or a toy he might have made out of paper and bottles.

"You can open your eyes now, mum."

I kept my eyes closed, savoring the 110 happy moment that only a mother can experience.

"Quick, mum!" he urged.

I opened my eyes on to what seemed at first like a meadow in springtime. It took me a moment to register that what my son was, in fact, holding in front of me was a bundle of green knitting wool.

"Do you like the color, mum?" he asked, looking at me expectantly.

Green was my favorite.

115 "Yes, very much! How did you know I like it?"

"You must have forgotten. You've always knitted me green clothes ever since I was little. I would be able to pick out the color among a thousand others." He must have wondered how I could even ask such a question.

"Did dad take you there?"

"No, I went by myself," he said proudly.

"Where did you get the money?" I asked in surprise.

120 He didn't answer, but stared at me motionlessly.

He could not have stolen it. The very thought of stealing was anathema to my young son. He must have got the money by recycling used paper or toothpaste tubes, but I hadn't noticed him returning home late with blackened fingers. Well, I'd have to ask him again.

"Tell me, where did you get the money?" I persisted, almost pleading with him to give me a satisfactory answer.

"I asked Fatty for it," he answered clearly.

"You asked who?" I couldn't believe my ears. It was impossible that he could have done something like that. He had always been so obedient.

"Fatty!" he repeated, staring at me 125 resolutely.

A loud buzzing sounded in my head. His bold expression seemed to come from a boy I didn't know.

"How did you get it from him?" I asked in a weak voice.

"The way those other people asked us for it," he said dismissively, as though I was being pernickety.

He saw my hand rise and, thinking I was about to stroke his head, moved in closer. But I slapped him. Remembering, in the split second before my arm descended, an article I had read somewhere warning parents never to hit their children on the head. But it was too late. My hand slanted at an angle and landed on his neck.

He didn't flinch, but merely looked at 130 me in astonishment.

I had never really hit him before, but now I felt certain that this would not be the last time.

Since then, every time a gust of wind pushes open the front door, I expect to see a little fellow with a round head appear. But Fatty has never been back. He paid for our Transformer and left it with us.

I fixed the big one with glue. Its bold appearance added a sense of wealth to our house.

Now we have two Transformers that do not transform.

My son has never touched them again. 135

·····▶*Your* Turn
Talking and Writing about Lit

1. Bi Shumin does an exceptional job of using sensory detail to reveal her characters. Analyze the use of imagery in "Broken Transformers."

2. Explain the use of symbolism in "Broken Transformers."

3. It is an aspect of Bi Shumin's style that she uses a great deal of figurative language. Analyze the use of figures of speech in "Broken Transformers."

4. **DIY** Bi Shumin's story is written from the first-person point of view of the mother. Rewrite any scene in the story from the point of view of the son.

Shirley Jackson (1919–1965)

Shirley Jackson was born in San Francisco and educated at Syracuse University in New York. She lived much of her adult life in Bennington, Vermont, where her husband taught at Bennington College and where she raised their three children. She is known for incorporating gothic elements and violence into her fiction. She has produced a number of lesser-known novels and two story collections, *The Lottery* (1944) and *The Magic of Shirley Jackson* (1966).

The Lottery (1948)

The morning of June 27th was clear and sunny, with the fresh warmth of a full-summer day; the flowers were blossoming profusely and the grass was richly green. The people of the village began to gather in the square, between the post office and the bank, around ten o'clock; in some towns there were so many people that the lottery took two days and had to be started on June 26th, but in this village, where there were only about three hundred people, the whole lottery took less than two hours, so it could begin at ten o'clock in the morning and still be through in time to allow the villagers to get home for noon dinner.

The children assembled first, of course. School was recently over for the summer, and the feeling of liberty sat uneasily on most of them; they tended to gather together quietly for a while before they broke into boisterous play, and their talk was still of the classroom and the teacher, of books and reprimands. Bobby Martin had already stuffed his pockets full of stones, and the other boys soon followed his example, selecting the smoothest and roundest stones; Bobby and Harry Jones and Dickie Delacroix—the villagers pronounced this name "Dellacroy"—eventually made a great pile of stones in one corner of the square and guarded it against the raids of the other boys. The girls stood aside, talking among themselves, looking over their shoulders at the boys, and the very small children rolled in the dust or clung to the hands of their older brothers or sisters.

Soon the men began to gather, surveying their own children, speaking of planting and rain, tractors and taxes. They stood together, away from the pile of stones in the corner, and their jokes were quiet and they smiled rather than laughed. The women, wearing faded house dresses and sweaters, came shortly after their menfolk. They greeted one another and exchanged bits of gossip as they went to join their husbands. Soon the women, standing by their husbands, began to call to their children, and the children came reluctantly, having to be called four or five times. Bobby Martin ducked under his mother's grasping hand and ran, laughing, back to the pile of stones. His father spoke up sharply, and Bobby came quickly and took his place between his father and his oldest brother.

The lottery was conducted—as were the square dances, the teen-age club, the Halloween program—by Mr. Summers, who had time and energy to devote to civic activities. He was a round-faced, jovial man and he ran the coal business, and people were sorry for him, because he had no children and his wife was a scold. When he arrived in the square, carrying the black wooden box, there was a murmur of conversation among the villagers, and he waved and called, "Little late today, folks." The postmaster, Mr. Graves, followed him, carrying a three-legged stool, and the stool was put in the center of the square and Mr. Summers set the black box down on it. The villagers kept their distance, leaving a space between themselves and the stool, and when Mr. Summers said, "Some of you fellows want to give me a hand?" there was a hesitation before two men, Mr. Martin and his oldest son, Baxter, came forward to hold the box steady on the stool while Mr. Summers stirred up the papers inside it.

5   The original paraphernalia for the lottery had been lost long ago, and the black box now resting on the stool had been put into use even before Old Man Warner, the oldest man in town, was born. Mr. Summers spoke frequently to the villagers about making a new box, but no one liked to upset even as much tradition as was represented by the black box. There was a story that the present box had been made with some pieces of the box that had preceded it, the one that had been constructed when the first people settled down to make a village here.

Every year, after the lottery, Mr. Summers began talking again about a new box, but every year the subject was allowed to fade off without anything's being done. The black box grew shabbier each year; by now it was no longer completely black but splintered badly along one side to show the original wood color, and in some places faded or stained.

Mr. Martin and his oldest son, Baxter, held the black box securely on the stool until Mr. Summers had stirred the papers thoroughly with his hand. Because so much of the ritual had been forgotten or discarded, Mr. Summers had been successful in having slips of paper substituted for the chips of wood that had been used for generations. Chips of wood, Mr. Summers had argued, had been all very well when the village was tiny, but now that the population was more than three hundred and likely to keep on growing, it was necessary to use something that would fit more easily into the black box. The night before the lottery, Mr. Summers and Mr. Graves made up the slips of paper and put them in the box, and it was then taken to the safe of Mr. Summers's coal company and locked up until Mr. Summers was ready to take it to the square next morning. The rest of the year, the box was put away, sometimes one place, sometimes another; it had spent one year in Mr. Graves's barn and another year underfoot in the post office, and sometimes it was set on a shelf in the Martin grocery and left there.

There was a great deal of fussing to be done before Mr. Summers declared the lottery open. There were the lists to make up— of heads of families, heads of households in each family, members of each household in each family. There was the proper swearing-in of Mr. Summers by the postmaster, as the official of the lottery; at one time, some people remembered, there had been a recital of some sort, performed by the official of the lottery, a perfunctory, tuneless chant that had been rattled off duly each year; some people believed that the official of the lottery used to stand just so when he said or sang it, others believed that he was supposed to walk among the people, but years and years ago this part of the ritual had been allowed to lapse. There had been, also, a ritual salute, which the official of the lottery had had to use in addressing each person who came up to draw from the box, but this also had changed with time, until now it was felt necessary only for the official to speak to each person approaching. Mr. Summers was very good at all this; in his clean white shirt and blue jeans, with one hand resting carelessly on the black box, he seemed very proper and important as he talked interminably to Mr. Graves and the Martins.

Just as Mr. Summers finally left off talking and turned to the assembled villagers, Mrs. Hutchinson came hurriedly along the path to the square, her sweater thrown over her shoulders, and slid into place in the back of the crowd. "Clean forgot what day it was," she said to Mrs. Delacroix, who stood next to her, and they both laughed softly. "Thought my old man was out back stacking wood," Mrs. Hutchinson went on, "and then I looked out the window and the kids were gone, and then I remembered it was the twenty-seventh and came a-running." She dried her hands on her apron, and Mrs. Delacroix said, "You're in time, though. They're still talking away up there."

Mrs. Hutchinson craned her neck to see through the crowd and found her husband and children standing near the front. She tapped Mrs. Delacroix on the arm as a farewell and began to make her way through the crowd. The people separated good-humoredly to let her through; two or three people said, in voices just loud enough to be heard across the crowd, "Here comes your Missus, Hutchinson," and "Bill, she made it

after all." Mrs. Hutchinson reached her husband, and Mr. Summers, who had been waiting, said cheerfully, "Thought we were going to have to get on without you, Tessie." Mrs. Hutchinson said, grinning, "Wouldn't have me leave m'dishes in the sink, now, would you, Joe?" and soft laughter ran through the crowd as the people stirred back into position after Mrs. Hutchinson's arrival.

"Well, now," Mr. Summers said 10 soberly, "guess we better get started, get this over with, so's we can go back to work. Anybody ain't here?"

"Dunbar," several people said. "Dunbar, Dunbar."

Mr. Summers consulted his list. "Clyde Dunbar," he said. "That's right. He's broke his leg, hasn't he? Who's drawing for him?"

"Me, I guess," a woman said, and Mr. Summers turned to look at her. "Wife draws for her husband," Mr. Summers said. "Don't you have a grown boy to do it for you, Janey?" Although Mr. Summers and everyone else in the village knew the answer perfectly well, it was the business of the official of the lottery to ask such questions formally. Mr. Summers waited with an expression of polite interest while Mrs. Dunbar answered.

"Horace's not but sixteen yet," Mrs. Dunbar said regretfully. "Guess I gotta fill in for the old man this year."

"Right," Mr. Summers said. He made a 15 note on the list he was holding. Then he asked, "Watson boy drawing this year?"

A tall boy in the crowd raised his hand. "Here," he said. "I'm drawing for m'mother and me." He blinked his eyes nervously and ducked his head as several voices in the crowd said things like "Good fellow, Jack," and "Glad to see your mother's got a man to do it."

"Well," Mr. Summers said, "guess that's everyone. Old Man Warner make it?"

"Here," a voice said, and Mr. Summers nodded.

A sudden hush fell on the crowd as Mr. Summers cleared his throat and looked at the list. "All ready?" he called. "Now, I'll read the names—heads of families first—and the men come up and take a paper out of the box. Keep the paper folded in your hand without looking at it until everyone has had a turn. Everything clear?"

20 The people had done it so many times that they only half listened to the directions; most of them were quiet, wetting their lips, not looking around. Then Mr. Summers raised one hand high and said, "Adams." A man disengaged himself from the crowd and came forward. "Hi, Steve," Mr. Summers said, and Mr. Adams said, "Hi, Joe." They grinned at one another humorlessly and nervously. Then Mr. Adams reached into the black box and took out a folded paper. He held it firmly by one corner as he turned and went hastily back to his place in the crowd, where he stood a little apart from his family, not looking down at his hand.

"Allen," Mr. Summers said. "Anderson . . . Bentham."

"Seems like there's no time at all between lotteries any more," Mrs. Delacroix said to Mrs. Graves in the back row. "Seems like we got through with the last one only last week."

"Time sure goes fast," Mrs. Graves said.

"Clark . . . Delacroix."

25 "There goes my old man," Mrs. Delacroix said. She held her breath while her husband went forward.

"Dunbar," Mr. Summers said, and Mrs. Dunbar went steadily to the box while one of the women said, "Go on, Janey," and another said, "There she goes."

"We're next," Mrs. Graves said. She watched while Mr. Graves came around from the side of the box, greeted Mr. Summers gravely, and selected a slip of paper from the box. By now, all through the crowd there were men holding the small folded papers in their large hands, turning them over and over nervously. Mrs. Dunbar and her two sons stood together, Mrs. Dunbar holding the slip of paper.

"Harburt . . . Hutchinson."

"Get up there, Bill," Mrs. Hutchinson said, and the people near her laughed.

"Jones." 30

"They do say," Mr. Adams said to Old Man Warner, who stood next to him, "that over in the north village they're talking of giving up the lottery."

Old Man Warner snorted. "Pack of crazy fools," he said. "Listening to the young folks, nothing's good enough for *them*. Next thing you know, they'll be wanting to go back to living in caves, nobody work any more, live *that* way for a while. Used to be a saying about 'Lottery in June, corn be heavy soon.' First thing you know, we'd all be eating stewed chickweed and acorns. There's *always* been a lottery," he added petulantly. "Bad enough to see young Joe Summers up there joking with everybody."

"Some places have already quit lotteries," Mrs. Adams said.

"Nothing but trouble in *that*," Old Man Warner said stoutly. "Pack of young fools."

"Martin." And Bobby Martin watched 35 his father go forward. "Overdyke . . . Percy."

"I wish they'd hurry," Mrs. Dunbar said to her older son. "I wish they'd hurry."

"They're almost through," her son said.

"You get ready to run tell Dad," Mrs. Dunbar said.

Mr. Summers called his own name and then stepped forward precisely and selected a slip from the box. Then he called, "Warner."

"Seventy-seventh year I been in the 40 lottery," Old Man Warner said as he went through the crowd. "Seventy-seventh time."

"Watson." The tall boy came awkwardly through the crowd. Someone said, "Don't be nervous, Jack," and Mr. Summers said, "Take your time, son."

"Zanini."

After that, there was a long pause, a breathless pause, until Mr. Summers, holding his slip of paper in the air, said, "All right, fellows." For a minute, no one moved, and then all the slips of paper were opened. Suddenly, all the women began to speak at once, saying, "Who is it?" "Who's got it?" "Is it the Dunbars?" "Is it the Watsons?" Then the voices began to say, "It's Hutchinson. It's Bill." "Bill Hutchinson's got it."

"Go tell your father," Mrs. Dunbar said to her older son.

45   People began to look around to see the Hutchinsons. Bill Hutchinson was standing quiet, staring down at the paper in his hand. Suddenly, Tessie Hutchinson shouted to Mr. Summers. "You didn't give him time enough to take any paper he wanted. I saw you. It wasn't fair."

"Be a good sport, Tessie," Mrs. Delacroix called, and Mrs. Graves said, "All of us took the same chance."

"Shut up, Tessie," Bill Hutchinson said.

"Well, everyone," Mr. Summers said, "that was done pretty fast, and now we've got to be hurrying a little more to get done in time." He consulted his next list. "Bill," he said, "you draw for the Hutchinson family. You got any other households in the Hutchinsons?"

"There's Don and Eva," Mrs. Hutchinson yelled. "Make *them* take their chance!"

50   "Daughters draw with their husband's families, Tessie," Mr. Summers said gently. "You know that as well as anyone else."

"It wasn't *fair*," Tessie said.

"I guess not, Joe," Bill Hutchinson said regretfully. "My daughter draws with her husband's family, that's only fair. And I've got no other family except the kids."

"Then, as far as drawing for families is concerned, it's you," Mr. Summers said in explanation, "and as far as drawing for households is concerned, that's you, too. Right?"

"Right," Bill Hutchinson said.

"How many kids, Bill?" Mr. Summers   55 asked formally.

"Three," Bill Hutchinson said. "There's Bill, Jr., and Nancy, and little Dave. And Tessie and me."

"All right, then," Mr. Summers said. "Harry, you got their tickets back?"

Mr. Graves nodded and held up the slips of paper. "Put them in the box, then," Mr. Summers directed. "Take Bill's and put it in."

"I think we ought to start over," Mrs. Hutchinson said, as quietly as she could. "I tell you it wasn't *fair*. You didn't give him time enough to choose. *Every*body saw that."

Mr. Graves had selected the five slips   60 and put them in the box, and he dropped all the papers but those onto the ground, where the breeze caught them and lifted them off.

"Listen, everybody," Mrs. Hutchinson was saying to the people around her.

"Ready, Bill?" Mr. Summers asked, and Bill Hutchinson, with one quick glance around at his wife and children, nodded.

"Remember," Mr. Summers said, "take the slips and keep them folded until each person has taken one. Harry, you help little Dave." Mr. Graves took the hand of the little boy, who came willingly with him up to the box. "Take a paper out of the box, Davy," Mr. Summers said. Davy put his hand into the box and laughed. "Take just *one* paper," Mr. Summers said. "Harry, you hold it for him." Mr. Graves took the child's hand and removed the folded paper from the tight fist and held it while little Dave stood next to him and looked up at him wonderingly.

"Nancy next," Mr. Summers said. Nancy was twelve, and her school friends breathed heavily as she went forward, switching her skirt, and took a slip daintily from the box. "Bill, Jr.," Mr. Summers said, and Billy, his face red and his feet over-large, nearly knocked the box over as he got a paper out. "Tessie," Mr. Summers said. She hesitated for a minute, looking around defiantly, and then set her lips and went up to the box. She snatched a paper out and held it behind her.

65 "Bill," Mr. Summers said, and Bill Hutchinson reached into the box and felt around, bringing his hand out at last with the slip of paper in it.

The crowd was quiet. A girl whispered, "I hope it's not Nancy," and the sound of the whisper reached the edges of the crowd.

"It's not the way it used to be," Old Man Warner said clearly. "People ain't the way they used to be."

"All right," Mr. Summers said. "Open the papers. Harry, you open little Dave's."

Mr. Graves opened the slip of paper and there was a general sigh through the crowd as he held it up and everyone could see that it was blank. Nancy and Bill, Jr., opened theirs at the same time, and both beamed and laughed, turning around to the crowd and holding their slips of paper above their heads.

70 "Tessie," Mr. Summers said. There was a pause, and then Mr. Summers looked at Bill Hutchinson, and Bill unfolded his paper and showed it. It was blank.

"It's Tessie," Mr. Summers said, and his voice was hushed. "Show us her paper, Bill."

Bill Hutchinson went over to his wife and forced the slip of paper out of her hand. It had a black spot on it, the black spot Mr. Summers had made the night before with the heavy pencil in the coal-company office. Bill Hutchinson held it up, and there was a stir in the crowd.

"All right, folks," Mr. Summers said. "Let's finish quickly."

Although the villagers had forgotten the ritual and lost the original black box, they still remembered to use stones. The pile of stones the boys had made earlier was ready; there were stones on the ground with the blowing scraps of paper that had come out of the box. Mrs. Delacroix selected a stone so large she had to pick it up with both hands and turned to Mrs. Dunbar. "Come on," she said. "Hurry up."

Mrs. Dunbar had small stones in both 75 hands, and she said, gasping for breath, "I can't run at all. You'll have to go ahead and I'll catch up with you."

The children had stones already, and someone gave little Davy Hutchinson a few pebbles.

Tessie Hutchinson was in the center of a cleared space by now, and she held her hands out desperately as the villagers moved in on her. "It isn't fair," she said. A stone hit her on the side of the head.

Old Man Warner was saying, "Come on, come on, everyone." Steve Adams was in front of the crowd of villagers, with Mrs. Graves beside him.

"It isn't fair, it isn't right," Mrs. Hutchinson screamed, and then they were upon her.

·····▶*Your* **Turn**
Talking and Writing about Lit

1. Are there any symbolic characters in "The Lottery"? What function does Old Man Warner serve? Are there any symbolic objects in the story?

2. Most people attribute positive associations to the word "lottery," expecting that a lottery will involve the bestowing of some sort of prize. Why does Shirley Jackson deliberately mislead the reader to expect a positive outcome?

3. Does the story contain any foreshadowing of its horrific ending?

4. **DIY** Part of the story's eeriness is achieved through the use of objective narration (we do not have access to the minds of any of the characters). Try rewriting a portion of the story from the point of view of a first-person narrator. Choose a character through whose eyes you'd like to re-imagine the story.

Talking Lit

In this "Talking Lit" section, Shirley Jackson writes about the rather startling public reaction to her startling story.

Shirley Jackson, Public Reception of "The Lottery"

On the morning of June 28, 1948, I walked down to the post office in our little Vermont town to pick up the mail. I was quite casual about it, as I recall—I opened the box, took out a couple of bills and a letter or two, talked to the postmaster for a few minutes, and left, never supposing that it was the last time for months that I was to pick up the mail without an active feeling of panic. By the next week I had had to change my mailbox to the largest one in the post office, and casual conversation with the postmaster was out of the question, because he wasn't speaking to me. June 28, 1948, was the day *The New Yorker* came out with a story of mine in it. It was not my first published story, nor my last, but I have been assured over and over that if it had been the only story I ever wrote or published, there would be people who would not forget my name.

I had written the story three weeks before, on a bright June morning when summer seemed to have come at last, with blue skies and warm sun and no heavenly signs to warn me that my morning's work was anything but just another story. The idea had come to me while I was pushing my daughter up the hill in her stroller—it was, as I say, a warm morning, and the hill was steep, and beside my daughter the stroller held the day's groceries—and perhaps the effort of that last fifty yards up the hill put an edge to the story; at any rate, I had the idea fairly clearly in my mind when I put my daughter in her playpen and the frozen vegetables in the refrigerator, and, writing the story, I found that it went quickly and easily, moving from beginning to end without pause. As a matter of fact, when I read it over later I decided that except for one or two minor corrections, it needed no changes, and the story I finally typed up and sent off to my agent the next day was almost word for word the original draft. This, as any writer of stories can tell you, is not a usual thing. All I know is that when I came to read the story over I felt strongly that I didn't want to fuss with it. It was, I thought, a serious, straightforward story, and I was pleased and a little surprised at the ease with which it had been written; I was reasonably proud of it, and hoped that my agent would sell it to some magazine and I would have the gratification of seeing it in print.

My agent did not care for the story, but—as she said in her note at the time— her job was to sell it, not to like it. She sent it at once to *The New Yorker*, and about a week after the story had been written I received a telephone call from the fiction editor of *The New Yorker*; it was quite clear that he did not really care for the story, either, but *The New Yorker* was going to buy it. He asked for one change—that the date mentioned in the story be changed to coincide with the date of the issue of the magazine in which the story would appear, and I said of course. He then asked, hesitantly, if I had any particular interpretation of my own for the story; Mr. Harold Ross, then the editor of *The New Yorker*, was not altogether sure that he understood the story, and wondered if I cared to enlarge upon its meaning. I said no. Mr. Ross, he said, thought that the story might be puzzling to some people, and in case anyone telephoned the magazine, as sometimes happened, or wrote in asking about the story, was there anything in particular I wanted them to say? No, I said, nothing in particular; it was just a story I wrote.

I had no more preparation than that. I went on picking up the mail every morning, pushing my daughter up and down the hill in her stroller, anticipating pleasurably the check from *The New Yorker*, and shopping for groceries. The weather stayed nice and it looked as thought it was going to be a good summer. Then, on June 28, *The New Yorker* came out with my story.

Things began mildly enough with a note from a friend at *The New Yorker*: "Your story has kicked up quite a fuss around the office," he wrote. I was flattered; it's nice to think that your friends notice what you write. Later that day there was a call from one of the magazine's editors; they had had a couple of people phone in about my story, he said, and was there anything I particularly wanted him to say if there were any more calls? No, I said, nothing particular; anything he chose to say was perfectly all right with me; it was just a story.

I was further puzzled by a cryptic note from another friend: "Heard a man talking about a story of yours on the bus this morning," she wrote. "Very exciting. I wanted to tell him I knew the author, but after I heard what he was saying I decided I'd better not."

One of the most terrifying aspects of publishing stories and books is the realization that they are going to be read, and read by strangers. I had never fully realized this before, although I had of course in my imagination dwelt lovingly upon the thought of the millions and millions of people who were going to be uplifted and enriched and delighted by the stories I wrote. It had simply never occurred to me that these millions and millions of people might be so far from being uplifted that they would sit down and write me letters I was downright scared to open; of the three-hundred-odd letters that I received that summer I can count only thirteen that spoke kindly to me, and they were mostly from friends. Even my mother scolded me: "Dad and I did not care at all for your story in *The New Yorker*," she wrote sternly, "it does seem, dear, that this gloomy kind of story is what all you young people think about these days. Why don't you write something to cheer people up?"

By mid-July I had begun to perceive that I was very lucky indeed to be safely in Vermont, where no one in our small town had ever heard of *The New Yorker*, much less read my story. Millions of people, and my mother, had taken a pronounced dislike to me.

The magazine kept no track of telephone calls, but all letters addressed to me care of the magazine were forwarded directly to me for answering, and all letters addressed to the magazine—some of them addressed to Harold Ross personally; these were the most vehement—were answered at the magazine and then the letters were sent me in great batches, along with carbons of the answers written at the magazine. I have all the letters still, and if they could be considered to give any accurate cross section of the reading public, or the reading public of *The New Yorker*, or even the reading public of one issue of *The New Yorker*, I would stop writing now.

Judging from these letters, people who read stories are gullible, rude, frequently illiterate, and horribly afraid of being laughed at. Many of the writers were positive that *The New Yorker* was going to ridicule them in print, and the most cautious letters were headed, in capital letters: NOT FOR PUBLICATION or PLEASE DO NOT PRINT THIS LETTER, or, at best, THIS LETTER MAY BE PUBLISHED AT YOUR USUAL RATES OF PAYMENT. Anonymous letters, of which there were a few, were destroyed. *The New Yorker* never published any comment of any kind about the story in the magazine, but did issue one publicity release saying that the story had received more mail than any piece of fiction they had ever published; this was after the newspapers had gotten into the act, in midsummer, with a front-page story in the San Francisco *Chronicle* begging to know what the story meant, and a series of columns in New York and Chicago papers pointing out that *New Yorker* subscriptions were being canceled right and left.

Curiously, there are three main themes which dominate the letters of that first summer—three themes which might be identified as bewilderment, speculation, and plain old-fashioned abuse. In the years since then, during which the story has been anthologized, dramatized, televised, and even—in one completely mystifying transformation—made into a ballet, the tenor of letters I receive has changed. I am addressed more politely, as a rule, and the letters largely confine themselves to questions like what does this story mean? The general tone of the early letters, however, was a kind of wide-eyed, shocked innocence. People at first were not so much concerned with what the story meant; what they wanted to know was where these lotteries were held, and whether they could go there and watch.

Student Essay

Of these two stories, student author Anita Shoup writes, "The authors seem to agree that when an individual or individuals are operating outside the bounds of reasonable behavior, most people will continue to play by the rules, and this will place them at a distinct disadvantage." Read Anita's interesting essay, "Fine Manners in the Face of Death: Shirley Jackson's 'The Lottery' and Flannery O'Connor's 'A Good Man Is Hard to Find,'" in Chapter 32.

MYTH AND FICTION

Even products use myth.

Nike, goddess of victory in Greek mythology, fought the god Zeus in her battle against the Titans. In Greek art she is sometimes represented as winged and carrying a wreath or palm of victory. She was chosen by one of the most successful tennis shoe companies in the world as the symbol of their products. In name and in logo, the company assumed the persona of the goddess. The famous Nike Swoosh Design logo was carefully crafted to echo the sleek, clean wing of the goddess winner. The company's hope, we might assume, is that consumers would associate Nike products with the strength, speed, and victory of Nike the goddess.

Mythological symbols are often used by corporations to help them establish an image, and with good reason. In addition to the particular heroic qualities of the Greek gods, consider the nature of myth in general: Myths are stories of universal appeal that offer some explanation or context for humanity's great themes. They transcend cultural, social, geographical, and temporal boundaries. Often, mythological symbols evoke those qualities, and companies use those symbols so that consumers will associate those qualities with the company and its products.

Myths are All Around Us

Myths are everywhere around us and are more familiar than we may realize, as shown in the pictures on the previous pages. As you read through the stories in this chapter, you may have a growing sense of how much you already know about **myth** through encounters with mythic stories and elements in everyday life. Myths are simply the stories we human beings have told ourselves to help us explain our world—the social context as well as the natural world. Some of these stories are also part of religious scriptures (from various of the world's religions), and some contain elements of magic, imagination, history, or moral or cultural teachings. They may also contain profound spiritual, social, or philosophical truths—but profound thoughts are made enjoyable by being embedded in a story.

What is Myth?

The impulse to create myths and stories to explain and illuminate our world is universal. Mythologists (people who study myths) and anthropologists (people who study human cultures and human development) have learned that these stories are created in every culture on earth and have been told since human beings learned how to communicate in language. Even before written language, mythic stories were part of the oral traditions of all human cultures. Myth crosses all cultural and religious boundaries, and it also crosses all disciplines (branches of knowledge and study). It relates to literature, languages, and linguistics (the study of language), sociology, anthropology, psychology, religion, history, philosophy, ethics, cosmology, astronomy, and even geology. These latter items on our list might seem far-fetched, but just consider what similar questions the cosmologist (a scientist who studies the nature and origins of the universe) and the theologian (a person who studies religions) ask. They both want to know (and have theories and beliefs about) how the world was created and how human life came to exist on the earth. Science and religion and mythology examine many of the same questions, questions we puzzle about as human beings in our everyday lives, as you will see in the stories that follow.

Mythic Patterns and Archetypes

The word **archetype** (in the context of mythology) is often used to refer to cross-cultural story patterns, or basic types of stories and concepts which recur in many different cultures. For example, peoples all over the earth tell stories about the creation of the world, of the hero's quest, of death and rebirth, of a supreme being or beings, of initiation (or coming-of-age), of the apocalypse (end of the world), and the afterlife. Flood stories (such as the story of Noah in Judeo-Christian scriptures) are also common to almost all cultures. The idea of the archetype, originally used by psychologist Carl Jung to signify the "collective unconscious" of humankind (our common dreams, elemental concepts, and stories), has influenced a number of fields of study, including the study of mythology.

In Gabriel García Márquez's story "A Very Old Man with Enormous Wings" (in this chapter), you will find an example of the archetypal pattern of death and rebirth, decay and renewal. When the angel (or the very old man with enormous wings) arrives, the newborn child has a dangerous fever, and the "neighbor woman who knew everything about life and death" believes his appearance means that the child is dying. "'He's an angel,' she told them. 'He must have been coming for the child, but the poor fellow is so old that the rain knocked him down'" (paragraph 3). However, this "wise" neighbor woman (like all of the other apparent authority figures in the story) turns out, ironically, not to be so wise. In the very next paragraph, we learn that the child has survived: "A short time afterward the child woke up without a fever and with a desire to eat." In addition, of course, the angel himself ends up near death and experiences a rebirth at the end of the story, ascending into the sky and flying over the houses and off into the horizon. Another familiar pattern in the story is that of the stranger in the community—the outsider and society. When the angel arrives and cannot speak their language (the villagers speak Spanish and the angel speaks Norwegian), how do the people treat this strange newcomer?

When Nathaniel Hawthorne's Young Goodman Brown (whom you'll read about in this chapter) ventures into the wilderness, he is undertaking a journey familiar to students of mythology—the journey quest of the hero. In this story pattern, common to all cultures, the hero (or heroine) journeys into the woods or the desert or the underworld. The hero's quest may involve a search for truth, for a lost loved one, for justice, or for eternal life, and in the end, the hero may succeed or he may fail. In "Young Goodman Brown," the wilderness into which the main character travels is a forest, which represents a moral wilderness that will present the hero with profound questions of good and evil. Hawthorne's description of the woods themselves indicates to us that his character has embarked on a dangerous path:

> He had taken a dreary road, darkened by all the gloomiest trees of the forest, which barely stood aside to let the narrow path creep through, and closed immediately behind. It was all as lonely as could be; and there is this peculiarity in such a solitude, that the traveler knows not who may be concealed by the innumerable trunks and the thick boughs overhead, so that with lonely footsteps he may be passing through an unseen multitude. (paragraph 8)

It is a moral wilderness indeed, and in it Brown soon confronts, perhaps, the devil himself. We say "perhaps" because many of this story's characters and events are invested with ambiguity. The traveler resembles the devil, but he also resembles Goodman's own father or grandfather. Also ambiguous is the traveler's staff (walking stick), "which bore the likeness of a great black snake, so curiously wrought that it might almost be seen to twist and wriggle itself like a living serpent. This, of course, must have been an ocular deception, assisted by the uncertain light" (paragraph 13). It might just be a walking staff, or it might be a snake (a creature often used to represent the devil or evil).

The Hero's Odyssey

As you read John Cheever's "The Swimmer" (in this chapter), watch for mythological references, and watch for the pattern of the hero's journey. The hero, Neddy Merrill, "had slid down his banister that morning and given the bronze backside of Aphrodite [Greek goddess of love] on the hall table a smack, as he jogged toward the smell of coffee in his dining room" (paragraph 2). Before beginning his journey, he imagines "that string of swimming pools, that quasi-subterranean stream that curved across the county" (paragraph 3). The mythical hero's quest often takes him into the subterranean, the underworld. This is true of such well-known mythological figures as the Greek Herakles (Roman name, Hercules), the Greek Orpheus, and the Mesopotamian Gilgamesh. But it is also true of many heroes and heroines lesser-known in the West—for example, the African heroine Wanjiru whose journey to the underworld helps save her people, and the Egyptian goddess Isis who travels to the underworld (and undertakes many other treacherous journeys) to rescue her husband, Osiris. In "The Swimmer," mythological allusions (references to mythic elements) abound. We are also told, in the same paragraph in which Neddy imagines his "subterranean" journey, that he "had a vague and modest idea of himself as a legendary figure."

More than any other myth, though, Neddy's journey resembles *The Odyssey*, the Greek poet Homer's story of the hero Odysseus (Roman name, Ulysses) and his long journey home from the Trojan War. Like Neddy's trip on the "Lucinda River" or the "subterranean stream," Odysseus's journey is over water, and along the way, he encounters numerous obstacles and adventures, including monsters, storms, and seductresses. Just as Odysseus tries to make his way home to Penelope, Neddy intends to swim back to Lucinda. It takes Odysseus ten long years to get home, but the duration of Neddy's journey is ambiguous. In a sense, it takes him one day, but we also recognize somewhere midway that his journey also represents the course of his entire life and the seasons of his life's passage.

Myths—Borderless and Timeless Stories

As well as having no cultural boundaries—emerging in astonishingly similar forms all over the earth—archetypal story patterns are also timeless. The same story patterns, which have existed and evolved throughout human history, were known in oral form long before they were recorded in written language. Some of these patterns have been around since the Egyptian Pyramid Texts (as early as 3000 B.C.E.), the Mesopotamian *Gilgamesh Epic* (fragments of the story have been found in writings on clay tablets dated as early as 2000 B.C.E.), the early writings of the Hebrew writers (fragments of Genesis may have been written down as early as 950 B.C.E.), and the works of Homer (as early as 900 B.C.E.). These early writings contain quest stories, stories of the hero's or heroine's journey, kidnapping and rescue (also called captivity narratives), death and rebirth, journey through the underworld, initiation of the young person, and many other patterns that are still prominent story patterns in modern literature as well as in such popular forms as movies, comic books, and video games.

In her story "Yellow Woman" (in this chapter), Leslie Marmon Silko incorporates the Yellow Woman, or Kochininako, stories of her Laguna Pueblo Native American ancestors. They are not just stories of the ancestors; they are stories while Silko heard as a girl growing up on the Laguna reservation west of Albuquerque, New Mexico. In "Yellow Woman," she represents the timelessness of myths and legends through the use of ambiguity. In a very real sense, we (the readers) do not know whether the myth is a thing of the past or whether the main character (Yellow Woman) is living the myth in the present day. Myth and present-day reality (and ordinary present-day details) are woven together in an intriguing story which appears to take place in two realms at once. At one moment Yellow Woman (our first-person narrator) is relating stories her grandpa told her—"My old grandpa liked to tell those stories best. There is one about Badger and Coyote who went hunting"—and the next moment, we're suddenly in the present time of the story, encountering things that are happening to the narrator right then and there! In the same paragraph quoted above, we read that in the Grandpa's story, Badger and Coyote find a house in which a girl is living (she is the Yellow Woman of the myth). Since Coyote likes her and wants to be with her, he persuades Badger to crawl into a hole in the ground, telling him that "he saw something in it":

> As soon as Badger crawled in, Coyote blocked up the entrance with rocks and hurried back to Yellow Woman.
>
> "Come here," he said gently.
>
> He touched my neck and I moved close to him to feel his breathing and to hear his heart. I was wondering if Yellow Woman had known who she was—if she knew that she would become part of the stories. (paragraphs 19–21)

As we read this, we are wondering whether the narrator has become part of the stories herself, part of the legend of Yellow Woman. The same ambiguity is created around the character of Silva—is he a Navajo named Silva who steals cattle from the ranchers in the present day, or is he a "ka'tsina" spirit, as told of in the ancient myths? The story doesn't say for sure, and the implication is that he is both and that he exists in the present as well as the past. Another implication of the story is that the old myths are still very much alive.

Readings

Gabriel García Márquez (b. 1928)

Born in the small coastal town of Aracataca, Colombia, Gabriel García Márquez has spent most of his writing life in Mexico City. He is widely credited with being the "father of magical realism," and his 1967 novel *One Hundred Years of Solitude* is the most widely read example of that school (a style of writing in which magical or fantastical details exist side by side with realistic, everyday details). He published a collection of short stories entitled *Leaf Storm and Other Stories* in 1955. His other novels include *The Autumn of the Patriarch* (1975), *Chronicle of a Death Foretold* (1981), and *Love in the Time of Cholera* (1985). García Márquez received the Nobel Prize for Literature in 1982.

A Very Old Man with Enormous Wings (1955)

On the third day of rain they had killed so many crabs inside the house that Pelayo had to cross his drenched courtyard and throw them into the sea, because the newborn child had a temperature all night and they thought it was due to the stench. The world had been sad since Tuesday. Sea and sky were a single ash-gray thing and the sands of the beach, which on March nights glimmered like powdered light, had become a stew of mud and rotten shellfish. The light was so weak at noon that when Pelayo was coming back to the house after throwing away the crabs, it was hard for him to see what it was that was moving and groaning in the rear of the courtyard. He had to go very close to see that it was an old man, a very old man, lying face down in the mud, who, in spite of his tremendous efforts, couldn't get up, impeded by his enormous wings.

Frightened by that nightmare, Pelayo ran to get Elisenda, his wife, who was putting compresses on the sick child, and he took her to the rear of the courtyard. They both looked at the fallen body with mute stupor. He was dressed like a ragpicker. There were only a few faded hairs left on his bald skull and very few teeth in his mouth, and his pitiful condition of a drenched great-grandfather had taken away any sense of grandeur he might have had. His huge buzzard wings, dirty and half-plucked, were forever entangled in the mud. They looked at him so long and so closely that Pelayo and Elisenda very soon overcame their surprise and in the end found him familiar. Then they dared speak to him, and he answered in an incomprehensible dialect with a strong sailor's voice. That was how they skipped over the inconvenience of the wings and quite intelligently concluded that he was a lonely castaway from some foreign ship wrecked by the storm. And yet, they called in a neighbor woman who knew everything about life and death to see him, and all she needed was one look to show them their mistake.

"He's an angel," she told them. "He must have been coming for the child, but the poor fellow is so old that the rain knocked him down."

On the following day everyone knew that a flesh-and-blood angel was held captive in Pelayo's house. Against the judgment of the wise neighbor woman, for whom angels in those times were the fugitive survivors of a celestial conspiracy, they did not have the heart to club him to death. Pelayo watched over him all afternoon from the kitchen, armed with his bailiff's club, and before going to bed he dragged him out of the mud and locked him up with the hens in the wire chicken coop. In the middle of the night, when the rain stopped, Pelayo and Elisenda were still killing crabs. A short time afterward the child woke up without a fever and with a desire to eat. Then they felt magnanimous and decided to put the angel on a raft with fresh water and provisions for three days and leave him to his fate on the high seas. But when they went out into the courtyard with the first light of dawn, they found the whole neighborhood in front of the chicken coop having fun with the angel, without the slightest reverence, tossing him things to eat through the openings in the wire as if he weren't a supernatural creature but a circus animal.

5   Father Gonzaga arrived before seven o'clock, alarmed at the strange news. By that time onlookers less frivolous than those at dawn had already arrived and they were making all kinds of conjectures concerning the captive's future. The simplest among them thought that he should be named mayor of the world. Others of sterner mind felt that he should be promoted to the rank of five-star general in order to win all wars. Some visionaries hoped that he could be put to stud in order to implant on earth a race of winged wise men who could take charge of the universe. But Father Gonzaga, before

becoming a priest, had been a robust woodcutter. Standing by the wire, he reviewed his catechism in an instant and asked them to open the door so that he could take a close look at that pitiful man who looked more like a huge decrepit hen among the fascinated chickens. He was lying in a corner drying his open wings in the sunlight among the fruit peels and breakfast leftovers that the early risers had thrown him. Alien to the impertinences of the world, he only lifted his antiquarian eyes and murmured something in his dialect when Father Gonzaga went into the chicken coop and said good morning to him in Latin. The parish priest had his first suspicion of an imposter when he saw that he did not understand the language of God or know how to greet His ministers. Then he noticed that seen close up he was much too human: he had an unbearable smell of the outdoors, the back side of his wings was strewn with parasites and his main feathers had been mistreated by terrestrial winds, and nothing about him measured up to the proud dignity of angels. Then he came out of the chicken coop and in a brief sermon warned the curious against the risks of being ingenuous. He reminded them that the devil had the bad habit of making use of carnival tricks in order to confuse the unwary. He argued that if wings were not the essential element in determining the difference between a hawk and an airplane, they were even less so in the recognition of angels. Nevertheless, he promised to write a letter to his bishop so that the latter would write to his primate so that the latter would write to the Supreme Pontiff in order to get the final verdict from the highest courts.

His prudence fell on sterile hearts. The news of the captive angel spread with such rapidity the after a few hours the courtyard had the bustle of a marketplace and they had to call in troops with fixed bayonets to disperse the mob that was about to knock the house down. Elisenda, her spine all twisted from sweeping up so much marketplace trash, then got the idea of fencing in the yard and charging five cents admission to see the angel.

The curious came from far away. A traveling carnival arrived with a flying acrobat who buzzed over the crowd several times, but no one paid any attention to him because his wings were not those of an angel but, rather, those of a sidereal bat. The most unfortunate invalids on earth came in search of health: a poor woman who since childhood had been counting her heartbeats and had run out of numbers; a Portuguese man who couldn't sleep because the noise of the stars disturbed him; a sleepwalker who got up at night to undo the things he had done while awake; and many others with less serious ailments. In the midst of that shipwreck disorder that made the earth tremble, Pelayo and Elisenda were happy with fatigue, for in less than a week they had crammed their rooms with money and the line of pilgrims waiting their turn to enter still reached beyond the horizon.

The angel was the only one who took no part in his own act. He spent his time trying to get comfortable in his borrowed nest, befuddled by the hellish heat of the oil lamps and sacramental candles that had been placed along the wire. At first they tried to make him eat some mothballs, which, according to the wisdom of the wise neighbor woman, were the food prescribed for angels. But he turned them down, just as he turned down the papal lunches that the penitents brought him, and they never found out whether it was because he was an angel or because he was an old man that in the end he ate nothing but eggplant mush. His only supernatural virtue seemed to be patience. Especially during the first days, when the hens pecked at him, searching for the stellar parasites that proliferated in his wings, and

the cripples pulled out feathers to touch their defective parts with, and even the most merciful threw stones at him, trying to get him to rise so they could see him standing. The only time they succeeded in arousing him was when they burned his side with an iron for branding steers, for he had been motionless for so many hours that they thought he was dead. He awoke with a start, ranting in his hermetic language and with tears in his eyes, and he flapped his wings a couple of times, which brought on a whirlwind of chicken dung and lunar dust and a gale of panic that did not seem to be of this world. Although many thought that his reaction had been one not of rage but of pain, from then on they were careful not to annoy him, because the majority understood that his passivity was not that of a hero taking his ease but that of a cataclysm in repose.

Father Gonzaga held back the crowd's frivolity with formulas of maidservant inspiration while awaiting the arrival of a final judgment on the nature of the captive. But the mail from Rome showed no sense of urgency. They spent their time finding out if the prisoner had a navel, if his dialect had any connection with Aramaic, how many times he could fit on the head of a pin, or whether he wasn't just a Norwegian with wings. Those meager letters might have come and gone until the end of time if a providential event had not put an end to the priests' tribulations.

It so happened that during those days, 10 among so many other carnival attractions, there arrived in town the traveling show of the woman who had been changed into a spider for having disobeyed her parents. The admission to see her was not only less than the admission to see the angel, but people were permitted to ask her all manner of questions about her absurd state and to examine her up and down so that no one would ever doubt the truth of her horror. She was a frightful tarantula the size of a ram and with the head of a sad maiden. What was most heartrending, however, was not her outlandish shape but the sincere affliction with which she recounted the details of her misfortune. While still practically a child she had sneaked out of her parents' house to go to a dance, and while she was coming back through the woods after having danced all night without permission, a fearful thunderclap rent the sky in two and through the crack came the lightning bolt of brimstone that changed her into a spider. Her only nourishment came from the meatballs that charitable souls chose to toss into her mouth. A spectacle like that, full of so much human truth and with such a fearful lesson, was bound to defeat without even trying that of a haughty angel who scarcely deigned to look at mortals. Besides, the few miracles attributed to the angel showed a certain mental disorder, like the blind man who didn't recover his sight but grew three new teeth, or the paralytic who didn't get to walk but almost won the lottery, and the leper whose sores sprouted sun flowers. Those consolation miracles, which were more like mocking fun, had already ruined the angel's reputation when the woman who had been changed into a spider finally crushed him completely. That was how Father Gonzaga was cured forever of his insomnia and Pelayo's courtyard went back to being as empty as during the time it had rained for three days and crabs walked through the bedrooms.

The owners of the house had no reason to lament. With the money they saved they built a two-story mansion with balconies and gardens and high netting so that crabs wouldn't get in during the winter, and with iron bars on the windows so that angels wouldn't get in. Pelayo also set up a rabbit warren close to town and gave up his job as bailiff for good, and Elisenda bought some satin pumps with high heels and many dresses of iridescent silk, the kind worn on Sunday by the most desirable women in those times. The chicken coop was the only thing that didn't receive any attention. If they washed it down with creolin and burned tears of myrrh inside it every so often, it was not in homage to the angel but to drive away the dungheap stench that still hung everywhere like a ghost and was turning the new house into an old one. At first, when the child learned to walk, they were careful that he not get too close to the chicken coop. But then they began to lose their fears and got used to the smell, and before the child got his second teeth he'd gone inside the chicken coop to play, where the wires were falling apart. The angel was no less standoffish with him than with other mortals, but he tolerated the most ingenious infamies with the patience of a dog who had no illusions. They both came down with chicken pox at the same time. The doctor who took care of the child couldn't resist the temptation to listen to the angel's heart, and he found so much whistling in the heart and so many sounds in his kidneys that it seemed impossible for him to be alive. What surprised him most, however, was the logic of his wings. They seemed so natural on that completely human organism that he couldn't understand why other men didn't have them too.

When the child began school it had been some time since the sun and rain had caused the collapse of the chicken coop. The angel went dragging himself about here and there like a stray dying man. They would drive him out of the bedroom with a broom and a moment later find him in the kitchen. He seemed to be in so many places at the same time that they grew to think that he'd been duplicated, that he was reproducing himself all through the house, and the exasperated and unhinged Elisenda shouted that it was awful living in that hell full of angels. He could scarcely eat and his antiquarian eyes had also become so foggy that he went about bumping into posts. All he had left were the bare cannulae[1] of his last feathers. Pelayo threw a blanket over him and extended him the charity of letting him sleep in the shed, and only then did they notice that he had a temperature at night, and was delirious with the tongue twisters of an old Norwegian. That was one of the few times they became alarmed, for they thought he was going to die and not even the wise neighbor woman had been able to tell them what to do with dead angels.

And yet he not only survived his worst winter, but seemed improved with the first sunny days. He remained motionless for several days in the farthest corner of the courtyard, where no one would see him, and at the beginning of December some large, stiff feathers began to grow on his wings, the feathers of a scarecrow, which looked more like another misfortune of decrepitude. But he must have known the

reason for those changes, for he was quite careful that no one should notice them, that no one should hear the sea chanteys that he sometimes sang under the stars. One morning Elisenda was cutting some bunches of onions for lunch when a wind that seemed to come from the high seas blew into the kitchen. Then she went to the window and caught the angel in his first attempts at flight. They were so clumsy that his fingernails opened a furrow in the vegetable patch and he was on the point of knocking the shed down with the ungainly flapping that slipped on the light and couldn't get a grip on the air. But he did manage to gain altitude. Elisenda let out a sigh of relief, for herself and for him, when she saw him pass over the last houses, holding himself up in some way with the risky flapping of a senile vulture. She kept watching him even when she was through cutting onions and she kept on watching until it was no longer possible for her to see him, because then he was no longer an annoyance in her life but an imaginary dot on the horizon of the sea.

------

[1] **cannulae:** the reedlike shafts of feathers.

····•►**Your Turn**
Talking and Writing about Lit

1. How has García Márquez used nonrealistic elements to help reveal themes in his story?

2. What is the narrative point of view used by the author in "A Very Old Man with Enormous Wings"? Does the narrative have access to any internal thoughts and feelings of the characters?

3. Can you identify examples of irony in the story? How does irony help García Márquez reveal his themes?

4. What is the function of the Spider Woman?

5. **DIY** One of the important things García Márquez is examining here is how strangers are treated in communities. Write a scene with dialogue in which you depict a character who enters a social situation. No one in your scene has ever laid eyes on this new character before and he or she is different. How will the people in your fictional community react to the stranger?

Nathaniel Hawthorne (1804–1864)

Nathaniel Hawthorne was born in Salem, Massachusetts. The fact that he was a descendent of a Puritan judge who had participated in the Salem witch trials caused Hawthorne considerable soul searching, and his exploration of related issues emerges in his fiction. Hawthorne's most important novel, *The Scarlet Letter* (1850), is widely regarded as a masterpiece of American literature. Another well-known novel of Hawthorne's is *The Blithedale Romance* (1852). His short stories are collected in two volumes—*Twice-Told Tales* (1837 and 1842) and *Mosses from an Old Manse* (1846).

Young Goodman Brown[1] (1835)

Young Goodman Brown came forth at sunset into the street of Salem village, but put his head back, after crossing the threshold, to exchange a parting kiss with his young wife. And Faith, as the wife was aptly named, thrust her own pretty head into the street, letting the wind play with the pink ribbons of her cap while she called to Goodman Brown.

"Dearest heart," whispered she softly and rather sadly when her lips were close to his ear, "prithee, put off your journey until sunrise, and sleep in your own bed tonight. A lone woman is troubled with such dreams and such thoughts that she's afeard of herself, sometimes. Pray, tarry with me this night, dear husband, of all nights in the year!"

"My love and my Faith," replied young Goodman Brown, "of all nights in the year this one must I tarry away from thee. My journey, as thou callest it, forth and back again must needs be done 'twixt now and sunrise. What, my sweet, pretty wife, dost thou doubt me already, and we but three months married!"

"Then God bless you!" said Faith with the pink ribbons, "and may you find all well when you come back."

"Amen!" cried Goodman Brown. "Say thy prayers, dear Faith, and go to bed at dusk, and no harm will come to thee."

So they parted; and the young man pursued his way until, being about to turn the corner by the meeting-house, he looked back and saw the head of Faith still peeping after him with a melancholy air in spite of her pink ribbons.

"Poor little Faith!" thought he, for his heart smote him. "What a wretch am I, to leave her on such an errand! She talks of dreams, too. Methought, as she spoke, there was trouble in her face, as if a dream had warned her what work is to be done tonight. But no, no! 'twould kill her to think it. Well; she's a blessed angel on earth and after this one night I'll cling to her skirts and follow her to Heaven."

With this excellent resolve for the future, Goodman Brown felt himself justified in making more haste on his present evil purpose. He had taken a dreary road, darkened by all the gloomiest trees of the forest, which barely stood aside to let the narrow path creep through, and closed immediately behind. It was all as lonely as could be; and there is this

---

[1]Deacon Gookin in the story is a historical personage (1612–1687), as are also Goody Cloyse, Goody Cory, and Martha Carrier, all three executed at the Salem witchcraft trials in 1692.

peculiarity in such a solitude, that the traveler knows not who may be concealed by the innumerable trunks and the thick boughs overhead, so that with lonely footsteps he may be passing through an unseen multitude.

"There may be a devilish Indian behind every tree," said Goodman Brown to himself; and he glanced fearfully behind him as he added, "What if the devil himself should be at my very elbow!"

10   His head being turned back, he passed a crook of the road, and looking forward again beheld the figure of a man in grave and decent attire, seated at the foot of an old tree. He rose at Goodman Brown's approach and walked onward side by side with him.

"You are late, Goodman Brown," said he. "The clock of the Old South was striking as I came through Boston, and that is full fifteen minutes agone."[2]

"Faith kept me back awhile," replied the young man with a tremor in his voice caused by the sudden appearance of his companion, though not wholly unexpected. It was now deep dusk in the forest, and deepest in that part of it where these two were journeying. As nearly as could be discerned, the second traveler was about fifty years old, apparently in the same rank of life as Goodman Brown, and bearing a considerable resemblance to him, though perhaps more in expression than features. Still, they might have been taken for father and son. And yet, though the elder person was as simply clad as the younger, and as simple in manner too, he had an indescribable air of one who knew the world and would not have felt abashed at the governor's dinner table or in King William's court,[3] were it possible that his affairs

should call him thither. But the only thing about him that could be fixed upon as remarkable was his staff, which bore the likeness of a great black snake, so curiously wrought that it might almost be seen to twist and wriggle itself like a living serpent. This, of course, must have been an ocular deception, assisted by the uncertain light.

"Come, Goodman Brown!" cried his fellow-traveler, "this is a dull pace for the beginning of a journey. Take my staff if you are so soon weary."

"Friend," said the other, exchanging   15 his slow pace for a full stop, "having kept covenant by meeting thee here, it is my purpose now to return whence I came. I have scruples touching the matter thou wot'st of."

"Sayest thou so?" replied he of the serpent, smiling apart. "Let us walk on nevertheless, reasoning as we go, and if I convince thee not, thou shalt turn back. We are but a little way in the forest yet."

"Too far, too far!" exclaimed the goodman, unconsciously resuming his walk. "My father never went into the woods on such an errand, nor his father before him. We have been a race of honest men and good Christians since the days of the martyrs. And shall I be the first of the name of Brown that ever took this path and kept—"

"Such company, thou wouldst say," observed the elder person interrupting his pause. "Well said, Goodman Brown! I have been as well acquainted with your family as with ever a one among the Puritans, and that's no trifle to say. I helped your grandfather the constable when he lashed the Quaker woman so smartly through the streets of Salem. And it was I that brought your father a pitch-pine knot kindled at my own hearth, to set fire to an Indian village, in King Philip's war.[4] They were my good

---

[2]**full fifteen minutes agone:** The distance from the center of Boston to the forest was over twenty miles.
[3]**King William's court:** William III, King of England, 1689–1702.

---

[4]**King Philip's War:** a war between the colonists and Indians, 1675–1676.

friends, both; and many a pleasant walk have we had along this path and returned merrily after midnight. I would fain be friends with you, for their sake."

"If it be as thou sayest," replied Goodman Brown, "I marvel they never spoke of these matters. Or, verily, I marvel not, seeing that the least rumor of the sort would have driven them from New England. We are a people of prayer, and good works to boot, and abide no such wickedness."

20 "Wickedness or not," said the traveler with twisted staff, "I have a general acquaintance here in New England. The deacons of many a church have drunk the communion wine with me, the selectmen of divers towns make me their chairman, and a majority of the Great and General Court[5] are firm supporters of my interest. The governor and I, too—but these are state secrets."

"Can this be so!" cried Goodman Brown with a stare of amazement at his undisturbed companion. "Howbeit, I have nothing to do with the governor and council; they have their own ways and are no rule for a simple husbandman like me. But were I to go on with thee, how should I meet the eye of that good old man, our minister, at Salem village? Oh, his voice would make me tremble, both Sabbath-day and lecture-day!"

Thus far, the elder traveler had listened with due gravity but now burst into a fit of irrepressible mirth, shaking himself so violently that his snakelike staff actually seemed to wriggle in sympathy.

"Ha! ha! ha!" shouted he, again and again; then composing himself, "Well, go on, Goodman Brown, go on; but prithee, don't kill me with laughing!"

"Well, then, to end the matter at once," said Goodman Brown, considerably nettled, "there is my wife, Faith. It would break her

dear little heart, and I'd rather break my own!"

"Nay, if that be the case," answered the 25 other, "e'en go thy ways, Goodman Brown. I would not for twenty old women like the one hobbling before us that Faith should come to any harm."

As he spoke he pointed his staff at a female figure on the path in whom Goodman Brown recognized a very pious and exemplary dame who had taught him his catechism in youth and was still his moral and spiritual adviser, jointly with the minister and Deacon Gookin.

"A marvel, truly, that Goody Cloyse should be so far in the wilderness at nightfall!" said he. "But with your leave, friend, I shall take a cut through the woods until we have left this Christian woman behind. Being a stranger to you, she might ask whom I was consorting with and whither I was going."

"Be it so," said his fellow-traveler. "Betake you to the woods and let me keep the path."

Accordingly, the young man turned aside, but took care to watch his companion who advanced softly along the road until he had come within a staff's length of the old dame. She, meanwhile, was making the best of her way, with singular speed for so aged a woman, and mumbling some indistinct words, a prayer, doubtless, as she went. The traveler put forth his staff and touched her withered neck with what seemed the serpent's tail.

"The devil!" screamed the pious old 30 lady.

"Then Goody Cloyse knows her old friend?" observed the traveler, confronting her and leaning on his writhing stick.

"Ah, forsooth, and is it your worship indeed?" cried the good dame. "Yea, truly is it, and in the very image of my old gossip, Goodman Brown, the grandfather of the silly

---

[5]**Great and General Court:** the legislature of the Massachusetts Bay Colony.

fellow that now is. But would your worship believe it? my broomstick hath strangely disappeared, stolen as I suspect by that unhanged witch, Goody Cory, and that, too, when I was all anointed with the juice of smallage and cinque-foil and wolf's-bane—"

"Mingled with fine wheat and the fat of a new-born babe," said the shape of old Goodman Brown.

"Ah, your worship knows the recipe," cried the old lady, cackling aloud. "So, as I was saying, being all ready for the meeting, and no horse to ride on, I made up my mind to foot it; for they tell me there is a nice young man to be taken into communion tonight. But now your good worship will lend me your arm and we shall be there in a twinkling."

35   "That can hardly be," answered her friend. "I may not spare you my arm, Goody Cloyse, but here is my staff, if you will."

So saying, he threw it down at her feet where, perhaps, it assumed life, being one of the rods which its owner had formerly lent to the Egyptian Magi. Of this fact, however, Goodman Brown could not take cognizance. He had cast up his eyes in astonishment, and looking down again beheld neither Goody Cloyse nor the serpentine staff, but his fellow-traveler alone, who waited for him as calmly as if nothing had happened.

"That old woman taught me my catechism!" said the young man, and there was a world of meaning in this simple comment.

They continued to walk onward while the elder traveler exhorted his companion to make good speed and persevere in the path, discoursing so aptly that his arguments seemed rather to spring up in the bosom of his auditor than to be suggested by himself. As they went he plucked a branch of maple to serve for a walking-stick, and began to strip it of the twigs and little boughs which were wet with evening dew. The moment his

fingers touched them they became strangely withered and dried up, as with a week's sunshine. Thus the pair proceeded at a good free pace, until suddenly, in a gloomy hollow of the road, Goodman Brown sat himself down on the stump of a tree and refused to go any farther.

"Friend," said he stubbornly, "my mind is made up. Not another step will I budge on this errand. What if a wretched old woman do choose to go to the devil when I thought she was going to Heaven! Is that any reason why I should quit my dear Faith and go after her?"

"You will think better of this by and by," said his acquaintance composedly. "Sit here and rest yourself awhile, and when you feel like moving again, there is my staff to help you along."

Without more words, he threw his companion the maple stick and was as speedily out of sight as if he had vanished into the deepening gloom. The young man sat a few moments by the roadside, applauding himself greatly and thinking with how clear a conscience he should meet the minister in his morning walk, nor shrink from the eye of good old Deacon Gookin. And what calm sleep would be his that very night, which was to have been spent so wickedly, but purely and sweetly now, in the arms of Faith! Amidst these pleasant and praiseworthy meditations, Goodman Brown heard the tramp of horses along the road and deemed it advisable to conceal himself within the verge of the forest, conscious of the guilty purpose that had brought him thither, though now so happily turned from it.

On came the hoof-tramps and the voices of the riders, two grave old voices conversing soberly as they drew near. These mingled sounds appeared to pass along the road within a few yards of the young man's hiding place; but owing, doubtless, to the depth of the gloom at that particular spot, neither the travelers nor their steeds were visible. Though their figures brushed the small boughs by the wayside, it could not be seen that they intercepted even for a moment the faint gleam from the strip of bright sky athwart which they must have passed. Goodman Brown alternately crouched and stood on tiptoe, pulling aside the branches and thrusting forth his head as far as he durst, without discerning so much as a shadow. It vexed him the more because he could have sworn, were such a thing possible, that he recognized the voices of the minister and Deacon Gookin, jogging along quietly as they were wont to do when bound to some ordination or ecclesiastical council. While yet within hearing, one of the riders stopped to pluck a switch.

"Of the two, reverend Sir," said the voice like the deacon's, "I had rather miss an ordination dinner than tonight's meeting. They tell me that some of our community are to be here from Falmouth and beyond, and others from Connecticut and Rhode Island, besides several of the Indian pow-wows who, after their fashion, know almost as much deviltry as the best of us. Moreover, there is a goodly young woman to be taken into communion."

"Mighty well, Deacon Gookin!" replied the solemn old tones of the minister. "Spur up, or we shall be late. Nothing can be done, you know, until I get on the ground."

45   The hoofs clattered again, and the voices talking so strangely in the empty air passed on through the forest where no church had ever been gathered nor solitary Christian prayed. Whither, then, could these holy men be journeying, so deep into the heathen wilderness? Young Goodman Brown caught hold of a tree for support, being ready to sink down on the ground, faint and over-burthened with the heavy sickness of his heart. He looked up to the sky, doubting whether there really was a Heaven above

him. Yet there was the blue arch, and the stars brightening in it.

"With Heaven above, and Faith below, I will yet stand firm against the devil!" cried Goodman Brown.

While he still gazed upward into the deep arch of the firmament and had lifted his hands to pray, a cloud, though no wind was stirring, hurried across the zenith and hid the brightening stars. The blue sky was still visible except directly overhead, where this black mass of cloud was sweeping swiftly northward. Aloft in the air, as if from the depths of the cloud, came a confused and doubtful sound of voices. Once the listener fancied that he could distinguish the accents of townspeople of his own, men and women, both pious and ungodly, many of whom he had met at the communion-table, and had seen others rioting at the tavern. The next moment, so indistinct were the sounds, he doubted whether he had heard aught but the murmur of the old forest whispering without a wind. Then came a stronger swell of those familiar tones heard daily in the sunshine at Salem village, but never, until now, from a cloud at night. There was one voice, of a young woman uttering lamentations yet with an uncertain sorrow, and entreating for some favor, which, perhaps, it would grieve her to obtain. And all the unseen multitude, both saints and sinners, seemed to encourage her onward.

"Faith!" shouted Goodman Brown in a voice of agony and desperation; and the echoes of the forest mocked him, crying "Faith! Faith!" as if bewildered wretches were seeking her all through the wilderness.

The cry of grief, rage, and terror was yet piercing the night when the unhappy husband held his breath for a response. There was a scream, drowned immediately in a louder murmur of voices fading into far-off laughter as the dark cloud swept away leaving the clear and silent sky above Goodman Brown. But something fluttered lightly down through the air and caught on the branch of a tree. The young man seized it and beheld a pink ribbon.

50 "My Faith is gone!" cried he, after one stupefied moment. "There is no good on earth, and sin is but a name. Come, devil! for to thee is this world given."

And maddened with despair, so that he laughed loud and long, did Goodman Brown grasp his staff and set forth again at such a rate that he seemed to fly along the forest path rather than to walk or run. The road grew wilder and drearier and more faintly traced, and vanished at length, leaving him in the heart of the dark wilderness, still rushing onward with the instinct that guides mortal man to evil. The whole forest was peopled with frightful sounds—the creaking of the trees, the howling of wild beasts, and the yell of Indians; while sometimes the wind tolled like a distant church bell, and sometimes gave a broad roar around the traveler, as if all Nature were laughing him to scorn. But he was himself the chief horror of the scene, and shrank not from its other horrors.

"Ha! ha! ha!" roared Goodman Brown when the wind laughed at him. "Let us hear which will laugh loudest! Think not to frighten me with your deviltry! come witch, come wizard, come Indian powwow, come devil himself! and here comes Goodman Brown. You may as well fear him as he fear you!"

In truth, all through the haunted forest there could be nothing more frightful than the figure of Goodman Brown. On he flew among the black pines, brandishing his staff with frenzied gestures, now giving vent to an inspiration of horrid blasphemy, and now shouting forth such laughter as set all the echoes of the forest laughing like demons around him. The fiend in his own

shape is less hideous than when he rages in the breast of man. Thus sped the demoniac on his course until, quivering among the trees, he saw a red light before him, as when the felled trunks and branches of a clearing have been set on fire and throw up their lurid blaze against the sky at the hour of midnight. He paused in a lull of the tempest that had driven him onward, and heard the swell of what seemed a hymn rolling solemnly from a distance with the weight of many voices. He knew the tune. It was a familiar one in the choir of the village meeting-house. The verse died heavily away, and was lengthened by a chorus not of human voices but of all the sounds of the benighted wilderness pealing in awful harmony together. Goodman Brown cried out, and his cry was lost to his own ear by its unison with the cry of the desert.

In the interval of silence he stole forward until the light glared full upon his eyes. At one extremity of an open space, hemmed in by the dark wall of the forest, arose a rock bearing some rude, natural resemblance either to an altar or a pulpit, and surrounded by four blazing pines, their tops aflame, their stems untouched, like candles at an evening meeting. The mass of foliage that had overgrown the summit of the rock was all on fire, blazing high into the night and fitfully illuminating the whole field. Each pendent twig and leafy festoon was in a blaze. As the red light arose and fell, a numerous congregation alternately shone forth, then disappeared in shadow, and again grew, as it were, out of the darkness, peopling the heart of the solitary woods at once.

"A grave and dark-clad company!" 55 quoth Goodman Brown.

In truth they were such. Among them, quivering to and fro between gloom and splendor, appeared faces that would be seen next day at the council-board of the province, and others which Sabbath after Sabbath looked devoutly heavenward and benignantly over the crowded pews from the holiest pulpits in the land. Some affirm that the lady of the governor was there. At least, there were high dames well known to her, and wives of honored husbands, and widows a great multitude, and ancient maidens, all of excellent repute, and fair young girls who trembled lest their mothers should espy them. Either the sudden gleams of light flashing over the obscure field bedazzled Goodman Brown, or he recognized a score of the church members of Salem village famous for their especial sanctity. Good old Deacon Gookin had arrived and waited at the skirts of that venerable saint, his reverend pastor. But irreverently consorting with these grave, reputable, and pious people, these elders of the church, these chaste dames and dewy virgins, there were men of dissolute lives and women of spotted fame, wretches given over to all mean and filthy vice and suspected even of horrid crimes. It was strange to see that the good shrank not from the wicked, nor were the sinners abashed by the saints. Scattered also among their pale-faced enemies were the Indian priests or powwows who had often scared their native forest with more hideous incantations than any known to English witchcraft.

"But where is Faith?" thought Goodman Brown; and as hope came into his heart he trembled.

Another verse of the hymn arose, a slow and mournful strain such as the pious love, but joined to words which expressed all that our nature can conceive of sin, and darkly hinted at far more. Unfathomable to mere mortals is the lore of fiends. Verse after verse was sung, and still the chorus of the desert swelled between, like the deepest tone of a mighty organ. And with the final peal of that dreadful anthem, there came a sound as if the roaring wind, the rushing streams, the howling beasts, and every other voice of the unconverted wilderness were mingling and according with the voice of guilty man in homage to the prince of all. The four blazing pines threw up a loftier flame and obscurely discovered shapes and visages of horror on the smoke-wreaths above the impious assembly. At the same moment the fire on the rock shot redly forth and formed a glowing arch above its base, where now appeared a figure. With reverence be it spoken, the apparition bore no slight similitude both in garb and manner to some grave divine of the New England churches.

"Bring forth the converts!" cried a voice that echoed through the field and rolled into the forest.

At the word, Goodman Brown stepped 60 forth from the shadow of the trees and approached the congregation, with whom he felt a loathful brotherhood by the sympathy of all that was wicked in his heart. He could have well-nigh sworn that the shape of his own dead father beckoned him to advance, looking downward from a smoke-wreath, while a woman with dim features of despair threw out her hand to warn him back. Was it his mother? But he had no power to retreat one step nor to resist, even in thought, when the minister and good old Deacon Gookin seized his arms and led him to the blazing rock. Thither came also the slender form of a veiled female led between Goody Cloyse, that pious teacher of the catechism, and Martha Carrier, who had received the devil's promise to be queen of hell. A rampant hag was she! And there stood the proselytes beneath the canopy of fire.

"Welcome, my children," said the dark figure, "to the communion of your race! Ye have found, thus young, your nature and your destiny. My children, look behind you!"

They turned, and flashing forth as it were in a sheet of flame, the fiend-worshippers were seen; the smile of welcome gleamed darkly on every visage.

"There," resumed the sable form, "are all whom ye have reverenced from youth. Ye deemed them holier than yourselves and shrank from your own sin, contrasting it with their lives of righteousness and prayerful aspirations heavenward. Yet here are they all in my worshipping assembly! This night it shall be granted you to know their secret deeds: how hoary-bearded elders of the church have whispered wanton words to the young maids of their households; how many a woman eager for widow's weeds has given her husband a drink at bedtime, and let him sleep his last sleep in her bosom; how beardless youths have made haste to inherit their father's wealth; and how fair damsels—blush not, sweet ones!—have dug little graves in the garden and bidden me, the sole guest, to an infant's funeral. By the sympathy of your human hearts for sin, ye shall scent out all the places—whether in church, bedchamber, street, field, or forest—where crime has been committed, and shall exult to behold the whole earth one stain of guilt, one mighty blood-spot. Far more than this! It shall be yours to penetrate in every bosom the deep mystery of sin, the fountain of all wicked arts, and which inexhaustibly supplies more evil impulses than human power—than my power, at its utmost!—can make manifest in deeds. And now, my children, look upon each other."

They did so, and by the blaze of the hell-kindled torches the wretched man beheld his Faith, and the wife her husband trembling before that unhallowed altar.

65 "Lo! there ye stand, my children," said the figure in a deep solemn tone, almost sad with its despairing awfulness, as if his once angelic nature could yet mourn for our miserable race. "Depending upon one another's hearts, ye had still hoped that virtue were not all a dream! Now are ye undeceived— Evil is the nature of mankind. Evil must be your only happiness. Welcome, again, my children, to the communion of your race!"

"Welcome!" repeated the fiend-worshippers in one cry of despair and triumph.

And there they stood, the only pair as it seemed who were yet hesitating on the verge of wickedness in this dark world. A basin was hollowed naturally in the rock. Did it contain water, reddened by the lurid light? or was it blood? or, perchance, a liquid flame? Herein did the Shape of Evil dip his hand and prepare to lay the mark of baptism upon their foreheads, that they might be partakers of the mystery of sin, more conscious of the secret guilt of others both in deed and thought than they could now be of their own. The husband cast one look at his pale wife, and Faith at him. What polluted wretches would the next glance show them to each other, shuddering alike at what they disclosed and what they saw!

"Faith! Faith!" cried the husband. "Look up to Heaven, and resist the Wicked One!"

Whether Faith obeyed he knew not. Hardly had he spoken when he found himself amid calm night and solitude, listening to a roar of the wind which died heavily away through the forest. He staggered against the rock and felt it chill and damp, while a hanging twig that had been all on fire besprinkled his cheek with the coldest dew.

The next morning, young Goodman 70 Brown came slowly into the street of Salem village staring around him like a bewildered man. The good old minister was taking a walk along the graveyard to get an appetite for breakfast and meditate his sermon, and bestowed a blessing as he passed on Goodman Brown. He shrank from the venerable saint as if to avoid an anathema. Old Deacon Gookin was at domestic worship, and the holy words of his prayer were heard through the open window. "What God doth the wizard pray to?" quoth Goodman Brown. Goody Cloyse, that excellent old Christian, stood in the early sunshine at her own lattice catechizing a little girl who had brought her a pint of morning's milk. Goodman Brown snatched away the child as from the grasp of the fiend himself. Turning the corner by the meeting-house, he spied the head of Faith with the pink ribbons gazing anxiously forth, and bursting into such joy at sight of him that she skipped along the street and almost kissed her husband before the whole village. But Goodman Brown looked sternly and sadly into her face and passed on without a greeting.

Had Goodman Brown fallen asleep in the forest and only dreamed a wild dream of a witch-meeting?

Be it so, if you will. But, alas! it was a dream of evil omen for young Goodman Brown. A stern, a sad, a darkly meditative, a distrustful, if not a desperate man did he become from the night of that fearful dream. On the Sabbath-day when the congregation were singing a holy psalm, he could not listen because an anthem of sin rushed loudly upon his ear and drowned all the blessed strain. When the minister spoke from the pulpit with power and fervid eloquence and with his hand on the open Bible, of the sacred truths of our religion, and of saint-like lives and triumphant deaths, and of future bliss or misery unutterable, then did Goodman Brown turn pale, dreading lest the roof should thunder down upon the gray blasphemer and his hearers. Often awaking suddenly at midnight, he shrank from the bosom of Faith, and at morning or eventide when the family knelt down at prayer, he scowled and muttered to himself and gazed sternly at his wife and turned away. And when he had lived long and was borne to his grave a hoary corpse, followed by Faith, an aged woman, and children and grandchildren, a goodly procession, besides neighbors not a few, they carved no hopeful verse upon his tombstone, for his dying hour was gloom.

·····➤*Your* **Turn**
Talking and Writing about Lit

1. In "Young Goodman Brown," could the characters themselves be seen as symbolic? What might the main characters represent?

2. This is a story in which the importance of setting is multifaceted. Explain how Hawthorne uses the historical context as well as the physical setting to reveal the story's characters and themes.

3. In what ways has Hawthorne used foreshadowing to prepare the reader for some of the events in the story?

4. **DIY** What would compel you to enter a totally unfamiliar setting or situation? What "errand into the wilderness" has compelled a friend or relative or yourself? Write a two-page plot sketch for a story in which a main character voluntarily heads into an unfamiliar and possibly dangerous or confusing setting.

John Cheever (1912–1982)

A chronicler of upper-middle-class lives in Manhattan and Greenwich, Connecticut, Cheever often published his short stories in *The New Yorker*, with which he had a long association. It was not unusual for his stories to be published only a few days after they were written. Though he wrote several novels, including *The Wapshot Chronicles* (1957), he was best known for his short fiction. He wrote over 200 short stories and won the Pulitzer Prize for his collection *The Stories of John Cheever* in 1978.

The Swimmer (1964)

It was one of those midsummer Sundays when everyone sits around saying "I *drank* too much last night." You might have heard it whispered by the parishioners leaving church, heard it from the lips of the priest himself, struggling with his cassock in the *vestiarium*, heard it from the golf links and the tennis courts, heard it from the wildlife preserve where the leader of the Audubon group was suffering from a terrible hangover. "I *drank* too much," said Donald Westerhazy. "We all *drank* too much," said Lucinda Merrill. "It must have been the wine," said Helen Westerhazy. "I *drank* too much of that claret."

This was at the edge of the Westerhazy's pool. The pool, fed by an artesian well with a high iron content, was a pale shade of green. It was a fine day. In the west there was a massive stand of cumulus clouds so like a city seen from a distance—from the bow of an approaching ship—that it might have had a name. Lisbon. Hackensack. The sun was hot. Neddy Merrill sat by the green water, one hand in it, one around a glass of gin. He was a slender man—he seemed to have the especial slenderness of youth—and while he was far from young he had slid down his

banister that morning and given the bronze backside of Aphrodite on the hall table a smack, as he jogged toward the smell of coffee in his dining room. He might have been compared to a summer's day, particularly the last hours of one, and while he lacked a tennis racket or a sail bag the impression was definitely one of youth, sport, and clement weather. He had been swimming and now he was breathing deeply, stertorously as if he could gulp into his lungs the components of that moment, the heat of the sun, the intenseness of his pleasure. It all seemed to flow into his chest. His own house stood in Bullet Park, eight miles to the south, where his four beautiful daughters would have had their lunch and might be playing tennis. Then it occurred to him that by taking a dogleg to the southwest he could reach his home by water.

His life was not confining and the delight he took in this observation could not be explained by its suggestion of escape. He seemed to see, with a cartographer's eye, that string of swimming pools, that quasi-subterranean stream that curved across the country. He had made a discovery, a contribution to modern geography; he would name the stream Lucinda after his wife. He was not a practical joker nor was he a fool but he was determinedly original and had a vague and modest idea of himself as a legendary figure. The day was beautiful and it seemed to him that a long swim might enlarge and celebrate its beauty.

He took off a sweater that was hung over his shoulders and dove in. He had an inexplicable contempt for men who did not hurl themselves into pools. He swam a choppy crawl, breathing either with every stroke or every fourth stroke and counting somewhere well in the back of his mind the one-two/one-two of a flutter kick. It was not a serviceable stroke for long distances but the domestication of swimming had saddled the sport with some customs and in his part of the world a crawl was customary. To be embraced and sustained by the light green water was less a pleasure, it seemed, than the resumption of a natural condition, and he would have liked to swim without trunks, but this was not possible, considering his project. He hoisted himself up on the far curb—he never used the ladder—and started across the lawn. When Lucinda asked where he was going he said he was going to swim home.

5   The only maps and charts he had to go by were remembered or imaginary but these were clear enough. First there were the Grahams, the Hammers, the Lears, the Howlands, and the Crosscups. He would cross Ditmar Street to the Bunkers and come, after a short portage, to the Levys, the Welchers, and the public pool in Lancaster. Then there were the Hallorans, the Sachses, the Biswangers, Shirley Adams, the Gilmartins, and the Clydes. The day was lovely, and that he lived in a world so generously supplied with water seemed like a clemency, a beneficence. His heart was high and he ran across the grass. Making his way home by an uncommon route gave him the feeling that he was a pilgrim, an explorer, a man with a destiny, and he knew that he would find friends all along the way; friends would line the banks of the Lucinda River.

He went through a hedge that separated the Westerhazys' land from the Grahams', walked under some flowering apple trees, passed the shed that housed their pump and filter, and came out at the Grahams' pool. "Why, Neddy," Mrs. Graham said, "what a marvelous surprise. I've been trying to get you on the phone all morning. Here, let me get you a drink." He saw then, like any explorer, that the hospitable customs and traditions of the natives would have to be handled with diplomacy if he was ever going to reach his destination. He did not want to mystify or seem rude to the Grahams nor did he have the time to linger there. He swam the length of their pool and joined them in the sun and was rescued, a few minutes later, by the arrival of two carloads of friends from Connecticut. During the uproarious reunions he was able to slip away. He went down by the front of the Grahams' house, stepped over a thorny hedge, and crossed a vacant lot to the Hammers'. Mrs. Hammer, looking up from her roses, saw him swim by although she wasn't quite sure who it was. The Lears heard him splashing past the open windows of their living room. The Howlands and the Crosscups were away. After leaving the Howlands' he crossed Ditmar Street and started for the Bunkers', where he could hear, even at that distance, the noise of a party.

The water refracted the sound of voices and laughter and seemed to suspend it in midair. The Bunkers' pool was on a rise and he climbed some stairs to a terrace where twenty-five or thirty men and women were drinking. The only person in the water was Rusty Towers, who floated there on a rubber raft. Oh, how bonny and lush were the banks of the Lucinda River! Prosperous men and women gathered by the sapphire-colored waters while caterer's men in white coats passed them cold gin. Overhead a red de Haviland trainer was circling around and around and around in the sky with something like the glee of a child in a swing. Ned felt a passing affection for the scene, a tenderness for the gathering, as if it was something he might touch. In the distance he heard thunder. As soon as Enid Bunker saw him she began to scream: "Oh, look who's here! What a marvelous surprise! When Lucinda said that you couldn't come I thought I'd *die*." She made her way to him through the crowd, and when they had finished kissing she led him to the bar, a progress that was slowed by the fact that he stopped to kiss eight or ten other women and shake the hands of as many men. A smiling bartender he had seen at a hundred parties gave him a gin and tonic and he stood by the bar for a moment, anxious not to get stuck in any conversation that would delay his voyage. When he seemed about to be surrounded he dove in and swam close to the side to avoid colliding with Rusty's raft. At the far end of the pool he bypassed the Tomlinsons with a broad smile and jogged up the garden path. The gravel cut his feet but this was the only unpleasantness. The party was confined to the pool, and as he went toward the house he heard the brilliant, watery sound of voices fade, heard the noise of a radio from the Bunkers' kitchen, where someone was listening to a ball game. Sunday afternoon. He made his way through the parked cars and down the grassy border of their driveway to Alewives Lane. He did not want to be seen on the road in his bathing trunks but there was no traffic and he made the short distance to the Levys' driveway, marked with a PRIVATE PROPERTY sign and a green tube for *The New York Times*. All the doors and windows of the big house were open but there were no signs of life; not even a dog barked. He went around the side of the house to the pool and saw that the Levys had only recently left. Glasses and bottles and dishes of nuts were on a table at the deep end, where there was a bathhouse or gazebo, hung with Japanese lanterns. After swimming the pool he got himself a glass and poured a drink. It was his fourth or fifth drink and he had swum nearly half the length of the Lucinda River. He felt tired, clean, and pleased at that moment to be alone; pleased with everything.

It would storm. The stand of cumulus cloud—that city—had risen and darkened, and while he sat there he heard the percussiveness of thunder again. The de Haviland trainer was still circling overhead and it seemed to Ned that he could almost hear the pilot laugh with pleasure in the afternoon; but when there was another peal of thunder he took off for home. A train whistle blew and he wondered what time it had gotten to be. Four? Five? He thought of the provincial station at that hour, where a waiter, his tuxedo concealed by a raincoat, a dwarf with some flowers wrapped in newspaper, and a woman who had been crying would be waiting for the local. It was suddenly growing dark; it was that moment when the pinheaded birds seem to organize their song into some acute and knowledgeable recognition of the storm's approach. Then there was a fine noise of rushing water from the crown of an oak at his back, as if a spigot there had been turned. Then the noise of fountains came from the crowns of all the tall trees. Why did he love storms, what was the meaning of his excitement when the door sprang open and the rain wind fled rudely up the stairs, why had the simple task of shutting the windows of an old house seemed fitting and urgent, why did the first watery notes of a storm wind have for him the unmistakable sound of good news, cheer, glad tidings? Then there was an explosion, a smell of cordite, and rain lashed the Japanese lanterns that Mrs. Levy had bought in Kyoto the year before last, or was it the year before that?

He stayed in the Levys' gazebo until the storm had passed. The rain had cooled the air and he shivered. The force of the wind had stripped a maple of its red and yellow leaves and scattered them over the grass and the water. Since it was midsummer the tree must be blighted, and yet he felt a peculiar sadness at this sign of autumn. He braced his shoulders, emptied his glass, and started for the Welchers' pool. This meant crossing the Lindleys' riding ring and he was surprised to find it overgrown with grass and all the jumps dismantled. He wondered if the Lindleys had sold their horses or gone away for the summer and put them out to board. He seemed to remember having heard something about the Lindleys and their horses but the memory was unclear. On he went, barefoot through the wet grass, to the Welchers', where he found their pool was dry.

10   This breach in his chain of water disappointed him absurdly, and he felt like some explorer who seeks a torrential headwater and finds a dead stream. He was disappointed and mystified. It was common enough to go away for the summer but no one ever drained his pool. The Welchers had definitely gone away. The pool furniture was folded, stacked, and covered with a tarpaulin. The bathhouse was locked. All the windows of the house were shut, and when he went around to the driveway in front he saw a FOR SALE sign nailed to a tree. When had he last heard from the Welchers—when, that is, had he and Lucinda last regretted an invitation to dine with them? It seemed only a week or so ago. Was his memory failing or had he so disciplined it in the repression of unpleasant facts that he had damaged his sense of the truth? Then in the distance he heard the sound of a tennis game. This cheered him, cleared away all his apprehensions and let him regard the overcast sky and the cold air with indifference. This was the day that Neddy Merrill swam across the county. That was the day! He started off then for his most difficult portage.

Had you gone for a Sunday afternoon ride that day you might have seen him, close to naked, standing on the shoulders of Route 424, waiting for a chance to cross. You might have wondered if he was the victim of foul play, had his car broken down, or was he merely a fool. Standing barefoot in the deposits of the highway—beer cans, rags, and blowout patches—exposed to all kinds of ridicule, he seemed pitiful. He had known when he started that this was a part of his journey—it had been on his maps—but confronted with the lines of traffic, worming through the summery light, he found himself unprepared. He was laughed at, jeered at, a beer can was thrown at him, and he had no dignity or humor to bring to the situation. He could have gone back, back to the Westerhazys', where Lucinda would still be sitting in the sun. He had signed nothing, vowed nothing, pledged nothing, not even to himself. Why, believing as he did, that all human obduracy was susceptible to common sense, was he unable to turn back? Why was he determined to complete his journey even if it meant putting his life in danger? At what point had this prank, this joke, this piece of horseplay become serious? He could not go back, he could not even recall with any clearness the green water at the Westerhazys', the sense of inhaling the day's components, the friendly and relaxed voices saying that they had *drunk* too much. In the space of an hour, more or less, he had covered a distance that made his return impossible.

An old man, tooling down the highway at fifteen miles an hour, let him get to the middle of the road, where there was a grass divider. Here he was exposed to the ridicule of the northbound traffic, but after ten or fifteen minutes he was able to cross. From here he had only a short walk to the Recreation Center at the edge of the village of Lancaster, where there were some handball courts and a public pool.

The effect of the water on voices, the illusion of brilliance and suspense, was the same here as it had been at the Bunkers' but the sounds here were louder, harsher, and more shrill, and as soon as he entered the crowded enclosure he was confronted with regimentation. "ALL SWIMMERS MUST TAKE A SHOWER BEFORE USING THE POOL. ALL SWIMMERS MUST USE THE FOOTBATH. ALL SWIMMERS MUST WEAR THEIR IDENTIFICATION DISKS." He took a shower, washed his feet in a cloudy and bitter solution, and made his way to the edge of the water. It stank of chlorine and looked to him like a sink. A pair of lifeguards in a pair of towers blew police whistles at what seemed to be regular intervals and abused the swimmers through a public address system. Neddy remembered the sapphire water at the Bunkers' with longing and thought that he might contaminate himself—damage his own prosperousness and charm—by swimming in this murk, but he reminded himself that he was an explorer, a pilgrim, and that this was merely a stagnant bend in the Lucinda River. He dove, scowling with distaste, into the chlorine and had to swim with his head above water to avoid collisions, but even so he was bumped into, splashed, and jostled. When he got to the shallow end both lifeguards were shouting at him: "Hey, you, you without the identification disk, get outa the water." He did, but they had no way of pursuing him and he went through the reek of suntan oil and chlorine out through the hurricane fence and passed the handball courts. By crossing the road he entered the wooded part of the

Halloran estate. The woods were not cleared and the footing was treacherous and difficult until he reached the lawn and the clipped beech hedge that encircled their pool.

The Hallorans were friends, an elderly couple of enormous wealth who seemed to bask in the suspicion that they might be Communists. They were zealous reformers but they were not Communists, and yet when they were accused, as they sometimes were, of subversion, it seemed to gratify and excite them. Their beech hedge was yellow and he guessed this had been blighted like the Levys' maple. He called hullo, hullo, to warn the Hallorans of his approach, to palliate his invasion of their privacy. The Hallorans, for reasons that had never been explained to him, did not wear bathing suits. No explanations were in order, really. Their nakedness was a detail in their uncompromising zeal for reform and he stepped politely out of his trunks before he went through the opening in the hedge.

Mrs. Halloran, a stout woman with white hair and a serene face, was reading the *Times*. Mr. Halloran was taking beech leaves out of the water with a scoop. They seemed not surprised or displeased to see him. Their pool was perhaps the oldest in the county, a fieldstone rectangle, fed by a brook. It had no filter or pump and its waters were the opaque gold of the stream.

"I'm swimming across the county," Ned said.

"Why, I didn't know one could," exclaimed Mrs. Halloran.

"Well, I've made it from the Westerhazys'," Ned said. "That must be about four miles."

He left his trunks at the deep end, walked to the shallow end, and swam this stretch. As he was pulling himself out of the water he heard Mrs. Halloran say, "We've been *terribly* sorry to hear about all your misfortunes, Neddy."

15

20 "My misfortunes?" Ned asked. "I don't know what you mean."

"Why, we heard that you'd sold the house and that your poor children . . ."

"I don't recall having sold the house," Ned said, "and the girls are at home."

"Yes," Mrs. Halloran sighed. "Yes . . ." Her voice filled the air with an unseasonable melancholy and Ned spoke briskly. "Thank you for the swim."

"Well, have a nice trip," said Mrs. Halloran.

25 Beyond the hedge he pulled on his trunks and fastened them. They were loose and he wondered if, during the space of an afternoon, he could have lost some weight. He was cold and he was tired and the naked Hallorans and their dark water had depressed him. The swim was too much for his strength but how could he have guessed this, sliding down the banister that morning and sitting in the Westerhazys' sun? His arms were lame. His legs felt rubbery and ached at the joints. The worst of it was the cold in his bones and the feeling that he might never be warm again. Leaves were falling down around him and he smelled wood smoke on the wind. Who would be burning wood at this time of year?

He needed a drink. Whiskey would warm him, pick him up, carry him through the last of his journey, refresh his feeling that it was original and valorous to swim across the county. Channel swimmers took brandy. He needed a stimulant. He crossed the lawn in front of the Hallorans' house and went down a little path to where they had built a house for their only daughter, Helen, and her husband, Eric Sachs. The Sachses' pool was small and he found Helen and her husband there.

"Oh, *Neddy*," Helen said. "Did you lunch at Mother's?"

"Not *really*," Ned said. "I *did* stop to see your parents." This seemed to be explanation enough. "I'm terribly sorry to break in on you like this but I've taken a chill and I wonder if you'd give me a drink."

"Why, I'd *love* to," Helen said, "but there hasn't been anything in this house to drink since Eric's operation. That was three years ago."

30 Was he losing his memory, had his gift for concealing painful facts let him forget that he had sold his house, that his children were in trouble, and that his friend had been ill? His eyes slipped from Eric's face to his abdomen, where he saw three pale, sutured scars, two of them at least a foot long. Gone was his navel, and what, Neddy thought, would the roving hand, bed-checking one's gifts at 3 A.M., make of a belly with no navel, no link to birth, this breach in the succession?

"I'm sure you can get a drink at the Biswangers'," Helen said. "They're having an enormous do. You can hear it from here. Listen!"

She raised her head and from across the road, the lawns, the gardens, the woods, the fields, he heard again the brilliant noise of voices over water. "Well, I'll get wet," he said, still feeling that he had no freedom of choice about his means of travel. He dove into the Sachses' cold water and, gasping, close to drowning, made his way from one end of the pool to the other. "Lucinda and I want *terribly* to see you," he said over his shoulder, his face set toward the Biswangers'. "We're sorry it's been so long and we'll call you *very* soon."

He crossed some fields to the Biswangers' and the sounds of revelry there. They would be honored to give him a drink, they would be happy to give him a drink. The Biswangers invited him and Lucinda for dinner four times a year, six weeks in advance. They were always rebuffed and yet they continued to send out their invitations, unwilling to comprehend the rigid and undemocratic realities of their society. They were the sort of people who discussed the price of things at cocktails, exchanged market tips during dinner, and after dinner told dirty stories to mixed company. They did not belong to Neddy's set—they were not even on Lucinda's Christmas card list. He went toward their pool with feelings of indifference, charity, and some unease, since it seemed to be getting dark and these were the longest days of the year. The party when he joined it was noisy and large. Grace Biswanger was the kind of hostess who asked the optometrist, the veterinarian, the real-estate dealer, and the dentist. No one was swimming and the twilight, reflected on the water of the pool, had a wintry gleam. There was a bar and he started for this. When Grace Biswanger saw him she came toward him, not affectionately as he had every right to expect, but bellicosely.

"Why, this party has everything," she said loudly, "including a gate crasher."

35 She could not deal him a social blow— there was no question about this and he did not flinch. "As a gate crasher," he asked politely, "do I rate a drink?"

"Suit yourself," she said. "You don't seem to pay much attention to invitations."

She turned her back on him and joined some guests, and he went to the bar and ordered a whiskey. The bartender served him but he served him rudely. His was a world in which the caterer's men kept the social score, and to be rebuffed by a part-time barkeep meant that he had suffered some loss of social esteem. Or perhaps the man was new and uninformed. Then he heard Grace at his back say: "They went for broke overnight— nothing but income—and he showed up drunk one Sunday and asked us to loan him five thousand dollars. . . ." She was always talking about money. It was worse than eating your peas off a knife. He dove into the pool, swam its length and went away.

The next pool on his list, the last but two, belonged to his old mistress, Shirley Adams. If he had suffered any injuries at the Biswangers'

they would be cured here. Love—sexual roughhouse in fact—was the supreme elixir, the pain killer, the brightly colored pill that would put the spring back into his step, the joy of life in his heart. They had had an affair last week, last month, last year. He couldn't remember. It was he who had broken it off, his was the upper hand, and he stepped through the gate of the wall that surrounded her pool with nothing so considered as self-confidence. It seemed in a way to be his pool, as the lover, particularly the illicit lover, enjoys the possessions of his mistress with an authority unknown to holy matrimony. She was there, her hair the color of brass, but her figure, at the edge of the lighted, cerulean water, excited in him no profound memories. It had been, he thought, a lighthearted affair, although she had wept when he broke it off. She seemed confused to see him and he wondered if she was still wounded. Would she, God forbid, weep again?

"What do you want?" she asked.

"I'm swimming across the county." 40

"Good Christ. Will you ever grow up?"

"What's the matter?"

"If you've come here for money," she said, "I won't give you another cent."

"You could give me a drink."

"I could but I won't. I'm not alone." 45

"Well, I'm on my way."

He dove in and swam the pool, but when he tried to haul himself up onto the curb he found that the strength in his arms and shoulders had gone, and he paddled to the ladder and climbed out. Looking over his shoulder he saw, in the lighted bathhouse, a young man. Going out onto the dark lawn he smelled chrysanthemums or marigolds— some stubborn autumnal fragrance—on the night air, strong as gas. Looking overhead he saw that the stars had come out, but why should he seem to see Andromeda, Cepheus, and Cassiopeia? What had become of the constellations of midsummer? He began to cry.

It was probably the first time in his adult life that he had ever cried, certainly the first time in his life that he had ever felt so miserable, cold, tired, and bewildered. He could not understand the rudeness of the caterer's barkeep or the rudeness of a mistress who had come to him on her knees and showered his trousers with tears. He had swum too long, he had been immersed too long, and his nose and his throat were sore from the water. What he needed then was a drink, some company, and some clean, dry clothes, and while he could have cut directly across the road to his home he went on to the Gilmartins' pool. Here, for the first time in his life, he did not dive but went down the steps into the icy water and swam a hobbled sidestroke that he might have learned as a youth. He staggered with fatigue on his way to the Clydes' and paddled the length of their pool, stopping again and again with his hand on the curb to rest. He climbed up the ladder and wondered if he had the strength to get home. He had done what he wanted, he had swum the county, but he was so stupefied with exhaustion that his triumph seemed vague. Stooped, holding on to the gateposts for support, he turned up the driveway of his own house.

The place was dark. Was it so late that they had all gone to bed? Had Lucinda stayed at the Westerhazys' for supper? Had the girls joined her there or gone someplace else? Hadn't they agreed, as they usually did on Sunday, to regret all their invitations and stay at home? He tried the garage doors to see what cars were in but the doors were locked and rust came off the handles onto his hands. Going toward the house, he saw that the force of the thunderstorm had knocked one of the rain gutters loose. It hung down over the front door like an umbrella rib, but it could be fixed in the morning. The house was locked, and he thought that the stupid cook or the stupid maid must have locked the place up until he remembered that it had been some time since they had employed a maid or a cook. He shouted, pounded on the door, tried to force it with his shoulder, and then, looking in at the windows, saw the place was empty.

····· ▶*Your* **Turn**
Talking and Writing about Lit

1. Explain how the Lucinda River, the season of the year, and the storm all serve as symbols in the story. What other elements of the story seem symbolic? How does this use of symbolism reveal themes?

2. How is social setting important in "The Swimmer"?

3. Does "The Swimmer" have a conventional plot? Does it have a climax or a turning point?

4. **DIY** Did you ever take a trip during which you encountered obstacles and adventures? Write a plot summary in which you sketch out a fictional story based on that experience. Remember that this is fiction, so you can make up scenes, characters, and incidents; it doesn't have to be a reportorial account of the experience, but it does need to be a story others might be interested in hearing or reading.

FROM PAGE TO SCREEN

Myth into Fiction into Film

e are told in the second paragraph of Cheever's "The Swimmer" that Neddy Merrill "had slid down his banister that morning and given the bronze backside of Aphrodite [goddess of love] on the hall table a smack" and we are told in the next paragraph that Neddy "had a

Leslie Marmon Silko (b. 1948)

Leslie Marmon Silko, who was born and raised on the Laguna Pueblo reservation west of Albuquerque, New Mexico, is a writer of mixed Laguna Pueblo, Mexican, and European ancestry. She and her husband and two children still live on the Laguna Pueblo reservation and she is a member of the tribe. Silko has published a number of collections of fiction and poetry, the best-known of which are *Ceremony* (1977), *Storyteller* (1981), and *The Almanac of the Dead* (1991).

Yellow Woman (1974)

I

My thigh clung to his with dampness, and I watched the sun rising up through the tamaracks and willows. The small brown water birds came to the river and hopped across the mud, leaving brown scratches in the alkali-white crust. They bathed in the river silently. I could hear the water, almost at our feet where the narrow fast channel bubbled and washed green ragged moss and fern

Burt Lancaster as Neddy Merrill

vague and modest idea of himself as a legendary figure." Like the classical Greek mythological hero Odysseus in Homer's *Odyssey*, Ned Merrill in "The Swimmer" braves an expanse of water (one he calls the "Lucinda River" after his wife—actually, it's a series of his suburbanite friends' swimming pools). Like Odysseus, Ned faces many obstacles in his watery quest. Unlike Odysseus, the end of Ned's journey quest is less than heroic. Cheever's short story was made into the movie *The Swimmer*, starring Burt Lancaster, in 1968.

leaves. I looked at him beside me, rolled in the red blanket on the white river sand. I cleaned the sand out of the cracks between my toes, squinting because the sun was above the willow trees. I looked at him for the last time, sleeping on the white river sand.

I felt hungry and followed the river south the way we had come the afternoon before, following our footprints that were already blurred by the lizard tracks and bug trails. The horses were still lying down, and the black one whinnied when he saw me but he did not get up—maybe it was because the corral was made out of thick cedar branches and the horses had not yet felt the sun like I had. I tried to look beyond the pale red mesas to the pueblo. I knew it was there, even if I could not see it, on the sand rock hill above the river, the same river that moved past me now and had reflected the moon last night.

The horse felt warm underneath me. He shook his head and pawed the sand. The bay whinnied and leaned against the gate trying to follow, and I remembered him asleep in the red blanket beside the river. I slid off the horse and tied him close to the other horse. I walked north with the river again, and the white sand broke loose in footprints over footprints.

"Wake up."

He moved in the blanket and turned his face to me with his eyes still closed. I knelt down to touch him.

"I'm leaving."

He smiled now, eyes still closed. "You are coming with me, remember?" He sat up now with his bare dark chest and belly in the sun.

"Where?"

"To my place."

"And will I come back?"

He pulled his pants on. I walked away from him, feeling him behind me and smelling the willows.

"Yellow Woman," he said.

I turned to face him. "Who are you?" I asked.

5

10

He laughed and knelt on the low, sandy bank, washing his face in the river. "Last night you guessed my name, and you knew why I had come."

15 I stared past him at the shallow moving water and tried to remember the night, but I could only see the moon in the water and remember his warmth around me.

"But I only said that you were him and that I was Yellow Woman—I'm not really her—I have my own name and I come from the pueblo on the other side of the mesa. Your name is Silva and you are a stranger I met by the river yesterday afternoon."

He laughed softly. "What happened yesterday has nothing to do with what you will do today, Yellow Woman."

"I know—that's what I'm saying—the old stories about the ka'tsina spirit[1] and Yellow Woman can't mean us."

My old grandpa liked to tell those stories best. There is one about Badger and Coyote who went hunting and were gone all day, and when the sun was going down they found a house. There was a girl living there alone, and she had light hair and eyes and she told them that they could sleep with her. Coyote wanted to be with her all night so he sent Badger into a prairie-dog hole, telling him he thought he saw something in it. As soon as Badger crawled in, Coyote blocked up the entrance with rocks and hurried back to Yellow Woman.

20 "Come here," he said gently.

He touched my neck and I moved close to him to feel his breathing and to hear his heart. I was wondering if Yellow Woman had known who she was—if she knew that she would become part of the stories. Maybe she'd had another name that her husband and relatives called her so that only the ka'tsina from the north and the storytellers would know her as Yellow Woman. But I

didn't go on; I felt him all around me, pushing me down into the white river sand.

Yellow Woman went away with the spirit from the north and lived with him and his relatives. She was gone for a long time, but then one day she came back and she brought twin boys.

"Do you know the story?"

"What story?" He smiled and pulled me close to him as he said this. I was afraid lying there on the red blanket. All I could know was the way he felt, warm, damp, his body beside me. This is the way it happens in the stories, I was thinking, with no thought beyond the moment she meets the ka'tsina spirit and they go.

25 "I don't have to go. What they tell in stories was real only then, back in time immemorial, like they say."

He stood up and pointed at my clothes tangled in the blanket. "Let's go," he said.

I walked beside him, breathing hard because he walked fast, his hand around my wrist. I had stopped trying to pull away from him, because his hand felt cool and the sun was high, drying the river bed into alkali. I will see someone, eventually I will see someone, and then I will be certain that he is only a man—some man from nearby—and I will be sure that I am not Yellow Woman. Because she is from out of time past and I live now and I've been to school and there are highways and pickup trucks that Yellow Woman never saw.

It was an easy ride north on horseback. I watched the change from the cottonwood trees along the river to the junipers that brushed past us in the foothills, and finally there were only piñons, and when I looked up at the rim of the mountain plateau I could see pine trees growing on the edge. Once I stopped to look down, but the pale sandstone had disappeared and the river was gone and the dark lava hills were all around. He touched my hand, not speaking,

---

[1]**ka'tsina spirit:** A mountain spirit of the Pueblo Indians.

but always singing softly a mountain song and looking into my eyes.

I felt hungry and wondered what they were doing at home now—my mother, my grandmother, my husband, and the baby. Cooking breakfast, saying, "Where did she go?—maybe kidnapped," and Al going to the tribal police with the details: "She went walking along the river."

30 The house was made with black lava rock and red mud. It was high above the spreading miles of arroyos and long mesas. I smelled a mountain smell of pitch and buck brush. I stood there beside the black horse, looking down on the small, dim country we had passed, and I shivered.

"Yellow Woman, come inside where it's warm."

II

He lit a fire in the stove. It was an old stove with a round belly and an enamel coffeepot on top. There was only the stove, some faded Navajo blankets, and a bedroll and cardboard box. The floor was made of smooth adobe plaster, and there was one small window facing east. He pointed at the box.

"There's some potatoes and the frying pan." He sat on the floor with his arms around his knees pulling them close to his chest and he watched me fry the potatoes. I didn't mind him watching me because he was always watching me—he had been watching me since I came upon him sitting on the river bank trimming leaves from a willow twig with his knife. We ate from the pan and he wiped the grease from his fingers on his Levis.

"Have you brought women here before?" He smiled and kept chewing, so I said, "Do you always use the same tricks?"

35 "What tricks?" He looked at me like he didn't understand.

"The story about being a ka'tsina from the mountains. The story about Yellow Woman."

Silva was silent; his face was calm.

"I don't believe it. Those stories couldn't happen now," I said.

He shook his head and said softly, "But someday they will talk about us, and they will say, 'Those two lived long ago when things like that happened.'"

He stood up and went out. I ate the 40 rest of the potatoes and thought about things—about the noise the stove was making and the sound of the mountain wind outside. I remembered yesterday and the day before, and then I went outside.

I walked past the corral to the edge where the narrow trail cut through the black rim rock. I was standing in the sky with nothing around me but the wind that came down from the blue mountain peak behind me. I could see faint mountain images in the distance miles across the vast spread of mesas and valleys and plains. I wondered who was over there to feel the mountain wind on those sheer blue edges—who walks on the pine needles in those blue mountains.

"Can you see the pueblo?" Silva was standing behind me.

I shook my head. "We're too far away."

"From here I can see the world." He stepped out on the edge. "The Navajo reservation begins over there." He pointed to the east. "The Pueblo boundaries are over here." He looked below us to the south, where the narrow trail seemed to come from. "The Texans have their ranches over there, starting with that valley, the Concho Valley. The Mexicans run some cattle over there too."

"Do you ever work for them?" 45

"I steal from them," Silva answered. The sun was dropping behind us and shadows were filling the land below. I turned away from the edge that dropped forever into the valleys below.

"I'm cold," I said; "I'm going inside." I started wondering about this man who could speak the Pueblo language so well but who lived on a mountain and rustled cattle. I decided that this man Silva must be Navajo, because Pueblo men didn't do things like that.

"You must be a Navajo."

Silva shook his head gently. "Little Yellow Woman," he said, "you never give up, do you? I have told you who I am. The Navajo people know me, too." He knelt down and unrolled the bedroll and spread the extra blankets out on a piece of canvas. The sun was down, and the only light in the house came from outside—the dim orange light from sundown.

50   I stood there and waited for him to crawl under the blankets.

"What are you waiting for?" he said, and I lay down beside him. He undressed me slowly like the night before beside the river—kissing my face gently and running his hands up and down my belly and legs. He took off my pants and then he laughed.

"Why are you laughing?"

"You are breathing so hard."

I pulled away from him and turned my back to him.

55   He pulled me around and pinned me down with his arms and chest. "You don't understand, do you, little Yellow Woman? You will do what I want."

And again he was all around me with his skin slippery against mine, and I was afraid because I understood that his strength could hurt me. I lay underneath him and I knew that he could destroy me. But later, while he slept beside me, I touched his face and I had a feeling—the kind of feeling for him that overcame me that morning along the river. I kissed him on the forehead and he reached out for me.

When I woke up in the morning he was gone. It gave me a strange feeling because

for a long time I sat there on the blankets and looked around the little house for some object of his—some proof that he had been there or maybe that he was coming back. Only the blankets and the cardboard box remained. The .30-30[2] that had been leaning in the corner was gone, and so was the knife I had used the night before. He was gone, and I had my chance to go now. But first I had to eat, because I knew it would be a long walk home.

I found some dried apricots in the cardboard box, and I sat down on a rock at the edge of the plateau rim. There was no wind and the sun warmed me. I was surrounded by silence. I drowsed with apricots in my mouth, and I didn't believe that there were highways or railroads or cattle to steal.

When I woke up, I stared down at my feet in the black mountain dirt. Little black ants were swarming over the pine needles around my foot. They must have smelled the apricots. I thought about my family far below me. They would be wondering about me, because this had never happened to me before. The tribal police would file a report. But if old Grandpa weren't dead he would tell them what happened—he would laugh and say, "Stolen by a ka'tsina, a mountain spirit. She'll come home—they usually do." There are enough of them to handle things. My mother and grandmother will raise the baby like they raised me. Al will find someone else, and they will go on like before, except that there will be a story about the day I disappeared while I was walking along the river. Silva had come for me; he said he had. I did not decide to go. I just went. Moonflowers blossom in the sand hills before dawn, just as I followed him. That's what I was thinking as I wandered along the trail through the pine trees.

---

[2]**.30-30:** A rifle.

60   It was noon when I got back. When I saw the stone house I remembered that I had meant to go home. But that didn't seem important any more, maybe because there were little blue flowers growing in the meadow behind the stone house and the gray squirrels were playing in the pines next to the house. The horses were standing in the corral, and there was a beef carcass hanging on the shady side of a big pine in front of the house. Flies buzzed around the clotted blood that hung from the carcass. Silva was washing his hands in a bucket full of water. He must have heard me coming because he spoke to me without turning to face me.

"I've been waiting for you."

"I went walking in the big pine trees."

I looked into the bucket full of bloody water with brown-and-white animal hairs floating in it. Silva stood there letting his hand drip, examining me intently.

"Are you coming with me?"

65   "Where ?" I asked him.

"To sell the meat in Marquez."

"If you're sure it's O.K."

"I wouldn't ask you if it wasn't," he answered.

He sloshed the water around in the bucket before he dumped it out and set the bucket upside down near the door. I followed him to the corral and watched him saddle the horses. Even beside the horses he looked tall, and I asked him again if he wasn't Navajo. He didn't say anything; he just shook his head and kept cinching up the saddle.

70   "But Navajos are tall."

"Get on the horse," he said, "and let's go."

The last thing he did before we started down the steep trail was to grab the .30-30 from the corner. He slid the rifle into the scabbard that hung from his saddle.

"Do they ever try to catch you?" I asked.

"They don't know who I am."

"Then why did you bring the rifle?"   75

"Because we are going to Marquez where the Mexicans live."

III

The trail leveled out on a narrow ridge that was steep on both sides like an animal spine. On one side I could see where the trail went around the rocky gray hills and disappeared into the southeast where the pale sandrock mesas stood in the distance near my home. On the other side was a trail that went west, and as I looked far into the distance I thought I saw the little town. But Silva said no, that I was looking in the wrong place, that I just thought I saw houses. After that I quit looking off into the distance; it was hot and the wildflowers were closing up their deep-yellow petals. Only the waxy cactus flowers bloomed in the bright sun, and I saw every color that a cactus blossom can be; the white ones and the red ones were still buds, but the purple and the yellow were blossoms, open full and the most beautiful of all.

Silva saw him before I did. The white man was riding a big gray horse, coming up the trail toward us. He was traveling fast and the gray horse's feet sent rocks rolling off the trail into the dry tumbleweeds. Silva motioned for me to stop and we watched the white man. He didn't see us right away, but finally his horse whinnied at our horses and he stopped. He looked at us briefly before he loped the gray horse across the three hundred yards that separated us. He stopped his horse in front of Silva, and his young fat face was shadowed by the brim of his hat. He didn't look mad, but his small, pale eyes moved from the blood-soaked gunny sacks hanging from my saddle to Silva's face and then back to my face.

"Where did you get the fresh meat?" the white man asked.

80   "I've been hunting," Silva said, and when he shifted his weight in the saddle the leather creaked.

    "The hell you have, Indian. You've been rustling cattle. We've been looking for the thief for a long time."

    The rancher was fat, and sweat began to soak through his white cowboy shirt and the wet cloth stuck to the thick rolls of belly fat. He almost seemed to be panting from the exertion of talking, and he smelled rancid, maybe because Silva scared him.

    Silva turned to me and smiled. "Go back up the mountain, Yellow Woman."

    The white man got angry when he heard Silva speak in a language he couldn't understand. "Don't try anything, Indian. Just keep riding to Marquez. We'll call the state police from there."

85   The rancher must have been unarmed because he was very frightened and if he had a gun he would have pulled it out then. I turned my horse around and the rancher yelled, "Stop!" I looked at Silva for an instant and there was something ancient and dark—something I could feel in my stomach—in his eyes, and when I glanced at his hand I saw his finger on the trigger of the .30-30 that was still in the saddle scabbard. I slapped my horse across the flank and the sacks of raw meat swung against my knees as the horse leaped up the trail. It was hard to keep my balance, and once I thought I felt the saddle slipping backward; it was because of this that I could not look back.

    I didn't stop until I reached the ridge where the trail forked. The horse was breathing deep gasps and there was a dark film of sweat on its neck. I looked down in the direction I had come from, but I couldn't see the place. I waited. The wind came up and pushed warm air past me. I looked up at the sky, pale blue and full of thin clouds and fading vapor trails left by jets.

    I think four shots were fired—I remember hearing four hollow explosions that reminded me of deer hunting. There could have been more shots after that, but I couldn't have heard them because my horse was running again and the loose rocks were making too much noise as they scattered around his feet.

    Horses have a hard time running downhill, but I went that way instead of uphill to the mountain because I thought it was safer. I felt better with the horse running southeast past the round gray hills that were covered with cedar trees and black lava rock. When I got to the plain in the distance I could see the dark green patches of tamaracks that grew along the river; and beyond the river I could see the beginning of the pale sandrock mesas. I stopped the horse and looked back to see if anyone was coming; then I got off the horse and turned the horse around, wondering if it would go back to its corral under the pines on the mountain. It looked back at me for a moment and then plucked a mouthful of green tumbleweeds before it trotted back up the trail with its ears pointed forward, carrying its head daintily to one side to avoid stepping on the dragging reins. When the horse disappeared over the last hill, the gunny sacks full of meat were still swinging and bouncing.

IV

I walked toward the river on a wood-hauler's road that I knew would eventually lead to the paved road. I was thinking about waiting beside the road for someone to drive by, but by the time I got to the pavement I had decided it wasn't very far to walk if I followed the river back the way Silva and I had come.

    The river water tasted good, and I sat 90 in the shade under a cluster of silvery willows. I thought about Silva, and I felt sad at leaving him; still, there was something strange about him, and I tried to figure it out all the way back home.

I came back to the place on the river bank where he had been sitting the first time I saw him. The green willow leaves that he had trimmed from the branch were still lying there, wilted in the sand. I saw the leaves and I wanted to go back to him—to kiss him and to touch him—but the mountains were too far away now. And I told myself, because I believe it, he will come back sometime and be waiting again by the river.

I followed the path up from the river into the village. The sun was getting low, and I could smell supper cooking when I got to the screen door of my house. I could hear their voices inside—my mother was telling my grandmother how to fix the Jell-O and my husband, Al, was playing with the baby. I decided to tell them that some Navajo had kidnapped me, but I was sorry that old Grandpa wasn't alive to hear my story because it was the Yellow Woman stories he liked to tell best.

· · · · · ▶ *Your* Turn
Talking and Writing about Lit

1. How important is setting in Silko's "Yellow Woman"? Give some examples to support your view.

2. Traditional (and contemporary) Native American belief systems put great emphasis on the way in which all life is connected—plant, animal, and human life. Look closely at Silko's depiction of animals in her story (for example, Silva's horse in the last scenes), and give two or three examples of her representation of the natural world (animals, plants, or landscape).

3. **DIY** Do you know any mythic stories that have been handed down in your family or legends or tales that represent your heritage in general? (If not, you can do a bit of research online or in the library to discover some.) Write a two- or three-page synopsis of a story that might be a myth representing some aspect of your heritage. If you feel stumped, talking to a family member might help. Is there someone in your family who tells stories?

Talking Lit

Leslie Marmon Silko writes about how the Kochininako stories were handed down in her family and about how she wrote "Yellow Woman."

Leslie Marmon Silko, "Myths of the Kochininako (Yellow Woman)"

When I was a little girl, Aunt Alice used to tell us kids the old-time stories, the "humma-hah" stories. Many of the stories were about the animals and birds and insects and reptiles who the old-time people believe are our sisters and brothers too, because Mother Earth's spirit gave birth to us all. But there were other stories too, about the Twin Brothers who went around saving people from giant monsters, about Salt Woman who gave her gift to the Parrot People because they invited her to share their food with them.

There is a whole cycle of Kochininako—Yellow Woman—stories which Aunt Alice seemed to enjoy a great deal. In most of the stories, Kochininako is a strong courageous woman, sometimes a hunter bringing home rabbits for her family to eat; other times she faces dangers or hardships and overcomes them. But in some of the stories Kochininako is swept away by forces and circumstances beyond her. All realms of possibility are open to Kochininako, even that of sorcery.

I wrote "Yellow-Woman" when I was 20 years old. I think it was the third short story I wrote for a class I took. Back then, I wasn't thinking about being a writer; writing was just something I loved to do. I planned to attend law school, and later I did attend for three semesters.

I did not know, at the time I began writing this story, what the story would be about; all I had was the notion of this sensuous woman who leaves her family responsibilities behind for a handsome stranger. Then, when I was about one-third of the way into the story, suddenly I remembered all the Kochininako–Yellow Woman stories I had heard while I was growing up. In one story a terrible drought has dried up all the nearby springs and so Kochininako must walk a great distance to find fresh water to carry home. At a distant water hole she encounters Buffalo Man, a supernatural being who is sometimes a handsome man and other times a buffalo. Although Kochininako leaves her husband and goes away with Buffalo Man, the outcome for Kochininako's people is life-saving; since Kochininako has now become their "sister-in-law," the Buffalo People agree to allow their meat to be harvested by Kochininako's starving people.

In another story, Kochininako meets Whirl-Wind Man at the water hole and goes away with him for a while. When Kochininako finally returns home months later, she is pregnant with twins who later grow up to be the Twin Brothers, who help the people in times of great trouble.

A warning has to go along with this story: in 1976, a Navajo woman who had been a student of mine reported that after six years trying and failing, she had become pregnant during the week our literature class had read and discussed "Yellow Woman."

Student Essay

Student Michelle Quinones writes about ambiguity and double meanings in "Young Goodman Brown."

Michelle Quinones
Prof. Barnard
English 102-JE

Into the Woods with Young Goodman Brown

The story of Young Goodman Brown is interestingly complex, in that my understanding of events and characters in the story evolved as I read. I often encountered elements of the story that seemed to clash with my previous assumptions about the events and characters. Throughout the story, many things seem contradictory or ambiguous. In the end, I came to the conclusion that the stranger in the forest was in fact the devil and the townspeople that Goodman knew were his worshipers.

Young Goodman Brown's name seems to be an example of what he stands for in the chain of events that take place in the forest. The words young and good in Young Goodman's name might represent strength, goodness, and possibly holiness as well. At the same time, he also seems to represent an "everyman." This sense is reinforced by the lower case representation of his name at times, for example in paragraph 17: "'Too far, too far!' exclaimed the goodman, unconsciously resuming his walk. 'My father never went into the woods on such an errand. . . . '" As Goodman Brown leaves his wife Faith to go into the forest, he is evidently letting go, not only of his wife, but also of his own faith in God. In this way, we can also see that her name, Faith, is symbolic here and throughout the story.

As he went into the forest, Goodman Brown appeared to know what he was going there to do. He knew of the evil that lay within this dark, treacherous forest that could strengthen or diminish his

Quinones 2

goodness as well as his faith in God. As he observes his surroundings, foreshadowing takes place when he suggests that the devil could be at his very elbow. Immediately following that, the traveler on the road appears, approaches Goodman, and begins to speak to him. Surprisingly, he is able to justify the fear within Goodman Brown. It is clear that this stranger who is astonishingly all knowing, is the one, among the many who appear in the forest, who is responsible for arranging the event that will take place. When they come across Goody Cloyse, it becomes even clearer who this traveler is and what he is capable of.

The description of the traveler's staff and the information he gives about all the people he knows in such high places (and even sacred places) suggests that he is very powerful and very accepted among many. As Goodman watches the events that take place in the forest, he suddenly sees his wife and begins to call out "faith" as though he is calling to his wife. However, during this time of trial I believe he is calling out to his own faith in God to save him from this moment of despair. As he awakes from what he thinks might be a dream, he seems a bit distrusting of Faith his wife, as well as all who occupy the streets of Salem whom he has known for so long and whom he may have observed as part of an apparent unholy communion.

Ultimately, it is clear he did not know his fellow neighbors as well as he thought he did. Although all the events seemed to be a dream when he suddenly awakes and everything he had seen vanishes, I think this was in fact reality. When Goodman started to call out "faith," this was a sign to all who had no faith in God that this was not a person that evil would successfully baptize into darkness and sin.

All of this causes me to speculate that perhaps Goodman was put under a spell in which he would wake up in the town wondering if what just happened was a dream or reality. The way he approaches his wife Faith and the way he now sees the townspeople differently suggests that the change inside him may be his own intuition telling him to be wary. Even though things appear to be a certain way, they are not always what they seem. Thus, irony figures prominently in the story. Also, the importance of ambiguity needs to be stressed. Often ambiguous or "double" meanings are possible in the story. In paragraph 71, we encounter this: "Had Goodman Brown fallen asleep in the forest and only dreamed a wild dream of a witch meeting?" And in paragraph 72, this: "Be it so, if you will. But, alas! It was a dream of evil omen of young Goodman Brown. A stern, a sad, a darkly meditative, a distrustful, if not a desperate man did he become from the night of that fearful dream."

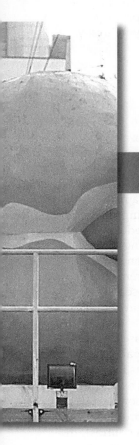

Even architecture uses theme. The architecture shown in these images evokes a theme in a playful way: The restaurants don't look like buildings, but instead like the food they advertise. The architecture itself symbolizes and evokes a mood or craving. The designers have tried to create in the viewer a positive feeling that will be associated with the actual product and may appeal to would-be patrons of the establishment. While looking at the pictures of these buildings, ask yourself the kind of questions you'd ask yourself about a work of fiction when trying to decipher theme: What do the designers of these buildings want us to understand after looking at them? What are the various paths to understanding? Are there multiple meanings, and if so, what are they? Buildings can symbolize the actual food offered, as does Tail 'O the Pup, or can symbolize fantasy as does Cinderalla's castle at Disney World. It can evoke happy feelings, like the ice cream cone stand might for children, or scary feelings, like a haunted house. How we interpret the signs is much the same for this type of architecture as it is for fiction.

Everyone knows how to talk about theme, in one way or another. We talk about what a movie was trying to say when we have different interpretations of it, or we talk about what an author might be saying when we discuss with a friend a book (or comic book) we've both read. For example, if you and a friend both watched the film version of John Cheever's "The Swimmer" (which you read in the previous chapter), you might have different opinions about what Cheever was trying to say.

Meaning and Interpretation

Theme refers to the meaning or interpretation of a work of literature. You might ask yourself: What does this story say about life? What does the writer want me to understand after reading this story? When discussing theme, you should always be aware of the possibilities for multiple meanings and for more than one interpretation. The most successful works of literature are often those with a richness of multiple meanings. Another concept to keep in mind when discussing theme is that an honest analysis of any work of literature involves asking good questions about what you have read. There are many pathways to discovering a story's meanings, and each of the previous chapters on the elements of fiction has introduced important pathways to interpretation. As readers, we want to remember to ask questions about *how* meanings are revealed in the story. We have seen that, in a given piece of fiction, some elements may be more important than others in revealing that particular story's themes.

What are the various pathways to the discovery of themes in Louise Erdrich's "The Red Convertible" (which you'll read in this chapter)? If you think about characterization (from Chapter 4), it could be pointed out that the story has two major characters: the two brothers. Henry, the brother who is changed by his experiences in the course of the story, is a dynamic character. Lyman, our first-person narrator, is fairly static in comparison, but he is a trustworthy observer of his brother's life and of their relationship and adventures together. The story sets up a contrast, in a number of ways, between the happy, adventurous, often carefree early scenes and the sadness of the scenes following Henry's return from the war in Vietnam. Two pathways through characterization to a discussion of themes are (1) the contrast between the two brothers and (2) the contrast between Henry's character in the early scenes and his transformed personality in the later scenes.

Image and Theme

The red convertible itself is our title image and serves symbolically throughout the story (see Chapter 8 for a discussion of symbolism). It is, so to speak, a vehicle for revealing the relationship between the two brothers and for showing the change taking place in Henry. Our son, Jake Winn, a college student himself, expresses it this way: "The red convertible is always there; it runs throughout the story, from the title to the ending. It gets the story everywhere it needs to go." Another pathway to discussion of themes in Erdrich's story is its chronological plot. The cluster of happy scenes which form the first half of "The Red Convertible," as well as the sad or tragic scenes which predominate in the latter part of the story, are carefully chosen and arranged by the author to lead us to an understanding of what the characters' experiences might mean. Additionally, you might approach themes by asking questions about point-of-view strategy. In what ways does it serve Erdrich's purposes thematically to tell the story from Lyman's point of view? Questions about voice and diction (Chapter 7) are also useful. Why does Erdrich let Lyman tell the story in his own words, rather than having him speak in formal standard English? Listen to the innocence and energy, the authenticity, of the resulting voice:

> The first time we saw it! I'll tell you when we first saw it. We had gotten a ride up to Winnipeg, and both of us had money. Don't ask me why, because we never mentioned a car or anything, we just had all our money. Mine was cash, a big bankroll from the Joliet's insurance. Henry had two checks—a week's pay for being laid off, and his regular check from the Jewel Bearing Plant. (paragraph 5)

Characterization, Plot, and Theme

In Gish Jen's "In the American Society" (in this chapter), characterization and plot structure converge to form an excellent pathway to the discovery of themes. The story is structured in two parts: "I. His Own Society" and "II. In the American Society." Considering the characterization of the father, Ralph Chang, how might the story's structure provide a pathway to a theme that could be phrased like this: How immigrants to the United States are transformed by their efforts to pursue the American Dream. Readers may hold different opinions regarding how much or how little Ralph Chang is changed by American society, and there are also some aspects of the country club society in which he finds himself at the end that many readers might want to question along with Mr. Chang.

Like most good stories, though, the theme suggested above is not the only meaning of Jen's story. A pathway to another of the story's themes might be obtained by a consideration of point of view (discussed in Chapter 6). The story is narrated by Ralph Chang's daughter, even though it is the father on whom the story focuses throughout. An interesting dynamic between the first-person narrator and her father has to do with questions of identity, finding one's identity, and balancing a concern for community (here represented as the Chinese way) and a concern for individual freedom (represented in the story as the American way). You may, of course, disagree with Jen's characterization of American society, and you may want to question any assumption that a country club is a typical

American social setting. One more pathway—if you were to approach Jen's story through a discussion of voice, tone, and style, you might find yourself mentioning the wonderful sense of humor with which she writes about these rather serious themes.

Other Pathways to Theme

Many of the elements of fiction—including character, plot, point of view, setting, irony, and imagery—could also be used as pathways to discovering themes in Anton Chekhov's "The Lady with the Pet Dog" (in this chapter). In addition, this story contains an example of the literary **epiphany** (also explained in the "Page to Screen" box in Chapter 7). The word epiphany is a religious term meaning a sudden spiritual insight or revelation of truth. James Joyce (an important Irish writer of the early twentieth century) brought this term from religion into literature and used it to describe such an experience depicted in fiction. Often, in Joyce's stories, it refers to a moment in which something quite commonplace and ordinary triggers an unusual emotional insight for a character. Certainly Chekhov, writing even before Joyce began to use the term epiphany in literary discourse, employs this type of sudden revelation in depicting the emotional journey of his character Dmitry Gurov. An example occurs in section III of "The Lady with the Pet Dog," when Gurov is startled into a new awareness of his situation by an offhand remark from a dinner companion about the fish they'd eaten:

> "You were quite right just now: the sturgeon wasn't fresh!"
> These words, in themselves so commonplace, for some reason aroused Gurov's indignation: they seemed somehow dirty and degrading. What savage manners, what awful faces! What wasted nights, what dull days devoid of interest! Frenzied card playing, gluttony, drunkenness, endless conversations about the same thing. Futile pursuits and conversations about the same topics taking up the greater part of the day and the greater part of a man's strength, so that he was left to live out a curtailed, bobtailed life with his wings clipped—an idiotic mess. (paragraphs 69–70)

Often an epiphany involves intensely felt emotion, as it does here. In fact, in the passage that follows, we find that "Gurov, boiling with indignation, did not sleep all night."

Another aspect of Chekhov's story which helps us recognize themes is that it is an open-ended story. It does not have a resolution in terms of the plot: We do not know what will happen to Gurov and Anna. It is also open ended in terms of its themes: The writer does not present us with a tidy "moral of the story" at the end, but instead he leaves the reader to draw his or her own conclusions and make his or her own judgments about what the characters should have done and what the story means. In writing to a critic, Aleksey S. Suvorin, in 1890, regarding another of his stories, Chekhov stated,

> You abuse me for objectivity, calling it indifference to good and evil, lack of ideals and ideas, and so on. You would have me, when I describe horse-thieves, say: "Stealing horses is an evil." But that has been known for ages without my saying so. Let the jury judge them; it's my job simply to show what sort of people they are. (from *Letters on the Short Story, the Drama and Other Literary Topics by Anton Chekhov*, 1924)

Likewise, in "The Lady with the Pet Dog," Chekhov chooses neither to approve nor to condemn the love affair which he depicts, preferring instead to let readers make those judgments for themselves. He does not sermonize. Indeed, in most modern fiction, multiple themes and interpretations are possible, and theme cannot be reduced to a simple "lesson" or "moral of the story." Often, something more complex is being revealed, and something more closely approximating real life (in which solutions are not always readily found) is the result.

What themes can you identify in Tillie Olsen's story "I Stand Here Ironing" (in this chapter)? You might want to look at the tone and style of the first-person narration and how this point-of-view strategy reveals both the mother's character and the daughter's and helps Olsen depict their evolving social and family situation over the years of Emily's life. Although the surface of the story takes place in one setting (the mother standing at her ironing board at home), the wide-ranging narration allows Olsen to depict also the historical backdrop of the Great Depression and World War II. Setting is, then, another rich aspect of the story and a pathway to meaning in this story as well as the other stories included in this chapter.

Readings

Louise Erdrich (b. 1954)

Louise Erdrich, who grew up on the Turtle Mountain Chippewa Reservation in southeastern North Dakota, is a Native American writer of mixed heritage. Her mother was Chippewa and her father German. Erdrich continues to add to her wonderful series of novels illuminating the Chippewa experience across many generations. These books could also be considered story cycles, in that each story or chapter is self-contained and can stand alone as a work of short fiction, but the characters also recur in story after story and book after book, and the family clans and characters' lives are depicted at different stages of experience and even different points in history. The books in Erdrich's Chippewa cycle are *Love Medicine* (1984), *The Beet Queen* (1986), *Tracks* (1988), *The Bingo Palace* (1994), *Tales of Burning Love* (1996), *The Antelope Wife* (1998), and *The Last Report on the Miracles at Little No Horse* (2001). Erdrich has also published children's books and books of nonfiction as well as poetry.

The Red Convertible (1984)

I was the first one to drive a convertible on my reservation. And of course it was red, a red Olds. I owned that car along with my brother Henry Junior. We owned it together until his boots filled with water on a windy night and he bought out my share. Now Henry owns the whole car, and his younger brother Lyman (that's myself), Lyman walks everywhere he goes.

How did I earn enough money to buy my share in the first place? My own talent was I could always make money. I had a touch for it, unusual in a Chippewa. From the first I was different that way, and everyone recognized it. I was the only kid they let in the American Legion Hall to shine shoes, for example, and one Christmas I sold spiritual bouquets for the mission door to door. The nuns let me keep a percentage. Once I started, it seemed the more money I made the easier the money came. Everyone encouraged it. When I was fifteen I got a job washing dishes at the Joliet Café, and that was where my first big break happened.

It wasn't long before I was promoted to busing tables, and then the short-order cook quit and I was hired to take her place. No sooner than you know it I was managing the Joliet. The rest is history. I went on managing. I soon became part owner, and of course there was no stopping me then. It wasn't long before the whole thing was mine.

After I'd owned the Joliet for one year, it blew over in the worst tornado ever seen around here. The whole operation was smashed to bits. A total loss! The fryalator was up in a tree, the grill torn in half like it was paper. I was only sixteen. I had it all in my mother's name, and I lost it quick, but before I lost it I had every one of my relatives, and their relatives, to dinner, and I also bought that red Olds I mentioned, along with Henry.

The first time we saw it! I'll tell you when we first saw it. We had gotten a ride up to Winnipeg, and both of us had money. Don't ask me why, because we never mentioned a car or anything, we just had all our money. Mine was cash, a big bankroll from the Joliet's insurance. Henry had two checks—a week's extra pay for being laid off, and his regular check from the Jewel Bearing Plant.

We were walking down Portage anyway, seeing the sights, when we saw it. There it was, parked, large as life. Really as *if* it was alive. I thought of the word *repose*, because the car wasn't simply stopped, parked, or whatever. That car reposed, calm and gleaming, a FOR SALE sign in its left front window. Then, before we had thought it over at all, the car belonged to us and our pockets were empty. We had just enough money for gas back home.

We went places in that car, me and Henry. We took off driving all one whole summer. We started off toward the Little Knife River and Mandaree in Fort Berthold and then we found ourselves down in Wakpala somehow, and then suddenly we were over in Montana on the Rocky Boy, and yet the summer was not even half over. Some people hang on to details when they travel, but we didn't let them bother us and just lived our everyday lives here to there.

I do remember this one place with willows. I remember I laid under those trees and it was comfortable. So comfortable. The branches bent down all around me like a tent or a stable. And quiet, it was quiet, even though there was a powwow close enough so I could see it going on. The air was not too still, not too windy either. When the dust rises up and hangs in the air around the dancers like that, I feel good. Henry was asleep with his arms thrown wide. Later on, he woke up and we started driving again. We were somewhere in Montana, or maybe on the Blood Reserve—it could have been anywhere. Anyway it was where we met the girl.

All her hair was in buns around her ears, that's the first thing I noticed about her. She was posed alongside the road with her arm out, so we stopped. That girl was short, so short her lumber shirt looked comical on her, like a nightgown. She had jeans on and fancy moccasins and she carried a little suitcase.

10   "Hop on in," says Henry. So she climbs in between us.

"We'll take you home," I says. "Where do you live?"

"Chicken," she says.

"Where the hell's that?" I ask her.

"Alaska."

15   "Okay," says Henry, and we drive. We got up there and never wanted to leave. The sun doesn't truly set there in summer, and the night is more a soft dusk. You might doze off, sometimes, but before you know it you're up again, like an animal in nature. You never feel like you have to sleep hard or put away the world. And things would grow up there. One day just dirt or moss, the next day flowers and long grass. The girl's name was Susy. Her family really took to us. They fed us and put us up. We had our own tent to live in by their house, and the kids would be in and out of there all day and night. They couldn't get over me and Henry being brothers, we looked so different. We told them we knew we had the same mother, anyway.

One night Susy came in to visit us. We sat around in the tent talking of this and that. The season was changing. It was getting darker by that time, and the cold was even getting just a little mean. I told her it was time for us to go. She stood up on a chair.

"You never seen my hair," Susy said.

That was true. She was standing on a chair, but still, when she unclipped her buns the hair reached all the way to the ground. Our eyes opened. You couldn't tell how much hair she had when it was rolled up so neatly. Then my brother Henry did something funny. He went up to the chair and said, "Jump on my shoulders." So she did that, and her hair reached down past his waist, and he started twirling, this way and that, so her hair was flung out from side to side.

"I always wondered what it was like to 20 have long pretty hair," Henry says. Well we laughed. It was a funny sight, the way he did it. The next morning we got up and took leave of those people.

On to greener pastures, as they say. It was down through Spokane and across Idaho then Montana and very soon we were racing the weather right along under the Canadian border through Columbus, Des Lacs, and then we were in Bottineau County and soon home. We'd made most of the trip, that summer, without putting up the car hood at all. We got home just in time, it turned out, for the army to remember Henry had signed up to join it.

I don't wonder that the army was so glad to get my brother that they turned him into a Marine. He was built like a brick outhouse anyway. We liked to tease him that they really wanted him for his Indian nose. He had a nose big and sharp as a hatchet, like the nose on Red Tomahawk, the Indian who killed Sitting Bull, whose profile is on signs all along the North Dakota highways. Henry went off to training camp, came home once during Christmas, then the next thing you know we got an overseas letter from him. It was 1970, and he said he was stationed up in the northern hill country. Whereabouts I did not know. He wasn't such a hot letter writer, and only got off two before the enemy caught him. I could never keep it straight, which direction those good Vietnam soldiers were from.

I wrote him back several times, even though I didn't know if those letters would get through. I kept him informed all about the car. Most of the time I had it up on blocks in the yard or half taken apart, because that long trip did a hard job on it under the hood.

I always had good luck with numbers, and never worried about the draft myself. I never even had to think about what my number was. But Henry was never lucky in the same way as me. It was at least three years before Henry came home. By then I guess the whole war was solved in the government's mind, but for him it would keep on going. In those years I'd put his car into almost perfect shape. I always thought of it as his car while he was gone, even though when he left he said, "Now it's yours," and threw me his key.

25   "Thanks for the extra key," I'd said. "I'll put it up in your drawer just in case I need it." He laughed.

When he came home, though, Henry was very different, and I'll say this: the change was no good. You could hardly expect him to change for the better, I know. But he was quiet, so quiet, and never comfortable sitting still anywhere but always up and moving around. I thought back to times we'd sat still for whole afternoons, never moving a muscle, just shifting our weight along the ground, talking to whoever sat with us, watching things. He'd always had a joke, then, too, and now you couldn't get

him to laugh, or when he did it was more the sound of a man choking, a sound that stopped up the throats of other people around him. They got to leaving him alone most of the time, and I didn't blame them. It was a fact: Henry was jumpy and mean.

I'd bought a color TV set for my mom and the rest of us while Henry was away. Money still came very easy. I was sorry I'd ever bought it though, because of Henry. I was also sorry I'd bought color, because with black-and-white the pictures seem older and farther away. But what are you going to do? He sat in front of it, watching it, and that was the only time he was completely still. But it was the kind of stillness that you see in a rabbit when it freezes and before it will bolt. He was not easy. He sat in his chair gripping the armrests with all his might, as if the chair itself was moving at a high speed and if he let go at all he would rocket forward and maybe crash right through the set.

Once I was in the room watching TV with Henry and I heard his teeth click at something. I looked over, and he'd bitten through his lip. Blood was going down his chin. I tell you right then I wanted to smash that tube to pieces. I went over to it but Henry must have known what I was up to. He rushed from his chair and shoved me out of the way, against the wall. I told myself he didn't know what he was doing.

My mom came in, turned the set off real quiet, and told us she had made something for supper. So we went and sat down. There was still blood going down Henry's chin, but he didn't notice it and no one said anything, even though every time he took a bit of his bread his blood fell onto it until he was eating his own blood mixed in with the food.

While Henry was not around we   30 talked about what was going to happen to him. There were no Indian doctors on the reservation, and my mom was afraid of trusting the old man, Moses Pillager, because he courted her long ago and was jealous of her husbands. He might take revenge through her son. We were afraid that if we brought Henry to a regular hospital they would keep him.

"They don't fix them in those places," Mom said; "they just give them drugs."

"We wouldn't get him there in the first place," I agreed, "so let's just forget about it."

Then I thought about the car.

Henry had not even looked at the car since he'd gotten home, though like I said, it was in tip-top condition and ready to drive. I thought the car might bring the old Henry back somehow. So I bided my time and waited for my chance to interest him in the vehicle.

35 One night Henry was off somewhere. I took myself a hammer. I went out to that car and I did a number on its underside. Whacked it up. Bent the tail pipe double. Ripped the muffler loose. By the time I was done with the car it looked worse than any typical Indian car that has been driven all its life on reservation roads, which they always say are like government promises—full of holes. It just about hurt me, I'll tell you that! I threw dirt in the carburetor and I ripped all the electric tape off the seats. I made it look just as beat up as I could. Then I sat back and waited for Henry to find it.

Still, it took him over a month. That was all right, because it was just getting warm enough, not melting, but warm enough to work outside.

"Lyman," he says, walking in one day, "that red car looks like shit."

"Well it's old," I says. "You got to expect that."

"No way!" says Henry. "That car's a classic! But you went and ran the piss right out of it, Lyman, and you know it don't deserve that. I kept that car in A-one shape. You don't remember. You're too young. But when I left, that car was running like a watch. Now I don't even know if I can get it to start again, let alone get it anywhere near its old condition."

"Well you try," I said, like I was getting 40 mad, "but I say it's a piece of junk."

Then I walked out before he could realize I knew he'd strung together more than six words at once.

After that I thought he'd freeze himself to death working on that car. He was out there all day, and at night he rigged up a little lamp, ran a cord out the window, and had himself some light to see by while he worked. He was better than he had been before, but that's still not saying much. It was easier for him to do the things the rest of us did. He ate more slowly and didn't jump up and down during the meal to get this or that or look out the window. I put my hand in the back of the TV set, I admit, and fiddled around with it good, so that it was almost impossible now to get a clear picture. He didn't look at it very often anyway. He was always out with that car or going off to get parts for it. By the time it was really melting outside, he had it fixed.

I had been feeling down in the dumps about Henry around this time. We had always been together before. Henry and Lyman. But he was such a loner now that I didn't know how to take it. So I jumped at the chance one day when Henry seemed friendly. It's not that he smiled or anything. He just said, "Let's take that old shitbox for a spin." Just the way he said it made me think he could be coming around.

We went out to the car. It was spring. The sun was shining very bright. My only sister, Bonita, who was just eleven years old, came out and made us stand together for a picture. Henry leaned his elbow on the red car's windshield, and he took his other arm and put it over my shoulder, very carefully, as though it was heavy for him to lift and he didn't want to bring the weight down all at once.

45   "Smile," Bonita said, and he did.

That picture, I never look at it anymore. A few months ago, I don't know why, I got his picture out and tacked it on the wall. I felt good about Henry at the time, close to him. I felt good having his picture on the wall, until one night when I was looking at television. I was a little drunk and stoned. I looked up at the wall and Henry was staring at me. I don't know what it was, but his smile had changed, or maybe it was gone. All I know is I couldn't stay in the same room with that picture. I was shaking. I got up, closed the door, and went into the kitchen. A little later my friend Ray came over and we both went back into that room. We put the picture in a brown bag, folded the bag over and over tightly, then put it way back in a closet.

I still see that picture now, as if it tugs at me, whenever I pass that closet door. The picture is very clear in my mind. It was so sunny that day Henry had to squint against the glare. Or maybe the camera Bonita held flashed like a mirror, blinding him, before she snapped the picture. My face is right out in the sun, big and round. But he might have drawn back, because the shadows on his face are deep as holes. There are two shadows curved like little hooks around the ends of his smile, as if to frame it and try to keep it there—that one, first smile that looked like it might have hurt his face. He has his field jacket on and the worn-in clothes he'd come back in and kept wearing ever since. After Bonita took the picture, she went into the house and we got into the car. There was a full cooler in the trunk. We started off, east, toward Pembina and the Red River because Henry said he wanted to see the high water.

The trip over there was beautiful. When everything starts changing, drying up, clearing off, you feel like your whole life is starting. Henry felt it, too. The top was down and the car hummed like a top. He'd really put it back in shape, even the tape on the seats was very carefully put down and glued back in layers. It's not that he smiled again or even joked, but his face looked to me as if it was clear, more peaceful. It looked as though he wasn't thinking of anything in particular except the bare fields and windbreaks and houses we were passing.

The river was high and full of winter trash when we got there. The sun was still out, but it was colder by the river. There were still little clumps of dirty snow here and there on the banks. The water hadn't gone over the banks yet, but it would, you could tell. It was just at its limit, hard swollen glossy like an old gray scar. We made ourselves a fire, and we sat down and watched the current go. As I watched it I felt something squeezing inside me and tightening and trying to let go all at the same time. I knew I was not just feeling it myself; I knew I was feeling what Henry was going through at that moment. Except that I couldn't stand it, the closing and opening. I jumped to my feet. I took Henry by the shoulders and I started shaking him. "Wake up," I says, "wake up, wake up, wake up!" I didn't know what had come over me. I sat down beside him again.

His face was totally white and hard.   50 Then it broke, like stones break all of a sudden when water boils up inside them.

"I know it," he says. "I know it. I can't help it. It's no use."

We start talking. He said he knew what I'd done with the car. It was obvious it had been whacked out of shape and not just neglected. He said he wanted to give the car to me for good now, it was no use. He said he'd fixed it just to give it back and I should take it.

"No way," I says, "I don't want it."

"That's okay," he says, "you take it."

55   "I don't want it, though," I says back to him, and then to emphasize, just to emphasize, you understand, I touch his shoulder. He slaps my hand off.

"Take that car," he says.

"No," I say. "Make me," I say, and then he grabs my jacket and rips the arm loose. That jacket is a class act, suede with tags and zippers. I push Henry backwards, off the log. He jumps up and bowls me over. We go down in a clinch and come up swinging hard, for all we're worth, with our fists. He socks my jaw so hard I feel like it swings loose. Then I'm at his rib cage and land a good one under his chin so his head snaps back. He's dazzled. He looks at me and I look at him and then his eyes are full of tears and blood and at first I think he's crying. But no, he's laughing. "Ha! Ha!" he says. "Ha! Ha! Take good care of it."

"Okay," I says, "okay, no problem. Ha! Ha!"

I can't help it, and I start laughing, too. My face feels fat and strange, and after a while I get a beer from the cooler in the trunk, and when I hand it to Henry he takes his shirt and wipes my germs off. "Hoof-and-mouth disease," he says. For some reason this cracks me up, and so we're really laughing for a while, and then we drink all the rest of the beers one by one and throw them in the river and see how far, how fast, the current takes them before they fill up and sink.

60   "You want to go on back?" I ask after a while. "Maybe we could snag a couple nice Kashpaw girls."

He says nothing. But I can tell his mood is turning again.

"They're all crazy, the girls up here, every damn one of them."

"You're crazy too," I say, to jolly him up. "Crazy Lamartine boys!"

He looks as though he will take this wrong at first. His face twists, then clears, and he jumps up on his feet. "That's right!" he says. "Crazier 'n hell. Crazy Indians!"

I think it's the old Henry again. He   65 throws off his jacket and starts swinging his legs out from the knees like a fancy dancer. He's down doing something between a grass dance and a bunny hop, no kind of dance I ever saw before, but neither has anyone else on all this green growing earth. He's wild. He wants to pitch whoopee! He's up and at me and all over. All this time I'm laughing so hard, so hard my belly is getting tied up in a knot.

"Got to cool me off!" he shouts all of a sudden. Then he runs over to the river and jumps in.

There's boards and other things in the current. It's so high. No sound comes from the river after the splash he makes, so I run right over. I look around. It's getting dark. I see he's halfway across the water already, and I know he didn't swim there but the current took him. It's far. I hear his voice, though, very clearly across it.

"My boots are filling," he says.

He says this in a normal voice, like he just noticed and he doesn't know what to think of it. Then he's gone. A branch comes by. Another branch. And I go in.

By the time I get out of the river, off the   70 snag I pulled myself onto, the sun is down. I walk back to the car, turn on the high beams, and drive it up the bank. I put it in first gear and then I take my foot off the clutch. I get out, close the door, and watch it plow softly into the water. The headlights reach in as they go down, searching, still lighted even after the water swirls over the back end. I wait. The wires short out. It is all finally dark. And then there is only the water, the sound of it going and running and going and running and running.

····•► *Your* **Turn**

Talking and Writing about Lit

1. How does Erdrich heighten the contrast between the way Henry Lamartine was before the war and the way he was when he returned from the war? How is the plot of "The Red Convertible" deliberately arranged to help us understand what has happened to Henry?

2. Do you agree that the red convertible itself serves as a symbol in the story? If so, what might it represent?

3. How do you interpret Lyman's actions in the end of the story? Why does he turn on the car's headlights before sending it into the river? Why do you think the story ends with the words "going and running and going and running and running?"

4. **DIY** How would this story be changed if the other brother were narrating it? Write two pages (depicting any scene from the story or a scene of your own creation), but write your scene from the point of view of Henry instead of Lyman.

Gish Jen (b. 1955)

Gish Jen's parents immigrated to the United States from China, and she grew up in Yonkers and Scarsdale, New York. She was educated at Harvard, Stanford, and the Iowa Writers Workshop. Her first novel was *Typical American* (1991). Like the story published here ("In the American Society," which first appeared in the *Sewanee Review*), most of Jen's work explores the identity struggles of immigrants, often with a touching and knowing sense of humor, and always (like Chekhov) with an affection for the humanness of the characters.

In the American Society (1991)

I. His Own Society

When my father took over the pancake house, it was to send my little sister Mona and me to college. We were only in junior high at the time, but my father believed in getting a jump on things. "Those Americans always saying it," he told us. "Smart guys thinking in advance." My mother elaborated, explaining that businesses took bringing up, like children. They could take years to get going, she said, years.

In this case, though, we got rich right away. At two months we were breaking even, and at four, those same hotcakes that could barely withstand the weight of butter and syrup were supporting our family with ease. My mother bought a station wagon with air conditioning, my father an oversized, red vinyl recliner for the back room; and as time went on and the business continued to thrive, my father started to talk about his grandfather and the village he had reigned over in China—things my father had never talked about when he worked for other people. He told us about the bags of rice his family would give out to the poor at New Year's, and about the people who came to beg, on their hands and knees, for his grandfather to intercede for the more wayward of their relatives. "Like that Godfather in the movie," he would tell us as, his feet up, he distributed paychecks. Sometimes an employee would get two green envelopes instead of one, which meant that Jimmy needed a tooth pulled, say, or that Tiffany's husband was in the clinker again.

"It's nothing, nothing," he would insist, sinking back into his chair. "Who else is going to take care of you people?"

My mother would mostly just sigh about it. "Your father thinks this is China," she would say, and then she would go back to her mending. Once in a while, though, when my father had given away a particularly large sum, she would exclaim, outraged, "But this here is the U—S—of—A!"— this apparently having been what she used to tell immigrant stock boys when they came in late.

5   She didn't work at the supermarket anymore; but she had made it to the rank of manager before she left, and this had given her not only new words and phrases, but new ideas about herself, and about America, and about what was what in general. She had opinions, now, on how downtown should be zoned; she could pump her own gas and check her own oil; and for all she used to chide Mona and me for being "copycats," she herself was now interested in espadrilles, and wallpaper, and most recently, the town country club.

"So join already," said Mona, flicking a fly off her knee.

My mother enumerated the problems as she sliced up a quarter round of watermelon: There was the cost. There was the waiting list. There was the fact that no one in our family played either tennis or golf.

"So what?" said Mona.

"It would be waste," said my mother.

"Me and Callie can swim in the pool."   10

"Plus you need that recommendation letter from a member."

"Come *on*," said Mona. "Annie's mom'd write you a letter in a *sec*."

My mother's knife glinted in the early summer sun. I spread some more newspaper on the picnic table.

"*Plus* you have to eat there twice a month. You know what that means." My mother cut another, enormous slice of fruit.

"No, I *don't* know what that means,"   15
said Mona.

"It means Dad would have to wear a jacket, dummy," I said.

"Oh! Oh! Oh!" said Mona, clasping her hand to her breast. "Oh! Oh! Oh! Oh! Oh!"

We all laughed: my father had no use for nice clothes, and would wear only ten-year-old shirts, with grease-spotted pants, to show how little he cared what anyone thought.

"Your father doesn't believe in joining the American society," said my mother. "He wants to have his own society."

20   "So go to dinner without him." Mona shot her seeds out in long arcs over the lawn. "Who cares what he thinks?"

    But of course we all did care, and knew my mother could not simply up and do as she pleased. For in my father's mind, a family owed its head a degree of loyalty that left no room for dissent. To embrace what he embraced was to love; and to embrace something else was to betray him.

    He demanded a similar sort of loyalty of his workers, whom he treated more like servants than employees. Not in the beginning, of course. In the beginning all he wanted was for them to keep on doing what they used to do, and to that end he concentrated mostly on leaving them alone. As the months passed, though, he expected more and more of them, with the result that for all his largesse, he began to have trouble keeping help. The cooks and busboys complained that he asked them to fix radiators and trim hedges, not only at the restaurant, but at our house; the waitresses that he sent them on errands and made them chauffeur him around. Our head waitress, Gertrude, claimed that he once even asked her to scratch his back.

    "It's not just the blacks don't believe in slavery," she said when she quit.

    My father never quite registered her complaint, though, nor those of the others who left. Even after Eleanor quit, then Tiffany, then Gerald, and Jimmy, and even his best cook, Eureka Andy, for whom he had bought new glasses, he remained mostly convinced that the fault lay with them.

25   "All they understand is that assembly line," he lamented. "Robots, they are. They want to be robots."

    There *were* occasions when the clear running truth seemed to eddy, when he would pinch the vinyl of his chair up into little peaks and wonder if he was doing things right. But with time he would always smooth the peaks back down; and when business started to slide in the spring, he kept on like a horse in his ways.

    By the summer our dishboy was overwhelmed with scraping. It was no longer just the hashbrowns that people were leaving for trash, and the service was as bad as the food. The waitresses served up French pancakes instead of German, apple juice instead of orange, spilt things on laps, on coats. On the Fourth of July some greenhorn sent an entire side of fries slaloming down a lady's *massif centrale*. Meanwhile in the back room, my father labored through articles on the economy.

    "What is housing starts?" he puzzled. "What is GNP?"

    Mona and I did what we could, filling in as busgirls and bookkeepers and, one afternoon, stuffing the comments box that hung by the cashier's desk. That was Mona's idea. We rustled up a variety of pens and pencils, checked boxes for an hour, smeared the cards up with coffee and grease, and waited. It took a few days for my father to notice that the box was full, and he didn't say anything about it for a few days more. Finally, though, he started to complain of fatigue; and then he began to complain that the staff was not what it could be. We encouraged him in this—pointing out, for instance, how many dishes got chipped—but in the end all that happened was that, for the first time since we took over the restaurant, my father got it into his head to fire someone. Skip, a skinny busboy who was saving up for a sportscar, said nothing as my father mumbled on about the price of dishes. My father's hands shook as he wrote out the severance check; and he spent the rest of the day napping in his chair once it was over.

    As it was going on midsummer, Skip 30 wasn't easy to replace. We hung a sign in the window and advertised in the paper, but no one called the first week, and the person who called the second didn't show up for his interview. The third week, my father phoned Skip to see if he would come back, but a friend of his had already sold him a Corvette for cheap.

Finally a Chinese guy named Booker turned up. He couldn't have been more than thirty, and was wearing a lighthearted seersucker suit, but he looked as though life had him pinned: his eyes were bloodshot and his chest sunken, and the muscles of his neck seemed to strain with the effort of holding his head up. In a single dry breath he told us that he had never bussed tables but was willing to learn, and that he was on the lam from the deportation authorities.

"I do not want to lie to you," he kept saying. He had come to the United States on a student visa, had run out of money, and was now in a bind. He was loath to go back to Taiwan, as it happened—he looked up at this point, to be sure my father wasn't pro-KMT—but all he had was a phony social security card and a willingness to absorb all blame, should anything untoward come to pass.

"I do not think, anyway, that it is against law to hire me, only to be me," he said, smiling faintly.

Anyone else would have examined him on this, but my father conceived of laws as speed bumps rather than curbs. He wiped the counter with his sleeve, and told Booker to report the next morning.

35 "I will be good worker," said Booker.

"Good," said my father.

"Anything you want me to do, I will do."

My father nodded.

Booker seemed to sink into himself for a moment. "Thank you," he said finally. "I am appreciate your help. I am very, very appreciate for everything." He reached out to shake my father's hand.

My father looked at him. "Did you eat 40 today?" he asked in Mandarin.

Booker pulled at the hem of his jacket.

"Sit down," said my father. "Please, have a seat."

My father didn't tell my mother about Booker, and my mother didn't tell my father about the country club. She would never have applied, except that Mona, while over at Annie's, had let it drop that our mother wanted to join. Mrs. Lardner came by the very next day.

"Why, I'd be honored and delighted to write you people a letter," she said. Her skirt billowed around her.

"Thank you so much," said my 45 mother. "But it's too much trouble for you, and also my husband is . . ."

"Oh, it's no trouble at all, no trouble at all. I tell you." She leaned forward so that her chest freckles showed. "I know just how it is. It's a secret of course, but you know, my natural father was Jewish. Can you see it? Just look at my skin."

"My husband," said my mother.

"I'd be honored and delighted," said Mrs. Lardner with a little wave of her hands. "Just honored and delighted."

Mona was triumphant. "See, Mom," she said, waltzing around the kitchen when Mrs. Lardner left. "What did I tell you? 'I'm just honored and delighted, just honored and delighted.'" She waved her hands in the air.

"You know, the Chinese have a say- 50 ing," said my mother. "To do nothing is better than to overdo. You mean well, but you tell me now what will happen."

"I'll talk Dad into it," said Mona, still waltzing. "Or I bet Callie can. He'll do anything Callie says."

"I can try, anyway," I said.

"Did you hear what I said?" said my mother. Mona bumped into the broom closet door. "You're not going to talk anything;

you've already made enough trouble." She started on the dishes with a clatter.

Mona poked diffidently at a mop.

55 I sponged off the counter. "Anyway," I ventured, "I bet our name'll never even come up."

"That's if we're lucky," said my mother.

"There's all these people waiting," I said.

"Good," she said. She started on a pot.

I looked over at Mona, who was still cowering in the broom closet. "In fact, there's some black family's been waiting so long, they're going to sue," I said.

60 My mother turned off the water. "Where'd you hear that?"

"Patty told me."

She turned the water back on, started to wash a dish, then put it back down and shut the faucet.

"I'm sorry," said Mona.

"Forget it," said my mother. "Just forget it."

65 Booker turned out to be a model worker, whose boundless gratitude translated into a willingness to do anything. As he also learned quickly, he soon knew not only how to bus, but how to cook, and how to wait table, and how to keep the books. He fixed the walk-in door so that it stayed shut, reupholstered the torn seats in the dining room, and devised a system for tracking inventory. The only stone in the rice was that he tended to be sickly; but, reliable even in illness, he would always send a friend to take his place. In this way we got to know Ronald, Lynn, Dirk, and Cedric, all of whom, like Booker, had problems with their legal status and were anxious to please. They weren't all as capable as Booker, though, with the exception of Cedric, whom my father often hired even when Booker was well. A round wag of a man who called

Mona and me *shou bou*—skinny monkeys—he was a professed nonsmoker who was nevertheless always begging drags off of other people's cigarettes. This last habit drove our head cook, Fernando, crazy, especially since, when refused a hit, Cedric would occasionally snitch one. Winking impishly at Mona and me, he would steal up to an ashtray, take a quick puff, and then break out laughing so that the smoke came rolling out of his mouth in a great incriminatory cloud. Fernando accused him of stealing fresh cigarettes too, even whole packs.

"Why else do you think he's weaseling around in the back of the store all the time," he said. His face was blotchy with anger. "The man is a frigging thief."

Other members of the staff supported him in this contention and joined in on an "Operation Identification," which involved numbering and initialing their cigarettes—even though what they seemed to fear for wasn't so much their cigarettes as their jobs. Then one of the cooks quit; and rather than promote someone, my father hired Cedric for the position. Rumors flew that he was taking only half the normal salary, that Alex had been pressured to resign, and that my father was looking for a position with which to placate Booker, who had been bypassed because of his health.

The result was that Fernando categorically refused to work with Cedric.

"The only way I'll cook with that piece of slime," he said, shaking his huge tattooed fist, "is if it's his ass frying on the grill."

70 My father cajoled and cajoled, to no avail, and in the end was simply forced to put them on different schedules.

The next week Fernando got caught stealing a carton of minute steaks. My father would not tell even Mona and me how he knew to be standing by the back door when Fernando was on his way out, but everyone suspected Booker. Everyone but Fernando, that is, who was sure Cedric had been the tip-off. My father held a staff meeting in which he tried to reassure everyone that Alex had left on his own, and that he had no intention of firing anyone. But though he was careful not to mention Fernando, everyone was so amazed that he was being allowed to stay that Fernando was incensed nonetheless.

"Don't you all be putting your bug eyes on me," he said. "*He's* the frigging crook." He grabbed Cedric by the collar.

Cedric raised an eyebrow. "Cook, you mean," he said.

At this Fernando punched Cedric in the mouth; and the words he had just uttered notwithstanding, my father fired him on the spot.

75   With everything that was happening, Mona and I were ready to be getting out of the restaurant. It was almost time: the days were still stuffy with summer, but our window shade had started flapping in the evening as if gearing up to go out. That year the breezes were full of salt, as they sometimes were when they came in from the East, and they blew anchors and docks through my mind like so many tumbleweeds, filling my dreams with wherries and lobsters and grainy-faced men who squinted, day in and day out, at the sky.

It was time for a change, you could feel it; and yet the pancake house was the same as ever. The day before school started my father came home with bad news.

"Fernando called police," he said, wiping his hand on his pant leg.

My mother naturally wanted to know what police; and so with much coughing and hawing, the long story began, the latest installment of which had the police calling immigration, and immigration sending an investigator. My mother sat stiff as whalebone as my father described how the man summarily refused lunch on the house and how my father had admitted, under pressure, that he knew there were "things" about his workers.

"So now what happens?"

My father didn't know. "Booker and 80 Cedric went with him to the jail," he said. "But me, here I am." He laughed uncomfortably.

The next day my father posted bail for "his boys" and waited apprehensively for something to happen. The day after that he waited again, and the day after that he called our neighbor's law student son, who suggested my father call the immigration department under an alias. My father took his advice; and it was thus that he discovered that Booker was right: it was illegal for aliens to work, but it wasn't to hire them.

In the happy interval that ensued, my father apologized to my mother, who in turn confessed about the country club, for which my father had no choice but to forgive her. Then he turned his attention back to "his boys."

My mother didn't see that there was anything to do.

"I like to talking to the judge," said my father.

"This is not China," said my mother.   85

"I'm only talking to him. I'm not give him money unless he wants it."

"You're going to land up in jail."

"So what else I should do?" My father threw up his hands. "Those are my boys."

"Your boys!" exploded my mother. "What about your family? What about your wife?"

My father took a long sip of tea. "You 90 know," he said finally, "in the war my father sent our cook to the soldiers to use. He always said it—the province comes before the town, the town comes before the family."

"A restaurant is not a town," said my mother.

My father sipped at his tea again. "You know, when I first come to the United States, I also had to hide-and-seek with those deportation guys. If people did not helping me, I'm not here today."

My mother scrutinized her hem.

After a minute I volunteered that before seeing a judge, he might try a lawyer.

95 He turned. "Since when did you become so afraid like your mother?"

I started to say that it wasn't a matter of fear, but he cut me off.

"What I need today," he said, "is a son."

My father and I spent the better part of the next day standing in lines at the immigration office. He did not get to speak to a judge, but with much persistence he managed to speak to a judge's clerk, who tried to persuade him that it was not her place to extend him advice. My father, though, shamelessly plied her with compliments and offers of free pancakes until she finally conceded that she personally doubted anything would happen to either Cedric or Booker.

"Especially if they're 'needed workers,'" she said, rubbing at the red marks her glasses left on her nose. She yawned. "Have you thought about sponsoring them to become permanent residents?"

100 Could he do that? My father was overjoyed. And what if he saw to it right away? Would she perhaps put in a good word with the judge?

She yawned again, her nostrils flaring. "Don't worry," she said. "They'll get a fair hearing."

My father returned jubilant. Booker and Cedric hailed him as their savior, their Buddha incarnate. He was like a father to them, they said; and laughing and clapping, they made him tell the story over and over, sorting over the details like jewels. And how old was the assistant judge? And what did she say?

That evening my father tipped the paperboy a dollar and bought a pot of mums for my mother, who suffered them to be placed on the dining room table. The next night he took us all out to dinner. Then on Saturday, Mona found a letter on my father's chair at the restaurant.

Dear Mr. Chang,
You are the grat boss. But, we do not like to trial, so will runing away now. Plese to excus us. People saying the law in America is fears like dragon. Here is only $140. We hope some day we can pay back the rest bale. You will getting intrest, as you diserving, so grat a boss you are. Thank you for every thing. In next life you will be burn in rich family, with no more pancaks.

Yours truley,
Booker + Cedric

In the weeks that followed my father went to the pancake house for crises, but otherwise hung around our house, fiddling idly with the sump pump and boiler in an effort, he said, to get ready for winter. It was as though he had gone into retirement, except that instead of moving South, he had moved to the basement. He even took to showering my mother with little attentions, and to calling her "old girl," and when we finally heard that the club had entertained all the applications it could for the year, he was so sympathetic that he seemed more disappointed than my mother.

II. In The American Society

Mrs. Lardner tempered the bad news with 105 an invitation to a bon voyage "bash" she was throwing for a friend of hers who was going to Greece for six months.

"Do come," she urged. "You'll meet everyone, and then, you know, if things open up in the spring . . ." She waved her hands.

My mother wondered if it would be appropriate to show up at a party for someone they didn't know, but "the honest truth" was that this was an annual affair. "If it's not Greece, it's Antibes," sighed Mrs. Lardner. "We really just do it because his wife left him and his daughter doesn't speak to him, and poor Jeremy just feels so *unloved*."

She also invited Mona and me to the goings on, as "*demi*-guests" to keep Annie out of the champagne. I wasn't too keen on the idea, but before I could say anything, she had already thanked us for so generously agreeing to honor her with our presence.

"A pair of little princesses, you are!" she told us. "A pair of princesses!"

110   The party was that Sunday. On Saturday, my mother took my father out shopping for a suit. As it was the end of September, she insisted that he buy a worsted rather than a seersucker, even though it was only ten, rather than fifty percent off. My father protested that it was as hot out as ever, which was true—a thick Indian summer had cozied murderously up to us—but to no avail. Summer clothes, said my mother, were not properly worn after Labor Day.

The suit was unfortunately as extravagant in length as it was in price, which posed an additional quandary, since the tailor wouldn't be in until Monday. The salesgirl, though, found a way of tacking it up temporarily.

"Maybe this suit not fit me," fretted my father.

"Just don't take your jacket off," said the salesgirl.

He gave her a tip before they left, but when he got home refused to remove the price tag.

"I like to asking the tailor about the size," he insisted.   115

"You mean you're going to *wear* it and then return it?" Mona rolled her eyes.

"I didn't say I'm return it," said my father stiffly. "I like to asking the tailor, that's all."

The party started off swimmingly, except that most people were wearing bermudas or wrap skirts. Still, my parents carried on, sharing with great feeling the complaints about the heat. Of course my father tried to eat a cracker full of shallots and burnt himself in an attempt to help Mr. Lardner turn the coals of the barbecue; but on the whole he seemed to be doing all right. Not nearly so well as my mother, though, who had accepted an entire cupful of Mrs. Lardner's magic punch, and seemed indeed to be under some spell. As Mona and Annie skirmished over whether some boy in their class inhaled when he smoked, I watched my mother take off her shoes, laughing and laughing as a man with a beard regaled her with navy stories by the pool. Apparently he had been stationed in the Orient and remembered a few words of Chinese, which made my mother laugh still more. My father excused himself to go to the men's room then drifted back and "dropped" anchor at the hors d'oeuvre table, while my mother sailed on to a group of women, who tinkled at length over the clarity of her complexion. I dug out a book I had brought.

Just when I'd cracked the spine, though, Mrs. Lardner came by to bewail her shortage of servers. Her caterers were criminals, I agreed; and the next thing I knew I was handing out bits of marine life, making the rounds as amicably as I could.

"Here you go, Dad," I said when I got   120 to the hors d'oeuvre table.

"Everything is fine," he said.

I hesitated to leave him alone; but then the man with the beard zeroed in on him, and though he talked of nothing but my mother, I thought it would be okay to get back to work. Just that moment, though, Jeremy Brothers lurched our way, an empty, albeit corked, wine bottle in hand. He was a slim, well-proportioned man, with a Roman nose and small eyes and a nice manly jaw that he allowed to hang agape.

"Hello," he said drunkenly. "Pleased to meet you."

"Pleased to meeting you," said my father.

125 "Right," said Jeremy. "Right. Listen. I have this bottle here, this most recalcitrant bottle. You see that it refuses to do my bidding. I bid it open sesame, please, and it does nothing." He pulled the cork out with his teeth, then turned the bottle upside down.

My father nodded.

"Would you have a word with it please?" said Jeremy. The man with the beard excused himself. "Would you please have a god-damned word with it?"

My father laughed uncomfortably.

"Ah!" Jeremy bowed a little. "Excuse me, excuse me, excuse me. You are not my man, not my man at all." He bowed again and started to leave, but then circled back. "Viticulture is not your forte, yes I can see that, see that plainly. But may I trouble you on another matter? Forget the damned bottle." He threw it into the pool, and winked at the people he splashed. "I have another matter. Do you speak Chinese?"

130 My father said he did not, but Jeremy pulled out a handkerchief with some characters on it anyway, saying that his daughter had sent it from Hong Kong and that he thought the characters might be some secret message.

"Long life," said my father.

"But you haven't looked at it yet."

"I know what it says without looking." My father winked at me.

"You do?"

"Yes, I do." 135

"You're making fun of me, aren't you?"

"No, no, no," said my father, winking again.

"Who are you anyway?" said Jeremy.

His smile fading, my father shrugged.

"Who are you?" 140

My father shrugged again.

Jeremy began to roar. "This is my party, *my party*, and I've never seen you before in my life." My father backed up as Jeremy came toward him. *"Who are you? WHO ARE YOU?"*

Just as my father was going to step back into the pool, Mrs. Lardner came running up. Jeremy informed her that there was a man crashing his party.

"Nonsense," said Mrs. Lardner. "This is Ralph Chang, who I invited extra especially so he could meet you." She straightened the collar of Jeremy's peach-colored polo shirt for him.

"Yes, well we've had a chance to chat," 145 said Jeremy.

She whispered in his ear; he mumbled something; she whispered something more.

"I do apologize," he said finally.

My father didn't say anything.

"I do." Jeremy seemed genuinely contrite. "Doubtless you've seen drunks before, haven't you? You must have them in China."

"Okay," said my father. 150

As Mrs. Lardner glided off, Jeremy clapped his arm over my father's shoulders. "You know, I really am quite sorry, quite sorry."

My father nodded.

"What can I do, how can I make it up to you?"

"No thank you."

"No, tell me, tell me," wheedled 155 Jeremy. "Tickets to casino night?" My father shook his head. "You don't gamble. Dinner at Bartholomew's?" My father shook his head again. "You don't eat." Jeremy scratched his chin. "You know, my wife was like you. Old Annabelle could never let me make things up—never, never, never, never, never."

My father wriggled out from under his arm.

"How about sport clothes? You are rather overdressed, you know, excuse me for saying so. But here." He took off his polo shirt and folded it up. "You can have this with my most profound apologies." He ruffled his chest hairs with his free hand.

"No thank you," said my father.

"No, take it, take it. Accept my apologies." He thrust the shirt into my father's arms. "I'm so very sorry, so very sorry. Please, try it on."

160 Helplessly holding the shirt, my father searched the crowd for my mother.

"Here, I'll help you off with your coat." My father froze.

Jeremy reached over and took his jacket off. "Milton's, one hundred twenty-five dollars reduced to one hundred twelve-fifty," he read. "What a bargain, what a bargain!"

"Please give it back," pleaded my father. "Please."

165 "Now for your shirt," ordered Jeremy. Heads began to turn.

"Take off your shirt."

"I do not take orders like a servant," announced my father.

"Take off your shirt, or I'm going to throw this jacket right into the pool, just right into this little pool here." Jeremy held it over the water.

170 "Go ahead."

"One hundred twelve-fifty," taunted Jeremy. "One hundred twelve . . ."

My father flung the polo shirt into the water with such force that part of it bounced back up into the air like a fluorescent fountain. Then it settled into a soft heap on top of the water. My mother hurried up.

"You're a sport!" said Jeremy, suddenly breaking into a smile and slapping my father on the back. "You're a sport! I like that. A man with spirit, that's what you are. A man with panache. Allow me to return to you your jacket." He handed it back to my father. "Good value you got on that, good value."

My father hurled the coat into the pool too. "We're leaving," he said grimly. "Leaving!"

"Now, Ralphie," said Mrs. Lardner, 175 bustling up; but my father was already stomping off.

"Get your sister," he told me. To my mother: "Get your shoes."

"That was *great*, Dad," said Mona as we walked down to the car. "You were *stupendous.*"

"Way to show 'em," I said.

"What?" said my father offhandedly.

Although it was only just dusk, we 180 were in a gulch, which made it hard to see anything except the gleam of his white shirt moving up the hill ahead of us.

"It was all my fault," began my mother.

"Forget it," said my father grandly. Then he said, "The only trouble is I left those keys in my jacket pocket."

"Oh *no*," said Mona.

"Oh no is right," said my mother.

"So we'll walk home," I said.   185

"But how're we going to get into the *house*," said Mona.

The noise of the party churned through the silence.

"Someone has to going back," said my father.

"Let's go to the pancake house first," suggested my mother. "We can wait there until the party is finished, and then call Mrs. Lardner."

190   Having all agreed that that was a good plan, we started walking again.

"God, just think," said Mona. "We're going to have to *dive* for them."

My father stopped a moment. We waited.

"You girls are good swimmers," he said finally. "Not like me."

Then his shirt started moving again, and we trooped up the hill after it, into the dark.

·····▶*Your* Turn

Talking and Writing about Lit

1. Does the reader feel differently about the narrator's father, Ralph Chang, by the end of the story than at the beginning? How does Gish Jen accomplish this?

2. How do the story's settings develop characterization? How does the writer's choice of settings help her develop her themes?

3. Like Jen's story, Gabriel García Márquez's story "A Very Old Man with Enormous Wings" (in Chapter 9) involves an "outsider" who comes into a community speaking a different language. Write an essay that explores the interesting comparisons and contrasts between these two stories and their two main characters.

4. DIY "Way to show 'em" says the narrator after her father Ralph throws Jeremy's peach-colored polo shirt into the swimming pool. Did you ever see a parent or other relative do something unexpected that made you feel surprised? Write a brief scene or plot sketch in which you depict this. If you don't want to write about a relative, make something up. It's okay, it's fiction!

Anton Chekhov (1860–1904)

Anton Chekhov, often referred to as the "father of the modern short story," is a figure of enormous importance to drama as well as fiction. He was raised in Taganrog, Russia, the son of a poor grocer and the grandson of a serf. His output of both fiction and drama was enormous, especially given that he died (a victim of tuberculosis) at the age of forty-four. Ironically, Chekhov was also a medical doctor. Many collections of Chekhov's stories have been compiled by others since his death. His best-known plays are *The Seagull* (1896), *Uncle Vanya* (1899), and *The Cherry Orchard* (1904).

The Lady with the Pet Dog (1899)

I

THEY were saying a new face had been seen on the esplanade: a lady with a pet dog. Dmitry Dmitrich Gurov, who had already spent two weeks in Yalta and regarded himself as an old hand, was beginning to show an interest in new faces. He was sitting in Vernet's coffeehouse when he saw a young lady, blonde and fairly tall, wearing a beret and walking along the esplanade. A white Pomeranian was trotting behind her.

Later he encountered her several times a day in the public gardens or in the square. She walked alone, always wearing the same beret, and always accompanied by the Pomeranian. No one knew who she was, and people called her simply "the lady with the pet dog."

"If she is here alone without a husband or any friends," thought Gurov, "then it wouldn't be a bad idea to make her acquaintance."

He was under forty, but he already had a twelve-year-old daughter and two boys at school. He had married young, when still a second-year student at college, and by now his wife looked nearly twice as old as he did. She was a tall, erect woman with dark eyebrows, dignified and imposing, who called herself a thinking person. She read a good deal, used simplified spelling in her letters, and called her husband Dimitry instead of Dmitry. Though he secretly regarded her as a woman of limited intelligence, narrow-minded and rather dowdy, he stood in awe of her and disliked being at home. Long ago he had begun being unfaithful to her, and he was now constantly unfaithful, and perhaps that was why he nearly always spoke ill of women, and whenever they were discussed in his presence he would call them "the lower race."

It seemed to him that he had been so schooled by bitter experience that he was entitled to call them anything he liked, but he was unable to live for even two days without "the lower race." In the company of men he was bored, cold, ill at ease, and uncommunicative, but felt at home among women, and knew what to say to them and how to behave; and even when he was silent in their presence he felt at ease. In his appearance, in his character, in his whole nature, there was something charming and elusive, which made him attractive to women and cast a spell over them. He knew this, and was himself attracted to them by some mysterious power.

Repeated and bitter experience had taught him that every fresh intimacy, which at first seems to give the spice of variety to life and a sense of delightful and easy conquest, inevitably ends by introducing excessively complicated problems, and creating intolerable situations—this is particularly true of the well-intentioned Moscow people, who are irresolute and slow to embark on adventures. But with every new encounter with an interesting woman he forgot all about his former experiences, and the desire to live surged in him, and everything suddenly seemed simple and amusing.

One evening when he was dining in the public gardens, the lady in the beret came strolling up and sat down at the next table. Her expression, her clothes, her way of walking, the way she did her hair, suggested that she belonged to the upper classes, that she was married, that she was paying her first visit to Yalta, and that she was alone and bored. . . . Stories told about immorality in Yalta are largely untrue, and for his part Gurov despised them, knowing they were mostly invented by people who were only too ready to sin, if they had the chance. . . . But when the lady sat down at the next table a few yards away from him, he remembered all those stories of easy conquests and trips to the mountains, and he was suddenly possessed with the tempting thought of a quick and temporary liaison, a romance with an unknown woman of whose very name he was ignorant.

He beckoned invitingly at the Pomeranian, and when the little dog came up to him, he shook his finger at it. The Pomeranian began to bark. Then Gurov wagged his finger again.

The lady glanced up at him and immediately lowered her eyes.

"He doesn't bite!" she said, and blushed.

"May I give him a bone?" Gurov said, and when she nodded, he asked politely: "Have you been long in Yalta?"

"Five days."

"And I am dragging through my second week."

There was silence for a while.

"Time passes so quickly, and it is so dull here," she said without looking at him.

"It's quite the fashion to say it is boring here," he replied. "People who live out their lives in places like Belevo or Zhizdro are not bored, but when they come here they say: 'How dull! All this dust!' One would think they live in Granada!"

She laughed. Then they both went on eating in silence, like complete strangers, but after dinner they walked off together and began to converse lightly and playfully like people who are completely at their ease and contented with themselves, and it is all the same to them where they go or what they talk about. They walked and talked about the strange light of the sea, the soft warm lilac color of the water, and the golden pathway made by the moonlight. They talked of how sultry it was after a hot day. Gurov told her he came from Moscow, that he had been trained as a philologist, though he now worked in a bank, that at one time he had trained to be an opera singer, but had given it up, and he told her about the two houses he owned in Moscow. From her he learned that she grew up in St. Petersburg and had been married in the town of S——, where she had been living for the past two years, that she would stay another month in Yalta, and perhaps her husband, who also needed a rest, would come to join her. She was not sure whether her husband was a member of a government board or on the zemstvo council, and this amused her. Gurov learned that her name was Anna Sergeyevna.

Afterwards in his room at the hotel he thought about her, and how they would surely meet on the following day. It was inevitable. Getting into bed, he recalled that only a little while ago she was a schoolgirl, doing lessons like his own daughter, and he remembered how awkward and timid she was in her laughter and in her manner of talking with a stranger—it was probably the first time in her life that she had found herself alone, in a situation where men followed her, gazed at her, and talked with her, always with a secret purpose she could not fail to guess. He thought of her slender and delicate throat and her lovely gray eyes.

"There's something pathetic about her," he thought, as he fell asleep.

II

A week had passed since they met. It was a holiday. Indoors it was oppressively hot, but the dust rose in clouds out of doors, and the people's hats whirled away. All day long

Gurov was plagued with thirst, and kept going to the soft-drink stand to offer Anna Sergeyevna a soft drink or an ice cream. There was no refuge from the heat.

In the evening when the wind dropped they walked to the pier to watch the steamer come in. There were a great many people strolling along the pier: they had come to welcome friends, and they carried bunches of flowers. Two peculiarities of a festive Yalta crowd stood out distinctly: the elderly ladies were dressed like young women, and there were innumerable generals.

Because there was a heavy sea, the steamer was late, and already the sun was going down. The steamer had to maneuver for a long time before it could take its place beside the jetty. Anna Sergeyevna scanned the steamer and the passengers through her lorgnette, as though searching for someone she knew, and when she turned to Gurov her eyes were shining. She talked a good deal, with sudden abrupt questions, and quickly forgot what she had been saying; and then she lost her lorgnette in the crush.

The smartly dressed people went away, and it was now too dark to recognize faces. The wind had dropped, but Gurov and Anna Sergeyevna still stood there as though waiting for someone to come off the steamer. Anna Sergeyevna had fallen silent, and every now and then she would smell her flowers. She did not look at Gurov.

"The weather is better this evening," he said. "Where shall we go now? We might go for a drive."

He gazed at her intently and suddenly embraced her and kissed her on the lips, overwhelmed by the perfume and moisture of the flowers. And then, frightened, he looked around—had anyone observed them?

"Let us go to your . . ." he said softly.

They walked away quickly.

Her room was oppressively hot, and there was the scent of the perfume she had bought at a Japanese shop. Gurov gazed at her, and all the while he was thinking: "How strange are our meetings!" Out of the past there came to him the memory of other careless, good-natured women, happy in their love-making, grateful for the joy he gave them, however short, and then he remembered other women, like his wife, whose caresses were insincere and who talked endlessly in an affected and hysterical manner, with an expression which said this was not love or passion but something far more meaningful; and then he thought of the few very beautiful cold women on whose faces there would suddenly appear the glow of a fierce flame, a stubborn desire to take, to wring from life more than it can give: women who were no longer in their first youth, capricious, imprudent, unreflecting, and domineering, and when Gurov grew cold to them, their beauty aroused his hatred, and the lace trimming of their lingerie reminded him of fish scales.

But here there was all the shyness and awkwardness of inexperienced youth: a feeling of embarrassment, as though someone had suddenly knocked on the door. Anna Sergeyevna, "the lady with the pet dog," accepted what had happened in her own special way, gravely and seriously, as though she had accomplished her own downfall, an attitude which he found odd and disconcerting. Her features faded and drooped away, and on both sides of her face the long hair hung mournfully down, while she sat musing disconsolately like an adulteress in an antique painting.

"It's not right," she said. "You're the first person not to respect me."

There was a watermelon on the table. Gurov cut off a slice and began eating it slowly. For at least half an hour they were silent.

There was something touching about Anna Sergeyevna, revealing the purity of a simple and naïve woman who knew very little about life. The single candle burning on the table barely illumined her face, but it was clear that she was deeply unhappy.

"Why should I not respect you?" Gurov said. "You don't know what you are saying."

"God forgive me!" she said, and her eyes filled with tears. "It's terrible!"

"You don't have to justify yourself."

"How can I justify myself? No, I am a wicked, fallen woman! I despise myself, and have no desire to justify myself! It isn't my husband I have deceived, but myself! And not only now, I have been deceiving myself for a long time. My husband may be a good, honest man, but he is also a flunky! I don't know what work he does, but I know he is a flunky! When I married him I was twenty. I was devoured with curiosity. I longed for something better! Surely, I told myself, there is another kind of life! I wanted to live! To live, only to live! I was burning with curiosity. You won't understand, but I swear by God I was no longer in control of myself! Something strange was going on in me. I could not hold back. I told my husband I was ill, and I came here. . . . And now I have been walking about as though in a daze, like someone who has gone out of his senses. . . . And now I am nothing else but a low, common woman, and anyone may despise me!"

Gurov listened to her, bored to death. He was irritated with her naïve tone, and with her remorse, so unexpected and so out of place. But for the tears in her eyes, he would have thought she was joking or playing a part.

"I don't understand," he said gently. "What do you want?"

She laid her face against his chest and pressed close to him.

"Believe me, believe me, I beg you," she said. "I love all that is honest and pure in life, and sin is hateful to me. I don't know

what I am doing. There are simple people who say: 'The Evil One led her astray,' and now I can say of myself that the Evil One has led me astray."

"Don't say such things," he murmured.

Then he gazed into her frightened, staring eyes, kissed her, spoke softly and affectionately, and gradually he was able to quieten her, and she was happy again; and then they both began to laugh.

Afterwards when they went out, there was not a soul on the esplanade. The town with its cypresses looked like a city of the dead, but the sea still roared and hurled itself against the shore. A single boat was rocking on the waves, and the lantern on it shone with a sleepy light.

They found a cab and drove to Oreanda.

"I discovered your name in the foyer just now," he said. "It was written up on the board—von Diederichs. Is your husband German?"

"No, I believe his grandfather was German, but he himself is an Orthodox Russian."

At Oreanda they sat on a bench not far from the church and gazed below at the sea and were lost in silence. Yalta was scarcely visible through the morning mist. Motionless white clouds covered the mountaintops. No leaves rustled, but the cicadas sang, and the monotonous muffled thunder of the sea, coming up from below, spoke of the peace, the eternal sleep awaiting us. This muffled thunder rose from the sea when neither Yalta nor Oreanda existed, and so it roars and will roar, dully, indifferently, after we have passed away. In this constancy of the sea, in her perfect indifference to our living and dying, there lies perhaps the promise of our eternal salvation, the unbroken stream of life on earth, and its unceasing movement toward perfection.

Sitting beside the young woman, who looked so beautiful in the dawn, Gurov was soothed and enchanted by the fairylike scene—the sea and the mountains, the clouds and the broad sky. He pondered how everything in the universe, if properly understood, would be entirely beautiful, but for our own thoughts and actions when we lose sight of the higher purposes of life and our human dignity.

Someone came up to them—probably a coast guard—looked at them and then walked away. His coming seemed full of mystery and beauty. Then in the glow of the early dawn they saw the steamer coming from Feodossia, its lights already doused.

"There is dew on the grass," said Anna Sergeyevna after a silence.

"Yes, it's time to go home."

They went back to the town.

Thereafter they met every day at noon on the esplanade, lunched and dined together, went out on excursions, and admired the sea. She complained of sleeping badly and of the violent beating of her heart, and she kept asking the same questions over and over again, alternately surrendering to jealousy and the fear that he did not really respect her. And often in the square or in the public gardens, when there was no one near, he would suddenly draw her to him and kiss her passionately. Their perfect idleness, those kisses in the full light of day, exchanged circumspectly and furtively for fear that anyone should see them, the heat, the smell of the sea, the continual glittering procession of idle, fashionable, well-fed people—all this seemed to give him a new lease of life. He kept telling Anna Sergeyevna how beautiful and seductive she was; he was impatient and passionate for her; and he never left her side, while she brooded continually, always trying to make him confess that he had no respect for her, did not love her at all, and saw in her nothing but a loose woman. Almost every evening at a late hour they would leave the town and drive out to Oreanda or to the waterfall, and these excursions were invariably a success, while the sensations they enjoyed were invariably beautiful and sublime.

All this time they were waiting for her husband to come, but he sent a letter saying he was having trouble with his eyes and imploring her to come home as soon as possible. Anna Sergeyevna made haste to obey.

"It's a good thing I am going away," she told Gurov. "It is fate."

She took a carriage to the railroad station, and he went with her. The drive took nearly a whole day. When she had taken her seat in the express train, and when the second bell had rung, she said: "Let me have one more look at you! Just one more! Like that!"

She did not cry, but looked sad and ill, and her face trembled.

"I shall always think of you and remember you," she said. "God be with you! Think kindly of me! We shall never meet again—that's all for the good, for we should never have met. God bless you!"

The train moved off rapidly, and soon its lights vanished, and in a few moments the sound of the engine grew silent, as though everything were conspiring to put an end to this sweet oblivion, this madness. Alone on the platform, gazing into the dark distance, Gurov listened to the crying of the cicadas and the humming of the telegraph wires with the feeling that he had only just this moment woken up. And he told himself that this was just one more of the many adventures in his life, and it was now over, and there remained only a memory. . . . He was confused, sad, and filled with a faint sensation of remorse. After all, this young woman whom he would never meet again, had not been happy with him. He had been affectionate and sincere, but in his manner, his tone, his caresses, there had always been a suggestion of irony, the insulting arrogance of a successful male who was almost twice her age. And always she had called him kind, exceptional, noble: obviously he had seemed to her different from what he really was, and unintentionally he had deceived her. . . .

Here at the railroad station there was the scent of autumn in the air; and the evening was cold.

"It's time for me to go north, too," Gurov thought as he left the platform. "High time!"

III

At home in Moscow winter was already at hand. The stoves were heated, and it was still dark when the children got up to go to school, and the nurse would light the lamp for a short while. Already there was frost. When the first snow falls, and people go out for the first time on sleighs, it is good to see the white ground, the white roofs: one breathes easily and lightly, and one remembers the days of one's youth. The old lime trees and birches have a kindly look about them: they lie closer to one's heart than cypresses and palms; and below their branches one has no desire to dream of mountains and the sea.

Gurov, a native of Moscow, arrived there on a fine, frosty day, and when he put on his fur coat and warm gloves and went for a stroll along the Petrovka, and when on Saturday evening he heard the church bells ringing, then his recent travels and all the places he had visited lost their charm for him. Little by little he became immersed in Moscow life, eagerly read three newspapers a day, and declared that on principle he never read Moscow newspapers. Once more he was caught up in a whirl of restaurants, clubs, banquets, and celebrations, and it was flattering to have famous lawyers and actors visiting his house, and flattering to play cards with a professor at the doctors' club. He could eat a whole portion of *selyanka*, a cabbage stew, straight off the frying pan. . . .

So a month would pass, and the image of Anna Sergeyevna, he thought, would vanish into the mists of memory, and only rarely would she visit his dreams with her touching smile, like the other women who appeared in his dreams. But more than a month went by, soon it was the dead of winter, and the memory of Anna Sergeyevna remained as vivid as if he had parted from her only the day before. And these memories kept glowing with an even stronger flame. Whether it was in the silence of the evening when he was in his study and heard the voices of his children preparing their lessons, or listening to a song or the music in a restaurant or a storm howling in the chimney, suddenly all his memories would spring to life again: what happened on the pier, the misty mountains in the early morning, the steamer coming in from Feodossia, their kisses. He would pace up and down the room for a long while, remembering it all and smiling to himself, and later these memories would fill his dreams, and in his imagination the past would mingle with the future. When he closed his eyes, he saw her as though she were standing before him in the flesh, younger, lovelier, tenderer than she had really been; and he imagined himself a finer person than he had been in Yalta. In the evenings she peered at him from the bookshelves, the fireplace, a corner of the room; he heard her breathing and the soft rustle of her skirts. In the street he followed the women with his eyes, looking for someone who resembled her.

He began to feel an overwhelming desire to share his memories with someone. But in his home it was impossible for him to talk of his love, and away from home—there was no one. The tenants who lived in his house and his colleagues at the bank were equally useless. And what could he tell them? Had he really been in love? Was there anything beautiful, poetic, edifying, or even interesting, in his relations with Anna Sergeyevna? He found himself talking about women and love in vague generalities, and nobody guessed what he meant, and only his wife twitched her dark eyebrows and said: "Really, Dimitry, the role of a coxcomb does not suit you at all!"

One evening he was coming out of the doctors' club with one of his card partners, a government official, and he could not prevent himself from saying: "If you only knew what a fascinating woman I met in Yalta!"

The official sat down in the sleigh, and was driving away when he suddenly turned round and shouted: "Dmitry Dmitrich!"

"What?"

"You were quite right just now! The sturgeon wasn't fresh!"

These words, in themselves so commonplace, for some reason aroused Gurov's indignation: they seemed somehow dirty and degrading. What savage manners, what awful faces! What wasted nights, what dull days devoid of interest! Frenzied card playing, gluttony, drunkenness, endless conversations about the same thing. Futile pursuits and conversations about the same topics taking up the greater part of the day and the greater part of a man's strength, so that he was left to live out a curtailed, bobtailed life with his wings clipped—an idiotic mess— impossible to run away or escape—one might as well be in a madhouse or a convict settlement.

Gurov, boiling with indignation, did not sleep a wink that night, and all the next day he suffered from a headache. On the following nights, too, he slept badly, sitting up in bed, thinking, or pacing the floor of his room. He was fed up with his children, fed up with the bank, and had not the slightest desire to go anywhere or talk about anything.

During the December holidays he decided to go on a journey and told his wife he had to go to St. Petersburg on some business connected with a certain young friend of his. Instead he went to the town of S——. Why? He hardly knew himself. He wanted to see Anna Sergeyevna and talk with her and if possible arrange a rendezvous.

He arrived at S—— during the morning and took the best room in the hotel, where the floor was covered with gray army cloth and on the table there was an inkstand, gray with dust, topped by a headless rider holding a hat in his raised hand. The porter gave him the necessary information: von Diederichs lived on Old Goncharnaya Street in a house of his own not far from the hotel; lived on a grand scale, luxuriously, and kept his own horses; the whole town knew him. The porter pronounced the name "Driderits."

He was in no hurry. He walked along Old Goncharnaya Street and found the house. In front of the house stretched a long gray fence studded with nails.

"You'd run away from a fence like that," Gurov thought, glancing now at the windows of the house, now at the fence.

He thought: "Today is a holiday, and her husband is probably at home. In any case it would be tactless to go up to the house and upset her. And if I sent her a note it might fall into her husband's hands and bring about a catastrophe! The best thing is to trust to chance." So he kept walking up and down the street by the fence, waiting for the chance. He saw a beggar entering the gates, only to be attacked by dogs, and about an hour later he heard someone playing on a piano, but the sounds were very faint and indistinct. Probably Anna Sergeyevna was playing. Suddenly the front door opened, and an old woman came out, followed by the familiar white Pomeranian. Gurov thought of calling out to the dog, but his heart suddenly began to beat violently and he was so excited he could not remember the dog's name.

As he walked on, he came to hate the gray fence more and more, and it occurred to him with a sense of irritation that Anna Sergeyevna had forgotten him and was perhaps amusing herself with another man, and that was very natural in a young woman who had nothing to look at from morning to night but that damned fence. He went back to his hotel room and for a long while sat on the sofa, not knowing what to do. Then he ordered dinner and took a long nap.

"How absurd and tiresome it is!" he thought when he woke and looked at the dark windows, for evening had fallen. "Well, I've had some sleep, and what is there to do tonight?"

He sat up in the bed, which was covered with a cheap gray blanket of the kind seen in hospitals, and he taunted himself with anger and vexation.

"You and your lady with the pet dog. . . . There's a fine adventure for you! You're in a nice fix now!"

However, at the railroad station that morning his eye had been caught by a playbill advertising in enormous letters the first performance of *The Geisha*. He remembered this, and drove to the theater.

"It's very likely that she goes to first nights," he told himself.

The theater was full. There, as so often in provincial theaters, a thick haze hung above the chandeliers, and the crowds in the gallery were fidgeting noisily. In the first row of the orchestra the local dandies were standing with their hands behind their backs, waiting for the curtain to rise, while in the governor's box the governor's daughter, wearing a boa, sat in front, the governor himself sitting modestly behind the drapes, with only his hands visible. The curtain was swaying; the orchestra spent a long time tuning up. While the audience was coming in and taking their seats, Gurov was looking impatiently around him.

And then Anna Sergeyevna came in. She sat in the third row, and when Gurov looked at her his heart seemed to stop, and he understood clearly that the whole world contained no one nearer, dearer, and more important than Anna. This slight woman, lost amid a provincial rabble, in no way remarkable, with her silly lorgnette in her hands, filled his whole life: she was his sorrow and his joy, the only happiness he desired for himself; and to the sounds of the wretched orchestra, with its feeble provincial violins, he thought how beautiful she was. He thought and dreamed.

There came with Anna Sergeyevna a young man with small side whiskers, very tall and stooped, who inclined his head at every step and seemed to be continually bowing. Probably this was the husband she once described as a flunky one day in Yalta when she was in a bitter mood. And indeed in his lanky figure, his side whiskers, his small bald patch, there was something of a flunky's servility. He smiled sweetly, and in his buttonhole there was an academic badge like the number worn by a waiter.

During the first intermission the husband went away to smoke, and she remained in her seat. Gurov, who was also sitting in the orchestra, went up to her and said in a trembling voice, with a forced smile: "How are you?"

She looked up at him and turned pale, then glanced at him again in horror, unable to believe her eyes, tightly gripping the fan and the lorgnette, evidently fighting to overcome a feeling of faintness. Both were silent. She sat, he stood, and he was frightened by her distress, and did not dare sit beside her. The violins and flutes sang out as they were tuned. Suddenly he was afraid, as it occurred to him that all the people in the boxes were staring down at them. She stood up and walked quickly to the exit; he followed her, and both of them walked aimlessly up and down the corridors, while crowds of lawyers, teachers, and civil servants, all wearing the appropriate uniforms and badges, flashed past; and the ladies, and the fur coats hanging from pegs, also flashed past; and the draft blew through the place, bringing with it the odor of cigar stubs. Gurov, whose heart was beating wildly, thought: "Oh Lord, why are these people here and this orchestra?"

At that moment he recalled how, when he saw Anna Sergeyevna off at the station in the evening, he had told himself it was all over and they would never meet again. But how far away the end seemed to be now!

Anna paused on a narrow dark stairway which bore the inscription: "This way to the upper balcony."

"How you frightened me!" she said, breathing heavily, pale and stunned. "How you frightened me! I am half dead! Why did you come? Why?"

"Do try to understand, Anna—please understand . . ." he said in a hurried whisper. "I implore you, please understand . . ."

She looked at him with dread, with entreaty, with love, intently, to retain his features all the more firmly in her memory.

"I've been so unhappy," she went on, not listening to him. "All this time I've thought only of you, I've lived on thoughts of you. I tried to forget, to forget—why, why have you come?"

A pair of schoolboys were standing on the landing above them, smoking and peering down, but Gurov did not care, and drawing Anna to him, he began kissing her face, her cheeks, her hands.

"What are you doing? What are you doing?" she said in terror, pushing him away from her. "We have both lost our senses! Go away now—tonight! . . . I implore you by everything you hold sacred. . . . Someone is coming!"

Someone was climbing up the stairs.

"You must go away . . ." Anna Sergeyevna went on in a whisper. "Do you hear, Dmitry Dmitrich? I'll come and visit you in Moscow. I have never been happy. I am miserable now, and I shall never be happy again, never! Don't make me suffer any more! I swear I'll come to Moscow! We must separate now. My dear precious darling, we have to separate!"

She pressed his hand and went quickly down the stairs, all the while gazing back at him, and it was clear from the expression in her eyes that she was miserable. For a while Gurov stood there, listening to her footsteps, and then all sounds faded away, and he went to look for his coat and left the theater.

IV

And Anna Sergeyevna began coming to see him in Moscow. Every two or three months she would leave the town of S— —, telling her husband she was going to consult a specialist in women's disorders, and her husband neither believed her nor disbelieved her. In Moscow she always stayed at the Slavyansky Bazaar Hotel, and the moment she arrived she would send a red-capped hotel messenger to Gurov. He would visit her, and no one in Moscow ever knew about their meetings.

One winter morning he was going to visit her as usual. (The messenger from the hotel had come the evening before, but he was out.) His daughter accompanied him. He was taking her to school, and the school lay on the way to the hotel. Great wet flakes of snow were falling.

"Three degrees above freezing, and it's still snowing," he told his daughter. "That's only the surface temperature of the earth— the other layers of the atmosphere have other temperatures."

"Yes, Papa. But why are there no thunderstorms in winter?"

He explained that, too. He talked, and all the while he was thinking about his meeting with the beloved, and not a living soul knew of it, and probably no one would ever know. He was living a double life: an open and public life visible to all who had any need to know, full of conventional truth and conventional lies, exactly like the lives of his friends and acquaintances, and another which followed a secret course. And by one of those strange and perhaps accidental circumstances everything that was to him meaningful, urgent, and important, everything about which he felt sincerely and did not deceive himself, everything that went to shape the very core of his existence, was concealed from others, while everything that was false and the shell where he hid in order to hide the truth about himself—his work at the bank, discussions at the club, conversations about women as "an inferior race," and attending anniversary celebrations with his wife—all this was on the surface. Judging others by himself, he refused to believe the evidence of his eyes, and therefore he imagined that all men led their real and meaningful lives under a veil of mystery and under cover of darkness. Every man's intimate existence revolved around mysterious secrets, and it was perhaps partly for this reason that all civilized men were so nervously anxious to protect their privacy.

Leaving his daughter at the school, Gurov went on to the Slavyansky Bazaar Hotel. He removed his fur coat in the lobby, and then went upstairs and knocked softly on the door. Anna Sergeyevna had been exhausted by the journey and the suspense of waiting for his arrival—she had in fact expected him the previous evening. She was wearing her favorite gray dress. She was pale, and she looked at him without smiling, and he had scarcely entered the room when she threw herself in his arms. Their kisses were lingering and prolonged, as though two years had passed since they had seen each other.

"How were things down there?" he said. "Anything new?"

"Please wait. . . . I'll tell you in a moment. . . . I can't speak yet!"

She could not speak because she was crying. She turned away from him, pressing a handkerchief to her eyes.

"Let her have her cry," he thought. "I'll sit down and wait." And he sat down in an armchair.

Then he rang and ordered tea, and while he drank the tea she remained standing with her face turned to the window. . . . She was crying from the depth of her emotions, in the bitter knowledge that their life together was so weighed down with sadness, because they could only meet in secret and were always hiding from people like thieves. And that meant surely that their lives were shattered!

"Oh, do stop crying!" he said.

It was evident to him that their love affair would not soon be over, and there was no end in sight. Anna Sergeyevna was growing more and more passionately fond of him, and it was beyond belief that he would ever tell her it must one day end; and if he had told her, she would not have believed him.

He went up to her and put his hands on her shoulders, intending to console her with some meaningless words and to fondle her; and then he saw himself in the mirror.

His hair was turning gray. It struck him as strange that he should have aged so much in these last years, and lost his good looks. Her shoulders were warm and trembling at his touch. Her felt pity for her, who was so warm and beautiful, though probably it would not be long before she would begin to fade and wither, as he had done. Why did she love him so much? Women had always believed him to be other than what he was, and they loved in him not himself but the creature who came to life in their imagination, the man they had been seeking eagerly all their lives, and when they had discovered their mistake, they went on loving him. And not one of them was ever happy with him. Time passed, he met other women, became intimate with them, parted from them, never having loved them. It was anything you please, but it was not love.

And now at last, when his hair was turning gray, he had fallen in love—real love—for the first time in his life.

Anna Sergeyevna and he loved one another as people who are very close and dear love one another: they were like deeply devoted friends, like husband and wife. It seemed to them that Fate had intended them for one another, and it was beyond understanding that one had a wife, the other a husband. It was as though they were two birds of passage, one male, one female, who had been trapped and were now compelled to live in different cages. They had forgiven one another for all they were ashamed of in the past, they forgave everything in the present, and felt that this love of theirs changed them both.

Formerly in moments of depression he had consoled himself with the first argument that came into his head, but now all such arguments were foreign to him. He felt a deep compassion for her, and desired to be tender and sincere. . . .

"Don't cry, my darling," he said. "You've cried enough. Now let us talk, and we'll think of something. . . ."

Then they talked it over for a long time, trying to discover some way of avoiding secrecy and deception, and living in different towns, and being separated for long periods. How could they free themselves from their intolerable chains?

"How? How?" he asked, holding his head in his hands. "How?"

And it seemed as though in a little while the solution would be found and a lovely new life would begin for them; and to both of them it was clear that the end was still very far away, and the hardest and most difficult part was only beginning.

····▶ *Your* Turn
Talking and Writing about Lit

1. "The Lady with the Pet Dog" contains four numbered sections and takes place in several different settings. How does Chekhov use the section breaks and shifts of setting to advance the plot and reveal themes?

2. Dmitri Gurov is a dynamic character. Analyze the change which takes place in him, and demonstrate how his transformation reveals themes.

3. Analyze Chekhov's use of narrative point of view in the story.

4. One of the important themes in the story has to do with the public life versus the private life. Find passages in the story that illuminate the way in which this theme is revealed in the experiences of Gurov.

5. **DIY** All of the events and characters in "The Lady with the Pet Dog" are seen through the filter of Dmitri Gurov's limited omniscient view. Often this "colors" or gives a certain spin to a scene or to our perception of other characters such as Anna. Write a scene (any scene) from the story from Anna's point of view instead of Gurov's.

Anton Chekhov: A Diviner with Words, a Healer with Medicine

When Anton Chekhov graduated from medical school in 1884 and began his medical practice, he was also beginning to experience success as a writer. Chekhov was fond of saying that medicine was his wife and literature was his mistress. He seemed to feel that while the practice of medicine was more important, the practice of literature was more fun. He also saw his involvement in science as a part of his humanitarian world view. Chekhov's own parents were serfs (peasants) and he worked hard to attain a medical degree.

Throughout his life, and in his writing, he strove to show accurately and realistically the conditions in which the poor lived. When Chekhov supposedly gave up his medical practice and moved to an estate outside Moscow in 1892, he

Tillie Olsen (b. circa 1912)

Tillie Olsen began writing in the 1930s, but the pressures of raising children while working outside the home and the deprivations of the Great Depression made it impossible for her to find time to continue. After raising four children, Olsen was able to return to her writing, and during the 1950s she wrote the stories collected in her best-known work, *Tell Me a Riddle* (1961). She has also published two other books, *Yonnondio* (1974) and *Silences* (1978). Because Olsen was unable to attend college as a young person, she acquired her education by herself in public libraries. Her work is now so highly respected that Olsen has received numerous honorary degrees from colleges and universities, and she has been the recipient of many grants, fellowships, and awards to support her writing. Olsen has been very involved in

nevertheless continued to be a doctor, offering free medical care to the peasants on his estate, and maintaining a clinic and dispensary for them at his own expense. When doctor characters appear in Chekhov's stories, they are inevitably level-headed types with a humanitarian outlook.

Chekhov sometimes drew material from his life as a doctor for use in his fictions. Sometimes even details from medical reports could become the stuff of fiction, reworked and re-imagined by his fertile mind. In an interview with Salon.com, contemporary fiction writer Tobias Wolff said he loved Anton Chekhov, and the interviewer asked, "What do you love about him?" Wolff replied: "His humanity, and at the same time his pitilessness. He's like a really good doctor— he's an expert diagnostician and at the same time he's very humane. But not soft. He knows where humans fit in the scale of things."

Anton Chekov with his friend, Russian writer Maxim Gorky, in Yalta, May 1900

feminist issues and labor rights issues. She was born in Omaha, Nebraska, circa 1912, and her parents were Jewish political refugees who fled the Russian Czarist repression after the revolution of 1905.

I Stand Here Ironing (1961)

I stand here ironing, and what you asked me moves tormented back and forth with the iron.

"I wish you would manage the time to come in and talk with me about your daughter. I'm sure you can help me understand her. She's a youngster who needs help and whom I'm deeply interested in helping."

"Who needs help." Even if I came, what good would it do? You think because I am her mother I have a key, or that in some way you could use me as a key? She has lived for nineteen years. There is all that life that has happened outside of me, beyond me.

And when is there time to remember, to sift, to weigh, to estimate, to total? I will start and there will be an interruption and I will have to gather it all together again. Or I will become engulfed with all I did or did not do, with what should have been and what cannot be helped.

She was a beautiful baby. The first and only one of our five that was beautiful at birth. You do not guess how new and uneasy her tenancy in her now-loveliness. You did not know her all those years she was thought homely, or see her poring over her baby pictures, making me tell her over and over how beautiful she had been—and would be, I would tell her—and was now, to the seeing eye. But the seeing eyes were few or nonexistent. Including mine.

I nursed her. They feel that's important nowadays. I nursed all the children, but with her, with all the fierce rigidity of first motherhood, I did like the books then said. Though her cries battered me to trembling and my breasts ached with swollenness, I waited till the clock decreed.

Why do I put that first? I do not even know if it matters, or if it explains anything.

She was a beautiful baby. She blew shining bubbles of sound. She loved motion, loved light, loved color and music and textures. She would lie on the floor in her blue overalls patting the surface so hard in ecstasy her hands and feet would blur. She was a miracle to me, but when she was eight months old I had to leave her daytimes with the woman downstairs to whom she was no miracle at all, for I worked or looked for work and for Emily's father, who "could no longer endure" (he wrote in his good-bye note) "sharing want with us."

I was nineteen. It was the pre-relief, pre-WPA world of the depression. I would start running as soon as I got off the street-car, running up the stairs, the place smelling sour, and awake or asleep to startle awake, when she saw me she would break into a clogged weeping that could not be comforted, a weeping I can hear yet.

10   After a while I found a job hashing at night so I could be with her days, and it was better. But it came to where I had to bring her to his family and leave her.

It took a long time to raise the money for her fare back. Then she got chicken pox and I had to wait longer. When she finally came, I hardly knew her, walking quick and nervous like her father, looking like her father, thin, and dressed in a shoddy red that yellowed her skin and glared at the pockmarks. All the baby loveliness gone.

She was two. Old enough for nursery school they said, and I did not know then what I know now—the fatigue of the long day, and the lacerations of group life in nurseries that are only parking places for children.

Except that it would have made no difference if I had known. It was the only place there was. It was the only way we could be together, the only way I could hold a job.

And even without knowing, I knew. I knew the teacher that was evil because all these years it has curdled into my memory, the little boy hunched in the corner, her rasp, "why aren't you outside, because Alvin hits you? that's no reason, go out, scaredy." I knew Emily hated it even if she did not clutch and implore "don't go Mommy" like the other children, mornings.

She always had a reason why we   15 should stay home. Momma, you look sick. Momma, I feel sick. Momma, the teachers aren't there today, they're sick. Momma, we can't go, there was a fire there last night. Momma, it's a holiday today, no school, they told me.

But never a direct protest, never rebellion. I think of our others in their three-, four-year-oldness—the explosions, the tempers, the denunciations, the demands—and I feel suddenly ill. I put the iron down. What in me demanded that goodness in her? And what was the cost, the cost to her of such goodness?

The old man living in the back once said in his gentle way: "You should smile at Emily more when you look at her." What *was* in my face when I looked at her? I loved her. There were all the acts of love.

It was only with the others I remembered what he said, and it was the face of joy, and not of care or tightness or worry I turned to them—too late for Emily. She does not smile easily, let alone almost always as her brothers and sisters do. Her face is closed and sombre, but when she wants, how fluid. You must have seen it in her pantomimes, you spoke of her rare gift for comedy on the stage that rouses a laughter out of the audience so dear they applaud and applaud and do not want to let her go.

Where does it come from, that comedy? There was none of it in her when she came back to me that second time, after I had had to send her away again. She had a new daddy now to learn to love, and I think perhaps it was a better time.

20   Except when we left her alone nights, telling ourselves she was old enough.

"Can't you go some other time, Mommy, like tomorrow?" she would ask. "Will it be just a little while you'll be gone? Do you promise?"

The time we came back, the front door open, the clock on the floor in the hall. She rigid awake. "It wasn't just a little while. I didn't cry. Three times I called you, just three times, and then I ran downstairs to open the door so you could come faster. The clock talked loud. I threw it away, it scared me what it talked."

She said the clock talked loud again that night I went to the hospital to have Susan. She was delirious with the fever that comes before red measles, but she was fully conscious all the week I was gone and the week after we were home when she could not come near the new baby or me.

She did not get well. She stayed skeleton thin, not wanting to eat, and night after night she had nightmares. She would call for me, and I would rouse from exhaustion to sleepily call back: "You're all right, darling, go to sleep, it's just a dream," and if she still called, in a sterner voice, "now go to sleep, Emily, there's

nothing to hurt you." Twice, only twice, when I had to get up for Susan anyhow, I went in to sit with her.

25   Now when it is too late (as if she would let me hold and comfort her like I do the others) I get up and go to her at once at her moan or restless stirring. "Are you awake, Emily? Can I get you something?" And the answer is always the same: "No, I'm all right, go back to sleep, Mother."

They persuaded me at the clinic to send her away to a convalescent home in the country where "she can have the kind of food and care you can't manage for her, and you'll be free to concentrate on the new baby." They still send children to that place. I see pictures on the society page of sleek young women planning affairs to raise money for it, or dancing at the affairs, or decorating Easter eggs or filling Christmas stockings for the children.

They never have a picture of the children so I do not know if the girls still wear those gigantic red bows and the ravaged looks on the every other Sunday when parents can come to visit "unless otherwise notified"—as we were notified the first six weeks.

Oh it is a handsome place, green lawns and tall trees and fluted flower beds. High up on the balconies of each cottage the children stand, the girls in their red bows and white dresses, the boys in white suits and giant red ties. The parents stand below shrieking up to be heard and the children shriek down to be heard, and between them the invisible wall "Not To Be Contaminated by Parental Germs or Physical Affection."

There was a tiny girl who always stood hand in hand with Emily. Her parents never came. One visit she was gone. "They moved her to Rose College," Emily shouted in explanation. "They don't like you to love anybody here."

30   She wrote once a week, the labored writing of a seven-year-old. "I am fine. How is the baby. If I write my leter nicly I will have a star. Love." There never was a star. We wrote every other day, letters she could never hold or keep but only hear read— once. "We simply do not have room for children to keep any personal possessions," they patiently explained when we pieced one Sunday's shrieking together to plead how much it would mean to Emily, who loved so to keep things, to be allowed to keep her letters and cards.

Each visit she looked frailer. "She isn't eating," they told us.

(They had runny eggs for breakfast or mush with lumps, Emily said later, I'd hold it in my mouth and not swallow. Nothing ever tasted good, just when they had chicken.)

It took us eight months to get her released home, and only the fact that she gained back so little of her seven lost pounds convinced the social worker.

I used to try to hold and love her after she came back, but her body would stay stiff, and after a while she'd push away. She ate little. Food sickened her, and I think much of life too. Oh she had physical lightness and brightness, twinkling by on skates, bouncing like a ball up and down up and down over the jump rope, skimming over the hill; but these were momentary.

35   She fretted about her appearance, thin and dark and foreign-looking at a time when every little girl was supposed to look or thought she should look a chubby blonde replica of Shirley Temple. The doorbell sometimes rang for her, but no one seemed to come and play in the house or be a best friend. Maybe because we moved so much.

There was a boy she loved painfully through two school semesters. Months later she told me how she had taken pennies from my purse to buy him candy. "Licorice was his favorite and I brought him some every day, but he still liked Jennifer better'n me. Why, Mommy?" The kind of question for which there is no answer.

School was a worry to her. She was not glib or quick in a world where glibness and quickness were easily confused with ability to learn. To her overworked and exasperated teachers she was an over-conscientious "slow learner" who kept trying to catch up and was absent entirely too often.

I let her be absent, though sometimes the illness was imaginary. How different from my now-strictness about attendance with the others. I wasn't working. We had a new baby, I was home anyhow. Sometimes, after Susan grew old enough, I would keep her home from school, too, to have them all together.

Mostly Emily had asthma, and her breathing, harsh and labored, would fill the house with a curiously tranquil sound. I would bring the two old dresser mirrors and her boxes of collections to her bed. She would select beads and single earrings, bottle tops and shells, dried flowers and pebbles, old postcards and scraps, all sorts of oddments; then she and Susan would play Kingdom, setting up landscapes and furniture, peopling them with action.

Those were the only times of peaceful 40 companionship between her and Susan. I have edged away from it, that poisonous feeling between them, that terrible balancing of hurts and needs I had to do between the two, and did so badly, those earlier years.

Oh there are conflicts between the others too, each one human, needing, demanding, hurting, taking—but only between Emily and Susan, no, Emily toward Susan that corroding resentment. It seems so obvious on the surface, yet it is not obvious. Susan, the second child, Susan, golden- and curly-haired and chubby, quick and articulate and assured, everything in appearance and manner Emily was not; Susan, not able to resist Emily's precious things, losing or sometimes clumsily breaking them; Susan telling jokes and riddles to company for applause while Emily sat silent (to say to me later: that was *my* riddle, Mother, I told it to Susan); Susan, who for all the five years' difference in age was just a year behind Emily in developing physically.

I am glad for that slow physical development that widened the difference between her and her contemporaries, though she suffered over it. She was too vulnerable for that terrible world of youthful competition, of preening and parading, of constant measuring of yourself against every other, of envy, "If I had that copper hair," "If I had that skin. . . ." She tormented herself enough about not looking like the others, there was enough of the unsureness, the having to be conscious of words before you speak, the constant caring—what are they thinking of me? without having it all magnified by the merciless physical drives.

Ronnie is calling. He is wet and I change him. It is rare there is such a cry now. That time of motherhood is almost behind me when the ear is not one's own but must always be racked and listening for the child cry, the child call. We sit for a while and I hold him, looking out over the city spread in charcoal with its soft aisles of light. "*Shoogily*," he breathes and curls closer. I carry him back to bed, asleep. *Shoogily*. A funny word, a family word, inherited from Emily, invented by her to say: *comfort*.

In this and other ways she leaves her seal, I say aloud. And startle at my saying it. What do I mean? What did I start to gather together, to try and make coherent? I was at the terrible, growing years. War years. I do not remember them well. I was working,

there were four smaller ones now, there was not time for her. She had to help be a mother, and housekeeper, and shopper. She had to set her seal. Mornings of crisis and near hysteria trying to get lunches packed, hair combed, coats and shoes found, everyone to school or Child Care on time, the baby ready for transportation. And always the paper scribbled on by a smaller one, the book looked at by Susan then mislaid, the homework not done. Running out to that huge school where she was one, she was lost, she was a drop; suffering over the unpreparedness, stammering and unsure in her classes.

There was so little time left at night 45 after the kids were bedded down. She would struggle over books, always eating (it was in those years she developed her enormous appetite that is legendary in our family) and I would be ironing, or preparing food for the next day, or writing V-mail to Bill, or tending the baby. Sometimes, to make me laugh, or out of her despair, she would imitate happenings or types at school.

I think I said once: "Why don't you do something like this in the school amateur show?" One morning she phoned me at work, hardly understandable through the weeping: "Mother, I did it. I won, I won; they gave me first prize; they clapped and clapped and wouldn't let me go."

Now suddenly she was Somebody, and as imprisoned in her difference as she had been in anonymity.

She began to be asked to perform at other high schools, even in colleges, then at city and statewide affairs. The first one we went to, I only recognized her that first moment when thin, shy, she almost drowned herself into the curtains. Then: Was this Emily? The control, the command, the convulsing and deadly clowning, the spell, then the roaring, stamping audience, unwilling to let this rare and precious laughter out of their lives.

Afterwards: You ought to do something about her with a gift like that—but without money or knowing how, what does one do? We have left it all to her, and the gift has as often eddied inside, clogged and clotted, as been used and growing.

50 She is coming. She runs up the stairs two at a time with her light graceful step, and I know she is happy tonight. Whatever it was that occasioned your call did not happen today.

"Aren't you ever going to finish the ironing, Mother? Whistler painted his mother in a rocker. I'd have to paint mine standing over an ironing board." This is one of her communicative nights and she tells me everything and nothing as she fixes herself a plate of food out of the icebox.

She is so lovely. Why did you want me to come in at all? Why were you concerned? She will find her way.

She starts up the stairs to bed. "Don't get me up with the rest in the morning." "But I thought you were having midterms." "Oh, those," she comes back in, kisses me, and says quite lightly, "in a couple of years when we'll all be atom-dead they won't matter a bit."

She has said it before. She *believes* it. But because I have been dredging the past, and all that compounds a human being is so heavy and meaningful in me, I cannot endure it tonight.

I will never total it all. I will never 55 come in to say: She was a child seldom smiled at. Her father left me before she was a year old. I had to work her first six years when there was work, or I sent her home and to his relatives. There were years she had care she hated. She was dark and thin and foreign-looking in a world where the prestige went to blondeness and curly hair and dimples, she was slow where glibness was prized. She was a child of anxious, not proud, love. We were poor and could not afford for her the soil of easy growth. I was a young mother, I was a distracted mother. There were the other children pushing up, demanding. Her younger sister seemed all that she was not. There were years she did not want me to touch her. She kept too much in herself, her life was such she had to keep too much in herself. My wisdom came too late. She has much to her and probably nothing will come of it. She is a child of her age, of depression, of war, of fear.

Let her be. So all that is in her will not bloom—but in how many does it? There is still enough left to live by. Only help her to know—help make it so there is cause for her to know—that she is more than this dress on the ironing board, helpless before the iron.

····▶ *Your* Turn
Talking and Writing about Lit

1. Who is telling the story; who is our narrator? Who is the "you" addressed by the first-person narrator? Do you think the mother will ever visit this "you," as referred to in the story?

2. Who is the main character—the mother or Emily? Support your view with details and quotations from the story.

3. Does our view of the mother change as we read the story? Compare Olsen's mother with Mrs. Johnson in "Everyday Use" (Chapter 8).

4. **DIY** The "interruptions" in the story serve more than one purpose. They serve as a sort of "list of difficulties faced," but they also may represent a dialogue with a potential critic, and they represent the narrator wrestling with her own self-doubt. Write two pages in which a narrator carries on a "monologue" (it appears to be just one voice speaking) which is interrupted by a second voice or by the narrator's own doubts or comments.

Talking Lit

Contemporary author Diane Johnson makes clear how even the author can be surprised by themes that emerge from a work he or she has completed, while nineteenth-century author Edgar Allan Poe asserts his belief that a story should aim for a unified effect.

Diane Johnson, "Pesky Themes Will Emerge When You're Not Looking"

I've been going around doing readings from a new novel ("Le Mariage"), and often, on these occasions, I've been asked surprising questions about its themes. At first I was somewhat confounded by this. The novelist may be the last to know the theme of her work, may even have avoided thinking about it too particularly, lest, like happiness, it disappear on too close examination or seem too thin and flimsy to live.

In Seattle a man asked me what the theme of rescued cats and dogs in my books meant. I had to think about that, because I hadn't really noticed they were there. Freud would say those cats and dogs are children, but that doesn't seem quite right to me.

Must a novel have a theme? If so, who is in charge of it?

You can't help but wonder if each writer has themes typical to him, if the themes are as particular to the writer as to the work. To read, as I have, of my own books, that they are full of desperate women fleeing their circumstances, greatly surprised this contented and settled housewife. Certainly I have never thought of them that way. To me, my heroines are interpretive consciousnesses through whom to observe external events, in Iran, California or France.

I have written elsewhere about the plight of the reliable female narrator, a modern innovation perhaps, for whom we are unprepared by a literary tradition of heroines who were only acted upon. My friend Max Byrd says that all fiction can be reduced to one of two plots: a stranger comes to town, or someone goes on a trip. And mine are the latter, that's all, about travelers to whom things happen, as things will.

But that's not all about them. Any novel has lots of themes, if I understand the word correctly. It seems like a holdover term from high school English class, useful for discussing novels, but not very relevant to the process of writing them. There's something too close to "thesis" about it; the idea of imposing a preconception is anathema to a novelist who likes to imagine she is observing life and manners without any didactic intention and without forcing her characters to follow a plan.

Of course a writer, like anybody, has a set of general ideas: the inhumanity of man to man, or that life is a struggle, or that nature is beautiful. Some of the ideas will be received ideas; some may be original or idiosyncratic or even suspect, as was said of Ayn Rand's, for instance, or some of T. S. Eliot's, or Pound's. Taken together, a writer's themes are thought to typify the writer despite him- or herself, except for protean geniuses like Shakespeare, invisible in the dense thicket of their contradictions.

I suppose the major theme of a given work is the sum of all its ideas. That's implicit in those joke contests on the Internet about Merged Novels, in which people compress the essence of two books into one, like "The Maltese Faulkner." ("Is the black bird a tortured symbol of Sam's struggles with race and family? Or is it merely a crow, mocking his attempts to understand? Or is it worth a cool mil?") Or "Catch-22 in the Rye." ("Holden learns that if you're insane, you'll probably flunk out of prep school, but if you're flunking out of prep school, you're probably not insane.")

But every novel is a "spongy tract," as E. M. Forster put it, a tissue of ideas so dense and various it would be impossible to tease them all out.

Too many themes and the novelist risks committing a "novel of ideas," a term that can conceal a note of reservation. As a phrase, "novel of ideas" is gathered from what seems now a somewhat dated typology used to categorize all novels as "of ideas," or as comedy of manners, or action, romance and so on, depending on the general effect. These were also shorthand ways of saying serious, boring, comic, moving account of personal anguish, love story, etc.

Even while there is a liking for the glib identification of themes, there is a resistance to the idea of ideas in novels. Two examples from my own experience:

The British publisher of "Le Divorce," a novel about a young woman's coming to worldliness in Paris, omitted an entire chapter wherein Americans in Paris in about 1995 fall into a bitter dispute about the Vietnam War, a subject still dividing us after 30 years. The publisher thought this would not be interesting to a British audience. Now people ask how I could have been so docile about allowing this omission, and the answer is, I don't know. Maybe I was still insecure about that theme.

Another time, a French translator, under the impression that "Persian Nights," a novel about the political situation in prerevolutionary Iran, was a bodice-ripper, a genre the French are fond of, omitted all the heroine's observations of the political scene and stressed all her moments of personal danger, preferably the risk of rape (which in fact never came up). Here I did protest, and the problem was partly fixed.

Several reviewers of Susan Sontag's new novel "In America" have used the expression "novel of ideas," perhaps because the characters have ideas about Fourier's utopianism, or methods of acting, and discuss them. But you have to wonder what a novel without ideas would be like? One idea or theme in, say, Forster's "Passage to India" is that people from different cultures rarely understand one another. Reduced to this simple statement, "Passage to India" has the same theme as many novels that many other writers, including me in "Le Mariage," have tried to write.

In its particulars of course "Passage to India" is utterly unlike any other novel. Is it a novel of ideas or a comedy of manners? The characters discuss philosophy. "When evil occurs, it expresses the whole of the universe," says the Indian Professor Godpole. Asked if he means that good and evil are the same, he says: "Oh, no . . . good and evil are different, as their names imply. But, in my humble opinion, they are both of them aspects of my Lord." He is talking to Fielding, for whom good and evil seem expressions of the indifference of the universe. Where does Forster stand in this difference of opinion? Does he take a stand?

Can the novelist entirely control the ideas in her text, or conceal herself among them? There's the phenomenon well known to writers whose characters, given their head, take off and do or say things the writer did not foresee. The writing has a Ouija board will of its own.

On the other hand there are the covert operations of your own character—your personal obsessions, perhaps—that ordain that, however you start out, you end up with the sort of novel only you would write. (Obviously these two are functions of each other: the unexpected crops up out of some less conscious realm of your self.) There's age, birth order, geography. Nationality is certainly part of the imperatives of our natures, something that we can't help and that has programmed us.

Of course you yourself can change with the years, with the events life deals you. I feel myself constantly struggling against some imperative of my own nature that dictates that no matter how much I want to write a serious, moving psychological novel, I end up with the sort of comic or tragicomic novel I have seen referred to as "of manners," reflecting my interest—and it is true that I'm interested in manners—in the way people behave and especially the way people behave when out of their own culture, or how people in other cultures behave.

But novels are never about what they are about; that is, there is always deeper, or more general, significance. The author may not be aware of this till she is pretty far along with it. A novel's whole pattern is rarely apparent at the outset of writing, or even at the end; that is when the writer finds out what a novel is about, and the job becomes one of understanding and deepening or sharpening what is already written. That is finding the theme.

If the writer is the last to identify the theme, probably we as readers don't consciously articulate the theme as we read either. When we are asked what a book is about, we tend to focus on some element of the plot, to say, "It's about a woman who was or wasn't molested in a cave in India," or "an orphan who has to work as a governess in a wild, remote house."

We fasten on the principal feature of the action. But what we get out of a book is the lesson or the theme: courage, the indomitability of the human spirit in the case of "Jane Eyre" (and all the works of Charlotte Brontë) and in "A Passage to India" things about integrity and pride, especially on the part of the misfit. These deep messages are the satisfying qualities that make us admire a book.

If a book had a wicked or meretricious message, we might reject or mistrust it, or in some way feel it to be subversive. Or we might be taken in by it, briefly. History is full of "dangerous" books, though they never prevail. But attempts to suppress them always eventually backfire, too. The moral careers of books are always fascinating.

Edgar Allan Poe, "The Short Story and the Single Effect," from a review of Hawthorne's *Twice-Told Tales*

The tale proper affords the fairest field which can be afforded by the wide domains of mere prose, for the exercise of the highest genius. Were I bidden to say how this genius could be most advantageously employed for the best display of its powers, I should answer, without hesitation, "in the composition of a rhymed poem not to exceed in length what might be perused in an hour."

Were I called upon, however, to designate that class of composition which, next to such a poem as I have suggested, should best fulfil the demands and serve the purposes of ambitious genius, should offer it the most advantageous field of exertion, and afford it the fairest opportunity of display, I should speak at once of the brief prose tale. History, philosophy, and other matters of that kind, we leave out of the question, of course. *Of course*, I say, and in spite of the gray-beards. These grave topics, to the end of time, will be best illustrated by what a discriminating world, turning up its nose at the drab pamphlets, has agreed to understand as *talent*. The ordinary novel is objectionable, from its length, for reasons analogous to those which render length objectionable in the poem. As the novel cannot be read at one sitting, it cannot avail itself of the immense benefit of *totality*. Worldly interests, intervening during the pauses of perusal, modify, counteract and annul the impressions intended. But simple cessation in reading would, of itself, be sufficient to destroy the true unity. In the brief tale, however, the author is enabled to carry out his full design without interruption. During the hour of perusal, the soul of the reader is at the writer's control.

A skilful artist has constructed a tale. He has not fashioned his thoughts to accommodate his incidents, but having deliberately conceived a certain *single effect* to be wrought, he then invents such incidents, he then combines such events, and discusses them in such tone as may best serve him in establishing this preconceived effect. If his very first sentence tend not to the outbringing of this effect, then in his very first step has he committed a blunder. In the whole composition there should be no word written of which the tendency, direct or indirect, is not to the one pre-established design. And by such means, with such care and skill, a picture is at length painted which leaves in the mind of him who contemplates it with a kindred art, a sense of the fullest satisfaction. The idea of the tale, its thesis, has been presented unblemished, because undisturbed—an end absolutely demanded, yet, in the novel, altogether unattainable.

CUTTING EDGES: METAFICTION AND AVANT-POP

Even Norman Rockwell uses metafiction.

A writer who uses metafiction creates a story aware of itself as a story. You can think of metafiction as a picture within a picture, and it is an idea illustrated with exceptional clarity by Norman Rockwell's *Triple Self Portrait*. In this self-portrait, Rockwell used metafiction by painting himself painting himself. The picture shows awareness that it is a portrait, and the artist captured his own conception of the process of creating art.

Consider the painting carefully and notice the juxtaposition of reality with fantasy. The props lend realism to the painting. The artist's tools at the bottom of the painting, the metal bucket emitting a tiny puff of smoke, the beverage that sits atop an open book on the chair that holds the mirror, and the small drawings and paintings tacked to the perimeter of the large canvas all ground the painting in reality. Then, notice the differences between the three Rockwells you see in the painting: the painter, with his back to the viewer, surrounded by his tools and his work; the bespectacled man in the mirror, the subject of the painting within the painting; and the dignified, wise gentleman on the canvas, the fictional character. By painting three versions of himself, he illustrated a disparity between reality and the human inter-pretation of reality, the various aspects of one man, and the variety of ways in which we perceive ourselves and our lives. *Triple Self Portrait* represents a challenge to perspective, a primary objective of any artist who uses metafiction or megaimage.

Rockwell's *Triple Self Portrait* appeared on the cover of the *Saturday Evening Post* on February 13, 1960, the issue that began a weekly series of articles drawn from Rockwell's autobiography, *My Adventures as an Illustrator*. He was 66 years old when he painted it. One of many self-portraits by Rockwell, *Triple Self Portrait* is the most famous, and most parodied.

The title of this chapter may look like a puzzler to you; however, if you've ever watched an interactive children's show like *Blue's Clues* or *Dora the Explorer*, you've experienced metafiction. If you've seen the movie *Roger Rabbit*, you're already attuned to avant-pop and its intertextual hijinx. Continue reading for a full explanation!

What is Metafiction?

Metafiction, an innovative point of view which most of us have encountered, means that the story is aware of itself as a story, just as Norman Rockwell is aware (in his *Triple Self Portrait* on the previous page) that he is looking in the mirror at a reflection of himself and at the same time painting a picture of himself painting himself. Likewise, in Tim O'Brien's "How to Tell a True War Story" (in this chapter), the narrator is aware that a story is being told: "In any war story, but especially a true one, it's difficult to separate what happened from what seemed to happen. What seems to happen becomes its own happening and has to be told that way. The angles of vision are skewed. . . . The pictures get jumbled." Throughout the story, and beginning even with the title, O'Brien's story is aware of itself as a fiction.

Metafiction is also sometimes called **self-reflexive narration** because it "reflects upon" the very act of telling a story and it does so *within* the story itself. This is especially true in Margaret Atwood's innovative story "There Was Once," which you'll read in this chapter. In Atwood's story a second voice argues with the narrator about how to tell the story. The story keeps folding back on itself as the narrator alters the details on the spot to satisfy the complaints of the listener. Don DeLillo's "Videotape" (also in this chapter) is self-reflexive in a different way: It uses the second person "you" to address both the viewer of the videotape and, in a sense, the reader of the story.

> You keep on looking not because you know something is going to happen—of course you do know something is going to happen and you do look for that reason but you might also keep on looking if you came across this footage for the first time without knowing the outcome. There is a crude power operating here. You keep on looking because things combine to hold you fast—a sense of the random, the amateurish, the accidental, the impending. (paragraph 13)

In a sense, the reader is also the viewer of the videotaped crime because the details of it (and of its videotaping by the child) are presented to us in the narration step by step (as if we were also watching it on the screen).

Another level of meaning in the story has to do with the reader/viewer as universal, as "every viewer," and the videotape as an example of the media or media coverage. Consider some of the video clips you've seen replayed again and again on television (and on the web): the assassination of John F. Kennedy and later of his assassin, Lee Harvey Oswald; the assassinations of Martin Luther King, Jr., Robert F. Kennedy, and Malcolm X; the planes hitting the twin towers of the World

Trade Center on 9/11 and the people leaping out of the windows of the towers. In "Videotape," the focus is more on the narrator watching the tape than it is on the girl doing the filming or even on the victim of the crime. The story is about the viewer; the story is about *you*. Charles Johnson pushes the metafictional envelope one step farther, as you'll read in this chapter. In "Moving Pictures," *you* are the reader, the narrator, the writer, all of us, the community, the society, the audience in the theater, the filmmaker, and the screenwriter! In a sense, the story (and its moving pictures) represents life in general, as well as *your* life.

Avant-Pop and Intertextuality

Avant-pop is a blending of two terms: avant-garde and pop culture. The concept of **avant-pop** has to do with the influence of media—television, comic books, and movies—and the borrowing of pop culture or common culture texts into the writing of fiction, poetry, or drama. We would call something **avant-garde** if it uses new techniques (cutting-edge techniques) in the creation of an art form; avant-pop uses cutting-edge techniques to blend in images, references, and sometimes whole passages from the media and pop culture into literary works. This can have startling and sometimes hilarious effects. The term **intertextuality** is also often used to refer to a text that incorporates snippets (or even whole chunks) of another text.

One interesting example of intertextuality is Robert Olen Butler's story "Jealous Husband Returns in Form of Parrot" (in this chapter), a takeoff on headlines gleaned from tabloid newspapers. Asked by an interviewer from the NuzDragon website how he got the idea to base works of fiction on headline stories taken from tabloids such as the *Weekly World News*, Butler replied,

> I got the idea at the 12th Street Kroger [grocery store in Lake Charles, Louisiana, where Butler lives]. It was about midnight, two years ago, and I was in the line, shifting a cold bottle of milk from hand to hand. There were two people ahead of me at the checkout counter and I was stalled in front of the tabloids. . . . I think the headline that night was "Boy Born With Tattoo of Elvis."

You will enjoy Butler's story, in which the narrator is a parrot. If it tickles your fancy, you might want to look for his book *Tabloid Dreams*, from which "Jealous Husband Returns in Form of Parrot" is taken.

The Real and The Nonreal In Fiction

The reader who enjoys Gish Jen's "In the American Society" or Anton Chekhov's "The Lady with the Pet Dog" (both in Chapter 10) is responding to the **realistic** model of human experience presented by these stories. The creation of this kind of fictional world, which is convincing because it resembles the details of real life, is also called **mimesis** (imitating natural life) or **verisimilitude** (appearing to be real). On the other hand, when one reads, in Gabriel García Márquez's "A Very Old Man with Enormous Wings" (Chapter 9), that "Pelayo . . . had to go very close to see that it was an old man, a very old man, lying face down in the mud, who, in spite of his tremendous efforts, couldn't get up, impeded by his enormous wings," it is obvious that the writer has landed us in a different model of reality. We know the story involves the use of **nonrealistic** elements or even **fantasy**. Either we are in an alternative reality—one different from our own—or the writer is proposing a new perspective on the everyday world.

The writer who employs nonrealistic elements in a story may, in fact, feel that the story is a more accurate, more complex, or more honest depiction of the real world because of the way in which this fiction shows the absurdity or contradictions of life as we know it. It may be nonrealistic to depict an old man who has wings on his back, but to the extent that the story of his experiences reveals truthfully the way in which a human community often treats a newcomer (especially one with a ragged appearance who speaks another language), it is real. And the way in which García Márquez shows the community to be searching for easy answers and shifting from one "carnival attraction" to another may rely on **hyperbole** (extravagant exaggeration) at times, but it does succeed in depicting some foibles of human behavior García Márquez wants to spotlight. Incidentally, García Márquez's particular brand of nonrealistic fiction is known as **magical realism**. This may seem to be a contradiction in terms; but, in fact, part of the charm of his fiction, and one of the ways in which he achieves his effects, is the **juxtaposition** (putting side by side) of ordinary, everyday details with fantastic details. This technique makes the story more "magical" and more convincingly real at the same time.

In Donald Barthelme's "The School" (as in García Márquez's story), we are confronted with some events and dialogue that we are not meant to take literally. Barthelme's stories often make mocking fun of their characters (and, by extension, of all of us), and when his schoolchildren suddenly start popping off with remarks like "isn't death, considered as the fundamental datum, the means by which the taken-for-granted mundanity of the everyday may be transcended," we know that this is nonrealistic and, in fact, **absurd** (ridiculous, illogical). Schoolchildren don't speak this way in the real world. Why, then, does Barthelme write this sort of thing? He wants to make us laugh, and he also perceives that the real world we live in every day contains more than a little absurdity and more than a few illogical systems with which we must cope (have you waited in line at the DMV lately?). Also, Barthelme wants to try something new. When you read John Barth's piece later in this chapter (in the "Talking Lit" section), you might chuckle at a Barthelme statement quoted by Barth: "'How come you write the way you do?' a Johns Hopkins apprentice writer once asked him. 'Because Samuel Beckett already wrote the way he did,' Barthelme replied."

You will notice that in the piece just mentioned, Barth refers (even in his title) to Barthelme as a **minimalist.** You might say that Barthelme is a man of few words. Minimalism in literature involves a spareness of style and an economy of form.

Barthelme (in addition to exposing what is ridiculous and absurd in our daily lives) is good at depicting all of this in plain language and in a story of economical length. Barth says (of Barthelme) that "he didn't waste words. . . . Donald barely indulged words—he valued them too much for that."

METAFICTION READINGS

Tim O'Brien (b. 1946)

Immediately after graduating from Macalester College in Minnesota in 1968, Tim O'Brien was drafted and sent to Vietnam where he served as an infantry combat soldier in the ill-fated Americal Division, 1969–1970. Despite the fact that O'Brien opposed the war in Vietnam, he served honorably and was awarded a Purple Heart. After his discharge, O'Brien spent some time at Harvard as a graduate student and then worked for a time as a journalist. His career as a writer of fiction and memoir began with the publication in 1973 of his memoir *If I Die in a Combat Zone, Box Me Up and Send Me Home*. O'Brien has since won many distinguished awards for his fiction and has published many successful works of fiction, among them, *Going After Cacciato* (1978), *The Nuclear Age* (1985), *In the Lake of the Woods* (1994), and *Tomcat in Love* (1998). The story below comes from *The Things They Carried* (1990).

How to Tell a True War Story (1987)

This is true.

I had a buddy in Vietnam. His name was Bob Kiley, but everybody called him Rat.

A friend of his gets killed, so about a week later Rat sits down and writes a letter to the guy's sister. Rat tells her what a great brother she had, how together the guy was, a number one pal and comrade. A real soldier's soldier, Rat says. Then he tells a few stories to make the point, how her brother would always volunteer for stuff nobody else would volunteer for in a million years, dangerous stuff, like doing recon or going out on these really badass night patrols. Stainless steel balls, Rat tells her. The guy was a little crazy, for sure, but crazy in a good way, a real daredevil, because he liked the challenge of it, he liked testing himself, just man against gook. A great, great guy, Rat says.

Anyway, it's a terrific letter, very personal and touching. Rat almost bawls writing it. He gets all teary telling about the good times they had together, how her brother made the war seem almost fun, always raising hell and lighting up villes and bringing smoke to bear every which way. A great sense of humor, too. Like the time at this river when he went fishing with a whole damn crate of hand grenades. Probably the funniest thing in world history, Rat says, all that gore, about twenty zillion dead gook fish. Her brother, he had the right attitude. He knew how to have a good time. On Halloween, this real hot spooky night,

POP CULTURE

What is Metafiction?

The Surreal and Outlandish Meditations of Mel Brooks and The Simpsons

In his "How to Tell a True War Story," Tim O'Brien reflects on the actual events he's writing about and on the parts he plays as the writer of his story and as a character in his story. O'Brien plays the story from three angles at once and acknowledges himself from each point. This kind of self-reflection is hardly comical in the context of the tragedies of the Vietnam War, but in other contexts, metafiction is often played for a laugh.

In Mel Brooks's films, for example, meta-moments frequently occur. In

A scene from Mel Brooks' *Spaceballs*

the dude paints up his body all different colors and puts on this weird mask and hikes over to a ville and goes trick-or-treating almost stark naked, just boots and balls and an M-16. A tremendous human being, Rat says. Pretty nutso sometimes, but you could trust him with your life.

5   And then the letter gets very sad and serious. Rat pours his heart out. He says he loved the guy. He says the guy was his best friend in the world. They were like soul mates, he says, like twins or something, they had a whole lot in common. He tells the guy's sister he'll look her up when the war's over.

So what happens?

Rat mails the letter. He waits two months. The dumb cooze never writes back.

A true war story is never moral. It does not instruct, nor encourage virtue, nor suggest models of proper human behavior, nor restrain men from doing the things men have always done. If a story seems moral, do not believe it. If at the end of a war story you feel uplifted, or if you feel that some small bit of rectitude has been salvaged from the larger waste, then you have been made the victim of a very old and terrible lie. There is no rectitude whatsoever.

Scene from *The Simpsons*

Brooks's *Star Wars* satire *SpaceBalls*, a light-saber battle results in the death of the film crew's boom operator. The camera pans over to the people shooting the film and pauses for a moment on their shocked faces before the sword-fighters shrug and resume battle. In the same film, the spoof character of *Star Wars'* Yoda (in *SpaceBalls*, he's Yogurt) discusses the merchandising opportunities for his own character. Definitely a metafictional moment.

The Simpsons TV series, another merchandising goldmine, ran an episode in which Bart Simpson becomes famous for a catchphrase, "I didn't do it." After the fad finally blows over, his sister Lisa expresses her relief at the demise of another pointless catchphrase. Immediately, each family member finds a reason to spout the gimmicky catchphrases for which he or she is known. Then neighbors appear in the living room, outside the window, and on the staircase, all belting out their various oft-said words. Nelson the Bully does his trademark nasally laugh, and Flanders pops from the bushes hailing them: "Hidely-Ho." *The Simpsons* abounds with meta-moments. The story is always aware of itself as a story; the script is commenting on itself as a script.

There is no virtue. As a first rule of thumb, therefore, you can tell a true war story by its absolute and uncompromising allegiance to obscenity and evil. Listen to Rat Kiley. Cooze, he says. He does not say bitch. He certainly does not say woman, or girl. He says cooze. Then he spits and stares. He's nineteen years old—it's too much for him— so he looks at you with those big sad gentle killer eyes and says cooze, because his friend is dead, and because it's so incredibly sad and true: she never wrote back.

You can tell a true war story if it embarrasses you. If you don't care for obscenity, you don't care for the truth; if you

don't care for the truth, watch how you vote. Send guys to war, they come home talking dirty.

Listen to Rat: "Jesus Christ, man, I write this beautiful fuckin' letter, I slave over it, and what happens? The dumb cooze never writes back." 10

The dead guy's name was Curt Lemon. What happened was, we crossed a muddy river and marched west into the mountains, and on the third day we took a break along a trail junction in deep jungle. Right away, Lemon and Rat Kiley started goofing. They didn't understand about the spookiness. They were kids; they just didn't know. A nature hike, they thought, not even a war, so they went off into the shade of some giant trees—quadruple canopy, no sunlight at all—and they were giggling and calling each other yellow mother and playing a silly game they'd invented. The game involved smoke grenades, which were harmless unless you did stupid things, and what they did was pull out the pin and stand a few feet apart and play catch under the shade of those huge trees. Whoever chickened out was a yellow mother. And if nobody chickened out, the grenade would make a light popping sound and they'd be covered with smoke and they'd laugh and dance around and then do it again.

It's all exactly true.

It happened, to *me*, nearly twenty years ago, and I still remember that trail junction and those giant trees and a soft dripping sound somewhere beyond the trees. I remember the smell of moss. Up in the canopy there were tiny white blossoms, but no sunlight at all, and I remember the shadows spreading out under the trees where Curt Lemon and Rat Kiley were playing catch with smoke grenades. Mitchell Sanders sat flipping his yo-yo. Norman Bowker and Kiowa and Dave Jensen were dozing, or half dozing, and all around us were those ragged green mountains.

Except for the laughter things were quiet.

15 At one point, I remember, Mitchell Sanders turned and looked at me, not quite nodding, as if to warn me about something, as if he already *knew*, then after a while he rolled up his yo-yo and moved away.

It's hard to tell you what happened next.

They were just goofing. There was a noise, I suppose, which must've been the detonator, so I glanced behind me and watched Lemon step from the shade into bright sunlight. His face was suddenly brown and shining. A handsome kid, really. Sharp gray eyes, lean and narrow-waisted, and when he died it was almost beautiful, the way the sunlight came around him and lifted him up and sucked him high into a tree full of moss and vines and white blossoms.

In any war story, but especially a true one, it's difficult to separate what happened from what seemed to happen. What seems to happen becomes its own happening and has to be told that way. The angles of vision are skewed. When a booby trap explodes, you close your eyes and duck and float outside yourself. When a guy dies, like Curt Lemon, you look away and then look back for a moment and then look away again. The pictures get jumbled; you tend to miss a lot. And then afterward, when you go to tell about it, there is always that surreal seemingness, which makes the story seem untrue, but which in fact represents the hard and exact truth as it *seemed*.

In many cases a true war story cannot be believed. If you believe it, be skeptical. It's a question of credibility. Often the crazy stuff is true and the normal stuff isn't, because the normal stuff is necessary to make you believe the truly incredible craziness.

In other cases you can't even tell a true 20 war story. Sometimes it's just beyond telling.

I heard this one, for example, from Mitchell Sanders. It was near dusk and we were sitting at my foxhole along a wide muddy river north of Quang Ngai. I remember how peaceful the twilight was. A deep pinkish red spilled out on the river, which moved without sound, and in the morning we would cross the river and march west into the mountains. The occasion was right for a good story.

"God's truth," Mitchell Sanders said. "A six-man patrol goes up into the mountains on a basic listening-post operation. The idea's to spend a week up there, just lie low and listen for enemy movement. They've got a radio along, so if they hear anything suspicious—anything—they're supposed to call in artillery or gunships, whatever it takes. Otherwise they keep strict field discipline. Absolute silence. They just listen."

Sanders glanced at me to make sure I had the scenario. He was playing with his yo-yo, dancing it with short, tight little strokes of the wrist.

His face was blank in the dusk.

25 "We're talking regulation, by-the-book LP. These six guys, they don't say boo for a solid week. They don't got tongues. *All* ears."

"Right," I said.

"Understand me?"

"Invisible."

Sanders nodded.

30 "Affirm," he said. "Invisible. So what happens is, these guys get themselves deep in the bush, all camouflaged up, and they lie down and wait and that's all they do, nothing else, they lie there for seven straight days and just listen. And man, I'll tell you—it's spooky. This is mountains. You don't *know* spooky till you been there. Jungle, sort of, except it's way up in the clouds and there's always this fog—like rain, except it's not raining—everything's all wet and swirly and tangled up and you can't see jack, you can't find your own pecker to piss with. Like you don't even have a body. Serious spooky. You just go with the vapors—the fog sort of takes you in . . . And the sounds, man. The sounds carry forever. You hear stuff nobody should *ever* hear."

Sanders was quiet for a second, just working the yo-yo, then he smiled at me.

"So after a couple days the guys start hearing this real soft, kind of wacked-out music. Weird echoes and stuff. Like a radio or something, but it's not a radio, it's this strange gook music that comes right out of the rocks. Faraway, sort of, but right up

close, too. They try to ignore it. But it's a listening post, right? So they listen. And every night they keep hearing that crazyass gook concert. All kinds of chimes and xylophones. I mean, this is wilderness—no way, it can't be real—but there it *is*, like the mountains are tuned in to Radio fucking Hanoi. Naturally they get nervous. One guy sticks Juicy Fruit in his ears. Another guy almost flips. Thing is, though, they can't report music. They can't get on the horn and call back to base and say, 'Hey, listen, we need some firepower, we got to blow away this weirdo gook rock band.' They can't do that. It wouldn't go down. So they lie there in the fog and keep their mouths shut. And what makes it extra bad, see, is the poor dudes can't horse around like normal. Can't joke it away. Can't even talk to each other except maybe in whispers, all hush-hush, and that just revs up the willies. All they do is listen."

Again there was some silence as Mitchell Sanders looked out on the river. The dark was coming on hard now, and off to the west I could see the mountains rising in silhouette, all the mysteries and unknowns.

"This next part," Sanders said quietly, "you won't believe."

"Probably not," I said. 35

"You won't. And you know why?" He gave me a long, tired smile. "Because it happened. Because every word is absolutely dead-on true."

Sanders made a sound in his throat, like a sigh, as if to say he didn't care if I believed him or not. But he did care. He wanted me to feel the truth, to believe by the raw force of feeling. He seemed sad, in a way.

"These six guys," he said, "they're pretty fried out by now, and one night they start hearing voices. Like at a cocktail party. That's what it sounds like, this big swank gook cocktail party somewhere out there in the fog. Music and chitchat and stuff. It's crazy, I know, but they hear the champagne corks. They hear the actual martini glasses. Real hoity-toity, all very civilized, except this isn't civilization. This is Nam.

"Anyway, the guys try to be cool. They just lie there and groove, but after a while they start hearing—you won't believe this—they hear chamber music. They hear violins and cellos. They hear this terrific mama-san soprano. Then after a while they hear gook opera and a glee club and the Haiphong Boys Choir and a barbershop quartet and all kinds of weird chanting and Buddha-Buddha stuff. And the whole time, in the background, there's still that cocktail party going on. All these different voices. Not human voices, though. Because it's the mountains. Follow me? The rock—it's *talking*. And the fog, too, and the grass and the goddamn mongooses. Everything talks. The trees talk politics, the monkeys talk religion. The whole country. Vietnam. The place talks. It talks. Understand? Nam—it truly *talks*.

40   "The guys can't cope. They lose it. They get on the radio and report enemy movement—a whole army, they say—and they order up the firepower. They get arty and gunships. They call in air strikes. And I'll tell you, they fuckin' crash that cocktail party. All night long, they just smoke those mountains. They make jungle juice. They blow away trees and glee clubs and whatever else there is to blow away. Scorch time. They walk napalm up and down the ridges. They bring in the Cobras and F-4s, they use Willie Peter and HE and incendiaries. It's all fire. They make those mountains burn.

"Around dawn things finally get quiet. Like you never even *heard* quiet before. One of those real thick, real misty days—just clouds and fog, they're off in this special zone—and the mountains are absolutely dead-flat silent. Like *Brigadoon*—pure vapor, you know? Everything's all sucked up inside the fog. Not a single sound, except they still *hear* it.

"So they pack up and start humping. They head down the mountain, back to base camp, and when they get there they don't say diddly. They don't talk. Not a word, like they're deaf and dumb. Later on this fat bird colonel comes up and asks what the hell happened out there. What'd they hear? Why all the ordnance? The man's ragged out, he gets down tight on their case. I mean, they spent six trillion dollars on firepower, and this fatass colonel wants answers, he wants to know what the fuckin' story is.

"But the guys don't say zip. They just look at him for a while, sort of funny like, sort of amazed, and the whole war is right there in that stare. It says everything you can't ever say. It says, man, you got *wax* in your ears. It says, poor bastard, you'll never know—wrong frequency—you don't *even* want to hear this. Then they salute the fucker and walk away, because certain stories you don't ever tell."

You can tell a true war story by the way it never seems to end. Not then, not ever. Not when Mitchell Sanders stood up and moved off into the dark.

It all happened.   45

Even now, at this instant, I remember that yo-yo. In a way, I suppose, you had to be there, you had to hear it, but I could tell how desperately Sanders wanted me to believe him, his frustration at not quite getting the details right, not quite pinning down the final and definitive truth.

And I remember sitting at my foxhole that night, watching the shadows of Quang Ngai, thinking about the coming day and how we would cross the river and march west into the mountains, all the ways I might die, all the things I did not understand.

Late in the night Mitchell Sanders touched my shoulder. "Just came to me," he whispered. "The moral, I mean. Nobody listens. Nobody hears nothin'. Like that fatass colonel. The politicians, all the civilian types. Your girlfriend. My girlfriend. Everybody's sweet little virgin girlfriend. What they need is to go out on LP. The vapors, man. Trees and rocks—you got to *listen* to your enemy."

And then again, in the morning, Sanders came up to me. The platoon was preparing to move out, checking weapons, going through all the little rituals that preceded a day's march. Already the lead squad had crossed the river and was filing off toward the west.

50 "I got a confession to make," Sanders said. "Last night, man, I had to make up a few things."

"I know that."

"The glee club. There wasn't any glee club."

"Right."

"No opera."

55 "Forget it, I understand."

"Yeah, but listen, it's still true. Those six guys, they heard wicked sound out there. They heard sound you just plain won't believe."

Sanders pulled on his rucksack, closed his eyes for a moment, then almost smiled at me. I knew what was coming.

"All right," I said, "what's the moral?"

"Forget it."

60 "No, go ahead."

For a long while he was quiet, looking away, and the silence kept stretching out until it was almost embarrassing. Then he shrugged and gave me a stare that lasted all day.

"Hear that quiet, man?" he said. "That quiet—just listen. There's your moral."

In a true war story, if there's a moral at all, it's like the thread that makes the cloth. You can't tease it out. You can't extract the meaning without unraveling the deeper meaning. And in the end, really, there's nothing much to say about a true war story, except maybe "Oh."

True war stories do not generalize. They do not indulge in abstraction or analysis.

65 For example: War is hell. As a moral declaration the old truism seems perfectly true, and yet because it abstracts, because it generalizes, I can't believe it with my stomach. Nothing turns inside.

It comes down to gut instinct. A true war story, if truly told, makes the stomach believe.

This one does it for me. I've told it before—many times, many versions—but here's what actually happened.

We crossed that river and marched west into the mountains. On the third day, Curt Lemon stepped on a booby-trapped 105 round. He was playing catch with Rat Kiley, laughing, and then he was dead. The trees were thick; it took nearly an hour to cut an LZ for the dustoff.

Later, higher in the mountains, we came across a baby VC water buffalo. What it was doing there I don't know—no farms or paddies—but we chased it down and got a rope around it and led it along to a deserted village where we set up for the night. After supper Rat Kiley went over and stroked its nose.

70 He opened up a can of C rations, pork and beans, but the baby buffalo wasn't interested.

Rat shrugged.

He stepped back and shot it through the right front knee. The animal did not make a sound. It went down hard, then got up again, and Rat took careful aim and shot off an ear. He shot it in the hindquarters and in the little hump at its back. He shot it twice in the flanks. It wasn't to kill; it was to hurt. He put the rifle muzzle up against the mouth and shot the mouth away. Nobody said much. The whole platoon stood there watching, feeling all kinds of things, but there wasn't a great deal of pity for the baby water buffalo. Curt Lemon was dead. Rat Kiley had lost his best friend in the world. Later in the week he would write a long personal letter to the guy's sister, who would not write back, but for now it was a question of pain. He shot off the tail. He shot away chunks of meat below the ribs. All around us there was the smell of smoke and filth and deep greenery, and the evening was humid and very hot. Rat went to automatic. He shot randomly, almost casually, quick little spurts in the belly and butt. Then he reloaded, squatted down, and shot it in the left front knee. Again the animal fell hard and tried to get up, but this time it couldn't quite make it. It wobbled and went down sideways. Rat shot it in the nose. He bent forward and whispered something, as if talking to a pet, then he shot it in the throat. All the while the baby buffalo was silent, or almost silent, just a light bubbling sound where the nose had been. It lay very still. Nothing moved except the eyes, which were enormous, the pupils shiny black and dumb.

Rat Kiley was crying. He tried to say something, but then cradled his rifle and went off by himself.

The rest of us stood in a ragged circle around the baby buffalo. For a time no one spoke. We had witnessed something essential, something brand-new and profound, a piece of the world so startling there was not yet a name for it.

75 Somebody kicked the baby buffalo.

It was still alive, though just barely, just in the eyes.

"Amazing," Dave Jensen said. "My whole life, I never seen anything like it."

"Never?"

"Not hardly. Not once."

Kiowa and Mitchell Sanders picked up 80 the baby buffalo. They hauled it across the open square, hoisted it up, and dumped it in the village well.

Afterward, we sat waiting for Rat to get himself together.

"Amazing," Dave Jensen kept saying. "A new wrinkle. I never seen it before."

Mitchell Sanders took out his yo-yo. "Well, that's Nam," he said. "Garden of Evil. Over here, man, every sin's real fresh and original."

How do you generalize?

War is hell, but that's not the half of it, 85 because war is also mystery and terror and adventure and courage and discovery and holiness and pity and despair and longing and love. War is nasty; war is fun. War is thrilling; war is drudgery. War makes you a man; war makes you dead.

The truths are contradictory. It can be argued, for instance, that war is grotesque. But in truth war is also beauty. For all its horror, you can't help but gape at the awful majesty of combat. You stare out at tracer rounds unwinding through the dark like brilliant red ribbons. You crouch in ambush as a cool, impassive moon rises over the nighttime paddies. You admire the fluid symmetries of troops on the move, the harmonies of sound and shape and proportion, the great sheets of metal-fire streaming down from a gunship, the illumination rounds, the white phosphorus, the purply orange glow of napalm, the rocket's red glare. It's not pretty, exactly. It's astonishing. It fills the eye. It commands you. You hate it, yes, but your eyes do not. Like a killer forest fire, like cancer under a microscope, any battle or bombing raid or artillery barrage has the aesthetic purity of absolute moral indifference—a powerful, implacable beauty— and a true war story will tell the truth about this, though the truth is ugly.

To generalize about war is like generalizing about peace. Almost everything is true. Almost nothing is true. At its core, perhaps, war is just another name for death, and yet any soldier will tell you, if he tells the truth, that proximity to death brings with it a corresponding proximity to life. After a firefight, there is always the immense pleasure of aliveness. The trees are alive. The grass, the soil—everything. All around you things are purely living, and you among them, and the aliveness makes you tremble. You feel an intense, out-of-the-skin awareness of your living self—your truest self, the human being you want to be and then become by the force of wanting it. In the midst of evil you want to be a good man. You want decency. You want justice and courtesy and human concord, things you never knew you wanted. There is a kind of largeness to it, a kind of godliness. Though it's odd, you're never more alive than when you're almost dead. You recognize what's valuable. Freshly, as if for the first time, you love what's best in yourself and in the world, all that might be lost. At the hour of dusk you sit at your foxhole and look out on a wide river turning pinkish red, and at the mountains beyond, and although in the morning you must cross the river and go into the mountains and do terrible things and maybe die, even so, you find yourself studying the fine colors on the river, you feel wonder and awe at the setting of the sun, and you are filled with a hard, aching love for how the world could be and always should be, but now is not.

Mitchell Sanders was right. For the common soldier, at least, war has the feel—the spiritual texture—of a great ghostly fog, thick and permanent. There is no clarity. Everything swirls. The old rules are no longer binding, the old truths no longer true. Right spills over into wrong. Order blends into chaos, love into hate, ugliness into beauty, law into anarchy, civility into savagery. The vapors suck you in. You can't tell where you are, or why you're there, and the only certainty is overwhelming ambiguity.

In war you lose your sense of the definite, hence your sense of truth itself, and therefore it's safe to say that in a true war story nothing is ever absolutely true.

Often in a true war story there is not even a point, or else the point doesn't hit you until twenty years later, in your sleep, and you wake up and shake your wife and start telling the story to her, except when you get to the end you've forgotten the point again. And then for a long time you lie there watching the story happen in your head. You listen to your wife's breathing. The war's over. You close your eyes. You smile and think, Christ, what's the *point*?

This one wakes me up.

In the mountains that day, I watched Lemon turn sideways. He laughed and said something to Rat Kiley. Then he took a peculiar half step, moving from shade into bright sunlight, and the booby-trapped 105 round blew him into a tree. The parts were just hanging there, so Dave Jensen and I were ordered to shinny up and peel him off. I remember the white bone of an arm. I remember pieces of skin and something wet and yellow that must've been the intestines. The gore was horrible, and stays with me. But what wakes me up twenty years later is Dave Jensen singing "Lemon Tree" as we threw down the parts.

You can tell a true war story by the questions you ask. Somebody tells a story, let's say, and afterward you ask, "Is it true?" and if the answer matters, you've got your answer.

For example, we've all heard this one. Four guys go down a trail. A grenade sails out. One guy jumps on it and takes the blast and saves his three buddies.

95   Is it true?

The answer matters.

You'd feel cheated if it never happened. Without the grounding reality, it's just a trite bit of puffery, pure Hollywood, untrue in the way all such stories are untrue. Yet even if it did happen—and maybe it did, anything's possible—even then you know it can't be true, because a true war story does not depend upon that kind of truth. Absolute occurrence is irrelevant. A thing may happen and be a total lie; another thing may not happen and be truer than the truth. For example: Four guys go down a trail. A grenade sails out. One guy jumps on it and takes the blast, but it's a killer grenade and everybody dies anyway. Before they die, though, one of the dead guys says, "The fuck you do *that* for?" and the jumper says, "Story of my life, man," and the other guy starts to smile but he's dead.

That's a true story that never happened.

Twenty years later, I can still see the sunlight on Lemon's face. I can see him turning, looking back at Rat Kiley, then he laughed and took that curious half step from shade into sunlight, his face suddenly brown and shining, and when his foot touched down, in that instant, he must've thought it was the sunlight that was killing him. It was not the sunlight. It was a rigged 105 round. But if I could ever get the story right, how the sun seemed to gather around him and pick him up and lift him high into a tree, if I could somehow re-create the fatal whiteness of that light, the quick glare, the obvious cause and effect, then you would believe the last thing Curt Lemon believed, which for him must've been the final truth.

Now and then, when I tell this story, 100 someone will come up to me afterward and say she liked it. It's always a woman. Usually it's an older woman of kindly temperament and humane politics. She'll explain that as a rule she hates war stories; she can't understand why people want to wallow in all the blood and gore. But this one she liked. The poor baby buffalo, it made her sad. Sometimes, even, there are little tears. What I should do, she'll say, is put it all behind me. Find new stories to tell.

I won't say it but I'll think it.

I'll picture Rat Kiley's face, his grief, and I'll think, *You dumb cooze.*

Because she wasn't listening.

It *wasn't* a war story. It was a *love* story.

But you can't say that. All you can do 105 is tell it one more time, patiently, adding and subtracting, making up a few things to get at the real truth. No Mitchell Sanders, you tell her. No Lemon, no Rat Kiley. No trail junction. No baby buffalo. No vines or moss or white blossoms. Beginning to end, you tell her, it's all made up. Every goddamn detail—the mountains and the river and especially that poor dumb baby buffalo. None of it happened. *None* of it. And even if it did happen, it didn't happen in the mountains, it happened in this little village on the Batangan Peninsula, and it was raining like crazy, and one night a guy named Stink Harris woke up screaming with a leech on his tongue. You can tell a true war story if you just keep on telling it.

And in the end, of course, a true war story is never about war. It's about sunlight. It's about the special way that dawn spreads out on a river when you know you must cross the river and march into the mountains and do things you are afraid to do. It's about love and memory. It's about sorrow. It's about sisters who never write back and people who never listen.

·····▶*Your* **Turn**
Talking and Writing about Lit

1. How would you describe the plot structure of "How to Tell a True War Story"? (Remember our discussion of chronological and nonchronological plots in Chapter 3.)

2. How doesn't narrative point of view relate to plot in this story? Note that the first-person narrator is looking back on his war experiences from the vantage point of twenty years later.

3. List several ways in which setting helps illuminate themes in the story.

4. **DIY** Write a brief story (four pages or less) in which the first-person narrator looks back on something in the past that affected her (or him) greatly.

Margaret Atwood (b. 1939)

Margaret Atwood grew up primarily in remote areas of northern Ontario and Quebec (in her native Canada), the daughter of an entomologist (a scientist who studies insects). She is a well-known and prolific writer whose novels include *The Edible Woman* (1969), *Surfacing* (1971), *Lady Oracle* (1976), *Life before Man* (1979), *Bodily Harm* (1982), *The Handmaid's Tale* (1985), and *Cat's Eye* (1988). Her short story collections are *Dancing Girls and Other Stories* (1978), *Murder in the Dark* (1983), and *Bluebeard's Egg* (1983). In an autobiographical statement about her development as a writer, she says that she realized in high school that writing was what she wanted to do as a profession.

About her college experience, she said, "After a year or two of keeping my head down and trying to pass myself off as a normal person, I made contact with the five other people at my university who were interested in writing; and through them, and some of my teachers, I discovered that there was a whole subterranean Wonderland of Canadian writing that was going on just out of general earshot and sight." (from a lecture delivered in Wales, 1995).

There Was Once (1992)

There was once a poor girl, as beautiful as she was good, who lived with her wicked stepmother in a house in the forest.

—Forest? *Forest* is passé, I mean, I've had it with all this wilderness stuff. It's not the right image of our society, today. Let's have some *urban* for a change.

—There was once a poor girl, as beautiful as she was good, who lived with her wicked stepmother in a house in the suburbs.

—That's better. But I have to seriously query this word *poor*.

5 —But she *was* poor!

—Poor is relative. She lived in a house, didn't she?
—Yes.

—Then socioeconomically speaking, she was not poor.

—But none of the money was *hers!* The whole point of the story is that the wicked stepmother makes her wear old clothes and sleep in the fireplace—

10 —Aha! They had a *fireplace!* With *poor*, let me tell you, there's no fireplace. Come down to the park, come to the subway stations after dark, come down to where they sleep in cardboard boxes, and I'll show you *poor!*

—There was once a middle-class girl, as beautiful as she was good—

—Stop right there. I think we can cut the *beautiful*, don't you? Women these days have to deal with too many intimidating physical role models as it is, what with those bimbos in the ads. Can't you make her, well, more average?

—There was once a girl who was a little overweight and whose front teeth stuck out, who—

—I don't think it's nice to make fun of people's appearances. Plus, you're encouraging anorexia.

—I wasn't making fun! I was just 15 describing—

—Skip the description. Description oppresses. But you can say what color she was.

—What color?

—You know. Black, white, red, brown, yellow. Those are the choices. And I'm telling you right now, I've had enough of white. Dominant culture this, dominant culture that—

—I don't know what color.

—Well, it would probably be *your* 20 color, wouldn't it?

—But this isn't *about* me! It's about this girl—

—Everything is about you.

—Sounds to me like you don't want to hear this story at all.

—Oh well, go on. You could make her ethnic. That might help.

—There was once a girl of indetermi- 25 nate descent, as average-looking as she was good, who lived with her wicked—

—Another thing. *Good* and *wicked*. Don't you think you should transcend those puritanical judgmental moralistic epithets? I mean, so much of that is conditioning, isn't it?

—There was once a girl, as average-looking as she was well-adjusted, who lived with her stepmother, who was not a very open and loving person because she herself had been abused in childhood.

—Better. But I am so *tired* of negative female images! And stepmothers—they always get it in the neck! Change it to step-*father*, why don't you? That would make more sense anyway, considering the bad behavior you're about to describe. And throw in some whips and chains. We all know what those twisted, repressed, middle-aged men are like—

—*Hey, just a minute! I'm a middle-aged*—

30   —Stuff it, Mister Nosy Parker. Nobody asked you to stick in your oar, or whatever you want to call that thing. This is between the two of us. Go on.

—There was once a girl—

—How old was she?

—I don't know. She was young.

—This ends with a marriage, right?

—Well, not to blow the plot, but—yes.   35

—Then you can scratch the condescending paternalistic terminology. It's *woman*, pal. *Woman.*

—There was once—

—What's this *was, once*? Enough of the dead past. Tell me about *now*.
—There—

—So?   40

—So, what?

—So, why not *here*?

◦◦◦◦◦▶ *Your* **Turn**
Talking and Writing about Lit

1. What sort of person do you think the criticizing voice in Atwood's "There Was Once" represents? Imagine who might be speaking and who might be replying.

2. Although both this story and Don DeLillo's "Videotape" can be said to be examples of satire as well as metafiction, the use of form in the two stories is quite different. Write an essay in which you compare the two stories.

3. **DIY** Write two pages in which one voice attempts to tell a story and another voice interrupts to make changes. You might simply use a familiar fairy tale (e.g., "Goldilocks and the Three Bears," "Jack and the Beanstalk," or "Little Red Riding Hood"), which the first voice tells and the second voice interrupts and "corrects."

Charles Johnson (b. 1948)

Charles Johnson was born in Evanston, Illinois. Before he became a writer, he was a cartoonist. In the course of his rich and varied professional and artistic life, Johnson has produced films and a television series, books of cartoons, essay collections, and an anthology, in addition to numerous works of fiction. His novels include *Faith and the Good Thing* (1974), *Oxherding Tale* (1982), *Middle Passage* (1990, awarded the National Book Award), and *Dreamer* (1998), and his short stories, including "Moving Pictures," are collected in *The Sorcerer's Apprentice* (1986). Charles Johnson is the Pollock Professor of English at the University of Washington, where he has taught fiction writing since 1976.

Moving Pictures (1985)

You sit in the Neptune Theater waiting for the thin, overhead lights to dim with a sense of respect, perhaps even reverence, for American movie houses are, as everyone knows, the new cathedrals, their stories better remembered than legends, totems, or mythologies, their directors more popular than novelists, more influential than saints—enough people, you've been told, have seen the James Bond adventures to fill the entire country of Argentina. Perhaps you have written this movie. Perhaps not. Regardless, you come to it as everyone does, as a seeker groping in the darkness for light, hoping something magical will be beamed from above, and no matter how bad this matinee is, or silly, something deep and maybe even too dangerous to talk loudly about will indeed happen to you and the others, before this drama reels to its last transparent frame.

Naturally, you have left your life outside the door. Like any life, it's a messy thing, hardly as orderly as art, what some call life in the fast lane: the Sanka and sugar-doughnut breakfasts, bumper-to-bumper traffic downtown, the business lunches, and a breakneck schedule not to get ahead but simply to stay in one place, which is peculiar, because you grew up in the sixties speeding on methadone and despising all this, knowing your Age (Aquarian) was made for finer stuff. But no matter. Outside, across town, you have put away for ninety minutes the tedious, repetitive job that is, obviously, beneath your talents, sensitivity, and education (a degree in English), the once beautiful woman—or wife—a former model (local), college dancer, or semiprofessional actress named Megan or Daphne, who has grown tired of you, or you of her, and talks now of legal separation and finding herself, the children from a former, frighteningly brief marriage whom you don't want to lose, the mortgage, alimony, IRS audit, the aging, gin-fattened face that once favored a rock star's but now frowns back at you in the bathroom mirror, the young woman at work born in 1960 and unable to recall John Kennedy who, after the Christmas party, took you to bed in her spacious downtown loft, perhaps out of pity because your mother, God bless her, died and left you with $1,000 in debt before you could get the old family house clear—all that shelved, mercifully, as the film starts, first that frosty mountaintop ringed by stars, or a lion roaring, or floodlights bathing the tips of buildings in a Hollywood skyline: stable trademarks in a world of flux, you think, surefire signs that whatever follows—tragedy or farce—is made by people who are accomplished dream merchants. Perhaps more: masters of vision, geniuses of the epistemological Murphy.

If you have written this film, which is possible, you look for your name in the credits, and probably frown at the names of the Crew, each recalling some disaster during the production, first at the studio, then later on location for five weeks in Oklahoma cow towns during the winter, which was worse than living on the moon, the days boiling and nights so cold. Nevertheless, you'd seen it as a miracle, an act of God when the director, having read your novel, called, offering you the project—a historical romance—then walked you patiently through the first eight drafts, suspicious of you at first (there was real money riding on this; it wasn't poetry), of your dreary, novelistic pretensions to Deep Profundity, and you equally suspicious of him, his background in sitcoms, obsession with "keeping it sexy," and love of Laurel and Hardy films. For this you wrote a dissertation on Derrida?[1] Yet you'd listened. He was right, in the end. He was good, you admitted, grudgingly. He knew, as you—with your liberal arts degree—didn't, the meaning of Entertainment. You'd learned. With his help, you got good, too. You gloated. And lost friends. "A movie?" said your poet friends. "That's wonderful, it's happening for you," and then they avoided you as if you had AIDS. What *was* happening was this:

You'd shelved the novel, the Big Book, for bucks monitored by the Writers Guild (West), threw yourself into fast-and-dirty scripts, the instant gratification of quick deadlines and fat checks because the Book, with its complexity and promise of critical praise, the Book, with its long-distance demands and no financial reward whatsoever, was impossible, and besides, you didn't have it anymore, not really, the gift for narrative or language, while the scripts were easy, like writing shorthand, and soon—way sooner than you thought—the films, with their life span shorter than a mayfly's, were all you could do. It's a living, you said. Nothing lasts forever. And you pushed on.

The credits crawl up against a montage of Oklahoma farm life, and in this you read a story, too, even before the film begins. For the audience, the actors are stars, the new Olympians, but oh, you know them, this one—the male lead—whose range is boundless, who could be a Brando, but who hadn't seen work in two years before this role and survived by doing voice-overs for a cartoon villain in *The Smurfs*; that one—the female supporting role—who can play the full scale of emotions, but whose last memorable performance was a commercial for Rolaids, all of them; all, including you, fighting for life in a city where the air is so corrupt joggers spit black after a two-mile run; failing, trying desperately to keep up the front of doing-well, these actors, treating you shabbily sometimes because your salary was bigger than theirs, even larger than the producer's, though he wasn't exactly hurting—no, he was richer than a medieval king, a complex man of remarkable charm and cunning, someone both to admire for his Horatio Alger orphan-boy success and to fear for his worship at the altar of power.

5

---

[1]**Derrida:** Jacques Derrida (b. 1930), French philosopher and founder of Deconstructionism.

You won't forget the evening he asked you to his home after a long conference, served you scotch, and then, from inside a drawer in his desk removed an envelope, dumped its contents out, and you saw maybe fifty snapshots of beautiful, naked women on his bed—all of them second-rate actresses, though the female supporting role was there, too—and he watched you closely for your reaction, sipping his drink, smiling, then asked, "You ever sleep with a woman like that?" No, you hadn't. And no, you didn't trust him either. You didn't turn your back. But, then again, nobody in this business did, and in some ways he was, you knew, better than most.

You'd compromised, given up ground, won a few artistic points, but generally you agreed to the producer's ideas—it *was* his show—and then the small army of badly paid performers and production people took over, you trailing behind them in Oklahoma, trying to look writerly, wearing a Panama hat, holding your notepad ready for rewrites, surviving the tedium of eight or nine takes for difficult scenes, the fights, fallings-out, bad catered food, and midnight affairs, watching your script change at each level of interpretation—director, actor— until it was unrecognizable, a new thing entirely, a celebration of the Crew. Not you. Does anyone suspect how bad this thing really looked in rough cut? How miraculous it is that its rags of shots, conflicting ideas, and scraps of footage actually cohere? You sneak a look around at the audience, the faces lit by the glow of the screen. No one suspects. You've managed to fool them again, you old fox.

No matter whether the film is yours or not, it pulls you in, reels in your perception like a trout. On the narrow screen, the story begins with an establishing wide shot of an Oklahoma farm, then in close-up shows the face of a big, tow-headed, brown-freckled boy named Bret, and finally settles on a two-shot of Bret and his blond, bosomy girlfriend, Bess. No margin for failure in a formula like that. In the opening funeral scene at a tiny whitewashed church, camera favors Bret, whose father has died. Our hero must seek his fortune in the city. Bess just hates to see him go. Dissolve to cemetery gate. As they leave the cemetery, and the coffin is lowered, she squeezes his hand, and something inside you shivers, the sense of ruin you felt at your own mother's funeral, the irreversible feeling of abandonment. There was no girl with you, but you wished to heaven there had been, the one named Sondra you knew in high school who wouldn't see you for squat, preferring basketball players to weird little wimps and geeks, which is pretty much what you were back then, a washout to those who knew you, but you give all that to Bret and Bess, the pain of parental loss, the hopeless, quiet love never to be, which thickens the screen so thoroughly that when Bess kisses Bret, your nose is clogged with tears and mucus, and then you have your handkerchief out, honking shamelessly, your eyes streaming, locked—even you— in a cycle of emotion (yours) which their images have borrowed, intensified, then given back to you, not because the images or sensations are sad, but because, at bottom, all you have known these last few minutes are the workings of your own nervous system. That is all you have ever known. You yourself have been supplying the grief and satisfaction all along, from within. But even that is not the true magic of film.

As Bret rides away, you remember sitting in the studio's tiny editing room amidst reels of film hanging like stockings in a bathroom, the editor, a fat, friendly man named Coates, tolerating your curiosity, letting you peer into his viewer as he patched the first reel together, figuring he owed you, a semifamous scriptwriter, that much. Each frame, you recall, was a single frozen image, like an individual thought, complete in itself, with no connection to the others, as if time stood still; but then the frames came faster as the viewer sped up, chasing each other, surging forward and creating a linear, continuous motion that outstripped your perception, and presto: a sensuously rich world erupted and took such nerve-knocking reality that you shielded your eyes when the harpsichord music came up and Bret stepped into a darkened Oklahoma shed seen only from his point of view—oh, yes, at times even your body responded, the sweat glands swaling,[2] but it was lunchtime then and Coates wanted to go to the cafeteria for coffee and clicked off his viewer; the images flipped less quickly, slowed finally to a stop, the drama disappearing again into frames, and you saw, pulling on your coat, the nerve racking, heart-thumping vision for what it really was: the illusion of speed.

But is even that the magic of film? Sitting back in your seat, aware of your right leg falling asleep, you think so, for the film has no capacity to fool you anymore. You do not give it your feelings to transfigure. All that you see with godlike detachment are your own decisions, the lines that were dropped, and the microphone just visible in a corner of one scene. Nevertheless, it's gratifying to see the audience laugh out loud at the funny parts, and blubber when Bret rides home at last to marry Bess (actually, they hated each other on the set), believing, as you can't, in a dream spun from accelerated imagery. It almost makes a man feel superior, like knowing how Uri Geller bends all those spoons.

And then it is done, the theater emptying, the hour and a half of illusion over. You file out with the others, amazed by how so much can be projected onto the tabula rasa of the Big Screen—grief, passion, fire, death—yet it remains, in the end, untouched. Dragging on your overcoat, the images still an afterglow in your thoughts, you step outside to the street. It takes your eyes, still in low gear, a moment to adjust to the light of late afternoon, traffic noise, and the things around you as you walk to your Fiat, feeling good, the objects on the street as flat and dimensionless at first as props on a stage. And then you stop.

The Fiat, you notice, has been broken into. The glove compartment has been rifled, and this is where you keep a checkbook, an extra key to the house, and where—you remember—you put the report due tomorrow at nine sharp. The glove compartment, how does it look? Like a part of your body, yes? A wound? From it spills a crumpled photo of your wife, who has asked you to move out so she can have the house, and another one of the children, who haven't the faintest idea how empty you feel getting up every morning to finance their lives at a job that is a ghastly joke, given your talents, where you can't slow down and at least four competitors stand waiting for you to step aside, fall on your face, or die, and the injustice of all this, what you see in the narrow range of radiation you call vision, in the velocity of thought, is necessary and sufficient—as some logicians say—to bring your fists down again and again on the Fiat's roof. You climb inside, sit, furiously cranking the starter, then swear and lower your forehead to the steering wheel, which is, as anyone in Hollywood can tell you, conduct unbecoming a triple-threat talent like yourself: producer, star, and director in the longest, most fabulous show of all.

10

---

[2]**swaling:** Burning.

····•▶ *Your* **Turn**

Talking and Writing about Lit

1. This story is an example of a seldom used narrative point of view, the second person. Who is the "you" in Johnson's story "Moving Pictures"? To whom does the pronoun refer?

2. Explain Johnson's use of symbolism in the story.

3. What is the purpose of having the story set largely in a movie theater? Do you think the name of the theater (the Neptune Theater) has any particular significance?

4. **DIY** Write a brief story (four pages or less) told in the second-person ("you") voice. Just as Charles Johnson begins his story in the Neptune Theater, begin your second-person story in a place that is familiar to you—a sports stadium, a favorite hangout, or a shopping mall, for example.

Don DeLillo (b. 1936)

Don DeLillo, the son of Italian immigrants, grew up in the Bronx, New York City. Some of his concerns as a fiction writer (over the span of thirteen successful novels) have been baseball, terrorism, paranoia, the media, and pop culture. Although some regard DeLillo's work as philosophical or theoretical, DeLillo himself says he works

"at street level." In an interview with *The Guardian Unlimited* in 2003, he said, "I listen to people. . . . I watch them walking, gesticulating. Everything stems from that." Some of DeLillo's best-known novels are *White Noise* (1985), *Libra* (1988), *Mao II* (1991), *Underworld* (1997), and *The Body Artist* (2001).

Videotape (1996)

It shows a man driving a car. It is the simplest sort of family video. You see a man at the wheel of a medium Dodge.

It is just a kid aiming her camera through the rear window of the family car at the windshield of the car behind her.

You know about families and their video cameras. You know how kids get involved, how the camera shows them that every subject is potentially charged, a million things they never see with the unaided eye. They investigate the meaning of inert objects and dumb pets and they poke at family privacy. They learn to see things twice.

It is the kid's own privacy that is being protected here. She is twelve years old and her name is being withheld even though she is neither the victim nor the perpetrator of the crime but only the means of recording it.

It shows a man in a sport shirt at the wheel of his car. There is nothing else to see. The car approaches briefly, then falls back. 5

You know how children with cameras learn to work the exposed moments that define the family cluster. They break every trust, spy out the undefended space, catching Mom coming out of the bathroom in her cumbrous robe and turbaned towel, looking bloodless and plucked. It is not a joke. They will shoot you sitting on the pot if they can manage a suitable vantage.

The tape has the jostled sort of non-eventness that marks the family product. Of course the man in this case is not a member of the family but a stranger in a car, a random figure, someone who has happened along in the slow lane.

It shows a man in his forties wearing a pale shirt open at the throat, the image washed by reflections and sunglint, with many jostled moments.

It is not just another video homicide. It is a homicide recorded by a child who thought she was doing something simple and maybe halfway clever, shooting some tape of a man in a car.

10 He sees the girl and waves briefly, wagging a hand without taking it off the wheel—an underplayed reaction that makes you like him.

It is unrelenting footage that rolls on and on. It has an aimless determination, a persistence that lives outside the subject matter. You are looking into the mind of home video. It is innocent, it is aimless, it is determined, it is real.

He is bald up the middle of his head, a nice guy in his forties whose whole life seems open to the hand-held camera.

But there is also an element of suspense. You keep on looking not because you know something is going to happen—of course you do know something is going to happen and you do look for that reason but you might also keep on looking if you came across this footage for the first time without knowing the outcome. There is a crude

power operating here. You keep on looking because things combine to hold you fast—a sense of the random, the amateurish, the accidental, the impending. You don't think of the tape as boring or interesting. It is crude, it is blunt, it is relentless. It is the jostled part of your mind, the film that runs through your hotel brain under all the thoughts you know you're thinking.

The world is lurking in the camera, already framed, waiting for the boy or girl who will come along and take up the device, learn the instrument, shooting old Granddad at breakfast, all stroked out so his nostrils gape, the cereal spoon baby-gripped in his pale fist.

15 It shows a man alone in a medium Dodge. It seems to go on forever.

There's something about the nature of the tape, the grain of the image, the sputtering black-and-white tones, the starkness—you think this is more real, truer-to-life, than anything around you. The things around you have a rehearsed and layered and cosmetic look. The tape is superreal, or maybe underreal is the way you want to put it. It is what lies at the scraped bottom of all the layers you have added. And this is another reason why you keep on looking. The tape has a searing realness.

It shows him giving an abbreviated wave, stiff-palmed, like a signal flag at a siding.

You know how families make up games. This is just another game in which the child invents the rules as she goes along. She likes the idea of videotaping a man in his car. She has probably never done it before and she sees no reason to vary the format or terminate early or pan to another car. This is her game and she is learning it and playing it at the same time. She feels halfway clever and inventive and maybe slightly intrusive as well, a little bit of brazenness that spices any game.

And you keep on looking. You look because this is the nature of the footage, to make a channeled path through time, to give things a shape and a destiny.

20   Of course if she had panned to another car, the right car at the precise time, she would have caught the gunman as he fired.

The chance quality of the encounter. The victim, the killer, and the child with a camera. Random energies that approach a common point. There's something here that speaks to you directly, saying terrible things about forces beyond your control, lines of intersection that cut through history and logic and every reasonable layer of human expectation.

She wandered into it. The girl got lost and wandered clear-eyed into horror. This is a children's story about straying too far from home. But it isn't the family car that serves as the instrument of the child's curiosity, her inclination to explore. It is the camera that puts her in the tale.

You know about holidays and family celebrations and how somebody shows up with a camcorder and the relatives stand around and barely react because they're numbingly accustomed to the process of being taped and decked and shown on the VCR with the coffee and cake.

He is hit soon after. If you've seen the tape many times you know from the hand-wave exactly when he will be hit. It is something, naturally, that you wait for. You say to your wife, if you're at home and she is there, Now here is where he gets it. You say, Janet, hurry up, this is where it happens.

25   Now here is where he gets it. You see him jolted, sort of wire-shocked—then he seizes up and falls toward the door or maybe leans or slides into the door is the proper way to put it. It is awful and unremarkable at the same time. The car stays in the slow lane. It approaches briefly, then falls back.

You don't usually call your wife over to the TV set. She has her programs, you have yours. But there's a certain urgency here. You want her to see how it looks. The tape has been running forever and now the thing is finally going to happen and you want her to be here when he's shot.

Here it comes, all right. He is shot, head-shot, and the camera reacts, the child reacts—there is a jolting movement but she keeps on taping, there is a sympathetic response, a nerve response, her heart is beating faster but she keeps the camera trained on the subject as he slides into the door and even as you see him die you're thinking of the girl. At some level the girl has to be present here, watching what you're watching, unprepared—the girl is seeing this cold and you have to marvel at the fact that she keeps the tape rolling.

It shows something awful and unaccompanied. You want your wife to see it because it is real this time, not fancy movie violence—the realness beneath the layers of cosmetic perception. Hurry up, Janet, here it comes. He dies so fast. There is no accompaniment of any kind. It is very stripped. You want to tell her it is realer than real but then she will ask what that means.

The way the camera reacts to the gunshot—a startled reaction that brings pity and terror into the frame, the girl's own shock, the girl's identification with the victim.

30   You don't see the blood, which is probably trickling behind his ear and down the back of his neck. The way his head is twisted away from the door, the twist of the head gives you only a partial profile and it's the wrong side, it's not the side where he was hit.

And maybe you're being a little aggressive here, practically forcing your wife to watch. Why? What are you telling her? Are you making a little statement? Like I'm going to ruin your day out of ordinary spite. Or a big statement? Like this is the risk of existing. Either way you're rubbing her face in this tape and you don't know why.

35   It shows the car drifting toward the guardrail and then there's a jostling sense of two other lanes and part of another car, a split-second blur, and the tape ends here, either because the girl stopped shooting or because some central authority, the police or the district attorney or the TV station, decided there was nothing else you had to see.

This is either the tenth or eleventh homicide committed by the Texas Highway Killer. The number is uncertain because the police believe that one of the shootings may have been a copycat crime.

And there is something about videotape, isn't there, and this particular kind of serial crime? This is a crime designed for random taping and immediate playing. You sit there and wonder if this kind of crime became more possible when the means of taping and playing an event—playing it immediately after the taping—became part of the culture. The principal doesn't necessarily commit the sequence of crimes in order to see them taped and played. He commits the crimes as if they were a form of taped-and-played event. The crimes are inseparable from the idea of taping and playing. You sit there thinking that this is a crime that has found its medium, or vice versa—cheap mass production, the sequence of repeated images and victims, stark and glary and more or less unremarkable.

It shows very little in the end. It is a famous murder because it is on tape and because the murderer has done it many times and because the crime was recorded by a child. So the child is involved, the Video Kid as she is sometimes called because they have to call her something. The tape is famous and so is she. She is famous in the modern manner of people whose names are strategically withheld. They are famous without names or faces, spirits living apart from their bodies, the victims and witnesses, the underage criminals, out there somewhere at the edges of perception.

Seeing someone at the moment he dies, dying unexpectedly. This is reason alone to stay fixed to the screen. It is instructional, watching a man shot dead as he drives along on a sunny day. It demonstrates an elemental truth, that every breath you take has two possible endings. And that's another thing. There's a joke locked away here, a note of cruel slapstick that you are completely willing to appreciate. Maybe the victim's a chump, a dope, classically unlucky. He had it coming, in a way, like an innocent fool in a silent movie.

You don't want Janet to give you any crap about it's on all the time, they show it a thousand times a day. They show it because it exists, because they have to show it, because this is why they're out there. The horror freezes your soul but this doesn't mean that you want them to stop.

Your Turn
Talking and Writing about Lit

1. Do the terms "protagonist" and "antagonist" (as discussed in Chapter 3) have any relevance in Don DeLillo's "Videotape"? If so, who would be the protagonist and who/what would be the antagonist?

2. Discuss the use of foreshadowing in "Videotape."

3. **DIY** Imagine this scene: Two friends are sitting on a couch watching a favorite movie video. Write two pages in which you alternate between description of what is on the screen and a depiction of the dialogue and the gestures of the two friends on the couch. What kind of commentary are they making about the scenes on the screen?

AVANT-POP READINGS

Robert Olen Butler (b. 1945)

Robert Olen Butler won the Pulitzer Prize in 1993 for his book *A Good Scent from a Strange Mountain*. In this short story collection, Butler imagines the voices of fifteen Vietnamese immigrants living in Louisiana. Butler, who served in the Vietnam War and speaks Vietnamese fluently, discovered a community of Vietnamese living in New Orleans. This was not the last book in which Butler gave voice to the experience of others different from himself. In an interview with Dave Weich of Powells.com, Butler confirmed that much of his work starts as playing with voices, imagining voices. According to Weich, Butler's work is also full of "outrageous humor and wild imagination." Butler's story "Jealous Husband Returns in Form of Parrot" comes from his book *Tabloid Dreams* (1996). Butler has also published ten novels and three collections of short fiction, and he has received numerous fellowships and awards.

Jealous Husband Returns in Form of Parrot (1996)

I never can quite say as much as I know. I look at other parrots and I wonder if it's the same for them, if somebody is trapped in each of them paying some kind of price for living their life in a certain way. For instance, "Hello," I say, and I'm sitting on a perch in a pet store in Houston and what I'm really thinking is Holy shit. It's you. And what's happened is I'm looking at my wife.

"Hello," she says, and she comes over to me and I can't believe how beautiful she is. Those great brown eyes, almost as dark as the center of mine. And her nose—I don't remember her for her nose but its beauty is clear to me now. Her nose is a little too long, but it's redeemed by the faint hook to it.

She scratches the back of my neck.

Her touch makes my tail flare. I feel the stretch and rustle of me back there. I bend my head to her and she whispers, "Pretty bird."

For a moment I think she knows it's 5 me. But she doesn't, of course. I say "Hello" again and I will eventually pick up "pretty bird." I can tell that as soon as she says it, but for now I can only give her another hello. Her fingertips move through my feathers and she seems to know about birds. She knows that to pet a bird you don't smooth his feathers down, you ruffle them.

But of course she did that in my human life, as well. It's all the same for her. Not that I was complaining, even to myself, at that moment in the pet shop when she found me like I presume she was supposed to. She said it again, "Pretty bird," and this brain that works like it does now could feel that tiny little voice of mine ready to shape itself around these sounds. But before I could get them out of my beak there was this guy at my wife's shoulder and all my feathers went slick flat like to make me small enough not to be seen and I backed away. The pupils of my eyes pinned and dilated and pinned again.

He circled around her. A guy that looked like a meat packer, big in the chest and thick with hair, the kind of guy that I always sensed her eyes moving to when I was alive. I had a bare chest and I'd look for little black hairs on the sheets when I'd come home on a day with the whiff of somebody else in the air. She was still in the same goddamn rut.

A "hello" wouldn't do and I'd recently learned "good night" but it was the wrong suggestion altogether, so I said nothing and the guy circled her and he was looking at me with a smug little smile and I fluffed up all my feathers, made myself about twice as big, so big he'd see he couldn't mess with me. I waited for him to draw close enough for me to take off the tip of his finger.

But she intervened. Those nut-brown eyes were before me and she said, "I want him."

10   And that's how I ended up in my own house once again. She bought me a large black wrought-iron cage, very large, convinced by some young guy who clerked in the bird department and who took her aside and made his voice go much too soft when he was doing the selling job. The meat packer didn't like it. I didn't either. I'd missed a lot of chances to take a bite out of this clerk in my stay at the shop and I regretted that suddenly.

But I got my giant cage and I guess I'm happy enough about that. I can pace as much as I want. I can hang upside down. It's full of bird toys. That dangling thing over there

with knots and strips of rawhide and a bell at the bottom needs a good thrashing a couple of times a day and I'm the bird to do it. I look at the very dangle of it and the thing is rough, the rawhide and the knotted rope, and I get this restlessness back in my tail, a burning thrashing feeling, and it's like all the times when I was sure there was a man naked with my wife. Then I go to this thing that feels so familiar and I bite and bite and it's very good.

I could have used the thing the last day I went out of this house as a man. I'd found the address of the new guy at my wife's office. He'd been there a month in the shipping department and three times she'd mentioned him. She didn't even have to work with him and three times I heard about him, just dropped into the conversation. "Oh," she'd say when a car commercial came on the television, "that car there is like the one the new man in shipping owns. Just like it." Hey, I'm not stupid. She said another thing about him and then another and right after the third one I locked myself in the bathroom because I couldn't rage about this anymore. I felt like a damn fool whenever I actually said anything about this kind of feeling and she looked at me like she could start hating me real easy and so I was working on saying nothing, even if it meant locking myself up. My goal was to hold my tongue about half the time. That would be a good start.

But this guy from shipping. I found out his name and his address and it was one of her typical Saturday afternoons of vague shopping. So I went to his house, and his car that was just like the commercial was outside. Nobody was around in the neighborhood and there was this big tree in the back of the house going up to a second floor window that was making funny little sounds. I went up. The shade was drawn but not quite all the way. I was holding on to a limb with arms and legs wrapped around it like it was her in those times when I could forget the others for a little while. But the crack in the shade was just out of view and I crawled on along till there was no limb left and I fell on my head. Thinking about that now, my wings flap and I feel myself lift up and it all seems so avoidable. Though I know I'm different now. I'm a bird.

Except I'm not. That's what's confusing. It's like those times when she would tell me she loved me and I actually believed her and maybe it was true and we clung to each other in bed and at times like that I was different. I was the man in her life. I was whole with her. Except even at that moment, holding her sweetly, there was this other creature inside me who knew a lot more about it and couldn't quite put all the evidence together to speak.

15   My cage sits in the den. My pool table is gone and the cage is sitting in that space and if I come all the way down to one end of my perch I can see through the door and down the back hallway to the master bedroom. When she keeps the bedroom door open I can see the space at the foot of the bed but not the bed itself. That I can sense to the left, just out of sight. I watch the men go in and I hear the sounds but I can't quite see. And they drive me crazy.

I flap my wings and I squawk and I fluff up and I slick down and I throw seed and I attack that dangly toy as if it was the guy's balls, but it does no good. It never did any good in the other life either, the thrashing around I did by myself. In that other life I'd have given anything to be standing in this den with her doing this thing with some other guy just down the hall and all I had to do was walk down there and turn the corner and she couldn't deny it anymore.

But now all I can do is try to let it go. I sidestep down to the opposite end of the cage and I look out the big sliding glass doors to the backyard. It's a pretty yard. There are great placid maple trees with good places to roost. There's a blue sky that plucks at the feathers on my chest. There are clouds. Other birds. Fly away. I could just fly away.

I tried once and I learned a lesson. She forgot and left the door to my cage open and I climbed beak and foot, beak and foot, along the bars and curled around to stretch sideways out the door and the vast scene of peace was there at the other end of the room. I flew.

And a pain flared through my head and I fell straight down and the room whirled around and the only good thing was she held me. She put her hands under my wings and lifted me and clutched me to her breast and I wish there hadn't been bees in my head at the time so I could have enjoyed that, but she put me back in the cage and wept awhile. That touched me, her tears. And I looked back to the wall of sky and trees. There was something invisible there between me and that dream of peace. I remembered, eventually, about glass, and I knew I'd been lucky, I knew that for the little fragile-boned skull I was doing all this thinking in, it meant death.

20   She wept that day but by the night she had another man. A guy with a thick Georgia truck-stop accent and pale white skin and an Adam's apple big as my seed ball. This guy has been around for a few weeks and he makes a whooping sound down the hallway, just out of my sight. At times like that I want to fly against the bars of the cage, but I don't. I have to remember how the world has changed.

She's single now, of course. Her husband, the man that I was, is dead to her. She does not understand all that is behind my "hello." I know many words, for a parrot. I am a yellow-nape Amazon, a handsome bird, I think, green with a splash of yellow at the back of my neck. I talk pretty well, but none of my words are adequate. I can't make her understand.

And what would I say if I could? I was jealous in life. I admit it. I would admit it to her. But it was because of my connection to her. I would explain that. When we held each other, I had no past at all, no present but her body, no future but to lie there and not let her go. I was an egg hatched beneath her crouching body, I entered as a chick into her wet sky of a body, and all that I wished was to sit on her shoulder and fluff my feathers and lay my head against her cheek, my neck exposed to her hand. And so the glances that I could see in her troubled me deeply, the movement of her eyes in public to other men, the laughs sent across a room, the tracking of her mind behind her blank eyes, pursuing images of others, her distraction even in our bed, the ghosts that were there of men who'd touched her, perhaps even that very day. I was not part of all those other men who were part of her. I didn't want to connect to all that. It was only her that I would fluff for but these others were there also and I couldn't put them aside. I sensed them inside her and so they were inside me. If I had the words, these are the things I would say.

But half an hour ago there was a moment that thrilled me. A word, a word we all knew in the pet shop, was just the right word after all. This guy with his cowboy belt buckle and rattlesnake boots and his pasty face and his twanging words of love trailed after my wife, through the den, past my cage, and I said, "Cracker." He even flipped his head back a little at this in surprise. He'd been called that before to his face, I realized. I said it again, "Cracker." But to him I was a bird and he let it pass. "Cracker," I said. "Hello, cracker." That was even better. They were out of sight through the hall doorway and I hustled along the perch and I caught a glimpse of them before they made the turn to the bed and I said, "Hello, cracker," and he shot me one last glance.

It made me hopeful. I eased away from that end of the cage, moved toward the scene of peace beyond the far wall. The sky is chalky blue today, blue like the brow of the blue-front Amazon who was on the perch next to me for about a week at the store. She was very sweet, but I watched her carefully for a day or two when she first came in. And it wasn't long before she nuzzled up to a cockatoo named Gordo and I knew she'd break my heart. But her color now in the sky is sweet, really. I left all those feelings behind me when my wife showed up. I am a faithful man, for all my suspicions. Too faithful, maybe. I am ready to give too much and maybe that's the problem.

The whooping began down the hall and I focused on a tree out there. A crow flapped down, his mouth open, his throat throbbing, though I could not hear his sound. I was feeling very odd. At least I'd made my point to the guy in the other room. "Pretty bird," I said, referring to myself. She called me "pretty bird," and I believed her and I told myself again, "Pretty bird."

But then something new happened, something very difficult for me. She appeared in the den naked. I have not seen her naked since I fell from the tree and had no wings to fly. She always had a certain tidiness in things. She was naked in the bedroom, clothed in the den. But now she appears from the hallway and I look at her and she is still slim and she is beautiful, I think—at least I clearly remember that as her husband I found her beautiful in this state. Now, though, she seems too naked. Plucked. I find that a sad thing. I am sorry for her and she goes by me and she disappears into the kitchen. I want to pluck some of my own feathers, the feathers from my chest, and give them to her. I love her more in that moment, seeing her terrible nakedness, than I ever have before.

And since I've had success in the last few minutes with words, when she comes back I am moved to speak. "Hello," I say, meaning, You are still connected to me, I still want only you. "Hello," I say again. Please listen to this tiny heart that beats fast at all times for you.

And she does indeed stop and she comes to me and bends to me. "Pretty bird," I say and I am saying, You are beautiful, my wife, and your beauty cries out for protection. "Pretty." I want to cover you with my own nakedness. "Bad bird," I say. If there are others in your life, even in your mind, then there is nothing I can do. "Bad." Your nakedness is touched from inside by the others. "Open," I say. How can we be whole together if you are not empty in the place that I am to fill?

She smiles at this and she opens the door to my cage. "Up," I say, meaning, Is there no place for me in this world where I can be free of this terrible sense of others?

30 She reaches in now and offers her hand and I climb onto it and I tremble and she says, "Poor baby."

"Poor baby," I say. You have yearned for wholeness too and somehow I failed you. I was not enough. "Bad bird," I say. I'm sorry.

And then the cracker comes around the corner. He wears only his rattlesnake boots. I take one look at his miserable, featherless body and shake my head. We keep our sexual parts hidden, we parrots, and this man is a pitiful sight. "Peanut," I say. I presume that my wife simply has not noticed. But that's foolish, of course. This is, in fact, what she wants. Not me. And she scrapes me off her hand onto the open cage door and she turns her naked back to me and embraces this man and they laugh and stagger in their embrace around the corner.

For a moment I still think I've been eloquent. What I've said only needs repeating for it to have its transforming effect. "Hello," I say. "Hello. Pretty bird. Pretty. Bad bird. Bad. Open. Up. Poor baby. Bad bird." And I am beginning to hear myself as I really sound to her. "Peanut." I can never say what is in my heart to her. Never.

I stand on my cage door now and my wings stir. I look at the corner to the hallway and down at the end the whooping has begun again. I can fly there and think of things to do about all this.

But I do not. I turn instead and I look at 35 the trees moving just beyond the other end of the room. I look at the sky the color of the brow of a blue-front Amazon. A shadow of birds spanks across the lawn. And I spread my wings. I will fly now. Even though I know there is something between me and that place where I can be free of all these feelings, I will fly. I will throw myself there again and again. Pretty bird. Bad bird. Good night.

······▶ *Your* **Turn**
Talking and Writing about Lit

1. To what degree is the narrator of "Jealous Husband Returns in Form of Parrot" reliable? In what ways is he unreliable?

2. Is this a nonrealistic story? Are there any ways in which you think it is realistic?

3. **DIY** Write a brief scene (two pages or less) from the point of view of any animal (perhaps a family pet). Give the animal a personality, as if it had a human consciousness, but retain enough of the realistic animal behavior to make the device convincing within the confines of your scene.

Donald Barthelme (1931–1989)

Donald Barthelme was born in Philadelphia, Pennsylvania, but was raised in Houston, Texas. In 1962 he moved to New York and began publishing short stories in *The New Yorker*. Barthelme authored fourteen books, including novels, essays, and the short story collections *Come Back, Dr. Caligari* (1964), *Unspeakable Practices, Unnatural Acts* (1968), *City Life* (1970), *Sixty Stories* (1982), *Overnight to Many Distant Cities* (1983), and *Forty Stories* (1987), from which "The School" is taken. For more information on Barthelme's work and life, see John Barth's article in the Talking Lit section.

The School (1981)

Well, we had all these children out planting trees, see, because we figured that . . . that was part of their education, to see how, you know, the root systems . . . and also the sense of responsibility, taking care of things, being individually responsible. You know what I mean. And the trees all died. They were orange trees. I don't know why they died, they just died. Something wrong with the soil possibly or maybe the stuff we got from the nursery wasn't the best. We complained about it. So we've got thirty kids there, each kid had his or her own little tree to plant and we've got these thirty dead trees. All these kids looking at these little brown sticks, it was depressing.

It wouldn't have been so bad except that just a couple of weeks before the thing with the trees, the snakes all died. But I think that the snakes—well, the reason that the snakes kicked off was that . . . you remember, the boiler was shut off for four days because of the strike, and that was explicable. It was something you could explain to the kids because of the strike. I mean, none of their parents would let them cross the picket line and they knew there was a strike going on and what it meant. So when things got started up again and we found the snakes they weren't too disturbed.

With the herb gardens it was probably a case of overwatering, and at least now they know not to overwater. The children were very conscientious with the herb gardens and some of them probably . . . you know, slipped them a little extra water when we weren't looking. Or maybe . . . well, I don't like to think about sabotage, although it did occur to us. I mean, it was something that crossed our minds. We were thinking that way probably because before that the gerbils had died, and the white mice had died, and the salamander . . . well, now they know not to carry them around in plastic bags.

Of course we expected the tropical fish to die, that was no surprise. Those numbers, you look at them crooked and they're belly-up on the surface. But the lesson plan called for a tropical fish input at that point, there was nothing we could do, it happens every year, you just have to hurry past it.

We weren't even supposed to have a puppy.   5

We weren't even supposed to have one, it was just a puppy the Murdoch girl found under a Gristede's truck one day and she was afraid the truck would run over it when the driver had finished making his delivery, so she stuck it in her knapsack and brought it to the school with her. So we had this puppy. As soon as I saw the puppy I thought, Oh Christ, I bet it will live for about two weeks and then . . . And that's what it did. It wasn't supposed to be in the classroom at all, there's some kind of regulation about it, but you can't tell them they can't have a puppy when the puppy is already there, right in front of them, running around on the floor and yap yap yapping. They named it Edgar—that is, they named it after me. They had a lot of fun running after it and yelling, "Here, Edgar! Nice Edgar!" Then they'd laugh like hell. They enjoyed the ambiguity. I enjoyed it myself. I don't mind being kidded. They made a little house for it in the supply closet and all that. I don't know what it died of. Distemper, I guess. It probably hadn't had any shots. I got it out of there before the kids got to school. I checked the supply closet each morning, routinely, because I knew what was going to happen. I gave it to the custodian.

And then there was this Korean orphan that the class adopted through the Help the Children program, all the kids brought in a quarter a month, that was the idea. It was an unfortunate thing, the kid's name was Kim and maybe we adopted him too late or something. The cause of death was not stated in the letter we got, they suggested we adopt another child instead and sent us some interesting case histories, but we didn't have the heart. The class took it pretty hard, they began (I think, nobody ever said anything to me directly) to feel that maybe there was something wrong with the school. But I don't think there's anything wrong with the school, particularly, I've seen better and I've seen worse.

It was just a run of bad luck. We had an extraordinary number of parents passing away, for instance. There were I think two heart attacks and two suicides, one drowning, and four killed together in a car accident. One stroke. And we had the usual heavy mortality rate among the grandparents, or maybe it was heavier this year, it seemed so. And finally the tragedy.

The tragedy occurred when Matthew Wein and Tony Mavrogordo were playing over where they're excavating for the new federal office building. There were all these big wooden beams stacked, you know, at the edge of the excavation. There's a court case coming out of that, the parents are claiming that the beams were poorly stacked. I don't know what's true and what's not. It's been a strange year.

I forgot to mention Billy Brandt's father who was knifed fatally when he grappled with a masked intruder in his home.

One day, we had a discussion in class. 10 They asked me, where did they go? The trees, the salamander, the tropical fish, Edgar, the poppas and mommas, Matthew and Tony, where did they go? And I said, I don't know, I don't know. And they said, who knows? and I said, nobody knows. And they said, is death that which gives meaning to life? And I said no, life is that which gives meaning to life. Then they said, but isn't death, considered as a fundamental datum, the means by which the taken-for-granted mundanity of the everyday may be transcended in the direction of—

I said, yes, maybe.

They said, we don't like it.

I said, that's sound.

They said, it's a bloody shame!

I said, it is. 15

They said, will you make love now with Helen (our teaching assistant) so that we can see how it is done? We know you like Helen.

I do like Helen but I said that I would not.

We've heard so much about it, they said, but we've never seen it.

I said I would be fired and that it was never, or almost never, done as a demonstration. Helen looked out the window.

20 They said, please, please make love with Helen, we require an assertion of value, we are frightened.

I said that they shouldn't be frightened (although I am often frightened) and that there was value everywhere. Helen came and embraced me. I kissed her a few times on the brow. We held each other. The children were excited. Then there was a knock on the door, I opened the door, and the new gerbil walked in. The children cheered wildly.

••••▶ *Your* **Turn**
Talking and Writing about Lit

1. In what ways do the events in Barthelme's "The School" seem real? In what ways do they seem unreal?

2. Did you find Barthelme's story humorous or tragic? Does it manage to be both? Write a paragraph either defending or criticizing Barthelme's blending of tragedy and comedy.

3. **DIY** Do you remember any time in your life when you had a ridiculously bad run of luck? Take that experience as a basic idea for your story, but exaggerate the events so that even though the story is depicting a string of bad luck, your reader might laugh at the fantastical degree of misfortune.

Talking Lit

In the reading selections below, Margaret Atwood (author of "There Was Once," above) explains why we sometimes need "bad" female characters, and John Barth—a master of metafiction himself—writes about his former friend Donald Barthelme ("The School").

Margaret Atwood, "Problems of Female Bad Behaviour in the Creation of Literature," from Spotty-Handed Villainesses

To summarize some of the benefits to literature of the Women's Movement—the expansion of the territory available to writers, both in character and in language; a sharp-eyed examination of the way power works in gender relations, and the exposure of much of this as socially constructed; a vigorous exploration of many hitherto-concealed areas of experience. But as with any political movement which comes out of real oppression—and I do emphasize the *real*—there was also, in the first decade at least of the present movement, a tendency to cookie-cut: that is, to write to a pattern and to oversugar on one side. Some writers tended to polarize morality by gender—that is, women were intrinsically good and men bad; to divide along allegiance lines—that is, women who slept with men were sleeping with the enemy; to judge by tribal markings—that is, women who wore high heels and makeup were instantly suspect, those in overalls were acceptable; and to make hopeful excuses: that is, defects in women were ascribable to the patriarchal system and would cure themselves once that system was abolished. Such oversimplifications may be necessary to some phases of political movements. But they are usually problematical for novelists, unless the novelist has a secret desire to be in billboard advertising.

If a novelist writing at that time was also a feminist, she felt her choices restricted. Were all heroines to be essentially spotless of soul—struggling against, fleeing from or done in by male oppression? Was the only plot to be The Perils of Pauline, with a lot of moustache-twirling villains but minus the rescuing hero? Did suffering prove you were good? (If so—think hard about this—wasn't it all for the best that women did so much of it?) Did we face a situation in which women could do no wrong, but could only have wrong done to them? Were women being confined yet again to that alabaster pedestal so beloved of the Victorian age, when Woman as better-than-man gave men a license to be gleefully and enjoyably worse than women, while all the while proclaiming that they couldn't help it because it was their nature? Were women to be condemned to virtue for life, slaves in the salt-mines of goodness? How intolerable.

Of course, the feminist analysis made some kinds of behaviour available to female characters which, under the old dispensation—the pre-feminist one—would have been considered bad, but under the new one were praiseworthy. A female character could rebel against social strictures without then having to throw herself in front of a train like Anna Karenina; she could think the unthinkable and say the unsayable; she could flout authority. She could do new bad-good things, such as leaving her husband and even deserting her children. Such activities and emotions, however, were—according to the new moral thermometer of the times—not really bad at all; they were good, and the women who did them were praiseworthy. I'm not against such plots. I just don't think they are the only ones.

And there were certain new no-no's. For instance: was it at all permissible, any more, to talk about women's will to power, because weren't women supposed by nature to be communal egalitarians? Could one depict the scurvy behaviour often practised by women against one another, or by little girls against other little girls? Could one examine the Seven Deadly Sins in their female version—to remind you, Pride, Anger, Lust, Envy, Avarice, Greed and Sloth—without being considered anti-feminist? Or was a mere mention of such things tantamount to aiding and abetting the enemy, namely the male power-structure? Were we to have a warning hand clapped over our mouths, yet once again, to prevent us from saying the unsayable—though the unsayable had changed? Were we to listen to our mothers, yet once again, as they intoned—If You Can't Say Anything Nice, Don't Say Anything At All? Hadn't men been giving women a bad reputation for centuries? Shouldn't we form a wall of silence around the badness of women, or at best explain it away by saying it was the fault of Big Daddy, or—permissible too, it seems—of Big Mom? Big Mom, that agent of the patriarchy, that pronatalist, got it in the neck from certain seventies feminists; though mothers were admitted into the fold again once some of these women turned into them. In a word: were women to be homogenized—one woman is the same as another—and deprived of free will—as in, *The patriarchy made her do it?*

Or, in another word—were men to get all the juicy parts? Literature cannot do without bad behaviour, but was all the bad behaviour to be reserved for men? Was it to be all Iago and Mephistopheles, and were Jezebel and Medea and Medusa and Delilah and Regan and Goneril and spotty-handed Lady Macbeth and Rider Haggard's powerful superfemme fatale in *She*, and Tony Morrison's mean Sula, to be banished from view? I hope not. Women characters, arise! Take back the night! In particular, take back The Queen of the Night, from Mozart's Magic Flute. It's a great part, and due for revision.

I have always known that there were spellbinding evil parts for women. For one thing, I was taken at an early age to see *Snow White and the Seven Dwarfs*. Never mind the Protestant work ethic of the dwarfs. Never mind the tedious housework-is-virtuous motif. Never mind the fact that Snow White is a vampire—anyone who lies in a glass coffin without decaying and then comes to life again must be. The truth is that I was paralysed by the scene in which the evil queen drinks the magic potion and changes her shape. What power, what untold possibilities!

Also, I was exposed to the complete, unexpurgated Grimm's Fairy Tales at an impressionable age. Fairy tales had a bad reputation among feminists for a while—partly because they'd been cleaned up, on the erroneous supposition that little children don't like gruesome gore, and partly because they'd been selected to fit the 'fifties Prince Charming Is Your Goal ethos. So Cinderella and the Sleeping Beauty were okay, though The Youth Who Set Out to Learn What Fear Was, which featured a good many rotting corpses, plus a woman who was smarter than her husband, were not. But many of these tales were originally told and retold by women, and these unknown women left their mark. There is a wide range of heroines in these tales; passive good girls, yes, but adventurous, resourceful women as well, and proud ones, and slothful ones, and foolish ones, and envious and greedy ones, and also many wise women and a variety of evil witches, both in disguise and not, and bad stepmothers and wicked ugly sisters and false brides as well. The stories, and the figures themselves, have immense vitality, partly because no punches are pulled—in the versions I read, the barrels of nails and the red-hot shoes were left intact—and also because no emotion is unrepresented. Singly, the female characters are limited and two-dimensional. But put all together, they form a rich five-dimensional picture.

Female characters who behave badly can of course be used as sticks to beat other women—though so can female characters who behave well, witness the cult of the Virgin Mary, better than you'll ever be, and the legends of the female saints and martyrs—just cut on the dotted line, and, minus one body part, there's your saint, and the only really good woman is a dead woman, so if you're so good why aren't you dead?

But female bad characters can also act as keys to doors we need to open, and as mirrors in which we can see more than just a pretty face. They can be explorations of moral freedom—because everyone's choices are limited, and women's choices have been more limited than men's, but that doesn't mean women can't make choices. Such characters can pose the question of responsibility, because if you want power you have to accept responsibility, and actions produce consequences. I'm not suggesting an agenda here, just some possibilities; nor am I prescribing, just wondering. If there's a closed-off road, the curious speculate about why it's closed off, and where it might lead if followed; and evil women have been, for a while recently, a somewhat closed-off road, at least for fiction-writers.

John Barth, Thinking Man's Minimalist: Honoring Barthelme

"The proper work of the critic is praise, and that which cannot be praised should be surrounded with a tasteful, well-thought-out silence."

This is to praise the excellent American writer Donald Barthelme, who, in a 1981 *Paris Review* interview, cited in passing that arguable proposition (by the music critic Peter Yates).

Donald worked hard on that anything-but-spontaneous interview—as wise, articulate and entertaining a specimen as can be found in the *Paris Review*'s long, ongoing series of shoptalks. He worked hard on all his printed utterance, to make it worth his and our whiles. His untimely death in July at the age of 58, like the untimely death of Raymond Carver just last summer at 50, leaves our literature—leaves Literature—bereft, wham-bang, of two splendid practitioners at the peak of their powers.

Polar opposites in some obvious respects (Carver's home-grown, blue-collar realism and programmatic unsophistication, Barthelme's urbane and urban semi-Surrealism), they shared an axis of rigorous literary craftsmanship, a preoccupation with the particulars of, shall we say, post-Eisenhower American life, and a late-modern conviction, felt to the bone, that less is more. For Carver, as for Jorge Luis Borges, the step from terse lyric poetry to terse short stories was temerity enough; neither, to my knowledge, ever attempted a novel. Barthelme was among us a bit longer than Carver and published three spare, fine specimens of that genre—all brilliant, affecting, entertaining and more deep than thick—but the short story was his long suit. Without underrating either Carver's intellectuality or Barthelme's emotional range, we nevertheless associate Raymond with reticent viscerality and may consider Donald the thinking man's—and woman's—

Minimalist. Opposing stars they became, in recent years, for hundreds of appren-tice writers in and out of our plenteous university writing programs; one has sometimes to remind student writers that there are expansive easts and wests in their literary heritage as well as those two magnetic poles.

His writing is not the only excellent thing that Donald Barthelme leaves those who knew him personally or professionally. He was by all accounts a first-rate lit-erary coach (most recently at the University of Houston), a conscientious literary citizen much involved with such organizations as PEN, and a gracious friend. But his fiction is our longest-lasting souvenir and the one that matters most to those of us who knew him mainly, if not only, as delighted readers.

"We like books that have a lot of dreck in them," remarks one of the urban dwarfs in Barthelme's first novel, "Snow White"; and included in that novel's mid-point questionnaire for the reader is the item, "Is there too much blague in the nar-ration? Not enough blague?" In fact the novel is blague-free, like all of Donald Barthelme's writing. Not enough to say that he didn't waste words; neither did extravagant Rabelais or apparently rambling Laurence Sterne. Donald barely indulged words—he valued them too much for that—and this rhetorical short leash makes his occasional lyric flights all the more exhilarating, like the sound of Hokie Mokie's trombone in Donald's short story, "The King of Jazz":

> "You mean that sound that sounds like the cutting edge of life? That sounds like polar bears crossing Arctic ice pans? That sounds like a herd of musk ox in full flight? That sounds like male walruses diving to the bottom of the sea? That sounds like fumaroles smoking on the slopes of Mt. Katmai? That sounds like the wild turkey walking through the deep, soft forest? That sounds like beavers chewing trees in an Appalachian marsh? That sounds like an oyster fungus growing on an aspen trunk? That sounds like a mule deer wandering a montane of the Sierra Nevada? That sounds like prairie dogs kissing? That sounds like witchgrass tum-bling or a river meandering? That sounds like manatees munching seaweed at Cape Sable? That sounds like coatimundis moving in packs across the face of Arkansas? That sounds like—"

More characteristic is the dispatch with which he ends "Snow White": a series of chapter-titles to which it would have been de trop to add the chapters themselves. THE FAILURE OF SNOW WHITE'S ARSE REVIRGINIZATION OF SNOW WHITE APOTHEOSIS OF SNOW WHITE SNOW WHITE RISES INTO THE SKY THE HEROES DEPART IN SEARCH OF A NEW PRINCIPLE HEIGH-HO. And at his tersest, with a single comma he can constrict your heart: "I visited the child's nursery school, once."

I have heard Donald referred to as essentially a writer of the American 1960's. It may be true that his alloy of irrealism and its opposite is more evocative of that fermentatious decade, when European formalism had its belated flowering in North American writing, than of the relatively conservative decades since. But his literary precursors antedate the century, not to mention its 60's, and are mostly non-American. "How come you write the way you do?" a Johns Hopkins apprentice writer once asked him. "Because Samuel Beckett already wrote the way he did," Barthelme replied. He then produced for the seminar his "short list": five books he recommended to the attention of aspiring American fiction writers. No doubt the list changed from time to time; just then it consisted of Rabelais's "Gargantua and Pantagruel," Laurence Sterne's "Tristram Shandy," the stories of Heinrich von Kleist, Flaubert's "Bouvard and Pecuchet" and Flann O'Brien's "At Swim-Two-Birds"—a fair sample of the kind of nonlinear narration, sportive form and cohabitation of radical fantasy with quotidian detail that mark his own fiction. He readily admired other, more "traditional" writers, but it is from the likes of these that he felt his genealogical descent.

Similarly, though he tsked at the critical tendency to group certain writers against certain others "as if we were football teams"—praising these as the true "post-contemporaries" or whatever, and consigning those to some outer darkness of the passe—he freely acknowledged his admiration for such of his "teammates," in those critics' view, as Robert Coover, Stanley Elkin, William Gaddis, William Gass, John Hawkes, Thomas Pynchon and Kurt Vonnegut, among others. A few springs ago, he and his wife, Marion, presided over a memorable Greenwich Village dinner party for most of these and their companions (together with his agent, Lynn Nesbit, whom Donald called "the mother of postmodernism"). In 1988, on the occasion of John Hawkes's academic retirement, Robert Coover impresarioed a more formal reunion of that team, complete with readings and symposia, at Brown University. Donald's throat cancer had by then already announced itself—another, elsewhere, would be the death of him—but he gave one more of his perfectly antitheatrical virtuoso readings.

How different from one another those above-mentioned teammates are! Indeed, other than their nationality and gender, their common inclination to some degree of irrealism and to the foregrounding of form and language, and the circumstance of their having appeared on the literary scene in the 1960's or thereabouts, it is not easy to see why their names should be so frequently linked (or why Grace Paley's, for example, is not regularly included in that all-male lineup). But if they constitute a team, it has no consistently brighter star than the one just lost.

Except for readers who require a new literary movement with each new network television season, the product of Donald Barthelme's imagination and artistry is an ongoing delight that we had looked forward to decades more of. Readers in the century to come (assuming etc.) will surely likewise prize that product—for its wonderful humor and wry pathos, for the cultural-historical interest its rich specificity will duly acquire, and—most of all, I hope and trust—for its superb verbal art.

Student Essay

Dominic Pignataro is interested in how two authors who had experiences in very different wars tell their stories using different point-of-view strategies. Read his essay "Two Authors, Two Ways to Tell a War Story: Point of View in 'Soldier's Home' and 'How to Tell a True War Story'" in Chapter 6.

A BOOKSHELF
OF SHORT FICTION

Chinua Achebe (b. 1930)

Dead Men's Path (1953/1972)

Michael Obi's hopes were fulfilled much earlier than he expected. He was appointed headmaster of Ndume Central School in January 1949. It had always been an unprogressive school, so the Mission authorities decided to send a young and energetic man to run it. Obi accepted this responsibility with enthusiasm. He had many wonderful ideas and this was an opportunity to put them into practice. He had had sound secondary school education which designated him a "pivotal teacher" in the official records and set him apart from the other headmasters in the mission field. He was outspoken in his condemnation of the narrow views of these older and often less-educated ones.

"We shall make a good job of it, shan't we?" he asked his young wife when they first heard the joyful news of his promotion.

"We shall do our best," she replied. "We shall have such beautiful gardens and everything will be just *modern* and delightful . . ." In their two years of married life she had become completely infected by his passion for "modern methods" and his denigration of "these old and superannuated people in the teaching field who would be better employed as traders in the Onitsha market." She began to see herself already as the admired wife of the young headmaster, the queen of the school.

The wives of the other teachers would envy her position. She would set the fashion in everything . . . Then, suddenly, it occurred to her that there might not be other wives. Wavering between hope and fear, she asked her husband, looking anxiously at him.

"All our colleagues are young and 5 unmarried," he said with enthusiasm which for once she did not share. "Which is a good thing," he continued.

"Why?"

"Why? They will give all their time and energy to the school."

Nancy was downcast. For a few minutes she became sceptical about the new school; but it was only for a few minutes. Her little personal misfortune could not blind her to her husband's happy prospects. She looked at him as he sat folded up in a chair. He was stoop-shouldered and looked frail. But he sometimes surprised people with sudden bursts of physical energy. In his present posture, however, all his bodily strength seemed to have retired behind his deep-set eyes, giving them an extraordinary power of penetration. He was only twenty-six, but looked thirty or more. On the whole, he was not unhandsome.

"A penny for your thoughts, Mike," said Nancy after a while, imitating the woman's magazine she read.

"I was thinking what a grand opportu- 10 nity we've got at last to show these people how a school should be run."

Ndume School was backward in every sense of the word. Mr. Obi put his whole life into the work, and his wife hers too. He had two aims. A high standard of teaching was insisted upon, and the school compound was to be turned into a place of beauty. Nancy's dream-gardens came to life with the coming of the rains, and blossomed. Beautiful hibiscus and allamanda hedges in brilliant red and yellow marked out the carefully tended school compound from the rank neighbourhood bushes.

One evening as Obi was admiring his work he was scandalized to see an old woman from the village hobble right across the compound, through a marigold flower-bed and the hedges. On going up there he found faint signs of an almost disused path from the village across the school compound to the bush on the other side.

"It amazes me," said Obi to one of his teachers who had been three years in the school, "that you people allowed the villagers to make use of this footpath. It is simply incredible." He shook his head.

"The path," said the teacher apologetically, "appears to be very important to them. Although it is hardly used, it connects the village shrine with their place of burial."

15   "And what has that got to do with the school?" asked the headmaster.

"Well, I don't know," replied the other with a shrug of the shoulders. "But I remember there was a big row some time ago when we attempted to close it."

"That was some time ago. But it will not be used now," said Obi as he walked away. "What will the Government Education Officer think of this when he comes to inspect the school next week? The villagers might, for all I know, decide to use the schoolroom for a pagan ritual during the inspection."

Heavy sticks were planted closely across the path at the two places where it entered and left the school premises. These were further strengthened with barbed wire.

Three days later the village priest of *Ani* called on the headmaster. He was an old man and walked with a slight stoop. He carried a stout walking-stick which he usually tapped on the floor, by way of emphasis, each time he made a new point in his argument.

"I have heard," he said after the usual 20 exchange of cordialities, "that our ancestral footpath has recently been closed . . ."

"Yes," replied Mr. Obi. "We cannot allow people to make a highway of our school compound."

"Look here, my son," said the priest bringing down his walking-stick, "this path was here before you were born and before your father was born. The whole life of this village depends on it. Our dead relatives depart by it and our ancestors visit us by it. But most important, it is the path of children coming in to be born . . ."

Mr. Obi listened with a satisfied smile on his face.

"The whole purpose of our school," he said finally, "is to eradicate just such beliefs as that. Dead men do not require footpaths. The whole idea is just fantastic. Our duty is to teach your children to laugh at such ideas."

"What you say may be true," replied 25 the priest, "but we follow the practices of our fathers. If you re-open the path we shall have nothing to quarrel about. What I always say is: let the hawk perch and let the eagle perch." He rose to go.

"I am sorry," said the young headmaster. "But the school compound cannot be a thoroughfare. It is against our regulations. I would suggest your constructing another path, skirting our premises. We can even get our boys to help in building it. I don't suppose the ancestors will find the little detour too burdensome."

"I have no more words to say," said the old priest, already outside.

Two days later a young woman in the village died in childbed. A diviner was immediately consulted and he prescribed heavy sacrifices to propitiate ancestors insulted by the fence.

Obi woke up next morning among the ruins of his work. The beautiful hedges were torn up not just near the path but right round the school, the flowers trampled to death and one of the school buildings pulled down . . . That day, the white Supervisor came to inspect the school and wrote a nasty report on the state of the premises but more seriously about the "tribal-war situation developing between the school and the village, arising in part from the misguided zeal of the new headmaster."

Kate Chopin (1850–1904)

The Story of an Hour (1894)

Knowing that Mrs. Mallard was afflicted with a heart trouble, great care was taken to break to her as gently as possible the news of her husband's death.

It was her sister Josephine who told her, in broken sentences; veiled hints that revealed in half concealing. Her husband's friend Richards was there, too, near her. It was he who had been in the newspaper office when intelligence of the railroad disaster was received, with Brently Mallard's name leading the list of "killed." He had only taken the time to assure himself of its truth by a second telegram, and had hastened to forestall any less careful, less tender friend in bearing the sad message.

She did not hear the story as many women have heard the same, with a paralyzed inability to accept its significance. She wept at once, with sudden, wild abandonment, in her sister's arms. When the storm of grief had spent itself she went away to her room alone. She would have no one follow her.

There stood, facing the open window, a comfortable, roomy armchair. Into this she sank, pressed down by a physical exhaustion that haunted her body and seemed to reach into her soul.

She could see in the open square 5 before her house the tops of trees that were all aquiver with the new spring life. The delicious breath of rain was in the air. In the street below a peddler was crying his wares. The notes of a distant song which some one was singing reached her faintly, and countless sparrows were twittering in the eaves.

There were patches of blue sky showing here and there through the clouds that had met and piled one above the other in the west facing her window.

She sat with her head thrown back upon the cushion of the chair, quite motionless, except when a sob came up into her throat and shook her, as a child who had cried itself to sleep continues to sob in its dreams.

She was young, with a fair, calm face, whose lines bespoke repression and even a certain strength. But now there was a dull stare in her eyes, whose gaze was fixed away off yonder on one of those patches of blue sky. It was not a glance of reflection, but rather indicated a suspension of intelligent thought.

There was something coming to her and she was waiting for it, fearfully. What was it? She did not know; it was too subtle and elusive to name. But she felt it, creeping out of the sky, reaching toward her through the sounds, the scents, the color that filled the air.

10 Now her bosom rose and fell tumultuously. She was beginning to recognize this thing that was approaching to possess her, and she was striving to beat it back with her will—as powerless as her two white slender hands would have been.

When she abandoned herself a little whispered word escaped her slightly parted lips. She said it over and over under her breath: "free, free, free!" The vacant stare and the look of terror that had followed it went from her eyes. They stayed keen and bright. Her pulses beat fast, and the coursing blood warmed and relaxed every inch of her body.

She did not stop to ask if it were or were not a monstrous joy that held her. A clear and exalted perception enabled her to dismiss the suggestion as trivial.

She knew that she would weep again when she saw the kind, tender hands folded in death; the face that had never looked save with love upon her, fixed and gray and dead. But she saw beyond that bitter moment a long procession of years to come that would belong to her absolutely. And she opened and spread her arms out to them in welcome.

There would be no one to live for her during those coming years: she would live for herself. There would be no powerful will bending hers in that blind persistence with which men and women believe they have a right to impose a private will upon a fellow-creature. A kind intention or a cruel intention made the act seem no less a crime as she looked upon it in that brief moment of illumination.

And yet she had loved him—some- 15 times. Often she had not. What did it matter! What could love, the unsolved mystery, count for in face of this possession of self-assertion which she suddenly recognized as the strongest impulse of her being!

"Free! Body and soul free!" she kept whispering.

Josephine was kneeling before the closed door with her lips to the keyhole, imploring for admission. "Louise, open the door! I beg; open the door—you will make yourself ill. What are you doing, Louise? For heaven's sake open the door."

"Go away. I am not making myself ill." No; she was drinking in a very elixir of life through that open window.

Her fancy was running riot along those days ahead of her. Spring days, and summer days, and all sorts of days that would be her own. She breathed a quick prayer that life might be long. It was only yesterday she had thought with a shudder that life might be long.

She arose at length and opened the 20 door to her sister's importunities. There was a feverish triumph in her eyes, and she carried herself unwittingly like a goddess of Victory. She clasped her sister's waist, and together they descended the stairs. Richards stood waiting for them at the bottom.

Some one was opening the front door with a latchkey. It was Brently Mallard who entered, a little travel-stained, composedly carrying his gripsack and umbrella. He had been far from the scene of accident, and did not even know there had been one. He stood amazed at Josephine's piercing cry; at Richards' quick motion to screen him from the view of his wife.

But Richards was too late.

When the doctors came they said she had died of heart disease—of joy that kills.

William Faulkner (1897–1962)

Barn Burning (1939)

The store in which the Justice of the Peace's court was sitting smelled of cheese. The boy, crouched on his nail keg at the back of the crowded room, knew he smelled cheese, and more: from where he sat he could see the ranked shelves close-packed with the solid, squat, dynamic shapes of tin cans whose labels his stomach read, not from the lettering which meant nothing to his mind but from the scarlet devils and the silver curve of fish— this, the cheese which he knew he smelled and the hermetic meat which his intestines believed he smelled coming in intermittent gusts momentary and brief between the other constant one, the smell and sense just a little of fear because mostly of despair and grief, the old fierce pull of blood. He could not see the table where the Justice sat and before which his father and his father's enemy (*our enemy* he thought in that despair; *ourn! mine and hisn both! He's my father!*) stood, but he could hear them, the two of them that is, because his father had said no word yet:

"But what proof have you, Mr. Harris?"

"I told you. The hog got into my corn. I caught it up and sent it back to him. He had no fence that would hold it. I told him so, warned him. The next time I put the hog in my pen. When he came to get it I gave him enough wire to patch up his pen. The next time I put the hog up and kept it. I rode down to his house and saw the wire I gave him still rolled on to the spool in his yard. I told him he could have the hog when he paid me a dollar pound fee. That evening a nigger came with the dollar and got the hog. He was a strange nigger. He said, 'He say to tell you wood and hay kin burn.' I said, 'What?' 'That whut he say to tell you,' the nigger said. 'Wood and hay kin burn.' That night my barn burned. I got the stock out but I lost the barn."

"Where is the nigger? Have you got him?"

"He was a strange nigger, I tell you. I don't know what became of him."

"But that's not proof. Don't you see that's not proof?"

"Get that boy up here. He knows." For a moment the boy thought too that the man meant his older brother until Harris said, "Not him. The little one. The boy," and, crouching, small for his age, small and wiry like his father, in patched and faded jeans even too small for him, with straight, uncombed, brown hair and eyes gray and wild as storm scud, he saw the men between himself and the table part and become a lane of grim faces, at the end of which he saw the Justice, a shabby, collarless, graying man in spectacles, beckoning him. He felt no floor under his bare feet; he seemed to walk beneath the palpable weight of the grim turning faces. His father, stiff in his black Sunday coat donned not for the trial but for the moving, did not even look at him. *He aims for me to lie*, he thought, again with that frantic grief and despair. *And I will have to do hit.*

"What's your name, boy?" the Justice said.

"Colonel Sartoris Snopes," the boy whispered.

10 "Hey?" the Justice said. "Talk louder. Colonel Sartoris? I reckon anybody named for Colonel Sartoris in this country can't help but tell the truth, can they?" The boy said nothing. *Enemy! Enemy!* he thought; for a moment he could not even see, could not see that the Justice's face was kindly nor discern that his voice was troubled when he spoke to the man named Harris: "Do you want me to question this boy?" But he could hear, and during those subsequent long seconds while there was absolutely no sound in the crowded little room save that of quiet and intent breathing it was as if he had swung outward at the end of a grape vine, over a ravine, and at the top of the swing had been caught in a prolonged instant of mesmerized gravity, weightless in time.

"No!" Harris said violently, explosively. "Damnation! Send him out of here!" Now time, the fluid world, rushed beneath him again, the voices coming to him again through the smell of cheese and sealed meat, the fear and despair and the old grief of blood:

"This case is closed. I can't find against you, Snopes, but I can give you advice. Leave this country and don't come back to it."

His father spoke for the first time, his voice cold and harsh, level, without emphasis: "I aim to. I don't figure to stay in a country among people who . . ." he said something unprintable and vile, addressed to no one.

"That'll do," the Justice said. "Take your wagon and get out of this country before dark. Case dismissed."

15 His father turned, and he followed the stiff black coat, the wiry figure walking a little stiffly from where a Confederate provost's man's musket ball had taken him in the heel on a stolen horse thirty years ago, followed the two backs now, since his older brother had appeared from somewhere in the crowd, no taller than the father but thicker, chewing tobacco steadily, between the two lines of grim-faced men and out of the store and across the worn gallery and down the sagging steps and among the dogs and half-grown boys in the mild May dust, where as he passed a voice hissed:

"Barn burner!"

Again he could not see, whirling; there was a face in a red haze, moonlike, bigger than the full moon, the owner of it half again his size, he leaping in the red haze toward the face, feeling no blow, feeling no shock when his head struck the earth, scrabbling up and leaping again, feeling no blow this time either and tasting no blood, scrabbling up to see the other boy in full flight and himself already leaping into pursuit as his father's hand jerked him back, the harsh, cold voice speaking above him: "Go get in the wagon."

It stood in a grove of locusts and mulberries across the road. His two hulking sisters in their Sunday dresses and his mother and her sister in calico and sunbonnets were already in it, sitting on and among the sorry residue of the dozen and more movings which even the boy could remember—the battered stove, the broken beds and chairs, the clock inlaid with mother-of-pearl, which would not run, stopped at some fourteen minutes past two o'clock of a dead and forgotten day and time, which had been his mother's dowry. She was crying, though when she saw him she drew her sleeve across her face and began to descend from the wagon. "Get back," the father said.

"He's hurt. I got to get some water and wash his . . ."

"Get back in the wagon," his father 20 said. He got in too, over the tail-gate. His father mounted to the seat where the older brother already sat and struck the gaunt mules two savage blows with the peeled willow, but without heat. It was not even sadistic; it was exactly that same quality which in later years would cause his descendants to over-run the engine before putting a motor car into motion, striking and reining back in the same movement. The wagon went on, the store with its quiet crowd of grimly watching men dropped behind; a curve in the road hid it. *Forever* he thought. *Maybe he's done satisfied now, now that he has* . . . stopping himself, not to say it aloud even to himself. His mother's hand touched his shoulder.

"Does hit hurt?" she said.

"Naw," he said. "Hit don't hurt. Lemme be."

"Can't you wipe some of the blood off before hit dries?"

"I'll wash to-night," he said. "Lemme be, I tell you."

25 The wagon went on. He did not know where they were going. None of them ever did or ever asked, because it was always somewhere, always a house of sorts waiting for them a day or two days or even three days away. Likely his father had already arranged to make a crop on another farm before he . . . Again he had to stop himself. He (the father) always did. There was something about his wolflike independence and even courage when the advantage was at least neutral which impressed strangers, as if they got from his latent ravening ferocity not so much a sense of dependability as a feeling that his ferocious conviction in the rightness of his own actions would be of advantage to all whose interest lay with his.

That night they camped, in a grove of oaks and beeches where a spring ran. The nights were still cool and they had a fire against it, of a rail lifted from a nearby fence and cut into lengths—a small fire, neat, niggard almost, a shrewd fire; such fires were his father's habit and custom always, even

in freezing weather. Older, the boy might have remarked this and wondered why not a big one; why should not a man who had not only seen the waste and extravagance of war, but who had in his blood an inherent voracious prodigality with material not his own, have burned everything in sight? Then he might have gone a step farther and thought that that was the reason: that niggard blaze was the living fruit of nights passed during those four years in the woods hiding from all men, blue or gray, with his strings of horses (captured horses, he called them). And older still, he might have divined the true reason: that the element of fire spoke to some deep mainspring of his father's being, as the element of steel or of powder spoke to other men, as the one weapon for the preservation of integrity, else breath were not worth the breathing, and hence to be regarded with respect and used with discretion.

But he did not think this now and he had seen those same niggard blazes all his life. He merely ate his supper beside it and was already half asleep over his iron plate when his father called him, and once more he followed the stiff back, the stiff and ruthless limp, up the slope and on to the starlit road where, turning, he could see his father against the stars but without face or depth— a shape black, flat, and bloodless as though cut from tin in the iron folds of the frockcoat which had not been made for him, the voice harsh like tin and without heat like tin:

"You were fixing to tell them. You would have told him." He didn't answer. His father struck him with the flat of his hand on the side of the head, hard but without heat, exactly as he had struck the two mules at the store, exactly as he would strike either of them with any stick in order to kill a horse fly, his voice still without heat or anger: "You're getting to be a man. You got to learn. You got to learn to stick to your own blood or you ain't going to have any blood to stick to you. Do you think either of them, any man there this morning, would? Don't you know all they wanted was a chance to get at me because they knew I had them beat? Eh?" Later, twenty years later, he was to tell himself, "If I had said they wanted only truth, justice, he would have hit me again." But now he said nothing. He was not crying. He just stood there. "Answer me," his father said.

"Yes," he whispered. His father turned.

30 "Get on to bed. We'll be there tomorrow."

Tomorrow they were there. In the early afternoon the wagon stopped before a paintless two-room house identical almost with the dozen others it had stopped before even in the boy's ten years, and again, as on the other dozen occasions, his mother and aunt got down and began to unload the wagon, although his two sisters and his father and brother had not moved.

"Likely hit ain't fitten for hawgs," one of the sisters said.

"Nevertheless, fit it will and you'll hog it and like it," his father said. "Get out of them chairs and help your Ma unload."

The two sisters got down, big, bovine, in a flutter of cheap ribbons; one of them drew from the jumbled wagon bed a battered lantern, the other a worn broom. His father handed the reins to the older son and began to climb stiffly over the wheel. "When they get unloaded, take the team to the barn and feed them." Then he said, and at first the boy thought he was still speaking to his brother: "Come with me."

35 "Me?" he said.

"Yes," his father said. "You."

"Abner," his mother said. His father paused and looked back—the harsh level stare beneath the shaggy, graying, irascible brows.

"I reckon I'll have a word with the man that aims to begin to-morrow owning me body and soul for the next eight months."

They went back up the road. A week ago—or before last night, that is—he would have asked where they were going, but not now. His father had struck him before last night but never before had he paused afterward to explain why; it was as if the blow and the following calm, outrageous voice still rang, repercussed, divulging nothing to him save the terrible handicap of being young, the light weight of his few years, just heavy enough to prevent his soaring free of the world as it seemed to be ordered but not heavy enough to keep him footed solid in it, to resist it and try to change the course of its events.

40 Presently he could see the grove of oaks and cedars and the other flowering trees and shrubs where the house would be, though not the house yet. They walked beside a fence massed with honeysuckle and Cherokee roses and came to a gate swinging open between two brick pillars, and now, beyond a sweep of drive, he saw the house for the first time and at that instant he forgot his father and the terror and despair both, and even when he remembered his father again (who had not stopped) the terror and despair did not return. Because, for all the twelve movings, they had sojourned until now in a poor country, a land of small farms and fields and houses, and he had never seen a house like this before. *Hit's big as a courthouse* he thought quietly, with a surge of peace and joy whose reason he could not have thought into words, being too young for that: *They are safe from him. People whose lives are a part of this peace and dignity are beyond his touch, he no more to them than a buzzing wasp: capable of stinging for a little moment but that's all; the spell of this peace and dignity rendering even the barns and stable and cribs which belong to it*

impervious to the puny flames he might contrive ... this, the peace and joy, ebbing for an instant as he looked again at the stiff black back, the stiff and implacable limp of the figure which was not dwarfed by the house, for the reason that it had never looked big anywhere and which now, against the serene columned backdrop, had more than ever that impervious quality of something cut ruthlessly from tin, depthless, as though, sidewise to the sun, it would cast no shadow. Watching him, the boy remarked the absolutely undeviating course which his father held and saw the stiff foot come squarely down in a pile of fresh droppings where a horse had stood in the drive and which his father could have avoided by a simple change of stride. But it ebbed only for a moment, though he could not have thought this into words either, walking on in the spell of the house, which he could ever want but without envy, without sorrow, certainly never with that ravening and jealous rage which unknown to him walked in the ironlike black coat before him: *Maybe he will feel it too. Maybe it will even change him now from what maybe he couldn't help but be.*

They crossed the portico. Now he could hear his father's stiff foot as it came down on the boards with clocklike finality, a sound out of all proportion to the displacement of the body it bore and which was not dwarfed either by the white door before it, as though it had attained to a sort of vicious and ravening minimum not to be dwarfed by anything—the flat, wide, black hat, the formal coat of broadcloth which had once been black but which had now that friction-glazed greenish cast of the bodies of old house flies, the lifted sleeve which was too large, the lifted hand like a curled claw. The door opened so promptly that the boy knew the Negro must have been watching them all the time, an old man with neat grizzled hair, in a linen jacket, who stood barring the door with his body, saying, "Wipe yo foots, white man, fo you come in here. Major ain't home nohow."

"Get out of my way, nigger," his father said, without heat too, flinging the door back and the Negro also and entering, his hat still on his head. And now the boy saw the prints of the stiff foot on the doorjamb and saw them appear on the pale rug behind the machinelike deliberation of the foot which seemed to bear (or transmit) twice the weight which the body compassed. The Negro was shouting "Miss Lula! Miss Lula!" somewhere behind them, then the boy, deluged as though by a warm wave by a suave turn of carpeted stair and a pendant glitter of chandeliers and a mute gleam of gold frames, heard the swift feet and saw her too, a lady—perhaps he had never seen her like before either—in a gray, smooth gown with lace at the throat and an apron tied at the waist and the sleeves turned back, wiping cake or biscuit dough from her hands with a towel as she came up the hall, looking not at his father at all but at the tracks on the blond rug with an expression of incredulous amazement.

"I tried," the Negro cried. "I tole him to ..."

"Will you please go away?" she said in a shaking voice. "Major de Spain is not at home. Will you please go away?"

His father had not spoken again. He did not speak again. He did not even look at her. He just stood stiff in the center of the rug, in his hat, the shaggy iron-gray brows twitching slightly above the pebble-colored eyes as he appeared to examine the house with brief deliberation. Then with the same deliberation he turned; the boy watched him pivot on the good leg and saw the stiff foot drag round the arc of the turning, leaving a final long and fading smear. His father never looked at it, he never once looked down at the rug. The Negro held the door. It

45

closed behind them, upon the hysteric and indistinguishable woman-wail. His father stopped at the top of the steps and scraped his boot clean on the edge of it. At the gate he stopped again. He stood for a moment, planted stiffly on the stiff foot, looking back at the house. "Pretty and white, ain't it?" he said. "That's sweat. Nigger sweat. Maybe it ain't white enough yet to suit him. Maybe he wants to mix some white sweat with it."

Two hours later the boy was chopping wood behind the house within which his mother and aunt and the two sisters (the mother and aunt, not the two girls, he knew that; even at this distance and muffled by walls the flat loud voices of the two girls emanated an incorrigible idle inertia) were setting up the stove to prepare a meal, when he heard the hooves and saw the linen-clad man on a fine sorrel mare, whom he recognized even before he saw the rolled rug in front of the Negro youth following on a fat bay carriage horse—a suffused, angry face vanishing, still at full gallop, beyond the corner of the house where his father and brother were sitting in the two tilted chairs; and a moment later, almost before he could have put the axe down, he heard the hooves again and watched the sorrel mare go back out of the yard, already galloping again. Then his father began to shout one of the sisters' names, who presently emerged backward from the kitchen door dragging the rolled rug along the ground by one end while the other sister walked behind it.

"If you ain't going to tote, go on and set up the wash pot," the first said.

"You, Sarty!" the second shouted. "Set up the wash pot!" His father appeared at the door, framed against that shabbiness, as he had been against that other bland perfection, impervious to either, the mother's anxious face at his shoulder.

"Go on," the father said. "Pick it up." The two sisters stooped, broad, lethargic; stooping, they presented an incredible expanse of pale cloth and a flutter of tawdry ribbons.

"If I thought enough of a rug to have to git hit all the way from France I wouldn't keep hit where folks coming in would have to tromp on hit," the first said. They raised the rug.

"Abner," the mother said. "Let me do it."

"You go back and git dinner," his father said. "I'll tend to this."

From the woodpile through the rest of the afternoon the boy watched them, the rug spread flat in the dust beside the bubbling wash pot, the two sisters stooping over it with that profound and lethargic reluctance, while the father stood over them in turn, implacable and grim, driving them though never raising his voice again. He could smell the harsh homemade lye they were using; he saw his mother come to the door once and look toward them with an expression not anxious now but very like despair; he saw his father turn, and he fell to with the axe and saw from the corner of his eye his father raise from the ground a flattish fragment of field stone and examine it and return to the pot, and this time his mother actually spoke: "Abner. Abner. Please don't. Please, Abner."

Then he was done too. It was dusk; the whippoorwills had already begun. He could smell coffee from the room where they would presently eat the cold food remaining from the mid-afternoon meal, though when he entered the house he realized they were having coffee again probably because there was a fire on the hearth, before which the rug now lay spread over the backs of the two chairs. The tracks of his father's foot were gone. Where they had been were now long, water-cloudy scoriations resembling the sporadic course of a lilliputian mowing machine.

55   It still hung there while they ate the cold food and then went to bed, scattered without order or claim up and down the two rooms, his mother in one bed, where his father would later lie, the older brother in the other, himself, the aunt, and the two sisters on pallets on the floor. But his father was not in bed yet. The last thing the boy remembered was the depthless, harsh silhouette of the hat and coat bending over the rug and it seemed to him that he had not even closed his eyes when the silhouette was standing over him, the fire almost dead behind it, the stiff foot prodding him awake. "Catch up the mule," his father said.

    When he returned with the mule his father was standing in the black door, the rolled rug over his shoulder. "Ain't you going to ride?" he said.

    "No. Give me your foot."

    He bent his knee into his father's hand, the wiry, surprising power flowed smoothly, rising, he rising with it, on to the mule's bare back (they had owned a saddle once; the boy could remember it though not when or where) and with the same effortlessness his father swung the rug up in front of him. Now in the starlight they retraced the afternoon's path, up the dusty road rife with honeysuckle, through the gate and up the black tunnel of the drive to the lightless house, where he sat on the mule and felt the rough warp of the rug drag across his thighs and vanish.

    "Don't you want me to help?" he whispered. His father did not answer and now he heard again that stiff foot striking the hollow portico with that wooden and clocklike deliberation, that outrageous overstatement of the weight it carried. The rug, hunched, not flung (the boy could tell that even in the darkness) from his father's shoulder struck the angle of wall and floor with a sound unbelievably loud, thunderous, then the foot again, unhurried and enormous; a light came on in the house and the boy sat, tense, breathing steadily and quietly and just a little fast, though the foot itself did not increase its beat at all, descending the steps now; now the boy could see him.

    "Don't you want to ride now?" he 60 whispered. "We kin both ride now," the light within the house altering now, flaring up and sinking. *He's coming down the stairs now*, he thought. He had already ridden the mule up beside the horse block; presently his father was up behind him and he doubled the reins over and slashed the mule across the neck, but before the animal could begin to trot the hard, thin arm came round him, the hard, knotted hand jerking the mule back to a walk.

    In the first red rays of the sun they were in the lot, putting plow gear on the mules. This time the sorrel mare was in the lot before he heard it at all, the rider collarless and even bareheaded, trembling, speaking in a shaking voice as the woman in the house had done, his father merely looking up once before stooping again to the hame he was buckling, so that the man on the mare spoke to his stooping back:

    "You must realize you have ruined that rug. Wasn't there anybody here, any of your women . . ." he ceased, shaking, the boy watching him, the older brother leaning now in the stable door, chewing, blinking slowly and steadily at nothing apparently. "It cost a hundred dollars. But you never had a hundred dollars. You never will. So I'm going to charge you twenty bushels of corn against your crop. I'll add it in your contract and when you come to the commissary you can sign it. That won't keep Mrs. de Spain quiet but maybe it will teach you to wipe your feet off before you enter her house again."

    Then he was gone. The boy looked at his father, who still had not spoken or even looked up again, who was now adjusting the logger-head in the hame.

"Pap," he said. His father looked at him—the inscrutable face, the shaggy brows beneath which the gray eyes glinted coldly. Suddenly the boy went toward him, fast, stopping as suddenly. "You done the best you could!" he cried. "If he wanted hit done different why didn't he wait and tell you how? He won't git no twenty bushels! He won't git none! We'll gether hit and hide hit! I kin watch . . ."

65   "Did you put the cutter back in that straight stock like I told you?"

"No, sir," he said.

"Then go do it."

That was Wednesday. During the rest of that week he worked steadily, at what was within his scope and some which was beyond it, with an industry that did not need to be driven nor even commanded twice; he had this from his mother, with the difference that some at least of what he did he liked to do, such as splitting wood with the half-size axe which his mother and aunt had earned, or saved money somehow, to present him with at Christmas. In company with the two older women (and on one afternoon, even one of the sisters), he built pens for the shoat and the cow which were a part of his father's contract with the landlord, and one afternoon, his father being absent, gone somewhere on one of the mules, he went to the field.

They were running a middle buster now, his brother holding the plow straight while he handled the reins, and walking beside the straining mule, the rich black soil shearing cool and damp against his bare ankles, he thought *Maybe this is the end of it. Maybe even that twenty bushels that seems hard to have to pay for just a rug will be a cheap price for him to stop forever and always from being what he used to be*; thinking, dreaming now, so that his brother had to speak sharply to him to mind the mule: *Maybe he even won't collect the twenty bushels. Maybe it will all add up and balance and vanish—corn, rug, fire; the terror and grief, the being pulled two ways like between two teams of horses—gone, done with for ever and ever.*

Then it was Saturday; he looked up 70 from beneath the mule he was harnessing and saw his father in the black coat and hat. "Not that," his father said. "The wagon gear." And then, two hours later, sitting in the wagon bed behind his father and brother on the seat, the wagon accomplished a final curve, and he saw the weathered paintless store with its tattered tobacco- and patent-medicine posters and the tethered wagons and saddle animals below the gallery. He mounted the gnawed steps behind his father and brother, and there again was the lane of quiet, watching faces for the three of them to walk through. He saw the man in spectacles sitting at the plank table and he did not need to be told this was a Justice of the Peace; he sent one glare of fierce, exultant, partisan defiance at the man in collar and cravat now, whom he had seen but twice before in his life, and that on a galloping horse, who now wore on his face an expression not of rage but of amazed unbelief which the boy could not have known was at the incredible circumstance of being sued by one of his own tenants, and came and stood against his father and cried at the Justice: "He ain't done it! He ain't burnt . . ."

"Go back to the wagon," his father said.

"Burnt?" the Justice said. "Do I understand this rug was burned too?"

"Does anybody here claim it was?" his father said. "Go back to the wagon." But he did not, he merely retreated to the rear of the room, crowded as that other had been, but not to sit down this time, instead, to stand pressing among the motionless bodies, listening to the voices:

"And you claim twenty bushels of corn is too high for the damage you did to the rug?"

75   "He brought the rug to me and said he wanted the tracks washed out of it. I washed the tracks out and took the rug back to him."

"But you didn't carry the rug back to him in the same condition it was in before you made the tracks on it."

His father did not answer, and now for perhaps half a minute there was no sound at all save that of breathing, the faint, steady suspiration of complete and intent listening.

"You decline to answer that, Mr. Snopes?" Again his father did not answer. "I'm going to find against you, Mr. Snopes. I'm going to find that you were responsible for the injury to Major de Spain's rug and hold you liable for it. But twenty bushels of corn seems a little high for a man in your circumstances to have to pay. Major de Spain claims it cost a hundred dollars. October corn will be worth about fifty cents. I figure that if Major de Spain can stand a ninety-five dollar loss on something he paid cash for, you can stand a five-dollar loss you haven't earned yet. I hold you in damages to Major de Spain to the amount of ten bushels of corn over and above your contract with him, to be paid to him out of your crop at gathering time. Court adjourned."

It had taken no time hardly, the morning was but half begun. He thought they would return home and perhaps back to the field, since they were late, far behind all other farmers. But instead his father passed on behind the wagon, merely indicating with his hand for the older brother to follow with it, and crossed the road toward the blacksmith shop opposite, pressing on after his father, overtaking him, speaking, whispering up at the harsh, calm face beneath the weathered hat: "He won't git no ten bushels neither. He won't git one. We'll . . ." until his father glanced for an instant down at him, the face absolutely calm, the grizzled eyebrows tangled above the cold eyes, the voice almost pleasant, almost gentle:

80   "You think so? Well, we'll wait till October anyway."

The matter of the wagon—the setting of a spoke or two and the tightening of the tires—did not take long either, the business of the tires accomplished by driving the wagon into the spring branch behind the shop and letting it stand there, the mules nuzzling into the water from time to time, and the boy on the seat with the idle reins, looking up the slope and through the sooty tunnel of the shed where the slow hammer rang and where his father sat on an upended cypress bolt, easily, either talking or listening, still sitting there when the boy brought the dripping wagon up out of the branch and halted it before the door.

"Take them on to the shade and hitch," his father said. He did so and returned. His father and the smith and a third man squatting on his heels inside the door were talking, about crops and animals; the boy, squatting too in the ammoniac dust and hoof-parings and scales of rust, heard his father tell a long and unhurried story out of the time before the birth of the older brother even when he had been a professional horsetrader. And then his father came up beside him where he stood before a tattered last year's circus poster on the other side of the store, gazing rapt and quiet at the scarlet horses, the incredible poisings and convolutions of tulle and tights and the painted leers of comedians, and said, "It's time to eat."

But not at home. Squatting beside his brother against the front wall, he watched his father emerge from the store and produce from a paper sack a segment of cheese and divide it carefully and deliberately into three with his pocket knife and produce crackers from the same sack. They all three squatted on the gallery and ate, slowly, without talking; then in the store again, they drank from a tin dipper tepid water smelling of the cedar bucket and of living beech trees. And still they did not go home. It was a horse lot this time, a tall rail fence upon and along which men stood and sat and out of which one by one horses were led, to be walked and trotted and then cantered back and forth along the road while the slow swapping and buying went on and the sun began to slant westward, they—the three of them—watching and listening, the older brother with his muddy eyes and his steady, inevitable tobacco, the father commenting now and then on certain of the animals, to no one in particular.

It was after sundown when they reached home. They ate supper by lamplight, then, sitting on the doorstep, the boy watched the night fully accomplish, listening to the whippoorwills and the frogs, when he heard his mother's voice: "Abner! No! No! Oh, God. Oh, God. Abner!" and he rose, whirled, and saw the altered light through the door where a candle stub now burned in a bottle neck on the table and his father, still in the hat and coat, at once formal and burlesque as though dressed carefully for some shabby and ceremonial violence, emptying the reservoir of the lamp back into the five-gallon kerosene can from which it had been filled, while the mother tugged at his arm until he shifted the lamp to the other hand and flung her back, not savagely or viciously, just hard, into the wall, her hands flung out against the wall for balance, her mouth open and in her face the same quality of hopeless despair as had been in her voice. Then his father saw him standing in the door.

85   "Go to the barn and get that can of oil we were oiling the wagon with," he said. The boy did not move. Then he could speak.

"What . . ." he cried. "What are you . . ."

"Go get that oil," his father said. "Go."

Then he was moving, running, outside the house, toward the stable: this the old habit, the old blood which he had not been permitted to choose for himself, which had been bequeathed him willy nilly and which

had run for so long (and who knew where, battening on what of outrage and savagery and lust) before it came to him. *I could keep on*, he thought. *I could run on and on and never look back, never need to see his face again. Only I can't. I can't*, the rusted can in his hand now, the liquid sploshing in it as he ran back to the house and into it, into the sound of his mother's weeping in the next room, and handed the can to his father.

"Ain't you going to even send a nigger?" he cried. "At least you sent a nigger before!"

This time his father didn't strike him.   90 The hand came even faster than the blow had, the same hand which had set the can on the table with almost excruciating care flashing from the can toward him too quick for him to follow it, gripping him by the back of his shirt and on to tiptoe before he had seen it quit the can, the face stooping at him in breathless and frozen ferocity, the cold, dead voice speaking over him to the older brother who leaned against the table, chewing with that steady, curious, sidewise motion of cows:

"Empty the can into the big one and go on. I'll catch up with you."

"Better tie him up to the bedpost," the brother said.

"Do like I told you," the father said. Then the boy was moving, his bunched shirt and the hard, bony hand between his shoulder-blades, his toes just touching the floor, across the room and into the other one, past the sisters sitting with spread heavy thighs in the two chairs over the cold hearth, and to where his mother and aunt sat side by side on the bed, the aunt's arms about his mother's shoulders.

"Hold him," the father said. The aunt made a startled movement. "Not you," the father said. "Lennie. Take hold of him. I want to see you do it." His mother took him by the wrist. "You'll hold him better than that. If he gets loose don't you know what he is going to do? He will go up yonder." He jerked his head toward the road. "Maybe I'd better tie him."

95   "I'll hold him," his mother whispered.

"See you do then." Then his father was gone, the stiff foot heavy and measured upon the boards, ceasing at last.

Then he began to struggle. His mother caught him in both arms, he jerking and wrenching at them. He would be stronger in the end, he knew that. But he had no time to wait for it. "Lemme go!" he cried. "I don't want to have to hit you!"

"Let him go!" the aunt said. "If he don't go, before God, I am going up there myself!"

"Don't you see I can't?" his mother cried. "Sarty! Sarty! No! No! Help me, Lizzie!"

100   Then he was free. His aunt grasped at him but it was too late. He whirled, running, his mother stumbled forward on to her knees behind him, crying to the nearest sister: "Catch him, Net! Catch him!" But that was too late too, the sister (the sisters were twins, born at the same time, yet either of them now gave the impression of being, encompassing as much living meat and volume and weight as any other two of the family) not yet having begun to rise from the chair, her head, face, alone merely turned, presenting to him in the flying instant an astonishing expanse of young female features untroubled by any surprise even, wearing only an expression of bovine interest. Then he was out of the room, out of the house, in the mild dust of the starlit road and the heavy rifeness of honeysuckle, the pale ribbon unspooling with terrific slowness under his running feet, reaching the gate at last and turning in, running, his heart and lungs drumming, on up the drive toward the lighted house, the lighted door. He did not knock, he burst in, sobbing for breath, incapable for the moment of speech;

he saw the astonished face of the Negro in the linen jacket without knowing when the Negro had appeared.

"De Spain!" he cried, panted. "Where's . . ." then he saw the white man too emerging from a white door down the hall. "Barn!" he cried. "Barn!"

"What?" the white man said. "Barn?"

"Yes!" the boy cried. "Barn!"

"Catch him!" the white man shouted.

But it was too late this time too. The 105 Negro grasped his shirt, but the entire sleeve, rotten with washing, carried away, and he was out that door too and in the drive again, and had actually never ceased to run even while he was screaming into the white man's face.

Behind him the white man was shouting, "My horse! Fetch my horse!" and he thought for an instant of cutting across the park and climbing the fence into the road, but he did not know the park nor how high the vine-massed fence might be and he dared not risk it. So he ran on down the drive, blood and breath roaring; presently he was in the road again though he could not see it. He could not hear either: the galloping mare was almost upon him before he heard her, and even then he held his course, as if the very urgency of his wild grief and need must in a moment more find him wings, waiting until the ultimate instant to hurl himself aside and into the weed-choked roadside ditch as the horse thundered past and on, for an instant in furious silhouette against the stars, the tranquil early summer night sky which, even before the shape of the horse and rider vanished, stained abruptly and violently upward: a long, swirling roar incredible and soundless, blotting the stars, and he springing up and into the road again, running again, knowing it was too late yet still running even after he heard the shot and, an instant later, two shots, pausing now without knowing he had ceased to run, crying "Pap! Pap!", running again before he knew he had begun to run, stumbling, tripping over something and scrabbling up again without ceasing to run, looking backward over his shoulder at the glare as he got up, running on among the invisible trees, panting, sobbing, "Father! Father!"

At midnight he was sitting on the crest of a hill. He did not know it was midnight and he did not know how far he had come. But there was no glare behind him now and he sat now, his back toward what he had called home for four days anyhow, his face toward the dark woods which he would enter when breath was strong again, small, shaking steadily in the chill darkness, hugging himself into the remainder of his thin, rotten shirt, the grief and despair now no longer terror and fear but just grief and despair. *Father. My father*, he thought. "He was brave!" he cried suddenly, aloud but not loud, no more than a whisper: "He was! He was in the war! He was in Colonel Sartoris' cav'ry!" not knowing that his father had gone to that war a private in the fine old European sense, wearing no uniform, admitting the authority of and giving fidelity to no man or army or flag, going to war as Malbrouck himself did: for booty—it meant nothing and less than nothing to him if it were enemy booty or his own.

The slow constellations wheeled on. It would be dawn and then sun-up after a while and he would be hungry. But that would be to-morrow and now he was only cold, and walking would cure that. His breathing was easier now and he decided to get up and go on, and then he found that he had been asleep because he knew it was almost dawn, the night almost over. He could tell that from the whippoorwills. They were everywhere now among the dark trees below him, constant and inflectioned and ceaseless, so that, as the instant for giving over to the day birds drew nearer and nearer, there was no interval at all between them. He got up. He was a little stiff, but walking would cure that too as it would the cold, and soon there would be the sun. He went on down the hill, toward the dark woods within which the liquid silver voices of the birds called unceasing—the rapid and urgent beating of the urgent and quiring heart of the late spring night. He did not look back.

James Joyce (1882–1941)

Araby (1914)

North Richmond Street, being blind, was a quiet street except at the hour when the Christian Brothers' School set the boys free. An uninhabited house of two storeys stood at the blind end, detached from its neighbours in a square ground. The other houses of the street, conscious of decent lives within them, gazed at one another with brown imperturbable faces.

The former tenant of our house, a priest, had died in the back drawing-room. Air, musty from having been long enclosed, hung in all the rooms, and the waste room behind the kitchen was littered with old useless papers. Among these I found a few paper-covered books, the pages of which were curled and damp: *The Abbot,* by Walter Scott, *The Devout Communicant* and *The Memoirs of Vidocq.* I liked the last best because its leaves were yellow. The wild garden behind the house contained a central apple-tree and a few straggling bushes under one of which I found the late tenant's rusty bicycle-pump. He had been a very charitable priest; in his will he had left all his money to institutions and the furniture of his house to his sister.

When the short days of winter came dusk fell before we had well eaten our dinners. When we met in the street the houses had grown sombre. The space of sky above us was the colour of ever-changing violet and towards it the lamps of the street lifted their feeble lanterns. The cold air stung us and we played till our bodies glowed. Our shouts echoed in the silent street. The career of our play brought us through the dark muddy lanes behind the houses where we ran the gauntlet of the rough tribes from the cottages, to the back doors of the dark dripping gardens where odours arose from the ashpits, to the dark odorous stables where a coachman smoothed and combed the horse or shook music from the buckled harness. When we returned to the street light from the kitchen windows had filled the areas. If my uncle was seen turning the corner we hid in the shadow until we had seen him safely housed. Or if Mangan's sister came out on the doorstep to call her brother in to his tea we watched her from our shadow peer up and down the street. We waited to see whether she would remain or go in and, if she remained, we left our shadow and walked up to Mangan's steps resignedly. She was waiting for us, her figure defined by the light from the half-opened door. Her brother always teased her before he obeyed and I stood by the railings looking at her. Her dress swung as she moved her body

and the soft rope of her hair tossed from side to side.

Every morning I lay on the floor in the front parlour watching her door. The blind was pulled down to within an inch of the sash so that I could not be seen. When she came out on the doorstep my heart leaped. I ran to the hall, seized my books and followed her. I kept her brown figure always in my eye and, when we came near the point at which our ways diverged, I quickened my pace and passed her. This happened morning after morning. I had never spoken to her, except for a few casual words, and yet her name was like a summons to all my foolish blood.

Her image accompanied me even in 5 places the most hostile to romance. On Saturday evenings when my aunt went marketing I had to go to carry some of the parcels. We walked through the flaring streets, jostled by drunken men and bargaining women, amid the curses of labourers, the shrill litanies of shop-boys who stood on guard by the barrels of pigs' cheeks, the nasal chanting of street-singers, who sang a *come-all-you* about O'Donovan Rossa, or a ballad about the troubles in our native land. These noises converged in a single sensation of life for me: I imagined that I bore my chalice safely through a throng of foes. Her name sprang to my lips at moments in strange prayers and praises which I myself did not understand. My eyes were often full of tears (I could not tell why) and at times a flood from my heart seemed to pour itself out into my bosom. I thought little of the future. I did not know whether I would ever speak to her or not or, if I spoke to her, how I could tell her of my confused adoration. But my body was like a harp and her words and gestures were like fingers running upon the wires.

One evening I went into the back drawing-room in which the priest had died.

It was a dark rainy evening and there was no sound in the house. Through one of the broken panes I heard the rain impinge upon the earth, the fine incessant needles of water playing in the sodden beds. Some distant lamp or lighted window gleamed below me. I was thankful that I could see so little. All my senses seemed to desire to veil themselves and, feeling that I was about to slip from them, I pressed the palms of my hands together until they trembled, murmuring: *O love! O love!* many times.

At last she spoke to me. When she addressed the first words to me I was so confused that I did not know what to answer. She asked me was I going to *Araby*. I forget whether I answered yes or no. It would be a splendid bazaar, she said; she would love to go.

—And why can't you? I asked.

While she spoke she turned a silver bracelet round and round her wrist. She could not go, she said, because there would be a retreat that week in her convent. Her brother and two other boys were fighting for their caps and I was alone at the railings. She held one of the spikes, bowing her head towards me. The light from the lamp opposite our door caught the white curve of her neck, lit up her hair that rested there and, falling, lit up the hand upon the railing. It fell over one side of her dress and caught the white border of a petticoat, just visible as she stood at ease.

10　　—It's well for you, she said.

—If I go, I said, I will bring you something.

What innumerable follies laid waste my waking and sleeping thoughts after that evening! I wished to annihilate the tedious intervening days. I chafed against the work of school. At night in my bedroom and by day in the classroom her image came between me and the page I strove to read. The syllables of the word *Araby* were called to me through the silence in which my soul luxuriated and cast an Eastern enchantment over me. I asked for leave to go to the bazaar on Saturday night. My aunt was surprised and hoped it was not some Freemason's affair. I answered few questions in class. I watched my master's face pass from amiability to sternness; he hoped I was not beginning to idle. I could not call my wandering thoughts together. I had hardly any patience with the serious work of life which, now that it stood between me and my desire, seemed to me child's play, ugly monotonous child's play.

On Saturday morning I reminded my uncle that I wished to go to the bazaar in the evening. He was fussing at the hallstand, looking for the hat-brush, and answered me curtly:

—Yes, boy, I know.

As he was in the hall I could not go 　15 into the front parlour and lie at the window. I left the house in bad humour and walked slowly towards the school. The air was pitilessly raw and already my heart misgave me.

When I came home to dinner my uncle had not yet been home. Still it was early. I sat staring at the clock for some time and, when its ticking began to irritate me, I left the room. I mounted the staircase and gained the upper part of the house. The high cold empty gloomy rooms liberated me and I went from room to room singing. From the front window I saw my companions playing below in the street. Their cries reached me weakened and indistinct and, leaning my forehead against the cool glass, I looked over at the dark house where she lived. I may have stood there for an hour, seeing nothing but the brown-clad figure cast by my imagination, touched discreetly by the lamplight at the curved neck, at the hand upon the railings and at the border below the dress.

When I came downstairs again I found Mrs. Mercer sitting at the fire. She was an old garrulous woman, a pawnbroker's widow, who collected used stamps for some pious purpose. I had to endure the gossip of the tea-table. The meal was prolonged beyond an hour and still my uncle did not come. Mrs. Mercer stood up to go: she was sorry she couldn't wait any longer, but it was after eight o'clock and she did not like to be out late, as the night air was bad for her. When she had gone I began to walk up and down the room, clenching my fists. My aunt said:

—I'm afraid you may put off your bazaar for this night of Our Lord.

At nine o'clock I heard my uncle's latchkey in the halldoor. I heard him talking to himself and heard the hallstand rocking when it had received the weight of his overcoat. I could interpret these signs. When he was midway through his dinner I asked him to give me the money to go to the bazaar. He had forgotten.

20 —The people are in bed and after their first sleep now, he said.

I did not smile. My aunt said to him energetically:

—Can't you give him the money and let him go? You've kept him late enough as it is.

My uncle said he was very sorry he had forgotten. He said he believed in the old saying: *All work and no play makes Jack a dull boy*. He asked me where I was going and, when I had told him a second time he asked me did I know *The Arab's Farewell to his Steed*. When I left the kitchen he was about to recite the opening line of the piece to my aunt.

I held a florin tightly in my hand as I strode down Buckingham Street towards the station. The sight of the streets thronged with buyers and glaring with gas recalled to me the purpose of my journey. I took my seat in a third-class carriage of a deserted train. After an intolerable delay the train moved out of the station slowly. It crept onward among ruinous houses and over the twinkling river. At Westland Row Station a crowd of people pressed to the carriage doors; but the porter moved them back, saying that it was a special train for the bazaar. I remained alone in the bare carriage. In a few minutes the train drew up beside an improvised wooden platform. I passed out on to the road and saw by the lighted dial of a clock that it was ten minutes to ten. In front of me was a large building which displayed the magical name.

I could not find any sixpenny entrance 25 and, fearing that the bazaar would be closed, I passed in quickly through a turnstile, handing a shilling to a weary-looking man. I found myself in a big hall girdled at half its height by a gallery. Nearly all the stalls were closed and the greater part of the hall was in darkness. I recognised a silence like that which pervades a church after a service. I walked into the centre of the bazaar timidly. A few people were gathered about the stalls which were still open. Before a curtain, over which the words *Café Chantant* were written in coloured lamps, two men were counting money on a salver. I listened to the fall of the coins.

Remembering with difficulty why I had come I went over to one of the stalls and examined porcelain vases and flowered tea-sets. At the door of the stall a young lady was talking and laughing with two young gentlemen. I remarked their English accents and listened vaguely to their conversation.

—O, I never said such a thing!

—O, but you did!

—O, but I didn't!

—Didn't she say that? 30

—Yes. I heard her.

—O, there's a . . . fib!

Observing me the young lady came over and asked me did I wish to buy anything. The tone of her voice was not encouraging; she seemed to have spoken to me out of a sense of duty. I looked humbly at the great jars that stood like eastern guards at either side of the dark entrance to the stall and murmured:

—No, thank you.

35   The young lady changed the position of one of the vases and went back to the two young men. They began to talk of the same subject. Once or twice the young lady glanced at me over her shoulder.

I lingered before her stall, though I knew my stay was useless, to make my interest in her wares seem the more real. Then I turned away slowly and walked down the middle of the bazaar. I allowed the two pennies to fall against the sixpence in my pocket. I heard a voice call from one end of the gallery that the light was out. The upper part of the hall was now completely dark.

Gazing up into the darkness I saw myself as a creature driven and derided by vanity; and my eyes burned with anguish and anger.

Jamaica Kincaid (b. 1949)

Girl (1978)

Wash the white clothes on Monday and put them on the stone heap; wash the color clothes on Tuesday and put them on the clothesline to dry; don't walk barehead in the hot sun; cook pumpkin fritters in very hot sweet oil; soak your little cloths right after you take them off; when buying cotton to make yourself a nice blouse, be sure that it doesn't have gum on it, because that way it won't hold up well after a wash; soak salt fish overnight before you cook it; is it true that you sing benna* in Sunday School?; always eat your food in such a way that it won't turn someone else's stomach; on Sundays try to walk like a lady and not like the slut you are so bent on becoming; don't sing benna in Sunday School; you mustn't speak to wharf-rat boys, not even to give directions; don't eat fruits on the street—flies will follow you; *but I don't sing benna[1] on Sundays at all and never in Sunday school*; this is how to sew on a button; this is how to make a buttonhole for the button you have just sewed on; this is how to hem a dress when you see the hem coming down and so to prevent yourself from looking like the slut I know you are so bent on becoming; this is how you iron your father's khaki shirt so that it doesn't have a crease; this is how you iron your father's khaki pants so that they don't have a crease; this is how you grow okra—far from the house, because okra tree harbors red ants; when you are growing dasheen,[2] make sure it gets plenty of water or else it makes your throat itch when you are eating it; this is how you sweep a corner; this is how you sweep a whole house; this is how you sweep a yard; this is how you smile to someone you don't like too much; this is how you smile to someone you don't like at all; this is how you smile to someone you like completely; this is how you set a table for tea; this is how you set a table for dinner; this is how you set a table for dinner with an

---

[1] **benna:** Calypso music.

[2] **dasheen:** The edible rootstock of taro, a tropical plant.

important guest; this is how you set a table for lunch; this is how you set a table for breakfast; this is how to behave in the presence of men who don't know you very well, and this way they won't recognize immediately the slut I have warned you against becoming; be sure to wash every day, even if it is with your own spit; don't squat down to play marbles—you are not a boy, you know; don't pick people's flowers—you might catch something; don't throw stones at blackbirds, because it might not be a blackbird at all; this is how to make a bread pudding; this is how to make doukona;[3] this is how to make pepper pot;[4] this is how to make a good medicine for a cold; this is how to make a good medicine to throw away a child before it even becomes a child; this is how to catch a fish; this is how to throw back a fish you don't like, and that way something bad won't fall on you; this is how to bully a man; this is how a man bullies you; this is how to love a man, and if this doesn't work there are other ways, and if they don't work don't feel too bad about giving up; this is how to spit up in the air if you feel like it, and this is how to move quick so that it doesn't fall on you; this is how to make ends meet; always squeeze bread to make sure it's fresh; *but what if the baker won't let me feel the bread?*; you mean to say that after all you are really going to be the kind of woman who the baker won't let near the bread?

---

[3]**doukona:** A spicy plantain pudding.
[4]**pepper pot:** A stew.

Joyce Carol Oates (b. 1938)

Where Are You Going, Where Have You Been? (1966)

FOR BOB DYLAN

Her name was Connie. She was fifteen and she had a quick, nervous giggling habit of craning her neck to glance into mirrors or checking other people's faces to make sure her own was all right. Her mother, who noticed everything and knew everything and who hadn't much reason any longer to look at her own face, always scolded Connie about it. "Stop gawking at yourself. Who are you? You think you're so pretty?" she would say. Connie would raise her eyebrows at these familiar old complaints and look right through her mother, into a shadowy vision of herself as she was right at that moment: she knew she was pretty and that was everything. Her mother had been pretty once too, if you could believe those old snapshots in the album, but now her looks were gone and that was why she was always after Connie.

"Why don't you keep your room clean like your sister? How've you got your hair fixed—what the hell stinks? Hair spray? You don't see your sister using that junk."

Her sister June was twenty-four and still lived at home. She was a secretary in the high school Connie attended, and if that wasn't bad enough—with her in the same building—she was so plain and chunky and steady that Connie had to hear her praised all the time by her mother and her mother's sisters. June did this, June did that, she saved money and helped clean the house and cooked and Connie couldn't do a thing, her mind was all filled with trashy daydreams. Their father was away at work most of the time and when he came home he wanted supper and he read the newspaper at supper and after supper he went to bed. He didn't bother talking much to them, but around his bent head Connie's mother kept picking at her until Connie wished her mother was dead and she herself was dead and it was all over. "She makes me want to throw up sometimes," she complained to her friends. She had a high, breathless, amused voice that made everything she said sound a little forced, whether it was sincere or not.

There was one good thing: June went places with girl friends of hers, girls who were just as plain and steady as she, and so when Connie wanted to do that her mother had no objections. The father of Connie's best girl friend drove the girls the three miles to town and left them at a shopping plaza so they could walk through the stores or go to a movie, and when he came to pick them up again at eleven he never bothered to ask what they had done.

5   They must have been familiar sights, walking around that shopping plaza in their shorts and flat ballerina slippers that always scuffed on the sidewalk, with charm bracelets jingling on their thin wrists; they would lean together to whisper and laugh secretly if someone passed who amused or interested them. Connie had long dark blond hair that drew anyone's eye to it, and she wore part of it pulled up on her head and puffed out and the rest of it she let fall down her back. She wore a pull-over jersey blouse that looked one way when she was at home and another way when she was away from home. Everything about her had two sides to it, one for home and one for any-

where that was not home: her walk, which could be childlike and bobbing, or languid enough to make anyone think she was hearing music in her head; her mouth, which was pale and smirking most of the time, but bright and pink on these evenings out; her laugh, which was cynical and drawling at home—"Ha, ha, very funny,"—but high-pitched and nervous anywhere else, like the jingling of the charms on her bracelet.

Sometimes they did go shopping or to a movie, but sometimes they went across the highway, ducking fast across the busy road, to a drive-in restaurant where older kids hung out. The restaurant was shaped like a big bottle, though squatter than a real bottle, and on its cap was a revolving figure of a grinning boy holding a hamburger aloft. One night in midsummer they ran across, breathless with daring, and right away someone leaned out a car window and invited them over, but it was just a boy from high school they didn't like. It made them feel good to be able to ignore him. They went up through the maze of parked and cruising cars to the bright-lit, fly-infested restaurant, their faces pleased and expectant as if they were entering a sacred building that loomed up out of the night to give them what haven and blessing they yearned for. They sat at the counter and crossed their legs at the ankles, their thin shoulders rigid with excitement, and listened to the music that made everything so good: the music was always in the background, like music at a church service; it was something to depend upon.

A boy named Eddie came in to talk with them. He sat backwards on his stool, turning himself jerkily around in semicircles and then stopping and turning again, and after a while he asked Connie if she would like something to eat. She said she would and so she tapped her friend's arm on her way out—her friend pulled her face up into a brave, droll look—and Connie said she would meet her at eleven, across the way. "I just hate to leave her like that," Connie said earnestly, but the boy said that she wouldn't be alone for long. So they went out to his car, and on the way Connie couldn't help but let her eyes wander over the windshields and faces all around her, her face gleaming with a joy that had nothing to do with Eddie or even this place; it might have been the music. She drew her shoulders up and sucked in her breath with the pure pleasure of being alive, and just at that moment she happened to glance at a face just a few feet away from hers. It was a boy with shaggy black hair, in a convertible jalopy painted gold. He stared at her and then his lips widened into a grin. Connie slit her eyes at him and turned away, but she couldn't help glancing back and there he was, still watching her. He wagged a finger and laughed and said, "Gonna get you, baby," and Connie turned away again without Eddie noticing anything.

She spent three hours with him, at the restaurant where they ate hamburgers and drank Cokes in wax cups that were always sweating, and then down an alley a mile or so away, and when he left her off at five to eleven only the movie house was still open at the plaza. Her girl friend was there, talking with a boy. When Connie came up, the two girls smiled at each other and Connie said, "How was the movie?" and the girl said, "*You* should know." They rode off with the girl's father, sleepy and pleased, and Connie couldn't help but look back at the darkened shopping plaza with its big empty parking lot and its signs that were faded and ghostly now, and over at the drive-in restaurant where cars were still circling tirelessly. She couldn't hear the music at this distance.

Next morning June asked her how the movie was and Connie said, "So-so."

She and that girl and occasionally another girl went out several times a week, and the rest of the time Connie spent around the house—it was summer vacation—getting in her mother's way and thinking, dreaming about the boys she met. But all the boys fell back and dissolved into a single face that was not even a face but an idea, a feeling, mixed up with the urgent insistent pounding of the music and the humid night air of July. Connie's mother kept dragging her back to the daylight by finding things for her to do or saying, suddenly, "What's this about the Pettinger girl?" 10

And Connie would say nervously, "Oh, her. That dope." She always drew thick clear lines between herself and such girls, and her mother was simple and kind enough to believe it. Her mother was so simple, Connie thought, that it was maybe cruel to fool her so much. Her mother went scuffling around the house in old bedroom slippers and complained over the telephone to one sister about the other, then the other called up and the two of them complained about the third one. If June's name was mentioned her mother's tone was approving, and if Connie's name was mentioned it was disapproving. This did not really mean she disliked Connie, and actually Connie thought that her mother preferred her to June just because she was prettier, but the two of them kept up a pretense of exasperation, a sense that they were tugging and struggling over something of little value to either of them. Sometimes, over coffee, they were almost friends, but something would come up—some vexation that was like a fly buzzing suddenly around their heads—and their faces went hard with contempt.

One Sunday Connie got up at eleven—none of them bothered with church—and washed her hair so that it could dry all day long, in the sun. Her parents and sister were going to a barbecue at an aunt's house and

Connie said no, she wasn't interested, rolling her eyes to let her mother know just what she thought of it. "Stay home alone then," her mother said sharply. Connie sat out back in a lawn chair and watched them drive away, her father quiet and bald, hunched around so that he could back the car out, her mother with a look that was still angry and not at all softened through the windshield, and in the back seat poor old June, all dressed up as if she didn't know what a barbecue was, with all the running yelling kids and the flies. Connie sat with her eyes closed in the sun, dreaming and dazed with the warmth about her as if this were a kind of love, the caresses of love, and her mind slipped over onto thoughts of the boy she had been with the night before and how nice he had been, how sweet it always was, not the way someone like June would suppose but sweet, gentle, the way it was in movies and promised in songs; and when she opened her eyes she hardly knew where she was, the back yard ran off into weeds and a fence-like line of trees and behind it the sky was perfectly blue and still. The asbestos "ranch house" that was now three years old startled her—it looked small. She shook her head as if to get awake.

It was too hot. She went inside the house and turned on the radio to drown out the quiet. She sat on the edge of her bed, barefoot, and listened for an hour and a half, to a program called XYZ Sunday Jamboree, record after record of hard, fast, shrieking songs she sang along with, interspersed by exclamations from "Bobby King": "An' look here, you girls at Napoleon's—Son and Charley want you to pay real close attention to this song coming up!"

And Connie paid close attention herself, bathed in a glow of slow-pulsed joy that seemed to rise mysteriously out of the music itself and lay languidly about the airless little room, breathed in and breathed out with each gentle rise and fall of her chest.

After a while she heard a car coming 15 up the drive. She sat up at once, startled, because it couldn't be her father so soon. The gravel kept crunching all the way in from the road—the driveway was long—and Connie ran to the window. It was a car she didn't know. It was an open jalopy, painted a bright gold that caught the sunlight opaquely. Her heart began to pound and her fingers snatched at her hair, checking it, and she whispered, "Christ, Christ," wondering how she looked. The car came to a stop at the side door and the horn sounded four short taps, as if this were a signal Connie knew.

She went into the kitchen and approached the door slowly, then hung out the screen door, her bare toes curling down off the step. There were two boys in the car and now she recognized the driver: he had shaggy, shabby black hair that looked crazy as a wig and he was grinning at her.

"I ain't late, am I?" he said.

"Who the hell do you think you are?" Connie said.

"Toldja I'd be out, didn't I?"

"I don't even know who you are."   20

She spoke sullenly, careful to show no interest or pleasure, and he spoke in a fast, bright monotone. Connie looked past him to the other boy, taking her time. He had fair brown hair, with a lock that fell onto his forehead. His sideburns gave him a fierce, embarrassed look, but so far he hadn't even bothered to glance at her. Both boys wore sunglasses. The driver's glasses were metallic and mirrored everything in miniature.

"You wanta come for a ride?" he said.

Connie smirked and let her hair fall loose over one shoulder.

"Don'tcha like my car? New paint job," he said. "Hey."

"What?"   25

"You're cute."

She pretended to fidget, chasing flies away from the door.

"Don'tcha believe me, or what?" he said.

"Look, I don't even know who you are," Connie said in disgust.

30 "Hey, Ellie's got a radio, see. Mine broke down." He lifted his friend's arm and showed her the little transistor the boy was holding, and now Connie began to hear the music. It was the same program that was playing inside the house.

"Bobby King?" she said.

"I listen to him all the time. I think he's great."

"He's kind of great," Connie said reluctantly.

"Listen, that guy's *great*. He knows where the action is."

35 Connie blushed a little, because the glasses made it impossible for her to see just what this boy was looking at. She couldn't decide if she liked him or if he was just a jerk, and so she dawdled in the doorway and wouldn't come down or go back inside. She said, "What's all that stuff painted on your car?"

"Can'tcha read it?" He opened the door very carefully, as if he were afraid it might fall off. He slid out just as carefully, planting his feet firmly on the ground, the tiny metallic world in his glasses slowing down like gelatine hardening, and in the midst of it Connie's bright green blouse. "This here is my name, to begin with," he said. ARNOLD FRIEND was written in tarlike black letters on the side, with a drawing of a round, grinning face that reminded Connie of a pumpkin, except it wore sunglasses. "I wanta introduce myself. I'm Arnold Friend and that's my real name and I'm gonna be your friend, honey, and inside the car's Ellie Oscar, he's kinda shy." Ellie brought his transistor radio up to his shoulder and

balanced it there. "Now these numbers are a secret code, honey," Arnold Friend explained. He read off the numbers 33, 19, 17 and raised his eyebrows at her to see what she thought of that, but she didn't think much of it. The left rear fender had been smashed and around it was written, on the gleaming gold background: DONE BY CRAZY WOMAN DRIVER. Connie had to laugh at that. Arnold Friend was pleased at her laughter and looked up at her. "Around the other side's a lot more—you wanta come and see them?"

"No."

"Why not?"

"Why should I?"

40 "Don'tcha wanta see what's on the car? Don'tcha wanta go for a ride?"

"I don't know."

"Why not?"

"I got things to do."

"Like what?"

45 "Things."

He laughed as if she had said something funny. He slapped his thighs. He was standing in a strange way, leaning back against the car as if he were balancing himself. He wasn't tall, only an inch or so taller than she would be if she came down to him. Connie liked the way he was dressed, which was the way all of them dressed: tight faded jeans stuffed into black, scuffed boots, a belt that pulled his waist in and showed how lean he was, and a white pull-over shirt that was a little soiled and showed the hard small muscles of his arms and shoulders. He looked as if he probably did hard work, lifting and carrying things. Even his neck looked muscular. And his face was a familiar face, somehow; the jaw and chin and cheeks slightly darkened because he hadn't shaved for a day or two, and the nose long and hawklike, sniffing as if she were a treat he was going to gobble up and it was all a joke.

"Connie, you ain't telling the truth. This is your day set aside for a ride with me and you know it," he said, still laughing. The way he straightened and recovered from his fit of laughing showed that it had been all fake.

"How do you know what my name is?" she said suspiciously.

"It's Connie."

50 "Maybe and maybe not."

"I know my Connie," he said, wagging his finger. Now she remembered him even better, back at the restaurant, and her cheeks warmed at the thought of how she sucked in her breath just at the moment she passed him—how she must have looked to him. And he had remembered her. "Ellie and I come out here especially for you," he said. "Ellie can sit in back. How about it?"

"Where?"

"Where what?"

"Where're we going?"

55 He looked at her. He took off the sunglasses and she saw how pale the skin around his eyes was, like holes that were not in shadow but instead in light. His eyes were chips of broken glass that catch the light in an amiable way. He smiled. It was as if the idea of going for a ride somewhere, to someplace, was a new idea to him.

"Just for a ride, Connie sweetheart."

"I never said my name was Connie," she said.

"But I know what it is. I know your name and all about you, lots of things," Arnold Friend said. He had not moved yet but stood still leaning back against the side of his jalopy. "I took a special interest in you, such a pretty girl, and found out all about you—like I know your parents and sister are gone somewheres and I know where and how long they're going to be gone, and I know who you were with last night, and your best girl friend's name is Betty. Right?"

He spoke in a simple lilting voice, exactly as if he were reciting the words to a song. His smile assured her that everything was fine. In the car Ellie turned up the volume on his radio and did not bother to look around at them.

"Ellie can sit in the back seat," Arnold 60 Friend said. He indicated his friend with a casual jerk of his chin, as if Ellie did not count and she should not bother with him.

"How'd you find out all that stuff?" Connie said.

"Listen: Betty Schultz and Tony Fitch and Jimmy Pettinger and Nancy Pettinger," he said, in a chant. "Raymond Stanley and Bob Hutter—"

"Do you know all those kids?"

"I know everybody."

"Look, you're kidding. You're not from 65 around here."

"Sure."

"But—how come we never saw you before?"

"Sure you saw me before," he said. He looked down at his boots, as if he were a little offended. "You just don't remember."

"I guess I'd remember you," Connie said.

"Yeah?" He looked up at this, beam- 70 ing. He was pleased. He began to mark time with the music from Ellie's radio, tapping his fists lightly together. Connie looked away from his smile to the car, which was painted so bright it almost hurt her eyes to look at it. She looked at that name, ARNOLD FRIEND. And up at the front fender was an expression that was familiar—MAN THE FLYING SAUCERS. It was an expression kids had used the year before but didn't use this year. She looked at it for a while as if the words meant something to her that she did not yet know.

"What're you thinking about? Huh?" Arnold Friend demanded. "Not worried about your hair blowing around in the car, are you?"

"No."

"Think I maybe can't drive good?"

"How do I know?"

75   "You're a hard girl to handle. How come?" he said. "Don't you know I'm your friend? Didn't you see me put my sign in the air when you walked by?"

"What sign?"

"My sign." And he drew an X in the air, leaning out toward her. They were maybe ten feet apart. After his hand fell back to his side the X was still in the air, almost visible. Connie let the screen door close and stood perfectly still inside it, listening to the music from her radio and the boy's blend together. She stared at Arnold Friend. He stood there so stiffly relaxed, pretending to be relaxed, with one hand idly on the door handle as if he were keeping himself up that way and had no intention of ever moving again. She recognized most things about him, the tight jeans that showed his thighs and buttocks and the greasy leather boots and the tight shirt, and even that slippery friendly smile of his, that sleepy dreamy smile that all the boys used to get across ideas they didn't want to put into words. She recognized all this and also the sing-song way he talked, slightly mocking, kidding, but serious and a little melancholy, and she recognized the way he tapped one fist against the other in homage to the perpetual music behind him. But all these things did not come together.

She said suddenly, "Hey, how old are you?"

His smile faded. She could see then that he wasn't a kid, he was much older— thirty, maybe more. At this knowledge her heart began to pound faster.

80   "That's a crazy thing to ask. Can'tcha see I'm your own age?"

"Like hell you are."

"Or maybe a coupla years older, I'm eighteen."

"Eighteen?" she said doubtfully.

He grinned to reassure her and lines appeared at the corners of his mouth. His teeth were big and white. He grinned so broadly his eyes became slits and she saw how thick the lashes were, thick and black as if painted with a black tarlike material. Then, abruptly, he seemed to become embarrassed, and looked over his shoulder at Ellie. "*Him*, he's crazy," he said. "Ain't he a riot? He's a nut, a real character." Ellie was still listening to the music. His sunglasses told nothing about what he was thinking. He wore a bright orange shirt unbuttoned halfway to show his chest, which was a pale, bluish chest and not muscular like Arnold Friend's. His shirt collar was turned up all around and the very tips of the collar pointed out past his chin as if they were protecting him. He was pressing the transistor radio up against his ear and sat there in a kind of daze, right in the sun.

"He's kinda strange," Connie said.   85

"Hey, she says you're kinda strange! Kinda strange!" Arnold Friend cried. He pounded on the car to get Ellie's attention. Ellie turned for the first time and Connie saw with shock that he wasn't a kid either— he had a fair, hairless face, cheeks reddened slightly as if the veins grew too close to the surface of his skin, the face of a forty-year-old baby. Connie felt a wave of dizziness rise in her at this sight and she stared at him as if waiting for something to change the shock of the moment, make it all right again. Ellie's lips kept shaping words, mumbling along with the words blasting in his ear.

"Maybe you two better go away," Connie said faintly.

"What? How come?" Arnold Friend cried. "We come out here to take you for a ride. It's Sunday." He had the voice of the man on the radio now. It was the same voice, Connie thought. "Don'tcha know it's Sunday all day? And honey, no matter who you were with last night, today you're with Arnold

Friend and don't you forget it! Maybe you better step out here," he said, and this last was in a different voice. It was a little flatter, as if the heat was finally getting to him.

"No. I got things to do."

90 "Hey."

"You two better leave."

"We ain't leaving until you come with us."

"Like hell I am—"

"Connie, don't fool around with me. I mean—I mean, don't fool *around*," he said, shaking his head. He laughed incredulously. He placed his sunglasses on top of his head, carefully, as if he were indeed wearing a wig, and brought the stems down behind his ears. Connie stared at him, another wave of dizziness and fear rising in her so that for a moment he wasn't even in focus but was just a blur, standing there against his gold car, and she had the idea that he had driven up the driveway all right but had come from nowhere before that and belonged nowhere and that everything about him and even about the music that was so familiar to her was only half real.

95 "If my father comes and sees you—"

"He ain't coming. He's at a barbecue."

"How do you know that?"

"Aunt Tillie's. Right now they're— uh—they're drinking. Sitting around," he said vaguely, squinting as if he were staring all the way to town and over to Aunt Tillie's back yard. Then the vision seemed to get clear and he nodded energetically. "Yeah. Sitting around. There's your sister in a blue dress, huh? And high heels, the poor sad bitch—nothing like you sweetheart! And your mother's helping some fat woman with the corn, they're cleaning the corn— husking the corn—"

"What fat woman?" Connie cried.

100 "How do I know what fat woman, I don't know every goddamn fat woman in the world!" Arnold Friend laughed.

"Oh, that's Mrs. Hornby. . . . Who invited her?" Connie said. She felt a little lightheaded. Her breath was coming quickly.

"She's too fat. I don't like them fat. I like them the way you are, honey," he said, smiling sleepily at her. They stared at each other for a while through the screen door. He said softly, "Now, what you're going to do is this: you're going to come out that door. You're going to sit up front with me and Ellie's going to sit in the back, the hell with Ellie, right? This isn't Ellie's date. You're my date. I'm your lover, honey."

"What? You're crazy—"

"Yes, I'm your lover. You don't know what that is but you will," he said. "I know that too. I know all about you. But look: it's real nice and you couldn't ask for nobody better than me, or more polite. I always keep my word. I'll tell you how it is, I'm always nice at first, the first time. I'll hold you so tight you won't think you have to try to get away or pretend anything because you'll know you can't. And I'll come inside you where it's all secret and you'll give in to me and you'll love me—"

"Shut up! You're crazy!" Connie said. 105 She backed away from the door. She put her hands up against her ears as if she'd heard something terrible, something not meant for her. "People don't talk like that, you're crazy," she muttered. Her heart was almost too big now for her chest and its pumping made sweat break out all over her. She looked out to see Arnold Friend pause and then take a step toward the porch, lurching. He almost fell. But, like a clever drunken man, he managed to catch his balance. He wobbled in his high boots and grabbed hold of one of the porch posts.

"Honey?" he said. "You still listening?"

"Get the hell out of here!"

"Be nice, honey. Listen."

"I'm going to call the police—"

He wobbled again and out of the side 110 of his mouth came a fast spat curse, an aside not meant for her to hear. But even this "Christ!" sounded forced. Then he began to smile again. She watched this smile come, awkward as if he were smiling from inside a mask. His whole face was a mask, she thought wildly, tanned down onto his throat but then running out as if he had plastered makeup on his face but had forgotten about his throat.

"Honey—? Listen, here's how it is. I always tell the truth and I promise you this: I ain't coming in that house after you."

"You better not! I'm going to call the police if you—if you don't—"

"Honey," he said, talking right through her voice, "honey. I'm not coming in there but you are coming out here. You know why?"

She was panting. The kitchen looked like a place she had never seen before, some room she had run inside but that wasn't good enough, wasn't going to help her. The kitchen window had never had a curtain, after three years, and there were dishes in the sink for her to do—probably—and if you ran your hand across the table you'd probably feel something sticky there.

115   "You listening, honey? Hey?"

"—going to call the police—"

"Soon as you touch the phone I don't need to keep my promise and can come inside. You won't want that."

She rushed forward and tried to lock the door. Her fingers were shaking. "But why lock it," Arnold Friend said gently, talking right into her face. "It's just a screen door. It's just nothing." One of his boots was at a strange angle, as if his foot wasn't in it. It pointed out to the left, bent at the ankle. "I mean, anybody can break through a screen door and glass and wood and iron or anything else if he needs to, anybody at all, and especially Arnold Friend. If the place got lit up with a fire, honey, you'd come runnin,' out into my arms, right into my arms an'

safe at home—like you knew I was your lover and'd stopped fooling around. I don't mind a nice shy girl but I don't like no fooling around." Part of those words were spoken with a slight rhythmic lilt, and Connie somehow recognized them—the echo of a song from last year, about a girl rushing into her boy friend's arms and coming home again—

Connie stood barefoot on the linoleum floor, staring at him. "What do you want?" she whispered.

"I want you," he said.   120

"What?"

"Seen you that night and thought, that's the one, yes sir. I never needed to look any more."

"But my father's coming back. He's coming to get me. I had to wash my hair first—" She spoke in a dry, rapid voice, hardly raising it for him to hear.

"No, your daddy is not coming and yes, you had to wash your hair and you washed it for me. It's nice and shining and all for me. I thank you sweetheart," he said with a mock bow, but again he almost lost his balance. He had to bend and adjust his boots. Evidently his feet did not go all the way down; the boots must have been stuffed with something so that he would seem taller. Connie stared out at him and behind him at Ellie in the car, who seemed to be looking off toward Connie's right, into nothing. This Ellie said, pulling the words out of the air one after another as if he were just discovering them, "You want me to pull out the phone?"

"Shut your mouth and keep it shut,"   125 Arnold Friend said, his face red from bending over or maybe from embarrassment because Connie had seen his boots. "This ain't none of your business."

"What—what are you doing? What do you want?" Connie said. "If I call the police they'll get you, they'll arrest you—"

"Promise was not to come in unless you touch that phone, and I'll keep that promise," he said. He resumed his erect position and tried to force his shoulders back. He sounded like a hero in a movie, declaring something important. But he spoke too loudly and it was as if he were speaking to someone behind Connie. "I ain't made plans for coming in that house where I don't belong but just for you to come out to me, the way you should. Don't you know who I am?"

"You're crazy," she whispered. She backed away from the door but did not want to go into another part of the house, as if this would give him permission to come through the door. "What do you . . . you're crazy, you . . ."

"Huh? What're you saying, honey?"

130 Her eyes darted everywhere in the kitchen. She could not remember what it was, this room.

"This is how it is, honey: you come out and we'll drive away, have a nice ride. But if you don't come out we're gonna wait till your people come home and then they're all going to get it."

"You want that telephone pulled out?" Ellie said. He held the radio away from his ear and grimaced, as if without the radio the air was too much for him.

"I toldja shut up, Ellie," Arnold Friend said, "you're deaf, get a hearing aid, right? Fix yourself up. This little girl's no trouble and's gonna be nice to me, so Ellie keep to yourself, this ain't your date—right? Don't hem in on me, don't hog, don't crush, don't bird dog, don't trail me," he said in a rapid, meaningless voice, as if he were running through all the expressions he'd learned but was no longer sure which of them was in style, then rushing on to new ones, making them up with his eyes closed. "Don't crawl under my fence, don't squeeze in my chipmunk hole, don't sniff my glue, suck my popsicle, keep your own greasy fingers on yourself!" He shaded his eyes and peered in at Connie, who was backed against the kitchen table. "Don't mind him, honey, he's just a creep. He's a dope. Right? I'm the boy for you and like I said, you come out here nice like a lady and give me your hand, and nobody else gets hurt, I mean, your nice old bald-headed daddy and your mummy and your sister in her high heels. Because listen: why bring them in this?"

"Leave me alone," Connie whispered.

"Hey, you know that old woman 135 down the road, the one with the chickens and stuff—you know her?"

"She's dead!"

"Dead? What? You know her?" Arnold Friend said.

"She's dead—"

"Don't you like her?"

"She's dead—she's—she isn't here any 140 more—"

"But don't you like her, I mean, you got something against her? Some grudge or something?" Then his voice dipped as if he were conscious of a rudeness. He touched the sunglasses perched up on top of his head as if to make sure they were still there. "Now, you be a good girl."

"What are you going to do?"

"Just two things, or maybe three," Arnold Friend said. "But I promise it won't last long and you'll like me that way you get to like people you're close to. You will. It's all over for you here, so come on out. You don't want your people in any trouble, do you?"

She turned and bumped against a chair or something, hurting her leg, but she ran into the back room and picked up the telephone. Something roared in her ear, a tiny roaring, and she was so sick with fear that she could do nothing but listen to it—the telephone was clammy and very heavy and her fingers groped down to the dial but were too weak to touch it. She began to scream into the phone, into the roaring. She cried out, she cried for her mother, she felt her breath start jerking back and forth in her lungs as if it were something Arnold Friend was stabbing her with again and again with no tenderness. A noisy sorrowful wailing rose all about her and she was locked inside it the way she was locked inside the house.

145   After a while she could hear again. She was sitting on the floor with her wet back against the wall.

Arnold Friend was saying from the door, "That's a good girl. Put the phone back."

She kicked the phone away from her.

"No, honey. Pick it up. Put it back right."

She picked it up and put it back. The dial tone stopped.

150   "That's a good girl. Now you come outside."

She was hollow with what had been fear but what was now just an emptiness. All that screaming had blasted it out of her. She sat, one leg cramped under her, and deep inside her brain was something like a pinpoint of light that kept going and would not let her relax. She thought, I'm not going to see my mother again. She thought, I'm not going to sleep in my bed again. Her bright green blouse was all wet.

Arnold Friend said, in a gentle-loud voice that was like a stage voice, "The place where you came from ain't there any more, and where you had in mind to go is cancelled out. This place you are now—inside your daddy's house—is nothing but a cardboard box I can knock down any time. You know that and always did know it. You hear me?"

She thought, I have got to think. I have got to know what to do.

"We'll go out to a nice field, out in the country here where it smells so nice and it's sunny," Arnold Friend said. "I'll have my arms tight around you so you won't need to try to get away and I'll show you what love is like, what it does. The hell with this house! It looks solid all right," he said. He ran a fingernail down the screen and the noise did not make Connie shiver, as it would have the day before. "Now put your hand on your heart, honey. Feel that? That feels solid too but we know better. Be nice to me, be sweet like you can because what else is there for a girl like you but to be sweet and pretty and give in?—and get away before her people get back?"

She felt her pounding heart. Her hand   155 seemed to enclose it. She thought for the first time in her life that it was nothing that was hers, that belonged to her, but just a pounding, living thing inside this body that wasn't really hers either.

"You don't want them to get hurt," Arnold Friend went on. "Now, get up, honey. Get up all by yourself."

She stood.

"Now, turn this way. That's right. Come over here to me—Ellie, put that away, didn't I tell you? You dope. You miserable creepy dope," Arnold Friend said. His words were not angry but only part of an incantation. The incantation was kindly. "Now come out through the kitchen to me, honey, and let's see a smile, try it, you're a brave, sweet little girl and now they're eating corn and hot dogs cooked to bursting over an outdoor fire, and they don't know one thing about you and never did and honey, you're better than them because not a one of them would have done this for you."

Connie felt the linoleum under her feet; it was cool. She brushed her hair back out of her eyes. Arnold Friend let go of the post tentatively and opened his arms for her, his elbows pointing in toward each other and his wrists limp, to show that this was an embarrassed embrace and a little mocking, he didn't want to make her self-conscious.

She put out her hand against the screen.   160 She watched herself push the door slowly open as if she were safe back somewhere in the other doorway, watching this body and this head of long hair moving out into the sunlight where Arnold Friend waited.

"My sweet little blue-eyed girl," he said in a half-sung sigh that had nothing to do with her brown eyes but was taken up just the same by the vast sunlit reaches of the land behind him and on all sides of him—so much land that Connie had never seen before and did not recognize except to know that she was going to it.

Edgar Allan Poe (1809–1849)

The Cask of Amontillado (1846)

The thousand injuries of Fortunato I had borne as I best could; but when he ventured upon insult, I vowed revenge. You, who so well know the nature of my soul, will not suppose, however, that I gave utterance to a threat. At length I would be avenged; this was a point definitively settled—but the very definitiveness with which it was resolved, precluded the idea of risk. I must not only punish, but punish with impunity. A wrong is unredressed when retribution overtakes its redresser. It is equally unredressed when the avenger fails to make himself felt as such to him who has done the wrong.

It must be understood, that neither by word nor deed had I given Fortunato cause to doubt my good-will. I continued, as was my wont, to smile in his face, and he did not perceive that my smile *now* was at the thought of his immolation.

He had a weak point—this Fortunato—although in other regards he was a man to be respected and even feared. He prided himself on his connoisseurship in wine. Few Italians have the true virtuoso spirit. For the most part their enthusiasm is adopted to suit the time and opportunity—to practice imposture upon the British and Austrian *millionaires*. In painting and gemmary Fortunato, like his countrymen, was a quack—but in the matter of old wines he was sincere. In this respect I did not differ from him materially: I was skilful in the Italian vintages myself, and bought largely whenever I could.

It was about dusk, one evening during the supreme madness of the carnival season, that I encountered my friend. He accosted me with excessive warmth, for he had been drinking much. The man wore motley. He had on a tight-fitting parti-striped dress, and his head was surmounted by the conical cap and bells. I was so pleased to see him, that I thought I should never have done wringing his hand.

I said to him: "My dear Fortunato, you 5 are luckily met. How remarkably well you are looking to-day! But I have received a pipe of what passes for Amontillado, and I have my doubts."

"How?" said he. "Amontillado? A pipe? Impossible! And in the middle of the carnival!"

"I have my doubts," I replied; "and I was silly enough to pay the full Amontillado price without consulting you in the matter. You were not to be found, and I was fearful of losing a bargain."

"Amontillado!"

"I have my doubts."

10   "Amontillado!"

"And I must satisfy them."

"Amontillado!"

"As you are engaged, I am on my way to Luchesi. If any one has a critical turn, it is he. He will tell me—"

"Luchesi cannot tell Amontillado from Sherry."

15   "And yet some fools will have it that his taste is a match for your own."

"Come, let us go."

"Whither?"

"To your vaults."

"My friend, no; I will not impose on your good nature. I perceive you have an engagement. Luchesi—"

20   "I have no engagement;—come."

"My friend, no. It is not the engagement, but the severe cold with which I perceive you are afflicted. The vaults are insufferably damp. They are encrusted with niter."

"Let us go, nevertheless. The cold is merely nothing. Amontillado! You have been imposed upon. And as for Luchesi, he cannot distinguish Sherry from Amontillado."

Thus speaking, Fortunato possessed himself of my arm. Putting on a mask of black silk, and drawing a *roquelaire* closely about my person, I suffered him to hurry me to my palazzo.

There were no attendants at home; they had absconded to make merry in honor of the time. I had told them that I should not return until the morning, and had given them explicit orders not to stir from the house. These orders were sufficient, I well knew, to insure their immediate disappearance, one and all, as soon as my back was turned.

25   I took from their sconces two flambeaux, and giving one to Fortunato, bowed him through several suites of rooms to the archway that led into the vaults. I passed down a long and winding staircase, requesting him to be cautious as he followed. We came at length to the foot of the descent and stood together on the damp ground of the catacombs of the Montresors.

The gait of my friend was unsteady, and the bells upon his cap jingled as he strode.

"The pipe?" said he.

"It is farther on," said I; "but observe the white web-work which gleams from these cavern walls."

He turned toward me, and looked into my eyes with two filmy orbs that distilled the rheum of intoxication.

"Nitre?" he asked, at length.   30

"Nitre," I replied. "How long have you had that cough?"

"Ugh! ugh! ugh!—ugh! ugh! ugh!—ugh! ugh! ugh!—ugh! ugh! ugh!—ugh! ugh! ugh!"

My poor friend found it impossible to reply for many minutes.

"It is nothing," he said, at last.

"Come," I said, with decision, "we will 35 go back; your health is precious. You are rich, respected, admired, beloved; you are happy, as once I was. You are a man to be missed. For me it is no matter. We will go back; you will be ill, and I cannot be responsible. Besides, there is Luchesi—"

"Enough," he said; "the cough is a mere nothing; it will not kill me. I shall not die of a cough."

"True—true," I replied; "and, indeed, I had no intention of alarming you unnecessarily; but you should use all proper caution. A draught of this Medoc will defend us from the damps."

Here I knocked off the neck a bottle which I drew from a long row of its fellows that lay upon the mould.

"Drink," I said, presenting him the wine.

40 He raised it to his lips with a leer. He paused and nodded to me familiarly, while his bells jingled.

"I drink," he said, "to the buried that repose around us."

"And I to your long life."

He again took my arm, and we proceeded.

"These vaults," he said, "are extensive."

45 "The Montresors," I replied, "were a great and numerous family."

"I forget your arms."

"A huge human foot d'or, in a field azure; the foot crushes a serpent rampant whose fangs are imbedded in the heel."

"And the motto?"

"Nemo me impune lacessit."

50 "Good!" he said.

The wine sparkled in his eyes and the bells jingled. My own fancy grew warm with the Medoc. We had passed through walls of piled bones, with casks and puncheons intermingling, into the inmost recesses of the catacombs. I paused again, and this time I made bold to seize Fortunato by an arm above the elbow.

"The niter!" I said; "see, it increases. It hangs like moss upon the vaults. We are below the river's bed. The drops of moisture trickle among the bones. Come, we will go back ere it is too late. Your cough—"

"It is nothing," he said; "let us go on. But first, another draught of the Medoc."

I broke and reached him a flacon of De Grâve. He emptied it at a breath. His eyes flashed with fierce light. He laughed and threw the bottle upward with a gesticulation I did not understand.

55 I looked at him in surprise. He repeated the movement—a grotesque one.

"You do not comprehend?" he said.

"Not I," I replied.

"Then you are not of the brotherhood."

"How?"

"You are not of the masons." 60

"Yes, yes," I said; "yes, yes."

"You? Impossible! A mason?"

"A mason," I replied.

"A sign," he said.

"It is this," I answered, producing a 65 trowel from beneath the folds of my *roquelaire.*

"You jest," he exclaimed, recoiling a few paces. "But let us proceed to the Amontillado."

"Be it so," I said, replacing the tool beneath the cloak, and again offering him my arm. He leaned upon it heavily. We continued our route in search of the Amontillado. We passed through a range of low arches, descended, passed on, and descending again, arrived at a deep crypt, in which the foulness of the air caused our flambeaux rather to glow than flame.

At the most remote end of the crypt there appeared another less spacious. Its walls had been lined with human remains, piled to the vault overhead, in the fashion of the great catacombs of Paris. Three sides of this interior crypt were still ornamented in this manner. From the fourth the bones had been thrown down, and lay promiscuously upon the earth, forming at one point a mound of some size. Within the wall thus exposed by the displacing of the bones, we perceived a still interior recess, in depth about four feet, in width three, in height six or seven. It seemed to have been constructed for no especial use within itself, but formed merely the interval between two of the colossal supports of the roof of the catacombs, and was backed by one of their circumscribing walls of solid granite.

It was in vain that Fortunato, uplifting his dull torch, endeavored to pry into the depth of the recess. Its termination the feeble light did not enable us to see.

70   "Proceed," I said; "herein is the Amontillado. As for Luchesi—"

"He is an ignoramus," interrupted my friend, as he stepped unsteadily forward, while I followed immediately at his heels. In an instant he had reached the extremity of the niche, and finding his progress arrested by the rock, stood stupidly bewildered. A moment more and I had fettered him to the granite. In its surface were two iron staples, distant from each other about two feet, horizontally. From one of these depended a short chain, from the other a padlock. Throwing the links about his waist, it was but the work of a few seconds to secure it. He was too much astounded to resist. Withdrawing the key I stepped back from the recess.

"Pass your hand," I said, "over the wall; you cannot help feeling the nitre. Indeed it is *very* damp. Once more let me *implore* you to return. No? Then I must positively leave you. But I must first render you all the little attentions in my power."

"The Amontillado!" ejaculated my friend, not yet recovered from his astonishment.

"True," I replied; "the Amontillado."

75   As I said these words I busied myself among the pile of bones of which I have before spoken. Throwing them aside, I soon uncovered a quantity of building stone and mortar. With these materials and with the aid of my trowel, I began vigorously to wall up the entrance of the niche.

I had scarcely laid the first tier of the masonry when I discovered that the intoxication of Fortunato had in a great measure worn off. The earliest indication I had of this was a low moaning cry from the depth of the recess. It was *not* the cry of a drunken man. There was then a long and obstinate silence. I laid the second tier, and the third, and the fourth; and then I heard the furious vibrations

of the chain. The noise lasted for several minutes, during which, that I might hearken to it with the more satisfaction, I ceased my labors and sat down upon the bones. When at last the clanking subsided, I resumed the trowel, and finished without interruption the fifth, the sixth, and the seventh tier. The wall was now nearly upon a level with my breast. I again paused, and holding the flambeaux over the mason-work, threw a few feeble rays upon the figure within.

A succession of loud and shrill screams, bursting suddenly from the throat of the chained form, seemed to thrust me violently back. For a brief moment I hesitated—I trembled. Unsheathing my rapier, I began to grope with it about the recess; but the thought of an instant reassured me. I placed my hand upon the solid fabric of the catacombs, and felt satisfied. I reapproached the wall. I replied to the yells of him who clamored. I re-echoed—I aided—I surpassed them in volume and in strength. I did this, and the clamorer grew still.

It was now midnight, and my task was drawing to a close. I had completed the eighth, the ninth, and the tenth tier. I had finished a portion of the last and the eleventh; there remained but a single stone to be fitted and plastered in. I struggled with its weight; I placed it partially in its destined position. But now there came from out the niche a low laugh that erected the hairs upon my head. It was succeeded by a sad voice, which I had difficulty in recognizing as that of the noble Fortunato. The voice said—

"Ha! ha! ha!—he! he!—a very good joke indeed—an excellent jest. We will have many a rich laugh about it at the palazzo—he! he! he!—over our wine—he! he! he!"

"The Amontillado!" I said.   80

"He! he! he!—he! he! he!—yes, the Amontillado. But is it not getting late? Will not they be awaiting us at the palazzo, the

Lady Fortunato and the rest? Let us be gone."

"Yes," I said, "let us be gone."
"For the love of God, Montresor!"
"Yes," I said, "for the love of God!"

85 But to these words I hearkened in vain for a reply. I grew impatient. I called aloud:

"Fortunato!"
No answer. I called again:
"Fortunato!"

No answer still. I thrust a torch through the remaining aperture and let it fall within. There came forth in return only a jingling of the bells. My heart grew sick—on account of the dampness of the catacombs. I hastened to make an end of my labor. I forced the last stone into its position; I plastered it up. Against the new masonry I re-erected the old rampart of bones. For the half of a century no mortal has disturbed them. *In pace requiescat!*

John Updike (b. 1932)

A & P (1961)

In walks these three girls in nothing but bathing suits. I'm in the third checkout slot, with my back to the door, so I don't see them until they're over by the bread. The one that caught my eye first was the one in the plaid green two-piece. She was a chunky kid, with a good tan and a sweet broad soft-looking can with those two crescents of white just under it, where the sun never seems to hit, at the top of the backs of her legs. I stood there with my hand on a box of HiHo crackers trying to remember if I rang it up or not. I ring it up again and the customer starts giving me hell. She's one of these cash-register-watchers, a witch about fifty with rouge on her cheekbones and no eyebrows, and I know it made her day to trip me up. She'd been watching cash registers for fifty years and probably never seen a mistake before.

By the time I got her feathers smoothed and her goodies into a bag—she gives me a little snort in passing, if she'd been born at the right time they would have burned her over in Salem[1]—by the time I get her on her way the girls had circled around the bread and were coming back, without a pushcart, back my way along the counters, in the aisle between the checkouts and the Special bins. They didn't even have shoes on. There was this chunky one, with the two-piece—it was bright green and the seams on the bra were still sharp and her belly was still pretty pale so I guessed she just got it (the suit)—there was this one, with one of those chubby berry-faces, the lips all bunched together under her nose, this one, and a tall one, with black hair that hadn't quite frizzed right, and one of these sunburns right across under the eyes, and a chin that was too long—you know, the kind of girl other girls think is very "striking" and "attractive" but never quite makes it, as they very well know, which is why they like her so much—and then the third one, that

---

[1]**Salem:** A seaport in Massachusetts, famous for the execution of "witches" in 1692.

wasn't quite so tall. She was the queen. She kind of led them, the other two peeking around and making their shoulders round. She didn't look around, not this queen, she just walked straight on slowly, on these long white primadonna legs. She came down a little hard on her heels, as if she didn't walk in bare feet that much, putting down her heels and then letting the weight move along to her toes as if she was testing the floor with every step, putting a little deliberate extra action into it. You never know for sure how girls' minds work (do you really think it's a mind in there or just a little buzz like a bee in a glass jar?) but you got the idea she had talked the other two into coming here with her, and now she was showing them how to do it, walk slow and hold yourself straight.

She had on a kind of dirty-pink—beige maybe, I don't know—bathing suit with a little nubble all over it and, what got me, the straps were down. They were off her shoulders looped loose around the cool tops of her arms, and I guess as a result the suit had slipped a little on her, so all around the top of the cloth there was this shining rim. If it hadn't been there you wouldn't have known there could have been anything whiter than those shoulders. With the straps pushed off, there was nothing between the top of the suit and the top of her head except just *her*, this clean bare plane of the top of her chest down from the shoulder bones like a dented sheet of metal tilted in the light. I mean, it was more than pretty.

She had a sort of oaky hair that the sun and salt had bleached, done up in a bun that was unravelling, and a kind of prim face. Walking into the A & P with your straps down, I suppose it's the only kind of face you *can* have. She held her head so high her neck, coming up out of those white shoulders, looked kind of stretched, but I didn't

mind. The longer her neck was, the more of her there was.

She must have felt in the corner of her eye me and over my shoulder Stokesie in the second slot watching, but she didn't tip. Not this queen. She kept her eyes moving across the racks, and stopped, and turned so slow it made my stomach rub the inside of my apron, and buzzed to the other two, who kind of huddled against her for relief, and then they all three of them went up the cat-and-dog-food-breakfast-cereal-macaroni-rice-raisins-seasonings-spreads-spaghetti-soft-drinks-crackers-and-cookies aisle. From the third slot I look straight up this aisle to the meat counter, and I watched them all the way. The fat one with the tan sort of fumbled with the cookies, but on second thought she put the packages back. The sheep pushing their carts down the aisle— the girls were walking against the usual traffic (not that we have one-way signs or anything)—were pretty hilarious. You could see them, when Queenie's white shoulders dawned on them, kind of jerk, or hop, or hiccup, but their eyes snapped back to their own baskets and on they pushed. I bet you could set off dynamite in an A & P and the people would by and large keep reaching and checking oatmeal off their lists and muttering "Let me see, there was a third thing, began with A, asparagus, no, ah, yes, applesauce!" or whatever it is they do mutter. But there was no doubt, this jiggled them. A few houseslaves in pin curlers even looked around after pushing their carts past to make sure what they had seen was correct.

You know, it's one thing to have a girl in a bathing suit down on the beach, where what with the glare nobody can look at each other much anyway, and another thing in the cool of the A & P, under the fluorescent lights, against all those stacked packages, with her feet paddling along naked over our checkerboard green-and-cream rubber-tile floor.

"Oh Daddy," Stokesie said beside me. "I feel so faint."

"Darling," I said. "Hold me tight." Stokesie's married, with two babies chalked up on his fuselage already, but as far as I can tell that's the only difference. He's twenty-two, and I was nineteen this April.

"Is it done?" he asks, the responsible married man finding his voice. I forgot to say he thinks he's going to be manager some sunny day, maybe in 1990 when it's called the Great Alexandrov and Petrooshki Tea Company or something.

10   What he meant was, our town is five miles from a beach, with a big summer colony out on the Point, but we're right in the middle of town, and the women generally put on a shirt or shorts or something before they get out of the car into the street. And anyway these are usually women with six children and varicose veins mapping their legs and nobody, including them, could care less. As I say, we're right in the middle of town, and if you stand at our front doors you can see two banks and the Congregational church and the newspaper store and three real-estate offices and about twenty-seven old freeloaders tearing up Central Street because the sewer broke again. It's not as if we're on the Cape;[2] we're north of Boston and there's people in this town haven't seen the ocean for twenty years.

The girls had reached the meat counter and were asking McMahon something. He pointed, they pointed, and they shuffled out of sight behind a pyramid of Diet Delight peaches. All that was left for us to see was old McMahon patting his mouth and looking

after them sizing up their joints. Poor kids, I began to feel sorry for them, they couldn't help it.

Now here comes the sad part of the story, at least my family says it's sad, but I don't think it's so sad myself. The store's pretty empty, it being Thursday afternoon, so there was nothing much to do except lean on the register and wait for the girls to show up again. The whole store was like a pinball machine and I didn't know which tunnel they'd come out of. After a while they come around out of the far aisle, around the light bulbs, records at discount of the Caribbean Six or Tony Martin Sings or some such gunk you wonder they waste the wax on, six-packs of candy bars, and plastic toys done up in cellophane that fall apart when a kid looks at them anyway. Around they come, Queenie still leading the way, and holding a little gray jar in her hand. Slots Three through Seven are unmanned and I could see her wondering between Stokes and me, but Stokesie with his usual luck draws an old party in baggy gray pants who stumbles up with four giant cans of pineapple juice (what do these bums *do* with all that pineapple juice? I've often asked myself) so the girls come to me. Queenie puts down the jar and I take it into my fingers icy cold. Kingfish Fancy Herring Snacks in Pure Sour Cream: 49¢. Now her hands are empty, not a ring or a bracelet, bare as God made them, and I wonder where the money's coming from. Still with that prim look she lifts a folded dollar bill out of the hollow at the center of her nubbled pink top. The jar went heavy in my hand. Really, I thought that was so cute.

Then everybody's luck begins to run out. Lengel comes in from haggling with a truck full of cabbages on the lot and is about to scuttle into that door marked MANAGER

---

[2] **The Cape:** Cape Cod, Massachusetts, a resort area where fashions of dress are usually informal.

behind which he hides all day when the girls touch his eye. Lengel's pretty dreary, teaches Sunday school and the rest, but he doesn't miss that much. He comes over and says, "Girls, this isn't the beach."

Queenie blushes, though maybe it's just a brush of sunburn I was noticing for the first time, now that she was so close. "My mother asked me to pick up a jar of herring snacks." Her voice kind of startled me, the way voices do when you see the people first, coming out so flat and dumb yet kind of tony, too, the way it ticked over "pick up" and "snacks." All of a sudden I slid right down her voice into her living room. Her father and the other men were standing around in ice-cream coats and bow ties and the women were in sandals picking up herring snacks on toothpicks off a big glass plate and they were all holding drinks the color of water with olives and sprigs of mint in them. When my parents have somebody over they get lemonade and if it's a real racy affair Schlitz in tall glasses with "They'll Do It Every Time" cartoons stenciled on.

15   "That's all right," Lengel said. "But this isn't the beach." His repeating this struck me as funny, as if it had just occurred to him, and he had been thinking all these years the A & P was a great big dune and he was the head lifeguard. He didn't like my smiling—as I say he doesn't miss much—but he concentrates on giving the girls that sad Sunday-school-superintendent stare.

Queenie's blush is no sunburn now, and the plump one in plaid, that I liked better from the back—a really sweet can—pipes up, "We weren't doing any shopping. We just came in for the one thing."

"That makes no difference," Lengel tells her, and I could see from the way his eyes went that he hadn't noticed she was wearing a two-piece before. "We want you decently dressed when you come in here."

"We *are* decent," Queenie says suddenly, her lower lip pushing, getting sore now that she remembers her place, a place from which the crowd that runs the A & P must look pretty crummy. Fancy Herring Snacks flashed in her very blue eyes.

"Girls, I don't want to argue with you. After this come in here with your shoulders covered. It's our policy." He turns his back. That's policy for you. Policy is what the kingpins want. What the others want is juvenile delinquency.

All this while, the customers had been   20 showing up with their carts but, you know, sheep, seeing a scene, they had all bunched up on Stokesie, who shook open a paper bag as gently as peeling a peach, not wanting to miss a word. I could feel in the silence everybody getting nervous, most of all Lengel, who asks me, "Sammy, have you rung up this purchase?"

I thought and said "No" but it wasn't about that I was thinking. I go through the punches, 4, 9, GROC, TOT—it's more complicated than you think, and after you do it often enough, it begins to make a little song, that you hear words to, in my case "Hello (*bing*) there, you (*gung*) hap-py *pee*-pul (*splat*)!"—the *splat* being the drawer flying out. I uncrease the bill, tenderly as you may imagine, it just having come from between the two smoothest scoops of vanilla I had ever known there were, and pass a half and a penny into her narrow pink palm, and nestle the herrings in a bag and twist its neck and hand it over, all the time thinking.

The girls, and who'd blame them, are in a hurry to get out, so I say "I quit" to Lengel quick enough for them to hear, hoping they'll stop and watch me, their unsuspected hero. They keep right on going, into the electric eye; the door flies open and they flicker across the lot to their car, Queenie and Plaid and Big Tall Goony-Goony (not that as raw material she was so bad), leaving me with Lengel and a kink in his eyebrow.

"Did you say something, Sammy?"

"I said I quit."

25   "I thought you did."

"You didn't have to embarrass them."

"It was they who were embarrassing us."

I started to say something that came out "Fiddle-de-do." It's a saying of my grandmother's, and I know she would have been pleased.

"I don't think you know what you're saying," Lengel said.

30   "I know you don't," I said. "But I do." I pull the bow at the back of my apron and start shrugging it off my shoulders. A couple of customers that had been heading for my slot begin to knock against each other, like scared pigs in a chute.

Lengel sighs and begins to look very patient and old and gray. He's been a friend of my parents for years. "Sammy, you don't want to do this to your Mom and Dad," he tells me. It's true, I don't. But it seems to me that once you begin a gesture it's fatal not to go through with it. I fold the apron, "Sammy" stitched in red on the pocket, and put it on the counter, and drop the bow tie on top of it.

The bow tie is theirs, if you've ever wondered. "You'll feel this for the rest of your life," Lengel says, and I know that's true, too, but remembering how he made that pretty girl blush makes me so scrunchy inside I punch the No Sale tab and the machine whirs "pee-pul" and the drawer splats out. One advantage to this scene taking place in summer, I can follow this up with a clean exit, there's no fumbling around getting your coat and galoshes, I just saunter into the electric eye in my white shirt that my mother ironed the night before, and the door heaves itself open, and outside the sunshine is skating around on the asphalt.

I look around for my girls, but they're gone, of course. There wasn't anybody but some young married screaming with her children about some candy they didn't get by the door of a powder-blue Falcon station wagon. Looking back in the big windows, over the bags of peat moss and aluminum lawn furniture stacked on the pavement, I could see Lengel in my place in the slot checking the sheep through. His face was dark gray and his back stiff, as if he's just had an injection of iron, and my stomach kind of fell as I felt how hard the world was going to be to me hereafter.

David Winn (b. 1945)

Temporary Duty (2006)

Jew Bread couldn't be sure that Nathan had actually been bitten.

"Look at his foot, Bread," Smalls said. "It all bloody an' swole up, man."

Bread poured water from a canteen over Nathan's foot. "You see the snake?" he asked Smalls.

"Hell yeah, I seen it. Hol' still, man."

Nathan wanted to get up and run. He 5 felt as if all his nerve endings were on fire.

"What'd it look like?"

"Look like a fuckin' *snake*, Bread. Long, skinny, no legs, you know. Was in the river where he standin'." Smalls poured water on a towel and mopped Nathan's face and forehead. "Then that gook girl show up and ever'one start shootin'."

Bread took the towel and wiped at the blood and river muck that coated Nathan's foot. "See the holes?" he asked.

Smalls bent over Nathan's foot and shaded his eyes with his palm. "Yeh, so he got bit, right?"

10 Bread shook his head. "There's four punctures there and the pattern don't fit—it don't show up in the book." He pulled a mini field manual from his shirt pocket.

Nathan started to scream. It was easier to breathe that way and the louder he screamed the less his heart seemed to race, his nerve endings burn. It felt like hot wires were being drawn through his veins. He flailed out with his arms and knocked the booklet out of Jew Bread's hands.

"Shit. I cannot work like this," Bread sighed and duck-walked over to the edge of the LZ and retrieved it just as the medevac touched down, the rotor wash kicking up wind and dust. He duck-walked back, one hand on his bush hat, stuck a morphine syrette in Nathan's thigh and drew a large 'M' on his forehead with a grease pencil.

"Calm the fuck down," he murmured soundlessly but the way his mouth shaped the words he might as well have been shouting. He circled several pages in the booklet with the pencil, tore them out and stuffed them in Nathan's shirt pocket. Then he and Smalls picked up the tarpaulin Nathan was lying on and rushed him through the medevac's cargo door.

Smalls stuck his head and patted Nathan's arm. "You gon' be okay, Schoolboy! Good dope, hunh?!" His teeth were white and brilliant against his dark skin, made even darker by the gloom of the cargo bay. His grin seemed to hover in the air, Cheshire like, in front of Nathan's face, even as Candle Ass's body, wrapped in a poncho, was slid in next to him. As the chopper pilot pulled pitch and lifted off, Candle Ass's closed eyelids slowly opened; his dead blue irises glared at Nathan.

As the helicopter gained altitude a 15 pair of boots came hurtling through the cargo door, startling the waist gunner who cursed and kicked them back out. Nathan tried to say, "Those are mine!" but his mouth was too dry and then he felt himself being rolled in clouds as the drug hit his veins. He grew calmer and happier by the minute, so much so, that the sound of Candle Ass's dead, booted feet drumming on the metal plating of the cargo deck began to sound musical.

The hospital had been built by the French as a resort hotel originally, so the grounds were green and landscaped with a view of the South China Sea. The building was a large white wedding cake surrounded by gardens and lawns. The nurses were pretty Filipina contract workers who had replaced the American medics as the war wound down and the Americans rotated home. The doctors were still Army and complained to each other about how much money they'd be making if they weren't stuck with a year's worth of duty in-country. Nathan thought they were odious. The nurses brought him ice cream and pizza, gave him sponge baths and massages. He fell in love with a girl who everyone called "Katie" because her last name was Katigbak and she hated her first name, which was Beatrice.

"Dante loved Beatrice," Nathan told her through his morphine mist on his first day in the ward.

"Sweetie, your name's Nathan, not Danny, an' you don' hardly know me. That foot starts to hurt, you hit the buzzer an' I'll get you more." She held up an ampoule of bright amber liquid. "Don' ask the doctors 'cause those *tangas* think pain is some kinda contest, unless they in pain." She flashed him a smile and moved on.

"Kinda makes you want to marry her and take her home, right?" The guy in the next bed said. He was Special Forces, his green beret hanging on his bed post. Nathan had the draftee's mixture of mistrust and awe for snake eaters; they were unlucky and brought trouble by definition. This guy had the front half of his left foot missing and he made Nathan wonder if he hadn't been placed in some special crip ward for the footless or soon-to-be. But there was a black kid in another bed in a coma who otherwise seemed perfectly whole and a First Infantry Division sergeant with a throat wound near the hallway door.

20   The hospital was a Joint Services Command facility so the place was full of interservice casualties and the doctors themselves were drawn from the Navy, Marine Corps and Air Force as well as the Army. They all came to look at Nathan's foot and examine the pages of Jew Bread's booklet and the illustrations he had circled in grease pencil. Nathan's toes had turned black and the foot itself had no more feeling than a block of wood, but Nathan's anxiety lay under a morphine haze of indifference and he was determined to say as little as possible to the doctors for fear that somehow he would betray just how doped up he was and the doctors would cut him off.

One of them, a fat marine captain named Fetters, kept coming back at odd times as if he were conducting surprise inspections.

"Who's this Biggleman, soldier?"

"That's Begelman, sir," Nathan said, trying not to slur his words and keep his eyelids from drooping. Jew Bread had

scrawled his name beneath the booklet's illustrations of poisonous snakes indigenous to South Vietnam and the bite patterns their fangs made. Cutler held the fanned pages against his chest like a poker hand.

"Your platoon medic?"

"Team medic, sir," Nathan nodded his   25 head. He closed his eyes and saw the Vietnamese girl step into the river from the opposite bank. She was carrying one of those shoulder-roll blivets the VC and NVA used to carry water or sticky rice. Nathan and Smalls had gone down to the river on water detail. Nathan needed to pee and went downstream to empty his bladder while Smalls filled the team's canteens.

He was unzipped, his dick hanging out like a flag on a pole, when the girl had come out of the tree line just above the riverbank and stepped into the shallows. She squatted in the water and unslung the blivet and submerged it to let it fill. There was an AKM strapped to her back, muzzle down and just out of the water. She hadn't seen Nathan, who had frozen the moment she appeared. His stream of urine had stopped. He slowly lowered his head to glance downward so that he could zip up and that's when he saw the snake. It was swimming in place just above his right foot, its body moving in long, sinuous s-curls, its flat, triangular head just above the river's surface.

Fuck me, oh fuck me, a voice sang in his head and it was his own voice. This can *not* be happening.

The girl was facing downstream. She wore a flat, round cap with a short bill, a black *bo doi* blouse and shorts. Nathan watched her take the cap off and toss it on the bank. She scooped water one-handed and bathed her face; the blivet was tethered to her other hand by a short length of rope looped around her wrist. Her black hair was braided and pinned to the back of her head.

Nathan looked down at his feet and the snake was still there. Shoo, Nathan thought. Go 'way. He had the insane urge to laugh. Bread had taken away his boots because both his feet were showing the first signs of immersion foot. He had gotten a lecture on field hygiene, both feet painted with gentian violet and a pair of sandals made out of truck tires. He was wearing them now so the tops of his feet were bare, exposed. The Ithaca 12 gauge he had carried for seven months of his tour was on the bank behind him. The girl seemed completely unaware of his presence. He tried turning his head to check the exact position of the shotgun, how far and in which direction he would have to lunge, but each time he started to turn his head he grew dizzy and felt he might lose his balance.

30   If he kept still, he thought, maybe the girl would fill the blivet and climb the bank and go away without ever looking in his direction. If the snake swam off, that would be good too. If the snake bit him—

He looked down and the snake was still suspended in the water above his foot. He (if it was a he) wasn't particularly large or long, but the orientation lectures on flora and fauna out in boonies that Nathan had largely slept through his first week in country had emphasized the particularly poisonous nature of the smaller varieties. There was a bamboo viper nicknamed "Mr. Two Step" by the grunts because, as Smalls had explained to Nathan his first day with the Team, "He bite you, you take two steps an' you gon', Schoolboy."

The Australian SAS officer who had given the one lecture Nathan remembered, had said that the bamboo viper was 'ubiquitous.' "This highly adaptive species thrives in a variety of environments including arboreal, riparian, marine and estuarine habitations. As a result, this little fellow's markings, shape and size vary in profusion. My advice, gentleman: avoid them all."

"Amen," someone had said in the back of the room.

Looking down at the snake, Nathan thought: you riparian motherfucker. Maybe it was harmless. The sunlight on the shallow water dappled the length of the snake's body so there was no telling what his coloring or markings were. You were supposed to look for pits on either side of the head with vipers, but Nathan could only see the top of the thing's skull, plus he was still holding his dick with his right hand and that partially obscured his view of the snake. Maybe if he peed on the thing it would swim away.

The girl had rolled up the sleeves of her 35 blouse and was washing her forearms. Nathan tried turning his head again to see where he'd propped the shotgun. Instead he saw Smalls' face peering through brush growing next to the bank, the muzzle of his M16 poking out below. He was drawing a bead on the girl. Nathan hissed and shook his head, terrified that the girl would hear him. He pointed downward with his free hand, jabbing at his left foot with his index finger. Smalls looked down and his eyes widened. He looked up at Nathan and nodded slowly. Then he grinned, the grin saying it all: you pathetic shit-for-brains-white-boy, what you got your pale-ass stupid self into now. He dropped his left hand from his rifle's foregrip and made a gesture that Nathan didn't understand until Smalls repeated it: put it back in your pants.

"Fuck is going on here?" Candle Ass's voice came crashing through the brush. Nathan felt an arm around his waist yanking him backward, the girl looked up and then seemed to disappear, the tree line behind her exploded, green tracer arcing out toward him, Smalls' M16 chattered, shells flying from the breech, something sharp and burning dragged across the top of Nathan's left foot.

"Go-Go-Go!!" Smalls yelled in his ear. Nathan stumbled, picked up his shotgun. Candle Ass grunted and fell in front of him. Nathan leaped over him and ran into the bush. His foot was on fire. Vines, leaves, tree branches fell from the canopy overhead, clipped by gunfire from the opposite bank. He looked back and saw Smalls trying to drag Candle Ass away. Nathan made himself stop and started to run back toward them, then realized that his genitals were still hanging out of his pants. He stuffed them back in and ran back.

"He gon'," Smalls said and waved him back. They left Candle Ass and ran back toward the trail. Nathan started to limp and then drool uncontrollably. When they reached the team's perimeter he collapsed, his muscles going spastic. Jew Bread and Smalls carried him to the LZ.

"So how are we today?" Fetters asked, addressing Nathan's foot. The green beret noncom in the bed next to Nathan started laughing.

40   "Something funny, Sergeant?" Cutler picked up Nathan's chart and began to read.

"I was just wondering if you were looking for souvenirs, sir, when you were going through the Corporal's personal effects earlier this morning while he was down in x-ray," the sergeant said. Nathan closed his eyes and pretended to sleep. He thought he heard Fetters walk out but when he peeked, he saw that the man had moved down the ward to the black kid's bed. The captain was in the habit of sticking needles into the soles of the kid's feet and poking him in various places to see if he could get a reaction. He was convinced the kid was

malingering, but Nathan knew the boy had been brought in over a week ago, days before he had arrived and had never opened his eyes or moved. The nurses fussed over him, bathed him and exercised his limbs. He was catheterized and they changed his dump bags in the mornings and afternoons. If the kid was faking it, Nathan thought, he deserved a medal. His name was Collingwood and he had been brought in from one of the Monitor flotillas down in the delta. No one knew what was wrong with him except that he was unconscious. Katie always brought him ice cream in the afternoon, as if he were awake, and then gave the extra bowl to Nathan or Grayles, the First Infantry Division sergeant with the throat wound. Montgomery, the green beret, never wanted his and some afternoons Nathan could score three bowls of the stuff.

She came into the ward now just as Fetters started in on Collingwood and began yelling at the captain that he had no business examining or touching the kid.

"I calling Major Naylor, now!" she threatened and snatched Nathan's chart out of Fetters' hands. He scuttled out and both Grayles and Montgomery applauded and whistled, Grayles through the hole in his throat.

"Is he going to cut my foot off?" Nathan asked her.

"Nobody cutting anything off any- 45 body. You need to get up, walk around." Katie came around to the side of Nathan's bed and lowered the rail. "Go to the bathroom by yourself today, I get you a beer. Them too." She pointed at Montgomery and Grayles.

"Whoa, kid." Montgomery sat up and swung his legs over the bed. "You got a mission. Don't let us down."

Nathan got up in stages and limped to the latrine at the end of the hallway, chaperoned by his IV stand. He sat, for the first time in months, on an actual toilet in a private stall with a door and the experience was so pleasurable he stayed for nearly twenty minutes, flushing every so often just to hear the rush of the water.

When he got back to the ward Montgomery presented him with an ornately carved Hmong walking stick that had been given to him after losing his foot. "You keep it," he said. "I'm getting far too much out of this as it is."

It struck Nathan as a curious thing to say but he knew enough not to press it. If the Army had taught him anything, it had taught him to wait. Since basic, he had learned to occupy a kind of "timeless time" (his own phrase) until the routine of military life presented whatever new variation of boredom, drudgery, nonsense or terror it seemed to possess in an endless rotating supply. The Vietnamese, Nathan soon realized, were masters of timeless time and were out-waiting the Americans; it was how you survived; it was how you won.

50   What Montgomery was getting far too much of was revealed that afternoon over the beers that Katie had promised and that, as good as her word, she delivered along with the afternoon ice cream and PX pizza that Nathan thought tasted like toasted cheese sandwich with tomato sauce poured over it but that he ate on principle anyway.

"Training and expertise; I'm full of it and I'm no good to anybody, now," Montgomery confessed. He sat on one of the cane backed chairs that were scattered throughout the ward as Nathan, Grayles, Katie, Katie's best friend, Becita, and Tired Dave the surgical orderly, drank beer and nibbled at the pizza.

Montgomery was from a wealthy Mobile, old-money Alabama family. He had flunked out of Princeton his freshman year and volunteered for the draft as a way of asserting his independence and deflecting his family's disappointment simultaneously. He was recruiting poster handsome, athletic, blond, and irresponsible without being a fuck-up about it, and to everyone's great surprise he took to the military life. He volunteered for airborne and aced jump school, took the Ranger course and got his patch, was tapped for Special Forces and was so outstanding there that they sent him to the Defense Language School in Monterey for a crash course in Vietnamese and Khmer. He ate it up. Ten days into his tour, he stepped over a log while on patrol in the highlands and set off a toe-popper: end of foot; end of military career.

Montgomery was obsessed with how much money it had taken to train him and furthermore, how much more the government would continue to spend compensating him for the loss of his foot. He kept a notebook at his bedside and filled it with figures. Next to the notebook was a 7.62 mm M-14 rifle round of the type that some 13-year-old VC had rigged as an antipersonnel device and dropped on the far side of the log that Montgomery had stepped over on his swift, expensive journey to crip-ville. Grayles was of the opinion (written in his own notebook because his voice box was shattered) that the U.S. Government's outlay for a single M-14 round was probably in the fraction-of-a-cent-category because they purchased so many of them in such large lots. Lay that against the likelihood that the round was filched by either VC cadre or black-market middleman, Grayles wrote, and therefore acquired gratis, and you added even further imbalance to an already one sided equation. It cost our side a huge amount of money to equip, train and transport Montgomery; it cost theirs next to nothing to render him useless.

This was somewhat of a surprise coming from Grayles because he was—as Montgomery put it—"the last of the true believers." Grayles believed in the war; he believed it was still winnable. Grayles' father had assaulted Omaha Beach with the Big Red One, his older brother had retreated from the Chosin Reservoir with the same division in Korea, and Grayles had been finishing his second tour as an advisor to the ARVN forces when a sniper gave him his throat wound, Grayles even then wearing the insignia of his family's adopted unit although said unit itself had departed Vietnam almost two years earlier. He was convinced the war could be won and would be won if the nation (the U.S.—not the RVN) simply showed some resolve.

55 "How many guys got Monty's training?" he scribbled on his notepad furiously and held it up for Nathan, Tired Dave, Katie, Becita and Monty to peruse. Nathan shrugged, Tired Dave put his arm around Becita and whispered something that made her giggle, Katie opened another beer and handed it to Montgomery—now dubbed Monty forever by Grayles' voiceless shorthand—and Montgomery took it, sipped and said, "There were maybe 40 other guys in my class at Monterey; what's your point?"

Grayles scribbled and then displayed his reply. "Attrition. They could kill half your class and we could still outspend and out-train them if we're willing to stay the course."

Nathan got another beer from Katie and tuned them out. It made him sleepy to watch Grayles scrawl his replies to Monty. His foot was getting better and they would send him back to the Team in a matter of days and he didn't want to go. He had five more months, one-hundred-and-fifty-some days. He couldn't conceive of the life he would lead when he returned home and that blankness had convinced him that if he returned to the Team he wouldn't survive. Tired Dave was the object lesson here. He had fallen in love with Becita and they planned to be married so he had voluntarily extended his tour in order to coincide with the termination of her contract. She would receive a work visa for her service and Tired Dave would get an early drop for staying on past his rotation date. He could leave the Army as soon as his feet touched American soil.

"Then we're goin' to Bolinas an' we're gonna be hippies for the rest of our lives."

"Then we are going to San Pedro to live with my uncle's family while you finish school and get a good job."

No matter what either of them said, or 60 which version of their future prevailed, they had plans, and Nathan envied them for that. Thinking of his own future was like thinking of a wall. It frightened him.

Nathan's mail had caught up with him and after months of isolation he now had some contact with his former life. His father, a widower, was getting married to a woman Nathan despised; his sister announced that she and her Quaker husband were contributing money to send medical supplies to North Vietnam in order to offset Nathan's participation in an unjust and immoral war (but he was not to take it personally). The girl he'd been sleeping with at school before he had been drafted had written to say that she had taken up again with the married Sociology professor she had been having an affair with when she'd first met Nathan and she needed to re-think their relationship. Finally, a Volkswagen dealership in East

Lansing had written demanding payment for a VW bus the dealership claimed Nathan had reserved for his return home. Nathan had no memory of doing any such thing, but the dealer's threats to write the Provost Marshall gave him pause. He couldn't think about any of it.

He thought, instead, of the dead. He dreamed about them at night. Lt. McCandless—Candle Ass—stood at the foot of his bed and glared at him disapprovingly. The Vietnamese girl held up the river water filled blivet and looked at Nathan with an expression of mourning and loss that made his throat close on itself. She had drowned, unable to loosen the thong that held the blivet to her wrist when the shooting started. The river had carried her off and she would never be found; no one she loved or who had loved her would ever know what had happened to her. In his dreams she explained all this to him in Vietnamese and he understood her perfectly.

It's not my fault, Nathan willed himself to tell them, but no words would come when he tried to speak.

Now, when he looked around at the hospital ward and saw its cleanliness, the privacy and hot water available in the bathrooms, the tender efficiency of the nurses and the supercilious attention of the doctors, it all forced his mind back on the past seven months. Much of what he had seen and done, he had forced into a compartment he could seal shut with exhaustion, fear and the routine of life in the field. His faith had been that those things would carry him through his tour and out the other end where there would be time to sort it all out or forget it altogether. Implicitly he had believed that if he weren't killed, maimed or driven crazy, he would find a way back to some idea of himself that connected his past and future and could even absorb what he had been through here.

But now he saw the very real possibility of permanent exile. Even if he went home physically whole, he would never retrieve any part of his old life. The thought ambushed him now and made him catch his breath.

"You okay?" Montgomery brought him out of his reverie. "Katie, I think Nathan's hurting." He pointed to Nathan's now bandaged foot, the blackened toes visible through the gauze. Katie got up from her seat on one of the empty beds and came toward him. Her hospital greens were freshly laundered and crisp, she smelled of soap and antiseptic, her face was set in an expression of concern that contained just a hint of pride: there was no situation in this hospital that she was not equal to. She sat next to Nathan and had him lift his foot so that his sole rested against her thigh. She pressed lightly on various parts of his foot with both hands, her fingers pressing gently against the ball of his foot, the instep, the arch, the ankle, the heel. Did it hurt here? No? Here? Here? No? Here?

Nathan burst into tears. It was profoundly humiliating and the kind of thing that he could not recall later in life without shuddering and forcing his mind away from the memory as quickly as possible. Katie gasped and pulled her hands away, thinking she had handled some tender spot roughly. Nathan tried to tell her that she wasn't responsible but he had begun to sob in the breathless, gasping way of very small children and he couldn't stop. He turned his face away from the others and was aware that he had ruined the get-together. He heard them shifting from their own places, gathering up the beer cans and bowls of melted ice cream. He got up and pushed off down the hall, his IV stand clattering next to him. When he got to the bathroom, he settled in one of the far stalls and waited for the blubbering to subside. It took a while because it came in waves, like an undulant fever. He would stop crying, catch his breath, wipe his face with his sleeve and start to get up but then the tears would start rolling from his eyes, his chest would begin to heave.

After a few minutes Katie's bleached white canvas shoes appeared beneath the transom of the stall. "You ok?"

"I'm all right."

70   "When you through, come back and go for a walk with Monty and Joe" (she meant Grayles). "They gonna go down to the beach with Dave. You need some air."

Nathan made himself breathe slowly for two minutes and count his breaths as he did so. When he was finished, he opened the stall door and walked back to the ward where Becita unhooked his IV and handed him soap, a towel and freshly laundered hospital greens. Then she and Katie wrapped his swollen foot, bandages and all in plastic and stood outside the shower stall (its curtain modestly drawn) while he soaked, soaped and rinsed himself. If he fell, they assured him, they would come right in and help. Nathan thought about falling down deliberately, a vivid tableau of his nude wet self intertwined with the two young women, nurses whites clinging soppily to their small bodies presented itself to his imagination in cinematic detail, but you can't be a cry-baby in the early part of the afternoon and a sex god in the latter, at least not all on the same day he concluded. He let himself stand underneath the stream of hot water for an extra two minutes and tried to think of the last time he had had a hot shower. When he was done, he toweled off, put on the clean greens and hopped out of the stall to the applause of both nurses who proceeded to dry his hair and comb it as if he were a five year old. They stripped the plastic off his sick foot, slipped a sandal on his good foot, gave him the Hmong walking stick that Monty had said was now his and led him to the French windows at the far end of the ward.

Beyond the coral and stone verandah was a garden filled with dwarf pines and bougainvillea that sloped down to a sun-colored beach. Beyond the beach was the South China Sea, an endless blue that stretched to the horizon.

Out on the verandah Monty, Grayles and Tired Dave were smoking, a white plume leaking from the hole in Grayles throat. Nathan limped out to join them, the breeze and salt smell from the sea displacing the hospital smell of ammonia and stale urine and hitting his nostrils with surprising force. For some reason all the sights and sounds of this new world made him think of the VW dealership in East Lansing, the threatening letter oddly juxtaposed with a number of brightly colored leaflets featuring attractive photographs of the model of the van the dealership insisted he had reserved. He saw himself in the van on a two lane highway, a beach like this on one side, mountains on the other, next to him a girl who, for a moment was Carla (minus her married sociology professor) who then became Becita who then became Katie: a possible future or a least a small chink in its wall.

Monty and Grayles were arguing about the war. The conversation had an odd, one-sided quality to it, since only Monty was speaking, followed by silences of varying lengths as Grayles scratched replies in his notebook. Decades later Nathan would have sudden, lurchingly vivid memories of their dialogues when cell phones became as ubiquitous as bamboo vipers and people conducted monologues on the street with the same lack of self-consciousness.

Tired Dave refused to make himself 75 part of the conversation. "You got to know how to pay out your energy reserves, man," he confided to Nathan as they walked down to the beach. "You can't be wasting 'em."

Tired Dave looked to Nathan like someone with absolutely no energy to waste and few reserves to draw on. There were rumors he was on his third tour. Nathan couldn't get his mind around the idea. They walked ahead of Monty and Joe Grayles down to the tide line where the beach sloped sharply down to the surf. Here the sea was green and very clear with a long swell that ran in a ruler-straight line from an offshore reef to the sand. Tired Dave pointed at the white caps that marked the reef. There were birds hovering above the water there, swooping low every so often to skim the tops of the waves. "Big fish chase the little fish from the reef to the surface an' the birds're just waitin'."

Nathan looked back toward the hospital and its neatly manicured grounds. Beyond the buildings and the LZ, past the French-built coastal road, stood a line of palms that made Nathan think of the tree line on the other side of the river where he had first seen the girl. Above the trees were forested hills, dark green and dotted with villas in pastel colors. They looked like petit-fours pastries set out on a dessert carousel. Nathan imagined American senior officers and civilian executives from the big contract companies living there now with their Vietnamese mistresses. Beyond the hills was the war although if you thought the war wasn't everywhere in this country, Nathan knew, you were kidding yourself.

"These people," Tired Dave said, apropos of nothing, "these people are totally fucked." He might have been talking about whoever lived in the villas but there was something to the note of exhaustion at the bottom of his voice that made Nathan think he was talking about the entire country.

Nathan suddenly saw the VW van he had ordered and forgotten pop to the surface of his mind like one of the reef fish. It was bright red with a white interior and tuck-and-roll upholstery; it carried the Porsche engine option, featured air conditioning and had been fitted with a stereo cassette system he had seen once in a speed shop on Woodward Avenue. He made a conscious effort not to carry the image any further but to hold onto it as it was. He was bringing it—or it was coming to him—from an enormous distance and Nathan knew instinctively that he must reel it in slowly and in stages in order for it to become real. He turned away from his contemplation of the hills and limped down to the surf until his feet were in the water. He expected Tired Dave to say something about ruining the bandages on his feet but instead he moved into the surf next to Nathan. The sky above the water had begun to darken, the horizon line beginning to smudge.

Nathan looked to his left and was surprised to see a line of soldiers, other ambulatory patients, in hospital greens or worn fatigues, whom the nurses had released into the relative cool of the late afternoon once the sun had gone behind the coastal hills. Nathan counted eight of them in addition to himself, Tired Dave, Monty and Joe Grayles. Everyone, it seemed, had decided to go wading in the South China Sea surf.

The water felt cold and astringent. He let his bandaged foot sink into it and for the first time in days he felt some sensation, a dull, throbbing ache near his ankle. It felt good and he kept his foot against the fine sand bottom.

One of the soldiers on his left suddenly pointed out toward the sea and Nathan watched the horizon line grow thick and dark in a way that he found oddly frightening. Then the sound came to him and the soldier who had pointed said, "Shit," in a tired voice and began backing out of the surf. Everyone else did the same and Nathan found himself leading the line of men up the beach. Monty caught up to him, his crutches making damp marks in the sand as he came even with Nathan. "Your first command?" he said, winking and jerking his thumb back at the line of men following them. Tired Dave broke out of the line and began sprinting toward the north end of the hospital wing just as the first V-line of gunships flew past them overhead. No one else ran but they all followed Nathan who followed Tired Dave to the hospital's landing zone, a wide apron of space hacked out of a date palm grove. The air was filled with the noise of helicopter rotors and Nathan could see two of them settling onto the LZ tarmac while others circled the hospital. When they reached the edge of the LZ, Tired Dave was squatting on his haunches talking to a very crisp looking officer in brand new battle fatigues and web gear. Tired Dave was pointing at the hospital and the officer—a major—was nodding and scribbling in a small, neat looking back notebook. Then he ran back to one of the gun ships and leaped past the door gunner into the ship's interior.

Tired Dave looked up at Nathan and said, "Motherfucking PIO," and Nathan had to think for a moment, sorting through the endless roster of military acronyms before coming upon Public Information Officer. By that time the major was back and said in a voice that suggested a good-humored father chiding a favorite son about a messy bedroom, "Corporal, I thought you were going to get these men formed up."

Tired Dave stood up, stared at the officer for a moment and then spat next to his spit-polished jump boots before turning and walking off.

"I want that man's name." The major 85 took out his small black notebook.

"Fetters," said Nathan and spelled it for him. The major wrote it down in his book. Nathan looked at the name tape sewn above his left breast pocket: Selwyn. He smelled of aftershave, his fatigues looked tailored and he wore a holstered pistol in the kind of combat shoulder rig issued to pilots. Nathan had a brief mental image of reaching out, grabbing the knurled walnut grips of the pistol, pulling it from the holster and shooting Major Selwyn. He pushed the image away by thinking about the red VW van. It would have a roof rack for surf boards and skis and he would learn to do both.

Something tapped him on the shoulder and he saw Grayles next to him, his hand on Nathan's shoulder, his arm fully extended to create the correct interval for parade inspection. Nathan turned to his right and put his hand on Monty's shoulder. Monty was doing the same to the soldier next to him: all the old training kicking in.

Major Selwyn had run back to the helicopter furthest from the line. Two other helicopters had landed and personnel were pouring out of them. Some of them were civilians. Monty said, "Fuck me. Reporters." There were clots of them, some of them women, running from the helicopters toward the line of men. They had cameras and the small cassette recorders Nathan had seen in shops and the open air markets in Saigon. There were military personnel as well and some of them had cameras and recorders too.

Major Selwyn stood with a large group of uniforms pointing at Nathan and the others and speaking animatedly to someone in the center of the group. Then the group began to move toward them with a tall senior officer at its center. Nathan recognized the man from a dozen yards off but it still took a moment for The General's face to register.

90   This was Theatre Commander, The Man-In-Charge, the man who would preside over the war's conclusion and after whom the Pentagon would name its latest generation of battle tanks. He started at the opposite end of the line, shaking hands and asking the soldiers' names, their hometowns. In spite of himself, Nathan was beginning to get nervous, his palms were sweaty. The general was asking some of the men about their wounds.

What would Nathan say? Well, sir, I was pissing in the river when I was attacked by this girl VC and her commie snake and the snake bit my foot.

Don't say anything, he told himself, just 'yes, sir, no, sir, Detroit, Michigan, sir.'

The general had reached Monty and was shaking his hand, a little tentatively because Monty was balanced on crutches. Monty was asking the general how much money the general thought it had taken to train him. The general looked a little confused and then said, "It doesn't matter, son, no amount is too much for you boys." Then he had pulled his hand away, a little too forcefully, and caused Monty to overbalance on his crutches and fall. There was confusion and shouting, reporters pressed in to take pictures and the small knot of Public Information Officers and body guards surged past them to surround the general. Nathan and the soldier on the other side of Monty helped him to his feet. Order was restored on the line and the general stepped forward to shake Nathan's hand. "Good work, son," he said, as if Nathan had just done something difficult and dangerous. "Where're you from?"

The blank wall of his future rose up in front of him once again, and Nathan had trouble remembering where he was from for a moment. "East Lansing, Michigan, sir," he blurted out, which was not where he was from at all.

"Keep up the good work son," the general replied and moved to Grayles, the last soldier in line, who saluted and whipped out his notebook and pencil all in one fluid motion.

95

The general asked for Grayles' hometown and Nathan, cutting his eyes sideways could see the answer, "Greenville, South Carolina, sir," scrawled on the page of Grayles' notebook. He handed it to the general, who took out his own pen and wrote beneath Grayles' scrawl, "A fine place, son, I know you'll be back home soon," and handed it back to Grayles who read it and wrote in turn, "General, this throat wound has affected my voice but my ears are okay and I can hear you just fine." He handed the notebook back to the general who read it and wrote, "That's great son, glad to hear it, keep up the good work!" and handed the notebook back to Grayles. Nathan turned for just a moment to look into Grayles' eyes as the general stepped back, came to attention and saluted Grayles. It was like watching the sun go down.

The general stood for a moment, uncertain, until Nathan realized he was expecting the requisite military courtesy. He snapped to attention himself and saluted the general, as did the other men in line, all except Grayles, who looked down at his notebook. Flash bulbs went off, the general about-faced and walked back to his helicopter, his entourage swarming around him, leaving Major Selwyn who rushed down the line of men handing each of them something. It was a signed photograph of the general. Grayles spat on his, crumpled it in his hand and tossed it away. None of the reporters or Public Information Officers seemed to notice; they had all gone haring after the general, who had returned to his helicopter.

In a matter of moments, the entire entourage was gone, the turbines of the heli-copters spooling up as they lifted off. Photographs of the general mixed with some of the men's hats in the rotor wash. Dust flew everywhere, coating the men. Nathan turned away and began walking back to the hospi-tal. He didn't want to look at Grayles' face.

" How does one go about such a poetry? I think it's like this: First there must be an experience, a sequence or constellation of perceptions of sufficient interest, felt by the poet intensely enough to demand of him their equivalence in words: he is *brought to speech*. Suppose there's the sight of the sky through a dusty window, birds and clouds and bits of paper flying through the sky, the sound of music from his radio, feelings of anger and love and amusement roused by a letter just received. . . . "

—Denise Levertov, from "Some Notes on Organic Form"

P A R T 2

Poetry

Long before the development of written language, human beings sang and chanted the stories of their lives, their sense of the world and the universe, and their beliefs about how those things came to be. They also created rhythmic expressions about everyday things—the killing of food in the hunt, the defeat of an enemy, the grinding of corn to prepare a meal, the initiation of boy-children and girl-children into adulthood. Poetry grows perhaps out of two ancient impulses: the use of rhythm, meter, and rhyme to record and memorialize the experience of the culture, and the equally important function of the chant to beseech the gods and effect contact between human beings and those forces that were believed to exist in the realm of the supernatural. So poetry has always been about everyday experience as well as a connection to the past or a link with invisible forces that move both the larger world and the inner realm of human nature and human impulse.

PROFILE OF A POET
Langston Hughes (1902–1967)

Langston Hughes was an eloquent voice for justice on the American home front, and he was also a writer of international stature. He traveled to Africa, the Caribbean, Mexico, and Europe, seeking out other poets and new subjects for his own writing. During the Spanish Civil War, he was an outspoken ally of the Loyalist government in Spain and an articulate and resolute opponent of fascism. He traveled to Spain and came under fire in Madrid and bombardment in Barcelona, where he wrote about the war and the American volunteers—white and black—in the Lincoln and Washington battalions of the International Brigade. This experience caused him problems later in the 1940s, as you can see in his poem "Un-American Investigators."

Un-American Investigators (1953)

The committee's fat,
Smug, almost secure
Co-religionists
Shiver with delight
In warm manure   5
As those investigated—
Too brave to name a name—
Have pseudonyms revealed
In Gentile game
    Of who,   10
    Born Jew,
    Is who?
Is not your name Lipshitz?
    Yes.
Did you not change it   15
For subversive purposes?
    No.
For nefarious gain?
    Not so.
Are you sure?   20
The committee shivers
With delight in
Its manure.

Langston Hughes was born in Joplin, Missouri, in 1902, when segregation was institutionalized and public racism was a fact of life for African Americans. In its 1896 decision *Plessy v. Ferguson,* the U.S. Supreme Court had handed down a doctrine of "separate but equal" which gave state and local governments a free hand to marginalize blacks and deny them the basic rights guaranteed to American citizens. This law, which formed the underpinnings of segregation, was not overturned until *Brown v. Board of Education* in 1954.

Langston as a boy in Lawrence, Kansas

Hughes's family, with its mixed heritage of African, Native American, and white blood, was strongly connected to the Abolitionist movement (an ancestor had fought and died with John Brown at Harper's Ferry in 1859), which made Hughes intensely aware from his youngest days of the issues of race and the dilemma of being black in an overwhelmingly white and largely intolerant society.

At a very young age, Hughes also found a vital connection between his love of language and the lives of black people as they were actually lived. His voice was the first American voice to sing not only of African American aspirations and the struggle for equality, it was a voice that narrated and described the close-to-the-bone existence of his people as they went about their daily lives.

What they did, what they saw, and what they encountered in the streets—at their jobs and in their homes—became the subjects of his plays, essays, and fiction, but primarily his poetry. His poems became both window and mirror for the day-to-day grief, joy, rage, and hopes of ordinary black Americans, and for that reason alone his work is significant. In Hughes's work, black readers saw themselves for the first time not only as they wished to be, but as they were. White readers were given a vivid glimpse into a world which, for most of them, was invisible and unknown.

However, Langston Hughes's value as a poet arises not only from his social commentary, but also from his unique marriage of mainstream American diction and the rhythms, patterns, and inflections of black English. His verse can be as "plain" and straightforward as the lines in the short, contemplative "Theme for English B," or they can be freighted with the raw expressive power of the Mississippi Delta, as in one of his earliest published poems, "The Weary Blues" (which appears later in this chapter).

A young Langston Hughes

Langston Hughes's poems became a window and a mirror for African Americans of all ages.

Theme for English B (1949)

The instructor said,

    Go home and write
    a page tonight.
    And let that page come out of you—
    Then, it will be true.   5

I wonder if it's that simple?
I am twenty-two, colored, born in Winston-Salem.
I went to school there, then Durham, then here
to this college on the hill above Harlem.
I am the only colored student in my class.   10
The steps from the hill lead down into Harlem,
through a park, then I cross St. Nicholas,
Eighth Avenue, Seventh, and I come to the Y,
the Harlem Branch Y, where I take the elevator
up to my room, sit down, and write this page: 15

It's not easy to know what is true for you or me
at twenty-two, my age. But I guess I'm what
I feel and see and hear, Harlem, I hear you:
hear you, hear me—we two—you, me, talk on this page.
(I hear New York, too.) Me—who?   20
Well, I like to eat, sleep, drink, and be in love.
I like to work, read, learn, and understand life.
I like a pipe for a Christmas present,
or records—Bessie, bop, or Bach.
I guess being colored doesn't make me *not* like   25
the same things other folks like who are other races.
So will my page be colored that I write?
Being me, it will not be white.
But it will be
a part of you, instructor.   30
You are white—
yet a part of me, as I am a part of you.
That's American.
Sometimes perhaps you don't want to be a part of me.
Nor do I often want to be a part of you.   35
But we are, that's true!
As I learn from you,
I guess you learn from me—
although you're older—and white—
and somewhat more free.   40

This is my page for English B.

Certainly Hughes was one of the first poets to connect the blues tradition
to the conventions and traditions of written poetic form. His consciousness
and awareness as a poet of color perhaps arises most significantly from his
identification with the anonymous black singers and musicians who first
defined the form for artists who would, over generations, accomplish the
migration of this new and original music from the fields and countryside into the

city streets where it would become jazz, rhythm & blues, rock 'n' roll, hip-hop, and rap.

Dream Boogie (1951)

Good morning, daddy!
Ain't you heard
The boogie-woogie rumble
Of a dream deferred?

Listen closely: 5
You'll hear their feet
Beating out and beating out a—

   You think
   It's a happy beat?

Listen to it closely: 10
Ain't you heard
something underneath
like a—

   What did I say?

Sure,   15
I'm happy!
Take it away!

   Hey, pop!
   Re-bop!
   Mop!   20

   Y-e-a-h!

It is fair to say that, without Hughes's voice, the journey might have been much longer, and whites would have been considerably less aware of the ways in which this music was touching their lives.

Hughes was also a significant public figure, and his poetry (as well as his plays, essays, and fiction) figures in the tumult and ferment of the American social scene, especially in the crucial first half of the twentieth century. Always on the left, his sympathies were with the downtrodden and mistreated. African American dramatist Lorraine Hansberry took the title of her celebrated play "A Raisin in the Sun" from a line of Hughes's powerful—and perhaps best known—poem "Harlem."

Harlem (A Dream Deferred) (1951)

What happens to a dream deferred?

    Does it dry up
    like a raisin in the sun?
    Or fester like a sore—
    And then run?   5
    Does it stink like rotten meat?
    Or crust and sugar over—
    like a syrupy sweet?

    Maybe it just sags
    like a heavy load.   10

    Or does it explode?

The question Hughes poses to the reader, "What happens to a dream deferred?" is a question still waiting for an answer. One possible answer that Hughes provides (". . . or does it explode?") is a powerful evocation of the racial violence of the past and a warning for the future.

A key figure in the Harlem Renaissance, Langston Hughes was often called the "poet laureate of Harlem."

Elements of Poetry

The **elements of poetry** are simply the techniques, strategies, and methods used by poets in practicing their craft. In the coming chapters, in the poetry unit of this book, you will find explanations of how the poet uses figurative language (metaphor, simile, personification, and so on), line breaks and other aspects of poetic form, sound, rhyme, rhythm and meter, symbolism, irony, imagery, and tone. Some of this discussion will sound familiar because it is related to our discussion of fiction, and some of the discussion might be new to you.

    Some of the new parts of the discussion are rhythm, rhyme, line breaks, and stanzas. Langston Hughes uses all four in his poem "Evenin' Air Blues." We will be exploring all of these aspects of poetry in the following chapters.

Evenin' Air Blues (1942)

Folks, I come up North
Cause they told me de North was fine.
I come up North
Cause they told me de North was fine.
Been up here six months—   5
I'm about to lose my mind.

This mornin' for breakfast
I chawed de mornin' air.
This mornin' for breakfast
Chawed de mornin' air.   10
But this evenin' for supper,
I got evenin' air to spare.

Believe I'll do a little dancin'
Just to drive my blues away—
A little dancin'   15
To drive my blues away,
Cause when I'm dancin'
De blues forgets to stay.

But if you was to ask me
How de blues they come to be,   20
Says if you was to ask me
How de blues they come to be—
You wouldn't need to ask me:
Just look at me and see!

   In poems like "Evenin' Air Blues," Hughes broke new ground, revealing connections between blues songs and poetry, jazz riffs, and the lives of ordinary people, and he put it all together. His poetry broke down barriers between popular culture and the arts, making him an especially appropriate poet to profile in this book.
   One of Hughes's recurring thematic motifs (recurring images or symbols) has to do with rivers.

The Negro Speaks of Rivers (1921)

I've known rivers:
I've known rivers ancient as the world and older than the flow of human
      blood in human veins.

My soul has grown deep like the rivers.

I bathed in the Euphrates when dawns were young.   5
I built my hut near the Congo and it lulled me to sleep.
I looked upon the Nile and raised the pyramids above it.
I heard the singing of the Mississippi when Abe Lincoln
      went down to New Orleans, and I've seen its muddy
      bosom turn all golden in the sunset.   10

I've known rivers:
Ancient, dusky rivers.

My soul has grown deep like the rivers.

The speaker of Hughes's poem here speaks not only of his own individual experience, but also of the experience of an entire people. In "Cross," since Hughes was a person of mixed racial heritage himself, he was able to speak to the experience of those many Americans whose identity is a mix of different racial and cultural heritages.

Cross (1925)

My old man's a white old man
And my old mother's black.
If ever I cursed my white old man
I take my curses back.

If ever I cursed my black old mother   5
And wished she were in hell,
I'm sorry for that evil wish
And now I wish her well.

My old man died in a fine big house.
My ma died in a shack.   10
I wonder where I'm gonna die,
Being neither white nor black?

In many of Hughes's poems, the speaker of the poem is an **eponymous** character—someone who represents not just his or her individual experience but the experience of an entire people or an entire cultural group. An example would be found in the speaker in Hughes's poem "Negro."

Negro (1926)

I am a Negro:
    Black as the night is black,
    Black like the depths of my Africa.

I've been a slave:
    Caesar told me to keep his door-steps clean. 5
    I brushed the boots of Washington.

I've been a worker:
    Under my hand the pyramids arose.
    I made mortar for the Woolworth Building.

I've been a singer: 10
    All the way from Africa to Georgia
    I carried my sorrow songs.
    I made ragtime.

I've been a victim:
    The Belgians cut off my hands in the Congo. 15
    They lynch me still in Mississippi.

I am a Negro:
    Black as the night is black,
    Black like the depths of my Africa.

    Langston Hughes also took on contemporary social issues of his day, as in "Ballad of the Landlord."

Ballad of the Landlord (1940)

Landlord, landlord,
My roof has sprung a leak.
Don't you 'member I told you about it
Way last week?

Landlord, landlord,   5
These steps is broken down.
When you come up yourself
It's a wonder you don't fall down.

Ten Bucks you say I owe you?
Ten Bucks you say is due?   10
Well, that's Ten Bucks more'n I'll pay you
Till you fix this house up new.

What? You gonna get eviction orders?
You gonna cut off my heat?
You gonna take my furniture and   15
Throw it in the street?

Um-huh! You talking high and mighty.
Talk on—till you get through.
You ain't gonna be able to say a word
If I land my fist on you.   20

Police! Police!
Come and get this man!
He's trying to ruin the government
And overturn the land!

Copper's whistle!   25
Patrol bell!
Arrest.

Precinct Station.
Iron cell.
Headlines in press: 30

MAN THREATENS LANDLORD
                              ∴
TENANT HELD NO BAIL
                              ∴
JUDGE GIVES NEGRO 90 DAYS IN COUNTY JAIL

Poems for Further Reading

I, Too (1925)

I, too, sing America.

I am the darker brother.
They send me to eat in the kitchen
When company comes,
But I laugh,   5
And eat well,
And grow strong.

Tomorrow,
I'll be at the table
When company comes.   10
Nobody'll dare
Say to me,
"Eat in the kitchen,"
Then.

Besides,   15
They'll see how beautiful I am
And be ashamed—

I, too, am America.

·····▷ *Your* **Turn**
Talking and Writing about Lit

1. Note Hughes's use of the word brother in "I, Too." The speaker of the poem
is not just a neighbor or a friend, but a brother. What is the significance of
this choice of words?

2. When Hughes's speaker says "Tomorrow" in line 8, does he mean the next
day? How do you interpret the word "Tomorrow" in the context of the poem?

Island (1951)

Wave of sorrow,
Do not drown me now:

I see the island
Still ahead somehow.

I see the island   5
And its sands are fair:

Wave of sorrow,
Take me there.

·····▷ *Your* **Turn**
Talking and Writing about Lit

1. What do you think the wave of sorrow represents?

2. What do you think the island represents?

Old Walt (1954)

Old Walt Whitman
Went finding and seeking,
Finding less than sought
Seeking more than found,
Every detail minding   5
Of the seeking or the finding.

Pleasured equally
In seeking as in finding,
Each detail minding,
Old Walt went seeking   10
And finding.

····▶ *Your* Turn
Talking and Writing about Lit

1. How does Hughes establish rhythm in "Old Walt"?

2. In what ways do the techniques of Hughes's "Old Walt" echo the techniques of Walt Whitman himself? (See Chapter 20.)

3. **DIY**   Write a brief poem (6–12 lines) in which you write about a poet you're interested in using that poet's style. You might like or *dis*like this poet's style (straight- shooting and satire are both welcome).

Democracy (1949)

Democracy will not come
Today, this year
        Nor ever
Through compromise and fear.

I have as much right   5
As the other fellow has
        To stand
On my two feet
And own the land.

I tire so of hearing people say,   10
Let things take their course.
Tomorrow is another day.
I do not need my freedom when I'm dead.
I cannot live on tomorrow's bread.

    Freedom   15
    Is a strong seed
    Planted
    In a great need.
    I live here, too.
    I want freedom   20
    Just as you.

·····➤ *Your* Turn
Talking and Writing about Lit

1. What images does Hughes use to make "Democracy" distinctly American?

2. How does the simplicity of Hughes's style work to simplify large and complex issues?

Mother to Son (1922, 1926)

Well, son, I'll tell you:
Life for me ain't been no crystal stair.
It's had tacks in it,
And splinters,
And boards torn up,   5
And places with no carpet on the floor—
Bare.
But all the time
I'se been a-climbin' on,
And reachin' landin's,   10
And turnin' corners,
And sometimes goin' in the dark
Where there ain't been no light.
So boy, don't you turn back.
Don't you set down on the steps   15
'Cause you finds it's kinder hard.
Don't you fall now—
For I'se still goin', honey,
I'se still climbin',
And life for me ain't been no crystal stair. 20

····► *Your* **Turn**
Talking and Writing about Lit

1. Does Hughes's conversational style help him convey his ideas in "Mother to Son"? Examples would include "Well, son, I'll tell you" and "I'se still climbin'."

2. **DIY** Write a brief poem (6–12 lines) in which you offer advice to someone less experienced than yourself (a younger sibling, a friend).

Same in Blues (1951)

I said to my baby,
Baby, take it slow.
I can't, she said, I can't!
I got to go!

    There's a certain   5
    amount of traveling
    in a dream deferred.

Lulu said to Leonard,
I want a diamond ring.
Leonard said to Lulu,   10
You won't get a goddamn thing!

    A certain
    amount of nothing
    in a dream deferred.

Daddy, daddy, daddy,   15
All I want is you.
You can have me, baby—
but my lovin' days is through.

    A certain
    amount of impotence   20
    in a dream deferred.

Three parties
On my party line—
But that third party,
Lord, ain't mine!   25

There's liable
to be confusion
in a dream deferred.

From river to river,
Uptown and down,   30
There's liable to be confusion
when a dream gets kicked around.

·····➤ *Your* Turn
Talking and Writing about Lit

1. What lines in "Same in Blues" refer to Hughes's own poem "Harlem" (above)?

2. When you look at the form of this poem, what aspects of our discussion of narrative point of view in fiction (Chapter 6) might be informative?

The Weary Blues (1926)

Droning a drowsy syncopated tune,
Rocking back and forth to a mellow croon,
     I heard a Negro play.
Down on Lenox Avenue the other night
By the pale dull pallor of an old gas light   5
     He did a lazy sway. . . .
     He did a lazy sway. . . .
To the tune o' those Weary Blues.
With his ebony hands on each ivory key
He made that poor piano moan with melody.   10
     O Blues!
Swaying to and fro on his rickety stool
He played that sad raggy tune like a musical fool.
     Sweet Blues!
Coming from a black man's soul.   15
     O Blues!
In a deep song voice with a melancholy tone
I heard that Negro sing, that old piano moan—
     "Ain't got nobody in all this world,
     Ain't got nobody but ma self.   20
     I's gwine to quit ma frownin'
     And put ma troubles on the shelf."
Thump, thump, thump, went his foot on the floor.
He played a few chords then he sang some more—

> "I got the Weary Blues   25
> And I can't be satisfied.
> Got the Weary Blues
> And can't be satisfied—
> I ain't happy no mo'
> And I wish that I had died."   30
> And far into the night he crooned that tune.
> The stars went out and so did the moon.
> The singer stopped playing and went to bed
> While the Weary Blues echoed through his head.
> He slept like a rock or a man that's dead.   35

····▶ *Your* **Turn**
Talking and Writing about Lit

1. What techniques of fiction does Hughes use in his narrative poem "The Weary Blues"?
2. What does this poem have in common with music and musical lyrics?

Dream Variations (1924, 1926)

> To fling my arms wide
> In some place of the sun,
> To whirl and to dance
> Till the white day is done.
> Then rest at cool evening   5
> Beneath a tall tree
> While night comes on gently,
>   Dark like me—
> That is my dream!
>
> To fling my arms wide   10
> In the face of the sun,
> Dance! Whirl! Whirl!
> Till the quick day is done.
> Rest at pale evening . . .
> A tall, slim tree . . .   15
> Night coming tenderly
>   Black like me.

····•▶ *Your* **Turn**
Talking and Writing about Lit

1. In Hughes's "Dream Variations," what is the function of "white" and what is the function of "black"?

2. **DIY**   The central action (and visual image) in "Dream Variations" is the whirling dance. Write a brief poem (6–12 lines) that has at its center a physical activity or action or gesture.

Subway Rush Hour (1951)

Mingled
breath and smell
so close
mingled
black and white   5
so near
no room for fear.

····•▶ *Your* **Turn**
Talking and Writing about Lit

1. Do you think the compactness of "Subway Rush Hour" serves Hughes well, or do you think the poem needs to be longer to get his idea across?

2. **DIY**   Write a simple poem in which you repeat a key word at least once and in which people either come together or come apart (it's your choice).

Lenox Avenue: Midnight (1926)

The rhythm of life
Is a jazz rhythm,
Honey.
The gods are laughing at us.

The broken heart of love,   5
The weary, weary heart of pain,—
  Overtones,
  Undertones,
To the rumble of street cars,
To the swish of rain.   10

Lenox Avenue,
Honey.
Midnight,
And the gods are laughing at us.

•••••• *Your* **Turn**
Talking and Writing about Lit

1. In what ways does "Lenox Avenue: Midnight" resemble musical lyrics?

2. **DIY** Write a short poem (6–14 lines) which contains at least three references to sounds (for example, "jazz rhythm," "rumble of street cars," "swish of rain" in Hughes's poem).

Talking Lit

In this "Talking Lit" you'll read an autobiographical excerpt as well as cultural commentary by Langston Hughes himself, and an analysis written by Gwendolyn Brooks—a context for reading Langston Hughes's work.

Langston Hughes, "Salvation"
from Hughes's autobiography,
***The Big Sea* (1940)**

I was saved from sin when I was going on thirteen. But not really saved. It happened like this. There was a big revival at my Auntie Reed's church. Every night for weeks there had been much preaching, singing, praying, and shouting, and some very hardened sinners had been brought to Christ, and the membership of the church had grown by leaps and bounds. Then just before the revival ended, they held a special meeting for children, "to bring

The young Langston Hughes portrayed by Gary Leroi Gray in the Wadsworth production of *Salvation.*

the young lambs to the fold." My aunt spoke of it for days ahead. That night I was escorted to the front row and placed on the mourners' bench with all the other young sinners, who had not yet been brought to Jesus.

My aunt told me that when you were saved you saw a light, and something happened to you inside! And Jesus came into your life! And God was with you from then on! She said you could see and hear and feel Jesus in your soul. I believed her. I had heard a great many old people say the same thing and it seemed to me they ought to know. So I sat there calmly in the hot, crowded church, waiting for Jesus to come to me.

The preacher preached a wonderful rhythmical sermon, all moans and shouts and lonely cries and dire pictures of hell, and then he sang a song about the ninety and nine safe in the fold, but one little lamb was left out in the cold. Then he said: "Won't you come? Won't you come to Jesus? Young lambs, won't you come?" And he held out his arms to all us young sinners there on the mourners' bench. And the little girls cried. And some of them jumped up and went to Jesus right away. But most of us just sat there.

A great many old people came and knelt around us and prayed, old women with jet-black faces and braided hair, old men with work-gnarled hands. And the church sang a song about the lower lights are burning, some poor sinners to be saved. And the whole building rocked with prayer and song.

Still I kept waiting to *see* Jesus.

Finally all the young people had gone to the altar and were saved, but one boy and me. He was a rounder's son named Westley. Westley and I were surrounded by sisters and deacons praying. It was very hot in the church, and getting late now. Finally Westley said to me in a whisper: "God damn! I'm tired o' sitting here. Let's get up and be saved." So he got up and was saved.

Then I was left all alone on the mourners' bench. My aunt came and knelt at my knees and cried, while prayers and songs swirled all around me in the little church. The whole congregation prayed for me alone, in a mighty wail of moans and voices. And I kept waiting serenely for Jesus, waiting, waiting—but he didn't come. I wanted to see him, but nothing happened to me. Nothing! I wanted something to happen to me, but nothing happened.

I heard the songs and the minister saying: "Why don't you come? My dear child, why don't you come to Jesus? Jesus is waiting for you. He wants you. Why don't you come? Sister Reed, what is this child's name?"

"Langston," my aunt sobbed.

"Langston, why don't you come? Why don't you come and be saved? Oh, Lamb of God! Why don't you come?"

Now it was really getting late. I began to be ashamed of myself, holding everything up so long. I began to wonder what God thought about Westley, who certainly hadn't seen Jesus either, but who was now sitting proudly on the platform, swinging his knickerbockered legs and grinning down at me, surrounded by deacons and old women on their knees praying. God had not struck Westley dead for taking his name in vain or for lying in the temple. So I decided that maybe to save further trouble, I'd better lie, too, and say that Jesus had come, and get up and be saved.

So I got up.

Suddenly the whole room broke into a sea of shouting, as they saw me rise. Waves of rejoicing swept the place. Women leaped in the air. My aunt threw her arms around me. The minister took me by the hand and led me to the platform.

When things quieted down, in a hushed silence, punctuated by a few ecstatic "Amens," all the new young lambs were blessed in the name of God. Then joyous singing filled the room.

That night, for the last time in my life but one—for I was a big boy twelve years old—I cried. I cried, in bed alone, and couldn't stop. I buried my head under the quilts, but my aunt heard me. She woke up and told my uncle I was crying because the Holy Ghost had come into my life, and because I had seen Jesus. But I was really crying because I couldn't bear to tell her that I had lied, that I had deceived everybody in the church, and I hadn't seen Jesus, and that now I didn't believe there was a Jesus any more, since he didn't come to help me.

Langston Hughes, "The Negro Artist and the Racial Mountain," (1926)

One of the most promising of the young Negro poets said to me once, "I want to be a poet—not a Negro poet," meaning, I believe, "I want to write like a white poet"; meaning subconsciously, "I would like to be a white poet"; meaning behind that, "I would like to be white." And I was sorry the young man said that, for no great poet has ever been afraid of being himself. And I doubted then that, with his desire to run away spiritually from his race, this boy would ever be a great poet. But this is the mountain standing in the way of any true Negro art in America—this urge within the race toward whiteness, the desire to pour racial individuality into the mold of American standardization, and to be as little Negro and as much American as possible.

But let us look at the immediate background of this young poet. His family is of what I suppose one would call the Negro middle class: people who are by no means rich yet never uncomfortable nor hungry—smug, contented, respectable folk, members of the Baptist church. The father goes to work every morning. He is a chief steward at a large white club. The mother sometimes does fancy sewing or supervises parties for the rich families of the town. The children go to a mixed school. In the home they read white papers and magazines. And the mother often says "Don't be like niggers" when the children are bad. A frequent phrase from the father is, "Look how well a white man does things." And so the word white comes to be unconsciously a symbol of all virtues. It holds for the children beauty, morality, and money. The whisper of "I want to be white" runs silently through their minds. This young poet's home is, I believe, a fairly typical home of the colored middle class. One sees immediately how difficult it would be for an artist born in such a home to interest himself in interpreting the beauty of his own people. He is never taught to see that beauty. He is taught rather not to see it, or if he does, to be ashamed of it when it is not according to Caucasian patterns.

For racial culture the home of a self-styled "high-class" Negro has nothing better to offer. Instead there will perhaps be more aping of things white than in a less cultured or less wealthy home. The father is perhaps a doctor, lawyer, landowner, or politician. The mother may be a social worker, or a teacher, or she may do nothing and have a maid. Father is often dark but he has usually married the lightest woman he could find. The family attend a fashionable church where few really colored faces are to be found. And they themselves draw a color line. In the North they go to white theaters and white movies. And in the South they have at least two cars and a house "like white folks." Nordic manners, Nordic faces, Nordic hair, Nordic art (if any), and an Episcopal heaven. A very high mountain indeed for the would-be racial artist to climb in order to discover himself and his people.

But then there are the low-down folks, the so-called common element, and they are the majority—may the Lord be praised! The people who have their hip of gin on Saturday nights and are not too important to themselves or the community, or too well fed, or too learned to watch the lazy world go round. They live on Seventh Street in Washington or State Street in Chicago and they do not particularly care whether they are like white folks or anybody else. Their joy runs, bang! into ecstasy. Their religion soars to a shout. Work maybe a little today, rest a little tomorrow. Play awhile. Sing awhile. O, let's dance! These common people are not afraid of spirituals, as for a long time their more intellectual brethren were, and jazz is their child. They furnish a wealth of colorful, distinctive material for any artist because they still hold their own individuality in the face of American standardizations. And perhaps these common people will give to the world its truly great Negro artist, the one who is not afraid to be himself. Whereas the better-class Negro would tell the artist what to do, the people at least let him alone when he does appear. And they are not ashamed of him—if they know he exists at all. And they accept what beauty is their own without question.

Certainly there is, for the American Negro artist who can escape the restrictions the more advanced among his own group would put upon him, a great field of unused material ready for his art. Without going outside his race, and even among the better classes with their "white" culture and conscious American manners, but still Negro enough to be different, there is sufficient matter to furnish a black artist with a lifetime of creative work. And when he chooses to touch on the relations between Negroes and whites in this country with their innumerable overtones and undertones surely, and especially for literature and the drama, there is an inexhaustible supply of themes at hand. To these the Negro artist can give his racial individuality, his heritage of rhythm and warmth, and his incongruous humor that so often, as in the Blues, becomes ironic laughter mixed with tears. But let us look again at the mountain.

A prominent Negro clubwoman in Philadelphia paid eleven dollars to hear Raquel Meller sing Andalusian popular songs. But she told me a few weeks before she would not think of going to hear "that woman," Clara Smith, a great black artist, sing Negro folksongs. And many an upper-class Negro church, even now, would not dream of employing a spiritual in its services. The drab melodies in white folks' hymnbooks are much to be preferred. "We want to worship the Lord correctly and quietly. We don't believe in 'shouting.' Let's be dull like the Nordics," they say, in effect.

The road for the serious black artist, then, who would produce a racial art is most certainly rocky and the mountain is high. Until recently he received almost no encouragement for his work from either white or colored people. The fine novels of Chesnutt go out of print with neither race noticing their passing. The quaint charm and humor of Dunbar's dialect verse brought to him, in his day, largely the same kind of encouragement one would give a sideshow freak (A colored man writing poetry! How odd!) or a clown (How amusing!).

The present vogue in things Negro, although it may do as much harm as good for the budding colored artist, has at least done this: it has brought him forcibly to the attention of his own people among whom for so long, unless the other race had noticed him beforehand, he was a prophet with little honor. I understand that Charles Gilpin acted for years in Negro theaters without any special acclaim from his own, but when Broadway gave him eight curtain calls, Negroes, too, began to beat a tin pan in his honor. I know a young colored writer, a manual worker by day, who had been writing well for the colored magazines for some years, but it was not until he recently broke into the white publications and his first book was accepted by a prominent New York publisher that the "best" Negroes in his city took the trouble to discover that he lived there. Then almost immediately they decided to give a grand dinner for him. But the society ladies were careful to whisper to his mother that perhaps she'd better not come. They were not sure she would have an evening gown.

The Negro artist works against an undertow of sharp criticism and misunderstanding from his own group and unintentional bribes from the whites. "Oh, be respectable, write about nice people, show how good we are," say the Negroes. "Be stereotyped, don't go too far, don't shatter our illusions about you, don't amuse us too seriously. We will pay you," say the whites. Both would have told Jean Toomer not to write *Cane*. The colored people did not praise it. The white people did not buy it. Most of the colored people who did read *Cane* hate it. They are afraid of it. Although the critics gave it good reviews the public remained indifferent. Yet (excepting the work of Du Bois) *Cane* contains the finest prose written by a Negro in America. And like the singing of Robeson, it is truly racial.

But in spite of the Nordicized Negro intelligentsia and the desires of some white editors we have an honest American Negro literature already with us. Now I await the rise of the Negro theater. Our folk music, having achieved world-wide fame, offers itself to the genius of the great individual American composer who is to come. And within the next decade I expect to see the work of a growing school of colored artists who paint and model the beauty of dark faces and create with new technique the expressions of their own soul-world. And the Negro dancers who will dance like flame and the singers who will continue to carry our songs to all who listen—they will be with us in even greater numbers tomorrow.

Most of my own poems are racial in theme and treatment, derived from the life I know. In many of them I try to grasp and hold some of the meanings and rhythms of jazz. I am as sincere as I know how to be in these poems and yet after every reading I answer questions like these from my own people: Do you think Negroes should always write about Negroes? I wish you wouldn't read some of your poems to white folks. How do you find anything interesting in a place like a cabaret? Why do you write about black people? You aren't black. What makes you do so many jazz poems?

But jazz to me is one of the inherent expressions of Negro life in America; the eternal tom-tom beating in the Negro soul—the tom-tom of revolt against weariness in a white world, a world of subway trains, and work, work, work; the tom-tom of joy and laughter, and pain swallowed in a smile. Yet the Philadelphia club-woman is ashamed to say that her race created it and she does not like me to write about it. The old subconscious "white is best" runs through her mind. Years of study under white teachers, a lifetime of white books, pictures, and papers, and white manners, morals, and Puritan standards made her dislike the spirituals. And now she turns up her nose at jazz and all its manifestations—likewise almost everything else distinctly racial. She doesn't care for the Winold Reiss portraits of Negroes because they are "too Negro." She does not want a true picture of herself from anybody. She wants the artist to flatter her, to make the white world believe that all Negroes are as smug and as near white in soul as she wants to be. But, to my mind, it is the duty of the younger Negro artist, if he accepts any duties at all from outsiders, to change through the force of his art that old whispering "I want to be white," hidden in the aspirations of his people, to "Why should I want to be white? I am a Negro—and beautiful".

So I am ashamed for the black poet who says, "I want to be a poet, not a Negro poet," as though his own racial world were not as interesting as any other world. I am ashamed, too, for the colored artist who runs from the painting of Negro faces to the painting of sunsets after the manner of the academicians because he fears the strange un-whiteness of his own features. An artist must be free to choose what he does, certainly, but he must also never be afraid to do what he might choose.

Let the blare of Negro jazz bands and the bellowing voice of Bessie Smith singing Blues penetrate the closed ears of the colored near-intellectuals until they listen and perhaps understand. Let Paul Robeson singing "Water Boy," and Rudolph Fisher writing about the streets of Harlem, and Jean Toomer holding the heart of Georgia in his hands, and Aaron Douglas drawing strange black fantasies cause the smug Negro middle class to turn from their white, respectable, ordinary books and papers to catch a glimmer of their own beauty. We younger Negro artists who create now intend to express our individual dark-skinned selves without fear or shame. If white people are pleased we are glad. If they are not, it doesn't matter. We know we are beautiful. And ugly too. The tom-tom cries and the tom-tom laughs. If colored people are pleased we are glad. If they are not, their displeasure doesn't matter either. We build our temples for tomorrow, strong as we know how, and we stand on top of the mountain, free within ourselves.

Gwendolyn Brooks, "The New Black: The Field of the Fever. The Time of the Tall-Walkers," from *Report from Part One* (1972)

Everybody has to go to the bathroom.
That's good.
That's a great thing.

If by some quirk of fate blacks had to go to the bathroom and whites didn't I shudder to think of the genocidal horrors that would be visited on the blacks of the whole world. Here is what my little green *Webster's New World* has to say about a world-shaking word:

black (blak), adj. (A S *blaec*) 1. opposite to white: see color. 2. dark-complexioned. 3. Negro. 4. without light; dark. 5. dirty. 6. evil; wicked. 7. sad; dismal. 8. sullen.

n.1. black pigment; opposite of white. 2. dark clothing, as for mourning. 3. a Negro. v.t.&v.i., to blacken.—black-out, to lose consciousness.—blackly, adv:—blackness, n.

Interestingly enough, we do not find that "white" is "opposite of black." That would "lift" black to the importance-level of white.

white (hwit), adj. (A S hwit). 1. having the color of pure snow or milk. 2. of a light or pale color. 3. pale; wan. 4. pure; innocent. 5. having a light-colored skin. n. 1. the color of pure snow or milk. 2. a white or light-colored thing, as the albumen of an egg, the white part of the eyeball, etc. 3. a person with a light-colored skin; Caucasian.—whiteness, n.

Until 1967 my own blackness did not confront me with a shrill spelling of itself. I knew that I was what most people were calling "a Negro"; I called myself that, although always the word fell awkwardly on a poet's ear; I had never liked the sound of it (Caucasian has an ugly sound, too, while the name Indian is beautiful to look at and to hear). *And* I knew that people of my coloration and distinctive history had been bolted to trees and sliced or burned or shredded; knocked to the back of the line; provided with separate toilets, schools, neighborhoods; denied, when possible, voting rights; hounded, hooted at, or shunned, or patronizingly patted (often the patting-hand was, I knew, surreptitiously wiped after the Kindness, so that unspeakable contamination might be avoided). America's social climate, it seemed, was trying to tell me something. It was trying to tell me something Websterian. Yet, although almost secretly, I had always felt that to be black was good. Sometimes, there would be an approximate whisper around me: *others* felt, it seemed, that to be black was good. The translation would have been something like "Hey—being black is *fun*." Or something like "Hey—our folks have got stuff to be proud of!" Or something like "Hey—since we are so good why aren't we treated like the other 'Americans'?"

Suddenly there was New Black to meet. In the spring of 1967 I met some of it at the Fisk University Writers' Conference in Nashville. Coming from white white white South Dakota State College I arrived in Nashville, Tennessee, to give one more "reading." But blood-boiling surprise was in store for me. First, I was aware of a general energy, an electricity, in look, walk, speech, *gesture* of the young blackness I saw all about me. I had been "loved" at South Dakota State College. Here, I was coldly Respected. Here, the heroes included the novelist-director, John Killens, editors David Llorens and Hoyt Fuller, playwright Ron Milner, historians John Henrik Clarke and Lerone Bennett (and even poor Lerone was taken to task, by irate members of a no-nonsense young audience, for affiliating himself with *Ebony Magazine*, considered at that time a traitor for allowing skin-bleach advertisements in its pages, and for over-featuring light-skinned women). Imamu Amiri Baraka, then "LeRoi Jones," was expected. He arrived in the middle of my own offering, and when I called attention to his presence there was jubilee in Jubilee Hall.

All that day and night, Margaret Danner Cunningham—another Old Girl, another coldly Respected old Has-been—and an almost hysterical Gwendolyn B. walked about in amazement, listening, looking, learning. *What was going on!*

In my cartoon basket I keep a cartoon of a stout, dowager-hatted, dowager-furred Helen Hokinson woman. She is on parade in the world. She is a sign-carrier in the wild world. Her sign says "Will someone please tell me what is going on?" Well, although I cannot give a full-blooded answer to that potent question, I have been supplied—the sources are plural—with helpful materials: hints, friendly *and* inimical clues, approximations, statistics, "proofs" of one kind and another; from these I am trying to weave the coat that I shall wear. In 1967's Nashville, however, the somewhat dotty expression in the eyes of the cartoon-woman, the *agapeness*, were certainly mine. I was in some inscrutable and uncomfortable wonderland. I didn't know what to make of what surrounded me, of what with hot sureness began almost immediately to invade me. *I* had never been, before, in the general presence of such insouciance, such live firmness, such confident vigor, such determination to mold or carve something DEFINITE.

Up against the wall, white man! was the substance of the Baraka shout, at the evening reading he shared with fierce Ron Milner among intoxicating drum-beats, heady incense and organic underhumming. Up against the wall! And a pensive (until that moment) white man of thirty or thirty three abruptly shot himself into the heavy air, screaming "Yeah! *Yeah!* Up against the wall, Brother! KILL 'EM ALL! KILL 'EM *ALL!*"

I thought that was interesting.

There is indeed a new black today. He is different from any the world has known. He's a tall-walker. Almost firm. By many of his own *brothers* he is not understood. And he is understood by *no* white. Not the wise white; not the Schooled white; not the Kind white. Your *least* pre-requisite toward an understanding of the new black is an exceptional Doctorate which can be conferred only upon those with the proper properties of bitter birth and intrinsic sorrow. I know this is infuriating, especially to those professional Negro-understanders, some of them so *very* kind, with special portfolio, special savvy. But I cannot say anything other, because nothing other is the truth.

I—who have "gone the gamut" from an almost angry rejection of my dark skin by some of my brainwashed brothers and sisters to a surprised queenhood in the new black sun—am qualified to enter at least the kindergarten of new consciousness now. New consciousness and trudge-toward-progress.

I have hopes for myself.

Student Essay

In this essay, a student gives her view of Langston Hughes and his work and times.

Nicole Halabuda
English 102-EN
Prof. Barnard
Essay #4

Harlem's Hughes

During the years 1902 to 1920 Langston Hughes lived in many different places such as: Missouri, Kansas, Illinois, Ohio and Mexico. In 1921, Hughes found himself in New York City attending Columbia University, the place where his literary career was launched. He committed himself to writing after the success of his first poem, "The Negro Speaks of Rivers." He left Columbia in 1922 and traveled abroad, and during this time and for the rest of his life Hughes continued to write. During his career he wrote numerous poems, plays and books. Most of his work emphasized lower-class black life. The two poems I have chosen to discuss are "Mother to Son" and "Cross." Both poems speak of his family, particularly his parents.

Hughes wrote his poem "Mother to Son" in 1922. The first line reads "Well, son, I'll tell you," and from the title and the first line it's obvious this poem represents the mother speaking to the son, though whether this comes from Hughes's own experience, we can't be sure. The poem continues and the mother tells the son how her life has not been a "crystal stair"; she says it's been wearing and is very treacherous. Using the metaphor "crystal stair" I think she is speaking of her life and the so-called path she has walked. By saying it has not been a "crystal stair" she's implying that her "path" has not been an easy, care-free life. Although her "stairs" have been beaten and bare, she never stopped climbing. Then she says that

Halabuda 2

she's proceeded to climb and reached landings, turned corners and sometimes she would even climb when she could not see. The mother then tells the son that he should never stop climbing his stairs, because she is still climbing hers, and her life has "been no crystal stair." Her description of the stairs is a metaphor for the troubles in her life. If you picture yourself starting at the bottom of stairs when you're born, then as you grow you would climb the stairs. With every new year or new day—however you look at it—you would ascend another stair. If your stairs happen to be crystal they would be easy and possibly enjoyable to climb, but if they're torn like she says hers are, they would be very difficult to climb. The splinters represent obstacles in her life. Even though her stairs were not easy to climb she still continued to climb them. Therefore, she overcame the obstacles in her path. Then when she tells Hughes to never stop climbing, she's saying that if she could do it so could he. When she repeats that her life has not been a crystal stair, I believe that she thinks his stairs are much better and easier to climb than hers were. So, if she can climb these rickety, ragged stairs, then he certainly can climb his and he best not stop. This poem is her advising and encouraging her son, just like the advice and encouragement most parents give their children today.

Langston Hughes wrote his poem entitled "Cross" in 1925. This is another poem involving his mother, but this time it also includes his father. This poem discusses the difficulty of being biracial in the 1920's. In the first stanza he says his "old man's a white old man" and his "old mother's black," which right away reveals he is biracial. "Old man" is a sarcastic nickname for father. He continues to say that, if he ever cursed his father or mother, that he now takes the curses back. In the second stanza he says he takes the curses

Halabuda 3

from his mother *and* wishes her well, but with his father he only takes back his curses. Then in the third stanza he explains that his father "died in a fine big house, my ma died in a shack." He then wonders where he will die, because he is neither black nor white, since his parents were of two different races. I think that Hughes has some resentment for his father, because if his father died in a house and his mother died in a shack, then obviously they did not live in the same place. Due to the discrimination at the time, his mother was not able to live in a nice house like his father. I see his resentment when he only takes his curses from his father and does not have any well wishes for him. He still takes the curses back out of respect for his father and his death. He seems to be sorrier that he ever cursed his mother because she cared for him and did not leave him like his father did. Then he wonders where he will die, because maybe by the time of his passing, discrimination will be a thing of the past. When Hughes wrote this poem, he was only twenty-three and he probably figured his death was at least forty years off. If there is still the same discrimination by that time, he wonders where he will die because he is both white and black; which side would take precedence?

Just by reading these two poems, it's obvious that at only the age of twenty, Langston Hughes was a very talented young poet. It's no wonder that he became as well known as he did. Today he is a very celebrated poet, and in February of 2002 he appeared on a stamp honoring African Americans for "Black History Month." Langston Hughes passed away in 1967, while living in a nice house that he purchased in Harlem. After all his success, I guess he took his mother's advice and continued to climb to the very top of his staircase.

Q U E S T I O N S

TO ASK ABOUT POETRY

Many concepts mentioned below have not yet been explained in this book. You will find useful discussions of them in the coming chapters, and you may find yourself looking back at this list of "Questions to Ask about Poetry" as you study and write about the poems in later chapters. We suggest putting a sticky note or a paper clip on this page so you can refer to it again and again.

1. Whose voice is speaking? Can you identify the speaker of the poem? Or, is the identity of the speaker ambiguous or veiled? Is the voice of the speaker addressing us in the present time, or is the speaker looking back to a past time? Is there a mix of time periods?

2. What is the nature of the speaker's voice? Does the poet use diction, word choice, or particular devices of sound to help reveal the speaker's character? Is the diction casual and conversational, speaking to us in the vernacular? Is it a more formal or distant voice? What is the level of diction the writer has chosen to use?

3. What choices has the poet made about the form of the poem? Is it a fixed-form poem or an open-form poem? Has the poet used word order or line breaks to help achieve the poem's effects?

4. Does the poet employ figurative language such as metaphor, simile, personfication, or hyperbole? Does the poet use imagery (language which appeals to the senses) to help reveal meaning?

5. What devices of sound does the poem employ (alliteration, assonance, etc.)? Does the poem make use of end rhyme, internal rhyme, or near rhyme? Can you identify a metrical pattern in the poem? Does it have a rhythm? If so, is the rhythm evoked through meter or through other devices?

6. Is irony an aspect of theme in the poem? What types of irony are present? Are there any allegorical or symbolic objects, images, characters, or events which seem to represent larger meanings, in addition to their literal significance in the poem? Does the title of the poem assist in revealing theme?

7. Does the poem contain any allusions to mythology, religious scriptures, or popular culture? Do these allusions enrich or help to reveal the poem's themes?

8. Can you characterize a particular tone in the poem? Does the tone change? How is tone revealed in the poem?

9. How do the various elements of the poem work together to reveal themes?

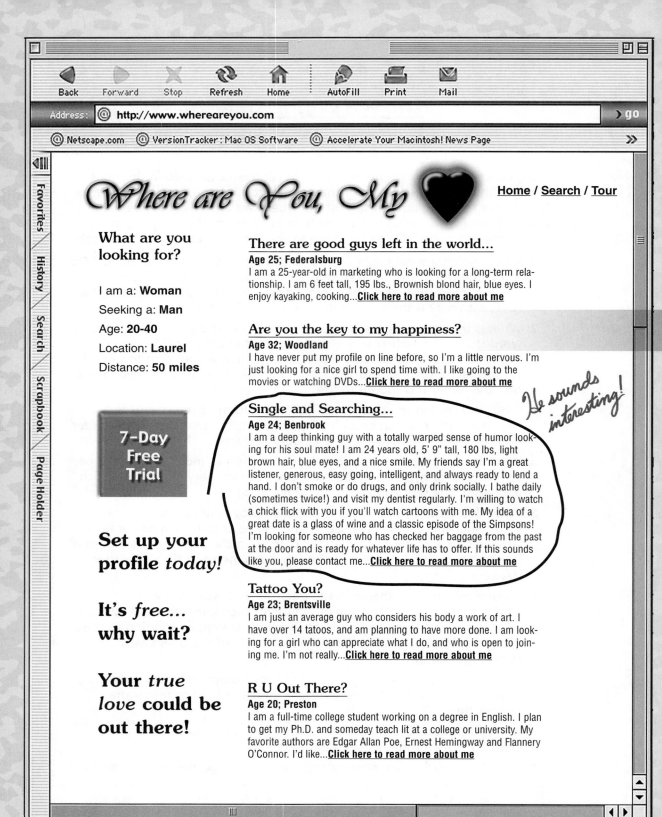

WORD CHOICE, WORD ORDER, AND TONE

Even personal ads use word choice, word order, and tone. The individual sitting at his or her computer to compose an ad for the personals section may not be a poet, but he or she is bound to be choosing words carefully. As the writer's hands hover over the keyboard, composing a personal profile attention is given to each and every word. *If, say I'm "down-to-earth and stable," will she think I'm boring?* or *If I say I'm "smart and sexy," will he think I'm too forward?* The writer is attentive to the connotations as well as the denotations of words (explanations to follow), just as the poet is. The writer might use word order and repeated constructions to establish a rhythm: "sweet, sexy, smart," "affectionate and attentive." The writer of a personal ad strives for the right tone. *If I say "I'm a deep thinking guy with a totally warped sense of humor," will she think I'm funny or will she think I have a screw loose? If sat "I'm ready to take care of you if you'll take care of me!! Let's go out and set the town on fire!" will he think I'm fun and call me, or will he think my tone is bossy?* Although we may not consider ourselves poets, we think about matters of word choice, word order, and tone in performing many everyday writing tasks.

You may never have written a personal ad, but you surely have worked hard sometimes to find the right words. Have you ever found yourself staring at the phone, trying to plan what you were going to say to the person on the other end of the line? Have you ever found yourself sitting in front of the computer, trying to write a difficult email message to a friend, a co-worker, a supervisor? We all struggle to find the right words sometimes—in speaking as well as in writing— but finding just the right words is the poet's life work. Native American writer Diane Glancy says this about the importance of choosing words:

> Isn't writing thinking? Aren't our lives made up of words? The ability to write clearly is the ability to think clearly. . . . Externalizing the thought process. Finding form for content. Using language for creative, expressive purposes. The revelation of words, their boldness, the imaginative impact of combined images, of seeing the familiar in a new way. That's what writing is. That's what living is. (from *Claiming Breath*)

In poetry more than any other type of writing, language is at the center of what's happening, and the poet's choice of words—*of every single word*—is crucial to meaning.

Denotative and connotative meanings

Meanings of words are themselves complex. Every word in a language has a **denotative** meaning, that is, the meaning or meanings as stated in a dictionary of that language. Many words have **connotative** meanings as well. The connotative meaning of a word has to do with the associations that word calls up in our minds, and these associations may range far afield from the actual denotative meaning of the word. The following poem by Puerto Rican–American poet Judith Ortiz Cofer describes the alternating journeys and homecomings that are the actual experience of the sailor and his family, but the poem is rich with connotative, or suggested, meanings as well.

Judith Ortiz Cofer (b. 1952)
My Father in the Navy: A Childhood Memory (1982)

Stiff and immaculate
in the white cloth of his uniform
and a round cap on his head like a halo,
he was an apparition on leave from a shadow-world
and only flesh and blood when he rose from below   5
the waterline where he kept watch over the engines
and dials making sure the ship parted the waters

on a straight course.
Mother, brother and I kept vigil
on the nights and dawns of his arrivals,   10
watching the corner beyond the neon sign of a quasar
for the flash of white our father like an angel
heralding a new day.
His homecomings were the verses
we composed over the years making up   15
the siren's song that kept him coming back
from the bellies of iron whales
and into our nights
like the evening prayer.

The cap "like a halo" in line 3, the "father like an angel" in line 12, and the mention of prayer, which ends the poem, all work to make the father seem almost holy and also might suggest an appeal to a higher power to protect him. In any case, here the use of "halo" and "prayer" suggests luminous and positive connotations. Words like "tyrant" or "devil" or even "cloven-hoofed," on the other hand, have negative connotations or associations beyond their dictionary definitions.

Words can have different connotations depending on their context. For instance, if we write, "Over the battlefield, a hush fell, and soon the large birds began to circle above," then the word "birds" certainly has a negative and menacing connotation. If, however, we write, "Her heart rose up like a bird riding the thermals when she saw the valley she once called home," the word "bird" has positive connotations. Cofer's poem is also rich in allusions, or **allusive** meanings, because elements of the poem may remind some readers of a familiar image or story from literature, myths, legends, or scriptures. In "My Father in the Navy," there are a number of allusions to the *Odyssey*—to the journeys, dangers, and homecoming of Homer's legendary hero. In line 17, there is also a Biblical allusion: "the bellies of iron whales" may remind many readers of the story of Jonah's captivity in the belly of the whale and his reluctant journey to Nineveh.

Who's Talking?—The Speaker of the Poem

Another thing that influences the poet's choice of words in a poem is the nature and perspective of the **speaker**. The speaker of the poem is the equivalent of the narrator of a work of fiction. Just as the narrator is not necessarily the author, the speaker of the poem does not necessarily represent the poet but can, instead, be an imagined voice. Who is the speaker of the poem? Whose voice are we hearing when we read it? From whose perspective is the poem spoken? In Cofer's poem, we recognize the voice of an adult speaker looking back on a childhood experience. The adult voice looks back in a thoughtful and searching way, in an almost reverent tone, as she tries to describe the nature of the experience as the child of a sailor. In contrast, the speaker of Robert Browning's "My Last Duchess" (see below) is the Duke, who doesn't go in much for soul searching or reverence but is more accustomed to command. Careful word choice allows the poet, through the Duke's own words, to make a chilling revelation about his last marriage, even as the listener (or reader) recognizes that he's planning to marry again.

Robert Browning (1812–1889)
My Last Duchess (1842)

Ferrara
That's my last Duchess painted on the wall,
Looking as if she were alive. I call
That piece a wonder, now: Frà Pandolf's[1] hands
Worked busily a day, and there she stands.   5
Will't please you sit and look at her? I said
"Frà Pandolf" by design, for never read
Strangers like you that pictured countenance,
The depth and passion of its earnest glance,
But to myself they turned (since none puts by   10
The curtain I have drawn for you, but I)
And seemed as they would ask me, if they durst,
How such a glance came there; so, not the first
Are you to turn and ask thus. Sir, 'twas not
Her husband's presence only, called that spot   15
Of joy into the Duchess' cheek: perhaps
Frà Pandolf chanced to say "Her mantle laps
Over my lady's wrist too much," or "Paint
Must never hope to reproduce the faint
Half-flush that dies along her throat": such stuff   20
Was courtesy, she thought, and cause enough
For calling up that spot of joy. She had
A heart—how shall I say?—too soon made glad,
Too easily impressed; she liked whate'er
She looked on, and her looks went everywhere.   25
Sir, 'twas all one! My favor at her breast,
The dropping of the daylight in the West,
The bough of cherries some officious fool
Broke in the orchard for her, the white mule
She rode with round the terrace—all and each   30

---

[1]**Frà Pandolf:** "Brother" Pandolf, a fictive painter.

Would draw from her alike the approving speech,
Or blush, at least. She thanked men—good! but thanked
Somehow—I know not how—as if she ranked
My gift of a nine-hundred-years-old name
With anybody's gift. Who'd stoop to blame   35
This sort of trifling? Even had you skill
In speech—(which I have not)—to make your will
Quite clear to such an one, and say, "Just this
Or that in you disgusts me; here you miss,
Or there exceed the mark"—and if she let   40
Herself be lessoned so, nor plainly set
Her wits to yours, forsooth, and made excuse
—E'en then would be some stooping; and I choose
Never to stoop. Oh sir, she smiled, no doubt,
Whene'er I passed her; but who passed without   45
Much the same smile? This grew; I gave commands;
Then all smiles stopped together. There she stands
As if alive. Will't please you rise? We'll meet
The company below, then. I repeat,
The Count your master's known munificence   50
Is ample warrant that no just pretense
Of mine for dowry will be disallowed;
Though his fair daughter's self, as I avowed
At starting, is my object. Nay, we'll go
Together down, sir. Notice Neptune,[2] though,   55
Taming a sea horse, thought a rarity,
Which Claus of Innsbruck[3] cast in bronze for me!

---

[2]**Neptune:** The God of the sea.
[3]**Claus of Innsbruck:** An imaginary—or unidentified—sculptor. The Count of Tyrol's capital was at Innsbruck, Austria.

Levels of Diction

Depending on who the speaker of the poem is, the poet might choose to use a certain level of **diction**. We can speak of formal diction, middle diction, informal diction, and mixed diction as ways of discussing different levels of formality or informality in the use of language. For instance, Browning's Duke, in "My Last Duchess," speaks in formal diction, using such words as "countenance" and "munificence." The poem also contains some archaic (old-fashioned or out-of-date) diction (like "'twas" and "durst") since it was written in 1842. On the other hand, a well-known poem written by Gwendolyn Brooks, "We Real Cool" (next page), is an example of informal diction, both in terms of its vocabulary and its grammar.

Gwendolyn Brooks (1917–2000)
We Real Cool (1960)

       The Pool Players.
   Seven at the Golden Shovel.

We real cool. We
Left school. We

Lurk late. We   5
Strike straight. We

Sing sin. We
Thin gin. We

Jazz June. We
Die soon.   10

    The poem below written by Ana Castillo is largely in middle diction—though we might want to say that it contains mixed diction since there are also some words or phrases which might be called informal or even slang.

Ana Castillo (b. 1953)
We Would Like You to Know (1995)

We would like you to know
we are not all
docile
nor revolutionaries
but we are all survivors.   5
We do not all carry
zip guns, hot pistols,
steal cars.
We do know how
to defend ourselves.   10

We do not all have
slicked-back hair
distasteful apparel
unpolished shoes
although the economy   15
doesn't allow everyone
a Macy's chargecard.

We do not all pick
lettuce, run
assembly lines, clean   20
restaurant tables, even
if someone has to do it.

We do not all sneak
under barbed wire or
wade the Rio Grande.   25

These are the facts.
We would like you to know
we are not all brown.
Genetic history has made
some of us blue eyed as any   30
German immigrant
and as black as a descendant
of an African slave.
We never claimed to be
a homogeneous race.   35

We are not all victims,
all loyal to one cause,
all perfect; it is a
psychological dilemma
no one has resolved.   40

We would like to give
a thousand excuses
as to why we all find
ourselves in a predicament
residents of a controversial   45
power
how we were all caught
with our pants down
and how petroleum was going
to change all that but   50
you've heard it all before and
with a wink and a snicker
left us babbling among
ourselves.
We would like you to know   55
guilt or apologetic gestures
won't revive the dead

redistribute the land
or natural resources.
We are left   60
with one final resolution
in our own predestined way,
we are going forward.
There is no going back.

In Castillo's poem, the words "docile" and "distasteful" would be examples of middle diction, whereas the words "zip gun," "slicked-back hair," and "charge-card" are informal. The level of diction helps set the tone of the poem, and it is also one means the poet has of characterizing the speaker.

Word Choice

The concepts just discussed also relate to the larger matter of **word choice**. Through all of the above techniques—and for all of the above reasons—the poet chooses words carefully to convey meaning in compact and effective ways. The following lyric comes from a collection of Sanskrit poetry compiled by the Indian poet Vidyākara around the year 1100. The original poet, Manovinoda, may have lived in the 10th or 11th century, though some scholars believe he lived earlier as early as the eighth century. Kāma is the Hindu god of love.

Manovinoda (c. 10th Century)
Kāma (324)

Shot from a stretched eyebrow-bow;
more beautiful than bees on waterlilies,
and swift as spotted antelope;
with pupils for their cruel tips to pierce the hearts of men;
feathered with the long angle of an eye   5
and hurtful with smiling venom:
may these, a woman's sidelong glances from thick lashes,
these hero-quelling, world-subduing arrows
of the five-arrowed god, protect you.

This lyric poem was originally written in Sanskrit, the ancient language of India. It is compact and emotionally expressive, and it achieves its effect partly through careful word choice. In the first line, the poet manages to suggest that the eyes of the beloved shoot arrows of love, without saying so explicitly. We get the idea instead through the reference to the "eyebrow-bow," an example of the poet's careful word choice. Also interesting here is the kinetic effect (a sense of motion) achieved with the words "bees," "swift," and "pierce." The word "feathered," on the other hand, conveys the image of soft eyelashes in a compact and visual way, with a single, carefully chosen word. And the poet makes a rather surprising connection between the pupils of the human eye, the spots on an antelope, and the sight of "bees on waterlilies," a comparison also achieved through careful word choice.

Words can also be chosen deliberately by the poet to convey **ambiguity**, or a double meaning. In Henry Reed's poem "Naming of Parts" (below), an intentional double meaning is developed through the use of such words as "spring," "parts," and "backwards and forwards." While the drill instructor explains the use of the rifle, the young recruit is thinking about spring happening all around him, about the birds and the bees.

Henry Reed (b. 1914)
Naming of Parts (1946)

Today we have naming of parts. Yesterday,
We had daily cleaning. And tomorrow morning,
We shall have what to do after firing. But today,
Today we have naming of parts. Japonica*
Glistens like coral in all of the neighboring gardens,   5
      And today we have naming of parts.

This is the lower sling swivel. And this
Is the upper sling swivel, whose use you will see,
When you are given your slings. And this is the piling swivel,
Which in your case you have not got. The branches   10
Hold in the gardens their silent, eloquent gestures,
      Which in our case we have not got.

This is the safety-catch, which is always released
With an easy flick of the thumb. And please do not let me
See anyone using his finger. You can do it quite easy   15
If you have any strength in your thumb. The blossoms
Are fragile and motionless, never letting anyone see
      Any of them using their finger.

And this you can see is the bolt. The purpose of this
Is to open the breech, as you see. We can slide it   20
Rapidly backwards and forwards: we call this

***Japonica:** A shrub having waxy flowers in a variety of colors.

Easing the spring. And rapidly backwards and forwards
The early bees are assaulting and fumbling the flowers:
    They call it easing the Spring.

They call it easing the Spring: it is perfectly easy   25
If you have any strength in your thumb: like the bolt,
And the breech, and the cocking-piece, and the point of balance,
Which in our case we have not got; and the almond-blossom
Silent in all of the gardens and the bees going backwards and forwards,
    For today we have naming of parts.   30

Word Order

In addition, **word order** can contribute to the rhythm of a poem as well as to its meaning. In Gwendolyn Brooks's "We Real Cool" (above), so much would be lost if the poet had used a more conventional, more predictable word order—if she had begun each line with the word "We," instead of placing most of these at the ends of her lines. Look for other ways in which these poets use word choice and word order to enhance sound, rhythm, and meaning.

A poet who is rather well-known for his innovative use of word choice and word order, as well as punctuation and other mechanics of the language, is e.e. cummings. This poet also preferred to have his name represented in lower-case letters. His poem "in Just-" is an example of the deliberate use of word order to convey meaning in the poem. How does the unusual form of the poem reflect the poet's themes here?

e.e. cummings (1894–1962)
in Just- (1923)

in Just-
spring when the world is mud-
luscious the little
lame balloonman
whistles   far   and wee   5

and eddieandbill come
running from marbles and
piracies and it's
spring

when the world is puddle-wonderful   10
the queer
old balloonman whistles
far   and   wee
and bettyandisbel come dancing

from hop-scotch and jump-rope and   15

it's
spring
and
    the
         goat-footed   20

balloonMan   whistles
far
and
wee

What's the Tone—Sad? Sarcastic? Pathetic? Playful?

Tone (also discussed in Chapter 7) is often defined as the author's attitude toward the subject, and this is a good, practical definition. So now we need to ask, *How* is the author's attitude toward the subject conveyed to the reader? What might lead us to describe the tone of "in Just-," for instance, as playful? Word choice and word order can certainly contribute to our sense of the speaker's tone in a poem. In cummings's playful poem, the words are scattered across the page, just as the children scatter across the playground at the end of winter, and just as the marbles are scattered across the ground. The innovative use of word choice and word order in cummings's made-up words such as "mud-luscious," "puddle-wonderful," and even "eddieandbill" also contribute to the fanciful tone of the poem.

Word choice can be used as a way of establishing tone in a poem, and it can also be used as a means of shifting the tone. Several poems in this chapter illustrate the interesting results that can be achieved by the coordinated effects of word choice, word order, and tone.

In "Flower Feet" (next) Ruth Fainlight uses careful word choice at the outset of the poem to establish a tone that conveys wonder, praise, and admiration for the beautiful details of the tiny shoes.

Ruth Fainlight (b. 1931)
Flower Feet (1989)

(SILK SHOES IN THE WHITWORTH ART GALLERY, MANCHESTER, ENGLAND)

Real women's feet wore these objects
that look like toys or spectacle cases stitched
from bands of coral, jade, and apricot silk
embroidered with twined sprays of flowers.
Those hearts, tongues, crescents, and disks, leather   5
shapes an inch across, are the soles of shoes
no wider or longer than the span of my ankle.
If the feet had been cut off and the raw stumps
thrust inside the openings, surely
it could not hurt more than broken toes, twisted   10
back and bandaged tight. An old woman,
leaning on a cane outside her door
in a Chinese village, smiled to tell how
she fought and cried, how when she stood on points
of pain that gnawed like fire, nurse and mother   15
praised her tottering walk on flower feet.
Her friends nodded, glad the times had changed.
Otherwise, they would have crippled their daughters.

In line 8, however, the tone abruptly shifts, and this shift is also accomplished through careful word choice. The beautiful images of lines 1–7 are suddenly replaced with violent images called up by such words and phrases as "raw stumps," "broken," "twisted," and "bandaged." The dramatic shift in tone serves the poet's purposes thematically—in other words, it increases the emotional power of Fainlight's point about the maiming of women's feet.

Maxine Kumin's "Woodchucks" uses the same techniques to establish and then shift the tone of the poem for thematic reasons.

Maxine Kumin (b. 1925)
Woodchucks (1972)

Gassing the woodchucks didn't turn out right.
The knockout bomb from the Feed and Grain Exchange
was featured as merciful, quick at the bone
and the case we had against them was airtight,
both exits shoehorned shut with puddingstone,*   5
but they had a sub-sub-basement out of range.

***puddingstone:** A mixture of cement, pebbles, and gravel.

Next morning they turned up again, no worse
for the cyanide than we for our cigarettes
and state-store Scotch, all of us up to scratch.
They brought down the marigolds as a matter of course   10
and then took over the vegetable patch
nipping the broccoli shoots, beheading the carrots.

The food from our mouths, I said, righteously thrilling
to the feel of the .22, the bullets' neat noses.
I, a lapsed pacifist falling from grace   15
puffed with Darwinian pieties for killing,
now drew a bead on the littlest woodchuck's face.
He died down in the everbearing roses.

Ten minutes later I dropped the mother. She
flipflopped in the air and fell, her needle teeth   20
still hooked in a leaf of early Swiss chard.
Another baby next. O one-two-three
the murderer inside me rose up hard,
the hawkeye killer came on stage forthwith.

There's one chuck left. Old wily fellow, he keeps   25
me cocked and ready day after day after day.
All night I hunt his humped-up form. I dream
I sight along the barrel in my sleep.
If only they'd all consented to die unseen
gassed underground the quiet Nazi way.   30

Juxtaposition and Contrast

In addition to these techniques, the second half of "Woodchucks"—after the tonal shift—provides many examples of the use of **juxtaposition** (the placing of different, often contrasting, images or words close together). Kumin deliberately gives the reader a shock by putting together "pieties" and "killing," "died" and "in the everbearing roses," "baby" and "murderer."

In Matthew Arnold's "Dover Beach" (next), word choice and imagery are again used to establish and to shift the tone.

Matthew Arnold (1822–1888)

Dover Beach (1867)

The sea is calm tonight.
The tide is full, the moon lies fair
Upon the straits;—on the French coast the light
Gleams and is gone; the cliffs of England stand,
Glimmering and vast, out in the tranquil bay.   5
Come to the window, sweet is the night-air!
Only, from the long line of spray
Where the sea meets the moon-blanched[1] land,
Listen! you hear the grating roar
Of pebbles which the waves draw back, and fling,   10
At their return, up the high strand,[2]
Begin, and cease, and then again begin,
With tremulous cadence slow, and bring
The eternal note of sadness in.

Sophocles[3] long ago   15
Heard it on the Aegean,[4] and it brought
Into his mind the turbid ebb and flow
Of human misery; we
Find also in the sound a thought,
Hearing it by this distant northern sea.   20

The Sea of Faith
Was once, too, at the full, and round earth's shore
Lay like the folds of a bright girdle furled.
But now I only hear
Its melancholy, long, withdrawing roar,   25
Retreating, to the breath
Of the night-wind, down the vast edges drear
And naked shingles[5] of the world.

Ah, love, let us be true
To one another! for the world, which seems   30
To lie before us like a land of dreams,
So various, so beautiful, so new,
Hath really neither joy, nor love, nor light,
Nor certitude, nor peace, nor help for pain;

---

[1]**Moon-blanched:** Whitened by the moon.
[2]**Strand:** Beach.
[3]**Sophocles:** Greek playwright (496–406 B.C.), author of tragedies including *Oedipus Rex* and *Antigone*.
[4]**Aegean:** Sea between Greece and Turkey.
[5]**Shingles:** Gravel beaches.

And we are here as on a darkling[6] plain   35
Swept with confused alarms of struggle and flight,
Where ignorant armies clash by night.

In Andrew Marvell's "To His Coy Mistress," we can describe three distinct sections, each of which has a distinct tone and a different purpose in terms of revealing theme.

Andrew Marvell (1621–1678)
To His Coy Mistress (1681)

Had we but world enough, and time,
This coyness, lady, were no crime.
We would sit down, and think which way
To walk, and pass our long love's day.
Thou by the Indian Ganges' side   5
Shouldst rubies find; I by the tide
Of Humber would complain. I would
Love you ten years before the Flood,
And you should, if you please, refuse
Till the conversion of the Jews.   10
My vegetable love should grow
Vaster than empires, and more slow;
An hundred years should go to praise
Thine eyes, and on thy forehead gaze;
Two hundred to adore each breast,   15
But thirty thousand to the rest;
An age at least to every part,
And the last age should show your heart.
For, lady, you deserve this state,
Nor would I love at lower rate.   20
　　　But at my back I always hear
Time's wingèd chariot hurrying near;
And yonder all before us lie
Deserts of vast eternity.
Thy beauty shall no more be found,   25
Nor, in thy marble vault, shall sound
My echoing song; then worms shall try
That long-preserved virginity,
And your quaint honor turn to dust,
And into ashes all my lust: 30

---

[6]**darkling:** Darkening.

The grave's a fine and private place,
But none, I think, do there embrace.
    Now therefore, while the youthful hue
Sits on thy skin like morning dew,
And while thy willing soul transpires   35
At every pore with instant fires,
Now let us sport us while we may,
And now, like amorous birds of prey,
Rather at once our time devour
Than languish in his slow-chapped power.   40
Let us roll all our strength and all
Our sweetness up into one ball,
And tear our pleasures with rough strife
Thorough* the iron gates of life.
Thus, though we cannot make our sun   45
Stand still, yet we will make him run.

---

*Thorough: through

Which of the techniques that we've just discussed can you spot in Wendy Cope's "Lonely Hearts"?

Wendy Cope (b. 1945)
LONELY HEARTS (1986)

Can someone make my simple wish come true?
Male biker seeks female for touring fun.
Do you live in North London? Is it you?

Gay vegetarian whose friends are few,
I'm into music, Shakespeare and the sun,   5
Can someone make my simple wish come true?

Executive in search of something new—
Perhaps bisexual woman, arty, young.
Do you live in North London? Is it you?

Successful, straight and solvent? I am too—   10
Attractive Jewish lady with a son.
Can someone make my simple wish come true?

I'm Libran, inexperienced and blue—
Need slim non-smoker, under twenty-one.
Do you live in North London? Is it you?   15

Please write (with photo) to Box 152.
Who knows where it may lead once we've begun?
Can someone make my simple wish come true?
Do you live in North London? Is it you?

Poems for Further Reading

Leonard Adamé (b. 1947)
My Grandmother Would Rock Quietly and Hum (1973)

in her house
she would rock quietly and hum
until her swelled hands
calmed

in summer   5
she wore thick stockings
sweaters
and grey braids
(when "el cheque"[1] came
we went to Payless   10
and I laughed greedily
when given a quarter)

mornings,
sunlight barely lit
the kitchen   15
and where
there were shadows
it was not cold

she quietly rolled
flour tortillas—   20
the "papas"[2]
cracking in hot lard
would wake me

---

[1]**"el cheque"**: The check
[2]**"papas"**: Potatoes

she had lost her teeth
and when we ate   25
she had bread
soaked in "café"[3]

always her eyes
were clear
and she could see   30
as I cannot yet see—
through her eyes
she gave me herself

she would sit
and talk   35
of her girlhood—
of things strange to me:
    México
    epidemics
    relatives shot   40
    her father's hopes
    of this country—
how they sank
with cement dust
to his insides   45
now
when I go
to the old house
the worn spots
by the stove   50
echo of her shuffling
and
México
still hangs in her
fading   55
calendar pictures

·····➤ *Your* Turn

Talking and Writing about Lit

1. Discuss Leonard Adamé's use of careful word choice to reveal the cultural heritage of the speaker and his grandmother.

---

[3]**"café"**: Coffee

2. The poet uses line breaks (where the poet decides to break the line) to create
many short lines. Consider some of his one-word lines and discuss what the
poet gains by having a single word standing alone on a line.

3. **DIY**   Write a brief paragraph about a favorite activity of a family
member (for example, your child or sibling playing soccer). Then
use line breaks to make a poem out of your paragraph.

Li-Young Lee (b. 1957)
My Father, in Heaven, Is Reading Out Loud (1990)

My father, in heaven, is reading out loud
to himself Psalms or news. Now he ponders what
he's read. No. He is listening for the sound
of children in the yard. Was that laughing
or crying? So much depends upon the   5
answer, for either he will go on reading,
or he'll run to save a child's day from grief.
As it is in heaven, so it was on earth.

Because my father walked the earth with a grave,
determined rhythm, my shoulders ached   10
from his gaze. Because my father's shoulders
ached from the pulling of oars, my life now moves
with a powerful back-and-forth rhythm:
nostalgia, speculation. Because he
made me recite a book a month, I forget   15
everything as soon as I read it. And knowledge
never comes but while I'm mid-stride a flight
of stairs, or lost a moment on some avenue.

A remarkable disappointment to him,
I am like anyone who arrives late   20
in the millennium and is unable
to stay to the end of days. The world's
beginnings are obscure to me, its outcomes
inaccessible. I don't understand
the source of starlight, or starlight's destinations.   25
And already another year slides out

of balance. But I don't disparage scholars;
my father was one and I loved him,
who packed his books once, and all of our belongings,
then sat down to await instruction   30

from his god, yes, but also from a radio.
At the doorway, I watched, and I suddenly
knew he was one like me, who got my learning
under a lintel; he was one of the powerless,
to whom knowledge came while he sat among   35
suitcases, boxes, old newspapers, string.

He did not decide peace or war, home or exile,
escape by land or escape by sea.
He waited merely, as always someone
waits, far, near, here, hereafter, to find out: 40
is it praise or lament hidden in the next moment?

·····▶ *Your* **Turn**
Talking and Writing about Lit

1. What kinds of concrete details does Li-Young Lee use to help characterize the father?

2. **DIY**   Write a poem of at least eight lines in which you provide four or more concrete details about a friend, family member, or family pet.

Rita Dove (b. 1952)
The Satisfaction Coal Company (1986)

1.
What to do with a day.
Leaf through *Jet*. Watch T.V.
Freezing on the porch
but he goes anyhow, snow too high
for a walk, the ice treacherous.   5
Inside, the gas heater takes care of itself;
he doesn't even notice being warm.

Everyone says he looks great.
Across the street a drunk stands smiling
at something carved in a tree.   10
The new neighbor with the floating hips
scoots out to get the mail
and waves once, brightly,
storm door clipping her heel on the way in.

2.
Twice a week he had taken the bus down Glendale hill   15
to the corner of Market. Slipped through
the alley by the canal and let himself in.
Started to sweep
with terrible care, like a woman
brushing shine into her hair,   20
same motion, same lullaby.
No curtains—the cop on the beat
stopped outside once in the hour
to swing his billy club and glare.

It was better on Saturdays   25
when the children came along:
he mopped while they emptied
ashtrays, clang of glass on metal
then a dry scutter. Next they counted
nailheads studding the leather cushions.   30
Thirty-four! they shouted,
that was the year and
they found it mighty amusing.

But during the week he noticed more—
lights when they gushed or dimmed   35
at the Portage Hotel, the 10:32
picking up speed past the B & O switchyard,
floorboards trembling and the explosive
kachook kachook kachook kachook
and the oiled rails ticking underneath.   40

3.
They were poor then but everyone had been poor.
He hadn't minded the sweeping,
just the thought of it—like now
when people ask him what he's thinking
and he says *I'm listening.*   45

Those nights walking home alone,
the bucket of coal scraps banging his knee,
he'd hear a roaring furnace
with its dry, familiar heat. Now the nights
take care of themselves—as for the days,   50
there is the canary's sweet curdled song,
the wino smiling through his dribble.
Past the hill, past the gorge

choked with wild sumac in summer,
the corner has been upgraded.   55
Still, he'd like to go down there someday
to stand for a while, and get warm.

•••••➤ *Your* Turn
Talking and Writing about Lit

1. How does Rita Dove clue us in that the poem takes place in more than one
time frame?

2. Compare Dove's poetic portrait of an older person with Li-Young Lee's. Do
you think that one is more effective than the other? Why?

e.e. cummings (1894–1962)
l(a (1958)

l(a

le
af
fa

ll   5

s)
one
l

iness

•••••➤ *Your* Turn
Talking and Writing about Lit

1. Did you put together the letters within the parentheses to see what words
they form? In what ways does the statement "a leaf falls" reflect other
aspects of the poem?

2. **DIY**   Write a brief poem that contains the words "a leaf blows."
Consider arranging the words on the page so that the form will
reflect what is being said.

William Carlos Williams (1883–1963)
This Is Just to Say (1934)

I have eaten
the plums
that were in
the icebox

and which   5
you were probably
saving
for breakfast

Forgive me
they were delicious   10
so sweet
and so cold

·····➤ *Your* Turn
Talking and Writing about Lit

1. Do you find William Carlos Williams's use of line breaks and short lines here effective?

2. **DIY**   Rearrange Williams's line breaks so that there are only six lines in the poem instead of twelve. Compare the original poem with your alteration. Which is more effective?

Helen Chasin (b. 1938)
The Word *Plum* (1968)

The word *plum* is delicious

pout and push, luxury of
self-love, and savoring murmur
full in the mouth and falling
like fruit   5

taut skin
pierced, bitten, provoked into
juice, and tart flesh

question
and reply, lip and tongue   10
of pleasure.

• • • • ◆▶ *Your* **Turn**

Talking and Writing about Lit

1. Compare Helen Chasin's "The Word *Plum*" with William Carlos Williams's "This Is Just to Say." How are they similar? How are they different? Which do you find more effective and why?

2. Compare Chasin's "The Word *Plum*" with Galway Kinnell's "Blackberry Eating" (Chapter 15).

Duane Esposito (b. 1965)
Love (2005)

Will you dance to Run
DMC & Public Enemy?

Will you draw, again,
that skinny chicken,

whose beak's tied on with string,   5
& the fat Turkey Hero

in sneakers & cape, who flies
to rescue the withering bird?

Are you falling or ascending?
Are you tiresome & cold?   10

Is God our awareness
inward of it

or its projection
outward into us,

blessed or mawkish hearts   15
silhouetted inside our chests?

Love, will you watch with me—
even while traffic & trains

whirl in the background—
geese at the end of winter   20

on the ball field out field,
& in the sumps?

Will you lean toward me
as we listen to the sound

of the shaping   25
of our grief?

····▶ *Your* **Turn**
Talking and Writing about Lit

1. How would you describe the level (or levels) of diction in Duane Esposito's
poem "Love"?

2. Take a close look at the verbs in Esposito's poem. How has he practiced careful word choice in terms of his use of verbs? How does that contribute to the
impact of the poem?

<u>**Richard Wilbur (b. 1921)**</u>
A Late Aubade (1968)

You could be sitting now in a carrel
Turning some liver-spotted page,
Or rising in an elevator-cage
Toward Ladies' Apparel.

You could be planting a raucous bed   5
Of salvia, in rubber gloves,
Or lunching through a screed of someone's loves
With pitying head,

Or making some unhappy setter
Heel, or listening to a bleak   10
Lecture on Schoenberg's serial technique.
Isn't this better?

Think of all the time you are not
Wasting, and would not care to waste,
Such things, thank God, not being to your taste.   15
Think what a lot

Of time, by woman's reckoning,
You've saved, and so may spend on this,
You who had rather lie in bed and kiss
Than anything.   20

It's almost noon, you say? If so,
Time flies, and I need not rehearse
The rosebuds-theme of centuries of verse.
If you *must* go,

Wait for a while, then slip downstairs   25
And bring us up some chilled white wine,
And some blue cheese, and crackers, and some fine
Ruddy-skinned pears.

·····▶ *Your* **Turn**
Talking and Writing about Lit

1. Discuss the use of diction in Wilbur's "A Late Aubade." Would you describe his use of diction as informal, middle, or formal?

2. Compare Wilbur's use of word choice and diction with Duane Esposito's in "Love."

<u>Simon J. Ortiz (b. 1941)</u>
When It Was Taking Place (1977)

This morning, the sun has risen
already to the midpoint of where
it will be at the center of the day.
The old man, Amado Quintana,
doesn't get up early anymore.   5
He still wakes early in the morning
but he can't see the clear things
in the dim light before the sun rises,
and he can't hear the clear sounds.
So he lies on his cot or he sits   10
in the wooden chair by the stove.
Sometimes he forgets he has not built
the fire in the stove and he wonders
why the weather has changed so early.

He is an old man.   15
The people in the village
call him Old Man Humped Back.
He has a hump on his back,
and the history about that

is he has lived a long time   20
and it has grown on him.

This morning at this moment,
Quintana is pointing to the river
below the hill on which he
and his grandson are standing.   25
He made his grandson help him
climb unto the hill and now
he is showing him the river
and the land before them.
The hill is not very high   30
and children climb it
to explore and look for things,
but from there you can see
the fields and the canals.

The old man cannot really see   35
those anymore; his eyes are cloudy
with a gray covering; the only thing
he can see is the sun when it is
at its brightest. Sometimes
he forgets, and he asks why   40
the weather has changed suddenly
and irisists that it must be the times
and the people that are the cause.
But he can see in his mind,
and he tells his grandson,   45
"You can see that canal that runs
from that gathering of cottonwoods
and then turns to the south
by Faustin's field, that canal
was dug by the first people   50
who came down from the Old Place.
It was dug then."

He had been a child then,
and he played most of the time,
but he can remember his father   55
and the others with him.
They dug the canal from the river
to the east and turned to the south,
and then it was easier
as the ground was softer   60
and the water found its own way.

They had worked and it was good.
They had talked a lot, laughed,
and they got so wearied.
At the end of the day, the men   65
drug themselves home,
and Amado can remember carrying
his father's handmade shovel
in his hands, and they would be
greeted at their home by his mother.   70
She would say, "Amo, my partner
and my son, have you worked so hard,"
and she would grab them and hold them
strongly to her.
She would especially make a fuss   75
over Amado, who, at the time,
was their only child.
At that time, they lived in a low
windcarved cave with a wall of stones
along the front of it.   80

Amado Quintana can see that,
and he points it all out to his grandson,
and he wants him to see all those things,
and he tells the boy, "I was your age then
when it was taking place."   85

·····➤ *Your* Turn
Talking and Writing about Lit

1. How does Ortiz clue us in that this poem takes place in more than one time
frame?

2. Compare Ortiz's "When It Was Taking Place" with Rita Dove's "The
Satisfaction Coal Company."

3. **DIY** Write a poem of twelve lines or more that refers to two different
time frames. Think about an incident or experience you had as a
child. Then think about how you interpret that incident now. Then write!

Emily Dickinson (1830–1886)
I'm Nobody! Who are you? (1891)

I'm Nobody! Who are you?
Are you—Nobody—too?

Then there's pair of us!
Don't tell! they'd banish us—you know!

How dreary—to be—Somebody!   5
How public—like a Frog—
To tell your name—the livelong June—
To an admiring Bog!

·····➤ *Your* Turn
Talking and Writing about Lit

1. Discuss the connotations of the word frog in Dickinson's "I'm Nobody! Who
are you?" Why do you think she has chosen this particular animal to refer to
in her poem?

2. **DIY**   Dickinson's tone is conversational, conspiratorial, personal, almost
as if she's confiding this advice to a friend. Can you think of some
advice you've recently given to a friend or family member? Use that idea to
write a poem. In your poem, you might even want to have the listener
answer the speaker back.

Randall Jarrell (1914–1965)
The Death of the Ball Turret Gunner (1945)

From my mother's sleep I fell into the State,
And I hunched in its belly till my wet fur froze.
Six miles from earth, loosed from its dream of life,
I woke to black flak and the nightmare fighters.
When I died they washed me out of the turret with a hose.   5

·····➤ *Your* Turn
Talking and Writing about Lit

1. Note that Jarrell's poem was published in 1945, at the end of World War II.
What is the effect of telling the poem in the voice of an aircraft gunner who
has been killed in battle?

2. In "The Death of the Ball Turret Gunner," what connotative meanings do you
see in the words "sleep," "State," "belly," and "fur"?

Robert Hayden (1913–1980)
Those Winter Sundays (1962)

Sundays too my father got up early
and put his clothes on in the blueblack cold,
then with cracked hands that ached
from labor in the weekday weather made
banked fires blaze. No one ever thanked him.   5

I'd wake and hear the cold splintering, breaking.
When the rooms were warm, he'd call,
and slowly I would rise and dress,
fearing the chronic angers of that house,

Speaking indifferently to him,   10
who had driven out the cold
and polished my good shoes as well.
What did I know, what did I know
of love's austere and lonely offices?

····•▶ *Your* Turn
Talking and Writing about Lit

1. Give four examples of careful word choice in Hayden's "Those Winter Sundays."

2. **DIY**   Write a two-part poem of any length. In the first stanza, reveal something that a relative or friend did in the past (this could be good or bad); in the second stanza, let the speaker reveal how he or she now sees this act differently.

Anthony Hecht (b. 1923)
The Dover Bitch (1968)

A Criticism of Life

So there stood Matthew Arnold and this girl
With the cliffs of England crumbling away behind them,
And he said to her, "Try to be true to me,
And I'll do the same for you, for things are bad
All over, etc., etc."   5

Well now, I knew this girl. It's true she had read
Sophocles in a fairly good translation
And caught that bitter allusion to the sea,*
But all the time he was talking she had in mind
The notion of what his whiskers would feel like   10
On the back of her neck. She told me later on
That after a while she got to looking out
At the lights across the channel, and really felt sad,
Thinking of all the wine and enormous beds
And blandishments in French and the perfumes.   15
And then she got really angry. To have been brought
All the way down from London, and then be addressed
As a sort of mournful cosmic last resort
Is really tough on a girl, and she was pretty.
Anyway, she watched him pace the room   20
And finger his watch-chain and seem to sweat a bit,
And then she said one or two unprintable things.
But you mustn't judge her by that. What I mean to say is,
She's really all right. I still see her once in a while
And she always treats me right. We have a drink   25
And I give her a good time, and perhaps it's a year
Before I see her again, but there she is,
Running to fat, but dependable as they come.
And sometimes I bring her a bottle of *Nuit d'Amour.*

Note: *The Dover Bitch:* A parody of Arnold's poem "Dover Beach" (see p. 600).
***And caught that bitter allusion to the sea:** Lines 9–18 in "Dover Beach" refer to Sophocles'
Antigone, lines 583–91.

····•▶ *Your* **Turn**
Talking and Writing about Lit

1. Anthony Hecht's poem is a **parody** (a spoof that pokes fun at the original)
   of Mathew Arnold's poem "Dover Beach," which appears earlier in
   this chapter. Why do you think Hecht uses the subtitle *"A Criticism of
   Life"*?

2. **DIY**   Write a parody of your own, satirizing any poem that appears in
           this book. You might choose Robert Browning's "My Last
   Duchess" or Andrew Marvell's "To His Coy Mistress," both of which
   appear earlier in this chapter.

Marianne Moore (1887–1972)
Poetry (1921)

I, too, dislike it: there are things that are important beyond all this fiddle.
    Reading it, however, with a perfect contempt for it, one discovers in
    it after all, a place for the genuine.
        Hands that can grasp, eyes
        that can dilate, hair that can rise   5
            if it must, these are important not because a

high-sounding interpretation can be put upon them but because they are
    useful. When they become so derivative as to become unintelligible,
    the same thing may be said for all of us, that we
        do not admire what   10
        we cannot understand: the bat
            holding on upside down or in quest of something to

eat, elephants pushing, a wild horse taking a roll, a tireless wolf under
    a tree, the immovable critic twitching his skin like a horse that feels a
        flea, the base-
    ball fan, the statistician—   15
    nor is it valid
        to discriminate against 'business documents and

school-books'; all these phenomena are important. One must make a dis-
    tinction however: when dragged into prominence by half poets, the
    result is not poetry,
    nor till the poets among us can be   20
    'literalists of
    the imagination'—above
        insolence and triviality and can present

for inspection, 'imaginary gardens with real toads in them', shall we have
    it. In the meantime, if you demand on the one hand,   25
    the raw material of poetry in
        all its rawness and
        that which is on the other hand
            genuine, you are interested in poetry.

·····▶ *Your* Turn
Talking and Writing about Lit

1. Marianne Moore refers, near the end of "Poetry" (line 26), to the "raw materials of poetry." Does she represent any of these "raw materials" in the poem
itself? Give examples.

2. What do you think makes a good poem? Write a poem about what makes a good poem.

Amy King (b. 1971)
Stay At Home (2004)

Outsourcing is a very cocktail
piano. I make the movies
embrace me. I force the t.v.
to taunt me. My days
should have been game   5
show contestants. The fork of childhood
asked why one road and not another alley.
Why, an assembly line.
I, the maker, am born from the taker
of plastic trains and hot wheels.   10
I lick melting suede feet.
Don't leave your teddy on the bedstand,
let's make out with one
less infringement. Wrap your sheet
around me and let the film begin   15
endlessly on the fingers of sleep.

·····▶ *Your* **Turn**
Talking and Writing about Lit

1. Amy King's lines may at first seem both appealing and confusing, but use both your heart and your head when you listen to her poem "Stay at Home." Express what you feel when you read the lines "Wrap your sheet/around me and let the film begin/endlessly in the fingers of sleep."

2. DIY Reread King's poem several times (at least four). Then write a poem of your own about something ordinary. Try to use images that explode previous ways of representing this kind of event or emotion.

Amy King (b. 1971)
My Panel at the Conference (2004)

I leak giraffes from my inner pores.
They feed on tree

leaves from my upper branches.
Public promoters of secrets
tell our skies to spread   5
over pausing smiles, chewing shadows in doubt.
Thus a postage stamp mind
much like the one I inhabit
follows the trappings of city-born flies.
These giraffes swallow my winged carcass   10
bark and reach toward the rafters
holding down each conference
member in fixed positions.
They spread their lips wide in reply
as if by nature's order they   15
form a panel,
napkin-folded boats on plates.

·····▶ *Your* Turn
Talking and Writing about Lit

1. As a poet, Amy King is interested in the evolution of language—how language changes over time and how we (as readers and writers) might even be agents of that change. In her Talking Lit article below, she advocates "putting new spins on the constructions of perception." Give three or four examples from her poem "My Panel at the Conference" that put a new spin on our perception of things.

2. Do the closing lines of the poem ("as if by nature's order they/form a panel,/ napkin-folded boats on plates.") make sense to you? Why or why not? Try to think of at least two possible meanings for these lines.

Talking Lit

Amy King speaks of our use of language as "revolutions, evolutions and revelations of the towns and communities we live in." Frank O'Hara proposes (somewhat tongue in cheek) a new poetic movement called "Personism." And William Wordsworth (writing 200 years ago) discusses poetic diction.

Amy King, "A Rose Is a Rose Is a Thorny Yellow Thing," 2005

When Gertrude Stein wrote, "A rose is a rose is a rose," she wanted readers to see that a rose is more than a rose. Stein's use of repetition brought the "wordness" of the rose to readers' awareness, thus implicating our active duty as constructors of meaning. Let me explain: we want the word "rose" to transparently link the pretty red flower in an author's mind to our own. However, a reader may begin thinking of the thorny yellow wilting rose she recently saw in her friend's lapel and never truly picture the intended rose the author first imagined. This simple example helps us to understand that language is not a mathematical equation in which a word can contain a whole, exact idea that is extracted by the reader-receiver. A word is understood to be a "stand-in" that only points at things and ideas elsewhere, outside of itself; it is a signpost that refers a reader to her own idea of a rose and can thus be "misinterpreted" as the author's original. Additionally, a word possesses its own tangible qualities such as acoustic and visual characteristics precisely because it is not a transparent entity, which is the "wordness" or materiality of language Stein wanted us to appreciate. At first glance, what we might consider to be a flaw in the mechanics of language, we can also embrace as a pleasant, necessary feature of our humanity upon closer inspection.

Ludwig Wittgenstein declared, "The limits of my language mean the limits of my world." Without language, we cannot think or share ideas or give commands. Language enables us to be communal beings and is always changing; new words pop up in public places, old words are used in uncustomary ways, and even the order of our exchanges evolves. The more familiar and accustomed we are with the syntactical constructions of our daily sentences, the less aware of language we are. Since language helps us to formulate ideas and is reflective of our independent and shared realities, a static language would mean that our world never changes and we would become a dull, boring species. Luckily, we are anything but unchanging and our use of language can refer to the daily revolutions, evolutions and revelations of the towns and communities we live in.

Poetry is a writing practice through which we can openly embrace and celebrate the changes we observe and participate in by putting new spins on the constructions of perception. We are not obligated to represent the world in any routine, socially-acceptable fashion under the guise of poetry. The very term gives us license to ignore the rules of grammar and syntax and to play with the reality within our own minds, since we acknowledge that language is a material medium we each possess and use at our individual discretion. Words comprise our private thoughts and are therefore available for personal interpretation and sculpting. Poetry allows such alterations to enter the public sphere. As readers and writers of poems, we are active in making and sharing meaning. Instead of passively absorbing the world and "taking it in," we help to create and change it through poetic means and in poetic ways.

Frank O'Hara, "Personism: A Manifesto," 1959

Everything is in the poems, but at the risk of sounding like the poor wealthy man's Allen Ginsberg I will write to you because I just heard that one of my fellow poets thinks that a poem of mine that can't be got at one reading is because I was confused too. Now, come on. I don't believe in god, so I don't have to make elaborately sounded structures. I have Vachel Lindsay, always have, I don't even like rhythm, assonance, all that stuff. You just go on your nerve. If someone's chasing you down the street with a knife you just run, you don't turn around and shout, "Give it up! I was a track star for Mineola Prep."

That's for the writing poems part. As for their reception, suppose you're in love and someone's mistreating (*mal aimé*) you, you don't say, "Hey, you can't hurt me this way, I *care*!" you just let all the different bodies fall where they may, and they always do may after a few months. But that's not why you fell in love in the first place, just to hang onto life, so you have to take your chances and try to avoid being logical. Pain always produces logic, which is very bad for you.

I'm not saying that I don't have practically the most lofty ideas of anyone writing today, but what difference does that make? they're just ideas. The only good thing about it is that when I get lofty enough I've stopped thinking and that's when refreshment arrives.

But how can you really care if anybody gets it, or gets what it means, or if it improves them. Improves them for what? for death? Why hurry them along? Too many poets act like a middle-aged mother trying to get her kids to eat too much cooked meat, and potatoes with drippings (tears). I don't give a damn whether they eat or not. Forced feeding leads to excessive thinness (effete). Nobody should experience anything they don't need to, if they don't need poetry bully for them, I like the movies too. And after all, only Whitman and Crane and Williams, of the American poets, are better than the movies. As for measure and other technical apparatus, that's just common sense: if you're going to buy a pair of pants you want them to be tight enough so everyone will want to go to bed with you. There's nothing metaphysical about it. Unless, of course, you flatter yourself into thinking that what you're experiencing is "yearning."

Abstraction in poetry, which Allen recently commented on in *It is*, is intriguing. I think it appears mostly in the minute particulars where decision is necessary. Abstraction (in poetry, not in painting) involves personal removal by the poet. For instance, the decision involved in the choice between "the nostalgia of the infinite" and "the nostalgia *for* the infinite" defines an attitude towards degree of abstraction. The nostalgia *of* the infinite representing the greater degree of abstraction, removal, and negative capability (as in Keats and Mallarmé). Personism, a movement which I recently founded and which nobody yet knows about, interests me a great deal, being so totally opposed to this kind of abstract removal that it is verging on a true abstraction for the first time, really, in the history of poetry. Personism is to Wallace Stevens what *la poésie pure* was to Béranger. Personism has nothing to do with philosophy, it's all art. It does not have to do with personality or intimacy, far from it! But to give you a vague idea, one of its minimal aspects is to address itself to one person (other than the poet himself), thus evoking overtones of love without destroying love's life-giving vulgarity, and sustaining the poet's feelings towards the poem while preventing love from distracting him into feeling about the person. That's part of personism. It was founded by me after lunch with LeRoi Jones on August 27, 1959, a day in which I was in love with someone (not Roi, by the way, a blond). I went back to work and wrote a poem for this person. While I was writing it I was realizing that if I wanted to I could use the telephone instead of writing the poem, and so Personism was born. It's a very exciting movement which will undoubtedly have lots of adherents. It puts the poem squarely between the poet and the person, Lucky Pierre style, and the poem is correspondingly gratified. The poem is at last between two persons instead of two pages. In all modesty, I confess that it may be the death of literature as we know it. While I have certain regrets, I am still glad I got there before Alain Robbe-Grillet did. Poetry being quicker and surer than prose, it is only just that poetry finish literature off. For a time people thought that Artaud was going to accomplish this, but actually, for all its magnificence, his polemical writings are not more outside literature than Bear Mountain is outside New York State. His relation is no more astounding than Dubuffet's to painting.

What can we expect of Personism? (This is getting good, isn't it?) Everything, but we won't get it. It is too new, too vital a movement to promise anything. But it, like Africa, is on the way. The recent propagandists for technique on the one hand, and for content on the other, had better watch out.

William Wordsworth, Appendix to the 1802 Preface of *Lyrical Ballads*

Perhaps, as I have no right to expect that attentive perusal, without which, confined, as I have been, to the narrow limits of a preface, my meaning cannot be thoroughly understood, I am anxious to give an exact notion of the sense in which the phrase poetic diction has been used; and for this purpose, a few words shall here be added, concerning the origin and characteristics of the phraseology, which I have condemned under that name.

The earliest poets of all nations generally wrote from passion excited by real events; they wrote naturally, and as men; feeling powerfully as they did, their language was daring, and figurative. In succeeding times, Poets, and Men ambitious of the fame of Poets, perceiving the influence of such language, and desirous of producing the same effect without being animated by the same passion, set themselves to a mechanical adoption of these figures of speech, and made use of them, sometimes with propriety, but much more frequently applied them to feelings and thoughts with which they had no natural connection whatsoever. A language was thus insensibly produced, differing materially from the real language of men in *any situation*. The Reader or Hearer of this distorted language found himself in a perturbed and unusual state of mind; when affected by the genuine language of passion he had been in a perturbed and unusual state of mind also: in both cases he was willing that his common judgment and understanding should be laid asleep, and he had no instinctive and infallible perception of the true to make him reject the false; the one served as a passport for the other. The emotion was in both cases delightful, and no wonder if he confounded the one with the other, and believed them both to be produced by the same, or similar causes. Besides, the Poet spake to him in the character of a man to be looked up to, a man of genius and authority. Thus, and from a variety of other causes, this distorted language was received with admiration; and Poets, it is probable, who had before contented themselves for the most part with misapplying only expressions which at first had been dictated by real passion, carried the abuse still further, and introduced phrases composed apparently in the spirit of the original figurative language of passion, yet altogether of their own invention, and characterized by various degrees of wanton deviation from good sense and nature.

It is indeed true, that the language of the earliest Poets was felt to differ materially from ordinary language, because it was the language of extraordinary occasions; but it was really spoken by men, language which the Poet himself had uttered when he had been affected by the events which he described, or which he had heard uttered by those around him. To this language it is probable that metre of some sort or other was early superadded. This separated the genuine language of Poetry still further from common life, so that whoever read or heard the poems of these earliest Poets felt himself moved in a way in which he had not been accustomed to be moved in real life, and by causes manifestly different from those which acted upon him in real life. This was the great temptation to all the corruptions which have followed: under the protection of this feeling succeeding Poets constructed a phraseology which had one thing, it is true, in common with the genuine language of poetry, namely, that it was not heard in ordinary conversation; that it was unusual. But the first Poets, as I have said, spake a language which, though unusual, was still the language of men. This circumstance, however, was disregarded by their successors; they found that they could please by easier means: they became proud of modes of expression which they themselves had invented, and which were uttered only by themselves. In process of time metre became a symbol or promise of this unusual language, and whoever took upon him to write in metre, according as he possessed more or less of true poetic genius, introduced less or more of this adulterated phraseology into his compositions, and the true and the false were inseparably interwoven until, the taste of men becoming gradually perverted, this language was received as a natural language: and at length, by the influence of books upon men, did to a certain degree really become so. Abuses of this kind were imported from one nation to another, and with the progress of refinement this diction became daily more and more corrupt, thrusting out of sight the plain humanities of nature by a motley masquerade of tricks, quaintnesses, hieroglyphics, and enigmas.

It would not be uninteresting to point out the causes of the pleasure given by this extravagant and absurd diction. It depends upon a great variety of causes, but upon none, perhaps, more than its influence in impressing a notion of the peculiarity and exaltation of the Poet's character, and in flattering the Reader's self-love by bringing him nearer to a sympathy with that character; an effect which is accomplished by unsettling ordinary habits of thinking, and thus assisting the Reader to approach to that perturbed and dizzy state of mind in which if he does not find himself, he imagines that he is *balked* of a peculiar enjoyment which poetry can and ought to bestow.

The sonnet quoted from Gray, in the Preface, except the lines printed in Italics, consists of little else but this diction, though not of the worst kind; and indeed, if one may be permitted to say so, it is far too common in the best writers both ancient and modern. Perhaps in no way, by positive example, could more easily be given a notion of what I mean by the phrase *poetic diction* than by referring to a comparison between the metrical paraphrases which we have of passages in the

Old and New Testament, and those passages as they exist in our common Translation. See Pope's "Messiah" throughout; Prior's "Did sweeter sounds adorn my flowing tongue," &c. &c. "Though I speak with the tongues of men and of angels," &c. &c. 1st Corinthians, chap. xiii. By way of immediate example, take the following of Dr. Johnson.[1]

> "Turn on the prudent Ant thy heedless eyes,
> Observe her labours, Sluggard, and be wise;
> No stern command, no monitory voice,
> Prescribes her duties, or directs her choice;
> Yet, timely provident, she hastes away
> To snatch the blessings of a plenteous day;
> When fruitful Summer loads the teeming plain,
> She crops the harvest, and she stores the grain.
> How long shall sloth usurp thy useless hours,
> Unnerve thy vigour, and enchain thy powers?
> While artful shades thy downy couch enclose,
> And soft solicitation courts repose,
> Amidst the drowsy charms of dull delight,
> Year chases year with unremitted flight,
> Till Want now following, fraudulent and slow,
> Shall spring to seize thee, like an ambush'd foe."

From this hubbub of words pass to the original. "Go to the Ant, thou Sluggard, consider her ways, and be wise: which having no guide, overseer, or ruler, provideth her meat in the summer, and gathereth her food in the harvest. How long wilt thou sleep, O Sluggard? when wilt thou arise out of thy sleep? Yet a little sleep, a little slumber, a little folding of the hands to sleep. So shall thy poverty come as one that travelleth, and thy want as an armed man." Proverbs, chap. vi.

One more quotation, and I have done. It is from Cowper's Verses supposed to be written by Alexander Selkirk:—

> "Religion! what treasure untold
> Resides in that heavenly word!
> More precious than silver and gold,
> Or all that this earth can afford.
> But the sound of the church-going bell
> These valleys and rocks never heard,
> Ne'er sighed at the sound of a knell,
> Or smiled when a sabbath appeared.

---

[1] **Pope's "Messiah"** combines paraphrase of several passages of Isaiah with imitation of Virgil's fourth eclogue; **Prior's "Charity"** is a paraphrase of I Corinthians 13, and Johnson's "The Ant" a paraphrase of Proverbs 6:6–11.

POP CULTURE

Gwendolyn Brooks, "South Side"

When you read Gwendolyn Brooks's "We Real Cool," it may have sounded familiar, especially in terms of word choice, order, and tone. Gwendolyn Brooks grew up in the South Side of Chicago in the 1920s, but her poetry is sometimes remarkably similar to a musical form that didn't surface until 1976 in the Bronx borough of New York—hip-hop.

Poet Gwendolyn Brooks

Take another look at the intonation, the words, and the rhythm of "We Real Cool" and you'll find the sentiments of the "Seven at the Golden Shovel" are largely the same as those of popular rap artists today. Some of the language needs to be

"Ye winds, that have made me your sport
Convey to this desolate shore
Some cordial endearing report
Of a land I must visit no more.
My Friends, do they now and then send
A wish or a thought after me?
O tell me I yet have a friend,
Though a friend I am never to see."

This passage is quoted as an instance of three different styles of composition. The first four lines are poorly expressed; some Critics would call the language prosaic; the fact is, it would be bad prose, so bad, that it is scarcely worse in metre. The epithet "church-going" applied to a bell, and that by so chaste a writer as Cowper, is an instance of the strange abuses which Poets have introduced into their language, till they and their Readers take them as matters of course, if they do not

Hip-hop artist 50 Cent performing

updated (We/Jazz June is more like "rocking a mike" today), but aside from that, the ideas are the same. The macho appeal of staying out late at clubs, drinking, talking hard, and dying young run throughout not only rap lyrics, but through down-and-out American youth culture—black and white, Latino and Asian.

Take a moment to compare "We Real Cool" to some selected lyrics from 50 Cent's "In Da Club":

You can find me in the club, bottle full of Bud . . .
When I roll 20 deep, it's 20 knives in the club . . .
If you watch how I move you'll mistake me for a playa or pimp
Been hit wit a few shells but I don't walk wit a limp

Even in these few, selected lyrics we can see the themes of drinking, playing, having a good time (instead of worrying about success), and dying young. Of course, while Brooks's speaker is trying to call attention to the dangers of this lifestyle, 50 Cent's lyrics are an uncritical celebration of it.

single them out expressly as objects of admiration. The two lines "Ne'er sighed at the sound," &c., are, in my opinion, an instance of the language of passion wrested from its proper use, and, from the mere circumstance of the composition being in metre, applied upon an occasion that does not justify such violent expressions; and I should condemn the passage, though perhaps few Readers will agree with me, as vicious poetic diction. The last stanza is throughout admirably expressed: it would be equally good whether in prose or verse, except that the Reader has an exquisite pleasure in seeing such natural language so naturally connected with metre. The beauty of this stanza tempts me to conclude with a principle which ought never to be lost sight of, and which has been my chief guide in all I have said,—namely, that in works *of imagination and sentiment*, for of these only have I been treating, in proportion as ideas and feelings are valuable, whether the composition be in prose or in verse, they require and exact one and the same language. Metre is but adventitious to composition, and the phraseology for which that passport is necessary, even where it may be graceful at all, will be little valued by the judicious.

IMAGERY AND SUMBOLISM

Even money uses imagery and symbolism.

Although five dollar bills may pass through our hands daily, we rarely stop to think about the images printed on them. The visual images on the dive dollar bill include the face of Abraham Lincoln; his features are square-jawed and clear eyed, and his expression in the artist's rendering is one of friendly certitude and determination. That is, if you will, the way we "read" this image on the literal level. But the image has symbolic meanings for us as well. We are meant, when looking at this representation of President Lincoln, to think of his championing of egalitarian ideals, of his conduct of the Civil War, of the Emancipation Proclamation, and Gettysburg Address. In other words, the very image of Lincoln's face is intended to symbolize American values and ideals. Other symbolic images on the front of the bill are the eagle on the Federal Reserve seal (symbolic of freedom) and the scales of justice on the Treasury Department seal. The representation of the Lincoln Memorial on the back of the bill is meant to symbolize many of the same ideas and ideals, and perhaps also to remind us of our nation's capitol.

What Is Imagery?

Have you ever tried to describe a special place or event to a friend? Maybe it was your favorite high school hangout, your grandmother's kitchen, or a great concert you attended. In your description, you likely tried to convey your feelings, the sights, the sounds, and the smells. If so, then you have used sensory detail. **Imagery** refers to language that appeals to the senses. While the most common sensory details in poetry are visual details (appealing to the sense of sight), a poem often seems most powerful and vivid when the poet has appealed to one or more of the other four senses as well (taste, smell, hearing, and touch). Pat Mora's poem "Curandera" (which means "healer") achieves an unusual clarity and vividness by appealing to all five of our senses.

Pat Mora (b. 1942)
Curandera (1985)

They think she lives alone
on the edge of town in a two-room house
where she moved when her husband died
at thirty-five of a gunshot wound
in the bed of another woman. The *curandera*   5
and house have aged together to the rhythm
of the desert.

She wakes early, lights candles before
her sacred statues, brews tea of *yerbabuena*.[1]
She moves down her porch steps, rubs   10
cool morning sand into her hands, into her arms.
Like a large black bird, she feeds on
the desert, gathering herbs for her basket.

Her days are slow, days of grinding
dried snake into powder, of crushing   15
wild bees to mix with white wine.
And the townspeople come, hoping
to be touched by her ointments
her hands, her prayers, her eyes.
She listens to their stories, and she listens   20
to the desert, always, to the desert.

Note: Curandera is a healer.
[1] **Yerbabuena:** Peppermint.

By sunset she is tired. The wind
strokes the strands of long gray hair,
the smell of drying plants drifts
into her blood, the sun seeps   25
into her bones. She dozes
on her back porch. Rocking, rocking.

At night she cooks chopped cactus
and brews more tea. She brushes a layer
of sand from her bed, sand which covers   30
the table, stove, floor. She blows
the statues clean, the candles out.
Before sleeping, she listens to the message
of the owl and the coyote. She closes her eyes
and breathes with the mice and snakes   35
and wind.

We may be led to imagine the taste of the curandera's healing herbs, her pep-permint (yerbabuena) tea, and her healing powders mixed with white wine. Smells are also present in the poem: "the smell of drying plants drifts/into her blood" and "At night she cooks chopped cactus/and brews more tea." Sounds are noted throughout the curandera's day, sounds of "grinding/dried snake into powder, of crushing/wild bees to mix with white wine." "Before sleeping, she listens to the message/of the owl and the coyote." Some of the most striking images in this poem are the tactile details (these appeal to the sense of touch, which includes sensations of movement, temperature, and texture). "She moves down her porch steps, rubs/cool morning sand into her hands, into her arms." "The wind/strokes the strands of long gray hair," "She brushes a layer/of sand from her bed," "she blows/the statues clean, the candles out."

Sensory Details

Such sensory details also involve the reader more directly in the emotional experience of the poem's speaker or subject. Martin Espada's "Who Burns for the Perfection of Paper" breaks into two sections. In the first section, the speaker is a high school student who is working at a factory that manufactures legal pads; in the second, the same speaker is a student in law school who knows the sweat of the workers who made the legal pad upon which he now writes. Sensory details draw the listener or reader into the speaker's emotional experience.

Martín Espada (b. 1957)
Who Burns for the Perfection of Paper (1993)

At sixteen, I worked after high school hours
at a printing plant
that manufactured legal pads:
Yellow paper
stacked seven feet high   5
and leaning
as I slipped cardboard
between the pages,
then brushed red glue
up and down the stack.   10
No gloves: fingertips required
for the perfection of paper,
smoothing the exact rectangle.
Sluggish by 9 PM, the hands
would slide along suddenly sharp paper,   15
and gather slits thinner than the crevices
of the skin, hidden.
Then the glue would sting,
hands oozing
till both palms burned   20
at the punchclock.

Ten years later, in law school,
I knew that every legal pad
was glued with the sting of hidden cuts,
that every open lawbook   25
was a pair of hands
upturned and burning.

Specific visual and tactile details help the reader imagine the feeling of the glue stinging in the paper cuts. In the second section, as well, visual and tactile images appeal to the reader emotionally.

In Czeslaw Milosz's "A Poor Christian Looks at the Ghetto," composed in 1943, the poet attempts to recreate the violent images of *Kristallnacht*, using sights and sounds and a wealth of active verbs: "tearing," "trampling," "breaking," "Engulfs," "torn," "collapse." *Kristallnacht*, "The Night of Broken Glass," took place in Germany on November 9, 1938. Following this night of terror and destruction against Jewish businesses, homes, and synagogues, many Jews fled from Germany and Austria.

Czeslaw Milosz (b. 1911)
A Poor Christian Looks at the Ghetto (1943)

TRANSLATED BY THE AUTHOR

Bees build around red liver,
Ants build around black bone.
It has begun: the tearing, the trampling on silks,
It has begun: the breaking of glass, wood, copper, nickel, silver, foam
Of gypsum, iron sheets, violin strings, trumpets, leaves, balls, crystals.   5
Poof! Phosphorescent fire from yellow walls
Engulfs animal and human hair.

Bees build around the honeycomb of lungs,
Ants build around white bone.
Torn is paper, rubber, linen, leather, flax,   10
Fiber, fabrics, cellulose, snakeskin, wire.
The roof and the wall collapse in flame and heat seizes
       the foundations.
Now there is only the earth, sandy, trodden down,
With one leafless tree.

Slowly, boring a tunnel, a guardian mole makes his way,   15
With a small red lamp fastened to his forehead.
He touches burned bodies, counts them, pushes on,
He distinguishes human ashes by their luminous vapor,
The ashes of each man by a different part of the spectrum.
Bees build around a red trace.   20
Ants build around the place left by my body.

I am afraid, so afraid of the guardian mole.
He has swollen eyelids, like a patriarch
Who has sat much in the light of candles
Reading the great book of the species.   25
What will I tell him, I, a Jew of the New Testament,
Waiting two thousand years for the second coming of Jesus?
My broken body will deliver me to his sight
And he will count me among the helpers of death:
The uncircumcised.   30

    Historical and physical setting also play a role in Susan Tichy's poem "At a P.C. Sergeant's House," although she relies on understated and implied images of violence, never overtly representing it. Her poem is set in Tarlac Province, Philippines, during the Philippine Insurrection (1899–1902). Colors and contrasts of light and dark play an important role in creating this poem's effects.

Susan Tichy (b. 1952)
At a P.C. Sergeant's House: Zambales Mountains (1988)

The food is good: beef, flat fish,
and dog, with vegetables—some of them
parts of trees—and fruit.
We sit under a tree whose branches shade
five hundred square feet of ground,   5
while the man who brought us tries to explain
who we are. We don't understand,
but they're laughing, just as
on the way here we were told
He is one of the most notorious, like a joke.   10
In the clearing that makes a barangay,
the jungle is not forgotten, neither
its presence, nor the colors
of its quickly receding face—
on open fires, the white   15
of rice in blackened pots;
and beside the green of palm leaves, cut
and laid over plates of food,
the red polka-dot dress
of the sergeant's wife. Above that,   20
her bashful but uncontrollable smile.
Her husband sits with his back to the house,
facing the ragged line
where jungle and the irrigated vines
of squash and eggplant meet.   25
He wears no uniform, just
a tee-shirt, white on the bulk of his skin.
And you have to admire how clean he looks
on this day of dry-season dust.
You have to admire the calm   30
with which he displays
no weapons, not even a knife.
"I'll tell you how much they hate him,"
said our friend as we entered the house.
"His wife can cook, but we will be   35
his only guests for fiesta."
And it's true. There's only us,
and behind the wide trunk of the tree
an old woman crouching
by a blue plastic tub. She washes our dishes   40
with her head tipped slightly back,

eyes closed, listening
to birds beyond the clearing,
cicadas overhead, and the bell-like laughter
of her two dead sons. The sergeant   45
never looks at her. His wife
taps one temple, to explain. We nod,
though we will never know
the sacred names of her sons, or
which side they were on. Our friend asks   50
with his eyes if we understand:
this is not the beginning
of policy; this is the end.
The sergeant eats. The woman
wears nothing under her thin dress   55
but the dry folds of her skin.
Who we are—he doesn't care.
His smile is vague. His eyes
look for something on the cleared ground
behind us. He ignores us   60
all—as a hunted animal listens
only for one sound.
We drop the name of his colonel
into the pool of talk
and it lands heavy, it lies there   65
like a murder weapon no one dares
retrieve though it's in plain sight.

Contrasting images of light and dark are also important in Yusef Komunyakaa's poem "Facing It," as his speaker views the polished wall of the Vietnam Memorial in Washington, D.C., covered with the 58,022 names of Americans who died in the Vietnam War.

Yusef Komunyakaa (b. 1947)
Facing It (1988)

My black face fades,
hiding inside the black granite.
I said I wouldn't,
dammit: No tears.
I'm stone. I'm flesh.   5
My clouded reflection eyes me
like a bird of prey, the profile of night
slanted against morning. I turn
this way—the stone lets me go.

I turn that way—I'm inside   10
the Vietnam Veterans Memorial
again, depending on the light
to make a difference.
I go down the 58,022 names,
half-expecting to find   15
my own in letters like smoke.
I touch the name Andrew Johnson;
I see the booby trap's white flash.
Names shimmer on a woman's blouse
but when she walks away   20
the names stay on the wall.
Brushstrokes flash, a red bird's
wings cutting across my stare.
The sky. A plane in the sky.
A white vet's image floats   25
closer to me, then his pale eyes
look through mine. I'm a window.
He's lost his right arm
inside the stone. In the black mirror
a woman's trying to erase names: 30
No, she's brushing a boy's hair.

In Chitra Banerjee Divakaruni's poem "Two Women Outside a Circus, Pushkar," village women, unable to afford the five rupee admission charge, peer in through the fence at the Nepal Circus. They are drawn especially to the female performers who seem to defy not only physical gravity, but also the social gravity which their society would ordinarily impose on their sex: "So the women/look and look/at the lighted sign of the lady acrobat.//In a short pink sequined skirt/she walks a tightrope/over gaping crocodile-jaws, twirling/her pink umbrella." Then, after taking in as much of the circus as they can through the fence slats, "The women gather their babies and head home," thinking of what they have seen.

Chitra Banerjee Divakaruni (b. 1956)
Two Women Outside a Circus, Pushkar (1977)

Faces pressed to the green stakes
of the circus fence, two village women
crouch low in the cloudy evening with their babies,
breathing in the odors of the beasts
painted on the canvas above: 5
great black snakes with ruby eyes,
tigers with stars sewn onto their skins.

Beyond, a tent translucent with sudden light,
bits of exotic sound: gunshots, growls,
a woman's raucous laugh.   10

The Nepal Circus demands five rupees
for entry to its neon world
of bears that dance, and porcupines
with arm-long poison quills. But five rupees
is a sack of *bajra*[1] from Ramdin's store,   15
a week's dinner for the family. So the women
look and look
at the lighted sign of the lady acrobat.

In a short pink sequined skirt
she walks a tightrope   20
over gaping crocodile-jaws, twirling
her pink umbrella. Inside the tent,
the crowd shrieks as Master Pinto the Boy Wonder
is hurled from a flaming cannon. The women
clutch each other and search the sky   25
for the thunder-sound. Ecstatic applause.
The band plays a hit from *Mera Naam Joker*[2]
and the crowd sings along.
The women gather their babies and head home
to the canvas of their lives: endless rounds of *rotis*[3]   30
rolled in smoky kitchens, whine of hungry children,
slaps or caresses from husbands with palm-wine breaths,
perhaps a new green skirt at harvest time.

But each woman
tending through burning noon the blinkered bull   35
that circles, all day, the *bajra*-crushing stones,
or wiping in dark the sweat
of unwanted sex from her body, remembers
in sparkling tights the woman acrobat
riding a one-wheeled cycle so immense   40
her head touches the stars. Remembers
the animal trainer in her leopard skins,
holding a blazing hoop through which leap
endless smiling lions.

---

[1] *bajra*: A grain similar to sorghum.
[2] *Mera Naam Joker*: A popular Hindi movie featuring circus performers.
[3] *roti*: Rolled-out Indian bread.

Clearly the female acrobats and lion tamers represent something larger than life—larger than their literal meaning in the poem. The women see in the acrobats a freedom they do not possess, and in the lion tamer they see the power to tame the most menacing beasts. When they dream of the female performers, they are also dreaming of a less earthbound life than the one they live in day to day, and so the acrobat and the lion tamer are **symbols** of the freedom and power longed for by the village women.

Symbolism

The "lady acrobat" is an example of a **contextual symbol** or a **literary symbol**. The acrobat has a particular meaning or meanings (freedom, mobility, power) within this particular work of literature; although, in other contexts, it might have a different meaning. A **universal symbol** or a **conventional symbol** would, on the other hand, be one which is recognized by most people within a culture to have a certain meaning wherever it appears; for example, a wedding ring, a Star of David, or a Christian cross.

Any image, object, or character within a poem can have a symbolic meaning in addition to its literal significance; as symbols, they may also have multiple possibilities for interpretation. In an allegorical work, on the other hand (John Bunyan's *The Pilgrim's Progress* is the most familiar example), each object, place, or character has exactly one corresponding meaning. Symbols may suggest, however, various meanings beyond the literal level, as does Divakaruni's "lighted sign of the lady acrobat." What do you think are the most interesting images in Divakaruni's "Tiger Mask Ritual" below? Do you think any elements of the poem are symbolic?

Chitra Banerjee Divakaruni (b. 1956)
Tiger Mask Ritual (1977)

When you put on the mask the thunder starts.
Through the nostril's orange you can smell
the far hope of rain. Up in the Nilgiris,
glisten of eucalyptus, drip of pine, spiders tumbling
from their silver webs.   5

The mask is raw and red as bark against your facebones.
You finger the stripes ridged like weals
out of your childhood. A wind is rising
in the north, a scarlet light
like a fire in the sky.   10

Note: The poem refers to a ritual performed by some Rajasthani hill tribes to ensure rain and a good harvest.

When you look through the eyeholes it is like falling.
Night gauzes you in black. You are blind
as in the beginning of the world. Sniff. Seek the moon.
After a while you will know
that creased musky smell is rising   15
from your skin.

Once you locate the ears the drums begin.
Your fur stiffens. A roar from the distant left,
like monsoon water. The air is hotter now
and moving. You swivel your sightless head.   20
Under your sheathed paw
the ground shifts wet.

What is that small wild sound
sheltering in your skull
against the circle that always closes in   25
just before dawn?

Likewise, in Robert Frost's poem "Acquainted with the Night," the concepts of "night," "rain," "walked out in rain," the "interrupted cry," "the watchman," and the "luminary clock" are not each limited to representing one fixed meaning but are the kind of rich symbols which might suggest a number of equally valid interpretations.

Robert Frost (1874–1963)
Acquainted with the Night (1928)

I have been one acquainted with the night.
I have walked out in rain—and back in rain.
I have outwalked the furthest city light.

I have looked down the saddest city lane.
I have passed by the watchman on his beat   5
And dropped my eyes, unwilling to explain.

I have stood still and stopped the sound of feet
When far away an interrupted cry
Came over houses from another street,

But not to call me back or say good-by;   10
And further still at an unearthly height,
One luminary clock against the sky

Proclaimed the time was neither wrong nor right.
I have been one acquainted with the night.

Robert Frost (1874–1963)
The Road Not Taken (1915)

Two roads diverged in a yellow wood,
And sorry I could not travel both
And be one traveler, long I stood
And looked down one as far as I could
To where it bent in the undergrowth;   5

Then took the other, as just as fair,
And having perhaps the better claim,
Because it was grassy and wanted wear;
Though as for that the passing there
Had worn them really about the same,   10

And both that morning equally lay
In leaves no step had trodden black.
Oh, I kept the first for another day!
Yet knowing how way leads on to way,
I doubted if I should ever come back   15

I shall be telling this with a sigh
Somewhere ages and ages hence:
Two roads diverged in a wood, and I—
I took the one less traveled by,
And that has made all the difference.   20

Allen Ginsberg (1926–1997)
A Supermarket in California (1956)

What thoughts I have of you tonight, Walt Whitman, for I walked down the streets under the trees with a headache self-conscious looking at the full moon.

In my hungry fatigue, and shopping for images, I went into the neon fruit supermarket, dreaming of your enumerations!

What peaches and what penumbras?[1] Whole families shopping at night! Aisles full of husbands! Wives in the avocados, babies in the tomatoes!— and you, García Lorca,[2] what were you doing down by the watermelons?

I saw you, Walt Whitman, childless, lonely old grubber, poking among the meats in the refrigerator and eyeing the grocery boys.

----
[1]**penumbras:** Partial shadows.
[2]**García Lorca:** Early twentieth-century Spanish poet and dramatist; like Ginsberg and Whitman, a homosexual.

I heard you asking questions of each: Who killed the pork chops?
What price bananas? Are you my Angel?   5
    I wandered in and out of the brilliant stacks of cans following you,
and followed in my imagination by the store detective.
    We strode down the open corridors together in our solitary fancy tasting
artichokes, possessing every frozen delicacy, and never passing the cashier.

    Where are we going, Walt Whitman? The doors close in an hour. Which
way does your beard point tonight?
    (I touch your book and dream of our odyssey in the supermarket and
feel absurd.)
    Will we walk all night through solitary streets? The trees add shade to
shade, lights out in the houses, we'll both be lonely.   10
    Will we stroll dreaming of the lost America of love past blue automobiles
in driveways, home to our silent cottage?
    Ah, dear father, graybeard, lonely old courage-teacher, what America did
you have when Charon quit poling his ferry and you got out on a smoking
bank and stood watching the boat disappear on the black waters of Lethe?[3]

---

[3]**Lethe:** One of the rivers of Hades (it means "forgetfulness"), across which Charon ferried the dead.

Octavio Paz (1914–1998)
The Street (1963)

A long silent street.
I walk in blackness and I stumble and fall
and rise, and I walk blind, my feet
stepping on silent stones and dry leaves.
Someone behind me also stepping on stones, leaves: 5
if I slow down, he slows;
if I run, he runs. I turn: nobody.
Everything dark and doorless.
Turning and turning among these corners
which lead forever to the street   10
where nobody waits for, nobody follows me,
where I pursue a man who stumbles
and rises and says when he sees me: nobody.

Galway Kinnell (b. 1927)
Blackberry Eating (1980)

I love to go out in late September
among the fat, overripe, icy, black blackberries
to eat blackberries for breakfast,
the stalks very prickly, a penalty

they earn for knowing the black art   5
of blackberry-making; and as I stand among them
lifting the stalks to my mouth, the ripest berries
fall almost unbidden to my tongue,
as words sometimes do, certain peculiar words
like *strengths* or *squinched*,   10
many-lettered, one-syllabled lumps,
which I squeeze, squinch open, and splurge well
in the silent, startled, icy, black language
of blackberry-eating in late September.

William Blake (1757–1828)
London (1794)

I wander thro' each charter'd[1] street,
Near where the charter'd Thames does flow,
And mark in every face I meet
Marks of weakness, marks of woe.

In every cry of every man,   5
In every Infant's cry of fear,
In every voice, in every ban,[2]
The mind-forg'd manacles I hear.

How the Chimney-sweeper's cry
Every blackning Church appalls;   10
And the hapless Soldier's sigh
Runs in blood down Palace walls.

But most thro' midnight streets I hear
How the youthful Harlot's curse
Blasts the new-born Infant's tear,   15
And blights with plagues the Marriage hearse.

---

[1]**charter'd:** Mapped out, legally defined, constricted.
[2]**ban:** A law or notice commanding or forbidding; a published penalty.

Poems for Further Reading

Ezra Pound (1885–1972)
In a Station of the Métro (1916)

The apparition of these faces in the crowd;
Petals on a wet, black bough.

······▸ *Your* **Turn**
Talking and Writing about Lit

1. The "Métro" in the title refers to the subway system in Paris. Look up the word "apparition," which appears in the first line. Why do you think Pound uses this word?

2. What feelings does it evoke when Pound uses the image of "Petals on a wet, black bough" (in line 2) to refer to human faces?

William Blake (1757–1828)
The Tyger (1794)

Tyger! Tyger! burning bright
In the forests of the night,
What immortal hand or eye
Could frame thy fearful symmetry?

In what distant deeps or skies   5
Burnt the fire of thine eyes?
On what wings dare he aspire?
What the hand, dare seize the fire?

And what shoulder, & what art,
Could twist the sinews of thy heart?   10
And when thy heart began to beat,
What dread hand? & what dread feet?

What the hammer? what the chain?
In what furnace was thy brain?
What the anvil? what dread grasp   15
Dare its deadly terrors clasp?

When the stars threw down their spears,
And water'd heaven with their tears,
Did he smile his work to see?
Did he who made the Lamb make thee?   20

Tyger! Tyger! burning bright
In the forests of the night,
What immortal hand or eye
Dare frame thy fearful symmetry?

·····▶ *Your* **Turn**
Talking and Writing about Lit

1. How has William Blake used careful word choice and connotative meanings to add vigor and energy (and a sense of awe and dread) to his depiction of the tiger? Give examples.

2. **DIY** Use vigorous verbs and strong images to characterize something or someone you find particularly powerful. This might be a sports team, a friend, a performer or actor, a musical artist or entertainer, or a family member. You may write this as a brief poem or as a paragraph.

William Blake (1757–1828)
The Lamb (1789)

> Little Lamb, who made thee?
> Dost thou know who made thee?
> Gave thee life & bid thee feed,
> By the stream & o'er the mead;
> Gave thee clothing of delight,   5
> Softest clothing wooly bright;
> Gave thee such a tender voice,
> Making all the vales rejoice!
> Little Lamb who made thee?
> Dost thou know who made thee?   10
>
> Little Lamb I'll tell thee,
> Little Lamb I'll tell thee!
> He* is calléd by thy name,
> For he calls himself a Lamb:
> He is meek & he is mild,   15
> He became a little child:
> I a child & thou a lamb,
> We are calléd by his name.
> Little Lamb God bless thee.
> Little Lamb God bless thee.   20

———————

***He:** Christ

······▶ *Your* **Turn**
Talking and Writing about Lit

1. Write a paragraph in which you compare and contrast the imagery and tone
of Blake's "The Lamb" and "The Tyger".

2. Write a paragraph or a brief poem in which you use tone and imagery to
characterize the gentleness and innocence of someone you know or have
seen in the media (a younger sibling, a child of your own, a friend, a grandparent, or an actor, actress, or entertainer).

T.S. Eliot (1888–1965)
The Love Song of J. Alfred Prufrock (1917)

> *S'io credesse che mia risposta fosse*
> *A persona che mai tornasse al mondo,*
> *Questa fiamma staria senza piu scosse.*
> *Ma perciocche giammai di questo fondo*
> *Non torno vivo alcun, s'i'odo il vero,*
> *Senza tema d'infamia ti rispondo.*

Let us go then, you and I,
When the evening is spread out against the sky
Like a patient etherized upon a table;
Let us go, through certain half-deserted streets,
The muttering retreats   5
Of restless nights in one-night cheap hotels
And sawdust restaurants with oyster-shells:
Streets that follow like a tedious argument
Of insidious intent
To lead you to an overwhelming question . . .   10
Oh, do not ask, "What is it?"
Let us go and make our visit.

   In the room the women come and go
Talking of Michelangelo.

   The yellow fog that rubs its back upon the window-panes,   15
The yellow smoke that rubs its muzzle on the window-panes
Licked its tongue into the corners of the evening,
Lingered upon the pools that stand in drains,
Let fall upon its back the soot that falls from chimneys,
Slipped by the terrace, made a sudden leap,   20
And seeing that it was a soft October night,
Curled once about the house, and fell asleep.

And indeed there will be time
For the yellow smoke that slides along the street,
Rubbing its back upon the window-panes;   25
There will be time, there will be time
To prepare a face to meet the faces that you meet;
There will be time to murder and create,
And time for all the works and days of hands
That lift and drop a question on your plate;   30
Time for you and time for me,
And time yet for a hundred indecisions,
And for a hundred visions and revisions,
Before the taking of a toast and tea.

    In the room the women come and go   35
Talking of Michelangelo.

    And indeed there will be time
To wonder, "Do I dare?" and "Do I dare?"
Time to turn back and descend the stair,
With a bald spot in the middle of my hair—   40
(They will say: "How his hair is growing thin!")
My morning coat, my collar mounting firmly to the chin,
My necktie rich and modest, but asserted by a simple pin—
(They will say: "But how his arms and legs are thin!")
Do I dare   45
Disturb the universe?
In a minute there is time
For decisions and revisions which a minute will reverse.

    For I have known them all already, known them all:—
Have known the evenings, mornings, afternoons,   50
I have measured out my life with coffee spoons;
I know the voices dying with a dying fall
Beneath the music from a farther room.
    So how should I presume?

    And I have known the eyes already, known them all—   55
The eyes that fix you in a formulated phrase,
And when I am formulated, sprawling on a pin,
When I am pinned and wriggling on the wall,
Then how should I begin
To spit out all the butt-ends of my days and ways?   60
    And how should I presume?

And I have known the arms already, known them all—
Arms that are braceleted and white and bare
(But in the lamplight, downed with light brown hair!)
Is it perfume from a dress   65
That makes me so digress?
Arms that lie along a table, or wrap about a shawl.
    And should I then presume?
    And how should I begin?

      •   •   •

Shall I say, I have gone at dusk through narrow streets   70
And watched the smoke that rises from the pipes
Of lonely men in shirt-sleeves, leaning out of windows? . . .

    I should have been a pair of ragged claws
Scuttling across the floors of silent seas.

      •   •   •

And the afternoon, the evening, sleeps so peacefully!   75
Smoothed by long fingers,
Asleep . . . tired . . . or it malingers,
Stretched on the floor, here beside you and me.
Should I, after tea and cakes and ices,
Have the strength to force the moment to its crisis?   80
But though I have wept and fasted, wept and prayed,
Though I have seen my head (grown slightly bald)
brought in upon a platter,
I am no prophet—and here's no great matter;
I have seen the moment of my greatness flicker,
And I have seen the eternal Footman hold my coat, and snicker,   85
And in short, I was afraid.

    And would it have been worth it, after all,
After the cups, the marmalade, the tea,
Among the porcelain, among some talk of you and me,
Would it have been worth while,   90
To have bitten off the matter with a smile,
To have squeezed the universe into a ball
To roll it toward some overwhelming question,
To say: "I am Lazarus, come from the dead,
Come back to tell you all, I shall tell you all"—   95
If one, settling a pillow by her head,
    Should say: "That is not what I meant at all.
    That is not it, at all."

    And would it have been worth it, after all,
Would it have been worth while,   100

After the sunsets and the dooryards and the sprinkled streets,
After the novels, after the teacups, after the skirts that trail along the
    floor—
And this, and so much more?—
It is impossible to say just what I mean!
But as if a magic lantern threw the nerves in patterns on a screen: 105
Would it have been worth while
If one, settling a pillow or throwing off a shawl,
And turning toward the window, should say:
     "That is not it at all,
     That is not what I meant, at all."   110

        •   •   •

No! I am not Prince Hamlet, nor was meant to be;
Am an attendant lord, one that will do
To swell a progress, start a scene or two,
Advise the prince; no doubt, an easy tool,
Deferential, glad to be of use,   115
Politic, cautious, and meticulous;
Full of high sentence, but a bit obtuse;
At times, indeed, almost ridiculous—
Almost, at times, the Fool.

    I grow old . . . I grow old . . .   120
I shall wear the bottoms of my trousers rolled.*

    Shall I part my hair behind? Do I dare to eat a peach?
I shall wear white flannel trousers, and walk upon the beach.
I have heard the mermaids singing, each to each.
    I do not think that they will sing to me.   125

    I have seen them riding seaward on the waves
Combing the white hair of the waves blown back
When the wind blows the water white and black.

    We have lingered in the chambers of the sea
By sea-girls wreathed with seaweed red and brown   130
Till human voices wake us, and we drown.

····► **Your Turn**
Talking and Writing about Lit

   1. In Eliot's "The Love Song of J. Alfred Prufrock," the speaker of the poem
    speaks freely, confiding to us his fears and shortcomings. What do you

---

*rolled: cuffed

suppose he means when he says (line 51): "I have measured out my life with coffee spoons"?

2. This poem abounds in intriguing images. Choose two more images and discuss what symbolic meanings they might suggest.

William Carlos Williams (1883–1963)
The Red Wheelbarrow (1923)

so much depends
upon

a red wheel
barrow

glazed with rain   5
water

beside the white
chickens.

·····▶ *Your* Turn
Talking and Writing about Lit

1. William Carlos Williams made some very careful choices here in creating his images and in deciding upon line breaks (where he would break a line and start a new line). Do you think the poet made the right choices? Why or why not?

2. **DIY**   Write a poem of your own that uses line breaks to fashion a single sentence into a poem. Use a moment, object, gesture, or action to be at the center of your poem, as the red wheelbarrow is at the center of Williams's poem.

Duane Esposito (b. 1965)
Open Window (2004)

You believe you are obese
at 96 pounds, refuse

to consume pleasure,
& because you're cold

our door isn't open,   5
our joy's untenable.

Love's memory scatters—
flat in me while you speak,

& I'm carefully distracted by
the sound of the sudden rain.   10

Your Turn
Talking and Writing about Lit

1. In Duane Esposito's "Open Window," a great deal goes on in only ten lines. In what ways is this poem simple? In what ways is this poem complex?

2. DIY   Write a brief poem in which the speaker of the poem is listening to someone speak while at the same time is being distracted by something else (perhaps more important).

Bart Edelman (b. 1951)
Photograph (Circa 1960) (2004)

You open the freezer one morning
In search of an onion bagel
To suppress last night's hunger
And find an old photograph
Hidden among the frozen foods.   5
You don't question how it got there—
Stranger things have happened;
Rather, you take it in stride
And begin the thawing process.
About an hour or two later   10
It all comes into focus:
The year is circa 1960,
Your family carefully posed
Around the backyard swimming pool
Which will one day swallow   15
Your younger brother, Herbert,
Who will lie, motionless,
At the bottom of the deep end,
Before he is discovered by you.
But in the photograph, of course,   20
There is no sign of this tragedy—
Just you two holding hands,
While your parents sit, lovingly,
On the edge of the diving board.
And that makes you wonder: 25
Who took this particular picture?

Any clue you hoped to find written
On the back of the snapshot
Has disappeared across the wet surface
And become, more or less, illegible.   30
This bothers you for a brief moment
Until you wash a week's worth of dishes
And place the photograph in the freezer, again.

·····➤ *Your* Turn
Talking and Writing about Lit

1. Bart Edelman's poem opens with a very ordinary image of someone ("You")
   opening the freezer one morning in search of an onion bagel and finding an
   old photograph instead. What do you think Edelman is trying to say in this
   poem?

2. What is the significance of the speaker's washing the dishes just now? What
   is the significance of his placing the photograph back in the freezer?

Theodore Roethke (1908–1963)
Root Cellar (1948)

Nothing would sleep in that cellar, dank as a ditch,
Bulbs broke out of boxes hunting for chinks in the dark,
Shoots dangled and drooped,
Lolling obscenely from mildewed crates,
Hung down long yellow evil necks, like tropical snakes.   5
And what a congress of stinks!—
Roots ripe as old bait,
Pulpy stems, rank, silo-rich,
Leaf-mold, manure, lime, piled against slippery planks.
Nothing would give up life: 10
Even the dirt kept breathing a small breath.

·····➤ *Your* Turn
Talking and Writing about Lit

1. After rereading the first line as well as the last two lines of the poem, articulate (in a brief paragraph) what you believe to be the poem's themes.

2. **DIY**   Write a brief poem that depicts simply the sensory detail of a
              place familiar to you: your favorite spot to relax, a musical venue,
   your bedroom, the house you grew up in.

Edgar Allan Poe (1809–1849)

The Raven (1845)

Once upon a midnight dreary, while I pondered, weak and weary,
Over many a quaint and curious volume of forgotten lore—
While I nodded, nearly napping, suddenly there came a tapping,
As of some one gently rapping, rapping at my chamber door.
"'Tis some visitor," I muttered, "tapping at my chamber door—   5
                                  Only this and nothing more."

Ah, distinctly I remember it was in the bleak December;
And each separate dying ember wrought its ghost upon the floor.
Eagerly I wished the morrow;—vainly I had sought to borrow
From my books surcease of sorrow—sorrow for the lost Lenore—   10
For the rare and radiant maiden whom the angels name Lenore—
                               Nameless *here* for evermore.

And the silken, sad, uncertain rustling of each purple curtain
Thrilled me—filled me with fantastic terrors never felt before;
So that now, to still the beating of my heart, I stood repeating   15
"'Tis some visitor entreating entrance at my chamber door;—
Some late visitor entreating entrance at my chamber door;—
                              This it is and nothing more."

Presently my soul grew stronger; hesitating then no longer,
"Sir," said I, "or Madam, truly your forgiveness I implore;   20
But the fact is I was napping, and so gently you came rapping,
And so faintly you came tapping, tapping at my chamber door,
That I scarce was sure I heard you"—here I opened wide the door;—
                             Darkness there and nothing more.

Deep into that darkness peering, long I stood there wondering,
    fearing,   25
Doubting, dreaming dreams no mortal ever dared to dream before;
But the silence was unbroken, and the stillness gave no token,
And the only word there spoken was the whispered word, "Lenore?"
This I whispered, and an echo murmured back the word, "Lenore!"
                         Merely this and nothing more.   30

Back into the chamber turning, all my soul within me burning,
Soon again I heard a tapping somewhat louder than before.
"Surely," said I, "surely that is something at my window lattice;
Let me see, then, what thereat is, and this mystery explore—
Let my heart be still a moment and this mystery explore;—   35
                       'Tis the wind and nothing more!"

Open here I flung the shutter, when, with many a flirt and flutter,
In there stepped a stately Raven of the saintly days of yore;
Not the least obeisance made he; not a minute stopped or stayed he;
But, with mien of lord or lady, perched above my chamber door—   40
Perched upon a bust of Pallas[1] just above my chamber door—
                    Perched, and sat, and nothing more.

Then this ebony bird beguiling my sad fancy into smiling,
By the grave and stern decorum of the countenance it wore,
"Though thy crest be shorn and shaven, thou," I said, "art sure
        no craven,   45
Ghastly grim and ancient Raven wandering from the Nightly shore—
Tell me what thy lordly name is on the Night's Plutonian[2] shore!"
                    Quoth the Raven, "Nevermore."

Much I marvelled this ungainly fowl to hear discourse so plainly,
Though its answer little meaning—little relevancy bore;   50
For we cannot help agreeing that no living human being
Ever yet was blessed with seeing bird above his chamber door—
Bird or beast upon the sculptured bust above his chamber door,
                    With such name as "Nevermore."

But the Raven, sitting lonely on the placid bust, spoke only   55
That one word, as if his soul in that one word he did outpour.
Nothing farther then he uttered—not a feather then he fluttered—
Till I scarcely more than muttered, "Other friends have flown before—
On the morrow *he* will leave me, as my Hopes have flown before."
                    Then the bird said, "Nevermore."   60

Startled at the stillness broken by reply so aptly spoken,
"Doubtless," said I, "what it utters is its only stock and store
Caught from some unhappy master whom unmerciful Disaster
Followed fast and followed faster till his songs one burden bore—
Till the dirges of his Hope that melancholy burden bore   65
                    Of 'Never—nevermore.'"

But the Raven still beguiling all my sad fancy into smiling,
Straight I wheeled a cushioned seat in front of bird and bust and door;
Then, upon the velvet sinking, I betook myself to linking
Fancy unto fancy, thinking what this ominous bird of yore—   70
What this grim, ungainly, ghastly, gaunt, and ominous bird of yore
                    Meant in croaking "Nevermore."

---

[1]**Pallas:** Athena, goddess of wisdom.
[2]**Plutonian:** after Pluto, Roman god of the underworld.

This I sat engaged in guessing, but no syllable expressing
To the fowl whose fiery eyes now burned into my bosom's core;
This and more I sat divining, with my head at ease reclining   75
On the cushion's velvet lining that the lamp-light gloated o'er,
But whose velvet-violet lining with the lamp-light gloating o'er,
                              She shall press, ah, nevermore!

Then, methought, the air grew denser, perfumed from an unseen censer
Swung by seraphim whose foot-falls tinkled on the tufted floor.   80
"Wretch," I cried, "thy God hath lent thee—by these angles he hath
       sent thee.
Respite—respite and nepenthe³ from thy memories of Lenore;
Quaff, oh quaff this kind nepenthe and forget this lost Lenore!"
                              Quoth the Raven, "Nevermore."

"Prophet!" said I, "thing of evil!—prophet still, if bird or devil!—   85
Whether Tempter sent, or whether tempest tossed thee here ashore,
Desolate yet all undaunted, on this desert land enchanted—
On this home by Horror haunted—tell me truly, I implore—
Is there—*is* there balm in Gilead?—tell me—tell me, I implore!"
                              Quoth the Raven, "Nevermore."   90

"Prophet!" said I, "thing of evil!—prophet still, if bird or devil!
By that Heaven that bends above us—by that God we both adore—
Tell this soul with sorrow laden if, within the distant Aidenn,⁴
It shall clasp a sainted maiden whom the angels name Lenore—
Clasp a rare and radiant maiden whom the angels name Lenore."   95
                              Quoth the Raven, "Nevermore."

"Be that word our sign of parting, bird or fiend!" I shrieked,
       upstarting—
"Get thee back into the tempest and the Night's Plutonian shore!
Leave no black plume as a token of that lie thy soul hath spoken!
Leave my loneliness unbroken—quit the bust above my door!   100
Take thy beak from out my heart, and take thy form from off my door!"
                              Quoth the Raven, "Nevermore."

And the Raven, never flitting, still is sitting, *still* is sitting
On the pallid bust of Pallas just above my chamber door;
And his eyes have all the seeming of a demon's that is dreaming,   105

---

³**Nepenthe:** drug that causes forgetfulness.
⁴**Aidenn:** Eden.

And the lamp-light o'er him streaming throws his shadow on the floor;
And my soul from out that shadow that lies floating on the floor
                                    Shall be lifted—nevermore!

·····➤ *Your* Turn
Talking and Writing about Lit

1. Name at least five images that contribute to the feeling of foreboding in
Edgar Allan Poe's "The Raven."

2. **DIY**   Write a tribute or a humorous parody of "The Raven" which
                makes use of at least some of its pattern of rhyming lines. Your
poem doesn't need to be as long as the original, but it needs to use some
images that create a tone or mood—either one of foreboding and dread, or
one that makes mocking fun of that familiar foreboding.

Elizabeth Barrett Browning (1806–1861)
Sonnets from the Portuguese, 43 (1845–46)

How do I love thee? Let me count the ways.
I love thee to the depth and breadth and height
My soul can reach, when feeling out of sight
For the ends of Being and ideal Grace.
I love thee to the level of everyday's   5
Most quiet need, by sun and candle-light.
I love thee freely, as men strive for Right;
I love thee purely, as they turn from Praise.
I love thee with the passion put to use
In my old griefs, and with my childhood's faith.   10
I love thee with a love I seemed to lose
With my lost saints—I love thee with the breath,
Smiles, tears, of all my life!—and, if God choose,
I shall but love thee better after death.

·····➤ *Your* Turn
Talking and Writing about Lit

1. List at least five of the specific images used by Browning's speaker to
characterize love.

2. This poem expresses a fervent love but in a relatively abstract way. Compare the use of imagery in Browning's poem to that in the following poem, Gary Snyder's "Pine Needles."

Gary Snyder (b. 1930)
Pine Needles (1968)

some raindrops still clinging
—I brought you these pine boughs

—you look like you'd jump up
& put your hot cheek against this green,
fiercely thrust your cheek   5
into the blue pine needles
greedily
—you're going to startle the others—
did you want to go to the woods
         that much?   10
burning with fever
tormented by sweat and pain

And me working happily in the sunlight
Thinking of you, walking slowly through the trees
"Oh I'm all right now   15
it's like you brought the
center of the forest right here . . ."

Like a bird or a squirrel
you long for the woods.
how you must envy me,   20
my sister, who this very day must
travel terribly far.
can you manage it alone?
ask me to go with you
crying—ask me—   25
your cheeks however
how beautiful they are.

I'll put these fresh pine boughs
on top of the mosquito net
they may drip a little   30
ah, a clean
smell like turpentine.

·····▶ *Your* **Turn**
Talking and Writing about Lit

1. How would you characterize the tone of Gary Snyder's "Pine Needles"? Give at least three examples (quotations) to support your view.

2. **DIY** In a simile in line 18, the speaker characterizes his lover as "a bird or a squirrel." Write a brief description (in the form of a paragraph or a poem) in which you characterize someone you know well, using characteristics of a familiar animal (this could be a domestic animal like a dog, cat, fish, or hamster, or it could be a farm animal or a wild animal).

Philip Levine (b. 1928)
Saturday Sweeping (1984)

Saturday sweeping
with an old broom
counting the strokes
back and forth.
The dust sprays   5
up silver in the
February sun
and comes down gray.
Soft straw muzzle
poking in and   10
bringing out
scraps of news,
little fingers
and signatures.
Everybody's   15
had this room
one time or another
and never thought
to sweep. Outside
the snows stiffen,   20
the roofs loosen
their last teeth
into the streets.
Outside it's
1952,   25
Detroit, unburned,
stumbles away
from my window

over the drained roofs
toward the river   30
to scald its useless
hands. Half
the men in this town
are crying in
the snow, their eyes   35
blackened like
Chinese soldiers.
The gates are closing
at Dodge Main
and Wyandotte   40
Chemical; they
must go home
to watch the kids
scrub their brown
faces or grease   45
cartridges for
the show down.
If anyone knocks
on your door
he'll be   50
oil flecked or
sea born, he'll
be bringing word
from the people
of the ice drifts   55
or the great talking dogs
that saved the Jews.
Meanwhile our masters
will come on
television   60
to ask for our help.
Here, the radiator's
working, stove says
Don't touch,
and the radio's crying,   65
I don't get enough.
I'm my keeper,
the only thing
I've got,
sweeping out   70
my one-room life
while the sun's
still up.

·····▶ *Your* **Turn**
Talking and Writing about Lit

1. Philip Levine's "Saturday Sweeping" is full of sensory images from beginning to end—from the dust motes spraying "up silver in the February sun" at the beginning to the speaker's sweeping out his "one-room life" at the end. Choose the two images you consider to be the most effective and explain why you think they work well.

2. Compare Levine's "Saturday Sweeping" with Rita Dove's "The Satisfaction Coal Company" (in Chapter 14).

Gerard Manley Hopkins (1844–1889)
Pied Beauty (1918)

Glory be to God for dappled things—
    For skies of couple-color as a brinded cow;
        For rose-moles all in stipple upon trout that swim;
Fresh-firecoal chestnut-falls; finches' wings;
    Landscape plotted and pieced—fold, fallow and plow;   5
        And all trades, their gear and tackle and trim.
All things counter, original, spare, strange;
    Whatever is fickle, freckled (who knows how?)
        With swift, slow; sweet, sour; adazzle, dim;
He fathers-forth whose beauty is past change: 10
        Praise him.

·····▶ *Your* **Turn**
Talking and Writing about Lit

1. *The American Heritage Dictionary* defines "pied" as "patchy in color, splotched or piebald." How would you interpret Hopkins's images here on the literal level? Do you think the poem's images have a symbolic meaning as well?

2. Compare the depiction of nature in Hopkins's poem with that in Gary Snyder's "Pine Needles".

Joseph Bruchac (b. 1942)
Ellis Island (1979)

Beyond the red brick of Ellis Island
where the two Slovak children
who became my grandparents
waited the long days of quarantine,

after leaving the sickness,   5
the old Empires of Europe,
a Circle Line[1] ship slips easily
on its way to the island
of the tall woman[2] green
as dreams of forests and meadows   10
waiting for those who'd worked
a thousand years
yet never owned their own.
Like millions of others,
I too come to this island,   15
nine decades the answerer
of dreams.

Yet only one part of my blood loves that memory.
Another voice speaks
of native lands   20
within this nation.
Lands invaded
when the earth became owned.
Lands of those who followed
the changing Moon,   25
knowledge of the seasons
in their veins.

·····▶ *Your* Turn
Talking and Writing about Lit

1. Joseph Bruchac's "Ellis Island" breaks neatly into two parts: one celebrates his Slovakian ancestors, who entered the United States through Ellis Island; the other celebrates his Native American (Abenaki tribe) ancestors, who were earlier inhabitants of this continent. What images in the poem help reveal this dual heritage?

2. **DIY** Think about your own heritage and your family's experience of the United States. Write a brief poem or a brief essay in which you use vivid description and images to depict the lives of your family forebears. They may represent more than one cultural background (like Bruchac's) or they may be of a single cultural heritage.

---

[1]**Circle Line:** A tour boat.
[2]**tall woman:** Statue of Liberty.

N. Scott Momaday (b. 1934)
Comparatives (1976)

Sunlit sea,
the drift of fronds,
and banners
of bobbing boats—
the seaside   5
of any day—
except: this
cold, bright body
of the fish
upon the planks,   10
the coil and
crescent of flesh
extending
just into death.

Even so,   15
in the distant,
inland sea,
a shadow runs,
radiant,
rude in the rock: 20
fossil fish,
fissure of bone
forever.
It is perhaps
the same thing,   25
an agony
twice perceived.

It is most like
wind on waves—
mere commotion,   30
mute and mean,
perceptible—
that is all.

·····▶ *Your* Turn
Talking and Writing about Lit

1. As does Bruchac's poem above, N. Scott Momaday's poem falls into two (or three) parts. Write two or three sentences summarizing the meaning of the first stanza. Write two or three sentences interpreting the second stanza. Write one or two sentences discussing the third stanza.

2. Momaday, of Kiowa (Native American) heritage, writes about the natural world in "Comparatives." Compare Momaday's depiction of the natural world with that of Gary Snyder's in "Pine Needles."

Talking Lit

N. Scott Momaday writes about his Kiowa heritage and his experience as an artist—poet, painter, storyteller, memoirist, dramatist, and novelist.

N. Scott Momaday, Preface to *In the Presence of the Sun* (1976)

The poems in this collection were written over a period of thirty years, the drawings drawn over something less than twenty. In the same span I have written a good many other things, novels, essays, an autobiographical narrative, a play. My drawings, paintings, and prints have been exhibited in galleries and museums in this country and abroad. I have been, from the time I was in my twenties, a productive artist, not a prolific one as I think of it, but neither a straggler. Deadlines are useful but in some sense alien to my work. I believe that poems and paintings are made as they are made. I like to work in different forms. When I knew what it was to write a poem, I wanted to know what it was to write a novel, then a travel piece, then a film script, then a play. When I had found my way with charcoal and graphite, I went to watercolor and acrylics, to oils, to printmaking. I was and remain a patient student. With every attempt to write a line or draw an image I have learned something. I have tried to keep my mind alive for the sake of learning, which is to say for its own sake. That is my reason for doing what I do and for being who I am.

Thirty years is a long time or not, depending upon your point of view. My point of view is a plateau from which I view the world in my fifty-seventh year. Below I can see, in the very far distance, the dim figures of my ancestors, entering upon this continent thirty thousand years ago. Closer I can see Columbus touching upon the island he named San Salvador, and closer and closer by degrees, such things as the founding of Harvard College and the publication of the first book on the first printing press in New England, the signing of the Declaration of Independence, the Battle of Gettysburg, the last Kiowa Sun Dance in 1887, the great influenza epidemic of 1918 in which my maternal grandmother died, the great World Wars (I was born between them), the civil rights movement, the assassinations of John and Robert Kennedy and of Martin Luther King, the footprints of man on the moon, the assault of AIDS upon the human race, the collapse of the Soviet Union, and a growing awareness, as yet vague, that human beings, for all their assumed superiority over the plants and animals of the earth, have inflicted wounds upon the environment that are surely much more serious than we have realized, that may indeed be mortal. As a poet, a painter, and a man I care about these things. My life is involved in them.

I have been called "the man made of words," a phrase that I myself coined some years ago in connection with a Kiowa folktale. It is an identity that pleases me. In a sense, a real sense, my life has been composed of words. Reading and writing, talking, telling stories, listening, remembering, and thinking (someone has said that thinking is talking to oneself) have been the cornerstones of my existence. Words inform the element in which I live my daily life.

Poetry is a very old and elemental expression, as venerable as song and prayer. In various times and languages we have tried to elevate it to our current notions of formality and eloquence. And we have succeeded, for language, by its nature, allows us to do so. But poetry remains elemental. In poetry we address ourselves really, without pretension or deceit, without the intervention of interest. At its best, poetry is an act of disinterested generosity. The poet gives his words to the world in the appropriate expression of his spirit. It belongs to none in particular and to everyone in general. "This is my letter to the world," Emily Dickinson wrote. It is a viable definition of poetry.

From the time I could first function in language, I have been in love with words. How I gloried to hear my father tell the old Kiowa stories, which existed only at the level of the human voice. And how I loved my mother to invent stories in which I played the principal part. In my earliest years I lived in a home that was informed by the imagination, by the telling of stories and the celebration of language. Not only that, but I lived on several American Indian reservations in those days. I fell in love with Tanoan and Athabascan and Spanish and English words. Even now I can hear old people conversing in *Diné bizaad*, the Navajo language, and I am thrilled; I am transported to a time when I was a child at Chinle and heard wonderful words echoing on the cliffs of Canyon de Chelly. When I attend the Gourd Dance at Carnegie, Oklahoma, in July, the Kiowa language buoys me up in my spirit, and my being is defined in ancestral voices.

Words are names. To write a poem is to practice a naming ceremony.

These figures moving in my rhyme,
Who are they? Death, and Death's dog, time.

And to confer a name is to confer being. We perceive existence by means of words and names. To this or that vague, potential thing I will give a name, and it will exist thereafter, and its existence will be clearly perceived. The name enables me to see it. I can call it by its name, and I can see it for what it is.

The poet says, Here, let me show you something. That is, let me help you to see something as you have not seen it before.

And so says the painter. My father was a painter, and I watched him paint as I was growing up. He belonged to that tradition of Plains Indian art which proceeds from rock paintings to hide paintings to ledgerbook drawings to modern art, so called. He was in line with Zo-tom and the Kiowa Five and Black Bear Bosin.

Joseph Bruchac

Poetry: The Heartbeat Knows No Borders

(from an international online chat interview with Joseph Bruchac, January 10, 2001)
Anu Garg (Moderator): I just received this in email from a linguaphile in Poland: "I am sorry, but I cannot enter the chat with the author which was translated and published in Poland, and whose words are always my escape from the hatred and brutality of day-to-day life. He is right that we see the same sky and touch the same earth by our feet everywhere, and that our imagination can see the same beautiful story despite different languages used by Abenaki, American or Polish people. I do not know why I couldn't meet you. I cry." Marek Nowocien, *Tawacin* editor, Poland.

His work was bright and two-dimensional, rich in detail. As he matured his work became mythical and abstract, moored to story and visions. His work became steadily more powerful. His last paintings were his best paintings.

I observed him at work. I learned to see the wonderful things in his mind's eye, how they were translated into images on the picture plane.

In 1974 I accepted an invitation to teach at Moscow State University, and I lived in Moscow, in what was then the U.S.S.R., for six months. It was an experience, a high point in my life. I had much more time to myself than I thought I would, and I spent many, many hours riding the trains and walking the streets with the Muscovites. Richard Nixon fell from power and Aleksandr Solzhenitsyn was expelled from his homeland in those days. Pretty girls asked me to secure banned books for them, and their parents prepared banquets for me.

Something about that time and place made for a surge in me, a kind of creative explosion. I wrote numerous poems, some on the landscapes of my native Southwest, urged, I believe, by an acute homesickness. And I began to sketch. Drawing became suddenly very important to me, and I haunted museums and galleries and looked into as many Russian sketchbooks as I could find. When I came out of the Soviet Union I brought with me a new way of seeing and a commitment

Joseph Bruchac (Guest Speaker): Marek, my friend, thank you for your words. You know, there are borders on human maps, but there are no such borders on the earth. The hawk in flight does not see national boundaries and the heartbeat is the same in all of our breasts.

miki-usa: How many revisions of a poem do you do? I often find the entire poem comes out at one time.

Bruchac: In terms of writing and revision, I have to admit that I am only a good writer. But I think I am a VERY GOOD rewriter. I revise everything I write many times. I read it aloud and listen to my own words. It is true of many of the best poets. I remember sitting behind my friend Galway Kinnell . . . (one of the truly great modern American poets) as he gave a reading. I could see the poem he was reading over his shoulder. He had a pencil in his hand and was making revisions as he was reading it!

Lynn: When teaching about Native Americans, what do you think teachers should emphasize? Please consider this question in light of the fact that Native Americans have been negatively portrayed and stereotyped in books, magazines, films, etc.

Bruchac: Lynn, I'd urge teachers to emphasize the fact that Native Americans/ American Indians are people, not cultural icons or clichés. They are not just in the past, but in the present day. And I'd urge them to read the work of contemporary Native Americans. I recommend the book *Through Indian Eyes* (Oyate Books, edited by Doris Seale and Beverly Slapin).

to record it. I moved from charcoal to paint, from black and white to color, from paper to canvas, and back again. In Europe I discovered painters who truly inspired me: Emil Nolde, Francis Bacon, Pablo Picasso (whose work I thought I knew but did not), Georg Baselitz.

I had my first show in 1979, at the University of North Dakota Art Galleries. As I write this, I am preparing for a show at the Wheelwright Museum in Santa Fe, a retrospective; after nearly two decades of work, it is time. I feel that I have finished the first chapter of life as a painter.

The poems and stories, the drawings here, express my spirit fairly, I believe. If you look closely into these pages, it is possible to catch a glimpse of me in my original being.

Even headlines use figures of speech.

Nearly every type of figurative language can be found in the headlines of any given newspaper on any given day. Metaphor, simile, personification, hyperbole, apostrophe, understatement, synecdoche, and metonymy are types of figurative language used routinely by newspapers. Consider some of the headlines shown here. The headline "Gender Gap Separates Harvard" metaphorically compares the figurative gap between males and females with the some sort of real gap related to sexes that exists in one of the country's top colleges.

Sometimes headlines combine two or more figures of speech. The headline, "Celtics Turn the Page, but the Story Remains the Same" employs metaphor and personification. Newspapers often use hyperbole in the their headlines to drive home a point. The headline above that screams "Fire Hell," metaphorically conveys the message that a building fire was more horrible than could be imagined. As you will see in the chapter that follows, figures of speech are used by writers to convey information without being taken literally, and they are used in headlines, as well as in all types of literature.

What are Figures of Speech?

In the previous chapter, we talked about how meaning can operate both on the literal level and beyond it (on the symbolic level). Another way poems may have meaning beyond the literal level is through the use of figurative language, or **figures of speech**. We speak of such an image or phrase as being meant figuratively, not literally (or in some cases, figuratively as well as literally). Figurative language is one of the ways used to infuse poems with imagination, often with emotion.

Metaphor and Simile

In Sylvia Plath's "Mirror," the speaker states, "I am silver and exact," "I am not cruel, only truthful—/The eye of a little god, four-cornered," and we realize that the speaker is a mirror. This figure of speech is a **metaphor**, an implicit (implied, indirect) comparison of two dissimilar things.

Sylvia Plath (1932–1963)
Mirror (1963)

I am silver and exact. I have no preconceptions.
Whatever I see I swallow immediately
Just as it is, unmisted by love or dislike.
I am not cruel, only truthful—
The eye of a little god, four-cornered.   5
Most of the time I meditate on the opposite wall.
It is pink, with speckles. I have looked at it so long
I think it is a part of my heart. But it flickers.
Faces and darkness separate us over and over.

Now I am a lake. A woman bends over me,   10
Searching my reaches for what she really is.
Then she turns to those liars, the candles or the moon.
I see her back, and reflect it faithfully.
She rewards me with tears and an agitation of hands.
I am important to her. She comes and goes.   15
Each morning it is her face that replaces the darkness.
In me she has drowned a young girl, and in me an old woman
Rises toward her day after day, like a terrible fish.

The speaker is also a lake (line 10), which mirrors the image of a woman who searches, like Narcissus in the Greek myth, for her reflection. Gradually we learn that the woman who gazes in the mirror is upset by what she sees. This anxiety is articulated powerfully in the final lines of the poem with another figure of speech, a **simile**: "Each morning it is her face that replaces the darkness./In me she has drowned a young girl, and in me an old woman/Rises toward her day after day, like a terrible fish." The simile "an old woman/Rises toward her . . . like a terrible fish" is an explicit (direct, clearly evident) comparison of two dissimilar things. A simile makes a more explicit comparison than a metaphor by using the words "like," "as," or other similar words of direct comparison.

Personification

Another example of the figurative use of language is **personification**. When the poet assigns human attributes to an object, animal, or other nonhuman element, we refer to this as personification. Personification is at work when the speaker of Plath's poem says, "I am not cruel, only truthful" and "I meditate on the opposite wall." In the second stanza, the speaker says of the woman, "then she turns to those liars, the candles or the moon," and the reader knows that literal lying is not being referred to, but instead that a softening of the woman's appearance in the dim light makes her age less obvious. The candles and the moon are metaphorical, not literal, liars.

Controlling Metaphor, Extended Metaphor

Poet Claribel Alegría was born in Nicaragua, raised in El Salvador, and educated in the United States. She has written many moving poems about the civil wars in Central America. The title of her poem "I Am Mirror" makes a statement which is both a metaphor and a use of personification. In addition, since the idea of the speaker as a mirror runs throughout the poem (as it does in Plath's "Mirror"), we can also call it a use of **extended metaphor** or **controlling metaphor**. These terms refer to a recurring use of a metaphor throughout all of (or a substantial portion of) a work.

<u>**Claribel Alegría (b. 1924)**</u>
I Am Mirror (1978)

Translated by Electa Arenal and Marsha Gabriela Dreyer

Water sparkles
on my skin
and I don't feel it
water streams
down my back   5
I don't feel it
I rub myself with a towel
I pinch myself in the arm
I don't feel
frightened I look at myself in the mirror   10
she also pricks herself
I begin to get dressed
stumbling
from the corners
shouts like lightning bolts   15
tortured eyes
scurrying rats
and teeth shoot forth
although I feel nothing
I wander through the streets: 20
children with dirty faces
ask me for charity
child prostitutes
who are not yet fifteen
the streets are paved with pain   25
tanks that approach
raised bayonets
bodies that fall
weeping
finally I feel my arm   30
I am no longer a phantom
I hurt
therefore I exist
I return to watch the scene:
children who run   35
bleeding
women with panic
in their faces
this time it hurts me less
I pinch myself again   40
and already I feel nothing

I simply reflect
what happens at my side
the tanks
are not tanks   45
nor are the shouts
shouts
I am a blank mirror
that nothing penetrates
my surface   50
is hard
is brilliant
is polished
I became a mirror
and I am fleshless   55
scarcely preserving
a vague memory
of pain.

Thematically, Alegría's poem evokes additional types of "reflection," since the poet's work in general reflects outward to the larger world the events of El Salvador's civil war, embodying them in the images that are the poet's tools of the trade.

Hyperbole

Hyperbole (pronounced "hi-PER-bo-lee") is a figure of speech which relies on exaggeration to achieve its effects. In Robert Burns's "Oh, My Love Is Like a Red, Red Rose" (which also contains many similes, including the one in the title), we encounter the following use of hyperbole.

Robert Burns (1759–1796)
Oh, My Love Is Like a Red, Red Rose (1796)

Oh, my love is like a red, red rose
    That's newly sprung in June;
My love is like the melody
    That's sweetly played in tune.

So fair art thou, my bonny lass,   5
    So deep in love am I;
And I will love thee still, my dear,
    Till a' the seas gang* dry.

***gang:** Go.

> Till a' the seas gang dry, my dear,
>   And the rocks melt wi' the sun;   10
> And I will love thee still, my dear,
>   While the sands o' life shall run.
>
> And fare thee weel, my only love!
>   And fare thee weel awhile!
> And I will come again, my love   15
>   Though it were ten thousand mile.

Sometimes the use of hyperbole is humorous, but as you see in Burns's well-known love poem, it can also be generous, or tender, or grand. The Scottish poet, writing in the 1790s, represents a speaker who will cherish his beloved until the seas go dry and the rocks melt—in other words, until the world as we know it comes to an end.

In a contemporary poem about love and death and the savoring of life, David Mura (in "Grandfather and Grandmother in Love") writes about "the bodies that begot the bodies that begot me" and uses hyperbole toward the end of the poem.

David Mura (b. 1952)
Grandfather and Grandmother in Love (1989)

Now I will ask for one true word beyond
betrayal, that creaks and buoys like the bedsprings
used by the bodies that begot the bodies that begot me.
Now I will think of the moon bluing the white
sheets soaked in sweat, that heard him whisper   5
haiku of clover, azaleas, the cry of the cuckoo:
complaints of moles and beetles,
blight and bad debts, as the *biwa*'s[1] spirit
bubbled up between them, its song quavering.
Now I take this word and crack it, like a seed   10
between the teeth, spit it out into the world,
and let it seek the loam that nourished his greenhouse
roses, sputtering petals of chrysanthemum:
let it leave the sweet taste of *teriyaki*,
and a grain of rice lodges in my molars,   15
and the faint breath of *sake*, hot in the nostrils.
Now the drifting before writhing, now Buddha
stand back, now he bumps beside her,
otoo-san,[2] *okaa-san*,[3] calling each other.

---

[1]**biwa:** A Japanese stringed instrument.
[2]**otoo-san:** AGrandfather.
[3]**okaa-san:** Grandmother.

Now there reverberates the *ran* of lovers,   20
and the bud of the past has burst through
into the other world,
where she, teasing, pushes him away, swats
his hand, like a pesky, tickling fly,
and then turns to his face that cries out   25
laughing, and he is hauling her in, trawling
the caverns of her flesh, gathering gift
after gift from a sea that seems endless,
depths a boy dreams of, where dolphins
and fluorescent fins and fish with wings   30
suddenly spill their glittering scales
before him, and he, who was always baffled by beauty,
lets slip the net and dives under, and the night
washes over them, slipping from sight,
just the soft shushing of waves, drifting ground   35
swells, echoing the knocking tide of morning.

Through this device of exaggeration, Mura is assisted in representing a lifetime of relationship within a few lines. Elizabeth Bishop's poem "The Fish" ends with a use of hyperbole—"until everything/was rainbow, rainbow, rainbow!/ And I let the fish go."—which is also a moment of epiphany (sudden realization; see Chapter 7) for the speaker.

Elizabeth Bishop (1911–1979)

The Fish (1946)

I caught a tremendous fish
and held him beside the boat
half out of water, with my hook
fast in a corner of his mouth.
He didn't fight.   5
He hadn't fought at all.
He hung a grunting weight,
battered and venerable
and homely. Here and there
his brown skin hung in strips   10
like ancient wall-paper,
and its pattern of darker brown
was like wall-paper:
shapes like full-blown roses
stained and lost through age.   15
He was speckled with barnacles,
fine rosettes of lime,

and infested
with tiny white sea-lice,
and underneath two or three   20
rags of green weed hung down.
While his gills were breathing in
the terrible oxygen
—the frightening gills,
fresh and crisp with blood,   25
that can cut so badly—
I thought of the coarse white flesh
packed in like feathers,
the big bones and the little bones,
the dramatic reds and blacks   30
of his shiny entrails,
and the pink swim-bladder
like a big peony.
I looked into his eyes
which were far larger than mine   35
but shallower, and yellowed,
the irises backed and packed
with tarnished tinfoil
seen through the lenses
of old scratched isinglass.   40
They shifted a little, but not
to return my stare.
—It was more like the tipping
of an object toward the light.
I admired his sullen face,   45
the mechanism of his jaw,
and then I saw
that from his lower lip
—if you could call it a lip—
grim, wet, and weapon-like,   50
hung five old pieces of fish-line,
or four and a wire leader
with the swivel still attached,
with all their five big hooks
grown firmly in his mouth.   55
A green line, frayed at the end
where he broke it, two heavier lines,
and a fine black thread
still crimped from the strain and snap
when it broke and he got away.   60
Like medals with their ribbons
frayed and wavering,
a five-haired beard of wisdom

trailing from his aching jaw.
I stared and stared   65
and victory filled up
the little rented boat,
from the pool of bilge
where oil had spread a rainbow
around the rusted engine   70
to the bailer rusted orange,
the sun-cracked thwarts,
the oarlocks on their strings,
the gunnels—until everything
was rainbow, rainbow, rainbow! 75
And I let the fish go.

Synecdoche and Metonymy

A less well-known figure of speech is the **synecdoche** (pronounced "sin-ek-da-kee"). Linda Hogan's poem "The Truth Is" begins, "In my left pocket a Chickasaw hand / rests on the bone of the pelvis. / In my right pocket / a white hand." In this use of figurative language, the two hands represent the whole person and the speaker's dual heritage. Thus, synecdoche is a figure of speech in which the part represents the whole.

Linda Hogan (b. 1947)
The Truth Is (1985)

In my left pocket a Chickasaw hand
rests on the bone of the pelvis.
In my right pocket
a white hand. Don't worry. It's mine
and not some thief's.   5
It belongs to a woman who sleeps in a twin bed
even though she falls in love too easily,
and walks along with hands
in her own empty pockets
even though she has put them in others   10
for love not money.

About the hands, I'd like to say
I am a tree, grafted branches
bearing two kinds of fruit,
apricots maybe and pit cherries.   15

It's not that way. The truth is
we are crowded together
and knock against each other at night.
We want amnesty.

Linda, girl, I keep telling you   20
this is nonsense
about who loved who
and who killed who.

Here I am, taped together
like some old civilian conservation corps   25
passed by from the great depression
and my pockets are empty.
It's just as well since they are masks
for the soul, and since coins and keys
both have the sharp teeth of property.   30

Metonymy is a similar figure in which an object associated with something represents the entire thing (or person or idea or institution). At the end of Hogan's poem, when the speaker says "and my pockets are empty./It's just as well since they are masks/for the soul, and since coins and keys/both have the sharp teeth of property," we understand that coins represent money or wealth, and keys represent houses or other real estate possessions.

Apostrophe and Understatement

Another interesting use of figurative language is the **apostrophe**, which is a speech addressed to an absent person, or to an idea, object, animal, or other nonhuman element. Pablo Neruda's "Sweetness, Always" slips into the device of apostrophe in the second half, when he addresses fellow poets from around the world: "Brother poets from here/and there, from earth and sky,/from Medellín, from Veracruz,/Abyssinia, Antofagasta,/do you know the recipe for honeycombs?"

Pablo Neruda (1904–1973)
Sweetness, Always (1958)

Translated by Alastair Reid

Why such harsh machinery?
Why, to write down the stuff

and people of every day,
must poems be dressed up in gold,
in old and fearful stone? 5

I want verses of felt or feather
which scarcely weigh, mild verses
with the intimacy of beds
where people have loved and dreamed.
I want poems stained 10
by hands and everydayness.

Verses of pastry which melt
into milk and sugar in the mouth,
air and water to drink,
the bites and kisses of love. 15
I long for eatable sonnets,
poems of honey and flour.

Vanity keeps prodding us
to lift ourselves skyward
or to make deep and useless 20
tunnels underground.
So we forget the joyous
love-needs of our bodies.
We forget about pastries.
We are not feeding the world. 25

In Madras a long time since,
I saw a sugary pyramid,
a tower of confectionery—
one level after another,
and in the construction, rubies, 30
and other blushing delights,
medieval and yellow.

Someone dirtied his hands
to cook up so much sweetness.

Brother poets from here 35
and there, from earth and sky,
from Medellín, from Veracruz,
Abyssinia, Antofagasta,
do you know the recipe for honeycombs?

Let's forget all about that stone. 40

Let your poetry fill up
the equinoctial pastry shop
our mouths long to devour—
all the children's mouths
and the poor adults' also.   45
Don't go on without seeing,
relishing, understanding
all these hearts of sugar.

Don't be afraid of sweetness.

With us or without us,   50
sweetness will go on living
and is infinitely alive,
forever being revived,
for it's in a man's mouth,
whether he's eating or singing,   55
that sweetness has its place.

Anne Bradstreet's entire poem "The Author to Her Book" is an apostrophe. It is addressed to her first book of poems (*The Tenth Muse*), which was published in 1650 by her brother-in-law, without her knowledge or permission.

Anne Bradstreet (1612–1672)
The Author to Her Book (1678)

Thou ill-formed offspring of my feeble brain,
Who after birth did'st by my side remain,
Till snatched from thence by friends, less wise than true,
Who thee abroad exposed to public view;
Made thee in rags, halting, to the press to trudge,   5
Where errors were not lessened, all may judge.
At thy return my blushing was not small,
My rambling brat (in print) should mother call;
I cast thee by as one unfit for light,
Thy visage was so irksome in my sight;   10
Yet being mine own, at length affection would
Thy blemishes amend, if so I could:
I washed thy face, but more defects I saw,
And rubbing off a spot, still made a flaw.
I stretched thy joints to make thee even feet,   15
Yet still thou run'st more hobbling than is meet;
In better dress to trim thee was my mind,

But nought save homespun cloth in the house I find.
In this array, 'mongst vulgars may'st thou roam;
In critics' hands beware thou dost not come;   20
And take thy way where yet thou are not known.
If for thy Father asked, say thou had'st none;
And for thy Mother, she alas is poor,
Which caused her thus to send thee out of door.

Understatement is a figure of speech in which the speaker says *less* than is actually meant. Bradstreet uses the device of understatement when the speaker says, in lines 4–6, "Who thee abroad exposed to public view;/Made thee in rags, halting, to the press to trudge,/Where errors were not lessened, all may judge." The speaker goes on to show, through the use of figurative language, the extent of the "errors" and "defects" not lessened by the "press," meaning the critics and published criticism of her work.

The above are only a few of the most commonly used types of **figurative language**. In general, any use of language in which what is said cannot be taken only literally, but is recognized to imply something beyond the literal level instead (or as well), is a figure of speech. Another way to express this general definition is to say that we are dealing with a figure of speech when the speaker means something other than (or more than, or less than) what is actually said. Can you spot the uses of figurative language in the following poems?

Mary Oliver (b. 1935)
The Black Snake (1979)

When the black snake
flashed onto the morning road,
and the truck could not swerve—
death, that is how it happens.

Now he lies looped and useless   5
as an old bicycle tire.
I stop the car
and carry him into the bushes.

He is as cool and gleaming
as a braided whip, he is as beautiful and quiet   10
as a dead brother.
I leave him under the leaves

and drive on, thinking,
about *death:* its suddenness,

its terrible weight,   15
its certain coming. Yet under

reason burns a brighter fire, which the bones
have always preferred.
It is the story of endless good fortune.
It says to oblivion: not me!   20

It is the light at the center of every cell.
It is what sent the snake coiling and flowing forward
happily all spring through the green leaves before
he came to the road.

Sappho (c. 612–c. 580 B.C.)
With his venom (6th century B.C.E.)

Translated by Mary Barnard

With his venom

Irresistible
and bittersweet

that loosener
of limbs, Love   5

reptile-like
strikes me down

Ron Padgett (b. 1942)
Metaphor of the Morning (2001)

The morning is as clean and bright
as a freshly shaved cheek splashed with water
and rubbed with a new white towel.
Ah, the joys of metaphor!

But what if the morning were as dirty as   5
an old hag with a wen for a head
that is licking its chops and drooling on you?
Ah, the joys of metaphor!

But what if a blank metaphor descended from the sky
and landed lightly in your living room,   10
a cloudy, shifting swirl of gray tones and smoke?
It would be a Greek god! It would scare you!

Poems for Further Reading

Billy Collins (b. 1941)
Picnic, Lightning (1998)

"My very photogenic mother died in a freak accident
(picnic, lightning) when I was three."

Lolita

It is possible to be struck by a meteor
or a single-engine plane
while reading in a chair at home.
Safes drop from rooftops
and flatten the odd pedestrian   5
mostly within the panels of the comics,
but still, we know it is possible,
as well as the flash of summer lightning,
the thermos toppling over,
spilling out on the grass.   10

And we know the message
can be delivered from within.
The heart, no valentine,
decides to quit after lunch,
the power shut off like a switch,   15
or a tiny dark ship is unmoored
into the flow of the body's rivers,
the brain a monastery,
defenseless on the shore.

This is what I think about   20
when I shovel compost
into a wheelbarrow,
and when I fill the long flower boxes,
then press into rows
the limp roots of red impatiens—   25
the instant hand of Death
always ready to burst forth
from the sleeve of his voluminous cloak.

Then the soil is full of marvels,
bits of leaf like flakes off a fresco,   30

red-brown pine needles, a beetle quick
to burrow back under the loam.
Then the wheelbarrow is a wilder blue,
the clouds a brighter white,

and all I hear is the rasp of the steel edge   35
against a round stone,
the small plants singing
with lifted faces, and the click
of the sundial
as one hour sweeps into the next.   40

····••▶ *Your* **Turn**
Talking and Writing about Lit

1. Make a list of the figures of speech Billy Collins uses in "Picnic, Lightning."
2. Collins's speaker has something to say about death here, and yet this is not a gloomy poem. Write three or four sentences explaining what you think Collins is expressing here.

Billy Collins (b. 1941)
Marginalia (1998)

Sometimes the notes are ferocious,
skirmishes against the author
raging along the borders of every page
in tiny black script.
If I could just get my hands on you,   5
Kierkegaard, or Conor Cruise O'Brien,
they seem to say,
I would bolt the door and beat some logic into your head.

Other comments are more offhand, dismissive—
"Nonsense." "Please!" "HA!!"—   10
that kind of thing.
I remember once looking up from my reading,
my thumb as a bookmark,
trying to imagine what the person must look like
who wrote "Don't be a ninny"   15
alongside a paragraph in *The Life of Emily Dickinson*.

Students are more modest
needing to leave only their splayed footprints
along the shore of the page.

One scrawls "Metaphor" next to a stanza of Eliot's.   20
Another notes the presence of "Irony"
fifty times outside the paragraphs of *A Modest Proposal*.

Or they are fans who cheer from the empty bleachers,
hands cupped around their mouths.
"Absolutely," they shout   25
to Duns Scotus and James Baldwin.
"Yes." "Bull's-eye." "My man!"
Check marks, asterisks, and exclamation points
rain down along the sidelines.

And if you have managed to graduate from college   30
without ever having written "Man vs. Nature"
in a margin, perhaps now
is the time to take one step forward.

We have all seized the white perimeter as our own
and reached for a pen if only to show   35
we did not just laze in an armchair turning pages;
we pressed a thought into the wayside,
planted an impression along the verge.

Even Irish monks in their cold scriptoria
jotted along the borders of the Gospels   40
brief asides about the pains of copying,
a bird singing near their window,
or the sunlight that illuminated their page—
anonymous men catching a ride into the future
on a vessel more lasting than themselves.   45

And you have not read Joshua Reynolds,
they say, until you have read him
enwreathed with Blake's furious scribbling.

Yet the one I think of most often,
the one that dangles from me like a locket,   50
was written in the copy of *Catcher in the Rye*
I borrowed from the local library
one slow, hot summer.
I was just beginning high school then,
reading books on a davenport in my parents' living room,   55
and I cannot tell you
how vastly my loneliness was deepened,
how poignant and amplified the world before me seemed,
when I found on one page

a few greasy looking smears   60
and next to them, written in soft pencil—
by a beautiful girl, I could tell,
whom I would never meet—
"Pardon the egg salad stains, but I'm in love."

·····▶ *Your* Turn
Talking and Writing about Lit

1. Personification, metaphor, and simile all abound in "Marginalia." Find, underline, and list at least one example of personification, one simile, and four metaphors.

2. **DIY**   In lines 39–45, Collins writes about notes jotted down by monks "along the borders of the Gospels." Lines 44–45 read, "anonymous men catching a ride into the future/on a vessel more lasting than themselves," representing religious scriptures as a ship. Write a poem of approximately twelve lines in which you use an extended metaphor of a ship, train, car, or airplane (or other means of transportation) to describe a sports event, concert, or party.

Linda Pastan (b. 1932)
Marks (1978)

My husband gives me an A
for last night's supper,
an incomplete for my ironing,
a B plus in bed.
My son says I am average,   5
an average mother, but if
I put my mind to it
I could improve.
My daughter believes
in Pass/Fail and tells me   10
I pass. Wait 'til they learn
I'm dropping out.

·····▶ *Your* Turn
Talking and Writing about Lit

1. Explain the extended metaphor in Linda Pastan's "Marks."

2. Write a brief poem in which you use sports rankings (like MVP, "top-ranked," "six under par," "first place," "placed last in a field of X") to "rank"

a particular group of teachers (for instance, all of your high school teachers, all of your elementary school teachers, or all of the teachers at a particular school you attended in the past).

William Carlos Williams (1883–1963)
To Waken an Old Lady (1921)

Old age is
a flight of small
cheeping birds
skimming
bare trees   5
above a snow glaze.
Gaining and failing
they are buffeted
by a dark wind—
But what?   10
On harsh weedstalks
the flock has rested,
the snow
is covered with broken
seedhusks   15
and the wind tempered
by a shrill
piping of plenty.

·····▶ *Your* Turn
Talking and Writing about Lit

1. How would you explain the use of figurative language in "To Waken an Old Lady?"

2. **DIY**   Write a poem that begins: "Youth is . . ." or "Childhood is . . ."
and find a controlling metaphor that helps capture what you want
to say about that period in life.

e. e. cummings (1894–1962)
the Cambridge ladies who live in furnished souls (1923)

the Cambridge ladies who live in furnished souls
are unbeautiful and have comfortable minds

(also, with the church's protestant blessings
daughters, unscented shapeless spirited)
they believe in Christ and Longfellow, both dead,   5
are invariably interested in so many things—
at the present writing one still finds
delighted fingers knitting for the is it Poles?
perhaps. While permanent faces coyly bandy
scandal of Mrs. N and Professor D   10
. . . . the Cambridge ladies do not care, above
Cambridge if sometimes in its box of
sky lavender and cornerless, the
moon rattles like a fragment of angry candy

·····▶ *Your* Turn
Talking and Writing about Lit

1. Summarize what you think e.e. cummings is trying to say about the "Cambridge ladies."
2. Take another look at the last four lines of the poem and offer several suggestions for what cummings might mean by the "fragment of angry candy" in the last line.

Margaret Atwood (b. 1939)
you fit into me (1971)

you fit into me
like a hook into an eye

a fish hook
an open eye

·····▶ *Your* Turn
Talking and Writing about Lit

1. What device of figurative language serves as the foundation of this poem?
2. **DIY**   Write a four-line poem that has at its core a metaphor or simile. Yours might present an idea of something frightening, irritating, joyful, tender . . . you get to choose the emotion you want to evoke.

Rosario Castellanos (1925–1974)
Chess (1971)

Translated by Maureen Ahern

Because we were friends and sometimes loved each other,
perhaps to add one more tie
to the many that already bound us,
we decided to play games of the mind.

We set up a board between us;   5
equally divided into pieces, values,
and possible moves.
We learned the rules, we swore to respect them,
and the match began.

We've been sitting here for centuries, meditating   10
ferociously
how to deal the one last blow that will finally
annihilate the other one forever.

·····▶ *Your* **Turn**
Talking and Writing about Lit

1. Who are the two players? Remember that there are often multiple possibilities for meaning in a successful poem.

2. **DIY** Can you think of anything else that reminds you of a chess game? Write a brief poem in which something dissimilar is represented as a chess game or any type of board game (Monopoly, Clue, Chutes and Ladders, Parcheesi, Sorry, Scrabble).

Seamus Heaney (b. 1939)
Digging (1966)

Between my finger and my thumb
The squat pen rests; snug as a gun.

Under my window, a clean rasping sound
When the spade sinks into gravelly ground:
My father, digging. I look down   5

Till his straining rump among the flowerbeds
Bends low, comes up twenty years away
Stooping in rhythm through potato drills
Where he was digging.

The coarse boot nestled on the lug, the shaft   10
Against the inside knee was levered firmly.
He rooted out tall tops, buried the bright edge deep
To scatter new potatoes that we picked
Loving their cool hardness in our hands.

By God, the old man could handle a spade.   15
Just like his old man.

My grandfather cut more turf in a day
Than any other man on Toner's bog.
Once I carried him milk in a bottle
Corked sloppily with paper. He straightened up   20
To drink it, then fell to right away

Nicking and slicing neatly, heaving sods
Over his shoulder, going down and down
For the good turf. Digging.
The cold smell of potato mould, the squelch and slap   25
Of soggy peat, the curt cuts of an edge
Through living roots awaken in my head.
But I've no spade to follow men like them.

Between my finger and my thumb
The squat pen rests.   30
I'll dig with it.

·····▶ *Your* Turn
Talking and Writing about Lit

1. What comparison is implied in the last stanza of "Digging"?

2. ⬭**DIY** Think of a task at which one of your parents (or another adult
close to you when you were growing up) was particularly good.
Write a brief poem about watching that person perform the task.

Robert Frost (1874–1963)
Mending Wall (1914)

Something there is that doesn't love a wall,
That sends the frozen-ground-swell under it,

And spills the upper boulders in the sun;
And makes gaps even two can pass abreast.
The work of hunters is another thing: 5
I have come after them and made repair
Where they have left not one stone on a stone,
But they would have the rabbit out of hiding,
To please the yelping dogs. The gaps I mean,
No one has seen them made or heard them made,   10
But at spring mending-time we find them there.
I let my neighbor know beyond the hill;
And on a day we meet to walk the line
And set the wall between us once again.
We keep the wall between us as we go.   15
To each the boulders that have fallen to each.
And some are loaves and some so nearly balls
We have to use a spell to make them balance:
"Stay where you are until our backs are turned!"
We wear our fingers rough with handling them.   20
Oh, just another kind of outdoor game,
One on a side. It comes to little more:
There where it is we do not need the wall:
He is all pine and I am apple orchard.
My apple trees will never get across   25
And eat the cones under his pines, I tell him.
He only says, "Good fences make good neighbors."
Spring is the mischief in me, and I wonder
If I could put a notion in his head:
"*Why* do they make good neighbors? Isn't it   30
Where there are cows? But here there are no cows.
Before I built a wall I'd ask to know
What I was walling in or walling out,
And to whom I was like to give offense.
Something there is that doesn't love a wall,   35
That wants it down." I could say "Elves" to him,
But it's not elves exactly, and I'd rather
He said it for himself. I see him there,
Bringing a stone grasped firmly by the top
In each hand, like an old-stone savage armed.   40
He moves in darkness as it seems to me,
Not of woods only and the shade of trees.
He will not go behind his father's saying,
And he likes having thought of it so well
He says again, "Good fences make good neighbors."   45

····•► *Your* **Turn**

Talking and Writing about Lit

1. In Frost's "Mending Wall," does the speaker of the poem feel differently about the wall than the neighbor? Explain.

2. What does the stone wall symbolize?

Emily Dickinson (1830–1886)
After great pain, a formal feeling comes— (ca. 1862)

After great pain, a formal feeling comes—
The Nerves sit ceremonious, like Tombs—
The stiff Heart questions was it He, that bore,
And Yesterday, or Centuries before?

The Feet, mechanical, go round—   5
Of Ground, or Air, or Ought—
A Wooden way
Regardless grown,
A Quartz contentment, like a stone—

This is the Hour of Lead—   10
Remembered, if outlived,
As Freezing Persons recollect the Snow—
First—Chill—then Stupor—then the letting go—

····•► *Your* **Turn**

Talking and Writing about Lit

1. Explain how imagery and sensory detail in Dickinson's poem help reveal its themes to us.

2. Concentrate on the last stanza, which begins with the memorable line, "This is the Hour of Lead—." For each of the four lines of that last stanza, write a sentence or more offering your interpretation of the line.

Derek Walcott
Frederiksted,[1] Dusk (1976)

Sunset, the cheapest of all picture-shows,
was all they waited for; old men like empties

---

[1]**Frederiksted:** City on the west coast of St. Croix, one of the Virgin Islands in the West Indies.

set down from morning outside the almshouse,[2]
to let the rising evening brim their eyes,
and, in one row, return the level stare   5
of light that shares its mortal properties
with the least stone in Frederiksted, as if
more than mortality brightened the air,
like a girl tanning on a rock alone
who fills with light. Whatever it is   10
that leaves bright flesh like sand and turns it chill,
not age alone, they were old, but a state
made possible by their collective will,
would shine in them like something between life
and death, our two concrete simplicities,   15
and waited too in, seeming not to wait,
substantial light and insubstantial stone.

---

[2]**Lines 2 and 3:** Poorhouse: "empties": that is, empty bottles to be picked up by the milk deliverer.

····▶ *Your* **Turn**
Talking and Writing about Lit

1. Walcott's seventeen-line poem comprises only two sentences. Why do you
think Walcott chose to use the long, winding syntax we encounter in this
poem? Do you think it serves his purposes here?

2. **DIY**   Write a six- to ten-line poem that is all one sentence. Use line
breaks to try different line lengths to achieve different pacing or
rhythm in your poem.

Sharon Olds (b. 1942)
Sex without Love (1984)

How do they do it, the ones who make love
without love? Beautiful as dancers,
gliding over each other like ice skaters
over the ice, fingers hooked
inside each other's bodies, faces   5
red as steak, wine, wet as the
children at birth whose mothers are going to
give them away. How do they come to the
come to the   come to the   God   come to the
still waters, and not love   10
the one who came there with them, light

rising slowly as steam off their joined
skin? These are the true religious,
the purists, the pros, the ones who will not
accept a false Messiah, love the   15
priest instead of the God. They do not
mistake the lover for their own pleasure,
they are like great runners: they know they are alone
with the road surface, the cold, the wind,
the fit of their shoes, their over-all cardio-   20
vascular health—just factors, like the partner
in the bed, and not the truth, which is the
single body alone in the universe
against its own best time.

····•► *Your* **Turn**
Talking and Writing about Lit

1. "Sex without Love" contains many complex and puzzling images. Analyze
   two of them.
2. Looking at the poem as a whole, what do you think Olds is trying to say
   about "Sex without Love"?

Anna Akhmatova (1889–1966)
Your Lynx-Eyes, Asia . . . (1945)

Translated by Stanley Kunitz

Your lynx-eyes, Asia,
spy on my discontent;
they lure into the light
my buried self,
something the silence spawned,   5
no more to be endured
than the noon sun in Termez.
Pre-memory floods the mind
like molten lava on the sands . . .
as if I were drinking my own tears   10
from the cupped palms of a stranger's hands.

····•► *Your* **Turn**
Talking and Writing about Lit

1. Identify two figures of speech in Akhmatova's "Your Lynx-Eyes, Asia . . . "
2. How many interpretations can you suggest for the final four lines of the poem?

Talking Lit

Stanley Kunitz, Pulitzer Prize–winner and former poet laureate of the United States, writes about his love of Anna Akhmatova's poetry and about the difficulties of translation.

Stanley Kunitz, from Preface to *Poems of Akhmatova*

In certain quarters the literal version of a poem is held sacred, though the term is definitely a misnomer. As Arthur Waley noted: "There are seldom sentences that have word-to-word equivalents in another language. It becomes a question of choosing between various approximations." Translation is a sum of approximations, but not all approximations are equal. Russian word-order, for example, says: "As if I my own sobs/out of another's hands were drinking." One has to rearrange the passage to make it sound idiomatic, and one may even have to sharpen the detail to make it work in English, but one is not at liberty to play arbitrarily with the given. The so-called literal version is already a radical reconstitution of the verbal ingredients of a poem into another linguistic system—at the expense of its secret life, its interconnecting psychic tissue, its complex harmonies. Let me illustrate with a close paraphrase (corrected for word-order) of one of Akhmatova's poems:

> It's your lynx's eyes, Asia,
> that have spied something in me,
> have ferreted out something buried,
> born of silence,
> and fatiguing and difficult,   5
> like midday Termez heat.
> As if the whole of proto-memory were flowing
> into the mind like molten lava,
> as if I were drinking my own sobs
> out of another's hands.   10

The rendering is conscientious, but the lines are only a shadow of the original text, incapable of producing its singular pleasures. The object is to produce an analogous poem in English out of available signs and sounds, a new poem sprung from the matrix of the old, drenched in memories of its former existence . . . what it said, how it breathed, the inflections of its voice. The Russian poet Nikolai Zabolotski had another figure for the process. He said it was like rebuilding a city out of the evidence of its ruins. To the best of my understanding, the version that follows—like its companions in the collection—is a translation from the Russian, not an adaptation or imitation:

> Your lynx-eyes, Asia,
> spy on my discontent;

Poets Laureate—
The People's Poets

The poet laureate of the United States is appointed by the Library of Congress. The official Library of Congress web site gives the following description of the purpose of the poet laureate position: "The Poet Laureate Consultant in Poetry to the Library of Congress serves as the nation's official lightning rod for the poetic impulse of Americans. During his or her term, the Poet Laureate seeks to raise the national consciousness to a greater appreciation of the reading and writing of poetry."

Billy Collins, Poet Laureate of United States, 2001–2003

> they lure into the light
> my buried self,
> something the silence spawned,   5
> no more to be endured
> than the noon sun in Termez.
> Pre-memory floods the mind
> like molten lava on the sands . . .
> as if I were drinking my own tears   10
> from the cupped palms of a stranger's hands.

Akhmatova is usually described as a formal poet, but in her later years she wrote more and more freely. Some of her poems, particularly the dramatic lyrics that developed out of her histrionic temperament, are so classically joined that they cannot be translated effectively without a considerable reconstruction of their architecture; others are much more fluid in their making. To insist on a universally rigid duplication of metrical or rhyming patterns is arbitrary and pointless, since the effects in any case are not mechanically transferable to another language. Instead of rhyme, our ear is often better pleased by an instrumentation of off-rhyme, assonance, consonance, and other linkages. Prosody is a manifold texture,

When Billy Collins was appointed to the position in 2001, the choice was praised by all those who were familiar with his poetry. Collins has a track record of attracting people from all walks of life and all cultural groups to his readings and to his poems. The reason he connects with so many people can be seen in his work. In "Picnic, Lightning" (above), he reveals his ideas to us through ordinary things: a pedestrian, comics, grass, a valentine, flower boxes, "a round stone." His poem "Marginalia" (also above) uses everyday language ("Yes." "Bull's-eye," "My man!") and images drawn from sports and the natural world ("cheer from the empty bleachers," "the shore of the page," "exclamation points/rain") to get his point across.

Other former poets laureate whose work is included in this book include Louise Glück (poet laureate for 2003–2004), Robert Pinsky (the first to serve three consecutive terms, 1997–2000), Rita Dove (1993–1995, two terms), Gwendolyn Brooks (1985–1986), Maxine Kumin (1981–1982), and Robert Frost (1958–1959). You can find a complete list of our poets laureate on the Library of Congress's Poet Laureate web page: http://www.loc.gov/poetry/laureate.html. The current poet laureate is Ted Kooser.

embodying the expressive range and variety of the human voice. In this connection Osip Mandelstam's widow offers a pertinent commentary:

> In the period when I lived with Akhmatova, I was able to watch her at work as well, but she was much less "open" about it than M., and I was not always even aware that she was "composing." She was, in general, much more withdrawn and reserved than M. and I was always struck by her self-control as a woman—it was almost a kind of asceticism. She did not even allow her lips to move, as M. did so openly, but rather, I think, pressed them tighter as she composed her poems, and her mouth became set in an even sadder way. M. once said to me before I had met Akhmatova—and repeated to me many times afterward—that looking at these lips you could hear her voice, that her poetry was made of it and was inseparable from it. Her contemporaries—he continued—who had heard this voice were richer than future generations who would not be able to hear it.

It may be some comfort to reflect that poets are not easily silenced, even in death. As Akhmatova herself wrote, towards the end, "On paths of air I seem to overhear/two friends, two voices, talking in their turn." Despite the passage of time, the ranks of listeners grow, and the names of Akhmatova and Pasternak and Mandelstam are familiar even on foreign tongues. Some of us are moved to record what we have heard, and to try to give it back in the language that we love.

Not many companies could get away with having only one word in their commercials, but that's what Meow Mix has done with its "Tastes so good, cats asks for it by name" campaign.

Generations later, kids are still wishing they were an Oscar Meyer wiener!

In 1974, Burger King launched one of its most enduring jingles: Hold the pickles, hold the lettuce. Special orders don't upset us. All we ask is that you let us serve it your way!

SOUND, RHYTHM, AND METER

Even jingles use sound, rhythm, and meter.

Even jingles use sound, rhythm, and meter. The sound, rhythm, and meter are what make these commercials memorable, in fact. While it is no longer on the air, the Burger King commercial that advertised the restaurant's willingness to accommodate special orders uses pleasing, repetitive sound to drive home the point that any ingredient can be removed from the standard menu items and to help the consumer remember that message. The use of alliteration in the first three lines makes the jingle easy to remember and repeat, and the repetitive use of the letters "l" and "s" make the jingle pleasing to the ear. The pattern of stressed and unstressed syllables creates rhythm. The metrical units are trochaic, with alternating stressed and unstressed syllables, beginning with a stressed syllable. The metrical units highlight the rhyming pattern, so that the syllables "let" from "lettuce," "set" from "upset us," and "let" from "let us" are rhymed. Similarly, the unstressed syllables in those phrases also rhyme: "uce" in "lettuce," "set" in "upset us" and "us" in "let us" all rhyme. Finally, every syllable of the last line is stressed, creating a spondee that deliberately disrupts the trochaic metrical pattern of the first three lines. The line thereby draws attention to itself, and drives home the message of the jingle.

Have you ever had the words to a song rolling around in your head all day? Even before human societies had written language, people took pleasure in the sound of words. Poetry had its origins in songs and chants which were passed on orally before they could be recorded in written form. It is thus not surprising that most poems still rely on the pleasures and devices of sound to help convey their effects.

Sound Effects

In William Carlos Williams's "The Dance," the poem's sounds almost seem to gather a physical, moving force equal to that of the dancers. This is achieved partly by the use of repetition, as in "the dancers go round, they go round and/around."

William Carlos Williams (1883–1963)
The Dance (1944)

In Breughel's* great picture, The Kermess,
the dancers go round, they go round and
around, the squeal and the blare and the
tweedle of bagpipes, a bugle and fiddles
tipping their bellies (round as the thick-   5
sided glasses whose wash they impound)
their hips and their bellies off balance
to turn them. Kicking and rolling about
the Fair Grounds, swinging their butts, those
shanks must be sound to bear up under such   10
rollicking measures, prance as they dance
in Breughel's great picture, The Kermess.

***Breughel's:** Pieter Breughel (died 1569), Flemish painter of peasant life.

The swinging sensation created by the repetition is also enhanced by **ono-matopoeia** (the use of words which approximate actual sounds; pronounced "ŏnă-mătă-pēē-ă"), such as "the squeal and the blare and the/tweedle of bag-pipes" and by the use of active, kinetic verbs: "Kicking and rolling," "swinging their butts," and "prance as they dance."

The poet Jean Toomer uses different devices of sound in "Reapers." **Alliteration** (the repetition of consonant sounds) and **assonance** (the repetition of vowel sounds) create pleasing or disturbing sounds in the piece, and they also echo the real-life sounds which are being described: "Black reapers with the sound of steel on stones/ Are sharpening scythes" and "And there, a field rat, startled, squealing bleeds."

Jean Toomer (1894–1967)
Reapers (1923)

Black reapers with the sound of steel on stones
Are sharpening scythes. I see them place the hones
In their hip-pockets as a thing that's done,
And start their silent swinging, one by one.
Black horses drive a mower through the weeds,   5
And there, a field rat, startled, squealing bleeds,
His belly close to ground. I see the blade,
Blood-stained, continue cutting weeds and shade.

Rhyme

In addition to the other sound devices mentioned, Toomer's poem above uses **end rhyme**: "stones . . . hones," "done . . . one," "weeds . . . bleeds," and "blade . . . shade." The use of such a precise **rhyme scheme** enhances the **rhythm** in the poem at the same time it creates a pleasing sound. The poet's scheme here comprises rhyming **couplets**, pairs of lines in which the last words rhyme with each other. All of the rhymes in this particular poem are examples of **exact rhyme** because the ending sounds are precisely the same.

When a poet uses endings that are almost the same, but not exactly, this is called **near rhyme** or **slant rhyme**. In Theodore Roethke's poem "My Papa's Waltz" (below), for instance, most of the end rhyme is exact, but two pairs of endings are examples of near rhyme: "dizzy . . . easy" and "pans . . . countenance." Traditional patterns of rhyme are discussed at greater length in Chapter 18, which explores fixed-form poetry.

Etheridge Knight uses a less common type of rhyme scheme in "A Watts Mother Mourns While Boiling Beans."

Etheridge Knight (b. 1931)
A Watts Mother Mourns While Boiling Beans (1973)

The blooming flower of my life is roaming
in the night, and I think surely
that never since he was born
have I been free from fright.
My boy is bold, and his blood   5
grows quickly hot / even now

he could be crawling in the street
bleeding out his life, likely as not.
Come home, my bold and restless son.—Stop
my heart's yearning! But I must quit   10
this thinking—my husband is coming
and the beans are burning.

While the poem is being read out loud, a pleasing echo of sound is noticeable. Only when the poem is studied more closely does the reader recognize the precise pattern of **internal rhyme** embedded in this poem: "night . . . fright," "hot . . . not," "yearning . . . burning." Some of the rhyming words appear internally, in the middle of a line, though their rhyming counterparts appear at the end of lines. If you underline the rhyming words, you can see the pattern visually. This poem contains other pleasing devices of sound in addition to its rhyme scheme. Here we also find examples of assonance, particularly many long "o" sounds, rich with emotion. The "o" sounds in "blooming," "flower," "roaming," "born," "bold," "blood," "hot," and "son" also serve a thematic purpose in helping to convey the mother's love for and fears for her son.

Patterns of Rhythm, called Metrical Patterns

Although it is a supremely compact poem, William Wordsworth's "My Heart Leaps Up" is rich in examples of the poet's devices of rhythm and meter.

William Wordsworth (1770–1850)
My Heart Leaps Up (1807)

My heart leaps up when I behold
    A rainbow in the sky:
So was it when my life began;
So is it now I am a man;
So be it when I shall grow old,
    Or let me die!   5
The Child is father of the Man;
And I could wish my days to be
Bound each to each by natural piety.

The use of a pattern of stressed and unstressed syllables to create rhythm is called **meter**. Scholars and poets have given names to different types of metrical units, called metrical **feet**. A pattern involving sets of unstressed syllables followed by stressed syllables, such as in Wordsworth's poem, is called an **iambic** foot, which can be represented by symbols to show the metrical pattern visually:

˘ ´ | ˘ ´ | ˘ ´ | ˘ ´

My heart   leaps up   when I   behold

The iambic foot is the most frequently used metrical unit in poetry. Other important types of metrical feet are given below, followed by words to illustrate the pattern of stressed and unstressed syllables:

Iambic	˘ ´	(ă—wáy)
Trochaic	´ ˘	(gó—iňg)
Anapestic	˘ ˘ ´	(ŭnděr—stánd)
Dactylic	´ ˘ ˘	(líke—ăblě)

The following two additional types of feet ordinarily would not be used as part of a metrical pattern but might instead be used to give special emphasis to a word or deliberately disrupt an established metrical pattern:

Spondee	´ ´	(deád sét)
Pyrrhic	˘ ˘	(ŭnděr)

Metrical patterns are further named according to the number of metrical feet in a line, in other words, the number of times that the pattern is repeated. In the example above from Wordsworth's first line, "My heárt | leăps úp | when Í | běhóld," this line is identified as iambic **tetrameter** because the iambic pattern is repeated four times. The following, then, are the names for these syllabic patterns and the number of feet per line that they represent:

Dimeter = two feet
Trimeter = three feet
Tetrameter = four feet
Pentameter = five feet
Hexameter = six feet
Heptameter = seven feet
Octameter = eight feet

About Wordsworth's "My Heart Leaps Up," we could say that iambic tetrameter (four iambic feet, as illustrated above in the first line) predominates in the poem. However, there are variations. The second line is in iambic trimeter (three iambic feet): "A rain | bow in | the sky." And the sixth line is in iambic dimeter (two iambic feet): "Or let | me die!"

Scanning a poem to determine its metrical pattern is called **scansion**. Although this is a useful exercise for looking more closely at how patterns of rhythm are established, it is not always exact. It is pretty common for two readers to analyze a line differently. For instance, the sixth line of Wordsworth's poem— "Or let me die!"—was read above as iambic diameter. It could also be identified as two spondee feet, with all four syllables being given equally strong emphasis. A reader reading the line this way might also want to assert that Wordsworth used every aspect of the line (spondees, shorter line, indentation, and exclamation point) to disrupt his established metrical pattern and get the listener's attention for this forceful thematic point: "Or let me die!" It is almost always useful to watch for connections between the poet's use of form and the themes embodied and expressed by the form. In other words, there is often a thematic reason for the choices a poet makes about form and technique.

Rhythm and Line Breaks

Line breaks (the poet's choice of where to break each line and begin a new line) can also influence a poem's rhythm, establishing it or disrupting it, in ways that engage the reader's attention, and often serving the theme. In "My Heart Leaps Up," there are both **end-stopped lines** (lines that come to a complete stop or long pause and that fall at the end of a complete thought grammatically) and **run-on lines** (lines that break without a full stop and that fall grammatically in the middle of a complete thought rather than at the end). An example of an end-stopped line would be the third line: "So was it when my life began;" and the fourth and seventh lines are end-stopped as well. The first line of the poem, on the other hand, is a run-on line because it is an unfinished thought that leans forward, drawing the reader down into the next line: "My heart leaps up when I behold / A rainbow in the sky:" The run-on line can also be referred to as **enjambment**, adapted from a French word meaning "to straddle." This is, in fact, a better way to think of the device, since the thought "straddles" two lines. In Wordsworth's poem, the first and second lines, the fifth and sixth lines, and the eighth and ninth lines are all examples of enjambment.

In "My Heart Leaps Up," it is evident that the poet found it thematically useful to establish a metrical pattern of rhythm and then disrupt it. In Theodore Roethke's "My Papa's Waltz," on the other hand, the poet does not choose to vary his rhythmic pattern but instead maintains it throughout the poem.

Theodore Roethke (1908–1963)
My Papa's Waltz (1948)

The whiskey on your breath
Could make a small boy dizzy;
But I hung on like death:
Such waltzing was not easy.

We romped until the pans   5
Slid from the kitchen shelf;
My mother's countenance
Could not unfrown itself.

The hand that held my wrist
Was battered on one knuckle;   10
At every step you missed
My right ear scraped a buckle.

You beat time on my head
With a palm caked hard by dirt,
Then waltzed me off to bed   15
Still clinging to your shirt.

Clearly, the sound of the waltz is echoed consistently in the waltz-like rhythm of the iambic trimeter lines. The strong rhythm created by the metrical pattern is also assisted by the consistent rhyme scheme. In each stanza, the first and third lines rhyme, as do the second and fourth lines.

There is little concern for end rhyme in Emily Dickinson's "Because I could not stop for Death," but the metrical pattern is of great importance.

Emily Dickinson (1830–1886)
Because I could not stop for Death (1863, 1890)

Because I could not stop for Death—
He kindly stopped for me—
The Carriage held but just Ourselves—
And Immortality.

We slowly drove—He knew no haste   5
And I had put away
My labor and my leisure too,
For His Civility—

We passed the School, where Children strove
At Recess—in the Ring—   10
We passed the Fields of Gazing Grain—
We passed the Setting Sun—

Or rather—He passed Us—
The Dews drew quivering and chill—
For only Gossamer, my Gown—   15
My Tippet—only Tulle—

We paused before a House that seemed
A Swelling of the Ground—
The Roof was scarcely visible—
The Cornice—in the Ground—   20

Since then—'tis Centuries—and yet
Feels shorter than the Day
I first surmised the Horses Heads
Were toward Eternity—

The predominant meter is a pattern of alternating lines of iambic tetrameter and iambic trimeter, within four-line stanzas (a stanza is a grouping of lines in a poem). This very regular pattern is disrupted, however, in the fourth stanza, when the speaker of the poem dies. Again, as we saw in Wordsworth's poem "My Heart Leaps Up," the poet has disrupted the metrical pattern for thematic reasons (reasons related to the poem's meaning). In Dickinson's fourth stanza, the meter breaks up as Death's carriage falls behind the setting sun, and the dying speaker's shroud-like garments are not adequate to protect her from the chill which descends on her. The regular meter resumes in the fifth stanza, in which they arrive at the grave, and continues in the sixth stanza, in which the speaker looks back from eternity (as you'll recall, we had learned in the first stanza that the speaker believes in an afterlife).

Simpler, perhaps, but no less powerful, is the kind of rhythm created by the repetition of words or phrases or grammatical patterns in a poem. Walt Whitman's influence is sometimes at work here, since so many modern and contemporary American poets have his sentence rhythms and enumerations (listing techniques) echoing in their heads. (See, for example, Whitman's poem included in Chapter 20). In Ana Castillo's "In My Country," most stanzas in the first half of the poem begin with the phrase "In my country"; whereas, in the remaining half of the poem's stanzas, the opening phrase "In my world" predominates. Also repeated within the stanzas are "I don't," "I do not," and "They do not." These and other uses of repetition not only establish a strong rhythm without the use of any fixed metrical pattern or rhyme scheme, but they also gather momentum and quicken the pace of the poem. The momentum which builds as the reader is drawn forward is both a momentum generated by form and also the force of an idea gathering speed. The repetitions are like successive waves of sound, propelling the ideas of the speaker foward—by turns forceful, wistful, hopeful.

Ana Castillo (b. 1953)

In My Country (1995)

This is not my country.
In my country, men
do not play at leaders
women do not play at men
there is no god   5
crucified to explain
the persistence of cruelty.

In my country
i don't hesitate to sit
alone in the park, to go   10
to the corner store at night
for my child's milk, to wear
anything that shows my breasts.

In my country
i do not stand for cutbacks,   15
layoffs, and pay union dues
companies do not close down
to open up again in far-off
places where eating is the
main objective.   20

In my country
men do not sleep with guns
beneath their pillows. They
do not accept jobs building weapons.
They don't lose their mortgages, pensions,   25
their faith or their dignity.

In my country
children are not abused
beaten into adulthood
left with sitters who resent them   30
for the meager salary a single parent
can afford. They do not grow up
to repeat the pattern.

In my country
i did not wait in line for milk   35
coupons for my baby, get the wrong
prescription at the clinic, was not

forced to give my ethnic origin,
nor died an unnatural death.

In my country, i am not exotic.   40
i do not have Asian eyes. i
was not raised on a reservation.
i do not go artificially blonde.
The sun that gravitates to my dark
pigmentation is not my enemy.   45

i do not watch television, entertain
myself at commercial movie houses,
invest in visual art or purchase
literature at grocery stores.

In my country, i do not stand   50
for the cold because i can't
afford the latest gas hike. i
am not expected to pay taxers
three times over.

This is not my world.   55
In my world, Mesoamerica
was a magnificent Quetzal,
Africa and its inhabitants
were left alone. Arab women
don't cover their faces or   60
allow their sexual parts to be
torn out. In my world,
no one is prey.

Death is not a relief.
i don't bet on reincarnation   65
or heaven, or lose the present
in apathy or oblivion.

i do not escape into my sleep.
Analysts are not made rich by
my discoveries therein. My   70
mother is not cursed for giving
birth. i am not made ashamed
for being.

In my world, i do not attend
conferences with academicians   75

who anthropologize my existence
dissect the simplicity of greed
and find the differences created
out of Babel interesting.

In my world   80
i am a poet
who can rejoice in the coming of
Halley's comet, the wonders
of Machu Picchu, and a sudden kiss.

In my world, i breathe clean air.   85
i don't anticipate nuclear war.
i speak all languages. i don't
negate aging, listen to myths
to explain my misery or create them.

In my world the poet sang loud   90
and clear and everyone heard
without recoiling. It was sweet
as harvest, sharp as tin, strong
as the northern wind, and all had
a coat warm enough to bear it.   95

Repetitions predominate in Joy Harjo's "She Had Some Horses," and the visual statement made on the page as it first catches the reader's eye is startling. Of the fifty-three lines of the poem, all but ten begin with the statement, "She had some horses." The statement stands alone, comprising its own stanza on eight of the lines.

Joy Harjo (b. 1951)
She Had Some Horses (1983)

She had some horses.

She had horses who were bodies of sand.
She had horses who were maps drawn of blood.
She had horses who were skins of ocean water.
She had horses who were the blue air of sky.   5

She had horses who were fur and teeth.
She had horses who were clay and would break.
She had horses who were splintered red cliff.

She had some horses.

She had horses with long, pointed breasts.   10
She had horses with full, brown thighs.
She had horses who laughed too much.
She had horses who threw rocks at glass houses.
She had horses who licked razor blades.

She had some horses.   15

She had horses who danced in their mothers' arms.
She had horses who thought they were the sun and their
bodies shone and burned like stars.
She had horses who waltzed nightly on the moon.
She had horses who were much too shy, and kept quiet   20
in stall of their own making.

She had some horses.

She had horses who liked Creek Stomp Dance songs.
She had horses who cried in their beer.
She had horses who spit at male queens who made   25
them afraid of themselves.
She had horses who said they weren't afraid.
She had horses who lied.

She had horses who told the truth, who were stripped
bare of their tongues.   30

She had some horses.

She had horses who called themselves, "horse."
She had horses who called themselves, "spirit," and kept
their voices secret and to themselves.
She had horses who had no names.   35
She had horses who had books of names.

She had some horses.

She had horses who whispered in the dark, who were afraid
to speak.
She had horses who screamed out of fear of the silence, who 40
carried knives to protect themselves from ghosts.
She had horses who waited for destruction.
She had horses who waited for resurrection.

She had some horses.

She had horses who got down on their knees for any savior.   45
She had horses who thought their high price had saved them.
She had horses who tried to save her, who climbed in her
bed at night and prayed as they raped her.

She had some horses.

She had some horses she loved.   50
She had some horses she hated.

These were the same horses.

    Because of the way in which the poem is structured, momentum builds in the longer stanzas, with enumerations following the core statement. Then the lines in which "She had some horses" stands alone bring the momentum to a halt and cause the reader to pause, breaking the rhythm and calling attention to the central statement in yet another way. The stopping of the rhythm regularly thus also becomes one aspect of the rhythm. And meaning gathers around the gathering up of sound—gradually, we come to know that the horses also represent people, and they also represent The People. Joy Harjo is of Creek, Cherokee, and French heritage.
    What devices of sound can be identified in Conrad Hilberry's painful poem "Tongue"?

Conrad Hilberry (b. 1928)
Tongue (1980)

He did not mean to test the cold
or his own daring. He did it idly,
not thinking, as he might suck
a little solace from his thumb.

Alone at recess, watching three boys   5
wrestle in the snow, he touched
his tongue to the cyclone fence
and it froze. The cold clanged shut.

With his fingers, he pulled at the tongue
as if it were a leech, sucking   10
the blood of his leg. But the ice held.
In panic, he tore away his mistake,

tore loose his tongue, leaving skin
like patches of rust on the metal.

What could he do with the torn and swollen   15
tongue, with shame that tasted like blood?

In school, he hid his mouth behind
his hands. He swallowed. He swallowed.

Describe the haunting cadences (rhythmic flow) of Denise Levertov's "The Ache of Marriage."

Denise Levertov (1923–1997)
The Ache of Marriage (1964)

The ache of marriage:

thigh and tongue, beloved,
are heavy with it,
it throbs in the teeth

We look for communion   5
and are turned away, beloved,
each and each

It is leviathan and we
in its belly
looking for joy, some joy   10
not to be known outside it

two by two in the ark of
the ache of it.

Examine the form of Richard Newman's "The Speed and Weight of Justice." How does the form of the poem help establish the rhythm? How does the use of enjambment help the poem gather momentum?

Richard Newman (b. 1962)
The Speed and Weight of Justice (2005)

You and I left this unfinished business
unfinished for too long, and now it's late.
Your flight leaves in two days. Tomorrow,

I have a date to help an old friend replace
china his ex-fiancée shattered against the wall   5
in their worst fight, which I witnessed. I'm

his lift to the warehouse, and then he
and his new girlfriend will join me
and my wife at our house for dinner.

You're smiling: Narrative always leads us away   10
from what our bodies lean towards.
I want you, I say. You whisper, *Where can we go?*

and it's so much more touch than words
that I carry the sounds with me on the train
the way I would've carried the texture   15

of your nipples on my palms. A man
parades in fatigues muttering *Kill
the bastards!*, pronouncing

each passenger *Dangerous!*
who dares to meet his gaze. I retreat   20
to where your question takes me:

The scene plays, my flesh rises, and the distance
this ride is putting between us vanishes
till the bell rings, the doors whoosh open

and I walk out squinting in sunlight   25
onto the streets of my marriage.
At the corner, the slow noise

where the justice is in our having met
now, when our separate lives separate us,
or, rather, we allow them to, so much   30

more effectively than the veils these women wore
protected them—to ask this is to ask what precisely?
I stand at my front door, the key still in my pocket,

and re-enter the room we never gave ourselves
the chance to find. Maybe someday we will,   35
but what would be different? I'd still arrive

here, home, in love; still feel myself there,
with you, coaxing, being coaxed, into presence,
until presence is all we know, and shadows

are what we are of the complex beings   40
we believe ourselves to be: the people
we need always to come back to.

Describe the uses of sound, rhythm, and meter found in the following two
poems.

Ben Jonson (1573–1637)
On My First Daughter (1616)

Here lies, to each her parents' ruth,*
Mary, the daughter of their youth;
Yet all heaven's gifts being heaven's due,
It makes the father less to rue,
At six months' end she parted hence   5
With safety of her innocence;
Whose soul heaven's queen, whose name she bears,
In comfort of her mother's tears,
Hath placed amongst her virgin-train:
Where, while that severed doth remain,   10
This grave partakes the fleshly birth;
Which cover lightly, gentle earth!

——————————

*ruth: sorrow

Robert Frost
The Secret Sits (1936)

We dance round in a ring and suppose,
But the Secret sits in the middle and knows.

Poems for Further Reading

Maxine Kumin (b. 1925)
Morning Swim

Into my empty head there come
a cotton beach, a dock wherefrom

I set out, oily and nude
through mist, in chilly solitude.

There was no line, no roof or floor   5
to tell the water from the air.

Night fog thick as terry cloth
closed me in its fuzzy growth.

I hung my bathrobe on two pegs.
I took the lake between my legs.   10

Invaded and invader, I
went overhand on that flat sky.

Fish twitched beneath me, quick and tame.
In their green zone they sang my name

and in the rhythm of the swim   15
I hummed a two-four-time slow hymn.

I hummed *Abide with Me*. The beat
rose in the fine thrash of my feet,

rose in the bubbles I put out
slantwise, trailing through my mouth.   20

My bones drank water; water fell
through all my doors. I was the well

that fed the lake that met my sea
in which I sang *Abide with Me*.

·····➤ *Your* Turn
Talking and Writing about Lit

1. How does the form of Maxine Kumin's "Morning Swim" help her establish
rhythm in the piece?

2. Describe the uses of rhyme in Kumin's poem.

Alfred, Lord Tennyson (1809–1892)
Break, Break, Break (1834)

Break, break, break,
    On thy cold gray stones, O sea!

And I would that my tongue could utter
    The thoughts that arise in me.

O, well for the fisherman's boy,   5
    That he shouts with his sister at play!
O, well for the sailor lad,
    That he sings in his boat on the bay!

And the stately ships go on
    To their haven under the hill;   10
But O for the touch of a vanished hand,
    And the sound of a voice that is still!

Break, break, break,
    At the foot of thy crags, O sea!
But the tender grace of a day that is dead   15
    Will never come back to me.

•••••▶ *Your* Turn
Talking and Writing about Lit

1. Describe at last three ways in which Tennyson establishes rhythm in "Break, Break, Break."

2. **DIY** **DIY:** Write a brief poem of your own (of ten to twelve lines) which begins with the same word repeated three times (for example "Wake, wake, wake" or "Pray, pray, pray" or "shake, shake, shake").

Alfred, Lord Tennyson (1809–1892)
The Eagle (1851)

He clasps the crag with crooked hands;
Close to the sun in lonely lands,
Ringed with the azure world, he stands.

The wrinkled sea beneath him crawls;
He watches from his mountain walls,   5
And like a thunderbolt he falls.

····•▶ *Your* **Turn**
Talking and Writing about Lit

1. How has Tennyson used careful word choice to characterize the eagle as powerful?

2. **DIY** Write a brief poem (of six to ten lines) in which you describe an animal. Settle on one or two important attributes of that animal and portray them using careful word choice and images.

<u>**Lewis Carroll (1832–1898)**</u>
Jabberwocky (1871)

'Twas brillig, and the slithy toves
    Did gyre and gimble in the wabe;
All mimsy were the borogoves,
      And the mome raths outgrabe.

"Beware the Jabberwock, my son!   5
    The jaws that bite, the claws that catch!
Beware the Jubjub bird, and shun
      The frumious Bandersnatch!"

He took his vorpal sword in hand:
    Long time the manxome foe he sought—   10
So rested he by the Tumtum tree,
      And stood awhile in thought.

And as in uffish thought he stood,
    The Jabberwock, with eyes of flame,
Came whiffling through the tulgey wood,   15
      And burbled as it came!

One, two! One, two! And through and through
    The vorpal blade went snicker-snack!
He left it dead, and with its head
      He went galumphing back.   20

"And hast thou slain the Jabberwock?
    Come to my arms, my beamish boy!
O frabjous day! Callooh! Callay!"
      He chortled in his joy.

'Twas brillig, and the slithy toves   25
    Did gyre and gimble in the wabe;
All mimsy were the borogoves,
      And the mome raths outgrabe.

····•▶ *Your* **Turn**
Talking and Writing about Lit

1. Although Lewis Carroll's "Jabberwocky" contains many "nonsense" words, these words tend to have strong connotations. Choose at least three of these words or phrases (such as "brillig," "Bandersnatch," or "Manxome foe") and discuss the connotations you associate with them. How do these connotative meanings lead one to interpret the words' meanings?

2. **DIY** Write at least four lines of poetry in which you use nonsense words or phrases that convey an emotion or a connotative meaning.

Philip Levine (b. 1928)
They Feed They Lion (1972)

Out of burlap sacks, out of bearing butter,
Out of black bean and wet slate bread,
Out of the acids of rage, the candor of tar,
Out of creosote, gasoline, drive shafts, wooden dollies,
They Lion grow.   5

      Out of the grey hills
Of industrial barns, out of rain, out of bus ride,
West Virginia to Kiss My Ass, out of buried aunties,
Mothers hardening like pounded stumps, out of stumps,
Out of the bones' need to sharpen and the muscles' to stretch,   10
They Lion grow.

      Earth is eating trees, fence posts,
Gutted cars, earth is calling her little ones,
"Come home, Come home!" From pig balls,
From the ferocity of pig driven to holiness,   15
From the furred ear and the full jowl come
The repose of the hung belly, from the purpose
They Lion grow.

From the sweet glues of the trotters
Come the sweet kinks of the fist, from the full flower   20
Of the hams the thorax of caves,
From "Bow Down" come "Rise Up,"
Come they Lion from the reeds of shovels,
The grained arm that pulls the hands,
They Lion grow.   25

From my five arms and all my hands,
From all my white sins forgiven, they feed,
From my car passing under the stars,
They Lion, from my children inherit,
From the oak turned to a wall, they Lion,   30
From they sack and they belly opened
And all that was hidden burning on the oil-stained earth
They feed they Lion and he comes.

·····➤ *Your* Turn
Talking and Writing about Lit

1. How does Philip Levine use connotative meanings to build an understanding of emotion and theme in "They Feed They Lion"?

2. Why do you think Levine uses nonstandard grammar in the poem (and even in the title)? How does his use of diction add to the rhythm and momentum of the piece?

Barbara Barnard (b. 1951)
Disguises (2003)

I am in disguise as a settled person.
inside, a gypsy struggles to get out.

I am in disguise as a proper person,
Inside, a girl in flame-lick boots shouts!

I am in disguise as a local person,   5
Inside, a hillbilly gal wants her say.

I am in disguise as a middle-class person,
Inside, the old ways pull strong and sure.

I am in disguise as a professional person,
Inside, it's hard to feel that I'm no longer poor.   10

I am in disguise as a well-spoken person,
Inside, my muse whispers ain'ts and double negatives
    to her heart's content!

I am in disguise as a carefully combed person.
Inside, a wild-haired mountain woman waits.   15

I am in disguise as a fixed-form person,
Inside, a free verse blossoms, pushing rhythm
    to the forefront like a field shout do!

·····▶ *Your* Turn
Talking and Writing about Lit

1. The author of "Disguises" (published in the *Nassau Review*, 2003) is the coauthor of this volume. In other words, I am writing questions for you about my own poem. Do you see the various devices I've used to establish the rhythm in this poem?

2. **DIY** The speaker of this poem feels the need to play down certain aspects of her heritage in her current social and professional context. Although I gave the speaker a particular cultural heritage, I see the poem as being rather universal. That is, most people use language in different ways depending on whom they're talking to (sociologists call this universal practice "code switching"). Write a poem in which your speaker uses two different levels of diction to portray two "sides" of his or her life experience. This might relate to two different "sides" of family heritage, two different schools you've attended, or the contrasting personalities of two parents or two siblings; the possibilities are endless.

Countee Cullen (1903–1946)
Incident (1925)

Once riding in old Baltimore
    Heart-filled, head-filled with glee,
I saw a Baltimorean
    Keep looking straight at me.

Now I was eight and very small,   5
      And he was no whit bigger,
And so I smiled, but he poked out
      His tongue, and called me, "Nigger."

I saw the whole of Baltimore
      From May until December;   10
Of all the things that happened there
      That's all that I remember.

····▶ *Your* Turn
Talking and Writing about Lit

1. Describe Countee Cullen's rhyme scheme in "Incident." How does the use of rhyme affect the sound of the speaker's "voice" (see Chapter 7)?

2. Reread the final stanza of "Incident." What multiple meanings do you think are implied in that last stanza?

Emily Dickinson (1830–1886)
There's a certain Slant of light (1861)

There's a certain Slant of light,
Winter Afternoons—
That oppresses, like the Heft
Of Cathedral Tunes—

Heavenly Hurt, it gives us—   5
We can find no scar,
But internal difference,
Where the Meanings, are—

None may teach it—Any—
'Tis the Seal Despair—   10
An imperial affliction
Sent us of the Air—

When it comes, the Landscape listens—
Shadows—hold their breath—
When it goes, 'tis like the Distance   15
On the look of Death—

·····▶ *Your* **Turn**

Talking and Writing about Lit

1. Looking beyond the literal level of the image, what do you think the "certain Slant of light,/Winter Afternoons—" might symbolize?
2. Dickinson chose to use a very precise pattern of rhyme here. Do you think this was a good choice?

Emily Dickinson (1830–1886)

The Bustle in a House (1866, 1890)

The Bustle in a House
The Morning after Death
Is solemnest of industries
Enacted upon Earth—

The Sweeping up the Heart   5
And putting Love away
We shall not want to use again
Until Eternity.

·····▶ *Your* **Turn**

Talking and Writing about Lit

1. This is another Dickinson poem about death, but "The Bustle in a House" takes a more practical turn than the previous poem. Summarize what you think Dickinson is trying to say here.
2. Compare the themes of this poem with those of Robert Frost's "Home Burial" or "Out, Out—" (both in Chapter 18).

Robert Herrick (1591–1674)

To the Virgins, to Make Much of Time (1646)

Gather ye rosebuds while ye may,
    Old Time is still a-flying;
And this same flower that smiles today
    Tomorrow will be dying.

The glorious lamp of heaven, the Sun,   5
    The higher he's a-getting,
The sooner will his race be run,
    And nearer he's to setting.

That age is best which is the first,
    When youth and blood are warmer;   10
But being spent, the worse, and worst
    Times still succeed the former.

Then be not coy, but use your time;
    And while ye may, go marry;
For having lost but once your prime,   15
    You may forever tarry.

·····▶ *Your* Turn
Talking and Writing about Lit

1. You will recognize a number of figures of speech here that, though they may have been fresh in the seventeenth century when Herrick first wrote them, have since become clichés. Point out at least two of these.

2. Compare the themes of Herrick's poem with those of Andrew Marvell's "To His Coy Mistress" (Chapter 14) or with Christopher Marlowe's "The Passionate Shepherd to His Love" and Sir Walter Raleigh's "The Nymph's Reply to the Shepherd" (both in Chapter 19).

William Butler Yeats (1865–1939)
The Lake Isle of Innisfree (1892)

I will arise and go now, and go to Innisfree,
And a small cabin build there, of clay and wattles made;
Nine bean-rows will I have there, a hive for the honey-bee,
And live alone in the bee-loud glade.

And I shall have some peace there, for peace comes dropping slow,   5
Dropping from the veils of the morning to where the cricket sings;
There midnight's all a glimmer, and noon a purple glow,
And evening full of the linnet's wings.

I will arise and go now, for always night and day
I hear lake water lapping with low sounds by the shore;   10

While I stand on the roadway, or on the pavements grey,
I hear it in the deep heart's core.

·····▶ *Your* **Turn**
Talking and Writing about Lit

1. Folk singer Judy Collins used this poem as song lyrics when she put "The Lake Isle of Innisfree" to music on her 1971 album *Judy Collins: Living*. How does the use of imagery and word choice in Yeats's famous poem contribute to its musical effects?

2. **DIY** Write a few lines of poetry or a prose poem that is a tribute to a place you know well and like to spend time (a park, your favorite bookstore, your room, a friend's house, your child's room).

William Carlos Williams (1883–1963)
A Sort of a Song (1944)

Let the snake wait under
his weed
and the writing
be of words, slow and quick, sharp
to strike, quiet to wait,   5
sleepless.

—through metaphor to reconcile
the people and the stones.
Compose. (No ideas
but in things) Invent!   10
Saxifrage is my flower that splits
the rocks.

·····▶ *Your* **Turn**
Talking and Writing about Lit

1. "No ideas but in things," William Carlos Williams famously said. Use examples from his poem "A Sort of a Song" to explain what he meant. Reading Charles Tomlinson's explanation (in Talking Lit) might help.

2. Compare Williams's "A Sort of a Song" to Marianne Moore's poem entitled "Poetry" (Chapter 14).

Talking Lit

Charles Tomlinson explains William Carlos Williams's famous statement, "No ideas but in things."

Charles Tomlinson, From the Introduction to *William Carlos Williams: Selected Poems* (1985)

On the face of it, the inheritance Williams brings to cubism seems to be very close in spirit not only to Whitman but also to Emerson and Thoreau. If "contact" is re-explored, so is Emerson's attachment to the vernacular: "the speech of Polish mothers" was where Williams insisted he got his English from. "Colleges and books only copy the language which the field and work-yard made," said Emerson. Williams's famous "flatness" comes not from the field, but from the urban "work-yard" of New Jersey. As Hugh Kenner writes of Williams's characteristic diction: "That words set in Jersey speech rhythms mean less but mean it with greater finality, is Williams's great technical perception."

Emerson seems to have prepared the ground for Williams's other war-cry, "No ideas but in things" with his "Ask the fact for the form." Thoreau sounds yet closer with: "The roots of letters are things." Again Emerson tells over things—"The meal in the firkin; the milk in the pan; the ballad in the street; the news of the boat . . ." —in the shape of a list very like Williams's "rigmaroles," as he calls his poems. "Bare lists of words," says Emerson, "are found suggestive to an imaginative mind." When Williams, long after Emerson and after Whitman's application of this, constructed "list" poems, he came in for suspicion, as in the interview which he prints as part of *Paterson 5* and in which, defending what amounts to a grocery list that forms the jagged pattern of one of his later poems, he concludes: "Anything is good material for poetry. Anything. I've said it time and time again."

Paterson 5 came out in 1958. Years before, Williams had formulated his kind of poem made out of anything and with a jagged pattern, in the 1920 preface to *Kora in Hell*, when he wrote that a poem is "tough by no quality it borrows from a logical recital of events nor from the events themselves but solely from the attenuated power which draws perhaps many broken things into a dance by giving them thus a full being." He was often to return to the idea of poem as dance. If, as with Emerson, Williams seems to "ask the fact for the form," the form, once it comes, is free of the fact, is a *dance above* the fact. After *Kora in Hell* he had another shot at the formula in the prose of *Spring and All*, where he concludes of John of Gaunt's speech in *Richard II* that "his words are related not to their sense as objects adherent to his son's welfare or otherwise, but as a dance over the body of his condition accurately accompanying it."

J. Hillis Miller in his book *Poets of Reality* has argued that Williams marks an historic moment for modern poetry in that his work sees the disappearance of all dualism. If it is not from dualism it is yet from a duality that much of the interest of his work arises: the words "accurately accompany" a perception of the forms of reality, they dance over or with these forms, but it is the gap between words and forms that gives poetry its chance to exist and to go on existing. Williams's most truncated and Zen-like expression of this fact comes in the tiny

> so much depends
> upon
>
> a red wheel
> barrow
>
> glazed with rain
> water
>
> beside the white
> chickens

What depends on the red wheelbarrow for Williams is the fact that its presence can be rendered over into words, that the perception can be slowed down and

POP CULTURE

Nü Metal, Nü Standard

Motley Crue

In the mid-to-late 1990s a number of new bands appeared touting a new hybrid of rock 'n' roll and rap. Using the basic instrumental structure of a rock band (bass, guitar, and drums) **like Motley Crue**, but taking the new vocal structure **and lyrical aggression** of hip-hop **groups like NWA**, bands like Korn and Limp Bizkit quickly rose through the ranks of popular music. The melding of these two musical genres soon formed its own structural habits.

This amalgamation took many of the staples of sound, rhythm, and meter from recent forms of rock 'n' roll. Along with the standard blaring guitar of heavy metal music, bands borrowed the "breakdown" from recent hard-core punk bands. Nü Metal often used this percussive guitar bridge in order to communicate an aggressive attitude. The heavy percussion only lends itself further to the rap-styled vocals. In this way both musical forms adapted to one another, bringing the more solidly rhythmic

meditated on by regulating, line by line, the gradual appearance of these words. The imagination "accurately accompanies" the wheelbarrow, or whatever facets of reality attract Williams, by not permitting too ready and emotional a fusion with them. When things go badly the imagination retreats into a subjective anguish—

> to an empty, windswept place
> without sun, stars or moon
> but a peculiar light as of thought
> that spins a dark fire—
> whirling upon itself . . .

But when the dance with facts suffices, syntax, the forms of grammar, puns, the ambiguous pull between words unpunctuated or divided by line-endings, these all contribute to—accompany—the richness of a reality one can never completely fuse with, but which affords a resistance whereby the I can know itself.

Rap group NWA

=

Limp Bizket band members

and metrical sound of hip-hop to added power with guitar. As pictured here, Motley Crue plus NWA equals Limp Bizkit. These bands were not the first to try such experiments. Run DMC, Ice-T, and, more contemporarily, Puff Daddy (P. Diddy) had all experimented with guitar and rock incorporation in order to add musical force to their songs. Perhaps the biggest change rap-metal bands have made is using rap's percussive strength to communicate young, white, middle-class angst. Often concentrating lyrically on personal pain and broken relationships, bands like Korn and Limp Bizkit brought an element of introspection often absent from two typically macho genres.

Pigtails
are just about
as much fun
as hair can have.

It's like a party for your head!

Things I've learned from the free lecture series at the public library:

A butterfly garden is a garden that attracts butterflies.

Not a tiny garden tended by butterflies.

THEME AND IRONY

Even greeting cards use theme and irony.

A well-known song by Irving Berlin extols the virtues about business and show people. "There's no people like show people," as the song goes. Show business and show people are special.

The themes of that song, that show business and show people are special, are used ironically in the greeting card. Here, two women dressed in glamorous, glittery costumes, posing for the camera on what appears to be a stage, smile brightly. They are obviously in show business, and appear to represent everything that's enviable about being in show business. Looking at the image, we might recall the Berlin song. But our positive associations with the image belie the message of the caption, and the caption uses irony, metaphor, and sensory language to convey that message. The message is that, indeed, show people are special, as the song says. The irony is that they are special in a satiric way.

The caption echoes the lyrics from the Berlin song, but changes the meaning of the lyrics so that they support a playfully sarcastic view of the women in the image. Use of sensory language and details also help to convey the theme. The expression, "show people creep me out," is an exaggerated, colloquial use of sensory language that effectively conveys the narrator's feeling with a tinge of humor and sarcasm. The slang also allows the card recipient to identify with the sender. Finally, after reading the caption, a second look at the image drives home the point of the caption: the smiles seem forced, the poses are exaggerated, and the costumes seem artificial and garish, and, in some respects, creepy. Now take a look at the other two cards. Where do you see the use of theme and irony?

for one,

m glad there

re no people

ke show people.

how people

reep me out.

How do we determine what the **theme** or themes (the meanings) of a poem are? Every preceding chapter in this unit helps us answer that question, and in every chapter we have been practicing that task. There are many pathways to discovering and describing themes. A writer may have used one or more of the many devices that help reveal meaning: symbolism, metaphor or other figures of speech, sensory language and exact detail, speaker and voice, tone, word choice and word order, ambiguity, irony, sound, rhythm and meter, or rhyme. Once again, it is clear that knowing how to ask good questions about a work of literature is the key to opening up its treasures of meaning or its interesting form.

Pathways to Meaning—Figurative Language

Sometimes a poem is obviously rich with ideas and emotions, but those ideas are difficult to pin down, difficult to articulate. "Spelling" by Margaret Atwood is just such a poem. When a work of literature seems complex, there are usually numerous possible pathways to meaning. The reader may proceed by placing a foot on any one of those paths—and one of those paths is the use of **metaphor**. The preceding sentence and the one before it contain metaphors, as does Atwood's poem.

Margaret Atwood (b. 1939)
Spelling (1981)

My daughter plays on the floor
with plastic letters,
red, blue & hard yellow,
learning how to spell,
spelling,   5
how to make spells.

I wonder how many women
denied themselves daughters,
closed themselves in rooms,
drew the curtains   10
so they could mainline words.

A child is not a poem,
a poem is not a child.
There is no either / or
However.   15

I return to the story
of the woman caught in the war
& in labour, her thighs tied
together by the enemy
so she could not give birth.   20

Ancestress: the burning witch,
her mouth covered by leather
to strangle words.

A word after a word
after a word is power.   25

At the point where language falls away
from the hot bones, at the point
where the rock breaks open and darkness
flows out of it like blood, at
the melting point of granite   30
when the bones know
they are hollow & the word
splits & doubles & speaks
the truth & the body
itself becomes a mouth.   35

This is a metaphor.

How do you learn to spell?
Blood, sky & the sun,
your own name first,
your first naming, your first name,   40
your first word.

    Exploring the use of metaphors in this piece would be one pathway to meaning. If someone is stumped by the opening of a poem (or uninterested in it), then it's good to begin somewhere else, with the lines that are powerful or puzzling. Most readers are startled, for instance, by lines 16–20 of Atwood's poem, with their disturbing description of the "woman caught in the war/& in labour, her thighs tied/together by the enemy/so she could not give birth." What does this have in common with the equally startling image that follows of the "Ancestress: the burning witch,/her mouth covered by leather/to strangle words." Both of these women have something locked inside that they need to bring forth, and both are prevented from doing so by other people (or by society).

    In the previous stanza (lines 12–15), the speaker says that "A child is not a poem,/a poem is not a child./There is no either/or. . . ." but then she adds, "However," and launches into the two images which seem in fact to compare the child trapped within to the words trapped within. Backtracking further brings us to the still previous stanza (lines 7–11) in which the speaker likens children to words in a different way: "I wonder how many women/denied themselves daughters,/closed themselves in rooms,/drew the curtains/so they could mainline words." This business of words and being able to use them is beginning to sound rather dangerous and also very potent: "A word after a word/after a word is power" (lines 24–25). In the longer stanza which follows this, there are more startling images: bones, heat, blood, darkness, "the melting point of granite," "the word," "the truth," and then "the body/itself becomes a mouth." This is followed by a surprisingly clear instruction to the reader: "This is a metaphor." The description of the sensations of childbirth above, then (lines 26–35), has to do with the birthing of words as well as the birthing of children.

Putting it all together, the reader is now able to tie in the first and last stanzas with confidence. The speaker's daughter on the floor with her plastic letters is the literal child the speaker/poet has given birth to, and as a poet/mother, she will teach her daughter "spelling," the power and magic of words: "learning how to spell,/spelling,/how to make spells." The last stanza returns to this idea of learning to spell. It is elemental ("Blood, sky & the sun,/your own name first") and it begins with the child's first development of language, usually assisted by the parent: "your first naming, your first name,/your first word." The poem comes full circle. The "Ancestress" of line 16 is forbidden to utter powerful words. But the speaker/poet in the present time of the poem not only gives birth to poems herself, but also will instruct her daughter in the powerful use of words. Teasing out the meanings of individual metaphors has led the reader to be able to make connections between the parts and ideas of the poem. The reader is now able to articulate several of the poem's central themes having to do with overcoming efforts to silence one's words, the particular ways in which women have been silenced, the likeness of giving birth to children and to poems, the legacy of knowing how to use words powerfully, and the pleasure of passing on that knowledge to the next generation.

Pathways to Meaning—Image, Detail, Story

In Tu Fu's strongly narrative poem "To Wei Pa, a Retired Scholar," the speaker of the poem is astonished by the powerful emotions he feels when he has a brief reunion with a long-ago classmate. Unlike Atwood above, Tu Fu (a classical Chinese poet of the T'ang Dynasty, who lived and wrote in the eighth century) does not rely much on figurative language. Instead he operates almost exclusively in the realm of the literal as he relates the story.

Tu Fu (713–770)
To Wei Pa, a Retired Scholar

Translated by Kenneth Rexroth

The lives of many men are
Shorter than the years since we have
Seen each other. Aldebaran
And Antares move as we have.
And now, what night is this? We sit   5
Here together in the candle
Light. How much longer will our prime
Last? Our temples are already
Grey. I visit my old friends.
Half of them have become ghosts.   10
Fear and sorrow choke me and burn
My bowels. I never dreamed I would
Come this way, after twenty years,
A wayfarer to your parlor.
When we parted years ago,   15
You were unmarried. Now you have
A row of boys and girls, who smile
And ask me about my travels.
How have I reached this time and place?
Before I can come to the end   20
Of an endless tale, the children
Have brought out the wine. We go
Out in the night and cut young
Onions in the rainy darkness.
We eat them with hot, steaming,   25
Yellow millet. You say, "It is
Sad, meeting each other again."
We drink ten toasts rapidly from
The rhinoceros horn cups.
Ten cups, and still we are not drunk.   30
We still love each other as
We did when we were schoolboys.
Tomorrow morning mountain peaks
Will come between us, and with them
The endless, oblivious   35
Business of the world.

The wonderful freshness and exactness of his details (images) capture the reader's attention in this poem, and strong emotions and ideas are conveyed through these **sensory details**. Tactile (including visceral) sensations are especially important here, along with the senses of sight and taste. The speaker does not mention the ages of his friends or himself, but he says instead, "Our temples are already/Grey." Thinking of friends he has lost, who have "become ghosts," the speaker says, "Fear and sorrow choke me and burn/My bowels," a startlingly visceral statement. The speaker does not mention the friend's offspring in the abstract by counting their number, but instead invites the reader to picture them: "Now you have/A row of boys and girls, who smile/And ask me about my travels." Since the friend had no children when they last saw each other, the "row" of children is also a way to make visual the fact that many years have passed. Lines 22–29 are especially rich in details of taste and touch: "the children/Have brought out the wine. We go/Out in the night and cut young/Onions in the rainy darkness./We eat them with hot, steaming,/Yellow millet. You say, 'It is/Sad, meeting each other again.'" The steaming millet and the rainy darkness make us feel the sadness of the aging speaker's lost time much more fully than any abstract generalization could. We come to know the themes of this poem because they are so vividly illustrated that we can't miss them.

Pathways to Meaning—The Speaker's Voice and Diction

In Lucille Clifton's narrative poem "For de Lawd," the speaker's **voice** is a pathway to theme. The first-person speaker tells her story in her own words (in casual diction), and her assertiveness and her bold insistence on telling things her own way help drive her ideas home.

Lucille Clifton (b. 1936)
For de Lawd (1969)

people say they have a hard time
understanding how i
go on about my business
playing my ray charles
hollering at the kids—   5
seem like my afro
cut off in some old image
would show I got a long memory
and I come from a line
of black and going on women   10

who got used to making it through murdered sons
and who grief kept on pushing
who fried chicken
ironed
swept off the back steps   15
who grief kept
for their still alive sons
for their sons coming
for their sons gone
just pushing   20
in the inner city
or
like we call it
home
we think a lot about uptown   25
and the silent nights
and the houses straight as
dead men
and the pastel lights
and we hang on to our no place   30
happy to be alive
and in the inner city
or
like we call it
home   35

As we move through the poem, we begin to perceive a contrast between the energy and activity of where the speaker lives and the way she sees a supposedly more well-to-do neighborhood: "we think a lot about uptown/and the silent nights/and the houses straight as/dead men/and the pastel lights." On the other hand, the speaker knows how to "go on about my business/playing my ray charles/hollering at the kids—," and this energy and determination is part of her legacy: "and I come from a line/of black and going on women/who got used to making it through murdered sons/and who grief kept on pushing/who fried chicken/ironed/swept off the back steps." The poem concludes with the speaker's restatement of her preference for the vigor of her own neighborhood: "and we hang on to our no place/happy to be alive/and in the inner city/or/like we call it/home[.]"

Readers may want to explore several other techniques used in Clifton's poem: the use of careful **word choice** to characterize the two neighborhoods she depicts and also the use of **line breaks** and the absence of end punctuation, even in the concluding line of the poem. This adds to the poem's momentum, to its determined way of "going on." Third, the **repetition** of "go on," "going on," and "kept on pushing" add force to the poem's voice as well.

Pathways to Meaning—Four Types of Irony

The title of Wilfred Owen's poem "Dulce et Decorum Est" is the first part of the Latin statement "dulce et decorum est pro patria mori," which means "it is sweet and fitting to die for one's country." As the reader encounters the violent and disturbing images of the poem, however, it becomes clear that the poet intends to show the opposite of the title's statement.

Wilfred Owen (1893–1918)
Dulce et Decorum Est (1920)

Bent double, like old beggars under sacks,
Knock-kneed, coughing like hags, we cursed through sludge,
Till on the haunting flares we turned our backs,
And towards our distant rest began to trudge.
Men marched asleep. Many had lost their boots,   5
But limped on, blood-shod. All went lame, all blind;
Drunk with fatigue; deaf even to the hoots
Of gas-shells dropping softly behind.

Gas! GAS! Quick, boys!—An ecstasy of fumbling,
Fitting the clumsy helmets just in time,   10
But someone still was yelling out and stumbling
And flound'ring like a man in fire or lime.—
Dim through the misty panes and thick green light,
As under a green sea, I saw him drowning.

In all my dreams before my helpless sight   15
He plunges at me, guttering, choking, drowning.

If in some smothering dreams, you too could pace
Behind the wagon that we flung him in,
And watch the white eyes writhing in his face,
His hanging face, like a devil's sick of sin,   20
If you could hear, at every jolt, the blood
Come gargling from the froth-corrupted lungs
Bitter as the cud
Of vile, incurable sores on innocent tongues,—
My friend, you would not tell with such high zest   25

To children ardent for some desperate glory,
The old lie: *Dulce et decorum est*
Pro patria mori.

Verbal Irony

This is an example of **verbal irony** (also often called sarcasm): meaning the oppo-site of what is said. The title reflects (as is evident in lines 25–29) the kind of prop-aganda ("the old lie") young men hear from politicians who want them to go to war. Owen, who himself served in the trenches and died in World War I, wants to show through careful word choice and exact imagery how un-sweet and un-glorious war is for those who have to fight it.

Likewise in Janice Mirikitani's "Recipe" for round eyes, the speaker does not actually want to recommend making Asian eyes look less like Asian eyes. Instead the speaker means to show how painful and "false" it is when one's heritage is not appreciated and respected.

Janice Mirikitani (b. 1942)
Recipe (1987)

Round Eyes
Ingredients: scissors, Scotch magic transparent tape,
              eyeliner—water based, black.
              Optional: false eyelashes.

Cleanse face thoroughly.   5

For best results, powder entire face, including eyelids.
    (lighter shades suited to total effect desired)

With scissors, cut magic tape $^1/_{16}$″ wide, $^3/_4$″–$^1/_2$″ long—
depending on length of eyelid.

Stick firmly onto mid-upper eyelid area   10
    (looking down into handmirror facilitates finding
    adequate surface)

If using false eyelashes, affix first on lid, folding any
excess lid over the base of eyelash with glue.

Paint black eyeliner on tape and entire lid.   15

Do not cry.

This poem, then, is also an example of verbal irony, of saying the opposite of what is meant.

David Huddle's poem "Holes Commence Falling" begins differently, with a careful **understatement** of how the town approved of the mining company's investment in "improvements" in the name of commerce. As one proceeds through the poem, however, it becomes evident that the enormous amount of damage being done to this community couldn't possibly be approved of by the people.

David Huddle (b. 1942)
Holes Commence Falling (1979)

The lead & zinc company
owned the mineral rights
to the whole town anyway,
and after drilling holes
for 3 or 4 years,   5
they finally found the right
place and sunk a mine shaft.
We were proud
of all that digging,
even though nobody from   10
town got hired. They
were going to dig right
under New River and hook up
with the mine at Austinville.
Then people's wells   15
started drying up just like
somebody'd shut off a faucet,
and holes commenced falling,
big chunks of people's yards
would drop 5 or 6 feet,   20
houses would shift and crack.
Now and then the company'd
pay out a little money
in damages; they got a truck
to haul water and sell it   25
to the people whose wells
had dried up, but most
everybody agreed the
situation wasn't
serious.   30

The final lines "but most/everybody agreed the/situation wasn't/serious" is clearly a use of verbal irony. The speaker has vividly shown the opposite of this throughout the poem. As is evident, when in the presence of irony, the reader must be careful to perceive it accurately in order to understand the poem's theme.

Situational Irony

A second type of irony, known as **situational irony**, is at work when there is a discrepancy between appearance and reality in the poem, or when what happens is not what we expected to happen. Both of these statements are true of Edwin Arlington Robinson's "Richard Cory." The speaker of the poem is the collective ("we") voice of the townspeople.

Edwin Arlington Robinson (1869–1935)
Richard Cory (1897)

Whenever Richard Cory went down town,
We people on the pavement looked at him:
He was a gentleman from sole to crown,
Clean favored, and imperially slim.

And he was always quietly arrayed,   5
And he was always human when he talked;
But still he fluttered pulses when he said,
"Good-morning," and he glittered when he walked.

And he was rich—yes, richer than a king—
And admirably schooled in every grace: 10
In fine, we thought that he was everything
To make us wish that we were in his place.

So on we worked, and waited for the light,
And went without the meat, and cursed the bread;
And Richard Cory, one calm summer night,   15
Went home and put a bullet through his head.

While Richard Cory's riches and good looks make him appear to be happy, evidently these things were not adequate for happiness. He comes to an ironic and unexpected end, an end the reader learns only in the last six words of the last line of the poem. This produces a **reversal** the reader probably had not expected. Other aspects of the poem that might be explored for their relation to the theme/s are sound, rhyme, rhythm and meter, and word choice. The poem is, in fact, in iambic pentameter and has a fixed rhyme scheme. It lends itself so easily to singing that the duo Simon and Garfunkel recorded it as a song in the 1970s.

Anna Akhmatova's poem "The First Long-Range Artillery Shell in Leningrad" is set in the Russian city of Leningrad in 1941, during the Nazi siege and bombardment of the city. One could, then, begin to explore this poem by following the pathway of **historical setting**. However, situational irony is also present here throughout the poem.

Anna Akhmatora
The First Long-Range Artillery Shell in Leningrad (1941)

Translated from the Russian by Lyn Coffin

A rainbow of people rushing around,
And suddenly everything changed completely,
This wasn't a normal city sound,
It came from unfamiliar country.
True, it resembled, like a brother,   5
One peal of thunder or another,
But every natural thunder contains
The moisture of clouds, fresh and high,
And the thirst of fields with drought gone dry,
A harbinger of happy rains,   10
And this was as arid as hell ever got,
And my distracted hearing would not
Believe it, if only because of the wild
Way it started, grew, and caught,
And how indifferently it brought   15
Death to my child.

Note the contrast between the seemingly normal and even lighthearted imagery of some lines ("rainbow of people," "like a brother," "moisture of clouds, fresh and high," "harbinger of happy rains") and the dark, foreboding imagery of others ("suddenly everything changed," "unfamiliar country," "as arid as hell ever got," "distracted hearing," "wild/Way it started, grew, and caught"). In fact, throughout much of the poem, images of happiness and dread alternate. The central irony (lines 5–6) of the sound of the first bomb reminding the speaker of the thunder that heralds a much-needed and welcome rain makes all the more poignant the death announced in the last line.

Dramatic Irony

In Elizabeth Bishop's "One Art," the poet's intention is not evident until the final stanza.

Elizabeth Bishop (1911–1979)

One Art (1976)

The art of losing isn't hard to master;
so many things seem filled with the intent
to be lost that their loss is no disaster.

Lose something every day. Accept the fluster
of lost door keys, the hour badly spent.   5
The art of losing isn't hard to master.

Then practice losing farther, losing faster:
places, and names, and where it was you meant
to travel. None of these will bring disaster.

I lost my mother's watch. And look! my last, or   10
next-to-last, of three loved houses went.
The art of losing isn't hard to master.

I lost two cities, lovely ones. And, vaster,
some realms I owned, two rivers, a continent.
I miss them, but it wasn't a disaster.   15

—Even losing you (the joking voice, a gesture
I love) I shan't have lied. It's evident
the art of losing's not too hard to master
though it may look like (*Write* it!) like disaster.

When readers encounter that last stanza, it becomes clear that Bishop means to show the opposite of what her speaker has been insisting upon. All losses are not the same, in fact; the loss of a loved one is indeed harder to master than any other. This poem is an example of **dramatic irony** because the reader comes to understand something that the speaker does not grasp. This poem also illustrates the fact that the **speaker** of the poem doesn't necessarily represent the poet. Here both the poet and the reader understand more than the speaker does. "One Art" is also an example of a **fixed-form** poem. It is a contemporary villanelle, meaning that the poet has modified the traditional form of the villanelle somewhat. The reader will notice a careful **rhyme scheme** throughout the poem, although some line endings employ near rhyme rather than exact rhyme.

Cosmic Irony

Stephen Crane's brief poem "A Man Said to the Universe" is an example of a less often encountered type of irony, **cosmic irony**.

Stephen Crane (1871–1900)
A Man Said to the Universe (1899)

A man said to the universe:
"Sir, I exist!"
"However," replied the universe,
"The fact has not created in me
A sense of obligation."   5

In these five lines, the character, "A man," insists to the universe, "Sir, I exist!" The universe, however, is indifferent to his existence. Thus there is a discrepancy between what the man expects (recognition and perhaps assistance) and what the universe is prepared to provide (in this case, nothing).

Dylan Thomas's "Fern Hill" presents an interesting example of the use of irony. It is interesting because it requires a bit more study and contemplation, perhaps, than the above examples. Read this poem out loud to enjoy the full experience of the **sound** of Dylan Thomas's lines. The freshness of his word choice and the extraordinary way in which he puts words together make this poem the kind of "lilting," "Flying," "Flashing" experience that the poem itself describes.

Dylan Thomas (1914–1953)
Fern Hill (1946)

Now as I was young and easy under the apple boughs
About the lilting house and happy as the grass was green,
⠀⠀⠀The night above the dingle starry,
⠀⠀⠀⠀⠀Time let me hail and climb
⠀⠀⠀Golden in the heydays of his eyes,   5
And honored among wagons I was prince of the apple towns
And once below a time I lordly had the trees and leaves
⠀⠀⠀⠀⠀Trail with daisies and barley
⠀⠀⠀Down the rivers of the windfall light.

And as I was green and carefree, famous among the barns   10
About the happy yard and singing as the farm was home,
⠀⠀⠀In the sun that is young once only,
⠀⠀⠀⠀⠀Time let me play and be
⠀⠀⠀Golden in the mercy of his means,
And green and golden I was huntsman and herdsman, the calves   15
Sang to my horn, the foxes on the hills barked clear and cold,
⠀⠀⠀⠀⠀And the sabbath rang slowly
⠀⠀⠀In the pebbles of the holy streams.

All the sun long it was running, it was lovely, the hay
Fields high as the house, the tunes from the chimneys, it was air   20

And playing, lovely and watery
    And fire green as grass.
And nightly under the simple stars
As I rode to sleep the owls were bearing the farm away,
All the moon long I heard, blessed among stables, the nightjars   25
    Flying with the ricks, and the horses
        Flashing into the dark.

And then to awake, and the farm, like a wanderer white
With the dew, come back, the cock on his shoulder: it was all
    Shining, it was Adam and maiden,   30
        The sky gathered again
    And the sun grew round that very day.
So it must have been after the birth of the simple light
In the first, spinning place, the spellbound horses walking warm
    Out of the whinnying green stable   35
        On to the fields of praise.

And honored among foxes and pheasants by the gay house
Under the new made clouds and happy as the heart was long,
    In the sun born over and over,
        I ran my heedless ways,   40
    My wishes raced through the house high hay
And nothing I cared, at my sky blue trades, that time allows
In all his tuneful turning so few and such morning songs
    Before the children green and golden
        Follow him out of grace,   45

Nothing I cared, in the lamb white days, that time would take me
Up to the swallow thronged loft by the shadow of my hand,
    In the moon that is always rising,
        Nor that riding to sleep
    I should hear him fly with the high fields   50
And wake to the farm forever fled from the childless land.
Oh as I was young and easy in the mercy of his means,
        Time held me green and dying
    Though I sang in my chains like the sea.

    Fern Hill was, in fact, the name of a farm where Thomas spent time in his boyhood, and here the innocence and the soaring, joyful memories of care-free youth predominate in the poem. Through four and a half stanzas, at least (some readers may argue for longer), the joy holds sway. Only in the last stanza, or stanza and a half, does the reader discover the note of irony and sadness in the poem. Even so, the voice of the poem continues to be suffused with energetic and figurative language until the end: "Oh as I was young and easy in the mercy of his means,/ Time held me green and dying/Though I sang in my chains like the sea." Readers may also be interested in the carefully constructed form of this much loved poem.

How would you explain the operation of irony and theme in William Hathaway's "Oh, Oh"?

William Hathaway (b. 1944)
Oh, Oh (1982)

My girl and I amble a country lane,
moo cows chomping daisies, our own
sweet saliva green with grass stems.
"Look, look," she says at the crossing,
"the choo-choo's light is on." And sure   5
enough, right smack dab in the middle
of maple dappled summer sunlight
is the lit headlight—so funny.
An arm waves to us from the black window.
We wave gaily to the arm. "When I hear   10
trains at night I dream of being president,"
I say dreamily. "And me first lady," she
says loyally. So when the last boxcars,
named after wonderful, faraway places,
and the caboose chuckle by we look   15
eagerly to the road ahead. And there,
poised and growling, are fifty Hell's Angels.

Poems for Further Reading

William Blake (1757–1827)
A Poison Tree (1794)

I was angry with my friend:
I told my wrath, my wrath did end.
I was angry with my foe:
I told it not, my wrath did grow.

And I waterd it in fears,   5
Night & morning with my tears;
And I sunnéd it with smiles,
And with soft deceitful wiles.

And it grew both day and night,
Till it bore an apple bright.   10
And my foe beheld it shine,
And he knew that it was mine,

And into my garden stole,
When the night had veild the pole;
In the morning glad I see   15
My foe outstretchd beneath the tree.

·····► *Your* Turn
Talking and Writing about Lit

1. Is "A Poison Tree" a lyric poem or a narrative poem?

2. What significance do you see in the fact that the speaker's foe picks
fruit off a tree in a garden, knowing it belongs to someone else and
he should not take it? If you read this as a biblical allusion, how does this
reference to the apple in the garden affect your interpretation of the poem?

William Blake (1757–1827)
The Chimney Sweeper (1789)

When my mother died I was very young,
And my father sold me while yet my tongue
Could scarcely cry "'weep! 'weep! 'weep! 'weep!"
So your chimneys I sweep, and in soot I sleep.

There's little Tom Dacre, who cried when his head,   5
That curled like a lamb's back, was shaved; so I said,
"Hush, Tom! never mind it, for, when your head's bare,
You know that the soot cannot spoil your white hair."

And so he was quiet, and that very night,
As Tom was asleeping, he had such a sight!   10
That thousands of sweepers, Dick, Joe, Ned, and Jack,
Were all of them locked up in coffins of black.

William Blake— Visual Artist and Verbal Artist

William Blake was an engraver and printer as well as a poet. This engraving of his poem "A Poison Tree" is typical of the engravings he created to illustrate his poems. Regarding theme and irony in this poem, the speaker may seem delighted to have held onto his "wrath" until it eventually poisoned his "foe." But however delighted the speaker may seem to be at the sight of his "foe outstretchd beneath the tree," the poet and the reader recognize that this is not the best way to conduct human relations. Hence, the reader knows more than the speaker does, and dramatic irony is at work here.

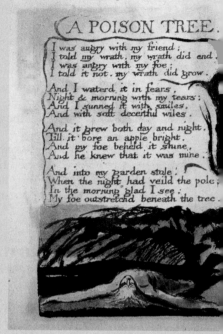

Blake's engraving for "A Poison Tree"

And by came an Angel who had a bright key,
And he opened the coffins and set them all free;
Then down a green plain leaping, laughing, they run,   15
And wash in a river, and shine in the sun.

Then naked and white, all their bags left behind,
They rise upon clouds and sport in the wind;
And the Angel told Tom, if he'd be a good boy,
He'd have God for his father, and never want joy.   20

And so Tom awoke, and we rose in the dark,
And got with our bags and our brushes to work.
Though the morning was cold, Tom was happy and warm;
So if all do their duty they need not fear harm.

•••••▶ *Your* **Turn**
Talking and Writing about Lit

   1. List the devices of sound that you recognize in "The Chimney Sweeper."

   2. What do you think the "coffins of black" (line 12) represent? How about the Angel (line 13)? Explain how irony operates in this poem.

e.e. cummings (1894–1962)
Buffalo Bill's (1923)

Buffalo Bill's
defunct
        who used to
        ride a watersmooth-silver
                   stallion   5
and break onetwothreefourfive pigeonsjustlikethat
                       Jesus
he was a handsome man
            and what i want to know is
how do you like your blueeyed boy   10
Mister Death

•••••▶ *Your* **Turn**
Talking and Writing about Lit

   1. What does cummings mean when he says in lines 1–2 that "Buffalo Bill's/ defunct"?

   2. Explain the contrast between the images in lines 4–8 and those in lines 9–11.

Wislawa Szymborska (b. 1923)
End and Beginning (1993)

Translated by Joseph Brodsky

After each war
somebody has to clear up
put things in order
by itself it won't happen.

Somebody's got to push   5
rubble to the highway shoulder
making way
for the carts filled up with corpses.

Someone might trudge
through muck and ashes,   10
sofa springs,
splintered glass
and blood-soaked rugs.

Somebody has to haul
beams for propping a wall,   15
another put glass in a window
and hang the door on hinges.

This is not photogenic
and takes years.
All the cameras have left already   20
for another war.

Bridges are needed
also new railroad stations.
Tatters turn into sleeves
for rolling up.   25

Somebody, broom in hand,
still recalls how it was,
Someone whose head was not
torn away listens nodding.
But nearby already   30
begin to bustle those
who'll need persuasion.

Somebody still at times
digs up from under the bushes
some rusty quibble   35
to add it to burning refuse.

Those who knew
what this was all about
must yield to those
who know little   40
or less than little
essentially nothing.

In the grass that has covered
effects in causes
somebody must recline,   45
a stalk of rye in the teeth,
ogling the clouds.

••••• *Your* **Turn**
Talking and Writing about Lit

1. Summarize Szymborska's principal themes in "End and Beginning." How do
you interpret the final stanza, in light of what comes before?

2. **DIY**   Szymborska creates a haunting kind of universality by beginning
   several stanzas with the word "somebody" or "someone." Write a
poem comprising four couplets (pairs of lines). The first three couplets
should begin with the word somebody. The last couplet should begin with
either "somebody" or "nobody." It's your call.

Emily Dickinson (1830–1886)
Tell all the Truth but tell it slant— (1868)

Tell all the Truth but tell it slant—
Success in Circuit lies
Too bright for our infirm Delight
The Truth's superb surprise
As Lightning to the Children eased   5
With explanation kind
The Truth must dazzle gradually
Or every man be blind—

••••• *Your* **Turn**
Talking and Writing about Lit

1. What do you think Dickinson means in this poem? After studying the poem,
explain the meaning of the first line.

2. If this poem can be taken to apply to poetry itself (as well as other kinds of
truth), then how do the themes here compare to those of Marianne Moore in

"Poetry" (in Chapter 14) and William Carlos Williams in "A Sort of a Song" (in Chapter 17)?

Emily Dickinson (1830–1886)
Some keep the Sabbath going to Church— (circa 1860)

Some keep the Sabbath going to Church—
I keep it, staying at Home—
With a Bobolink for a Chorister—
And an Orchard, for a Dome—

Some keep the Sabbath in Surplice*   5
I just wear my Wings—
And instead of tolling the Bell, for Church,
Our little Sexton—sings.

God preaches, a noted Clergyman—
And the sermon is never long,   10
So instead of getting to Heaven, at last—
I'm going, all along.

····•▶ *Your* Turn
Talking and Writing about Lit

1. Summarize what you think Dickinson is saying in "Some keep the Sabbath going to Church—." How do others keep the Sabbath? How does the speaker keep the Sabbath?

2. **DIY** Structure a brief poem in a similar way: "Some do X," "I do Y." Alternate between what "some do" and what your speaker does throughout your piece. You may shift tone and attitude at the end if you want, but you don't have to. It's your call.

—————————
*Surplice: holy robes

James Dickey (1923–1997)
The Leap (1967)

The only thing I have of Jane MacNaughton
Is one instant of a dancing-class dance.

She was the fastest runner in the seventh grade,
My scrapbook says, even when boys were beginning
To be as big as the girls,   5
But I do not have her running in my mind,
Though Frances Lane is there, Agnes Fraser,
Fat Betty Lou Black in the boys-against-girls
Relays we ran at recess: she must have run

Like the other girls, with her skirts tucked up   10
So they would be like bloomers,
But I cannot tell; that part of her is gone.
What I do have is when she came,
With the hem of her skirt where it should be
For a young lady, into the annual dance   15
Of the dancing class we all hated, and with a light
Grave leap, jumped up and touched the end
Of one of the paper-ring decorations

To see if she could reach it. She could,
And reached me now as well, hanging in my mind   20
From a brown chain of brittle paper, thin
And muscular, wide-mouthed, eager to prove
Whatever it proves when you leap
In a new dress, a new womanhood, among the boys
Whom you easily left in the dust   25
Of the passionless playground. If I said I saw
In the paper where Jane MacNaughton Hill,

Mother of four, leapt to her death from a window
Of a downtown hotel, and that her body crushed-in
The top of a parked taxi, and that I held   30
Without trembling a picture of her lying cradled
In that papery steel as though lying in the grass,
One shoe idly off, arms folded across her breast,
I would not believe myself. I would say
The convenient thing, that it was a bad dream   35
Of maturity, to see that eternal process

Most obsessively wrong with the world
Come out of her light, earth-spurning feet
Grown heavy: would say that in the dusty heels
Of the playground some boy who did not depend   40
On speed of foot, caught and betrayed her.
Jane, stay where you are in my first mind:
It was odd in that school, at that dance.

I and the other slow-footed yokels sat in corners
Cutting rings out of drawing paper   45

Before you leapt in your new dress
And touched the end of something I began,
Above the couples struggling on the floor,
New men and women clutching at each other
And prancing foolishly as bears: hold on   50
To that ring I made for you, Jane—
My feet are nailed to the ground
By dust I swallowed thirty years ago—
While I examine my hands.

····•▶ *Your* **Turn**
Talking and Writing about Lit

1. "The Leap" is a narrative poem. Explain how the poem builds an important
   contrast through two parts of the narrative.

2. **DIY** Think of an event (or, like Dickey, just a moment or image) from
         the past that has particular significance for you. Reinterpret that
   moment—or reilluminate that moment—in light of what you know now.
   You may use prose or poetry to examine this moment from past and present
   perspectives.

Emily Dickinson (1830–1886)
Much madness is divinest sense (1862)

Much madness is divinest sense
To a discerning eye,
Much sense, the starkest madness.
'Tis the majority
In this, as all, prevail: 5
Assent, and you are sane;
Demur, you're straightway dangerous
And handled with a chain.

····•▶ *Your* **Turn**
Talking and Writing about Lit

1. How could the themes of "Much madness is divinest sense—" be summarized as a statement about the artist (including poets and writers) and
   conventional society?

2. Dickinson uses a loose rhyme scheme in this poem. Do you think this serves her purpose well? Why might she want a less rigid scheme of end rhyme for this particular poem?

Robert Herrick (1591–1674)
Delight in Disorder (1648)

A sweet disorder in the dress
Kindles in clothes a wantonness.
A lawn[1] about the shoulders thrown
Into a fine distractión;
An erring lace, which here and there   5
Enthralls the crimson stomacher;[2]
A cuff neglectful, and thereby
Ribbons to flow confusedly;
A winning wave, deserving note,
In the tempestuous petticoat;   10
A careless shoestring, in whose tie
I see a wild civility;
Do more bewitch me than when art
Is too precise in every part.

---

[1]**lawn:** A shawl made of fine fabric.
[2]**stomacher:** A heavily embroidered garment worn by females over the chest and stomach.

·····▶ *Your* Turn
Talking and Writing about Lit

1. How does Robert Herrick use specific detail to make his theme vivid? Give examples.

2. **DIY** Describe the clothing of someone in such a way that it reveals the personality of that person. You may use prose or poetry as a vehicle for what you want to show.

Percy Bysshe Shelley (1792–1822)
Ozymandias (1818)

I met a traveler from an antique land
Who said: Two vast and trunkless legs of stone
Stand in the desert. Near them, on the sand,
Half sunk, a shattered visage lies, whose frown,
And wrinkled lip, and sneer of cold command,   5

Tell that its sculptor well those passions read
Which yet survive, stamped on these lifeless things,
The hand that mocked them, and the heart that fed;
And on the pedestal these words appear:
"My name is Ozymandias,* king of kings: 10
Look on my works, ye Mighty, and despair!"
Nothing beside remains. Round the decay
Of that colossal wreck, boundless and bare
The lone and level sands stretch far away.

---

*Ozymandias: Greek name for Ramses II, ruler of Egypt in the thirteenth century B.C.

·····➤ *Your* Turn
Talking and Writing about Lit

1. Explain the irony of lines 9–14 in Shelley's "Ozymandias."

2. **DIY** Write a poem (or a paragraph of prose) using some other man-made object or event to show the vanity possible in human beings. You might choose the *Titanic* or the *Hindenburg*, for example. Also, wars in general or one war in particular might lend itself to this type of ironic treatment.

Gary Snyder (b. 1930)
Moon, Son of Heaven (1957)

When I was a child
in all sorts of magazines and newspapers
        —how many—photographs of the moon;
face scarred by jagged craters.
I clearly saw that the sun light strikes it.   5
later I learned it's terribly cold
                and no air.
maybe three times I saw it eclipsed—
the earth's shadow
slipped over it, clearly.   10
next, that it probably broke off from earth.
and last, a fellow I met during rice planting
        from the Morioka meteorological observatory
        once showed me that heavenly body through
        a something-mm little telescope   15
        and explained how its orbit and motions
accord with a simple formula.

However. ah,
for me in the end there's no obstacle
to reverently titling that heavenly body   20
Emperor Moon.
if someone says
    man is his body
    that's a mistake.
    and if someone says   25
    man is body and mind
    that too is an error
    and if one says man is mind,
    still it's wrong.
so—I—   30
hail the moon as Emperor Moon.
this is not mere personification.

····➤ *Your* Turn
Talking and Writing about Lit

1. What do you think Gary Snyder is trying to say in his poem "Moon, Son of Heaven"?

2. **DIY** What is your strongest (or most interesting) memory of a moment during which you enjoyed the natural world? This might be an experience of a particular pet (dog, cat, bird) or it might be an experience in a natural place (a lake, a city park, the ocean, the woods, your back yard, someone else's back yard, the beach, looking out your window at the sky, driving in a rain storm). Write a poem or a paragraph of prose about this experience.

Thomas Hardy (1840–1928)
The Convergence of the Twain[1] (1912)

Lines on the Loss of the "Titanic"

I

In a solitude of the sea
Deep from human vanity,
And the Pride of Life that planned her, stilly couches she.

---

[1]**The Convergence of the Twain:** The luxury liner *Titanic*, supposedly unsinkable, went down in 1912 after striking an iceberg on its first Atlantic voyage.

II

Steel chambers, late the pyres
Of her salamandrine fires,[2]
Cold currents thrid,[3] and turn to rhythmic tidal lyres.

5

III

Over the mirrors meant
To glass the opulent
The sea-worm crawls—grotesque, slimed, dumb, indifferent.

IV

Jewels in joy designed
To ravish the sensuous mind
Lie lightless, all their sparkles bleared and black and blind.

10

V

Dim moon-eyed fishes near
Gaze at the gilded gear
And query: "What does this vaingloriousness down here?" . . .

15

VI

Well: while was fashioning
This creature of cleaving wing,
The Immanent Will that stirs and urges everything

VII

Prepared a sinister mate
For her—so gaily great—
A Shape of Ice, for the time far and dissociate.

20

VIII

And as the smart ship grew
In stature, grace, and hue,
In shadowy silent distance grew the Iceberg too.

IX

Alien they seemed to be:
No mortal eye could see
The intimate welding of their later history,

25

---

[2]**salamandrine:** like the salamander, a lizard that supposedly thrives in fires, or like a spirit of the same name that inhabits fire (according to alchemists).
[3]**thrid:** *thread*

X
Or sign that they were bent
By paths coincident
On being anon twin halves of one august event,   30

XI
Till the Spinner of the Years
Said "Now!" And each one hears,
And consummation comes, and jars two hemispheres.

·····➤ *Your* **Turn**
Talking and Writing about Lit

1. Describe the rhyme scheme used by Hardy in "The Convergence of the Twain."

2. Write an essay comparing Hardy's "The Convergence of the Twain" with Shelley's "Ozymandias."

Theodore Roethke (1908–1963)
Night Crow (1944)

When I saw that clumsy crow
Flap from a wasted tree,
A shape in the mind rose up:
Over the gulfs of dream
Flew a tremendous bird   5
Further and further away
Into a moonless black,
Deep in the brain, far back.

·····➤ *Your* **Turn**
Talking and Writing about Lit

1. Why is the "clumsy crow" of line 1 characterized so differently than the "tremendous bird" in line 5?

2. What do you think the crow in "Night Crow" symbolizes?

Theodore Roethke (1908–1963)
River Incident (1948)

A shell arched under my toes,
Stirred up a whirl of silt
That riffled around my knees.

Whatever I owed to time
Slowed in my human form;   5
Sea water stood in my veins,
The elements I kept warm
Crumbled and flowed away,
And I knew I had been there before,
In that cold, granitic slime,   10
In the dark, in the rolling water.

·····► **Your Turn**
Talking and Writing about Lit

1. How many concrete images can you spot in this poem?

2. How would you relate the themes of "Night Crow" to the themes of "River Incident?"

Randall Schroth (b. 1946)
Certain Scenes May Be Offensive (1989)

Certain scenes may depict the antagonist
exercising various measures of violence
against our hero in ascending orders
of intensity, or afflicting assorted
premeditated cruelties on the actress   5
who plays our *anima*, chained to a wall,
drill, power saw, or tied, as now,
in scanty attire to iron rails, vibrating
in front of the oncoming locomotive.
    This is nothing. These early situations   10
are easily resolved; but first, in a flashback,
Roy recalls his original meeting with Diana,
their first space-probe together,
how they vowed to love each other forever
there in the supermarket. Now, sweating,   15
bleeding from the corner of his mouth
and panting hard, he cuts, cuts, cuts
the heavy chords with a rock and drags her
at the last possible instant from the path
of the blind clash of iron wheels—while Bart   20
antagonistically fires his highly technological
gun from a space-chopper, laughing
hysterically among the clatter of blades,

hitting Roy's former foil and loyal sidekick,
Jack, in the throat. Here we get a closeup   25
of Jack's nearly severed neck, the big artery
pumping his last few quarts of blood
into the indifferent desert sand.
As Roy attempts to comfort Jack, Bart's henchman
Burt loads the helpless Diana into another ORV   30
to rendezvous with the chopper before Roy
can drag himself to the new location—
no longer stoically, but shouting obscenities
(thus the R rating) in grief and futile rage
as it disappears in the infinite sky.   35
        In the next scene, a nuclear power plant,
a swarthy Bart is threatening to atomize
Diana (chained to a reactor, tormented by Bart
in even more scanty attire) unless she
reveals certain female secrets Bart thinks   40
have been hidden from him all his life.
Of course she refuses, knowing the terrible
damage they can do in the wrong hands.
Bart slaps her around some more.
Her blouse becomes more appealingly torn.   45
Roy, showered and freshly shaved,
is seen driving a fresh Ford Bronco
at lunatic speeds across the dunes.
And this is where we came in, during the explosion,
so we know the horrible after-effects   50
of the radiation: Diana's breasts bulging
even more enormous, Roy's ears deformed
beyond surgery below his mutating cowlick,
Bart's demented grimace overlapping the margins
of the wide screen, his internal machinery   55
growing exponentially more evil.
        And we know the scene, more poignant
with each viewing, where Diana Anima
tells her therapist, the handsome doctor
Luke Dupree, who's been replaced, by this time,   60
with one of Bart's robots, that Roy's protruding
ears, along with this distressing
lapse in action, caused her to become
less responsive, and wonder if perhaps
their engagement isn't a mistake.   65
Here the bogus Luke lays a cloned hand
on his alleged favorite portions of Diana,
who smiles into his sad electronic eyes.

His mechanical lips, programmed for
maximum titilation, pulsate toward her   70
impressive cleavage as the camera pans
her sensational mouth, draws back to her whole
face in ecstatic abandonment and cuts to Roy,
working out in the gym, preparing
for new, unavoidable confrontations   75
containing scenes that may certainly be offensive
as they all move into the foreseeable future.

···· ➤ *Your* **Turn**

Talking and Writing about Lit

1. What do you think Randall Schroth's poem means to say about popular
action/romance/adventure films?

2. How well do the title and first lines work to frame the ideas to come in the
piece?

Lyn Hejinian (b. 1941)

As for we who "love to be astonished" (1987)

You spill the sugar when you lift the spoon. My father had filled an old
apothecary jar with what he called "sea glass," bits of old bottles rounded
and textured by the sea, so abundant on beaches. There is no solitude. It
buries itself in veracity. It is as if one splashed in the water lost by one's
tears. My mother had climbed into the garbage can in order to stamp
down the accumulated trash, but the can was knocked off balance, and
when she fell she broke her arm. She could only give a little shrug. The
family had little money but plenty of food. At the circus only the elephants
were greater than anything I could have imagined. The egg of Columbus,
landscape and grammar. She wanted one where the playground was dirt,
with grass, shaded by a tree, from which would hang a rubber tire as a
swing, and when she found it she sent me. These creatures are compound
and nothing they do should surprise us. I don't mind, or I won't mind,
where the verb "to care" might multiply. The pilot of the little airplane had
forgotten to notify the airport of his approach, so that when the lights of
the plane in the night were first spotted, the air raid sirens went off, and
the entire city on that coast went dark. He was taking a drink of water and
the light was growing dim. My mother stood at the window watching the
only lights that were visible, circling over the darkened city in search of
the hidden airport. Unhappily, time seems more normative than place.
Whether breathing or holding the breath, it was the same thing, driving
through the tunnel from one sun to the next under a hot brown hill. She

sunned the baby for sixty seconds, leaving him naked except for a blue cotton sunbonnet. At night, to close off the windows from view of the street, my grandmother pulled down the window shades, never loosening the curtains, a gauze starched too stiff to hang properly down. I sat on the windowsill singing sunny lunny teena, ding-dang-dong. Out there is an aging magician who needs a tray of ice in order to turn his bristling breath into steam. He broke the radio silence. Why would anyone find astrology interesting when it is possible to learn about astronomy. What one passes in the Plymouth. It is the wind slamming the doors. All that is nearly incommunicable to my friends. Velocity and throat verisimilitude. Were we seeing a pattern or merely an appearance of small white sailboats on the bay, floating at such a distance from the hill that they appeared to be making no progress. And for once to a country that did not speak another language. To follow the progress of ideas, or that particular line of reasoning, so full of surprises and unexpected correlations, was somehow to take a vacation. Still, you had to wonder where they had gone, since you could speak of reappearance. A blue room is always dark. Everything on the boardwalk was shooting toward the sky. It was not specific to any year, but very early. A German goldsmith covered a bit of metal with cloth in the 14th century and gave mankind its first button. It was hard to know this as politics, because it plays like the work of one person, but nothing is isolated in history—certain humans are situations. Are your fingers in the margin. Their random procedures make monuments to fate. There is something still surprising when the green emerges. The blue fox has ducked its head. The front rhyme of harmless with harmony. Where is my honey running. You cannot linger "on the lamb." You cannot determine the nature of progress until you assemble all of the relatives.

·····➤ *Your* Turn
Talking and Writing about Lit

1. Why is "As for we who 'love to be astonished'" a prose poem and not just a passage of prose?

2. In her Talking Lit piece "The Rejection of Closure" (at the end of this chapter), Lyn Hejinian writes, "Two dangers never cease threatening in the world: order and disorder." Do you feel that she has provided the right balance of "order and disorder" in her prose poem?

Robert Frost (1874–1963)
Home Burial (1914)

He saw her from the bottom of the stairs
Before she saw him. She was starting down,

Looking back over her shoulder at some fear.
She took a doubtful step and then undid it
To raise herself and look again. He spoke   5
Advancing toward her: "What is it you see
From up there always—for I want to know."
She turned and sank upon her skirts at that,
And her face changed from terrified to dull.
He said to gain time: "What is it you see,"   10
Mounting until she cowered under him.
"I will find out now—you must tell me, dear."
She, in her place, refused him any help
With the least stiffening of her neck and silence.
She let him look, sure that he wouldn't see,   15
Blind creature; and awhile he didn't see.
But at last he murmured, "Oh," and again, "Oh."

"What is it—what?" she said.

                         "Just that I see."

"You don't," she challenged. "Tell me what it is."

"The wonder is I didn't see at once.   20
I never noticed it from here before.
I must be wonted to it—that's the reason.
The little graveyard where my people are!
So small the window frames the whole of it.
Not so much larger than a bedroom, is it?   25
There are three stones of slate and one of marble,
Broad-shouldered little slabs there in the sunlight
On the sidehill. We haven't to mind *those*.
But I understand: it is not the stones,
But the child's mound—"

                         "Don't, don't, don't,
     don't," she cried.   30

She withdrew, shrinking from beneath his arm
That rested on the banister, and slid downstairs;
And turned on him with such a daunting look,
He said twice over before he knew himself:
"Can't a man speak of his own child he's lost?"   35

"Not you! Oh, where's my hat? Oh, I don't need it!
I must get out of here. I must get air.

I don't know rightly whether any man can."

"Amy! Don't go to someone else this time.
Listen to me. I won't come down the stairs."   40
He sat and fixed his chin between his fists.
"There's something I should like to ask you, dear."

"You don't know how to ask it."

                              "Help me, then."

Her fingers moved the latch for all reply.

"My words are nearly always an offense.   45
I don't know how to speak of anything
So as to please you. But I might be taught,
I should suppose. I can't say I see how.
A man must partly give up being a man
With women-folk. We could have some arrangement   50
By which I'd bind myself to keep hands off
Anything special you're a-mind to name.
Though I don't like such things 'twixt those that love.
Two that don't love can't live together without them.
But two that do can't live together with them."   55
She moved the latch a little. "Don't—don't go.
Don't carry it to someone else this time.
Tell me about it if it's something human.
Let me into your grief. I'm not so much
Unlike other folks as your standing there   60
Apart would make me out. Give me my chance.
I do think, though, you overdo it a little.
What was it brought you up to think it the thing
To take your mother-loss of a first child
So inconsolably—in the face of love.   65
You'd think his memory might be satisfied—"

"There you go sneering now!"

                              "I'm not, I'm not!
You make me angry. I'll come down to you.
God, what a woman! And it's come to this,
A man can't speak of his own child that's dead."   70

"You can't because you don't know how to speak.
If you had any feelings, you that dug

With your own hand—how could you?—his little grave;
I saw you from that very window there,
Making the gravel leap and leap in air,   75
Leap up, like that, like that, and land so lightly
And roll back down the mound beside the hole.
I thought, Who is that man? I didn't know you.
And I crept down the stairs and up the stairs
To look again, and still your spade kept lifting.   80
Then you came in. I heard your rumbling voice
Out in the kitchen, and I don't know why,
But I went near to see with my own eyes.
You could sit there with the stains on your shoes
Of the fresh earth from your own baby's grave   85
And talk about your everyday concerns.
You had stood the spade up against the wall
Outside there in the entry, for I saw it."

"I shall laugh the worst laugh I ever laughed.
I'm cursed. God, if I don't believe I'm cursed."   90

"I can repeat the very words you were saying:
'Three foggy mornings and one rainy day
Will rot the best birch fence a man can build.'
Think of it, talk like that at such a time!
What had how long it takes a birch to rot   95
To do with what was in the darkened parlor?
You *couldn't* care! The nearest friends can go
With anyone to death, comes so far short
They might as well not try to go at all.
No, from the time when one is sick to death,   100
One is alone, and he dies more alone.
Friends make pretense of following to the grave,
But before one is in it, their minds are turned
And making the best of their way back to life
And living people, and things they understand.   105
But the world's evil. I won't have grief so
If I can change it. Oh, I won't, I won't!"

"There, you have said it all and you feel better.
You won't go now. You're crying. Close the door.
The heart's gone out of it: why keep it up?   110
Amy! There's someone coming down the road!"

"*You*—oh, you think the talk is all. I must go—
Somewhere out of this house. How can I make you—"
"If—you—do!" She was opening the door wider.

·····➤ *Your* Turn
Talking and Writing about Lit

1. What aspects of "Home Burial" make it a narrative poem?

2. **DIY** Write a narrative poem of your own which tells a story of an
incident in a family. Your poem does not need to be as long as
Frost's, and it doesn't have to involve death.

Robert Frost (1874–1963)
"Out, Out—" (1916)

The buzz-saw snarled and rattled in the yard
And made dust and dropped stove-length sticks of wood,
Sweet-scented stuff when the breeze drew across it.
And from there those that lifted eyes could count
Five mountain ranges one behind the other   5
Under the sunset far into Vermont.
And the saw snarled and rattled, snarled and rattled,
As it ran light, or had to bear a load.
And nothing happened: day was all but done.
Call it a day, I wish they might have said   10
To please the boy by giving him the half hour
That a boy counts so much when saved from work.
His sister stood beside them in her apron
To tell them "Supper." At the word, the saw,
As if to prove saws knew what supper meant,   15
Leaped out at the boy's hand, or seemed to leap—
He must have given the hand. However it was,
Neither refused the meeting. But the hand!
The boy's first outcry was a rueful laugh,
As he swung toward them holding up the hand   20
Half in appeal, but half as if to keep
The life from spilling. Then the boy saw all—
Since he was old enough to know, big boy
Doing a man's work, though a child at heart—
He saw all spoiled. "Don't let him cut my hand off—   25
The doctor, when he comes. Don't let him, sister!"
So. But the hand was gone already.
The doctor put him in the dark of ether.
He lay and puffed his lips out with his breath.
And then—the watcher at his pulse took fright.   30
No one believed. They listened at his heart.

Little—less—nothing!—and that ended it.
No more to build on there. And they, since they
Were not the one dead, turned to their affairs.

·····▶ *Your* **Turn**
Talking and Writing about Lit

1. How do you interpret the last two lines of Frost's "Out, Out—"?
2. Compare Frost's poems "Home Burial" and "Out, Out—."

Talking Lit

Lyn Hejinian explains that language is ever changing; in fact, "Language itself is never in a state of rest."

Lyn Hejinian, from "The Rejection of Closure" (1984)

My title, "The Rejection of Closure," sounds judgmental, which is a little misleading—though only a little—since I am a happy reader of detective novels and an admiring, a very admiring, reader of Charles Dickens' novels.

Nevertheless, whatever the pleasures, in a fundamental way closure is a fiction—one of the amenities that fantasy or falsehood provides.

What then is the fundamental necessity for openness? Or, rather, what is there in language itself that compels and implements the rejection of closure?

I perceive the world as vast and overwhelming; each moment stands under an enormous vertical and horizontal pressure of information, potent with ambiguity, meaning-full, unfixed, and certainly incomplete. What saves this from becoming a vast undifferentiated mass of data and situation is one's ability to make distinctions. Each written text may act as a distinction, may be a distinction. The experience of feeling overwhelmed by undifferentiated material is like claustrophobia. One feels panicky, closed in. The open text is one which both acknowledges the vastness of the world and is formally differentiating. It is the form that opens it, in that case.

• • •

Two dangers never cease threatening in the world: order and disorder.

Language discovers what one might know. Therefore, the limits of language are the limits of what we might know. We discover the limits of language early, as children. Anything with limits can be imagined (correctly or incorrectly) as an object, by analogy with other objects—balls and rivers. Children objectify language when they render it their plaything, in jokes, puns, and riddles, or in glossolaliac chants and rhymes. They discover that words are not equal to the world, that a shift, analogous to parallax in photography, occurs between things (events, ideas, objects) and the words for them—a displacement that leaves a gap. Among the most prevalent and persistent category of joke is that which identifies and makes use of the fallacious comparison of words to the world and delights in the ambiguity resulting from the discrepancy:

> Why did the moron eat hay?
> To feed his hoarse voice.

Because we have language we find ourselves in a peculiar relationship to the objects, events, and situations which constitute what we imagine of the world. Language generates its own characteristics in the human psychological and spiritual condition. This psychology is generated by the struggle between language and that which it claims to depict or express, by our overwhelming experience of the vastness and uncertainty of the world and by what often seems to be the inadequacy of the imagination that longs to know it, and, for the poet, the even greater inadequacy of the language that appears to describe, discuss, or disclose it.

This inadequacy, however, is merely a disguise for other virtues.

"What mind worthy of the name," said Flaubert, "ever reached a conclusion?"

Language is one of the principal forms our curiosity takes. It makes us restless. As Francis Ponge puts it, "Man is a curious body whose center of gravity is not in himself." Instead it seems to be located in language, by virtue of which we negotiate our mentalities and the world; off-balance, heavy at the mouth, we are pulled forward.

> She is lying on her stomach with one eye closed, driving a toy truck along the road she has cleared with her fingers. Then the tantrum broke out, blue, without a breath of air. . . . You could increase the height by making lateral additions and building over them a sequence of steps, leaving tunnels, or windows, between the blocks, and I did. I made signs to them to be as quiet as possible. But a word is a bottomless pit. It became magically pregnant and one day split open, giving birth to a stone egg, about as big as a football.
>
> —*My Life*

Language itself is never in a state of rest. And the experience of using it, which includes the experience of understanding it, either as speech or as writing, is inevitably active. I mean both intellectually and emotionally active.

The progress of a line or sentence, or a series of lines or sentences, has spatial properties as well as temporal properties. The spatial density is both vertical and horizontal. The meaning of a word in its place derives both from the word's lateral reach, its contacts with its neighbors in a statement, and from its reach through and out of the text into the other world, the matrix of its contemporary and historical reference. The very idea of reference is spatial: over here is word, over there is thing at which word is shooting amiable love-arrows.

• • •

Writing develops subjects that mean the words we have for them.

Even words in storage, in the dictionary, seem frenetic with activity, as each individual entry attracts to itself other words as definition, example, and amplification. Thus, to open the dictionary at random, mastoid attracts nipplelike, temporal, bone, ear, and behind. Then turning to temporal we find that the definition includes time, space, life, world, transitory, and near the temples, but, significantly, not mastoid. There is no entry for nipplelike, but the definition for nipple brings protuberance, breast, udder, the female, milk, discharge, mouthpiece, and nursing bottle, and not mastoid, nor temporal, nor time, bone, ear, space, or world, etc. It is relevant that the exchanges are incompletely reciprocal.

> and how did this happen like an excerpt
>   beginning in a square white boat abob on a gray sea
>   tootling of another message by the hacking lark
> as a child to the rescue and its spring
>   many comedies emerge and in particular a group of girls   5
>   in a great lock of letters
>   like knock look
> a restless storage of a thousand boastings
> but cow dull bulge clump
>   slippage thinks random patterns through wishes   10
>   I intend greed as I intend pride
>   patterns of roll extend over the wish
>   —*Writing is an Aid to Memory*

The "rage to know" is one expression of restlessness produced by language.

> As long as man keeps hearing words
> He's sure that there's a meaning somewhere

says Mephistopheles in Goethe's *Faust*.

It's in the nature of language to encourage, and in part to justify, such Faustian longings. The notion that language is the means and medium for attaining knowledge, and, concomitantly, power, is old, of course. The knowledge towards which we seem to be driven by language, or which language seems to promise, is inherently sacred as well as secular, redemptive as well as satisfying. The *nomina sint numina* position (i.e., that there is an essential identity between name and thing, that the real nature of a thing is immanent and present in its name, that nouns are numinous) suggests that it is possible to find a language which will meet its object with perfect identity. If this were the case, we could, in speaking or in writing, achieve the at-oneness with the universe, at least in its particulars, that is the condition of paradise, or complete and perfect knowing—or of perfect mental health.

But if in the Edenic scenarios we acquired knowledge of the animals by naming them, it was not by virtue of any numinous immanence in the name but because Adam was a taxonomist. He distinguished the individual animals, discovered the concept of categories, and then organized the species according to their functions and relationships in a system.

What the naming provides is structure, not individual words.

Student Essay

Nicole Callan examines what Robert Frost has to say about death in his poems "Out, Out—" and "Home Burial."

Nicole Callan

Prof. Barnard

English 102-JE

Dealing with Death

Although death tends to be looked at as being negative and people don't usually like to think about death and dying, it is reality. Some people can't even think or talk about death without becoming depressed. Others feel that it is natural and are unafraid (so they say) of dying. One poet who writes about death and coping with death is Robert Frost. Frost lost his father at the age of eleven, and perhaps writing about death was a way of releasing his thoughts about the experience he went through at such a young age. Two poems that are related to death are "Out, Out—" and "Home Burial." "Out, Out—" deals with the experience of a child's death

Callan 2

from the point of view of the child, at the moment of accidental death, and "Home Burial" deals with coping with the loss of a child, from the point of view of the parents.

We know that the death in "Out, Out—" is accidental because in lines 14–17 Frost writes, "As if to prove saws knew what supper meant, / Leaped out at the boy's hand, or seemed to leap— / He must have given the hand." This is a very detailed scene and it makes the reader feel like he or she is standing in front of the boy watching this chain saw whip across his hand while it bleeds uncontrollably. From the very beginning of the poem I could tell that the saw was going to be a negative object because Frost wrote, "The buzz-saw snarled and rattled in the yard." When I think of something snarling I think of a negative image, like a dog growling and showing its teeth. After the saw takes the boy's hand, "The boy's first outcry was a rueful laugh." When I read this I imagined a boy in a complete shock and scared for his life. Sometimes after something so shocking happens to you, you are unable to express any emotions because you are in disbelief. This is what I think the boy was feeling. I also found it interesting that the boy in the poem was from Vermont because Frost was named Poet Laureate of Vermont (in addition to being a Poet Laureate of the U.S.). This makes me wonder if maybe, while living in Vermont, he witnessed a tragic death like this.

The title of this poem carries a lot of meaning and helps the reader to understand what Frost is possibly trying to say. The title, "Out, Out—" is from *Macbeth* (Act V, Scene v), written by William Shakespeare. Life is compared to a "brief candle." The line implies that life has no meaning to it and death can come at any moment, so one should feel comfortable about living. In this passage he is

Callan 3

describing how life really doesn't have any meaning and how death surrounds us every day. I think this is a perfect title for this poem because the tragic death of this boy was very unpredictable and his life was taken away in a flash. He never saw this coming; all he was thinking about was eating supper, and moments later he was thoughtless. The ending of this poem is also interesting. Frost writes: "Little—less—nothing!—and that ended it. / No more to build on there. And they, since they / Were not the one dead, turned to their affairs." "Little—less—nothing" symbolizes the candle in Macbeth's hand. When a candle starts to go out it takes a while and flutters just like his heart. Another line in the poem that relates to the candle is line 29, "He lay and puffed his lips out with his breath." When I read this line I imagined someone blowing out a candle, which symbolizes life in the passage from *Macbeth*. The ending— "And then, since they / were not the one dead, turned to their affairs"—made me think of the old saying "Life goes on." Even though they had to cope with the death of the boy, their lives were still not over and they still were able to move forward.

Another poem that is about death is "Home Burial." This poem is slightly different from "Out, Out—" because this poem describes the relationship between a father and mother and how they both are trying to cope with the death of their first born child. This poem is written as a dialogue between two people (the mother and father) and is in all quotations, unlike "Out, Out—," which is a narrative poem with one speaker.

In this poem, the father seems to be the stronger one of the couple. He is able to speak of the death, but the mother isn't having as easy a time of it. She feels that he speaks too freely of the whole thing and she probably doesn't understand how he was able to

Callan 4

cope with it because she is not psychologically healthy. He is trying to move to the next level of coping, but the mother is not. The mother feels that he doesn't talk about the death "properly." He says, "Help me, then. / My words are nearly always an offense. / I don't know how to speak of anything / So as to please you." He is trying to help his wife out with the grieving process, but she won't let him try or know what she is thinking. He goes on to say, "Don't carry it to someone else this time." Maybe this is implying another man or just that she doesn't feel comfortable enough with her own husband that she has to go to someone else to talk.

The window in the poem shows the grave, where the child is buried. It is a constant reminder of the death and the sight of it makes it very difficult for the mother to walk down the steps without seeing and remembering her child. In the beginning of the poem, Frost writes, "So small the window frames the whole of it. / Not so much larger than a bedroom, is it?" The first time I read this poem it didn't dawn on me, but on a second reading, I thought, maybe the grave symbolizes a crib and the window symbolizes the entranceway into the child's room. So every time she walks down the step, it is as if she is looking into her child's bedroom, which is now a graveyard.

When reading this poem, I sympathized with both characters, but more with the wife. I feel badly for both of them because they lost their first child. I feel badly for the father because he feels helpless when it comes to his wife and I feel badly for the mother because she is not dealing with death in a healing way. Some people are able to overcome the loss of a loved one more quickly than others. Some people like to talk about it, some like to write about it, and others are never able to face the reality that the person is gone.

Callan 5

Death isn't an easy topic to talk about, but unfortunately there is going to be a time in every person's life when he or she is faced with death. Both poems showed different views about death and coping with it. "Out, Out—" was more about the process of living and not knowing when death will come, and "Home Burial" was about the different ways people try to get over a death. Frost's use of figurative language and details really pulls the reader into the poems and brings us along on the journey of the characters.

FIXED FORMS

Even sports arenas use fixed form.

Players of the various sports follow the rules of the games, and the fields and courts on which the sports are played are built according to fixed dimensions. In the fan-shaped baseball field, for example home plate area is always a perfect 26 foot circle. The pitcher's mound is 60 feet, 6 inches from home plate, and there are exactly 90 feet between first and second base, second and third base, and third base and home plate. The distance between home plate and second base, and between first and third bases, is exactly 127 feet, 3 3/8 inches.

Moreover, the games themselves follow well-defined rules, and players that transgress are penalized. In some sports, the bodies of the participants must follow a specified form. Olympic swimmers, for example, must not only be fast, but must properly execute a particular stroke.

While not nearly as rigid in application, some poetry also follows a fixed, traditional form. Some poetry, on the other hand, deviates from traditional form entirely, and is not judged to be poor for its non-compliance. As you will see, a poet's deviation from traditional form often yields spectacular results. The same cannot be said with regard to sports: a tennis player who refuses to engage in a volley won't enjoy a long or lustrous career.

If you've played a sport or been a spectator at a sporting event, you are already familiar with fixed forms. Just as baseball diamonds, football fields, tennis or basketball courts are always configured in the same basic way, certain types of poems have a fixed form too. The term **fixed form** in poetry refers to poems that use rhyme, rhythm, word choice, meter (see Chapter 17), or stanzaic arrangements in patterns that are repeated. A poet may create a new pattern for use in a particular poem, or poets may use traditional fixed forms that are familiar and recognizable— for instance, the ballad stanza, the sonnet, the villanelle, the sestina, the pantoum, the tanka, and the haiku. The Western forms that we will discuss are also examples of **stanzaic forms**, that is, poetic forms based on a pattern of stanzas. The haiku, however, a traditional Japanese form, involves a syllabic pattern (a pattern based on the number of syllables per line) rather than a stanzaic pattern.

The Ballad Stanza

In the discussion of poetic form, the pattern of end rhyme is usually represented using letters of the alphabet to correspond to the ending sounds of lines. Dudley Randall's "Ballad of Birmingham," below, has the pattern *abcb*, *efgf*, and so on. In other words, the second and fourth lines in each stanza rhyme, but the first and third do not. The letters we assign represent the ending sounds of lines. If it is an ending sound appearing for the first time in a given poem, it gets a new letter. If it is a repeated sound, the corresponding letter is used again.

Dudley Randall (1914–2000)
Ballad of Birmingham (1969)

(On the bombing of a church in Birmingham, Alabama, 1963)

"Mother dear, may I go downtown
Instead of out to play,
And march the streets of Birmingham
In a Freedom March today?"

"No, baby, no, you may not go,   5
For the dogs are fierce and wild,
And clubs and hoses, guns and jails
Aren't good for a little child."

"But, mother, I won't be alone.
Other children will go with me,   10
And march the streets of Birmingham
To make our country free."

"No, baby, no, you may not go,
For I fear those guns will fire.
But you may go to church instead   15
And sing in the children's choir."

She has combed and brushed her night-dark hair,
And bathed rose petal sweet,
And drawn white gloves on her small brown hands,
And white shoes on her feet.   20

The mother smiled to know her child
Was in the sacred place,
But that smile was the last smile
To come upon her face.

For when she heard the explosion,   25
Her eyes grew wet and wild.
She raced through the streets of Birmingham
Calling for her child.

She clawed through bits of glass and brick,
Then lifted out a shoe.   30
"Oh, here's the shoe my baby wore,
But, baby, where are you?"

"Ballad of Birmingham" is an example of the **ballad stanza** form. When composing a ballad stanza poem, the poet maintains the traditional pattern of end rhyme in the second and fourth lines of each stanza throughout the poem, as Randall has done above.

Mother dear, may I go downtown	*a*
Instead of out to play,	*b*
And march the streets of Birmingham	*c*
In a freedom march today?	*b*

Another fixed characteristic of the ballad stanza is its syllabic pattern. Each stanza has eight syllables each in the first and third lines, and six syllables each in the second and fourth lines. One might also refer to this as alternating lines of tetrameter and trimeter (see Chapter 17 for a discussion of meter), though the pattern of stresses may vary (in other words, it may not always be composed of iambic feet). When read aloud, the syllabic pattern, combined with the pattern of end rhyme, creates a strong rhythm in the poem reminiscent of lyrics set to music. Indeed the original folk ballad form evolved to be sung, sometimes accompanied by a musical instrument. Before written literature was widely available, the bard or balladeer was an important transmitter of folk narratives, stories embodying the experiences of the people. The use of rhyme and rhythm in folk ballads helped people to remember the lines at a time when there was no written text. An oral tradition of this kind has been important in every human culture.

The Italian Sonnet

The **sonnet** is a fixed form which always employs a total of fourteen lines and uses a rather elaborate pattern of end rhyme. Although there are no space breaks between the stanzas of a sonnet, it does indeed have stanzas and is considered a stanzaic form. There are two basic types of sonnets. The **Italian sonnet** (also called the **Petrarchan sonnet**, after the fourteenth-century Italian poet Petrarch) is composed of an **octave** (an eight-line stanza) followed by a **sestet** (a six-line stanza). Although there is no space break between the two, there is usually a thematic turn at the shift from the octave to the sestet. Often the octave poses a problem or question and the sestet answers or responds to it in some way. Again, we see that poetic form is employed to serve the thematic intentions of the poet.

The rhyming pattern of the Italian sonnet further defines its stanzaic form. The octave contains two **quatrains** (four-line stanzas), with the rhyming pattern *abba, abba.*

William Wordsworth (1770–1850)
The World Is Too Much with Us (1807)

The world is too much with us; late and soon,
Getting and spending, we lay waste our powers;
Little we see in Nature that is ours;
We have given our hearts away, a sordid boon!*,
This Sea that bares her bosom to the moon,   5
The winds that will be howling at all hours,
And are up-gathered now like sleeping flowers,
For this, for everything, we are out of tune;
It moves us not.—Great God! I'd rather be

***boon:** gift

A Pagan suckled in a creed outworn;   10
So might I, standing on this pleasant lea,
Have glimpses that would make me less forlorn;
Have sight of Proteus rising from the sea;
Or hear old Triton blow his wreathéd horn.

The sestet often follows the rhyming pattern *cdcdcd* (as in Wordsworth's "The World Is Too Much with Us"); however, other possible patterns for the sestet are *cdecde* or *cdedce*. The poet may choose to make additional slight variations on the basic form. For instance, Wordsworth's "The World Is Too Much with Us" makes its thematic turn in the middle of the sestet's first line, rather than at the beginning of it. John Keats's "On First Looking into Chapman's Homer," on the other hand, follows the traditional form of the Italian sonnet exactly.

John Keats (1795–1821)
On First Looking into Chapman's Homer[1] (1816)

Much have I traveled in the realms of gold,
    And many goodly states and kingdoms seen;
    Round many western islands have I been
Which bards in fealty[2] to Apollo[3] hold.
Oft of one wide expanse had I been told   5
    That deep-browed Homer ruled as his demesne;[4]
    Yet did I never breathe its pure serene[5]
Till I heard Chapman speak out loud and bold:
Then felt I like some watcher of the skies
    When a new planet swims into his ken;   10
Or like stout Cortez[6] when with eagle eyes
    He stared at the Pacific—and all his men
Looked at each other with a wild surmise—
    Silent, upon a peak in Darien.

---

[1]**Chapman's Homer:** Translation of Homer's *Iliad* by George Chapman, a contemporary of Shakespeare's.
[2]**fealty:** allegiance
[3]**Apollo:** God of poetic inspiration.
[4]**demesne:** domain
[5]**serene:** atmosphere
[6]**Cortez:** Spanish conqueror of Mexico; in fact, Balboa, not Cortez, was the first European to see the Pacific, from Darien, in Panama.

Remember Gwendolyn Brooks's poem "We Real Cool" from Chapter 14? In "First Fight. Then Fiddle," a sonnet by Gwendolyn Brooks, the rhyme scheme of the sestet is *cddcee*, a slight variation on the traditional patterns. Some poets have made more substantial alterations to the traditional sonnet form, and these are often called **contemporary sonnets**.

Gwendolyn Brooks (1917–2000)
First Fight. Then Fiddle. (1949)

First fight. Then fiddle. Ply the slipping string
With feathery sorcery; muzzle the note
With hurting love; the music that they wrote
Bewitch, bewilder. Qualify to sing
Threadwise. Devise no salt, no hempen thing   5
For the dear instrument to bear. Devote
The bow to silks and honey. Be remote
A while from malice and from murdering.
But first to arms, to armor. Carry hate
In front of you and harmony behind.   10
Be deaf to music and to beauty blind.
Win war. Rise bloody, maybe not too late
For having first to civilize a space
Wherein to play your violin with grace.

The English Sonnet

The second traditional type of sonnet is the **English sonnet** (also called the **Shakespearean sonnet** for its most well-known practitioner). The English sonnet also contains a total of fourteen lines. The main body of the poem is composed of three quatrains. Usually the thematic turn comes at the end of the third quatrain, which is followed by a **couplet** (a pair of lines which are linked by rhyme and by thematic thrust). The couplet typically answers or responds to—or provides a thematic reversal of—the subject of the preceding quatrains. The rhyme scheme of the English sonnet is *abab, cdcd, efef, gg*. Sometimes near rhyme, as well as exact rhyme, is used. The three Shakespearean sonnets below provide examples of these variations.

William Shakespeare (1564–1616)
My mistress' eyes are nothing like the sun (1609)

My mistress' eyes are nothing like the sun;
Coral is far more red than her lips' red;
If snow be white, why then her breasts are dun;[1]
If hairs be wires, black wires grow on her head.

---

[1]**dun:** Mouse-colored.

I have seen roses damasked[2] red and white,   5
But no such roses see I in her cheeks;
And in some perfumes is there more delight
Than in the breath that from my mistress reeks.
I love to hear her speak, yet well I know
That music hath a far more pleasing sound;   10
I grant I never saw a goddess go;[3]
My mistress, when she walks, treads on the ground.
And yet, by heaven, I think my love as rare
As any she belied with false compare.

------

[2]**damasked:** Variegated,
[3]**go:** Walk.

William Shakespeare (1564–1616)
Shall I compare thee to a summer's day? (1609)

Shall I compare thee to a summer's day?
Thou art more lovely and more temperate:
Rough winds do shake the lovely buds of May,
And summer's lease hath all too short a date.
Sometimes too hot the eye of heaven shines,   5
And often is his gold complexion dimmed;
And every fair[1] from fair sometimes declines
By chance or nature's changing course untrimmed[2];
But thy eternal summer shall not fade
Nor lose possession of that fair thou ow'st[3],   10
Nor shall death brag thou wand'rest in his shade
When in eternal lines to time thou grow'st.
So long as men can breathe or eyes can see,
So long lives this[4], and this gives life to thee.

------

[1]**fair:** beauty
[2]**untrimmed:** stripped bare
[3]**ow'st:** own
[4]**this:** this poem

William Shakespeare (1564–1616)
When, in disgrace with fortune and men's eyes (1609)

When, in disgrace with Fortune and men's eyes,
I all alone beweep my outcast state,
And trouble deaf heaven with my bootless[1] cries,

------

[1]**bootless:** Futile.

And look upon myself and curse my fate,
Wishing me like to one more rich in hope,   5
Featured like him, like him with friends possessed,
Desiring this man's art, and that man's scope,
With what I most enjoy contented least,
Yet in these thoughts myself almost despising,
Haply[2] I think on thee, and then my state,   10
Like to the lark at break of day arising
From sullen earth, sings hymns at heaven's gate;
  For thy sweet love rememb'red such wealth brings
  That then I scorn to change my state with kings.

---

[2]**Haply:** Luckily.

The Villanelle, the Sestina, and the Pantoum

The **villanelle** (a form first used by French balladeers in the Middle Ages) is a nineteen-line poem composed of five **tercets** (three-line stanzas) and a final quatrain. In this form entire lines are repeated as refrains (like a chorus in song lyrics), which creates a strong rhythm and an echoing pattern of end rhyme. Line 1 is repeated as lines 6, 12, and 18. Line 3 is repeated as lines 9, 15, and 19. Only two different rhyming endings appear throughout the poem, and the lines repeated as refrains reappear also in the final quatrain. Dylan Thomas's "Do Not Go Gentle into That Good Night" is an example of the traditional villanelle form.

Dylan Thomas (1914–1953)
Do Not Go Gentle into That Good Night (1952)

Do not go gentle into that good night,
Old age should burn and rave at close of day;
Rage, rage against the dying of the light.

Though wise men at their end know dark is right,
Because their words had forked no lightning they   5
Do not go gentle into that good night.

Good men, the last wave by, crying how bright
Their frail deeds might have danced in a green bay,
Rage, rage against the dying of the light.

Wild men who caught and sang the sun in flight,   10
And learn, too late, they grieved it on its way,
Do not go gentle into that good night.

Grave men, near death, who see with blinding sight
Blind eyes could blaze like meteors and be gay,
Rage, rage against the dying of the light.   15

And you, my father, there on the sad height,
Curse, bless, me now with your fierce tears, I pray.
Do not go gentle into that good night.
Rage, rage against the dying of the light.

Because of its length, the **sestina** may be considered an even more demand-ing form. It contains six six-line stanzas and a concluding three-line stanza, called an **envoi**. As illustrated by Alberto Alvaro Ríos's poem "Nani," the endings of the first six lines are repeated throughout the poem. Note that the six key words are all repeated in the final three-line stanza, one at the end of each half line.

Alberto Alvaro Ríos (b. 1952)

Nani (1982)

Sitting at her table, she serves
the sopa de arroz[1] to me
instinctively, and I watch her,
the absolute *mamá*, and eat words
I might have had to say more   5
out of embarrassment. To speak,
now-foreign words I used to speak,
too, dribble down her mouth as she serves
me albóndigas.[2] No more
than a third are easy to me.   10
By the stove she does something with words
and looks at me only with her
back. I am full. I tell her
I taste the mint, and watch her speak
smiles at the stove. All my words   15
make her smile. Nani[3] never serves
herself, she only watches me
with her skin, her hair. I ask for more.

---

[1]**sopa de arroz:** rice soup
[2]**albóndigas:** spiced meatballs
[3]**Nani:** granny

I watch the *mamá* warming more
tortillas for me. I watch her   20
fingers in the flame for me.
Near her mouth, I see a wrinkle speak
of a man whose body serves
the ants like she serves me, then more words
from more wrinkles about children, words   25
about this and that, flowing more
easily from these other mouths. Each serves
as a tremendous string around her,
holding her together. They speak
nani was this and that to me   30
and I wonder just how much of me
will die with her, what were the words
I could have been, was. Her insides speak
through a hundred wrinkles, now, more
than she can bear, steel around her,   35
shouting, then, What is this thing she serves?

She asks me if I want more.
I own no words to stop her.
Even before I speak, she serves.

Clement Long's "Always the One Who Loves His Father Most" is a **pantoum**. Note how this verse form resembles a relay race, with lines (and ideas) being handed off from one quatrain to the next. This makes possible the sound of a refrain (resembling a song's refrain) and also the interconnectedness of thematic echoes in the poem.

Clement Long
Always the One Who Loves His Father Most (1986)

Always the one who loves his father most,
the one the father loves the most in turn,
will fight against his father as he must.
Neither knows what he will come to learn.

The one the father loves the most in turn   5
tells the father no and no and no,
but neither knows what he will come to learn
nor cares a lot what that could be, and so

tells his father no and no and no,
is ignorant of what the years will teach   10
nor cares a lot what that could be, and so
unties the knot that matters most, while each

is ignorant of what the years will teach,
they'll learn how pride—if each lives out his years—
unties the knot that matters most, while each   15
will feel a sadness, feel the midnight fears.

They'll learn how pride—if each lives out his years—
will lose the aging other as a friend,
will feel a sadness, feel the midnight fears.
The child and then the father, world without end,   20

will lose the aging other as a friend.
And then the child of that one, too, will grow—
the child and then the father, world without end—
in turn to fight his father, *comme il faut,*

will fight against his father, as he must,   25
always, the one who loves his father most.

Syllabic Forms—Haiku and Tanka

The **tanka** and the **haiku** are Japanese syllabic forms which have attracted readers and practitioners worldwide. The tanka is a poem of thirty-one syllables. The haiku has seventeen syllables that appear in three lines of five, seven, and five syllables each. Although these syllabic forms have their precursors in Japanese poetry written as early as the eighth century, the haiku form (the most popular of the two) came to full flower in the seventeenth century in the work of Japanese poet Matsuo Bashō.

Haiku and tanka poets often compose works in response to one another. For instance, Bashō composed the following poem after reading a tanka poem (thirty-one syllables) in which the eight views of Lake Ōmi were represented. Bashō then represented all eight views in a haiku (seventeen syllables). The mention of "Mii-dera's bell" serves as one "view" of the lake, from the Mii-dera temple.

Matsuo Bashō (1644–1694)
Eight Views of Lake Ōmi (17th Century)

Eight Views?—Ah, well;
    mist hid seven when I heard
        Mii-dera's bell.

A haiku often involves this kind of word play or clever turn. In addition, it is typical to strive for nuances of meaning and philosophical significance in the poem, and this is most often accomplished by using sharply focused images of nature. For instance, Bashō wrote the following haiku after traveling in the Kiso mountains, where he had to cross a deep gorge on a rather precarious rope bridge. In only seventeen syllables, the poet manages to suggest a connection between the risk of crossing the bridge and the risks inherent in human life.

Matsuo Bashō
Around Existence Twine (17th Century)

Around existence twine
    (Oh, bridge that hangs across the gorge!)
        ropes of twisted vine.

It should be noted that, in the translation of such precise and delicate poems from Japanese to English, a great deal is often lost. The Japanese ideographs (graphic representations of words and meanings) may not translate into the same number of syllables in English. Also some clever word play and double meanings or allusions in the Japanese cannot be represented in English.

Below is a haiku written by African American poet Etheridge Knight. Knight wrote primarily open form poetry, but he enjoyed trying his hand at the haiku form. Knight was one of many African American writers whose work was first published by fellow poet Dudley Randall through his Broadside Press in Detroit. Randall succeeded in bringing to the attention of American readers many previously unrecognized poets of color, including some who were serving prison terms, when he first published their work.

Etheridge Knight (1931–1991)
Eastern Guard Tower (1968)

Eastern guard tower
glints in sunset; convicts rest
like lizards on rocks.

The Poet's Use of Form

In the following poem, William Wordsworth devised his own individual form for the poem and then used it consistently throughout, repeating the pattern in each stanza. Analyze Wordsworth's use of form here, pointing out aspects of the poem that resemble the fixed forms we have studied in this chapter. In the following chapter, "Open Form," we will be looking at poems that go farther down this road of devising a new form to fit what the poet wants to say.

William Wordsworth (1770–1850)
I Wandered Lonely as a Cloud (1807)

I wandered lonely as a cloud
That floats on high o'er vales and hills,
When all at once I saw a crowd,
A host, of golden daffodils;
Beside the lake, beneath the trees,   5
Fluttering and dancing in the breeze.

Continuous as the stars that shine
And twinkle on the milky way,
They stretched in never-ending line
Along the margin of a bay: 10
Ten thousand saw I at a glance,
Tossing their heads in sprightly dance.

The waves beside them danced; but they
Outdid the sparkling waves in glee;
A poet could not but be gay,   15
In such a jocund company;
I gazed—and gazed—but little thought
What wealth the show to me had brought:

For oft, when on my couch I lie
In vacant or in pensive mood,   20
They flash upon that inward eye
Which is the bliss of solitude;
And then my heart with pleasure fills,
And dances with the daffodils.

Poems for Further Reading

Sonnet (1999)

All we need is fourteen lines, well, thirteen now,
and after this one just a dozen
to launch a little ship on love's storm-tossed seas,
then only ten more left like rows of beans.
How easily it goes unless you get Elizabethan   5
and insist the iambic bongos must be played
and rhymes positioned at the ends of lines,
one for every station of the cross.
But hang on here while we make the turn
into the final six where all will be resolved,   10
where longing and heartache will find an end,
where Laura will tell Petrarch to put down his pen,
take off those crazy medieval tights,
blow out the lights, and come at last to bed.

·····▶ *Your* Turn
Talking and Writing about Lit

1. Think back to our discussion of metafiction in Chapter 11. Why might Billy Collin's "Sonnet" be called a metapoem, or even a metasonnet?

2. **DIY** Write a poem of from six to fourteen lines which expresses your views about writing poetry.

William Shakespeare (1564–1616)
Th' expense of spirit in a waste of shame (1609)

Th' expense of spirit in a waste of shame
Is lust in action; and till action, lust
Is perjured, murderous, bloody, full of blame,
Savage, extreme, rude, cruel, not to trust;
Enjoyed no sooner but despiséd straight: 5
Past reason hunted; and no sooner had,
Past reason hated, as a swallowed bait,

On purpose laid to make the taker mad:
Mad in pursuit, and in possession so;
Had, having, and in quest to have, extreme;   10
A bliss in proof,* and proved, a very woe;
Before, a joy proposed; behind, a dream.
All this the world well knows; yet none knows well
To shun the heaven that leads men to this hell.

A bliss in proof: I.e., in the experience.

·····▶ *Your* Turn
Talking and Writing about Lit

1. In two or three sentences, paraphrase (summarize in your own words) the poem's meaning.

2. Find two metaphors in the poem and explain their meaning.

e.e. cummings (1894–1962)
next to of course god america i (1926)

"next to of course god america i
love you land of the pilgrims' and so forth oh
say can you see by the dawn's early my
country 'tis of centuries come and go
and are no more what of it we should worry   5
in every language even deafanddumb
thy sons acclaim your glorious name by gorry
by jingo by gee by gosh by gum
why talk of beauty what could be more beautiful than these heroic happy dead   10
who rushed like lions to the roaring slaughter
they did not stop to think they died instead
then shall the voice of liberty be mute?"

He spoke. And drank rapidly a glass of water

·····▶ *Your* Turn
Talking and Writing about Lit

1. Who is the speaker of the poem in e.e. cummings's "next to of course god america i"? Note that most of the poem is enclosed in quotation marks; only the last line is outside the quotation marks.

2. This poem has fourteen lines. Is it a sonnet?

Countee Cullen (1903–1946)
Yet Do I Marvel (1925)

I doubt not God is good, well-meaning, kind,
And did He stoop to quibble could tell why
The little buried mole continues blind,
Why flesh that mirrors Him must some day die,
Make plain the reason tortured Tantalus*   5
Is baited by the fickle fruit, declare
If merely brute caprice dooms Sisyphus
To struggle up a never-ending stair.
Inscrutable His ways are, and immune
To catechism by a mind too strewn   10
With petty cares to slightly understand
What awful brain compels His awful hand.
Yet do I marvel at this curious thing:
To make a poet black, and bid him sing!

*__Tantalus:__ Tantalus, and Sisyphus in lines 5 and 7, are figures in Greek mythology who were pun-
ished in Hades for crimes committed on earth. Tantalus's punishment was to be offered food and
water that was then instantly snatched away. Sisyphus's torment was to roll a heavy stone to the top
of a hill and, after it rolled back down, to repeat the ordeal perpetually.

····· ▶ *Your* Turn
Talking and Writing about Lit

1. In his sonnet "Yet Do I Marvel," Harlem renaissance poet Countee Cullen
   compares the task of the black poet in 1920s America and the tasks of
   Tantalus and Sisyphus in Greek mythology. Look up these two mythological
   figures and explain the comparison. If you use the Internet, you might try
   searching the Greek and Roman Mythology pages of the Bulfinch's
   Mythology site (http://www.bulfinch.org/fables/).
2. Compare and contrast "Yet Do I Marvel" with any poem written by
   Langston Hughes (see Chapter 13). Consider form as well as themes.

Barbara Horn
Midnight Blue: Ray Charles and Roy Orbison Select Their Wardrobes (2003)

We need the ones in blacks and blues
  Who sing sad songs that last for years.
They shake our hearts out, air our views.

That they sound mournful and confused
    Makes those of us inept at tears   5
More crazy 'bout those blacks. And blues

Can help spurned lovers bear old news:
"That's just the way life goes, my dears."
Let's stake our hearts, declare our views

That we, the lovelorn, mend, though bruised.   10
    If proud ones scorn, we'll face down jeers
        By list'ning to the blacks and blues.

    We crave their crooning "Born to Lose"
        And "Crying" tunes 'til it appears
They've sung their hearts out, bared our views.   15

        In words not hopeful but that fuse
    The pains of Ray with Roy's deep fears,
    They sing to us—in blacks and blues—
And put our hearts back, share our views.

·····▶ *Your* Turn
Talking and Writing about Lit

1. Barbara Horn's "Midnight Blue: Ray Charles and Roy Orbison Select Their Wardrobes" is a contemporary villanelle; that is, it uses the basic pattern of the traditional villanelle, but it includes some variations on the form as well. Identify ways in which the poem adheres to the traditional form and ways in which it innovates on the form. You might compare this poem with Dylan Thomas's "Do Not Go Gentle into That Good Night," which follows the traditional form exactly.

2. **DIY** Write a traditional or contemporary villanelle of your own. You may choose your own subject, or you may write about a family member (Thomas's famous villanelle was composed as his own father was dying), or you might write a poem that is a tribute (or critique) of a well-known figure or figures (like Ray Charles and Roy Orbison).

Theodore Roethke (1908–1963)
The Waking (1953)

I wake to sleep, and take my waking slow.
I feel my fate in what I cannot fear.
I learn by going where I have to go.

We think by feeling. What is there to know?
I hear my being dance from ear to ear.   5
I wake to sleep, and take my waking slow.

Of those so close beside me, which are you?
God bless the Ground! I shall walk softly there,
And learn by going where I have to go.

Light takes the Tree; but who can tell us how?   10
The lowly worm climbs up a winding stair;
I wake to sleep, and take my waking slow.

Great Nature has another thing to do
To you and me; so take the lively air,
And, lovely, learn by going where to go.   15

This shaking keeps me steady. I should know.
What falls away is always. And is near.
I wake to sleep, and take my waking slow.
I learn by going where I have to go.

·······► *Your* Turn
Talking and Writing about Lit

1. Is Theodore Roethke's "The Waking" a traditional or contemporary villanelle?

2. Compare and contrast form and themes in Roethke's "The Waking" and Dylan Thomas's "Do Not Go Gentle into That Good Night" (above).

Barbara Barnard (b. 1951)
Hillbilly Daughter (2003)

What's a hillbilly daughter got to lose?
'Fore God there ain't nothing left for you to say;
Got me my heaven, got my walking shoes.

You tell me it's not my place to choose?
Think how long you kept me from the light of day;   5
What's a hillbilly daughter got to lose?

You got your achy heart, you got your booze,
What right you got to tell me stay,
Got me my heaven, got my walking shoes.

Whose rights you talking about, say whose?   10
You with your cold heart like a manta ray;
What's a hillbilly daughter got to lose?

Go ahead put your feet up, go ahead take your snooze.
I'll just off and leave you where you lay,
Got me my heaven, got my walking shoes.   15

Where I'm going, you won't have no clues,
Ain't going to come to you however hard you pray.
What's a hillbilly daughter got to lose?
Got me my heaven, got my walking shoes.

·····► *Your* Turn
Talking and Writing about Lit

1. The first thing you notice about this poem is that it is written in dialect, in the nonstandard vocabulary and grammar of Appalachian English. Compare the use of voice (dialect) and themes in Langston Hughes's "Mother to Son" (Chapter 13) or Gwendolyn Brooks's "We Real Cool" (Chapter 14). In all three of these poems, the speaker of the poem is not necessarily the poet but may be an imagined voice.

2. This poem is also a villanelle. Did I follow the traditional form exactly in "Hillbilly Daughter" or did I use variations on the form? Support your answer, using examples from the poem.

Gerard Manley Hopkins (1844–1889)
God's Grandeur (1877)

The world is charged with the grandeur of God.
        It will flame out, like shining from shook foil;
        It gathers to a greatness, like the ooze of oil
Crushed. Why do men then now not reck his rod?
Generations have trod, have trod, have trod;   5
        And all is seared with trade; bleared, smeared with toil;
        And wears man's smudge and shares man's smell: the soil
Is bare now, nor can foot feel, being shod.

And for all this, nature is never spent;
        There lives the dearest freshness deep down things;   10
And though the last lights off the black West went

Oh, morning, at the brown brink eastward, springs—
Because the Holy Ghost over the bent
World broods with warm breast and with ah! bright wings.

····▶ *Your* Turn

Talking and Writing about Lit

1. Notice the pattern of rhyme and the thematic grouping of lines in Hopkins's "God's Grandeur." Which of the fixed forms described above has Hopkins followed here?

2. **DIY** Hopkins refers to some aspects of the natural world that delight him. Hopkins was a deeply religious person ordained as a Jesuit priest, and his praise of nature is expressed in religious language. Write a brief poem (in fixed form or open) which names some of the things you enjoy in the natural world. Your poem may use religious language to do this or not—that's your call.

Christopher Marlowe (1564–1593)

The Passionate Shepherd to His Love (1600)

Come live with me and be my love,
And we will all the pleasures prove[1]
That valleys, groves, hills, and fields,
Woods, or steepy mountain yields.

And we will sit upon the rocks,   5
Seeing the shepherds feed their flocks,
By shallow rivers to whose falls
Melodious birds sing madrigals.

And I will make thee beds of roses
And a thousand fragrant posies,   10
A cap of flowers, and a kirtle[2]
Embroidered all with leaves of myrtle;

A gown made of the finest wool
Which from our pretty lambs we pull;
Fair lined slippers for the cold,   15
With buckles of the purest gold;

---

[1]**prove:** Try.
[2]**kirtle:** Gown.

A belt of straw and ivy buds,
With coral clasps and amber studs;
And if these pleasures may thee move,
Come live with me, and be my love.   20

The shepherd swains[3] shall dance and sing
For thy delight each May morning:
If these delights thy mind may move,
Then live with me and be my love.

----

[3]**swains:** Youths.

····•► *Your* **Turn**
Talking and Writing about Lit

1. "The Passionate Shepherd to His Love" is a lyric poem in which Marlowe
   did not use a traditional fixed pattern but instead established a pattern of his
   own. Describe Marlowe's use of form in the poem.

2. Compare imagery and themes in this poem and Richard Wilbur's "A Late
   Aubade" (Chapter 14).

Sir Walter Raleigh (1552–1618)
The Nymph's Reply to the Shepherd (1600)

If all the world and love were young,
And truth in every shepherd's tongue,
These pretty pleasures might me move
To live with thee and be thy love.

Time drives the flocks from field to fold,   5
When rivers rage, and rocks grow cold,
And Philomel becometh dumb;
The rest complain of cares to come.

The flowers do fade, and wanton fields
To wayward winter reckoning yields: 10
A honey tongue, a heart of gall,
Is fancy's spring, but sorrow's fall.

Thy gowns, thy shoes, thy beds of roses,
Thy cap, thy kirtle, and thy posies
Soon break, soon wither, soon forgotten;   15
In folly ripe, in reason rotten.

Thy belt of straw and ivy buds,
Thy coral clasps and amber studs,
All these in me no means can move
To come to thee and be thy love.   20

But could youth last, and love still breed,
Had joys no date, nor age no need,
Then these delights my mind might move
To live with thee and be thy love.

·····•▶ *Your* **Turn**
Talking and Writing about Lit

1. Analyze the themes of Raleigh's "The Nymph's Reply to the Shepherd," a playful parody of Marlowe's "The Passionate Shepherd to His Love."

2. **DIY** In Raleigh's parody, he imagines the voice of the nymph herself, replying to the shepherd. Using an up-to-date setting and in contemporary language, write a brief poem in which the speaker tries to woo a potential sweetheart. Then write a brief poem in reply from the point of view of the "sweetheart." Your poems do not need to be the same form or length as Marlowe's and Ralegh's. Also, yours may be serious or satirical.

William Shakespeare (1564–1616)
That time of year thou mayst in me behold (1609)

That time of year thou mayst in me behold
When yellow leaves, or none, or few, do hang
Upon those boughs which shake against the cold,
Bare ruined choirs where late the sweet birds sang.
In me thou see'st the twilight of such day   5
As after sunset fadeth in the west,
Which by and by black night doth take away,
Death's second self, that seals up all in rest.
In me thou see'st the glowing of such fire,
That on the ashes of his youth doth lie   10
As the deathbed whereon it must expire,
Consumed with that which it was nourished by.
This thou perceivest, which makes thy love more strong,
To love that well which thou must leave ere long.

·····▶ Your Turn
Talking and Writing about Lit

1. Explain the use of the extended metaphor (see Chapter 16) in this Shakespearean sonnet.
2. To whom does the speaker address the poem?

William Shakespeare (1564–1616)
Let me not to the marriage of true minds (1609)

Let me not to the marriage of true minds
Admit impediments. Love is not love
Which alters when it alteration finds,
Or bends with the remover to remove.
O no! it is an ever-fixèd mark   5
That looks on tempests and is never shaken;
It is the star to every wandering bark,
Whose worth's unknown, although his height be taken.
Love's not Time's fool, though rosy lips and cheeks
Within his bending sickle's compass come;   10
Love alters not with his brief hours and weeks,
But bears it out even to the edge of doom.
If this be error and upon me proved,
I never writ, nor no man ever loved.

·····▶ Your Turn
Talking and Writing about Lit

1. Paraphrase the definition of love offered by Shakespeare in "Let me not to the marriage of true minds." What are love's characteristics, according to the speaker?

2. **DIY** Can you recall any current song lyrics that offer a definition of love? Write a brief poem of your own, in any style or form, which tries to say what love is.

John Donne (1572–1631)
Death, be not proud (circa 1610)

Death, be not proud, though some have callèd thee
Mighty and dreadful, for thou art not so;

For those whom thou think'st thou dost overthrow
Die not, poor death, nor yet canst thou kill me.
From rest and sleep, which but thy pictures be,   5
Much pleasure—then, from thee much more must flow;
And soonest* our best men with thee do go,
Rest of their bones and soul's delivery.
Thou art slave to fate, chance, kings, and desperate men,
And dost with poison, war, and sickness dwell;   10
And poppy or charms can make us sleep as well,
And better than thy stroke. Why swell'st thou then?
One short sleep passed, we wake eternally,
And death shall be no more; death, thou shalt die.

---

*soonest: readiest

·····▶ *Your* Turn
Talking and Writing about Lit

1. Explain the speaker's main idea in John Donne's "Death, be not proud." Is the speaker a person who feels certain of his religious beliefs or a person who doubts them? Paraphrase the meaning of the last two lines of the poem in contemporary English.

2. Look at the rhyme scheme and form of this poem and identify the type of fixed form used by Donne.

Elizabeth Bishop (1911–1979)
Sestina (1965)

September rain falls on the house.
In the failing light, the old grandmother
sits in the kitchen with the child
beside the Little Marvel Stove,
reading the jokes from the almanac,   5
laughing and talking to hide her tears.

She thinks that her equinoctial tears
and the rain that beats on the roof of the house
were both foretold by the almanac,
but only known to a grandmother.   10
The iron kettle sings on the stove.
She cuts some bread and says to the child,

It's time for tea now; but the child
is watching the teakettle's small hard tears
dance like mad on the hot black stove,   15
the way the rain must dance on the house.
Tidying up, the old grandmother
hangs up the clever almanac

on its string. Birdlike, the almanac
hovers half open above the child,   20
hovers above the old grandmother
and her teacup full of dark brown tears.
She shivers and says she thinks the house
feels chilly, and puts more wood in the stove.

It was to be, says the Marvel Stove.   25
I know what I know, says the almanac.
With crayons the child draws a rigid house
and a winding pathway. Then the child
puts in a man with buttons like tears
and shows it proudly to the grandmother.   30

But secretly, while the grandmother
busies herself about the stove,
the little moons fall down like tears
from between the pages of the almanac
into the flower bed the child   35
has carefully placed in the front of the house.

Time to plant tears, says the almanac.
The grandmother sings to the marvellous stove
and the child draws another inscrutable house.

······▶**Your** Turn
Talking and Writing about Lit

1. The sestina is a fixed form that has been used since medieval times (the Middle Ages). Review the definition of a sestina. Has Elizabeth Bishop followed the form exactly, or has she made any variations in the traditional form?

2. Read the poem again. Could you identify differences between the child's perception of things and the grandmother's perception? Do you think the images of tears have any special significance to the meaning of the poem?

Talking Lit

In "To Define," Robert Creeley is still pushing the boundaries of poetry. In his "The Problem of Form," J. V. Cunningham asks whether the next step forward should be a step back to traditional forms.

Robert Creeley, "To Define" (1953)

The process of definition is the intent of the poem, or is to that sense—"Peace comes of communication." Poetry stands in no need of any sympathy, or even goodwill. One acts from bottom, the root is the purpose quite beyond any kindness.

A poetry can act on this: "A poem is energy transferred from where the poet got it (he will have some several causations), by way of the poem itself to, all the way over to, the reader." One breaks the line of aesthetics, or that outcrop of a general division of knowledge. A sense of the KINETIC impels recognition of force. Force is, and therefore stays.

The means of a poetry are, perhaps, related to Pound's sense of the *increment of association;* usage coheres value. Tradition is an aspect of what anyone is now thinking—not what someone once thought. We make with what we have, and in this way anything is worth looking at. A tradition becomes inept when it blocks the necessary conclusion; it says we have felt nothing, it implies others have felt more.

A poetry denies its end in any *descriptive* act, I mean any act which leaves the attention outside the poem. Our anger cannot exist usefully without its objects, but a description of them is also a perpetuation. There is that confusion—one wants the thing to act on, and yet hates it. *Description* does nothing, it includes the object—it neither hates nor loves.

If one can junk these things, of the content which relates only to denial, the negative, the impact of dissolution—act otherwise, on other things. There is no country. Speech is an assertion of one man, by one man. "Therefore each speech having its own character the poetry it engenders will be peculiar to that speech also in its own intrinsic form."

Form

The Whip
I spent a night turning in bed,
my love was a feather, a flat

sleeping thing. She was
very white

and quiet, and above us on
the roof, there was another woman I

also loved, had
addressed myself to in

a fit she
returned. That

encompasses it. But now I was
lonely, I yelled,

but what is that? Ugh,
she said, beside me, she put

her hand on
my back, for which act

I think to say this
wrongly.

Form has such a diversity of associations and it seems obvious enough that it
would have—like *like*. Like a girl of my generation used to get a formal for the big
dance, or else it could be someone's formalizing the situation, which was a little
more serious. Form a circle, etc.

It was something one intended, clearly, that came of defined terms. But in what
respect, of course, made a great difference. As advice for editing a magazine,
Pound wrote, "Verse consists of a constant and a variant . . . " His point was that
any element might be made the stable, recurrent event, and that any other might
be let to go "hog wild," as he put it, and such a form could prove "a center around
which, not a box within which, every item . . . "

Pound was of great use to me as a young writer, as were also Williams and
Stevens. I recall the latter's saying there were those who thought of form as a variant of plastic shape. Pound's point was that poetry is a form cut in time as sculpture is a form cut in space. Williams' introduction to *The Wedge* (1944) I took as
absolute credo.

"The Whip" was written in the middle fifties, and now reading it I can vividly
remember the bleak confusion from which it moves emotionally. There is a parallel, a story called "The Musicians," and if one wants to know more of the implied
narrative of the poem, it's in this sad story. The title is to the point, because it is
music, specifically jazz, that informs the poem's manner in large part. Not that it's
jazzy, or about jazz—rather, it's trying to use a rhythmic base much as jazz of this
time would—or what was especially characteristic of Charlie Parker's playing, or
Miles Davis', Thelonious Monk's, or Milt Jackson's. That is, the beat is used to

delay, detail, prompt, define the content of the statement or, more aptly, the emotional field of the statement. It's trying to do this while moving in time to a set periodicity—durational units, call them. It will say as much as it can, or as little, in the "time" given. So each line is figured as taking the same time, like they say, and each line ending works as a distinct pause. I used to listen to Parker's endless variations on "I Got Rhythm" and all the various times in which he'd play it, all the tempi, up, down, you name it. What fascinated me was that he'd write silences as actively as sounds, which of course they were. Just so in poetry.

So it isn't writing like jazz, trying to be some curious social edge of that imagined permission. It's a time one's keeping, which could be the variations of hopscotch, or clapping, or just traffic's blurred racket. It was what you could do with what you got, or words to that effect.

Being shy as a young man, I was very formal, and still am. I make my moves fast but very self-consciously. I would say that from "Ugh . . . " on the poem moves as cannily and as solidly as whatever. "Listen to the sound that it makes," said Pound. Fair enough.

J. V. Cunningham, "The Problem of Form" (1963)

I shall stipulate that there is a problem of form in the poetry of our day, but I shall treat *form*, for the moment, as an undefined term, and I shall not until later specify the nature of some of the problems. I am, at the outset, interested in pointing to certain generalities, and to certain broad, simpleminded, pervasive attitudes and dualisms, of which the problem in poetry is to a large extent only a localization. These will give in outline the larger context of the problem.

To begin with, it is apparent that in our society we have too many choices. When we ask the young what they are going to do when they grow up, we should not be surprised or amused that the answers are whimsical and bewildered. The young poet today has a large and not too discriminated anthology of forms to realize; only illiterate ignorance or having made the pilgrimage to Gambier or to Los Altos will reduce the scope of options to manageable size—and even then there will be a hankering for further options. On the other hand, the young poet 250 years ago had it easy in this respect. He wrote octosyllabic or decasyllabic couplets, and the rhetoric and areas of experience of each were fairly delimited. For recreation he wrote a song in quatrains, and once or twice in a lifetime a Pindaric ode.

We come now to those attitudes and dualisms that make the problem of particular forms peculiarly our problem. We are a democratic society and give a positive value to informality, though some of the ladies still like to dress up. We will have nothing to do with the formal language and figured rhetoric of the *Arcadia*, for that is the language and rhetoric of a hierarchical and authoritarian society in which ceremony and formality were demanded by and accorded to the governing class. Instead, we praise, especially in poetry, what we call the accents of real speech—that is, of uncalculated and casual utterance, and sometimes even of vulgar impropriety. Now, if this attitude is a concomitant of the Democratic Revolution, the value we give to antiformality, to the deliberate violation of form and decorum, is a concomitant of its sibling, the Romantic Revolution. The measured, or formal, the contrived, the artificial are, we feel, insincere; they are perversions of the central value of our life, genuineness of feeling. "At least I was honest," we say with moral benediction as we leave wife and child for the sentimental empyrean.

If informality and antiformality are positive values, then the problem of form is how to get rid of it. But to get rid of it we must keep it; we must have something to get rid of. To do this we need a method, and we have found it in our dualisms of science and art, of intellectual and emotional, of regularity and irregularity, of norm and variation. We have been convinced, without inquiry or indeed adequate knowledge, that the regularities of ancient scientific law, of Newton's law of motion, are regularities of matter, not of spirit, and hence are inimical to human significance. And so we embrace the broad, pervasive, simpleminded, and scarcely scrutinized proposition that regularity is meaningless and irregularity is meaningful—to the subversion of Form. For one needs only so much regularity as will validate irregularity. But Form is regularity.

So we come to definition. The customary distinctions of form and matter, or form and content, are in the discussion of writing at least only usable on the most rudimentary level. For it is apparent to any poet who sets out to write a sonnet that the form of the sonnet is the content, and its content the form. This is not a profundity, but the end of the discussion. I shall define form, then, without a contrasting term. It is that which remains the same when everything else is changed. This is not at all, I may say, a Platonic position. It is rather a mathematical and, as it should be, linguistic notion: $a^2 - b^2 = (a + b)(a - b)$ through all the potentialities of a and b. The form of the simple declarative sentence in English is in each of its realizations.

It follows, then, that form is discoverable by the act of substitution. It is what has alternative realizations. And the generality or particularity of a form lies in the range or restriction of alternatives. It follows, also, that the form precedes its realization, even in the first instance, and that unique form, or organic form in the sense of unique form, is a contradiction in terms. For it is the essence of form to be repetitive, and the repetitive is form. It follows, further, that there may be in a given utterance simultaneously a number of forms, so that the common literary question, What is the form of this work? can only be answered by a tacit disregard of all the forms other than the one we are momently concerned with.

It is time for illustration. Donne has a little epigram on Hero and Leander:

> Both robbed of air, we both lie in one ground,
> Both whom one fire had burnt, one water drowned.

What are the forms of this poem? First, both lines are decasyllabic in normal iambic pattern. Second, they rhyme. Third, it is phrased in units of four and six syllables in chiasmic order. Fourth, there are three "both's" and three "one's" in overlapping order. Fifth, the whole story of the lovers is apprehended, summarized, and enclosed in the simple scheme or form of the four elements. Finally, it is recognizably an epigram. Now Sir Philip Sidney, a few years earlier, in one of the *Arcadia* poems has the following lines:

> Man oft is plagued with air, is burnt with fire,
> In water drowned, in earth his burial is.

POP CULTURE

Dee Dee and the Slam Dance Sonnet

The cover image for the Ramones debut album

Sometimes, with the evolution of poetry, it's hard to conceive of wanting to write a poem in fixed form. It seems as though all the poetic rules have been broken since these traditional forms were devised. We know that we don't need a rhyme scheme; we don't have to meter; we can put our line breaks anywhere it suits us. After e.e. cummings, it seems like writing in a fixed form would restrict us more than help us.

Consider this equation: verse, chorus, verse, chorus, verse. Feel

The lines are decasyllabic in normal iambic pattern. The adjacent lines do not rhyme, for the form of the poem is terza rima, an alternative form. It is phrased in units of six and four in chiasmic order. The first line repeats "with," the second "in." Man, not Hero and Leander, is apprehended in the scheme of the four elements, and in both cases the order of the elements is not formally predetermined. Finally, it is not an epigram, but part of an eclogue.

I have illustrated in these examples and in this analysis something of the variety of what may be distinguished as form: literary kind, conceptual distinctions, and all the rhetorical figures of like ending, equal members, chiasmus, and the various modes of verbal repetition. That some of the forms of Sidney's lines are repeated in Donne's, with the substitution of Hero and Leander for man, shows they have alternate realizations, and that so many operate simultaneously shows, not that a literary work has form, but that it is a convergence of forms, and forms of disparate orders. It is the coincidence of forms that locks in the poem.

Indeed, it is the inherent coincidence of forms in poetry, in metrical writing, that gives it its place and its power—a claim for poetry perhaps more accurate and

free to throw a musical variation in between a chorus and a verse, maybe a guitar solo or a breakdown, and you have the basic fixed form for nearly a century of popular music. Of course, many songs have been written way outside this structure, but this is a structure we can understand and one that is still used today. Any person who enjoys music from the blues to nü metal and everything in between can probably think of a favorite song that fits this pattern. But does the fixed form make a song better or worse?

It depends on what you're conveying. On the one hand, fixed forms are more restrictive to the author, but they may be more accessible to readers, in comparison to trying to wrap their heads around eccentric line breaks and creative free forms. The masters of using the simplicity of pop music's fixed form are the Ramones. Nearly every Ramones song follows a strict fixed form of verse/chorus three times, uses only three chords, and follows a simple rhyme scheme (usually *aabb* or *abab*). With this simple stripped-down form, the Ramones invented an entirely new and successful genre of music called punk which has been expanded upon to a wide variety of different creative methods. All the same, any Ramones fan will tell you that it's hard to beat the straight-to-the-point methods of the pop forms embraced by the Ramones.

certainly more modest than is customary. For this is the poet's *Poetics:* prose is written in sentences; poetry in sentences and lines. It is encoded not only in grammar, but also simultaneously in meter, for meter is the principle or set of principles, whatever they may be, that determines the line. And as we perceive of each sentence that it is grammatical or not, so the repetitive perception that this line is metrical or that it is not, that it exemplifies the rules or that it does not, is the metrical experience. It is the ground base of all poetry.

And here in naked reduction is the problem of form in the poetry of our day. It is before all a problem of meter. We have lost the repetitive harmony of the old tradition, and we have not established a new. We have written to vary or violate the old line, for regularity we feel is meaningless and irregularity meaningful. But a generation of poets, acting on the principles and practice of significant variation, have at last nothing to vary from. The last variation is regularity.

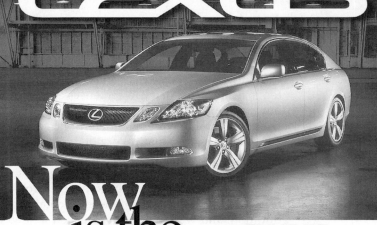

OPEN FORM

Even car ads use line breaks.

A poet carefully considers each line break because the line break can affect the poem's rhythm by either establishing or disrupting it in ways that engage the reader's attention. The Mercedes ad shown here uses enjambment, which are lines that break without a full stop, and which fall grammatically in the middle of a complete thought rather than at the end. The ad consists of two lines only, the first of which teases the reader into thinking that the second line provides the answer to a question shared by most people: Where can I find my soul mate? The second line finishes the thought, and while it's important to the car company that the reader see images of the Mercedes, the images are not required for the reader to understand the message.

The Audi ad, on the other hand, uses images to complete the thought. The line breaks are end-stopped lines, but while each line is a complete thought in itself, the two lines together present a clearer sense of the whole ad, and the full meaning can only be gleaned by moving from the second line to the images.

The Lexus ad uses enjambment, and the main message straddles many lines. The ad also uses other aspects of open-form poetry: it stacks lines and varies font size and color to set rhythm and pace and to emphasize the words and symbols that are most important to the ad. It even sets the word "new" on its side, which is particularly memorable.

What Is Open Form?

Just as ad writers think consciously about how line breaks, careful word choice, rhyme, rhythm, and sound appeal to the reader, so do poets think consciously about these matters of form. Poets who compose poems in **open form**, or **free verse**, do not usually think of their poems as being without form; instead, they think of an open-form poem as assuming a natural shape—some would say an organic form.

> The rhyme and uniformity of perfect poems show the free growth of metrical laws and bud from them as unerringly and loosely as lilacs or roses on a bush, and take shapes as compact as the shapes of chestnuts and oranges and melons and pears, and shed the perfume impalpable to form.—Walt Whitman (from the 1855 Preface to *Leaves of Grass*)

Whitman's passage above uses the natural growth of flowers and fruits as an analogy to explain the way he conceives of a poem's being created by the poet. The poem assumes (or grows into) that form which most naturally fits the material the poet wishes to embody in language. Or, we might say, the poet decides to dress the poem in a certain suit of clothes because that style of dressing fits that particular poem best. Remember also Pablo Neruda's poetic manifesto in "Sweetness, Always" (Chapter 16):

> Why such harsh machinery?
> Why, to write down the stuff
> And people of every day,
> Must poems be dressed up in gold,
> In old and fearful stone?   5
>
> I want verses of felt or feather
> Which scarcely weigh, mild verses
> With the intimacy of beds
> Where people have loved and dreamed.
> I want poems stained   10
> By hands and everydayness.

The poems "dressed up in gold" would be those heavy with ornamentation, those weighed down by a rigid and unnatural form. Many poets, however, have written both fixed-form and open-form poems and see no need to choose between the two on a permanent basis. Instead, these versatile poets decide the form of each poem, as Whitman advises that they do, based on the natural shape the material of the poem seeks to assume—choosing the suit of clothes that best fits that body, so to speak.

One such versatile poet is Dudley Randall. We read his fixed-form ballad stanza poem "Ballad of Birmingham" in the previous chapter. Here is another poem by Dudley Randall, written in open form.

Dudley Randall (1914–2000)
A Poet Is Not a Jukebox (1981)

A poet is not a jukebox, so don't tell me what to write.
I read a dear friend a poem about love, and she said,
"You're in to that bag now, for whatever it's worth,
But why don't you write about the riot in Miami?"[1]

I didn't write about Miami because I didn't know about Miami.   5
I've been so busy working for the Census, and listening to music all night,
    and making new poems
That I've broken my habit of watching TV and reading newspapers.
So it wasn't absence of Black Pride that caused me not to write about Miami,
But simple ignorance.

Telling a Black poet what he ought to write   10
Is like some Commissar of Culture in Russia telling a poet
He'd better write about the new steel furnaces in the Novobigorsk region,
Or the heroic feats of Soviet labor in digging the trans-Caucausus Canal,
Or the unprecedented achievement of workers in the sugar beet industry
    who exceeded their quota by 400 per cent (it was later discovered to
    be a typist's error).

Maybe the Russian poet is watching his mother die of cancer,   15
Or is bleeding from an unhappy love affair,
Or is bursting with happiness and wants to sing of wine, roses, and
    nightingales.

I'll bet that in a hundred years the poems the Russian people will read,
    sing, and love
Will be the poems about his mother's death, his unfaithful mistress, or his
    wine, roses, and nightingales,
Not the poems about steel furnaces, the trans-Caucausus Canal, or the   20
    sugar beet industry.
A poet writes about what he feels, what agitates his heart and sets his pen
    in motion.

---

[1]**the riot in Miami:** In 1980, perhaps one of the severest race riots of the century, in which Blacks took revenge for the killing of a Black man by four white policemen.

Not what some apparatchnik[2] dictates, to promote his own career of theories.

Yeah, maybe I'll write about Miami, as I wrote about Birmingham,[3]
But it'll be because I want to write about Miami, not because somebody
  says I ought to.

Yeah, I write about love. What's wrong with love?   25
If we had more loving, we'd have more Black babies to become Black
  brothers and sisters and build the Black family.

When people love, they bathe with sweet-smelling soap, splash their
  bodies with perfume or cologne,
Shave, and comb their hair, and put on gleaming silken garments,
Speak softly and kindly and study their beloved to anticipate and satisfy
  her every desire.
After loving they're relaxed and happy and friends with all the world.   30
What's wrong with love, beauty, joy, or peace?

If Josephine had given Napoleon more loving, he wouldn't have sown the
  meadows of Europe with skulls.
If Hitler had been happy in love, he wouldn't have baked people in ovens.[4]
So don't tell me it's trivial and a cop-out to write about love and not about
  Miami.

A poet is not a jukebox.   35
A poet is not a jukebox.
I repeat, A poet is not a jukebox for someone to shove a quarter in his ear
  and get the tune they want to hear.
Or to pat on the head and call "a good little Revolutionary,"
Or to give a Kuumba Liberation Award.[5]

A poet is not a *jukebox*.   40
A poet is *not* a jukebox.
A *poet* is not a jukebox.

So don't tell *me* what to write.

---

[2]**apparatchnik:** Flunky, minor civil servant.
[3]**Birmingham:** See note 1, above.
[4]**Lines 32–33:** Napoleon, French conqueror of Europe, married Josephine in 1796 and divorced her in 1809; gas ovens were only one feature of Adolf Hitler's extermination camps.
[5]**Kuumba Liberation Award:** Randall received a Kuumba Award in 1973.

Clearly, the use of open form here suits the defiant, playful, and self-assertive intentions of this particular poem. The poet declares that he is both formally and politically free to write what he likes (and how he likes). Just as certainly, though, the fixed form of the ballad stanza served Randall well for embodying the material of "Ballad of Birmingham," given that poem's narrative needs and the poet's desire to memorialize the tragic deaths of the young children. The ballad form has traditionally been used for remembering important stories and events, and Randall shows that the ballad stanza is still an excellent vehicle for collective memory. "Ballad of Birmingham" is Randall's most widely anthologized poem.

Using Conventional Techniques in the Open-Form Poem

Despite the fact that we characterize it as an open-form poem, "A Poet Is Not a Jukebox" does employ formal devices in achieving its effects. In fact, poets who write in open form typically insist, with Whitman, that these poems are not without form, but are simply written in the form that most naturally and effectively embodies that particular material. One device Randall uses, of course, is the phrasing accomplished by use of line breaks, spacing, and enjambment (run-on lines). For instance, in the movement from line 8 to line 9, the use of enjambment to draw us down to line 9 helps create a humorous emphasis on "But simple ignorance," which is in a sense the punch line. In addition, Randall effectively establishes and then changes pace in the poem by using long Whitmanesque lines throughout most of the piece and then shifting (in lines 35–43) to the short, insistent lines that predominate in the final stanzas.

Randall also effectively establishes rhythm in the poem, not through the use of a fixed metrical pattern such as we would find in the ballad stanza, but instead through the repetition of words and phrases ("A poet is not a jukebox" being the most prevalent of these, of course) and through repetition of grammatical constructions. For example, in lines 13–17, several lines begin with a similar construction: "Or the heroic feats," "Or the unprecedented achievement," "Or is bleeding," "Or is bursting."

Walt Whitman's Long-Lasting Influence

These devices for establishing rhythm in open-form poetry are not new, and in fact we need to go back again to the grandfather of open-form poetry, Walt Whitman, to see how he sowed the seeds of open form. Read the following excerpt from Whitman's poem "Song of Myself," keeping in mind how the rhythm might be created. The excerpt below is the twenty-first section of "Song of Myself," which is a long poem with fifty-two sections.

Walt Whitman (1819–1892)
From "Song of Myself" (1855)

21

I am the poet of the Body and I am the poet of the Soul,
The pleasures of heaven are with me and the pains of hell are with me,
The first I graft and increase upon myself, the latter I translate into a new
    tongue.

I am the poet of the woman the same as the man,
And I say it is as great to be a woman as to be a man,   5
And I say there is nothing greater than the mother of men.

I chant the chant of dilation or pride,
We have had ducking and deprecating about enough,
I show that size is only development.

Have you outstript the rest? are you the President?   10
It is a trifle, they will more than arrive there every one, and still pass on.

I am he that walks with the tender and growing night,
I call to the earth and sea half-held by the night.

Press close bare-bosom'd night—press close magnetic nourishing night!
Night of south winds—night of the large few stars!   15
Still nodding night—mad naked summer night.

Smile O voluptuous cool-breath'd earth!
Earth of the slumbering and liquid trees!
Earth of departed sunset—earth of the mountains misty-topt!
Earth of the vitreous pour of the full moon just tinged with blue!   20
Earth of shine and dark mottling the tide of the river!
Earth of the limpid gray of clouds brighter and clearer for my sake!
Far-swooping elbow'd earth—rich apple-blossom'd earth!
Smile, for your lover comes.

Prodigal, you have given me love—therefore I to you give love!   25
O unspeakable passionate love.

    The sensuous language here is typical of Whitman's work, and the devices for establishing rhythm are also characteristic of his poems, particularly of the longer works such as "Song of Myself." Rhythm results from the repetition of single words and of phrases and grammatical constructions: "I am," "I am," "I chant," "I show," "I call," and "Earth of the slumbering," "Earth of departed," "Earth of the vitreous." Additionally, there is sometimes an effect of listing things, which in itself contributes to the rhythm (for example, in lines 18–23). There is occasionally a repeated metrical scheme, although it is not part of any overall metrical pattern. An example is line 23: "Far-swooping elbow'd earth—rich apple-blossom'd earth!" Here a pattern of iambic trimeter is repeated within the line, accomplishing a pleasingly musical effect, though it is a pattern repeated only once within the poem. So, we might say that while metrical patterns are sometimes used to good effect, they are flexible, not fixed, in Whitman's work.

Many modern and contemporary poets have been influenced by the work of Walt Whitman. Analyze the following two contemporary works in light of what you know about Whitman's techniques.

Nazik al-Mălă'ika (b. 1923)
I Am (1949)

Translated by Kamal Boullata

The night asks me who I am
    Its impenetrable black, its unquiet secret
                               I am
    Its lull rebellious.
    I veil myself with silence   5
    Wrapping my heart with doubt
    Solemnly, I gaze
    While ages ask me
       who I am.

The wind asks me who I am   10
    Its bedevilled spirit I am
    Denied by Time, going nowhere
    I journey on and on
    Passing without a pause
    And when reaching an edge   15
    I think it may be the end
    Of suffering, but then:
       the void.

Time asks me who I am
    A giant enfolding centuries I am   20
    Later to give new births.
    I have created the dim past
    From the bliss of unbound hope
    I push it back into its grave
    To make a new yesterday, its tomorrow   25
       is ice.

The self asks me who I am
    Baffled, I stare into the dark
    Nothing brings me peace
    I ask, but the answer   30
    Remains hooded in mirage
    I keep thinking it is near
    Upon reaching it, it dissolves.

Tato LaViera (b. 1951)

AmeRícan (1985)

we gave birth to a new generation,
AmeRícan, broader than lost gold
never touched, hidden inside the
puerto rican mountains.

we gave birth to a new generation,   5
AmeRícan, it includes everything
imaginable you-name-it-we-got-it
society.

we gave birth to a new generation,
AmeRícan salutes all folklores,   10
european, indian, black, spanish,
and anything else compatible:

AmeRícan, singing to composer pedro flores' palm
    trees high up in the universal sky!

AmeRícan, sweet soft spanish danzas gypsies   15
    moving lyrics la espanola cascabelling
    presence always singing at our side!

AmeRícan, beating jibaro modern troubadours[1]
    crying guitars romantic continental
    bolero[2] love songs!   20

AmeRícan, across forth and across back
    back across and forth back
    forth across and back and forth
    our trips are walking bridges!

---

[1]**troubadours:** Puerto Rican mountain folk.
[2]**bolero:** Slow tropical dance.

it all dissolved into itself, the attempt   25
was truly made, the attempt was truly
absorbed, digested, we spit out
the poison, we spit out the malice,
we stand, affirmative in action,
to reproduce a broader answer to the   30
marginality that gobbled us up abruptly!

AmeRícan, walking plena[3]-rhythms in new york,
    strutting beautifully alert, alive,
    many turning eyes wondering,
    admiring!   35

AmeRícan, defining myself my own way any way many
    ways Am e Rícan, with the big R and the
    accent on the i!

AmeRícan, like the soul gliding talk of gospel
    boogie music!   40

AmeRícan, speaking new words in spanglish tenements.
    fast tongue moving street corner "que
    corta"[4] talk being invented at the insistence
    of a smile!

AmeRícan, abounding inside so many ethnic english   45
    people, and out of humanity, we blend
    and mix all that is good!

AmeRícan, integrating in new york and defining our
    own destino,[5] our own way of life,

AmeRícan, defining the new america, humane america,   50
    admired america, loved america, harmonious
    america, the world in peace, our energies
    collectively invested to find other civili-
    zations, to touch God, further and further,
    to dwell in the spirit of divinity!   55

AmeRícan, yes, for now, for i love this, my second
    land, and i dream to take the accent from

---

[3]**plena:** An Afro–Puerto Rican dance.
[4]**que corta:** That cuts.
[5]**destino:** Destiny.

the altercation, and be proud to call
myself AmeRícan, in the U.S. sense of the
word, AmeRícan, America!   60

As you can see, al-Mălă'ika's poem contains many repeated words and phrases that help create the haunting rhythm of the poem. LaViera's long lines, repetitions, and enumerations, as well as his gathering momentum as we move through the poem, are all reminiscent of Whitman's use of open form. At the same time, LaViera has made his own innovations here which uniquely fit this particular poem. The poem employs two strings of stanzas with two different patterns. The three quatrains at the outset are followed by a string of variable stanzas with the word "AmeRícan" standing alone at the beginning of each first line. That is, all stanzas in that string are introduced this way except one. Did LaViera have a thematic purpose for leaving the word "AmeRícan" off the stanza which begins on line 25? It is useful here to remember the discussion of Emily Dickinson's "Because I could not stop for Death" (Chapter 17). There it was noted that a poet often has thematic reasons for disrupting a poem's pattern. In Dickinson's poem, the stanza in which the speaker dies is the only stanza that breaks from the established metrical scheme. In LaViera's poem, as well as in Dickinson's, a shift in form is used to suggest a thematic shift. This is one of many ways in which the poet uses form to reflect meaning.

Open Form Can be Compact or Diffuse

The poem below, Carolyn Forché's "The Colonel," is called a prose poem because it does not use poetic line breaks and thus looks much like prose on the page. It is as if the influence of Whitman's long lines was taken to its greatest extreme, resulting in lines that fill the page like prose. What makes the following poem different from a regular passage of prose? What aspects of the piece would lead us to think of it as a poem?

Carolyn Forché (b. 1950)
The Colonel (1978)

What you have heard is true. I was in his house. His wife carried
a tray of coffee and sugar. His daughter filed her nails, his son went
out for the night. There were daily papers, pet dogs, a pistol on the
cushion beside him. The moon swung bare on its black cord over
the house. On the television was a cop show. It was in English.   5
Broken bottles were embedded in the walls around the house to
scoop the kneecaps from a man's legs or cut his hands to lace. On
the windows there were gratings like those in liquor stores. We had

dinner, rack of lamb, good wine, a gold bell was on the table for
calling the maid. The maid brought green mangoes, salt, a type of   10
bread. I was asked how I enjoyed the country. There was a brief
commercial in Spanish. His wife took everything away. There was
some talk then of how difficult it had become to govern. The parrot
said hello on the terrace. The colonel told it to shut up, and pushed
himself from the table. My friend said to me with his eyes: say   15
nothing. The colonel returned with a sack used to bring groceries
home. He spilled many human ears on the table. They were like
dried peach halves. There is no other way to say this. He took one
of them in his hands, shook it in our faces, dropped it into a water
glass. It came alive there. I am tired of fooling around he said. As   20
for the rights of anyone, tell your people they can go fuck themselves. He swept the ears to the floor with his arm and held the last
of his wine in the air. Something for your poetry, no? he said. Some
of the ears on the floor caught this scrap of his voice. Some of the
ears on the floor were pressed to the ground.   25

    The absence of line breaks in "The Colonel" enhances the poet's dramatic use of juxtaposition (using contrasting images side by side), as we move from the ordinary and mundane ("daily papers, pet dogs") to the violent and startling ("a pistol on the cushion beside him") without any breaks or transitions. In addition, the use of figurative, allusive, and symbolic language in the piece (discussed in Chapters 15 and 16), as well as its compactness, all cause us to think of this as a poetic use of language.

    At the opposite extreme from the relative density of the prose poem form is the scattering of words on the page, practiced most strikingly by e.e. cummings. For instance, in his poem "in Just-" (in Chapter 14), words are playfully strewn down the page to illustrate the joyfulness of spring and of children running onto the playground after a winter's confinement. Here is another poem that employs similar open-form techniques to achieve its effects, both musically and thematically.

Leslie Marmon Silko (b. 1948)
Where Mountain Lion Lay Down with Deer (1973)

I climb the black rock mountain
    stepping from day to day
            silently.
I smell the wind for my ancestors
    pale blue leaves   5
    crushed wild mountain smell.
Returning
    up the gray stone cliff
    where I descended
        a thousand years ago.   10

Returning to faded black stone.
    where mountain lion lay down with deer.
It is better to stay up here
    watching wind's reflection
    in tall yellow flowers.   15
The old ones who remember me are gone
    the old songs are all forgotten
And the story of my birth.
How I danced in snow-frost moonlight
    distant stars to the end of the Earth,   20
How I swam away
    in freezing mountain water
    narrow mossy canyon tumbling down
        out of the mountain
        out of the deep canyon stone   25
    down
      the memory
       spilling out
       into the world.

Silko's arrangement of lines on the page reflects theme, but it serves a different thematic purpose (or, rather, purposes). In the first thirteen lines, the speaker is "stepping from day to day," climbing both literally and metaphorically, climbing the "black rock mountain" and also climbing through time, to the time of the ancestors. The arrangement of lines like steps reflects the theme here. Also, when the speaker says "Returning" and again "Returning," a new line is begun, returning to the margin as the speaker speaks of returning to the ancestors—to the place of the ancestors—but also to the lore and legends and cultural legacy of those who went before on the land.

Line breaks go hand in hand with theme in the closing lines (19–29) in a different way, as they mirror the gathering momentum of the speaker's journey and as they also reflect the tumbling of the "freezing mountain water" and the "canyon tumbling down" and "down," "the memory/spilling out/into the world." In the final lines, the speaker may be referring to the lost traditions lamented earlier and perhaps, in a sense, the diaspora of the scattered people as well as the scattered memories.

The Potential for Playfulness in Poetic Form

"O sweet spontaneous" by e.e. cummings is another poem celebrating nature, but in it the human participants behave less kindly toward the earth than does Silko's speaker. However—cummings's poem suggests—the earth knows how to answer back cheerfully with, once again, spring!

e.e. cummings (1894–1962)

O sweet spontaneous (1923)

O sweet spontaneous
earth how often have
the
doting

        fingers of   5
prurient philosophers pinched
and
poked

thee
, has the naughty thumb   10
of science prodded
thy

    beauty   . how
often have religions taken
thee upon their scraggy knees   15
squeezing and

buffeting thee that thou mightest conceive
gods
    (but
true   20

to the incomparable
couch of death thy
rhythmic
lover

      thou answerest   25

them only with

      spring)

As we've noticed in looking at e.e. cummings's work before—in our discussion of "l(a" and "in Just-" (in Chapter 14)—his playful use of punctuation as well as line breaks is fun, but it's also another case of the poet choosing a form to reflect the meaning. The final lines of "O sweet spontaneous" (19–27) are both parenthetical and playful, teasing the reader (and the irreverent humans of lines 1–18) with the whispered reversal of the last three lines.

Discover and discuss the kinds of techniques used by writers of the following open-form poems in achieving their effects. In what way does the theme of William Stafford's poem below resemble that of cummings's "O sweet spontaneous?" Are any similar techniques or themes present in Pablo Neruda's "The United Fruit Co." or Howard Nemerov's "Life Cycle of Common Man?" How do the poems by Knight, Rutsala, Williams, and Olds use techniques of open-form poetry to illustrate their various themes regarding ancestry, family, and personal identity?

William Stafford (b. 1914)
Traveling through the Dark (1960)

Traveling through the dark I found a deer
dead on the edge of the Wilson River road.
It is usually best to roll them into the canyon:
that road is narrow; to swerve might make more dead.

By glow of the tail-light I stumbled back of the car   5
and stood by the heap, a doe, a recent killing;
she had stiffened already, almost cold.
I dragged her off; she was large in the belly.

My fingers touching her side brought me the reason—
her side was warm; her fawn lay there waiting,   10
alive, still, never to be born.
Beside that mountain road I hesitated.

The car aimed ahead its lowered parking lights;
under the hood purred the steady engine.
I stood in the glare of the warm exhaust turning red;   15
around our group I could hear the wilderness listen.

I thought hard for us all—my only swerving—,
then pushed her over the edge into the river.

Pablo Neruda (1904–1973)
The United Fruit Co. (1950)

Translated by Robert Bly

When the trumpet sounded, it was
all prepared on the earth,

and Jehovah parceled out the earth
to Coca-Cola, Inc., Anaconda,
Ford Motors, and other entities: 5
The Fruit Company, Inc.
reserved for itself the most succulent,
the central coast of my own land,
the delicate waist of America.
It rechristened its territories   10
as the "Banana Republics"
and over the sleeping dead,
over the restless heroes
who brought about the greatness,
the liberty and the flags,   15
it established the comic opera:
abolished the independencies,
presented crowns of Caesar,
unsheathed envy, attracted
the dictatorship of the flies,   20
Trujillo flies, Tacho flies,
Carias flies, Martinez flies,
Ubico flies, damp flies
of modest blood and marmalade,
drunken flies who zoom   25
over the ordinary graves,
circus flies, wise flies
well trained in tyranny.

Among the bloodthirsty flies
the Fruit Company lands its ships,   30
taking off the coffee and the fruit;
the treasure of our submerged
territories flows as though
on plates into the ships.

Meanwhile Indians are falling   35
into the sugared chasms
of the harbors, wrapped
for burial in the mist of the dawn:
a body rolls, a thing
that has no name, a fallen cipher,   40
a cluster of dead fruit
thrown down on the dump.

<u>**Howard Nemerov (b. 1920)**</u>
Life Cycle of Common Man (1960)

Roughly figured, this man of moderate habits,
This average consumer of the middle class,
Consumed in the course of his average life span
Just under half a million cigarettes,
Four thousand fifths of gin and about   5
A quarter as much vermouth; he drank
Maybe a hundred thousand cups of coffee,
And counting his parents' share it cost
Something like half a million dollars
To put him through life. How many beasts   10
Died to provide him with meat, belt and shoes
Cannot be certainly said.
                              But anyhow,
It is in this way that a man travels through time,
Leaving behind him a lengthening trail   15
Of empty bottles and bones, of broken shoes,
Frayed collars and worn out or outgrown
Diapers and dinnerjackets, silk ties and slickers.

Given the energy and security thus achieved,
He did . . . ? What? The usual things, of course,   20
The eating, dreaming, drinking and begetting,
And he worked for the money which was to pay
For the eating, et cetera, which were necessary
If he were to go on working for the money, et cetera,
But chiefly he talked. As the bottles and bones   25
Accumulated behind him, the words proceeded
Steadily from the front of his face as he
Advanced into the silence and made it verbal.
Who can tally the tale of his words? A lifetime
Would barely suffice for their repetition;   30
If you merely printed all his commas the result
Would be a very large volume, and the number of times
He said "thank you" or "very little sugar, please,"
Would stagger the imagination. There were also
Witticisms, platitudes, and statements beginning   35
"It seems to me" or "As I always say."

Consider the courage in all that, and behold the man
Walking into deep silence, with the ectoplastic
Cartoon's balloon of speech proceeding
Steadily out of the front of his face, the words   40

Borne along on the breath which is his spirit
Telling the numberless tale of his untold Word
Which makes the world his apple, and forces him to eat.

Etheridge Knight (1931–1991)
The Idea of Ancestry (1968)

1

Taped to the wall of my cell are 47 pictures: 47 black
faces: my father, mother, grandmothers (1 dead), grandfathers (both dead), brothers, sisters, uncles, aunts,
cousins (1st and 2nd), nieces, and nephews. They stare
across the space at me sprawling on my bunk. I know   5
their dark eyes, they know mine. I know their style,
they know mine. I am all of them, they are all of me;
they are farmers, I am a thief, I am me, they are thee.

I have at one time or another been in love with my mother,
1 grandmother, 2 sisters, 2 aunts (1 went to the asylum),   10
and 5 cousins. I am now in love with a 7-yr-old niece
(she sends me letters in large block print, and
her picture is the only one that smiles at me).

I have the same name as 1 grandfather, 3 cousins, 3 nephews,
and 1 uncle. The uncle disappeared when he was 15, just took   15
off and caught a freight (they say). He's discussed each year
when the family has a reunion, he causes uneasiness in
the clan, he is an empty space. My father's mother, who is 93
and who keeps the Family Bible with everbody's birth dates
(and death dates) in it, always mentions him. There is no   20
place in her Bible for "whereabouts unknown."

2

Each fall the graves of my grandfathers call me, the brown
hills and red gullies of mississippi send out their electric
messages, galvanizing my genes. Last yr/like a salmon quitting
the cold ocean-leaping and bucking up his birth stream/I   25
hitchhiked my way from LA with 16 caps in my pocket and a
monkey on my back. And I almost kicked it with the kinfolks.
I walked barefooted in my grandmother's backyard/I smelled the old
land and the woods/I sipped cornwhiskey from fruit jars with the men/
I flirted with the women/I had a ball till the caps ran out   30
and my habit came down. That night I looked at my grandmother
and split/my guts were screaming for junk/but I was almost

contented/I had almost caught up with me.
(The next day in Memphis I cracked a croaker's crib for a fix.)

This yr there is a gray stone wall damming my stream, and when   35
the falling leaves stir my genes, I pace my cell or flop on my bunk
and stare at 47 black faces across the space. I am all of them,
they are all of me, I am me, they are thee, and I have no children
to float in the space between.

Vern Rutsala (b. 1934)
Words (1981)

We had more than
we could use.
They embarrassed us,
our talk fuller than our
rooms. They named   5
nothing we could see—
dining room, study,
mantel piece, lobster
thermidor. They named
things you only   10
saw in movies—
the thin flicker Friday
nights that made us
feel empty in the cold
as we walked home   15
through our only great
abundance, snow.
This is why we said "ain't"
and "he don't."
We wanted words to fit   20
our cold linoleum,
our oil lamps, our
outhouse. We knew
better but it was wrong
to use a language   25
that named ghosts,
nothing you could touch.
We left such words at school
locked in books
where they belonged.   30
It was the vocabulary
of our lives that was

so thin. We knew this
and grew to hate
all the words that named   35
the vacancy of our rooms—
looking here we said
studio couch and saw cot;
looking there we said
venetian blinds and saw only the yard;   40
brick meant tarpaper,
fireplace meant wood stove.
And this is why we came to love
the double negative.

Miller Williams (b. 1930)
Ruby Tells All (1985)

When I was told, as Delta children were,
that crops don't grow unless you sweat at night,
I thought that it was my own sweat they meant.
I have never felt as important again
as on those early mornings, waking up,   5
my body slick, the moon full on the fields.
That was before air conditioning.
Farm girls sleep cool now and wake up dry,
but still the cotton overflows the fields.
We lose everything that's grand and foolish;   10
it all becomes something else. One by one,
butterflies turn into caterpillars
and we grow up, or more or less we do,
and, Lord, we do lie then. We lie so much
the truth has a false ring and it's hard to tell.   15
I wouldn't take crap off anybody
if I just knew that I was getting crap
in time not to take it. I could have won
a small one now and then if I was smarter,
but I've poured coffee here too many years   20
for men who rolled in in Peterbilts,
and I have gotten into bed with some
if they could talk and seemed to be in pain.
I never asked for anything myself;
giving is more blessed and leaves you free.   25
There was a man, married and fond of whiskey.
Given the limitations of men, he loved me.
Lord, we laid concern upon our bodies

but then he left. Everything has its time.
We used to dance. He made me feel the way   30
a human wants to feel and fears to.
He was a slow man and didn't expect.
I would get off work and find him waiting.
We'd have a drink or two and kiss awhile.
Then a bird-loud morning late one April   35
we woke up naked. We had made a child.
She's grown up now and gone though god knows where.
She ought to write, for I do love her dearly
who raised her carefully and dressed her well.

Everything has its time. For thirty years   40
I never had a thought about time.
Now, turning through newspapers, I pause
to see if anyone who passed away
was younger than I am. If one was
I feel hollow for a little while   45
but then it passes. Nothing matters enough
to stay bent down about. You have to see
that some things matter slightly and some don't.
Dying matters a little. So does pain.
So does being old. Men do not.   50
Men live by negatives, like don't give up,
don't be a coward, don't call me a liar,
don't ever tell me don't. If I could live
two hundred years and had to be a man
I'd take my grave. What's a man but a match,   55
a little stick to start a fire with?
My daughter knows this, if she's alive.
What could I tell her now, to bring her close,
something she doesn't know, if we met somewhere?
Maybe that I think about her father,   60
maybe that my fingers hurt at night,
maybe that against appearances
there is love, constancy, and kindness,
that I have dresses I have never worn.

Sharon Olds (b. 1942)
The Elder Sister (1984)

When I look at my elder sister now
I think how she had to go first, down through the
birth canal, to force her way
head-first through the tiny channel,

the pressure of Mother's muscles on her brain,   5
the tight walls scraping her skin.
Her face is still narrow from it, the long
hollow cheeks of a Crusader on a tomb,
and her inky eyes have the look of someone who has
been in prison a long time and   10
knows they can send her back. I look at her
body and think how her breasts were the first to
rise, slowly, like swans on a pond.
By the time mine came along, they were just
two more birds in the flock, and when the hair   15
rose on the white mound of her flesh, like
threads of water out of the ground, it was the
first time, but when mine came
they knew about it. I used to think
only in terms of her harshness, sitting and   20
pissing on me in bed, but now I
see I had her before me always
like a shield. I look at her wrinkles, her clenched
jaws, her frown-lines—I see they are
the dents on my shield, the blows that did not reach me.   25
She protected me, not as a mother
protects a child, with love, but as a
hostage protects the one who makes her
escape as I made my escape, with my sister's
body held in front of me.   30

Poems for Further Reading

Michael Harper (b. 1938)
Makin' Jump Shots (1973, 1977)

He waltzes into the lane
'cross the free-throw line,
fakes a drive, pivots,
floats from the asphalt turf
in an arc of black light,   5
and sinks two into the chains.*

---

*chains: That is, of the basketball net.

One on one he fakes
down the main, passes
into the free lane
and hits the chains.   10

A sniff in the fallen air—
he stuffs it through the chains
riding high:
"traveling" someone calls—
and he laughs, stepping   15
to a silent beat, gliding
as he sinks two into the chains.

·····▶ *Your* **Turn**
Talking and Writing about Lit

1. How does Michael Harper's use of line breaks in "Makin' Jump Shots"
   serve the purposes of his material, of the images and ideas he wants to
   convey, of the action he wants us to "see"?

2. **DIY** Write a brief poem in which you depict some action—playing a
   sport, dancing, swimming, driving, cleaning house, shopping. This
   might be an action or activity you enjoy or one you dislike.

Michael Harper (b. 1938)
Dear John, Dear Coltrane (1978)

a love supreme, a love supreme[1]
a love supreme, a love supreme

Sex fingers toes
in the marketplace
near your father's church
in Hamlet, North Carolina—[2]
witness to this love   5
in this calm fallow
of these minds,

---

[1]**a love supreme:** Coltrane wrote "A Love Supreme" in response to a spiritual experience in 1957,
which led to his quitting heroin and alcohol. The record was released in 1965.
[2]**Hamlet, North Carolina:** Coltrane's birthplace. His family shared a house with Coltrane's grandfather, who was the minister of St. Stephen's AME Zion Church there.

there is no substitute for pain:
genitals gone or going,
seed burned out,   10
you tuck the roots in the earth,
turn back, and move
by river through the swamps,
singing: *a love supreme, a love supreme;*
what does it all mean?   15
Loss, so great each black
woman expects your failure
in mute change, the seed gone.
You plod up into the electric city—
your song now crystal and   20
the blues. You pick up the horn
with some will and blow
into the freezing night:
a love supreme, a love supreme—

Dawn comes and you cook   25
up the thick sin 'tween
impotence and death, fuel
the tenor sax cannibal
heart, genitals and sweat
that makes you clean—   30
a love supreme, a love supreme—

Why you so black?
cause I am
why you so funky?
cause I am   35
why you so black
cause I am
why you so sweet?
cause I am
why you so black?   40
cause I am
a love supreme, a love supreme:

So sick
you couldn't play *Naima,*[3]
so flat we ached   45
for song you'd concealed

---

[3] *Naima:* A song Coltrane wrote for and named after his wife, recorded in 1959.

with your own blood,
your diseased liver gave
out its purity,
the inflated heart   50
pumps out, the tenor kiss,
tenor love:
a love supreme, a love supreme—
a love supreme, a love supreme—

·····▶ **Your Turn**
Talking and Writing about Lit

1. How does Michael Harper establish rhythm in "Dear John, Dear Coltrane"?
   John Coltrane was, of course, a jazz musician. How is this aspect of
   Coltrane's life represented in the poem?
2. How would you summarize the many themes and ideas suggested in
   Harper's poem?

William Carlos Williams (1883–1963)
To Elsie (1923)

The pure products of America
go crazy—
mountain folk from Kentucky

or the ribbed north end of
Jersey   5
with its isolate lakes and

valleys, its deaf-mutes, thieves
old names
and promiscuity between

devil-may-care men who have taken   10
to railroading
out of sheer lust of adventure—

and young slatterns, bathed
in filth
from Monday to Saturday   15

to be tricked out that night
with gauds
from imaginations which have no

peasant traditions to give them
character   20
but flutter and flaunt

sheer rags—succumbing without
emotion
save numbed terror

under some hedge of choke-cherry   25
or viburnum—
which they cannot express—

Unless it be that marriage
perhaps
with a dash of Indian blood   30

will throw up a girl so desolate
so hemmed round
with disease or murder

that she'll be rescued by an
agent—   35
reared by the state and

sent out at fifteen to work in
some hard-pressed
house in the suburbs—

some doctor's family, some Elsie—   40
voluptuous water
expressing with broken

brain the truth about us—
her great
ungainly hips and flopping breasts   45

addressed to cheap
jewelry
and rich young men with fine eyes

as if the earth under our feet
were   50
an excrement of some sky

and we degraded prisoners
destined
to hunger until we eat filth

while the imagination strains   55
after deer
going by fields of goldenrod in

the stifling heat of September
Somehow
it seems to destroy us   60

It is only in isolate flecks that
something
is given off

No one
to witness   65
and adjust, no one to drive the car

·····➤ *Your* Turn
Talking and Writing about Lit

1. Elsie was a retarded nursemaid from the state orphanage who worked for
the Williams family. How do you interpret lines 49–58? Whose "imagination
strains/after deer/going by fields of goldenrod"?

2. **DIY** Write a brief poem (or prose poem) that depicts someone you feel
sympathy for but do not necessarily like.

Philip Appleman (b. 1926)
Desire (1991)

1

The body
tugged like a tide, a pull
stronger than
the attraction of stars.

2

Moons   5
circling their planets,
planets
rounding their suns.

3

Nothing is what
we cannot imagine: 10
all that we know we know
moves in the muscles.

4

Undertow:
I reach for you,
oceans away.   15

•••••➤ *Your* Turn
Talking and Writing about Lit

1. Explain the use of figurative language in Philip Appleman's "Desire."

2. This poem is a good example of an open-form poem that uses a very precise (and original) form. How do Appleman's choices about the form of the poem suit his purposes in conveying his ideas and feelings?

Miller Williams (b. 1930)
Ruby Tells All (1985)

When I was told, as Delta children were,
that crops don't grow unless you sweat at night,
I thought that it was my own sweat they meant,
I have never felt as important again
as on those early mornings, waking up,   5
my body slick, the moon full on the fields.
That was before air conditioning.
Farm girls sleep cool now and wake up dry.
but still the cotton overflows the fields.
We lose everything that's grand and foolish;   10
it all becomes something else. One by one,
butterflies turn into caterpillars
and we grow up, or more or less we do,
and, Lord, we do lie then. We lie so much
the truth has a false ring and it's hard to tell. 15

I wouldn't take crap off anybody
if I just knew that I was getting crap
in time not to take it. I could have won
a small one now and then if I was smarter,
but I've poured coffee here too many years   20
for men who rolled in in Peterbilts,
and I have gotten into bed with some
if they could talk and seemed to be in pain.
I never asked for anything myself;
giving is more blessed and leaves you free.   25
There was a man, married and fond of whiskey.
Given the limitations of men, he loved me.
Lord, we laid concern upon our bodies
but then he left. Everything has its time.
We used to dance. He made me feel the way   30
a human wants to feel and fears to.
He was a slow man and didn't expect.
I would get off work and find him waiting.
We'd have a drink or two and kiss awhile.
Then a bird-loud morning late one April   35
we woke up naked. We had made a child.
She's grown up now and gone though god knows where.
She ought to write, for I do love her dearly
who raised her carefully and dressed her well.

Everything has its time. For thirty years   40
I never had a thought about time.
Now, turning through newspaper, I pause
to see if anyone who passed away
was younger than I am. If one was
I feel hollow for a little while   45
but then it passes. Nothing matters enough
to stay bent down about. You have to see
that some things matter slightly and some don't.
Dying matters a little. So does pain.
So does being old. Men do not.   50
Men live by negatives, like don't give up,
don't be a coward, don't call me a liar,
don't ever tell me don't. If I could live
two hundred years and had to be a man
I'd take my grave. What's a man but a match,   55
a little stick to start a fire with?
My daughter knows this, if she's alive.
What could I tell her now, to bring her close,
something she doesn't know, if we met somewhere?

Maybe that I think about her father,   60
maybe that against appearances
there is love, constancy, and kindness,
that I have dresses I have never worn.

Your Turn
Talking and Writing about Lit

1. How would you describe the diction (use of language) in Miller Williams's
"Ruby Tells All"?

2. This is a narrative poem (it tells a story). Like a work of fiction, does this
poem have plot? Characterization? Setting?

Diane Ackerman (b. 1948)
A Fine, a Private Place (1983)

He took her one day
under the blue horizon
where long sea fingers
parted like beads
hitched in the doorway   5
of an opium den,
and canyons mazed the deep
reef with hollows,
cul-de-sacs, and narrow boudoirs,
and had to ask twice   10
before she understood
his stroking her arm
with a marine feather
slobbery as aloe pulp
was wooing, or saw the octopus   15
in his swimsuit
stretch one tentacle
and ripple its silky bag.

While bubbles rose
like globs of mercury,   20
they made love
mask to mask, floating
with oceans of air between them,
she his sea-geisha
in an orange kimono   25
of belts and vests,

her lacquered hair waving,
as Indigo Hamlets
tattooed the vista,
and sunlight   30
cut through the water,
twisting its knives
into corridors of light.

His sandy hair
and sea-blue eyes,   35
his kelp-thin waist
and chest ribbed wider
than a sandbar
where muscles domed
clear and taut as shells   40
(freckled cowries,
flat, brawny scallops
the color of dawn),
his sea-battered hands
gripping her thighs   45
like tawny starfish
and drawing her close
as a pirate vessel
to let her board:
who was this she loved?   50

Overhead, sponges
sweating raw color
jutted from a coral arch,
Clown Wrasses*
hovered like fireworks,   55
and somewhere an abalone opened
its silver wings.
Part of a lusty dream
under aspic, her hips rolled
like a Spanish galleon,   60
her eyes swam
and chest began to heave.
Gasps melted on the tide.
Knowing she would soon be
breathless as her tank,   65
he pumped his brine
deep within her,

***Clown Wrasses:** brightly colored tropical fish

letting sea water drive it
through petals
delicate as anemone veils   70
to the dark purpose
of a conch-shaped womb.
An ear to her loins
would have heard the sea roar.

When panting ebbed,   75
and he signaled *Okay?*
as lovers have asked,
land or waterbound
since time heaved ho,
he led her to safety;   80
shallower realms,
heading back toward
the boat's even keel,
though ocean still petted her
cell by cell, murmuring   85
along her legs and neck,
caressing her
with pale, endless arms.

Later, she thought often
of that blue boudoir,   90
pillow-soft and filled
with cascading light,
where together
they'd made a bell
that dumbly clanged   95
beneath the waves
and minutes lurched
like mountain goats.
She could still see
the quilted mosaics   100
that were fish
twitching spangles overhead,
still feel the ocean
inside and out, turning her
evolution around.   105

She thought of it miles
and fathoms away, often,
at odd moments: watching
the minnow snowflakes

dip against the windowframe,   110
holding a sponge
idly under tap-gush,
sinking her teeth
into the cleft
of a voluptuous peach.   115

•••••▶ *Your* **Turn**
Talking and Writing about Lit

1. Give at least five examples of figurative language in Diane Ackerman's "A Fine, a Private Place."

2. **DIY** Use figurative language to depict an intense emotional experience. This might be a religious experience, a moment of triumph in sports, a reunion with a loved one, the birth of a child—any experience in which intense emotion is felt.

Yevgeny Yevtushenko (b. 1933)
People (1962)

Translated by Robin Milner-Gulland and Peter Levi

No people are uninteresting.
Their fate is like the chronicle of planets.

Nothing in them is not particular,
and planet is dissimilar from planet.

And if a man lived in obscurity   5
making his friends in that obscurity
obscurity is not uninteresting.

To each his world is private,
and in that world one excellent minute.

And in that world one tragic minute.   10
These are private.

In any man who dies there dies with him
his first snow and kiss and fight.
It goes with him.

They are left books and bridges   15
and painted canvas and machinery.

Whose fate is to survive.
But what has gone is also not nothing:

by the rule of the game something has gone.
Not people die but worlds die in them.   20

Whom we knew as faulty, the earth's creatures.
Of whom, essentially, what did we know?

Brother of a brother? Friend of friends?
Lover of lover?

We who knew our fathers   25
in everything, in nothing.

They perish. They cannot be brought back.
The secret worlds are not regenerated.

And every time again and again
I make my lament against destruction.   30

·····▶ *Your* Turn
Talking and Writing about Lit

1. How would you summarize Yevgeny Yevtushenko's principle theme/s in "People"? How do the last two lines (29–30) add dimension to the argument made by the rest of the poem?
2. Look at the choices Yevtushenko has made about form in this open-form poem. How has he crafted the form to suit his material?

Richard Newman (b. 1962)
Blank Verse in a Time of War (2004)

1.

Today you stayed at home to tend our son.
Two days from now, I leave to see the show
my music was commissioned for. Tonight,
you'll be in class till seven forty five,
and if I'm lucky I'll be sound asleep   5
when you get in, our boy as well, curled
into dreams that keep him warm and happy
till morning. Maybe you'll wake me into sex.
Probably not. Instead, you'll want to know

how high his fever was and when he took   10
his medication last, and if he asked
for you, and whether we did more than watch
Aladdin for the hundred and first time.
Yesterday, a woman younger than you were
when I met you made me the second person   15
to learn she's a lesbian. Another came
to my office after class to tell me how
when she was five no one believed she wasn't
fantasizing the man's hands on her sex,
and then he raped her sister. And someone   20
just told me a friend's daughter killed herself;
and a colleague's mother died of pneumonia;
and another one's father, somebody else's
husband. It's been a semester of loss.
When I tell her her friend David is gone,   25
my grandmother can't remember who he is.

2.

I wake to moonlight through the open blinds
and three stars in the window's top right pane,
jewels that from this angle echo the line
the glowing edge of the cat's black fur stains   30
the dark with. I'm dreaming—I've never owned
a black cat—while at the same time, within
the sleep my dreamed self inhabits, I watch
the dream unfold, wanting and wanting not
to know before it happens what comes next.   35
What comes next: I kneel at your naked breasts,
tease a nipple into my mouth and hope
the moans I draw from you reach no one's ears
but ours. Then, footsteps in the hall, a woman's
shoes ticking off the seconds we have left,   40
and the office gets busy. Someone's dead,
no, more than one, and their death certificates
need to be signed. These you lift from your desk
but they're in a language neither of us can read
and the translator is on extended leave.   45
Perhaps, you suggest, *they're not really gone,*
but if they are, we have all the time in the world.

3.

Before you took him with you to Iran,
Shahob drew a map connecting here
to wherever he imagined there was,   50

tracing each part of the journey on its own
sheet of paper. This way, he explained,
I could find you in an emergency,
and you would not get lost on your way home.
He mixed and matched the sections till the contours   55
fit the shape the trip made in his mind;
then we taped them together, and he smiled,
and he kissed me, *Now I can leave*, and I'm thinking
how every day since he was born has mapped
our lives for us, and will until we die;   60
and I remember watching the columns
of white smoke rising into the skyline
from what had been the World Trade Center;
and the moment the child safety bars
we'd had such difficulty installing   65
resolved themselves in my field of vision
into the bars of a locked cage; the smug
voice of the TV news commentator
describing for his audience the bombs
we were sending *to teach our enemies*   70
the true meaning of terror; and the clipart
map of Afghanistan he used to show
where *our fine young men in uniform*—
he'd forgotten there are women pilots too—
would drop their load. I listened while Shahob   75
and I dug through the rock he imagined
held in his room the dinosaur fossils
we had to find before he could go to sleep,
and no differently than I am now,
I was afraid, except now it's official,   80
it has colors—orange, green, yellow, red—
and so we talk about stocking up on food
and bottled water, and batteries, and since
we should have a first aid kit anyway,
we tell ourselves it's time. We buy one.   85

4.

A father pulls his son into his arms
and runs. The boy, too young to fathom war,
cries for the game this sudden flight destroys,
falls silent at the rhyme his mother sings
the way she does when she puts him to bed   90
and then screams what he hopes is loud enough—
though he doesn't really think of it as hope—
to make the world stop booming in his ears.

As way leads onto way, his sister trips,
and the wall of fire forces her to run   95
back up the stairs she thought would lead her down,
reborn into the rest of her years. People
watching below don't know it's her out there
on the window sill, holding a stranger's hand,
saying who-knows-what to comfort him   100
before they jump, but what she says works,
and he steps off the edge of his world at peace,
though his son, shooting wildly at men
whose occupying bullets stop his heart,
will never know he's been forgiven,   105
just as the one enemy he hits will die
shivering in his buddy's arms, not knowing
his sister was arrested days before
carrying a sign that said *Impeach Bush!*,
while her husband tried to comfort their two kids   110
at the hospital where doctors finished the job
the unexploded yellow ordnance
did on their uncle's left leg, on which he'd bounced
the week before his new niece, whose hands slapped
the face of the woman sitting opposite   115
on the train after the bomb blew them off
and before the roof caved in and crushed them both,
whose cousin lay halfway around the world
dying in his uniform much too soon,
the way the soldiers in our war movies   120
who aren't supposed to die die, except
the blood bubbling up into his throat
chokes off the last words the scriptwriters
would have given him.
     I have none to replace them.   125

• • • • • ➤ *Your* Turn
Talking and Writing about Lit

1. Like Philip Appleman ("Desire"), Richard Newman has chosen to arrange his open-form poem into four numbered sections; however, the results are quite different. Compare and contrast the poets' techniques in these two pieces. Why do you think each poet has made the choices he has made about form?

2. Another difference between the two poems is that Appleman's "Desire" is a lyric poem; Newman's "Blank Verse in a Time of War" is a narrative poem. Use these two equally successful works to discuss the characteristics of lyric and narrative poetry.

Carl Sandburg (1878–1967)
Chicago (1916)

Hog Butcher for the World,
Tool Maker, Stacker of Wheat,
Player with Railroads and the Nation's Freight Handler;
Stormy, husky, brawling,
City of the Big Shoulders: 5

They tell me you are wicked and I believe them, for I have seen your
  painted women under the gas lamps luring the farm boys.
And they tell me you are crooked and I answer: Yes, it is true I have seen
  the gunman kill and go free to kill again.
And they tell me you are brutal and my reply is: On the faces of women
  and children I have seen the marks of wanton hunger.
And having answered so I turn once more to those who sneer at this my
  city, and I give them back the sneer and say to them:
Come and show me another city with lifted head singing so proud to be   10
  alive and coarse and strong and cunning.
Flinging magnetic curses amid the toil of piling job on job, here is a tall
  bold slugger set vivid against the little soft cities;
Fierce as a dog with tongue lapping for action, cunning as a savage pitted
  against the wilderness,
      Bareheaded,
      Shoveling,
      Wrecking,   15
      Planning,
      Building, breaking, rebuilding,
Under the smoke, dust all over his mouth, laughing with white teeth,
Under the terrible burden of destiny laughing as a young man laughs,
Laughing even as an ignorant fighter laughs who has never lost a battle,   20
Bragging and laughing that under his wrist is the pulse, and under his ribs
  the heart of the people,
      Laughing!
Laughing the stormy, husky, brawling laughter of Youth, half-naked, sweat-
  ing, proud to be Hog Butcher, Tool Maker, Stacker of Wheat, Player with
  Railroads and Freight Handler to the Nation.

····▶ *Your* **Turn**
Talking and Writing about Lit

1. Explain the use of extended metaphor in Carl Sandburg's "Chicago."

2. **DIY** Write a brief poem or prose poem that characterizes your hometown, village, or city (or where you live now, if you prefer).

Amy Clampitt (b. 1920)
Nothing Stays Put (1989)

The strange and wonderful are too much with us.
The protea of the antipodes—a great,
globed, blazing honeybee of a bloom—
for sale in the supermarket! We are in
our decadence, we are not entitled.   5
What have we done to deserve
all the produce of the tropics—
this fiery trove, the largesse of it
heaped up like cannonballs, these pineapples, bossed
and crested, standing like troops at attention,   10
these tiers, these balconies of green, festoons
grown sumptuous with stoop labor?

The exotic is everywhere, it comes to us
before there is a yen or a need for it. The green-
grocers, uptown and down, are from South Korea.   15
Orchids, opulence by the pailful, just slightly
fatigued by the plane trip from Hawaii, are
disposed on the sidewalks; alstroemerias, freesias
flattened a bit in translation from overseas; gladioli
likewise estranged from their piercing ancestral crimson;   20
as well as, less altered from the original blue cornflower
of the roadsides and railway embankments of Europe, these
bachelor's buttons. But it isn't the railway embankments
their featherweight wheels of cobalt remind me of—it's
a row of them among prim colonnades of cosmos,   25
snapdragon, nasturtium, bloodsilk red poppies
in my grandmother's garden; a prairie childhood,
the grassland shorn, overlaid with a grid,
unsealed, furrowed, harrowed, and sown with immigrant grasses,
their massive corduroy, their wavering feltings embroidered   30
here and there by the scarlet shoulder patch of cannas
on a courthouse lawn, by a love knot, a cross-stitch
of living matter, sown and tended by women,
nurturers everywhere of the strange and wonderful,
beneath whose hands what had been alien begins,   35
as it alters, to grow as though it were indigenous.

But at this remove what I think of as
strange and wonderful—strolling the side streets of Manhattan
on an April afternoon, seeing hybrid pear trees in blossom,
a tossing, vertiginous colonnade of foam up above—   40

is the white petalfall, the warm snowdrift
of the indigenous wild plum of my childhood.
Nothing stays put. The world is a wheel.
All that we know, that we're
made of, is motion.   45

·····► *Your* Turn
Talking and Writing about Lit

1. How would you summarize the theme/s of Amy Clampitt's "Nothing Stays
Put"?

2. Explain your interpretation of the last three lines (43–45) and then compare
this poem to Theodore Roethke's "Root Cellar" (Chapter 15).

Gwendolyn Brooks (1917–2000)
The Mother (1945)

Abortions will not let you forget.
You remember the children you got that you did not get,
The damp small pulps with a little or with no hair,
The singers and workers that never handled the air.
You will never neglect or beat   5
them, or silence or buy with a sweet.
You will never wind up the sucking-thumb
Or scuttle off ghosts that come.
You will never leave them, controlling your luscious sigh,
Return for a snack of them, with gobbling mother-eye.   10

I have heard in the voices of the wind the voices of my dim killed children.
I have contracted. I have eased
My dim dears at the breasts they could never suck.
I have said, Sweets, if I sinned, if I seized
Your luck   15
And your lives from your unfinished reach,
If I stole your births and your names,
Your straight baby tears and your games,
Your stilted or lovely loves, your tumults, your marriages, aches, and your
    deaths,
If I poisoned the beginnings of your breaths,   20
Believe that even in my deliberateness I was not deliberate.
Though why should I whine,
Whine that the crime was other than mine?—
Since anyhow you are dead.
Or rather, or instead,   25

You were never made.
But that too, I am afraid,
Is faulty: oh, what shall I say, how is the truth to be said?
You were born, you had body, you died.
It is just that you never giggled or planned or cried.   30

Believe me, I loved you all.
Believe me, I knew you, though faintly, and I loved, I loved you
All.

•·····▶ *Your* Turn

Talking and Writing about Lit

1. Who is the speaker in Gwendolyn Brooks's "The Mother" and to whom is she addressing herself? How effective are the poet's choices regarding speaker and voice?

2. **DIY** Write a brief poem or prose poem addressed to someone who is no longer living or someone you never knew (for example, a brother you never had although you sometimes wish you'd had a brother).

Galway Kinnell (b. 1927)
After Making Love We Hear Footsteps (1980)

For I can snore like a bullhorn
or play loud music
or sit up talking with any reasonably sober Irishman
and Fergus will only sink deeper
into his dreamless sleep, which goes by all in one flash,   5
but let there be that heavy breathing
or a stifled come-cry anywhere in the house
and he will wrench himself awake
and make for it on the run—as now, we lie together,
after making love, quiet, touching along the length of our bodies,   10
familiar touch of the long-married,
and he appears—in his baseball pajamas, it happens,
the neck opening so small
he has to screw them on, which one day may make him wonder
about the mental capacity of baseball players—   15
and says, "Are you loving and snuggling? May I join?"
He flops down between us and hugs us and snuggles himself to sleep,
his face gleaming with satisfaction at being this very child.

In the half darkness we look at each other
and smile   20
and touch arms across his little, startlingly muscled body—
this one whom habit of memory propels to the ground of his making,
sleeper only the mortal sounds can sing awake,
this blessing love gives again into our arms.

·····▶ *Your* Turn
Talking and Writing about Lit

1. Is Galway Kinnell's poem "After Making Love We Hear Footsteps" a lyric
   poem or a narrative poem? Use specific examples from the poem to defend
   your answer.
2. Theodore Roethke's "My Papa's Waltz" (in Chapter 17) is another poem that
   features a mother, father, and son. Compare and contrast the two poems in
   terms of both themes and poetic techniques.

Amy King (b. 1971)
The Late Show Effect (2004)

I swallowed hard the whole bottle of your footsteps
and slipped into the cup of a nightingale's tear—

Will you become my fragrant flash in the pan,
my dusted desire to be right up against it

Feeding on ears of popcorn, pull the blinds, am now in disguise   5
beneath the covers, one leg stretches beside a leg outstretched

We transform into the middle of morning's minutes
accepting the fat of the wing & a blank nun's humming cargo

It has often been Jesus who attacks on-screen, one without
the other I, in turn, played Geppetto for the duration of the film,   10

Besides, all future visions are off. Watching the death of someone
close by, our close-captioned feet couldn't get traction.

Over there, an elbow girl spends her time with lotions and days
alone inside her iridescent character lining, considering revisions.

·····▶ *Your* **Turn**
Talking and Writing about Lit

1. Reread Amy King's "Talking Lit" piece in Chapter 14 ("A Rose Is a Rose Is a Thorny Yellow Thing"). Apply the ideas she discusses in her essay as you write a paragraph discussing her poetic techniques in "The Late Show Effect."

2. **DIY** Try your hand at creating lines of poetry that juxtapose unlikely words. Reach for unusual combinations of images that nevertheless say something (though they may say it ambiguously and may leave open the possibility of many different meanings). For example, "I tried to slip the/glass slipper of your love/onto my/ungainly foot." Or, "Don't speak to me with those/lampshade eyes." Write at least twelve lines of a poem.

Barbara Barnard (b. 1951)
Legacy (2004)

Things I can use:
The warmth of your smile, when you showed it,
Instructions on outsmarting rattlesnakes
    of the human variety,

Things I can't use: 5
Your cowboy-booted swagger, when it led to a fight,
Instructions on outsmarting rattlesnakes
    of the reptilian variety,
The Colt 45 you left me in your will,
    now that I'm a Quaker,   10

Things I can use:
Your way of looking up when you had to,
    though you felt low down,
The way you could look folks straight in the eye and stay on,
    when they didn't want your *kind* around.   15

Things I can't use:
Your habit of punching folks in the face
    who went one step too far messing with you,
Your habit of punching folks in the face
    who controlled your, and your family's, livelihood,   20
Your habit of drinking a bottle of good whiskey,
    then getting behind the wheel.
Your habit of pulling out the big belt to whomp on us,
    for some small infraction.

Things I can use: 25
Your love of music of all kinds,
    especially fiddle music,
The way you favored a good pair of boots
    over any shoe,
The way the lines crinkled at the corners   30
    of your eyes when you smiled real big,
The way you'd say to me, "Girl,
    I got a bone to pick with you,"
    with a grin on your face, sometimes.

·····▶ *Your* **Turn**
Talking and Writing about Lit

1. In this poem by the coauthor of this volume, two key ideas were important. First, that the "Legacy" of a parent (or other close relative) might be a mixed bag of good traits and bad. Second, we all have the option to pick and choose which traits we want to be part of our own character—we can reject what is bad and keep what is good. Do you think the form I chose for this open-form poem works well, given what I hoped to convey? Why do you think I structured the poem the way I did?

2. **DIY** I give you permission to "borrow" the basic idea of my poem. Write a poem of your own in which you enumerate things about a person (perhaps a parent or grandparent, though it could instead be a celebrity or a politician) who might be an influence on you. Let the poem reflect how you would separate the influences or traits of that person you would embrace and the traits you would reject. You are in control; you decide what to keep and what to throw out.

Gary Snyder (b. 1930)
Looking at Pictures to Be Put Away (1968)

Who was this girl
In her white night gown
Clutching a pair of jeans

On a foggy redwood deck.
She looks up at me tender,   5
Calm, surprised,

What will we remember
Bodies thick with food and lovers
After twenty years.

····•► *Your* Turn
Talking and Writing about Lit

1. Gary Snyder's "Looking at Pictures to Be Put Away" is a lyric poem that is compact in its form and economical in its phrasing. Summarize in a sentence or two what the speaker is feeling as he looks at this picture. Do you think the form of the poem serves his purpose well?

2. **DIY** Find a photograph of someone you know well and write a poem as compact as Snyder's—three three-line stanzas—which conveys thoughts and feelings about the photograph. Your poem might be pensive and serious like Snyder's, or it might be funny or satirical.

Robert Pinsky (b. 1940)
ABC (2000)

Any body can die, evidently. Few
Go happily, irradiating joy,

Knowledge, love. Many
Need oblivion, painkillers,
Quickest respite.   5

Sweet time unafflicted,
Various world:

X = your zenith.

····•► *Your* Turn
Talking and Writing about Lit

1. Examine Robert Pinsky's "ABC" and explain how the form of the poem works.

2. **DIY** Write a compact poem of your own that uses words beginning with each letter of the alphabet. Have fun; you may find this easier than you think. Don't worry if you are not sure what the poem says until you are finished with it.

Talking Lit

Here is an excerpt from Walt Whitman's manifesto about open-form poetry, along with a poem written by Native American writer Sherman Alexie in which he imagines Walt Whitman's appreciation of a reservation basketball game.

Walt Whitman, from the Preface to *Leaves of Grass*

The poetic quality is not marshalled in rhyme or uniformity or abstract addresses to things nor in melancholy complaints or good precepts, but is the life of these and much else and is in the soul. The profit of rhyme is that it drops seeds of a sweeter and more luxuriant rhyme, and of uniformity that it conveys itself into its own roots in the ground out of sight. The rhyme and uniformity of perfect poems show the free growth of metrical laws and bud from them as unerringly and loosely as lilacs or roses on a bush, and take shapes as compact as the shapes of chestnuts and oranges and melons and pears, and shed the perfume impalpable to form. The fluency and ornaments of the finest poems or music or orations or recitations are not independent but dependent. All beauty comes from beautiful blood and a beautiful brain. If the greatnesses are in conjunction in a man or woman it is enough . . . the fact will prevail through the universe . . . but the gaggery and gilt of a million years will not prevail. Who troubles himself about his ornaments or fluency is lost. This is what you shall do: Love the earth and sun and the animals, despise riches, give alms to every one that asks, stand up for the stupid and crazy, devote your income and labor to others, hate tyrants, argue not concerning God, have patience and indulgence toward the people, take off your hat to nothing known or unknown or to any man or number of men, go freely with powerful uneducated persons and with the young and with the mothers of families, read these leaves in the open air every season of every year of your life, reexamine all you have been told at school or church or in any book, dismiss whatever insults your own soul, and your very flesh shall be a great poem and have the richest fluency not only in its words but in the silent lines of its lips and face and between the lashes of your eyes and in every motion and joint of your body. . . .

Sherman Alexie, "Defending Walt Whitman," 1996

Basketball is like this for young Indian boys, all arms and legs
and serious stomach muscles. Every body is brown!
These are the twentieth-century warriors who will never kill,
although a few sat quietly in the deserts of Kuwait,
waiting for orders to do something, do something.   5

God, there is nothing as beautiful as a jump shot
on a reservation summer basketball court
where the ball is moist with sweat
and makes a sound when it swishes through the net
that causes Walt Whitman to weep because it is so perfect.   10

There are veterans of foreign wars here,
whose bodies are still dominated
by collarbones and knees, whose bodies still respond
in the ways that bodies are supposed to respond when we are young.
Every body is brown! Look there, that boy can run   15

POP CULTURE

Open Form Film: Tarantino Chops up Chronology

One of the great joys of working in any art form is breaking the rules of that art form. Poets have broken the traditions of structure, meter, and punctuation, but artists in every medium constantly create new methods of artistic communication by trampling over that medium's typical way of doing things.

In 1992 Quentin Tarantino made his first widely received film, *Reservoir Dogs*. Despite being filmed out of chronological sequence (beginning in the middle, flashing back to the beginning, and then forward to the end), *Reservoir Dogs*

up and down this court forever. He can leap for a rebound
with his back arched like a salmon, all meat and bone
synchronized, magnetic, as if the court were a river,
as if the rim were a dam, as if the air were a ladder
leading the Indian boy toward home.   20

Some of the Indian boys still wear their military haircuts
while a few have let their hair grow back.
It will never be the same as it was before!
One Indian boy has never cut his hair, not once, and he braids it
into wild patterns that do not measure anything.   25
He is just a boy with too much time on his hands.
Look at him. He wants to play this game in bare feet.

God, the sun is so bright! There is no place like this.
Walt Whitman stretches his calf muscles
on the sidelines. He has the next game.   30
His huge beard is ridiculous on the reservation.
Some body throws a crazy pass and Walt Whitman catches
      it with quick hands.
He brings the ball close to his nose
and breathes in all of its smells: leather, brown skin, sweat, black hair,
burning oil, twisted ankle, long drink of warm water,   35
gunpowder, pine tree. Walt Whitman squeezes the ball tightly.
He wants to run. He hardly has the patience to wait for his turn.
"What's the score?" he asks. He asks, "What's the score?"

Quentin Tarantino

fully communicated a story and was well liked by audiences and critics. Since that first film, Tarantino has made something of a tradition of chronologically disordered films which are action packed, entertaining, and exciting.

Chronology isn't the only rule that Tarantino plays with in cinema. In his recent *Kill Bill* epic he avoids mentioning the main character's real name until the middle of the second film, he nonchalantly includes wildly cartoonish violence, and he has his main character speak directly into the camera, addressing the audience (a tradition from the French New Wave directors).

Basketball is like this for Walt Whitman. He watches these Indian boys
as if they were the last bodies on earth. Every body is brown! 40
Walt Whitman shakes because he believes in God.
Walt Whitman dreams of the Indian boy who will defend him,
trapping him in the corner, all flailing arms and legs
and legendary stomach muscles. Walt Whitman shakes
because he believes in God. Walt Whitman dreams 45
of the first jump shot he will take, the ball arcing clumsily
from his fingers, striking the rim so hard that it sparks.
Walt Whitman shakes because he believes in God.
Walt Whitman closes his eyes. He is a small man and his beard
is ludicrous on the reservation, absolutely insane. 50
His beard makes the Indian boys laugh righteously. His beard frightens
the smallest Indian boys. His beard tickles the skin
of the Indian boys who dribble past him. His beard, his beard!

God, there is beauty in every body. Walt Whitman stands
at center court while the Indian boys run from basket to basket. 55
Walt Whitman cannot tell the difference between
offense and defense. He does not care if he touches the ball.
Half of the Indian boys wear T-shirts damp with sweat
and the other half are barebacked, skin slick and shiny.
There is no place like this. Walt Whitman smiles. 60
Walt Whitman shakes. This game belongs to him.

MYTH AND POETRY

Even fashion uses myth.

Myths are the stories we tell ourselves to explain the world around us. Common to all cultures, they share many of the same themes. Mythical figures, or archetypes, which serve as a fundamental story patterns across cultures, attempt to explain aspects of the natural world or define the psychology, customs, or ideals of a society. While myths are, by definition, traditional and ancient, they remain relevant today and influence us in our day-to-day living. Goth teenagers wear black makeup, black outfits and black combat boots or sneakers, often accessorized with black leather armbands and multiple piercings. The term "Gothic" refers to medieval times. Gothic style in architecture and fiction typically emphasizes the desolate, grotesque, and mysterious, and Goth fashion evokes the same themes. Similarly, Jennifer Lopez in her Grecian-style dress, cuts a romantic figure evocative of a Greek goddesses. Do you think that Punk style has mythic associations? How would you describe the mythic appeal of punk? In short, each fashion style shown here is an archetype of a particular worldview, a certain sentiment, representative of a particular cultural or social value just as mythological archetypes are symbols of particular points of view.

If you have enjoyed movies like *Star Wars*, *The Lord of the Rings*, *The Warriors*, *Princess Bride*, or *The Labyrinth*, then you have experienced the power and pervasiveness of myths. As illustrated in the opening pages of this chapter, myth shows up in many contexts, and often we are not aware of how ever-present myths are in our daily lives. We discussed myth in Chapter 9 where we gave a general description of what myth is and what kinds of mythic patterns (such as the hero's quest) routinely turn up in literary works.

Myths of Love and Myths of Ancestors

Of course, many mythic patterns or archetypes (story patterns common across cultures) deal with romance. In the following poem, you may recognize the familiar pattern of two lovers whose families forbid them to be together because of feuds or cultural differences. Our best-known example of this pattern in the English language is William Shakespeare's *Romeo and Juliet*. Poet Ana Castillo grew up in Chicago, but her family heritage is Mexican, and her more distant heritage is Aztec, as well as the Toltec people who were ancestors of the Aztecs. In the following poem, Castillo depicts the Toltec myth of two volcanic mountains who were once a warrior and a princess longing for forbidden love.

Ana Castillo (b. 1953)
Ixtacihuatl Died in Vain* (1988)

I

Hard are the women of my family,
hard on the mothers who've died on us
and the daughters born to us,
hard on all except sacred husbands
and the blessings of sons.   5
We are Ixtacihuatls,
sleeping, snowcapped volcanoes
buried alive in myths
princesses with the name of a warrior
on our lips.   10

*****Ixtacihuatl:** The legend of the twin volcanoes Popocatepetl and Ixtacihuatl in Puebla, Mexico, has it that these were once a warrior and princess of rivaling tribes who came to an end similar to that of the two lovers of Shakespeare's *Romeo and Juliet*.

II

You, my impossible bride,
at the wedding where our mothers
were not invited,
our fathers, the fourteen
stations of the cross—   15

You, who are not my bride,
have loved too vast, too wide.
Yet I dare to steal you
from your mother's house.

It is you   20
I share my son with
to whom I offer up
his palpitating heart
so that you may breathe,
and replenish yourself,   25
you alone, whom I forgive.

III

Life is long enough
to carry all things
to their necessary end. So
if i am with you   30
only this while,
or until our hair goes white,
our mothers have died,
children grown,
their children been born,   35
or when you spy someone
who is me
but with fresh eyes that see
you as Coatlicue once did—
and my heart   40
shrivels with vanity;
or a man takes me out to dance
and i leave you at the table
ice melting in your glass;
or all the jasmine in the world   45
has lost its scent,
let us place this born of us
at Ixtacihuatl's grave:
a footnote in the book of myths

sum of our existence—   50
"Even the greatest truths
contain the tremor of a lie."

Note how Castillo shifts voices here. Section II is in the voice of the warrior,
and section III is in the voice of the princess. From what perspective does the voice
in section I speak?

Castillo's use of speaker and voice in the following poem is also interesting.

Ana Castillo
Our Tongue Was Nahuatl (1974)

You.
We have never met
yet
we know each other
well.   5
i recognized
your high
          set
               cheekbones,
slightly rounded   10
             nose,
the deep brown of your hardened
face, soft
full lips.

Your near-slanted eyes   15
follow me—
sending flashback memories
to your so-called
primitive mind.
And i know   20
you remember . . .

It was a time
of turquoise blue green,
sky topped mountains,
god-suns, wind-swept rains;   25
oceanic deities
naked children running
in the humid air.

i ground corn
upon a slab of stone   30
while you bargained
at the market
dried skins
and other things
that were our own.   35

i watched our small sons
chase behind your bare legs
when you came home those days.
We sat, ate,
gave thanks to our golden Earth.   40
Our tongue was Nahuatl.
We were content—
with the generosity
of our gods and our kings,
knowing nothing of the world   45
across the bitter waters—
Until they came . . .

White foreign strangers
riding high
            on four-legged   50
              creatures;
that made us bow to them.
In our ignorance of the unknown
they made us bow.

They made us bow—   55
until our skin became
the color of caramel
and nothing anymore
was our own.

Raped of ourselves,   60
our civilization,
even our gods turned away
from us in shame . . .

Yet we bowed,
            as we do now—   65

On buses
       going to factories

where "No Help Wanted" signs
laugh at our faces,
stare at our hungry eyes.   70

Yet we bow . . .
                    WE BOW!
It was a time
much different
                    than now.   75

In this poem, Castillo's speaker first addresses the ancestor as "you" (in lines 1–21); then in the following stanza (lines 22–28), she makes a transition into the past time; and in the central stanzas of the poem (lines 29–64), the speaker is as one with the ancestor, speaking in the first-person voice of the ancestor. How would you describe the shift in voice that occurs in line 65? Do you think the shift to the final perspective of the poem (lines 65–75) is effective?

Fairy Tales

Although many critics would categorize fairy tales as folklore rather than myth, both are often used for instructive purposes, to pass on knowledge to the next generation, or as cautionary tales telling us what not to do. Little Red Riding Hood is a cautionary tale about young girls going alone into the woods, and Hansel and Gretel warns us against not only the dark forest but also strangers offering sweets. Louise Glück's poem, an interesting takeoff on the familiar Hansel and Gretel story, imagines the thoughts and life of Gretel years after she survived the incident with the witch.

Louise Glück (b. 1943)
Gretel in Darkness (1971)

This is the world we wanted.
All who would have seen us dead
are dead. I hear the witch's cry
break in the moonlight through a sheet
of sugar: God rewards.   5
Her tongue shrivels into gas. . . .

    Now, far from women's arms
and memory of women, in our father's hut

we sleep, are never hungry.
Why do I not forget?   10
My father bars the door, bars harm
from this house, and it is years.

No one remembers. Even you, my brother,
summer afternoons you look at me as though
you meant to leave,   15
as though it never happened.
But I killed for you. I see armed firs,
the spires of that gleaming kiln—

Nights I turn to you to hold me
but you are not there.   20
Am I alone? Spies
hiss in the stillness, Hansel,
we are there still and it is real, real,
that black forest and the fire in earnest.

    In this imaginative poem, Gretel seems to have mixed feelings about being safe in her father's hut. "My father bars the door, bars harm/from this house, and it is years. // No one remembers." It seems only Gretel remembers that adventure into the woods and the discovery of evil there. But she also remembers her own bravery and the fact that she was equal to the task of dispatching the witch. Now, shut up in her father's house, she displays a note of regret in her voice, even from the first line: "This is the world we wanted." Ironically, she escaped the witch's confinement only to face confinement of a different sort.

    Anne Sexton's "Cinderella" is as funny as Glück's "Gretel" is melancholy. To generate a humorous effect, Sexton puts the details of the familiar fairy tale, set in an earlier time, side by side with details from modern, everyday life or recent cultural history (again, juxtaposition is at work here). In fact, the Cinderella story pattern dates back at least to the fifth century and has been a popular tale not only in Europe, but also in Greece, India, China, and elsewhere around the world.

Anne Sexton (1928–1974)
Cinderella (1970)

You always read about it:
the plumber with twelve children
who wins the Irish Sweepstakes.
From toilets to riches.
That story.   5

Or the nursemaid,

some luscious sweet from Denmark
who captures the oldest son's heart.
From diapers to Dior.
That story.   10

Or a milkman who serves the wealthy,
eggs, cream, butter, yogurt, milk,
the white truck like an ambulance
who goes into real estate
and makes a pile.   15
From homogenized to martinis at lunch.

Or the charwoman
who is on the bus when it cracks up
and collects enough from the insurance.
From mops to Bonwit Teller.   20
That story.

Once
the wife of a rich man was on her deathbed
and she said to her daughter Cinderella:
Be devout. Be good. Then I will smile   25
down from heaven in the seam of a cloud.
The man took another wife who had
two daughters, pretty enough
but with hearts like blackjacks.
Cinderella was their maid.   30
She slept on the sooty hearth each night
and walked around looking like Al Jolson.
Her father brought presents home from town,
jewels and gowns for the other women
but the twig of a tree for Cinderella.   35
She planted that twig on her mother's grave
and it grew to a tree where a white dove sat.
Whenever she wished for anything the dove
would drop it like an egg upon the ground.
The bird is important, my dears, so heed him.   40

Next came the ball, as you all know.
It was a marriage market.
The prince was looking for a wife.
All but Cinderella were preparing
and gussying up for the big event.   45
Cinderella begged to go too.
Her stepmother threw a dish of lentils

into the cinders and said: Pick them
up in an hour and you shall go.
The white dove brought all his friends;   50
all the warm wings of the fatherland came,
and picked up the lentils in a jiffy.
No, Cinderella, said the stepmother,
you have no clothes and cannot dance.
That's the way with stepmothers.   55

Cinderella went to the tree at the grave
and cried forth like a gospel singer:
Mama! Mama! My turtledove,
send me to the prince's ball!
The bird dropped down a golden dress   60
and delicate little gold slippers.
Rather a large package for a simple bird.
So she went. Which is no surprise.
Her stepmother and sisters didn't
recognize her without her cinder face   65
and the prince took her hand on the spot
and danced with no other the whole day.

As nightfall came she thought she'd
better get home. The prince walked her home
and she disappeared into the pigeon house   70
and although the prince took an axe and broke
it open she was gone. Back to her cinders.
These events repeated themselves for three days.
However on the third day the prince
covered the palace steps with cobbler's wax   75
And Cinderella's gold shoe stuck upon it.

Now he would find whom the shoe fit
and find his strange dancing girl for keeps.
He went to their house and the two sisters
were delighted because they had lovely feet.   80
The eldest went into a room to try the slipper on
but her big toe got in the way so she simply
sliced it off and put on the slipper.
The prince rode away with her until the white dove
told him to look at the blood pouring forth.   85
That is the way with amputations.
They don't just heal up like a wish.
The other sister cut off her heel
but the blood told as blood will.

The prince was getting tired. 90
He began to feel like a shoe salesman.
But he gave it one last try.
This time Cinderella fit into the shoe
like a love letter into its envelope.

At the wedding ceremony 95
the two sisters came to curry favor
and the white dove pecked their eyes out.
Two hollow spots were left
like soup spoons.

Cinderella and the prince 100
lived, they say, happily ever after,
like two dolls in a museum case
never bothered by diapers or dust,
never arguing over the timing of an egg,
never telling the same story twice, 105
never getting a middle-aged spread,
their darling smiles pasted on for eternity
Regular Bobbsey Twins.
That story.

Contextual Mythic Allusions

In Adrienne Rich's "Diving into the Wreck," there are references to "the book of myths" (line 1), "the thing itself and not the myth" (line 63), "mermaid" and "merman" (lines 72–73), and "a book of myths/in which/our names do not appear" (lines 92–94). In addition to all of these specific references to myth, there are allusions such as "the body-armor of black rubber" (line 5), "[t]he words are maps" (line 54), and "the treasures that prevail" (line 56). As you read the poem, pay attention to the voice of the speaker and the nuances of the speaker's perspective.

Adrienne Rich (b. 1929)
Diving into the Wreck (1972)

First having read the book of myths,
and loaded the camera,
and checked the edge of the knife-blade,
I put on

the body-armor of black rubber   5
the absurd flippers
the grave and awkward mask.
I am having to do this
not like Cousteau with his
assiduous team   10
aboard the sun-flooded schooner
but here alone.

There is a ladder.
The ladder is always there
hanging innocently   15
close to the side of the schooner.
We know what it is for,
we who have used it.
Otherwise
it's a piece of maritime floss   20
some sundry equipment.

I go down.
Rung after rung and still
the oxygen immerses me
the blue light   25
the clear atoms
of our human air.
I go down.
My flippers cripple me,
I crawl like an insect down the ladder   30
and there is no one
to tell me when the ocean
will begin.

First the air is blue and then
it is bluer and then green and then   35
black I am blacking out and yet
my mask is powerful
it pumps my blood with power
the sea is another story
the sea is not a question of power   40
I have to learn alone
to turn my body without force
in the deep element.

And now: it is easy to forget
what I came for   45

among so many who have always
lived here
swaying their crenellated fans
between the reefs
and besides   50
you breathe differently down here.

I came to explore the wreck.
The words are purposes.
The words are maps.
I came to see the damage that was done   55
and the treasures that prevail.
I stroke the beam of my lamp
slowly along the flank
of something more permanent
than fish or weed   60

the thing I came for:
the wreck and not the story of the wreck
the thing itself and not the myth
the drowned face always staring
toward the sun   65
the evidence of damage
worn by salt and sway into this threadbare beauty
the ribs of the disaster
curving their assertion
among the tentative haunters.   70

This is the place.
And I am here, the mermaid whose dark hair
streams black, the merman in his armored body
We circle silently
about the wreck   75
we dive into the hold.
I am she: I am he
whose drowned face sleeps with open eyes
whose breasts still bear the stress
whose silver, copper, vermeil cargo lies   80
obscurely inside barrels
half-wedged and left to rot
we are the half-destroyed instruments
that once held to a course
the water-eaten log   85
the fouled compass

We are, I am, you are
by cowardice or courage
the one who find our way
back to this scene   90
carrying a knife, a camera
a book of myths
in which
our names do not appear.

As you see, the speaker is sometimes singular but sometimes represents both herself and a male partner, "mermaid" and "merman" (lines 72–73), "I am she: I am he" (line 77), exploring the wreck of their past together. Some of the mythic allusions in this poem are "contextual," that is, they are specific to this literary context. Without the biographical information we just provided about the author, we might not perceive some of the specific nuances of the mythological allusions in the poem.

Cultural Mythic Allusions

Ishmael Reed's allusions to Egyptian myths, gods, and goddesses is not specific only to the context of his poem "I Am a Cowboy in the Boat of Ra." His references to Isis, Ra, Osiris, Set, the conflict between the mythic god-brothers Osiris and Set . . . all of this is drawn directly from Egyptian mythology. Specifically, these mythic stories are recounted in the Pyramid Texts (dating back to 3000–2200 B.C.E.) and Coffin Texts (2134–1660 B.C.E.) and the *Book of the Dead* (1550 B.C.E.). The meanings suggested by the references to these figures and stories would be interpreted fairly uniformly by readers familiar with the Egyptian material. They are not specific to this work alone, but have broader, more universal significance. What is new and innovative in this poem, of course, is the way in which Reed blends allusions to ancient Egyptian mythology with the details, diction, and lore of the American West and cowboy culture. As we see even in the title of this poem, what delights is the mixing of the ancient myths of one continent with the swaggering tone of the Chisholm Trail, Wild West outlaws, the Bowie knife, and the Loup Garou Kid.

Ishmael Reed (b. 1938)
I Am a Cowboy in the Boat of Ra (1969)

The devil must be forced to reveal any such physical evil (potions, charms, fetishes, etc.) still outside the body and these must be burned.
—*Rituale Romanum*, published 1947, endorsed by the coat of
      arms and introduction letter from Francis Cardinal Spellman

I am a cowboy in the boat of Ra,[1]
sidewinders in the saloons of fools
bit my forehead   like   O
the untrustworthiness of Egyptologists
Who do not know their trips. Who was that   5
dog-faced man?[2] they asked, the day I rode
from town.

School marms with halitosis cannot see
the Nefertiti[3] fake chipped on the run by slick
germans, the hawk behind Sonny Rollins' head or   10
the ritual beard of his axe,[4] a longhorn winding
its bells thru the Field of Reeds.

I am a cowboy in the boat of Ra. I bedded
down with Isis,[5] Lady of the Boogaloo, dove
down deep in her horny, stuck up her Wells-Far-ago   15
in daring midday get away. "Start grabbing the
blue," i said from top of my double crown.

I am a cowboy in the boat of Ra. Ezzard Charles[6]
of the Chisholm Trail. Took up the bass but they
blew off my thumb. Alchemist in ringmanship but a   20
sucker for the right cross.

I am a cowboy in the boat of Ra. Vamoosed from
the temple i bide my time. The price on the wanted
poster was a-going down, outlaw alias copped my stance
and moody greenhorns were making me dance; while my mouth's   25
shooting iron got its chambers jammed.

I am a cowboy in the boat of Ra. Boning-up in
the ol West i bide my time. You should see
me pick off these tin cans whippersnappers. I
write the motown long plays for the comeback of   30
Osiris.[7] Make them up when stars stare at sleeping
steer out here near the campfire. Women arrive

---

[1]**Ra:** Chief of the ancient Egyptian gods, creator and protector of humans and vanquisher of Evil.

[2]**dog-faced man:** The Egyptian god of the dead, Anubis was usually depicted as a man with the head of a dog or jackal.

[3]**Nefertiti:** Fourteenth-century B.C. Egyptian queen; elsewhere Reed says that German scholars are responsible for the notion that her dynasty was white.

[4]**axe:** Saxophone. *Sonny Rollins:* jazz great of the late 1950s and early 1960s.

[5]**Isis:** Principal goddess of ancient Egypt.

[6]**Ezzard Charles:** World heavyweight boxing champion, 1949–51.

[7]**Osiris:** Husband of Isis and constant foe of his brother Set (line 48). Tricked by Set, he died violently but later rose from the dead.

on the backs of goats and throw themselves on
my Bowie.[8]

I am a cowboy in the boat of Ra. Lord of the lash,   35
the Loup Garou[9] Kid. Half breed son of Pisces and
Aquarius. I hold the souls of men in my pot. I do
the dirty boogie with scorpions. I make the bulls
keep still and was the first swinger to grape the taste.

I am a cowboy in his boat. Pope Joan[10] of the   40
Ptah Ra. C/mere a minute willya doll?
Be a good girl and
Bring me my Buffalo horn of black powder
Bring me my headdress of black feathers
Bring me my bones of Ju-Ju snake   45
Go get my eyelids of red paint.
Hand me my shadow
I'm going into town after Set

I am a cowboy in the boat of Ra
look out Set   here i come Set   50
to get Set   to sunset Set
to unseat Set   to Set down Set
            usurper of the Royal couch
            imposter RAdio of Moses' bush[11]
            party pooper O hater of dance   55
            vampire outlaw of the milky way

---

[8]**Bowie:** Large hunting knife.
[9]**Loup Garou:** French for werewolf; in voodoo, a priest who has run amok or gone mad.
[10]**Pope Joan:** Mythical female pope, supposed to have succeeded to the papacy in 855. *Ptah Ra:*
chief god of Memphis, capital of ancient Egypt.
[11]**Moses' bush:** Which, according to Exodus 3:2, burned but was not consumed and from which
Moses heard the voice of God telling him to lead the Israelites out of Egypt.

Do you think Reed is also trying to say something about his (or, we might
say, his speaker's) experience as an American of African descent?

In Aron Keesbury's "The Echo and Narcissus Equation," you may recognize
the references to the Greek myth of Echo and Narcissus. The wood nymph Echo
was in love with Narcissus, but because the goddess Juno had removed her ability
to speak for herself, she could only echo the words of others. She repeats Narcissus's
words (as a poor substitute for communication), but she is rejected by him since he
is able to love only himself. Eventually, Echo wastes away, becoming only a voice
(an echo); and of course, while admiring his own beloved self, Narcissus falls into
the lake and drowns, thus becoming nothing as well. Remembering these details
about the mythological characters, how would you interpret this poem? How do
the "You and I" of the title offer the solution to the "Echo and Narcissus Equation"?

Aron Keesbury (b. 1971)
The Echo and Narcissus Equation
(to Which You and I Offer the Solution)

If love is the completion from two of one,
then adding only unto him, himself, his love
diminishes off into nothingness. Her love,

denied, diminishes off into nothingness as well.
Her self, as his was, only half enough   5
to fill the whole. But you and I: Though true

that I'm a whole glass half filled, and
true that you're a whole glass half filled too,
in yours is the reflection of me. And I fill the echo of you.

In another Greek myth, the god Zeus, in the form of a swan, overpowers the
mortal girl Leda and impregnates her. She later gives birth to the fatally beautiful
Helen over whom the Trojan War is later fought, hence the reference in lines 10–11
to "The broken wall, the burning roof and tower / And Agamemnon dead."

William Butler Yeats (1865–1939)
Leda and the Swan[1] (1923, 1924)

A sudden blow: the great wings beating still
Above the staggering girl, her thighs caressed
By the dark webs, her nape caught in his bill,
He holds her helpless breast upon his breast.

How can those terrified vague fingers push   5
The feathered glory from her loosening thighs?
And how can body, laid in that white rush,
But feel the strange heart beating where it lies?

A shudder in the loins engenders there
The broken wall, the burning roof and tower   10
And Agamemnon dead.
                              Being so caught up,
So mastered by the brute blood of the air,
Did she put on his knowledge with his power
Before the indifferent beak could let her drop?   15

---

[1]**Leda and the Swan:** Leda, possessed by Zeus in the guise of a swan, gave birth to Helen of Troy and
the twins Castor and Pollux. (Leda was also the mother of Clytemnestra, Agamemnon's wife, who
murdered him on his return from the war at Troy.) Helen's abduction by Paris from her husband,
Menelaus, brother of Agamemnon, was the cause of the Trojan war. Yeats saw Leda as the recipient of an
annunciation that would found Greek civilization, as the Annunciation to Mary would found Christianity.

Ulysses is the Roman name for the Greek mythological character Odysseus, whose story is told in Homer's *The Iliad* and *The Odyssey*. Tennyson's speaker imagines the life of Ulysses after his return from the Trojan War (his ten-year journey home is the story presented in *The Odyssey*). His feelings (as Tennyson depicts them) might best be summed up by the poem's twenty-second and twenty-third lines: "How dull it is to pause, to make an end, / To rust unburnished, not to shine in use!"

Alfred, Lord Tennyson (1809–1892)

Ulysses[1] (1833, 1842)

It little profits that an idle king,
By this still hearth, among these barren crags,
Matched with an aged wife, I mete and dole
Unequal laws unto a savage race,
That hoard, and sleep, and feed, and know not me.   5
I cannot rest from travel; I will drink
Life to the lees. All times I have enjoyed
Greatly, have suffered greatly, both with those
That loved me, and alone; on shore, and when
Through scudding drifts the rainy Hyades[2]   10
Vext the dim sea. I am become a name;
For always roaming with a hungry heart
Much have I seen and known—cities of men
And manners, climates, councils, governments,
Myself not least, but honored of them all,—   15
And drunk delight of battle with my peers,
Far on the ringing plains of windy Troy.
I am a part of all that I have met;
Yet all experience is an arch wherethrough
Gleams that untraveled world whose margin fades   20
For ever and for ever when I move.
How dull it is to pause, to make an end,
To rust unburnished, not to shine in use!
As though to breathe were life! Life piled on life
Were all too little, and of one to me   25
Little remains; but every hour is saved
From that eternal silence, something more,
A bringer of new things; and vile it were
For some three suns to store and hoard myself,
And this gray spirit yearning in desire   30

---

[1]**Ulysses:** Tennyson's Ulysses (Greek *Odysseus*), restless after his return to Ithaca, eager to renew the life of great deeds he had known during the Trojan war and the adventures of his ten-year journey home, resembles the figure of Ulysses presented by Dante, *Inferno* XXVI.
[2]**Hyades:** A group of stars in the constellation Taurus, believed to foretell the coming of rain when they rose with the sun.

To follow knowledge like a sinking star,
Beyond the utmost bound of human thought.
    This is my son, mine own Telemachus,
To whom I leave the scepter and the isle,
Well-loved of me, discerning to fulfill   35
This labor, by slow prudence to make mild
A rugged people, and through soft degrees
Subdue them to the useful and the good.
Most blameless is he, centered in the sphere
Of common duties, decent not to fail   40
In offices of tenderness, and pay
Meet adoration to my household gods,
When I am gone. He works his work, I mine.
    There lies the port; the vessel puffs her sail;
There gloom the dark, broad seas. My mariners,   45
Souls that have toiled, and wrought, and thought with me,
That ever with a frolic welcome took
The thunder and the sunshine, and opposed
Free hearts, free foreheads—you and I are old;
Old age hath yet his honor and his toil.   50
Death closes all; but something ere the end,
Some work of noble note, may yet be done,
Not unbecoming men that strove with gods.
The lights begin to twinkle from the rocks;
The long day wanes; the slow moon climbs; the deep   55
Moans round with many voices. Come, my friends,
'Tis not too late to seek a newer world.
Push off, and sitting well in order smite
The sounding furrows; for my purpose holds
To sail beyond the sunset, and the baths   60
Of all the western stars, until I die.
It may be that the gulfs will wash us down;
It may be we shall touch the Happy Isles,[3]
And see the great Achilles, whom we knew.
Though much is taken, much abides; and though   65
We are not now that strength which in old days
Moved earth and heaven, that which we are, we are,
One equal temper of heroic hearts,
Made weak by time and fate, but strong in will
To strive, to seek, to find, and not to yield.   70

---

[3]**Happy Isles:** The Islands of the Blessed, or Elysium, the abode after death of those favored by the gods, especially heroes and patriots: supposed, in earlier myth, to be located beyond the western limits of the

Marilyn Hacker makes more playful use of mythological characters in her poem "Mythology," mixing details of classical (Greek and Roman) myths with contemporary details. However, she also has a point to make about all of this. How would you interpret her last line?

Marilyn Hacker (b. 1942)
Mythology (1986)

Penelope as a *garçon manqué*
weaves sonnets on a barstool among sailors,
tapping her iambs out on the brass rail.[1] Ours
is not the high-school text. Persephone
a.k.a. Télémaque-who-tagged-along,[2]   5
sleeps off her lunch on an Italian train
headed for Paris, while Ulysse-Maman[3]
plugs into the Shirelles singing her song
("What Does a Girl Do?"). What *does* a girl do
but walk across the world, her kid in tow,   10
stopping at stations on the way, with friends
to tie her to the mast when she gets too
close to the edge? And when the voyage ends,
what does a girl do? Girl, that's up to you.

---

[1]**Lines 1–3:** Penelope, in Homer's *Odyssey*, is the name of the wife Odysseus left behind; *garçon manqué*: that is, a boy in a girl's body; literally, a boy just lacking in "boyness"; "iambs": metrical feet. The incident may allude to the story of the German poet Goethe making love while composing a poem and tapping out the rhythm on his lover's backside.
[2]**Lines 4–5:** Persephone, in classical mythology, was the daughter of Ceres, the earth-goddess; abducted by Pluto, king of the underworld, Persephone spent the spring and summer on earth, the fall and winter in the underworld. "A.k.a.": also known as; *Télémaque* is the French form of Telemachus, the name of the diffident son of Odysseus, who accompanies his father on the last part of his wanderings.
[3]**Ulysse-Maman:** That is, Mama-Odysseus.

Poems for Further Reading

Robert Hayden (1913–1980)
O Daedalus,[1] Fly Away Home (1966)

Drifting night in the Georgia pines,
coonskin drum and jubilee banjo.
      Pretty Malinda, dance with me.

---

[1]**Daedalus:** In Greek legend, Daedalus is the great artificer and craftsman who built the labyrinth for King Minos of Crete, and was himself imprisoned there. Daedalus and his son Icarus fashioned wings for themselves to escape the labyrinth. Daedalus succeeded, but Icarus, ignoring his father's warning not to fly too near the sun (the wings were held together with wax), perished in the sea.

Night is juba,[2] night is conjo.[3]
　　Pretty Malinda, dance with me.　　　5

Night is an African juju man[4]
weaving a wish and a weariness together
　　to make two wings.

　　O fly away home fly away

Do you remember Africa?　　　　10

　　O cleave the air fly away home

My gran, he flew back to Africa,
just spread his arms and
　　flew away home.

Drifting night in the windy pines;　　15
night is a laughing, night is a longing.
　　Pretty Malinda, come to me.

Night is a mourning juju man
weaving a wish and a weariness together
　　to make two wings.　　　　20
　　O fly away home fly away

····▶ *Your* Turn

Talking and Writing about Lit

1. In "O Daedalus, Fly Away Home," African American poet Robert Hayden
incorporates ideas from African American folktales in which people suffering
under slavery rise up and fly back home to Africa. Look up the Greek myth
about Daedalus and Icarus. Why does Hayden choose to center his poem
around the character of Daedalus rather than Icarus?

---

[2]**juba:** A dance popular among Negro slaves in their quarters.
[3]**conjo:** Perhaps a corruption of *conjure*.
[4]**juju man:** Magician or conjurer who uses jujus, or charms and fetishes.

2. How do your interpret the last stanza of Hayden's poem (lines 18–21)? How
do you visualize them?

<u>**Seamus Heaney (b. 1939)**</u>
Hercules and Antaeus (1975)

Sky-born and royal,
snake-choker, dung-heaver,
his mind big with golden apples,
his future hung with trophies,

Hercules has the measure   5
of resistance and black powers
feeding off the territory.
Antaeus, the mould-hugger,

is weaned at last:
a fall was a renewal   10
but now he is raised up—
the challenger's intelligence

is a spur of light,
a blue prong graiping him
out of his element   15
into a dream of loss

and origins—the cradling dark,
the river-veins, the secret gullies
of his strength,
the hatching grounds   20

of cave and souterrain,
he has bequeathed it all
to elegists. Balor will die
and Byrthnoth and Sitting Bull.

Hercules lifts his arms   25
in a remorseless V,
his triumph unassailed
by the powers he has shaken,

and lifts and banks Antaeus
high as a profiled ridge,   30
a sleeping giant,
pap for the dispossessed.

·····▶ *Your* **Turn**
Talking and Writing about Lit

1. Look up the mythological figures Hercules and Antaeus. What elements of the mythic stories about these heroes has Seamus Heaney incorporated into "Hercules and Antaeus"?

2. Examine the very precise and regular form of "Hercules and Antaeus." What decisions has Heaney made about form here? Do you think they serve the poem well?

3. **DIY** Write a brief poem in which you recount a heroic deed performed by a friend or relative.

John Keats (1795–1821)
Ode on a Grecian Urn (1819)

Thou still unravished bride of quietness,
    Thou foster-child of silence and slow time,
Sylvan historian, who canst thus express
    A flowery tale more sweetly than our rhyme:
What leaf-fringed legend haunts about thy shape   5
    Of deities or mortals, or of both,
        In Tempe or the dales of Arcady?
    What men or gods are these? What maidens loth?
What mad pursuit? What struggle to escape?
    What pipes and timbrels? What wild ecstasy?   10

Heard melodies are sweet, but those unheard
    Are sweeter; therefore, ye soft pipes, play on;
Not to the sensual ear, but, more endeared,
    Pipe to the spirit ditties of no tone:
Fair youth, beneath the trees, thou canst not leave   15
    Thy song, nor ever can those trees be bare;
        Bold lover, never, never canst thou kiss,
Though winning near the goal—yet, do not grieve;
        She cannot fade, though thou hast not thy bliss,
    For ever wilt thou love, and she be fair!   20

Ah, happy, happy boughs! that cannot shed
    Your leaves, nor ever bid the spring adieu;
And, happy melodist, unwearièd,
    For ever piping songs for ever new;
More happy love! more happy, happy love!   25

For ever warm and still to be enjoyed,
    For ever panting and for ever young;
All breathing human passion far above,
    That leaves a heart high-sorrowful and cloyed,
        A burning forehead, and a parching tongue.   30

Who are these coming to the sacrifice?
    To what green altar, O mysterious priest,
Lead'st thou that heifer lowing at the skies,
    And all her silken flanks with garlands drest?
What little town by river or sea shore,   35
    Or mountain-built with peaceful citadel,
        Is emptied of its folk, this pious morn?
And, little town, thy streets for evermore
    Will silent be; and not a soul to tell
        Why thou are desolate, can e'er return.   40

O Attic shape! Fair attitude! with brede
    Of marble men and maidens overwrought,
With forest branches and the trodden weed;
    Thou, silent form, dost tease us out of thought
As doth eternity: Cold Pastoral!   45
    When old age shall this generation waste,
        Thou shalt remain, in midst of other woe
    Than ours, a friend to man, to whom thou say'st,
Beauty is truth, truth beauty,—that is all
        Ye know on earth, and all ye need to know.   50

·····➤ *Your* Turn
Talking and Writing about Lit

1. One of the striking things about this poem is the speaker's focus on the "freeze frame" of the lover pursuing his beloved. Have you ever paused a video or DVD at a moment that seemed particularly captivating? Describe that moment.

2. **DIY** Write a brief poem that depicts a "screen shot" of a moment in a film you found particularly meaningful.

Note: (49–50) In the 1820 edition of Keats's poems the words "Beauty is truth, truth beauty" were enclosed in quotation marks, and the poem is often reprinted that way. It is now generally agreed, however, on the basis of contemporary transcripts of Keats's poem, that Keats intended the entire last two lines to be spoken by the urn.

H.D. (1886–1961)
Adonis (1916)

1.

Each of us like you
has died once,
each of us like you
has passed through drift of wood-leaves
cracked and bent   5
and tortured and unbent
in the winter-frost,
then burnt into gold points,
lighted afresh,
crisp amber, scales of gold-leaf,   10
gold turned and re-welded
in the sun-heat

each of us like you
has died once,
each of us has crossed an old wood-path   15
and found the winter-leaves
so golden in the sun-fire
that even the live wood-flowers
were dark

2.

Not the gold on the temple-front   20
where you stand
is as gold as this
not the gold that fastens your sandal,
nor the gold, reft
through your chiseled locks,   25
is as gold as this last year's leaf,
not all the gold hammered and wrought
and beaten
on your lover's face,
brow and bare breast   30
is as golden as this.

each of us like you
has died once,
each of us like you
stands apart, like you   35
fit to be worshipped.

·····▶ *Your* Turn
Talking and Writing about Lit

1. In the Greek myth, the goddess Aphrodite falls in love with Adonis. He, however, is killed in a hunting accident. Afterward, a lovely blood-red flower springs up from the earth where he died. Identify the lines in the poem "Adonis" that refer to the myth.

2. How does H.D. carry the meaning of the poem beyond the myth itself? Why does the speaker repeat the refrain "Each of us like you . . . "?

Conrad Aiken (1889–1973)
The Wedding (1925)

At noon, Tithonus,[1] withered by his singing,
Climbing the oatstalk with his hairy legs,
Met gray Arachne,[2] poisoned and shrunk down
By her own beauty; pride had shriveled both.
In the white web—where seven flies hung wrapped—   5
She heard his footstep; hurried to him; bound him;
Enshrouded him in silk; then poisoned him.
Twice shrieked Tithonus, feebly; then was still.
Arachne loved him. Did he love Arachne?
She watched him with red eyes, venomous sparks,   10
And the furred claws outspread . . . "O sweet Tithonus!
Darling! Be kind, and sing that song again!
Shake the bright web again with that deep fiddling!
Are you much poisoned? sleeping? do you dream?
Darling Tithonus!"   15

            And Tithonus, weakly
Moving one hairy shin against the other
Within the silken sack, contrived to fiddle
A little tune, half-hearted: "Shrewd Arachne!
Whom pride in beauty withered to this shape   20
As pride in singing shriveled me to mine—
Unwrap me, let me go—and let me limp,

---

[1]**Tithonus:** In Greek legend, Tithonus, a beautiful and musically gifted youth, at the plea of his wife, Aurora, goddess of the dawn, to Zeus, was given eternal life but, unfortunately, without eternal youth. After many years and progressive aging, Tithonus was turned into a cicada by the pitying gods.
[2]**Arachne:** Arachne was a superb weaver who angered Athena by weaving a better tapestry than the goddess. Arachne tried to hang herself because of Athena's anger, but was spared and turned into a spider.

With what poor strength your venom leaves me, down
This oatstalk, and away."

Arachne, angry, 25
Stung him again, twirling him with rough paws,
The red eyes keen. "What! You would dare to leave me?
Then let you go. But sing that tune again—
So plaintive was it!"

And Tithonus faintly 30
Moved the poor fiddles, which were growing cold,
And sang: "Arachne, goddess envied of gods,
Beauty's eclipse eclipsed by angry beauty,
Have pity, do not ask the withered heart
To sing too long for you! My strength goes out, 35
Too late we meet for love. O be content
With friendship, which the noon sun once may kindle
To give one flash of passion, like a dewdrop,
Before it goes! . . . Be reasonable, Arachne!"

Arachne heard the song grow weaker, dwindle 40
To first a rustle, and then half a rustle,
And last a tick, so small no ear could hear it
Save hers, a spider's ear. And her small heart,
(Rusted away, like his, to a pinch of dust,)
Gleamed once, like his, and died. She clasped him tightly 45
And sunk her fangs in him. Tithonus dead,
She slept awhile, her last sensation gone;
Woke from the nap, forgetting him; and ate him.

•••••▶ *Your* Turn
Talking and Writing about Lit

1. Look up the stories of Tithonus and Arachne from Greek mythology.
   Summarize the two mythic tales.

2. After reading the poem and also the two characters' myths, do you have any
   more sympathy for Arachne, as Aiken presents her?

Sappho (c. 615 BC)
Invocation to Aphrodite (6th Century B.C.E.)

Translated by Richard Lattimore (1955)

Throned in splendor, deathless, O Aphrodite,
child of Zeus, charm-fashioner, I entreat you

not with griefs and bitternesses to break my
    spirit, O goddess;

standing by me rather, if once before now   5
far away you heard, when I called upon you,
left your father's dwelling place and descended,
    yoking the golden

chariot to sparrows, who fairly drew you
down in speed aslant the black world, the bright   10
trembling at the heart to the pulse of countless
    fluttering wingbeats.

Swiftly then they came, and you, blessed lady,
smiling on me out of immortal beauty,
asked me what affliction was on me, why I   15
    called thus upon you,

what beyond all else I would have befall my
tortured heart: "Whom then would you have
    Persuasion
force to serve desire in your heart? Who is it,   20
    Sappho, that hurt you?

Though she now escape you, she soon will follow;
though she take not gifts from you, she will give
    them:
though she love not, yet she will surely love you   25
    even unwilling."

In such guise come even again and set me
free from doubt and sorrow; accomplish all those
things my heart desires to be done; appear and
    stand at my shoulder.   30

·····▶ *Your* Turn
Talking and Writing about Lit

1. The speaker (evidently the poet Sappho herself) recalls an earlier time when
she called on the goddess Aphrodite to assist her in love. What is it the goddess promised to do for Sappho in the past? What does the speaker (Sappho)
want the goddess Aphrodite to do for her now?

2. Do you think that "Invocation to Aphrodite" is a lyric poem or a narrative poem?

Gary Soto (b. 1952)
The Skeptics (1995)

Pyrrho of Elis and Sextus Empiricus were Skeptics,
Two big-shot thinkers who argued
Over figs, wine, and the loveliness of their sex.
I crowed to my brother about them,
And one evening, with Fig Newton crumbs in our mouths,   5
I was Pyrrho and Rick was Sextus,
Both of us skeptical about getting good jobs.
I said, "Brother Sextus, what will you render on the canvas
When you're all grown up?" He chewed
On his Fig Newton and answered, "Pyrrho,   10
My young flame, I will draw the reality
Of dead dogs with their feet in the air."
I crowed, "Wow, Rick—I mean Sextus—that's pretty good."
In sandals, we went down to the liquor store,
Each of us in our imaginary Greek robes,   15
And stole a quart of beer. Neither of us was a skeptic
When we swigged on that quart
And walked by the house with a woman hammering walnuts,
The rise and fall of her buttery hand quivering
The two hairs on my chest. We had our figs and wine,   20
And what we Skeptics needed,
Or at least I, was three strokes of that hammering.
I flowed over in my robe and said, "We're Brothers Skeptic,
Ruled by cautious truths." She smiled,
Hammer raised, and said, "Sure you are."   25
Right away we got along, a womanly skeptic
With a nice swing. I sat on the steps,
A young man with his figs, his wine,
And, with my Greek name shed,
A reverent believer in a woman with hammer in hand.   30

•••••▶ *Your* Turn
Talking and Writing about Lit

1. In Gary Soto's "The Skeptics," Pyrrho and Sextus are historical figures, not mythological characters. Are there any mythological connotations to the hammer wielded by the walnut-cracking woman?

2. **DIY** Write a humorous poem (or prose poem) in which your speaker
pretends to be a historical or mythological figure.

Constantine Cavafy (1863–1933)
Ithaca (1894)

TRANSLATED BY BARRY B. POWELL

As you set out on your journey to Ithaca,
pray that your journey be a long one,
filled with adventure, filled with discovery.
Laestrygonians and Cyclopes,
the angry Poseidon—do not fear them: 5
you'll never find such things on your way
unless your sight is set high, unless a rare
excitement stirs your spirit and your body.
The Laestrygonians and Cyclopes,
the savage Poseidon—you won't meet them   10
so long as you do not admit them to your soul,
as long as your soul does not set them before you.
Pray that your road is a long one.
May there be many summer mornings
when with what pleasure, with what joy,   15
you enter harbors never seen before;
may you stop at Phoenician trading stations
to buy fine things,
mother of pearl and coral, amber and ebony,
and voluptuous perfumes of every kind   20
—buy as many voluptuous perfumes as you can;
and may you go to many Egyptian cities
to learn and learn from those who know.
Always keep Ithaca in your mind.
You are destined to arrive there.   25
But don't hurry your journey at all.
Far better if it takes many years,
and if you are old when you anchor at the island,
rich with all you have gained on the way,
not expecting that Ithaca will give you wealth.   30
Ithaca has given you a beautiful journey.
Without her you would never have set out.
She has no more left to give you.
And if you find her poor, Ithaca has not mocked you.
As wise as you have become, so filled with experience,   35
you will have understood what these Ithacas signify.

·····➤ *Your* Turn
Talking and Writing about Lit

1. How would you summarize what the speaker of Constantine Cavafy's poem "Ithaca" is saying to the Greek mythic hero Odysseus at the outset of his journey home? Does the speaker advise him to rush home to Ithaca or to enjoy the adventure?

2. How do Cavafy's imagined instructions to Odysseus at the outset of his journey fit with Tennyson's imagined description of Odysseus upon his return to Ithaca in "Ulysses" (see above). (Note that Ulysses is simply the Roman name for the Greek hero Odysseus; they are the same character.)

T.S. Eliot (1888–1965)
Journey of the Magi[1] (1927)

'A cold coming we had of it,[2]
Just the worst time of the year
For a journey, and such a long journey:
The ways deep and the weather sharp,
The very dead of winter.'   5
And the camels galled, sore-footed, refractory,
Lying down in the melting snow.
There were times we regretted
The summer palaces on slopes, the terraces,
And the silken girls bringing sherbet.   10
Then the camel men cursing and grumbling
And running away, and wanting their liquor and women,
And the night-fires going out, and the lack of shelters,
And the cities hostile and the towns unfriendly
And the villages dirty and charging high prices: 15
A hard time we had of it.
At the end we preferred to travel all night,
Sleeping in snatches,
With the voices singing in our ears, saying
That this was all folly.   20

---

[1]**Journey of the Magi:** The poem recreates the recollections of one of the three Wise Men, or Magi, who, guided by the star, had come to Bethlehem to witness the birth of Christ, as told in Matthew ii.1–2.
[2]**Lines 1–5:** The first five lines are adapted from the sermon preached at Christmas, 1622, by Bishop Lancelot Andrewes: "Last, we consider the *time* of their coming, the season of the yeare. It was no *summer Progresse.* A cold comming they had of it, at this time of the year; just, the worst time of the yeare, to take a journey, and specially a long journey, in. The waies deep, the weather sharp, the daies short, the sunn farthest off . . . , the very dead of *Winter.*"

Then at dawn we came down to a temperate valley,
Wet, below the snow line, smelling of vegetation;
With a running stream and a water-mill beating the darkness,
And three trees on the low sky,[3]
And an old white horse galloped away in the meadow.   25
Then we came to a tavern with vine-leaves over the lintel,
Six hands at an open door dicing for pieces of silver,
And feet kicking the empty wine-skins.
But there was no information, and so we continued
And arrived at evening, not a moment too soon   30
Finding the place; it was (you may say) satisfactory.

All this was a long time ago, I remember,
And I would do it again, but set down
This set down
This: were we led all that way for   35
Birth or Death? There was a Birth, certainly,
We had evidence and no doubt. I had seen birth and death,
But had thought they were different; this Birth was
Hard and bitter agony for us, like Death, our death.
We returned to our places, these Kingdoms,   40
But no longer at ease here, in the old dispensation,
With an alien people clutching their gods.
I should be glad of another death.

·····➤ *Your* Turn
Talking and Writing about Lit

1. Eliot's "Journey of the Magi" imagines, from the point of view of one of
   the Magi (wise men), the events related in the Bible's New Testament
   (Matthew 2:1–2): "Now when Jesus was born in Bethlehem of Judea in
   the days of Herod the king, behold, wise men from the East came to
   Jerusalem, saying, "Where is he who has been born king of the Jews? For
   we have seen his star in the East, and have come to worship him." What
   does Eliot's poem imply about the circumstances and experiences of the
   wise men?

2. How do you interpret the last line of Eliot's poem?

---

[3]**three trees on the low sky:** The image prefigures the three crosses of the Crucifixion, as line 27
suggests the Roman soldiers dicing for Christ's robe, as well as the pieces of silver paid to Judas for
betraying Christ.

Louise Glück (b. 1943)
The Magi (1975)

Toward world's end, through the bare
beginnings of winter, they are traveling again.
How many winters have we seen it happen,
watched the same sign come forward as they pass
cities sprung around this route their gold   5
engraved on the desert, and yet
held our peace, these
being the Wise, come to see at the accustomed hour
nothing changed: roofs, the barn
blazing in darkness, all they wish to see.   10

· · · · · ·▶ *Your* Turn
Talking and Writing about Lit

1. In Louise Glück's "The Magi," what does the word "again," in line 2 imply?

2. Compare Glück's "The Magi" with Eliot's "Journey of the Magi."

John Keats (1795–1821)
Ode to Psyche[1] (1819, 1820)

O Goddess! hear these tuneless numbers, wrung
   By sweet enforcement and remembrance dear,
And pardon that thy secrets should be sung
   Even into thine own soft-conchéd[2] ear;
Surely I dreamt today, or did I see   5
   The wingéd Psyche with awakened eyes?
I wandered in a forest thoughtlessly,
   And, on the sudden, fainting with surprise,
Saw two fair creatures, couchéd side by side
   In deepest grass, beneath the whisp'ring roof   10
   Of leaves and trembled blossoms, where there ran
      A brooklet, scarce espied:

'Mid hushed, cool-rooted flowers, fragrant-eyed,
   Blue, silver-white, and budded Tyrian,[3]

---

[1]**Ode to Psyche:** In Greek legend, Psyche (meaning "soul") was loved in secret and in darkness by Cupid, the "wingéd" son of the goddess Venus. After many trials Psyche was united with Cupid in immortality.
[2]**soft-conchéd:** shell-like
[3]**Tyrian:** Purple or red, as in the "royal" dye made in ancient Tyre.

They lay calm-breathing on the bedded grass;   15
    Their arms embracéd, and their pinions[4] too;
    Their lips touched not, but had not bade adieu,
As if disjoinéd by soft-handed slumber,
And ready still past kisses to outnumber
    At tender eye-dawn of aurorean[5] love: 20
       The wingéd boy I knew;
    But who wast thou, O happy, happy dove?
       His Psyche true!

O latest born and loveliest vision far
    Of all Olympus' faded hierarchy![6]   25
Fairer than Phoebe's[7] sapphire-regioned star,
    Or Vesper;[8] amorous glowworm of the sky;
Fairer than these, though temple thou hast none,
    Nor altar heaped with flowers;
Nor virgin choir to make delicious moan   30
    Upon the midnight hours;
No voice, no lute, no pipe, no incense sweet
    From chain-swung censer teeming;
No shrine, no grove, no oracle, no heat
    Of pale-mouthed prophet dreaming.   35

O brightest! though too late for antique vows,
    Too, too late for the fond believing lyre,
When holy were the haunted forest boughs,
    Holy the air, the water, and the fire;
Yet even in these days so far retired   40
    From happy pieties, thy lucent fans,[9]
    Fluttering among the faint Olympians,
I see, and sing, by my own eyes inspired.
So let me be thy choir, and make a moan
    Upon the midnight hours;   45
Thy voice, thy lute, thy pipe, thy incense sweet
    From swingéd censer teeming;
Thy shrine, thy grove, thy oracle, thy heat
    Of pale-mouthed prophet dreaming.

Yes, I will be thy priest, and build a fane[10]   50
    In some untrodden region of my mind,

---

[4]**pinions:** wings
[5]**aurorean:** dawning
[6]**Lines 24–25:** last of the deities to be added to the company of the Greek Olympian gods.
[7]**Phoebe's:** the moon's
[8]**Vesper:** the evening star
[9]**fans:** wings
[10]**fane:** temple

Where branchéd thoughts, new grown with pleasant pain,
 Instead of pines shall murmur in the wind:
Far, far around shall those dark-clustered trees
 Fledge the wild-ridgéd mountains steep by steep;   55
And there by zephyrs,[11] streams, and birds, and bees,
 The moss-lain Dryads[12] shall be lulled to sleep;
And in the midst of this wide quietness
A rosy sanctuary will I dress
With the wreathed trellis of a working brain,   60
 With buds, and bells, and stars without a name,
With all the gardener Fancy e'er could feign,
 Who breeding flowers, will never breed the same:
And there shall be for thee all soft delight
 That shadowy thought can win,   65
A bright torch, and a casement ope at night,
 To let the warm Love[13] in!

---

[11]**zephyrs:** breezes
[12]**Dryads:** tree-nymphs
[13]**Love:** i.e., Cupid.

• • • • •▶ *Your* **Turn**
Talking and Writing about Lit

1. John Keats represents the happy ending to Psyche and Cupid's romance. The earlier part of their story involves a truly vengeful "mother-in-law" (Venus,

The Myth of Icarus, Imagined by Poet and Painter

Landscape with the Fall of Icarus by Pieter Brue the Elder

The Greek myth of Icarus actually begins on the island of Crete, with a powerful king (Minos), a formidable monster (the Minotaur), and a maze (the

a.k.a. Aphrodite), who, out of jealousy, inflicts incredible tortures and torments on poor Psyche. In choosing to relate the happier portion of the story, instead of the tormenting of Psyche, what do you think is Keats's purpose?

2. **DIY**   Research any Greek or Roman myth and write a poem that incorporates elements of the myth.

W. H. Auden (1907–1973)
Musée des Beaux Arts[1] (1938)

About suffering they were never wrong,
The Old Masters: how well they understood
Its human position; how it takes place
While someone else is eating or opening a window or just
 walking dully along;
How, when the aged are reverently, passionately waiting   5
For the miraculous birth, there always must be
Children who did not specially want it to happen, skating
On a pond at the edge of the wood:
They never forgot
That even the dreadful martyrdom must run its course   10
Anyhow in a corner, some untidy spot
Where the dogs go on with their doggy life and the torturer's horse
Scratches its innocent behind on a tree.

---

[1]**Musée des Beaux Arts:** The Museum of the Fine Arts, in Brussels.

Labyrinth). The story includes Icarus's loving father Daedalus (see Robert Hayden's poem "O Daedalus, Fly Away Home"). Daedalus had constructed the Labyrinth for the tyrant King Minos, but now he and his son, Icarus, were being held prisoner there, trapped by the fearsome Minotaur (who was half-bull). Daedalus—a crafty inventor—fashioned wings for himself and his son, made of feathers and held together with wax. Before they took flight from the Labyrinth, Daedalus warned his son not to dip down too close to the sea where he might accidentally wet his wings, and he warned him not to fly too high where proximity to the sun might melt the wax holding the wings together. Icarus tragically forgot his father's warnings as he thrilled to the sensations of soaring high in the sky, and he flew too close to the sun. His death is depicted in Brueghel's painting.

In Brueghel's *Icarus*,[2] for instance: how everything turns away
Quite leisurely from the disaster; the plowman may   15
Have heard the splash, the forsaken cry,
But for him it was not an important failure; the sun shone
As it had to on the white legs disappearing into the green
Water; and the expensive delicate ship that must have seen
Something amazing, a boy falling out of the sky,   20
Had somewhere to get to and sailed calmly on.

---

[2]**Brueghel's *Icarus*:** *Landscape with the Fall of Icarus*, by Pieter Brueghel the elder (1525?–1569), located in the Brussels Museum. According to Greek myth, Daedalus and his son Icarus escaped from imprisonment by using homemade wings of wax; but Icarus flew too near the sun, the wax melted, and he fell into the sea and drowned. In the Brueghel painting the central figure is a peasant plowing, and several other figures are more immediately noticeable than Icarus who, disappearing into the sea, is easy to miss in the lower right-hand corner. Equally ignored by the figures is a dead body in the woods.

·····▶ *Your* **Turn**
Talking and Writing about Lit

1. How does Auden, in his poem "Musée des Beaux Arts," manage to link ancient myth and everyday life?
2. What details in Auden's poem help to make the drowning of Icarus seem like a real event that might elicit our sympathy?

Talking Lit

Judith Ortiz Cofer explains how she later discovered that the Puerto Rican stories her mother used to tell her as a child were actually "ancient folklore brought to the colonies by Spaniards from their own versions of even older myths of Greek and Roman origins." Renee Shea explains the importance of storytelling to Ana Castillo's poetry.

Judith Ortiz Cofer, "Tales Told under the Mango Tree," from *Silent Dancing: A Remembrance of a Puerto Rican Childhood* (1990)

"Colorín, colorado este cuento se ha acabado."[1] Mamá would slap her knees with open palms and say this little rhyme to indicate to the children sitting around her under the giant mango tree that the story was finished. It was time for us to go play and leave the women alone to embroider in the shade of the tree and to talk about serious things.

I remember that tree as a natural wonder. It was large, with a trunk that took four or five children holding hands to reach across. Its leaves were so thick that the shade it cast made a cool room where we took refuge from the hot sun. When an

---

[1]**"Colorín, colorado este cuento se ha acabado":** "Colorin colorado [nonsense syllables], this story has ended."

unexpected shower caught us there, the women had time to gather their embroidery materials before drops came through the leaves. But the most amazing thing about that tree was the throne it had made for Mamá. On the trunk there was a smooth seat-like projection. It was perfect for a story-teller. She would take her place on the throne and lean back. The other women—my mother and her sisters—would bring towels to sit on; the children sat anywhere. Sometimes we would climb to a thick branch we called "the ship," to the right of the throne, and listen there. "The ship" was a thick limb that hung all the way down to the ground. Up to three small children could straddle this branch while the others bounced on the end that sat near the ground making it sway like a ship. When Mamá told her stories, we sat quietly on our crow's nest because if anyone interrupted her narrative she should stop talking and no amount of begging would persuade her to finish the story that day.

The first time my mother took my brother and me back to Puerto Rico, we were stunned by the heat and confused by a houseful of relatives. Mamá's *casa* was filled to capacity with grandchildren, because two of the married daughters had come to stay there until their husbands sent for them: my mother and the two of us and her oldest sister with her five children. Mamá still had three of her own children at home, ranging in age from a teenage daughter to my favorite uncle who was six months older than me.

Our solitary life in New Jersey, where we spent our days inside a small dark apartment watching television and waiting for our father to come home on leave from the navy, had not prepared us for life in Mamá's house or for the multitude of cousins, aunts and uncles pulling us into their loud conversations and rough games. For the first few days my little brother kept his head firmly buried in my mother's neck, while I stayed relatively close to her; but being nearly six, and able to speak as loudly as anyone, I soon joined Mamá's tribe.

In the last few weeks before the beginning of school, when it was too hot for cooking until it was almost dark and when mothers would not even let their boys go to the playgrounds and parks for fear of sunstroke, Mamá would lead us to the mango tree, there to spin the web of her *cuentos*[2] over us, making us forget the heat, the mosquitoes, our past in a foreign country, and even the threat of the first day of school looming just ahead.

It was under that mango tree that I first began to feel the power of words. I cannot claim to have always understood the point of the stories I heard there. Some of these tales were based on ancient folklore brought to the colonies by Spaniards from their own versions of even older myths of Greek and Roman origins—which, as I later discovered through my insatiable reading—had been modified in clever ways to fit changing times. María Sabida became the model Mamá used for the "prevailing woman"—the woman who "slept with one eye open"—whose wisdom was gleaned through the senses: from the natural world and from ordinary experiences. Her main virtue was that she was always alert and never a victim. She was by implication contrasted to María La Loca, that poor girl who gave it all up for love, becoming a victim of her own foolish heart.

[. . .] To entertain myself, I would make up stories about the smartest girl in all of Puerto Rico.

---

[2] **cuentos:** Stories.

When María Sabida was only six years old, I began, she saved her little brother's life. He was dying of a broken heart, you see, for he desperately wanted some sweet guavas that grew at the top of a steep, rocky hill near the lair of a fierce dragon. No one had ever dared to climb that hill, though everyone could see the huge guava tree and the fruit, as big as pears, hanging from its branches. María Sabida's little brother had stared at the tree until he had made himself sick from yearning for the forbidden fruit.

Everyone knew that the only way to save the boy was to give him one of the guavas. María Sabida's parents were frantic with worry. The little boy was fading fast. The father tried climbing the treacherous hill to the guava tree, but the rocks were loose and for every step forward he took, he slipped back three. He returned home. The mother spent her days cooking delicious meals with which to tempt her little son to eat, but he just turned his sad eyes to the window in his room from where he could see the guava tree loaded with the only food he wanted. The doctor came to examine the boy and pronounced him as good as gone. The priest came and told the women they should start making their black dresses. All hope seemed lost when María Sabida, whose existence everyone seemed to have forgotten, came up with an idea to save her brother one day while she was washing her hair in the special way her grandmother had taught her.

Her Mamá had shown her how to collect rainwater—water from the sky—into a barrel, and then, when it was time to wash her hair, how to take a fresh coconut and draw the oil from its white insides. You then took a bowl of clear rainwater and added the coconut oil, using the mixture to rinse your hair. Her Mamá had shown her how the rainwater, coming as it did from the sky, had little bits of starshine in it. This starstuff was what made your hair glossy, the oil was to make it stick.

It was while María Sabida was mixing the starshine that she had the brilliant idea which saved her brother. She ran to her father who was in the stable feeding the mule and asked if she could borrow the animal that night. The man, startled by his daughter's wild look (her hair was streaming wet and she still held the coconut scraps in her hands) at first just ordered his daughter into the house, thinking that she had gone crazy with grief over her brother's imminent death. But María Sabida could be stubborn, and she refused to move until her parents heard what she had to say. The man called his wife to the stable, and when María Sabida had finished telling them her plan, he still thought she had lost her mind. He agreed with his desperate wife that at this point anything was worth trying. They let María Sabida have the mule to use that night.

María Sabida then waited until it was pitch black. She knew there would be no moon that night. Then she drew water from her rainbarrel and mixed it with plenty of coconut oil and plastered her mule's hoofs with it. She led the animal to the bottom of the rocky hill where the thick, sweet smell of ripe guavas was irresistible. María Sabida felt herself caught in the spell. Her mouth watered and she felt drawn to the guava tree. The mule must have felt the same thing because it started walking ahead of the girl with quick, sure steps. Though rocks came tumbling down, the animal found footing, and in so doing, left a shiny path with the bits of starshine that María Sabida had glued to its hoofs. María Sabida kept her eyes on the bright trail because it was a dark, dark night.

As she approached the guava tree, the sweet aroma was like a liquid that she drank through her nose. She could see the fruit within arms-reach when the old mule stretched her neck to eat one and a horrible scaly arm reached out and yanked the animal off the path. María Sabida quickly grabbed three guavas and ran down the golden trail all the way back to her house.

When she came into her little brother's room, the women had already gathered around the bed with their flowers and their rosaries, and because María Sabida was a little girl herself and could not see past the crowd she thought for one terrible minute that she was too late. Luckily, her brother smelled the guavas from just this side of death and he sat up in bed. María Sabida pushed her way through the crowd and gave him one to eat. Within minutes the color returned to his cheeks. Everyone rejoiced remembering other wonderful things that she had done, and why her middle name was "Sabida."

And, yes, María Sabida ate one of the enchanted guavas herself and was never sick a day in her long life. The third guava was made into a jelly that could cure every childhood illness imaginable, from a toothache to the chicken pox.

"Colorín, colorado . . . " I must have said to myself, "Colorín colorado . . . " as I embroidered my own fable, listening all the while to that inner voice which, when I was very young, sounded just like Mamá's when she told her stories in the parlor or under the mango tree. And later, as I gained more confidence in my own ability, the voice telling the story became my own.

Renee H. Shea, "No Silence for This Dreamer: The Stories of Ana Castillo" (2000)

While, of course, Castillo would like for her work to be admired and to have a wide readership, what is most important to her is for it to be understood, particularly by the brown women who are so much like her—the audience she imagines when she is writing and an audience she feels has been overlooked and undervalued. She has made these ideas quite explicit in her ground-breaking theoretical work, *Massacre of the Dreamers: Essays on Xicanisma* (University of New Mexico, 1994), in which she defines the "Mestiza/Mexic Amerindian woman's identity" through the concept of "Xicanisma," a term she coined to capture the concept of Chicana feminism. Writing against an Anglocentric perspective and carefully distinguishing her concerns and position from those of white feminists, Castillo's essay collection is a manifesto on racism, machisma, sexuality, mothering, spirituality, and language. The title derives from the legend that the Aztec ruler Montezuma sought out the people who he had heard dreamed of the fall of his empire and had them massacred. No one, after that, dared tell of their dreams. Castillo includes herself in "we, the silenced dreamers" who must reclaim the vision of wholeness—a spiritually grounded self defined apart from "the greed on which patriarchy is based" and living in harmony with the natural world. In this work, she analyzes the forces that have instilled self-contempt in the mestiza and calls for recognition of the vast difference between the reality of the mestiza and that of the dominant cultures. Castillo intends for this collection, as she writes in her introduction, to be a contribution to "the ongoing polemic of our 500-year status as countryless residents on land that is now the United States."

Massacre of the Dreamers made her Dr. Castillo. The University of Bremen in Germany awarded her a Doctorate in American Studies in 1991, accepting this collection in lieu of a conventional doctoral dissertation. Castillo explains that since the 1970s, European academics have taken an interest in Native American and Chicano studies, and by the 1980s had become interested in women within these groups. Dieter Herms, former dean of the American Studies Program at the University of Bremen, had traveled to the U.S., where he met Castillo and invited her to give a keynote address for an annual conference of German Americanists. *My Father Was a Toltec* and *The Mixquiahuala Letters* were being used in Germany as Chicana feminist theory, and when Castillo told Herms that one day she was going to sit down and write her ideas out in essay form, he told her that when she did, she should submit it as a formal dissertation.

In the tradition of the academic world, the approval process was lengthy and often contentious, but Herms, who became very ill with cancer, remained Castillo's champion and shepherded the book through the necessary channels. Castillo traveled to Germany, where she successfully defended the work a few months before Herms's death. While *Massacre of the Dreamers* has the requisite theoretical underpinnings expected of a dissertation in interdisciplinary studies, including references to critical work in social sciences, history, and literature, the stark difference is in approach. Subverting the objective voice of an allegedly impartial researcher, this work, as Castillo announces in her introduction, "directed itself to the subject of this thesis rather than to the academy." This is a dissertation by, for, and about Chicanas. It seeks to raise consciousness of their history and to incite change in their self-awareness and, thus, their future. In the call for inclusion, its message is a revolutionary one calling for change throughout the culture.

Not surprisingly, one of those changes, Castillo argues, will come about through a "re-visioning" of language. Not interested in becoming part of an existing discourse, Castillo looks toward creating a new, more inclusive one. She calls for a critical understanding of the consequences of being marginalized from the language of the dominant society and writes of the need to take on "the re-visioning of our own culture's metaphors"—not only to understand but to act on the bone-and-blood link between language and identity, the topic of an earlier poem, "A Christmas Gift for the President of the United States, Chicano Poets, and a Marxist or Two I've Known in My Time":

> My verses have no legitimacy.
> A white woman inherits
> her father's library,
> her brother's friends, Privilege
> gives language that escapes me.
> Past my Nahua eyes
> and Spanish surname, English syntax
> makes its way to my mouth
> with the grace of a club foot.

Castillo writes and publishes some poetry in Spanish, but she writes mostly in English, a decision, she says, she made over 20 years ago—"not because I was trying to reach a gringo audience. But I was raised in Chicago without the privilege of bilingual education, so the people I thought would read my work would be the Chicanos who read English. I didn't learn to write in Spanish." She has stated in interviews that the English she writes is not "white standard English" and that an essential element of her work is the distinctive language of the narrator, particularly in *Sapagonia*, where the narrator's pretentiousness is signaled by the second-language English he proudly uses.

When she sits down to write, language is not the only choice Castillo has to make, since she feels equally at home in poetry, fiction, and nonfiction. She claims that the choice is sometimes hers, sometimes not—"Sometimes with poetry, it's like a meteorite"—and that sometimes there is no real need for choice: "I have what people have told me is a quick left brain/right brain switch. I have worked, for example, on *Massacre of the Dreamers* with *So Far From God*, then the short stories, then back to painting, then some poetry—and that was all in one day! At some point, I say, 'Enough is enough,' go back to the easel, and spend the rest of the day painting." Although Castillo originally intended to be a visual artist, she had stopped painting for over 17 years, then resumed around 1990 when she was in New Mexico and a friend gave her a box of paints and brushes, along with the encouragement to take up art again: "I felt confident enough in my writing at that time that it didn't matter what people thought of me as a painter. I paint for myself." And she paints herself: "My son has gotten me to do a couple of him, but very rarely. Usually, I paint myself in whatever is going on at the moment. Then, I don't necessarily put that in my writing."

Castillo is never alone in her creative process. One of the key chapters in *Massacre of the Dreamers* is about spirituality. In the doctrine of Xicanisma, spirituality involves acceptance of self in the context of forces that Western thought might consider "supernatural" and requires rejection of the hierarchical thinking characteristic of Western culture. In Chicana culture, spiritualism is embodied in *curanderas* and *brujas*, the latter spiritual healers or psychics, by Castillo's definition, the former "specialized healers, learned in the knowledge of specifically healing the body." Castillo is the granddaughter of a *curandera*, and it is she, Castillo says, "who taught me how to love and care for other living things. We lived in the heart of Chicago in a flat in the back with a kitchen looking out into a nasty, rat-infested alley. Yet she grew her herbs there, in coffee cans." In the introduction to *Toltec*, Castillo tells a moving story of beginning to write at age nine when this grandmother, her *abuelita*, died. "My lines were short, roughly whittled *saetas* [flamenco-style songs] of sorrow spun out of the biting late winter of Chicago," she writes—and so Ana the writer was born out of the death of the woman who was and is her spiritual guide.

Castillo is herself a *curandera*, but explains that she has been reluctant to take on that lifestyle. In 1997, she was crowned "a *curandera* and hail-maker by the Nahua people of Central Mexico, the region of my ancestry." She believes this is work she is destined to do, but chooses not to elaborate on what that means: "I'm not trying to be mysterious, but as I learn and accept my responsibilities and duties, I must humbly keep them private."

CUTTING EDGES:
Protest and
Performance Poetry

 graffiti uses elements
of protest and performance.

SPEAKING OUT with style—that's what the spoken word or
hip-hop poet does in performance, and it's also what the graffiti artist does in spray paint on city walls, the visual equivalent
of the verbal message conveyed by the performance poet. The
graffiti artist also often mixes pictures and text (visual and verbal messages) like the designer of a web page might do, and
sometimes with equally startling colors to please the eye and
get our attention for the message.

That message might be militant, sexy or poignant—like
the graffito here reading "We Love You Miguel," a tribute to a
friend who died at the age of 20, or the one reading "Brothers
We Lost." The message might incorporate pop culture images
or everyday images—as in the street mural here with elaborate
tags (artists' stylized graffiti signatures) that also picture
lipstick, a hairbrush brushing long hair and messages added
later by others (graffiti commenting on graffiti)—"Raw Power,"
"2-Tone!!" and "Shock and Bore."

Whatever the content, these visual "spoken words" are
messages from (and to and about) ordinary people, which is also
a characteristic of the poetry to which they are a counterpart.

Walt Whitman refers to the voice of his poetry as "my barbaric yawp"

> I too am not a bit tamed, I too am untranslatable,
> I sound my barbaric yawp over the roofs of the world.
> ("Song of Myself," section 52)

"Barbaric" suggests someone uneducated and unlettered, and "yawp" is the sound of a sound itself: a cry, a shout, a yelling out, without a specific meaning. Yet no one would accuse Whitman of being too ignorant, too uneducated, or too unsophisticated to be a serious poet. Whitman wrote his poems in the vernacular (the everyday language of ordinary people), and he intended for his work to be a democratizing force. It's not surprising, then, that some spoken word poets (such as Tato LaViera) have acknowledged his influence.

The most authentic, exciting poetry has always come up from the streets, the fields, and the workplaces. Whitman himself sought inspiration in those city streets and workshops, in factories, in fields, and in the neighborhoods and households of ordinary working people. He didn't need a Harvard education or a formal grounding in academic tradition to master his craft or to understand its traditions and conventions. Whitman read and studied and went out into the world to observe and experience it because he wanted his voice to reflect that world and the lives of the ordinary Americans in it. His poetry is an expression of that world and those lives, and it enters the American tradition with perhaps greater force than any other because it confers and affirms the integrity and legitimacy of any poet's right to "cry out" and write about what she or he sees and feels and thinks.

The poets in this chapter belong very much to the tradition established by Whitman. They are free voices, steeped in an intense awareness of life lived at the level of the common exchange of work and dreams, of the interplay between hope and what is risked each day on the street, between the next paycheck and the rent.

Slam, Hip-Hop, and Spoken Word Poetry

If any development emphasizes and reaffirms the vital connection and relationship between song and poetry in recent years, it is the emergence of poetry slams, hip-hop, and spoken word poetry.

The slams (competitive poetry reading events) have grown out of street corner traditions such as "toasting" or "the dozens" in which contestants strive to outdo one another in word invention, insult, rhyme, and meter to celebrate the prowess, inventiveness, and wit of the composer while denigrating those who are competing against him or her.

Hip-hop (and to an extent rap) has its roots in the same tradition. The addition of instrumentation and musical arrangements has created an entirely new genre of popular music. Spoken word poetry carries many of the same qualities of hip-hop and slam into the venue of poetry as performance and not just as poetry to be read on the page. Spoken word attempts to infuse the language of the poem with the same feeling of immediacy and sense of spontaneity.

Suheir Hammad's poem "First Writing Since" refers very directly to the events of September 11, 2001, and the days that followed the attacks. The poet, who is a Palestinian American, began her life in the refugee camps in Jordan; spent her early childhood years in Beirut, Lebanon, while the civil war there was growing in intensity and viciousness; but grew to maturity in Crown Heights, Brooklyn, after she immigrated with her parents to the United States.

Suheir Hammad (b. 1972)
First Writing Since (2001)

1. there have been no words.
i have not written one word.
no poetry in the ashes south of canal street.
no prose in the refrigerated trucks driving debris and dna.
not one word.   5

today is a week, and seven is of heavens, gods, science.
evident out my kitchen window is an abstract reality.
sky where once was steel.
smoke where once was flesh.

fire in the city air and i feared for my sister's life in a way never   10
before. and then, and now, i fear for the rest of us.

first, please god, let it be a mistake, the pilot's heart failed, the
plane's engine died.
then please god, let it be a nightmare, wake me now.
please god, after the second plane, please, don't let it be anyone   15
who looks like my brothers.

i do not know how bad a life has to break in order to kill.
i have never been so hungry that i willed hunger
i have never been so angry as to want to control a gun over a pen.
not really.   20
even as a woman, as a palestinian, as a broken human being.
never this broken.

more than ever, i believe there is no difference.
the most privileged nation, most americans do not know the difference
between indians, afghanis, syrians, muslims, sikhs, hindus.   25
more than ever, there is no difference.

2. thank you korea for kimchi and bibim bob, and corn tea and the
genteel smiles of the wait staff at wonjo—smiles never revealing
the heat of the food or how tired they must be working long midtown
shifts. thank you korea, for the belly craving that brought me into   30
the city late the night before and diverted my daily train ride into
the world trade center.

there are plenty of thank yous in ny right now. thank you for my
lazy procrastinating late ass. thank you to the germs that had me
call in sick. thank you, my attitude, you had me fired the week   35
before. thank you for the train that never came, the rude nyer who
stole my cab going downtown. thank you for the sense my mama
     gave me
to run. thank you for my legs, my eyes, my life.

3. the dead are called lost and their families hold up shaky
printouts in front of us through screens smoked up.   40

we are looking for iris, mother of three. please call with any
information. we are searching for priti, last seen on the 103rd
floor. she was talking to her husband on the phone and the line
went. please help us find george, also known as adel. his family is
waiting for him with his favorite meal. i am looking for my son, who   45
was delivering coffee. i am looking for my sister girl, she started
her job on monday.

i am looking for peace. i am looking for mercy. i am looking for
evidence of compassion. any evidence of life. i am looking for
life.   50

4. ricardo on the radio said in his accent thick as yuca, "i will
feel so much better when the first bombs drop over there. and my
friends feel the same way."

on my block, a woman was crying in a car parked and stranded in hurt.
i offered comfort, extended a hand she did not see before she said,   55
"we're gonna burn them so bad, i swear, so bad." my hand went to my
head and my head went to the numbers within it of the dead iraqi
children, the dead in nicaragua. the dead in rwanda who had to vie
with fake sport wrestling for america's attention.

yet when people sent emails saying, this was bound to happen, lets   60
not forget u.s. transgressions, for half a second i felt resentful.
hold up with that, cause i live here, these are my friends and fam,
and it could have been me in those buildings, and we're not bad

people, do not support america's bullying. can i just have a half
second to feel bad?   65

if i can find through this exhaust people who were left behind to
mourn and to resist mass murder, i might be alright.

thank you to the woman who saw me brinking my cool and
        blinking back
tears. she opened her arms before she asked "do you want a hug?" a
big white woman, and her embrace was the kind only people with the   70
warmth of flesh can offer. i wasn't about to say no to any comfort.
"my brother's in the navy," i said. "and we're arabs." "wow, you
got double trouble." word.

5. one more person ask me if i knew the hijackers.
one more motherfucker ask me what navy my brother is in.   75
one more person assume no arabs or muslims were killed.
one more person assume they know me, or that i represent a people.
or that a people represent an evil. or that evil is as simple as a
flag and words on a page.

we did not vilify all white men when mcveigh bombed oklahoma.   80
america did not give out his family's addresses or where he went to
church. or blame the bible or pat robertson.

and when the networks air footage of palestinians dancing in the
street, there is no apology that hungry children are bribed with
sweets that turn their teeth brown. that correspondents edit images.   85
that archives are there to facilitate lazy and inaccurate
journalism.

and when we talk about holy books and hooded men and death,
        why do we
never mention the kkk?

if there are any people on earth who understand how new york is   90
feeling right now, they are in the west bank and the gaza strip.

6. today it is ten days. last night bush waged war on a man once
openly funded by the
cia. i do not know who is responsible. read too many books, know
too many people to believe what i am told. i don't give a fuck about   95
bin laden. his vision of the world does not include me or those i
love. and petitions have been going around for years trying to get

the u.s. sponsored taliban out of power. shit is complicated, and i
don't know what to think.

but i know for sure who will pay.   100

in the world, it will be women, mostly colored and poor. women will
have to bury children, and support themselves through grief. "either
you are with us, or with the terrorists"—meaning keep your people
under control and your resistance censored. meaning we got the loot
and the nukes.   105

in america, it will be those amongst us who refuse blanket attacks on
the shivering. those of us who work toward social justice, in
support of civil liberties, in opposition to hateful foreign
policies.

i have never felt less american and more new yorker—particularly   110
brooklyn, than these past days. the stars and stripes on all these
cars and apartment windows represent the dead as citizens first—not
family members, not lovers.

i feel like my skin is real thin, and that my eyes are only going to
get darker. the future holds little light.   115

my baby brother is a man now, and on alert, and praying five times a
day that the orders he will take in a few days time are righteous and
will not weigh his soul down from the afterlife he deserves.

both my brothers—my heart stops when i try to pray—not a beat to
disturb my fear. one a rock god, the other a sergeant, and both   120
palestinian, practicing muslim, gentle men. both born in brooklyn
and their faces are of the archetypal arab man, all eyelashes and
nose and beautiful color and stubborn hair.

what will their lives be like now?

over there is over here.   125

7. all day, across the river, the smell of burning rubber and limbs
floats through. the sirens have stopped now. the advertisers are
back on the air. the rescue workers are traumatized. the skyline is
brought back to human size. no longer taunting the gods with its
height.   130

i have not cried at all while writing this. i cried when i saw those
buildings collapse on themselves like a broken heart. i have never
owned pain that needs to spread like that. and i cry daily that my
brothers return to our mother safe and whole.

there is no poetry in this. there are causes and effects. there are   135
symbols and ideologies. mad conspiracy here, and information we will
never know. there is death here, and there are promises of more.

there is life here. anyone reading this is breathing, maybe hurting,
but breathing for sure. and if there is any light to come, it will
shine from the eyes of those who look for peace and justice after the   140
rubble and rhetoric are cleared and the phoenix has risen.

affirm life.
affirm life.
we got to carry each other now.
you are either with life, or against it.   145
affirm life.

    As the poet herself has said, she received her education as much on the
streets and through the sounds and language of popular music as from the New
York City Public School system. Her embrace of those rhythms and that vocabulary can be seen to combine here with her own awareness of herself and her family, divided between identities more crucially than ever before after the towers fell.
In presenting that division she also describes the rich diversity of the city and its
cohesiveness in the aftermath of disaster. At the same time, the poem poses important questions about the motivations for judging people and the consequences of
stereotyping: "one more person assume they know me, or that I represent a people/
or that a people represent an evil. Or that evil is as simple as a/flag and words on
a page." The poem's immediacy and freshness is still evident, even as the horrific
source of its inspiration is receding into history.
    Regie Cabico, a national poetry slam champion, personifies poems them-
selves by imagining them as himself and imagining them as women and
goddesses.

Regie Cabico
tribute: the poet is shiva isis mothermary nefertiti & judy garland (1998)

together they got a 9 octave range/
keepin' the whole world hummin'

i gotta to write
　　how beautiful it must be
　　　　to leave apparition on tile &　　　　　　5

ride down the nile wit' crocodile lightin'
　　fireflies 'n cattails

sometimes i wear isis bracelets
& sashay down the streets like shiva/

& i deliver my fierceness　　　　　　　　　10

shoot/id marry 'em all / be out predictin'
disasters/be my own fortune teller
have
　　　　　　　　a 1-man show at carnegie hall

my poems'll clap so loud fo' me & dey　　　15
gonna take care of me when I'm old/

dey'll be datin' other psalms

the boys like ntozake & the girls like allen ginsberg
cuz ever since dey was little
you'd swear their skirts were high & raunchy　　20

& when i'm 95 & my back be hurtin'
& i can't pick no letters
no more/

　　my little great haiku child/
　　wd've grown to be sestina & ask me　　　25
　　to march her down the aisle

so i'll pull out mary's wedding gown & veil/
& I'll hand her nefertiti's ring &
ol' judy's gonna be there/ yr gonna luv to hear hr
sing　　　　　　　　　　　　　　　　　30

Toward the poem's conclusion, the poet sees his own work as a father might see a daughter: "& when i'm 95 & my back be hurtin'/& i can't pick no letters/no more/my little great haiku child/wd've grown to be sestina & ask me/to march her down the aisle."

In "built like that," Alix Olson examines with rap-like relentlessness the varieties of artistic presentations in a search for a way in which to define and describe her own art.

Alix Olson
Built Like That (2001)

some art's just like a teacup,
when you're looking for a beer
some art, some art, it scares you and some,
some art's about the fear.
some art is a highbrow thing   5
some art's about the eyebrow ring
some art's about the tattoo
some art's about the artist
and that art's not meant for you:

but my art's not made like that   10
my art's not meant for that
no, my art's not built like that
my art's not dressed for that.

some art's ecclesiastes,
some art's about the sin   15
some art it seems just heavenly
and that's great if it lets you in.
some art's all multi-colored til it goes behind the scene
it comes out all multi-corporate
then it only comes in green: 20

but my art's not made like that
my art's not meant for that
my art's not built like that
my art's not dressed for that.

some art's a one-hit wonder why   25
they think we're deaf and dumb
it's like the disciples at the last supper
if God fed 'em bubble gum.
some art's a pedigree whitewash,
a cryptic clean cover-up   30
my art don't need no ivory badge to back up
what's in its gut:

my art's not made like that
my art's not meant for that
no, my art's not built like that   35
my art's not dressed for that.

some art don't care about you,
what you say or what you do
my art's the Mona Lisa
and she's looking straight at you.   40
my art wears the same clothes seven days a week
cause my art don't seem to care about
what other people think.

some art's real nice to look at,
some art's all neat and clean   45
my art forgot her tampon
and she's bleeding through her jeans.
my art forgot her tampon
and she's bleeding through her jeans
yeah, my art don't need no tampon   50
she'll just bleed through your dreams:

my art's just made like that
my art's just meant for that
my art's just built like that
yeah, my art's just dressed for that   55
my art's just made like that
my art's just meant for that
my art's just built like that
my heart's just
built like that.   60

The poem proposes, examines, considers, and dismisses "art" as a number of possibilities ("some art's just like a teacup,/when you're looking for a beer/some art, some art, it scares you and some,/some art's about the fear."). Near the poem's conclusion, Olson defines her own art: "some art's real nice to look at,/some art's all neat and clean/my art forgot her tampon/and she's bleeding through her jeans./yeah, my art don't need no tampon/she'll just bleed through your dreams."

Tato LaViera
boricua (1985)

we are a people
who love to love
we are loving
lovers who love

Note: Boricua is a Puerto Rican word referring to the Indian name of the Island.

to love respect,   5
the best intentions
of friendship,
and we judge from
the moment on, no
matter who you are,   10
and, if we find
sincere smiles,
we can be friends,
and, if we have a
drink together,   15
we can be brothers,
on the spot, no
matter who you are,
and we have a lot
of black & white   20
& yellow & red
people whom we
befriend, we're
ready to love
with you, that's   25
why we
say, let there
be no prejudice,
on race, color is
generally color-blind   30
with us, that's our
contribution, all
the colors are tied
to our one,
but we must fight   35
the bad intentions,
we must respect
each other's values,
but guess what,
we're not the only ones,   40
and we offer what your
love has taught us,
and what you're worth
in our self-respect,
we are a people   45
who love to love
who are loving
lovers who love
to love respect.

····•▶ *Your* **Turn**
Talking and Writing about Lit

1. What does Tato LaViera mean in "boricua" when he says that "all/the colors are tied/to our one"? If you read the poem carefully, you should be able to determine this from the details given in the poem itself.

2. This poem is written in simple diction without much use of figurative language. Do you think the poem succeeds on the page, as a written work, as well as it might succeed in oral performance?

Miguel Algarín (b. 1941)
Tato—Reading at the Nuyorican Poets' Cafe (1980)

Sentimientos pour from your teeth
just like señoritas arouse in a bolero
a solas sin que haya nadie en casa,
sentimientos coming through the fuerza espíritu
de leche agria en senos de hielo,   5
the darkest part of my spirit
radiates ordering fears,
not against but towards a balance,
no hay que dejar que el meñique
se pierda ya que hemos encontrado   10
el contacto de una nenita
mirándome mientras escribo,
esperando que el sonero llegue
aunque su voz esté encarcelada,
pero Tato lo celebra y suda palabras   15
en su memoria, cucándole el ritmo,
sacándole el jugo universal, musical
Tato sudando palabras,
salpicando, arrojando su negreza
into the field of electricity he has created   20
between himself and Liz Sánchez,
esa palabra o coro coroso,
esa palabra o coro coroso,
trucutú, trucutú, trucutú,
pracatú, trucutuuuuuuuuuu,   25
no nos dejes, danos aliento,
trucutú, pracatú, trucutuuuuuuuuuuuuuu.

····▶ *Your* **Turn**
Talking and Writing about Lit

1. Miguel Algarín writes about Tato LaViera reading his poetry at the Nuyorican Poets' Cafe, on the Lower East Side in New York. What do you think about the way Algarín mixes Spanish and English words in the poem? Do you think enough meaning is revealed to the English-speaking reader who does not understand Spanish?

2. **DIY** Do you speak or write in another language other than English? Whether you learned this language at home or in school, construct a brief poem which incorporates words from the second language as well as words in English. Your poem might be about an event—as Algarín has written about his friend Tato LaViera's reading—or you may choose to write about your two languages themselves. Or you may write on a topic of your choice.

Protest Poetry

Ginsberg's "Howl" is, literally, a howl—a cry of the heart and a yelp of pain and frustration. Ginsberg's intent here is not simply to express his rage and pain, but to shape those feelings into a set of values opposed to what he regards to be the failed values of American culture of the mid-twentieth century. One of the interesting aspects of the poem, apart from its intense musicality and speech-like rhythms, is that it presents a kind of "negative portrait" of that era. A close reading will reveal that much of what the poet describes as suppressed and marginalized in the America of the post–World War II 1950s has emerged into the mainstream awareness of the culture today.

Allen Ginsberg (1926–1997)
from Howl (1956)

For Carl Solomon

I

I saw the best minds of my generation destroyed by madness, starving
    hysterical naked,
dragging themselves through the negro streets at dawn looking for an
    angry fix,

angelheaded hipsters burning for the ancient heavenly connection to
the starry dynamo in the machinery of night,
who poverty and tatters and hollow-eyed and high sat up smoking in
the supernatural darkness of cold-water flats floating across
the tops of cities contemplating jazz,
who bared their brains to Heaven under the El and saw Mohammedan   5
angels staggering on tenement roofs illuminated,
who passed through universities with radiant cool eyes hallucinating
Arkansas and Blake-light tragedy among the scholars of war,
who were expelled from the academies for crazy & publishing obscene
odes on the windows of the skull,
who cowered in unshaven rooms in underwear, burning their money
in wastebaskets and listening to the Terror through the wall,
who got busted in their pubic beards returning through Laredo with a
belt of marijuana for New York,
who ate fire in paint hotels or drank turpentine in Paradise Alley, death,   10
or purgatoried their torsos night after night
with dreams, with drugs, with waking nightmares, alcohol and cock and
endless balls,
incomparable blind streets of shuddering cloud and lightning in the
mind leaping toward poles of Canada & Paterson, illuminating
all the motionless world of Time between,
Peyote solidities of halls, backyard green tree cemetery dawns, wine
drunkenness over the roof tops, storefront boroughs of teahead
joyride neon blinking traffic light, sun and moon and tree
vibrations in the roaring winter dusks of Brooklyn, ashcan
rantings and kind king light of mind,
who chained themselves to subways for the endless ride from Battery
to holy Bronx on benzedrine until the noise of wheels and
children brought them down shuddering mouth-wracked
and battered bleak of brain all drained of brilliance in the
drear light of Zoo,
who sank all night in submarine light of Bickford's floated out and   15
sat through the stale beer afternoon in desolate Fugazzi's,
listening to the crack of doom on the hydrogen jukebox,
who talked continuously seventy hours from park to pad to bar to
Bellevue to museum to the Brooklyn Bridge,
a lost battalion of platonic conversationalists jumping down the stoops
off fire escapes off windowsills off Empire State out of
the moon,
yacketayakking screaming vomiting whispering facts and memories
and anecdotes and eyeball kicks and shocks of hospitals and jails
and wars,
whole intellects disgorged in total recall for seven days and nights
with brilliant eyes, meat for the Synagogue cast on the pavement,

who vanished into nowhere Zen New Jersey leaving a trail of   20
    ambiguous picture postcards of Atlantic City Hall,
suffering Eastern sweats and Tangerian bone-grindings and migraines
    of China under junk-withdrawal in Newark's bleak furnished
    room,
who wandered around and around at midnight in the railroad yard
    wondering where to go, and went, leaving no broken hearts,
who lit cigarettes in boxcars boxcars boxcars racketing through snow
    toward lonesome farms in grandfather night,
who studied Plotinus Poe St. John of the Cross telepathy and bop
    kabbalah because the cosmos instinctively vibrated at their
    feet in Kansas,
who loned it through the streets of Idaho seeking visionary indian   25
    angels who were visionary indian angels,
who thought they were only mad when Baltimore gleamed in
    supernatural ecstasy,
who jumped in limousines with the Chinaman of Oklahoma on the
    impulse of winter midnight streetlight smalltown rain,
who lounged hungry and lonesome through Houston seeking jazz or
    sex or soup, and followed the brilliant Spaniard to converse
    about America and Eternity, a hopeless task, and so took ship
    to Africa,
who disappeared into the volcanoes of Mexico leaving behind
    nothing but the shadow of dungarees and the lava and ash of poetry
    scattered in fireplace Chicago,
who reappeared on the West Coast investigating the FBI in beards and   30
    shorts with big pacifist eyes sexy in their dark skin passing
    out incomprehensible leaflets,
who burned cigarette holes in their arms protesting the narcotic
    tobacco haze of Capitalism,
who distributed Supercommunist pamphlets in Union Square weeping
    and undressing while the sirens of Los Alamos wailed them
    down, and wailed down Wall, and the Staten Island ferry also
    wailed,
who broke down crying in white gymnasiums naked and trembling
    before the machinery of other skeletons,
who bit detectives in the neck and shrieked with delight in
    policecars for committing no crime but their own wild
    cooking pederasty and intoxication,
who howled on their knees in the subway and were dragged off the   35
    roof waving genitals and manuscripts,
who let themselves be fucked in the ass by saintly motorcyclists,
    and screamed with joy,
who blew and were blown by those human seraphim, the sailors,
    caresses of Atlantic and Caribbean love,

who balled in the morning in the evenings in rosegardens and
    the grass of public parks and cemeteries scattering their semen
    freely to whomever come who may,
who hiccuped endlessly trying to giggle but wound up with a sob behind
    a partition in a Turkish Bath when the blond & naked angel came to
    pierce them with a sword,
who lost their loveboys to the three old shrews of fate the one eyed   40
    shrew of the heterosexual dollar the one eyed shrew that winks
    out of the womb and the one eyed shrew that does nothing but sit
    on her ass and snip the intellectual golden threads of the
    craftsman's loom,
who copulated ecstatic and insatiate with a bottle of beer a sweetheart
    a package of cigarettes a candle and fell off the bed, and
    continued along the floor and down the hall and ended
    fainting on the wall with a vision of ultimate cunt and come
    eluding the last gyzym of consciousness,
who sweetened the snatches of a million girls trembling in the sunset, and
    were red eyed in the morning but prepared to sweeten the snatch
    of the sunrise, flashing buttocks under barns and naked in the lake,
who went out whoring through Colorado in myriad stolen
    night-cars, N.C., secret hero of these poems, cocksman and
    Adonis of Denver—joy to the memory of his innumerable lays
    of girls in empty lots & diner backyards, moviehouses' rickety
    rows, on mountaintops in caves or with gaunt waitresses in
    familiar roadside lonely petticoat upliftings & especially
    secret gas-station solipsisms of johns, & hometown alleys too,
who faded out in vast sordid movies, were shifted in dreams, woke
    on a sudden Manhattan, and picked themselves up out of
    basements hungover with heartless Tokay and horrors of Third
    Avenue iron dreams & stumbled to unemployment offices,
who walked all night with their shoes full of blood on the   45
    snowbank docks waiting for a door in the East River to open
    to a room full of steam-heat and opium,
who created great suicidal dramas on the apartment cliff-banks of the
    Hudson under the wartime blue floodlight of the moon &
    their heads shall be crowned with laurel in oblivion,
who ate the lamb stew of the imagination or digested the crab at the
    muddy bottom of the rivers of Bowery,
who wept at the romance of the streets with their pushcarts full
    of onions and bad music,
who sat in boxes breathing in the darkness under the bridge, and rose
    up to build harpsichords in their lofts,
who coughed on the sixth floor of Harlem crowned with flame under   50
    the tubercular sky surrounded by orange crates of theology,

who scribbled all night rocking and rolling over lofty
  incantations which in the yellow morning were stanzas of gibberish,

who cooked rotten animals lung heart feet tail borsht & tortillas
  dreaming of the pure vegetable kingdom,

who plunged themselves under meat trucks looking for an egg,

who threw their watches off the roof to cast their ballot for
  Eternity outside of Time, & alarm clocks fell on their heads
  every day for the next decade,

who cut their wrists three times successively unsuccessfully, gave up   55
  and were forced to open antique stores where they thought they
  were growing old and cried,

who were burned alive in their innocent flannel suits on Madison
  Avenue amid blasts of leaden verse & the tanked-up clatter of the
  iron regiments of fashion & the nitroglycerine shrieks of the fairies
  of advertising & the mustard gas of sinister intelligent editors,
  or were run down by the drunken taxicabs of Absolute Reality,

who jumped off the Brooklyn Bridge this actually happened and walked
  away unknown and forgotten into the ghostly daze of Chinatown
  soup alleyways & firetrucks, not even one free beer,

who sang out of their windows in despair, fell out of the subway
  window, jumped in the filthy Passaic, leaped on negroes, cried
  all over the street, danced on broken wineglasses barefoot
  smashed phonograph records of nostalgic European 1930s
  German jazz finished the whiskey and threw up groaning
  into the bloody toilet, moans in their ears and the blast of
  colossal steamwhistles,

who barreled down the highways of the past journeying to each other's
  hotrod-Golgotha jail-solitude watch of Birmingham jazz incarnation,

who drove crosscountry seventytwo hours to find out if I had a vision   60
  or you had a vision or he had a vision to find out Eternity,

who journeyed to Denver, who died in Denver, who came back to
  Denver & waited in vain, who watched over Denver & brooded &
  loned in Denver and finally went away to find out the Time, & now
  Denver is lonesome for her heroes,

who fell on their knees in hopeless cathedrals praying for each
  other's salvation and light and breasts, until the soul illuminated its
  hair for a second,

who crashed through their minds in jail waiting for impossible
  criminals with golden heads and the charm of reality in their
  hearts who sang sweet blues to Alcatraz,

who retired to Mexico to cultivate a habit, or Rocky Mount to
  tender Buddha or Tangiers to boys or Southern Pacific to
  the black locomotive or Harvard to Narcissus to Woodlawn
  to the daisychain or grave,

who demanded sanity trials accusing the radio of hypnotism &
    were left with their insanity & their hands & a hung jury,   65

who threw potato salad at CCNY lecturers on Dadaism and
    subsequently presented themselves on the granite steps of the
    madhouse with shaven heads and harlequin speech of suicide,
    demanding instantaneous lobotomy,

and who were given instead the concrete void of insulin Metrazol
    electricity hydrotherapy psychotherapy pingpong & amnesia,

who in humorless protest overturned only one symbolic pingpong
    table, resting briefly in catatonia,

returning years later truly bald except for a wig of blood, and
    tears and fingers, to the visible madman doom of the wards
    of the madtowns of the East,

Pilgrim State's Rockland's and Greystone's foetid halls, bickering   70
    with the echoes of the soul, rocking and rolling in the
    midnight solitude-bench dolmen-realms of love, dream of
    life a nightmare, bodies turned to stone as heavy as
    the moon,

with mother finally ° ° ° ° ° °, and the last fantastic book
    flung out of the tenement window, and the last door
    closed at 4 A.M. and the last telephone slammed
    at the wall in reply and the last furnished room emptied
    down to the last piece of mental furniture, a yellow paper
    rose twisted on a wire hanger in the closet, and even that
    imaginary, nothing but a hopeful little bit of hallucination—

ah, Carl, while you are not safe I am not safe, and now you're really
    in the total animal soup of time—

and who therefore ran through the icy streets obsessed with a
    sudden flash of the alchemy of the use of the ellipsis catalog a
    variable measure and the vibrating plane,

who dreamt and made incarnate gaps in Time & Space through
    images juxtaposed, and trapped the archangel of the soul
    between 2 visual images and joined the elemental verbs and
    set the noun and dash of consciousness together jumping
    with sensation of Pater Omnipotens Aeterne Deus

to recreate the syntax and measure of poor human prose and stand   75
    before you speechless and intelligent and shaking with shame,
    rejected yet confessing out the soul to conform to the rhythm
    of thought in his naked and endless head,

the madman bum and angel beat in Time, unknown, yet putting
    down here what might be left to say in time come after death,

and rose reincarnate in the ghostly clothes of jazz in the goldhorn
    shadow of the band and blew the suffering of America's naked
    mind for love into an eli eli lamma lamma sabacthani saxophone
    cry that shivered the cities down to the last radio

with the absolute heart of the poem of life butchered out of their
        own bodies good to eat a thousand years.

What common themes and rhythms can you identify in Ginsberg's poem
"America," below?

Allen Ginsberg (1926–1997)
America (1956)

America I've given you all and now I'm nothing.
America two dollars and twentyseven cents January 17, 1956.
I can't stand my own mind.
America when will we end the human war?
Go fuck yourself with your atom bomb.   5
I don't feel good don't bother me.
I won't write my poem till I'm in my right mind.
America when will you be angelic?
When will you take off your clothes?
When will you look at yourself through the grave?   10
When will you be worthy of your million Trotskyites?
America why are your libraries full of tears?
America when will you send your eggs to India?
I'm sick of your insane demands.
When can I go into the supermarket and buy what I need with my
        good looks?   15
America after all it is you and I who are perfect not the next world.
Your machinery is too much for me.
You made me want to be a saint.
There must be some other way to settle this argument.
Burroughs is in Tangiers I don't think he'll come back it's sinister.   20
Are you being sinister or is this some form of practical joke?
I'm trying to come to the point.
I refuse to give up my obsession.
America stop pushing I know what I'm doing.
America the plum blossoms are falling.   25
I haven't read the newspapers for months, everyday somebody
        goes on trial for murder.
America I feel sentimental about the Wobblies.
America I used to be a communist when I was a kid I'm not sorry.
I smoke marijuana every chance I get.
I sit in my house for days on end and stare at the roses in the closet. 30
When I go to Chinatown I get drunk and never get laid.

My mind is made up there's going to be trouble.
You should have seen me reading Marx.
My psychoanalyst thinks I'm perfectly right.
I won't say the Lord's Prayer.   35
I have mystical visions and cosmic vibrations.
America I still haven't told you what you did to Uncle Max after he
    came over from Russia.

I'm addressing you.
Are you going to let your emotional life be run by Time Magazine?
I'm obsessed by Time Magazine.   40
I read it every week.
Its cover stares at me every time I slink past the corner candystore.
I read it in the basement of the Berkeley Public Library.
It's always telling me about responsibility. Businessmen are serious.
    Movie producers are serious. Everybody's serious but me.   45
It occurs to me that I am America.
I am talking to myself again.

Asia is rising against me.
I haven't got a chinaman's chance.
I'd better consider my national resources.   50
My national resources consist of two joints of marijuana millions of
    genitals an unpublishable private literature that jetplanes
    1400 miles an hour and twentyfive-thousand mental
    institutions.
I say nothing about my prisons nor the millions of underprivileged
    who live in my flowerpots under the light of five hundred suns.
I have abolished the whorehouses of France, Tangiers is the next to go.
My ambition is to be President despite the fact that I'm a Catholic.

America how can I write a holy litany in your silly mood?   55
I will continue like Henry Ford my strophes are as individual as
    his automobiles more so they're all different sexes.
America I will sell you strophes $2500 apiece $500 down on your
    old strophe
America free Tom Mooney
America save the Spanish Loyalists
America Sacco & Vanzetti must not die   60
America I am the Scottsboro boys.
America when I was seven momma took me to Communist Cell
    meetings they sold us garbanzos a handful per ticket a ticket
    costs a nickel and the speeches were free everybody was
    angelic and sentimental about the workers it was all so sincere
    you have no idea what a good thing the party was in 1835 Scott

Nearing was a grand old man a real mensch Mother Bloor the
    Silk-strikers' Ewig-Weibliche made me cry I once saw the
    Yiddish orator Israel Amter plain. Everybody must have
    been a spy.
America you don't really want to go to war.
America it's them bad Russians.
Them Russians them Russians and them Chinamen. And them Russians.   65
The Russia wants to eat us alive. The Russia's power mad. She
    wants to take our cars from out our garages.
Her wants to grab Chicago. Her needs a Red *Reader's Digest.* Her
    wants our auto plants in Siberia. Him big bureaucracy running our
    fillingstations.
That no good. Ugh. Him make Indians learn read. Him need big
    black niggers. Hah. Her make us all work sixteen hours a day. Help.
America this is quite serious.
America this is the impression I get from looking in the television set.   70
America is this correct?
I'd better get right down to the job.
It's true I don't want to join the Army or turn lathes in precision parts
    factories, I'm nearsighted and psychopathic anyway.
America I'm putting my queer shoulder to the wheel.

   In the tone of a letter or a note, Ishmael Reed's "voice" is the voice of a
runaway slave who is addressing his former master from the safe haven of
Canada. The former slave mocks his master. The poem seems to echo in many
ways the voices of the rap artists who speak out of their own experiences to a white
world.

Ishmael Reed (b. 1938)
Flight to Canada (1976)

Dear Massa Swille:
What it was?
I have done my Liza Leap
& am safe in the arms
of Canada, so   5
Ain't no use your Slave
Catchers waitin on me
At Trailways
I won't be there

I flew in non-stop   10
Jumbo jet this A.M. Had
Champagne

Compliments of the Cap'n
Who announced that a
Runaway Negro was on the   15
Plane. Passengers came up
And shook my hand
& within 10 min. I had
Signed up for 3 anti-slavery
Lectures. Remind me to get an   20
Agent

    Traveling in style
Beats craning your neck after
The North Star and hiding in
Bushes anytime, Massa   25
Besides, your Negro dogs
Of Hays & Allen stock can't
Fly

    By now I s'pose that
Yellow Judas Cato done tole   30
You that I snuck back to
The plantation 3 maybe 4 times
Since I left the first time

    Last visit I slept in
Your bed and sampled your   35
Cellar. Had your prime
Quadroon give me
She-Bear. Yes, yes

    You was away at a
Slave auction at Ryan's Mart   40
In Charleston & so I knowed
You wouldn't mind
Did you have a nice trip, Massa?

    I borrowed your cotton money
to pay for my ticket & to get   45
Me started in this place called
Saskatchewan Brrrrrrr!
It's cold up here but least
Nobody is collaring hobbling gagging
Handcuffing yoking chaining & thumbscrewing   50
You like you is they hobby horse

The Mistress Ms. Lady
Gived me the combination
To your safe, don't blame
The feeble old soul, Cap'n   55
I told her you needed some

More money to shop with &
You sent me from Charleston
To get it. Don't worry
Your employees won't miss   60
It & I accept it as a
Down payment on my back
Wages

     I must close now
Massa, by the time you gets   65
This letter old Sam will have
Probably took you to the
Deep Six

That was rat poison I left
In your Old Crow   70
     Your boy
     Quickskill

Denise Levertov's "At the Justice Department, November 15, 1969," is a kind of real-time account of the protest experience. The issue at hand, of course, is the Vietnam War, but the poet grounds her description of frustration and moral outrage in a vivid physical sensation of confrontation and being gassed.

Denise Levertov (1923–1997)
At the Justice Department (1970)
November 15, 1969

Brown gas-fog, white
beneath the street lamps.
Cut off on three sides, all space filled
with our bodies.
     Bodies that stumble   5
in brown airlessness, whitened
in light, a mildew glare,
     that stumble

hand in hand, blinded, retching.
Wanting it, wanting   10
to be here, the body believing it's
dying in its nausea, my head
clear in its despair, a kind of joy,
knowing this is by no means death,
is trivial, an incident, a   15
fragile instant.   Wanting it, wanting
  with all my hunger this anguish,
  this knowing in the body
the grim odds we're
up against, wanting it real.   20
Up that bank where gas
curled in the ivy, dragging each other
up, strangers, brothers
and sisters.   Nothing
will do but   25
to taste the bitter
taste. No life
other, apart from.

Amiri Baraka (LeRoi Jones) (b. 1934)
Political Poem (1964)

(for Basil)

Luxury, then, is a way of
being ignorant, comfortably
An approach to the open market
of least information. Where theories
can thrive, under heavy tarpaulins   5
without being cracked by ideas.

(I have not seen the earth for years
and think now possibly "dirt" is
negative, positive, but clearly
social. I cannot plant a seed, cannot   10
recognize the root with clearer dent
than indifference. Though I eat
and shit as a natural man. (Getting up
from the desk to secure a turkey sandwich
and answer the phone: the poem undone 15
undone by my station, by my station,
and the bad words of Newark.) Raised up

to the breech, we seek to fill for this
crumbling century. The darkness of love,
in whose sweating memory all error is forced.   20

Undone by the logic of any specific death. (Old gentlemen
who still follow fires, tho are quieter
and less punctual. It is a polite truth
we are left with. Who are you? What are you
saying? Something to be dealt with, as easily.   25
The noxious game of reason, saying, "No, No,
you cannot feel," like my dead lecturer
lamenting thru gipsies his fast suicide.

·····▶ *Your* Turn
Talking and Writing about Lit

1. What do you make of Amiri Baraka's statement in "Political Poem" that
"Luxury . . . is a way of / being ignorant, comfortably"? What do you think
the "tarpaulins" that protect "theories" and prevent the entry of "ideas"
might represent in lines 4–6?

2. **DIY** Write a political poem of your own. It might be a poem of only
six lines (the length of Baraka's first stanza). In your poem, make a
statement about some political view of your own. Try to use at least one figure of speech (like Baraka's "tarpaulins").

Wanda Coleman (b. 1946)
the ISM (1983)

tired i count the ways in which it determines my life
permeates everything. it's in the air
lives next door to me in stares of neighbors
meets me each day in the office. its music comes out the radio
drives beside me in my car. strolls along with me   5
down supermarket aisles
it's on television
and in the streets even when my walk is casual/undefined
it's overhead flashing lights
i find it in my mouth   10
when i would speak of other things

····•▶ *Your* **Turn**

Talking and Writing about Lit

1. Wanda Coleman has chosen to use no capitalization in her poem "the ISM," aside from the "ISM" itself. Do you think this choice fits well with her subject matter and purpose here, or do you think the poem would succeed better if it used conventional capitalization?

2. **DIY** Write a brief poem (6–12 lines) in which you drop at least one convention of punctuation or spelling or capitalization. You may drop them all if you wish, but eliminate at least one.

Legacy: The Beats and Other Voices

The Beat Movement was a youth counter-culture movement that came into full flower in the 1950s. Beat poetry was characterized by sound, spontaneity, and opposition to conventional society. Jack Spicer, an early friend and close associate of many of the poets who were later to become the Beat Poets (for example, Corso, Kerouac, and Ginsberg) and poets of the San Francisco Renaissance (including Ferlinghetti), wrote, in 1949, that

> Live poetry is a kind of singing. It differs from prose, as song does, in its complexity of stress and intonation. Poetry demands a human voice to sing it and demands an audience to hear it. Without these it is naked, pure, and incomplete—a bore.
>
> If plays were only printed and never acted, who would read them? If songs were only printed on song sheets, who would read them? It would be like playing a football game on paper.—(from "On Spoken Poetry," in *The House That Jack Built*)

As you read these poets' words on the page, imagine them being performed, being spoken aloud. If you can, read them aloud yourself. Gregory Corso's poem "Marriage" is a series of questions and what-ifs posed humorously but with some seriousness as well. They take the form of daydream-like fantasies which might be imagined by any young man or woman in terms of the tension created by an awareness of what one ought to do and what one wants to do.

Gregory Corso (1930–2001)
Marriage (1960)

Should I get married? Should I be good?
Astound the girl next door with my velvet suit and faustus hood?
Don't take her to movies but to cemeteries
tell all about werewolf bathtubs and forked clarinets

then desire her and kiss her and all the preliminaries   5
and she going just so far and I understanding why
not getting angry saying You must feel! It's beautiful to feel!
Instead take her in my arms lean against an old crooked tombstone
and woo her the entire night the constellations in the sky—

When she introduces me to her parents   10
back straightened, hair finally combed, strangled by a tie,
should I sit knees together on their 3rd degree sofa
and not ask Where's the bathroom?
How else to feel other than I am,
often thinking Flash Gordon soap—   15
O how terrible it must be for a young man
seated before a family and the family thinking
We never saw him before! He wants our Mary Lou!
After tea and homemade cookies they ask What do you do for a
                                                                            living?

Should I tell them: Would they like me then?   20
Say All right get married, we're losing a daughter
but we're gaining a son—
And should I then ask Where's the bathroom?

O God, and the wedding! All her family and her friends
and only a handful of mine all scroungy and bearded   25
just wait to get at the drinks and food—
And the priest! he looking at me as if I masturbated
asking me Do you take this woman for your lawful wedded wife?
And I trembling what to say say Pie Glue!
I kiss the bride all those corny men slapping me on the back   30
She's all yours, boy! Ha-ha-ha!
And in their eyes you could see some obscene honeymoon going
on—

Then all that absurd rice and clanky cans and shoes
Niagara Falls! Hordes of us! Husbands! Wives! Flowers!
                                                                   Chocolates!

All streaming into cozy hotels   35
All going to do the same thing tonight
The indifferent clerk he knowing what was going to happen
The lobby zombies they knowing what
The whistling elevator man he knowing
The winking bellboy knowing   40
Everybody knowing! I'd be almost inclined not to do anything!
Stay up all night! Stare that hotel clerk in the eye!
Screaming: I deny honeymoon! I deny honeymoon!

running rampant into those almost climactic suites
yelling Radio belly! Cat shovel!   45

O I'd live in Niagara forever! in a dark cave beneath the Falls
I'd sit there the Mad Honeymooner
devising ways to break marriages, a scourge of bigamy
a saint of divorce—

But I should get married I should be good   50
How nice it'd be to come home to her
and sit by the fireplace and she in the kitchen
aproned young and lovely wanting my baby
and so happy about me she burns the roast beef
and comes crying to me and I get up from my big papa chair   55
saying Christmas teeth! Radiant brains! Apple deaf!
God what a husband I'd make! Yes, I should get married!
So much to do! like sneaking into Mr Jones' house late at night
and cover his golf clubs with 1920 Norwegian books
Like hanging a picture of Rimbaud on the lawnmower   60
like pasting Tannu Tuva postage stamps all over the picket fence
like when Mrs Kindhead comes to collect for the Community Chest
grab her and tell her There are unfavorable omens in the sky!
And when the mayor comes to get my vote tell him
When are you going to stop people killing whales!   65
And when the milkman comes leave him a note in the bottle
Penguin dust, bring me penguin dust, I want penguin dust—

Yet if I should get married and it's Connecticut and snow
and she gives birth to a child and I am sleepless, worn,
up for nights, head bowed against a quiet window, the past behind
me,   70

finding myself in the most common of situations a trembling man
knowledged with responsibility not twig-smear nor Roman coin
soup—

O what would that be like!
Surely I'd give it for a nipple a rubber Tacitus
For a rattle a bag of broken Bach records   75
Tack Della Francesca all over its crib
Sew the Greek alphabet on its bib
And build for its playpen a roofless Parthenon

No, I doubt I'd be that kind of father
not rural not snow no quiet window   80
but hot smelly tight New York City

seven flights up, roaches and rats in the walls
a fat Reichian wife screeching over potatoes Get a job!
And five nose running brats in love with Batman
And the neighbors all toothless and dry haired   85
like those hag masses of the 18th century
all wanting to come in and watch TV
The landlord wants his rent
Grocery store Blue Cross Gas & Electric Knights of Columbus
Impossible to lie back and dream Telephone snow, ghost parking—   90
No! I should not get married I should never get married!
But—imagine if I were married to a beautiful sophisticated woman
tall and pale wearing an elegant black dress and long black gloves
holding a cigarette holder in one hand and a highball in the other
and we lived high up in a penthouse with a huge window   95
from which we could see all of New York and ever farther on
                                                        clearer days
No, can't imagine myself married to that pleasant prison dream—

O but what about love? I forget love
not that I am incapable of love
it's just that I see love as odd as wearing shoes—   100
I never wanted to marry a girl who was like my mother
And Ingrid Bergman was always impossible
And there's maybe a girl now but she's already married
And I don't like men and—
but there's got to be somebody!   105
Because what if I'm 60 years old and not married,
all alone in a furnished room with pee stains on my underwear
and everybody else is married! All the universe married but me!

Ah, yet well I know that were a woman possible as I am possible
then marriage would be possible—   110
Like SHE in her lonely alien gaud waiting her Egyptian lover
so I wait—bereft of 2,000 years and the bath of life.

Lawrence Ferlinghetti likens the task and role of the poet to that of the high-wire acrobat. The lines of his poem themselves seem to be arranged to mimic the movement of a performer on a tight rope or a trapeze.

Lawrence Ferlinghetti (b. 1919)
Constantly Risking Absurdity (1958)

Constantly risking absurdity
                        and death
        whenever he performs

                        above the heads
                                      of his audience   5
            the poet like an acrobat
                        climbs on rime
                              to a high wire of his own making
         and balancing on eyebeams
                                      above a sea of faces   10
                  paces his way
                              to the other side of day
            performing entrechats
                              and sleight-of-foot tricks
            and other high theatrics   15
                              and all without mistaking
                  any thing
                              for what it may not be

         For he's the super realist
                              who must perforce perceive   20
                  taut truth
                              before the taking of each stance or step
            in his supposed advance
                              toward that still higher perch
         where Beauty stands and waits   25
                              with gravity
                                      to start her death-defying leap
            And he
                  a little charleychaplin man
                              who may or may not catch   30
                  her fair eternal form
                              spreadeagled in the empty air
                  of existence

Amiri Baraka looks at the routine of a big city street as it empties out for the night and asks the reader to consider the purposes of human beings as they go about their daily lives ("Those who realize / how fitful and indecent consciousness is / stare solemnly out on the emptying street"). A kind of consciousness and awareness, apart from the normal rounds of workaday demands and preoccupations, is what the poet proposes here.

Amiri Baraka (LeRoi Jones) (b. 1934)
The New World (1969)

The sun is folding, cars stall and rise
beyond the window. The workmen leave
the street to the bums and painters' wives

pushing their babies home. Those who realize
how fitful and indecent consciousness is   5
stare solemnly out on the emptying street.
The mourners and soft singers. The liars,
and seekers after ridiculous righteousness. All
my doubles, and friends, whose mistakes cannot
be duplicated by machines, and this is all of our   10
arrogance. Being broke or broken, dribbling
at the eyes. Wasted lyricists, and men
who have seen their dreams come true, only seconds
after they knew those dreams to be horrible conceits
and plastic fantasies of gesture and extension,   15
shoulders, hair and tongues distributing misinformation
about the nature of understanding. No one is that simple
or priggish, to be alone out of spite and grown strong
in its practice, mystics in two-pants suits. Our style,
and discipline, controlling the method of knowledge.   20
Beatniks, like Bohemians, go calmly out of style. And boys
are dying in Mexico, who did not get the word.
The lateness of their fabrication: mark their holes
with filthy needles. The lust of the world. This will not
be news. The simple damning lust,   25

                         float flat magic in low changing
                         evenings. Shiver your hands
                         in dance. Empty all of me for
                         knowing, and will the danger
                         of identification,   30

        Let me sit and go blind in my dreaming
        and be that dream in purpose and device.

        A fantasy of defeat, a strong strong man
        older, but no wiser than the defect of love.

Jack Kerouac (1922–1969)
"113th Chorus," from *Mexico City Blues* (1959)

Got up and dressed up
        and went out & got laid
Then died and got buried
        in a coffin in the grave,
Man—   5
        Yet everything is perfect,
Because it is empty,
Because it is perfect

with emptiness,
Because it's not even happening.   10

Everything
Is Ignorant of its own emptiness—
Anger
Doesn't like to be reminded of fits—

You start with the Teaching   15
     Inscrutable of the Diamond
And end with it, your goal
     is your startingplace,
No race was run, no walk
     of prophetic toenails   20
Across Arabies of hot
     meaning—you just
     numbly don't get there

Your Turn

• • • • ▶ **Talking and Writing about Lit**

1. Can you imagine Jack Kerouac's "113th Chorus" from *Mexico City Blues* being performed aloud? Try reading it aloud yourself. What elements or techniques in this poem help Kerouac establish the rhythm?

2. **DIY** Write a brief poem that begins with a gesture or action, as Kerouac's "113th Chorus" begins with "Got up and dressed up." After the opening action or gesture, you may take the poem anywhere you like.

Allen Ginsberg (1926–1997)
Europe! Europe! (1958)

World world world
I sit in my room
imagine the future
sunlight falls on Paris
I am alone there is no   5
one whose love is perfect
man has been mad man's
love is not perfect I
have not wept enough

my breast will be heavy   10
till death the cities
are specters of cranks
of war the cities are
work & brick & iron &
smoke of the furnace of   15
selfhood makes tearless
eyes red in London but
no eye meets the sun

Flashed out of sky it
hits Lord Beaverbrook's   20
white modern solid
paper building leaned
in London's street to
bear last yellow beams
old ladies absently gaze   25
thru fog toward heaven
poor pots on windowsills
snake flowers to street
Trafalgar's fountains splash
on noon-warmed pigeons   30
Myself beaming in ecstatic
wilderness on St. Paul's dome
seeing the light on London
or here on a bed in Paris
sunglow through the high   35
window on plaster walls

Meek crowd underground
saints perish creeps
streetwomen meet lacklove
under gaslamp and neon   40
no woman in house loves
husband in flower unity
nor boy loves boy soft
fire in breast politics
electricity scares downtown   45
radio screams for money
police light on TV screens
laughs at dim lamps in
empty rooms tanks crash
thru bombshell no dream   50
of man's joy is made movie
think factory pushes junk

autos tin dreams of Eros
mind eats its flesh in
geekish starvation and no   55
man's fuck is holy for
man's work is most war

Bony China hungers brain
wash over power dam and
America hides mad meat   60
in refrigerator Britain
cooks Jerusalem too long
France eats oil and dead
salad arms & legs in Africa
loudmouth devours Arabia   65
negro and white warring
against the golden nuptial
Russia manufacture feeds
millions but no drunk can
dream Mayakovsky's suicide   70
rainbow over machinery
and backtalk to the sun

I lie in bed in Europe
alone in old red under
wear symbolic of desire   75
for union with immortality
but man's love's not perfect
in February it rains
as once for Baudelaire
one hundred years ago   80
planes roar in the air
cars race thru streets
I know where they go
to death but that is OK
it is that death comes   85
before life that no man
has loved perfectly no one
gets bliss in time new
mankind is not born that
I weep for this antiquity   90
and herald the Millenium
for I saw the Atlantic sun
rayed down from a vast cloud
at Dover on the sea cliffs
tanker size of ant heaved   95

up on ocean under shining
cloud and seagull flying
thru sun light's endless
ladders streaming in Eternity
to ants in the myriad fields   100
of England to sun flowers
bent up to eat infinity's
minute gold dolphins leaping
thru Mediterranean rainbow
White smoke and steam in Andes   105
Asia's rivers glittering
blind poets deep in lone
Apollonic radiance on hillsides
littered with empty tombs

Your Turn

•••••▶ Talking and Writing about Lit

1. The lines in "Europe! Europe!" are shorter than those in most of Ginsberg's poems. What is the effect of these line breaks? Try reading the poem aloud.

2. **DIY** Write a poem in which short lines predominate (three to five words per line).

Talking Lit

Jerome Rothenberg quotes Tristan Tzara as saying "Thought is made in the mouth," and Rothenberg believes that the stiffer conventions of Western literature have been touted at the expense of the "thought . . . made in the mouth" of "pre-literate and oral cultures." Denise Levertov writes about the "artist as explorer in language."

Jerome Rothenberg, "New Models, New Visions: Some Notes Toward a Poetics of Performance" (1977)

The fact of performance now runs through all our arts, and the arts themselves begin to merge and lose their old distinctions, till it's apparent that we're no longer where we were to start with. The Renaissance is over or it begins again with us. Yet the origins we seek—the frame that bounds our past, that's set against an open-ended future—are no longer Greek, nor even Indo-European, but take in all times and places. To say this isn't to deny history, for we're in fact involved with history, with the sense of ourselves "in time" and in relation to other forms of human experience besides our own. The model—or better, the vision—has shifted: away from a "great tradition" centered in a single stream of art and literature in the West, to a *greater* tradition that includes, sometimes as its central fact, preliterate and oral cultures throughout the world, with a sense of their connection to subterranean but literate traditions in civilizations both East and West. "Thought is made in the mouth," said Tristan Tzara, and Edmond Jabès: "The book is as old as fire and water"—and both, we know, are right.

The change of view, for those who have experienced it, is by now virtually paradigmatic. We live with it in practice and find it more and more difficult to communicate with those who still work with the older paradigm. Thus, what appears to us as essentially creative—how can we doubt it?—carries for others the threat that was inherent when Tzara, as arch Dadaist, called *circa* 1917, for "a great negative work of destruction" against a late, overly textualized derivation from the Renaissance paradigm of culture and history. No longer viable, that great Western thesis was already synthesizing, setting the stage for its own disappearance. The other side of Tzara's work—and increasingly that of other artists within the several avant-gardes, the different, often conflicted sides of "modernism"—was, we now see clearly, a great positive work of construction/synthesis. With Tzara it took the form of a projected anthology. *Poèmes nègres*, a gathering of African and Oceanic poems culled from existing ethnographies and chanted at Dada performances in Zurich's Cabaret Voltaire. To the older brokers of taste—the bearers of Western values in an age of chaos—this may have looked like yet another Dada gag, but seeing it now in its actual publication six decades after the fact, it reads like a first, almost too serious attempt at a new classic anthology. In circulation orally, it formed with Tzara's own poetry—the process of a life and its emergence as performance in the soundworks and simultaneities of the dada soirées, etc.—one of the prophetic statements of where our work was to go.

Sixty years after Dada, a wide range of artists have been making deliberate and increasing use of ritual models for performance, have swept up arts like painting, sculpture, poetry (if those terms still apply) long separated from their origins in performance. (Traditional performance arts—music, theater, dance—have undergone similarly extreme transformations: often, like the others, toward a virtual liberation from the dominance of text.) The principal function here may be viewed as that of mapping and exploration, but however defined or simplified (text, e.g., doesn't vanish but is revitalized; so, likewise, the Greco-European past itself), the performance/ritual impulse seems clear throughout: in "happenings" and related event pieces (particularly those that involve participatory performance), in meditative works (often on an explicitly mantric model), in earthworks (derived from monumental American Indian structures), in dreamworks that play off trance and ecstasy, in bodyworks (including acts of self-multilation and edurance that seem to test the model), in a range of healing events as literal explorations of the shaman-istic premise, in animal language pieces related to the new ethology, etc.

Note: When I made a similar point in *Technicians of the Sacred* ten years earlier, I attributed the relation between "primitive" ritual and contemporary art and performance to an implicit coincidence of attitudes, where today the relation seems up-front, explicit, and increasingly comparable to the Greek and Roman model in Renaissance Europe, the Chinese model in medieval Japan, the Toltec model among the Aztecs, etc.; i.e., an overt influence but alive enough to work a series of distortions conditioned by the later culture and symptomatic of the obvious differences between the two. (Rothenberg's note.)

Denise Levertov, Preface to *To Stay Alive* (1971)

As one goes on living and working, themes recur, transposed into another key perhaps. Single poems that seemed isolated perceptions when one wrote them prove to have struck the first note of a scale or a melody. I have heard professors of literature snicker with embarrassment because a poet quoted himself: they thought it immodest, narcis-sistic. Their attitude, a common one, reveals a failure to understand that though *the artist as craftsman* is engaged in making discrete and autonomous works—each of which, like a chair or a table, will have, as Ezra Pound said, the requisite number of legs and not wobble—yet at the same time, more unconsciously, as these attempts accumulate over the years, *the artist as explorer in language of the experiences of his or her life* is, willy-nilly, weaving a fabric, building a whole in which each discrete work is a part that functions in some way in relation to all the others. It happens at times that the poet becomes aware of the relationships that exist between poem and poem; is conscious, after the act, of one poem, one line or stanza, having been the precursor of another. It may be years later; and then, to get the design clear—'for himself and *thereby* for others,' Ibsen put it—he must in honesty pick up that thread, bring the cross reference into its rightful place in the inscape, the Gestalt of his life (his work)/his work (his life).

In *Relearning the Alphabet* I published some sections of a poem then called, as a working title, 'From a Notebook,' which I was aware was 'unfinished,' open-ended. In pursuing it further I came to realize that the long poem 'An Interim,' published in a different section of the same volume, was really a prelude or intro-duction to the Notebook poem. And Mitch Goodman and Hayden Carruth, on reading new parts of the Notebook, showed me that other, earlier poems—such as those I had written about my sister Olga after her death in 1964, and included in *The Sorrow Dance*—had a relation to it that seemed to demand their reissue in juxtaposition. It was Hayden who, years ago, pointed out to me how, in writing about my childhood in England, my diction became English—and this fact becomes itself one of the themes of the Notebook poem; for the sense my individ-ual history gives me of being straddled between *places* extends to the more uni-versal sense any writer my age—rooted in a cultural past barely shared by younger readers, yet committed to a solidarity of hope and struggle with the revolutionary young—must have of being almost unbearably, painfully, straddled across *time*.

In the pendant to 'Olga Poems'—'A Note to Olga, 1966,' two years after her death—occurs the first mention in my work of one of those public occasions, demonstrations, that have become for many of us such familiar parts of our lives. Later, not as a deliberate repetition but because the events were of importance to me, other such occasions were spoken of in other poems. The sense of community, of fellowship, experienced in the People's Park in Berkeley in 1969, deepened and intensified under the vicious police attack that, for middle-class whites especially, was so instructive. The personal response that moves from the identification of my lost sister, as a worker for human rights, with the pacifists 'going limp' as they are dragged to the paddy-wagon in Times Square in 1966, to the understanding by 1970 that 'there comes a time when only anger/is love,' is one shared by many of us who have come bit by bit to the knowledge that opposition to war, whose foul air we have breathed so long that by now we are almost choked forever by it, cannot be separated from opposition to the whole system of insane greed, of racism and imperialism, of which war is only the inevitable expression. In 'Prologue: An Interim' some of my heroes—that is, those who stand for integrity, honesty, love of life—are draft resisters who go to jail in

POP CULTURE

Music without Music— Artists Cross from Music to Spoken Word

The link between music and poetry is an ancient one. Songs and lyrical chants have always been a way of passing down stories in rhythmic, rhyming formats which are easier to remember. In this way, from the earliest experience of humans with spoken language, oral traditions have been shared and passed on to the young in every culture on earth. Early Gaelic-speaking people passed on cultural information this way, as did the griot storytellers of Africa as well as Native American tribal elders. In the Middle Ages in Europe, traveling minstrels composed poetry with rhyme and meter to be accompanied by lutes, mandolins, and other instruments. In ancient Greece, singer-storytellers, to the accompaniment of the lyre, passed on the oral tradition that was later written down by the Greek poet Homer (and we now refer to as Greek mythology).

In the 1960s, Bob Dylan was heralded as a poet as well as a musician. And poets from the Beat generation had close links to the music scene. Allen Ginsberg wrote the liner notes for a band called The Fugs and released an album on the same label. Beat writer William Borroughs was actively involved in the early punk music scene in

testimony of their refusal to take part in carnage. In the same poem I invoked the self-immolators—Vietnamese and American—not as models but as flares to keep us moving in the dark. I spoke with love—a love I still feel—of those who 'disdain to kill.' But later I found that Gandhi himself had said it was better to 'cultivate the art of killing and being killed rather than in a cowardly manner to flee from danger.' In the later sections of the Notebook the sense of who the guardians of life, of integrity, are, is extended to include not only those who 'disdain to kill' but all who struggle, violently if need be, to pull down this obscene system before it destroys all life on earth.

The justification, then, of including in a new volume poems which are available in other collections, is esthetic—it assembles separated parts of a whole. And I am given courage to do so by the hope of that whole being seen as having some value not as mere 'confessional' autobiography, but as a document of some historical value, a record of one person's inner/outer experience in America during the '60's and the beginning of the '70's, an experience which is shared by so many and transcends the peculiar details of each life, though it can only be expressed in and through such details.

Beat Writer William Burroughs with artist Jean Michael Basquait and Debby Harry, singer of Blondie

his later years. In fact, two of the hardcore music scene's foremost front men in the 1980s went on to become popular spoken word artists. Both Henry Rollins of Black Flag and Jello Biafra of the Dead Kennedys composed a number of albums and tours around their respective spoken word performances.

Perhaps most successful, though, has been hip-hop's crossover into spoken word poetry, which popularized the new spoken word form of slam poets. Russel Simmons, himself a prominent figure in the hip-hop movement, coproduced Def Poetry Jam, which became a series of specials on HBO and launched a long and successful run on Broadway. It also launched the career of poet Saul Williams, the focus of the film *Slam!* (which won the 1998 Sundance Film Festival grand jury prize), thus carrying slam poetry from coffeehouses and poetry events into the larger world of the movies.

C H A P T E R 23

A BOOKSHELF
OF POETRY

Claribel Alegría (b. 1924)
Documentary (1989)

Come, be my camera.
Let's photograph the ant heap
the queen ant
extruding sacks of coffee,
my country.   5
It's the harvest.
Focus on the sleeping family
cluttering the ditch.
Now, among trees:
rapid,   10
dark-skinned fingers
stained with honey.
Shift to a long shot:
the file of ant men
trudging down the ravine   15
with sacks of coffee.
A contrast:
girls in colored skirts
laugh and chatter,
filling their baskets   20
with berries.
Focus down.
A close-up of the pregnant mother
dozing in the hammock.
Hard focus on the flies   25
spattering her face.
Cut.
The terrace of polished mosaics
protected from the sun.
Maids in white aprons   30
nourish the ladies
who play canasta,
celebrate invasions
and feel sorry for Cuba.
Izalco sleeps   35
beneath the volcano's eye.
A subterranean growl
makes the village tremble.
Trucks and ox-carts
laden with sacks   40
screech down the slopes.
Besides coffee

they plant angels in my country.
A chorus of children
and women   45
with the small white coffin
move politely aside
as the harvest passes by.
The riverside women,
naked to the waist,   50
wash clothing.
The truck drivers
exchange jocular obscenities
for insults.
In Panchimalco,   55
waiting for the ox-cart to pass by,
a peasant
with hands bound behind him
by the thumbs
and his escort of soldiers   60
blinks at the airplane:
a huge bee
bulging with coffee growers
and tourists.
The truck stops in the marketplace.   65
A panorama of iguanas,
chickens,
strips of meat,
wicker baskets,
piles of *nances*,   70
nisperos,
oranges,
zunzas,
zapotes,
cheeses,   75
bananas,
dogs, *pupusas, jocotes*,
acrid odors,
taffy candies,
urine puddles, tamarinds.   80
The virginal coffee
dances in the millhouse.
They strip her,
rape her,
lay her out on the patio   85
to doze in the sun.
The dark storage sheds

glimmer.
The golden coffee
sparkles with malaria,   90
blood,
illiteracy,
tuberculosis,
misery.
A truck roars   95
out of the warehouse.
It bellows uphill
drowning out the lesson:
A for alcoholism,
B for batalions   100
C for corruption
D for dictatorship
E for exploitation
F for the feudal power
of fourteen families   105
and etcetera, etcetera, etcetera.
My etcetera country,
my wounded country,
my child,
my tears,   110
my obsession.

When do you catch sight of the promised land?

Anonymous
Western Wind (circa 1500)

Western wind, when wilt thou blow,
The* small rain down can rain?
Christ, if my love were in my arms,
And I in my bed again!

_____

*The: [So that] the.

W. H. Auden (1907–1973)
The Unknown Citizen (1939)

(To JS/07/M/378 This Marble Monument Is Erected by the State)

He was found by the Bureau of Statistics to be
One against whom there was no official complaint,
And all the reports on his conduct agree

That, in the modern sense of an old-fashioned word, he was a saint,
For in everything he did he served the Greater Community.   5
Except for the War till the day he retired
He worked in a factory and never got fired,
But satisfied his employers, Fudge Motors Inc.
Yet he wasn't a scab or odd in his views,
For his Union reports that he paid his dues   10
(Our report on his Union shows it was sound),
And our Social Psychology workers found
That he was popular with his mates and liked a drink.
The Press are convinced that he bought a paper every day
And that his reactions to advertisements were normal in every way.   15
Policies taken out in his name prove that he was fully insured,
And his Health-card shows he was once in hospital but left it cured.
Both Producers Research and High-Grade Living declare
He was fully sensible to the advantages of the Installment Plan
And had everything necessary to the Modern Man,   20
A phonograph, a radio, a car and a frigidaire.
Our researchers into Public Opinion are content
That he held the proper opinions for the time of year;
When there was peace, he was for peace; when there was war, he went.
He was married and added five children to the population,   25
Which our Eugenist says was the right number for a parent of his
        generation,
And our teachers report that he never interfered with their education.
Was he free? Was he happy? The question is absurd:
Had anything been wrong, we should certainly have heard.

John Berryman (1914–1972)
from *The Dream Songs* (1964)

14

Life, friends, is boring. We must not say so.
After all, the sky flashes, the great sea yearns,
we ourselves flash and yearn,
and moreover my mother told me as a boy
(repeatedly) 'Ever to confess you're bored   5
means you have no
Inner Resources.' I conclude now I have no
inner resources, because I am heavy bored.
Peoples bore me,
literature bores me, especially great literature,   10
Henry bores me, with his plights & gripes

as bad as achilles,*
who loves people and valiant art, which bores me.
And the tranquil hills, & gin, look like a drag
and somehow a dog   15
has taken itself & its tail considerably away
into mountains or sea or sky, leaving
behind: me, wag.

*****achilles:** Achilles, the Greek warrior whose strength was needed if the Trojans were to be defeated, withdrew from fighting over a slight from the Greeks' general, King Agamemnon.

William Blake (1757–1827)
The Sick Rose (1794)

O Rose, thou art sick!
The invisible worm
That flies in the night,
In the howling storm,

Has found out thy bed   5
Of crimson joy,
And his dark secret love
Does thy life destroy.

Gwendolyn Brooks (b. 1917–2000)
from *The Children of the Poor* (1949)

11
Life for my child is simple, and is good.
He knows his wish. Yes, but that is not all.
Because I know mine too.
And we both want joy of undeep and unabiding things,
Like kicking over a chair or throwing blocks out of a window   5
Or tipping over an icebox pan
Or snatching down curtains or fingering an electric outlet
Or a journey or a friend or an illegal kiss.
No. There is more to it than that.
It is that he has never been afraid.   10
Rather, he reaches out and lo the chair falls with a beautiful crash,
And the blocks fall, down on the people's heads,

And the water comes slooshing sloppily out across the floor.
And so forth.
Not that success, for him, is sure, infallible.   15
But never has he been afraid to reach.
His lesions are legion.
But reaching is his rule.

Raymond Carver (1938–1988)
Photograph of My Father in His Twenty-Second Year (1983)

October. Here in this dank, unfamiliar kitchen
I study my father's embarrassed young man's face.
Sheepish grin, he holds in one hand a string
Of spiny yellow perch, in the other
A bottle of Carlsbad beer.   5

In jeans and denim shirt, he leans
Against the front fender of a Ford *circa* 1934.
He would like to pose bluff and hearty for his posterity,
Wear his old hat cocked over his ear, stick out his
tongue . . .   10
All his life my father wanted to be bold.

But the eyes give him away, and the hands
That limply offer the string of dead perch
And the bottle of beer. Father, I loved you,
Yet how can I say thank you,   15
    I who cannot hold my liquor either,
And do not even know the places to fish?

Samuel Taylor Coleridge (1772–1834)
Kubla Khan (1797, 1798)

In Xanadu did Kubla Khan
A stately pleasure-dome decree:
Where Alph, the sacred river, ran
Through caverns measureless to man
    Down to a sunless sea.   5
So twice five miles of fertile ground
With walls and towers were girdled round:

And here were gardens bright with sinuous rills,
Where blossomed many an incense-bearing tree;
And here were forests ancient as the hills,   10
Enfolding sunny spots of greenery.

But oh! that deep romantic chasm which slanted
Down the green hill athwart a cedarn cover!
A savage place! as holy and enchanted
As e'er beneath a waning moon was haunted   15
By woman wailing for her demon-lover!
And from this chasm, with ceaseless turmoil seething,
As if this earth in fast thick pants were breathing,
A mighty fountain momently was forced:
Amid whose swift half-intermitted burst   20
Huge fragments vaulted like rebounding hail,
Or chaffy grain beneath the thresher's flail:
And 'mid these dancing rocks at once and ever
It flung up momently the sacred river.
Five miles meandering with a mazy motion   25
Through wood and dale the sacred river ran,
Then reached the caverns measureless to man,
And sank in tumult to a lifeless ocean:
And 'mid this tumult Kubla heard from far
Ancestral voices prophesying war!   30

    The shadow of the dome of pleasure
    Floated midway on the waves;
    Where was heard the mingled measure
    From the fountain and the caves.
It was a miracle of rare device,   35
A sunny pleasure-dome with caves of ice!

    A damsel with a dulcimer
    In a vision once I saw:
    It was an Abyssinian maid,
    And on her dulcimer she played,   40
    Singing of Mount Abora.
    Could I revive within me
    Her symphony and song,
    To such a deep delight, 'twould win me,
That with music loud and long,   45
I would build that dome in air,
That sunny dome! those caves of ice!
And all who heard should see them there,

And all should cry, Beware! Beware!
His flashing eyes, his floating hair!   50
Weave a circle round him thrice,
And close your eyes with holy dread,
For he on honey-dew hath fed,
And drunk the milk of Paradise.

Billy Collins (b. 1941)
The City of Tomorrow (1995)

No matter which illustrator was called on
during the 1930s, '40s or '50s
to squint into the world of tomorrow
and render his impression,
the resulting drawing was always the same.   5
A city of tall, streamlined buildings,
bubble-shaped elevators running up the sides,
spiraling towers, vast oval terminals,
transparent pavilions, glassy arcades,
all connected by a complicated network   10
of ramps, monorails, and vaulted walkways,
and above it all, a sky busy with the traffic of strange craft:
jet dirigibles, flying omnibuses,
jumbo helicopters, and one-man winged torpedoes.
Even the air they flew in looked futuristic.   15

I would linger on these magazine pages
studying the brushed aluminum surface of things,
the little pen strokes indicating plate glass,
the perfectly artificial environment
completely enclosed in a huge dome   20
as if it were a city brought to your table,
a delicacy for the imagination to savor,
for this, I believed, was the city of my future.

I focused on the tiny human figures
waiting at a rooftop heliport or drifting along   25
an electronic sidewalk, heading for the office,
and I knew some day I would be one of them.
This city of clean lines was my inheritance,
and it would fall into my outstretched arms
as soon as the present grew old and died in its sleep.   30

But time never advanced, only turned
like the slow blades of the summer fan
over my bed where I would lie imagining
what it would be like to drive a plastic car,
speed lines coming off a giant fin,   35
to wear a chromium rocket on my back,
yes, wondering what it would be like
to recline high up in an apartment of the future,
pushing the buttons on a bedside console
while stroking the forehead of a beautiful robot.   40

I didn't know that the city of tomorrow
was not a place we would come to inhabit
but a place that inhabits us, a phantom
that draftsmen with rulers and India ink
would soon lose interest in drawing.   45

Never mind.
The city of the future I now envision
could be a city of ice, a city of candles,
a city of shoe horns or empty frames,
a city of desire and facing it,   50
across a river, a city of no desire.
It might not be a city at all, but a meadow of grass
where the horses of tomorrow will lower
their mild heads to graze,
or a vaporous landscape, the valleys flooded   55
with the dolorous chords of unwritten songs,
the mountain tops cold and forbidding,
waiting for the climbers of the future to seek them out.

Billy Collins (b. 1941)
The Many Faces of Jazz (1998)

There's the one where you scrunch up
your features into a look of pained concentration,
every riff a new source of agony,

and there's the look of existential bemusement,
eyebrows lifted, chin upheld by a thumb,   5
maybe a swizzle stick oscillating in the free hand.

And, of course, for ballads,
you have the languorous droop,

her eyes half-closed, lips slightly parted,
the head lolling back, flower on a stem,   10
exposing plenty of turtleneck.

There's the everything-but-the-instrument look
on the fellow at the front table,
the one poised to mount the bandstand,
and the classic crazy-man-crazy face,   15
where the fixed grin joins the menacing stare,
especially suitable for long drum solos.

And let us not overlook the empathetic
grimace of the listener
who has somehow located the body   20
of cold rage dammed up behind the playing
and immersed himself deeply in it.

As far as my own jazz face goes—
and don't tell me you don't have one—
it hasn't changed that much   25
since its debut in 1957.
It's nothing special, easy enough to spot
in a corner of any club on any given night.
You know it—the reptilian squint,
lips pursed, jaw clenched tight,   30
and, most essential, the whole
head furiously, yet almost imperceptibly
nodding
in total and absolute agreement.

William Cowper (1731–1800)
Epitaph on a Hare (1783, 1784)

Here lies, whom hound did ne'er pursue,
   Nor swifter greyhound follow,
Whose foot ne'er tainted[1] morning dew,
   Nor ear heard huntsman's hallo',

---

[1]**tainted:** left a scent on

Old Tiney, surliest of his kind,   5
    Who, nursed with tender care,
And to domestic bounds confined,
    Was still a wild jack-hare.

Though duly from my hand he took
    His pittance every night,   10
He did it with a jealous look,
    And, when he could, would bite.

His diet was of wheaten bread,
    And milk, and oats, and straw,
Thistles, or lettuces instead,   15
    With sand to scour his maw.

On twigs of hawthorn he regaled,[2]
    On pippins' russet peel;
And, when his juicy salads failed,
    Sliced carrot pleased him well.   20

A Turkey carpet was his lawn,[3]
    Whereon he loved to bound,
To skip and gambol like a fawn,
    And swing his rump around.

His frisking was at evening hours,   25
    For then he lost his fear;
But most before approaching showers,
    Or when a storm drew near.

Eight years and five round-rolling moons
    He thus saw steal away,   30
Dozing out all his idle noons,
    And every night at play.

I kept him for his humor's sake,
    For he would oft beguile
My heart of thoughts that made it ache,   35
    And force me to a smile.

---

[2]**regaled:** feasted
[3]**Line 21:** Cowper exercised his hares on his parlor carpet of Turkey red.

But now, beneath this walnut-shade
 He finds his long, last home,
And waits in snug concealment laid,
 Till gentler Puss shall come.   40

He,[4] still more agéd, feels the shocks
 From which no care can save,
And, partner once of Tiney's box,
 Must soon partake his grave.

---

[4]**He:** Puss, the longest-lived of Cowper's three hares.

Hart Crane (1899–1932)
from *The Bridge* (1930)

Proem: To Brooklyn Bridge

How many dawns, chill from his rippling rest
The seagull's wings shall dip and pivot him,
Shedding white rings of tumult, building high
Over the chained bay waters Liberty—

Then, with inviolate curve, forsake our eyes 5
As apparitional as sails that cross
Some page of figures to be filed away;
—Till elevators drop us from our day . . .

I think of cinemas, panoramic sleights
With multitudes bent toward some flashing scene 10
Never disclosed, but hastened to again,
Foretold to other eyes on the same screen;

And Thee,[1] across the harbor, silver-paced
As though the sun took step of thee, yet left
Some motion ever unspent in thy stride— 15
Implicitly thy freedom staying thee!

Out of some subway scuttle, cell or loft
A bedlamite[2] speeds to thy parapets,
Tilting there momently, shrill shirt ballooning,
A jest falls from the speechless caravan. 20

---

[1]**Thee:** I.e., Brooklyn Bridge.
[2]**bedlamite:** madman

Down Wall, from girder into street noon leaks,
A rip-tooth of the sky's acetylene,
All afternoon the cloud-flown derricks turn . . .
Thy cables breathe the North Atlantic still.

And obscure as that heaven of the Jews,   25
Thy guerdon . . . Accolade thou dost bestow
Of anonymity time cannot raise:
Vibrant reprieve and pardon thou dost show.

O harp and altar, of the fury fused,
(How could mere toil align thy choiring strings!)   30
Terrific threshold of the prophet's pledge,
Prayer of pariah, and the lover's cry—

Again the traffic lights that skim thy swift
Unfractioned idiom, immaculate sigh of stars,
Beading thy path—condense eternity: 35
And we have seen night lifted in thine arms.

Under thy shadow by the piers I waited;
Only in darkness is thy shadow clear.
The City's fiery parcels all undone,
Already snow submerges an iron year . . .   40

O Sleepless as the river under thee,
Vaulting the sea, the prairies' dreaming sod,
Unto us lowliest sometime sweep, descend
And of the curveship lend a myth to God.

e.e. cummings (1894–1962)

since feeling is first (1926)

since feeling is first
who pays any attention
to the syntax of things
will never wholly kiss you;
wholly to be a fool   5
while Spring is in the world

my blood approves,
and kisses are a better fate
than wisdom
lady i swear by all flowers. Don't cry   10
—the best gesture of my brain is less than
your eyelids' flutter which says

we are for each other: then
laugh, leaning back in my arms
for life's not a paragraph   15

And death i think is no parenthesis

Emily Dickinson (1830–1886)
A Bird came down the Walk— (1862, 1891)

A Bird came down the Walk—
He did not know I saw—
He bit an Angleworm in halves
And ate the fellow, raw,

And then he drank a Dew   5
From a convenient Grass—
And then hopped sidewise to the Wall
To let a Beetle pass—

He glanced with rapid eyes
That hurried all around—   10
They looked like frightened Beads, I thought—
He stirred his Velvet Head

Like one in danger, Cautious,
I offered him a Crumb
And he unrolled his feathers   15
And rowed him softer home—

Than Oars divide the Ocean,
Too silver for a seam—
Or Butterflies, off Banks of Noon
Leap, plashless as they swim.   20

Emily Dickinson (1830–1886)
A narrow Fellow in the Grass (1866, 1891)

A narrow Fellow in the Grass
Occasionally rides—
You may have met Him—did you not
His notice sudden is—

The Grass divides as with a Comb—   5
A spotted shaft is seen—

And then it closes at your feet
And opens further on—

He likes a Boggy Acre
A Floor too cool for Corn— 10
Yet when a Boy, and Barefoot—
I more than once at Noon
Have passed, I thought, a Whip lash
Unbraiding in the Sun
When stooping to secure it 15
It wrinkled, and was gone—

Several of Nature's People
I know, and they know me—
I feel for them a transport
Of cordiality— 20

But never met this Fellow
Attended, or alone
Without a tighter breathing
And Zero at the Bone—

Emily Dickinson (1830–1886)
Apparently with no surprise (circa 1884)

Apparently with no surprise
To any happy Flower
The Frost beheads it at its play—
In accidental power—
The blonde Assassin passes on— 5
The Sun proceeds unmoved
To measure off another Day
For an Approving God.

Emily Dickinson (1830–1886)
I dwell in Possibility— (1862)

I dwell in Possibility—
A fairer House than Prose—
More numerous of Windows—
Superior—for Doors—

Of Chambers as the Cedars— 5
Impregnable of Eye—

And for an Everlasting Roof
The Gambrels* of the Sky—
Of Visitors—the fairest—
For Occupation—This—   10
The spreading wide my narrow Hands
To gather Paradise—

Gambrels: Roofs with double slopes

Emily Dickinson (1830–1886)
I felt a Funeral, in my Brain (circa 1861)

I felt a Funeral, in my Brain,
And Mourners to and fro
Kept treading—treading—till it seemed
That Sense was breaking through—

And when they all were seated,   5
A Service, like a Drum—
Kept beating—beating—till I thought
My Mind was going numb—

And then I heard them lift a Box
And creak across my Soul   10
With those same Boots of Lead, again,
Then Space—began to toll,

As all the Heavens were a Bell,
And Being, but an Ear,
And I, and Silence, some strange Race   15
Wrecked, solitary, here—

And then a Plank in Reason, broke,
And I dropped down, and down—
And hit a World, at every plunge,
And Finished knowing—then—   20

Emily Dickinson (1830–1886)
I heard a Fly buzz—when I died— (1862?, 1896)

I heard a Fly buzz—when I died—
The Stillness in the Room
Was like the Stillness in the Air—
Between the Heaves of Storm—

The Eyes around—had wrung them dry—   5
And Breaths were gathering firm
For that last Onset—when the King
Be witnessed—in the Room—

I willed my Keepsakes—Signed away
What portion of me be   10
Assignable—and then it was
There interposed a Fly—

With Blue—uncertain stumbling Buzz—
Between the light—and me—
And then the Windows failed—and then   15
I could not see to see—

Emily Dickinson (1830–1886)
Wild Nights—Wild Nights! (1861)

Wild Nights—Wild Nights!
Were I with thee
Wild Nights should be
Our luxury!

Futile—the Winds—   5
To a Heart in port—
Done with the Compass—
Done with the Chart!

Rowing in Eden—
Ah, the Sea!   10
Might I but moor—Tonight—
In Thee!

John Donne (1572–1631)
A Valediction: Forbidding Mourning (1633)

As virtuous men pass mildly' away,
    And whisper to their souls to go,
Whilst some of their sad friends do say
    The breath goes now, and some say, No;

So let us melt, and make no noise,   5
    No tear-floods, nor sigh-tempests move,
'Twere profanation of our joys
    To tell the laity our love.

Moving of th' earth brings harms and fears,
    Men reckon what it did and meant;   10
But trepidation of the spheres,[1]
    Though greater far, is innocent.

Dull sublunary[2] lovers' love
    (Whose soul is sense) cannot admit
Absence, because it doth remove   15
    Those things which elemented it.

But we by'a love so much refined
    That our selves know not what it is,
Inter-assuréd of the mind,
    Care less, eyes, lips, and hands to miss.   20

Our two souls therefore, which are one,
    Though I must go, endure not yet
A breach, but an expansion,
    Like gold to airy thinness beat.

If they be two, they are two so   25
    As stiff twin compasses are two;
Thy soul, the fixed foot, makes no show
    To move, but doth, if th' other do.

And though it in the center sit,
    Yet when the other far doth roam,   30
It leans and hearkens after it,
    And grows erect, as that comes home.

Such wilt thou be to me, who must
    Like th' other foot, obliquely run;
Thy firmness makes my circle[3] just,   35
    And makes me end where I begun.

---

[1]**trepidation of the spheres:** A trembling of the celestial spheres, hypothesized by Ptolemaic astronomers to account for unpredicted variations in the paths of the heavenly bodies.
[2]**sublunary:** Beneath the moon; earthly—hence, changeable.
[3]**circle:** The circle was a symbol of perfection; with a dot in the middle, it was also the alchemist's symbol for gold.

John Donne (1572–1631)
Batter my heart, three-personed God; for You (Holy Sonnets 14) (1633)

Batter my heart, three-personed God; for You
As yet but knock, breathe, shine, and seek to mend;
That I may rise and stand, o'erthrow me,'and bend
Your force to break, blow, burn, and make me new.
I, like an usurped town, to'another due,   5
Labor to'admit You, but O, to no end;
Reason, Your viceroy'in me, me should defend,
But is captíved, and proves weak or untrue.
Yet dearly'I love You,'and would be lovéd fain,
But am betrothed unto Your enemy.   10
Divorce me,'untie or break that knot again;
Take me to You, imprison me, for I,
Except You'enthrall me, never shall be free,
Nor ever chaste, except You ravish me.

John Donne (1572–1631)
The Flea (1633)

Mark but this flea, and mark in this
How little that which thou deny'st me is;
It sucked me first, and now sucks thee,
And in this flea our two bloods mingled be;
Thou know'st that this cannot be said   5
A sin, nor shame, nor loss of maidenhead;
    Yet this enjoys before it woo,
      And pampered swells with one blood made of two,
      And this, alas, is more than we would do.

Oh stay, three lives in one flea spare,   10
Where we almost, yea more than married are.
This flea is you and I, and this
Our marriage bed and marriage temple is;
Though parents grudge, and you, we are met
And cloistered in these living walls of jet.   15
    Though use[1] make you apt to kill me,

---

[1]**use:** habit

Let not to that, self-murder added be,
And sacrilege, three sins in killing three.

Cruel and sudden, hast thou since
Purpled[2] thy nail in blood of innocence?   20
Wherein could this flea guilty be,
Except in that drop which it sucked from thee?
Yet thou triumph'st and say'st that thou
Find'st not thyself, nor me, the weaker now.
    'Tis true. Then learn how false fears be: 25
    Just so much honor, when thou yield'st to me,
    Will waste, as this flea's death took life from thee.

---

[2]**Purpled:** crimsoned

John Donne (1572–1631)
The Sun Rising (1633)

    Busy old fool, unruly sun,
      Why dost thou thus
Through windows and through curtains call on us?
Must to thy motions lovers' seasons run?
    Saucy pedantic wretch, go chide   5
    Late schoolboys and sour 'prentices,
  Go tell court-huntsmen that the king will ride,
  Call country ants to harvest offices;
Love, all alike, no season knows, nor clime,
Nor hours, days, months, which are the rags of time.   10

    Thy beams so reverend and strong
      Why shouldst thou think?
I could eclipse and cloud them with a wink,
But that I would not lose her sight so long;
    If her eyes have not blinded thine,   15
    Look, and tomorrow late tell me
  Whether both th' Indias of spice and mine
  Be where thou left'st them, or lie here with me.
Ask for those kings whom thou saw'st yesterday,
And thou shalt hear, "All here in one bed lay."   20

    She's all states, and all princes I;
      Nothing else is.

Princes do but play us; compared to this,
All honor's mimic, all wealth alchemy.
    Thou, sun, art half as happy as we,   25
      In that the world's contracted thus;
    Thine age asks ease, and since thy duties be
    To warm the world, that's done in warming us.
Shine here to us, and thou art everywhere;
This bed thy center is, these walls thy sphere.   30

Paul Laurence Dunbar (1872–1906)
We Wear the Mask (1896)

We wear the mask that grins and lies,
It hides our cheeks and shades our eyes—
This debt we pay to human guile;
With torn and bleeding hearts we smile,
And mouth with myriad subtleties.   5

Why should the world be over-wise,
In counting all our tears and sighs?
Nay, let them only see us, while
    We wear the mask.

We smile, but, O great Christ, our cries   10
To thee from tortured souls arise.
We sing, but oh the clay is vile
Beneath our feet, and long the mile;
But let the world dream otherwise,
    We wear the mask!   15

Robert Frost (1874–1963)
Birches (1915)

When I see birches bend to left and right
Across the lines of straighter darker trees,
I like to think some boy's been swinging them.
But swinging doesn't bend them down to stay
As ice-storms do. Often you must have seen them   5
Loaded with ice a sunny winter morning

After a rain. They click upon themselves
As the breeze rises, and turn many-colored
As the stir cracks and crazes their enamel.
Soon the sun's warmth makes them shed crystal shells   10
Shattering and avalanching on the snow-crust—
Such heaps of broken glass to sweep away
You'd think the inner dome of heaven had fallen.
They are dragged to the withered bracken by the load,
And they seem not to break; though once they are bowed   15
So low for long, they never right themselves:
You may see their trunks arching in the woods
Years afterwards, trailing their leaves on the ground
Like girls on hands and knees that throw their hair
Before them over their heads to dry in the sun.   20
But I was going to say when Truth broke in
With all her matter-of-fact about the ice-storm
I should prefer to have some boy bend them
As he went out and in to fetch the cows—
Some boy too far from town to learn baseball,   25
Whose only play was what he found himself,
Summer or winter, and could play alone.
One by one he subdued his father's trees
By riding them down over and over again
Until he took the stiffness out of them,   30
And not one but hung limp, not one was left
For him to conquer. He learned all there was
To learn about not launching out too soon
And so not carrying the tree away
Clear to the ground. He always kept his poise   35
To the top branches, climbing carefully
With the same pains you use to fill a cup
Up to the brim, and even above the brim.
Then he flung outward, feet first, with a swish,
Kicking his way down through the air to the ground.   40
So was I once myself a swinger of birches.
And so I dream of going back to be.
It's when I'm weary of considerations,
And life is too much like a pathless wood
Where your face burns and tickles with the cobwebs   45
Broken across it, and one eye is weeping
From a twig's having lashed across it open.
I'd like to get away from earth awhile
And then come back to it and begin over.
May no fate willfully misunderstand me   50
And half grant what I wish and snatch me away

Not to return. Earth's the right place for love:
I don't know where it's likely to go better.
I'd like to go by climbing a birch tree,
And climb black branches up a snow-white trunk   55
Toward heaven, till the tree could bear no more,
But dipped its top and set me down again.
That would be good both going and coming back.
One could do worse than be a swinger of birches.

Robert Frost (1874–1963)
Design (1936)

I found a dimpled spider, fat and white,
On a white heal-all, holding up a moth
Like a white piece of rigid satin cloth—
Assorted characters of death and blight
Mixed ready to begin the morning right,   5
Like the ingredients of a witches' broth—
A snow-drop spider, a flower like a froth,
And dead wings carried like a paper kite.

What had that flower to do with being white,
The wayside blue and innocent heal-all?   10
What brought the kindred spider to that height,
Then steered the white moth thither in the night?
What but design of darkness to appall?—
If design govern in a thing so small.

Robert Frost (1874–1963)
Fire and Ice (1923)

Some say the world will end in fire,
Some say in ice.
From what I've tasted of desire
I hold with those who favor fire.
But if it had to perish twice,   5
I think I know enough of hate
To say that for destruction ice
Is also great
And would suffice.

Tu Fu (712–770)
Loneliness

A hawk hovers in air.
Two white gulls float on the stream.
Soaring with the wind, it is easy
To drop and seize
Birds who foolishly drift with the current.   5
Where the dew sparkles in the grass,
The spider's web waits for its prey.
The processes of nature resemble the business of men.
I stand alone with ten thousand sorrows.

Seamus Heaney (b. 1939)
Mid-Term Break (1966)

I sat all morning in the college sick bay
Counting bells knelling classes to a close.
At two o'clock our neighbours drove me home.

In the porch I met my father crying—
He had always taken funerals in his stride—   5
And Big Jim Evans saying it was a hard blow.

The baby cooed and laughed and rocked the pram
When I came in, and I was embarrassed
By old men standing up to shake my hand

And tell me they were 'sorry for my trouble'.   10
Whispers informed strangers I was the eldest,
Away at school, as my mother held my hand

In hers and coughed out angry tearless sighs.
At ten o'clock the ambulance arrived
With the corpse, stanched and bandaged by the nurses. 15

Next morning I went up into the room. Snowdrops
And candles soothed the bedside; I saw him
For the first time in six weeks. Paler now,

Wearing a poppy bruise on his left temple,
He lay in the four-foot box as in his cot.   20
No gaudy scars, the bumper knocked him clear.

A four-foot box, a foot for every year.

Robert Herrick (1591–1674)
Upon Julia's Clothes (1648)

Whenas in silks my Julia goes
Then, then, methinks, how sweetly flows
That liquefaction of her clothes.

Next, when I cast mine eyes, and see
That brave* vibration, each way free,   5
O, how that glittering taketh me!

*brave: Handsome, showy.

John Hollander (b. 1929)
A State of Nature (1969)

Some broken
Iroquois adze
pounded southward
and resembled this
outline once But now   5
boundaries foul-lines
and even sea-coasts are
naturally involved with
mappers and followers of
borders So that we who grew   10
up here might think That steak is
shaped too much like New York to be real And like
the shattered flinty implement whose ghost lives
inside our sense of what this rough chunk should
by right of history recall the language spoken by   15
its shapers now inhabits only streams and lakes and
hills The natural names are only a chattering and mean
only the land they label How shall we live in a forest of
such murmurs with
no ideas but in   20
forms a state
whose name
passes
for
a city   25

Gerard Manley Hopkins (1844–1889)
The Windhover[1] (1877, 1918)

To Christ Our Lord

I caught this morning morning's minion,[2] king-
  dom of daylight's dauphin,[3] dapple-dawn-drawn Falcon, in his riding
  Of the rolling level underneath him steady air, and striding
High there, how he rung upon the rein of a wimpling[4] wing
In his ecstasy! then off, off forth on swing,   5
  As a skate's heel sweeps smooth on a bow-bend: the hurl and gliding
  Rebuffed the big wind. My heart in hiding
Stirred for a bird,—the achieve of, the mastery of the thing!

Brute beauty and valour and act, oh, air, pride, plume, here
  Buckle![5] AND the fire that breaks from thee then, a billion
Times told lovelier, more dangerous, O my chevalier![6]   10

  No wonder of it: shéer plód makes plough down sillion[7]
Shine, and blue-bleak embers, ah my dear,
  Fall, gall themselves, and gash gold-vermilion.

---

[1]**Windhover:** "A name for the kestrel [a species of small hawk], from its habit of hovering or hanging with its head to the wind" [O.E.D.].
[2]**minion:** darling, favorite
[3]**dauphin:** The eldest son of the king of France was called the *dauphin*: hence, the word here means heir to a splendid, kingly condition.
[4]**wimpling:** rippling
[5]**Buckle:** The word "buckle" brings to a single focus the several elements of line 8, in both their literal sense, as descriptive of a single, sudden movement of the airborne bird, and in their symbolic sense as descriptive of Christ and with further reference to the poet himself and the lesson he draws from his observation. It may be read either as indicative or imperative, and in one or another of its possible meanings: "to fasten," "to join closely," "to equip for battle," "to grapple with, engage," but also "to cause to bend, give way, crumple."
[6]**chevalier:** Knight, nobleman, champion.
[7]**sillion:** furrow

A. E. Housman (1859–1936)
"Terence,[1] This Is Stupid Stuff . . ." (1896)

  "Terence, this is stupid stuff:
You eat your victuals fast enough;

---

[1]**Terence:** Housman had at first planned to call the volume in which this poem appeared *The Poems of Terence Hearsay.*

There can't be much amiss, [2]tis clear,
To see the rate you drink your beer.
But oh, good Lord, the verse you make, 5
It gives a chap the belly-ache.
The cow, the old cow, she is dead;
It sleeps well, the hornéd head:
We poor lads, 'tis our turn now
To hear such tunes as killed the cow. 10
Pretty friendship 'tis to rhyme
Your friends to death before their time
Moping melancholy mad:
Come, pipe a tune to dance to, lad."

    Why, if 'tis dancing you would be, 15
There's brisker pipes than poetry.
Say, for what were hop-yards meant,
Or why was Burton built on Trent?[2]
Oh many a peer of England brews
Livelier liquor than the Muse, 20
And malt does more than Milton can
To justify God's ways to man.
Ale, man, ale's the stuff to drink
For fellows whom it hurts to think:
Look into the pewter pot 25
To see the world as the world's not.
And faith, 'tis pleasant till 'tis past:
The mischief is that 'twill not last.
Oh I have been to Ludlow[3] fair
And left my necktie God knows where, 30
And carried halfway home, or near,
Pints and quarts of Ludlow beer:
Then the world seemed none so bad,
And I myself a sterling lad;
And down in lovely muck I've lain, 35
Happy till I woke again.
Then I saw the morning sky:
Heigho, the tale was all a lie;
The world, it was the old world yet,
I was I, my things were wet, 40

---

[2]**Burton built on Trent:** Burton-on-Trent, a town in Staffordshire whose principal industry is the brewing of ale.
[3]**Ludlow:** A town in Shropshire.

And nothing now remained to do
But begin the game anew.

    Therefore, since the world has still
Much good, but much less good than ill,
And while the sun and moon endure   45
Luck's a chance, but trouble's sure,
I'd face it as a wise man would,
And train for ill and not for good.
'Tis true, the stuff I bring for sale
Is not so brisk a brew as ale: 50
Out of a stem that scored the hand
I wrung it in a weary land.
But take it: if the smack is sour,
The better for the embittered hour;
It should do good to heart and head   55
When your soul is in my soul's stead;
And I will friend you, if I may,
In the dark and cloudy day.

    There was a king reigned in the East:
There, when kings will sit to feast,   60
They get their fill before they think
With poisoned meat and poisoned drink.
He gathered all that springs to birth
From the many-venomed earth;
First a little, thence to more,   65
He sampled all her killing store;
And easy, smiling, seasoned sound,
Sate the king when healths went round.
They put arsenic in his meat
And stared aghast to watch him eat;   70
They poured strychnine in his cup
And shook to see him drink it up:
They shook, they stared as white's their shirt:
Them it was their poison hurt.
—I tell the tale that I heard told.   75
Mithridates, he died old.[4]

---

[4]**Line 76:** Mithridates VI, king of Pontus in Asia Minor in the first century B.C., produced in himself an immunity to certain poisons by administering them to himself in small, gradual doses.

A. E. Housman (1859–1936)
To an Athlete Dying Young (1896)

The time you won your town the race
We chaired you through the market-place;
Man and boy stood cheering by,
And home we brought you shoulder-high.

Today, the road all runners come,   5
Shoulder-high, we bring you home,
And set you at your threshold down,
Townsman of a stiller town.

Smart lad, to slip betimes away
From fields where glory does not stay   10
And early though the laurel grows
It withers quicker than the rose.

Eyes the shady night has shut
Cannot see the record cut,
And silence sounds no worse than cheers   15
After earth has stopped the ears:

Now you will not swell the rout
Of lads that wore their honors out,
Runners whom renown outran
And the name died before the man.   20

So set, before its echoes fade,
The fleet foot on the sill of shade,
And hold to the low lintel up
The still-defended challenge-cup.

And round that early-laureled head   25
Will flock to gaze the strengthless dead,
And find unwithered on its curls
The garland briefer than a girl's.

Ben Jonson (1572–1637)
Still to Be Neat[1] (1609)

Still[2] to be neat, still to be dressed,
As you were going to a feast;

---

[1]**Still to Be Neat:** A song from Jonson's play *The Silent Woman* (1609–1610).
[2]**Still:** Continually.

Still to be powdered, still perfumed;
Lady, it is to be presumed,
Though art's hid causes are not found,   5
All is not sweet, all is not sound.

Give me a look, give me a face
That makes simplicity a grace;
Robes loosely flowing, hair as free;
Such sweet neglect more taketh me   10
Than all th' adulteries of art.
They strike mine eyes, but not my heart.

John Keats (1795–1821)

Ode to a Nightingale (1819, 1820)

1

My heart aches, and a drowsy numbness pains
    My sense, as though of hemlock[1] I had drunk.
Or emptied some dull opiate to the drains
    One minute past, and Lethe-wards[2] had sunk:
'Tis not through envy of thy happy lot,   5
    But being too happy in thine happiness—
        That thou, light-wingéd Dryad of the trees,
        In some melodious plot
Of beechen green, and shadows numberless,
    Singest of summer in full-throated ease.   10

2

O, for a draught of vintage! that hath been
    Cooled a long age in the deep-delvéd earth,
Tasting of Flora[3] and the country green,
    Dance, and Provençal song,[4] and sunburnt mirth!
O for a beaker full of the warm South,   15
    Full of the true, the blushful Hippocrene,[5]
        With beaded bubbles winking at the brim,

---

[1] **hemlock:** Opiate made from a poisonous herb.
[2] **Lethe-wards:** Towards the river Lethe, whose waters in Hades bring the dead forgetfulness.
[3] **Flora:** Roman goddess of springtime and flowers.
[4] **Provençal song:** Of the late-medieval troubadours of Provence, in southern France.
[5] **Hippocrene:** The fountain of the Muses (goddesses of poetry and the arts) on Mt. Helicon in Greece; its waters induce poetic inspiration.

And purple-stainéd mouth;
   That I might drink, and leave the world unseen,
      And with thee fade away into the forest dim: 20
   3
Fade far away, dissolve, and quite forget
   What thou among the leaves hast never known,
The weariness, the fever, and the fret
   Here, where men sit and hear each other groan;
Where palsy shakes a few, sad, last gray hairs,   25
   Where youth grows pale, and specter-thin, and dies,
      Where but to think is to be full of sorrow
         And leaden-eyed despairs,
   Where Beauty cannot keep her lustrous eyes,
      Or new Love pine at them beyond tomorrow.   30
   4
Away! away! for I will fly to thee,
   Not charioted by Bacchus and his pards,[6]
But on the viewless[7] wings of Poesy,
   Though the dull brain perplexes and retards:
Already with thee! tender is the night,   35
   And haply the Queen-Moon is on her throne,
      Clustered around by all her starry Fays;[8]
         But here there is no light,
   Save what from heaven is with the breezes blown
      Through verdurous glooms and winding mossy ways.   40
   5
I cannot see what flowers are at my feet,
   Nor what soft incense hangs upon the boughs,
But, in embalméd[9] darkness, guess each sweet
   Wherewith the seasonable month endows
The grass, the thicket, and the fruit tree wild;   45
   White hawthorn, and the pastoral eglantine;[10]
      Fast fading violets covered up in leaves;
         And mid-May's eldest child,
   The coming musk-rose, full of dewy wine,
      The murmurous haunt of flies on summer eves.   50

---

[6]**Bacchus and his pards:** "Bacchus": god of wine, often depicted in a chariot drawn by leopards ("pards").
[7]**viewless:** invisible
[8]**Fays:** fairies
[9]**embalméd:** perfumed
[10]**eglantine:** Sweetbrier; wood roses.

6
Darkling[11] I listen; and for many a time
I have been half in love with easeful Death,
Called him soft names in many a muséd rhyme,
To take into the air my quiet breath;
Now more than ever seems it rich to die,   55
To cease upon the midnight with no pain,
While thou art pouring forth thy soul abroad
In such an ecstasy!
Still wouldst thou sing, and I have ears in vain—
To thy high requiem become a sod.   60

7
Thou wast not born for death, immortal Bird!
No hungry generations tread thee down;
The voice I hear this passing night was heard
In ancient days by emperor and clown:
Perhaps the selfsame song that found a path   65
Through the sad heart of Ruth,[12] when, sick for home,
She stood in tears amid the alien corn;
The same that ofttimes hath
Charmed magic casements, opening on the foam
Of perilous seas, in faery lands forlorn.   70

8
Forlorn! the very word is like a bell
To toll me back from thee to my sole self!
Adieu! the fancy cannot cheat so well
As she is famed to do, deceiving elf.
Adieu! adieu! thy plaintive anthem fades   75
Past the near meadows, over the still stream,
Up the hill side; and now 'tis buried deep
In the next valley-glades:
Was it a vision, or a waking dream?
Fled is that music:—Do I wake or sleep?   80

---

[11]**Darkling:** in darkness
[12]**Ruth:** In the Old Testament, a woman of great loyalty and modesty who, as a stranger in Judah, won a husband while gleaning in the barley-fields ("the alien corn," line 67).

Amy King (b. 1971)
Love, without Its Name (2005)

Something recognizable like
knowing a city by its street
people faraway in an instant

on the grass of breeze olive
country pauses in the freeze,   5
the fresco taking smaller
strokes as part of a mountain
cutaway to be hung later on
dining room walls. Words
between centuries are forever   10
closing. Laws eat mathematics.
Man stands in for the lava
of creation, the never-was
and never-being. Alternate
an explanation for why there   15
is so much, angled reason.
Our tired sheep settle closer
to the ground and wool clothing
echoes painted clouds, now fading.

Etheridge Knight (1931–1991)
For Malcolm, a Year After (1966)

Compose for Red a proper verse;
Adhere to foot and strict iamb;
Control the burst of angry words
Or they might boil and break the dam.
Or they might boil and overflow   5
And drench me, drown me, drive me mad.
So swear no oath, so shed no tear,
And sing no song blue Baptist sad.
Evoke no image, stir no flame,
And spin no yarn across the air.   10
Make empty anglo tea lace words—
Make them dead and white and dry bone bare.

Compose a verse for Malcolm man,
And make it rime and make it prim.
The verse will die—as all men do—   15
But not the memory of him!
Death might come singing sweet like C,
Or knocking like the old folk say,
The moon and stars may pass away,
But not the anger of that day.   20

D. H. Lawrence (1885–1930)

Snake (1923)

A snake came to my water-trough
On a hot, hot day, and I in pajamas for the heat,
To drink there.

In the deep, strange-scented shade of the great dark carob-tree
I came down the steps with my pitcher   5
And must wait, must stand and wait, for there he was at the trough
    before me.

He reached down from a fissure in the earth-wall in the gloom
And trailed his yellow-brown slackness soft-bellied down, over
    the edge of the stone trough
And rested his throat upon the stone bottom,
And where the water had dripped from the tap, in a small clearness,   10
He sipped with his straight mouth,
Softly drank through his straight gums, into his slack long body,
Silently.

Someone was before me at my water-trough,
And I, like a second comer, waiting.   15

He lifted his head from his drinking, as cattle do,
And looked at me vaguely, as drinking cattle do,
And flickered his two-forked tongue from his lips, and mused a moment,
And stooped and drank a little more,
Being earth-brown, earth-golden from the burning bowels of the earth   20
On the day of Sicilian July, with Etna smoking.

The voice of my education said to me
He must be killed,
For in Sicily the black, black snakes are innocent, the gold are venomous.

And voices in me said, If you were a man   25
You would take a stick and break him now, and finish him off.

But must I confess how I liked him,
How glad I was he had come like a guest in quiet, to drink at my
    water-trough

And depart peaceful, pacified, and thankless,
Into the burning bowels of this earth?   30

Was it cowardice, that I dared not kill him?
Was it perversity, that I longed to talk to him?
Was it humility, to feel so honored?
I felt so honored.

And yet those voices:
If you were not afraid, you would kill him!   35

And truly I was afraid, I was most afraid,
But even so, honored still more
That he should seek my hospitality
From out the dark door of the secret earth.

He drank enough   40
And lifted his head, dreamily, as one who has drunken,
And flickered his tongue like a forked night on the air, so black,
Seeming to lick his lips,
And looked around like a god, unseeing, into the air,
And slowly turned his head,   45
And slowly, very slowly, as if thrice adream,
Proceeded to draw his slow length curving round
And climb again the broken bank of my wall-face.

And as he put his head into that dreadful hole,
And as he slowly drew up, snake-easing his shoulders, and
        entered farther,   50
A sort of horror, a sort of protest against his withdrawing into that
        horrid black hole,
Deliberately going into the blackness, and slowly drawing himself after,
Overcame me now his back was turned.

I looked round, I put down my pitcher,
I picked up a clumsy log   55
And threw it at the water-trough with a clatter.

I think it did not hit him,
But suddenly that part of him that was left behind convulsed in
        undignified haste
Writhed like lightning, and was gone
Into the black hole, the earth-lipped fissure in the wall-front, 60
At which, in the intense still noon, I stared with fascination.

And immediately I regretted it.
I thought how paltry, how vulgar, what a mean act!
I despised myself and the voices of my accursed human education.

And I thought of the albatross*   65
And I wished he would come back, my snake.

For he seemed to me again like a king,
Like a king in exile, uncrowned in the underworld,
Now due to be crowned again.

And so, I missed my chance with one of the lords   70
Of life.
And I have something to expiate;
A pettiness.

---

*albatross:** In Samuel Taylor Coleridge's *Rime of the Ancient Mariner.*

Richard Lovelace (1618–1658)
To Lucasta, Going to the Wars (1649)

Tell me not, Sweet, I am unkind
    That from the nunnery
Of thy chaste breast and quiet mind,
    To war and arms I fly.

True, a new mistress now I chase,   5
    The first foe in the field;
And with a stronger faith embrace
    A sword, a horse, a shield.

Yet this inconstancy is such
    As you too shall adore;   10
I could not love thee, Dear, so much,
    Loved I not Honor more.

Edna St. Vincent Millay (1892–1950)
What lips my lips have kissed, and where, and why (1923)

What lips my lips have kissed, and where, and why,
I have forgotten, and what arms have lain
Under my head till morning; but the rain
Is full of ghosts tonight, that tap and sigh
Upon the glass and listen for reply,   5

And in my heart there stirs a quiet pain
For unremembered lads that not again
Will turn to me at midnight with a cry.
Thus in the winter stands the lonely tree,
Nor knows what birds have vanished one by one,   10
Yet knows its boughs more silent than before:
I cannot say what loves have come and gone;
I only know that summer sang in me
A little while, that in me sings no more.

Robert Morgan (b. 1944)
Mountain Graveyard (1979)

for the author of "Slow Owls"

Spōre Prose

stone	notes	
slate	rales	
sacred	cedars	
heart	earth	
asleep	please	5
hated	death	

Charles Olson (1910–1970)
Maximus, to Himself (1966)

I have had to learn the simplest things
last. Which made for difficulties.
Even at sea I was slow, to get the hand out, or to cross
a wet deck.
          The sea was not, finally, my trade.   5
But even my trade, at it, I stood estranged
from that which was most familiar. Was delayed,
and not content with the man's argument
that such postponement
is now the nature of   10
obedience,
          that we are all late
          in a slow time,

that we grow up many
And the single
is not easily   15
known

It could be, though the sharpness (the *achiote*)
I note in others,
makes more sense   20
than my own distances. The agilities

        they show daily
        who do the world's
        businesses
        And who do nature's   25
        as I have no sense
        I have done either

I have made dialogues,
have discussed ancient texts,
have thrown what light I could, offered   30
what pleasures
doceat allows

        But the known?
This, I have had to be given,
a life, love, and from one man   35
the world.

        Tokens.
        But sitting here
        I look out as a wind
        and water man, testing   40
        And missing
        some proof

I know the quarters
of the weather, where it comes from,
where it goes. But the stem of me,   45
this I took from their welcome,
or their rejection, of me

        And my arrogance
        was neither diminished
        nor increased,   50
        by the communication

2

It is undone business
I speak of, this morning,
with the sea
stretching out   55
from my feet

Marge Piercy (b. 1936)
Barbie Doll (1973)

This girlchild was born as usual
and presented dolls that did pee-pee
and miniature GE stoves and irons
and wee lipsticks the color of cherry candy.
Then in the magic of puberty, a classmate said: 5
You have a great big nose and fat legs.

She was healthy, tested intelligent,
possessed strong arms and back,
abundant sexual drive and manual dexterity.
She went to and fro apologizing.   10
Everyone saw a fat nose on thick legs.

She was advised to play coy,
exhorted to come on hearty,
exercise, diet, smile and wheedle.
Her good nature wore out   15
like a fan belt.
So she cut off her nose and her legs
and offered them up.

In the casket displayed on satin she lay
with the undertaker's cosmetics painted on,   20
a turned-up putty nose,
dressed in a pink and white nightie.
Doesn't she look pretty? everyone said.
Consummation at last.
To every woman a happy ending.   25

Edgar Allan Poe (1809–1849)
Annabel Lee* (1849)

It was many and many a year ago,
    In a kingdom by the sea
That a maiden there lived whom you may know
    By the name of ANNABEL LEE;
And this maiden she lived with no other thought   5
    Than to love and be loved by me.

I was a child and *she* was a child,
    In this kingdom by the sea;
But we loved with a love that was more than love—
    I and my ANNABEL LEE—   10
With a love that the wingèd seraphs of heaven
    Coveted her and me.

And this was the reason that, long ago,
    In this kingdom by the sea,
A wind blew out of a cloud, chilling   15
    My beautiful ANNABEL LEE;
So that her highborn kinsmen came
    And bore her away from me,
To shut her up in a sepulchre
    In this kingdom by the sea.   20

The angels, not half so happy in heaven,
    Went envying her and me—
Yes!—that was the reason (as all men know,
    In this kingdom by the sea)
That the wind came out of the cloud by night,   25
    Chilling and killing my ANNABEL LEE.

But our love it was stronger by far than the love
    Of those who were older than we—
    Of many far wiser than we—
And neither the angels in heaven above,   30
    Nor the demons down under the sea,
Can ever dissever my soul from the soul
    Of the beautiful ANNABEL LEE:

---

*Annabel Lee: The text is that of the first printing, in Rufus Griswold's article in the New York *Tribune* (October 9, 1849), signed "Ludwig."

For the moon never beams, without bringing me dreams
    Of the beautiful ANNABEL LEE;   35
And the stars never rise, but I feel the bright eyes
    Of the beautiful ANNABEL LEE:
And so, all the night tide, I lie down by the side
Of my darling—my darling—my life and my bride,
    In her sepulchre there by the sea—   40
    In her tomb by the sounding sea.

Ishmael Reed (b. 1938)
beware : do not read this poem (1970)

tonite   ,   thriller was
abt an ol woman   , so vain she
surrounded herself w/
    many mirrors

it got so bad that finally she   5
locked herself indoors & her
whole life became the
    mirrors

one day the villagers broke
into her house   ,   but she was too   10
swift for them   .   she disappeared
    into a mirror

each tenant who bought the house
after that   ,   lost a loved one to
    the ol woman in the mirror :   15
    first a little girl
    then a young woman
    then the young woman/s husband

the hunger of this poem is legendary
it has taken in many victims   20
back off from this poem
it has drawn in yr feet
back off from this poem
it has drawn in yr legs

back off from this poem   25
it is a greedy mirror

you are into this poem   .   from
        the waist down
nobody can hear you can they?
this poem has had you up to here   30
        belch
this poem aint got no manners
you cant call out frm this poem
relax now & go w / this poem
move & roll on to this poem   35
do not resist this poem
this poem has yr eyes
this poem has his head
this poem has his arms
this poem has his fingers   40
this poem has his fingertips
this poem is the reader & the
reader this poem

statistic   :   the us bureau of missing persons reports
                that in 1968 over 100,000 people disappeared   45
                leaving no solid clues
                        nor trace   only
    a space   in the lives of their friends

Adrienne Rich (b. 1929)
Aunt Jennifer's Tigers (1951)

Aunt Jennifer's tigers prance across a screen,
Bright topaz denizens of a world of green.
They do not fear the men beneath the tree;
They pace in sleek chivalric certainty.

Aunt Jennifer's fingers fluttering through her wool   5
Find even the ivory needle hard to pull.
The massive weight of Uncle's wedding band
Sits heavily upon Aunt Jennifer's hand.

When Aunt is dead, her terrified hands will lie
Still ringed with ordeals she was mastered by.   10
The tigers in the panel that she made
Will go on prancing, proud and unafraid.

Adrienne Rich (b. 1929)
Living in Sin (1955)

She had thought the studio would keep itself;
no dust upon the furniture of love.
Half heresy, to wish the taps less vocal,
the panes relieved of grime. A plate of pears,
a piano with a Persian shawl, a cat   5
stalking the picturesque amusing mouse
had risen at his urging.
Not that at five each separate stair would writhe
under the milkman's tramp; that morning light
so coldly would delineate the scraps   10
of last night's cheese and three sepulchral bottles;
that on the kitchen shelf among the saucers
a pair of beetle-eyes would fix her own—
envoy from some village in the moldings . . .
Meanwhile, he, with a yawn,   15
sounded a dozen notes upon the keyboard,
declared it out of tune, shrugged at the mirror,
rubbed at his beard, went out for cigarettes;
while she, jeered by the minor demons,
pulled back the sheets and made the bed and found   20
a towel to dust the table-top,
and let the coffee-pot boil over on the stove.
By evening she was back in love again,
though not so wholly but throughout the night
she woke sometimes to feel the daylight coming   25
like relentless milkman up the stairs.

Edwin Arlington Robinson (1869–1935)
Miniver Cheevy (1910)

Miniver Cheevy, child of scorn,
    Grew lean while he assailed the seasons;
He wept that he was ever born,
    And he had reasons.

Miniver loved the days of old   5
    When swords were bright and steeds were prancing;
The vision of a warrior bold
    Would set him dancing.

Miniver sighed for what was not,
    And dreamed, and rested from his labors;   10
He dreamed of Thebes and Camelot,
    And Priam's neighbors.[1]

Miniver mourned the ripe renown
    That made so many a name so fragrant;
He mourned Romance, now on the town,   15
    And Art, a vagrant.

Miniver loved the Medici,[2]
    Albeit he had never seen one;
He would have sinned incessantly
    Could he have been one.   20

Miniver cursed the commonplace
    And eyed a khaki suit with loathing;
He missed the medieval grace
    Of iron clothing.

Miniver scorned the gold he sought,   25
    But sore annoyed was he without it;
Miniver thought, and thought, and thought,
    And thought about it.

Miniver Cheevy, born too late,
    Scratched his head and kept on thinking;   30
Miniver coughed, and called it fate,
    And kept on drinking.

---

[1]**Lines 11–12:** Thebes was a Greek city, anciently famous in history and legend; Camelot is said to have been the site of King Arthur's court; Priam was king of Troy during the Trojan War.
[2]**Medici:** A family of merchant-princes of the Italian Renaissance, rulers of Florence for nearly two centuries; they were known both for cruelty and for their support of learning and art.

Charles Simic (b. 1938)
Stone (1971)

Go inside a stone
That would be my way.
Let somebody else become a dove
Or gnash with a tiger's tooth.
I am happy to be a stone.   5

From the outside the stone is a riddle:
No one knows how to answer it.
Yet within, it must be cool and quiet
Even though a cow steps on it full weight,
Even though a child throws it in a river;   10
The stone sinks, slow, unperturbed
To the river bottom
Where the fishes come to knock on it
And listen.

I have seen sparks fly out   15
When two stones are rubbed,
So perhaps it is not dark inside after all;
Perhaps there is a moon shining
From somewhere, as though behind a hill—
Just enough light to make out   20
The strange writings, the star-charts
On the inner walls.

Wallace Stevens (1879–1955)
Anecdote of the Jar (1923)

I placed a jar in Tennessee,
And round it was, upon a hill.
It made the slovenly wilderness
Surround that hill.

The wilderness rose up to it,   5
And sprawled around, no longer wild.
The jar was round upon the ground
And tall and of a port in air.

It took dominion everywhere.
The jar was gray and bare.   10
It did not give of bird or bush,
Like nothing else in Tennessee.

Wallace Stevens (1879–1955)
Sunday Morning (1915, 1923)

1

Complacencies of the peignoir, and late
Coffee and oranges in a sunny chair,
And the green freedom of a cockatoo

Upon a rug mingle to dissipate
The holy hush of ancient sacrifice.   5
She dreams a little, and she feels the dark
Encroachment of that old catastrophe,
As a calm darkens among water-lights.
The pungent oranges and bright, green wings
Seem things in some procession of the dead,   10
Winding across wide water, without sound.
The day is like wide water, without sound,
Stilled for the passing of her dreaming feet
Over the seas, to silent Palestine,
Dominion of the blood and sepulchre.   15

2

Why should she give her bounty to the dead?
What is divinity if it can come
Only in silent shadows and in dreams?
Shall she not find in comforts of the sun,
In pungent fruit and bright, green wings, or else   20
In any balm or beauty of the earth,
Things to be cherished like the thought of heaven?
Divinity must live within herself:
Passions of rain, or moods in falling snow;
Grievings in loneliness, or unsubdued   25
Elations when the forest blooms; gusty
Emotions on wet roads on autumn nights;
All pleasures and all pains, remembering
The bough of summer and the winter branch.
These are the measures destined for her soul.   30

3

Jove in the clouds had his inhuman birth.
No mother suckled him, no sweet land gave
Large-mannered motions to his mythy mind.
He moved among us, as a muttering king,
Magnificent, would move among his hinds,   35
Until our blood, commingling, virginal,
With heaven, brought such requital to desire
The very hinds discerned it, in a star.
Shall our blood fail? Or shall it come to be
The blood of paradise? And shall the earth   40
Seem all of paradise that we shall know?
The sky will be much friendlier then than now,
A part of labor and a part of pain,

And next in glory to enduring love,
Not this dividing and indifferent blue.   45

4

She says, "I am content when wakened birds,
Before they fly, test the reality
Of misty fields, by their sweet questionings;
But when the birds are gone, and their warm fields
Return no more, where, then, is paradise?"   50
There is not any haunt of prophecy,
Nor any old chimera of the grave,
Neither the golden underground, nor isle
Melodious, where spirits gat them home,
Nor visionary south, nor cloud palm   55
Remote on heaven's hill, that has endured
As April's green endures; or will endure
Like her remembrance of awakened birds,
Or her desire for June and evening, tipped
By the consummation of the swallow's wings.   60

5

She says, "But in contentment I still feel
The need of some imperishable bliss."
Death is the mother of beauty; hence from her,
Alone, shall come fulfillment to our dreams
And our desires. Although she strews the leaves   65
Of sure obliteration on our paths,
The path sick sorrow took, the many paths
Where triumph rang its brassy phrase, or love
Whispered a little out of tenderness,
She makes the willow shiver in the sun   70
For maidens who were wont to sit and gaze
Upon the grass, relinquished to their feet.
She causes boys to pile new plums and pears
On disregarded plate. The maidens taste
And stray impassioned in the littering leaves.   75

6

Is there no change of death in paradise?
Does ripe fruit never fall? Or do the boughs
Hang always heavy in that perfect sky,
Unchanging, yet so like our perishing earth,
With rivers like our own that seek for seas   80

They never find, the same receding shores
That never touch with inarticulate pang?
Why set the pear upon those river-banks
Or spice the shores with odors of the plum?
Alas, that they should wear our colors there,   85
The silken weavings of our afternoons,
And pick the strings of our insipid lutes!
Death is the mother of beauty, mystical,
Within whose burning bosom we devise
Our earthly mothers waiting, sleeplessly.   90

7

Supple and turbulent, a ring of men
Shall chant in orgy on a summer morn
Their boisterous devotion to the sun,
Not as a god, but as a god might be,
Naked among them, like a savage source.   95
Their chant shall be a chant of paradise,
Out of their blood, returning to the sky;
And in their chant shall enter, voice by voice,
The windy lake wherein their lord delights,
The trees, like serafin, and echoing hills,   100
That choir among themselves long afterward.
They shall know well the heavenly fellowship
Of men that perish and of summer morn.
And whence they came and whither they shall go
The dew upon their feet shall manifest.   105

8

She hears, upon that water without sound,
A voice that cries, "The tomb in Palestine
Is not the porch of spirits lingering.
It is the grave of Jesus, where he lay."
We live in an old chaos of the sun,   110
Or old dependency of day and night,
Or island solitude, unsponsored, free,
Of that wide water, inescapable.
Deer walk upon our mountains, and the quail
Whistle about us their spontaneous cries;   115
Sweet berries ripen in the wilderness;
And, in the isolation of the sky,
At evening, casual flocks of pigeons make
Ambiguous undulations as they sink,
Downward to darkness, on extended wings.   120

Dylan Thomas (1914–1953)
The Force That Through the Green Fuse Drives the Flower (1934)

The force that through the green fuse drives the flower
Drives my green age; that blasts the roots of trees
Is my destroyer.
And I am dumb to tell the crooked rose
My youth is bent by the same wintry fever.   5

The force that drives the water through the rocks
Drives my red blood; that dries the mouthing streams
Turns mine to wax.
And I am dumb to mouth unto my veins
How at the mountain spring the same mouth sucks.   10

The hand that whirls the water in the pool
Stirs the quicksand; that ropes the blowing wind
Hauls my shroud sail.
And I am dumb to tell the hanging man
How of my clay is made the hangman's lime.   15

The lips of time leech to the fountain head;
Love drips and gathers, but the fallen blood
Shall calm her sores.
And I am dumb to tell a weather's wind
How time has ticked a heaven round the stars.   20

And I am dumb to tell the lover's tomb
How at my sheet goes the same crooked worm.

Phyllis Wheatley (1735–1784)
On Being Brought from Africa to America (1773)

'Twas mercy brought me from my pagan land,
Taught my benighted soul to understand
That there's a God, that there's a Savior too:
Once I redemption neither sought nor knew.
Some view our sable[1] race with scornful eye.   5
"Their color is a diabolic dye."
Remember, Christians, Negroes, black as Cain.[2]
May be refined, and join the angelic train.

---

[1]**sable:** Black.
[2]**Cain:** Cain slew his brother Abel and was "marked" by God for doing so. This mark has sometimes been taken to be the origin of the Negro (Genesis 4: 1–15).

Walt Whitman (1819–1892)
A Noiseless Patient Spider (1868, 1881)

A noiseless patient spider,
I mark'd where on a little promontory it stood isolated,
Mark'd how to explore the vacant vast surrounding,
It launch'd forth filament, filament, filament, out of itself,
Ever unreeling them, ever tirelessly speeding them.   5

And you O my soul where you stand,
Surrounded, detached, in measureless oceans of space,
Ceaselessly musing, venturing, throwing, seeking the spheres
    to connect them,
Till the bridge you will need be form'd, till the ductile anchor hold,
Till the gossamer thread you fling catch somewhere, O my soul.   10

Walt Whitman (1819–1892)
I Hear America Singing (1860)

I hear America singing, the varied carols I hear,
Those of mechanics, each one singing his as it should be blithe and strong,
The carpenter singing his as he measures his plank or beam,
The mason singing his as he makes ready for work, or leaves off work,
The boatman singing what belongs to him in his boat, the deck-hand   5
    singing on the steamboat deck,
The shoemaker singing as he sits on his bench, the hatter singing as
    he stands,
The wood-cutter's song, the ploughboy's on his way in the morning, or at
    noon intermission or at sundown,
The delicious singing of the mother, or of the young wife at work, or of
    the girl sewing or washing.
Each singing what belongs to him or her and to none else,
The day what belongs to the day—at night the party of young fellows,   10
    robust, friendly,
Singing with open mouths their strong melodious songs.

Walt Whitman (1819–1892)
One's-Self I Sing (1867)

One's-self I sing, a simple separate person,
Yet utter the word Democratic, the word En-Masse.

Of physiology from top to toe I sing,
Not physiognomy alone nor brain alone is worthy for the Muse,
   I say the
   Form complete is worthier far,   5
The Female equally with the Male I sing.

Of Life immense in passion, pulse, and power,
Cheerful, for freest action form'd under the laws divine,
The Modern Man I sing.

Walt Whitman (1819–1892)
There Was a Child Went Forth (1855, 1871)

There was a child went forth every day,
And the first object he look'd upon, that object he became,
And that object became part of him for the day or a certain part of the day,
Or for many years or stretching cycles of years.

The early lilacs became part of this child,   5
And grass and white and red morning-glories, and white and
   red clover, and the song of the phoebe-bird,
And the Third-month lambs and the sow's pink-faint litter, and the mare's
   foal and the cow's calf,
And the noisy brood of the barnyard or by the mire of the pond-side,
And the fish suspending themselves so curiously below there, and the
   beautiful curious liquid,
And the water-plants with their graceful flat heads, all became
   part of him.   10

The field-sprouts of Fourth-month and Fifth-month became part of him,
Winter-grain sprouts and those of the light-yellow corn, and the esculent
   roots of the garden,
And the apple-trees cover'd with blossoms and the fruit afterward, and
   wood-berries, and the commonest weeds by the road,
And the old drunkard staggering home from the outhouse of the tavern
   whence he had lately risen,
And the schoolmistress that pass'd on her way to the school,   15
And the friendly boys that pass'd, and the quarrelsome boys,
And the tidy and fresh-cheek'd girls, and the barefoot negro boy and girl,
And all the changes of city and country wherever he went.

Note: This poem was first published in the 1855 edition of *Leaves of Grass* as *Poem of the Child That Went Forth, and Always Goes Forth, Forever and Forever,* then subsequently published under other titles until the present one was reached in the 1871 edition.

His own parents, he that had father'd him and she that had conceiv'd
    him in her womb and birth'd him,
They gave this child more of themselves than that,   20
They gave him afterward every day, they became part of him.
The mother at home quietly placing the dishes on the supper-table,
The mother with mild words, clean her cap and gown, a wholesome
    odor falling off her person and clothes as she walks by,
The father, strong, self-sufficient, manly, mean, anger'd, unjust,
The blow, the quick loud word, the tight bargain, the crafty lure,   25
The family usages, the language, the company, the furniture, the
    yearning and swelling heart,
Affection that will not be gainsay'd, the sense of what is real, the
    thought if after all it should prove unreal,
The doubts of day-time and the doubts of night-time, the curious
    whether and how,
Whether that which appears so is so, or is it all flashes and specks?
Men and women crowding fast in the streets, if they are not flashes
    and specks what are they?   30
The streets themselves and the façades of houses, and goods in the
    windows,
Vehicles, teams, the heavy-plank'd wharves, the huge crossing at
    the ferries,
The village on the highland seen from afar at sunset, the river
    between,
Shadows, aureola and mist, the light falling on roofs and gables of
    white or brown two miles off,
The schooner near by sleepily dropping down the tide, the little
    boat slack-tow'd astern,   35
The hurrying tumbling waves, quick-broken crests, slapping,
The strata of color'd clouds, the long bar of maroon-tint away solitary
    by itself, the spread of purity it lies motionless in,
The horizon's edge, the flying sea-crow, the fragrance of salt marsh
    and shore mud,
These became part of that child who went forth every day, and who
    now goes, and will always go forth every day.

Walt Whitman (1819–1892)
When I Heard the Learn'd Astronomer (1865)

When I heard the learn'd astronomer,
When the proofs, the figures, were ranged in columns before me,
When I was shown the charts and diagrams, to add, divide, and
    measure them,

When I sitting heard the astronomer where he lectured with much
    applause in the lecture-room,
How soon unaccountable I became tired and sick,   5
Till rising and gliding out I wander'd off by myself,
In the mystical moist night-air, and from time to time,
Look'd up in perfect silence at the stars.

Mitsuye Yamada (b. 1923)
Desert Run (1988)

I

I return to the desert
where criminals
were abandoned to wander
away to their deaths
where scorpions   5
spiders
snakes
lizards
and rats
live in outcast harmony   10
where the sculptor's wreck
was reclaimed
by the gentle drifting sands.

We approach the dunes while
the insistent flies bother our ears   15
the sound of crunching gravel under
our shoes cracks the desolate stillness
and opens our way.

Everything is done in silence here:
the wind fingers fluted stripes   20
over mounds and mounds of sand
the swinging grasses sweep
patterns on the slopes
the sidewinder passes out of sight.
I was too young to hear silence before.   25

II

I spent 547 sulking days here
in my own dreams

there was not much to marvel at
I thought
only miles of sagebrush and   30
lifeless sand.

I watched the most beautiful
sunsets in the world and saw nothing
forty years ago
I wrote my will here   35
my fingers moved slowly in the
hot sand the texture of whole wheat flour
three words: I died here
the winds filed them away.

I am back to claim my body   40
my carcass lies
between the spiny branches
of two creosote bushes
it looks strangely like a small calf
left to graze and die   45
half of its bones are gone
after all these years

but no matter
I am satisfied
I take a dry stick   50
and give myself
a ritual burial.

III

Like the bull snakes brought
into this desert by the soldiers
we were transported here   55
to drive away rattlers
in your nightmares
we were part of some one's plan
to spirit away spies
in your peripheral vision.   60

My skin turned pink brown
in the bright desert light
I slithered in the matching sand
doing what you put me here to do
we were predators at your service   65
I put your mind at ease.

I am that odd creature
the female bull snake
I flick my tongue in your face
an image trapped in your mirror.   70
You will use me or
you will honor me in a shrine
to keep me pure.

IV

At night the outerstellar darkness
above is only an arm's length away   75
I am pressed by the silence around me
the stars are bold as big as quarters
against the velvet blue sky
their beams search for the marrow
of my bones   80
I shiver as I stumble my way to
the outhouse.

In the morning we find
kangaroo rats
have built mounds of messy homes   85
out of dry sticks and leavings
behind our wagon
They have accepted our alien presence.
The night creatures keep a discreet
distance.   90

V

The desert is the lungs of the world.
This land of sudden lizards and nappy ants
is only useful when not used
We must leave before we feel we can
change it.   95

When we leave the dirt roads
my body is thankful for the
paved ride the rest of the way
home.
Rows of yucca trees with spiked crowns   100
wave stiffly at us
Some watch us arms akimbo.

I cannot stay in the desert
where you will have me nor

will I be brought back in a cage   105
to grace your need for exotica.
I write these words at night
for I am still a night creature
but I will not keep a discreet distance
If you must fit me to your needs   110
I will die
and so will you.

William Butler Yeats (1865–1939)

Easter 1916[1] (1916)

I have met them at close of day
Coming with vivid faces
From counter or desk among gray
Eighteenth-century houses.
I have passed with a nod of the head   5
Or polite meaningless words,
Or have lingered awhile and said
Polite meaningless words,
And thought before I had done
Of a mocking tale or a gibe   10
To please a companion
Around the fire at the club,
Being certain that they and I
But lived where motley is worn:
All changed, changed utterly: 15
A terrible beauty is born.

That woman's days were spent
In ignorant good will,

---

[1]**Easter 1916:** An Irish Nationalist uprising had been planned for Easter Sunday 1916, and although the German ship which was bringing munitions had been intercepted by the British, attempts to postpone the uprising failed; it began in Dublin on Easter Monday. "Fifteen hundred men seized key points and an Irish republic was proclaimed from the General Post Office. After the initial surprise prompt British military action was taken, and when over 300 lives had been lost the insurgents were forced to surrender on 29 April * * * The seven signatories of the republican proclamation, including [Pádraic] Pearse and [James] Connolly, and nine others were shot after court martial between 3 and 12 May; 75 were reprieved and over 2000 held prisoners" [From "Ireland: History," by D. B. Quinn, in *Chambers's Encyclopedia*].

Her nights in argument
Until her voice grew shrill.   20
What voice more sweet than hers
When, young and beautiful,
She rode to harriers?[2]
This man had kept a school
And rode our wingéd horse,[3]   25
This other his helper and friend
Was coming into his force;
He might have won fame in the end,
So sensitive his nature seemed,
So daring and sweet his thought.   30
This other man I had dreamed
A drunken, vainglorious lout.[4]
He had done most bitter wrong
To some who are near my heart,
Yet I number him in the song;   35
He, too, has resigned his part
In the casual comedy;
He, too, has been changed in his turn,
Transformed utterly:
A terrible beauty is born.   40

Hearts with one purpose alone
Through summer and winter seem
Enchanted to a stone
To trouble the living stream.
The horse that comes from the road,   45
The rider, the birds that range
From cloud to tumbling cloud,
Minute by minute they change;
A shadow of cloud on the stream
Changes minute by minute;   50
A horse-hoof slides on the brim,
And a horse plashes within it;
The long-legged moor-hens dive,

----

[2]Countess Constance Georgina Markiewicz, *née* Gore-Booth, about whom Yeats wrote *On a Political Prisoner* and a later poem, *In Memory of Eva Gore-Booth and Con Markiewicz.*
[3]Pádraic Pearse, headmaster of St. Enda's School, and a prolific writer of poems, plays, and stories as well as of essays on Irish politics and Gaelic literature. "This other" was Thomas MacDonough, also a schoolteacher.
[4]Major John MacBride, who had married Maud Gonne (the woman with whom Yeats had for years been hopelessly in love) in 1903 and separated from her in 1905.

And hens to moor-cocks call;
Minute by minute they live: 55
The stone's in the midst of all.

Too long a sacrifice
Can make a stone of the heart.
O when may it suffice?
That is Heaven's part, our part   60
To murmur name upon name,
As a mother names her child
When sleep at last has come
On limbs that had run wild.
What is it but nightfall?   65
No, no, not night but death;
Was it needless death after all?
For England may keep faith
For all that is done and said.
We know their dream; enough   70
To know they dreamed and are dead;
And what if excess of love
Bewildered them till they died?
I write it out in a verse—
MacDonagh and MacBride   75
And Connolly and Pearse
Now and in time to be,
Wherever green is worn,
Are changed, changed utterly:
A terrible beauty is born.   80

William Butler Yeats (1865–1939)
Sailing to Byzantium (1927)

That is no country for old men. The young
In one another's arms, birds in the trees
—Those dying generations—at their song,
The salmon-falls, the mackerel-crowded seas,
Fish, flesh, or fowl, commend all summer long   5
Whatever is begotten, born, and dies.
Caught in that sensual music all neglect
Monuments of unaging intellect.

An aged man is but a paltry thing,
A tattered coat upon a stick, unless   10

Soul clap its hands and sing, and louder sing
For every tatter in its mortal dress,
Nor is there singing school but studying
Monuments of its own magnificence;
And therefore I have sailed the seas and come   15
To the holy city of Byzantium.

O sages standing in God's holy fire
As in the gold mosaic of a wall,
Come from the holy fire, perne in a gyre,
And be the singing-masters of my soul.   20
Consume my heart away; sick with desire
And fastened to a dying animal
It knows not what it is; and gather me
Into the artifice of eternity.

Once out of nature I shall never take   25
My bodily form from any natural thing,
But such a form as Grecian goldsmiths make
Of hammered gold and gold enameling
To keep a drowsy Emperor awake;
Or set upon a golden bough to sing   30
To lords and ladies of Byzantium
Of what is past, or passing, or to come.

William Butler Yeats (1865–1939)
The Second Coming[1] (1921)

Turning and turning in the widening gyre[2]
The falcon cannot hear the falconer;
Things fall apart; the center cannot hold;
Mere anarchy is loosed upon the world,
The blood-dimmed tide is loosed, and everywhere   5
The ceremony of innocence is drowned;
The best lack all conviction, while the worst
Are full of passionate intensity.[3]

---

[1]**The Second Coming:** The Second Coming usually refers to the return of Christ. Yeats theorized cycles of history much like the turning of a wheel. Here he offers a poetic comment on his view of the dissolution of civilization at the end of one such cycle.
[2]**gyre:** Spiral.
[3]Lines 4–8 refer to the Russian Revolution (1917).

Surely some revelation is at hand;
Surely the Second Coming is at hand;   10
The Second Coming! Hardly are those words out
When a vast image out of *Spiritus Mundi*[4]
Troubles my sight: somewhere in sands of the desert
A shape with lion body and the head of a man,
A gaze blank and pitiless as the sun,   15
Is moving its slow thighs, while all about it
Reel shadows of the indignant desert birds.
The darkness drops again; but now I know
That twenty centuries[5] of stony sleep
Were vexed to nightmare by a rocking cradle,   20
And what rough beast, its hour come round at last,
Slouches towards Bethlehem to be born?

---

[4]***Spiritus Mundi:*** The Spirit of the World. Yeats believed all souls to be connected by a "Great Memory."
[5]**twenty centuries:** The centuries since the birth of Christ.

CHAPTER **24**

THE
LIVES
OF THE
POETS

Biographical notes are included here for poets with two or more poems in *Access Literature*.

Anna Andreyevna Akhmatova (1889–1966)

was born in Odessa, the Ukraine, in 1889. She was born Anna Gorenko but assumed Akhmatova as her pen name at her father's request because he disapproved of her poetic aspirations. The name she chose was that of her maternal great-grandmother. Akhmatova became part of the literary scene in Saint Petersburg after her first book *Evening* was published in 1912. Her second book, *Rosary*, published in 1914, was critically acclaimed and established her reputation. With her husband, she became a leader of acmeism, a movement which praised the virtues of lucid, carefully crafted verse in reaction to the vagueness of the symbolist style which dominated the Russian literary scene of the period.

Gumilev was executed in 1921 by the Bolsheviks, and even though Akhmatova and Gumilev had divorced in 1918, her association with him prompted an unofficial ban on her poetry from 1925 until 1940. Although Akhmatova was frequently confronted by official government opposition to her work during her lifetime, she was deeply loved by the Russian people. Her most accomplished works, "Requiem" (which was not published in its entirety in Russia until 1987) and "Poem without a Hero," are reactions to the horror of the Stalinist Terror, during which time she endured artistic repression as well as tremendous personal loss. Akhmatova died in Leningrad, where she had spent most of life, in 1966.

Claribel Alegría (b. 1924)

was born in Nicaragua and raised in El Salvador. She received her college education in the United States, but she returned to El Salvador to live. She received the Casa de las Americas Prize for her book *I Survive*. A bilingual edition of her major works, entitled *Flowers from the Volcano*, was published in 1982. In addition to poetry, Alegría has written books on Latin American politics, civil war, and culture (some are coauthored with her late husband, Darwin Flakoll).

Margaret Atwood (b. 1939)

grew up largely in remote areas of northern Ontario and Quebec (in her native Canada), the daughter of an entomologist. A well-known and prolific writer, her novels include *The Edible Woman* (1969), *Surfacing* (1971),

Lady Oracle (1976), *Life Before Man* (1979), *Bodily Harm* (1982), *The Handmaid's Tale* (1985), and *Cat's Eye* (1988). Her short story collections are *Dancing Girls and Other Stories* (1978), *Murder in the Dark* (1983), and *Bluebeard's Egg* (1983).

W. H. Auden (1907–1973)

Wystan Hugh Auden was born in York, England, in 1907. He was educated at Christ's Church, Oxford, where his ability as a poet was immediately recognized. Auden's first book of verse was published in 1928, and his collection *Poems*, published in 1930, established him as a leading voice of a new generation. Since that time, he has been admired for his unsurpassed technical virtuosity and an ability to write poems in nearly every imaginable verse form. He is also known for his ability to incorporate popular culture, current events, and common language in his work.

Auden traveled widely, and his poetry frequently recounts, literally or metaphorically, a journey or quest. He visited Germany, Iceland, and China, served in the Spanish civil war, and in 1939 moved to the United States where he met his lover, Chester Kallman, and became an American citizen. Auden was a chancellor of the Academy of American Poets from 1954 to 1973, and he divided most of the second half of his life between residences in New York City and Austria. He died in Vienna in 1973. A prolific writer, Auden was also a noted playwright, editor, and essayist. He is considered by some to be the greatest English poet of the twentieth century, and his work has exerted a major influence on succeeding generations of poets on both sides of the Atlantic.

Amiri Baraka (LeRoi Jones) (b. 1934)

was born Everett LeRoi Jones in Newark, New Jersey, on October 7, 1934. He earned his B.A. in English from Howard University in 1954, served in the U.S. Air Force from 1954 until 1957, and then moved to the Lower East Side of Manhattan where he joined a loose circle of Greenwich Village artists, musicians, and writers. He published his first volume of poetry, *Preface to a Twenty-Volume Suicide Note*, in 1961. His increasing hostility toward white society was reflected in two plays, *The Slave* and *The Toilet*, both written in 1962. 1963 saw the publication of *Blues People: Negro Music in White America*, which he wrote, and *The Moderns: An Anthology of New Writing in America*, which he edited and introduced. His reputation as a playwright was established with the production of *Dutchman* at the Cherry Lane Theatre in New York on March 24, 1964. The controversial play subsequently won an Obie Award (for best off-Broadway play) and was made into a film.

In 1965, after the assassination of Malcolm X, Jones repudiated his former life and ended his marriage. He later married a second time, to a woman now known as Amina Baraka. In 1968 he coedited *Black Fire: An Anthology of Afro-American Writing* with Larry Neal, and his play *Home on the Range* was performed as a benefit for the Black Panther party. That same year he became a Muslim and changed his name to Imamu Amiri Baraka ("Imamu" means "spiritual leader"). Amiri Baraka's literary prizes and honors include fellowships from the Guggenheim Foundation and the National Endowment for the Arts, the PEN/Faulkner Award, the Rockefeller Foundation Award for Drama, the Langston Hughes Award from the City College of New York, and a lifetime achievement award from the Before Columbus Foundation. Since 1985 he has been a professor of Africana Studies at the State University of New York in Stony Brook. He is codirector, with his wife, of Kimako's Blues People, a community arts space. Amiri and Amina Baraka live in Newark, New Jersey.

Barbara Barnard (b. 1951)

has published fiction and poetry in various literary magazines, including *The Cimarron Review, New Letters, The Nassau Review* and *Gallimaufry*, and she has worked as an editor of both commercial and literary publications. She has also published numerous book reviews and has just completed a novel entitled *Long Devil's Fork*. Recent awards include *The Nassau Review* Poetry Award (2002) and the Bridge Fund Fellowship for poetry and fiction (2004). Although Barbara was born in Arkansas, she grew up as a Navy brat, living all over the United States. She has taught literature and creative writing at various two-year and four-year colleges in California and New York. Currently, she teaches at Nassau Community College/SUNY in Garden City, New York. Barbara Barnard is also co-author of this text, *Access Literature*.

Matsuo Bashō (1644–1694)

is the pseudonym of Matsuo Munefusa. His acute observations of the world's appearance and meaning led him eventually to Zen Buddhism. For a period of time, Bashō lived as a hermit in a hut. His poems never preach to the reader but, instead, reveal the world through sharply meaningful images. Bashō is the best-known writer in the Japanese haiku form.

Elizabeth Bishop (1911–1979)

was born in Worcester, Massachusetts, and grew up in New England and Nova Scotia. She spent a great deal of time in her life traveling, and many of her poems concern travel and exile. She received the Pulitzer Prize in poetry for a 1955 compilation of two of her books, *North & South* (1946) and *A Cold Spring* (1955). Late in her life, from 1970 to 1977, she taught at Harvard University. Her other books include *Questions of Travel* (1965), *Complete Poems* (1969, for which she won a National Book Award), *Geography III* (1979), *The Complete Poems 1929–1979*, and *The Collected Prose*.

William Blake (1757–1828)

In addition to his poems, William Blake created many drawings, paintings, and engravings and was a pioneer in combining textual and visual art. Blake's best-known collections of poems, among the many he produced, are *Songs of Innocence* (1789) and *Songs of Experience* (1794). In these, as in most of his books, he experimented with "illuminated printing," interspersing printings of his engravings with the poems themselves. Among his other books of poems are *The Marriage of Heaven and Hell* (1793) and *Jerusalem* (1809).

Gwendolyn Brooks (b. 1917)

was born in Topeka, Kansas, and grew up in Chicago. Her first book of poems (1945) was *A Street in Bronzeville*. Her second book of poems, *Annie Allen* (1949), won the Pulitzer Prize for poetry. Brooks was the first African American poet to win this prestigious prize. Her work, recognized internationally, has been widely anthologized and is widely read.

Ana Castillo (b. 1953)

Born and raised in Chicago, Ana Castillo has become one of the most widely admired Mexican American poets writing today. She has published the novels *The Mixquiahuala Letters* (1986), *Sapagonia* (1994), and *So Far from God* (1993). Her collections of poetry are *My Father Was a Toltec* (1988) and *Peel My Love Like an Onion* (1999).

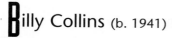

Billy Collins (b. 1941)

was born in New York City in 1941. He is the author of several books of poetry, including *Nine Horses* (2002), *Sailing Alone around the Room: New and Selected Poems* (2001), *Picnic, Lightning* (1998), *The Art of Drowning* (1995, a finalist for the Lenore Marshall Poetry Prize), *Questions about Angels* (1991, selected by Edward Hirsch for the National Poetry Series), *The Apple That Astonished Paris* (1988), *Video Poems* (1980), and *Pokerface* (1977). A recording of Collins reading thirty-three of his poems, *The Best Cigarette*, was released in 1997. Collins's poetry has appeared in anthologies, textbooks, and a variety of periodicals, including *Poetry, American Poetry Review, American Scholar, Harper's, Paris Review*, and the *New Yorker*. His work has been featured in the *Pushcart Prize* anthology and the *Best American Poetry* for 1992, 1993, 1997, and 2004. Collins has received fellowships from the New York Foundation for the Arts, the National Endowment for the Arts, and the Guggenheim Foundation. In 1992 he was chosen by the New York Public Library to serve as "literary lion" and, in 2001, he served as the U.S. poet laureate. For several years he has conducted summer poetry workshops in Ireland at University College Galway. He is a professor of English at Lehman College, City University of New York, and lives in Somers, New York.

Countee Cullen (1903–1946)

was born in 1903 in New York City and began to write poetry at the age of fourteen. In 1922 Cullen entered New York University, and during his college years, his poems were published in *The Crisis*, under the leadership of W. E. B. Du Bois, and *Opportunity*, a magazine of the National Urban League. He was soon after published in *Harper's*, the *Century Magazine*, and *Poetry*. He won several awards for his poem "Ballad of the Brown Girl." In 1925 he graduated from New York University. That same year, Harper published his first volume of verse, *Color*, and he was admitted to Harvard University, where he completed a master's degree.

His second volume of poetry, *Copper Sun* (1927), met with controversy in the black community because Cullen did not focus as intently on the subject of race as he had in *Color*. He was raised and educated in a primarily white community, and because of that he differed from other poets of the Harlem Renaissance, such as Langston Hughes. An imaginative lyric poet, he wrote in the tradition of Keats and Shelley and was resistant to the new poetic techniques of the Modernists.

e.e. cummings (1894–1962)

Edward Estlin Cummings, the quintessential iconoclastic poet, preferred that his name be written in lower case letters with only his initials. Cummings, the son of a Unitarian minister in Cambridge, Massachusetts, is known for his idiosyncratic use of spelling, line breaks, and punctuation, as well as for the exuberant and spontaneous character of his poems.

Emily Dickinson (1830–1886)

was born in Amherst, Massachusetts, and was educated at schools for females. She returned home to live after her education and became famously reclusive until her death. Although she wrote over 2,000 poems, only two were published during her lifetime. She is recognized, along with Walt Whitman, as a leading figure in nineteenth-century American poetry. Her poems are distinguished by their novel use of dashes and capitalization and by their startlingly honest (and often ironic) views of inner experience.

Chitra Banerjee Divakaruni (b. 1956)

lives in Sunnyvale, California, with her husband and two children and teaches creative writing at Foothill College. Her fiction and poetry have won many prizes and awards, including a Pushcart Prize, two PEN syndicated fiction awards, and an American Book Award (for her fiction collection *Arranged Marriage*). A recent collection of her poetry is *Leaving Yuba City, New and Selected Poems* (1997).

John Donne (1572–1631)

trained in the law with the intention that he would pursue a career in government service. Instead, he became one of the best-known Anglican preachers of his day. At the end of his life, he was dean of Saint Paul's Cathedral in London. Only a few of his poems and sermons were published during his lifetime, but his reputation as a poet was already substantial. He is now considered the first great English metaphysical poet.

T.S. Eliot (1888–1965)

Thomas Stearns Eliot was born in Missouri on September 26, 1888. He lived in Saint Louis during the first eighteen years of his life, and then attended Harvard University where he earned undergraduate and master's degrees. In 1910 he left the United States for the Sorbonne. After a year in Paris, he returned to Harvard to pursue a doctorate in philosophy. He returned to Europe and settled in England in 1914. The following year, he married Vivienne Haigh-Wood and began working in London, first as a teacher, and later for Lloyd's Bank.

It was in London that Eliot came under the influence of his contemporary Ezra Pound, who recognized his poetic genius at once and assisted Eliot in the publication of his work in a number of magazines, most notably "The Love Song of J. Alfred Prufrock" in *Poetry* in 1915. His first book of poems, *Prufrock and Other Observations*, which was published in 1917, immediately established him as a leading poet of the avant-garde. With the publication of *The Waste Land* in 1922, now considered by many to be the single most influential poetic work of the twentieth century, Eliot's reputation began to grow to nearly mythic proportions. By 1930, and for the next thirty years, he was the most dominant figure in poetry and literary criticism in the English-speaking world.

Eliot became a British citizen in 1927. As an associate with the publishing house of Faber & Faber, he published many younger poets and eventually became director of the firm. After a notoriously unhappy first marriage, Eliot separated from his wife in 1933. He married Valerie Fletcher in 1956. Eliot received the Nobel Prize for Literature in 1948 and died in London in 1965.

Duane Esposito (b. 1965)

is an assistant professor of English at Nassau Community College in Garden City, New York. He has an M.A. from SUNY Brockport and an M.F.A. from the University of Arizona. In 1994, in conjunction with the University of Arizona Poetry Center, Esposito was given the Academy of American Poets Award, selected by Diane Glancy. His poems have appeared in numerous literary journals, including *Rattle, Fence, Wisconsin Review, Spinning Jenny, Faultline, Can We Have Our Ball Back,* and *BlazeVOX.* His poems are forthcoming in *Snow Monkey.* He has published two books of poetry: *The Book of Bubba* (1998) and *Cadillac Battleship* (2005). Esposito was nominated for a 2003 Pushcart Prize. He lives on Long Island with his wife, their cat, and fish.

Robert Frost (1874–1963)

was born in San Francisco, but his family moved to New England when he was a child. He attended Dartmouth and Harvard without completing degrees. His poems reflect the life and people of New England but also deeply probe the philosophical and emotional questions fundamental to human experience, often viewed through the prism of the natural world. Frost received four Pulitzer Prizes and many other awards, and he read his poem "The Gift Outright" at President John F. Kennedy's inauguration in 1961. Frost was a prolific writer, and the 1994 Library of America compilation of his *Collected Poems, Prose & Plays* is 1,036 pages in length.

Tu Fu (713–770)

A Chinese poet of the T'ang Dynasty, Tu Fu is thought by many to be the finest lyric poet in the Chinese language and is thought by some to be the finest lyric poet in any language. Tu Fu was born into a family of scholars, officials, and landowners, and he rose to a minor position in the emperor's court. Later, due to political turmoil in the imperial court, he was dismissed and endured a period of wandering, trouble, and exile. For many years, he lived in a thatched hut in Szechuan Province. Further political changes some years later sent him wandering again, and he lived for a time on a houseboat. Tu Fu died at the age of 59, apparently on his houseboat. He left behind a treasure trove of lyric poetry, notable for its reverence for life, the clarity of its details, and the loving light with which it illuminates human experience.

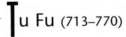

Allen Ginsberg (1926–1997)

was born in Newark, New Jersey, in 1926. As a student at Columbia University in the 1940s, he began close friendships with William S. Burroughs, Neal Cassady, and Jack Kerouac, all of whom later became leading figures of the Beat movement. In 1954 Ginsberg moved to San Francisco. His first book of poems, *Howl*, overcame censorship trials to become one of the most widely read books of poems of the century, translated into more than twenty-two languages. Ginsberg cofounded and directed the Jack Kerouac School of Disembodied Poetics at the Naropa Institute in Colorado. In his later years, he was a Distinguished Professor at Brooklyn College. He died in 1997 in New York City.

Louise Glück (b. 1943)

was born in New York City in 1943 and grew up on Long Island. Her many books of poetry include *The Seven Ages* (2001); *Vita Nova* (1999), winner of Boston Book Review's Bingham Poetry Prize; *Meadowlands* (1996); *The Wild Iris* (1992), which received the Pulitzer Prize and the Poetry Society of America's William Carlos Williams Award; *Ararat* (1990), for which she received the Rebekah Johnson Bobbitt National Prize for Poetry; and *The Triumph of Achilles* (1985), which received the National Book Critics Circle Award, the Boston Globe Literary Press Award, and the Poetry Society of America's Melville Kane Award. She has also published a collection of essays, *Proofs and Theories: Essays on Poetry* (1994), which won the PEN/Martha Albrand Award for Nonfiction. Her other honors include the Bollingen Prize in Poetry, the Lannan Literary Award for Poetry, and fellowships from the Guggenheim and Rockefeller foundations, and from the National Endowment for the Arts. She teaches at Williams College and lives in Cambridge, Massachusetts. In 1999 she was elected a chancellor of the Academy of American Poets. In the fall of 2003, Glück assumed her duties as the Library of Congress's twelfth poet laureate consultant in poetry.

Michael Harper (b. 1938)

was born in Brooklyn, New York, in 1938. He earned his B.A. and M.A. degrees from what is now known as California State University and an M.F.A. from the University of Iowa. He has published more than ten books of poetry, including *Songlines in Michaeltree: New and Collected Poems* (2000); *Honorable Amendments* (1995); *Healing Song for the Inner Ear* (1985); *Images of Kin* (1977), which won the Melville-Cane Award from the Poetry Society of America and was nominated for the National Book Award; *Nightmare Begins Responsibility* (1975); *History Is Your Heartbeat* (1971), which won the Black Academy of Arts & Letters Award for poetry; and *Dear John, Dear Coltrane* (1970), which was nominated for the National Book Award. Harper was the first poet laureate of the state of Rhode Island (1988–1993) and has received many other honors, including a fellowship from the Guggenheim Foundation and a National Endowment for the Arts Creative Writing Award. He is University Professor and a professor of English at Brown University, where he has taught since 1970. He lives in Barrington, Rhode Island.

Robert Hayden (1913–1980)

Born Asa Bundy Sheffey in 1913, Robert Hayden was raised in a poor neighborhood in Detroit. He had an emotionally tumultuous childhood and was shuttled between the home of his parents and that of a foster family, who lived next door. In 1932 he graduated from high school and, on scholarship, attended Detroit City College (later Wayne State University).

Hayden published his first book of poems, *Heart-Shape in the Dust*, in 1940. He enrolled in a graduate English literature program at the University of Michigan where he studied with W. H. Auden. Auden became an influential critical guide in the development of Hayden's writing. Hayden admired the work of Edna St. Vincent Millay, Elinor Wiley, Carl Sandburg, and Hart Crane, as well as the poets of the Harlem Renaissance, Langston Hughes, Countee Cullen, and Jean Toomer. He had an interest in African American history and explored racial issues in his writing.

Hayden's poetry gained international recognition in the 1960s, and in 1966 he was awarded the grand prize for poetry at the First World Festival of Negro Arts in Dakar, Senegal, for his book *Ballad of Remembrance*. In 1976 he became the first black American to be appointed as consultant in poetry to the Library of Congress (later called the poet laureate). He died in Ann Arbor, Michigan, in 1980.

Seamus Heaney (b. 1939)

was born on April 13, 1939, in Castledawson, County Derry, Northern Ireland. He earned a teacher's certificate in English at St. Joseph's College in Belfast, and in 1963 he took a position as a lecturer in English at that school. While at St. Joseph's he began to write and joined a poetry workshop with Derek Mahon, Michael Longley, and others under the guidance of Philip Hobsbaum. In 1965 he married Marie Devlin, and the following year he published "Death of a Naturalist."

Since then he has published widely in collections, including *Opened Ground* (1999), which was named a New York Times Notable Book of the Year; *The Spirit Level* (1996); *Selected Poems 1966–1987* (1990); and *Sweeney Astray* (1984). He has also written several volumes of criticism, including *The Redress of Poetry* (1995). Heaney's most recent translation is *Beowulf* (2000), which won the Whitbread Book of the Year Award. He is also cotranslator, with Stanislaw Baranczak, of *Laments: Poems of Jan Kochanowski* (1995) and coauthor, with Joseph Brodsky and Derek Walcott, of a collection of essays entitled *Homage to Robert Frost* (1996). In 1995 Heaney received the Nobel

Prize in literature. He has been a resident of Dublin since 1976, but since 1981 he has spent part of each year teaching at Harvard University where, in 1984, he was elected the Boylston Professor of Rhetoric and Oratory.

Robert Herrick (1591–1674)

was an Anglican clergyman who secretly wrote exotic poems about imaginary mistresses, while also writing more publicly available poems on religious themes. He was a royalist during the Puritan and Parliamentarian revolution and lost his post at his Devonshire parish during Cromwell's Protectorate. He was able to return to his parish after the restoration of Charles II. In 1648 he published more than 1,400 poems under two titles, *Hesperides* for the secular poems and *Noble Numbers* for the poems on religious themes.

Gerard Manley Hopkins (1844–1889)

was born the eldest son of an Anglican clergyman. He thrived in the intellectual atmosphere at Oxford and, while studying there, he was befriended by Walter Pater and John (later Cardinal) Newman. He determined that he would convert to Catholicism, and this he did, with the sponsorship of Cardinal Newman and against the wishes of his parents. When he later entered the Jesuit order as a priest, he burned all of the final copies of his poems, fearing that the aesthetic life was incompatible with the spiritual life. Later he resumed writing poetry on religious themes and accepted a teaching post at University College, Dublin. There, he evidently felt isolated from his native culture, and he died of typhoid in 1889.

A. E. Housman (1859–1936)

Alfred Edward Housman was born in Fockbury, Worcestershire, England, on March 26, 1859. He attended St. John's College, Oxford, but left school to work as a clerk in the Patent Office in London for ten years. During this time he studied Greek and Roman classics intensively, and in 1892 Housman was appointed professor of Latin at University College, London. In 1911 he became professor of Latin at Trinity College, Cambridge, a post he held until his death.

Housman published only two volumes of poetry during his life: *A Shropshire Lad* (1896) and *Last Poems* (1922). The majority of the poems in *A*

Shropshire Lad were written after the death of Adalbert Jackson, Housman's friend and companion, in 1892. These poems focus thematically on pastoral beauty, unrequited love, fleeting youth, grief, death, and the patriotism of the common soldier. While *A Shropshire Lad* was slow to gain in popularity, the advent of war, first in the Boer War and then in World War I, gave the book widespread appeal. *Last Poems* was an immediate success upon its release. Despite acclaim as a scholar and a poet, Housman lived as a recluse, rejecting honors and avoiding the public eye. He died in 1936 in Cambridge.

Langston Hughes (1902–1967)

is of African American and Cherokee ancestry and was born in Joplin, Missouri and largely raised in Lawrence, Kansas, as detailed in his autobiography *The Big Sea* (1940). After moving to New York's Harlem, Hughes became a central figure in the Harlem Renaissance, writing plays, short stories, essays, opera librettos, histories, documentaries, autobiographies, biographies, anthologies, children's books, translations, and novels, as well as poetry. One might almost say he wrote music as well, since many of his poems are influenced by the rhythms and diction of blues and jazz. A few of his many works are *The Weary Blues* (1926), *Montage of a Dream Deferred* (1951), *Ask Your Mama: 12 Moods for Jazz* (1961), and *The Panther and the Lash: Poems of Our Time* (1961). Langston Hughes had a tremendous influence on African American writers and poets who came after him, and was also a significant influence on Caribbean and African literature.

Ben Jonson (1572–1637)

was born in 1572 in London, England. His father, a minister, died shortly before his birth and his mother later married a bricklayer. Jonson was raised in Westminster and attended St. Martin's parish school and Westminster School, where he came under the influence of the classical scholar William Camden. He left the Westminster school in 1589, worked briefly in his step-father's trade, and served briefly in the army. In 1598 he wrote what many consider his first great play, *Every Man in His Humor*. Under James I, Jonson received royal favor and patronage. Over the next fifteen years, many of his most famous plays, including *Volpone* (1606) and *The Alchemist* (1610), were produced for the London stage. In 1616 he was appointed poet laureate and received a substantial pension. His circle of admirers and friends, who called themselves "the Tribe of Ben," met regularly at the Mermaid Tavern and later at the Devil's Tavern. Among "the Tribe of Ben" were nobles, such as the Duke and Duchess of Newcastle, and writers, including James Howell and Thomas Carew. Jonson was also friendly with many of the writers of his day, and many of his best-known poems include tributes to friends such as William Shakespeare, John Donne, and Francis Bacon. Jonson died in Westminster in 1637. A tremendous crowd of mourners attended his burial at Westminster Abbey. He is regarded as one of the major dramatists and poets of the seventeenth century.

John Keats (1795–1821)

English Romantic poet John Keats was born in London on October 31, 1795. His father, a livery-stable keeper, died when Keats was eight, and his mother died of tuberculosis six years later. Around 1816, Keats met Leigh Hunt, an influential editor of the *Examiner*, who published his sonnets "On First Looking into Chapman's Homer" and "O Solitude." Hunt also introduced Keats to a circle of literary men, including the poets Percy Bysshe Shelley and William Wordsworth. The group's influence enabled Keats to see his first volume, *Poems by John Keats*, published in 1817.

In 1819 Keats contracted tuberculosis, and by the following February he felt that death was already upon him, referring to the present as his "posthumous existence." In July 1820, he published his third and best volume of poetry, *Lamia, Isabella, The Eve of St. Agnes, and Other Poems*. The three title poems, dealing with mythical and legendary themes of ancient, medieval, and Renaissance times, are rich in imagery and phrasing. The volume also contains the unfinished "Hyperion," and three poems considered among the finest in the English language: "Ode on a Grecian Urn," "Ode on Melancholy," and "Ode to a Nightingale." The book received enthusiastic praise from Hunt, Shelley, Charles Lamb, and others. Under his doctor's orders to seek a warm climate for the winter, Keats went to Rome with a friend, the painter Joseph Severn. He died there on February 23, 1821, at the age of twenty-five.

Amy King (b. 1971)

received her M.F.A. degree in poetry from Brooklyn College/CUNY and an M.A. in poetics from SUNY Buffalo. In 1999 she received a MacArthur Scholarship for Poetry. King's book, *Antidotes for an Alibi*, was published in the fall of 2004. Her poems can be found in *Aphrodite of the Spangled Mind* (New York), *Combo* (Pennsylvania), *furniture press* (Maryland), the *Mississippi Review, nthposition* (London), and *Shampoo Poetry*. Her photos appear sporadically at *Unpleasant Event Schedule*. Her ebook, *The Citizen's Dilemma*, is available at Duration Press. King currently teaches English at Nassau Community College. Please visit her website at http://www.amyking.org for more information.

Galway Kinnell (b. 1927)

was born in Providence, Rhode Island, and earned his B.A. at Princeton and his M.A. at the University of Rochester. He worked early on as a journalist and civil rights field worker, and he has worked for many years as a professor of English at numerous colleges and universities. He currently teaches poetry in the Graduate Creative Writing Program at New York University. Kinnell's early poems are collected in *First Poems 1946–1954* (1970). Other collections are *Body Rags* (1969), *The Past* (1985), *Selected Poems* (1982), and a recent compilation entitled *Three Books: Body Rags; Mortal Acts—Mortal Words; and The Past* (1993).

Etheridge Knight (1931–1991)

was born in Corinth, Mississippi, in 1931. He dropped out of school at the age of fourteen and continued his education in the love of language in pool halls, juke joints, and poker parlors. From 1947 to 1951, Knight served in the U.S. Army in Korea; he suffered a shrapnel wound that may have contributed to the drug problem he experienced on returning to the United States. In 1960 Knight was arrested for robbery and was sentenced to eight years in the Indiana State Prison. While in prison, he honed his poetry, and his love of language only increased. Such established African American poets as Dudley Randall (publisher of the Broadside Press in Detroit) and Gwendolyn Brooks visited him in prison and encouraged him in his craft. In 1968 Broadside Press published *Poems from Prison*, Knight's first book. This was followed by *Belly Song and Other Poems* (1973), after Knight was released from prison in 1969. Knight earned awards and fellowships from the Guggenheim Foundation, the National Endowment for the Arts, and the Poetry Society of America. In 1970 he edited a collection entitled *Black Voices from Prison*.

Maxine Kumin (b. 1925)

was born in Philadelphia in 1925. Her eleven books of poetry include *Connecting the Dots* (1996); *Looking for Luck* (1992), which received the Poets' Prize; *Nurture* (1989); *The Long Approach* (1986); *Our Ground Time Here Will Be Brief: New and Selected Poems* (1982); *House, Bridge, Fountain, Gate* (1975); and *Up Country: Poems of New England* (1972), for which she received the Pulitzer Prize. She is also the author of a memoir, *Inside the Halo and*

Beyond: The Anatomy of a Recovery (2000); four novels; a collection of short stories; more than twenty children's books; and four books of essays, most recently *Always Beginning: Essays on a Life in Poetry* (2000) and *Women, Animals, and Vegetables* (1994). She has received the Aiken Taylor Award for Modern Poetry, an American Academy of Arts and Letters Award, the Sarah Joseph Hale Award, the Levinson Prize, a National Endowment for the Arts grant, the Eunice Tietjens Memorial Prize for Poetry, and fellowships from the Academy of American Poets and the National Council on the Arts. She has served as consultant in poetry to the Library of Congress and poet laureate of New Hampshire, and she is a former chancellor of the Academy of American Poets. She lives in New Hampshire.

Tato LaViera (b. 1951)

is one of the most influential voices in Puerto Rican poetry in the United States. His poetry and plays traverse the cultural and linguistic borders that separate Spanish and English. He is one of the key figures in the development of the Nuyorican sensibility in literature, and his poetry encodes the history of the Puerto Rican diaspora as a way to remain culturally mobile between the island and the mainland. His work documents the lives of those who have arduously carved a Caribbean space out of the concrete urban jungle. The rhythms in his poems fuse Spanish, English, and Spanglish together to illustrate a transnational and transcultural identity.

Denise Levertov (1923–1997)

was born in Ilford, Essex, England, on October 24, 1923. She was educated entirely at home and claimed to have decided to become a writer at the age of five. At age seventeen, her first poem was published in *Poetry Quarterly*.

In 1947 Levertov married Mitchell Goodman, an American writer, and a year later they moved to America. They settled in New York City, and Levertov became a naturalized U.S. citizen in 1956. Once in New York, she became associated with the Black Mountain group of poets, particularly Creeley, Charles Olson, and Robert Duncan, who had formed a short-lived but groundbreaking school in 1933 in North Carolina. Some of her work was published in the 1950s in the *Black Mountain Review*. Levertov acknowledged these influences but disclaimed membership in any poetic school. She moved away from the fixed forms of English practice and developed an open, experimental style. With the publication of her first American book, *Here and Now*

(1956), she became an important voice in the American avant-garde. Her poems of the 1950s and 1960s won her immediate recognition, not just from peers like Creeley and Duncan, but also from the avant-garde poets of an earlier generation, such as Kenneth Rexroth and William Carlos Williams.

Levertov went on to publish more than twenty volumes of poetry, including *Freeing the Dust* (1975), which won the Lenore Marshall Poetry Prize. She was also the author of four books of prose, most recently *Tesserae* (1995), and translator of three volumes of poetry, among them Jean Joubert's *Black Iris* (1989). From 1982 to 1993, she taught at Stanford University. She spent the last decade of her life in Seattle, Washington, during which time she published *Poems 1968–1972* (1987), *Breathing the Water* (1987), *A Door in the Hive* (1989), *Evening Train* (1992), and *The Sands of the Well* (1996). In December 1997, Levertov, at age seventy-four, died from complications of lymphoma. *This Great Unknowing: Last Poems* was published by New Directions in 1999.

Philip Levine (b. 1928)

was born in Detroit, Michigan, in 1928. He is the author of sixteen books of poetry, including *Breath* (2004); *The Mercy* (1999); *The Simple Truth* (1994), which won the Pulitzer Prize; *What Work Is* (1991), which won the National Book Award; *New Selected Poems* (1991); *Ashes: Poems New and Old* (1979), which received the National Book Critics Circle Award and the first American Book Award for Poetry; *7 Years from Somewhere* (1979), which won the National Book Critics Circle Award; and *The Names of the Lost* (1975), which won the Lenore Marshall Poetry Prize. He also published a collection of essays, *The Bread of Time: Toward an Autobiography* (1994). He has received the Ruth Lilly Poetry Prize, the Harriet Monroe Memorial Prize for Poetry, the Frank O'Hara Prize, and two Guggenheim Foundation fellowships. He served as chair of the Literature Panel of the National Endowment for the Arts for two years, and he was elected a chancellor of the Academy of American Poets in 2000. He lives in New York City and Fresno, California, and teaches at New York University.

Pablo Neruda (1904–1973)

is the most widely read Chilean poet and was a central figure in the Latin American Renaissance. During the 1920s and 1930s, Neruda was a political activist and Chilean diplomat, and in 1971, he was awarded the Nobel Prize for literature. Neruda was killed in 1973 when dictator Augusto Pinochet seized power in a military coup. In addition to being a poet, Neruda was an essayist, short story writer, and dramatist. His many works include *Twenty Love Poems and a Song of Despair* (1924), *Residence on Earth* (three series,

1925–1945), *Spain in the Heart* (1937), *The Captain's Verses* (1952), and *Memorial of Isla Negra* (1964).

Richard Newman (b. 1962)

is a poet and essayist who has been publishing essays on gender and male sexuality since 1988. His work, prose and poetry, has appeared in *Changing Men, Salon.com*, the *American Voice, On the Issues, The Pedestal* (thepedestal-magazine.com), *Prairie Schooner, ACM*, and other literary journals. His literary translation of selections from Saadi's *Gulistan*, a classic from thirteenth-century Persia, was published in 2004 by Global Scholarly Publications and the International Society for Iranian Culture. It is the first new translation to include portions of the whole book in more than 100 years. He is an associate professor in the English Department of Nassau Community College.

Sharon Olds (b. 1942)

was born in San Francisco and studied at Stanford and Columbia universities. She settled in New York City, where she teaches poetry in the Graduate Creative Writing Program at New York University. Her poetry collections include *Satan Says* (1980), *The Dead and the Living* (1983, awarded the National Book Critics Circle Award), *The Gold Cell* (1987), and *The Father* (1992).

Edgar Allan Poe (1809–1849)

was born in Boston, Massachusetts, on January 19, 1809. Poe's father and mother, both professional actors, died before he was three, and John and Frances Allan raised him as a foster child in Richmond, Virginia. John Allan, a prosperous tobacco exporter, sent Poe to the best boarding schools and later to the University of Virginia, where Poe excelled academically. After less than one year of school, however, he was forced to leave the university when Allan refused to pay his gambling debts. In 1827 Poe's first collection of poems, *Tamerlane, and Other Poems*, was published. Poe began to sell short stories to magazines at around this time, and, in 1835, he became the editor of the *Southern Literary Messenger* in Richmond. He edited a number of literary journals over the next ten years, including *Burton's Gentleman's Magazine* and *Graham's Magazine*, in Philadelphia, and the *Broadway Journal*, in New York City. During these years he also established himself as a poet and short story writer and published some of his best-known stories and poems including "The Fall of the House of Usher," "The Tell-Tale Heart," "The Murders in the Rue Morgue," and "The Raven." After his wife, Virginia, died from tuberculosis in 1847, Poe's depression and alcoholism worsened. He returned briefly to Richmond in 1849 and then set out for an editing job in Philadelphia. For unknown reasons, he stopped in Baltimore where, on October 3, 1849, he was found in a state of semiconsciousness. Poe died four days later of "acute congestion of the brain."

Poe is considered one of the first American writers to become a major figure in world literature. His stories mark the beginning of both horror and detective fiction. Many critics credit him as an "architect" of the modern short story. He was also one of the first critics to focus primarily on the effect of style and structure in a literary work; as such, he has been regarded as a forerunner to the "art for art's sake" movement.

Dudley Randall (b. 1914)

was born in Washington, D.C., but has spent most of his life in Detroit. In his early adult years, he was a foundry worker for Ford Motor Company, and later he held jobs as a clerk and a letter carrier for the U.S. Postal Service. He served in the U.S. Army in the South Pacific during World War II, and upon returning he resumed his work at the post office while pursuing a degree at Wayne State University. After receiving his B.A. at Wayne, he earned an M.A. in library science from the University of Michigan and subsequently worked as a librarian, first outside Michigan, and then in Detroit, holding increasingly important positions in the public library system there. In 1969 he assumed the post of reference librarian and poet in residence at the University of Detroit. He has also taught at the University of Michigan. In 1965 Randall established the Broadside Press, which grew to become the most influential publisher of contemporary black poetry. He helped to discover and publish many young African American poets, including Etheridge Knight and others who have served time in the prison system.

Ishmael Reed (b. 1938)

was born in 1938 in Chattanooga, Tennessee, was raised in Buffalo, New York, and attended the University of New York at Buffalo. He has written five collections of poetry: *New and Collected Poems* (1988), *A Secretary to the Spirits* (1978), *Chattanooga* (1973), *Conjure* (1972), and *Catechism of D Neoamerican HooDoo Church* (1970). Reed has also written nine novels: *Japanese by Spring* (1993), *The Terrible Twos* (1982), *Flight to Canada* (1976), *The*

Last Days of Louisiana Red (1974), *Yellow Back Radio Broke Down* (1969), and *The Free-Lance Pallbearers* (1967). His plays include *Mother Hubbard* (1982) and *The Ace Boons* (1980). He is also the author of four collections of essays: *Airing Dirty Laundry* (1993), *Writin' Is Fightin': Thirty-Seven Years of Boxing on Paper* (1988), *God Made Alaska for the Indians: Selected Essays* (1982), and *Shrovetide in Old New Orleans* (1978). Reed was a cofounder of Yardbird Publishing in 1971 and also founded Reed, Cannon, and Johnson Communications in 1973. With Al Young, he cofounded *Quilt* magazine. His many honors and awards include the Richard and Hinda Rosenthal Foundation award, a Guggenheim Foundation award, the Lewis Michaux Award, an American Civil Liberties award, and fellowships from the National Endowment for the Arts, the American Civil Liberties Union, and the California Arts Council. Reed has lectured at numerous colleges and universities. For the past twenty years, he has been a lecturer at the University of California at Berkeley. He lives in Oakland, California.

Adrienne Rich (b. 1929)

was born in Baltimore, Maryland, in 1929. Her nearly twenty volumes of poetry include *Fox: Poems 1998–2000* (2001), *Midnight Salvage: Poems 1995–1998* (1999), *Dark Fields of the Republic: Poems 1991–1995* (1995), *Collected Early Poems: 1950–1970* (1993), *An Atlas of the Difficult World: Poems 1988–1991* (1991), *Time's Power: Poems 1985–1988* (1989), *The Fact of a Doorframe: Poems Selected and New 1950–1984* (1984), *The Dream of a Common Language* (1978), and *Diving into the Wreck* (1973). She is also the author of several books of nonfiction prose, including *Arts of the Possible: Essays and Conversations* (2001), *What Is Found There: Notebooks on Poetry and Politics* (1993), and *Of Woman Born: Motherhood as Experience and Institution* (1986). Rich has received the Bollingen Prize, the Lannan Lifetime Achievement Award, the Academy of American Poets Fellowship, the Ruth Lilly Poetry Prize, the Lenore Marshall Poetry Prize, the National Book Award, and a MacArthur Fellowship. In 1997 Rich was awarded the Wallace Stevens Award for outstanding and proven mastery in the art of poetry. She lives in northern California.

Edwin Arlington Robinson (1869–1935)

was born on December 22, 1869, in Head Tide, Maine (the same year as W. B. Yeats). His family moved to Gardiner, Maine, in 1870, which became the backdrop for many of Robinson's poems, renamed "Tilbury Town." Robinson spent two years studying at Harvard University as a special student, and his first poems were published in the *Harvard Advocate*.

In 1896 Robinson privately printed and released his first volume of poetry, *The Torrent and the Night Before*, at his own expense. The collection was extensively revised and published in 1897 as *The Children of the Night*. Unable to make a living as a writer, he got a job as an inspector for the New York City subway system. In 1902 he published *Captain Craig and Other Poems*. This work received little attention until President Theodore Roosevelt wrote a magazine article praising it and Robinson. Roosevelt also offered Robinson a sinecure in a U.S. Customs House, a job he held from 1905 to 1910. Robinson dedicated his next work, *The Town down the River* (1910), to Roosevelt. Robinson was awarded Pulitzer Prizes for *Collected Poems* (1921) in 1922 and *The Man Who Died Twice* (1924) in 1925. His first major success was *The Man against the Sky* (1916). He also wrote a trilogy based on Arthurian legend: *Merlin* (1917), *Lancelot* (1920), and *Tristram* (1927), which also won a Pulitzer Prize, in 1928. For the last twenty-five years of his life, Robinson spent his summers at the MacDowell Colony of artists and musicians in Peterborough, New Hampshire. Robinson never married and led a notoriously solitary lifestyle. He died in New York City on April 6, 1935.

Theodore Roethke (1908–1963)

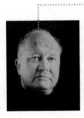

was born in Saginaw, Michigan, and grew up around his father and grandfather's greenhouse business. The greenhouses became a rich source of imagery for his poems. Roethke taught for a time at Lafayette College in Pennsylvania, where he was professor of English and the tennis coach. Later he taught at the University of Washington, where he was also appointed poet-in-residence. Roethke's books include *Open House* (1942), *Praise to the End!* (1951), and *The Far Field* (1964), which received the National Book Award posthumously.

Sappho (b. circa 615 B.C.E.)

was born to an aristocratic family on the Greek island of Lesbos. Evidence suggests that she had several brothers, married a wealthy man named Cercylas, and had a daughter named Cleis. She spent most of her adult life in the city of Mytilene on Lesbos where she ran an academy for unmarried young women. It is unclear whether she invented or simply refined the meter of her day, but today it is known as "Sapphic" meter. Her poems were first collected into nine volumes around the third century B.C.E., but her work was lost almost entirely for many years. Only one of her poems has survived in its entirety; she was known principally through quotations found in the works of other authors until the nineteenth century. In 1898 scholars unearthed papyri that contained fragments of her other poems. In 1914, in Egypt, archeologists discovered papier-mâché coffins made from scraps of paper which contained more verse fragments attributed to Sappho.

Sappho is one of the few women poets we know of from antiquity and one of the greatest lyric poets from any age. Most of her poems were meant to be sung by one person to the accompaniment of the lyre (hence the name, "lyric" poetry). Rather than addressing the gods or recounting epic narratives such as those of Homer, Sappho's verses take form as speech by one individual to another. They speak simply and directly to the joys and difficulties of love.

William Shakespeare (1564–1616)

was born at Stratford-on-Avon, the son of a prosperous English businessman and a gentlewoman whose family were large landowners, although evidently the Shakespeares' financial situation later became precarious. At the age of eighteen, William Shakespeare struck out on his own and married twenty-six-year-old Anne Hathaway. They soon had three children, and before he was twenty-one, Shakespeare had a family to support. By 1600, however, when he was only thirty-four years old, Shakespeare had become the fore-most playwright of his age, was the author of fourteen plays and numerous sonnets, and an owner (along with other shareholders) of the Globe Theater, where he directed and acted in his own dramatic works. His early plays include the histories *Richard II* (1597) and *I Henry IV* (1598); the comedies *A Midsummer Night's Dream* (1595), *The Merchant of Venice* (1596), and *Much Ado about Nothing* (1598); and the early tragedies *Romeo and Juliet* (1594) and *Julius Caesar* (1600). After 1600 Shakespeare devoted most of his time to writing his great tragedies, *Hamlet* (1602), *Othello* (1604), *King Lear* (1606), *Macbeth* (1606), and *Antony and Cleopatra* (1606), as well as other dramatic works. After 1608, following a number of personal tragedies, including the death of his illegiti-mate son and a younger brother, Shakespeare spent more time at home in Stratford. He died there in 1616, the author of 154 sonnets and 37 plays.

Leslie Marmon Silko (b. 1948)

was born and raised on the Laguna Pueblo reservation west of Albuquerque, New Mexico, and she is a writer of mixed Laguna Pueblo, Mexican, and European ancestry. She and her husband and two children still live on the Laguna Pueblo reservation and she is a member of the tribe. Silko has published a number of collections of fiction and poetry, the best-known of which are *Ceremony* (1988), *Storyteller* (1989), and *The Almanac of the Dead* (1992).

Wallace Stephens (1879–1955)

Born in Reading, Pennsylvania, Wallace Stephens later attended Harvard University and New York University Law School. He was admitted to the New York bar in 1904, and he later became a successful executive of an insurance company. Stephens's first volume of poetry was *Harmonium* (1923). His other books of poetry include *Ideas of Order* (1935), *The Man with the Blue Guitar* (1937), *Transport to Summer* (1947), *Collected Poems* (1954), and *Opus Posthumous* (1957).

Gary Snyder (b. 1930)

was born in San Francisco. He has published sixteen books of poetry and prose, including *The Gary Snyder Reader (1952–1998)* (1999); *Mountains and Rivers without End* (1997); *No Nature: New and Selected Poems* (1993), which was a finalist for the National Book Award; *The Practice of the Wild* (1990); *Left out in the Rain, New Poems 1947–1985* (1988); *Axe Handles* (1983), for which he received an American Book Award; *Turtle Island* (1974), which won the Pulitzer Prize for poetry; *Regarding Wave* (1970); and *Myths & Texts* (1960). His awards include an American Academy of Arts and Letters award, the Bollingen Prize, a Guggenheim Foundation fellowship, the Bess Hokin Prize and the Levinson Prize for Poetry, the Robert Kirsch Lifetime Achievement Award from the Los Angeles Times, and the Shelley Memorial Award. Snyder was elected a chancellor of the Academy of American Poets in 2003. He is a professor of English at the University of California, Davis.

Alfred, Lord Tennyson (1809–1892)

was born on August 6, 1809, in Somersby, Lincolnshire, England. He is considered one of the most well-loved Victorian poets. In 1827 Tennyson began to study at Trinity College, Cambridge. In that same year, he and his brother Charles published *Poems by Two Brothers*. The poems in the book attracted the attention of the "Apostles," an undergraduate literary club led by Arthur Hallam. The "Apostles" provided Tennyson, who was tremendously shy, with much needed friendship and confidence as a poet. In 1830 Tennyson published *Poems, Chiefly Lyrical* and, in 1832, published a second volume, *Poems*. Neither book received good reviews, and because of this, Tennyson did not publish another book for nine years. In 1842, however, Tennyson's *Poems in Two Volumes* was hailed as a critical and popular success. After the publication of "In Memoriam" in 1850, Tennyson became one of Britain's most popular poets. He was selected poet laureate, succeeding William Wordsworth. In that same year, he married Emily Sellwood. They had two sons, Hallam and Lionel.

At the age of forty-one, Tennyson had established himself as the most popular poet of the Victorian era. In 1859 he published the first poems of *Idylls of the King*, which sold more than 10,000 copies in one month. In 1884 he became Alfred, Lord Tennyson. Tennyson died in 1892 and was buried in Westminster Abbey.

Dylan Thomas (1914–1953)

was born in Swansea, a small town in Wales, and was largely self-educated. His first book of poems, *18 Poems*, was published in 1934 when he was twenty years old. Considered one of the most important twentieth-century poets in the English language, Thomas went on to publish many more collections of poetry, as well as short stories and plays. His best-known play is *Under Milk Wood* (1954, published posthumously). Thomas had a chronic drinking problem, and he died from the effects of alcoholism in 1953.

Walt Whitman (1819–1892)

Born on a Long Island farm to a Dutch mother and a British father, Walt Whitman began his writing career in the field of journalism. He also worked at a variety of manual jobs during his life, including service as a nurse during the Civil War. One of the journalistic positions he held before the war was the editorship of the Brooklyn *Eagle*. He was later fired from this position for allying himself with "free soilers," that is, the political movement opposed to admitting any more states to the union that permitted slavery. After that time, he began to focus more on his poetry, bringing out the first edition of his beloved *Leaves of Grass* in 1855. In later editions, he added new poems and revised old ones but kept the original title. Often controversial in his own time, many of Whitman's poems explore themes related to sexuality (he was himself homosexual) and the interrelatedness of the spiritual and physical selves, as well as themes related to his passionate feelings about American diversity, democracy, and equality. Walt Whitman, along with Emily Dickinson, is considered one of the two greatest American poets of the nineteenth century.

William Carlos Williams (1883–1963)

was born in Rutherford, New Jersey, of a father who was British and a mother (from Puerto Rico) who was Spanish, Basque, Dutch, and Jewish. Although Williams traveled abroad as a young person, he spent most of his life in the town of his birth. Williams became a medical doctor in private practice in Rutherford, and it is said that he delivered nearly 2,000 babies in that community during the course of his medical career. All the while, he was also giving birth to many great poems, cherished for their warm humanity and their precise attention to detail. His first book, *Poems*, was published in 1909, and two more early collections came out in the following few years. His greatest work is the epic poem *Paterson* (1946–1963), published in five books (he was working on a sixth when he died). In addition to poetry, Williams published short stories, novels, essays, and an autobiography.

William Wordsworth (1770–1850)

Born in Cockermouth, England, in the area known as the Lake District, Wordsworth spent his youth in close contact with nature, a feature of his experience that would figure prominently in his poetry. Together with Samuel Taylor Coleridge, Wordsworth published *Lyrical Ballads* in 1798, an event which launched the Romantic Period in English literature. In reaction against what they saw as the elitist and academic preoccupations of the eighteenth-century Classicist poets, Wordsworth's and Coleridge's poems pursued signal romantic themes related to the natural world and to human emotional experience, imagination, and creativity. Along with Coleridge, Percy Bysshe Shelley, John Keats, and George Gordon Lord Byron, Wordsworth was one of the foremost poets of the Romantic Period.

William Butler Yeats (1865–1939)

One of the greatest modern poets, William Butler Yeats was born in Dublin. His father was the well-known painter John Butler Yeats. His family were Irish Protestants, and he grew up moving between London and the Irish countryside. Yeats began to publish early in life and achieved widespread fame as a poet within his lifetime. In 1889 he met and fell in love with Maud Gonne, an Irish radical figure. Several times in the years following, Yeats asked her to marry him, but she did not share his feelings and turned him down each time. He married Georgie Hyde-Lees in 1917, and this marriage was evidently helpful to his work. Yeats was primarily a poet, but he also had interests in theater, politics, philosophy, folklore, magic, and the occult. He wrote a number of plays, and, with the help of his wife, he wrote *A Vision*, a volume that presents his philosophy and systematic worldview. Yeats's collections of poetry and his plays are too numerous to list here. He received the Nobel Prize in 1923.

" Faced with chaos, [Father Henkel] laid the textbook down, climbed up onto his desk, and stood on his head. We all stopped horsing around and stared him in stupefaction. Henkel then climbed back down, picked up the book, and said, "Let's get back to 'Beauty be not caused—it is,' page 388. It was probably my first glimpse of the power of the theatrical: you gather an audience, you do a headstart to get everyone's attention, and then you're free to explore beauty, poetry, truth, the human condition, what you will. Now that's an education. "

—(David Ives, from his Preface to All in the Timing)

PART 3

Getting Into Drama

As you move into this section of the book, you'll be reading some of Ives's work. comment above is humorous, but at the same time it is quite serious. Ives is being funny but he is also being straightforward and truthful about the force and immedi acy of drama and how it distinguishes itself from all the other forms of literature.

We read poems, stories, and novels (and plays, for that matter) and we create our minds a visual sense of what is happening. Language makes an agreement with our imaginations and, if we are paying attention and the author is doing her or his job, the story or feeling unfolds in our mind's eye: our imagination is the stage.

But seeing live actors on the stage in "real time," acting out the words and action of a playwright is a unique and powerful experience. The characters who populate the landscape or scene the author had created are personified before our eyes. The confli in which they engage and the fates that befall them are seen by the audience in the space of however many acts the playwright has allotted them. And it is important to note that we are not alone, as we so often are when we read. Even in a crowded subway, bus, or room full of people, when our eyes are on the page and our minds a absorbed by the words we are reading, we are in isolation.

In the theater we are in an audience—one among many. This is what Ives me when he talks about "(his) first glimpse of the power of the theatrical." His teache headstand is opening line, the first gripping scene, the "hook" if you will, that gath the attention and focus of the audience and brings them into the world he is abou create.

PROFILE OF A PLAYWRIGHT—
DAVID IVES (b. 1950)

Three monkeys sitting at typewriters trying to write *Hamlet;* people speaking in a new "universal language" in which a word processor is a "verboblender," "velcro" means welcome, and when you're "spinichless," you're speechless; and characters waking up to find themselves located in states of mind rather than geographical locations—these are some of the zany, and usually hilarious, scenarios David Ives's characters find themselves.

David Ives was born in Chicago and received his education at Northwestern University and the Yale Drama School. He writes for television, film and opera as well as for the stage, and many of his plays have enjoyed on- and off-Broadway productions in New York City. His one-act play *Sure Thing*, which appears below, was first produced in 1988 as part of the annual comedy festival of the Manhattan Punch Line Theatre. It was also performed as part of a production of several plays from Ives's book *All in the Timing* at Primary Stages in New York City in 1993.

That production was so successful, that it subsequently moved to the John Houseman theatre in New York City. *The Philadelphia*, also below, was part of the same production of six one-act comedies from *All in the Timing*. Before opening at Primary Stages and then the John Houseman theatre, it had premiered at the 1992 New Hope Performing Arts Festival in New Hope, Pennsylvania.

Frolics in Ivesland

In Stephanie Coen's interview with David Ives (reprinted in this chapter's "Talking Lit"), she points out to him that one critic, in discussing his work, used words like "Ivesian" and "Ivesland" and that in his plays, "the ordinary seems fantastical and the fantastical somehow seems ordinary." She also states that "[t]he short comedies . . . have sent critics to their thesauri for variations on the word *hilarious*." Indeed, Ives's work is hilarious; it's hard not to chuckle while reading his plays, and seeing them on the stage is pure delight.

What, then, accounts for the humorous effect of Ives's plays? He uses devices, like the ringing bell in *Sure Thing*, which are funny in themselves. He also makes good use of a standard device of comedy: juxtaposition (placing seemingly incongruous things side by side). He puts realistic and fantastical elements side by side in a way that makes us laugh. We have in *Words, Words, Words,* for instance, monkeys eating bananas and doing various monkey-like things, but they are also reciting lines from Milton's *Paradise Lost* and from Shakespeare's *Hamlet*.

Ives also uses anachronisms (details inconsistent with the time frame in which the action is taking place) for humorous effect. For example, in *Variations on the Death of Trotsky*, another of the one-act plays in *All in the Timing*, Trotsky's wife notices that the date on the spine of an encyclopedia volume is 1994; however, Leon Trotsky died on August 20, 1940, and the date on the calendar in the room where the scene takes place is August 21,

All in the Timing

Three monkeys Swift, Milton, and Kafka (Robert Stanton, Michael Countryman, and Nancy Opel), perform for the unseen Dr. Rosenbaum, who hopes to prove that three monkeys typing randomly will, eventually, produce *Hamlet*. Photo from the Primary Stages production in New York City.

1940, one day after the date of his death. (Leon Trotsky, an original founder of the Soviet Communist government, later came into disfavor with Joseph Stalin and lived in exile in Mexico City, until he was assassinated in 1940.) In another anachronistic moment, Trotsky says that ice picks will not be allowed in the house (he was killed with an ice pick), but ice cube trays will be allowed, "if they've been invented yet."

Plot and Form

Ives's departure from convention is not confined to his humor. Even the form and plot of David Ives's plays are innovative. *Sure Thing*, for example, does not for a moment follow the traditional arc of a plot (rising action, climax, falling action, resolution). You might argue that it has a resolution in the end, but the circular nature of the plot— repeating itself, folding back on itself, questioning itself—doesn't follow the traditional structure. Also, the circularity of the struc-

Betty and Bill (Played by actors Nancy Opel and Robert Stanton) try to get their romantic timing right, in the premiere production of *Sure Thing* at the Manhattan Punchline Theater (1993).

ture here contributes to the existence of multiple possibilities for meaning. The playwright might have in mind a number of intentions as to what the play "means." Does the interaction between Betty and Bill represent the ups and downs of one relationship, the similarities among a number of relationships, the searching through various relationships before finding the right one, or just a funny spoof on the "dating game"? The answer is that it could represent any or all of these possible meanings, and that's part of what's interesting about Ives's innovative use of plot.

Characterization and Theme

In *Sure Thing*, we clearly do not have conventional characterization. Instead, these characters may actually be regarded as eponymous (representing all women and all men). The characterization is somewhat more conventional in *The Philadelphia*— certainly we get a better sense of the characters as individuals, although the terse, funny dialogue through which they are revealed is hardly typical. In a sense, the cities mentioned as states of mind (Philadelphia, Los Angeles, Cleveland, Baltimore) are "characterized" in a humorous way by the properties jokingly attributed to them. Are there ways, though, in which this humorous theme (of states of mind which somehow resemble stereotypes about cities) also touches on common experiences that we have in everyday life? For instance, is going to the DMV (Department of Motor Vehicles) like "being in a Philadelphia," as Ives's play "defines" it?

Mark (Danny Burstein) finds his day takes a turn for the better when his waitress (Kathy Morath) joins him for a cheese steak in the 1993 production of *The Philadelphia* at Primary Stages in New York City.

Of course, in addition to these possible themes and ideas, the play is fun to read just because of the absurd situation. We have to chuckle when the waitress again and again offers the opposite of what she is asked to serve, and Al and Mark begin to ask for the opposite of what they actually want.

Setting and Staging

The stage sets for these two plays by Ives are quite simple and also similar. In both one-act plays, the characters are sitting in a simple interior setting, a table at a bar/restaurant or a café. In many plays, however, the instructions for setting and staging are much more elaborate and extensive. Some playwrights choose to use longer blocks of initial stage directions (which precede the body of the play), or to write more extensive parenthetical, italicized stage directions which appear in quotation marks within the dialogue. August Wilson, for example, in *Fences* (Chapter 26) uses rather lengthy initial stage directions in order to put the play in historical and cultural context. It is important to Wilson—given the fact that this play is part of a cycle of plays which represent various periods in African American history—to let the reader know how the events depicted in the play reflect that history and how they fit in with the whole progression of the black experience in American society.

Readings

David Ives (b. 1950)

Sure Thing (1988)

CHARACTERS:
BILL AND BETTY,   *both in their late twenties*

SETTING: *A café table, with a couple of chairs*

Betty, reading at the table. An empty chair opposite her. Bill enters.

BILL: Excuse me. Is this chair taken?
BETTY: Excuse me?
BILL: Is this taken?
BETTY: Yes it is.
5 BILL: Oh. Sorry.
BETTY: Sure thing. (*A bell rings softly.*)
BILL: Excuse me. Is this chair taken?
BETTY: Excuse me?
BILL: Is this taken?
10 BETTY: No, but I'm expecting somebody in a
    minute.
BILL: Oh. Thanks anyway.
BETTY: Sure thing. (*A bell rings softly.*)
BILL: Excuse me. Is this chair taken?
BETTY: No, but I'm expecting somebody
    very shortly.
15 BILL: Would you mind if I sit here till he or
    she or it comes?
BETTY: (*glances at her watch*): They seem to
    be pretty late. . . .
BILL: You never know who you might be
    turning down.
BETTY: Sorry. Nice try, though.
BILL: Sure thing. (*Bell.*) Is this seat taken?
20 BETTY: No it's not.
BILL: Would you mind if I sit here?
BETTY: Yes I would.

BILL: Oh. (*Bell.*) Is this chair taken?
BETTY: No it's not.
BILL: Would you mind if I sit here?   25
BETTY: No. Go ahead.
BILL: Thanks. (*He sits. She continues reading.*)
    Everyplace else seems to be taken.
BETTY: Mm-hm.
BILL: Great place.
BETTY: Mm-hm.   30
BILL: What's the book?
BETTY: I just wanted to read in quiet, if you
    don't mind.
BILL: No. Sure thing. (*Bell.*)
BILL: Everyplace else seems to be taken.
BETTY: Mm-hm.   35
BILL: Great place for reading.
BETTY: Yes, I like it.
BILL: What's the book?
BETTY: *The Sound and the Fury.*
BILL: Oh. Hemingway. (*Bell.*) What's the   40
    book?
BETTY: *The Sound and the Fury.*
BILL: Oh. Faulkner.
BETTY: Have you read it?
BILL: Not . . . actually. I've sure read *about* . . .
    it, though. It's supposed to be great.
BETTY: It is great.   45
BILL: I hear it's great. (*Small pause.*) Waiter?
    (*Bell.*) What's the book?
BETTY: *The Sound and the Fury.*
BILL: Oh. Faulkner.

BETTY: Have you read it?

50 BILL: I'm a Mets fan, myself. (*Bell.*)

BETTY: Have you read it?

BILL: Yeah, I read it in college.

BETTY: Where was college?

BILL: I went to Oral Roberts University. (*Bell.*)

55 BETTY: Where was college?

BILL: I was lying. I never really went to college. I just like to party. (*Bell.*)

BETTY: Where was college?

BILL: Harvard.

BETTY: Do you like Faulkner?

60 BILL: I love Faulkner. I spent a whole winter reading him once.

BETTY: I've just started.

BILL: I was so excited after ten pages that I went out and bought everything else he wrote. One of the greatest reading experiences of my life. I mean, all that incredible psychological understanding. Page after page of gorgeous prose. His profound grasp of the mystery of time and human existence. The smells of the earth . . . What do you think?

BETTY: I think it's pretty boring. (*Bell.*)

BILL: What's the book?

65 BETTY: *The Sound and the Fury.*

BILL: Oh! Faulkner!

BETTY: Do you like Faulkner?

BILL: I love Faulkner.

BETTY: He's incredible.

70 BILL: I spent a whole winter reading him once.

BETTY: I was so excited after ten pages that I went out and bought everything else he wrote.

BILL: All that incredible psychological understanding.

BETTY: And the prose is so gorgeous.

BILL: And the way he's grasped the mystery of time—

75 BETTY: —and human existence. I can't believe I've waited this long to read him.

BILL: You never know. You might not have liked him before.

BETTY: That's true.

BILL: You might not have been ready for him. You have to hit these things at the right moment or it's no good.

BETTY: That's happening to me.

BILL: It's all in the timing. (*Small pause.*) My   80
name's Bill, by the way.

BETTY: I'm Betty.

BILL: Hi.

BETTY: Hi. (*Small pause.*)

BILL: Yes I thought reading Faulkner was . . .
a great experience.

BETTY: Yes. (*Small pause.*)   85

BILL: *The Sound and the Fury* . . . (*Another small pause.*)

BETTY: Well. Onwards and upwards. (*She goes back to her book.*)

BILL: Waiter—? (*Bell.*) You have to hit these things at the right moment or it's no good.

BETTY: That's happened to me.

BILL: It's all in the timing. My name's Bill,   90
by the way.

BETTY: I'm Betty.

BILL: Hi.

BETTY: Hi.

BILL: Do you come in here a lot?

BETTY: Actually I'm just in town for two   95
days from Pakistan.

BILL: Oh. Pakistan. (*Bell.*) My name's Bill,
by the way.

BETTY: I'm Betty.

BILL: Hi.

BETTY: Hi.

BILL: Do you come here a lot?   100

BETTY: Every once in a while. Do you?

BILL: Not much anymore. Not as much as I used to. Before my nervous breakdown. (*Bell.*) Do you come in here a lot?

BETTY: Why are you asking?

BILL: Just interested.

BETTY: Are you really interested, or do you   105
just want to pick me up?

BILL: No, I'm really interested.

BETTY: Why would you be interested in whether I come in here a lot?

BILL: Just . . . getting acquainted.

BETTY: Maybe you're only interested for the sake of making small talk long enough to ask me back to your place to listen to some music, or because you've just rented some great tape for your VCR, or because you've got some terrific unknown Django Reinhardt record, only all you'll really want to do is fuck—which you won't do very well—after which you'll go into the bathroom and pee very loudly, then pad into the kitchen and get yourself a beer from the refrigerator without asking me whether I'd like anything, and then you'll proceed to lie back down beside me and confess that you've got a girlfriend named Stephanie who's away at medical school in Belgium for a year, and that you've been involved with her—*off and on*—in what you'll call a very "intricate" relationship, for about *seven YEARS*. None of which *interests* me, mister!

110 BILL: Okay. (*Bell.*) Do you come in here a lot?

BETTY: Every other day, I think.

BILL: I come in here quite a lot and I don't remember seeing you.

BETTY: I guess we must be on different schedules.

BILL: Missed connections.

115 BETTY: Yes. Different time zones.

BILL: Amazing how you can live right next door to somebody in this town and never even know it.

BETTY: I know.

BILL: City life.

BETTY: It's crazy.

120 BILL: We probably pass each other in the street every day. Right in front of this place, probably.

BETTY: Yep.

BILL (*looks around*): Well, the waiters here sure seem to be in some different time zone. I can't seem to locate one anywhere . . . Waiter! (*He looks back.*) So what do you— (*He sees that she's gone back to her book.*)

BETTY: I beg pardon?

BILL: Nothing. Sorry. (*Bell.*)

BETTY: I guess we must be on different schedules.　　125

BILL: Missed connections.

BETTY: Yes. Different time zones.

BILL: Amazing how you can live right next door to somebody in this town and never even know it.

BETTY: I know.

BILL: City life.　　130

BETTY: It's crazy.

BILL: You weren't waiting for somebody when I came in, were you?

BETTY: Actually, I was.

BILL: Oh. Boyfriend?

BETTY: Sort of.　　135

BILL: What's a sort-of boyfriend?

BETTY: My husband.

BILL: Ah-ha. (*Bell.*) You weren't waiting for somebody when I came in, were you?

BETTY: Actually I was.

BILL: Oh. Boyfriend?　　140

BETTY: Sort of.

BILL: What's a sort-of boyfriend?

BETTY: We were meeting here to break up.

BILL: Mm-hm . . . (*Bell.*) What's a sort-of boyfriend?

BETTY: My lover. Here she comes right now!　　145 (*Bell.*)

BILL: You weren't waiting for somebody when I came in, were you?

BETTY: No, just reading.

BILL: Sort of a sad occupation for a Friday night, isn't it? Reading here, all by yourself?

BETTY: Do you think so?

BILL: Well sure. I mean, what's a good-　　150 looking woman like you doing out alone on a Friday night?

BETTY: Trying to keep away from lines like that.

BILL: No, listen— (*Bell.*) You weren't waiting for somebody when I came in, were you?

BETTY: No, just reading.

BILL: Sort of a sad occupation for a Friday night, isn't it? Reading here all by yourself?

155 BETTY: I guess it is, in a way.

BILL: What's a good-looking woman like you doing out alone on a Friday night anyway? No offense, but . . .

BETTY: I'm out alone on a Friday night for the first time in a very long time.

BILL: Oh.

BETTY: You see, I just recently ended a relationship.

160 BILL: Oh.

BETTY: Of rather long standing.

BILL: I'm sorry. (*Small pause.*) Well listen, since reading by yourself *is* such a sad occupation for a Friday night, would you like to go elsewhere?

BETTY: No . . .

BILL: Do something else?

165 BETTY: No thanks.

BILL: I was headed out to the movies in a while anyway.

BETTY: I don't think so.

BILL: Big chance to let Faulkner catch his breath. All those long sentences get him pretty tired.

BETTY: Thanks anyway.

170 BILL: Okay.

BETTY: I appreciate the invitation.

BILL: Sure thing. (*Bell.*) You weren't waiting for somebody when I came in, were you?

BETTY: No, just reading.

BILL: Sort of a sad occupation for a Friday night, isn't it? Reading here all by yourself?

175 BETTY: I guess I was trying to think of it as existentially romantic. You know— cappuccino, great literature, rainy night . . .

BILL: That only works in Paris. We *could* hop the late plane to Paris. Get on a Concorde. Find a café . . .

BETTY: I'm a little short on plane fare tonight.

BILL: Darn it, so am I.

BETTY: To tell you the truth, I was headed to the movies after I finished this section.

Would you like to come along? Since you   180 can't locate a waiter?

BILL: That's a very nice offer, but . . .

BETTY: Uh-huh. Girlfriend?

BILL: Two, actually. One of them's pregnant, and Stephanie— (*Bell.*)

BETTY: Girlfriend?

BILL: No, I don't have a girlfriend. Not if   185 you mean the castrating bitch I dumped last night. (*Bell.*)

BETTY: Girlfriend?

BILL: Sort of. Sort of.

BETTY: What's a sort-of girlfriend?

BILL: My mother. (*Bell.*) I just ended a relationship, actually.

BETTY: Oh.   190

BILL: Of rather long standing.

BETTY: I'm sorry to hear it.

BILL: This is my first night out alone in a long time. I feel a little bit at sea, to tell you the truth.

BETTY: So you didn't stop to talk because you're a Moonie, or you have some weird political affiliation—?

BILL: Nope. Straight-down-the-ticket   195 Republican. (*Bell.*) Straight-down-the-ticket Democrat. (*Bell.*) Can I tell you something about politics? (*Bell.*) I like to think of myself as a citizen of the universe. (*Bell.*) I'm unaffiliated.

BETTY: That's a relief. So am I.

BILL: I vote my beliefs.

BETTY: Labels are not important.

BILL: Labels are not important, exactly. Like me, for example. I mean, what does it matter if I had a two-point at—(*bell*)— three-point at (*bell*)—four-point at college, or if I did come from Pittsburgh— (*bell*)—Cleveland—(*bell*)—Westchester County?

BETTY: Sure.   200

BILL: I believe that a man is what he is. (*Bell.*) A person is what he is. (*Bell.*) A person is . . . what they are.

BETTY: I think so too.

BILL: So what if I admire Trotsky? (*Bell.*) So what if I once had a total-body liposuction? (*Bell.*) So what if I don't have a penis? (*Bell.*) So what if I once spent a year in the Peace Corps? I was acting on my convictions.

BETTY: Sure.

205 BILL: You can't just hang a sign on a person.

BETTY: Absolutely. I'll bet you're a Scorpio. (*Many bells ring.*) Listen, I was headed to the movies after I finished this section. Would you like to come along?

BILL: That sounds like fun. What's playing?

BETTY: A couple of the really early Woody Allen movies.

BILL: Oh.

210 BETTY: Don't you like Woody Allen?

BILL: Sure. I like Woody Allen.

BETTY: But you're not crazy about Woody Allen.

BILL: Those early ones kind of get on my nerves.

BETTY: Uh-huh. (*Bell.*)

215 BILL: Y'know I was—(*simultaneously*)— heading to the—

BETTY: I was thinking about—

BILL: I'm sorry.

BETTY: No, go ahead.

BILL: I was going to say that I was headed to the movies in a little while, and . . .

220 BETTY: So was I.

BILL: The Woody Allen festival?

BETTY: Just up the street.

BILL: Do you like the early ones?

BETTY: I think anybody who doesn't ought to be run off the planet.

BILL: How many times have you seen *Bananas*?   225

BETTY: Eight times.

BILL: Twelve. So are you still interested? (*Long pause.*)

BETTY: Do you like Entenmann's crumb cake . . . ?

BILL: Last night I went out at two in the morning to get one. (*Small pause.*) Did you have an Etch-a-Sketch as a child?

BETTY: Yes! And do you like Brussels sprouts? (*Small pause.*)   230

BILL: I think they're gross.

BETTY: They *are* gross!

BILL: Do you still believe in marriage in spite of current sentiments against it?

BETTY: Yes.

BILL: And children?   235

BETTY: Three of them.

BILL: Two girls and a boy.

BETTY: Harvard, Vassar, and Brown.

BILL: And will you love me?

BETTY: Yes.   240

BILL: And cherish me forever?

BETTY: Yes.

BILL: Do you still want to go the movies?

BETTY: Sure thing.

BILL and BETTY (*together*): Waiter!   245

BLACKOUT

····· ▶ *Your* **Turn**
Talking and Writing about Lit

1. David Ives's *Sure Thing* is a play that might have multiple interpretations. What do you think it means?

2. What purpose does the bell serve in the play? What would be missing (in terms of meaning, in terms of humor, in terms of characterization) if the bell were not used?

3. At the end of *Sure Thing*, everything seems to be coming together for Betty and Bill. Do you think this is a good ending for Ives's play? How do you interpret the ending, in terms of its meaning?

4. **DIY** Write a page or two of dialogue between two characters who are coming from quite different perspectives. Then add a ringing bell which interrupts their conversation. Your bell might serve the same function as Ives's, or it might have a different purpose.

The Philadelphia (1989)

CHARACTERS:
AL
WAITRESS
MARK

A bar/restaurant. A table, red-checked cloth, two chairs, and a specials board. At lights up, AL *is at the restaurant table, with the* WAITRESS.

WAITRESS: Can I help you?

AL: Do you know you would look fantastic on a wide screen?

WAITRESS: Uh-huh.

AL: Seventy millimeters.

5 WAITRESS: Look. Do you want to see a menu, or what?

AL: Let's negotiate, here. What's the soup du jour today?

WAITRESS: Soup of the day, you got a choice of Polish duck blood or cream of kidney.

AL: Beautiful. Beautiful! Kick me in a kidney.

WAITRESS: (*writes it down*): You got it.

10 AL: Any oyster crackers on your seabed?

WAITRESS: Nope. All out.

AL: How about the specials today? Spread out your options.

WAITRESS: You got your deep-fried gizzards.

AL: Fabulous.

15 WAITRESS: Calves' brains with okra.

AL: You are a *temptress*.

WAITRESS: And pickled pigs' feet.

AL: Pigs' feet. *I love it*. Put me down for a quadruped.

WAITRESS: If you say so.

AL: Any sprouts to go on those feet? 20

WAITRESS: Iceberg.

AL: So be it.

(WAITRESS *exits, as* MARK *enters, looking shaken and bedraggled.*)

MARK: Al!

AL: Hey there, Marcus. What's up?

MARK: Jesus! 25

AL: What's going on, buddy?

MARK: Oh, man . . . !

AL: What's the matter? Sit down.

MARK: I don't get it, Al. I don't understand it.

AL: You want something? You want a 30
drink? I'll call the waitress—

MARK (*desperate*): *No!* No! Don't even try. (*Gets a breath.*) I don't know what's going on today, Al. It's really weird.

AL: What, like . . . ?

MARK: Right from the time I got up.

AL: What is it? What's the story?

MARK: Well—just for an example. This 35
morning I stopped off at a drugstore to buy some aspirin. This is at a big drugstore, right?

AL: Yeah . . .

MARK: I go up to the counter, the guy says what can I do for you, I say, Give me a bottle of aspirin. The guy gives me this funny look and he says, "Oh we don't have *that*, sir." I said to him, You're a drugstore and you don't have any *aspirin*?

AL: Did they have Bufferin?

MARK: Yeah!

40 AL: Advil?

MARK: Yeah!

AL: Extra-strength Tylenol?

MARK: Yeah!

AL: But no aspirin.

45 MARK: No!

AL: Wow . . .

MARK: And that's the kind of weird thing that's been happening all day. It's like, I go to a newsstand to buy the *Daily News*, the guy never even *heard* of it.

AL: Could've been a misunderstanding.

MARK: I asked everyplace—*nobody* had the *News*! I had to read the *Toronto Hairdresser*. Or this. I go into a deli at lunchtime to buy a sandwich, the guy tells me they don't have any *pastrami*. How can they be a deli if they don't have pastrami?

50 AL: Was this a Korean deli?

MARK: This was a kosher-from-*Jerusalem* deli. "Oh we don't carry *that*, sir," he says to me. "Have some tongue."

AL: Mmm.

MARK: I just got into a cab, the guy says he doesn't go to Fifty-sixth Street! He offers to take me to Newark instead!

AL: Mm-hm.

55 MARK: Looking at me like I'm an alien or something!

AL: Mark. Settle down.

MARK: "Oh I don't go *there*, sir."

AL: Settle down. Take a breath.

MARK: Do you know what this is?

60 AL: Sure.

MARK: What is it? What's happening to me?

AL: Don't panic. You're in a Philadelphia.

MARK: I'm in a what?

AL: You're in a Philadelphia. That's all.

MARK: But I'm in—   65

AL: Yes, physically you're in New York. But *meta*physically you're in a Philadelphia.

MARK: I've never heard of this!

AL: You see, inside of what we know as reality there are these pockets, these black holes called Philadelphias. If you fall into one, you run up against exactly the kinda shit that's been happening to you all day.

MARK: Why?

AL: Because in a Philadelphia, no matter   70 what you ask for, you can't get it. You ask for something, they're not gonna have it. You want to do something, it ain't gonna get done. You want to go somewhere, you can't get there from here.

MARK: Good God. So this is very serious.

AL: Just remember, Marcus. This is a condition named for the town that invented the *cheese steak*. Something that nobody in his right mind would willingly ask for.

MARK: And I thought I was just having a very bad day. . . .

AL: Sure. Millions of people have spent entire lifetimes inside a Philadelphia and never even knew it. Look at the city of Philadelphia itself. Hopelessly trapped forever inside a Philadelphia. And do they know it?

MARK: Well what can I do? Should I just kill   75 myself now and get it over with?

AL: You try to kill yourself in a Philadelphia, you're only gonna get hurt, babe.

MARK: So what do I do?

AL: Best thing to do is wait it out. Someday the great cosmic train will whisk you outta the City of Brotherly Love and off to someplace happier.

MARK: *You're* pretty goddamn mellow today.

80 AL: Yeah well. Everybody has to be
    someplace.
    (WAITRESS *enters.*)
    WAITRESS: Is your name Allen Chase?
    AL: It is indeed.
    WAITRESS: There was a phone call for you.
        Your boss?
    AL: Okay.
85 WAITRESS: He says you're fired.
    AL: Cool! Thanks. (WAITRESS *exits.*) So
        anyway, you have this problem . . .
    MARK: Did she just say you got *fired*?
    AL: Yeah. I wonder what happened to my
        pigs' feet. . . .
    MARK: Al—!? You *loved* your job!
90 AL: Hey. No sweat.
    MARK: How can you be so calm?
    AL: Easy. You're in a Philadelphia? *I* woke
        up in a Los Angeles. And life is beautiful!
        You know Susie packed up and left me
        this morning.
    MARK: Susie left you?
    AL: And frankly, Scarlett, I don't give a shit.
        I say, go and God bless and may your
        dating pool be Olympic-sized.
95 MARK: But your job? The garment district is
        your life!
    AL: So I'll turn it into a movie script and sell
        it to Paramount. Toss in some sex, add a
        little emotional blah-blah-*blah*, pitch it to
        Jack and Dusty, you got a buddy movie
        with a garment background. Not relevant
        enough? We'll throw in the hole in the
        ozone, make it E.C.
    MARK: E.C.?
    AL: Environmentally correct. Have you
        heard about this hole in the ozone?
    MARK: Sure.
100 AL: Marcus, I *love* this concept. I *embrace*
        this ozone. Sure, some people are gonna
        get hurt in the process. Meantime, every-
        body else'll tan a little faster.
    MARK (*quiet horror*): So this is a Los
        Angeles . . .
    AL: Well. Everybody has to be someplace.

MARK: Wow.
AL: You want my advice? *Enjoy your
    Philadelphia*. Sit back and order yourself a
    beer and a burger and chill out for a
    while.
MARK: But I can't order anything. Life is   105
    great for you out there on the cosmic
    beach. Whatever *I* ask for, I'll get a cheese
    steak or something.
AL: No. There's a very simple rule of
    thumb in a Philadelphia. *Ask for the
    opposite.*
MARK: What?
AL: If you can't get what you ask for, ask for
    the opposite and you'll get what you
    want. You want the *Daily News*, ask for the
    Times. You want pastrami, ask for tongue.
MARK: Oh.
AL: Works great with women. What is more   110
    opposite than the opposite sex?
MARK: Uh-huh.
AL: So. Would you like a Bud?
MARK: I sure could use a—
AL: No. Stop. (*Very deliberately.*) Do you
    want . . . a Bud?
MARK (*also deliberately*): No. I *don't* want a   115
    Bud.
(WAITRESS *enters and goes to the specials board.*)
AL: Good. Now there's the waitress. Order
    yourself a Bud and a burger. But don't
    ask for a Bud and a burger.
MARK: Waitress!
AL: Don't call her. She won't come.
MARK: Oh.
AL: You're in a Philadelphia, so just figure,   120
    fuck her.
MARK: Fuck *her*.
AL: You don't need that waitress.
MARK: *Fuck* that waitress.
AL: And everything to do with her.
MARK: *Hey, waitress! FUCK YOU!*   125
(WAITRESS *turns to him.*)
WAITRESS: Can I help you, sir?
AL: *That's* how you get service in a
    Philadelphia.

WAITRESS: Can I help you?

MARK: Uh—no thanks.

130 WAITRESS: Okay, what'll you have? (*Takes out her pad.*)

AL: Excellent.

MARK: Well—how about some O.J.?

WAITRESS: Sorry. Squeezer's broken.

MARK: A glass of milk?

135 WAITRESS: Cow's dry.

MARK: Egg nog?

WAITRESS: Just ran out.

MARK: Cuppa coffee?

WAITRESS: Oh we don't have *that*, sir. (MARK *and* AL *exchange a look and nod. The* WAITRESS *has spoken the magic words.*)

140 MARK: Got any ale?

WAITRESS: Nope.

MARK: Stout?

WAITRESS: Nope.

MARK: Porter?

145 WAITRESS: Just beer.

MARK: That's too bad. How about a Heineken?

WAITRESS: Heineken? Try again.

MARK: Rolling Rock?

WAITRESS: Outta stock.

150 MARK: Schlitz?

WAITRESS: Nix.

MARK: Beck's?

WAITRESS: Next.

MARK: Sapporo?

155 WAITRESS: Tomorrow.

MARK: Lone Star?

WAITRESS: Hardy-har.

MARK: Bud Lite?

WAITRESS: Just plain Bud is all we got.

160 MARK: No thanks.

WAITRESS (*calls*): *Gimme a Bud!* (*To* MARK) Anything to eat?

MARK: Nope.

WAITRESS: Name it.

MARK: Pork chops.

165 WAITRESS (*writes down*): Hamburger . . .

MARK: Medium.

WAITRESS: Well done . . .

MARK: Baked potato.

WAITRESS: Fries . . .

170 MARK: And some zucchini.

WAITRESS: Slice of raw. (*Exits, calling.*) Burn one!

AL: Marcus, that was excellent.

MARK: Thank you.

AL: *Excellent.* You sure you've never done this before?

175 MARK: I've spent so much of my life asking for the wrong thing without knowing it, doing it on purpose comes easy.

AL: I hear you.

MARK: I could've saved myself a lot of trouble if I'd screwed up on purpose all those years. Maybe I was in a Philadelphia all along and never knew it!

AL: You might've been in a Baltimore. They're practically the same.

(WAITRESS *enters with a glass of beer and a plate.*)

WAITRESS: Okay. Here's your Bud. (*Sets that in front of* MARK.) And one cheese steak. (*She sets that in front of* AL *and starts to go.*)

180 AL: Excuse me. Hey. Wait a minute. What is that?

WAITRESS: It's a cheese steak.

AL: No. I ordered cream of kidney and two pairs of feet.

WAITRESS: Oh we don't have *that*, sir.

AL: I beg your pardon?

185 WAITRESS: We don't have that, sir. (*Small pause.*)

AL (*to* MARK): You son of a bitch! *I'm in your Philadelphia!*

MARK: I'm sorry, Al.

AL: You brought me into your fucking Philadelphia!

MARK: I didn't know it was contagious.

190 AL: Oh God, please don't let me be in a Philadelphia! Don't let me be in a—

MARK: Shouldn't you ask for the opposite? I mean, since you're in a Philad—

AL: Don't you tell *me* about life in a Philadelphia.

MARK: Maybe you're not really—

AL: I taught you everything you know about Philly, asshole. Don't tell *me* how to act in a Philadelphia!

195 MARK: But maybe you're not really in a Philadelphia!

AL: Do you see the cheese on that steak? What do I need for proof? The fucking *Liberty Bell*? Waitress, bring me a glass of water.

WAITRESS: Water? Don't have that, sir.

AL (*to* MARK): "We don't have *water*"—? What, you think we're in a sudden drought or something? (*Suddenly realizes.*) Holy shit, I just lost my job. . . . ! Susie left me! I gotta make some phone calls! (*To* WAITRESS.) 'Scuse me, where's the payphone?

WAITRESS: Sorry, we don't have a payph—

200 AL: Of *course* you don't have a payphone, of *course* you don't! Oh shit, let me outta here! (*Exits.*)

MARK: I don't know. It's not that bad in a Philadelphia.

WAITRESS: Could be worse. I've been in a Cleveland all week.

MARK: A Cleveland. What's that like?

WAITRESS: It's like death, without the advantages.

MARK: Really. Care to stand?   205

WAITRESS: Don't mind if I do. (*She sits.*)

MARK: I hope you won't reveal your name.

WAITRESS: Sharon.

MARK (*holds out his hand*): Good-bye.

WAITRESS: Hello. (*They shake.*)   210

MARK (*indicating the cheese steak*): Want to starve?

WAITRESS: Thanks. (*She picks up the cheese steak and starts eating.*)

MARK: Yeah, everybody has to be some-place. . . . (*Leans across the table with a smile.*) So.

BLACKOUT

• • • • •➤ *Your Turn*

Talking and Writing about Lit

1. Does *The Philadelphia* have conventional sources of dramatic conflict? Is there a protagonist; is there an antagonist? Does it fit into any of the traditional categories of conflict: character versus character, character versus environment, or character versus himself or herself?

2. What is the matter with Al? What condition is he suffering from? How does he end up coping with the problem?

3. Although David Ives's plays seem similarly satirical and irreverent, do you notice a common characteristic regarding the ending of the two plays in this chapter, a characteristic that might undercut the earlier satire to a certain extent?

4. **DIY** This play is set in New York with New Yorkers as characters. If the scenario in *The Philadelphia* plays on stereotypes of Philadelphia, how would you envision a play which placed characters into "a New York"? What would the characteristics be of that state of mind? Write one or two pages of dialogue in which characters are stuck in a New York, or choose another city which you would like to characterize.

Talking Lit

In his preface, David Ives enumerates forty-one things that have warped him to become the person he is today. Stephanie Coen tries to make sense of all this. Ives writes in "Some Origins" about how he gets his zany ideas.

David Ives, Preface to *All in the Timing* (1994)

Thank you for your very kind letter about my plays. Here are the answers to your questions:

Time Flies

1. Longhand, with Bic blue medium-point pens.

2. Mornings from 9:00 till lunch, and again in the evenings if I'm really onto something. *Sure Thing* got written in two successive nights between about 11:00 P.M. and 3 A.M. (and then, of course, much *re*written in rehearsal). *Long Ago and Far Away* took months.

3. The South Side of Chicago.

4. Yes.

5. No.

6. "Pinocchio."

7. Absolutely not.

8. My aunt Jo.

9. I was about nine or ten. I found an antiquated, bloody thriller called *Mr. Strang* on my parents' bookshelves and turned its three hundred pages of mayhem into a headlong fifteen-minute play. (Obviously the short form attracted me from a tender age.) What I didn't know at age ten was that everybody in the cast had to get a copy of the script, so after learning my lines I passed my handwritten pages on to Johnny Stanislawski down the block, and he lost them. Probably my greatest work.

10. Ironically, my first date was with a girl whose last name was Kafka, and I took her to see *The Sound of Music*. God knows how that experience warped me, but several therapists have turned me down for treatment on the basis of it.

11. Anchovies.

12. By moistening the tip and saying, "Wankel Rotary Engine," of course.

13. I think Father Henkel did it. He was my English teacher in the rather peculiar, old-fashioned high school I attended (Catholic, all boys, jackets and ties, four years of Latin, the works). One particular afternoon Henkel was trying to focus our young attentions on Emily Dickinson. Unfortunately for Henkel (and Emily Dickinson) it was a warm spring day and we boys were feeling, well, boisterous. Faced with chaos, he laid the textbook down, climbed up onto his desk, and stood on his head. We all stopped horsing around and stared at him in stupefaction. Henkel then climbed back down, picked up the book, and said, "Let's get back to 'Beauty be not caused—it is,' page 388." It was probably my first glimpse of the power of the theatrical: you gather an audience, you do a headstand to get everyone's attention, and then you're free to explore beauty, poetry, truth, the human condition, what you will. NOW *that's* an education.

14. No, I never have. Too messy.

15. It happened right around the same time as Henkel's headstand. I was about sixteen and had bought a balcony ticket to see a matinee of *A Delicate Balance* with Hume Cronyn and Jessica Tandy. I remember sitting in the balcony that afternoon watching Hume Cronyn do the speech about the cat (in my memory, I'm sitting in the first row of the balcony staring down at the stage as if I were in the first car of a roller coaster) and thinking that there couldn't be anyplace in the world more thrilling than where I was right then. Maybe the height just made me dizzy. Anyway, that day I started writing plays in earnest, so by the time I reached college I was already in my fertile middle period.

16. Frankly, I don't think it's any of your business.

17. When I was twenty-one, a grant got me my first professional production in a remote area of Los Angeles at America's smallest, and possibly worst theater, in a storefront that had a pillar dead center in the middle of the stage. That play was called *Canvas*, and it catapulted me into immediate and total obscurity.

18. Panty hose.

19. Very often. In fact during my twenties I left the theater not once but twice—only to come back when I realized that nobody knew I'd left. (What are you leaving, when you "leave" the theater? It's the kind of question a Buddhist monk answers by hitting you on the head with a plank.)

20. Probably the production in which the actress playing the lead made her entrance on opening night and the door came off the hinges. I walked out at intermission and came back three years later.

21. (a) Yale Drama School, and (b) not really, what with the head of the playwriting department busy digging trenches outside the cherry orchard trying to keep Sam Shepard out. Yale was a blissful time for me, in spite of the fact that there is slush on the ground in New Haven 238 days a year.

22. The Manhattan Punch Line Theatre, on West Forty-second Street. Much reviled then, much missed now, the Punch Line went bankrupt several years ago. Steve Kaplan, God bless him, ran it with an air of inimitable, hopeless gloom, and always found a place in his annual one-act festival for one or more of my pieces. Unpaid interns, an asthmatic Xerox machine, seething actors—it was real theater. The kind of place where the shows have to be good, because the bathrooms aren't working.

23. Yes.

24. Yes.

25. Yes I said yes I will Yes.

26. *All in the Timing* was the collective title for the Primary Stages production of *Sure Thing, Words, Words, Words, The Universal Language, Philip Glass Buys a Loaf of Bread, The Philadelphia*, and *Variations on the Death of Trotsky*. It was directed by the brilliant Jason McConnell Buzas, who also directed the premieres of several other of these plays and whose stamp (a rare Polynesian first-class airmail) is on practically every one.

27. Mrs. Peacock, in the library, with the lead pipe.

28. The great crested orc.

29. Did you mean "bunion" or "onion"? The difference is, of course, crucial.

30. *Variations on the Death of Trotsky* was not originally intended for production. I wrote it as a birthday gift for Fred Sanders, who directed the first production of *Words, Words, Words*. I had seen an article in the *Times* about Trotsky which mentioned that after being hit in the head with a mountain-climber's axe, Trotsky lived on for thirty-six hours. I thought it was the funniest thing I'd ever heard, and I got very taken with the question of what one does for thirty-six hours with a mountain-climber's axe in one's head. What kind of food do you eat? (Fast food, naturally.)

31. *Mere Mortals* was inspired by an article in a New Jersey newspaper about a guy in an old-folks home who was trying to claim the Lindbergh baby's inheritance. I originally intended to call the play "Perkin Warbeck," but a rioting mob stopped me.

32. *The Philadelphia* was my affectionate revenge on the City of Brotherly Love after I'd spent many miserable months there working on an opera commission and finding myself up against that town's peculiar metaphysical, ah, peculiarities. Bakeries that didn't have any bread on the shelves, for example. Magazine stands that didn't sell *Time* magazine. Or the morning when I tried to get a cheese omelette for breakfast at a restaurant.

> Me: I'll have a cheese omelette, please.
> Waitress: Sure, what kinda cheese you want?
> Me: What kind do you have?
> Waitress: Any kinda cheese. You name it.

ME: Okay, I'll have Swiss.
WAITRESS: Sorry. We don't have any Swiss.
ME: Oh. Cheddar, then.
WAITRESS: No cheddar.
ME: Monterey jack?
WAITRESS: Just ran out.
ME: Jarlsberg . . . ?
WAITRESS: What's that?

33. Yes, *Sure Thing* was written several years before the movie *Groundhog Day*, which bears it a superficial resemblance. Originally I planned to set the play at a bus stop, and I wanted to write something that would trace all the possible routes the answer to a simple question could take. As for *Foreplay*, I was overdosing on Glenn Gould's recording of *The Well-Tempered Clavier* and had an idea for a play that worked like a fugue. Originally it was to be four secretaries at four desks with four telephones, but somehow a miniature-golf course suggested itself as richer ground.

34. Love. What else?

35. Oop scoopa wee-bop, bonk, *deek!*

36. *The Universal Language* started life as a twenty-minute opera for three singers as part of a commission in dreaded Philadelphia. (Jarlsberg? What's that?) I had long wanted to try writing a play in a language I myself made up, so the composer and I wrote several scenes and presented it in front of an audience as a work in progress. Somehow the piece didn't work, though it was interesting enough. Years later I realized that it hadn't worked because the music was redundant. Unamunda, the made-up language, *was* the music. I took the basic idea, the names of Don and Dawn, and started from scratch, with better results.

37. Does it ever strike you that life is like a list of answers, in which you have to glean or even make up the questions yourself? Just asking.

38. Two reams of paper, several bottles of Jim Beam, and a seemingly indestructible copy of Bizet's *The Pearl Fishers*.

39. Martha Stoberock, who keeps me reminded that the really important things in life don't have anything to do with the theater.

40. Lithuanian chutney.

41. Panty hose.

Sincerely,

DAVID IVES
JUNE 1994

Stephanie Coen "No Comparisons: An Interview with the Playwright"

David Ives and I met in a New York restaurant not unlike the café where Bill and Betty work out their future in *Sure Thing*, the first play in this collection. Our conversation initially seemed like a parody of his signature piece; a bell didn't ring, but the 43-year-old author called for the check anytime he wanted to change the subject. Ives has been writing for more than 20 years: plays, screenplays, an opera, fiction and journalism. He describes his early, full-length works as "terrible plays that nobody even knows about anymore," but the short comedies collected here have sent critics to their thesauri for variations on the word hilarious.

When the *New Criterion* reviewed *All in the Timing*, the reviewer used words like "Ivesian" and "Ivesland." How would you define Ivesland?
Oh my God. What's your next question?

I'm not equipped to answer that. I've been reading all these reviews and critiques of my work, and being wonderfully enlightened about what these plays are actually about. I thought they were just harmless little skits, and here they are saying "Ivesland" and "Ivesian." For me to consider what these plays are about would probably cripple me irredeemably in trying to write any more of them. You have to write innocently, up to a certain point. What does Ivesland mean to *you*?

Well, for one thing, the ordinary seems fantastical and the fantastical somehow seems ordinary.
I've never known the difference between those two things. I don't honestly try to be fantastical. I don't honestly try to be anything.

I write these things so that someone will write the sort of play that I'd like to go and see. Too much in theatre to me is literal and boring and unimaginative and untheatrical. My own interest in going to the theatre sort of slackened off when I finally started writing plays that I liked.

I think Ivesland is also a place where, if people try hard enough, or simply stick around long enough, they can get things right. Are you as much of a romantic as your plays?
I've heard that word bandied about about me, and I want to stop this rumor immediately. I am a dark, troubled, angst-ridden, misanthropic writer about the dark side of the human condition.

Am I a romantic? Seeing all of these plays together surprised me. The one thing that I learned was how weirdly optimistic they are. Something that audiences must find so appealing about them is that people overcome the most insuperable difficulties in these plays: Trying to write *Hamlet* when you don't know what *Hamlet* is, or learning a language that you're creating as you go along, or living with a mountain climber's axe in your head for 36 hours. I don't know if romantic is the word. But a lot of guys do end up getting the girl, and vice versa, so there must be something there.

There is, in all of your work, a sense of possibility. Do you think that's true of theatre as an art form?

I think of theatre as an arena for communal empathy. To write for the theatre, you have to have a kind of imaginative empathy for people in order to understand how and what they feel. You then bring that to an audience. The audience has to empathize with what you're saying, and the actors have to empathize with what you've written, and all the people who put a production together have to empathize with each other for the space of four or eight weeks. I think of theatre as this great civilizing arena where people find a common ground. It's where, in one way or another, we realize that we're in the same leaky boat, and we realize it in person.

You've been compared to Beckett, Ionesco, Pinter, Stoppard. In a not-unimaginable Ivesian situation, what would you say to them?

What could I possibly say to them—little did you know you were like me. Do you mean, what would I say to them about their plays?

Anything. Let's say you're in a room, and in walks Beckett.

I'd tell him, *You're dead, Sam, go home.* Then I'd say, *Oh, by the way, lighten up.*

I'm abjectly grateful to these people for writing the good plays they have, but I don't really see the justice of the comparison. I don't know why people say Harold Pinter. And Samuel Beckett? Three monkeys typing in a room trying to write *Hamlet*—does that sound like something Beckett would write? Maybe I'm just resisting being compared to anybody. I don't take these plays as seriously as these reviewers have. I'm just trying to make good jokes.

What would you do if you weren't a playwright?

At last, an easy question. I'd not be a playwright. Wittgenstein would approve of that answer.

What would I do? I'd spend all my time in museums looking at paintings. Much more fun than being a playwright. To me the theatre is about necessity, and painting is somehow or other, in a way that I can't define, about freedom. I think that my resistance to Beckett, Pinter, Ionesco, Stoppard, that nonsense—I think that resistance actually comes because I don't think that I'm influenced by those people, even though I somehow seem to be like them. The effect that I want these plays to have isn't a theatrical effect; it's about painting and music. The best theatre I've seen in years was the Lucian Freud exhibit.

Is there anything you want to ask me?

Are you paying for this meal?

David Ives, *Some Origins* (2001)

Some origins, for anyone interested in such things. "Dr. Fritz" was sparked by a story in *The New York Times* about a South American mechanic-turned-healer who performs gruesome medical operations without anesthesia and using the crudest of tools while under the spiritual influence of a German doctor who died in 1912. Apparently, this works, so it may be the answer to America's health crisis. The idea for "Degas" simply came to me out of the blue as I woke up one Sunday morning. The moment I opened my eyes, the sentence *I decided to be Degas for a day* sounded in the porches of my ears. (All those delicious D's!) I went straight to my writing table and wrote the idea up as a 1,000-word humor piece. The day the piece appeared in the *Times* Magazine, John Guare called me up and said: "How could you waste this idea on *The New York Times*?" So I turned it into a play.

"Soap Opera" popped into my head as I stood on a totally empty street in Independence, Kansas—again on an early Sunday morning, interestingly enough—looking into an old shop window that had a poster of the weeping Maytag Repairman on display. Suddenly that well-known TV-commercial face seemed pathetic, even tragic—human. I did the instinctive human thing and tried to help turn his pain comedywards. My old David Mamet, um, *hommage* "Speed-the-Play" got updated, rethought, rehauled and rewritten thoroughly for the evening called "Mere Mortals." That revised version is included here for all disciples of The Fuckin' Master.

By now I've amassed pages and pages of ideas for plays—many too many plays for me to live long enough to write. But then, Cato The Elder had some excellent agricultural advice circa 200 B.C.: *Sterquilinium magnum stude ut habeas*, or: "Make sure you've got a nice big dungheap." Advice as valuable to writers as to farmers. (*Sterquilinium*'s a handsome word to throw around your next literary tea.) On an opposite advisory tack is another line I often ponder, which a priest in my high school used to quote with pointed relish. It's part of a letter Cicero sent to a servant who was getting the Roman politico's country house ready for the summer and works as well for playwrights chewing their pens as for sophomores chewing their futures: *Si aqua in balnia non sit, fac sit.* "If there's no water in the bath, put it there."

In a world where millions of people a night watch "Kojak" reruns in distant, silent communion every evening, one wonders about the future of a local, hand-made art like theatre which can only touch, tickle or appall a roomful of people at a time. Independent movies have invaded and coopted the exotic psychic and existential terrain that once belonged solely to good theatre. Smart young writers bypass the boards and head straight for Gomorrah, to set up shop in an office in West Hollywood. In New York it's practically impossible to cast a play these days, when movie, TV and commercial commitments mean that only three unsuitable actors over the age of twenty-three are available and willing to commit to four weeks of rehearsal and a limited run at insulting wages. "The theatre," a notable Hollywood producer is reputed to have said, "is nothing but a flea up an elephant's ass." And yet somehow fine plays still get written and good theatre continues to get made and actors still come back to speak lines in front of that handful of diehards. Must be one hell of a flea.

In the several years since my last anthology of short plays, Eugene Ionesco died, still a wildly undervalued poet of the theatre. One obituary quoted his own reasons for still sitting down to work in this wacky masochistic business: "To allow others to share in the astonishment of being, the dazzlement of existence, and to shout to God and other human beings our anguish, letting it be known that we were there."

Now pardon me while I go tend my dungheap and fill up the bath.

Student Essay

Student Adam Marchbein explores some of the most hilarious and interesting aspects of three plays by David Ives.

Adam Marchbein

English 102-EN

Professor Barnard

Essay 5

From the Mind of David Ives

Many people try to write about topics in life that affect us all, such as dating, and society in general. Few, however, are able to put such a unique comedic twist on life as David Ives has. As unique as his plays were that I decided to read, some of them irritated me so badly I had to stop reading them; when reading others, I couldn't stop laughing. Not everyone will like the plays one writes nor understand them, but I guess that is one of the things that makes us all unique, our sense of humor. In an interview with Ives by Stephanie Coen, he said, "I thought they were just harmless little skits," basically saying not to analyze them, just to enjoy them. "I write these things so that someone will write the sort of play that I'd like to go and see." Maybe that's why I enjoyed them so much because I wasn't trying to analyze them, I was enjoying them for the innovative comedies that they are.

Have you ever wondered, what if you had said something different? How could that have changed the whole outcome of that

Marchbein 2

situation? Well, in Ives's *Sure Thing* he takes a glimpse at the meeting of
Bill, a man in his late twenties, and Betty, a woman in her late twenties.
These characters are able to go back in time briefly to change their
response to the other's questions and vice versa every time a bell
sounds. A little weird, but certain television shows—such as *The Drew
Carey Show*—have used this strategy. When that type of episode is on, I
have to watch it. Bill and Betty discuss certain things like background
and literature, and every time they don't like the answer they are given
or the answer they gave themselves, a bell sounds, making them able
to go one or a few phrases back and change what they had said. Bill
tries to initiate the conversation and at one point is bombarded with a
verbal assault accusing him of only wanting sex from Betty. Naturally
the bell sounds soon afterward. Not many writers would put such
things in their plays like Ives has decided to but it worked quite well.
One part I couldn't stop laughing at was when the characters are discussing school and Bill says "what does it matter if I had a two-point
at—(*Bell*)—three-point at—(*Bell*)—four-point at college? Or if I did
come from Pittsburgh—(*Bell*)—Cleveland—(*Bell*)—Westchester
County?" The use of the question shows that not even Bill was sure
what he should say, like in improv theatre. This next part I couldn't
stop laughing at. Bill says "so what if I admire Trotsky? (*Bell*) So what if
I once had total-body liposuction? (*Bell*) So what if I don't have a
penis? (*Bell*) So what if I once spent a year in the Peace Corps?" It
seems like the characters are rewriting the play as it progresses. At the
end, because of all the bells, they soon are able to find out that they
are perfect for each other. But couldn't anyone be perfect for you with
that bell? I know I could've used that bell a couple times in my life.

There is an old saying that "three monkeys typing into infinity
will sooner or later produce *Hamlet*." Ives decides to do just that. In

Marchbein 3

the comedy *Words, Words, Words*, we have our three main characters—Swift, Kafka, and Milton. There is also the unseen character Rosenbaum, the man performing the experiment. The monkeys are discussing what they have written—critiquing each other—and some of the writing isn't even English; it's just sounds or gibberish. "How are we supposed to write *Hamlet* if we don't even know what it is?" Kafka points out. Aside from not knowing *Hamlet* they don't even know Shakespeare. By doing a trick and motioning a cigarette to his mouth Milton receives one and proceeds to smoke it. Swift says, "They should have thrown in a kewpie doll for that performance." "It got results, didn't it?" says Milton. Swift then states how he had broken a typewriter and gotten a carton of Marlboros. But he didn't smoke them, he "took a crap on them" as "political statement." Swift is definitely the thinker of the group; he wants to know what happens if they actually come up with *Hamlet*. Or, why even *Hamlet* in general? In the midst of the typing Swift gets fed up. "That's it! Forget this random *Hamlet* crap. What about revenge?" Sound familiar? Revenge, Hamlet, wink wink. While discussing how to get revenge, Swift actually mentions details reminiscent of death plots in Shakespeare's plays, such as "poisoning the typewriter keys" (as Claudius and Laertes poison the sword in *Hamlet*). Swift then suggests challenging Rosenbaum to a duel, "in the course of combat, I casually graze my rapier over the poisoned typewriter keys, and (*Jabs*) a hit! A palpable hit! For a reserve, we lay a cup with some venomous distilment." As a joke Ives has Swift mention two ways that death had occurred in other Shakespeare plays. After all the commotion, Kafka returns to typing, as does Milton. Kafka types Act one, scene one, Elsinore Castle, Denmark. Enter Bernardo and Francisco. Bernardo says, "Who's there?" as the comedy ends. This is such a classic example of dramatic and comedic irony that Kafka had actually stumbled on Hamlet after typing twenty lines of just K. The reason I chose to discuss this comedy was to show that Ives wasn't afraid to touch upon the extreme. As I said before, not too many playwrights would write about three monkeys typing. This play gets into the mind of the monkey, having Swift complain that he should be in Africa digging for anis. Honestly, there probably aren't many plays I could sit through, but if I had the chance to go see one of Ives's I would in a heartbeat.

The last play I want to discuss is *The Philadelphia*. Have you ever had one of *those* days? You know which one I'm talking about. The one where you can't get anything that you're looking for and everything seems backwards. Well, what if each day had its own name, and was a separate place for that matter. Philadelphia is the name given to the day where no matter what you are looking for, you can't find it. The comedy begins in a New York restaurant with Al who is apparently having a Los Angeles day; everything is fabulous, surreal, and movie-like. He gives the waitress his order for soup, pig's feet and lettuce. In comes Mark, one of Al's friends. Mark complains that wherever he went that day, no one had what he wanted. He went to a kosher deli and they said they didn't carry pastrami. He went to a newsstand and they said they had never heard of the *Daily News*. Al, having had experience in this, explains the theory of the black holes in our reality, Philadelphia being one of them. During the meal, Al gets fired from his job and his wife leaves him, but he doesn't mind because in Los Angeles nothing is real. Al explains to Mark how to handle talking in Philadelphia. After "not ordering" what he wanted they began to analyze Mark's life, "I could have saved myself a lot of trouble if I'd screwed up on purpose all those years. Maybe I was in Philadelphia all along and never knew it!" Al then says that he might have been in Baltimore because they are practically the same. The waitress then brings out a cheese steak and a beer for Al. Knowing he didn't order this he tells the waitress what he ordered, and she tells him that they don't have that. Al then realizes that he has been pulled into Mark's Philadelphia. Some of us can relate to this, when one of our friends has a bad day we begin to—not on purpose, just lucky I guess. As you can imagine, Al freaks out realizing that he really did lose his job and his wife in one day, and he leaves. I think we've all had one of those days—and maybe it wasn't my fault, maybe I was really in Philadelphia. Thank G-d it wasn't a Seattle day (I made that one up).

By use of Ives's innovative and strange idea of comedy we are able to take a look at our own lives and question certain things. I think the common theme of these comedies is "what if?" What if your bad day wasn't your fault? What if you could change what you'd said to get that better response? As for the monkeys, well I think that was just funny, but if you need a what if, here's one: "what if a researcher had that much free time to see if three monkeys eventually would type *Hamlet*! Would those monkeys try to kill him?" Maybe it's true that some things need to he analyzed, but we don't need to analyze everything; some things are just meant to be funny.

Works Cited

Ives, David. "All in the Timing: Six One-Act Comedies." *American Theatre*, July/August 1994. 25–42.

Ives, David. "No Comparisons: An Interview with the Playwright." Interview. By Stephanie Coen. *American Theatre* March 1994: 26.

Ives, David. *Sure Thing, Access Literature* by Barbara Barnard and David Winn (Wadsworth, 2005).

Q U E S T I O N S

TO ASK ABOUT DRAMA

1. Who is the central character? Might there be two main characters, or does this play have a single central character? What kinds of conflict reveal character here? Are there external conflicts (between characters, between a character and his or her environment)? Are there internal conflicts (within the main character or characters)? What methods of character development does the playwright use?

2. What level (or levels) of diction has the writer chosen to use? Is the use of language casual and conversational, speaking to us in the vernacular? Is it a more formal or distant voice? Is the level of diction the same in the characters' dialogue, or is dialogue one way in which the playwright has individuated the characters?

3. What kind of plot strategy has the playwright chosen to use? Does the story take place in more than one time frame? Do events in the drama begin at the beginning? Or does the story begin in medias res, in the middle of things? Does the writer employ flashbacks or foreshadowing? Is the plot structured traditionally, with rising action, a climax, and a dénouement, or has the dramatist used an innovative structure?

4. Has the writer used setting to help reveal characters in the play? Does setting play a role in revealing themes? What aspects of setting are important in this particular work (interior or exterior physical settings, social setting, historical time and place, climate and seasons)? Do the stage directions give precise instructions for the staging of the play, or has the playwright offered more interpretive leeway to the director, set designer, and actors?

5. What is the tone of the play? Is irony an aspect of characterization or theme here? Are there any symbolic objects, characters, or events which seem to represent larger meanings, in addition to their literal significance in the play?

6. Does the writer make use of figurative language (metaphor, simile, etc.), in dialogue or in stage directions, to convey ideas and emotions? Are there any thematic motifs in the play, any "systems" of imagery, or recurring or related symbols? Does the play's title reflect its theme/s?

7. Is this a realistic drama, or does the writer also use some nonrealistic or fantastic details? How do these nonrealistic elements work across the span of the play, and how do they enhance the play's meaning or themes?

PLOT
AND FORM

Even the World Wrestling Federation uses plot and form.

Each wrestling match is a story with conflict between characters. The wrestlers adopt nicknames and personas that establish character, and their characteristics interplay with the plot to make the drama more entertaining for the audience. "Stone Cold" Steve Austin is stoic and merciless and "The Rock" is immovable and dense.

The plot of the match follows conventional structure. The wrestlers often engage in pre-match fanfare that sets the stage for the story. Stone Cold proclaims himself the tougher wrestler. The Rock does the same. This is the exposition. It is during the exposition that the wrestlers establish their characters, their bonds with the audience, and their opinions of their opponents, thus setting up the conflict. As the wrestlers engage the audience, and their speeches become more and more inflammatory, seeming to enrage their opponents, the grudge between them becomes apparent. The conflict thus intensifies. When the match begins, the audience clearly understands what each wrestler wants and that he'll have to overcome a formidable opponent to get what he wants. The conflicts in wrestling matches are external, and pit antagonist against protagonist. The plot of the match moves from rising action, through climax, and into denouement. The conflict, the match itself in this case, is central to the plot. During the match, the wrestlers always trade winning and losing moves, but the plot can vary among matches. One wrestler might attack the referee or some innocent bystander, for example, thereby further developing character (the character of the wrestler, that is) and building conflict. The end of the match provides resolution of the central conflict, clearly establishing the victor and the fate of the loser.

The Importance of Plot

Whether we're talking about a story line that enlivens the contest between two wrestlers by fictionalizing their lives and powers . . . or whether we're talking about a "serious" work of literature (like a play by Shakespeare), an interesting plot is essential in order to capture and maintain the audience's (or reader's) interest. Playwright John Galsworthy expressed it this way:

> The plot! A good plot is that sure edifice which slowly rises out of the interplay of circumstance on temperament, and temperament on circumstance, within the enclosing atmosphere of an idea. A human being is the best plot there is. . . . He is organic. And so it must be with a good play. Reason alone produces no good plots; they come by original sin, sure conception, and instinctive after-power of selecting what benefits the germ. A bad plot, on the other hand, is simply a row of stakes, with a character impaled on each.
>
> —John Galsworthy, "Some Platitudes Concerning Drama"

Galsworthy was right to emphasize the interplay of plot and characterization. As was noted in our discussion of fiction, plot is the author's arrangement of incidents in the story (or play). We also noted that the author—here, the playwright—deliberately selects which events will be depicted, out of an infinite number of possible scenes.

The Shape of a Conventional Plot

The conception of the traditional plot structure of a short story (which we represented visually as a parabola) actually grows out of the conception of the shape of a traditionally plotted play. The traditional plot in drama is usually represented as a triangle.

As with fiction, of course, modern and contemporary playwrights have not always chosen to follow the traditional structure,

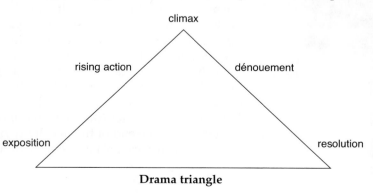

Drama triangle

and many have made innovations to it. In our discussion of the modern short story, we noted the leadership of Anton Chekhov in making such innovations as the open-ended story and the slice-of-life story. The development of drama in the early modern period (the last quarter of the nineteenth century) paralleled that of the short story, and both Anton Chekhov (see his short story in Chapter 10) and Henrik Ibsen (see his play in Chapter 27) were in the forefront of these innovations.

Shakespeare's *Othello* provides a good example of the traditional plot structure in drama, progressing deliberately and skillfully through each of the stages represented on our triangle. The five acts of the play may even be said to correspond to the five stages illustrated: exposition, rising action, climax, dénouement, and resolution. The Shakespearean critic A. L. Rowse, writing about this particular period in Shakespeare's working life, has this to say about the purity and force of *Othello*'s plot:

> [T]he first work of this time, *Othello*, rushes through breathless and inspired, from beginning to end, with one impulse. . . . All the world recognizes *Othello* as an inspired play, written with one continuous impulse like *Romeo and Juliet* a decade before. . . . *Othello* is the most concentrated of the plays: no subsidiary focus of interest is permitted, all our attention is fixed upon the drama of the three characters, Othello, Desdemona and Iago. The conflict of good and evil . . . is here at its simplest and most intense.
>
> —A. L. Rowse, *William Shakespeare, a Biography*, 380–81

So, here, given Shakespeare's focus and intentions for the play, the conventional plot structure has served him well. Indeed, this plot structure dominated in dramatic works of the Elizabethan period, and this dramatic shape had been inherited rather generally in Western culture from the form of the classical Greek drama, as defined by Aristotle and others.

Individualizing the Structure of Plot

August Wilson, in *Fences*, skillfully makes use of the power of the form learned from the traditional playwrights, but he alters this pattern whenever it suits his purposes. Thus, in the beginning of his play, we find not only a careful (and dramatically compelling) exposition of the situation of the individual characters, but also a lengthy passage of stage directions (a part of the exposition as well) which casts the present action in the context of the migration of African American people from the Southern states to the Northern states. *Fences* is a part of August Wilson's ambitious cycle of plays about the African American experience, and he wants to suggest to us at the outset that while these are vivid and individualized characters, they are also in many ways representative of their people's experience. Wilson reminds us of the big picture.

August Wilson's play is an example of a contemporary work of drama which makes use of the old form, while feeling free to change it to fit the playwright's material. *Fences* is a play in two acts (not the typical Elizabethan five acts), but the climax of the conflict does come rather precisely in the middle. Act I has four scenes, and Act II has five scenes. Act II, scene one, which is at the center of the play structurally, also contains the climax and the turning point of the plot.

Most of the concepts discussed in the chapter on fictional plot apply to dramatic plot as well. **Flashbacks**, although not used in either of the plays presented in this chapter, can be an important part of the plot strategy. A classic example would be Arthur Miller's *Death of a Salesman* (Chapter 28), in which scenes occurring in the present time alternate with scenes taking place in the past. **Foreshadowing**, however, is a device much used in Wilson's *Fences*. Examples would be Troy's story about wrestling with Mr. Death in Act I, scene one (a foreshadowing of the ending in Act II, scene five), and also the scenes of conflict with Cory (strike one and strike two) as foreshadowings of Act II, scene four (strike three). Wilson uses baseball as a metaphor throughout the play for various aspects of Troy's life and experience.

Conflict in the Dramatic Plot

In drama, the concepts of protagonist and antagonist and the necessity of conflict are of obvious importance. Conflict can be of any one of the three types noted in our discussion of fictional conflict:

- A character in conflict with another character
- A character in conflict with the environment (physical or social)
- A character in conflict with herself or himself.

The first two types of conflict are types of external conflict, and the last is called internal conflict (or inner conflict) because it takes place within the character. The torment which Iago puts Othello through may be one of the most agonizing examples of internal conflict in Western literature. A. L. Rowse has this to say about the nature and intensity of Othello's internal conflict:

> Shakespeare—evidently as much beyond conventional racial prejudices with Othello as with Shylock—depicts him as the heroic soldier he is, "great of heart," a leader of men who easily towers above his environment. The mutual passion of Othello and Desdemona surmounts all obstacles—to be shipwrecked in the event by the natal difference: Othello does not really understand her and so his natural confiding trust and simplicity of nature can be worked upon and overthrown by the evil mind of

Iago. Hence the absoluteness of Othello's reaction, the priest-like murder, the native ferocity and tenderness.

(A. L. Rowse, *William Shakespeare, a Biography*, 381–82)

And so, as Rowse subsequently notes, Shakespeare has also—in his typically forward-looking way—raised important questions about racial identity and cross-cultural misunderstandings.

Inner conflict is important, certainly, in *Fences*; but external conflicts are very much in the forefront, in terms of what serves to show forth the play's major themes. Troy is in conflict with himself, yes, but he is also in conflict with Cory, with Lyons, with Rose, sometimes with Bono, with Death, and—most crucially for Wilson—with the larger society (his social environment). There are metaphorical "fences" separating family members from one another, but that literal fence around the yard also symbolizes Troy's wish to be able to "fence out" the larger society, especially white American society. While Rose, Cory, and Bono try to remind him that some changes have begun to take place in society (e.g., Jackie Robinson's debut in the major leagues), Troy resists recognizing these changes. This is true in spite of the fact that he helped to bring about change himself, having challenged the color line in his city's Sanitation Department to become its first African American driver.

Perhaps Troy's difficulty in giving society credit for some change is that he is still justifiably angry about the unfairness of those obstacles having been put in his own and his people's way in the first place. Also, of course, he understands that there is still much to do to acquire truly equal opportunity. He sings his happy song about the dog "Blue" on the day he learns that he won his appeal and will be made a driver, and his children Raynell and Cory sing that same song of triumph in the last scene of the play, on the day of Troy's funeral. Although there is a sense of loss in the final scene, it is overshadowed by the feeling of hope represented by the two young characters as they sing Troy's "best song." Hope is also represented by Gabriel's dance in the final moments of the scene, and the opening of the gates, as well as Gabriel's final exclamatory statement: "That's the way that go!" These are all matters that you would want to look at if you were discussing the conflicts that drive the plot and deciding whether the ending of the play provides resolution or whether it is open ended (providing multiple possibilities for meaning and multiple possibilities for what happens next).

A Final Note on Plot and Conflict

Most critics and playwrights feel that conflict is so central to what drama is about that even when a play appears to have an entirely unconventional plot, it still contains some kind of conflict. An example would be David Ives's play *Sure Thing* (Chapter 25). While some readers might be tempted to say that this play has no plot—and others would say instead that it has an intentionally fragmented and circular plot—surely all would agree that it has conflict. The conflict between the male and female characters, arising out of misunderstandings and assumptions, is unmistakable.

Readings

William Shakespeare (1564–1616)

William Shakespeare was born at Stratford-on-Avon, the son of a prosperous English businessman and a gentlewoman whose family were large landowners, although evidently the Shakespeares' financial situation later became precarious. At the age of eighteen, Shakespeare struck out on his own and married twenty-six-year-old Anne Hathaway. The couple quickly had three children, and, before he was twenty-one, Shakespeare had a family to support. By 1600, at the age of thirty-four, Shakespeare had become the foremost playwright of his age, was already the author of fourteen plays and numerous sonnets, and was an owner (along with other shareholders) of the Globe Theater, where he directed and acted in his own dramatic works. His early plays include the histories *Richard II*

William Shakespeare

and *I Henry IV;* the comedies *A Midsummer Night's Dream, The Merchant of Venice,* and *Much Ado about Nothing;* and the early tragedies *Romeo and Juliet* and *Julius Caesar.* After 1600 Shakespeare devoted most of his time to writing his great tragedies, *Hamlet* (1602), *Othello* (1604), *King Lear* (1606), *Macbeth* (1606), and *Antony and Cleopatra* (1606), as well as other dramatic works. After 1608, following a number of personal tragedies, including the death of his illegitimate son and also a younger brother, Shakespeare spent more time at home in Stratford. He died there in 1616.

Othello, the Moor of Venice

CHARACTERS:

DUKE OF VENICE
BRABANTIO, *a Senator*
OTHER SENATORS
GRATIANO, *brother to Brabantio*

LODOVICO, *kinsman to Brabantio*

OTHELLO, *a noble Moor in the service of the Venetian state*

CASSIO, *his lieutenant*

IAGO, *his ensign*

MONTANO, *Othello's predecessor in the government of Cyprus*

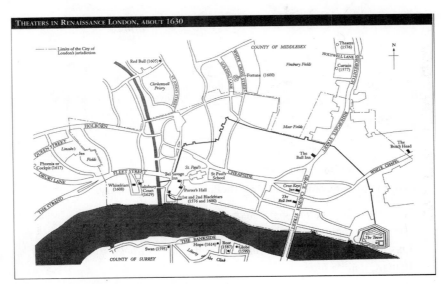

Theaters in Renaissance London, about 1630

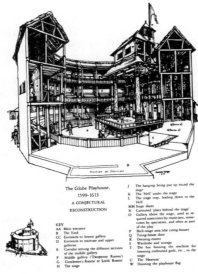

Globe Playhouse

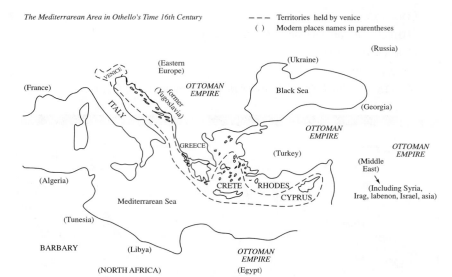

The Mediterrarean Area in Othello's Time 16th Century

– – – Territories held by venice
( ) Modern places names in parenthesis

Map of the Mediterranean area in Othello's time, 16th century.

RODERIGO, *a Venetian gentleman*

CLOWN, *servant to Othello*

DESDEMONA, *daughter to Brabantio and wife to Othello*

EMILIA, *wife to Iago*

BIANCA, *mistress to Cassio*

SAILOR, MESSENGER, HERALD, OFFICERS, GENTLEMEN, MUSICIANS, *and*
ATTENDANTS

SCENE. *Venice, a seaport in Cyprus.*

⎯⎯⎯⎯⎯(**ACT 1**)⎯⎯⎯⎯⎯

SCENE 1. *Venice. A street.*

Enter RODERIGO *and* IAGO.

1 RODERIGO.   Tush, never tell me! I take it
much unkindly
That thou, Iago, who hast had my purse
As if the strings were thine, shouldst
5   know of this.
IAGO.   'Sblood, but you will not hear me.

The version presented here is that of G. B. Harrison,
from *Shakespeare: The Complete Works* (New York:
Harcourt, 1952).

If ever I did dream of such a matter,
Abhor me.
RODERIGO.   Thou told'st me thou didst
hold him in thy hate.   10
IAGO.   Despise me if I do not. Three great
ones of the city,
In personal suit to make me his
Lieutenant,
Off-capped to him. And, by the faith   15
of man,
I know my price, I am worth no worse
a place.
But he, as loving his own pride and
purposes,   20
Evades them, with a bombast circumstance
Horribly stuffed with epithets of war.
And, in conclusion,

Nonsuits[1] my mediators, for, "Certes,"
25   says he,
"I have already chose my officer."
And what was he?
Forsooth, a great arithmetician,[2]
One Michael Cassio, a Florentine,
30   A fellow almost damned in a fair wife,[3]
That never set a squadron in the field,
Nor the division of a battle knows
More than a spinster, unless the bookish
theoric,
35   Wherein the toged Consuls can propose
As masterly as he—mere prattle without
practice
Is all his soldiership. But he, sir, had the
election.
40   And I, of whom his eyes had seen the
proof
At Rhodes, at Cyprus, and on other
grounds
Christian and heathen, must be beleed[4]
45   and calmed
By debitor and creditor. This countercaster,[5]
He, in good time,[6] must his Lieutenant be,
And I—God bless the mark!—his
Moorship's Ancient.[7]
50   RODERIGO.   By Heaven, I rather would
have been his hangman.
IAGO.   Why, there's no remedy. 'Tis the
curse of service,
Preferment goes by letter and affection,

And not by old gradation,[8] where each   55
second
Stood heir to the first. Now, sir, be judge
yourself
Whether I in any just term am affined[9]
To love the Moor.   60
RODERIGO.   I would not follow him, then.
IAGO.   Oh, sir, content you,
I follow him to serve my turn upon him.
We cannot all be masters, nor all masters
Cannot be truly followed. You shall mark   65
Many a duteous and knee-crooking knave
That doting on his own obsequious
bondage
Wears out his time, much like his
master's ass,   70
For naught but provender, and when he's
old, cashiered.
Whip me such honest knaves. Others
there are
Who, trimmed in forms and visages of   75
duty,
Keep yet their hearts attending on
themselves,
And throwing but shows of service on
their lords   80
Do well thrive by them, and when they
have lined their coats
Do themselves homage. These fellows
have some soul,
And such a one do I profess myself.   85
For, sir,
It is as sure as you are Roderigo,
Were I the Moor, I would not be Iago.
In following him, I follow but myself.
Heaven is my judge, not I for love and   90
duty,
But seeming so, for my peculiar end.
For when my outward action doth
demonstrate

---

[1]**Nonsuits:** rejects the petition of
[2]**arithmetician:** Contemporary books on military tactics are full of elaborate diagrams and numerals to explain military formations. Cassio is a student of such books.
[3]**almost . . . wife:** A much-disputed phrase. There is an Italian proverb, "You have married a fair wife? You are damned." If Iago has this in mind, he means by *almost* that Cassio is about to marry.
[4]**beleed:** placed on the lee (or unfavorable) side
[5]**countercaster:** calculator (repeating the idea of arithmetician). Counters were used in making calculations.
[6]**in good time:** a phrase expressing indignation
[7]**Ancient:** ensign, the third officer in the company of which Othello is Captain and Cassio Lieutenant

---

[8]**Preferment . . . gradation:** Promotion comes through private recommendation and favoritism and not by order of seniority.
[9]**affined:** tied by affection

95 The native act and figure of my heart
In compliment extern, 'tis not long after
But I will wear my heart upon my sleeve
For daws to peck at. I am not what I am.

RODERIGO.   What a full fortune does the
100 thick-lips owe[10]
If he can carry 't thus![11]

IAGO.   Call up her father,
Rouse him. Make after him, poison his delight,
105 Proclaim him in the streets. Incense her kinsmen,
And though he in a fertile climate dwell,
Plague him with flies. Though that his joy be joy,
110 Yet throw such changes of vexation on 't
As it may lose some color.

RODERIGO.   Here is her father's house, I'll call aloud.

IAGO.   Do, with like timorous[12] accent and
115 dire yell
As when, by night and negligence, the fire
Is spied in populous cities.

RODERIGO.   What ho, Brabantio! Signior Brabantio, ho!

120 IAGO.   Awake! What ho, Brabantio!
Thieves! Thieves! Thieves!
Look to your house, your daughter and your bags![13]
Thieves! Thieves! (BRABANTIO *appears*
125 *above, at a window.*)

BRABANTIO.   What is the reason of this terrible summons?
What is the matter there?

RODERIGO.   Signior, is all your family
130 within?

IAGO.   Are your doors locked?

BRABANTIO.   Why, wherefore ask you this?

IAGO.   'Zounds, sir, you're robbed. For shame, put on your gown,

Your heart is burst, you have lost half   135
your soul.
Even now, now, very now, an old
black ram
Is tupping your white ewe. Arise, arise,
Awake the snorting[14] citizens with   140
the bell,
Or else the Devil[15] will make a grandsire
of you.
Arise, I say.

BRABANTIO.   What, have you lost your wits?   145

RODERIGO.   Most reverend signior, do you
know my voice?

BRABANTIO.   Not I. What are you?

RODERIGO.   My name is Roderigo.

BRABANTIO.   The worser welcome.   150
I have charged thee not to haunt about
my doors.
In honest plainness thou hast heard
me say
My daughter is not for thee, and now, in   155
madness,
Being full of supper and distempering
draughts,
Upon malicious bravery[16] dost thou
come   160
To start[17] my quiet.

RODERIGO.   Sir, sir, sir—

BRABANTIO.   But thou must needs be sure
My spirit and my place have in them
power   165
To make this bitter to thee.

RODERIGO.   Patience, good sir.

BRABANTIO.   What tell'st thou me of
robbing? This is Venice,
My house is not a grange.[18]   170

RODERIGO.   Most grave Brabantio,
In simple and pure soul I come to you.

---

[10]**owe:** own
[11]**carry 't thus:** i.e., bring off this marriage
[12]**timorous:** terrifying
[13]**bags:** moneybags

[14]**snorting:** snoring
[15]**Devil:** The Devil in old pictures and woodcuts was represented as black.
[16]**bravery:** defiance
[17]**start:** startle
[18]**grange:** lonely farm

IAGO. 'Zounds, sir, you are one of those
that will not serve God if the Devil bid
175   you. Because we come to do you service
and you think we are ruffians, you'll
have your daughter covered with a
Barbary[19] horse, you'll have your
nephews[20] neigh to you, you'll have
180   coursers for cousins,[21] and jennets[22] for
germans.[23]
  BRABANTIO.   What profane wretch art thou?
  IAGO.   I am one, sir, that comes to tell you
your daughter and the Moor are now
185   making the beast with two backs.
  BRABANTIO.   Thou art a villain.
  IAGO.   You are—a Senator.
  BRABANTIO.   This thou shalt answer.
  I know thee, Roderigo.
190 RODERIGO.   Sir, I will answer anything. But
I beseech you
If 't be your pleasure and most wise
consent,
As partly I find it is, that your fair
195   daughter,
At this odd-even[24] and dull watch o' the
night,
Transported with no worse nor better
guard
200   But with a knave of common hire, a
gondolier,
To the gross clasps of a lascivious Moor—
If this be known to you, and your
allowance,[25]
205   We then have done you bold and saucy
wrongs.
But if you know not this, my manners
tell me
We have your wrong rebuke. Do not
210   believe

That, from the sense of all civility,
I thus would play and trifle with your
reverence.
Your daughter, if you have not given
her leave,   215
I say again, hath made a gross revolt,
Tying her duty, beauty, wit, and fortunes
In an extravagant[26] and wheeling[27]
stranger
Of here and everywhere. Straight satisfy   220
yourself.
If she be in her chamber or your house,
Let loose on me the justice of the state
For thus deluding you.
  BRABANTIO.   Strike on the tinder,[28] ho!   225
Give me a taper![29] Call up all my people!
This accident is not unlike my dream.
Belief of it oppresses me already.
Light, I say! Light! (*Exit above.*)
  IAGO.   Farewell, for I must leave you,   230
It seems not meet, nor wholesome to
my place,[30]
To be produced—as if I stay I shall—
Against the Moor. For I do know the
state,   235
However this may gall him with some
check,
Cannot with safety cast[31] him. For he's
embarked
With such loud reason to the Cyprus   240
wars,
Which even now stand in act,[32] that, for
their souls,
Another of his fathom they have none
To lead their business. In which regard,   245
Though I do hate him as I do Hell pains,
Yet for necessity of present life

---

[19]**Barbary:** Moorish
[20]**nephews:** grandsons
[21]**cousins:** near relations
[22]**jennets:** Moorish ponies
[23]**germans:** kinsmen
[24]**odd-even:** about midnight
[25]**your allowance:** by your permission

[26]**extravagant:** vagabond
[27]**wheeling:** wandering
[28]**tinder:** the primitive method of making fire, used
before the invention of matches
[29]**taper:** candle
[30]**place:** i.e., as Othello's officer
[31]**cast:** dismiss from service
[32]**stand in act:** are under way [Eds.]

I must show out a flag and sign of love,
Which is indeed but sign. That you shall
250 surely find him,
Lead to the Sagittary[33] the raisèd search,
And there will I be with him. So farewell.
(*Exit* IAGO. *Enter, below,* BRABANTIO, *in his
nightgown, and* SERVANTS *with torches.*)
255 BRABANTIO.   It is too true an evil. Gone
she is,
And what's to come of my despisèd time
Is naught but bitterness. Now, Roderigo,
Where didst thou see her? Oh, unhappy
260 girl!
With the Moor, say'st thou? Who would
be a father!
How didst thou know 'twas she? Oh, she
deceives me
265 Past thought! What said she to you? Get
more tapers.
Raise all my kindred. Are they married,
think you?
RODERIGO.   Truly, I think they are.
270 BRABANTIO.   Oh Heaven! How got she out?
Oh, treason of the blood!
Fathers, from hence trust not your
daughters' minds
By what you see them act. Are there not
275 charms[34]
By which the property[35] of youth and
maidhood
May be abused?[36] Have you not read,
Roderigo,
280 Of some such thing?
RODERIGO.   Yes, sir, I have indeed.
BRABANTIO.   Call up my brother.—Oh,
would you had had her!—
Some one way, some another.—Do you
285 know
Where we may apprehend her and the
Moor?

RODERIGO.   I think I can discover him, if
you please
To get good guard and go along with me. 290
BRABANTIO.   Pray you, lead on. At every
house I'll call,
I may command[37] at most. Get
weapons, ho!
And raise some special officers of night. 295
On, good Roderigo, I'll deserve your
pains.[38] (*Exeunt.*)

SCENE 2. *Another street.*

Enter OTHELLO, IAGO, *and* ATTENDANTS
with torches.

IAGO.   Though in the trade of war I have
slain men,
Yet do I hold it very stuff o' the conscience 300
To do no contrivèd murder. I lack iniquity
Sometimes to do me service. Nine or ten
times
I had thought to have yerked him[39] here
under the ribs. 305
OTHELLO.   'Tis better as it is.
IAGO.   Nay, but he prated
And spoke such scurvy and provoking
terms
Against your honor 310
That, with the little godliness I have,
I did full hard forbear him. But I pray
you, sir,
Are you fast married? Be assured of this,
That the Magnifico is much beloved, 315
And hath in his effect a voice potential
As double as[40] the Duke's. He will
divorce you,
Or put upon you what restraint and
grievance 320
The law, with all his might to enforce it on,
Will give him cable.

---

[33]**Sagittary:** presumably some inn in Venice [Eds.]
[34]**charms:** magic spells
[35]**property:** nature
[36]**abused:** deceived

[37]**command:** find supporters
[38]**deserve your pains:** reward your labor
[39]**yerked him:** stabbed Brabantio [Eds.]
[40]**potential . . . as:** twice as powerful as

OTHELLO.   Let him do his spite.
My services which I have done the
325 signiory[41]
Shall out-tongue his complaints. 'Tis yet
to know[42]—
Which, when I know that boasting is
an honor,
330 I shall promulgate—I fetch my life and
being
From men of royal siege,[43] and my
demerits[44]
May speak unbonneted to as proud a
335 fortune
As this that I have reached. For know,
Iago,
But that I love the gentle Desdemona,
I would not my unhousèd[45] free condition
340 Put into circumscription and confine
For the sea's worth. But look! What lights
come yond?
IAGO.   Those are the raisèd father and his
friends.
345 You were best go in.
OTHELLO.   Not I, I must be found.
My parts, my title, and my perfect soul
Shall manifest me rightly. Is it they?
IAGO.   By Janus, I think no.
350 (*Enter* CASSIO, *and certain* OFFICERS *with*
torches.)
OTHELLO.   The servants of the Duke, and
my Lieutenant.
The goodness of the night upon you,
355 friends!
What is the news?
CASSIO.   The Duke does greet you,
General,
And he requires your haste-posthaste
360 appearance,
Even on the instant.

OTHELLO.   What is the matter, think you?
CASSIO.   Something from Cyprus, as I may
divine.
It is a business of some heat. The galleys   365
Have sent a dozen sequent messengers
This very night at one another's heels,
And many of the consuls, raised and met,
Are at the Duke's already. You have been
hotly called for   370
When, being not at your lodging to be
found,
The Senate hath sent about three several[46]
quests
To search you out.   375
OTHELLO.   'Tis well I am found by you.
I will but spend a word here in the house
And go with you. (*Exit.*)
CASSIO.   Ancient, what makes he here?
IAGO.   Faith, he tonight hath boarded a   380
land carrack.[47]
If it prove lawful prize, he's made forever.
CASSIO.   I do not understand.
IAGO.   He's married.
CASSIO.   To who? (*Re-enter* OTHELLO.)   385
IAGO.   Marry, to—Come, Captain, will
you go?
OTHELLO.   Have with you.
CASSIO.   Here comes another troop to seek
for you.   390
IAGO.   It is Brabantio. General, be advised,
He comes to bad intent.
(*Enter* BRABANTIO, RODERIGO, *and* OFFICERS
with torches and weapons.)
OTHELLO.   Holloa! Stand there!   395
RODERIGO.   Signior, it is the Moor.
BRABANTIO.   Down with him, thief!
(*They draw on both sides.*)
IAGO.   You, Roderigo! Come, sir, I am
for you.   400
OTHELLO.   Keep up[48] your bright swords,
for the dew will rust them.

---

[41]**signiory:** state of Venice
[42]**yet to know:** not widely known [Eds.]
[43]**siege:** rank [Eds.]
[44]**demerits:** deserts
[45]**unhousèd:** unmarried

---

[46]**several:** separate
[47]**carrack:** large merchant ship
[48]**Keep up:** sheathe

Good signior, you shall more command
with years
405 Than with your weapons.

BRABANTIO.   O thou foul thief, where hast
thou stowed my daughter?
Damned as thou art, thou hast
enchanted her.
410 For I'll refer me to all things of sense
If she in chains of magic were not bound,
Whether a maid so tender, fair, and
happy,
So opposite to marriage that she shunned
415 The wealthy curlèd darlings of our
nation,
Would ever have, to incur a general
mock,
Run from her guardage[49] to the sooty
420 bosom
Of such a thing as thou, to fear, not to
delight.
Judge me the world if 'tis not gross in
sense
425 That thou hast practiced on her with foul
charms,
Abused her delicate youth with drugs or
minerals
That weaken motion. I'll have 't
430 disputed on,
'Tis probable, and palpable to thinking.
I therefore apprehend and do attach[50]
thee
For an abuser of the world, a practicer
435 Of arts inhibited and out of warrant.
Lay hold upon him. If he do resist,
Subdue him at his peril.

OTHELLO.   Hold your hands,
Both you of my inclining and the rest.
440 Were it my cue to fight, I should have
known it
Without a prompter. Where will you
that I go
To answer this your charge?

BRABANTIO.   To prison, till fit time   445
Of law and course of direct session
Call thee to answer.

OTHELLO.   What if I do obey?
How may the Duke be therewith satisfied,
Whose messengers are here about my side   450
Upon some present business of the state
To bring me to him?

FIRST OFFICER.   'Tis true, most worthy
signior.
The Duke's in council, and your noble self   455
I am sure is sent for.

BRABANTIO.   How? The Duke in council?
In this time of the night? Bring him away.
Mine's not an idle cause. The Duke
himself,   460
Or any of my brothers of the state,
Cannot but feel this wrong as 'twere
their own.
For if such actions may have passage
free,   465
Bondslaves and pagans shall our
statesmen be. (*Exeunt.*)

SCENE 3. *A council chamber.*
The DUKE *and* SENATORS *sitting at a table,*
OFFICERS *attending.*

DUKE.   There is no composition[51] in these
news[52]
That gives them credit.   470

FIRST SENATOR.   Indeed they are
disproportioned.
My letters say a hundred and seven
galleys.

DUKE.   And mine, a hundred and forty.   475

SECOND SENATOR.   And mine, two
hundred.
But though they jump not on a just
account[53]—

---

[49]**guardage:** guardianship
[50]**attach:** arrest

[51]**composition:** agreement
[52]**news:** reports
[53]**jump . . . account:** do not agree with an exact
estimate

480 As in these cases, where the aim reports,[54]
'Tis oft with difference—yet do they all confirm
A Turkish fleet, and bearing up to Cyprus.

485 DUKE.   Nay, it is possible enough to judgment.
I do not so secure me in the error,[55]
But the main article[56] I do approve
In fearful[57] sense.

490 SAILOR (*within*).   What ho! What ho! What ho!

FIRST OFFICER.   A messenger from the galleys. (*Enter* SAILOR.)

DUKE.   Now, what's the business?

495 SAILOR.   The Turkish preparation makes for Rhodes.
So was I bid report here to the state
By Signior Angelo.

DUKE.   How say you by this charge?

500 FIRST SENATOR.   This cannot be,
By no assay of reason. 'Tis a pageant
To keep us in false gaze. When we consider
The importancy of Cyprus to the Turk,

505 And let ourselves again but understand
That as it more concerns the Turk than Rhodes,
So may he with more facile question bear it,[58]

510 For that it stands not in such warlike brace
But altogether lacks the abilities
That Rhodes is dressed in—if we make thought of this,

515 We must not think the Turk is so unskillful
To leave that latest which concerns him first,

Neglecting an attempt of ease and gain
To wake and wage a danger profitless.

DUKE.   Nay, in all confidence, he's not for Rhodes.   520

FIRST OFFICER.   Here is more news. (*Enter a* MESSENGER.)

MESSENGER.   The Ottomites,[59] Reverend and Gracious,   525
Steering with due course toward the isle of Rhodes,
Have there injointed[60] them with an after-fleet.[61]

FIRST SENATOR.   Aye, so I thought. How   530
many, as you guess?

MESSENGER.   Of thirty sail. And now they do restem[62]
Their backward course, bearing with frank appearance   535
Their purposes toward Cyprus. Signior Montano,
Your trusty and most valiant servitor,
With his free duty recommends you thus,
And prays you to believe him.   540

DUKE.   'Tis certain then for Cyprus.
Marcus Luccicos, is not he in town?

FIRST SENATOR.   He's now in Florence.

DUKE.   Write from us to him,
post-posthaste dispatch.   545

FIRST SENATOR.   Here comes Brabantio and the valiant Moor.
(*Enter* BRABANTIO, OTHELLO, IAGO, RODERIGO, *and* OFFICERS.)

DUKE.   Valiant Othello, we must straight   550
employ you
Against the general enemy Ottoman.
(*To* BRABANTIO) I did not see you.
Welcome, gentle signior,
We lacked your counsel and your help   555
tonight.

---

[54]**aim reports:** i.e., intelligence reports of an enemy's intention often differ in the details
[55]**I . . . error:** I do not consider myself free from danger, because the reports may not all be accurate.
[56]**main article:** general report
[57]**fearful:** to be feared
[58]**with . . . it:** take it more easily

---

[59]**Ottomites:** Turks
[60]**injointed:** joined
[61]**after-fleet:** second fleet
[62]**restem:** steer again

BRABANTIO.   So did I yours. Good your
    Grace, pardon me,
    Neither my place nor aught I heard of
560   business
    Hath raised me from my bed, nor doth
    the general care
    Take hold on me. For my particular[63]
    grief
565   Is of so floodgate and o'erbearing nature
    That it engluts and swallows other
    sorrows,
    And it is still itself.
    DUKE.   Why, what's the matter?
570 BRABANTIO.   My daughter! Oh, my
    daughter!
    ALL.   Dead?
    BRABANTIO.   Aye, to me.
    She is abused, stol'n from me and
575   corrupted
    By spells and medicines bought of
    mountebanks.
    For nature so preposterously to err,
    Being not deficient, blind, or lame of
580   sense,
    Sans[64] witchcraft could not.
    DUKE.   Whoe'er he be that in this foul
    proceeding
    Hath thus beguiled your daughter of
585   herself
    And you of her, the bloody book of law
    You shall yourself read in the bitter letter
    After your own sense—yea, though our
    proper[65] son
590   Stood in your action.
    BRABANTIO.   Humbly I thank your Grace.
    Here is the man, this Moor, whom now,
    it seems,
    Your special mandate for the state affairs
595   Hath hither brought.
    ALL.   We are very sorry for 't.

DUKE (*to* OTHELLO).   What in your own
    part can you say to this?
BRABANTIO.   Nothing but this is so.
OTHELLO.   Most potent, grave, and   600
    reverend signiors,
    My very noble and approved good
    masters,
    That I have ta'en away this old man's
    daughter,   605
    It is most true—true, I have married her.
    The very head and front of my offending
    Hath this extent, no more. Rude am I in
    my speech,
    And little blest with the soft phrase of   610
    peace,
    For since these arms of mine had seven
    years' pith
    Till now some nine moons wasted, they
    have used   615
    Their dearest action in the tented field;
    And little of this great world can I speak,
    More than pertains to feats of broil and
    battle,
    And therefore little shall I grace my cause 620
    In speaking for myself. Yet, by your
    gracious patience,
    I will a round unvarnished tale[66] deliver
    Of my whole course of love—what
    drugs, what charms,   625
    What conjuration and what mighty
    magic—
    For such proceeding I am charged
    withal—
    I won his daughter.   630
BRABANTIO.   A maiden never bold,
    Of spirit so still and quiet that her motion
    Blushed at herself, and she—in spite of
    nature,
    Of years, of country, credit,[67]   635
    everything—
    To fall in love with what she feared
    to look on!

---

[63]**particular:** personal
[64]**Sans:** without
[65]**proper:** own

[66]**round . . . tale:** direct, unadorned account
[67]**credit:** reputation

640   It is a judgment maimed and most
      imperfect
      That will confess perfection so could err
      Against all rules of nature, and must be
      driven
645   To find out practices of cunning Hell
      Why this should be. I therefore vouch
      again
      That with some mixtures powerful o'er
      the blood,
650   Or with some dram conjured to this
      effect,
      He wrought upon her.
        DUKE.   To vouch this is no proof
        Without more certain and more overt test
655   Than these thin habits and poor
      likelihoods
      Of modern seeming do prefer against
      him.
        FIRST SENATOR.   But, Othello, speak.
660   Did you by indirect and forcèd courses
      Subdue and poison this young maid's
      affections?
      Or came it by request, and such fair
      question
665   As soul to soul affordeth?
        OTHELLO.   I do beseech you
        Send for the lady to the Sagittary,
        And let her speak of me before her father.
        If you do find me foul in her report,
670   The trust, the office I do hold of you,
        Not only take away, but let your sentence
        Even fall upon my life.
        DUKE.   Fetch Desdemona hither.
        OTHELLO.   Ancient, conduct them, you best
675   know the place.
        (*Exeunt* IAGO *and* ATTENDANTS.)
        And till she come, as truly as to Heaven
        I do confess the vices of my blood,
        So justly to your grave ears I'll present
680   How I did thrive in this fair lady's love
      And she in mine.
        DUKE.   Say it, Othello.
        OTHELLO.   Her father loved me, oft
        invited me,

Still[68] questioned me the story of my life
From year to year, the battles, sieges,   685
fortunes,
That I have passed
I ran it through, even from my boyish
days
To the very moment that he bade me   690
tell it.
Wherein I spake of most disastrous
chances,
Of moving accidents by flood and field,
Of hairbreadth 'scapes i' the imminent   695
deadly breach,
Of being taken by the insolent foe
And sold to slavery, of my redemption
thence,
And portance in my travels' history.   700
Wherein of antres[69] vast and deserts idle,
Rough quarries, rocks, and hills whose
heads touch heaven,
It was my hint to speak . . . such was the
process.   705
And of the cannibals that each other eat,
The anthropophagi,[70] and men whose
heads
Do grow beneath their shoulders. This
to hear   710
Would Desdemona seriously incline.
But still the house affairs would draw
her thence,
Which ever as she could with haste
dispatch,   715
She'd come again, and with a greedy ear
Devour up my discourse. Which I
observing,
Took once a pliant hour and found good
means   720
To draw from her a prayer of earnest
heart
That I would all my pilgrimage dilate,

---

[68]**Still:** always
[69]**antres:** caves
[70]**anthropophagi:** cannibals

725 Whereof by parcels she had something heard,
But not intentively. I did consent,
And often did beguile her of her tears
When I did speak of some distressful
730 stroke
That my youth suffered. My story being done,
She gave me for my pains a world of sighs.
735 She swore, in faith, 'twas strange, 'twas passing strange,
'Twas pitiful, 'twas wondrous pitiful.
She wished she had not heard it, yet she wished
740 That Heaven had made her such a man. She thanked me,
And bade me, if I had a friend that loved her,
I should but teach him how to tell my
745 story
And that would woo her. Upon this hint I spake.
She loved me for the dangers I had passed,
750 And I loved her that she did pity them.
This only is the witchcraft I have used.
Here comes the lady, let her witness it.
(*Enter* DESDEMONA, IAGO, *and*
ATTENDANTS.)
755 DUKE.   I think this tale would win my daughter too.
Good Brabantio,
Take up this mangled matter at the best.[71]
Men do their broken weapons rather use
760 Than their bare hands.
BRABANTIO.   I pray you hear her speak.
If she confess that she was half the wooer,
Destruction on my head if my bad blame
765 Light on the man! Come hither, gentle mistress.

Do you perceive in all this noble company
Where most you owe obedience?
DESDEMONA.   My noble father,
I do perceive here a divided duty.
To you I am bound for life and education, 770
My life and education both do learn me
How to respect you; you are the lord of duty,
I am hitherto your daughter. But here's my husband, 775
And so much duty as my mother showed
To you, preferring you before her father,
So much I challenge that I may profess
Due to the Moor my lord.
BRABANTIO.   God be with you! I have done. 780
Please it your Grace, on to the state affairs.
I had rather to adopt a child than get[72] it.
Come hither, Moor.
I here do give thee that with all my heart 785
Which, but thou hast already, with all my heart
I would keep from thee. For your sake, jewel,
I am glad at soul I have no other child, 790
For thy escape would teach me tyranny,
To hang clogs on them. I have done, my lord.
DUKE.   Let me speak like yourself, and lay a sentence[73] 795
Which, as a grise[74] or step, may help these lovers
Into your favor.
When remedies are past, the griefs are ended 800
By seeing the worst, which late on hopes depended.
To mourn a mischief that is past and gone
Is the next way to draw new mischief on. 805

---

[71]**Take . . . best:** make the best settlement you can of this confused business

[72]**get:** beget
[73]**sentence:** proverbial saying
[74]**grise:** degree

What cannot be preserved when fortune takes,
Patience her injury a mockery makes.
810 The robbed that smiles steals something from the thief.
He robs himself that spends a bootless grief.

BRABANTIO.   So let the Turk of Cyprus us beguile,
815 We lose it not so long as we can smile.
He bears the sentence well that nothing bears
But the free comfort which from thence he hears.
820 But he bears both the sentence and the sorrow
That, to pay grief, must of poor patience borrow.
These sentences, to sugar or to gall,
825 Being strong on both sides, are equivocal.
But words are words. I never yet did hear
That the bruisèd heart was piercèd through the ear.
I humbly beseech you, proceed to the
830 affairs of state.

DUKE.   The Turk with a most mightly preparation makes for Cyprus. Othello, the fortitude of the place is best known to you, and though we have there a
835 substitute[75] of most allowed sufficiency, yet opinion, a sovereign mistress of effects, throws a more safer voice on you. You must therefore be content to slubber[76] the gloss of your new fortunes with this
840 more stubborn and boisterous expedition.

OTHELLO.   The tyrant custom, most grave Senators,
Hath made the flinty and steel couch of war
845 My thrice-driven bed of down. I do agnize[77]

A natural and prompt alacrity
I find in hardness,[78] and do undertake
These present wars against the Ottomites.
850 Most humbly therefore bending to your state,
I crave fit disposition for my wife,
Due reference of place and exhibition,[79]
With such accommodation and besort[80]
855 As levels with her breeding.

DUKE.   If you please,
Be 't at her father's.

BRABANTIO.   I'll not have it so.

OTHELLO.   Nor I.

DESDEMONA.   Nor I. I would not there
860 reside,
To put my father in impatient thoughts
By being in his eye. Most gracious Duke,
To my unfolding lend your prosperous[81]
865 ear,
And let me find a charter in your voice
To assist my simpleness.

DUKE.   What would you, Desdemona?

DESDEMONA.   That I did love the Moor to
870 live with him,
My downright violence and storm of fortunes
May trumpet to the world. My heart's subdued
875 Even to the very quality[82] of my lord.
I saw Othello's visage in his mind,
And to his honors and his valiant parts[83]
Did I my soul and fortunes consecrate.
So that, dear lords, if I be left behind,
880 A moth of peace, and he go to the war,
The rites for which I love him are bereft me,
And I a heavy interim shall support
By his dear absence. Let me go with him.

---

[75]**substitute:** deputy commander
[76]**slubber:** tarnish
[77]**agnize:** confess

[78]**hardness:** hardship
[79]**exhibition:** allowance
[80]**besort:** attendants
[81]**prosperous:** favorable
[82]**quality:** profession
[83]**parts:** qualities

885 OTHELLO.   Let her have your voices.
Vouch with me, Heaven, I therefore beg
it not
To please the palate of my appetite,
Nor to comply with heat—the young
890 affects
In me defunct[84]—and proper satisfaction,
But to be free and bounteous to her
mind.[85]
And Heaven defend your good souls,
895 that you think
I will your serious and great business
scant
For she is with me. No, when light-
winged toys
900 Of feathered Cupid seel[86] with wanton
dullness
My speculative and officed instruments,[87]
That my disports[88] corrupt and taint my
business,
905 Let housewives make a skillet of my helm,
And all indign[89] and base adversities
Make head against my estimation![90]
DUKE.   Be it as you shall privately
determine,
910 Either for her stay or going. The affair
cries haste,
And speed must answer 't. You must
hence tonight.
DESDEMONA.   Tonight, my lord?
915 DUKE.   This night.
OTHELLO.   With all my heart.
DUKE.   At nine i' the morning here we'll
meet again.
Othello, leave some officer behind,

And he shall our commission bring to you, 920
With such things else of quality and
respect
As doth import you.
OTHELLO.   So please your Grace, my
Ancient, 925
A man he is of honesty and trust.
To his conveyance I assign my wife,
With what else needful your good Grace
shall think
To be sent after me. 930
DUKE.   Let it be so.
Good night to everyone. (*To* BRABANTIO)
And, noble signior,
If virtue no delighted beauty lack,
Your son-in-law is far more fair than 935
black.[91]
FIRST SENATOR.   Adieu, brave Moor. Use
Desdemona well.
BRABANTIO.   Look to her, Moor, if thou hast
eyes to see. 940
She has deceived her father, and may
thee.
(*Exeunt* DUKE, SENATORS, OFFICERS, *etc.*)
OTHELLO.   My life upon her faith! Honest
Iago, 945
My Desdemona must I leave to thee.
I prithee, let thy wife attend on her,
And bring them after in the best
advantage.
Come, Desdemona, I have but an hour 950
Of love, of worldly matters and direction,
To spend with thee. We must obey the
time.
(*Exeunt* OTHELLO *and* DESDEMONA.)
RODERIGO.   Iago! 955
IAGO.   What sayest thou, noble heart?
RODERIGO.   What will I do, thinkest thou?
IAGO.   Why, go to bed and sleep.
RODERIGO.   I will incontinently[92] drown
myself. 960

---

[84]**young . . . defunct:** in me the passion of youth is dead.
[85]**to . . . mind:** Othello repeats Desdemona's claim that this is a marriage of minds.
[86]**seel:** close up
[87]**speculative . . . instruments:** powers of sight and action; i.e., my efficiency as your general
[88]**disports:** amusements
[89]**indign:** unworthy
[90]**estimation:** reputation

[91]**If . . . black:** If worthiness is a beautiful thing in itself, your son-in-law, though black, has beauty.
[92]**incontinently:** immediately

IAGO.   If thou dost, I shall never love thee
    after. Why, thou silly gentleman!

RODERIGO.   It is silliness to live when to live
    is torment, and then have we a prescrip-
965   tion to die when death is our physician.

IAGO.   Oh, villainous! I have looked upon
    the world for four times seven years, and
    since I could distinguish betwixt a benefit
    and an injury I never found man that
970   knew how to love himself. Ere I would
    say I would drown myself for the love of
    a guinea hen, I would change my
    humanity with a baboon.

RODERIGO.   What should I do? I confess it
975   is my shame to be so fond, but it is not in
    my virtue to amend it.

IAGO.   Virtue! A fig! 'Tis in ourselves that
    we are thus or thus. Our bodies are gar-
    dens, to the which our wills are gardeners.
980   So that if we will plant nettles or sow
    lettuce, set hyssop and weed up thyme,
    supply it with one gender of herbs or
    distract it with many, either to have it
    sterile with idleness or manured with
985   industry—why, the power and corrigible[93]
    authority of this lies in our wills. If the
    balance of our lives had not one scale of
    reason to poise another of sensuality, the
    blood and baseness of our natures would
990   conduct us to most preposterous conclu-
    sions. But we have reason to cool our
    raging motions, our carnal stings, our
    unbitted lusts, whereof I take this that
    you call love to be a sect or scion.[94]

995 RODERIGO.   It cannot be.

IAGO.   It is merely a lust of the blood and a
    permission of the will. Come, be a man!
    Drown thyself? Drown cats and blind
    puppies! I have professed me thy friend,
1000   and I confess me knit to thy deserving
    with cables of perdurable toughness.

I could never better stead thee than now.
Put money in thy purse, follow thou the
wars, defeat thy favor with an usurped
beard[95]—I say put money in thy purse. It   1005
cannot be that Desdemona should long
continue her love to the Moor—put
money in thy purse—nor he his to her. It
was a violent commencement, and thou
shalt see an answerable sequestration[96]—   1010
put but money in thy purse. These Moors
are changeable in their wills.—Fill thy
purse with money. The food that to him
now is as luscious as locusts shall be to
him shortly as bitter as coloquintida. She   1015
must change for youth. When she is
sated with his body, she will find the
error of her choice. She must have
change, she must—therefore put money
in thy purse. If thou wilt needs damn   1020
thyself, do it a more delicate way than
drowning. Make all the money thou
canst.[97] If sanctimony and a frail vow
betwixt an erring[98] barbarian and a
supersubtle Venetian be not too hard for   1025
my wits and all the tribe of Hell, thou
shalt enjoy her—therefore make money.
A pox of drowning thyself! It is clean out
of the way. Seek thou rather to be hanged
in compassing thy joy than to be   1030
drowned and go without her.

RODERIGO.   Wilt thou be fast to my hopes if
    I depend on the issue?

IAGO.   Thou art sure of me. Go, make
    money. I have told thee often, and I retell   1035
    thee again and again, I hate the Moor. My
    cause is hearted,[99] thine hath no less
    reason. Let us be conjunctive in our
    revenge against him. If thou canst

---

[93]**corrigible:** correcting, directing
[94]**sect or scion:** Both words mean a slip taken from
a tree and planted to produce a new growth.

[95]**defeat . . . beard:** disguise your face by growing
a beard
[96]**answerable sequestration:** corresponding separation; i.e., reaction
[97]**Make . . . canst:** turn all you can into ready cash
[98]**erring:** vagabond
[99]**hearted:** heartfelt

1040 cuckold him thou dost thyself a pleasure,
me a sport. There are many events in the
womb of time which will be delivered.
Traverse, go, provide thy money. We will
have more of this tomorrow. Adieu.

1045 RODERIGO.   Where shall we meet i' the
morning?

IAGO.   At my lodging.

RODERIGO.   I'll be with thee betimes.

IAGO.   Go to, farewell. Do you hear,
1050 Roderigo?

RODERIGO.   What say you?

IAGO.   No more of drowning, do you hear?

RODERIGO.   I am changed. I'll go sell all my
land. (*Exit.*)

1055 IAGO.   Thus do I ever make my fool my
purse,
For I mine own gained knowledge
should profane
If I would time expend with such a snipe
1060 But for my sport and profit. I hate the
Moor,
And it is thought abroad that 'twixt my
sheets
He's done my office. I know not if 't be
1065 true,
But I for mere suspicion in that kind
Will do as if for surety. He holds me well,
The better shall my purpose work on
him.
1070 Cassio's a proper[100] man. Let me see now,
To get his place, and to plume up[101] my
will
In double knavery—How, how?—Let's
see.—
1075 After some time, to abuse Othello's ear
That he is too familiar with his wife.
He hath a person and a smooth dispose
To be suspected,[102] framed to make
women false.

---

[100]**proper:** handsome
[101]**plume up:** glorify
[102]**He . . . suspected:** an easy way about him that is
naturally suspected

The Moor is of a free and open nature   1080
That thinks men honest that but seem to
be so,
And will as tenderly be led by the nose
As asses are.
I have't. It is engendered. Hell and night   1085
Must bring this monstrous birth to the
world's light. (*Exit.*)

────────(**ACT 2**)────────

SCENE 1. *A seaport in Cyprus. An open place
near the wharf.*

Enter MONTANO *and two* GENTLEMEN.

MONTANO.   What from the cape can you   1
discern at sea?

FIRST GENTLEMAN.   Nothing at all. It is a
high-wrought flood.
I cannot 'twixt the heaven and the main   5
Descry a sail.

MONTANO.   Methinks the wind hath spoke
aloud at land,
A fuller blast ne'er shook our
battlements.   10
If it hath ruffianed so upon the sea,
What ribs of oak, when mountains melt
on them,
Can hold the mortise? What shall we
hear of this?   15

SECOND GENTLEMAN.   A segregation[103] of
the Turkish fleet.
For do but stand upon the foaming shore,
The chidden billow seems to pelt the
clouds,   20
The wind-shaked surge, with high and
monstrous mane,
Seems to cast water on the burning Bear,
And quench the guards of the ever-fixèd
Pole.   25
I never did like molestation view
On the enchafèd flood.

MONTANO.   If that the Turkish fleet

---

[103]**segregation:** separation

30 Be not ensheltered and embayed, they
are drowned.
It is impossible to bear it out. (*Enter a*
THIRD GENTLEMAN.)
THIRD GENTLEMAN.   News, lads! Our wars
35 are done.
The desperate tempest hath so banged
the Turks
That their designment halts. A noble ship
of Venice
40 Hath seen a grievous wreck and
sufferance[104]
On most part of their fleet.
MONTANO.   How! Is this true?
THIRD GENTLEMAN.   The ship is here put in,
45 A Veronesa. Michael Cassio,
Lieutenant to the warlike Moor Othello,
Is come on shore, the Moor himself
at sea,
And is in full commission here for Cyprus.
50 MONTANO.   I am glad on 't. 'Tis a worthy
governor.
THIRD GENTLEMAN.   But this same Cassio,
though he speak of comfort
Touching the Turkish loss, yet he looks
55 sadly
And prays the Moor be safe, for they
were parted
With foul and violent tempest.
MONTANO.   Pray Heavens he be,
60 For I have served him, and the man
commands
Like a full soldier. Let's to the seaside, ho!
As well to see the vessel that's come in
As to throw out our eyes for brave
65 Othello,
Even till we make the main and the aerial
blue
An indistinct regard.
THIRD GENTLEMAN.   Come, let's do so.
70 For every minute is expectancy
Of more arrivance. (*Enter* CASSIO.)

CASSIO.   Thanks, you the valiant of this   75
warlike isle
That so approve the Moor! Oh, let the
heavens
Give him defense against the elements,
For I have lost him on a dangerous sea.   80
MONTANO.   Is he well shipped?
CASSIO.   His bark is stoutly timbered, and
his pilot
Of very expert and approved allowance.
Therefore my hopes, not surfeited to   85
death,
Stand in bold cure.
(*A cry within:* "A sail, a sail, a sail!" *Enter
a* FOURTH GENTLEMAN.)
What noise?   90
FOURTH GENTLEMAN.   The town is empty.
On the brow o' the sea
Stand ranks of people and they cry
"A sail!"
CASSIO.   My hopes do shape him for the   95
governor. (*Guns heard.*)
SECOND GENTLEMAN.   They do discharge
their shot of courtesy.
Our friends, at least.
CASSIO.   I pray you, sir, go forth,   100
And give us truth who 'tis that is arrived.
SECOND GENTLEMAN.   I shall. (*Exit.*)
MONTANO.   But, good Lieutenant, is your
General wived?
CASSIO.   Most fortunately. He hath   105
achieved a maid
That paragons description and wild
fame,
One that excels the quirks of blazoning
pens   110
And in the essential vesture of creation
Does tire the ingener.[105] (*Re-enter* SECOND
GENTLEMAN.) How now! Who has put in?

---

[104]**sufferance:** damage

[105]**One . . . ingener:** one that is too good for the fancy
phrases (*quirks*) of painting pens (i.e., poets) and in
her absolute perfection wearies the artist (i.e., the
painter) **ingener:** inventor

SECOND GENTLEMAN.   'Tis one Iago,
115   Ancient to the General.
CASSIO.   He has had most favorable and
happy speed.
Tempests themselves, high seas, and
howling winds,
120   The guttered rocks, and congregated
sands,
Traitors ensteeped to clog the guiltless
keel,
As having sense of beauty, do omit
125   Their mortal[106] natures, letting go safely by
The divine Desdemona.
MONTANO.   What is she?
CASSIO.   She that I spake of, our great
Captain's captain,
130   Left in the conduct of the bold Iago,
Whose footing here anticipates our
thoughts
A sennight's[107] speed. Great Jove, Othello
guard,
135   And swell his sail with thine own power-
ful breath,
That he may bless this bay with his tall
ship,
Make love's quick pants in Desdemona's
140   arms,
Give renewed fire to our extincted spirits,
And bring all Cyprus comfort.
(*Enter* DESDEMONA, EMILIA, IAGO,
RODERIGO, *and* ATTENDANTS.)
145   Oh, behold,
The riches of the ship is come on shore!
Ye men of Cyprus, let her have your
knees.
Hail to thee, lady! And the grace of
150   Heaven,
Before, behind thee, and on every hand,
Enwheel thee round!
DESDEMONA.   I thank you, valiant Cassio.
What tidings can you tell me of my lord?

CASSIO.   He is not yet arrived, nor know   155
I aught
But that he's well and will be shortly
here.
DESDEMONA.   Oh, but I fear—How lost you
company?   160
CASSIO.   The great contention of the sea
and skies
Parted our fellowship.—But hark! A sail.
(*A cry within:* "A sail, a sail!" *Guns heard.*)
SECOND GENTLEMAN.   They give their   165
greeting to the citadel.
This likewise is a friend.
CASSIO.   See for the news. (*Exit*
GENTLEMAN.)
Good Ancient, you are welcome. (*To*   170
EMILIA) Welcome, mistress.
Let it not gall your patience, good Iago,
That I extend my manners. 'Tis my
breeding
That gives me this bold show of courtesy.   175
(*Kissing her.*)
IAGO.   Sir, would she give you so much of
her lips
As of her tongue she oft bestows on me,
You'd have enough.   180
DESDEMONA.   Alas, she has no speech.
IAGO.   In faith, too much,
I find it still when I have list[108] to sleep.
Marry, before your ladyship, I grant,
She puts her tongue a little in her heart   185
And chides with thinking.
EMILIA.   You have little cause to say so.
IAGO.   Come on, come on. You are
pictures[109] out of doors,
Bells[110] in your parlors, wildcats in your   190
kitchens,
Saints in your injuries,[111] devils being
offended,

---

[106]**mortal:** deadly
[107]**sennight's:** week's

[108]**list:** desire
[109]**pictures:** i.e., painted and dumb
[110]**Bells:** i.e., ever clacking
[111]**Saints . . . injuries:** saints when you hurt anyone else

Players in your housewifery, and
195   housewives in your beds.

DESDEMONA.   Oh, fie upon thee, slanderer!

IAGO.   Nay, it is true, or else I am a Turk.
You rise to play, and go to bed to work.

EMILIA.   You shall not write my praise.

200   IAGO.   No, let me not.

DESDEMONA.   What wouldst thou write of
me if thou shouldst praise me?

IAGO.   O gentle lady, do not put me to 't,
For I am nothing if not critical.

205   DESDEMONA.   Come on, assay.[112]—There's
one gone to the harbor?

IAGO.   Aye, madam.

DESDEMONA (*aside*).   I am not merry, but I
do beguile
210   The thing I am by seeming otherwise.—
Come, how wouldst thou praise me?

IAGO.   I am about it, but indeed my
invention
Comes from my pate as birdlime does
215   from frieze[113]—
It plucks out brains and all. But my Muse
labors,
And thus she is delivered:
If she be fair and wise, fairness and wit,
220   The one's for use, the other useth it.

DESDEMONA.   Well praised! How if she be
black and witty?

IAGO.   If she be black, and thereto have a wit,
She'll find a white[114] that shall her black-
225   ness fit.

DESDEMONA.   Worse and worse.

EMILIA.   How if fair and foolish?

IAGO.   She never yet was foolish that was
fair,
230   For even her folly helped her to an heir.

DESDEMONA.   These are old fond paradoxes
to make fools laugh i' the alehouse. What

miserable praise hast thou for her that's
foul and foolish?

IAGO.   There's none so foul, and foolish   235
thereunto,
But does foul pranks which fair and wise
ones do.

DESDEMONA.   Oh, heavy ignorance! Thou
praisest the worst best. But what praise   240
couldst thou bestow on a deserving
woman indeed, one that in the authority
of her merit did justly put on the vouch
of very malice itself?[115]

IAGO.   She that was ever fair and never   245
proud,
Had tongue at will[116] and yet was never
loud,
Never lacked gold and yet went never
gay,   250
Fled from her wish and yet said "Now
I may";
She that, being angered, her revenge
being nigh,
Bade her wrong stay and her displeasure   255
fly;
She that in wisdom never was so frail
To change the cod's head for the salmon's
tail;[117]
She that could think and ne'er disclose   260
her mind,
See suitors following and not look
behind;
She was a wight, if ever such wight
were—   265

DESDEMONA.   To do what?

IAGO.   To suckle fools and chronicle small
beer.

DESDEMONA.   Oh, most lame and impotent
conclusion! Do not learn of him, Emilia,   270
though he be thy husband. How say you,

---

[112]**assay:** try
[113]**my . . . frieze:** my literary effort (*invention*) is as
hard to pull out of my head as frieze (cloth with a nap)
stuck to birdlime
[114]**white:** with a pun on *wight* (line 156), man, person

---

[115]**one . . . itself:** one so deserving that even malice
would declare her good
[116]**tongue . . . will:** a ready flow of words
[117]**To . . . tail:** to prefer the tail end of a good thing to
the head of a poor thing

Cassio? Is he not a most profane and
liberal[118] counselor?

CASSIO.   He speaks home, madam. You
275 may relish him more in the soldier than
in the scholar.

IAGO (*aside*).   He takes her by the palm.
Aye, well said, whisper. With as little a
web as this will I ensnare as great a fly as
280 Cassio. Aye, smile upon her, do, I will
gyve thee in thine own courtship. You
say true, 'tis so indeed. If such tricks as
these strip you out of your Lieutenantry,
it had been better you had not kissed
285 your three fingers[119] so oft, which now
again you are most apt to play the sir[120]
in. Very good, well kissed! An excellent
courtesy! 'Tis so indeed. Yet again your
fingers to your lips? Would they were
290 clyster pipes[121] for your sake! (*Trumpet
within.*) The Moor! I know his trumpet.

CASSIO.   'Tis truly so.

DESDEMONA.   Let's meet him and receive
him.

295 CASSIO.   Lo where he comes! (*Enter
OTHELLO and ATTENDANTS.*)

OTHELLO.   O my fair warrior![122]

DESDEMONA.   My dear Othello!

OTHELLO.   It gives me wonder great as my
300 content
To see you here before me. O my soul's
joy!
If after every tempest come such calms,
May the winds blow till they have
305 wakened death!
And let the laboring bark climb hills
of seas
Olympus-high, and duck again as low
As Hell's from Heaven! If it were now
310 to die,

'Twere now to be most happy, for I fear
My soul hath her content so absolute
That not another comfort like to this
Succeeds in unknown fate.

DESDEMONA.   The Heavens forbid   315
But that our loves and comforts should
increase,
Even as our days do grow!

OTHELLO.   Amen to that, sweet powers!
I cannot speak enough of this content.   320
It stops me here,[123] it is too much of joy.
And this, and this, the greatest discords
be (*Kissing her.*)
That e'er our hearts shall make!

IAGO (*aside*).   Oh, you are well tuned now,   325
But I'll set down the pegs[124] that make
this music,
As honest as I am.

OTHELLO.   Come, let us to the castle.
News, friends! Our wars are done, the   330
Turks are drowned.
How does my old acquaintance of this
isle?
Honey, you shall be well desired in
Cyprus,   335
I have found great love amongst them.
O my sweet,
I prattle out of fashion, and I dote
In mine own comforts. I prithee, good
Iago,   340
Go to the bay and disembark my coffers.[125]
Bring thou the master[126] to the citadel.
He is a good one, and his worthiness
Does challenge much respect. Come,
Desdemona,   345
Once more well met at Cyprus. (*Exeunt
all but IAGO and RODERIGO.*)

IAGO.   Do thou meet me presently at the
harbor. Come hither. If thou beest

---

[118]**liberal:** gross
[119]**kissed . . . fingers:** a gesture of gallantry
[120]**play the sir:** act the fine gentleman
[121]**clyster pipes:** an enema syringe
[122]**warrior:** because she is a soldier's wife

---

[123]**here:** i.e., in the heart
[124]**set . . . pegs:** i.e., make you sing out of tune. A
stringed instrument was tuned by the pegs.
[125]**coffers:** trunks
[126]**master:** captain of the ship

350 valiant—as they say base men being in
love have then a nobility in their natures
more than is native to them—list me. The
Lieutenant tonight watches on the court
of guard. First, I must tell thee this.
355 Desdemona is directly in love with him.
RODERIGO. With him! Why, 'tis not
possible.
IAGO. Lay thy finger thus,[127] and let thy
soul be instructed. Mark me with what
360 violence she first loved the Moor, but for
bragging and telling her fantastical lies.
And will she love him still for prating?
Let not thy discreet heart think it. Her
eye must be fed, and what delight shall
365 she have to look on the Devil? When the
blood is made dull with the act of sport,
there should be, again to inflame it and
to give satiety a fresh appetite, loveliness
in favor,[128] sympathy in years, manners,
370 and beauties, all which the Moor is
defective in. Now, for want of these
required conveniences, her delicate tenderness will find itself abused, begin to
heave the gorge, disrelish and abhor the
375 Moor. Very nature will instruct her in it
and compel her to some second choice.
Now, sir, this granted—as it is a most
pregnant and unforced position[129]—who
stands so eminently in the degree of this
380 fortune as Cassio does? A knave very
voluble, no further conscionable[130] than
in putting on the mere form of civil and
humane seeming[131] for the better compassing of his salt[132] and most hidden loose
385 affection? Why, none, why, none. A
slipper[133] and subtle knave, a finder-out

of occasions, that has an eye can stamp
and counterfeit advantages,[134] though
true advantage never present itself. A
devilish knave! Besides, the knave is   390
handsome, young, and hath all those
requisites in him that folly and green
minds look after. A pestilent complete
knave, and the woman hath found him
already.   395
RODERIGO. I cannot believe that in her.
She's full of most blest condition.
IAGO. Blest fig's-end! The wine she drinks
is made of grapes. If she had been blest,
she would never have loved the Moor.   400
Blest pudding! Didst thou not see her
paddle with the palm of his hand? Didst
not mark that?
RODERIGO. Yes, that I did, but that was but
courtesy.   405
IAGO. Lechery, by his hand, an index and
obscure prologue to the history of lust
and foul thoughts. They met so near with
their lips that their breaths embraced
together. Villainous thoughts, Roderigo!   410
When these mutualities so marshal the
way, hard at hand comes the master and
main exercise, the incorporate[135]
conclusion. Pish! But, sir, be you ruled by
me. I have brought you from Venice.   415
Watch you tonight. For the command, I'll
lay 't upon you. Cassio knows you not.
I'll not be far from you. Do you find
some occasion to anger Cassio, either by
speaking too loud, or tainting[136] his   420
discipline, or from what other course you
please which the time shall more
favorably minister.
RODERIGO. Well.
IAGO. Sir, he is rash and very sudden in   425
choler,[137] and haply may strike at you.

---

[127]**thus:** i.e., on the lips
[128]**favor:** face
[129]**pregnant . . . position:** very significant and probable argument
[130]**no . . . conscionable:** who has no more conscience
[131]**humane seeming:** courteous appearance
[132]**salt:** lecherous
[133]**slipper:** slippery

---

[134]**stamp . . . advantages:** forge false opportunities
[135]**incorporate:** bodily
[136]**tainting:** disparaging
[137]**choler:** anger

Provoke him, that he may, for even out of
that will I cause these of Cyprus to
mutiny, whose qualification shall come
430   into no true taste again but by the
displanting of Cassio. So shall you have a
shorter journey to your desires by the
means I shall then have to prefer[138] them,
and the impediment most profitably
435   removed without the which there were
no expectation of our prosperity.
   RODERIGO.   I will do this, if I can bring it to
any opportunity.
   IAGO.   I warrant thee. Meet me by and by
440   at the citadel. I must fetch his necessaries
ashore. Farewell.
   RODERIGO.   Adieu. (*Exit.*)
   IAGO.   That Cassio loves her, I do well
believe it.
445   That she loves him, 'tis apt and of great
credit.[139]
   The Moor, howbeit that I endure him not,
Is of a constant, loving, noble nature,
And I dare think he'll prove to
450   Desdemona
A most dear husband. Now, I do love
her too,
Not out of absolute lust, though
peradventure
455   I stand accountant for as great a sin,
But partly led to diet[140] my revenge
For that I do suspect the lusty Moor
Hath leaped into my seat. The thought
whereof
460   Doth like a poisonous mineral gnaw my
inwards,
And nothing can or shall content my soul
Till I am evened with him, wife for wife.
Or failing so, yet that I put the Moor
465   At least into a jealousy so strong
That judgment cannot cure. Which thing
to do,

If this poor trash of Venice, whom I trash
For his quick hunting, stand the
putting-on,   470
I'll have our Michael Cassio on the hip,
Abuse him to the Moor in the rank
garb[141]—
For I fear Cassio with my nightcap too—
Make the Moor thank me, love me, and   475
reward me
For making him egregiously an ass
And practicing upon his peace and
quiet
Even to madness. 'Tis here, but yet   480
confused.
Knavery's plain face is never seen till
used. (*Exit.*)

SCENE 2. A street.

Enter a HERALD *with a proclamation,* PEOPLE
following.

HERALD.   It is Othello's pleasure, our noble
and valiant General, that upon certain   485
tidings now arrived, importing the mere
perdition[142] of the Turkish fleet, every
man put himself into triumph[143]—some
to dance, some to make bonfires, each
man to what sport and revels his   490
addiction leads him. For, besides these
beneficial news, it is the celebration of
his nuptial. So much was his pleasure
should be proclaimed. All offices[144] are
open, and there is full liberty of feasting   495
from this present hour of five till the bell
have told eleven. Heaven bless the isle of
Cyprus and our noble General Othello!
(*Exeunt.*)

---

[138]**prefer:** promote
[139]**apt . . . credit:** likely and very creditable
[140]**diet:** feed

---

[141]**rank garb:** gross manner; i.e., by accusing him of
being Desdemona's lover
[142]**mere perdition:** absolute destruction
[143]**put . . . triumph:** celebrate
[144]**offices:** the kitchen and buttery—i.e., free food and
drink for all

SCENE 3. A hall in the castle.

Enter OTHELLO, DESDEMONA, CASSIO, *and*
ATTENDANTS.

500 OTHELLO.   Good Michael, look you to the
guard tonight.
Let's teach ourselves that honorable stop,
Not to outsport discretion.[145]
CASSIO.   Iago hath directions what to do,
505 But notwithstanding with my personal
eye
Will I look to 't.
OTHELLO.   Iago is most honest.
Michael, good night. Tomorrow with
510 your earliest
Let me have speech with you. (*To*
DESDEMONA) Come, my dear love,
The purchase made, the fruits are to
ensue—
515 That profit's yet to come 'tween me and
you.
Good night. (*Exeunt all but* CASSIO. *Enter*
IAGO.)
CASSIO.   Welcome, Iago. We must to the
520 watch.
IAGO.   Not this hour, Lieutenant, 'tis not
yet ten o'clock. Our General cast[146] us
thus early for the love of his Desdemona,
who let us not therefore blame. He hath
525 not yet made wanton the night with her,
and she is sport for Jove.
CASSIO.   She's a most exquisite lady.
IAGO.   And, I'll warrant her, full of game.
CASSIO.   Indeed she's a most fresh and del-
530 icate creature.
IAGO.   What an eye she has! Methinks it
sounds a parley to provocation.
CASSIO.   An inviting eye, and yet methinks
right modest.
535 IAGO.   And when she speaks, is it not an
alarum to love?

CASSIO.   She is indeed perfection.
IAGO.   Well, happiness to their sheets!
Come, Lieutenant, I have a stoup of wine,
and there without are a brace of Cyprus   540
gallants that would fain have a measure
to the health of black Othello.
CASSIO.   Not tonight, good Iago. I have
very poor and unhappy brains for
drinking. I could well wish courtesy   545
would invent some other custom of
entertainment.
IAGO.   Oh, they are our friends. But one
cup—I'll drink for you.
CASSIO.   I have drunk but one cup tonight,   550
and that was craftily qualified too, and
behold what innovation it makes here. I
am unfortunate in the infirmity, and dare
not task my weakness with any more.
IAGO.   What, man! 'Tis a night of revels.   555
The gallants desire it.
CASSIO.   Where are they?
IAGO.   Here at the door. I pray you call
them in.
CASSIO.   I'll do 't, but it dislikes me. (*Exit.*) 560
IAGO.   If I can fasten but one cup upon
him,
With that which he hath drunk tonight
already,
He'll be as full of quarrel and offense   565
As my young mistress' dog. Now my
sick fool Roderigo,
Whom love hath turned almost the
wrong side out,
To Desdemona hath tonight caroused   570
Potations pottle-deep, and he's to watch.
Three lads of Cyprus, noble swelling
spirits
That hold their honors in a wary distance,
The very elements[147] of this warlike isle,   575
Have I tonight flustered with flowing
cups,
And they watch too. Now, 'mongst this
flock of drunkards,

---

[145]**outsport discretion:** let the fun go too far.
[146]**cast:** dismissed

[147]**very elements:** typical specimens

580 Am I to put our Cassio in some action
That may offend the isle. But here they
come.
If consequence do but approve my
dream,
585 My boat sails freely, both with wind and
stream.

(*Re-enter* CASSIO, *with him* MONTANO *and*
GENTLEMEN, SERVANTS *following with wine.*)

CASSIO. 'Fore God, they have given me a
590 rouse already.

MONTANO. Good faith, a little one—not
past a pint, as I am a soldier.

IAGO. Some wine, ho! (*Sings*)
"And let me the cannikin clink, clink
595 And let me the cannikin clink.
  A soldier's a man,
  A life's but a span.[148]
Why, then let a soldier drink."
Some wine, boys!

600 CASSIO. 'Fore God, an excellent song.

IAGO. I learned it in England, where
indeed they are most potent in potting.[149]
Your Dane, your German, and your
swag-bellied Hollander—Drink, ho!—are
605 nothing to your English.

CASSIO. Is your Englishman so expert in
his drinking?

IAGO. Why, he drinks you with facility
your Dane dead drunk, he sweats not to
610 overthrow your Almain,[150] he gives your
Hollander a vomit[151] ere the next pottle
can be filled.

CASSIO. To the health of our General!

MONTANO. I am for it, Lieutenant, and I'll
615 do you justice.

IAGO. O sweet England! (*Sings*)
"King Stephen was a worthy peer,
  His breeches cost him but a crown.

---

[148]**span:** lit., the measure between the thumb and little
finger of the outstretched hand; about 9 inches
[149]**potting:** drinking
[150]**Almain:** German
[151]**gives . . . vomit:** drinks as much as will make a
Dutchman throw up

He held them sixpence all too dear,
  With that he called the tailor lown.[152]   620

"He was a wight of high renown,
  And thou art but of low degree.
'Tis pride that pulls the country down.
  Then take thine auld cloak about thee."
Some wine, ho!   625

CASSIO. Why, this is a more exquisite song
than the other.

IAGO. Will you hear 't again?

CASSIO. No, for I hold him to be unworthy
of his place that does those things. Well,   630
God's above all, and there be souls must
be saved and there be souls must not be
saved.

IAGO. It's true, good Lieutenant.

CASSIO. For mine own part—no offense to   635
the General, nor any man of quality—
I hope to be saved.

IAGO. And so do I too, Lieutenant.

CASSIO. Aye, but, by your leave, not
before me. The Lieutenant is to be saved   640
before the Ancient. Let's have no more of
this, let's to our affairs. God forgive us
our sins! Gentlemen, let's look to our
business. Do not think, gentlemen, I am
drunk. This is my Ancient, this is my   645
right hand and this is my left. I am not
drunk now, I can stand well enough and
speak well enough.

ALL. Excellent well.

CASSIO. Why, very well, then, you must   650
not think then that I am drunk. (*Exit.*)

MONTANO. To the platform, masters.
Come, let's set the watch.

IAGO. You see this fellow that is gone
before.   655
He is a soldier fit to stand by Caesar
And give direction. And do but see
his vice.
'Tis to his virtue a just equinox,

---

[152]**lown:** lout

660 The one as long as the other. 'Tis pity of him.
I fear the trust Othello puts him in
On some odd time of his infirmity
Will shake this island.

665 MONTANO. But is he often thus?

IAGO. 'Tis evermore the prologue to his sleep.
He'll watch the horologe a double set,[153]
If drink rock not his cradle.

670 MONTANO. It were well
The General were put in mind of it.
Perhaps he sees it not, or his good nature
Prizes the virtue that appears in Cassio
And looks not on his evils. Is not this

675 true? (*Enter* RODERIGO.)

IAGO (*aside to him*). How now, Roderigo!
I pray you, after the Lieutenant. Go.
(*Exit* RODERIGO.)

MONTANO. And 'tis great pity that the

680 noble Moor
Should hazard such a place as his own second
With one of an ingraft infirmity.
It were an honest action to say

685 So to the Moor.

IAGO. Not I, for this fair island.
I do love Cassio well, and would do much
To cure him of this evil—But hark! What noise?

690 (*A cry within:* "Help! Help!" *Re-enter*
CASSIO, *driving in* RODERIGO.)

CASSIO. 'Zounds! You rogue! You rascal!

MONTANO. What's the matter, Lieutenant?

CASSIO. A knave teach me my duty! But

695 I'll beat the knave into a wicker bottle.

RODERIGO. Beat me!

CASSIO. Does thou prate, rogue? (*Striking* RODERIGO.)

MONTANO. Nay, good Lieutenant (*staying*

700 *him*),
I pray you sir, hold your hand.

CASSIO. Let me go, sir, or I'll knock you o'er the mazzard.[154]

MONTANO. Come, come, you're drunk.

CASSIO. Drunk! (*They fight.*) 705

IAGO (*aside to* RODERIGO). Away, I say. Go out and cry a mutiny.
(*Exit* RODERIGO.)
Nay, good Lieutenant! God's will, gentlemen! 710
Help, ho!—Lieutenant—sir—Montano—sir—
Help, masters!—Here's a goodly watch indeed! (*A bell rings.*)
Who's that that rings the bell?— 715
Diablo, ho!
The town will rise. God's will, Lieutenant, hold—
You will be ashamed forever. (*Re-enter*
OTHELLO *and* ATTENDANTS.) 720

OTHELLO. What is the matter here?

MONTANO. 'Zounds, I bleed still, I am hurt to death. (*Faints.*)

OTHELLO. Hold, for your lives!

IAGO. Hold, ho! Lieutenant—sir— 725
Montano—gentlemen—
Have you forgot all sense of place and duty?
Hold! The General speaks to you. Hold, hold, for shame! 730

OTHELLO. Why, how now, ho! From whence ariseth this?
Are we turned Turks, and to ourselves do that
Which Heaven hath forbid the 735
Ottomites?
For Christian shame, put by this barbarous brawl.
He that stirs next to carve for his own rage 740
Holds his soul light, he dies upon his motion.
Silence that dreadful bell. It frights the isle

---

[153]**watch . . . set:** stay awake the clock twice round

[154]**mazzard:** head

745 From her propriety. What is the matter, masters?
Honest Iago, that look'st dead with grieving,
Speak, who began this? On thy love, I
750 charge thee.

IAGO.   I do not know. Friends all but now, even now,
In quarter and in terms like bride and groom
755 Devesting them for bed. And then, but now,
As if some planet had unwitted men,
Swords out, and tilting one at other's breast
760 In opposition bloody. I cannot speak
Any beginning to this peevish odds,
And would in action glorious I had lost
Those legs that brought me to a part of it!

OTHELLO.   How comes it, Michael, you are
765 thus forgot?[155]

CASSIO.   I pray you, pardon me, I cannot speak.

OTHELLO.   Worthy Montano, you were wont be civil.
770 The gravity and stillness of your youth
The world hath noted, and your name is great
In mouths of wisest censure.[156] What's the matter
775 That you unlace your reputation thus
And spend your rich opinion for the name
Of a night brawler? Give me answer to it.

MONTANO.   Worthy Othello, I am hurt to
780 danger.
Your officer, Iago, can inform you—
While I spare speech, which something now offends me—
Of all that I do know. Nor know I aught
785 By me that's said or done amiss this night,

Unless self-charity[157] be sometimes a vice,
And to defend ourselves it be a sin
When violence assails us.

OTHELLO.   Now, by Heaven,   790
My blood begins my safer guides to rule,
And passion, having my best judgment collied,[158]
Assays to lead the way. If I once stir,
Or do but lift this arm, the best of you   795
Shall sink in my rebuke. Give me to know
How this foul rout began, who set it on,
And he that is approved[159] in this offense,
Though he had twinned with me, both at   800
a birth,
Shall lose me. What! In a town of war,
Yet wild, the people's hearts brimful of fear,
To manage private and domestic quarrel,   805
In night, and on the court and guard of safety!
'Tis monstrous. Iago, who began 't?

MONTANO.   If partially affined or leagued in office,   810
Thou dost deliver more or less than truth,
Thou art no soldier.

IAGO.   Touch me not so near.
I had rather have this tongue cut from my mouth   815
Than it should do offense to Michael Cassio.
Yet I persuade myself to speak the truth
Shall nothing wrong him. Thus it is, General.   820
Montano and myself being in speech,
There comes a fellow crying out for help,
And Cassio following him with determined sword
To execute upon him. Sir, this gentleman   825
Steps in to Cassio and entreats his pause.

---

[155]**are thus forgot:** have so forgotten yourself
[156]**censure:** judgment

[157]**self-charity:** love for oneself
[158]**collied:** darkened
[159]**approved:** proved guilty

Myself the crying fellow did pursue
Lest by his clamor—as it so fell out—
The town might fall in fright. He, swift of
830   foot,
Outran my purpose, and I returned the
rather
For that I heard the clink and fall of
swords,
835   And Cassio high in oath, which till
tonight
I ne'er might say before. When I came
back—
For this was brief—I found them close
840   together,
At blow and thrust, even as again they
were
When you yourself did part them.
More of this matter cannot I report.
845   But men are men, the best sometimes
forget.
Though Cassio did some little wrong to
him,
As men in rage strike those that wish
850   them best,
Yet surely Cassio, I believe, received
From him that fled some strange
indignity,
Which patience could not pass.

855 OTHELLO.   I know, Iago,
Thy honesty and love doth mince this
matter,
Making it light to Cassio. Cassio, I love
thee,
860   But never more be officer of mine.
(*Re-enter* DESDEMONA, *attended*.)
Look, if my gentle love be not raised up!
I'll make thee an example.

    DESDEMONA.   What's the matter?

865 OTHELLO.   All's well now, sweeting. Come
away to bed.
(*To* MONTANO, *who is led off*)
Sir, for your hurts, myself will be your
surgeon.
870   Lead him off.
Iago, look with care about the town,

And silence those whom this vile brawl
distracted.
Come, Desdemona. 'Tis the soldier's life
To have their balmy slumbers waked   875
with strife.
(*Exeunt all but* IAGO *and* CASSIO.)

IAGO.   What, are you hurt, Lieutenant?

CASSIO.   Aye, past all surgery.

IAGO.   Marry, Heaven forbid!   880

CASSIO.   Reputation, reputation,
reputation! Oh, I have lost my reputation!
I have lost the immortal part of myself,
and what remains is bestial. My
reputation, Iago, my reputation!   885

IAGO.   As I am an honest man, I thought
you had received some bodily wound.
There is more sense in that than in
reputation. Reputation is an idle and
most false imposition, oft got without   890
merit and lost without deserving. You
have lost no reputation at all unless you
repute yourself such a loser. What, man!
There are ways to recover the General
again. You are but now cast in his   895
mood,[160] a punishment more in policy[161]
than in malice—even so as one would
beat his offenseless dog to affright an
imperious lion.[162] Sue to him again and
he's yours.   900

CASSIO.   I will rather sue to be despised
than to deceive so good a commander
with so slight, so drunken, and so indiscreet an officer. Drunk? And speak
parrot[163]? And squabble? Swagger?   905
Swear? And discourse fustian[164] with
one's own shadow? O thou invisible

---

[160]**cast . . . mood:** dismissed because he is in a bad mood
[161]**in policy:** i.e., because he must appear to be angry before the Cypriots
[162]**even . . . lion:** A proverb meaning that when the lion sees the dog beaten, he will know what is coming to him
[163]**speak parrot:** babble
[164]**fustian:** nonsense

spirit of wine, if thou hast no name to be
known by, let us call thee devil!

910 IAGO.   What was he that you followed
with your sword? What had he done
to you?

CASSIO.   I know not.

IAGO.   Is 't possible?

915 CASSIO.   I remember a mass of things, but
nothing distinctly—a quarrel, but nothing wherefore. Oh God, that men should
put an enemy in their mouths to steal
away their brains! That we should, with

920 joy, pleasance, revel, and applause, transform ourselves into beasts!

IAGO.   Why, but you are now well enough.
How came you thus recovered?

CASSIO.   It hath pleased the devil drunken-

925 ness to give place to the devil wrath. One
unperfectness shows me another, to make
me frankly despise myself.

IAGO.   Come, you are too severe a moraler.
As the time, the place, and the condition

930 of this country stands, I could heartily
wish this had not befallen. But since it is
as it is, mend it for your own good.

CASSIO.   I will ask him for my place again,
he shall tell me I am a drunkard! Had I as

935 many mouths as Hydra, such an answer
would stop them all. To be now a sensible man, by and by a fool, and presently
a beast! Oh, strange! Every inordinate
cup is unblest, and the ingredient is a

940 devil.

IAGO.   Come, come, good wine is a good
familiar creature, if it be well used.
Exclaim no more against it. And, good
Lieutenant, I think you think I love you.

945 CASSIO.   I have well approved it, sir.
I drunk!

IAGO.   You or any man living may be
drunk at some time, man. I'll tell you
what you shall do. Our General's wife is

950 now the General. I may say so in this
respect, for that he hath devoted and
given up himself to the contemplation,

mark, and denotement of her parts and
graces. Confess yourself freely to her,
importune her help to put you in your   955
place again. She is of so free, so kind, so
apt, so blessed a disposition, she holds it
a vice in her goodness not to do more
than she is requested. This broken joint
between you and her husband entreat   960
her to splinter[165] and, my fortunes against
any lay[166] worth naming, this crack of
your love shall grow stronger than it was
before.

CASSIO.   You advise me well.   965

IAGO.   I protest, in the sincerity of love and
honest kindness.

CASSIO.   I think it freely, and betimes in the
morning I will beseech the virtuous
Desdemona to undertake for me. I am   970
desperate of my fortunes if they check
me here.

IAGO.   You are in the right. Good night,
Lieutenant, I must to the watch.

CASSIO.   Good night, honest Iago. (*Exit*.)   975

IAGO.   And what's he then that says I play
the villain?
When this advice is free I give and honest,
Probal[167] to thinking, and indeed the
course   980
To win the Moor again? For 'tis most
easy
The inclining Desdemona to subdue
In any honest suit. She's framed as fruitful
As the free elements. And then for her   985
To win the Moor, were 't to renounce his
baptism,
All seals and symbols of redeemed sin,
His soul is so enfettered to her love
That she may make, unmake, do what   990
she list,
Even as her appetite shall play the god

---

[165]**splinter:** put in splints
[166]**lay:** bet
[167]**Probal:** probable

With his weak function. How am I then
a villain

995   To counsel Cassio to this parallel course,
Directly to his good? Divinity of Hell!
When devils will the blackest sins put on,
They do suggest at first with heavenly
shows,

1000   As I do now. For whiles this honest fool
Plies Desdemona to repair his fortunes,
And she for him pleads strongly to the
Moor,
I'll pour this pestilence into his ear,

1005   That she repeals[168] him for her body's
lust,
And by how much she strives to do
him good,
She shall undo her credit with the Moor.

1010   So will I turn her virtue into pitch,
And out of her own goodness make
the net
That shall enmesh them all. (*Enter*
RODERIGO.)

1015   How now, Roderigo!

  RODERIGO.   I do follow here in the chase,
not like a hound that hunts but one that
fills up the cry. My money is almost
spent, I have been tonight exceedingly

1020   well cudgeled, and I think the issue will
be I shall have so much experience from
my pains and so, with no money at all
and a little more wit, return again to
Venice.

1025   IAGO.   How poor are they that have not
patience!
What wound did ever heal but by
degrees?
Thou know'st we work by wit and not by

1030   witchcraft,
And wit depends on dilatory Time.
Does 't not go well? Cassio hath beaten
thee,
And thou by that small hurt hast

1035   cashiered Cassio.

---

[168]**repeals:** calls back

Though other things grow fair against
the sun,
Yet fruits that blossom first will first be
ripe.

1040   Content thyself awhile. By the mass, 'tis
morning.
Pleasure and action make the hours seem
short.
Retire thee, go where thou art billeted.

1045   Away, I say. Thou shalt know more
hereafter.
Nay, get thee gone. (*Exit* RODERIGO.)
Two things are to be done:
My wife must move for Cassio to her

1050   mistress,
I'll set her on,
Myself the while to draw the Moor apart
And bring him jump[169] when he may
Cassio find

1055   Soliciting his wife. Aye, that's the way.
Dull not device by coldness and delay.
(*Exit.*)

(ACT 3)

SCENE 1. Before the castle.

Enter CASSIO *and some* MUSICIANS.

CASSIO.   Masters, play here, I will content   1
your pains[170]—
Something that's brief, and bid "Good
morrow, General."[171]
(*Music. Enter* CLOWN.)   5

CLOWN.   Why, masters, have your instruments been in Naples, that they speak i'
the nose thus?

FIRST MUSICIAN.   How, sir, how?

CLOWN.   Are these, I pray you, wind   10
instruments?

---

[169]**jump:** at the moment

[170]**content your pains:** reward your labor

[171]**bid . . . General:** It was a common custom to play
or sing a song beneath the bedroom window of a distinguished guest or of a newly wedded couple on the
morning after their wedding night.

FIRST MUSICIAN.   Aye, marry are they, sir.
CLOWN.   Oh, thereby hangs a tail.
FIRST MUSICIAN.   Whereby hangs a tale, sir?
15 CLOWN.   Marry, sir, by many a wind
    instrument that I know. But, masters,
    here's money for you. And the General so
    likes your music that he desires you, for
    love's sake, to make no more noise with it.
20 FIRST MUSICIAN.   Well, sir, we will not.
CLOWN.   If you have any music that may
    not be heard, to 't again. But, as they say,
    to hear music the General does not
    greatly care.
25 FIRST MUSICIAN.   We have none such, sir.
CLOWN.   Then put up your pipes in your
    bag, for I'll away. Go, vanish into air,
    away! (*Exeunt* MUSICIANS.)
CASSIO.   Dost thou hear, my honest friend?
30 CLOWN.   No, I hear not your honest friend,
    I hear you.
CASSIO.   Prithee keep up thy quillets.[172]
    There's a poor piece of gold for thee. If
    the gentlewoman that attends the
35 General's wife be stirring, tell her there's
    one Cassio entreats her a little favor of
    speech. Wilt thou do this?
CLOWN.   She is stirring, sir. If she will stir
    hither, I shall seem to notify unto her.
40 CASSIO.   Do, good my friend. (*Exit* CLOWN.
    Enter IAGO.)
    In happy time, Iago.
IAGO.   You have not been abed, then?
CASSIO.   Why, no, the day had broke
45   Before we parted. I have made bold, Iago,
    To send in to your wife. My suit to her
    Is that she will to virtuous Desdemona
    Procure me some access.
IAGO.   I'll send her to you presently,
50   And I'll devise a mean to draw the Moor
    Out of the way, that your convérse and
    business
    May be more free.

CASSIO.   I humbly thank you for 't. (*Exit*   55
IAGO.)
    I never knew
    A Florentine more kind and honest.
    (*Enter* EMILIA.)
EMILIA.   Good morrow, good Lieutenant.   60
    I am sorry
    For your displeasure, but all will sure
    be well.
    The General and his wife are talking of it,
    And she speaks for you stoutly. The   65
    Moor replies
    That he you hurt is of great fame in
    Cyprus
    And great affinity,[173] and that in
    wholesome wisdom   70
    He might not but refuse you. But he
    protests he loves you,
    And needs no other suitor but his likings
    To take the safest occasion by the front
    To bring you in again.   75
CASSIO.   Yet I beseech you
    If you think fit, or that it may be done,
    Give me advantage of some brief
    discourse
    With Desdemona alone.   80
EMILIA.   Pray you, come in.
    I will bestow you where you shall have
    time
    To speak your bosom freely.
CASSIO.   I am much bound to you.   85
    (*Exeunt.*)

SCENE 2. A room in the castle.

Enter OTHELLO, IAGO, *and* GENTLEMEN.

OTHELLO.   These letters give, Iago, to the
    pilot,
    And by him do my duties to the Senate.
    That done, I will be walking on the   90
    works.[174]

---

[172]**keep . . . quillets:** put away your wisecracks

[173]**affinity:** kindred
[174]**works:** fortifications

Repair there to me.

IAGO.   Well, my good lord, I'll do 't.

OTHELLO.   This fortification, gentlemen, shall we see 't?

95 GENTLEMEN.   We'll wait upon your lordship. (*Exeunt.*)

SCENE 3. *The garden of the castle.*

Enter DESDEMONA, CASSIO, *and* EMILIA.

DESDEMONA.   Be thou assured, good Cassio, I will do
All my abilities in thy behalf.

100 EMILIA.   Good madam, do. I warrant it grieves my husband
As if the case were his.

DESDEMONA.   Oh, that's an honest fellow. Do not doubt, Cassio,

105 But I will have my lord and you again
As friendly as you were.

CASSIO.   Bounteous madam,
Whatever shall become of Michael Cassio,

110 He's never anything but your true servant.

DESDEMONA.   I know 't. I thank you. You do love my lord.
You have known him long, and be you well assured

115 He shall in strangeness stand no farther off
Than in a politic distance.[175]

CASSIO.   Aye, but lady,
That policy may either last so long,

120 Or feed upon such nice and waterish diet,
Or breed itself so out of circumstance,
That, I being absent and my place supplied,

125 My General will forget my love and service.

DESDEMONA.   Do not doubt[176] that. Before Emilia here
I give thee warrant of thy place. Assure thee,   130
If I do vow a friendship, I'll perform it
To the last article. My lord shall never rest.
I'll watch him tame and talk him out of patience,   135
His bed shall seem a school, his board a shrift.
I'll intermingle every thing he does
With Cassio's suit. Therefore be merry, Cassio,   140
For thy solicitor shall rather die
Than give thy cause away. (*Enter* OTHELLO *and* IAGO, *at a distance.*)

EMILIA.   Madam, here comes my lord.

CASSIO.   Madam, I'll take my leave.   145

DESDEMONA.   Nay, stay and hear me speak.

CASSIO.   Madam, not now. I am very ill at ease,
Unfit for mine own purposes.

DESDEMONA.   Well, do your discretion.   150
(*Exit* CASSIO.)

IAGO.   Ha! I like not that.

OTHELLO.   What dost thou say?

IAGO.   Nothing, my lord. Or if—I know not what.   155

OTHELLO.   Was not that Cassio parted from my wife?

IAGO.   Cassio, my lord! No, sure, I cannot think it,
That he would steal away so guilty-like,   160
Seeing you coming.

OTHELLO.   I do believe 'twas he.

DESDEMONA.   How now, my lord!
I have been talking with a suitor here,
A man that languishes in your displeasure.   165

OTHELLO.   Who is 't you mean?

DESDEMONA.   Why, your Lieutenant, Cassio. Good my lord,

---

[175]**He . . . distance:** i.e., his apparent coldness to you shall only be so much as his official position demands for reasons of policy

[176]**doubt:** fear

If I have any grace or power to move you,
170 His present reconciliation take.[177]
For if he be not one that truly loves you,
That errs in ignorance and not in cunning,
I have no judgment in an honest face.
I prithee call him back.
175 OTHELLO.   Went he hence now?
DESDEMONA.   Aye, sooth, so humbled
That he hath left part of his grief with me,
To suffer with him. Good love, call him
back.
180 OTHELLO.   Not now, sweet Desdemona,
some other time.
DESDEMONA.   But shall 't be shortly?
OTHELLO.   The sooner, sweet, for you.
DESDEMONA.   Shall 't be tonight at supper?
185 OTHELLO.   No, not tonight.
DESDEMONA.   Tomorrow dinner then?
OTHELLO.   I shall not dine at home.
I meet the captains at the citadel.
DESDEMONA.   Why, then tomorrow night or
190 Tuesday morn,
On Tuesday noon, or night, on
Wednesday morn.
I prithee name the time, but let it not
Exceed three days. In faith, he's penitent,
195 And yet his trespass, in our common
reason—
Save that, they say, the wars must make
examples
Out of their best—is not almost[178] a fault
200 To incur a private check.[179] When shall he
come?
Tell me, Othello. I wonder in my soul
What you would ask me that I should
deny,
205 Or stand so mammering[180] on. What!
Michael Cassio,

That came a-wooing with you, and so
many a time
When I have spoke of you
dispraisingly   210
Hath ta'en your part—to have so much to
do
To bring him in! Trust me, I could do
much—
OTHELLO.   Prithee, no more. Let him come   215
when he will.
I will deny thee nothing.
DESDEMONA.   Why, this is not a boon.
'Tis as I should entreat you wear your
gloves,   220
Or feed on nourishing dishes, or keep
you warm,
Or sue to you to do a peculiar profit
To your own person. Nay, when I have
a suit   225
Wherein I mean to touch your love
indeed,
It shall be full of poise and difficult
weight,
And fearful to be granted.   230
OTHELLO.   I will deny thee nothing.
Whereon I do beseech thee grant me this,
To leave me but a little to myself.
DESDEMONA.   Shall I deny you? No.
Farewell, my lord.   235
OTHELLO.   Farewell, my Desdemona.
I'll come to thee straight.
DESDEMONA.   Emilia, come. Be as your
fancies teach you.
Whate'er you be, I am obedient.   240
(*Exeunt* DESDEMONA *and* EMILIA.)
OTHELLO.   Excellent wretch! Perdition
catch my soul
But I do love thee! And when I love
thee not,   245
Chaos is come again.
IAGO.   My noble lord—
OTHELLO.   What dost thou say, Iago?
IAGO.   Did Michael Cassio, when you
wooed my lady,   250
Know of your love?

---

[177]**His . . . take:** accept his immediate apology and forgive him
[178]**not almost:** hardly
[179]**check:** rebuke
[180]**mammering:** hesitating

OTHELLO.   He did, from first to last. Why
   dost thou ask?

255 IAGO.   But for a satisfaction of my thought,
   No further harm.

OTHELLO.   Why of thy thought, Iago?

IAGO.   I did not think he had been
   acquainted with her.

OTHELLO.   Oh yes, and went between us
260   very oft.

IAGO.   Indeed!

OTHELLO.   Indeed! Aye, indeed. Discern'st
   thou aught in that?
   Is he not honest?

265 IAGO.   Honest, my lord!

OTHELLO.   Honest! Aye, honest.

IAGO.   My lord, for aught I know.

OTHELLO.   What dost thou think?

IAGO.   Think, my lord!

270 OTHELLO.   Think, my lord! By Heaven, he
   echoes me
   As if there were some monster in his
   thought
   Too hideous to be shown. Thou dost
275   mean something.
   I heard thee say even now that thou
   likedst not that
   When Cassio left my wife. What didst
   not like?
280   And when I told thee he was of my
   counsel
   In my whole course of wooing, thou
   criedst "Indeed!"
   And didst contract and purse thy brow
285   together
   As if thou then hadst shut up in thy brain
   Some horrible conceit. If thou dost love me,
   Show me thy thought.

IAGO.   My lord, you know I love you.

290 OTHELLO.   I think thou dost,
   And for I know thou'rt full of love and
   honesty
   And weigh'st thy words before thou
   givest them breath,
295   Therefore these stops of thine fright me
   the more.

For such things in a false disloyal knave
Are tricks of custom, but in a man that's
   just
They're close delations,[181] working from   300
   the heart,
That passion cannot rule,

IAGO.   For Michael Cassio,
   I dare be sworn I think that he is honest.

OTHELLO.   I think so too.   305

IAGO.   Men should be what they seem,
   Or those that be not, would they might
   seem none![182]

OTHELLO.   Certain, men should be what
   they seem.   310

IAGO.   Why, then I think Cassio's an
   honest man.

OTHELLO.   Nay, yet there's more in this.
   I prithee speak to me as to thy thinkings,
   As thou dost ruminate, and give thy   315
   worst of thoughts
   The worst of words.

IAGO.   Good my lord, pardon me.
   Though I am bound to every act of duty,
   I am not bound to that all slaves are   320
   free to.
   Utter my thoughts? Why, say they are
   vile and false,
   As where's that palace whereinto foul
   things   325
   Sometimes intrude not? Who has a breast
   so pure
   But some uncleanly apprehensions
   Keep leets[183] and law days, and in
   session sit   330
   With meditations lawful?

OTHELLO.   Thou dost conspire against thy
   friend, Iago,
   If thou but think'st him wronged and
   makest his ear   335
   A stranger to thy thoughts.

IAGO.   I do beseech you—

---

[181]**close delations:** concealed accusations
[182]**seem none:** i.e., not seem to be honest men
[183]**leets:** courts

Though I perchance am vicious in my guess,

340 As, I confess, it is my nature's plague
To spy into abuses, and oft my jealousy[184]
Shapes faults that are not—that your wisdom yet,
From one that so imperfectly conceits,[185]

345 Would take no notice, nor build yourself a trouble
Out of his scattering and unsure observance.[186]
It were not for your quiet nor your good,

350 Nor for my manhood, honesty, or wisdom,
To let you know my thoughts.
OTHELLO.   What dost thou mean?
IAGO.   Good name in man and woman, dear my lord,

355 Is the immediate jewel of their souls.
Who steals my purse steals trash—'tis something, nothing,
'Twas mine, 'tis his, and has been slave to thousands—

360 But he that filches from me my good name
Robs me of that which not enriches him
And makes me poor indeed.
OTHELLO.   By Heaven, I'll know thy

365 thoughts.
IAGO.   You cannot, if my heart were in your hand,
Nor shall not, whilst 'tis in my custody.
OTHELLO.   Ha!

370 IAGO.   Oh, beware, my lord, of jealousy.
It is the green-eyed monster which doth mock
The meat it feeds on. That cuckold lives in bliss

375 Who, certain of his fate, loves not his wronger.[187]

But, oh, what damnèd minutes tells he o'er
Who dotes, yet doubts, suspects, yet strongly loves! 380
OTHELLO.   Oh misery!
IAGO.   Poor and content is rich, and rich enough,
But riches fineless[188] is as poor as winter
To him that ever fears he shall be poor. 385
Good God, the souls of all my tribe defend
From jealousy!
OTHELLO.   Why, why is this?
Think'st thou I'd make a life of jealousy, 390
To follow still the changes of the moon
With fresh suspicions? No, to be once in doubt
Is once to be resolved.[189] Exchange me for a goat 395
When I shall turn the business of my soul
To such exsufflicate[190] and blown surmises,
Matching thy inference.[191] 'Tis not to make me jealous 400
To say my wife is fair, feeds well, loves company,
Is free of speech, sings, plays, and dances well.
Where virtue is, these are more virtuous. 405
Nor from mine own weak merits will I draw
The smallest fear or doubt of her revolt,
For she had eyes, and chose me. No, Iago, 410
I'll see before I doubt, when I doubt, prove,
And on the proof, there is no more but this—

---

[184]**jealousy:** suspicion
[185]**conceits:** conceives
[186]**observance:** observation
[187]**That . . . wronger:** i.e., the cuckold who hates his wife and knows her falseness is not tormented by suspicious jealousy.

[188]**fineless:** limitless
[189]**to . . . resolved:** whenever I find myself in doubt I at once seek out the truth.
[190]**exsufflicate:** blown up like a bubble
[191]**When . . . inference:** when I shall allow that which concerns me most dearly to be influenced by such trifling suggestions as yours.

415   Away at once with love or jealousy!
IAGO.   I am glad of it, for now I shall have
      reason
      To show the love and duty that I bear
      you
420   With franker spirit. Therefore, as I am
      bound,
      Receive it from me. I speak not yet of
      proof.
      Look to your wife. Observe her well with
425   Cassio.
      Wear your eye thus, not jealous nor
      secure.[192]
      I would not have your free and noble
      nature
430   Out of self-bounty[193] be abused. Look to 't.
      I know our country disposition well.
      In Venice[194] they do let Heaven see the
      pranks
      They dare not show their husbands.
435   Their best conscience
      Is not to leave 't undone, but keep 't
      unknown.
      OTHELLO.   Dost thou say so?
      IAGO.   She did deceive her father, marry-
440   ing you,
      And when she seemed to shake and fear
      your looks,
      She loved them most.
      OTHELLO.   And so she did.
445 IAGO.   Why, go to, then.
      She that so young could give out such a
      seeming
      To seel[195] her father's eyes up close as
      oak—
450   He thought 'twas witchcraft—but I am
      much to blame.

I humbly do beseech you of your pardon
For too much loving you.
OTHELLO.   I am bound to thee forever.
IAGO.   I see this hath a little dashed your   455
      spirits.
OTHELLO.   Not a jot, not a jot.
IAGO.   I' faith, I fear it has.
      I hope you will consider what is spoke
      Comes from my love. But I do see you're   460
      moved.
      I am to pray you not to strain my speech
      To grosser issues nor to larger reach
      Than to suspicion.
OTHELLO.   I will not.   465
IAGO.   Should you do so, my lord,
      My speech should fall into such vile
      success
      As my thoughts aim not at. Cassio's my
      worthy friend.—   470
      My lord, I see you're moved.
OTHELLO.   No, not so much moved.
      I do not think but Desdemona's honest.[196]
IAGO.   Long live she so! And long live you
      to think so!   475
OTHELLO.   And yet, how nature erring
      from itself—
IAGO.   Aye, there's the point. As—to be
      bold with you—
      Not to affect[197] many proposèd matches   480
      Of her own clime, complexion, and
      degree,
      Whereto we see in all things nature
      tends[198]—
      Foh! One may smell in such a will most   485
      rank,[199]
      Foul disproportion, thoughts unnatural.
      But pardon me. I do not in position

---

[192]**secure:** overconfident

[193]**self-bounty:** natural goodness

[194]**In Venice:** Venice was notorious for its loose women; the Venetian courtesans were among the sights of Europe and were much commented upon by travelers.

[195]**seel:** blind

---

[196]**honest:** When applied to Desdemona, "honest" means "chaste," but applied to Iago it has the modern meaning of "open and sincere."

[197]**affect:** be inclined to

[198]**in . . . tends:** i.e., a woman naturally marries a man of her own country, color, and rank.

[199]**will . . . rank:** desire most lustful

Distinctly speak of her, though I may fear
490 Her will, recoiling to her better judgment,
May fall to match[200] you with her country forms,[201]
And happily[202] repent.

OTHELLO.   Farewell, farewell.
495 If more thou dost perceive, let me know more.
Set on thy wife to observe. Leave me, Iago.

IAGO. (*going*),   My lord, I take my leave.

500 OTHELLO.   Why did I marry? This honest creature doubtless
Sees and knows more, much more, than he unfolds.

IAGO. (*returning*).   My lord, I would I
505 might entreat your honor
To scan this thing no further. Leave it to time.
Though it be fit that Cassio have his place,
510 For sure he fills it up with great ability,
Yet if you please to hold him off awhile,
You shall by that perceive him and his means.
Note if your lady strain his
515 entertainment[203]
With any strong or vehement importunity—
Much will be seen in that. In the meantime,
520 Let me be thought too busy in my fears—
As worthy cause I have to fear I am—
And hold her free, I do beseech your Honor.

OTHELLO.   Fear not my government.[204]

525 IAGO.   I once more take my leave. (*Exit.*)

OTHELLO.   This fellow's of exceeding honesty,

And knows all qualities, with a learned spirit,
Of human dealings. If I do prove her   530
haggard,[205]
Though that her jesses[206] were my dear heartstrings,
I'd whistle her off and let her down the wind   535
To prey at fortune.[207] Haply, for I am black
And have not those soft parts of conversation
That chamberers[208] have, or for I am   540
declined
Into the vale of years—yet that's not much—
She's gone, I am abused, and my relief   545
Must be to loathe her. Oh, curse of marriage,
That we can call these delicate creatures ours,
And not their appetites! I had rather be a toad   550
And live upon the vapor of a dungeon
Than keep a corner in the thing I love
For others' uses. Yet, 'tis the plague of great ones,
Prerogatived are they less than the base.   555
'Tis destiny unshunnable, like death.
Even then this forkèd plague[209] is fated to us
When we do quicken.[210] Desdemona comes.   560
(*Re-enter* DESDEMONA *and* EMILIA.)
If she be false, oh, then Heaven mocks itself!

---

[200]**match:** compare
[201]**country forms:** the appearance of her countrymen, i.e., white men
[202]**happily:** haply, by chance
[203]**strain his entertainment:** urge you to receive him
[204]**government:** self-control

[205]**haggard:** a wild hawk
[206]**jesses:** the straps attached to a hawk's legs
[207]**If . . . fortune:** Othello keeps up the imagery of falconry throughout. He means: If I find that she is wild, I'll whistle her off the game and let her go where she will, for she's not worth keeping.
[208]**chamberers:** playboys
[209]**forkèd plague:** i.e., to be a cuckold
[210]**quicken:** stir in our mother's womb

I'll not believe 't.

565 DESDEMONA.   How now, my dear Othello!
Your dinner, and the generous[211] islanders
By you invited, do attend your presence.

OTHELLO.   I am to blame.

570 DESDEMONA.   Why do you speak so faintly?
Are you not well?

OTHELLO.   I have a pain upon my forehead
here.

DESDEMONA.   Faith, that's with watch-
575 ing,[212] 'twill away again.
Let me but bind it hard, within this hour
It will be well.

OTHELLO.   Your napkin[213] is too little,
(*He puts the handkerchief from him, and it*
580 *drops.*)
Let it alone. Come, I'll go in with you.

DESDEMONA.   I am very sorry that you are
not well.

(*Exeunt* OTHELLO *and* DESDEMONA.)

585 EMILIA.   I am glad I have found this napkin.
This was her first remembrance from the
Moor.
My wayward[214] husband hath a hundred
times
590 Wooed me to steal it, but she so loves the
token,
For he conjured[215] her she should ever
keep it,
That she reserves it evermore about her
595 To kiss and talk to. I'll have the work
ta'en out,[216]
And give 't to Iago. What he will do
with it
Heaven knows, not I.
600 I nothing know, but for his fantasy.[217]
(*Re-enter* IAGO.)

IAGO.   How now! What do you here alone?

EMILIA.   Do not you chide, I have a thing
for you.

IAGO.   A thing for me? It is a common
605 thing—

EMILIA.   Ha!

IAGO.   To have a foolish wife.

EMILIA.   Oh, is that all? What will you give
me now
610 For that same handkerchief?

IAGO.   What handkerchief?

EMILIA.   What handkerchief!
Why, that the Moor first gave to
Desdemona,
615 That which so often you did bid me steal.

IAGO.   Hast stol'n it from her?

EMILIA.   No, faith, she let it drop by
negligence,
And, to the advantage, I being here
620 took 't up.
Look, here it is.

IAGO.   A good wench. Give it me.

EMILIA.   What will you do with 't, that you
have been so earnest
625 To have me filch it?

IAGO. (*snatching it*).   Why, what's that to
you?

EMILIA.   If 't be not for some purpose of
import,
630 Give 't me again. Poor lady, she'll run
mad
When she shall lack it.

IAGO.   Be not acknown on 't,[218] I have use
for it.
635 Go, leave me. (*Exit* EMILIA.)
I will in Cassio's lodging lose this napkin,
And let him find it. Trifles light as air
Are to the jealous confirmations strong
As proofs of Holy Writ. This may do
640 something.
The Moor already changes with my
poison.

---

[211]**generous:** noble
[212]**watching:** lack of sleep
[213]**napkin:** handkerchief
[214]**wayward:** unaccountable
[215]**conjured:** begged with an oath
[216]**work . . . out:** pattern copied
[217]**fantasy:** whim

---

[218]**Be . . . 't:** Know nothing about it

645 Dangerous conceits are in their natures poisons,
Which at the first are scarce found to distaste,
But, with a little, act upon the blood,
650 Burn like the mines of sulphur. I did say so.[219]
Look where he comes! (*Re-enter* OTHELLO.)
Not poppy,[220] nor mandragora,[221]
Nor all the drowsy syrups of the world,
655 Shall ever medicine thee to that sweet sleep
Which thou owedst[222] yesterday,
OTHELLO.   Ha! Ha! False to me?
IAGO.   Why, how now, General! No more
660 of that.
OTHELLO.   Avaunt! Be gone! Thou hast set me on the rack.
I swear 'tis better to be much abused
Than but to know 't a little.
665 IAGO.   How now, my lord!
OTHELLO.   What sense had I of her stol'n hours of lust?
I saw 't not, thought it not, it harmed not me.
670 I slept the next night well, was free and merry.
I found not Cassio's kisses on her lips.
He that is robbed, not wanting[223] what is stol'n,
675 Let him not know 't and he's not robbed at all.
IAGO.   I am sorry to hear this.
OTHELLO.   I had been happy if the general camp,

680 Pioners[224] and all, had tasted her sweet body,
So I had nothing known. Oh, now forever
Farewell the tranquil mind! Farewell content
685 Farewell the plumèd troop and the big wars
That make ambition virtue! Oh farewell,
Farewell the neighing steed and the shrill trump,
690 The spirit-stirring drum, the ear-piercing fife,
The royal banner, and all quality,
Pride, pomp, and circumstance of glorious war!
695 And, O you mortal engines,[225] whose rude throats
The immortal Jove's dread clamors counterfeit,
Farewell! Othello's occupation's gone!
700 IAGO.   Is 't possible, my lord?
OTHELLO.   Villain, be sure thou prove my love a whore,
Be sure of it, give me the ocular proof.
Or by the worth of man's eternal soul,
705 Thou hadst been better have been born a dog
Than answer my waked wrath!
IAGO.   Is 't come to this?
OTHELLO.   Make me to see 't, or at the least
710 so prove it
That the probation[226] bear no hinge nor loop
To hang a doubt on, or woe upon thy life!
IAGO.   My noble lord—
715 OTHELLO.   If thou dost slander her and torture me,
Never pray more, abandon all remorse.[227]
On horror's head horrors accumulate,

---

[219]**I . . . so:** As Iago says this, Othello is seen approaching, with all the signs of his agitation outwardly visible.
[220]**poppy:** opium
[221]**mandragora:** called also mandrake—a root used as a drug to bring sleep
[222]**owedst:** owned
[223]**wanting:** missing

---

[224]**Pioners:** pioneers, the lowest type of soldier
[225]**mortal engines:** deadly cannon
[226]**probation:** proof
[227]**remorse:** pity

720 Do deeds to make Heaven weep, all earth
amazed,
For nothing canst thou to damnation add
Greater than that.

    IAGO.   Oh, grace! Oh, Heaven defend me!

725 Are you a man? Have you a soul or
sense?
God be wi' you, take mine office. O
wretched fool,
That livest to make thine honesty a vice!

730 O monstrous world! Take note, take note,
O world,
To be direct and honest is not safe.
I thank you for this profit, and from
hence

735 I'll love no friend, sith[228] love breeds such
offense.

    OTHELLO.   Nay, stay. Thou shouldst be
honest.

    IAGO.   I should be wise, for honesty's a

740 fool,
And loses that it works for.

    OTHELLO.   By the world,
I think my wife be honest, and think she
is not.

745 I think that thou are just, and think thou
art not.
I'll have some proof. Her name, that was
as fresh
As Dian's[229] visage, is now begrimed and

750 black
As mine own face. If there be cords, or
knives,
Poison, or fire, or suffocating streams,
I'll not endure it. Would I were satisfied!

755 IAGO.   I see, sir, you are eaten up with
passion.
I do repent me that I put it to you.
You would be satisfied?

    OTHELLO.   Would! Nay, I will.

760 IAGO.   And may, but how? How satisfied,
my lord?

---

[228]**sith:** since
[229]**Dian:** Diana, goddess of chastity

Would you, the supervisor,[230] grossly
gape on?
Behold her topped?

    OTHELLO.   Death and damnation! Oh!

IAGO.   It were a tedious difficulty, I think, 765
To bring them to that prospect. Damn
them then,
If ever mortal eyes do see them bolster[231]
More than their own! What then? How
then? 770
What shall I say? Where's satisfaction?
It is impossible you should see this,
Were they as prime[232] as goats, as hot as
monkeys,
As salt[233] as wolves in pride,[234] and fools 775
as gross
As ignorance made drunk. But yet I say
If imputation[235] and strong
circumstances,
Which lead directly to the door of truth, 780
Will give you satisfaction, you may have 't.

    OTHELLO.   Give me a living reason she's
disloyal.

IAGO.   I do not like the office.
But sith I am entered in this cause so far, 785
Pricked to 't by foolish honesty and love,
I will go on. I lay with Cassio lately,
And being troubled with a raging tooth,
I could not sleep.
There are a kind of men so loose of soul 790
That in their sleeps will mutter their
affairs.
One of this kind is Cassio.
In sleep I heard him say "Sweet
Desdemona,
Let us be wary, let us hide our loves." 795
And then, sir, would he gripe[236] and
wring my hand,

---

[230]**supervisor:** looker-on
[231]**bolster:** sleep together
[232]**prime:** lustful
[233]**salt:** eager
[234]**pride:** in heat
[235]**imputation:** probability
[236]**gripe:** grip

800 Cry "O sweet creature!" and then kiss
me hard,
As if he plucked up kisses by the roots
That grew upon my lips. Then laid his leg
Over my thigh, and sighed and kissed,
805 and then
Cried "Cursed-fate that gave thee to the
Moor!"
OTHELLO.   Oh, monstrous! Monstrous!
IAGO.   Nay, this was but his dream.
810 OTHELLO.   But this denoted a foregone
conclusion.
'Tis a shrewd doubt,[237] though it be but a
dream.
IAGO.   And this may help to thicken other
815 proofs
That do demonstrate thinly.
OTHELLO.   I'll tear her all to pieces.
IAGO.   Nay, but be wise. Yet we see
nothing done.
820 She may be honest yet. Tell me this:
Have you not sometimes seen a
handkerchief
Spotted with strawberries in your wife's
hand?
825 OTHELLO.   I gave her such a one, 'twas my
first gift.
IAGO.   I know not that. But such a
handkerchief—
I am sure it was your wife's—did I today
830 See Cassio wipe his beard with.
OTHELLO.   If it be that—
IAGO.   If it be that, or any that was hers,
It speaks against her with the other
proofs.
835 OTHELLO.   Oh, that the slave had forty
thousand lives!
One is too poor, too weak, for my
revenge.
Now do I see 'tis true. Look here, Iago,
840 All my fond love thus do I blow to
Heaven—
'Tis gone.

Arise, black Vengeance, from thy hollow
cell!
Yield up, O Love, thy crown and hearted
throne   845
To tyrannous hate! Swell, bosom, with
thy fraught,[238]
For 'tis of aspics'[239] tongues!
IAGO.   Yet be content.
OTHELLO.   Oh, blood, blood, blood!   850
IAGO.   Patience, I say. Your mind perhaps
may change.
OTHELLO.   Never, Iago. Like to the Pontic
Sea,
Whose icy current and compulsive   855
course
Ne'er feels retiring ebb but keeps due on
To the Propontic and the Hellespont;
Even so my bloody thoughts, with
violent pace,   860
Shall ne'er look back, ne'er ebb to
humble love,
Till that a capable[240] and wide revenge
Swallow them up. Now, by yond marble
Heaven,   865
In the due reverence of a sacred vow
(*kneels*)
I here engage my words.
IAGO.   Do not rise yet. (*Kneels.*)
Witness, you ever burning lights above,   870
You elements that clip[241] us round about,
Witness that here Iago doth give up
The execution of his wit, hands, heart,
To wronged Othello's service! Let him
command,   875
And to obey shall be in me remorse,[242]
What bloody business ever. (*They rise.*)
OTHELLO.   I greet thy love,
Not with vain thanks, but with accept-
ance bounteous,   880

---

[238]**fraught:** freight
[239]**aspics':** asps'
[240]**capable:** comprehensive
[241]**clip:** embrace
[242]**remorse:** solemn obligation

---

[237]**shrewd doubt:** bitter suspicion

And will upon the instant put thee to 't.
Within these three days let me hear
thee say
That Cassio's not alive.

885 IAGO.   My friend is dead. 'Tis done at your
request.
But let her live.

OTHELLO.   Damn her, lewd minx! Oh,
damn her!

890 Come, go with me apart. I will
withdraw,
To furnish me with some swift means
of death
For the fair devil. Now art thou my

895 Lieutenant.

IAGO.   I am your own forever. (*Exeunt.*)

SCENE 4. Before the castle.

Enter DESDEMONA, EMILIA, *and* CLOWN.

DESDEMONA.   Do you know, sirrah, where
Lieutenant Cassio lies?

CLOWN.   I dare not say he lies anywhere.

900 DESDEMONA.   Why, man?

CLOWN.   He's a soldier, and for one to say
a soldier lies is stabbing.

DESDEMONA.   Go to. Where lodges he?

CLOWN.   To tell you where he lodges is to

905 tell you where I lie.

DESDEMONA.   Can anything be made
of this?

CLOWN.   I know not where he lodges, and
for me to devise a lodging, and say he

910 lies here or he lies there, were to lie in
mine own throat.

DESDEMONA.   Can you inquire him out and
be edified by report?[243]

CLOWN.   I will catechize the world for him;

915 that is, make questions and by them
answer.

DESDEMONA.   Seek him, bid him come
hither. Tell him I have moved my lord on
his behalf and hope all will be well.

CLOWN.   To do this is within the compass   920
of man's wit, and therefore I will attempt
the doing it. (*Exit.*)

DESDEMONA.   Where should I lose that
handkerchief, Emilia?

EMILIA.   I know not, madam.   925

DESDEMONA.   Believe me, I had rather have
lost my purse
Full of crusados. And, but my noble
Moor
Is true of mind and made of no such   930
baseness
As jealous creatures are, it were enough
To put him to ill thinking.

EMILIA.   Is he not jealous?

DESDEMONA.   Who, he? I think the sun   935
where he was born
Drew all such humors from him.

EMILIA.   Look where he comes.

DESDEMONA.   I will not leave him now till
Cassio   940
Be called to him. (*Enter* OTHELLO.)
How is 't with you, my lord?

OTHELLO.   Well, my good lady. (*Aside*) Oh,
hardness to dissemble!
How do you, Desdemona?   945

DESDEMONA.   Well, my good lord.

OTHELLO.   Give me your hand. This hand
is moist,[244] my lady.

DESDEMONA.   It yet has felt no age nor
known no sorrow.   950

OTHELLO.   This argues fruitfulness and
liberal heart.
Hot, hot, and moist—this hand of yours
requires
A sequester from liberty, fasting and   955
prayer,
Much castigation, exercise devout.

---

[243]**edified by report:** enlightened by the information.
Desdemona speaks with mock pomposity.

[244]**moist:** A hot moist palm was believed to show
desire.

For here's a young and sweating devil here,

960   That commonly rebels. 'Tis a good hand,
A frank one.

DESDEMONA.   You may indeed say so,
For 'twas that hand that gave away my heart.

965 OTHELLO.   A liberal[245] hand. The hearts of
old gave hands,
But our new heraldry is hands, not hearts.[246]

DESDEMONA.   I cannot speak of this. Come
970   now, your promise.

OTHELLO.   What promise, chuck?[247]

DESDEMONA.   I have sent to bid Cassio
come speak with you.

OTHELLO.   I have a salt and sorry rheum
975   offends me.
Lend me thy handkerchief.

DESDEMONA.   Here, my lord.

OTHELLO.   That which I gave you.

DESDEMONA.   I have it not about me.

980 OTHELLO.   Not?

DESDEMONA.   No indeed, my lord.

OTHELLO.   That's a fault. That handkerchief
Did an Egyptian to my mother give.
She was a charmer, and could almost read
985 The thoughts of people. She told her
while she kept it
'Twould make her amiable and subdue
my father
Entirely to her love, but if she lost it
990 Or made a gift of it, my father's eye
Should hold her loathèd and his spirits
should hunt
After new fancies. She dying gave it me,

And bid me, when my fate would have   995
me wive,
To give it her. I did so. And take heed on 't,
Make it a darling like your precious eye.
To lose 't or give 't away were such
perdition   1000
As nothing else could match.

DESDEMONA.   Is 't possible?

OTHELLO.   'Tis true. There's magic in the
web of it.
A sibyl that had numbered in the world   1005
The sun to course two hundred
compasses
In her prophetic fury sewed the work.
The worms were hallowed that did breed
the silk,   1010
And it was dyed in mummy which the
skillful
Conserved[248] of maiden's hearts.

DESDEMONA.   Indeed! Is 't true?

OTHELLO.   Most veritable, therefore look   1015
to 't well.

DESDEMONA.   Then would God that I had
never seen 't.

OTHELLO.   Ha! Wherefore?

DESDEMONA.   Why do you speak so start-   1020
ingly and rash?

OTHELLO.   Is 't lost? Is 't gone? Speak, is it
out o' the way?

DESDEMONA.   Heaven bless us!

OTHELLO.   Say you?   1025

DESDEMONA.   It is not lost, but what an if it
were?

OTHELLO.   How!

DESDEMONA.   I say it is not lost.

OTHELLO.   Fetch 't, let me see it.   1030

DESDEMONA.   Why, so I can, sir, but I will
not now.
This is a trick to put me from my suit.
Pray you let Cassio be received again.

OTHELLO.   Fetch me the handkerchief. My   1035
mind misgives.

---

[245]**liberal:** overgenerous
[246]**The . . . hearts:** Once love and deeds went
together, but now it is all deeds (i.e., faithlessness)
and no love.
[247]**chuck:** A term of affection, but not the kind of word
with which a person of Othello's dignity would normally
address his wife. He is beginning to treat her with
contemptuous familiarity.

---

[248]**Conserved:** prepared

DESDEMONA. Come, come,
    You'll never meet a more sufficient man.
OTHELLO. The handkerchief!
DESDEMONA. I pray talk me of Cassio.
1040 OTHELLO. The handkerchief!
DESDEMONA. A man that all this time
    Hath founded his good fortunes on your
    love,
    Shared dangers with you—
1045 OTHELLO. The handkerchief!
DESDEMONA. In sooth, you are to blame.
OTHELLO. Away! (*Exit.*)
EMILIA. Is not this man jealous?
DESDEMONA. I ne'er saw this before.
1050   Sure there's some wonder in this
    handkerchief.
    I am most unhappy in the loss of it.
EMILIA. 'Tis not a year or two shows
    us a man.[249]
1055   They are all but stomachs and we all but
    food.
    They eat us hungerly, and when they
    are full
    They belch us. Look you, Cassio and my
1060   husband.
    (*Enter* CASSIO *and* IAGO.)
IAGO. There is no other way, 'tis she
    must do 't.
    And, lo, the happiness![250] Go and impór-
1065   tune her.
DESDEMONA. How now, good Cassio!
    What's the news with you?
CASSIO. Madam, my former suit. I do
    beseech you
1070   That by your virtuous means I may again
    Exist, and be a member of his love
    Whom I with all the office of my heart
    Entirely honor. I would not be delayed.
    If my offense be of such mortal kind

    That nor my service past nor present 1075
    sorrows
    Nor purposed merit in futurity
    Can ransom me into his love again,
    But to know so must be my benefit.
    So shall I clothe me in a forced content 1080
    And shut myself up in some other course
    To Fortune's aims.
DESDEMONA. Alas, thrice-gentle Cassio!
    My advocation[251] is not now in tune.
    My lord is not my lord, nor should I 1085
    know him
    Were he in favor as in humor altered.
    So help me every spirit sanctified,
    As I have spoken for you all my best
    And stood within the blank[252] of his 1090
    displeasure
    For my free speech! You must awhile be
    patient.
    What I can do I will, and more I will
    Than for myself I dare. Let that 1095
    suffice you.
IAGO. Is my lord angry?
EMILIA. He went hence but now,
    And certainly in strange unquietness.
IAGO. Can he be angry? I have seen the 1100
    cannon
    When it hath blown his ranks into the air,
    And, like the Devil, from his very arm
    Puffed his own brother, and can he be
    angry? 1105
    Something of moment then. I will go
    meet him.
    There's matter in 't indeed if he be angry.
DESDEMONA. I prithee do so. (*Exit* IAGO.)
    Something sure of state, 1110
    Either from Venice, or some unhatched
    practice
    Made demonstrable[253] here in Cyprus
    to him,

---

[249]**Tis . . . man:** It does not take a couple of years to discover the nature of a man; i.e., he soon shows his real nature.
[250]**And . . . happiness:** what good luck, here she is

[251]**advocation:** advocacy
[252]**blank:** aim
[253]**unhatched . . . demonstrable:** some plot, not yet matured, which has been revealed

1115 Hath puddled his clear spirit. And in such cases
Men's natures wrangle with inferior things,
Though great ones are their object. 'Tis
1120 even so,
For let our finger ache and it indues
Our other healthful members even to that sense
Of pain. Nay, we must think men are
1125 not gods,
Nor of them look for such observancy
As fits the bridal.[254] Beshrew me much, Emilia,
I was, unhandsome warrior[255] as I am,
1130 Arraigning his unkindness with my soul,
But now I find I had suborned the witness,
And he's indicted falsely.

EMILIA. Pray Heaven it be state matters, as
1135 you think,
And no conception nor no jealous toy[256]
Concerning you.

DESDEMONA. Alas the day, I never gave him cause!

1140 EMILIA. But jealous souls will not be answered so.
They are not ever jealous for the cause,
But jealous for they are jealous. 'Tis a monster
1145 Begot upon itself, born on itself.

DESDEMONA. Heaven keep that monster from Othello's mind!

EMILIA. Lady, amen.

DESDEMONA. I will go seek him. Cassio,
1150 walk hereabout.
If I do find him fit, I'll move your suit,
And seek to effect it to my uttermost.

CASSIO. I humbly thank your ladyship.

254**bridal:** honeymoon
255**unhandsome warrior:** clumsy soldier. Desdemona continually thinks of herself as Othello's companion in arms. Cf. 1.3.248 ff.
256**jealous toy:** silly suspicion

(*Exeunt* DESDEMONA *and* EMILIA. *Enter* 1155
BIANCA.)

BIANCA. Save you, friend Cassio!

CASSIO. What make you from home?
How is it with you, my most fair Bianca?
I' faith, sweet love, I was coming to your 1160
house.

BIANCA. And I was going to your lodging, Cassio.
What, keep a week away? Seven days and nights?
1165
Eightscore eight hours? And lovers' absent hours,
More tedious than the dial eightscore times?
Oh, weary reckoning! 1170

CASSIO. Pardon me, Bianca.
I have this while with leaden thoughts been pressed,
But I shall in a more continuate time
Strike off this score of absence. Sweet 1175
Bianca,
(*Giving her* DESDEMONA'S *handkerchief*)
Take me this work out.

BIANCA. O Cassio, whence came this?
This is some token from a newer friend. 1180
To the felt absence now I feel a cause.
Is 't come to this? Well, well.

CASSIO. Go to, woman!
Throw your vile guesses in the Devil's teeth,
1185
From whence you have them. You are jealous now
That this is from some mistress, some remembrance.
No, by my faith, Bianca. 1190

BIANCA. Why, whose is it?

CASSIO. I know not, sweet. I found it in my chamber.
I like the work well. Ere it be demanded—
1195
As like enough it will—I'd have it copied.
Take it, and do 't, and leave me for this time.

BIANCA.   Leave you! Wherefore?
1200 CASSIO.   I do attend here on the General,
    And think it no addition,[257] nor my wish
    To have him see me womaned.[258]
    BIANCA.   Why, I pray you?
    CASSIO.   Not that I love you not.
1205 BIANCA.   But that you do not love me.
    I pray you bring me on the way a little,
    And say if I shall see you soon at night.
    CASSIO.   'Tis but a little way that I can
    bring you,
1210 For I attend here. But I'll see you soon.
    BIANCA.   'Tis very good, I must be circum-
    stanced.[259] (*Exeunt.*)

────────(ACT 4)────────

SCENE 1. Cyprus. Before the castle.

Enter OTHELLO *and* IAGO.

1 IAGO.   Will you think so?
    OTHELLO.   Think so, Iago!
    IAGO.   What,
    To kiss in private?
5 OTHELLO.   An unauthorized kiss.
    IAGO.   Or to be naked with her friend
    in bed
        An hour or more, not meaning any
        harm?
10 OTHELLO.   Naked in bed, Iago, and not
    mean harm!
        It is hypocrisy against the Devil.
        They that mean virtuously and yet do so,
        The Devil their virtue tempts and they
15   tempt Heaven.
    IAGO.   So they do nothing, 'tis a venial[260]
    slip.
        But if I give my wife a handkerchief—
    OTHELLO.   What then?
20 IAGO.   Why, then, 'tis hers, my lord, and
    being hers,

She may, I think, bestow 't on any man.
OTHELLO.   She is protectress of her honor
    too.
    May she give that?   25
IAGO.   Her honor is an essence that's
    not seen.
    They have it very oft that have it not.
    But for the handkerchief—
OTHELLO.   By Heaven, I would most   30
    gladly have forgot it.
    Thou said'st—oh, it comes o'er my
    memory,
    As doth the raven o'er the infected house
    Boding to all—he had my handkerchief.   35
IAGO.   Aye, what of that?
OTHELLO.   That's not so good now.
IAGO.   What
    If I had said I had seen him do you
    wrong?   40
    Or heard him say—as knaves be such
    abroad,
    Who having, by their own importunate
    suit,
    Or voluntary dotage of some mistress,   45
    Convincèd or supplied[261] them, cannot
    choose
    But they must blab—
OTHELLO.   Hath he said anything?
IAGO.   He hath, my lord, but be you well   50
    assured,
    No more than he'll unswear.
OTHELLO.   What hath he said?
IAGO.   Faith, that he did—I know not what
    he did.   55
OTHELLO.   What? What?
IAGO.   Lie—
OTHELLO.   With her?
IAGO.   With her, on her, what you will.
OTHELLO.   Lie[262] with her! Lie on her!—We   60
    say lie on her when they belie her.—Lie

───────────

[257]**addition:** honor
[258]**womaned:** with a woman
[259]**circumstanced:** put off
[260]**venial:** pardonable

[261]**Convincèd or supplied:** overcome or satisfied
their desires
[262]**Lie . . . devil:** Othello breaks into incoherent
muttering before he falls down in a fit.

with her. 'Zounds, that's fulsome![263]
Handkerchief—confessions—
handkerchief!—To confess, and be
65 hanged for his labor. First to be hanged,
and then to confess. I tremble at it. Nature
would not invest herself in such
shadowing passion without some
instruction.[264] It is not words that shake
70 me thus. Pish! Noses, ears, and lips. Is 't
possible?—Confess?—Handkerchief?—
Oh, devil! (*Falls in a trance.*)
IAGO.   Work on,
My medicine, work! Thus credulous fools
75 are caught,
And many worthy and chaste dames
even thus,
All guiltless, meet reproach. What ho!
My lord!
80 My lord, I say! Othello! (*Enter* CASSIO.)
How now, Cassio!
CASSIO.   What's the matter?
IAGO.   My lord is fall'n into an epilepsy.
This is his second fit, he had one yesterday.
85 CASSIO.   Rub him about the temples.
IAGO.   No, forbear,
The lethargy[265] must have his quiet
course.
If not, he foams at mouth and by and by
90 Breaks out to savage madness. Look, he
stirs.
Do you withdraw yourself a little while,
He will recover straight. When he is
gone,
95 I would on great occasion speak with
you. (*Exit* CASSIO.)
How is it, General? Have you not hurt
your head?[266]
OTHELLO.   Dost thou mock me?

IAGO.   I mock you! No, by Heaven.   100
Would you would bear your fortune like
a man!
OTHELLO.   A hornèd man's a monster and
a beast.
IAGO.   There's many a beast, then, in a   105
populous city,
And many a civil monster.
OTHELLO.   Did he confess it?
IAGO.   Good sir, be a man.
Think every bearded fellow that's but   110
yoked[267]
May draw with you.[268] There's millions
now alive
That nightly lie in those unproper beds
Which they dare swear peculiar.[269] Your   115
case is better.
Oh, 'tis the spite of Hell, the Fiend's
arch-mock,
To lip[270] a wanton in a secure couch[271]
And to suppose her chaste! No, let me   120
know,
And knowing what I am, I know what
she shall be.
OTHELLO.   Oh, thou art wise, 'tis certain.
IAGO.   Stand you awhile apart,   125
Confine yourself but in a patient list.[272]
Whilst you were here o'erwhelmèd with
your grief—
A passion most unsuiting such a
man—   130
Cassio came hither. I shifted him away,
And laid good 'scuse upon your
ecstasy,[273]
Bade him anon return and here speak
with me,   135

---

[263]**fulsome:** disgusting
[264]**Nature . . . instruction:** Nature would not fill me
with such overwhelming emotion unless there was
some cause.
[265]**lethargy:** epileptic fit
[266]**Have . . . head:** With brutal cynicism Iago asks
whether Othello is suffering from cuckold's headache.

[267]**yoked:** married
[268]**draw with you:** be your yoke fellow
[269]**That . . . peculiar:** that lie nightly in beds which they
believe are their own but which others have shared
[270]**lip:** kiss
[271]**secure couch:** lit., a carefree bed; i.e., a bed which
has been used by the wife's lover, but secretly
[272]**patient list:** confines of patience
[273]**ecstasy:** fit

The which he promised. Do but encave
yourself,
And mark the fleers, the gibes, and
notable scorns,
140 That dwell in every region of his face.
For I will make him tell the tale anew,
Where, how, how oft, how long ago, and
when
He hath and is again to cope[274] your wife.
145 I say but mark his gesture. Marry,
patience,
Or I shall say you are all in all in spleen,
And nothing of a man.
OTHELLO.   Dost thou hear, Iago?
150 I will be found most cunning in my
patience,
But—dost thou hear?—most bloody.
IAGO.   That's not amiss.
But yet keep time in all. Will you with-
155 draw? (OTHELLO *retires*.)
Now will I question Cassio of Bianca,
A housewife[275] that by selling her desires
Buys herself bread and clothes. It is a
creature
160 That dotes on Cassio, as 'tis the strum-
pet's plague
To beguile many and be beguiled by one.
He, when he hears of her, cannot refrain
From the excess of laughter. Here he
165 comes. (*Re-enter* CASSIO.)
As he shall smile, Othello shall go mad,
And his unbookish[276] jealousy must
construe
Poor Cassio's smiles, gestures, and light
170 behavior
Quite in the wrong. How do you now,
Lieutenant?
CASSIO.   The worser that you give me the
addition[277]
175 Whose want even kills me.

IAGO.   Ply Desdemona well, and you are
sure on 't.
Now, if this suit lay in Bianca's power,
How quickly should you speed!
CASSIO.   Alas, poor caitiff![278]   180
OTHELLO.   Look how he laughs already!
IAGO.   I never knew a woman love man so.
CASSIO.   Alas, poor rogue! I think i' faith,
she loves me.
OTHELLO.   Now he denies it faintly and   185
laughs it out.
IAGO.   Do you hear, Cassio?
OTHELLO.   Now he impórtunes him
To tell it o'er. Go to. Well said, well said.
IAGO.   She gives it out that you shall   190
marry her.
Do you intend to?
CASSIO.   Ha, ha, ha!
OTHELLO.   Do you triumph, Roman?[279] Do
you triumph?   195
CASSIO.   I marry her! What, a customer![280] I
prithee bear some charity to my wit. Do
not think it so unwholesome. Ha, ha, ha!
OTHELLO.   So, so, so, so. They laugh
that win.   200
IAGO.   Faith, the cry goes that you shall
marry her.
CASSIO.   Prithee say true.
IAGO.   I am a very villain else.
OTHELLO.   Have you scored[281] me? Well.   205
CASSIO.   This is the monkey's own giving
out. She is persuaded I will marry her
out of her own love and flattery, not out
of my promise.
OTHELLO.   Iago beckons me, now he begins   210
the story.
CASSIO.   She was here even now. She
haunts me in every place. I was the other

---

[274]**cope:** encounter
[275]**housewife:** hussy
[276]**unbookish:** unlearned
[277]**addition:** title (Lieutenant) which he has lost

---

[278]**caitiff:** wretch
[279]**triumph, Roman:** The word "triumph" suggests
"Roman" because the Romans celebrated their victories with triumphs, elaborate shows, and processions.
[280]**customer:** harlot
[281]**scored:** marked, as with a blow from a whip

215 day talking on the sea bank with certain Venetians, and thither comes the bauble, and, by this hand, she falls me thus about my neck—

OTHELLO.   Crying "O dear Cassio!" as it were. His gesture imports it.

220 CASSIO.   So hangs and lolls and weeps upon me, so hales and pulls me. Ha, ha, ha!

OTHELLO.   Now he tells how she plucked him to my chamber. Oh, I see that nose of yours, but not that dog I shall throw it to.

225 CASSIO.   Well, I must leave her company.

IAGO.   Before me![282] Look where she comes.

CASSIO.   'Tis such another fitchew![283] Marry, a perfumed one.

230 (*Enter* BIANCA.)

What do you mean by this haunting of me?

BIANCA.   Let the Devil and his dam haunt you! What did you mean by that same handkerchief you gave me even now? I

235 was a fine fool to take it. I must take out the work? A likely piece of work, that you should find it in your chamber and not know who left it there! This is some minx's token, and I must take out the

240 work? There, give it your hobbyhorse. Wheresoever you had it, I'll take out no work on 't.

CASSIO.   How now, my sweet Bianca! How now! How now!

245 OTHELLO.   By Heaven, that should be my handkerchief!

BIANCA.   An[284] you'll come to supper tonight, you may. An you will not, come when you are next prepared for. (*Exit.*)

250 IAGO.   After her, after her.

CASSIO.   Faith, I must, she'll rail i' the street else.

IAGO.   Will you sup there?

CASSIO.   Faith, I intend so.

IAGO.   Well, I may chance to see you, for I 255 would very fain speak with you.

CASSIO.   Prithee, come, will you?

IAGO.   Go to. Say no more. (*Exit* CASSIO.)

OTHELLO (*advancing*).   How shall I murder him, Iago? 260

IAGO.   Did you perceive how he laughed at his vice?

OTHELLO.   Oh, Iago!

IAGO.   And did you see the handkerchief?

OTHELLO.   Was that mine? 265

IAGO.   Yours, by this hand. And to see how he prizes the foolish woman your wife? She gave it him, and he hath given it his whore.

OTHELLO.   I would have him nine years 270 a-killing. A fine woman! A fair woman! A sweet woman!

IAGO.   Nay, you must forget that.

OTHELLO.   Aye, let her rot, and perish, and be damned tonight, for she shall not live. 275 No, my heart is turned to stone, I strike it and it hurts my hand. Oh, the world hath not a sweeter creature. She might lie by an emperor's side, and command him tasks. 280

IAGO.   Nay, that's not your way.[285]

OTHELLO.   Hang her! I do but say what she is, so delicate with her needle, an admirable musician—oh, she will sing the savageness out of a bear—of so high 285 and plenteous wit and invention—

IAGO.   She's the worse for all this.

OTHELLO.   Oh, a thousand times. And then, of so gentle a condition!

IAGO.   Aye, too gentle. 290

OTHELLO.   Nay, that's certain. But yet the pity of it, Iago! O Iago, the pity of it, Iago!

IAGO.   If you are so fond over her iniquity, give her patent to offend, for if it touch not you, it comes near nobody. 295

OTHELLO.   I will chop her into messes. Cuckold me!

---

[282]**Before me:** by my soul
[283]**fitchew:** polecat
[284]**An:** if

[285]**Nay . . . way:** i.e., don't get soft thoughts about her

IAGO.   Oh, 'tis foul in her.

OTHELLO.   With mine officer!

300 IAGO.   That's fouler.

OTHELLO.   Get me some poison, Iago, this night. I'll not expostulate with her, lest her body and beauty unprovide my mind again. This night, Iago.

305 IAGO.   Do it not with poison, strangle her in her bed, even the bed she hath contaminated.

OTHELLO.   Good, good. The justice of it pleases. Very good.

310 IAGO.   And for Cassio, let me be his undertaker.[286]
You shall hear more by midnight.

OTHELLO.   Excellent good. (*A trumpet within.*) What trumpet is that same?

315 IAGO.   Something from Venice, sure. 'Tis Lodovico
Come from the Duke. And see, your wife is with him.
(*Enter* LODOVICO, DESDEMONA, *and*
320   ATTENDANTS.)

LODOVICO.   God save the worthy General!

OTHELLO.   With all my heart, sir.

LODOVICO.   The Duke and Senators of Venice greet you. (*Gives him a letter.*)

325 OTHELLO.   I kiss the instrument of their pleasures.
(*Opens the letter, and reads.*)

DESDEMONA.   And what's the news, good Cousin Lodovico?

330 IAGO.   I am very glad to see you, signior. Welcome to Cyprus.

LODOVICO.   I thank you. How does Lieutenant Cassio?

IAGO.   Lives, sir.

335 DESDEMONA.   Cousin, there's fall'n between him and my lord
An unkind breach, but you shall make all well.

OTHELLO.   Are you sure of that?

DESDEMONA.   My lord?   340

OTHELLO   (*reads*). "This fail you not to do, as you will—"

LODOVICO.   He did not call, he's busy in the paper.
Is there division 'twixt my lord and   345
Cassio?

DESDEMONA.   A most unhappy one.
I would do much
To atone[287] them, for the love I bear to
Cassio.   350

OTHELLO.   Fire and brimstone!

DESDEMONA.   My lord?

OTHELLO.   Are you wise?[288]

DESDEMONA.   What, is he angry?

LODOVICO.   Maybe the letter moved him,   355
For, as I think, they do command him home,
Deputing Cassio in his government.

DESDEMONA.   By my troth, I am glad on 't.

OTHELLO.   Indeed!   360

DESDEMONA.   My lord?

OTHELLO.   I am glad to see you mad.

DESDEMONA.   Why, sweet Othello?

OTHELLO.   Devil! (*Striking her.*)

DESDEMONA.   I have not deserved this.   365

LODOVICO.   My lord, this would not be believed in Venice
Though I should swear I saw 't. 'Tis very much.
Make her amends, she weeps.   370

OTHELLO.   O devil, devil!
If that the earth could teem with a woman's tears,
Each drop she falls would prove a crocodile.[289]   375

---

[286]**be his undertaker:** undertake to manage his business. In Shakespeare's plays the word does *not* mean "mortician."

[287]**atone:** reconcile

[288]**Are you wise:** i.e., in saying you bear love to Cassio

[289]**If . . . crocodile:** If the earth could breed from woman's tears, each tear that she lets fall would become a crocodile. It was believed that the crocodile would cry and sob to attract the sympathetic passer-by, who was then snapped up.

Out of my sight!

DESDEMONA.   I will not stay to offend you.
(*Going*.)

LODOVICO.   Truly, an obedient lady.

380   I do beseech your lordship, call her back.

OTHELLO.   Mistress!

DESDEMONA.   My lord?

OTHELLO.   What would you with her, sir?

LODOVICO.   Who, I, my lord?

385   OTHELLO.   Aye, you did wish that I would
make her turn.
Sir, she can turn and turn, and yet go on
And turn again. And she can weep, sir,
weep.

390   And she's obedient, as you say, obedient,
Very obedient.—Proceed you in your
tears—
Concerning this, sir—oh, well-painted
passion!—

395   I am commanded home.—Get you away.
I'll send for you anon.—Sir, I obey the
mandate,
And will return to Venice.—Hence,
avaunt! (*Exit* DESDEMONA.)

400   Cassio shall have my place. And, sir,
tonight,
I do entreat that we may sup together.
You are welcome, sir, to Cyprus.—Goats
and monkeys! (*Exit*.)

405   LODOVICO.   Is this the noble Moor whom
our full Senate
Call all-in-all sufficient? This the nature
Whom passion could not shake? Whose
solid virtue

410   The shot of accident nor dart of chance
Could neither graze nor pierce?

IAGO.   He is much changed.

LODOVICO.   Are his wits safe? Is he not
light of brain?

415   IAGO.   He's that he is. I may not breathe
my censure
What he might be. If what he might he
is not,
I would to Heaven he were!

420   LODOVICO.   What, strike his wife!

IAGO.   Faith, that was not so well, yet
would I knew
That stroke would prove the worst!

LODOVICO.   Is it his use?
Or did the letters work upon his blood,   425
And new-create this fault?

IAGO.   Alas, alas!
It is not honesty in me to speak
What I have seen and known. You shall
observe him,   430
And his own courses will denote him so
That I may save my speech. Do but
go after,
And mark how he continues.

LODOVICO.   I am sorry that I am deceived   435
in him. (*Exeunt*.)

SCENE 2. *A room in the castle.*

Enter OTHELLO *and* EMILIA.

OTHELLO.   You have seen nothing, then?

EMILIA.   Nor ever heard, nor ever did
suspect.

OTHELLO.   Yes, you have seen Cassio and   440
she together.

EMILIA.   But then I saw no harm, and then
I heard
Each syllable that breath made up
between them.   445

OTHELLO.   What, did they never whisper?

EMILIA.   Never, my lord.

OTHELLO.   Nor send you out o' the way?

EMILIA.   Never.

OTHELLO.   To fetch her fan, her gloves, her   450
mask, nor nothing?

EMILIA.   Never, my lord.

OTHELLO.   That's strange.

EMILIA.   I durst, my lord, to wager she is
honest,   455
Lay down my soul at stake. If you think
other,
Remove your thought, it doth abuse your
bosom.
If any wretch have put this in your   460
head,

Let Heaven requite it with the serpent's
curse!
For if she be not honest, chaste, and true,
465 There's no man happy, the purest of their
wives
Is foul as slander.
OTHELLO.   Bid her come hither. Go. (*Exit*
EMILIA.)
470 She says enough. Yet she's a simple bawd
That cannot say as much. This is a subtle
whore,
A closet lock and key of villainous
secrets.
475 And yet she'll kneel and pray, I have seen
her do 't.
(*Enter* DESDEMONA *with* EMILIA.)
DESDEMONA.   My lord, what is your will?
OTHELLO.   Pray, chuck, come hither.
480 DESDEMONA.   What is your pleasure?
OTHELLO.   Let me see your eyes.
Look in my face.
DESDEMONA.   What horrible fancy's this?
OTHELLO (*to* EMILIA).   Some of your
485 function,[290] mistress.
Leave procreants alone and shut the
door,
Cough, or cry hem, if anybody come.
Your mystery,[291] your mystery. Nay,
490 dispatch. (*Exit* EMILIA.)
DESDEMONA.   Upon my knees, what doth
your speech import?
I understand a fury in your words,
But not the words.
495 OTHELLO.   Why, what art thou?
DESDEMONA.   Your wife, my lord, your
true and loyal wife.
OTHELLO.   Come, swear it, damn thyself,
Lest, being like one of Heaven,[292] the
500 devils themselves

---

[290]**Some . . . function:** Get about your business, i.e.,
prostitution. Othello pretends that Emilia is keeper of a
brothel and Desdemona one of the women.
[291]**mystery:** profession
[292]**being . . . Heaven:** because you look like an angel

Should fear to seize thee. Therefore be
double-damned.
Swear thou art honest.
DESDEMONA.   Heaven doth truly know it.
OTHELLO.   Heaven truly knows that thou   505
art false as Hell.
DESDEMONA.   To whom, my lord? With
whom? How am I false?
OTHELLO.   O Desdemona! Away! Away!
Away!   510
DESDEMONA.   Alas the heavy day! Why
do you weep!
Am I the motive of these tears, my lord?
If haply you my father do suspect
An instrument of this your calling-back,   515
Lay not your blame on me. If you have
lost him,
Why, I have lost him too.
OTHELLO.   Had it pleased Heaven
To try me with affliction, had they rained   520
All kinds of sores and shames on my
bare head,
Steeped me in poverty to the very lips,
Given to captivity me and my utmost
hopes,   525
I should have found in some place of
my soul
A drop of patience. But, alas, to make me
A fixèd figure for the time of scorn
To point his slow unmoving finger at!   530
Yet could I bear that too, well, very well.
But there where I have garnered up my
heart,
Where either I must live or bear no life,
The fountain from the which my current   535
runs
Or else dries up—to be discarded thence!
Or keep it as a cistern for foul toads
To knot and gender in! Turn thy com-
plexion there,   540
Patience, thou young and rose-lipped
cherubin—
Aye, there, look grim as Hell!
DESDEMONA.   I hope my noble lord
esteems me honest.   545

OTHELLO.   Oh, aye, as summer flies are in the shambles,[293]
That quicken even with blowing,[294] O thou weed,
550 Who art so lovely fair and smell'st so sweet
That the sense aches at thee, would thou hadst ne'er been born!
DESDEMONA.   Alas, what ignorant sin have
555 I committed?
OTHELLO.   Was this fair paper,[295] this most goodly book,
Made to write "whore" upon? What committed!
560 Committed! O thou public commoner![296]
I should make very forges of my cheeks
That would to cinders burn up modesty
Did I but speak thy deeds. What committed!
565 Heaven stops the nose at it, and the moon winks.
The bawdy wind, that kisses all it meets,
Is hushed within the hollow mine of earth
570 And will not hear it. What committed!
Impudent strumpet!
DESDEMONA.   By Heaven, you do me wrong.
OTHELLO.   Are not you a strumpet?
575 DESDEMONA.   No, as I am a Christian.
If to preserve this vessel for my lord
From any other foul unlawful touch
Be not to be a strumpet, I am none.
OTHELLO.   What, not a whore?
580 DESDEMONA.   No, as I shall be saved.
OTHELLO.   Is 't possible?
DESDEMONA.   Oh, Heaven forgive us!
OTHELLO.   I cry you mercy, then.

I took you for that cunning whore of Venice 585
That married with Othello. (*Raising his voice*) You mistress,
That have the office opposite to Saint Peter,
And keep the gate of Hell! (*Re-enter* 590
EMILIA.)
You, you, aye, you!
We have done our course, there's money for your pains.
I pray you turn the key, and keep our 595
counsel. (*Exit.*)
EMILIA.   Alas, what does this gentleman conceive?
How do you, madam? How do you, my good lady? 600
DESDEMONA.   Faith, half-asleep.
EMILIA.   Good madam, what's the matter with my lord?
DESDEMONA.   With who?
EMILIA.   Why, with my lord, madam. 605
DESDEMONA.   Who is thy lord?
EMILIA.   He that is yours, sweet lady.
DESDEMONA.   I have none. Do not talk to me, Emilia.
I cannot weep, nor answer have I none 610
But what should go by water.[297] Prithee tonight
Lay on my bed my wedding sheets. Remember,
And call thy husband hither. 615
EMILIA.   Here's a change indeed! (*Exit.*)
DESDEMONA.   'Tis meet I should be used so, very meet.
How have I been behaved that he might stick 620
The small'st opinion on my least misuse?[298]
(*Re-enter* EMILIA *with* IAGO.)
IAGO.   What is your pleasure, madam? How is 't with you? 625

---

[293]**shambles:** slaughterhouse
[294]**quicken . . . blowing:** come to life as soon as the eggs are laid
[295]**fair paper:** i.e., her white body
[296]**public commoner:** one who offers herself to all comers

[297]**go by water:** be expressed in tears
[298]**misuse:** mistake

DESDEMONA.   I cannot tell. Those that do teach young babes
Do it with gentle means and easy tasks.
630   He might have chid me so, for, in good faith,
I am a child to chiding.
IAGO.   What's the matter, lady?
EMILIA.   Alas, Iago, my lord hath so bewhored her,
635   Thrown such despite and heavy terms upon her,
As true hearts cannot bear.
DESDEMONA.   Am I that name, Iago?
IAGO.   What name, fair lady?
640   DESDEMONA.   Such as she says my lord did say I was.
EMILIA.   He called her whore. A beggar in his drink
Could not have laid such terms upon
645   his callet.
IAGO.   Why did he so?
DESDEMONA.   I do not know. I am sure I am none such.
IAGO.   Do not weep, do not weep. Alas
650   the day!
EMILIA.   Hath she forsook so many noble matches,
Her father and her country and her friends,
To be called whore? Would it not make
655   one weep?
DESDEMONA.   It is my wretched fortune.
IAGO.   Beshrew him for 't!
How comes this trick upon him?
DESDEMONA.   Nay, Heaven doth know.
660   EMILIA.   I will be hanged if some eternal villain,
Some busy and insinuating rogue,
Some cogging, cozening slave, to get some office,
665   Have not devised this slander. I'll be hanged else.
IAGO.   Fie, there is no such man, it is impossible.
DESDEMONA.   If any such there be, heaven
670   pardon him!

EMILIA.   A halter pardon him! And Hell gnaw his bones!
Why should he call her whore? Who keeps her company?
675   What place? What time? What form? What likelihood?
The Moor's abused by some most villain-ous knave,
Some base notorious knave, some scurvy
680   fellow.
O Heaven, that such companions[299] Thou'dst unfold,[300]
And put in every honest hand a whip
To lash the rascals naked through the
685   world
Even from the east to the west!
IAGO.   Speak withindoor.[301]
EMILIA.   Oh, fie upon them! Some such squire he was
690   That turned your wit the seamy side without,
And made you to suspect me with the Moor.
IAGO.   You are a fool. Go to.[302]
695   DESDEMONA.   O good Iago,
What shall I do to win my lord again?
Good friend, go to him, for, by this light of Heaven,
I know not how I lost him. Here I kneel.
700   If e'er my will did trespass 'gainst his love
Either in discourse of thought or actual deed,
Or that mine eyes, mine ears, or any sense
705   Delighted them in any other form,
Or that I do not yet, and ever did,
And ever will, though he do shake me off
To beggarly divorcement, love him dearly,

---

[299]**companions:** low creatures
[300]**unfold:** bring to light
[301]**Speak withindoor:** Don't shout so loud that all the street will hear you.
[302]**Go to:** an expression of derision

710 Comfort forswear me! Unkindness may
do much,
And his unkindness may defeat my life,
But never taint my love. I cannot say
"whore,"
715 It doth abhor me now I speak the word.
To do the act that might the addition[303] earn
Not the world's mass of vanity[304] could
make me.

IAGO.   I pray you be content, 'tis but his
720 humor.
The business of the state does him
offense,
And he does chide with you.

DESDEMONA.   If 'twere no other—

725 IAGO.   'Tis but so, I warrant. (*Trumpets
within*.)
Hark how these instruments summon to
supper!
The messengers of Venice stay the meat.[305]
730 Go in, and weep not, all things shall be
well.
(*Exeunt* DESDEMONA *and* EMILIA. *Enter*
RODERIGO.)
How now, Roderigo!

735 RODERIGO.   I do not find that thou dealest
justly with me.

IAGO.   What in the contrary.

RODERIGO.   Every day thou laffest me with
some device, Iago, and rather, as it seems
740 to me now, keepest from me all conve-
niency than suppliest me with the least
advantage of hope. I will indeed no
longer endure it, nor am I yet persuaded
to put up in peace what already I have
745 foolishly suffered.

IAGO.   Will you hear me, Roderigo?

RODERIGO.   Faith, I have heard too much,
for your words and performances are no
kin together.

750 IAGO.   You charge me most unjustly.

RODERIGO.   With naught but truth. I have
wasted myself out of my means. The
jewels you have had from me to deliver
to Desdemona would half have cor-
rupted a votarist.[306] You have told me she 755
hath received them, and returned me
expectations and comforts of sudden
respect and acquaintance, but I find none.

IAGO.   Well, go to, very well.

RODERIGO.   Very well! Go to! I cannot go to, 760
man, nor 'tis not very well. By this hand, I
say 'tis very scurvy, and begin to find
myself fopped in it.

IAGO.   Very well.

RODERIGO.   I tell you 'tis not very well. I 765
will make myself known to Desdemona.
If she will return me my jewels, I will
give over my suit and repent my
unlawful solicitation. If not, assure
yourself I will seek satisfaction of you. 770

IAGO.   You have said now.[307]

RODERIGO.   Aye, and said nothing but what
I protest intendment of doing.

IAGO.   Why, now I see there's mettle in
thee, and even from this instant do build 775
on thee a better opinion than ever before.
Give me thy hand, Roderigo. Thou hast
taken against me a most just exception,
but yet I protest I have dealt most
directly in thy affair. 780

RODERIGO.   It hath not appeared.

IAGO.   I grant indeed it hath not appeared,
and your suspicion is not without wit
and judgment. But, Roderigo, if thou hast
that in thee indeed which I have greater 785
reason to believe now than ever—I mean
purpose, courage, and valor—this night
show it. If thou the next might following
enjoy not Desdemona, take me from this
world with treachery and devise 790
engines[308] for my life.

---

[303]**addition:** title
[304]**vanity:** i.e., riches
[305]**meat:** serving of supper

---

[306]**votarist:** nun
[307]**You . . . now:** or in modern slang, "Oh yeah."
[308]**engines:** instruments of torture

RODERIGO. Well, what is it? Is it within reason and compass?

IAGO. Sir, there is especial commission
795 come from Venice to depute Cassio in Othello's place.

RODERIGO. Is that true? Why, then Othello and Desdemona return again to Venice.

IAGO. Oh, no. He goes into Mauritania, and
800 takes away with him the fair Desdemona, unless his abode be lingered here by some accident, wherein none can be so determinate as the removing of Cassio.

RODERIGO. How do you mean, "removing
805 of" him?

IAGO. Why, by making him uncapable of Othello's place, knocking out his brains.

RODERIGO. And that you would have me to do?

810 IAGO. Aye, if you dare do yourself a profit and a right. He sups tonight with a harlotry,[309] and thither will I go to him. He knows not yet of his honorable fortune. If you will watch his going thence, which I
815 will fashion to fall out between twelve and one, you may take him at your pleasure. I will be near to second your attempt, and he shall fall between us. Come, stand not amazed at it, but go along with me. I
820 will show you such a necessity in his death that you shall think yourself bound to put it on him. It is now high suppertime and the night grows to waste. About it.

RODERIGO. I will hear further reason for this.
825 IAGO. And you shall be satisfied. (*Exeunt.*)

SCENE 3. *Another room in the castle.*

Enter OTHELLO, LODOVICO, DESDEMONA, EMILIA, *and* ATTENDANTS.

LODOVICO. I do beseech you, sir, trouble yourself no further.

OTHELLO. Oh, pardon me, 'twill do me good to walk.

LODOVICO. Madam, good night. I humbly
830 thank your ladyship.

DESDEMONA. Your Honor is most welcome.

OTHELLO. Will you walk, sir?
Oh—Desdemona—

DESDEMONA. My lord?   835

OTHELLO. Get you to bed on the instant, I will be returned forthwith.
Dismiss your attendant there. Look it be done.

DESDEMONA. I will, my lord,   840
(*Exeunt* OTHELLO, LODOVICO, *and* ATTENDANTS.)

EMILIA. How goes it now? He looks gentler than he did.

DESDEMONA. He says he will return
incontinent.[310]   845
He hath commanded me to go to bed,
And bade me to dismiss you.

EMILIA. Dismiss me!

DESDEMONA. It was his bidding, therefore,   850
good Emilia,
Give me my nightly wearing, and adieu.
We must not now displease him.

EMILIA. I would you had never seen him!

DESDEMONA. So would not I. My love   855
doth so approve him
That even his stubbornness, his checks, his frowns—
Prithee, unpin me—have grace and favor in them.   860

EMILIA. I have laid those sheets you bade me on the bed.

DESDEMONA. All's one. Good faith, how foolish are our minds!
If I do die before thee, prithee shroud me   865
In one of those same sheets.

EMILIA. Come, come, you talk.

DESDEMONA. My mother had a maid called Barbary.

---

[309]**harlotry:** harlot

[310]**incontinent:** immediately

870 She was in love, and he she loved
proved mad
And did forsake her. She had a song of
"willow"[311]—
An old thing 'twas, but it expressed her
875 fortune,
And she died singing it. That song
tonight
Will not go from my mind. I have much
to do
880 But to go hang my head all at one side
And sing it like poor Barbary. Prithee,
dispatch.
EMILIA.   Shall I go fetch your nightgown?
DESDEMONA.   No, unpin me here.
885 This Lodovico is a proper man.
EMILIA.   A very handsome man.
DESDEMONA.   He speaks well.
EMILIA.   I know a lady in Venice would
have walked barefoot to Palestine for a
890 touch of his nether lip.
DESDEMONA (*singing*).
"The poor soul sat sighing by a sycamore
tree,
Sing all a green willow.
895 Her hand on her bosom, her head on
her knee,
Sing willow, willow, willow.
The fresh streams ran by her, and mur-
mured her moans,
900 Sing willow, willow, willow.
Her salt tears fell from her, and softened
the stones—"
Lay by these—(*singing*)
"Sing willow, willow, willow,"
905 Prithee, hie thee, he'll come anon.—
(*singing*)
"Sing all a green willow must be my
garland.
Let nobody blame him, his scorn
910 I approve—"
Nay, that's not next. Hark! Who is 't that
knocks?

EMILIA.   It's the wind.
DESDEMONA (*singing*).
"I called my love false love, but what   915
said he then?
Sing willow, willow, willow.
If I court moe[312] women, you'll couch
with moe men."
So get thee gone, good night. Mine eyes   920
do itch.
Doth that bode weeping?
EMILIA.   'Tis neither here nor there.
DESDEMONA.   I have heard it said so. Oh,
these men, these men!   925
Dost thou in conscience think—tell me,
Emilia—
That there be women do abuse their
husbands
In such gross kind?   930
EMILIA.   There be some such, no question.
DESDEMONA.   Wouldst thou do such a deed
for all the world?
EMILIA.   Why, would not you?
DESDEMONA.   No, by this heavenly light!   935
I might do 't as well i' the dark.
DESDEMONA.   Would thou do such a deed
for all the world?
EMILIA.   The world's a huge thing. It is a
great price   940
For a small vice.
DESDEMONA.   In troth, I think thou wouldst
not.
EMILIA.   In troth, I think I should, and
undo 't when I had done. Marry, I would   945
not do such a thing for a joint ring, nor
for measures of lawn, nor for gowns,
petticoats, nor caps, nor any petty
exhibition;[313] but for the whole world—
why, who would not make her husband a   950
cuckold to make him a monarch? I
should venture Purgatory for 't.
DESDEMONA.   Beshrew me if I would do
such a wrong for the whole world.

---

[311]**willow:** the emblem of the forlorn lover

[312]**moe:** more
[313]**petty exhibition:** small allowance of money

955 EMILIA.   Why, the wrong is but a wrong i'
   the world, and having the world for your
   labor, 'tis a wrong in your own world
   and you might quickly make it right.
   DESDEMONA.   I do not think there is any
960   such woman.
   EMILIA.   Yes, a dozen, and as many to the
   vantage as would store the world they
   played for.
   But I do think it is their husbands' faults
965 If wives do fall. Say that they slack their
   duties
   And pour our treasures into foreign laps,
   Or else break out in peevish jealousies,
   Throwing restraint upon us, or say they
970 strike us,
   Or scant our former having in despite,[314]
   Why, we have galls,[315] and though we
   have some grace,
   Yet have we some revenge. Let husbands
975 know
   Their wives have sense like them. They
   see and smell
   And have their palates both for sweet
   and sour,
980 As husbands have. What is it that
   they do
   When they change us for others? Is it
   sport?
   I think it is. And doth affection breed it?
985 I think it doth. Is 't frailty that thus errs?
   It is so too. And have not we affections,
   Desires for sport, and frailty, as men
   have?
   Then let them use us well. Else let them
990 know
   The ills we do, their ills instruct us so.
   DESDEMONA.   Good night, good night.
   Heaven me such uses send,
   Not to pick bad from bad, but by bad
995 mend! (*Exeunt.*)

(**ACT 5**)

SCENE 1. Cyprus. A street.

Enter IAGO *and* RODERIGO.

IAGO.   Here, stand behind this bulk,   1
   straight will he come.
   Wear thy good rapier bare, and put it
   home.
   Quick, quick, fear nothing. I'll be at thy   5
   elbow.
   It makes us, or it mars us. Think on that,
   And fix most firm thy resolution.
RODERIGO.   Be near at hand. I may
   miscarry in 't.   10
IAGO.   Here, at thy hand. Be bold, and take
   thy stand. (*Retires.*)
RODERIGO.   I have no great devotion to
   the deed,
   And yet he hath given me satisfying   15
   reasons.
   'Tis but a man gone. Forth, my sword.
   He dies.
IAGO.   I have rubbed this young quat[316]
   almost to the sense,[317]   20
   And he grows angry. Now, whether he
   kill Cassio,
   Or Cassio him, or each do kill the other,
   Every way makes my gain. Live
   Roderigo,   25
   He calls me to a restitution large
   Of gold and jewels that I bobbed
   from him
   As gifts to Desdemona.
   It must not be. If Cassio do remain,   30
   He hath a daily beauty in his life
   That makes me ugly,[318] and besides,
   the Moor
   May unfold me to him. There stand I
   in much peril.   35

314**scant . . . despite:** for spite cut down our allowance
315**galls:** bile, the cause of bitterness

316**quat:** pimple
317**sense:** quick
318**He . . . ugly:** by comparison with him I am a poor
thing. Iago is conscious of his lack of social graces.

No, he must die. Be 't so. I hear him coming. (*Enter* CASSIO.)

RODERIGO.   I know his gait, 'tis he. Villain, thou diest!

40   (*Makes a pass at* CASSIO.)

CASSIO.   That thrust had been mine enemy indeed

But that my coat is better than thou know'st.

45   I will make proof of thine. (*Draws, and wounds* RODERIGO.)

RODERIGO.   Oh, I am slain!

(IAGO *from behind wounds* CASSIO *in the leg, and exit.*)

50   CASSIO.   I am maimed for ever. Help, ho! Murder! Murder!

(*Falls. Enter* OTHELLO.)

OTHELLO.   The voice of Cassio. Iago keeps his word.

55   RODERIGO.   Oh, villain that I am!

OTHELLO.   It is even so.

CASSIO.   Oh, help, ho! Light! A surgeon!

OTHELLO.   'Tis he. O brave Iago, honest and just,

60   That hast such noble sense of thy friend's wrong!

Thou teachest me. Minion,[319] your dear friend lies dead,

And your unblest fate hies. Strumpet,

65   I come!

Forth of my heart those charms, thine eyes, are blotted.

Thy bed lust-stained shall with lust's blood be spotted.

70   (*Exit. Enter* LODOVICO *and* GRATIANO.)

CASSIO.   What ho! No watch?[320] No passage?[321] Murder! Murder!

GRATIANO.   'Tis some mischance, the cry is very direful.

75   CASSIO.   Oh, help!

LODOVICO.   Hark!

RODERIGO.   Oh, wretched villain!

LODOVICO.   Two or three groan. It is a heavy[322] night.

These may be counterfeits. Let's think 't   80
unsafe

To come in to the cry without more help.

RODERIGO.   Nobody come? Then I shall bleed to death.

LODOVICO.   Hark! (*Re-enter* IAGO, *with a*   85
light.)

GRATIANO.   Here's one comes in his shirt, with light and weapons.

IAGO.   Who's there? Whose noise is this that cries on murder?   90

LODOVICO.   We do not know.

IAGO.   Did not you hear a cry?

CASSIO.   Here, here! For Heaven's sake, help me!

IAGO.   What's the matter?   95

GRATIANO.   This is Othello's Ancient, as I take it.

LODOVICO.   The same indeed, a very valiant fellow.

IAGO.   What are you here that cry so   100
grievously?

CASSIO.   Iago? Oh, I am spoiled, undone by villains! Give me some help.

IAGO.   Oh me, Lieutenant! What villains have done this?   105

CASSIO.   I think that one of them is hereabout,

And cannot make away.

IAGO.   Oh, treacherous villains!

(*To* LODOVICO *and* GRATIANO) What are   110
you there?

Come in and give some help.

RODERIGO.   Oh, help me here!

CASSIO.   That's one of them.

IAGO.   Oh, murderous slave! Oh, villain!   115

(*Stabs* RODERIGO.)

RODERIGO.   Oh, damned Iago! Oh, inhuman dog!

---

[319]**Minion:** darling, in a bad sense
[320]**watch:** police
[321]**No passage:** Nobody passing

[322]**heavy:** thick

IAGO. Kill men i' the dark! Where be these
120 bloody thieves?
How silent is this town! Ho! Murder!
Murder!
What may you be? Are you of good or
evil?
125 LODOVICO. As you shall prove us, praise us.
IAGO. Signior Lodovico?
LODOVICO. He, sir.
IAGO. I cry your mercy. Here's Cassio hurt
by villains.
130 GRATIANO. Cassio!
IAGO. How is 't, brother?
CASSIO. My leg is cut in two.
IAGO. Marry, Heaven forbid!
Light, gentlemen. I'll bind it with my
135 shirt. (*Enter* BIANCA.)
BIANCA. What is the matter, ho? Who is 't
that cried?
IAGO. Who is 't that cried!
BIANCA. Oh, my dear Cassio! My sweet
140 Cassio!
Oh, Cassio, Cassio, Cassio!
IAGO. Oh, notable strumpet! Cassio, may
you suspect
Who they should be that have thus
145 mangled you?
CASSIO. No.
GRATIANO. I am sorry to find you thus. I
have been to seek you.
IAGO. Lend me a garter. Oh, for a chair,
150 To bear him easily hence!
BIANCA. Alas, he faints! Oh, Cassio,
Cassio, Cassio!
IAGO. Gentlemen all, I do suspect this
trash
155 To be a party in this injury.
Patience awhile, good Cassio. Come,
come
Lend me a light. Know we this face or no?
Alas, my friend and my dear countryman
160 Roderigo? No—yes, sure. Oh Heaven!
Roderigo.
GRATIANO. What, of Venice?
IAGO. Even he, sir. Did you know him?

GRATIANO. Know him! Aye.
IAGO. Signior Gratiano? I cry you gentle 165
pardon.
These bloody accidents must excuse my
manners,
That so neglected you.
GRATIANO. I am glad to see you. 170
IAGO. How do you, Cassio? Oh, a chair, a
chair!
GRATIANO. Roderigo!
IAGO. He, he, 'tis he. (*A chair brought in.*)
Oh, that's well said, the chair. 175
Some good man bear him carefully
from hence.
I'll fetch the General's surgeon.
(*To* BIANCA) For you, mistress,
Save you your labor. He that lies slain 180
here, Cassio,
Was my dear friend. What malice
between you?
CASSIO. None in the world, nor do I know
the man. 185
IAGO (*to* BIANCA). What, look you pale?
Oh, bear him out o' the air.
(CASSIO *and* RODERIGO *are borne off.*)
Stay you, good gentlemen. Look you
pale, mistress? 190
Do you perceive the gastness of her eye?
Nay, if you stare, we shall hear more
anon.
Behold her well, I pray you look upon her.
Do you see, gentlemen? Nay, guiltiness 195
will speak,
Though tongues were out of use. (*Enter*
EMILIA.)
EMILIA. 'Las, what's the matter? What's
the matter, husband? 200
IAGO. Cassio hath here been set on in the
dark
By Roderigo and fellows that are 'scaped.
He's almost slain, and Roderigo dead.
EMILIA. Alas, good gentleman! Alas, good 205
Cassio!
IAGO. This is the fruit of whoring. Prithee,
Emilia,

Go know of Cassio where he supped
210   tonight.
       What, do you shake at that?
       BIANCA.   He supped at my house, but I
       therefore shake not.
       IAGO.   Oh, did he so? I charge you, go
215   with me.
       EMILIA.   Fie, fie upon thee, strumpet!
       BIANCA.   I am no strumpet, but of life as
       honest
       As you that thus abuse me.
220   EMILIA.   As I! Foh! Fie upon thee!
       IAGO.   Kind gentlemen, let's go see poor
       Cassio dressed.[323]
       Come, mistress, you must tell's another
       tale.
225   Emilia, run you to the citadel,
       And tell my lord and lady what hath
       happened!
       Will you go on afore? I pray. (*Aside*) This
       is the night
230   That either makes me or fordoes me
       quite. (*Exeunt.*)

       SCENE 2. *A bedchamber in the castle.*
       DESDEMONA *in bed asleep, a light burning.*

       Enter OTHELLO.

       OTHELLO.   It is the cause,[324] it is the cause,
       my soul.
       Let me not name it to you, you chaste
235   stars!
       It is the cause. Yet I'll not shed her blood,
       Nor scar that whiter skin of hers than
       snow
       And smooth as monumental alabaster.
240   Yet she must die, else she'll betray
       more men.

---

[323]**dressed:** i.e., his wound dressed
[324]**It . . . cause:** The meaning of the opening lines of
this speech has been much discussed. The *cause* is
Desdemona's supposed faithlessness; Othello, at this
moment, sees himself as embodied justice, the
avenger of man betrayed by woman.

Put out the light, and then put out the
light.
If I quench thee, thou flaming minister,[325]
I can again thy former light restore,   245
Should I repent me. But once put out
thy light,
Thou cunning'st[326] pattern of excelling
nature,
I know not where is that Promethean heat 250
That can thy light relume. When I have
plucked the rose,
I cannot give it vital growth again,
It needs must wither. I'll smell it on the
tree. (*Kissing her*)   255
Ah, balmy breath, that dost almost
persuade
Justice to break her sword! One more,
one more.
Be thus when thou art dead, and I will   260
kill thee,
And love thee after. One more, and this
the last.
So sweet was ne'er so fatal. I must weep,
But they are cruel tears. This sorrow's   265
heavenly,
It strikes where it doth love. She wakes.
DESDEMONA.   Who's there? Othello?
OTHELLO.   Aye, Desdemona.
DESDEMONA.   Will you come to bed, my   270
lord?
OTHELLO.   Have you prayed tonight,
Desdemona?
DESDEMONA.   Aye, my lord.
OTHELLO.   If you bethink yourself of any   275
crime
Unreconciled as yet to Heaven and grace,
Solicit for it straight.
DESDEMONA.   Alas, my lord, what may you
mean by that?   280
OTHELLO.   Well, do it, and be brief. I will
walk by.
I would not kill thy unpreparèd spirit.

---

[325]**minister:** servant
[326]**cunning'st:** most skillfully made

No, Heaven forfend! I would not kill
285 thy soul.
DESDEMONA.   Talk you of killing?
OTHELLO.   Aye, I do.
DESDEMONA.   Then Heaven
Have mercy on me!
290 OTHELLO.   Amen, with all my heart!
DESDEMONA.   If you say so, I hope you will
not kill me.
OTHELLO.   Hum!
DESDEMONA.   And yet I fear you, for you
295 are fatal then
When your eyes roll so. Why I should
fear I know not,
Since guiltiness I know not, but yet I feel
I fear.
300 OTHELLO.   Think on thy sins.
DESDEMONA.   They are loves I bear to you.
OTHELLO.   Aye, and for that thou diest.
DESDEMONA.   That death's unnatural that
kills for loving.
305 Alas, why gnaw you so your nether lip?
Some bloody passion shakes your very
frame.
These are portents, but yet I hope, I hope,
They do not point on me.
310 OTHELLO.   Peace, and be still!
DESDEMONA.   I will so. What's the matter?
OTHELLO.   That handkerchief which I so
loved and gave thee
Thou gavest to Cassio.
315 DESDEMONA.   No, by my life and soul!
Send for the man, and ask him.
OTHELLO.   Sweet soul, take heed,
Take heed of perjury, thou art on thy
deathbed.
320 DESDEMONA.   Aye, but not yet to die.
OTHELLO.   Yes, presently.[327]
Therefore confess thee freely of thy sin,
For to deny each article with oath
Cannot remove nor choke the strong
325 conception
That I do groan withal. Thou art to die.

DESDEMONA.   Then Lord have mercy on me!
OTHELLO.   I say amen.
DESDEMONA.   And have you mercy too! I
never did   330
Offend you in my life, never loved Cassio
But with such general warranty of Heaven
As I might love. I never gave him token.
OTHELLO.   By Heaven, I saw my
handkerchief in 's hand.   335
O perjured woman! Thou dost stone[328]
my heart,
And makest me call what I intend to do
A murder, which I thought a sacrifice.
I saw the handkerchief.   340
DESDEMONA.   He found it, then,
I never gave it him. Send for him hither.
Let him confess a truth.
OTHELLO.   He hath confessed.
DESDEMONA.   What, my lord?   345
OTHELLO.   That he hath used thee.
DESDEMONA.   How? Unlawfully?
OTHELLO.   Aye.
DESDEMONA.   He will not say so.
OTHELLO.   No, his mouth is stopped.   350
Honest Iago hath ta'en order for 't.
DESDEMONA.   Oh, my fear interprets! What,
is he dead?
OTHELLO.   Had all his hairs been lives, my
great revenge   355
Had stomach for them all.
DESDEMONA.   Alas, he is betrayed, and I
undone!
OTHELLO.   Out, strumpet! Weep'st thou for
him to my face?   360
DESDEMONA.   Oh, banish me, my lord, but
kill me not!
OTHELLO.   Down, strumpet!
DESDEMONA.   Kill me tomorrow, let me live
tonight!   365
OTHELLO.   Nay, if you strive—
DESDEMONA.   But half an hour!
OTHELLO.   Being done, there is no pause.
DESDEMONA.   But while I say one prayer!

---

[327]**presently:** at once

[328]**stone:** turn to stone

370 OTHELLO.   It is too late. (*He stifles her.*)

EMILIA (*within*).   My lord, my lord! What
  ho! My lord, my lord!

OTHELLO.   What noise is this? Not dead?
  Not yet quite dead?

375 I that am cruel am yet merciful,
  I would not have thee linger in thy pain.
  So, so.

EMILIA (*within*).   What ho! My lord, my lord!

OTHELLO.   Who's there?

380 EMILIA (*within*).   Oh, good my lord, I
  would speak a word with you!

OTHELLO.   Yes, 'tis Emilia. By and by.
  She's dead.
  'Tis like she comes to speak of Cassio's

385 death.
  The noise was here. Ha! No more moving?
  Still as the grave. Shall she come in?
  Were 't good?
  I think she stirs again. No. What's best to

390 do?
  If she come in, she'll sure speak to my wife.
  My wife! My wife! What wife? I have no
  wife.
  Oh, insupportable! Oh, heavy hour!

395 Methinks it should be now a huge eclipse
  Of sun and moon, and that the affrighted
  globe
  Should yawn[329] at alteration.

EMILIA (*within*).   I do beseech you

400 That I may speak with you, O good my
  lord!

OTHELLO.   I had forgot thee. Oh, come in,
  Emilia.
  Soft, by and by. Let me the curtains[330] draw.

405 What art thou? (*Unlocks the door. Enter
  EMILIA.*) What's the matter with thee now?

EMILIA.   Oh, my good lord, yonder's foul
  murders done!

OTHELLO.   What, now?

410 EMILIA.   But now, my lord.

OTHELLO.   It is the very error of the moon.
  She comes more nearer earth than she
  was wont
  And makes men mad.

EMILIA.   Cassio, my lord, hath killed a   415
  young Venetian
  Called Roderigo.

OTHELLO.   Roderigo killed!
  And Cassio killed!

EMILIA.   No, Cassio is not killed.   420

OTHELLO.   Not Cassio killed! Then
  murder's out of tune,
  And sweet revenge grows harsh.

DESDEMONA.   Oh, falsely, falsely
  murdered!   425

EMILIA.   Alas, what cry is that?

OTHELLO.   That! What?

EMILIA.   Out and alas! That was my lady's
  voice.
  Help! Help, ho! Help! O lady, speak again!   430
  Sweet Desdemona! O sweet mistress,
  speak!

DESDEMONA.   A guiltless death I die.

EMILIA.   Oh, who hath done this deed?

DESDEMONA.   Nobody, I myself. Farewell.   435
  Commend me to my kind lord. Oh,
  farewell! (*Dies.*)

OTHELLO.   Why, how should she be
  murdered?

EMILIA.   Alas, who knows?   440

OTHELLO.   You heard her say herself it was
  not I.

EMILIA.   She said so. I must needs report
  the truth.

OTHELLO.   She's like a liar gone to burning   445
  Hell.
  'Twas I that killed her.

EMILIA.   Oh, the more angel she,
  And you the blacker devil!

OTHELLO.   She turned to folly, and she was   450
  a whore.

EMILIA.   Thou dost belie her, and thou art a
  devil.

OTHELLO.   She was false as water.

EMILIA.   Thou art rash as fire to say   455
  That she was false. Oh, she was heavenly
  true!

---

[329]**yawn:** split open in an earthquake [Eds.]
[330]**curtains:** i.e., of the bed

OTHELLO. Cassio did top her, ask thy husband else.

460 Oh, I were damned beneath all depth in Hell
But that I did proceed upon just grounds
To this extremity. Thy husband knew it all.

EMILIA. My husband!

465 OTHELLO. Thy husband.

EMILIA. That she was false to wedlock?

OTHELLO. Aye, with Cassio. Nay, had she been true,
If Heaven would make me such another

470 world
Of one entire and perfect chrysolite,
I'd not have sold her for it.

EMILIA. My husband!

OTHELLO. Aye, 'twas he that told me first.

475 An honest man he is, and hates the slime
That sticks on filthy deeds.

EMILIA. My husband!

OTHELLO. What needs this iteration, woman? I say thy husband.

480 EMILIA. Oh, mistress, villainy hath made mocks with love!
My husband say that she was false!

OTHELLO. He, woman.
I say thy husband. Dost understand the

485 word?
My friend, thy husband, honest, honest Iago.

EMILIA. If he say so, may his pernicious soul
Rot half a grain a day! He lies to the

490 heart.
She was too fond of her most filthy bargain.

OTHELLO. Ha!

EMILIA. Do thy worst.

495 This deed of thine is no more worthy Heaven
Than thou wast worthy her.

OTHELLO. Peace, you were best.

EMILIA. Thou hast not half that power to

500 do me harm
As I have to be hurt. O gull! O dolt!
As ignorant as dirt! Thou hast done a deed—

I care not for thy sword, I'll make thee known,   505
Though I lost twenty lives. Help! Help! ho! Help!
The Moor hath killed my mistress! Murder! Murder!
(*Enter* MONTANO, GRATIANO, IAGO, *and*   510
others.)

MONTANO. What is the matter? How now, General!

EMILIA. Oh, are you come, Iago? You have done well,   515
That men must lay their murders on your neck.

GRATIANO. What is the matter?

EMILIA. Disprove this villain, if thou be'st a man.   520
He says thou told'st him that his wife was false.
I know thou didst not, thou'rt not such a villain.
Speak, for my heart is full.   525

IAGO. I told him what I thought, and told no more
Than what he found himself was apt and true.

EMILIA. But did you ever tell him she was   530
false?

IAGO. I did.

EMILIA. You told a lie, an odious, damnèd lie,
Upon my soul, a lie, a wicked lie!   535
She false with Cassio! Did you say with Cassio?

IAGO. With Cassio, mistress. Go to, charm your tongue.[331]

EMILIA. I will not charm my tongue, I am   540
bound to speak.
My mistress here lies murdered in her bed.

ALL. Oh, Heavens forfend!

EMILIA. And your reports have set the murder on.   545

OTHELLO. Nay, stare not, masters. It is true indeed.

---

[331]**charm your tongue:** be silent

GRATIANO. 'Tis a strange truth.

MONTANO. Oh, monstrous act!

550 EMILIA. Villainy, villainy, villainy!
  I think upon 't. I think I smell 't. Oh, villainy!
  I thought so then. I'll kill myself for grief.
  Oh, villainy, villainy!

555 IAGO. What, are you mad? I charge you, get you home.

  EMILIA. Good gentlemen, let me have leave to speak.
  'Tis proper I obey him, but not now.

560 Perchance, Iago, I will ne'er go home.

  OTHELLO. Oh! Oh! Oh! (*Falling on the bed.*)

  EMILIA. Nay, lay thee down and roar,
  For thou has killed the sweetest innocent
  That e'er did lift up eye.

565 OTHELLO (*rising*). Oh, she was foul!
  I scarce did know you, Uncle. There lies your niece,
  Whose breath indeed these hands have newly stopped.

570 I know this act shows horrible and grim.

  GRATIANO. Poor Desdemona! I am glad thy father's dead.
  Thy match was mortal to him, and pure grief

575 Shore his old thread in twain. Did he live now,
  This sight would make him do a desperate turn—
  Yea, curse his better angel from his side,

580 And fall to reprobation.[332]

  OTHELLO. 'Tis pitiful, but yet Iago knows
  That she with Cassio hath the act of shame
  A thousand times committed. Cassio

585 confessed it.
  And she did gratify his amorous works
  With that recognizance and pledge of love
  Which I first gave her, I saw it in his hand.
  It was a handkerchief, an antique token

590 My father gave my mother.

EMILIA. Oh, Heaven! Oh, heavenly powers!

IAGO. 'Zounds! Hold your peace.

EMILIA. 'Twill out, 'twill out. I peace!
  No, I will speak as liberal as the north.[333]
  Let Heaven and men and devils, let them 595
  all,
  All, all, cry shame against me, yet I'll speak.

IAGO. Be wise, and get you home.

EMILIA. I will not.
  (IAGO *offers to stab* EMILIA.) 600

GRATIANO. Fie!
  Your sword upon a woman!

EMILIA. O thou dull Moor! That handker-
  chief thou speak'st of
  I found by fortune and did give my 605
  husband,
  For often with a solemn earnestness,
  More than indeed belonged to such a trifle,
  He begged of me to steal it.

IAGO. Villainous whore! 610

EMILIA. She give it Cassio! No, alas,
  I found it,
  And I did give 't my husband.

IAGO. Filth, thou liest!

EMILIA. By Heaven, I do not, I do not, 615
  gentlemen.
  Oh, murderous coxcomb! What should such a fool
  Do with so good a wife!

OTHELLO. Are there no stones[334] in Heaven 620
  But what serve for the thunder? Precious villain!
  (*He runs at* IAGO. IAGO, *from behind, stabs* EMILIA, *and exits.*)

GRATIANO. The woman falls. Sure, he hath 625
  killed his wife.

EMILIA. Aye. Aye. Oh, lay me by my mistress' side.

GRATIANO. He's gone, but his wife's killed.

MONTANO. 'Tis a notorious villain. Take 630
  you this weapon,

---

[332]**reprobation:** damnation; i.e., by self-murder

[333]**liberal . . . north:** as freely as the north wind, which is loud and bitter

[334]**stones:** thunderbolts

Which I have here recovered from the Moor.
Come, guard the door without, let him
635 not pass,
But kill him rather. I'll after that same villain,
For 'tis a damnèd slave. (*Exeunt all but*
OTHELLO *and* EMILIA.)
640 OTHELLO.   I am not valiant neither,
But every puny whipster gets my sword.
But why should honor outlive honesty?
Let it go all.
EMILIA.   What did thy song bode, lady?
645 Hark, canst thou hear me? I will play the swan,
And die in music. (*Singing*)
"Willow, willow, willow."
Moor, she was chaste. She loved thee,
650 cruel Moor,
So come my soul to bliss as I speak true.
So speaking as I think, I die, I die. (*Dies.*)
OTHELLO.   I have another weapon in this chamber.
655 It is a sword of Spain, the ice brook's temper.—
Oh, here it is. Uncle, I must come forth.
GRATIANO (*within*).   If thou attempt it, it will cost thee dear.
660 Thou hast no weapon, and perforce must suffer.
OTHELLO.   Look in upon me then, and speak with me,
Or, naked[335] as I am, I will assault thee.
665 (*Re-enter* GRATIANO.)
GRATIANO.   What is the matter?
OTHELLO.   Behold, I have a weapon,
A better never did itself sustain
Upon a soldier's thigh. I have seen the day
670 That with this little arm and this good sword
I have made my way through more impediments

Than twenty times your stop. But, oh,
vain boast! 675
Who can control his fate? 'Tis not so now.
Be not afraid, though you do see me weaponed.
Here is my journey's end, here is
my butt[336] 680
And very sea mark of my utmost sail.
Do you go back dismayed? 'Tis a lost fear.
Man but a rush[337] against Othello's breast,
And he retires. Where should Othello go?
Now, how dost thou look now? 685
O ill-starred wench!
Pale as thy smock! When we shall meet
at compt,[338]
This look of thine will hurl my soul from
Heaven 690
And fiends will snatch at it. Cold, cold,
my girl!
Even like thy chastity. Oh, cursèd slave!
Whip me, ye devils,
From the possession of this heavenly sight! 695
Blow me about in winds! Roast me in sulphur!
Wash me in steep-down gulfs of liquid fire!
O Desdemona! Desdemona! Dead! 700
Oh! Oh! Oh!
(*Enter* LODOVICO, MONTANO, CASSIO *carried
in a chair, and* OFFICERS *with* IAGO,
prisoner.)
LONOVICO.   Where is this rash and most 705
unfortunate man?
OTHELLO.   That's he that was Othello. Here
I am.
LODOVICO.   Where is the viper? Bring the
villain forth. 710
OTHELLO.   I look down toward his feet,[339]
but that's a fable.

---

[335]**naked:** unarmed

[336]**butt:** aim
[337]**Man . . . rush:** Attack with only a reed
[338]**compt:** account; i.e., the Day of Judgment
[339]**toward his feet:** i.e., to see if he has the cloven hoof of a devil

If that thou be'st a devil, I cannot kill
thee. (*Wounds* IAGO.)

715 LODOVICO.   Wrench his sword from him.

IAGO.   I bleed, sir, but not killed.

OTHELLO.   I am not sorry neither. I'd have
thee live,
For, in my sense, 'tis happiness to die.

720 LODOVICO.   O thou Othello, that wert once
so good,
Fall'n in the practice[340] of a damnèd slave,
What shall be said to thee?

OTHELLO.   Why, anything.

725 An honorable murderer, if you will,
For naught did I in hate, but all in honor.

LODOVICO.   This wretch hath part
confessed his villainy.
Did you and he consent in Cassio's death?

730 OTHELLO.   Aye.

CASSIO.   Dear General, I never gave you
cause.

OTHELLO.   I do believe it, and I ask your
pardon.

735 Will you, I pray, demand that demi-devil
Why he hath thus ensnared my soul and
body?

IAGO.   Demand me nothing. What you
know, you know.

740 From this time forth I never will speak
word.

LODOVICO.   What, not to pray?

GRATIANO.   Torments will ope your lips.

OTHELLO.   Well, thou dost best.

745 LODOVICO.   Sir, you shall understand what
hath befall'n,
Which, as I think, you know not. Here is
a letter
Found in the pocket of the slain Roderigo,

750 And here another. The one of them imports
The death of Cassio to be undertook
By Roderigo.

OTHELLO.   Oh, villain!

CASSIO.   Most heathenish and most gross!

755 LODOVICO.   Now here's another discon-
tented paper,

Found in his pocket too. And this, it seems,
Roderigo meant to have sent this
damnèd villain
But that, belike, Iago in the interim   760
Came in and satisfied him.

OTHELLO.   Oh, the pernicious caitiff!
How come you, Cassio, by that
handkerchief
That was my wife's?   765

CASSIO.   I found it in my chamber.
And he himself confessed but even now
That there he dropped it for a special
purpose
Which wrought to his desire.   770

OTHELLO.   O fool! Fool! Fool!

CASSIO.   There is besides in Roderigo's letter
How he upbraids Iago, that he made him
Brave[341] me upon the watch, whereon it
came   775
That I was cast.[342] And even but now he
spake
After long seeming dead, Iago hurt him,
Iago set him on.

LODOVICO.   You must forsake this room,   780
and go with us.
Your power and your command is
taken off,
And Cassio rules in Cyprus. For this slave,
If there be any cunning cruelty   785
That can torment him much and hold
him long,[343]
It shall be his. You shall close prisoner rest
Till that the nature of your fault be
known   790
To the Venetian state. Come, bring away.

OTHELLO.   Soft you, a word or two before
you go.
I have done the state some service, and
they know 't.   795
No more of that. I pray you, in your letters,
When you shall these unlucky deeds relate,
Speak of me as I am, nothing extenuate,

---

[340]**Fall'n . . . practice:** destroyed by the plotting

[341]**Brave:** insult
[342]**cast:** dismissed
[343]**long:** i.e., in dying

Nor set down aught in malice. Then must
800 you speak
Of one that loved not wisely but too well;
Of one not easily jealous, but, being
wrought,
Perplexed in the extreme; of one whose
805 hand,
Like the base Indian, threw a pearl away
Richer than all his tribe; of one whose
subdued eyes,
Albeit unusèd to the melting mood,
810 Drop tears as fast as the Arabian trees
Their medicinable gum. Set you down this,
And say besides that in Aleppo once,
Where a malignant and a turbaned Turk
Beat a Venetian and traduced the state,
815 I took by the throat the circumcisèd dog
And smote him, thus. (*Stabs himself.*)

LODOVICO.   Oh, bloody period!

GRATIANO.   All that's spoke is marred.

OTHELLO.   I kissed thee ere I killed thee.
820 No way but this,
Killing myself, to die upon a kiss. (*Falls
on the bed, and dies.*)

CASSIO.   This did I fear, but thought he had
no weapon,
For he was great of heart.   825

LODOVICO (*to* IAGO).   O Spartan[344] dog,
More fell[345] than anguish, hunger, or the
sea!
Look on the tragic loading of this bed:
This is thy work. The object poisons sight, 830
Let it be hid.[346] Gratiano, keep the house,
And seize upon the fortunes of the Moor,
For they succeed on you. To you, Lord
Governor,
Remains the censure of this hellish villain, 835
The time, the place, the torture.
Oh, enforce it!
Myself will straight aboard, and to the state
This heavy act with heavy heart relate.
(*Exeunt.*)   840

---

[344]**Spartan:** i.e., hardhearted
[345]**fell:** cruel
[346]**Let . . . hid:** At these words the curtains are closed
across the inner stage (or chamber, if this scene was
acted aloft), concealing all three bodies.

····•▶ *Your* **Turn**
Talking and Writing about Lit

1. How does Shakespeare establish the noble character of Othello in Act I?

2. Analyze the ways in which Iago's use of language differs from that of the other characters in Act I.

3. Three great themes of Shakespeare's *Othello* are deception, judgment, and jealousy. Show how these themes are sounded decisively beginning in the early scenes of Act I and then throughout the play.

4. What does Brabantio accuse Othello of in the Senate chamber (1.3)? How does Othello defend himself?

5. How has Shakespeare established Desdemona's character in Act I, scene 3?

6. Shakespeare depicts varying degrees of racial bias (or lack of racial bias) among his characters. What is Iago's attitude toward Othello and Desdemona's marriage? How does it compare to Brabantio's view? How does the Duke view the union of Othello and Desdemona? What other characters demonstrate the varying degrees of racial bias in Renaissance society?

7. What significance do you see in the shift of settings from Venice (the center of the Venetian Empire) to Cyprus (a militarily contested outpost in the Mediterranean Sea)? How is the storm important thematically? Do you see a parallel between the storm at sea and the storm Iago is brewing in the characters' relationships?

8. In Act II, scene one, Shakespeare accomplishes the important characterization of Cassio. How does Cassio view his general, Othello? How does he view Othello and Desdemona's marriage? How do Montano and the other gentlemen of Cyprus regard Othello?

9. What plots do Iago and Roderigo collaborate on in Act II? How is Iago able to get Cassio removed from his position as Othello's lieutenant?

10. Elizabethans believed that reason (or judgment or conscience) should rule over the will (or ambitions or desire for worldly status) and the will should rule over the passions (or "blood" or "appetites"). What is the significance of Othello's declaration in Act II, scene three, lines 183–85 that "Now, by Heaven,/My blood begins my safer guides to rule,/And passion, having my best judgment collied,/Assays to lead the way"?

11. There has been much discussion about whether Shakespeare made it believable in the crucial Act III that Othello was so completely taken in by Iago's lies about Desdemona and Cassio. One problem, of course, is that Othello's nobility and strength of character might seem to make such a radical change implausible. Shakespeare is said to have revealed the changes taking place in Othello in four ways: the pollution of his use of language (which comes to resemble Iago's), the ascendance of passion over reason in Act II, Othello's trances, and the change in his behavior toward Desdemona. Do you find the transformation of Othello convincing?

12. Act III, scene three is sometimes referred to as the "Temptation Scene" for its resemblance to the Biblical scene of the temptation of Christ by Satan. Do you find this a valid comparison?

13. Explain the significance of the handkerchief in terms of the play's plot. What is its significance symbolically?

14. Othello demands "ocular proof" of Desdemona's unfaithfulness. What so-called proofs does Iago provide?

15. In important ways, Desdemona and Emilia are allies, especially in the play's tragic conclusion. In some respects, however, Emilia also serves as a foil to Desdemona's character. Analyze Shakespeare's use of Emilia as a foil character, considering especially her conversation with Desdemona at the end of Act IV (4.3.53–101).

16. Describe the sequence of events in Act I, scene one. Who stabs Cassio? Who kills Roderigo?

17. What does Othello mean when he declares in Act V, scene two (5.2.7–15) that "I know not where is that Promethean heat/That can thy light relume" and "When I have plucked the rose,/It needs must wither"? Looking at the entire

passage, how does it illuminate the difference between Othello's view of the value of human life and that of Iago or Roderigo?

18. How do the characters assembled in the bedchamber (5.2.220–329) learn the truth about the events leading up to the murders? How is Othello's noble character reasserted in the end of the play (5.2.220–361)?

August Wilson (b. 1945)

August Wilson was born in Pittsburgh to an impoverished family. He dropped out of school at the age of sixteen, and while working at low-paying jobs to support himself, he began to write poetry. Later he moved to Saint Paul, Minnesota, where he founded the Black Horizons Theatre Company. In the 1980s Wilson began writing plays, first producing *The Jitney* (1982) in Pittsburgh. Since then, he has been crafting one play after another, building an ambitious cycle of dramas depicting the black experience in American society. Two plays in the series, *Fences* (1986) and *Piano Lesson* (1990), have been awarded Pulitzer Prizes. All of Wilson's plays in this series have premiered at the Yale Repertory Theater under the direction of Lloyd Richards, and all of them have had subsequent successful runs on Broadway.

Fences (1985)

CHARACTERS:

TROY MAXSON

JIM BONO, *Troy's friend*

ROSE, *Troy's wife*

LYONS, *Troy's oldest son by previous marriage*

GABRIEL, *Troy's brother*

CORY, *Troy and Rose's son*

RAYNELL, *Troy's daughter*

The setting is the yard which fronts the only entrance to the Maxson household, an ancient two-story brick house set back off a small alley in a big-city neighborhood. The entrance to the house is gained by two or three steps leading to a wooden porch badly in need of paint.

A relatively recent addition to the house and running its full width, the porch lacks congruence. It is a sturdy porch with a flat roof. One or two chairs of dubious value sit at one end where the kitchen window opens onto the porch. An old-fashioned icebox stands silent guard at the opposite end.

The yard is a small dirt yard, partially fenced, except for the last scene, with a wooden sawhorse, a pile of lumber, and other fence-building equipment set off to the side. Opposite is a tree from which hangs a ball made of rags. A baseball bat leans against the tree. Two oil drums serve as garbage receptacles and sit near the house at right to complete the setting.

Near the turn of the century, the destitute of Europe sprang on the city with tenacious claws and an honest and solid dream. The city devoured them. They swelled its belly until it burst into a thousand furnaces and sewing machines, a thousand butcher shops and bakers' ovens, a thousand churches and hospitals and funeral parlors and money-lenders. The city grew. It nourished itself and offered each man a partnership limited only by his talent, his guile, and his willingness and capacity for hard work. For the immigrants of Europe, a dream dared and won true.

The descendants of African slaves were offered no such welcome or participation. They came from places called the Carolinas and the Virginias, Georgia, Alabama, Mississippi, and Tennessee. They came strong, eager, searching. The city rejected them and they fled and settled along the riverbanks and under bridges in shallow, ramshackle houses made of sticks and tarpaper. They collected rags and wood. They sold the use of their muscles and their bodies. They cleaned houses and washed clothes, they shined shoes, and in quiet desperation and vengeful pride, they stole, and lived in pursuit of their own dream: that they could breathe free, finally, and stand to meet life with the force of dignity and whatever eloquence the heart could call upon.

By 1957, the hard-won victories of the European immigrants had solidified the industrial might of America. War had been confronted and won with new energies that used loyalty and patriotism as its fuel. Life was rich, full, and flourishing. The Milwaukee Braves won the World Series, and the hot winds of change that would make the sixties a turbulent, racing, dangerous, and provocative decade had not yet begun to blow full.

───────────(**ACT 1**)───────────

SCENE 1

It is 1957. TROY *and* BONO *enter the yard, engaged in conversation.* TROY *is fifty-three years old, a large man with thick, heavy hands; it is this largeness that he strives to fill out and make an accommodation with. Together with his blackness, his largeness informs his sensibilities and the choices he has made in his life.*

Of the two men, BONO *is obviously the follower. His commitment to their friendship of thirty-odd years is rooted in his admiration of* TROY'S *honesty, capacity for hard work, and his strength, which* BONO *seeks to emulate.*

It is Friday night, payday, and the one night of the week the two men engage in a ritual of talk and drink. TROY *is usually the most talkative and at times he can be crude and almost vulgar, though he is capable of rising to profound heights of expression. The men carry lunch buckets and wear or carry burlap aprons and are dressed in clothes suitable to their jobs as garbage collectors.*

BONO.   Troy, you ought to stop that lying!

TROY.   I ain't lying! The nigger had a watermelon this big. (*He indicates with his hands.*) Talking about . . . "What watermelon, Mr. Rand?" I liked to fell out! "What watermelon, Mr. Rand?" . . . And it sitting there big as life.

BONO.   What did Mr. Rand say?

TROY.   Ain't said nothing. Figure if the nigger too dumb to know he carrying a watermelon, he wasn't gonna get much sense out of him. Trying to hide that great big watermelon under his coat. Afraid to let the white man see him carry it home.

BONO.   I'm like you . . . I ain't got no time   5
for them kind of people.

TROY. Now what he look like getting mad cause he see the man from the union talking to Mr. Rand?

BONO. He come to me talking about . . . "Maxson gonna get us fired." I told him to get away from me with that. He walked away from me calling you a troublemaker. What Mr. Rand say?

TROY. Ain't said nothing. He told me to go down the Commissioner's office next Friday. They called me down there to see them.

BONO. Well, as long as you got your complaint filed, they can't fire you. That's what one of them white fellows tell me.

10 TROY. I ain't worried about them firing me. They gonna fire me 'cause I asked a question? That's all I did. I went to Mr. Rand and asked him, "Why? Why you got the white mens driving and the colored lifting?" Told him, "what's the matter, don't I count? You think only white fellows got sense enough to drive a truck. That ain't no paper job! Hell, anybody can drive a truck. How come you got all whites driving and the colored lifting?" He told me "take it to the union." Well, hell, that's what I done! Now they wanna come up with this pack of lies.

BONO. I told Brownie if the man come and ask him any questions . . . just tell the truth! It ain't nothing but something they done trumped up on you cause you filed a complaint on them.

TROY. Brownie don't understand nothing. All I want them to do is change the job description. Give everybody a chance to drive the truck. Brownie can't see that. He ain't got that much sense.

BONO. How you figure he be making out with that gal be up at Taylors' all the time . . . that Alberta gal?

TROY. Same as you and me. Getting just as much as we is. Which is to say nothing.

BONO. It is, huh? I figure you doing a little 15 better than me . . . and I ain't saying what I'm doing.

TROY. Aw, nigger, look here . . . I know you. If you had got anywhere near that gal, twenty minutes later you be looking to tell somebody. And the first one you gonna tell . . . that you gonna want to brag to . . . is me.

BONO. I ain't saying that. I see where you be eyeing her.

TROY. I eye all the women. I don't miss nothing. Don't never let nobody tell you Troy Maxson don't eye the women.

BONO. You been doing more than eyeing her. You done bought her a drink or two.

TROY. Hell yeah, I bought her a drink! 20 What that mean? I bought you one, too. What that mean cause I buy her a drink? I'm just being polite.

BONO. It's all right to buy her one drink. That's what you call being polite. But when you wanna be buying two or three . . . that's what you call eyeing her.

TROY. Look here, as long as you known me . . . you ever known me to chase after women?

BONO. Hell yeah! Long as I done known you. You forgetting I knew you when.

TROY. Naw, I'm talking about since I been married to Rose?

BONO. Oh, not since you been married to 25 Rose. Now, that's the truth, there. I can say that.

TROY. All right then! Case closed.

BONO. I see you be walking up around Alberta's house. You supposed to be at Taylors' and you be walking up around there.

TROY. What you watching where I'm walking for? I ain't watching after you.

BONO. I seen you walking around there more than once.

30 TROY.   Hell, you liable to see me walking anywhere! That don't mean nothing cause you see me walking around there.

BONO.   Where she come from anyway? She just kinda showed up one day.

TROY.   Tallahassee. You can look at her and tell she one of them Florida gals. They got some big healthy women down there. Grow them right up out the ground. Got a little bit of Indian in her. Most of them niggers down in Florida got some Indian in them.

BONO.   I don't know about that Indian part. But she damn sure big and healthy. Woman wear some big stockings. Got them great big old legs and hips as wide as the Mississippi River.

TROY.   Legs don't mean nothing. You don't do nothing but push them out of the way. But them hips cushion the ride!

35 BONO.   Troy, you ain't got no sense.

TROY.   It's the truth! Like you riding on Goodyears!

(ROSE *enters from the house. She is ten years younger than* TROY; *her devotion to him stems from her recognition of the possibilities of her life without him: a succession of abusive men and their babies, a life of partying and running the streets, the Church, or aloneness with its attendant pain and frustration. She recognizes* TROY'S *spirit as a fine and illuminating one and she either ignores or forgives his faults, only some of which she recognizes. Though she doesn't drink, her presence is an integral part of the Friday night rituals. She alternates between the porch and the kitchen, where supper preparations are under way.*)

ROSE.   What you all out here getting into?

TROY.   What you worried about what we getting into for? This is men talk, woman.

ROSE.   What I care what you all talking about? Bono, you gonna stay for supper?

40 BONO.   No, I thank you, Rose. But Lucille says she cooking up a pot of pigfeet.

TROY.   Pigfeet! Hell, I'm going home with you! Might even stay the night if you got some pigfeet. You got something in there to top them pigfeet, Rose?

ROSE.   I'm cooking up some chicken. I got some chicken and collard greens.

TROY.   Well, go on back in the house and let me and Bono finish what we was talking about. This is men talk. I got some talk for you later. You know what kind of talk I mean. You go on and powder it up.

ROSE.   Troy Maxson, don't you start that now!

TROY (*puts his arms around her*).   Aw, woman . . . come here. Look here, Bono . . . when I met this woman . . . I got out that place, say, "Hitch up my pony, saddle up my mare . . . there's a woman out there for me somewhere. I looked here. Looked there. Saw Rose and latched on to her." I latched on to her and told her—I'm gonna tell you the truth—I told her, "Baby, I don't wanna marry, I just wanna be your man." Rose told me . . . tell him what you told me, Rose.

ROSE.   I told him if he wasn't the marrying kind, then move out the way so the marrying kind could find me.

TROY.   That's what she told me. "Nigger, you in my way. You blocking the view! Move out the way so I can find me a husband." I thought it over two or three days. Come back—

ROSE.   Ain't no two or three days nothing. You was back the same night.

TROY.   Come back, told her . . . "Okay, baby . . . but I'm gonna buy me a banty rooster and put him out there in the backyard . . . and when he see a stranger come, he'll flap his wings and crow . . ." Look here, Bono, I could watch the front door by myself . . . it was that back door I was worried about.

ROSE.   Troy, you ought not talk like that. Troy ain't doing nothing but telling a lie.

45

50

TROY.   Only thing is . . . when we first got married . . . forget the rooster . . . we ain't had no yard!

BONO.   I hear you tell it. Me and Lucille was staying down there on Logan Street. Had two rooms with the outhouse in the back. I ain't mind the outhouse none. But when that goddamn wind blow through there in the winter . . . that's what I'm talking about! To this day I wonder why in the hell I ever stayed down there for six long years. But see, I didn't know I could do no better. I thought only white folks had inside toilets and things.

ROSE.   There's a lot of people don't know they can do no better than they doing now. That's just something you got to learn. A lot of folks still shop at Bella's.

TROY.   Ain't nothing wrong with shopping at Bella's. She got fresh food.

55 ROSE.   I ain't said nothing about if she got fresh food. I'm talking about what she charge. She charge ten cents more than the A&P.

TROY.   The A&P ain't never done nothing for me. I spends my money where I'm treated right. I go down to Bella, say, "I need a loaf of bread, I'll pay you Friday." She give it to me. What sense that make when I got money to go and spend it somewhere else and ignore the person who done right by me? That ain't in the Bible.

ROSE.   We ain't talking about what's in the Bible. What sense it make to shop there when she overcharge?

TROY.   You shop where you want to. I'll do my shopping where the people been good to me.

ROSE.   Well, I don't think it's right for her to overcharge. That's all I was saying.

60 BONO.   Look here . . . I got to get on. Lucille going be raising all kind of hell.

TROY.   Where you going, nigger? We ain't finished this pint. Come here, finish this pint.

BONO.   Well, hell, I am . . . if you ever turn the bottle loose.

TROY (*hands him the bottle*).   The only thing I say about the A&P is I'm glad Cory got that job down there. Help him take care of his school clothes and things. Gabe done moved out and things getting tight around here. He got that job. . . . He can start to look out for himself.

ROSE.   Cory done went and got recruited by a college football team.

TROY.   I told that boy about that football   65 stuff. The white man ain't gonna let him get nowhere with that football. I told him when he first come to me with it. Now you come telling me he done went and got more tied up in it. He ought to go and get recruited in how to fix cars or something where he can make a living.

ROSE.   He ain't talking about making no living playing football. It's just something the boys in school do. They gonna send a recruiter by to talk to you. He'll tell you he ain't talking about making no living playing football. It's a honor to be recruited.

TROY.   It ain't gonna get him nowhere. Bono'll tell you that.

BONO.   If he be like you in the sports . . . he's gonna be all right. Ain't but two men ever played baseball as good as you. That's Babe Ruth and Josh Gibson. Them's the only two men ever hit more home runs than you.

TROY.   What it ever get me? Ain't got a pot to piss in or a window to throw it out of.

ROSE.   Times have changed since you was   70 playing baseball, Troy. That was before the war. Times have changed a lot since then.

TROY.   How in hell they done changed?

ROSE.   They got lots of colored boys playing ball now. Baseball and football.

BONO.   You right about that, Rose. Times have changed, Troy. You just come along too early.

TROY.   There ought not never have been no time called too early! Now you take that fellow . . . what's that fellow they had playing right field for the Yankees back then? You know who I'm talking about, Bono. Used to play right field for the Yankees.

75 ROSE.   Selkirk?

TROY.   Selkirk! That's it! Man batting .269, understand? .269. What kind of sense that make? I was hitting .432 with thirty-seven home runs! Man batting .269 and playing right field for the Yankees! I saw Josh Gibson's daughter yesterday. She walking around with raggedy shoes on her feet. Now I bet you Selkirk's daughter ain't walking around with raggedy shoes on her feet! I bet you that!

ROSE.   They got a lot of colored baseball players now. Jackie Robinson was the first. Folks had to wait for Jackie Robinson.

TROY.   I done seen a hundred niggers play baseball better than Jackie Robinson. Hell, I know some teams Jackie Robinson couldn't even make! What you talking about Jackie Robinson. Jackie Robinson wasn't nobody. I'm talking about if you could play ball then they ought to have let you play. Don't care what color you were. Come telling me I come along too early. If you could play . . . then they ought to have let you play. (TROY *takes a long drink from the bottle.*)

ROSE.   You gonna drink yourself to death. You don't need to be drinking like that.

80 TROY.   Death ain't nothing. I done seen him. Done wrassled with him. You can't tell me nothing about death. Death ain't nothing but a fastball on the outside corner. And you know what I'll do to that! Lookee here, Bono . . . am I lying?

You get one of them fastballs, about waist high, over the outside corner of the plate where you can get the meat of the bat on it . . . and good god! You can kiss it goodbye. Now, am I lying?

BONO.   Naw, you telling the truth there. I seen you do it.

TROY.   If I'm lying . . . that 450 feet worth of lying! (*Pause.*) That's all death is to me. A fastball on the outside corner.

ROSE.   I don't know why you want to get on talking about death.

TROY.   Ain't nothing wrong with talking about death. That's part of life. Everybody gonna die. You gonna die, I'm gonna die. Bono's gonna die. Hell, we all gonna die.

ROSE.   But you ain't got to talk about it. I   85 don't like to talk about it.

TROY.   You the one brought it up. Me and Bono was talking about baseball . . . you tell me I'm gonna drink myself to death. Ain't that right, Bono? You know I don't drink this but one night out of the week. That's Friday night. I'm gonna drink just enough to where I can handle it. Then I cuts it loose. I leave it alone. So don't you worry about me drinking myself to death. 'Cause I ain't worried about Death. I done seen him. I done wrestled with him.

Look here, Bono . . . I looked up one day and Death was marching straight at me. Like Soldiers on Parade! The Army of Death was marching straight at me. The middle of July, 1941. It got real cold just like it be winter. It seem like Death himself reached out and touched me on the shoulder. He touch me just like I touch you. I got cold as ice and Death standing there grinning at me.

ROSE.   Troy, why don't you hush that talk.

TROY.   I say . . . what you want, Mr. Death? You be wanting me? You done brought your army to be getting me? I looked him dead in the eye. I wasn't fearing nothing. I was ready to tangle. Just like I'm ready to tangle now. The Bible say be ever vigilant. That's why I don't get but so drunk. I got to keep watch.

ROSE. Troy was right down there in Mercy Hospital. You remember he had pneumonia? Laying there with a fever talking plumb out of his head.

90 TROY. Death standing there staring at me . . . carrying that sickle in his hand. Finally he say, "You want bound over for another year?" See, just like that . . . "You want bound over for another year?" I told him, "Bound over hell! Let's settle this now!"

It seem like he kinda fell back when I said that, and all the cold went out of me. I reached down and grabbed that sickle and threw it just as far as I could throw it . . . and me and him commenced to wrestling.

We wrestled for three days and three nights. I can't say where I found the strength from. Every time it seemed like he was gonna get the best of me, I'd reach way down deep inside myself and find the strength to do him one better.

ROSE. Every time Troy tell that story he find different ways to tell it. Different things to make up about it.

TROY. I ain't making up nothing. I'm telling you the facts of what happened. I wrestled with Death for three days and three nights and I'm standing here to tell you about it. (*Pause.*) All right. At the end of the third night we done weakened each other to where we can't hardly move. Death stood up, throwed on his robe . . . had him a white robe with a hood on it. He throwed on that robe and went off to look for his sickle. Say, "I'll be back." Just like that. "I'll be back." I told him, say, "Yeah, but . . . you gonna have to find me!" I wasn't no fool. I wasn't

going looking for him. Death ain't nothing to play with. And I know he's gonna get me. I know I got to join his army . . . his camp follower. But as long as I keep my strength and see him coming . . . as long as I keep up my vigilance . . . he's gonna have to fight to get me. I ain't going easy.

BONO. Well, look here, since you got to keep up your vigilance . . . let me have the bottle.

TROY. Aw hell, I shouldn't have told you that part. I should have left out that part.

ROSE. Troy be talking that stuff and half the time don't even know what he be talking about.

95

TROY. Bono know me better than that.

BONO. That's right. I know you. I know you got some Uncle Remus* in your blood. You got more stories than the devil got sinners.

TROY. Aw hell, I done seen him too! Done talked with the devil.

ROSE. Troy, don't nobody wanna be hearing all that stuff. (LYONS *enters the yard from the street. Thirty-four years old,* TROY'S *son by a previous marriage, he sports a neatly trimmed goatee, sport coat, white shirt, tieless and buttoned at the collar. Though he fancies himself a musician, he is more caught up in the rituals and "idea" of being a musician than in the actual practice of the music. He has come to borrow money from* TROY, *and while he knows he will be successful, he is uncertain as to what extent his lifestyle will be held up to scrutiny and ridicule.*)

LYONS. Hey, Pop.

100

TROY. What you come "Hey, Popping" me for?

LYONS. How you doing, Rose? (*He kisses her.*) Mr. Bono. How you doing?

BONO. Hey, Lyons . . . how you been?

*****Uncle Remus:** black narrator of folk tales in a series of books by Joel Chandler Harris (1848–1908).

TROY.   He must have been doing all right. I ain't seen him around here last week.

105   ROSE.   Troy, leave your boy alone. He come by to see you and you wanna start all that nonsense.

TROY.   I ain't bothering Lyons. (*Offers him the bottle.*) Here . . . get you a drink. We got an understanding. I know why he come by to see me and he know I know.

LYONS.   Come on, Pop . . . I just stopped by to say hi . . . see how you was doing.

TROY.   You ain't stopped by yesterday.

ROSE.   You gonna stay for supper, Lyons? I got some chicken cooking in the oven.

110   LYONS.   No, Rose . . . thanks. I was just in the neighborhood and thought I'd stop by for a minute.

TROY.   You was in the neighborhood all right, nigger. You telling the truth there. You was in the neighborhood cause it's my payday.

LYONS.   Well, hell, since you mentioned it . . . let me have ten dollars.

TROY.   I'll be damned! I'll die and go to hell and play blackjack with the devil before I give you ten dollars.

BONO.   That's what I wanna know about . . . that devil you done seen.

115   LYONS.   What . . . Pop done seen the devil? You too much, Pops.

TROY.   Yeah, I done seen him. Talked to him too!

ROSE.   You ain't seen no devil. I done told you that man ain't had nothing to do with the devil. Anything you can't understand, you want to call it the devil.

TROY.   Look here, Bono . . . I went down to see Hertzberger about some furniture. Got three rooms for two-ninety-eight. That what it say on the radio. "Three rooms . . . two-ninety-eight." Even made up a little song about it. Go down there . . . man tell me I can't get no credit. I'm working every day and can't get no credit. What to do? I got an empty house with some raggedy furniture in it. Cory ain't got no bed. He's sleeping on a pile of rags on the floor. Working every day and can't get no credit. Come back here—Rose'll tell you—madder than hell. Sit down . . . try to figure what I'm gonna do. Come a knock on the door. Ain't been living here but three days. Who know I'm here? Open the door . . . devil standing there bigger than life. White fellow . . . white fellow . . . got on good clothes and everything. Standing there with a clipboard in his hand. I ain't had to say nothing. First words come out of his mouth was . . . "I understand you need some furniture and can't get no credit." I liked to fell over. He say, "I'll give you all the credit you want, but you got to pay the interest on it." I told him, "Give me three rooms worth and charge whatever you want." Next day a truck pulled up here and two men unloaded them three rooms. Man what drove the truck give me a book. Say send ten dollars, first of every month to the address in the book and everything will be all right. Say if I miss a payment the devil was coming back and it'll be hell to pay. That was fifteen years ago. To this day . . . the first of the month I send my ten dollars, Rose'll tell you.

ROSE.   Troy lying.

TROY.   I ain't never seen that man since. Now you tell me who else that could have been but the devil? I ain't sold my soul or nothing like that, you understand. Naw, I wouldn't have truck with the devil about nothing like that. I got my furniture and pays my ten dollars the first of the month just like clockwork.   120

BONO.   How long you say you been paying this ten dollars a month?

TROY.   Fifteen years!

BONO.   Hell, ain't you finished paying for it yet? How much the man done charged you?

TROY. Ah hell, I done paid for it. I done paid for it ten times over! The fact is I'm scared to stop paying it.

125 ROSE. Troy lying. We got that furniture from Mr. Glickman. He ain't paying no ten dollars a month to nobody.

TROY. Aw hell, woman. Bono know I ain't that big a fool.

LYONS. I was just getting ready to say . . . I know where there's a bridge for sale.

TROY. Look here, I'll tell you this . . . it don't matter to me if he was the devil. It don't matter if the devil give credit. Somebody has got to give it.

ROSE. It ought to matter. You going around talking about having truck with the devil . . . God's the one you gonna have to answer to. He's the one gonna be at the Judgment.

130 LYONS. Yeah, well, look here, Pop . . . let me have that ten dollars. I'll give it back to you. Bonnie got a job working at the hospital.

TROY. What I tell you, Bono? The only time I see this nigger is when he wants something. That's the only time I see him.

LYONS. Come on, Pop, Mr. Bono don't want to hear all that. Let me have the ten dollars. I told you Bonnie working.

TROY. What that mean to me? "Bonnie working." I don't care if she working. Go ask her for the ten dollars if she working. Talking about "Bonnie working." Why ain't you working?

LYONS. Aw, Pop, you know I can't find no decent job. Where am I gonna get a job at? You know I can't get no job.

135 TROY. I told you I know some people down there. I can get you on the rubbish if you want to work. I told you that the last time you came by here asking me for something.

LYONS. Naw, Pop . . . thanks. That ain't for me. I don't wanna be carrying nobody's rubbish. I don't wanna be punching nobody's time clock.

TROY. What's the matter, you too good to carry people's rubbish? Where you think that ten dollars you talking about come from? I'm just supposed to haul people's rubbish and give my money to you cause you too lazy to work. You too lazy to work and wanna know why you ain't got what I got.

ROSE. What hospital Bonnie working at? Mercy?

LYONS. She's down at Passavant working in the laundry.

140 TROY. I ain't got nothing as it is. I give you that ten dollars and I got to eat beans the rest of the week. Naw . . . you ain't getting no ten dollars here.

LYONS. You ain't got to be eating no beans. I don't know why you wanna say that.

TROY. I ain't got no extra money. Gabe done moved over to Miss Pearl's paying her the rent and things done got tight around here. I can't afford to be giving you every payday.

LYONS. I ain't asked you to give me nothing. I asked you to loan me ten dollars. I know you got ten dollars.

TROY. Yeah, I got it. You know why I got it? Cause I don't throw my money away out there in the streets. You living the fast life . . . wanna be a musician . . . running around in them clubs and things . . . then, you learn to take care of yourself. You ain't gonna find me going and asking nobody for nothing. I done spent too many years without.

145 LYONS. You and me is two different people, Pop.

TROY. I done learned my mistake and learned to do what's right by it. You still trying to get something for nothing. Life don't owe you nothing. You owe it to yourself. Ask Bono. He'll tell you I'm right.

LYONS. You got your way of dealing with the world . . . I got mine. The only thing that matters to me is the music.

TROY. Yeah, I can see that! It don't matter how you gonna eat . . . where your next dollar is coming from. You telling the truth there.

LYONS. I know I got to eat. But I got to live too. I need something that gonna help me to get out of the bed in the morning. Make me feel like I belong in the world. I don't bother nobody. I just stay with the music 'cause that's the only way I can find to live in the world. Otherwise there ain't no telling what I might do. Now I don't come criticizing you and how you live. I just come by to ask you for ten dollars. I don't wanna hear all that about how I live.

150 TROY. Boy, your mamma did a hell of a job raising you.

LYONS. You can't change me, Pop. I'm thirty-four years old. If you wanted to change me, you should have been there when I was growing up. I come by to see you . . . ask for ten dollars and you want to talk about how I was raised. You don't know nothing about how I was raised.

ROSE. Let the boy have ten dollars, Troy.

TROY (*to* LYONS). What the hell you looking at me for? I ain't got no ten dollars. You know what I do with my money. (*To* ROSE) Give him ten dollars if you want him to have it.

ROSE. I will. Just as soon as you turn it loose.

155 TROY (*handing* ROSE *the money*). There it is. Seventy-six dollars and forty-two cents. You see this, Bono? Now, I ain't gonna get but six of that back.

ROSE. You ought to stop telling that lie. Here, Lyons. (*She hands him the money.*)

LYONS. Thanks, Rose. Look . . . I got to run . . . I'll see you later.

TROY. Wait a minute. You gonna say, "thanks, Rose" and ain't gonna look to see where she got that ten dollars from? See how they do me, Bono?

LYONS. I know she got it from you, Pop. Thanks. I'll give it back to you.

TROY. There he go telling another lie. Time 160
I see that ten dollars . . . he'll be owing me thirty more.

LYONS. See you, Mr. Bono.

BONO. Take care, Lyons!

LYONS. Thanks, Pop. I'll see you again. (LYONS *exits the yard.*)

TROY. I don't know why he don't go and get him a decent job and take care of that woman he got.

BONO. He'll be all right, Troy. The boy is 165
still young.

TROY. The *boy* is thirty-four years old.

ROSE. Let's not get off into all that.

BONO. Look here . . . I got to be going. I got to be getting on. Lucille gonna be waiting.

TROY (*puts his arm around* ROSE). See this woman, Bono? I love this woman. I love this woman so much it hurts. I love her so much . . . I done run out of ways of loving. So I got to go back to basics. Don't you come by my house Monday morning talking about time to go to work . . . 'cause I'm still gonna be stroking!

ROSE. Troy! Stop it now! 170

BONO. I ain't paying him no mind, Rose. That ain't nothing but gin-talk. Go on, Troy. I'll see you Monday.

TROY. Don't you come by my house, nigger! I done told you what I'm gonna be doing. (*The lights go down to black.*)

SCENE 2

The lights come up on ROSE *hanging up clothes. She hums and sings softly to herself. It is the following morning.*

ROSE (*sings*). Jesus, be a fence all around me every day

Jesus, I want you to protect me as I travel
on my way.
Jesus, be a fence all around me every day.
(TROY *enters from the house.*)
Jesus, I want you to protect me
As I travel on my way.
(*To* TROY) 'Morning. You ready for break-
fast? I can fix it soon as I finish hanging
up these clothes.

TROY.   I got the coffee on. That'll be all
right. I'll just drink some of that this
morning.

175 ROSE.   That 651 hit yesterday. That's the
second time this month. Miss Pearl hit
for a dollar . . . seem like those that need
the least always get lucky. Poor folks
can't get nothing.

TROY.   Them numbers don't know nobody.
I don't know why you fool with them.
You and Lyons both.

ROSE.   It's something to do.

TROY.   You ain't doing nothing but
throwing your money away.

ROSE.   Troy, you know I don't play
foolishly. I just play a nickel here and
nickel there.

180 TROY.   That's two nickels you done thrown
away.

ROSE.   Now I hit sometimes . . . that makes
up for it. It always comes in handy when
I do hit. I don't hear you complaining
then.

TROY.   I ain't complaining now. I just say
it's foolish. Trying to guess out of six
hundred ways which way the number
gonna come. If I had all the money
niggers, these Negroes, throw away on
numbers for one week—just one week—
I'd be a rich man.

ROSE.   Well, you wishing and calling it foolish ain't gonna stop folks from playing
numbers. That's one thing for sure.
Besides . . . some good things come from
playing numbers. Look where Pope done
bought him that restaurant off of numbers.

TROY.   I can't stand niggers like that. Man
ain't had two dimes to rub together. He
walking around with his shoes all run
over bumming money for cigarettes. All
right. Got lucky there and hit the
numbers . . .

ROSE.   Troy, I know all about it.   185

TROY.   Had good sense, I'll say that for
him. He ain't throwed his money away.
I seen niggers hit the numbers and go
through two thousand dollars in four
days. Man bought him that restaurant
down there . . . fixed it up real nice . . .
and then didn't want nobody to come in
it! A Negro go in there and can't get no
kind of service. I seen a white fellow
come in there and order a bowl of stew.
Pope picked all the meat out the pot for
him. Man ain't had nothing but a bowl of
meat! Negro come behind him and ain't
got nothing but the potatoes and carrots.
Talking about what numbers do for
people, you picked a wrong example.
Ain't done nothing but make a worser
fool out of him than he was before.

ROSE.   Troy, you ought to stop worrying
about what happened at work yesterday.

TROY.   I ain't worried. Just told me to be
down there at the Commissioner's office
on Friday. Everybody think they gonna
fire me. I ain't worried about them firing
me. You ain't got to worry about that.
(*Pause.*) Where's Cory? Cory in the
house? (*Calls*) Cory?

ROSE.   He gone out.

TROY.   Out, huh? He gone out 'cause he   190
know I want him to help me with this
fence. I know how he is. That boy scared
of work. (GABRIEL *enters. He comes halfway
down the alley and, hearing* TROY'S *voice,
stops.*) He ain't done a lick of work in his
life.

ROSE.   He had to go to football practice.
Coach wanted them to get in a little extra
practice before the season start.

TROY.   I got his practice . . . running out of here before he get his chores done.

ROSE.   Troy, what is wrong with you this morning? Don't nothing set right with you. Go on back in there and go to bed . . . get up on the other side.

TROY.   Why something got to be wrong with me? I ain't said nothing wrong with me.

195 ROSE.   You got something to say about everything. First it's the numbers . . . then it's the way the man runs his restaurant . . . then you done got on Cory. What's it gonna be next? Take a look up there and see if the weather suits you . . . or is it gonna be how you gonna put up the fence with the clothes hanging in the yard.

TROY.   You hit the nail on the head then.

ROSE.   I know you like I know the back of my hand. Go on in there and get you some coffee . . . see if that straighten you up. 'Cause you ain't right this morning. (TROY *starts into the house and sees* GABRIEL. GABRIEL *starts singing.* TROY'S *brother, he is seven years younger than* TROY. *Injured in World War II, he has a metal plate in his head. He carries an old trumpet tied around his waist and believes with every fiber of his being that he is the Archangel Gabriel. He carries a chipped basket with an assortment of discarded fruits and vegetables he has picked up in the strip district and which he attempts to sell.*)

GABRIEL (*singing*).   Yes, ma'am, I got plums
You ask me how I sell them
Oh ten cents apiece
Three for a quarter
Come and buy now
'Cause I'm here today
And tomorrow I'll be gone
(GABRIEL *enters the yard.*) Hey, Rose!

ROSE.   How you doing, Gabe?

200 GABRIEL.   There's Troy . . . Hey, Troy!

TROY.   Hey, Gabe. (*Exit into kitchen.*)

ROSE (*to* GABRIEL).   What you got there?

GABRIEL.   You know what I got, Rose. I got fruits and vegetables.

ROSE (*looking in basket*).   Where's all these plums you talking about?

GABRIEL.   I ain't got no plums today, Rose. 205
I was just singing that. Have some tomorrow. Put me in a big order for plums. Have enough plums tomorrow for St. Peter and everybody. (TROY *reenters from kitchen, crosses to steps.*) Troy's mad at me.

TROY.   I ain't mad at you. What I got to be mad at you about? You ain't done nothing to me.

GABRIEL.   I just moved over to Miss Pearl's to keep out from in your way. I ain't mean no harm by it.

TROY.   Who said anything about that? I ain't said anything about that.

GABRIEL.   You ain't mad at me, is you?

TROY.   Naw . . . I ain't mad at you, Gabe. If 210
I was mad at you I'd tell you about it.

GABRIEL.   Got me two rooms. In the basement. Got my own door too. Wanna see my key? (*He holds up a key.*) That's my own key! Ain't nobody else got a key like that. That's my key! My two rooms!

TROY.   Well, that's good, Gabe. You got your own key . . . that's good.

ROSE.   You hungry, Gabe? I was just fixing to cook Troy his breakfast.

GABRIEL.   I'll take some biscuits. You got some biscuits? Did you know when I was in heaven . . . every morning me and St. Peter would sit down by the gate and eat some big fat biscuits? Oh, yeah! We had us a good time. We'd sit there and eat us them biscuits and then St. Peter would go off to sleep and tell me to wake him up when it's time to open the gates for the judgment.

ROSE.   Well, come on . . . I'll make up a 215
batch of biscuits. (*Exits into the house.*)

GABRIEL.   Troy . . . St. Peter got your name in the book. I seen it. It say . . . Troy

Maxson. I say . . . I know him! He got the same name like what I got. That's my brother!

TROY.   How many times you gonna tell me that, Gabe?

GABRIEL.   Ain't got my name in the book. Don't have to have my name. I done died and went to heaven. He got your name though. One morning St. Peter was looking at his book . . . marking it up for the judgment . . . and he let me see your name. Got it in there under M. Got Rose's name . . . I ain't seen it like I seen yours . . . but I know it's in there. He got a great big book. Got everybody's name what was ever been born. That's what he told me. But I seen your name. Seen it with my own eyes.

TROY.   Go on in the house there. Rose going to fix you something to eat.

220 GABRIEL.   Oh, I ain't hungry. I done had breakfast with Aunt Jemimah. She come by and cooked me up a whole mess of flapjacks. Remember how we used to eat them flapjacks?

TROY.   Go on in the house and get you something to eat now.

GABRIEL.   I got to sell my plums. I done sold some tomatoes. Got me two quarters. Wanna see? (*He shows* TROY *his quarters.*) I'm gonna save them and buy me a new horn so St. Peter can hear me when it's time to open the gates. (GABRIEL *stops suddenly. Listens.*) Hear that? That's the hellhounds. I got to chase them out of here. Go on get out of here! Get out! (GABRIEL *exits singing.*)

> Better get ready for the judgment
> Better get ready for the judgment
> My Lord is coming down

(ROSE *enters from the house.*)

TROY.   He's gone off somewhere.

GABRIEL (*offstage*).   Better get ready for the judgment

Better get ready for the judgment morning

> Better get ready for the judgment
> My God is coming down.

ROSE.   He ain't eating right. Miss Pearl say   225
she can't get him to eat nothing.

TROY.   What you want me to do about it, Rose? I done did everything I can for the man. I can't make him get well. Man got half his head blown away . . . what you expect?

ROSE.   Seem like something ought to be done to help him.

TROY.   Man don't bother nobody. He just mixed up from that metal plate he got in his head. Ain't no sense for him to go back into the hospital.

ROSE.   Least he be eating right. They can help him take care of himself.

TROY.   Don't nobody wanna be locked up,   230
Rose. What you wanna lock him up for? Man go over there and fight the war . . . messin' around with them Japs, get half his head blown off . . . and they give him a lousy three thousand dollars. And I had to swoop down on that.

ROSE.   Is you fixing to go into that again?

TROY.   That's the only way I got a roof over my head . . . 'cause of that metal plate.

ROSE.   Ain't no sense you blaming yourself for nothing. Gabe wasn't in no condition to manage that money. You done what was right by him. Can't nobody say you ain't done what was right by him. Look how long you took care of him . . . till he wanted to have his own place and moved over there with Miss Pearl.

TROY.   That ain't what I'm saying, woman! I'm just stating the facts. If my brother didn't have that metal plate in his head . . . I wouldn't have a pot to piss in or a window to throw it out of. And I'm fifty-three years old. Now see if you can understand that! (TROY *gets up from the porch and starts to exit the yard.*)

235 ROSE.   Where you going off to? You been running out of here every Saturday for weeks. I thought you was gonna work on this fence?

TROY.   I'm gonna walk down to Taylors'. Listen to the ball game. I'll be back in a bit. I'll work on it when I get back. (*He exits the yard. The lights go to black.*)

SCENE 3

The lights come up on the yard. It is four hours later. ROSE *is taking down the clothes from the line.* CORY *enters carrying his football equipment.*

ROSE.   Your daddy like to had a fit with you running out of here this morning without doing your chores.

CORY.   I told you I had to go to practice.

ROSE.   He say you were supposed to help him with this fence.

240 CORY.   He been saying that the last four or five Saturdays, and then he don't never do nothing, but go down to Taylors'. Did you tell him about the recruiter?

ROSE.   Yeah, I told him.

CORY.   What he say?

ROSE.   He ain't said nothing too much. You get in there and get started on your chores before he gets back. Go on and scrub down them steps before he gets back here hollering and carrying on.

CORY.   I'm hungry. What you got to eat, Mama?

245 ROSE.   Go on and get started on your chores. I got some meat loaf in there. Go on and make you a sandwich . . . and don't leave no mess in there. (CORY *exits into the house.* ROSE *continues to take down the clothes.* TROY *enters the yard and sneaks up and grabs her from behind.*) Troy! Go on, now. You liked to scared me to death. What was the score of the game? Lucille had me on the phone and I couldn't keep up with it.

TROY.   What I care about the game? Come here, woman. (*He tries to kiss her.*)

ROSE.   I thought you went down Taylors' to listen to the game. Go on, Troy! You supposed to be putting up this fence.

TROY.   (*attempting to kiss her again.*) I'll put it up when I finish with what is at hand.

ROSE.   Go on, Troy. I ain't studying you.

250 TROY.   (*chasing after her*). I'm studying you . . . fixing to do my homework!

ROSE.   Troy, you better leave me alone.

TROY.   Where's Cory? That boy brought his butt home yet?

ROSE.   He's in the house doing his chores.

TORY (*calling*).   Cory! Get your butt out here, boy! (ROSE *exits into the house with the laundry.* TROY *goes over to the pile of wood, picks up a board, and starts sawing.* CORY *enters from the house.*) You just now coming in here from leaving this morning?

255 CORY.   Yeah, I had to go to football practice.

TROY.   Yeah, what?

CORY.   Yessir.

TROY.   I ain't but two seconds off you noway. The garbage sitting in there overflowing . . . you ain't done none of your chores . . . and you come in here talking about "Yeah."

CORY.   I was just getting ready to do my chores now, Pop . . .

260 TROY.   Your first chore is to help me with this fence on Saturday. Everything else come after that. Now get that saw and cut them boards. (CORY *takes the saw and begins cutting the boards.* TROY *continues working. There is a long pause.*)

CORY.   Hey, Pop . . . why don't you buy a TV?

TROY.   What I want with a TV? What I want one of them for?

CORY.   Everybody got one. Earl, Ba Bra . . . Jesse!

TROY.   I ain't asked you who had one. I say what I want with one?

265 CORY. So you can watch it. They got lots of things on TV. Baseball games and everything. We could watch the World Series.

TROY. Yeah . . . and how much this TV cost?

CORY. I don't know. They got them on sale for around two hundred dollars.

TROY. Two hundred dollars, huh?

CORY. That ain't that much, Pop.

270 TROY. Naw, it's just two hundred dollars. See that roof you got over your head at night? Let me tell you something about that roof. It's been over ten years since that roof was last tarred. See now . . . the snow come this winter and sit up there on that roof like it is . . . and it's gonna seep inside. It's just gonna be a little bit . . . ain't gonna hardly notice it. Then the next thing you know, it's gonna be leaking all over the house. Then the wood rot from all that water and you gonna need a whole new roof. Now, how much you think it cost to get that roof tarred?

CORY. I don't know.

TROY. Two hundred and sixty-four dollars . . . cash money. While you thinking about a TV, I got to be thinking about the roof . . . and whatever else go wrong here. Now if you had two hundred dollars, what would you do . . . fix the roof or buy a TV?

CORY. I'd buy a TV. Then when the roof started to leak . . . when it needed fixing . . . I'd fix it.

TROY. Where you gonna get the money from? You done spent it for a TV. You gonna sit up and watch the water run all over your brand new TV.

275 CORY. Aw, Pop. You got money. I know you do.

TROY. Where I got it at, huh?

CORY. You got it in the bank.

TROY. You wanna see my bankbook? You wanna see that seventy-three dollars and twenty-two cents I got sitting up in there.

CORY. You ain't got to pay for it all at one time. You can put a down payment on it and carry it on home with you.

TROY. Not me. I ain't gonna owe nobody 280 nothing if I can help it. Miss a payment and they come and snatch it right out your house. Then what you got? Now, soon as I get two hundred dollars clear, then I'll buy a TV. Right now, as soon as I get two hundred and sixty-four dollars, I'm gonna have this roof tarred.

CORY. Aw . . . Pop!

TROY. You go on and get you two hundred dollars and buy one if ya want it. I got better things to do with my money.

CORY. I can't get no two hundred dollars. I ain't never seen two hundred dollars.

TROY. I'll tell you what . . . you get you a hundred dollars and I'll put the other hundred with it.

CORY. All right, I'm gonna show you. 285

TROY. You gonna show me how you can cut them boards right now. (CORY begins to cut the boards. There is a long pause.)

CORY. The Pirates won today. That makes five in a row.

TROY. I ain't thinking about the Pirates. Got an all-white team. Got that boy . . . that Puerto Rican boy . . . Clemente. Don't even half-play him. That boy could be something if they give him a chance. Play him one day and sit him on the bench the next.

CORY. He gets a lot of chances to play.

TROY. I'm talking about playing regular. 290 Playing every day so you can get your timing. That's what I'm talking about.

CORY. They got some white guys on the team that don't play every day. You can't play everybody at the same time.

TROY. If they got a white fellow sitting on the bench . . . you can bet your last dollar he can't play! The colored guy got to be twice as good before he get on the team. That's why I don't want you to get all tied up in them sports. Man on the team and what it get him? They got colored on the team and don't use them. Same as not having them. All them teams the same.

CORY.   The Braves got Hank Aaron and Wes Covington. Hank Aaron hit two home runs today. That makes forty-three.

TROY.   Hank Aaron ain't nobody. That what you supposed to do. That's how you supposed to play the game. Ain't nothing to it. It's just a matter of timing . . . getting the right follow-through. Hell, I can hit forty-three home runs right now!

295 CORY.   Not off no major-league pitching, you couldn't.

TROY.   We had better pitching in the Negro leagues. I hit seven home runs off of Satchel Paige. You can't get no better than that!

CORY.   Sandy Koufax. He's leading the league in strikeouts.

TROY.   I ain't thinking of no Sandy Koufax.

CORY.   You got Warren Spahn and Lew Burdette. I bet you couldn't hit no home runs off of Warren Spahn.

300 TROY.   I'm through with it now. You go on and cut them boards. (*Pause.*) Your mama tell me you done got recruited by a college football team? Is that right?

CORY.   Yeah. Coach Zellman say the recruiter gonna be coming by to talk to you. Get you to sign the permission papers.

TROY.   I thought you supposed to be working down there at the A&P. Ain't you suppose to be working down there after school?

CORY.   Mr. Stawicki say he gonna hold my job for me until after the football season. Say starting next week I can work weekends.

TROY.   I thought we had an understanding about this football stuff? You suppose to

keep up with your chores and hold that job down at the A&P. Ain't been around here all day on a Saturday. Ain't none of your chores done . . . and now you telling me you done quit your job.

CORY.   I'm going to be working weekends.   305

TROY.   You damn right you are! And ain't no need for nobody coming around here to talk to me about signing nothing.

CORY.   Hey, Pop . . . you can't do that. He's coming all the way from North Carolina.

TROY.   I don't care where he coming from. The white man ain't gonna let you get nowhere with that football noway. You go on and get your book-learning so you can work yourself up in that A&P or learn how to fix cars or build houses or something; get you a trade. That way you have something can't nobody take away from you. You go on and learn how to put your hands to some good use. Besides hauling people's garbage.

CORY.   I get good grades, Pop. That's why the recruiter wants to talk with you. You got to keep up your grades to get recruited. This way I'll be going to college. I'll get a chance . . .

TROY.   First you gonna get your butt down   310 there to the A&P and get your job back.

CORY.   Mr. Stawicki done already hired somebody else 'cause I told him I was playing football.

TROY.   You a bigger fool than I thought . . . to let somebody take away your job so you can play some football. Where you gonna get your money to take out your girlfriend and whatnot? What kind of foolishness is that to let somebody take away your job?

CORY.   I'm still gonna be working weekends.

TROY.   Naw . . . naw. You getting your butt out of here and finding you another job.

CORY.   Come on, Pop! I got to practice. I   315 can't work after school and play football too. The team needs me. That's what Coach Zellman say . . .

TROY. I don't care what nobody else say. I'm the boss . . . you understand? I'm the boss around here. I do the only saying what counts.

CORY. Come on, Pop!

TROY. I asked you . . . did you understand?

CORY. Yeah . . .

320 TROY. What?!

CORY. Yessir.

TROY. You go on down there to that A&P and see if you can get your job back. If you can't do both . . . then you quit the football team. You've got to take the crookeds with the straights.

CORY. Yessir. (*Pause.*) Can I ask you a question?

TROY. What the hell you wanna ask me? Mr. Stawicki the one you got the questions for.

325 CORY. How come you ain't never liked me?

TROY. Liked you? Who the hell say I got to like you? What law is there say I got to like you? Wanna stand up in my face and ask a damn fool-ass question like that. Talking about liking somebody. Come here, boy, when I talk to you. (CORY *comes over to where* TROY *is working. He stands slouched over and* TROY *shoves him on his shoulder.*) Straighten up, goddammit! I asked you a question . . . what law is there say I got to like you?

CORY. None.

TROY. Well, all right then! Don't you eat every day? (*Pause.*) Answer me when I talk to you! Don't you eat every day?

CORY. Yeah.

330 TROY. Nigger, as long as you in my house, you put that sir on the end of it when you talk to me!

CORY. Yes . . . sir.

TROY. You eat every day.

CORY. Yessir!

TROY. Got a roof over your head.

CORY. Yessir! 335

TROY. Got clothes on your back.

CORY. Yessir.

TROY. Why you think that is?

CORY. 'Cause of you.

TROY. Ah, hell I know it's 'cause of me . . . but why do you think that is? 340

CORY (*hesitant*). 'Cause you like me.

TROY. Like you? I go out of here every morning . . . bust my butt . . . putting up with them crackers every day . . . 'cause I like you? You are the biggest fool I ever saw. (*Pause.*) It's my job. It's my responsibility! You understand that? A man got to take care of his family. You live in my house . . . sleep you behind on my bedclothes . . . fill you belly up with my food . . . 'cause you my son. You my flesh and blood. Not 'cause I like you! 'Cause it's my duty to take care of you. I owe a responsibility to you! Let's get this straight right here . . . before it go along any further . . . I ain't got to like you. Mr. Rand don't give me my money come payday 'cause he likes me. He give me 'cause he owe me. I done give you everything I had to give you. I gave you your life! Me and your mama worked that out between us. And liking your black ass wasn't part of the bargain. Don't you try and go through life worrying about if somebody like you or not. You best be making sure they doing right by you. You understand what I'm saying, boy?

CORY. Yessir.

TROY. Then get the hell out of my face, and get on down to that A&P. (ROSE *has been standing behind the screen door for much of the scene. She enters as* CORY *exits.*)

ROSE. Why don't you let the boy go ahead 345 and play football, Troy? Ain't no harm in that. He's just trying to be like you with the sports.

TROY. I don't want him to be like me! I want him to move as far away from my life as he can get. You the only decent thing that ever happened to me. I wish him that. But I don't wish him a thing else from my life. I decided seventeen years ago that boy wasn't getting involved in no sports. Not after what they did to me in the sports.

ROSE. Troy, why don't you admit you was too old to play in the major leagues? For once . . . why don't you admit that?

TROY. What do you mean too old? Don't come telling me I was too old. I just wasn't the right color. Hell, I'm fifty-three years old and can do better than Selkirk's .269 right now!

ROSE. How's was you gonna play ball when you were over forty? Sometimes I can't get no sense out of you.

350 TROY. I got good sense, woman. I got sense enough not to let my boy get hurt over playing no sports. You been mothering that boy too much. Worried about if people like him.

ROSE. Everything that boy do . . . he do for you. He wants you to say "Good job, son." That's all.

TROY. Rose, I ain't got time for that. He's alive. He's healthy. He's got to make his own way. I made mine. Ain't nobody gonna hold his hand when he get out there in that world.

ROSE. Times have changed from when you was young, Troy. People change. The world's changing around you and you can't even see it.

TROY (slow, methodical). Woman . . . I do the best I can do. I come in here every Friday. I carry a sack of potatoes and a bucket of lard. You all line up at the door with your hands out. I give you the lint from my pockets. I give you my sweat and my blood. I ain't got no tears. I done spent them. We go upstairs in that room at night . . . and I fall down on you and try to blast a hole into forever. I get up Monday morning . . . find my lunch on the table. I go out. Make my way. Find my strength to carry me through to the next Friday. (Pause.) That's all I got, Rose. That's all I got to give. I can't give nothing else. (TROY exits into the house. The lights go down to black.)

SCENE 4

It is Friday. Two weeks later. CORY starts out of the house with his football equipment. The phone rings.

CORY (calling). I got it! (He answers the phone and stands in the screen door talking.) Hello? Hey, Jesse. Naw . . . I was just getting ready to leave now. 355

ROSE (calling). Cory!

CORY. I told you, man, them spikes is all tore up. You can use them if you want, but they ain't no good. Earl got some spikes.

ROSE (calling). Cory!

CORY (calling to ROSE). Mam? I'm talking to Jesse. (Into phone) When she say that? (Pause.) Aw, you lying, man. I'm gonna tell her you said that.

ROSE (calling). Cory, don't you go nowhere! 360

CORY. I got to go to the game, Ma! (Into the phone) Yeah, hey, look, I'll talk to you later. Yeah, I'll meet you over Earl's house. Later. Bye, Ma. (CORY exits the house and starts out the yard.)

ROSE. Cory, where you going off to? You got that stuff all pulled out and thrown all over your room.

CORY (in the yard). I was looking for my spikes. Jesse wanted to borrow my spikes.

ROSE. Get up there and get that cleaned up before your daddy get back in here.

CORY. I got to go to the game! I'll clean it up when I get back. (CORY exits.) 365

ROSE. That's all he need to do is see that room all messed up. (ROSE *exits into the house.* TROY *and* BONO *enter the yard.* TROY *is dressed in clothes other than his work clothes.*)

BONO. He told him the same thing he told you. Take it to the union.

TROY. Brownie ain't got that much sense. Man wasn't thinking about nothing. He wait until I confront them on it . . . then he wanna come crying seniority. (*Calls*) Hey, Rose!

BONO. I wish I could have seen Mr. Rand's face when he told you.

370 TROY. He couldn't get it out of his mouth! Liked to bit his tongue! When they called me down there to the Commissioner's office . . . he thought they was gonna fire me. Like everybody else.

BONO. I didn't think they was gonna fire you. I thought they was gonna put you on the warning paper.

TROY. Hey, Rose! (*To* BONO) Yeah, Mr. Rand like to bit his tongue. (TROY *breaks the seal on the bottle, takes a drink, and hands it to* BONO.)

BONO. I see you run right down to Taylors' and told that Alberta gal.

TROY (*calling*). Hey Rose! (*To* BONO) I told everybody. Hey, Rose! I went down there to cash my check.

375 ROSE (*entering from the house*). Hush all that hollering, man! I know you out here. What they say down there at the Commissioner's office?

TROY. You supposed to come when I call you, woman. Bono'll tell you that. (*To* BONO) Don't Lucille come when you call her?

ROSE. Man, hush your mouth. I ain't no dog . . . talk about "come when you call me."

TROY (*puts his arm around* ROSE). You hear this, Bono? I had me an old dog used to get uppity like that. You say, "C'mere,

Blue!" . . . and he just lay there and look at you. End up getting a stick and chasing him away trying to make him come.

ROSE. I ain't studying you and your dog. I remember you used to sing that old song.

TROY (*he sings*). Hear it ring! Hear it ring! 380 I had a dog his name was Blue.

ROSE. Don't nobody wanna hear you sing that old song.

TROY (*sings*). You know Blue was mighty true.

ROSE. Used to have Cory running around here singing that song.

BONO. Hell, I remember that song myself.

TROY (*sings*). You know Blue was a good 385 old dog.
Blue treed a possum in a hollow log.
That was my daddy's song. My daddy made up that song.

ROSE. I don't care who made it up. Don't nobody wanna hear you sing it.

TROY (*makes a song like calling a dog*). Come here, woman.

ROSE. You come in here carrying on, I reckon they ain't fired you. What they say down there at the Commissioner's office?

TROY. Look here, Rose . . . Mr. Rand called me into his office today when I got back from taking to them people down there . . . it come from up top . . . he called me in and told me they was making me a driver.

ROSE. Troy, you kidding! 390

TROY. No I ain't. Ask Bono.

ROSE. Well, that's great, Troy. Now you don't have to hassle them people no more. (LYONS *enters from the street.*)

TROY. Aw hell, I wasn't looking to see you today. I thought you was in jail. Got it all over the front page of the *Courier* about them raiding Sefus's place . . . where you be hanging out with all them thugs.

LYONS. Hey, Pop . . . that ain't got nothing to do with me. I don't go down there gambling. I go down there to sit in with the band. I ain't got nothing to do with the gambling part. They got some good music down there.

395 TROY. They got some rogues . . . is what they got.

LYONS. How you been, Mr. Bono? Hi, Rose.

BONO. I see where you playing down at the Crawford Grill tonight.

ROSE. How come you ain't brought Bonnie like I told you? You should have brought Bonnie with you, she ain't been over in a month of Sundays.

LYONS. I was just in the neighborhood . . . thought I'd stop by.

400 TROY. Here he come . . .

BONO. Your daddy got a promotion on the rubbish. He's gonna be the first colored driver. Ain't got to do nothing but sit up there and read the paper like them white fellows.

LYONS. Hey, Pop . . . if you knew how to read you'd be all right.

BONO. Naw . . . naw . . . you mean if the nigger knew how to *drive* he'd be all right. Been fighting with them people about driving and ain't even got a license. Mr. Rand know you ain't got no driver's license?

TROY. Driving ain't nothing. All you do is point the truck where you want it to go. Driving ain't nothing.

405 BONO. Do Mr. Rand know you ain't got no driver's license? That's what I'm talking about. I ain't asked if driving was easy. I asked if Mr. Rand know you ain't got no driver's license.

TROY. He ain't got to know. The man ain't got to know my business. Time he find out, I have two or three driver's licenses.

LYONS (*going into his pocket*). Say, look here, Pop . . .

TROY. I knew it was coming. Didn't I tell you, Bono? I know what kind of "Look

here, Pop" that was. The nigger fixing to ask me for some money. It's Friday night. It's my payday. All them rogues down there on the avenue . . . the ones that ain't in jail . . . and Lyons is hopping in his shoes to get down there with them.

LYONS. See, Pop . . . if you give somebody else a chance to talk sometimes, you'd see that I was fixing to pay you back your ten dollars like I told you. Here . . . I told you I'd pay you when Bonnie got paid.

TROY. Naw . . . you go ahead and keep   410
that ten dollars. Put it in the bank. The next time you feel like you wanna come by here and ask me for something . . . you go on down there and get that.

LYONS. Here's your ten dollars, Pop. I told you I don't want you to give me nothing. I just wanted to borrow ten dollars.

TROY. Naw . . . you go on and keep that for the next time you want to ask me.

LYONS. Come on, Pop . . . here go your ten dollars.

ROSE. Why don't you go on and let the boy pay you back, Troy?

LYONS. Here you go, Rose. If you don't   415
take it I'm gonna have to hear about it for the next six months. (*He hands her the money.*)

ROSE. You can hand yours over here too, Troy.

TROY. You see this, Bono. You see how they do me.

BONO. Yeah, Lucille do me the same way. (GABRIEL *is heard singing offstage. He enters.*)

GABRIEL. Better get ready for the Judgment! Better get ready for . . . Hey! . . . Hey! There's Troy's boy!

LYONS. How are you doing, Uncle Gabe!   420

GABRIEL. Lyones . . . The King of the Jungle! Rose . . . hey, Rose. Got a flower for you. (*He takes a rose from his pocket.*) Picked it myself. That's the same rose like you is!

ROSE.   That's right nice of you, Gabe.

LYONS.   What you been doing, Uncle Gabe?

GABRIEL.   Oh, I been chasing hellhounds and waiting on the time to tell St. Peter to open the gates.

425   LYONS.   You been chasing hellhounds, huh? Well . . . you doing the right thing, Uncle Gabe. Somebody got to chase them.

GABRIEL.   Oh, yeah . . . I know it. The devil's strong. The devil ain't no pushover. Hellhounds snipping at everybody's heels. But I got my trumpet waiting on the judgment time.

LYONS.   Waiting on the Battle of Armageddon, huh?

GABRIEL.   Ain't gonna be too much of a battle when God get to waving that Judgment sword. But the people's gonna have a hell of a time trying to get into heaven if them gates ain't open.

LYONS (*putting his arm around* GABRIEL).   You hear this, Pop. Uncle Gabe, you all right!

430   GABRIEL. (*laughing with* LYONS).   Lyons! King of the Jungle.

ROSE.   You gonna stay for supper, Gabe? Want me to fix you a plate?

GABRIEL.   I'll take a sandwich, Rose. Don't want no plate. Just wanna eat with my hands. I'll take a sandwich.

ROSE.   How about you. Lyons? You staying? Got some short ribs cooking.

LYONS.   Naw, I won't eat nothing till after we finished playing. (*Pause.*) You ought to come down and listen to me play, Pop.

435   TROY.   I don't like that Chinese music. All that noise.

ROSE.   Go on in the house and wash up, Gabe . . . I'll fix you a sandwich.

GABRIEL (*to* LYONS, *as he exits*).   Troy's mad at me.

LYONS.   What you mad at Uncle Gabe for, Pop?

ROSE.   He thinks Troy's mad at him 'cause he moved over to Miss Pearl's.

TROY.   I ain't mad at the man. He can live   440 where he want to live at.

LYONS.   What he move over there for? Miss Pearl don't like nobody.

ROSE.   She don't mind him none. She treats him real nice. She just don't allow all that singing.

TROY.   She don't mind that rent he be paying . . . that's what she don't mind.

ROSE.   Troy, I ain't going through that with you no more. He's over there 'cause he want to have his own place. He can come and go as he please.

TROY.   Hell, he could come and go as he   445 please here. I wasn't stopping him. I ain't put no rules on him.

ROSE.   It ain't the same thing, Troy. And you know it. (GABRIEL *comes to the door.*) Now, that's the last I wanna hear about that. I don't wanna hear nothing else about Gabe and Miss Pearl. And next week . . .

GABRIEL.   I'm ready for my sandwich, Rose.

ROSE.   And next week . . . when that recruiter come from that school . . . I want you to sign that paper and go on and let Cory play football. Then that'll be the last I have to hear about that.

TROY (*to* ROSE *as she exits into the house*).   I ain't thinking about Cory nothing.

LYONS.   What . . . Cory got recruited? What   450 school he going to?

TROY.   That boy walking around here smelling his piss . . . thinking he's grown. Thinking he's gonna do what he want, irrespective of what I say. Look here, Bono . . . I left the Commissioner's office and went down to the A&P . . . that boy ain't working down there. He lying to me. Telling me he got his job back . . . telling me he working weekends . . . telling me he working after school . . . Mr. Stawicki tell me he ain't working down there at all!

LYONS.   Cory just growing up. He's just busting at the seams trying to fill out your shoes.

TROY.   I don't care what he's doing. When he get to the point where he wanna disobey me . . . then it's time for him to move on. Bono'll tell you that. I bet he ain't never disobeyed his daddy without paying the consequences.

BONO.   I ain't never had a chance. My daddy came on through . . . but I ain't never knew him to see him . . . or what he had on his mind or where he went. Just moving on through. Searching out the New Land. That's what the old folks used to call it. See a fellow moving around from place to place . . . woman to woman . . . called it searching out the New Land. I can't say if he ever found it. I come along, didn't want no kids. Didn't know if I was gonna be in one place long enough to fix on them right as their daddy. I figured I was going searching too. As it turned out I been hooked up with Lucille near about as long as your daddy been with Rose. Going on sixteen years.

455 TROY.   Sometimes I wish I hadn't known my daddy. He ain't cared nothing about no kids. A kid to him wasn't nothing. All he wanted was for you to learn how to walk so he could start you to working. When it come time for eating . . . he ate first. If there was anything left over, that's what you got. Man would sit down and eat two chickens and give you the wing.

LYONS.   You ought to stop that, Pop. Everybody feed their kids. No matter how hard times is . . . everybody care about their kids. Make sure they have something to eat.

TROY.   The only thing my daddy cared about was getting them bales of cotton in to Mr. Lubin. That's the only thing that mattered to him. Sometimes I used to wonder why he was living. Wonder why the devil hadn't come and got him. "Get them bales of cotton in to Mr. Lubin" and find out he owe him money . . .

LYONS.   He should have just went on and left when he saw he couldn't get nowhere. That's what I would have done.

TROY.   How he gonna leave with eleven kids? And where he gonna go? He ain't knew how to do nothing but farm. No, he was trapped and I think he knew it. But I'll say this for him . . . he felt a responsibility toward us. Maybe he ain't treated us the way I felt he should have . . . but without that responsibility he could have walked off and left us . . . made his own way.

BONO.   A lot of them did. Back in those 460 days what you talking about . . . they walk out their front door and just take on down one road or another and keep on walking.

LYONS.   There you go! That's what I'm talking about.

BONO.   Just keep on walking till you come to something else. Ain't you never heard of nobody having the walking blues? Well, that's what you call it when you just take off like that.

TROY.   My daddy ain't had them walking blues! What you talking about? He stayed right there with his family. But he was just as evil as he could be. My mama couldn't stand him. Couldn't stand that evilness. She run off when I was about eight. She sneaked off one night after he had gone to sleep. Told me she was coming back for me. I ain't never seen her no more. All his women run off and left him. He wasn't good for nobody.

   When my turn come to head out, I was fourteen and got to sniffing around Joe Canewell's daughter. Had us an old mule we called Greyboy. My daddy sent me out to do some plowing and I tied up Greyboy and went to fooling around with Joe Canewell's daughter. We done found us a nice little spot, got real cozy with each other. She about thirteen and we done figured we was grown anyway . . . so we down there enjoying ourselves . . . ain't thinking about nothing. We didn't know Greyboy had got loose and wandered back to the house and my daddy was looking for me. We down there by the creek enjoying ourselves when my daddy come up on us. Surprised us. He had them leather straps off the mule and commenced to whupping me like there was no tomorrow. I jumped up, mad and embarrassed. I was scared of my daddy. When he commenced to whupping on me . . . quite naturally I run to get out of the way. (*Pause.*) Now I thought he was mad 'cause I ain't done my work. But I see where he was chasing me off so he could have the gal for himself. When I see what the matter of it was, I lost all fear of my daddy. Right there is where I become a man . . . at fourteen years of age. (*Pause.*) Now it was my turn to run him off. I picked up them same reins that he had used on me. I picked up them reins and commenced to whupping on him. The gal jumped up and run off . . . and when my daddy turned to face me, I could see why the devil had never come to get him . . . 'cause he was the devil himself. I don't know what happened. When I woke up, I was laying right there by the creek, and Blue . . . this old dog we had . . . was licking my face. I thought I was blind. I couldn't see nothing. Both my eyes were swollen shut. I laid there and cried. I didn't know what I was gonna do. The only thing I knew was the time had come for me to leave my daddy's house. And right there the world suddenly got big.

And it was a long time before I could cut it down to where I could handle it.

Part of that cutting down was when I got to the place where I could feel him kicking in my blood and knew that the only thing that separated us was the matter of a few years. (GABRIEL *enters from the house with a sandwich.*)

LYONS. What you got there, Uncle Gabe?

GABRIEL. Got me a ham sandwich. Rose gave me a ham sandwich. 465

TROY. I don't know what happened to him. I done lost touch with everybody except Gabriel. But I hope he's dead. I hope he found some peace.

LYONS. That's a heavy story, Pop. I didn't know you left home when you was fourteen.

TROY. I didn't know nothing. The only part of the world I knew was the forty-two acres of Mr. Lubin's land. That's all I knew about life.

LYONS. Fourteen's kinda young to be out on your own. (*Phone rings.*) I don't even think I was ready to be out on my own at fourteen. I don't know what I would have done.

TROY. I got up from the creek and walked on down to Mobile. I was through with farming. Figured I could do better in the city. So I walked the two hundred miles to Mobile. 470

LYONS. Wait a minute . . . you ain't walked no two hundred miles, Pop. Ain't nobody gonna walk no two hundred miles. You talking about some walking there.

BONO. That's the only way you got anywhere back in them days.

LYONS. Shhh. Damn if I wouldn't have hitched a ride with somebody!

TROY. Who you gonna hitch it with? They ain't had no cars and things like they got now. We talking about 1918.

ROSE (*entering*). What you all out here getting into? 475

TROY (*to* ROSE). I'm telling Lyons how good he got it. He don't know nothing about this I'm talking.

ROSE. Lyons, that was Bonnie on the phone. She say you supposed to pick her up.

LYONS. Yeah, okay, Rose.

TROY. I walked on down to Mobile and hitched up with some of them fellows that was heading this way. Got up here and found out . . . not only couldn't you get a job . . . you couldn't find no place to live. I thought I was in freedom. Shhh. Colored folks living down there on the riverbanks in whatever kind of shelter they could find for themselves. Right down there under the Brady Street Bridge. Living in shacks made of sticks and tarpaper. Messed around there and went from bad to worse. Start stealing. First it was food. Then I figured, hell, if I steal money I can buy me some food. Buy me some shoes too! One thing led to another. Met your mama. I was young and anxious to be a man. Met your mama and had you. What I do that for? Now I got to worry about feeding you and her. Got to steal three times as much. Went out one day looking for somebody to rob . . . that's what I was, a robber. I'll tell you the truth. I'm ashamed of it today. But it's the truth. Went to rob this fellow . . . pulled out my knife . . . and he pulled out a gun. Shot me in the chest. I felt just like somebody had taken a hot branding iron and laid it on me. When he shot me I jumped at him with my knife. They told me I killed him and they put me in the penitentiary and locked me up for fifteen years. That's where I met Bono. That's where I learned how to play baseball. Got out that place and your mama had taken you and went on to make life without me. Fifteen years was a long time for her to wait. But that fifteen years

cured me of that robbing stuff. Rose'll tell you. She asked me when I met her if I had gotten all that foolishness out of my system. And I told her, "Baby, it's you and baseball all what count with me." You hear me, Bono? I mean it too. She say, "Which one comes first?" I told her, "Baby, ain't no doubt it's baseball . . . but you stick and get old with me and we'll both outlive this baseball." Am I right, Rose? And it's true.

ROSE. Man, hush your mouth. You ain't   480
said no such thing. Talking about, "Baby, you know you'll always be number one with me." That's what you was talking.

TROY. You hear that, Bono. That's why I love her.

BONO. Rose'll keep you straight. You get off the track, she'll straighten you up.

ROSE. Lyons, you better get on up and get Bonnie. She waiting on you.

LYONS (*gets up to go*). Hey, Pop, why don't you come on down to the Grill and hear me play?

TROY. I ain't going down there. I'm too   485
old to be sitting around in them clubs.

BONO. You got to be good to play down at the Grill.

LYONS. Come on, Pop . . .

TROY. I got to get up in the morning.

LYONS. You ain't got to stay long.

TROY. Naw, I'm gonna get my supper and   490
go on to bed.

LYONS. Well, I got to go. I'll see you again.

TROY. Don't you come around my house on my payday.

ROSE. Pick up the phone and let somebody know you coming. And bring Bonnie with you. You know I'm always glad to see her.

LYONS. Yeah, I'll do that, Rose. You take care now. See you, Pop. See you, Mr. Bono. See you, Uncle Gabe.

GABRIEL. Lyons! King of the Jungle!   495
(LYONS *exits.*)

TROY. Is supper ready, woman? Me and you got some business to take care of. I'm gonna tear it up too.

ROSE. Troy, I done told you now!

TROY (*puts his arm around* BONO). Aw hell, woman . . . this is Bono. Bono like family. I done known this nigger since . . . how long I done know you?

BONO. It's been a long time.

500 TROY. I done know this nigger since Skippy was a pup. Me and him done been through some times.

BONO. You sure right about that.

TROY. Hell, I done know him longer than I known you. And we still standing shoulder to shoulder. Hey, look here, Bono . . . a man can't ask for no more than that. (*Drinks to him.*) I love you, nigger.

BONO. Hell, I love you too . . . I got to get home see my woman. You got yours in hand. I got to go get mine. (BONO *starts to exit as* CORY *enters the yard, dressed in his football uniform. He gives* TROY *a hard, uncompromising look.*)

CORY. What you do that for, Pop? (*He throws his helmet down in the direction of* TROY.)

505 ROSE. What's the matter? Cory . . . what's the matter?

CORY. Papa done went up to the school and told Coach Zellman I can't play football no more. Wouldn't even let me play the game. Told him to tell the recruiter not to come.

ROSE. Troy . . .

TROY. What you Troying me for. Yeah, I did it. And the boy know why I did it.

CORY. Why you wanna do that to me? That was the one chance I had.

510 ROSE. Ain't nothing wrong with Cory playing football, Troy.

TROY. The boy lied to me. I told the nigger if he wanna play football . . . to keep up his chores and hold down that job at the A&P. That was the conditions. Stopped down there to see Mr. Stawicki . . .

CORY. I can't work after school during the football season, Pop! I tried to tell you that Mr. Stawicki's holding my job for me. You don't never want to listen to nobody. And then you wanna go and do this to me!

TROY. I ain't done nothing to you. You done it to yourself.

CORY. Just 'cause you didn't have a chance! You just scared I'm gonna be better than you, that's all.

TROY. Come here.   515

ROSE. Troy . . . (CORY *reluctantly crosses over to* TROY.)

TROY. All right! See. You done made a mistake.

CORY. I didn't even do nothing!

TROY. I'm gonna tell you what your mistake was. See . . . you swung at the ball and didn't hit it. That's strike one. See, you in the batter's box now. You swung and you missed. That's strike one. Don't you strike out! (*Lights fade to black.*)

─────(**ACT 2**)─────

SCENE 1

The following morning. CORY *is at the tree hitting the ball with the bat. He tries to mimic* TROY, *but his swing is awkward, less sure.* ROSE *enters from the house.*

ROSE. Cory, I want you to help me with this cupboard.

CORY. I ain't quitting the team. I don't care what Poppa say.

ROSE. I'll talk to him when he gets back. He had to go see about your Uncle Gabe. The police done arrested him. Say he was disturbing the peace. He'll be back directly. Come on in here and help me clean out the top of this cupboard. (CORY *exits into the house.* ROSE *sees* TROY *and*

BONO *coming down the alley.*) Troy . . . what they say down there?

TROY.   Ain't said nothing. I give them fifty dollars and they let him go. I'll talk to you about it. Where's Cory?

5 ROSE.   He's in there helping me clean out these cupboards.

TROY.   Tell him to get his butt out here. (TROY *and* BONO *go over to the pile of wood.* BONO *picks up the saw and begins sawing.* To BONO) All they want is the money. That makes six or seven times I done went down there and got him. See me coming they stick out their *hands*.

BONO.   Yeah. I know what you mean. That's all they care about . . . that money. They don't care about what's right. (*Pause.*) Nigger, why you got to go and get some hard wood? You ain't doing nothing but building a little old fence. Get you some soft pine wood. That's all you need.

TROY.   I know what I'm doing. This is outside wood. You put pine wood inside the house. Pine wood is inside wood. This here is outside wood. Now you tell me where the fence is gonna be?

BONO.   You don't need this wood. You can put it up with pine wood and it'll stand as long as you gonna be here looking at it.

10 TROY.   How you know how long I'm gonna be here, nigger? Hell, I might just live forever. Live longer than old man Horsely.

BONO.   That's what Magee used to say.

TROY.   Magee's a damn fool. Now you tell me who you ever heard of gonna pull their own teeth with a pair of rusty pliers.

BONO.   The old folks . . . my granddaddy used to pull his teeth with pliers. They ain't had no dentists for the colored folks back then.

TROY.   Get clean pliers! You understand? Clean pliers! Sterilize them! Besides we

ain't living back then. All Magee had to do was walk over to Doc Goldblum's.

BONO.   I see where you and that Tallahassee gal . . . that Alberta . . . I see where you all done got tight.   15

TROY.   What you mean "got tight"?

BONO.   I see where you be laughing and joking with her all the time.

TROY.   I laughs and jokes with all of them, Bono. You know me.

BONO.   That ain't the kind of laughing and joking I'm talking about. (CORY *enters from the house.*)

CORY.   How you doing, Mr. Bono?   20

TROY.   Cory? Get that saw from Bono and cut some wood. He talking about the wood's too hard to cut. Stand back there, Jim, and let that young boy show you how it's done.

BONO.   He's sure welcome to it. (CORY *takes the saw and begins to cut the wood.*) Whew-e-e! Look at that. Big old strong boy. Look like Joe Louis. Hell, must be getting old the way I'm watching that boy whip through that wood.

CORY.   I don't see why Mama want a fence around the yard noways.

TROY.   Damn if I know either. What the hell she keeping out with it? She ain't got nothing nobody want.

BONO.   Some people build fences to keep people out . . . and other people build fences to keep people in. Rose wants to hold on to you all. She loves you.   25

TROY.   Hell, nigger, I don't need nobody to tell me my wife loves me. Cory . . . go on in the house and see if you can find that other saw.

CORY.   Where's it at?

TROY   I said find it! Look for it till you find it! (CORY *exits into the house.*) What's that supposed to mean? Wanna keep us in?

BONO.   Troy . . . I done known you seem like damn near my whole life. You and Rose both. I done know both of you all for a long time. I remember when you met Rose. When you was hitting them baseball out the park. A lot of them old gals was after you then. You had the pick of the litter. When you picked Rose, I was happy for you. That was the first time I knew you had any sense. I said . . . My man Troy knows what he's doing . . . I'm gonna follow this nigger . . . he might take me somewhere. I been following you too. I done learned a whole heap of things about life watching you. I done learned how to tell where the shit lies. How to tell it from the alfalfa. You done learned me a lot of things. You showed me how to not make the same mistakes . . . to take life as it comes along and keep putting one foot in front of the other. (*Pause.*) Rose a good woman, Troy.

30 TROY.   Hell, nigger, I know she a good woman. I been married to her for eighteen years. What you got on your mind, Bono?

BONO.   I just say she a good woman. Just like I say anything. I ain't got to have nothing on my mind.

TROY.   You just gonna say she a good woman and leave it hanging out there like that? Why you telling me she a good woman?

BONO.   She loves you, Troy. Rose loves you.

TROY.   You saying I don't measure up. That's what you trying to say. I don't measure up 'cause I'm seeing this other gal. I know what you trying to say.

35 BONO.   I know what Rose means to you, Troy. I'm just trying to say I don't want to see you mess up.

TROY.   Yeah, I appreciate that, Bono. If you was messing around on Lucille I'd be telling you the same thing.

BONO.   Well, that's all I got to say. I just say that because I love you both.

TROY.   Hell, you know me . . . I wasn't out there looking for nothing. You can't find a better woman than Rose. I know that. But seems like this woman just stuck onto me where I can't shake her loose. I done wrestled with it, tried to throw her off me . . . but she just stuck on tighter. Now she's stuck on for good.

BONO.   You's in control . . . that's what you tell me all the time. You responsible for what you do.

TROY.   I ain't ducking the responsibility of 40 it. As long as it sets right in my heart . . . then I'm okay. 'Cause that's all I listen to. It'll tell me right from wrong every time. And I ain't talking about doing Rose no bad turn. I love Rose. She done carried me a long ways and I love and respect her for that.

BONO.   I know you do. That's why I don't want to see you hurt her. But what you gonna do when she find out? What you got then? If you try and juggle both of them . . . sooner or later you gonna drop one of them. That's common sense.

TROY.   Yeah, I hear what you saying, Bono. I been trying to figure a way to work it out.

BONO.   Work it out right, Troy. I don't want to be getting all up between you and Rose's business . . . but work it so it come out right.

TROY.   Ah hell, I get all up between you and Lucille's business. When you gonna get that woman that refrigerator she been wanting? Don't tell me you ain't got no money now. I know who your banker is. Mellon don't need that money bad as Lucille want that refrigerator. I'll tell you that.

BONO.   Tell you what I'll do . . . when you 45 finish building this fence for Rose . . . I'll buy Lucille that refrigerator.

TROY.   You done stuck your foot in your mouth now! (*Grabs up a board and begins to saw.* BONO *starts to walk out of the yard.*) Hey, nigger . . . where you going?

BONO.   I'm going home. I know you don't expect me to help you now. I'm protecting my money. I wanna see you put that fence up by yourself. That's what I want to see. You'll be here another six months without me.

TROY.   Nigger, you ain't right.

BONO.   When it comes to my money . . . I'm right as fireworks on the Fourth of July.

50 TROY.   All right, we gonna see now. You better get out your bankbook. (BONO *exits, and* TROY *continues to work.* ROSE *enters from the house.*)

ROSE.   What they say down there? What's happening with Gabe?

TROY.   I went down there and got him out. Cost me fifty dollars. Say he was disturbing the peace. Judge set up a hearing for him in three weeks. Say to show cause why he shouldn't be recommitted.

ROSE.   What was he doing that cause them to arrest him?

TROY.   Some kids was teasing him and he run them off home. Say he was howling and carrying on. Some folks seen him and called the police. That's all it was.

55 ROSE.   Well, what's you say? What'd you tell the judge?

TROY.   Told him I'd look after him. It didn't make no sense to recommit the man. He stuck out his big greasy palm and told me to give him fifty dollars and take him on home.

ROSE.   Where's he at now? Where'd he go off to?

TROY.   He's gone about his business. He don't need nobody to hold his hand.

ROSE.   Well, I don't know. Seem like that would be the best place for him if they did put him into the hospital. I know what you're gonna say. But that's what I think would be best.

60 TROY.   The man done had his life ruined fighting for what? And they wanna take and lock him up. Let him be free. He don't bother nobody.

ROSE.   Well, everybody got their own way of looking at it I guess. Come on and get your lunch. I got a bowl of lima beans and some cornbread in the oven. Come and get something to eat. Ain't no sense you fretting over Gabe. (*Turns to go into the house.*)

TROY.   Rose . . . got something to tell you.

ROSE.   Well, come on . . . wait till I get this food on the table.

TROY.   Rose! (*She stops and turns around.*) I don't know how to say this. (*Pause.*) I can't explain it none. It just sort of grows on you till it gets out of hand. It starts out like a little bush . . . and the next thing you know it's a whole forest.

ROSE.   Troy . . . what is you talking about?   65

TROY.   I'm talking, woman, let me talk. I'm trying to find a way to tell you . . . I'm gonna be a daddy. I'm gonna be somebody's daddy.

ROSE.   Troy . . . you're not telling me this? You're gonna be . . . what?

TROY.   Rose . . . now . . . see . . .

ROSE.   You telling me you gonna be somebody's daddy? You telling your *wife* this? (GABRIEL *enters from the street. He carries a rose in his hand.*)

GABRIEL.   Hey, Troy! Hey, Rose!   70

ROSE.   I have to wait eighteen years to hear something like this.

GABRIEL.   Hey, Rose . . . I got a flower for you. (*He hands it to her.*) That's a rose. Same rose like you is.

ROSE.   Thanks, Gabe.

GABRIEL.   Troy, you ain't mad at me is you? Them bad mens come and put me away. You ain't mad at me is you?

TROY.   Naw, Gabe, I ain't mad at you.   75

ROSE.   Eighteen years and you wanna come with this.

GABRIEL (*takes a quarter out of his pocket*). See what I got? Got a brand new quarter.

TROY.   Rose . . . it's just . . .

ROSE.   Ain't nothing you can say, Troy. Ain't no way of explaining that.

80 GABRIEL.   Fellow that give me this quarter had a whole mess of them. I'm gonna keep this quarter till it stop shining.

ROSE.   Gabe, go on in the house there. I got some watermelon in the Frigidaire. Go on and get you a piece.

GABRIEL.   Say, Rose . . . you know I was chasing hellhounds and them bad mens come and get me and take me away. Troy helped me. He come down there and told them they better let me go before he beat them up. Yeah, he did!

ROSE.   You go on and get you a piece of watermelon, Gabe. Them bad mens is gone now.

GABRIEL.   Okay, Rose . . . gonna get me some watermelon. The kind with the stripes on it. (GABRIEL *exits into the house.*)

85 ROSE.   Why, Troy? Why? After all these years to come dragging this in to me now. It don't make no sense at your age. I could have expected this ten or fifteen years ago, but not now.

TROY.   Age ain't got nothing to do with it, Rose.

ROSE.   I done tried to be everything a wife should be. Everything a wife could be. Been married eighteen years and I got to live to see the day you tell me you been seeing another woman and done fathered a child by her. And you know I ain't never wanted no half nothing in my family. My whole family is half. Everybody got different fathers and mothers . . . my two sisters and my brother. Can't hardly tell who's who. Can't never sit down and talk about Papa and Mama. It's your papa and your mama and my papa and my mama . . .

TROY.   Rose . . . stop it now.

ROSE.   I ain't never wanted that for none of my children. And now you wanna drag your behind in here and tell me something like this.

TROY.   You ought to know. It's time for you 90 to know.

ROSE.   Well, I don't want to know, goddamn it!

TROY.   I can't just make it go away. It's done now. I can't wish the circumstance of the thing away.

ROSE.   And you don't want to either. Maybe you want to wish me and my boy away. Maybe that's what you want? Well, you can't wish us away. I've got eighteen years of my life invested in you. You ought to have stayed upstairs in my bed where you belong.

TROY.   Rose . . . now listen to me . . . we can get a handle on this thing. We can talk this out . . . come to an understanding.

ROSE.   All of a sudden it's "we." Where 95 was "we" at when you was down there rolling around with some godforsaken woman? "We" should have come to an understanding before you started making a damn fool of yourself. You're a day late and a dollar short when it comes to an understanding with me.

TROY.   It's just . . . She gives me a different idea . . . a different understanding about myself. I can step out of this house and get away from the pressures and problems . . . be a different man. I ain't got to wonder how I'm gonna pay the bills or get the roof fixed. I can just be a part of myself that I ain't never been.

ROSE.   What I want to know . . . is do you plan to continue seeing her. That's all you can say to me.

TROY.   I can sit up in her house and laugh. Do you understand what I'm saying? I can laugh out loud . . . and it feels good. It reaches all the way down to the bottom of my shoes. (*Pause.*) Rose, I can't give that up.

ROSE.   Maybe you ought to go on and stay down there with her . . . if she's a better woman than me.

100 TROY.   It ain't about nobody being a better woman or nothing. Rose, you ain't the blame. A man couldn't ask for no woman to be a better wife than you've been. I'm responsible for it. I done locked myself into a pattern trying to take care of you all that I forgot about myself.

ROSE.   What the hell was I there for? That was my job, not somebody else's.

TROY.   Rose, I done tried all my life to live decent . . . to live a clean . . . hard . . . useful life. I tried to be a good husband to you. In every way I knew how. Maybe I come into the world backwards, I don't know. But . . . you born with two strikes on you before you come to the plate. You got to guard it closely . . . always looking for the curve ball on the inside corner. You can't afford to let none get past you. You can't afford a call strike. If you going down . . . you going down swinging. Everything lined up against you. What you gonna do? I fooled them, Rose. I bunted. When I found you and Cory and a halfway decent job . . . I was safe. Couldn't nothing touch me. I wasn't gonna strike out no more. I wasn't going back to the penitentiary. I wasn't gonna lay in the streets with a bottle of wine. I was safe. I had me a family. A job. I wasn't gonna get that last strike. I was on first looking for one of them boys to knock me in. To get me home.

ROSE.   You should have stayed in my bed, Troy.

TROY.   Then when I saw that gal . . . she firmed up my backbone. And I got to thinking that if I tried . . . I just might be able to steal second. Do you understand after eighteen years I wanted to steal second.

105 ROSE.   You should have held me tight. You should have grabbed me and held on.

TROY.   I stood on first base for eighteen years and I thought . . . well, goddamn it . . . go on for it!

ROSE.   We're not talking about baseball! We're talking about you going off to lay in bed with another woman . . . and then bring it home to me. That's what we're talking about. We ain't talking about no baseball.

TROY.   Rose, you're not listening to me. I'm trying the best I can to explain it to you. It's not easy for me to admit that I been standing in the same place for eighteen years.

ROSE.   I been standing with you! I been right here with you, Troy. I got a life too. I gave eighteen years of my life to stand in the same spot with you. Don't you think I ever wanted other things? Don't you think I had dreams and hopes? What about my life? What about me. Don't you think it ever crossed my mind to want to know other men? That I wanted to lay up somewhere and forget about my responsibilities? That I wanted someone to make me laugh so I could feel good? You not the only one who's got wants and needs. But I held on to you, Troy. I took all my feelings, my wants and needs, my dreams . . . and buried them inside you. I planted a seed and watched and prayed over it. I planted myself inside you and waited to bloom. And it didn't take me no eighteen years to find out the soil was hard and rocky and it wasn't never gonna bloom.

But I held on to you, Troy. I held you tighter. You was my husband. I owed you everything I had. Every part of me I could find to give you. And upstairs in that room . . . with the darkness falling in on me . . . I gave everything I had to try and erase the doubt that you wasn't the finest man in the world. And wherever you was going . . . I wanted to be there with you. 'Cause you was my husband.

'Cause that's the only way I was gonna survive as your wife. You always talking about what you give . . . and what you don't have to give. But you take too. You take . . . and don't even know nobody's giving! (*Turns to exit into the house;* TROY *grabs her arm.*)

110 TROY. You say I take and don't give!

ROSE. Troy! You're hurting me!

TROY. You say I take and don't give!

ROSE. Troy . . . you're hurting my arm! Let go!

TROY. I done give you everything I got. Don't you tell that lie on me.

115 ROSE. Troy!

TROY. Don't you tell that lie on me! (CORY *enters from the house.*)

CORY. Mama!

ROSE. Troy. You're hurting me.

TROY. Don't you tell me about my taking and giving. (CORY *comes up behind* TROY *and grabs him.* TROY, *surprised, is thrown off balance just as* CORY *throws a glancing blow that catches him on the chest and knocks him down.* TROY *is stunned, as is* CORY.)

120 ROSE. Troy, Troy. No! (TROY *gets to his feet and starts at* CORY.) Troy . . . no. Please! Troy! (ROSE *pulls on* TROY *to hold him back.* TROY *stops himself.*)

TROY (*to* CORY). All right. That's strike two. You stay away from around me, boy. Don't you strike out. You living with a full count. Don't you strike out. (TROY *exits out the yard as the lights go down.*)

SCENE 2

It is six months later, early afternoon. TROY *enters from the house and starts to exit the yard.* ROSE *enters from the house.*

ROSE. Troy, I want to talk to you.

TROY. All of a sudden, after all this time, you want to talk to me, huh? You ain't wanted to talk to me for months. You ain't wanted to talk to me last night. You ain't wanted no part of me then. What you wanna talk to me about now?

ROSE. Tomorrow's Friday.

TROY. I know what day tomorrow is. You 125 think I don't know tomorrow's Friday? My whole life I ain't done nothing but look to see Friday coming and you got to tell me it's Friday.

ROSE. I want to know if you're coming home.

TROY. I always come home, Rose. You know that. There ain't never been a night I ain't come home.

ROSE. That ain't what I mean . . . and you know it. I want to know if you're coming straight home after work.

TROY. I figure I'd cash my check . . . hang out at Taylors' with the boys . . . maybe play a game of checkers . . .

ROSE. Troy, I can't live like this. I won't 130 live like this. You livin' on borrowed time with me. It's been going on six months now you ain't been coming home.

TROY. I be here every night. Every night of the year. That's 365 days.

ROSE. I want you to come home tomorrow after work.

TROY. Rose . . . I don't mess up my pay. You know that now. I take my pay and I give it to you. I don't have no money but what you give me back. I just want to have a little time to myself . . . a little time to enjoy life.

ROSE. What about me? When's my time to enjoy life?

TROY. I don't know what to tell you, Rose. 135 I'm doing the best I can.

ROSE. You ain't been home from work but time enough to change your clothes and run out . . . and you wanna call that the best you can do?

TROY. I'm going over to the hospital to see Alberta. She went into the hospital this afternoon. Look like she might have the baby early. I won't be gone long.

ROSE.   Well, you ought to know. They
   went over to Miss Pearl's and got Gabe
   today. She said you told them to go
   ahead and lock him up.

TROY.   I ain't said no such thing.
   Whoever told you that is telling a lie.
   Pearl ain't doing nothing but telling a big
   fat lie.

140 ROSE.   She ain't had to tell me. I read it on
   the papers.

TROY.   I ain't told them nothing of the
   kind.

ROSE.   I saw it right there on the papers.

TROY.   What it say, huh?

ROSE.   It said you told them to take him.

145 TROY.   Then they screwed that up, just the
   way they screw up everything. I ain't
   worried about what they got on the
   paper.

ROSE.   Say the government send part of his
   check to the hospital and the other part
   to you.

TROY.   I ain't got nothing to do with that if
   that's the way it works. I ain't made up
   the rules about how it work.

ROSE.   You did Gabe just like you did
   Cory. You wouldn't sign the paper for
   Cory . . . but you signed for Gabe. You
   signed that paper. (*The telephone is heard
   ringing inside the house.*)

TROY.   I told you I ain't signed nothing,
   woman! The only thing I signed was the
   release form. Hell, I can't read, I don't
   know what they had on that paper! I
   ain't signed nothing about sending Gabe
   away.

150 ROSE.   I said send him to the hospital . . .
   you said let him be free . . . now you
   done went down there and signed him to
   the hospital for half his money. You went
   back on yourself, Troy. You gonna have to
   answer for that.

TROY.   See now . . . you been over there
   talking to Miss Pearl. She done got mad
   'cause she ain't getting Gabe's rent

money. That's all it is. She's liable to say
   anything.

ROSE.   Troy, I seen where you signed the
   paper.

TROY.   You ain't seen nothing I signed.
   What she doing got papers on my
   brother anyway? Miss Pearl telling a big
   fat lie. And I'm gonna tell her about it
   too! You ain't seen nothing I signed.
   Say . . . you ain't seen nothing I signed.
   (ROSE *exits into the house to answer the
   telephone. Presently she returns.*)

ROSE.   Troy . . . that was the hospital.
   Alberta had the baby.

TROY.   What she have? What is it?   155

ROSE.   It's a girl.

TROY.   I better get on down to the hospital
   to see her.

ROSE.   Troy . . .

TROY.   Rose . . . I got to go see her now.
   That's only right . . . what's the matter . . .
   the baby's all right, ain't it?

ROSE.   Alberta died having the baby.   160

TROY.   Died . . . you say she's dead?
   Alberta's dead?

ROSE.   They said they done all they could.
   They couldn't do nothing for her.

TROY.   The baby? How's the baby?

ROSE.   They say it's healthy. I wonder
   who's gonna bury her.

TROY.   She had family, Rose. She wasn't   165
   living in the world by herself.

ROSE.   I know she wasn't living in the
   world by herself.

TROY.   Next thing you gonna want to
   know if she had any insurance.

ROSE.   Troy, you ain't got to talk like that.

TROY.   That's the first thing that jumped
   out your mouth. "Who's gonna bury
   her?" Like I'm fixing to take on that task
   for myself.

ROSE.   I am your wife. Don't push me   170
   away.

TROY.   I ain't pushing nobody away. Just
   give me some space. That's all. Just give

me some room to breathe. (ROSE *exits into the house.* TROY *walks about the yard. With a quiet rage that threatens to consume him.*) All right . . . Mr. Death. See now . . . I'm gonna tell you what I'm gonna do. I'm gonna take and build me a fence around this yard. See? I'm gonna build me a fence around what belongs to me. And then I want you to stay on the other side. See? You stay over there until you're ready for me. Then you come on. Bring your army. Bring your sickle. Bring your wrestling clothes. I ain't gonna fall down on my vigilance this time. You ain't gonna sneak up on me no more. When you ready for me . . . when the top of your list say Troy Maxson . . . that's when you come around here. You come up and knock on the front door. Ain't nobody else got nothing to do with this. This is between you and me. Man to man. You stay on the other side of that fence until you ready for me. Then you come up and knock on the front door. Anytime you want. I'll be ready for you. (*The lights go down to black.*)

SCENE 3

The lights come up on the porch. It is late evening three days later. ROSE *sits listening to the ball game waiting for* TROY. *The final out of the game is made and* ROSE *switches off the radio.* TROY *enters the yard carrying an infant wrapped in blankets. He stands back from the house and calls.*

ROSE *enters and stands on the porch. There is a long, awkward silence, the weight of which grows heavier with each passing second.*

TROY. Rose . . . I'm standing here with my daughter in my arms. She ain't but a wee bittie little old thing. She don't know nothing about grownups' business. She innocent . . . and she ain't got no mama.

ROSE. What you telling me for, Troy? (*She turns and exits into the house.*)

TROY. Well . . . I guess we'll just sit out here on the porch. (*He sits down on the porch. There is an awkward indelicateness about the way he handles the baby. His largeness engulfs and seems to swallow it. He speaks loud enough for* ROSE *to hear*) A man's got to do what's right for him. I ain't sorry for nothing I done. It felt right in my heart. (*To the baby*) What you smiling at? Your daddy's a big man. Got these great big old hands. But sometimes he's scared. And right now your daddy's scared 'cause we sitting out here and ain't got no home. Oh, I been homeless before. I ain't had no little baby with me. But I been homeless. You just be out on the road by your lonesome and you see one of them trains coming and you just kinda go like this . . . (*He sings as a lullaby.*)

> Please, Mr. Engineer let a man ride the
> line
> Please, Mr. Engineer let a man ride the
> line
> I ain't got no ticket please let me ride
> the blinds

(ROSE *enters from the house.* TROY, *hearing her steps behind him, stands and faces her.*) She's my daughter, Rose. My own flesh and blood. I can't deny her no more than I can deny them boys. (*Pause.*) You and them boys is my family. You and them and this child is all I got in the world. So I guess what I'm saying is . . . I'd appreciate it if you'd help me take care of her.

ROSE. Okay, Troy . . . you're right. I'll take care of your baby for you 'cause . . . like you say . . . she's innocent . . . and you can't visit the sins of the father upon the child. A motherless child has got a hard time. (*She takes the baby from him.*) From right now . . . this child got a mother. But you a woman-less man. (ROSE *turns and exits into the house with the baby. Lights go down to black.*)

175

SCENE 4

It is two months later. LYONS *enters from the street. He knocks on the door and calls.*

LYONS.   Hey, Rose! (*Pause*) Rose!

ROSE (*from inside the house*).   Stop that yelling. You gonna wake up Raynell. I just got her to sleep.

LYONS.   I just stopped by to pay Papa this twenty dollars I owe him. Where's Papa at?

ROSE.   He should be here in a minute. I'm getting ready to go down to the church. Sit down and wait on him.

180 LYONS.   I got to go pick up Bonnie over her mother's house.

ROSE.   Well, sit it down there on the table. He'll get it.

LYONS (*enters the house and sets the money on the table*). Tell Papa I said thanks. I'll see you again.

ROSE.   All right, Lyons. We'll see you.

(LYONS *starts to exit as* CORY *enters.*)

CORY.   Hey, Lyons.

185 LYONS.   What's happening, Cory? Say man, I'm sorry I missed your graduation. You know I had a gig and couldn't get away. Otherwise, I would have been there, man. So what you doing?

CORY.   I'm trying to find a job.

LYONS.   Yeah I know how that go, man. It's rough out here. Jobs are scarce.

CORY.   Yeah, I know.

LYONS.   Look here, I got to run. Talk to Papa . . . he know some people. He'll be able to help you get a job. Talk to him . . . see what he say.

190 CORY.   Yeah . . . all right, Lyons.

LYONS.   You take care. I'll talk to you soon. We'll find some time to talk. (LYONS *exits the yard.* CORY *wanders over to the tree, picks up the bat, and assumes a batting stance. He studies an imaginary pitcher and swings. Dissatisfied with the result, he tries again.* TROY *enters. They eye each other for a beat.* CORY *puts the bat down and exits the yard.* TROY *starts into the house as* ROSE *exits with* RAYNELL. *She is carrying a cake.*)

TROY.   I'm coming in and everybody's going out.

ROSE.   I'm taking this cake down to the church for the bake sale. Lyons was by to see you. He stopped by to pay you your twenty dollars. It's laying in there on the table.

TROY (*going into his pocket*).   Well . . . here go this money.

ROSE.   Put it in there on the table, Troy. I'll   195 get it.

TROY.   What time you coming back?

ROSE.   Ain't no use in you studying me. It don't matter what time I come back.

TROY.   I just asked you a question, woman. What's the matter . . . can't I ask you a question?

ROSE.   Troy, I don't want to go into it. Your dinner's in there on the stove. All you got to do is heat it up. And don't you be eating the rest of them cakes in there. I'm coming back for them. We having a bake sale at the church tomorrow. (ROSE *exits the yard.* TROY *sits down on the step, takes a pint bottle from his pocket, opens it, and drinks. He begins to sing.*)

TROY.   Hear it ring! Hear it ring!   200
Had an old dog his name was Blue
You know Blue was mighty true
You know Blue was a good old dog
Blue trees a possum in a hollow log
You know from that he was a good old
dog (BONO *enters the yard.*)

BONO.   Hey, Troy.

TROY.   Hey, what's happening, Bono?

BONO.   I just thought I'd stop by to see you.

TROY.   What you stop by and see me for? You ain't stopped by in a month of Sundays. Hell, I must owe you money or something.

BONO.   Since you got your promotion I   205
can't keep up with you. Used to see you

every day. Now I don't even know what
route you working.

TROY.   They keep switching me around.
Got me out in Greentree now . . . hauling
white folks' garbage.

BONO.   Greentree, huh? You lucky, at least
you ain't got to be lifting them barrels.
Damn if they ain't getting heavier. I'm
gonna put in my two years and call it
quits.

TROY.   I'm thinking about retiring myself.

BONO. You got it easy. You can *drive* for
another five years.

210 TROY.   It ain't the same, Bono. It ain't like
working the back of the truck. Ain't got
nobody to talk to . . . feel like you
working by yourself. Naw, I'm thinking
about retiring. How's Lucille?

BONO.   She all right. Her arthritis get to
acting up on her sometime. Saw Rose on
my way in. She going down to the
church, huh?

TROY.   Yeah, she took up going down
there. All them preachers looking for
somebody to fatten their pockets. (*Pause.*)
Got some gin here.

BONO.   Naw, thanks. I just stopped by to
say hello.

TROY.   Hell, nigger . . . you can take a
drink. I ain't never known you to say
no to a drink. You ain't got to work
tomorrow.

215 BONO.   I just stopped by. I'm fixing to go
over to Skinner's. We got us a domino
game going over his house every Friday.

TROY.   Nigger, you can't play no
dominoes. I used to whup you four
games out of five.

BONO.   Well, that learned me. I'm getting
better.

TROY.   Yeah? Well, that's all right.

BONO.   Look here . . . I got to be getting on.
Stop by sometime, huh?

220 TROY.   Yeah, I'll do that, Bono. Lucille told
Rose you bought her a new refrigerator.

BONO.   Yeah, Rose told Lucille you had
finally built your fence . . . so I figured
we'd call it even.

TROY.   I knew you would.

BONO.   Yeah . . . okay. I'll be talking to you.

TROY.   Yeah, take care, Bono. Good to see
you. I'm gonna stop over.

BONO.   Yeah. Okay, Troy. (BONO *exits.* TROY   225
drinks from the bottle.)

TROY.   Old Blue died and I dig his grave
Let him down with a golden chain
Every night when I hear old Blue bark
I know Blue treed a possum in Noah's
Ark.
Hear it ring! Hear it ring!

(CORY *enters the yard. They eye each other for a
beat.* TROY *is sitting in the middle of the
steps.* CORY *walks over.*)

CORY.   I got to get by.

TROY.   Say what? What's you say?

CORY.   You in my way. I got to get by.

TROY.   You got to get by where? This is my   230
house. Bought and paid for. In full. Took
me fifteen years. And if you wanna go in
my house and I'm sitting on the steps . . .
you say excuse me. Like your mama
taught you.

CORY.   Come on, Pop . . . I got to get by.

(CORY *starts to maneuver his way past* TROY.
TROY *grabs his leg and shoves him back.*)

TROY.   You just gonna walk over top of
me?

CORY.   I live here too!

TROY (*advancing towards him*).   You just
gonna walk over top of me in my own
house?

CORY.   I ain't scared of you.   235

TROY.   I ain't asked if you was scared of
me. I asked you if you was fixing to
walk over top of me in my own house?
That's the question. You ain't gonna say
excuse me? You just gonna walk over top
of me?

CORY.   If you wanna put it like that.

TROY.   How else am I gonna put it?

CORY.   I was walking by you to go into the house 'cause you sitting on the steps drunk, singing to yourself. You can put it like that.

240 TROY.   Without saying excuse me??? (CORY *doesn't respond.*) I asked you a question. Without saying excuse me???

CORY.   I ain't got to say excuse me to you. You don't count around here no more.

TROY.   Oh, I see . . . I don't count around here no more. You ain't got to say excuse me to your daddy. All of a sudden you done got so grown that your daddy don't count around here no more . . . Around here in his own house and yard that he done paid for with the sweat of his brow. You done got so grown to where you gonna take over. You gonna take over my house. Is that right? You gonna wear my pants. You gonna go in there and stretch out on my bed. You ain't got to say excuse me 'cause I don't count around here no more. Is that right?

CORY.   That's right. You always talking this dumb stuff. Now, why don't you just get out my way?

TROY.   I guess you got someplace to sleep and something to put in your belly. You got that, huh? You got that? That's what you need. You got that, huh?

245 CORY.   You don't know what I got. You ain't got to worry about what I got.

TROY.   You right! You one hundred percent right! I done spent the last seventeen years worrying about what you got. Now it's your turn, see? I'll tell you what to do. You grown . . . we done established that. You a man. Now, let's see you act like one. Turn your behind around and walk out this yard. And when you get out there in the alley . . . you can forget about this house. See? 'Cause this is my house. You go on and be a man and get your own house. You can forget about this. 'Cause this is mine. You go on and

get yours 'cause I'm through with doing for you.

CORY.   You talking about what you did for me . . . what'd you ever give me?

TROY.   Them feet and bones! That pumping heart, nigger! I give you more than anybody else is ever gonna give you.

CORY.   You ain't never gave me nothing! You ain't never done nothing but hold me back. Afraid I was gonna be better than you. All you ever did was try and make me scared of you. I used to tremble every time you called my name. Every time I heard your footsteps in the house. Wondering all the time . . . what's Papa gonna say if I do this? . . . What's he gonna say if I do that? . . . What's Papa gonna say if I turn on the radio? And Mama, too . . . she tries . . . but she's scared of you.

TROY.   You leave your mama out of this.   250 She ain't got nothing to do with this.

CORY.   I don't know how she stand you . . . after what you did to her.

TROY.   I told you to leave your mama out of this! (*He advances toward* CORY.)

CORY.   What you gonna do . . . give me a whupping? You can't whup me no more. You're too old. You just an old man.

TROY (*shoves him on his shoulder*).   Nigger! That's what you are. You just another nigger on the street to me!

CORY.   You crazy! You know that?   255

TROY.   Go on now! You got the devil in you. Get on away from me!

CORY.   You just a crazy old man . . . talking about I got the devil in me.

TROY.   Yeah, I'm crazy! If you don't get on the other side of that yard . . . I'm gonna show you how crazy I am! Go on . . . get the hell out of my yard.

CORY.   It ain't your yard. You took Uncle Gabe's money he got from the army to buy this house and then you put him out.

260 TROY (*advances on* CORY).   Get your black
ass out of my yard! (TROY'S *advance backs*
CORY *up against the tree.* CORY *grabs up the
bat.*)

CORY.   I ain't going nowhere! Come on . . .
put me out! I ain't scared of you.

TROY.   That's my bat!

CORY.   Come on!

TROY.   Put my bat down!

265 CORY.   Come on, put me out. (*Swings at*
TROY, *who backs across the yard.*) What's
the matter? you so bad . . . put me out!
(TROY *advances toward* CORY. *Backing up*)
Come on! Come on!

TROY.   You're gonna have to use it! You
wanna draw that bat back on me . . .
you're gonna have to use it.

CORY.   Come on! . . . Come on! (CORY
swings the bat at TROY *a second time. He
misses.* TROY *continues to advance toward
him.*)

TROY.   You're gonna have to kill me! You
wanna draw that bat back on me. You're
gonna have to kill me. (CORY, *backed up
against the tree, can go no farther.* TROY
*taunts him. He sticks out his head and offers
him a target.*) Come on! Come on! (CORY *is
unable to swing the bat.* TROY *grabs it.*)
Then I'll show you. (CORY *and* TROY
*struggle over the bat. The struggle is fierce
and fully engaged.* TROY *ultimately is the
stronger and takes the bat from* CORY *and
stands over him ready to swing. He stops
himself.*) Go on and get away from
around my house. (CORY, *stung by his
defeat, picks himself up, walks slowly out of
the yard and up the alley.*)

CORY.   Tell Mama I'll be back for my
things.

270 TROY.   They'll be on the other side of that
fence. (CORY *exits.*) I can't taste nothing.
Hallelujah! I can't taste nothing no more.
(TROY *assumes a batting posture and begins
to taunt Death, the fastball on the outside
corner.*) Come on! It's between you and

me now! Come on! Anytime you want!
Come on! I be ready for you . . . but I
ain't gonna be easy. (*The lights go down on
the scene.*)

SCENE 5

*The time is 1965. The lights come up in the
yard. It is the morning of* TROY'S *funeral. A
funeral plaque with a light hangs beside the
door. There is a small garden plot off to the
side. There is noise and activity in the house
as* ROSE *and* BONO *have gathered. The door
opens and* RAYNELL, *seven years old, enters
dressed in a flannel nightgown. She crosses to
the garden and pokes around with a stick.*
ROSE *calls from the house.*

ROSE.   Raynell!

RAYNELL.   Mam?

ROSE.   What you doing out there?

RAYNELL.   Nothing. (ROSE *comes to the door.*)

ROSE.   Girl, get in here and get dressed.   275
What you doing?

RAYNELL.   Seeing if my garden growed.

ROSE.   I told you it ain't gonna grow
overnight. You got to wait.

RAYNELL.   It don't look like it never gonna
grow. Dag!

ROSE.   I told you a watched pot never
boils. Get in here and get dressed.

RAYNELL.   This ain't even no pot, Mama.   280

ROSE.   You just have to give it a chance.
It'll grow. Now you come on and do
what I told you. We got to be getting
ready. This ain't no morning to be
playing around. You hear me?

RAYNELL.   Yes, mam. (ROSE *exits into the
house.* RAYNELL *continues to poke at her
garden with a stick.* CORY *enters. He is dressed
in a Marine corporal's uniform, and carries a
duffel bag. His posture is that of a military
man, and his speech has a clipped sternness.*)

CORY (*to* RAYNELL).   Hi. (*Pause.*) I bet your
name is Raynell.

RAYNELL.   Uh huh.

285 CORY.   Is your mama home? (RAYNELL *runs up on the porch and calls through the screen door.*)

RAYNELL.   Mama . . . there's some man out here. Mama? (ROSE *comes to the door.*)

ROSE.   Cory? Lord have mercy! Look here, you all! (ROSE *and* CORY *embrace in a tearful reunion as* BONO *and* LYONS *enter from the house dressed in funeral clothes.*)

BONO.   Aw, looka here . . .

ROSE.   Done got all grown up!

290 CORY.   Don't cry, Mama. What you crying about?

ROSE.   I'm just so glad you made it.

CORY.   Hey Lyons. How you doing, Mr. Bono. (LYONS *goes to embrace* CORY.)

LYONS.   Look at you, man. Look at you. Don't he look good, Rose. Got them Corporal stripes.

ROSE.   What took you so long?

295 CORY.   You know how the Marines are, Mama. They got to get all their paperwork straight before they let you do anything.

ROSE.   Well, I'm sure glad you made it. They let Lyons come. Your Uncle Gabe's still in the hospital. They don't know if they gonna let him out or not. I just talked to them a little while ago.

LYONS.   A Corporal in the United States Marines.

BONO.   Your daddy knew you had it in you. He used to tell me all the time.

LYONS.   Don't he look good, Mr. Bono?

300 BONO.   Yeah, he remind me of Troy when I first met him. (*Pause.*) Say, Rose, Lucille's down at the church with the choir. I'm gonna go down and get the pallbearers lined up. I'll be back to get you all.

ROSE.   Thanks, Jim.

CORY.   See you, Mr. Bono.

LYONS (*with his arm around* RAYNELL).   Cory . . . look at Raynell. Ain't she precious? She gonna break a whole lot of hearts.

ROSE.   Raynell, come and say hello to your brother. This is your brother, Cory. You remember Cory?

RAYNELL.   No, Mam. 305

CORY.   She don't remember me, Mama.

ROSE.   Well, we talk about you. She heard us talk about you. (*To* RAYNELL) This is your brother, Cory. Come on and say hello.

RAYNELL.   Hi.

CORY.   Hi. So you're Raynell. Mama told me a lot about you.

ROSE.   You all come on into the house and 310 let me fix you some breakfast. Keep up your strength.

CORY.   I ain't hungry, Mama.

LYONS.   You can fix me something, Rose. I'll be in there in a minute.

ROSE.   Cory, you sure you don't want nothing? I know they ain't feeding you right.

CORY.   No, Mama . . . thanks. I don't feel like eating. I'll get something later.

ROSE.   Raynell . . . get on upstairs and get 315 that dress on like I told you. (ROSE *and* RAYNELL *exit into the house.*)

LYONS.   So . . . I hear you thinking about getting married.

CORY.   Yeah, I done found the right one, Lyons. It's about time.

LYONS.   Me and Bonnie been split up about four years now. About the time Papa retired. I guess she just got tired of all them changes I was putting her through. (*Pause.*) I always knew you was gonna make something out yourself. Your head was always in the right direction. So . . . you gonna stay in . . . make it a career . . . put in your twenty years?

CORY.   I don't know. I got six already, I think that's enough.

LYONS.   Stick with Uncle Sam and retire 320 early. Ain't nothing out here. I guess Rose told you what happened with me. They got me down the workhouse. I thought I was being slick cashing other people's checks.

CORY.   How much time you doing?

LYONS.   They give me three years. I got that beat now. I ain't got but nine more

months. It ain't so bad. You learn to deal
with it like anything else. You got to take
the crookeds with the straights. That's
what Papa used to say. He used to say that
when he struck out. I seen him strike out
three times in a row . . . and the next time
up he hit the ball over the grandstand.
Right out there in Homestead Field. He
wasn't satisfied hitting in the seats . . .
he want to hit it over everything! After
the game he had two hundred people
standing around waiting to shake his
hand. You got to take the crookeds with
the straights. Yeah, Papa was something
else.

CORY.   You still playing?

LYONS.   Cory . . . you know I'm gonna do
that. There's some fellows down there we
got us a band . . . we gonna try and stay
together when we get out . . . but yeah,
I'm still playing. It still helps me to get
out of bed in the morning. As long as it
do that I'm gonna be right there playing
and trying to make some sense out of it.

325 ROSE (*calling*).   Lyons, I got these eggs in
the pan.

LYONS.   Let me go on and get these eggs,
man. Get ready to go bury Papa.
(*Pause.*) How you doing? You doing all
right? (CORY *nods.* LYONS *touches him on
the shoulder and they share a moment of
silent grief.* LYONS *exits into the house.*
CORY *wanders about the yard.* RAYNELL
enters.)

RAYNELL.   Hi.

CORY.   Hi.

RAYNELL.   Did you used to sleep in my
room?

330 CORY.   Yeah . . . that used to be my room.

RAYNELL.   That's what Papa call it. "Cory's
room." It got your football in the closet.
(ROSE *comes to the door.*)

ROSE.   Raynell, get in there and get them
good shoes on.

RAYNELL.   Mama, can't I wear these? Them
other one hurt my feet.

ROSE.   Well, they just gonna have to hurt
your feet for a while. You ain't said they
hurt your feet when you went down to
the store and got them.

RAYNELL.   They didn't hurt then. My feet   335
done got bigger.

ROSE.   Don't you give me no backtalk now.
You get in there and get them shoes on.
(RAYNELL *exits into the house.*) Ain't too
much changed. He still got that piece of
rag tied to that tree. He was out here
swinging that bat. I was just ready to go
back in the house. He swung that bat and
then he just fell over. Seem like he swung
it and stood there with this grin on his
face . . . and then he just fell over. They
carried him on down to the hospital, but
I knew there wasn't no need . . . why
don't you come on in the house?

CORY.   Mama . . . I got something to tell
you. I don't know how to tell you this . . .
but I've got to tell you . . . I'm not going
to Papa's funeral.

ROSE.   Boy, hush your mouth. That's your
daddy you talking about. I don't want to
hear that kind of talk this morning. I
done raised you to come to this? You
standing there all healthy and grown
talking about you ain't going to your
daddy's funeral?

CORY.   Mama . . . listen . . .

ROSE.   I don't want to hear it, Cory. You   340
just get that thought out of your head.

CORY.   I can't drag Papa with me
everywhere I go. I've got to say no to him.
One time in my life I've got to say no.

ROSE.   Don't nobody have to listen to
nothing like that. I know you and your
daddy ain't seen eye to eye, but I ain't
got to listen to that kind of talk this
morning. Whatever was between you
and your daddy . . . the time has come to
put it aside. Just take it and set it over
there on the shelf and forget about it.
Disrespecting your daddy ain't gonna
make you a man, Cory. You got to find a

way to come to that on your own. Not going to your daddy's funeral ain't gonna make you a man.

CORY.   The whole time I was growing up . . . living in his house . . . Papa was like a shadow that followed you everywhere. It weighed on you and sunk into your flesh. It would wrap around you and lay there until you couldn't tell which one was you anymore. That shadow digging in your flesh. Trying to crawl in. Trying to live through you. Everywhere I looked, Troy Maxson was staring back at me . . . hiding under the bed . . . in the closet. I'm just saying I've got to find a way to get rid of that shadow, Mama.

ROSE.   You just like him. You got him in you good.

345 CORY.   Don't tell me that, Mama.

ROSE.   You Troy Maxson all over again.

CORY.   I don't want to be Troy Maxson. I want to be me.

ROSE.   You can't be nobody but who you are, Cory. That shadow wasn't nothing but you growing into yourself. You either got to grow into it or cut it down to fit you. But that's all you got to make life with. That's all you got to measure yourself against that world out there. Your daddy wanted you to be everything he wasn't . . . and at the same time he tried to make you into everything he was. I don't know if he was right or wrong . . . but I do know he meant to do more good than he meant to do harm. He wasn't always right. Sometimes when he touched he bruised. And sometimes when he took me in his arms he cut.

   When I first met your daddy I thought . . . Here is a man I can lay down with and make a baby. That's the first thing I thought when I seen him. I was thirty years old and had done seen my share of men. But when he walked up to me and said, "I can dance a waltz that'll make you dizzy," I thought, Rose Lee, here is a man that you can open yourself up to and be filled to bursting. Here is a man that can fill all them empty spaces you been tipping around the edges of. One of them empty spaces was being somebody's mother.

   I married your daddy and settled down to cooking his supper and keeping clean sheets on the bed. When your daddy walked through the house he was so big he filled it up. That was my first mistake. Not to make him leave some room for me. For my part in the matter. But at that time I wanted that. I wanted a house that I could sing in. And that's what your daddy gave me. I didn't know to keep up his strength I had to give up little pieces of mine. I did that. I took on his life as mine and mixed up the pieces so that you couldn't hardly tell which was which anymore. It was my choice. It was my life and I didn't have to live it like that. But that's what life offered me in the way of being a woman and I took it. I grabbed hold of it with both hands.

   By the time Raynell came into the house, me and your daddy had done lost touch with one another. I didn't want to make my blessing off of nobody's misfortune . . . but I took on to Raynell like she was all them babies I had wanted and never had. (*The phone rings.*) Like I'd been blessed to relive a part of my life. And if the Lord see fit to keep up my strength . . . I'm gonna do her just like your daddy did you . . . I'm gonna give her the best of what's in me.

RAYNELL (*entering, still with her old shoes*).   Mama . . . Reverend Tollivier on the phone. (ROSE *exits into the house.*)

RAYNELL.   Hi.

CORY.   Hi.   350

RAYNELL.   You in the Army or the Marines?

CORY.   Marines.

RAYNELL.   Papa said it was the Army. Did you know Blue?

355   CORY.   Blue? Who's Blue?

RAYNELL.   Papa's dog what he sing about all the time.

CORY (*singing*).   Hear it ring! Hear it ring!
   I had a dog his name was Blue
   You know Blue was mighty true
   You know Blue was a good old dog
   Blue treed a possum in a hollow log
   You know from that he was a good old dog.
   Hear it ring! Hear it ring! (RAYNELL *joins in singing.*)

CORY *and* RAYNELL.   Blue treed a possum out on a limb
   Blue looked at me and I looked at him
   Grabbed that possum and put him in a sack
   Blue stayed there till I came back
   Old Blue's feets was big and round
   Never allowed a possum to touch the ground.

   Old Blue died and I dug his grave
   I dug his grave with a silver spade
   Let him down with a golden chain
   And every night I call his name
   Go on Blue, you good dog you
   Go on Blue, you good dog you

RAYNELL.   Blue laid down and died like a man
   Blue laid down and died . . .

360   BOTH.   Blue laid down and died like a man
   Now he's treeing possums in the Promised Land
   I'm gonna tell you this to let you know
   Blue's gone where the good dogs go
   When I hear old Blue bark
   When I hear old Blue bark
   Blue treed a possum in Noah's Ark
   Blue treed a possum in Noah's Ark.

(ROSE *comes to the screen door.*)

ROSE.   Cory, we gonna be ready to go in a minute.

CORY (*to* RAYNELL).   You go on in the house and change them shoes like Mama told you so we can go to Papa's funeral.

RAYNELL.   Okay, I'll be back. (RAYNELL *exits into the house.* CORY *gets up and crosses over to the tree.* ROSE *stands in the screen door watching him.* GABRIEL *enters from the alley.*)

GABRIEL (*calling*).   Hey, Rose!

ROSE.   Gabe?   365

GABRIEL.   I'm here, Rose. Hey Rose, I'm here! (ROSE *enters from the house.*)

ROSE.   Lord . . . Look here, Lyons!

LYONS.   See, I told you, Rose . . . I told you they'd let him come.

CORY.   How you doing, Uncle Gabe?

LYONS.   How you doing, Uncle Gabe?   370

GABRIEL.   Hey, Rose. It's time. It's time to tell St. Peter to open the gates. Troy, you ready? You ready, Troy. I'm gonna tell St. Peter to open the gates. You get ready now. (GABRIEL, *with great fanfare, braces himself to blow. The trumpet is without a mouthpiece. He puts the end of it into his mouth and blows with great force, like a man who has been waiting some twenty-odd years for this single moment. No sound comes out of the trumpet. He braces himself and blows again with the same result. A third time he blows. There is a weight of impossible description that falls away and leaves him bare and exposed to a frightful realization. It is a trauma that a sane and normal mind would be unable to withstand. He begins to dance. A slow, strange dance, eeril, and life-giving. A dance of atavistic signature and ritual.* LYONS *attempts to embrace him.* GABRIEL *pushes* LYONS *away. He begins to howl in what is an attempt at song, or perhaps a song turning back into itself in an attempt at speech. He finishes his dance and the gates of heaven stand open as wide as God's closet.*) That's the way that go!

····· ▶ *Your* Turn

Talking and Writing about Lit

1. The playwright's plotting of a drama is as deliberate as the fiction writer's arrangement of events in a story or novel. Analyze August Wilson's plot structure in *Fences*.

2. How does the play's title point to an important theme in the play? What are some of the fences (literal and symbolic) you recognize in the play?

3. The physical fence around the Maxson's yard serves different purposes for different characters. What does the fence mean to Troy? To Rose? To Cory?

4. Analyze Wilson's use of the baseball metaphor as a way of illuminating Troy's life and worldview.

5. If Troy's life is revealed in terms of the game of baseball, Rose's and Raynell's are related more to the metaphor of gardening. Describe the metaphor of garden, gardening, and cultivating as it relates to Rose's and Raynell's functions in the play.

6. Wilson remarked in an interview that "Troy's flaw is that he did not recognize that the world was changing." How is this revealed in the play? What is its importance to the overall themes in the play?

7. Do other characters in the play succeed in recognizing changes in society which Troy refuses to acknowledge? How do the various characters (Rose, Troy, Bono, Cory) view change?

8. What is the turning point in the life of Troy and the plot of *Fences?*

9. Compare and contrast how two playwrights, August Wilson in *Fences* and Arthur Miller in *Death of a Salesman,* deal with the idea of "the American Dream."

10. Explain the meaning of strike one, strike two, and strike three.

11. What is the importance of Troy's singing the song about the dog Blue the first time we hear it? What is the significance of Cory and Raynell's singing the Blue song together in the last scene?

12. How do you interpret Gabriel's dance in the final scene of *Fences*?

Talking Lit

A book of popular Italian tales was one of Shakespeare's sources in conceiving the story of *Othello*. In an interview, Wilson makes clear his thematic intentions in *Fences*.

Giovanni Battista Giraldi Cinthio From *Gli Hecatommithi,* 1565

Translated by Geoffrey Bullough

Not long afterwards the Moor deprived the Corporal [the equivalent to Cassio] of his rank for having drawn his sword and wounded a soldier while on guard-duty. Disdemona was grieved by this and tried many times to reconcile the Moor with him. Whereupon the Moor told the rascally Ensign [the equivalent to Iago] that his wife importuned him so much for the Corporal that he feared he would be obliged to reinstate him. The evil man saw in this a hint for setting in train the deceits he had planned, and said: "Perhaps Disdemona has good cause to look on him so favourably!" "Why is that?" asked the Moor. "I do not wish," said the Ensign, "to come between man and wife, but if you keep your eyes open you will see for your-self." Nor for all the Moor's inquiries would the Ensign go beyond this: nonethe-less his words left such a sharp thorn in the Moor's mind, that he gave himself up to pondering intensely what they could mean. He became quite melancholy, and one day, when his wife was trying to soften his anger towards the Corporal, beg-ging him not to condemn to oblivion the loyal service and friendship of many years just for one small fault, especially since the Corporal had been reconciled to the man he had struck, the Moor burst out in anger and said to her, "There must be a very powerful reason why you take such trouble for this fellow, for he is not your brother, nor even a kinsman, yet you have him so much at heart!"

The lady, all courtesy and modesty, replied: "I should not like you to be angry with me. Nothing else makes me do it but sorrow to see you deprived of so dear a friend as you have shown that the Corporal was to you. He has not committed so serious an offence as to deserve such hostility.[1] But you Moors are so hot by nature that any little thing moves you to anger and revenge."

Still more enraged by these words the Moor answered: "Anyone who does not believe that may easily have proof of it! I shall take such revenge for any wrongs done to me as will more than satisfy me!" The lady was terrified by these words, and seeing her husband angry with her, quite against his habit, she said humbly: "Only a very good purpose made me speak to you about this, but rather than have you angry with me I shall never say another word on the subject."

The Moor, however, seeing the earnestness with which his wife had again pleaded for the Corporal, guessed that the Ensign's words had been intended to suggest that Disdemona was in love with the Corporal, and he went in deep depression to the scoundrel and urged him to speak more openly. The Ensign, intent on injuring this unfortunate lady, after pretending not to wish to say any-thing that might displease the Moor, appeared to be overcome by his entreaties and said: "I must confess that it grieves me greatly to have to tell you something that must be in the highest degree painful to you; but since you wish me to tell you, and the regard that I must have of your honour as my master spurs me on, I shall not

---

[1]Cf. *Othello* 3.3.63–67.

fail in my duty to answer your request. You must know therefore that it is hard for your Lady to see the Corporal in disgrace for the simple reason that she takes her pleasure with him whenever he comes to your house. The woman has come to dislike your blackness."

David Savran

An Interview with August Wilson, 1987

Savran: In reading *Fences,* I came to view Troy more and more critically as the play progressed, sharing Rose's point of view. We see that Troy has been crippled by his father. That's being replayed in Troy's relationship with Cory. Do you think there'a a way out of that cycle?

Wilson: Surely. First of all, we're all like our parents. The things we are taught early in life, how to respond to the world, our sense of morality—everything, we get from them. Now you can take that legacy and do with it anything you want to do. It's in your hands. Cory is Troy's son. How can he be Troy's son without sharing Troy's values? I was trying to get at why Troy made the choices he made, how they have influenced his values, and how he attempts to pass those along to his son. Each generation gives the succeeding generation what they think they need. One question in the play is "Are the tools we are given sufficient to compete in a world that is different from the one our parents knew?" I think they are—it's just that we have to do different things with the tools. That's all Troy has to give. Troy's flaw is that he does not recognize that the world was changing. That's because he spent fifteen years in a penitentiary.

As African-Americans, we should demand to participate in society as Africans. That's the way out of the vicious cycle of poverty and neglect that exists in 1987 in America, where you have a huge percentage of blacks living in the equivalent of South African townships, in housing projects. No one is inviting these people to participate in society. Look at the poverty levels—$8,500 for a family of four, if you have $8,501 you're not counted. Those statistics would go up enormously if we had an honest assessment of the cost of living in America. I don't know how anybody can support a family of four on $8,500. What I'm saying is that 85 or 90 percent of blacks in America are living in abject poverty and, for the most part, are crowded into what amount to concentration camps. The situation for blacks in America is worse than it was forty years ago. Some sociologists will tell you about the tremendous progress we've made. They didn't put me out when I walked in the door. And you can always point to someone who works on Wall Street, or is a doctor. But they don't count in the larger scheme of things.

Savran: Do you have any idea how these political changes could take place?

Wilson: I'm not sure. I know that blacks must be allowed their cultural differences. I think the process of assimilation to white American society was a big mistake. We don't want to be like you. Blacks living in housing projects are isolated from the society, for the most part—living as they choose, as Africans. Only they don't realize the value in what they're doing because they have accepted their victimization. They've marked themselves as victims. Once they recognize that, they can begin to move through society in a different manner, from a stronger position, and claim what is theirs.

Savran: A project of yours is to point up what happens when oppression is internalized.

Wilson: Yes, transfer of aggression to the wrong target. I think it's interesting that the two roads open to blacks for "full participation" are entertainment and sports. *Ma Rainey* and *Fences*, and I didn't plan it that way. I don't think that they're the correct roads. I think Troy's right. Now with the benefit of historical perspective, I can say that the athletic scholarship was actually a way of exploiting. Now you've got two million kids who think they're going to play in the NBA. In the sixties the universities made a lot of money off of athletics. You had kids playing for free who, by and large, were not getting educated, were taking courses in basketweaving. Some of them could barely read.

Savran: Troy may be right about that issue, but it seems that he has passed on certain destructive traits in spite of himself. Take the hostility between father and son.

Wilson: I think every generation says to the previous generation: you're in my way, I've got to get by. The father-son conflict is actually a normal generational conflict that happens all the time.

Savran: So it's a healthy and a good thing?

Wilson: Oh, sure. Troy is seeing this boy walk around, smelling his piss. Two men cannot live in the same household. Troy would have been tremendously disappointed if Cory had not challenged him. Troy knows that this boy has to go out and do battle with that world: "So I had best prepare him because I know that's a harsh, cruel place out there. But that's going to be easy compared to what he's getting here. Ain't nobody gonna whip your ass like I'm gonna whip it." He has a tremendous love for the kid. But he's not going to say, "I love you," he's going to demonstrate it. He's carrying garbage for seventeen years just for the kid. The only world Troy knows is the one that he made. Cory's going to go on to find another one, he's going to arrive at the same place as Troy. I think one of the most important lines in the play is when Troy is talking about his father: "I got to the place where I could feel him kicking in my blood and knew that the only thing that separated us was the matter of a few years."

Hopefully, Cory will do things a bit differently with his son. For Troy, sports was not the way to go, the white man wouldn't let him get away with that. "Get you a job, with your hands, something that nobody can take away from you." The idea of school—he doesn't know what that is. That's for white folks. Very few blacks had paperwork jobs. But if you knew how to fix cars, you could always make some money. That's what Troy wants for Cory. There aren't many people who ever jumped up in Troy's face. So he's proud of the kid at the same time that he expresses a hurt that all men feel. You got to cut your kid loose at some point. There's that sense of loss and separation. You find out how Troy left his father's house and you see how Cory leaves his house. I suspect with Cory it will repeat with some differences and maybe, after five or six generations, they'll find a different way to do it.

Savran: Where Cory ends up is very ambiguous, as a marine in 1965.

Wilson: Yes. For the average black kid on the street, that was an alternative. You went into the army because you could learn how to do something. I can remember my parents talking about the son of some friends: "He's in the navy. He *did* something"—as opposed to standing on the street corner, shooting drugs, drinking wine, and robbing stores. Lyons says to Cory, "I always knew you were going to make something out of yourself." It really wounds me. He's a corporal in the marines. For blacks, that is a sense of accomplishment. Therein lies one of the tragedies of blacks in America. Cory says, "I don't know. I put in six years. That's enough." Anyone who goes into the army and makes a career out of it is a loser. They sit there and are nurtured by the army and they don't have to confront life. Then they get out of the army and find there's nothing to do. They didn't learn any skills. And if they did, they can't find a job. Four months later, they're shooting dope. In the sixties a whole bunch of blacks went over, fought, and died in the Vietnam War. The survivors came back to the same street corners and found out nothing had changed. They still couldn't get a job.

At the end of *Fences* every person, with the exception of Raynell, is institutionalized. Rose is in a church, Lyons is in a penitentiary, Gabriel's in a mental hospital, and

POP CULTURE

Plot And Form: Slasher Flicks Self-Recognize

William Shakespeare

Genre-based work often gets a bad rap. Works that fall into a popular genre can be considered somehow limited or restricted. It is often assumed that such work follows a formula. Mystery novels, science-fiction films, and reality TV often get the academic short end of the stick. Consider, however, that even Shakespeare's works are genre based. Some of his comedies might remind you of modern teen-comedy films. In fact, all of Shakespeare's comedies end traditionally with everyone getting married, the sixteenth century equivalent of the prom night ending of our modern high school–based films. *Othello* and Shakespeare's other tragedies bear a close resemblance to our bio-pic entertainment like VH1's *Behind the Music* or films like *Supermodel: Gia*. The protagonist's quick rise to power is always followed by a tragic fall; the stage is littered with bodies. Swords and poison were more popular in Renaissance times than drugs and bad agents, but the result is the same.

Cory's in the marines. The only free person is the girl, Troy's daughter, the hope for the future. That was conscious on my part because in '57 that's what I saw. Blacks have relied on institutions which are really foreign—except for the black church, which has been our saving grace. I have some problems with it but I recognize it as a central social organization and sometimes an economic organization for the black community. I would like to see blacks develop their own institutions that respond to their needs.

From *In Their Own Voices*

Student Essay

Student D. Scott Humphries wrote about what he perceives as internalized racism in Shakespeare's *Othello*.

D. Scott Humphries, "More or Less a Moor: Racism in Othello" (see Chapter 32)

masked figure from the *Scream* movie

Sometimes great genre-based work is achieved through self-acknowledgement. The blockbuster horror film *Scream* reinvented the small but popular horror subgenre of the "teen slasher flick" by giving its formulaic trappings a voice through its killer and resident horror film buff. "You should never say 'Who's there?' Don't you watch scary movies? It's a death wish. You might as well just come out here to investigate a strange noise or something," our killer says to a victim in the film's opening sequence. Later, our video store employee and horror film fan gives us the three rules for surviving a scary movie: (1) never have sex, (2) never do drugs (the "sin factor"), and (3) "never, ever, ever, under any circumstances, say 'I'll be right back,' because you won't be." The film lays down a number of references to its predecessors, including *Halloween*, *Friday the Thirteenth*, and *Nightmare on Elm Street*, and its brilliance is in its self-referential quality. In literature or any medium, it is not the genre framework that determines the quality of a piece, but the form and style within the work that makes it either formulaic or freshly original.

C H A P T E R **27**

CHARACTERIZATION
AND THEME

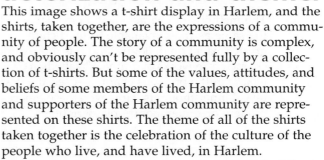

Even t-shirts use characterization and theme.

This image shows a t-shirt display in Harlem, and the shirts, taken together, are the expressions of a community of people. The story of a community is complex, and obviously can't be represented fully by a collection of t-shirts. But some of the values, attitudes, and beliefs of some members of the Harlem community and supporters of the Harlem community are represented on these shirts. The theme of all of the shirts taken together is the celebration of the culture of the people who live, and have lived, in Harlem.

The characters on the t-shirts include Lady Liberty and the African Continent sporting dreadlocks. One significance of Lady Liberty might be that she represents freedom for all people in the United States. The image of the African Continent with dreadlocks suggests the musical roots of reggae, jazz, and soul, and calls to mind the rich artistic history of Harlem. The t-shirts with messages opposing racism express a broadly shared goal, and another theme of the display. Other t-shirts just celebrate the community by displaying its name, boldly and brightly. In short, the images of characters and thematic messages on the shirts help to tell the story of the people who created the shirts and who live in the community. Increasingly, t-shirt displays and projects are being used in communities around the country to depict characters and situations and to express themes common to political and cultural groups within our society.

Characterization in Drama

Novelist John Gardner's words about the importance of character in fiction apply equally well to characterization in drama. Until a human being comes on stage to give life to the story, the other elements only seem preliminary.

> Character is the very life of fiction. Setting exists so that the character has someplace to stand, something that can help define him, something he can pick up and throw, if necessary, or eat, or give to his girlfriend. Plot exists so the character can discover for himself (and in the process reveal to the reader) what he, the character, is really like: plot forces the character to choice and action, transforms him from a static construct to a lifelike human being making choices and paying for them or reaping the rewards. And theme exists only to make the character stand up and be somebody: theme is elevated critical language for what the character's main problem is.
>
> —John Gardner, *On Becoming a Novelist*, page 52

The methods of characterization available to the dramatist (playwright) are largely the same as those available to the fiction writer; however, the dramatist relies to a greater extent on dialogue, and it is more difficult to convey the internal thoughts of characters in works of drama. Elizabethan dramatists—as illustrated in Shakespeare's *Othello* in the previous chapter—used the devices of the **soliloquy** and the **aside**, to reveal inner thoughts. However, these devices are not usually viable options for the modern or contemporary playwright.

What Is Modern Drama?

It is important to make a few general statements about **modern drama** before examining characterization in Henrik Ibsen's play *A Doll's House*. Modern drama, which refers to dramatic works written during and since the last quarter of the nineteenth century, typically shares certain broad characteristics. Ibsen's *A Doll's House*, for instance, was written in 1879. Just as Anton Chekhov is credited with being the "father of the modern short story," so Henrik Ibsen is often said to be the "father of modern drama." Both Chekhov and Ibsen emphasized the writer's responsibility to pose good questions through the work of literature, while not necessarily providing answers to those questions. In other words, Chekhov's modern innovation of the open-ended story has its equivalent in Ibsen's open-ended plays. These writers resisted the use of clearly resolved endings, preferring to let the reader wrestle with the ambiguities and dilemmas that are so often a part of real life. Thus, the modern period in literature is characterized by a greater willingness to grapple with social issues and with the realistic problems of everyday life and ordinary people. **Realism** became the order of the day, and characters were more likely to be drawn from the middle class or working classes—ordinary people— rather than the wealthy or aristocratic classes. Correspondingly, diction became more relaxed. Characters no longer spoke in couplets but in the **vernacular**, the language of everyday speech.

Along with the language of the people, modern playwrights adopted more realistic sets. **Verisimilitude** (the appearance of being real) was desirable, and stage sets began to look like living rooms, kitchens, town squares—a far cry from the simple Elizabethan staging, and an even greater distance from the Greek amphitheater of classical drama. Stage directions are often used, of course, to convey setting in the written play, providing for the director and actors a sense of the playwright's intentions for how the set should look and giving instructions as to how the actors should move about in the space. *A Doll's House* opens in the parlor, or living room, of the Helmers' home, where most of the action takes place.

Dialogue is the predominant vehicle for conveying characterization in drama. Helmer's repeated use of diminutive words to refer to his wife Nora ("lark," "squirrel," "squanderbird") provides more characterization of the speaker (Helmer) than of the subject (Nora). It is also through dialogue and in dramatic **scenes** that the reader or audience begins to develop an understanding of the Helmers' relationship. Although Ibsen's play is not divided into numbered scenes within its three acts, it moves through successive scenes, which are delineated by shifts of time and setting, as well as by shifting pairs and groups of characters on stage. For instance, the transition into the final scene of Act I begins at the stage direction: *"The Maid, who has set the tree down, goes out."* Nora then mutters to herself as she begins to trim the Christmas tree. Then: *"Helmer comes in from the hall, with a sheaf of papers under his arm,"* and the scene is under way.

How Theme Is Revealed

During this interaction between Torvald Helmer and Nora Helmer, which forms the last scene of Act I, several of the play's **themes** (or ideas, or meanings) are either restated or more clearly articulated, and others arise for the first time. Nora has, in the previous scene, been talking with Nils Krogstad, and when she denies to Helmer that anyone has been there, she is caught in a lie. This restates Nora's tendency to bend the truth, but it also restates Helmer's assumption that he should control every aspect of her life. Also, the audience will recall that the dilemma she finds herself in with Krogstad is solely a result of her efforts to save Torvald's life. An example of a new idea (or theme, or meaning), which is articulated during this scene, would be connected to the metaphor of masks. Helmer states that Krogstad has damaged his home and children by wearing a mask (covering up his earlier crime of forgery), and we see that Nora takes this personally, given her own situation (the document she has forged to get the loan to save her husband's life). The audience recognizes Nora's plight here, but Helmer does not, so this exchange is also an example of **dramatic irony**, a situation in which the audience knows more than a character or characters do.

Other Aspects of Characterization

Many of the other aspects of characterization that were discussed in relation to fiction also apply here. Characters in drama need to have plausible **motivation**. If they are **major characters** who are **round** and fully developed, the audience will understand more about their motives. If they are **minor characters**, they may remain **flat** (less fully developed) characters because the audience does not need to understand their motives. Additionally, one often has characters who serve as **foils** to one another in drama, as in fiction. Certainly, Kristine Linde is a foil to Nora Helmer, since the contrasts between their personalities and their life experiences highlight the characteristics of each and assist in developing themes.

Other methods of characterization common to dramatic writing as well as the writing of fiction involve depiction of the character through **actions**, **behavior**, and **physical appearance**, although these are often accomplished in different ways in drama. In the text of the play, these aspects of characterization may be described in stage directions or referred to in dialogue. In the play as it is being performed, of course, these aspects of characterization are physically and dramatically depicted to the audience by the live actors on stage.

Reading

Henrik Ibsen (1828–1906)

Ibsen was born in Skien, Norway. His parents, though previously wealthy, had lost their money, and Ibsen was at first apprenticed to a pharmacist. At the age of 22, he had completed his first play, and he subsequently became involved in theater work in Norway, Denmark and Germany. Several less successful plays were produced early on, but his real success began with his "social problem plays," realistic

works dealing boldly with modern social situations and issues. Among these most important of his plays are *A Doll's House* (1879), *Ghosts* (1881), *An Enemy of the People* (1884), and *Hedda Gabler* (1890). Ibsen is often credited with being the "father of modern drama" for his pioneering realism, his focus on the lives of ordinary people, and his willingness to depict controversial social issues in plays that were open-ended rather than didactic.

HENRIK IBSEN

A Doll's House (1879)

Translated by Rolf Fjelde

THE CHARACTERS

TORVALD HELMER, *a lawyer*
NORA, *his wife*
DR. RANK
MRS. LINDE
NILS KROGSTAD, *a bank clerk*
The HELMERS' three small children
ANNE-MARIE, *their nurse*
HELENE, *a maid*
A DELIVERY BOY
SCENE: *The action takes place in Helmer's residence.*

ACT I

A comfortable room, tastefully but not expensively furnished. A door to the right in the back wall leads to the entryway; another to the left leads to Helmer's study. Between these doors, a piano. Midway in the left-hand wall a door, and further back a window. Near the window a round table with an armchair and a small sofa. In the right-hand wall, toward the rear, a door, and nearer the foreground a porcelain stove with two armchairs and a rocking chair beside it. Between the stove and the side door, a small table. Engravings on the walls. An etagère with china figures and other small art objects; a small bookcase with richly bound books; the floor carpeted; a fire burning in the stove. It is a winter day.

A bell rings in the entryway; shortly after we hear the door being unlocked. Nora comes into the room, humming happily to herself; she is wearing street clothes and carries an armload of packages, which she puts down on the table to the right. She has left the hall door open; and through it a Delivery Boy is seen, holding a Christmas tree and a basket, which he gives to the Maid who let them in.

NORA: Hide the tree well, Helene. The children mustn't get a glimpse of it till this evening, after it's trimmed. (*To the Delivery Boy, taking out her purse.*) How much?

DELIVERY BOY: Fifty, ma'am.

NORA: There's a crown. No, keep the change. (*The Boy thanks her and leaves. Nora shuts the door. She laughs softly to herself while taking off her street things. Drawing a bag of macaroons from her pocket, she eats a couple, then steals over and listens at her husband's study door.)* Yes, he's home. *(Hums again as she moves to the table right.)*

HELMER (*from the study*):   Is that my little lark twittering out there?

5 NORA (*busy opening some packages*):   Yes, it is.

HELMER: Is that my squirrel rummaging around?

NORA: Yes!

HELMER: When did my squirrel get in?

NORA: Just now. *(Putting the macaroon bag in her pocket and wiping her mouth.)* Do come in, Torvald, and see what I've bought.

10 HELMER: Can't be disturbed. *(After a moment he opens the door and peers in, pen in hand.)* Bought, you say? All that there? Has the little spendthrift been out throwing money around again?

NORA: Oh, but Torvald, this year we really should let ourselves go a bit. It's the first Christmas we haven't had to economize.

HELMER: But you know we can't go squandering.

NORA: Oh yes, Torvald, we can squander a little now. Can't we? Just a tiny, wee bit. Now that you've got a big salary and are going to make piles and piles of money.

HELMER: Yes—starting New Year's. But then it's a full three months till the raise comes through.

15 NORA: Pooh! We can borrow that long.

HELMER: Nora! *(Goes over and playfully takes her by the ear.)* Are your scatterbrains off again? What if today I borrowed a thousand crowns, and you squandered them over Christmas week, and then on New Year's Eve a roof tile fell on my head and I lay there—

NORA (*putting her hand on his mouth*):   Oh! Don't say such things!

HELMER: Yes, but what if it happened— then what?

NORA: If anything so awful happened, then it just wouldn't matter if I had debts or not.

HELMER: Well, but the people I'd borrowed from?   20

NORA: Them? Who cares about them! They're strangers.

HELMER: Nora, Nora, how like a woman! No, but seriously, Nora, you know what I think about that. No debts! Never borrow! Something of freedom's lost—and something of beauty, too—from a home that's founded on borrowing and debt. We've made a brave stand up to now, the two of us; and we'll go right on like that the little while we have to.

NORA (*going toward the stove*):   Yes, whatever you say, Torvald.

HELMER (*following her*):   Now, now, the little lark's wings mustn't droop. Come on, don't be a sulky squirrel. *(Taking out his wallet.)* Nora, guess what I have here.

NORA (*turning quickly*):   Money!   25

HELMER: There, see. *(Hands her some notes.)* Good grief, I know how costs go up in a house at Christmastime.

NORA: Ten—twenty—thirty—forty. Oh, thank you, Torvald; I can manage no end on this.

HELMER: You really will have to.

NORA: Oh yes, I promise I will! But come here so I can show you everything I bought. And so cheap! Look, new clothes for Ivar here—and a sword. Here a horse and a trumpet for Bob. And a doll and a doll's bed here for Emmy; they're nothing much, but she'll tear them to bits in no time anyway. And here I have dress material and handkerchiefs for the maids. Old Anne-Marie really deserves something more.

HELMER: And what's in that package there?   30

NORA (*with a cry*):   Torvald, no! You can't see that till tonight!

HELMER: I see. But tell me now, you little prodigal, what have you thought of for yourself?

NORA: For myself? Oh, I don't want anything at all.

HELMER: Of course you do. Tell me just
what—within reason—you'd most like to
have.

35 NORA: I honestly don't know. Oh, listen,
Torvald—

HELMER: Well?

NORA (*fumbling at his coat buttons, without
looking at him*):   If you want to give me
something, then maybe you could—you
could—

HELMER: Come on, out with it.

NORA (*hurriedly*):   You could give me
money, Torvald. No more than you think
you can spare; then one of these days I'll
buy something with it.

40 HELMER: But Nora—

NORA: Oh please, Torvald darling,
do that! I beg you, please. Then I
could hang the bills in pretty gilt
paper on the Christmas tree. Wouldn't
that be fun?

HELMER: What are those little birds called
that always fly through their fortunes?

NORA: Oh yes, spendthrifts: I know
all that. But let's do as I say, Torvald;
then I'll have time to decide what I
really need most. That's very sensible,
isn't it?

HELMER (*smiling*):   Yes, very—that is, if
you actually hung onto the money I
give you, and you actually used it to
buy yourself something. But it goes for
the house and for all sorts of foolish
things, and then I only have to lay out
some more.

45 NORA: Oh, but Torvald—

HELMER: Don't deny it, my dear little
Nora. (*Putting his arm around her waist.*)
Spendthrifts are sweet, but they use up a
frightful amount of money. It's incredible
what it costs a man to feed such birds.

NORA: Oh, how can you say that! Really,
I save everything I can.

HELMER (*laughing*):   Yes, that's the truth.
Everything you can. But that's nothing
at all.

NORA (*humming, with a smile of quiet satisfaction*):   Hm, if you only knew what
expenses we larks and squirrels have,
Torvald.

HELMER: You're an odd little one. Exactly   50
the way your father was. You're never at
a loss for scaring up money; but the
moment you have it, it runs right out
through your fingers; you never know
what you've done with it. Well, one takes
you as you are. It's deep in your blood.
Yes, these things are hereditary, Nora.

NORA: Ah, I could wish I'd inherited
many of Papa's qualities.

HELMER: And I couldn't wish you anything but just what you are, my sweet little lark. But wait; it seems to me you
have a very—what should I call it?—a
very suspicious look today—

NORA: I do?

HELMER: You certainly do. Look me
straight in the eye.

NORA (*looking at him*):   Well?   55

HELMER (*shaking an admonitory finger*):
Surely my sweet tooth hasn't been running riot in town today, has she?

NORA: No. Why do you imagine that?

HELMER: My sweet tooth really didn't make
a little detour through the confectioner's?

NORA: No, I assure you, Torvald—

HELMER: Hasn't nibbled some pastry?   60

NORA: No, not at all.

HELMER: Not even munched a macaroon
or two?

NORA: No, Torvald, I assure you, really—

HELMER: There, there now. Of course I'm
only joking.

NORA (*going to the table, right*):   You know I   65
could never think of going against you.

HELMER: No, I understand that; and you
have given me your word. (*Going over to
her.*) Well, you keep your little Christmas

secrets to yourself, Nora darling. I expect they'll come to light this evening, when the tree is lit.

NORA: Did you remember to ask Dr. Rank?

HELMER: No. But there's no need for that: it's assumed he'll be dining with us. All the same, I'll ask him when he stops by here this morning. I've ordered some fine wine. Nora, you can't imagine how I'm looking forward to this evening.

NORA: So am I. And what fun for the children, Torvald!

70 HELMER: Ah, it's so gratifying to know that one's gotten a safe, secure job, and with a comfortable salary. It's a great satisfaction, isn't it?

NORA: Oh, it's wonderful!

HELMER: Remember last Christmas? Three whole weeks before, you shut yourself in every evening till long after midnight, making flowers for the Christmas tree, and all the other decorations to surprise us. Ugh, that was the dullest time I've ever lived through.

NORA: It wasn't at all dull for me.

HELMER (*smiling*):   But the outcome *was* pretty sorry, Nora.

75 NORA: Oh, don't tease me with that again. How could I help it that the cat came in and tore everything to shreds.

HELMER: No, poor thing, you certainly couldn't. You wanted so much to please us all, and that's what counts. But it's just as well that the hard times are past.

NORA: Yes, it's really wonderful.

HELMER: Now I don't have to sit here alone, boring myself, and you don't have to tire your precious eyes and your fair little delicate hands—

NORA (*clapping her hands*):   No, is it really true, Torvald, I don't have to? Oh, how wonderfully lovely to hear! (*Taking his arm.*) Now I'll tell you just how I've thought we should plan things. Right after Christmas— (*The doorbell rings.*) Oh,

the bell. (*Straightening the room up a bit.*) Somebody would have to come. What a bore!

HELMER: I'm not home to visitors, don't   80 forget.

MAID (*from the hall doorway*):   Ma'am, a lady to see you—

NORA: All right, let her come in.

MAID (*to Helmer*):   And the doctor's just come too.

HELMER: Did he go right to my study?

MAID: Yes, he did.   85

HELMER *goes into his room. The* MAID *shows in* MRS. LINDE, *dressed in traveling clothes, and shuts the door after her.*

MRS. LINDE (*in a dispirited and somewhat hesitant voice*):   Hello, Nora.

NORA (*uncertain*):   Hello—

MRS. LINDE: You don't recognize me.

NORA: No, I don't know—but wait, I think— (*Exclaiming.*) What! Kristine! Is it really you?

MRS. LINDE: Yes, it's me.   90

NORA: Kristine! To think I didn't recognize you. But then, how could I? (*More quietly.*) How you've changed, Kristine!

MRS. LINDE: Yes, no doubt I have. In nine—ten long years.

NORA: Is it so long since we met! Yes, it's all of that. Oh, these last eight years have been a happy time, believe me. And so now you've come in to town, too. Made the long trip in the winter. That took courage.

MRS. LINDE: I just got here by ship this morning.

NORA: To enjoy yourself over Christmas,   95 of course. Oh, how lovely! Yes, enjoy ourselves, we'll do that. But take your coat off. You're not still cold? (*Helping her.*) There now, let's get cozy here by the stove. No, the easy chair there! I'll take the rocker here. (*Seizing her hands.*) Yes, now you have your old look again; it was only in that first moment. You're a bit more pale, Kristine—and maybe a bit thinner.

MRS. LINDE: And much, much older, Nora.

NORA: Yes, perhaps a bit older: a tiny, tiny bit; not much at all. (*Stopping short; suddenly serious.*) Oh, but thoughtless me, to sit here, chattering away. Sweet, good Kristine, can you forgive me?

MRS. LINDE: What do you mean, Nora?

NORA (*softly*):   Poor Kristine, you've become a widow.

100   MRS. LINDE: Yes, three years ago.

NORA: Oh, I knew it, of course: I read it in the papers. Oh, Kristine, you must believe me; I often thought of writing you then, but I kept postponing it, and something always interfered.

MRS. LINDE: Nora dear, I understand completely.

NORA: No, it was awful of me, Kristine. You poor thing, how much you must have gone through. And he left you nothing?

MRS. LINDE: No.

105   NORA: And no children?

MRS. LINDE: No.

NORA: Nothing at all, then?

MRS. LINDE: Not even a sense of loss to feed on.

NORA (*looking incredulously at her*):   But Kristine, how could that be?

110   MRS. LINDE (*smiling wearily and smoothing her hair*):   Oh, sometimes it happens, Nora.

NORA: So completely alone. How terribly hard that must be for you. I have three lovely children. You can't see them now; they're out with the maid. But now you must tell me everything—

MRS. LINDE: No, no, no, tell me about yourself.

NORA: No, you begin. Today I don't want to be selfish. I want to think only of you today. But there *is* something I must tell you. Did you hear of the wonderful luck we had recently?

MRS. LINDE: No, what's that?

115   NORA: My husband's been made manager in the bank, just think!

MRS. LINDE: Your husband? How marvelous!

NORA: Isn't it? Being a lawyer is such an uncertain living, you know, especially if one won't touch any cases that aren't clean and decent. And of course Torvald would never do that, and I'm with him completely there. Oh, we're simply delighted, believe me! He'll join the bank right after New Year's and start getting a huge salary and lots of commissions. From now on we can live quite differently—just as we want. Oh, Kristine, I feel so light and happy! Won't it be lovely to have stacks of money and not a care in the world?

MRS. LINDE: Well, anyway, it would be lovely to have enough for necessities.

NORA: No, not just for necessities, but stacks and stacks of money!

120   MRS. LINDE (*smiling*):   Nora, Nora, aren't you sensible yet? Back in school you were such a free spender.

NORA (*with a quiet laugh*):   Yes, that's what Torvald still says. (*Shaking her finger.*) But "Nora, Nora" isn't as silly as you all think. Really, we've been in no position for me to go squandering. We've had to work, both of us.

MRS. LINDE: You too?

NORA: Yes, at odd jobs—needlework, crocheting, embroidery, and such— (*Casually.*) and other things too. You remember that Torvald left the department when we were married? There was no chance of promotion in his office, and of course he needed to earn more money. But that first year he drove himself terribly. He took on all kinds of extra work that kept him going morning and night. It wore him down, and then he fell deathly ill. The doctors said it was essential for him to travel south.

MRS. LINDE: Yes, didn't you spend a whole year in Italy?

125 NORA: That's right. It wasn't easy to get away, you know. Ivar had just been born. But of course we had to go. Oh, that was a beautiful trip, and it saved Torvald's life. But it cost a frightful sum, Kristine.

MRS. LINDE: I can well imagine.

NORA: Four thousand, eight hundred crowns it cost. That's really a lot of money.

MRS. LINDE: But it's lucky you had it when you needed it.

NORA: Well, as it was, we got it from Papa.

130 MRS. LINDE: I see. It was just about the time your father died.

NORA: Yes, just about then. And, you know, I couldn't make that trip out to nurse him. I had to stay here, expecting Ivar any moment, and with my poor sick Torvald to care for. Dearest Papa, I never saw him again, Kristine. Oh, that was the worst time I've known in all my marriage.

MRS. LINDE: I know how you loved him. And then you went off to Italy?

NORA: Yes. We had the means now, and the doctors urged us. So we left a month after.

MRS. LINDE: And your husband came back completely cured?

135 NORA: Sound as a drum!

MRS. LINDE: But—the doctor?

NORA: Who?

MRS. LINDE: I thought the maid said he was a doctor, the man who came in with me.

NORA: Yes, that was Dr. Rank—but he's not making a sick call. He's our closest friend, and he stops by at least once a day. No, Torvald hasn't had a sick

moment since, and the children are fit and strong, and I am, too. (*Jumping up and clapping her hands.*) Oh, dear God, Kristine, what a lovely thing to live and be happy! But how disgusting of me—I'm talking of nothing but my own affairs. (*Sits on a stool close by Kristine, arms resting across her knees.*) Oh, don't be angry with me! Tell me, is it really true that you weren't in love with your husband? Why did you marry him, then?

MRS. LINDE: My mother was still alive, but 140 bedridden and helpless—and I had my two younger brothers to look after. In all conscience, I didn't think I could turn him down.

NORA: No, you were right there. But was he rich at the time?

MRS. LINDE: He was very well off, I'd say. But the business was shaky, Nora. When he died, it all fell apart, and nothing was left.

NORA: And then—?

MRS. LINDE: Yes, so I had to scrape up a living with a little shop and a little teaching and whatever else I could find. The last three years have been like one endless workday without a rest for me. Now it's over, Nora. My poor mother doesn't need me, for she's passed on. Nor the boys, either; they're working now and can take care of themselves.

NORA: How free you must feel— 145

MRS. LINDE: No—only unspeakably empty. Nothing to live for now. (*Standing up anxiously.*) That's why I couldn't take it any longer out in that desolate hole. Maybe here it'll be easier to find something to do and keep my mind occupied. If I could only be lucky enough to get a steady job, some office work—

NORA: Oh, but Kristine, that's so dreadfully tiring, and you already look so tired. It would be much better for you if you could go off to a bathing resort.

MRS. LINDE (*going toward the window*):   I have no father to give me travel money, Nora.

NORA (*rising*):   Oh, don't be angry with me.

150 MRS. LINDE (*going to her*):   Nora dear, don't you be angry with me. The worst of my kind of situation is all the bitterness that's stored away. No one to work for, and yet you're always having to snap up your opportunities. You have to live; and so you grow selfish. When you told me the happy change in your lot, do you know I was delighted less for your sakes than for mine?

NORA: How so? Oh, I see. You think maybe Torvald could do something for you.

MRS. LINDE: Yes, that's what I thought.

NORA: And he will, Kristine! Just leave it to me; I'll bring it up so delicately—find something attractive to humor him with. Oh, I'm so eager to help you.

MRS. LINDE: How very kind of you, Nora, to be so concerned over me—doubly kind, considering you really know so little of life's burdens yourself.

155 NORA: I—? I know so little—?

MRS. LINDE (*smiling*):   Well, my heavens—a little needlework and such—Nora, you're just a child.

NORA (*tossing her head and pacing the floor*): You don't have to act so superior.

MRS. LINDE: Oh?

NORA: You're just like the others. You all think I'm incapable of anything serious—

160 MRS. LINDE: Come now—

NORA: That I've never had to face the raw world.

MRS. LINDE: Nora dear, you've just been telling me all your troubles.

NORA: Hm! Trivia! (*Quietly.*) I haven't told you the big thing.

MRS. LINDE: Big thing? What do you mean?

NORA: You look down on me so, Kristine, 165 but you shouldn't. You're proud that you worked so long and hard for your mother.

MRS. LINDE: I don't look down on a soul. But it *is* true: I'm proud—and happy, too—to think it was given to me to make my mother's last days almost free of care.

NORA: And you're also proud thinking of what you've done for your brothers.

MRS. LINDE: I feel I've a right to be.

NORA: I agree. But listen to this, Kristine—I've also got something to be proud and happy for.

MRS. LINDE: I don't doubt it. But whatever 170 do you mean?

NORA: Not so loud. What if Torvald heard! He mustn't, not for anything in the world. Nobody must know, Kristine. No one but you.

MRS. LINDE: But what is it, then?

NORA: Come here. (*Drawing her down beside her on the sofa.*) It's true—I've also got something to be proud and happy for. I'm the one who saved Torvald's life.

MRS. LINDE: Saved—? Saved how?

NORA: I told you about the trip to Italy. 175 Torvald never would have lived if he hadn't gone south—

MRS. LINDE: Of course; your father gave you the means—

NORA (*smiling*):   That's what Torvald and all the rest think, but—

MRS. LINDE: But—?

NORA: Papa didn't give us a pin. I was the one who raised the money.

MRS. LINDE: You? That whole amount? 180

NORA: Four thousand, eight hundred crowns. What do you say to that?

MRS. LINDE: But Nora, how was it possible? Did you win the lottery?

NORA (*disdainfully*):   The lottery? Pooh! No art to that.

MRS. LINDE: But where did you get it from then?

185 NORA (*humming, with a mysterious smile*): Hmm, tra-la-la-la.

MRS. LINDE: Because you couldn't have borrowed it.

NORA: No? Why not?

MRS. LINDE: A wife can't borrow without her husband's consent.

NORA (*tossing her head*):   Oh, but a wife with a little business sense, a wife who knows how to manage—

190 MRS. LINDE: Nora, I simply don't understand—

NORA: You don't have to. Whoever said I *borrowed* the money? I could have gotten it other ways. (*Throwing herself back on the sofa.*) I could have gotten it from some admirer or other. After all, a girl with my ravishing appeal—

MRS. LINDE: You lunatic.

NORA: I'll bet you're eaten up with curiosity, Kristine.

MRS. LINDE: Now listen here, Nora—you haven't done something indiscreet?

195 NORA (*sitting up again*):   Is it indiscreet to save your husband's life?

MRS. LINDE: I think it's indiscreet that without his knowledge you—

NORA: But that's the point: he mustn't know! My Lord, can't you understand? He mustn't ever know the close call he had. It was to *me* the doctors came to say his life was in danger—that nothing could save him but a stay in the south. Didn't I try strategy then! I began talking about how lovely it would be for me to travel abroad like other young wives; I begged and I cried; I told him please to remember my condition, to be kind and indulge me; and then I dropped a hint that he could easily take out a loan. But at that, Kristine, he nearly exploded. He said I was frivolous, and it was his duty as man of the house not to indulge me in whims and fancies—as I think he called them. Aha, I thought, now you'll just have to be saved—and that's when I saw my chance.

MRS. LINDE: And your father never told Torvald the money wasn't from him?

NORA: No, never. Papa died right about then. I'd considered bringing him into my secret and begging him never to tell. But he was too sick at the time—and then, sadly, it didn't matter.

MRS. LINDE: And you've never confided 200 in your husband since?

NORA: For heaven's sake, no! Are you serious? He's so strict on that subject. Besides—Torvald, with all his masculine pride—how painfully humiliating for him if he ever found out he was in debt to me. That would just ruin our relationship. Our beautiful, happy home would never be the same.

MRS. LINDE: Won't you ever tell him?

NORA (*thoughtfully, half smiling*):   Yes— maybe sometime, years from now, when I'm no longer so attractive. Don't laugh! I only mean when Torvald loves me less than now, when he stops enjoying my dancing and dressing up and reciting for him. Then it might be wise to have something in reserve— (*Breaking off.*) How ridiculous! That'll never happen—Well, Kristine, what do you think of my big secret? I'm capable of something too, hm? You can imagine, of course, how this thing hangs over me. It really hasn't been easy meeting the payments on time. In the business world there's what they call quarterly interest and what they call amortization, and these are always so terribly hard to manage. I've had to skimp a little here and there, wherever I could, you know. I could hardly spare anything from my house allowance, because Torvald has to live well. I couldn't let the children go poorly dressed; whatever I got for them, I felt I had to use up completely—the darlings!

MRS. LINDE: Poor Nora, so it had to come out of your own budget, then?

205 NORA: Yes, of course. But I was the one most responsible, too. Every time Torvald gave me money for new clothes and such, I never used more than half; always bought the simplest, cheapest outfits. It was a godsend that everything looks so well on me that Torvald never noticed. But it did weigh me down at times, Kristine. It *is* such a joy to wear fine things. You understand.

MRS. LINDE: Oh, of course.

NORA: And then I found other ways of making money. Last winter I was lucky enough to get a lot of copying to do. I locked myself in and sat writing every evening till late in the night. Ah, I was tired so often, dead tired. But still it was wonderful fun, sitting and working like that, earning money. It was almost like being a man.

MRS. LINDE: But how much have you paid off this way so far?

NORA: That's hard to say, exactly. These accounts, you know, aren't easy to figure. I only know that I've paid out all I could scrape together. Time and again I haven't known where to turn. (*Smiling.*) Then I'd sit here dreaming of a rich old gentleman who had fallen in love with me—

210 MRS. LINDE: What! Who is he?

NORA: Oh, really! And that he'd died, and when his will was opened, there in big letters it said, "All my fortune shall be paid over in cash, immediately, to that enchanting Mrs. Nora Helmer."

MRS. LINDE: But Nora dear—who *was* this gentleman?

NORA: Good grief, can't you understand? The old man never existed; that was only something I'd dream up time and again whenever I was at my wits' end for

money. But it makes no difference now; the old fossil can go where he pleases for all I care; I don't need him or his will— because now I'm free. (*Jumping up.*) Oh, how lovely to think of that, Kristine! Carefree! To know you're carefree, utterly carefree; to be able to romp and play with the children, and to keep up a beautiful, charming home—everything just the way Torvald likes it! And think, spring is coming, with big blue skies. Maybe we can travel a little then. Maybe I'll see the ocean again. Oh yes, it *is* so marvelous to live and be happy!

The front doorbell rings.

MRS. LINDE (*rising*):   There's the bell. It's probably best that I go.

NORA: No, stay. No one's expected. It   215 must be for Torvald.

MAID (*from the hall doorway*):   Excuse me, ma'am—there's a gentleman here to see Mr. Helmer, but I didn't know—since the doctor's with him—

NORA: Who is the gentleman?

KROGSTAD (*from the doorway*):   It's me, Mrs. Helmer.

MRS. LINDE *starts and turns away toward the window.*

NORA (*stepping toward him, tense, her voice a whisper*):   You? What is it? Why do you want to speak to my husband?

KROGSTAD: Bank business—after a fashion.   220 I have a small job in the investment bank, and I hear now your husband is going to be our chief—

NORA: In other words, it's—

KROGSTAD: Just dry business, Mrs. Helmer. Nothing but that.

NORA: Yes, then please be good enough to step into the study. (*She nods indifferently as she sees him out by the hall door, then returns and begins stirring up the stove.)*

MRS. LINDE: Nora—who was that man?

225 NORA: That was a Mr. Krogstad—a lawyer.

MRS. LINDE: Then it really was him.

NORA: Do you know that person?

MRS. LINDE: I did once—many years ago. For a time he was a law clerk in our town.

NORA: Yes, he's been that.

230 MRS. LINDE: How he's changed.

NORA: I understand he had a very unhappy marriage.

MRS. LINDE: He's a widower now.

NORA: With a number of children. There now, it's burning. (*She closes the stove door and moves the rocker a bit to one side.*)

MRS. LINDE: They say he has a hand in all kinds of business.

235 NORA: Oh? That may be true; I wouldn't know. But let's not think about business. It's so dull.

DR. RANK *enters from* HELMER'S *study.*

RANK (*still in the doorway*): No, no really— I don't want to intrude, I'd just as soon talk a little while with your wife. (*Shuts the door, then notices* MRS. LINDE.) Oh, beg pardon. I'm intruding here too.

NORA: No, not at all. (*Introducing him.*) Dr. Rank, Mrs. Linde.

RANK: Well now, that's a name much heard in this house. I believe I passed the lady on the stairs as I came.

MRS. LINDE: Yes, I take the stairs very slowly. They're rather hard on me.

240 RANK: Uh-hm, some touch of internal weakness?

MRS. LINDE: More overexertion, I'd say.

RANK: Nothing else? Then you're probably here in town to rest up in a round of parties?

MRS. LINDE: I'm here to look for work.

RANK: Is that the best cure for overexertion?

MRS. LINDE: One has to live, Doctor. 245

RANK: Yes, there's a common prejudice to that effect.

NORA: Oh, come on, Dr. Rank—you really do want to live yourself.

RANK: Yes, I really do. Wretched as I am, I'll gladly prolong my torment indefinitely. All my patients feel like that. And it's quite the same, too, with the morally sick. Right at this moment there's one of those moral invalids in there with Helmer—

MRS. LINDE (*softly*): Ah!

NORA: Who do you mean? 250

RANK: Oh, it's a lawyer, Krogstad, a type you wouldn't know. His character is rotten to the root—but even he began chattering all-importantly about how he had to *live.*

NORA: Oh? What did he want to talk to Torvald about?

RANK: I really don't know. I only heard something about the bank.

NORA: I didn't know that Krog—that this man Krogstad had anything to do with the bank.

RANK: Yes, he's gotten some kind of berth 255 down there. (*To* MRS. LINDE.) I don't know if you also have, in your neck of the woods, a type of person who scuttles about breathlessly, sniffing out hints of moral corruption, and then maneuvers his victim into some sort of key position where he can keep an eye on him. It's the healthy these days that are out in the cold.

MRS. LINDE: All the same, it's the sick who most need to be taken in.

RANK (*with a shrug*): Yes, there we have it. That's the concept that's turning society into a sanatorium.

NORA, *lost in her thoughts, breaks out into quiet laughter and claps her hands.*

RANK: Why do you laugh at that? Do you have any real idea of what society is?

NORA: What do I care about dreary old society? I was laughing at something quite different—something terribly funny. Tell me, Doctor—is everyone who works in the bank dependent now on Torvald?

260 RANK: Is that what you find so terribly funny?

NORA (*smiling and humming*): Never mind, never mind! (*Pacing the floor.*) Yes, that's really immensely amusing: that we—that Torvald has so much power now over all those people. (*Taking the bag out of her pocket.*) Dr. Rank, a little macaroon on that?

RANK: See here, macaroons! I thought they were contraband here.

NORA: Yes, but these are some that Kristine gave me.

MRS. LINDE: What? I—?

265 NORA: Now, now, don't be afraid. You couldn't possibly know that Torvald had forbidden them. You see, he's worried they'll ruin my teeth. But hmp! Just this once! Isn't that so, Dr. Rank? Help yourself! (*Puts a macaroon in his mouth.*) And you too, Kristine. And I'll also have one, only a little one—or two, at the most. (*Walking about again.*) Now I'm really tremendously happy. Now there's just one last thing in the world that I have an enormous desire to do.

RANK: Well! And what's that?

NORA: It's something I have such a consuming desire to say so Torvald could hear.

RANK: And why can't you say it?

NORA: I don't dare. It's quite shocking.

270 MRS. LINDE: Shocking?

RANK: Well, then it isn't advisable. But in front of us you certainly can. What do you have such a desire to say so Torvald could hear?

NORA: I have such a huge desire to say— to hell and be damned!

RANK: Are you crazy?

MRS. LINDE: My goodness, Nora!

RANK: Go on, say it. Here he is. 275

NORA (*hiding the macaroon bag*): Shh, shh, shh!

HELMER *comes in from his study, hat in hand, overcoat over his arm.*

NORA (*going toward him*): Well, Torvald dear, are you through with him?

HELMER: Yes, he just left.

NORA: Let me introduce you—this is Kristine, who's arrived here in town.

HELMER: Kristine—? I'm sorry, but I don't 280 know—

NORA: Mrs. Linde, Torvald dear. Mrs. Kristine Linde.

HELMER: Of course. A childhood friend of my wife's, no doubt?

MRS. LINDE: Yes, we knew each other in those days.

NORA: And just think, she made the long trip down here in order to talk with you.

HELMER: What's this? 285

MRS. LINDE: Well, not exactly—

NORA: You see, Kristine is remarkably clever in office work, and so she's terribly eager to come under a capable man's supervision and add more to what she already knows—

HELMER: Very wise, Mrs. Linde.

NORA: And then when she heard that you'd become a bank manager—the story was wired out to the papers—then she came in as fast as she could and—Really, Torvald, for my sake you can do a little something for Kristine, can't you?

HELMER: Yes, it's not at all impossible. 290 Mrs. Linde, I suppose you're a widow?

MRS. LINDE: Yes.

HELMER: Any experience in office work?

MRS. LINDE: Yes, a good deal.

HELMER: Well, it's quite likely that I can make an opening for you—

295 NORA (*clapping her hands*):   You see, you see!

HELMER: You've come at a lucky moment, Mrs. Linde.

MRS. LINDE: Oh, how can I thank you?

HELMER: Not necessary. (*Putting his overcoat on.*) But today you'll have to excuse me—

RANK: Wait, I'll go with you. (*He fetches his coat from the hall and warms it at the stove.*)

300 NORA: Don't stay out long, dear.

HELMER: An hour; no more.

NORA: Are you going too, Kristine?

MRS. LINDE (*putting on her winter garments*): Yes, I have to see about a room now.

HELMER: Then perhaps we can all walk together.

305 NORA (*helping her*):   What a shame we're so cramped here, but it's quite impossible for us to—

MRS. LINDE: Oh, don't even think of it! Good-bye, Nora dear, and thanks for everything.

NORA: Good-bye for now. Of course you'll be back this evening. And you too, Dr. Rank. What? If you're well enough? Oh, you've got to be! Wrap up tight now.

In a ripple of small talk the company moves out into the hall; children's voices are heard outside on the step

NORA: There they are! There they are! (*She runs to open the door. The children come in with their nurse, Anne-Marie.*) Come in, come in! (*Bends down and kisses them.*) Oh, you darlings—! Look at them, Kristine. Aren't they lovely!

RANK: No loitering in the draft here.

310 HELMER: Come, Mrs. Linde—this place is unbearable now for anyone but mothers.

DR. RANK, HELMER, *and* MRS. LINDE *go down the stairs.* ANNE-MARIE *goes into the living room with the children.* NORA *follows, after closing the hall door.*

NORA: How fresh and strong you look. Oh, such red cheeks you have! Like apples and roses. (*The children interrupt her throughout the following.*) And it was so much fun? That's wonderful. Really? You pulled both Emmy and Bob on the sled? Imagine, all together! Yes, you're a clever boy, Ivar. Oh, let me hold her a bit, Anne-Marie. My sweet little doll baby! (*Takes the smallest from the nurse and dances with her.*) Yes, yes, Mama will dance with Bob as well. What? Did you throw snowballs? Oh, if I'd only been there! No, don't bother, Anne-Marie—I'll undress them myself. Oh yes, let me. It's such fun. Go in and rest; you look half frozen. There's hot coffee waiting for you on the stove. (*The nurse goes into the room to the left. Nora takes the children's winter things off, throwing them about, while the children talk to her all at once.*) Is that so? A big dog chased you? But it didn't bite? No, dogs never bite little, lovely doll babies. Don't peek in the packages, Ivar! What is it? Yes, wouldn't you like to know. No, no, it's an ugly something. Well? Shall we play? What shall we play? Hide-and-seek? Yes, let's play hide-and-seek. Bob must hide first. I must? Yes, let me hide first. (*Laughing and shouting, she and the children play in and out of the living room and the adjoining room to the right. At last* NORA *hides under the table. The children come storming in, search, but cannot find her, then hear her muffled laughter, dash over to the table, lift the cloth up and find her. Wild shouting. She creeps forward as if to scare them. More shouts. Meanwhile, a knock at the hall door; no one has noticed it. Now the door half opens, and* KROGSTAD *appears. He waits a moment; the game goes on.*)

KROGSTAD: Beg pardon, Mrs. Helmer—

NORA (*with a strangled cry, turning and scrambling to her knees*):   Oh! What do you want?

KROGSTAD: Excuse me. The outer door was ajar; it must be someone forgot to shut it—

315 NORA (*rising*):   My husband isn't home, Mr. Krogstad.

KROGSTAD: I know that.

NORA: Yes—then what do you want here?

KROGSTAD: A word with you.

NORA: With—? (*To the children, quietly.*) Go in to Anne-Marie. What? No, the strange man won't hurt Mama. When he's gone, we'll play some more. (*She leads the children into the room to the left and shuts the door after them. Then, tense and nervous:*) You want to speak to me?

320 KROGSTAD: Yes, I want to.

NORA: Today? But it's not yet the first of the month—

KROGSTAD: No, it's Christmas Eve. It's going to be up to you how merry a Christmas you have.

NORA: What is it you want? Today I absolutely can't—

KROGSTAD: We won't talk about that till later. This is something else. You do have a moment to spare, I suppose?

325 NORA: Oh yes, of course—I do, except—

KROGSTAD: Good. I was sitting over at Olsen's Restaurant when I saw your husband go down the street—

NORA: Yes?

KROGSTAD: With a lady.

NORA: Yes. So?

330 KROGSTAD: If you'll pardon my asking: wasn't that lady a Mrs. Linde?

NORA: Yes.

KROGSTAD: Just now come into town?

NORA: Yes, today.

KROGSTAD: She's a good friend of yours?

335 NORA: Yes, she is. But I don't see—

KROGSTAD: I also knew her once.

NORA: I'm aware of that.

KROGSTAD: Oh? You know all about it. I thought so. Well, then let me ask you short and sweet: is Mrs. Linde getting a job in the bank?

NORA: What makes you think you can cross-examine me, Mr. Krogstad—you, one of my husband's employees? But since you ask, you might as well know— yes, Mrs. Linde's going to be taken on at the bank. And I'm the one who spoke for her, Mr. Krogstad. Now you know.

KROGSTAD: So I guessed right.   340

NORA (*pacing up and down*):   Oh, one does have a tiny bit of influence, I should hope. Just because I am a woman, don't think it means that—When one has a subordinate position, Mr. Krogstad, one really ought to be careful about pushing somebody who—hm—

KROGSTAD: Who has influence?

NORA: That's right.

Krogstad (in a different tone):   Mrs. Helmer, would you be good enough to use your influence on my behalf?

NORA: What? What do you mean?   345

KROGSTAD: Would you please make sure that I keep my subordinate position in the bank?

NORA: What does that mean? Who's thinking of taking away your position?

KROGSTAD: Oh, don't play the innocent with me. I'm quite aware that your friend would hardly relish the chance of running into me again; and I'm also aware now whom I can thank for being turned out.

NORA: But I promise you—

KROGSTAD: Yes, yes, yes, to the point: 350 there's still time, and I'm advising you to use your influence to prevent it.

NORA: But Mr. Krogstad, I have absolutely no influence.

KROGSTAD: You haven't? I thought you were just saying—

NORA: You shouldn't take me so literally. I! How can you believe that I have any such influence over my husband?

KROGSTAD: Oh, I've known your husband from our student days. I don't think the great bank manager's more steadfast than any other married man.

355 NORA: You speak insolently about my husband, and I'll show you the door.

KROGSTAD: The lady has spirit.

NORA: I'm not afraid of you any longer. After New Year's, I'll soon be done with the whole business.

KROGSTAD (*restraining himself*):   Now listen to me, Mrs. Helmer. If necessary, I'll fight for my little job in the bank as if it were life itself.

NORA: Yes, so it seems.

360 KROGSTAD: It's not just a matter of income; that's the least of it. It's something else— All right, out with it! Look, this is the thing. You know, just like all the others, of course, that once, a good many years ago, I did something rather rash.

NORA: I've heard rumors to that effect.

KROGSTAD: The case never got into court; but all the same, every door was closed in my face from then on. So I took up those various activities you know about. I had to grab hold somewhere; and I dare say I haven't been among the worst. But now I want to drop all that. My boys are growing up. For their sakes, I'll have to win back as much respect as possible here in town. That job in the bank was like the first rung in my ladder. And now your husband wants to kick me right back down in the mud again.

NORA: But for heaven's sake, Mr. Krogstad, it's simply not in my power to help you.

KROGSTAD: That's because you haven't the will to—but I have the means to make you.

NORA: You certainly won't tell my hus-   365 band that I owe you money?

KROGSTAD: Hm—what if I told him that?

NORA: That would be shameful of you. (*Nearly in tears.*) This secret—my joy and my pride—that he should learn it in such a crude and disgusting way—learn it from you. You'd expose me to the most horrible unpleasantness—

KROGSTAD: Only unpleasantness?

NORA (*vehemently*):   But go on and try. It'll turn out the worse for you, because then my husband will really see what a crook you are, and then you'll *never* be able to hold your job.

KROGSTAD: I asked if it was just domestic   370 unpleasantness you were afraid of?

NORA: If my husband finds out, then of course he'll pay what I owe at once, and then we'd be through with you for good.

KROGSTAD (*a step closer*):   Listen, Mrs. Helmer—you've either got a very bad memory, or else no head at all for business. I'd better put you a little more in touch with the facts.

NORA: What do you mean?

KROGSTAD: When your husband was sick, you came to me for a loan of four thousand, eight hundred crowns.

NORA: Where else could I go?   375

KROGSTAD: I promised to get you that sum—

NORA: And you got it.

KROGSTAD: I promised to get you that sum, on certain conditions. You were so involved in your husband's illness, and so eager to finance your trip, that I guess you didn't think out all the details. It might just be a good idea to remind you. I promised you the money on the strength of a note I drew up.

NORA: Yes, and that I signed.

KROGSTAD: Right. But at the bottom I   380 added some lines for your father to guarantee the loan. He was supposed to sign down there.

NORA: Supposed to? He did sign.

KROGSTAD: I left the date blank. In other words, your father would have dated his signature himself. Do you remember that?

NORA: Yes, I think—

KROGSTAD: Then I gave you the note for you to mail to your father. Isn't that so?

385 NORA: Yes.

KROGSTAD: And naturally you sent it at once—because only some five, six days later you brought me the note, properly signed. And with that, the money was yours.

NORA: Well, then; I've made my payments regularly, haven't I?

KROGSTAD: More or less. But—getting back to the point—those were hard times for you then, Mrs. Helmer.

NORA: Yes, they were.

390 KROGSTAD: Your father was very ill, I believe.

NORA: He was near the end.

KROGSTAD: He died soon after?

NORA: Yes.

KROGSTAD: Tell me, Mrs. Helmer, do you happen to recall the date of your father's death? The day of the month, I mean.

395 NORA: Papa died the twenty-ninth of September.

KROGSTAD: That's quite correct; I've already looked into that. And now we come to a curious thing—(*Taking out a paper.*) which I simply cannot comprehend.

NORA: Curious thing? I don't know—

KROGSTAD: This is the curious thing: that your father co-signed the note for your loan three days after his death.

NORA: How—? I don't understand.

400 KROGSTAD: Your father died the twenty-ninth of September. But look. Here your father dated his signature October second. Isn't that curious, Mrs. Helmer? (NORA *is silent.*) Can you explain it to me?

(NORA *remains silent.*) It's also remarkable that the words "October second" and the year aren't written in your father's hand, but rather in one that I think I know. Well, it's easy to understand. Your father forgot perhaps to date his signature, and then someone or other added it, a bit sloppily, before anyone knew of his death. There's nothing wrong in that. It all comes down to the signature. And there's no question about *that*, Mrs. Helmer. It really *was* your father who signed his own name here, wasn't it?

NORA (*after a short silence, throwing her head back and looking squarely at him*):   No, it wasn't. *I* signed Papa's name.

KROGSTAD: Wait, now—are you fully aware that this is a dangerous confession?

NORA: Why? You'll soon get your money.

KROGSTAD: Let me ask you a question— why didn't you send the paper to your father?

NORA: That was impossible. Papa was so 405 sick. If I'd asked him for his signature, I also would have had to tell him what the money was for. But I couldn't tell him, sick as he was, that my husband's life was in danger. That was just impossible.

KROGSTAD: Then it would have been better if you'd given up the trip abroad.

NORA: I couldn't possibly. The trip was to save my husband's life. I couldn't give that up.

KROGSTAD: But didn't you ever consider that this was a fraud against me?

NORA: I couldn't let myself be bothered by that. You weren't any concern of mine. I couldn't stand you, with all those cold complications you made, even though you knew how badly off my husband was.

KROGSTAD: Mrs. Helmer, obviously you 410 haven't the vaguest idea of what you've involved yourself in. But I can tell you this: it was nothing more and nothing worse that I once did—and it wrecked my whole reputation.

NORA: You? Do you expect me to believe that you ever acted bravely to save your wife's life?

KROGSTAD: Laws don't inquire into motives.

NORA: Then they must be very poor laws.

KROGSTAD: Poor or not—if I introduce this paper in court, you'll be judged according to law.

415 NORA: This I refuse to believe. A daughter hasn't a right to protect her dying father from anxiety and care? A wife hasn't a right to save her husband's life? I don't know much about laws, but I'm sure that somewhere in the books these things are allowed. And you don't know anything about it—you who practice the law? You must be an awful lawyer, Mr. Krogstad.

KROGSTAD: Could be. But business—the kind of business we two are mixed up in—don't you think I know about that? All right. Do what you want now. But I'm telling you *this*; if I get shoved down a second time, you're going to keep me company. (*He bows and goes out through the hall.*)

NORA (*pensive for a moment, then tossing her head*): Oh, really! Trying to frighten me! I'm not so silly as all that. (*Begins gathering up the children's clothes, but soon stops.*) But—? No, but that's impossible! I did it out of love.

THE CHILDREN (*in the doorway, left*): Mama, that strange man's gone out the door.

NORA: Yes, yes, I know it. But don't tell anyone about the strange man. Do you hear? Not even Papa!

420 THE CHILDREN: No, Mama. But now will you play again?

NORA: No, not now.

THE CHILDREN: Oh, but Mama, you promised.

NORA: Yes, but I can't now. Go inside; I have too much to do. Go in, go in, my sweet darlings. (*She herds them gently back in the room and shuts the door after them. Settling on the sofa, she takes up a piece of embroidery and makes some stitches, but soon stops abruptly.*) No! (*Throws the work aside, rises, goes to the hall door and calls out.*) Helene! Let me have the tree in here. (*Goes to the table, left, opens the table drawer, and stops again.*) No, but that's utterly impossible!

MAID (*with the Christmas tree*): Where should I put it, ma'am?

NORA: There. The middle of the floor. 425

MAID: Should I bring anything else?

NORA: No, thanks. I have what I need.

The MAID, *who has set the tree down, goes out.*

NORA (*absorbed in trimming the tree*): Candles here—and flowers here. That terrible creature! Talk, talk, talk! There's nothing to it at all. The tree's going to be lovely. I'll do anything to please you, Torvald. I'll sing for you, dance for you—

HELMER *comes in from the hall, with a sheaf of papers under his arm.*

NORA: Oh! You're back so soon?

HELMER: Yes. Has anyone been here? 430

NORA: Here? No.

HELMER: That's odd. I saw Krogstad leaving the front door.

NORA: So? Oh yes, that's true. Krogstad was here a moment.

HELMER: Nora, I can see by your face that he's been here, begging you to put in a good word for him.

NORA: Yes. 435

HELMER: And it was supposed to seem like your own idea? You were to hide it from me that he'd been here. He asked you that, too, didn't he?

NORA: Yes, Torvald, but—

HELMER: Nora, Nora, and you could fall for that? Talk with that sort of person and promise him anything? And then in the bargain, tell me an untruth.

NORA: An untruth—?

440 HELMER: Didn't you say that no one had been here? (*Wagging his finger.*) My little songbird must never do that again. A songbird needs a clean beak to warble with. No false notes. (*Putting his arm about her waist.*) That's the way it should be, isn't it? Yes, I'm sure of it. (*Releasing her.*) And so, enough of that. (*Sitting by the stove.*) Ah, how snug and cozy it is here. (*Leafing among his papers.*)

NORA (*busy with the tree, after a short pause*):   Torvald!

HELMER: Yes.

NORA: I'm so much looking forward to the Stenborgs' costume party, day after tomorrow.

HELMER: And I can't wait to see what you'll surprise me with.

445 NORA: Oh, that stupid business!

HELMER: What?

NORA: I can't find anything that's right. Everything seems so ridiculous, so inane.

HELMER: So my little Nora's come to *that* recognition?

NORA (*going behind his chair, her arms resting on its back*):   Are you very busy, Torvald?

450 HELMER: Oh—

NORA: What papers are those?

HELMER: Bank matters.

NORA: Already?

HELMER: I've gotten full authority from the retiring management to make all necessary changes in personnel and procedure. I'll need Christmas week for that. I want to have everything in order by New Year's.

455 NORA: So that was the reason this poor Krogstad—

HELMER: Hm.

NORA (*still leaning on the chair and slowly stroking the nape of his neck*):   If you weren't so very busy, I would have asked you an enormous favor, Torvald.

HELMER: Let's hear. What is it?

NORA: You know, there isn't anyone who has your good taste—and I want so much to look well at the costume party. Torvald, couldn't you take over and decide what I should be and plan my costume?

HELMER: Ah, is my stubborn little creature 460 calling for a lifeguard?

NORA: Yes, Torvald, I can't get anywhere without your help.

HELMER: All right—I'll think it over. We'll hit on something.

NORA: Oh, how sweet of you. (*Goes to the tree again. Pause.*) Aren't the red flowers pretty—? But tell me, was it really such a crime that this Krogstad committed?

HELMER: Forgery. Do you have any idea what that means?

NORA: Couldn't he have done it out of 465 need?

HELMER: Yes, or thoughtlessness, like so many others. I'm not so heartless that I'd condemn a man categorically for just one mistake.

NORA: No, of course not, Torvald!

HELMER: Plenty of men have redeemed themselves by openly confessing their crimes and taking their punishment.

NORA: Punishment—?

HELMER: But now Krogstad didn't go that 470 way. He got himself out by sharp practices, and that's the real cause of his moral breakdown.

NORA: Do you really think that would—?

HELMER: Just imagine how a man with that sort of guilt in him has to lie and cheat and deceive on all sides, has to wear a mask even with the nearest and dearest he has, even with his own wife and children. And with the children, Nora—that's where it's most horrible.

NORA: Why?

HELMER: Because that kind of atmosphere of lies infects the whole life of a home. Every breath the children take in is filled with the germs of something degenerate.

475 NORA (*coming closer behind him*):   Are you sure of that?

HELMER: Oh, I've seen it often enough as a lawyer. Almost everyone who goes bad early in life has a mother who's a chronic liar.

NORA: Why just—the mother?

HELMER: It's usually the mother's influence that's dominant, but the father's works in the same way, of course. Every lawyer is quite familiar with it. And still this Krogstad's been going home year in, year out, poisoning his own children with lies and pretense; that's why I call him morally lost. (*Reaching his hands out toward her.*) So my sweet little Nora must promise me never to plead his cause. Your hand on it. Come, come, what's this? Give me your hand. There, now. All settled. I can tell you it'd be impossible for me to work alongside of him. I literally feel physically revolted when I'm anywhere near such a person.

NORA (*withdraws her hand and goes to the other side of the Christmas tree*):   How hot it is here! And I've got so much to do.

480 HELMER (*getting up and gathering his papers*): Yes, and I have to think about getting some of these read through before dinner. I'll think about your costume, too. And something to hang on the tree in gilt paper, I may even see about that. (*Putting his hand on her head.*) Oh you, my darling little songbird. (*He goes into his study and closes the door after him.*)

NORA (*softly, after a silence*):   Oh, really! It isn't so. It's impossible. It must be impossible.

ANNE-MARIE (*in the doorway, left*):   The children are begging so hard to come in to Mama.

NORA: No, no, no, don't let them in to me! You stay with them, Anne-Marie.

ANNE-MARIE: Of course, ma'am. (*Closes the door.*)

NORA (*pale with terror*):   Hurt my children—! Poison my home? (*A moment's pause; then she tosses her head.*) That's not true. Never. Never in all the world.   485

(ACT II)

Same room. Beside the piano the Christmas tree now stands stripped of ornament, burned-down candle stubs on its ragged branches. NORA'S *street clothes lie on the sofa.* NORA, *alone in the room, moves restlessly about; at last she stops at the sofa and picks up her coat.*

NORA (*dropping the coat again*):   Someone's coming! (*Goes toward the door, listens.*) No—there's no one. Of course—nobody's coming today, Christmas Day—or tomorrow, either. But maybe— (*Opens the door and looks out.*) No, nothing in the mailbox. Quite empty. (*Coming forward.*) What nonsense! He won't do anything serious. Nothing terrible could happen. It's impossible. Why, I have three small children.

ANNE-MARIE, *with a large carton, comes in from the room to the left.*

ANNE-MARIE: Well, at last I found the box with the masquerade clothes.

NORA: Thanks. Put it on the table.

ANNE-MARIE (*does so*):   But they're all pretty much of a mess.

NORA: Ahh! I'd love to rip them in a million pieces!   5

ANNE-MARIE: Oh, mercy, they can be fixed right up. Just a little patience.

NORA: Yes, I'll go get Mrs. Linde to help me.

ANNE-MARIE: Out again now? In this nasty weather? Miss Nora will catch cold—get sick.

NORA: Oh, worse things could happen. How are the children?

10 ANNE-MARIE: The poor mites are playing with their Christmas presents, but—

NORA: Do they ask for me much?

ANNE-MARIE: They're so used to having Mama around, you know.

NORA: Yes, but Anne-Marie, I *can't* be together with them as much as I was.

ANNE-MARIE: Well, small children get used to anything.

15 NORA: You think so? Do you think they'd forget their mother if she was gone for good?

ANNE-MARIE: Oh, mercy—gone for good!

NORA: Wait, tell me, Anne-Marie—I've wondered so often—how could you ever have the heart to give your child over to strangers?

ANNE-MARIE: But I had to, you know, to become little Nora's nurse.

NORA: Yes, but how could you *do* it?

20 ANNE-MARIE: When I could get such a good place? A girl who's poor and who's gotten in trouble is glad enough for that. Because that slippery fish, he didn't do a thing for me, you know.

NORA: But your daughter's surely forgotten you.

ANNE-MARIE: Oh, she certainly has not. She's written to me, both when she was confirmed and when she was married.

NORA (*clasping her about the neck*):   You old Anne-Marie, you were a good mother for me when I was little.

ANNE-MARIE: Poor little Nora, with no other mother but me.

25 NORA: And if the babies didn't have one, then I know that you'd—What silly talk! (*Opening the carton.*) Go in to them. Now

I'll have to—Tomorrow you can see how lovely I'll look.

ANNE-MARIE: Oh, there won't be anyone at the party as lovely as Miss Nora. (*She goes off into the room, left.*)

NORA (*begins unpacking the box, but soon throws it aside*):   Oh, if I dared to go out. If only nobody would come. If only nothing would happen here while I'm out. What craziness—nobody's coming. Just don't think. This muff—needs a brushing. Beautiful gloves, beautiful gloves. Let it go. Let it go! One, two, three, four, five, six—(*With a cry.*) Oh, there they are! (*Poises to move toward the door, but remains irresolutely standing.* MRS. LINDE *enters from the hall, where she has removed her street clothes.*)

NORA: Oh, it's you, Kristine. There's no one else out there? How good that you've come.

MRS. LINDE: I hear you were up asking for me.

30 NORA: Yes, I just stopped by. There's something you really can help me with. Let's get settled on the sofa. Look, there's going to be a costume party tomorrow evening at the Stenborgs' right above us, and now Torvald wants me to go as a Neapolitan peasant girl and dance the tarantella that I learned in Capri.

MRS. LINDE: Really, are you giving a whole performance?

NORA: Torvald says yes, I should. See, here's the dress. Torvald had it made for me down there; but now it's all so tattered that I just don't know—

MRS. LINDE: Oh, we'll fix that up in no time. It's nothing more than the trimmings—they're a bit loose here and there. Needle and thread? Good, now we have what we need.

NORA: Oh, how sweet of you!

35 MRS. LINDE (*sewing*):   So you'll be in disguise tomorrow, Nora. You know what?

I'll stop by then for a moment and have a look at you all dressed up. But listen, I've absolutely forgotten to thank you for that pleasant evening yesterday.

NORA (*getting up and walking about*):   I don't think it was as pleasant as usual yesterday. You should have come to town a bit sooner, Kristine—Yes, Torvald really knows how to give a home elegance and charm.

MRS. LINDE: And you do, too, if you ask me. You're not your father's daughter for nothing. But tell me, is Dr. Rank always so down in the mouth as yesterday?

NORA: No, that was quite an exception. But he goes around critically ill all the time—tuberculosis of the spine, poor man. You know, his father was a disgusting thing who kept mistresses and so on—and that's why the son's been sickly from birth.

MRS. LINDE (*lets her sewing fall to her lap*):   But my dearest Nora, how do you know about such things?

40 NORA (*walking more jauntily*):   Hmp! When you've had three children, then you've had a few visits from—from women who know something of medicine, and they tell you this and that.

MRS. LINDE (*resumes sewing; a short pause*):   Does Dr. Rank come here every day?

NORA: Every blessed day. He's Torvald's best friend from childhood, and *my* good friend, too. Dr. Rank almost belongs to this house.

MRS. LINDE: But tell me—is he quite sincere? I mean, doesn't he rather enjoy flattering people?

NORA: Just the opposite. Why do you think that?

45 MRS. LINDE: When you introduced us yesterday, he was proclaiming that he'd often heard my name in this house; but later I noticed that your husband hadn't the slightest idea who I really was. So how could Dr. Rank—?

NORA: But it's all true, Kristine. You see, Torvald loves me beyond words, and, as he puts it, he'd like to keep me all to himself. For a long time he'd almost be jealous if I even mentioned any of my old friends back home. So of course I dropped that. But with Dr. Rank I talk a lot about such things, because he likes hearing about them.

MRS. LINDE: Now listen, Nora; in many ways you're still like a child. I'm a good deal older than you, with a little more experience. I'll tell you something: you ought to put an end to all this with Dr. Rank.

NORA: What should I put an end to?

MRS. LINDE: Both parts of it, I think. Yesterday you said something about a rich admirer who'd provide you with money—

NORA: Yes, one who doesn't exist—worse   50
luck. So?

MRS. LINDE: Is Dr. Rank well off?

NORA: Yes, he is.

MRS. LINDE: With no dependents?

NORA: No, no one. But—

MRS. LINDE: And he's over here every   55
day?

NORA: Yes, I told you that.

MRS. LINDE: How can a man of such refinement be so grasping?

NORA: I don't follow you at all.

MRS. LINDE: Now don't try to hide it, Nora. You think I can't guess who loaned you the forty-eight hundred crowns?

NORA: Are you out of your mind? How   60
could you think such a thing! A friend of ours, who comes here every single day. What an intolerable situation that would have been!

MRS. LINDE: Then it really wasn't him.

NORA: No, absolutely not. It never even crossed my mind for a moment—And he had nothing to lend in those days; his inheritance came later.

MRS. LINDE: Well, I think that was a stroke of luck for you, Nora dear.

NORA: No, it never would have occurred to me to ask Dr. Rank—Still, I'm quite sure that if I had asked him—

65 MRS. LINDE: Which you won't, of course.

NORA: No, of course not. I can't see that I'd ever need to. But I'm quite positive that if I talked to Dr. Rank—

MRS. LINDE: Behind your husband's back?

NORA: I've got to clear up this other thing; *that's* also behind his back. I've *got* to clear it all up.

MRS. LINDE: Yes, I was saying that yesterday, but—

70 NORA (*pacing up and down*): A man handles these problems so much better than a woman—

MRS. LINDE: One's husband does, yes.

NORA: Nonsense. (*Stopping.*) When you pay everything you owe, then you get your note back, right?

MRS. LINDE: Yes, naturally.

NORA: And can rip it into a million pieces and burn it up—that filthy scrap of paper!

75 MRS. LINDE (*looking hard at her, laying her sewing aside, and rising slowly*): Nora, you're hiding something from me.

NORA: You can see it in my face?

MRS. LINDE: Something's happened to you since yesterday morning. Nora, what is it?

NORA (*hurrying toward her*): Kristine! (*Listening.*) Shh! Torvald's home. Look, go in with the children a while. Torvald can't bear all this snipping and stitching. Let Anne-Marie help you.

MRS. LINDE (*gathering up some of the things*): All right, but I'm not leaving here until we've talked this out. (*She disappears into the room, left, as Torvald enters from the hall.*)

80 NORA: Oh, how I've been waiting for you, Torvald dear.

HELMER: Was that the dressmaker?

NORA: No, that was Kristine. She's helping me fix up my costume. You know, it's going to be quite attractive.

HELMER: Yes, wasn't that a bright idea I had?

NORA: Brilliant! But then wasn't I good as well to give in to you?

HELMER: Good—because you give in to 85 your husband's judgment? All right, you little goose, I know you didn't mean it like that. But I won't disturb you. You'll want to have a fitting, I suppose.

NORA: And you'll be working?

HELMER: Yes. (*Indicating a bundle of papers.*) See. I've been down to the bank. (*Starts toward his study.*)

NORA: Torvald.

HELMER (*stops*): Yes.

NORA: If your little squirrel begged 90 you, with all her heart and soul, for something—?

HELMER: What's that?

NORA: Then would you do it?

HELMER: First, naturally, I'd have to know what it was.

NORA: Your squirrel would scamper about and do tricks, if you'd only be sweet and give in.

HELMER: Out with it. 95

NORA: Your lark would be singing high and low in every room—

HELMER: Come on, she does that anyway.

NORA: I'd be a wood nymph and dance for you in the moonlight.

HELMER: Nora—don't tell me it's that same business from this morning?

NORA (*coming closer*): Yes, Torvald, I beg 100 you, please!

HELMER: And you actually have the nerve to drag that up again?

NORA: Yes, yes, you've got to give in to me; you *have* to let Krogstad keep his job in the bank.

HELMER: My dear Nora, I've slated his job for Mrs. Linde.

NORA: That's awfully kind of you. But you could just fire another clerk instead of Krogstad.

105   HELMER: This is the most incredible stubbornness! Because you go and give an impulsive promise to speak up for him, I'm expected to—

NORA: That's not the reason, Torvald. It's for your own sake. That man does writing for the worst papers; you said it yourself. He could do you any amount of harm. I'm scared to death of him—

HELMER: Ah, I understand. It's the old memories haunting you.

NORA: What do you mean by that?

HELMER: Of course, you're thinking about your father.

110   NORA: Yes, all right. Just remember how those nasty gossips wrote in the papers about Papa and slandered him so cruelly. I think they'd have had him dismissed if the department hadn't sent you up to investigate, and if you hadn't been so kind and open-minded toward him.

HELMER: My dear Nora, there's a notable difference between your father and me. Your father's official career was hardly above reproach. But mine is; and I hope it'll stay that way as long as I hold my position.

NORA: Oh, who can ever tell what vicious minds can invent? We could be so snug and happy now in our quiet, carefree home—you and I and the children, Torvald! That's why I'm pleading with you so—

HELMER: And just by pleading for him you make it impossible for me to keep him on. It's already known at the bank that I'm firing Krogstad. What if it's rumored around now that the new bank manager was vetoed by his wife—

NORA: Yes, what then—?

115   HELMER: Oh yes—as long as our little bundle of stubbornness gets her way—! I

should go and make myself ridiculous in front of the whole office—give people the idea I can be swayed by all kinds of outside pressure. Oh, you can bet I'd feel the effects of that soon enough! Besides— there's something that rules Krogstad right out at the bank as long as I'm the manager.

NORA: What's that?

HELMER: His moral failings I could maybe overlook if I had to—

NORA: Yes, Torvald, why not?

HELMER: And I hear he's quite efficient on the job. But he was a crony of mine back in my teens—one of those rash friendships that crop up again and again to embarrass you later in life. Well, I might as well say it straight out: we're on a first-name basis. And that tactless fool makes no effort at all to hide it in front of others. Quite the contrary—he thinks that entitles him to take a familiar air around me, and so every other second he comes booming out with his "Yes, Torvald!" and "Sure thing, Torvald!" I tell you, it's been excruciating for me. He's out to make my place in the bank unbearable.

NORA: Torvald, you can't be serious about   120 all this.

HELMER: Oh no? Why not?

NORA: Because these are such petty considerations.

HELMER: What are you saying? Petty? You think I'm petty!

NORA: No, just the opposite, Torvald dear. That's exactly why—

HELMER: Never mind. You call my   125 motives petty; then I might as well be just that. Petty! All right! We'll put a stop to this for good. (*Goes to the hall door and calls.*) Helene!

NORA: What do you want?

HELMER (*searching among his papers*):   A decision. (*The* MAID *comes in.*) Look here; take this letter; go out with it at once. Get hold of a messenger and have him deliver it. Quick now. It's already addressed. Wait, here's some money.

MAID: Yes, sir. (*She leaves with the letter.*)

HELMER (*straightening his papers*):   There, now, little Miss Willful.

130 NORA (*breathlessly*):   Torvald, what was that letter?

HELMER: Krogstad's notice.

NORA: Call it back, Torvald! There's still time. Oh, Torvald, call it back! Do it for my sake—for your sake, for the children's sake! Do you hear, Torvald; do it! You don't know how this can harm us.

HELMER: Too late.

NORA: Yes, too late.

135 HELMER: Nora dear, I can forgive you this panic, even though basically you're insulting me. Yes, you are! Or isn't it an insult to think that *I* should be afraid of a courtroom hack's revenge? But I forgive you anyway, because this shows so beautifully how much you love me. (*Takes her in his arms.*) This is the way it should be, my darling Nora. Whatever comes, you'll see; when it really counts, I have strength and courage enough as a man to take on the whole weight myself.

NORA (*terrified*):   What do you mean by that?

HELMER: The whole weight, I said.

NORA (*resolutely*):   No, never in all the world.

HELMER: Good. So we'll share it, Nora, as man and wife. That's as it should be. (*Fondling her.*) Are you happy now? There, there, there—not these frightened dove's eyes. It's nothing at all but empty fantasies—Now you should run through your tarantella and practice your tambourine. I'll go to the inner office and shut both doors, so I won't hear a thing; you can make all the noise you like. (*Turning in the doorway.*) And when Rank comes, just tell him where he can find

me. (*He nods to her and goes with his papers into the study, closing the door.*)

NORA (*standing as though rooted, dazed with   140 fright, in a whisper*):   He really could do it. He will do it. He'll do it in spite of everything. No, not that, never, never! Anything but that! Escape! A way out— (*The doorbell rings.*) Dr. Rank! Anything but that! *Anything*, whatever it is! (*Her hands pass over her face, smoothing it; she pulls herself together, goes over and opens the hall door. DR. RANK stands outside, hanging his fur coat up. During the following scene, it begins getting dark.*)

NORA: Hello, Dr. Rank. I recognized your ring. But you mustn't go in to Torvald yet; I believe he's working.

RANK: And you?

NORA: For you, I always have an hour to spare—you know that. (*He has entered, and she shuts the door after him.*)

RANK: Many thanks. I'll make use of these hours while I can.

NORA: What do you mean by that? While   145 you can?

RANK: Does that disturb you?

NORA: Well, it's such an odd phrase. Is anything going to happen?

RANK: What's going to happen is what I've been expecting so long—but I honestly didn't think it would come so soon.

NORA (*gripping his arm*):   What is it you've found out? Dr. Rank, you have to tell me!

Rank (*sitting by the stove*):   It's all over for   150 me. There's nothing to be done about it.

NORA (*breathing easier*):   Is it you—then—?

RANK: Who else? There's no point in lying to one's self. I'm the most miserable of all my patients, Mrs. Helmer. These past few days I've been auditing my internal accounts. Bankrupt! Within a month I'll probably be laid out and rotting in the churchyard.

NORA: Oh, what a horrible thing to say.

RANK: The thing itself is horrible. But the worst of it is all the other horror before it's over. There's only one final examination left; when I'm finished with that, I'll know about when my disintegration will begin. There's something I want to say. Helmer with his sensitivity has such a sharp distaste for anything ugly. I don't want him near my sickroom.

155 NORA: Oh, but Dr. Rank—

RANK: I won't have him in there. Under no condition. I'll lock my door to him— As soon as I'm completely sure of the worst, I'll send you my calling card marked with a black cross, and you'll know then the wreck has started to come apart.

NORA: No, today you're completely unreasonable. And I wanted you so much to be in a really good humor.

RANK: With death up my sleeve? And then to suffer this way for somebody else's sins. Is there any justice in that? And in every single family, in some way or another, this inevitable retribution of nature goes on—

NORA (*her hands pressed over her ears*):   Oh, stuff! Cheer up! Please—be gay!

160 RANK: Yes, I'd just as soon laugh at it all. My poor, innocent spine, serving time for my father's gay army days.

NORA (*by the table, left*):   He was so infatuated with asparagus tips and pâté de foie gras, wasn't that it?

RANK: Yes—and with truffles.

NORA: Truffles, yes. And then with oysters, I suppose?

RANK: Yes, tons of oysters, naturally.

165 NORA: And then the port and champagne to go with it. It's so sad that all these delectable things have to strike at our bones.

RANK: Especially when they strike at the unhappy bones that never shared in the fun.

NORA: Ah, that's the saddest of all.

RANK (*looks searchingly at her*):   Hm.

NORA (*after a moment*):   Why did you smile?

RANK: No, it was you who laughed.   170

NORA: No, it was you who smiled, Dr. Rank!

RANK (*getting up*):   You're even a bigger tease than I'd thought.

NORA: I'm full of wild ideas today.

RANK: That's obvious.

NORA (*putting both hands on his shoulders*):   175
Dear, dear Dr. Rank, you'll never die for Torvald and me.

RANK: Oh, that loss you'll easily get over. Those who go away are soon forgotten.

NORA (*looks fearfully at him*):   You believe that?

RANK: One makes new connections, and then—

NORA: Who makes new connections?

RANK: Both you and Torvald will when   180
I'm gone. I'd say you're well under way already. What was that Mrs. Linde doing here last evening?

NORA: Oh, come—you can't be jealous of poor Kristine?

RANK: Oh yes, I am. She'll be my successor here in the house. When I'm down under, that woman will probably—

NORA: Shh! Not so loud. She's right in there.

RANK: Today as well. So you see.

NORA: Only to sew on my dress. Good   185
gracious, how unreasonable you are. (*Sitting on the sofa.*) Be nice now, Dr. Rank. Tomorrow you'll see how beautifully I'll dance; and you can imagine then that I'm dancing only for you— yes, and of course for Torvald, too— that's understood. (*Takes various items out of the carton.*) Dr. Rank, sit over here and I'll show you something.

RANK (*sitting*):   What's that?

NORA: Look here. Look.

RANK: Silk stockings.

NORA: Flesh-colored. Aren't they lovely? Now it's so dark here, but tomorrow— No, no, no, just look at the feet. Oh well, you might as well look at the rest.

190 RANK: Hm—

NORA: Why do you look so critical? Don't you believe they'll fit?

RANK: I've never had any chance to form an opinion on that.

NORA (*glancing at him a moment*): Shame on you. (*Hits him lightly on the ear with the stockings.*) That's for you. (*Puts them away again.*)

RANK: And what other splendors am I going to see now?

195 NORA: Not the least bit more, because you've been naughty. (*She hums a little and rummages among her things.*)

RANK (*after a short silence*): When I sit here together with you like this, completely easy and open, then I don't know—I simply can't imagine—whatever would have become of me if I'd never come into this house.

NORA (*smiling*): Yes, I really think you feel completely at ease with us.

RANK (*more quietly, staring straight ahead*): And then to have to go away from it all—

NORA: Nonsense, you're not going away.

200 RANK (*his voice unchanged*): —and not even be able to leave some poor show of gratitude behind, scarcely a fleeting regret— no more than a vacant place that anyone can fill.

NORA: And if I asked you now for—? No—

RANK: For what?

NORA: For a great proof of your friendship—

RANK: Yes, yes?

205 NORA: No, I mean—for an exceptionally big favor—

RANK: Would you really, for once, make me so happy?

NORA: Oh, you haven't the vaguest idea what it is.

RANK: All right, then tell me.

NORA: No, but I can't, Dr. Rank—it's all out of reason. It's advice and help, too— and a favor—

RANK: So much the better. I can't fathom 210 what you're hinting at. Just speak out. Don't you trust me?

NORA: Of course. More than anyone else. You're my best and truest friend, I'm sure. That's why I want to talk to you. All right, then, Dr. Rank: there's something you can help me prevent. You know how deeply, how inexpressibly dearly Torvald loves me; he'd never hesitate a second to give up his life for me.

RANK (*leaning close to her*): Nora—do you think he's the only one—

NORA (*with a slight start*): Who—

RANK: Who'd gladly give up his life for you.

NORA (*heavily*): I see. 215

RANK: I swore to myself you should know this before I'm gone. I'll never find a better chance. Yes, Nora, now you know. And also you know now that you can trust me beyond anyone else.

NORA (*rising, natural and calm*): Let me by.

RANK (*making room for her, but still sitting*): Nora—

NORA (*in the hall doorway*): Helene, bring the lamp in. (*Goes over to the stove.*) Ah, dear Dr. Rank, that was really mean of you.

RANK (*getting up*): That I've loved you just 220 as deeply as somebody else? Was *that* mean?

NORA: No, but that you came out and told me. That was quite unnecessary—

RANK: What do you mean? Have you known—?

The MAID *comes in with the lamp, sets it on the table, and goes out again.*

RANK: Nora—Mrs. Helmer—I'm asking you: have you known about it?

NORA: Oh, how can I tell what I know or don't know? Really, I don't know what to say—Why did you have to be so clumsy, Dr. Rank! Everything was so good.

225 RANK: Well, in any case, you now have the knowledge that my body and soul are at your command. So won't you speak out?

NORA (*looking at him*): After that?

RANK: Please, just let me know what it is.

NORA: You can't know anything now.

RANK: I have to. You mustn't punish me like this. Give me the chance to do whatever is humanly possible for you.

230 NORA: Now there's nothing you can do for me. Besides, actually, I don't need any help. You'll see—it's only my fantasies. That's what it is. Of course! (*Sits in the rocker, looks at him, and smiles.*) What a nice one you are, Dr. Rank. Aren't you a little bit ashamed, now that the lamp is here?

RANK: No, not exactly. But perhaps I'd better go—for good?

NORA: No, you certainly can't do that. You must come here just as you always have. You know Torvald can't do without you.

RANK: Yes, but *you?*

NORA: You know how much I enjoy it when you're here.

235 RANK: That's precisely what threw me off. You're a mystery to me. So many times I've felt you'd almost rather be with me than with Helmer.

NORA: Yes—you see, there are some people that one loves most and other people that one would almost prefer being with.

RANK: Yes, there's something to that.

NORA: When I was back home, of course I loved Papa most. But I always thought it was so much fun when I could sneak down to the maids' quarters, because they never tried to improve me, and it

was always so amusing, the way they talked to each other.

RANK: Aha, so it's *their* place that I've filled.

NORA (*jumping up and going to him*): Oh, 240 dear, sweet Dr. Rank, that's not what I meant at all. But you can understand that with Torvald it's just the same as with Papa—

The MAID *enters from the hall.*

MAID: Ma'am—please! (*She whispers to* NORA *and hands her a calling card.*)

NORA (*glancing at the card*): Ah! (*Slips it into her pocket.*)

RANK: Anything wrong?

NORA: No, no, not at all. It's only some— it's my new dress—

RANK: Really? But—there's your dress. 245

NORA: Oh, that. But this is another one—I ordered it—Torvald mustn't know—

RANK: Ah, now we have the big secret.

NORA: That's right. Just go in with him— he's back in the inner study. Keep him there as long as—

RANK: Don't worry. He won't get away. (*Goes into the study.*)

NORA (*to the* MAID): And he's standing 250 waiting in the kitchen?

MAID: Yes, he came up by the back stairs.

NORA: But didn't you tell him somebody was here?

MAID: Yes, but that didn't do any good.

NORA: He won't leave?

MAID: No, he won't go till he's talked 255 with you, ma'am.

NORA: Let him come in, then—but quietly. Helene, don't breathe a word about this. It's a surprise for my husband.

MAID: Yes, yes, I understand— (*Goes out.*)

NORA: This horror—it's going to happen. No, no, no, it can't happen, it mustn't. (*She goes and bolts* HELMER'S *door. The* MAID *opens the hall door for* KROGSTAD *and shuts it behind him. He is dressed for travel in a fur coat, boots, and a fur cap.*)

NORA (*going toward him*): Talk softly. My husband's home.

260 KROGSTAD: Well, good for him.

NORA: What do you want?

KROGSTAD: Some information.

NORA: Hurry up, then. What is it?

KROGSTAD: You know, of course, that I got my notice.

265 NORA: I couldn't prevent it, Mr. Krogstad. I fought for you to the bitter end, but nothing worked.

KROGSTAD: Does your husband's love for you run so thin? He knows everything I can expose you to, and all the same he dares to—

NORA: How can you imagine he knows anything about this?

KROGSTAD: Ah, no—I can't imagine it either, now. It's not at all like my fine Torvald Helmer to have so much guts—

NORA: Mr. Krogstad, I demand respect for my husband!

270 KROGSTAD: Why, of course—all due respect. But since the lady's keeping it so carefully hidden, may I presume to ask if you're also a bit better informed than yesterday about what you've actually done?

NORA: More than you could ever teach me.

KROGSTAD: Yes, I *am* such an awful lawyer.

NORA: What is it you want from me?

KROGSTAD: Just a glimpse of how you are, Mrs. Helmer. I've been thinking about you all day long. A cashier, a night-court scribbler, a—well, a type like me also has a little of what they call a heart, you know.

275 NORA: Then show it. Think of my children.

KROGSTAD: Did you or your husband ever think of mine? But never mind. I simply wanted to tell you that you don't need to take this thing too seriously. For the present, I'm not proceeding with any action.

NORA: Oh no, really! Well—I knew that.

KROGSTAD: Everything can be settled in a friendly spirit. It doesn't have to get around town at all; it can stay just among us three.

NORA: My husband must never know anything of this.

KROGSTAD: How can you manage that? 280 Perhaps you can pay me the balance?

NORA: No, not right now.

KROGSTAD: Or you know some way of raising the money in a day or two?

NORA: No way that I'm willing to use.

KROGSTAD: Well, it wouldn't have done you any good, anyway. If you stood in front of me with a fistful of bills, you still couldn't buy your signature back.

NORA: Then tell me what you're going to 285 do with it.

KROGSTAD: I'll just hold onto it—keep it on file. There's no outsider who'll even get wind of it. So if you've been thinking of taking some desperate step—

NORA: I have.

KROGSTAD: Been thinking of running away from home—

NORA: I have!

KROGSTAD: Or even of something worse— 290

NORA: How could you guess that?

KROGSTAD: You can drop those thoughts.

NORA: How could you guess I was thinking of *that*?

KROGSTAD: Most of us think about *that* at first. I thought about it too, but I discovered I hadn't the courage—

NORA (*lifelessly*): I don't either. 295

Krogstad (*relieved*): That's true, you haven't the courage? You too?

NORA: I don't have it—I don't have it.

KROGSTAD: It would be terribly stupid, anyway. After that first storm at home blows out, why, then—I have here in my pocket a letter for your husband—

NORA: Telling everything?

300 KROGSTAD: As charitably as possible.

NORA (*quickly*):   He mustn't ever get that letter. Tear it up. I'll find some way to get money.

KROGSTAD: Beg pardon, Mrs. Helmer, but I think I just told you—

NORA: Oh, I don't mean the money I owe you. Let me know how much you want from my husband, and I'll manage it.

KROGSTAD: I don't want money from your husband.

305 NORA: What do you want, then?

KROGSTAD: I'll tell you what. I want to recoup, Mrs. Helmer; I want to get on in the world—and there's where your husband can help me. For a year and a half I've kept myself clean of anything disreputable—all that time struggling with the worst conditions; but I was satisfied, working my way up step by step. Now I've been written right off, and I'm just not in the mood to come crawling back. I tell you, I want to move on. I want to get back in the bank—in a better position. Your husband can set up a job for me—

NORA: He'll never do that!

KROGSTAD: He'll do it. I know him. He won't dare breathe a word of protest. And once I'm in there together with him, you just wait and see! Inside of a year, I'll be the manager's right-hand man. It'll be Nils Krogstad, not Torvald Helmer, who runs the bank.

NORA: You'll never see the day!

310 KROGSTAD: Maybe you think you can—

NORA: I have the courage now—for *that*.

KROGSTAD: Oh, you don't scare me. A smart, spoiled lady like you—

NORA: You'll see; you'll see!

KROGSTAD: Under the ice, maybe? Down in the freezing coal-black water? There, till you float up in the spring, ugly, unrecognizable, with your hair falling out—

NORA: You don't frighten me.   315

KROGSTAD: Nor do you frighten me. One doesn't do these things, Mrs. Helmer. Besides, what good would it be? I'd still have him safe in my pocket.

NORA: Afterwards? When I'm no longer—?

KROGSTAD: Are you forgetting that *I'll* be in control then over your final reputation? (NORA *stands speechless, staring at him.*) Good; now I've warned you. Don't do anything stupid. When Helmer's read my letter, I'll be waiting for his reply. And bear in mind that it's your husband himself who's forced me back to my old ways. I'll never forgive him for that. Good-bye, Mrs. Helmer. (*He goes out through the hall.*)

NORA (*goes to the hall door, opens it a crack, and listens*):   He's gone. Didn't leave the letter. Oh no, no, that's impossible too! (*Opening the door more and more.*) What's that? He's standing outside—not going downstairs. He's thinking it over? Maybe he'll—? (*A letter falls in the mailbox; then* KROGSTAD'S *footsteps are heard, dying away down a flight of stairs.* NORA *gives a muffled cry and runs over toward the sofa table. A short pause.*) In the mailbox. (*Slips warily over to the hall door.*) It's lying there. Torvald, Torvald—now we're lost!

MRS. LINDE (*entering with costume from the*   320
room, left):   There now, I can't see anything else to mend. Perhaps you'd like to try—

NORA (*in a hoarse whisper*):   Kristine, come here.

MRS. LINDE (*tossing the dress on the sofa*):   What's wrong? You look upset.

NORA: Come here. See that letter? *There!* Look—through the glass in the mailbox.

MRS. LINDE: Yes, yes, I see it.

NORA: That letter's from Krogstad—   325

MRS. LINDE: Nora—it's Krogstad who loaned you the money!

NORA: Yes, and now Torvald will find out everything.

MRS. LINDE: Believe me, Nora, it's best for both of you.

NORA: There's more you don't know. I forged a name.

330 MRS. LINDE: But for heaven's sake—?

NORA: I only want to tell you that, Kristine, so that you can be my witness.

MRS. LINDE: Witness? Why should I—?

NORA: If I should go out of my mind—it could easily happen—

MRS. LINDE: Nora!

335 NORA: Or anything else occurred—so I couldn't be present here—

MRS. LINDE: Nora, Nora, you aren't yourself at all!

NORA: And someone should try to take on the whole weight, all of the guilt, you follow me—

MRS. LINDE: Yes, of course, but why do you think—?

NORA: Then you're the witness that it isn't true, Kristine. I'm very much myself; my mind right now is perfectly clear; and I'm telling you: nobody else has known about this; I alone did everything. Remember that.

340 MRS. LINDE: I will. But I don't understand all this.

NORA: Oh, how could you ever understand it? It's the miracle now that's going to take place.

MRS. LINDE: The miracle?

NORA: Yes, the miracle. But it's so awful, Kristine. It mustn't take place, not for anything in the world.

MRS. LINDE: I'm going right over and talk with Krogstad.

345 NORA: Don't go near him; he'll do you some terrible harm!

MRS. LINDE: There was a time once when he'd gladly have done anything for me.

NORA: He?

MRS. LINDE: Where does he live?

NORA: Oh, how do I know? Yes. (*Searches in her pocket.*) Here's his card. But the letter, the letter—!

HELMER (*from the study, knocking on the door*):   350 Nora!

NORA (*with a cry of fear*):   Oh! What is it? What do you want?

HELMER: Now, now, don't be so frightened. We're not coming in. You locked the door—are you trying on the dress?

NORA: Yes, I'm trying it. I'll look just beautiful, Torvald.

MRS. LINDE (*who has read the card*):   He's living right around the corner.

NORA: Yes, but what's the use? We're lost.   355 The letter's in the box.

MRS. LINDE: And your husband has the key?

NORA: Yes, always.

MRS. LINDE: Krogstad can ask for his letter back unread; he can find some excuse—

NORA: But it's just this time that Torvald usually—

MRS. LINDE: Stall him. Keep him in there.   360 I'll be back as quick as I can. (*She hurries out through the hall entrance.*)

NORA (*goes to* HELMER'S *door, opens it, and peers in*):   Torvald!

HELMER (*from the inner study*):   Well—does one dare set foot in one's own living room at last? Come on, Rank, now we'll get a look— (*In the doorway.*) But what's this?

NORA: What, Torvald dear?

HELMER: Rank had me expecting some grand masquerade.

RANK (*in the doorway*):   That was my   365 impression, but I must have been wrong.

NORA: No one can admire me in my splendor—not till tomorrow.

HELMER: But Nora dear, you look so exhausted. Have you practiced too hard?

NORA: No, I haven't practiced at all yet.

HELMER: You know, it's necessary—

370 NORA: Oh, it's absolutely necessary, Torvald. But I can't get anywhere without your help. I've forgotten the whole thing completely.

HELMER: Ah, we'll soon take care of that.

NORA: Yes, take care of me, Torvald, please! Promise me that? Oh, I'm so nervous. That big party—You must give up everything this evening for me. No business—don't even touch your pen. Yes? Dear Torvald, promise?

HELMER: It's a promise. Tonight I'm totally at your service—you little helpless thing. Hm—but first there's one thing I want to—(*Goes toward the hall door.*)

NORA: What are you looking for?

375 HELMER: Just to see if there's any mail.

NORA: No, no, don't do that, Torvald!

HELMER: Now what?

NORA: Torvald, please. There isn't any.

HELMER: Let me look, though. (*Starts out. NORA, at the piano, strikes the first notes of the tarantella. HELMER, at the door, stops.*) Aha!

380 NORA: I can't dance tomorrow if I don't practice with you.

HELMER (*going over to her*): Nora dear, are you really so frightened?

NORA: Yes, so terribly frightened. Let me practice right now; there's still time before dinner. Oh, sit down and play for me, Torvald. Direct me. Teach me, the way you always have.

HELMER: Gladly, if it's what you want. (*Sits at the piano.*)

NORA (*snatches the tambourine up from the box, then a long, varicolored shawl, which she throws around herself, whereupon she springs forward and cries out*): Play for me now! Now I'll dance!

HELMER *plays and* NORA *dances.* RANK *stands behind* HELMER *at the piano and looks on.*

385 HELMER (*as he plays*): Slower. Slow down.

NORA: Can't change it.

HELMER: Not so violent, Nora!

NORA: Has to be just like this.

HELMER (*stopping*): No, no, that won't do at all.

390 NORA (*laughing and swinging her tambourine*): Isn't that what I told you?

RANK: Let me play for her.

HELMER (*getting up*): Yes, go on. I can teach her more easily then.

RANK *sits at the piano and plays;* NORA *dances more and more wildly.* HELMER *has stationed himself by the stove and repeatedly gives her directions; she seems not to hear them; her hair loosens and falls over her shoulders; she does not notice, but goes on dancing.* MRS. LINDE *enters.*

MRS. LINDE (*standing dumbfounded at the door*): Ah—!

NORA (*still dancing*): See what fun, Kristine!

395 HELMER: But Nora darling, you dance as if your life were at stake.

NORA: And it is.

HELMER: Rank, stop! This is pure madness. Stop it, I say!

RANK *breaks off playing, and* NORA *halts abruptly.*

HELMER (*going over to her*): I never would have believed it. You've forgotten everything I taught you.

NORA (*throwing away the tambourine*): You see for yourself.

400 HELMER: Well, there's certainly room for instruction here.

NORA: Yes, you see how important it is. You've got to teach me to the very last minute. Promise me that, Torvald?

HELMER: You can bet on it.

NORA: You mustn't, either today or tomorrow, think about anything else but

me; you mustn't open any letters—or the
mailbox—

HELMER: Ah, it's still the fear of that man—

405 NORA: Oh yes, yes, that too.

HELMER: Nora, it's written all over you—
there's already a letter from him out
there.

NORA: I don't know. I guess so. But you
mustn't read such things now; there
mustn't be anything ugly between us
before it's all over.

RANK (*quietly to* HELMER):   You shouldn't
deny her.

HELMER (*putting his arms around her*):   The
child can have her way. But tomorrow
night, after you've danced—

410 NORA: Then you'll be free.

MAID (*in the doorway, right*):   Ma'am,
dinner is served.

NORA: We'll be wanting champagne,
Helene.

MAID: Very good, ma'am. (*Goes out.*)

HELMER: So—a regular banquet, hm?

415 NORA: Yes, a banquet—champagne till
daybreak! (*Calling out.*) And some
macaroons, Helene. Heaps of them—just
this once.

HELMER (*taking her hands*):   Now, now,
now—no hysterics. Be my own little lark
again.

NORA: Oh, I will soon enough. But go on
in—and you, Dr. Rank. Kristine, help me
put up my hair.

RANK (*whispering, as they go*):   There's
nothing wrong—really wrong, is there?

HELMER: Oh, of course not. It's nothing
more than this childish anxiety I was
telling you about. (*They go out, right.*)

420 NORA: Well?

MRS. LINDE: Left town.

NORA: I could see by your face.

MRS. LINDE: He'll be home tomorrow
evening. I wrote him a note.

NORA: You shouldn't have. Don't try to
stop anything now. After all, it's a

wonderful joy, this waiting here for the
miracle.

MRS. LINDE: What is it you're waiting for?   425

NORA: Oh, you can't understand that. Go
in to them; I'll be along in a moment.

MRS. LINDE *goes into the dining room.* NORA
*stands a short while as if composing herself;
then she looks at her watch.*

NORA: Five. Seven hours to midnight.
Twenty-four hours to the midnight after,
and then the tarantella's done. Seven and
twenty-four? Thirty-one hours to live.

HELMER (*in the doorway, right*):   What's
become of the little lark?

NORA (*going toward him with open arms*):
Here's your lark!

⟨ACT III⟩

*Same scene. The table, with chairs around it,
has been moved to the center of the room. A
lamp on the table is lit. The hall door stands
open. Dance music drifts down from the floor
above.* MRS. LINDE *sits at the table, absently
paging through a book, trying to read, but
apparently unable to focus her thoughts.
Once or twice she pauses, tensely listening
for a sound at the outer entrance.*

MRS. LINDE (*glancing at her watch*):   Not
yet—and there's hardly any time left. If
only he's not— (*Listening again.*) Ah,
there he is. (*She goes out in the hall and
cautiously opens the outer door. Quiet footsteps are heard on the stairs. She whispers:*)
Come in. Nobody's here.

KROGSTAD (*in the doorway*):   I found a note
from you at home. What's back of all
this?

MRS. LINDE: I just *had* to talk to you.

KROGSTAD: Oh? And it just *had* to be here
in this house?

MRS. LINDE: At my place it was impossible;   5
my room hasn't a private entrance.

Come in; we're all alone. The maid's asleep, and the Helmers are at the dance upstairs.

KROGSTAD (*entering the room*): Well, well, the Helmers are dancing tonight? Really?

MRS. LINDE: Yes, why not?

KROGSTAD: How true—why not?

MRS. LINDE: All right, Krogstad, let's talk.

10 KROGSTAD: Do we two have anything more to talk about?

MRS. LINDE: We have a great deal to talk about.

KROGSTAD: I wouldn't have thought so.

MRS. LINDE: No, because you've never understood me, really.

KROGSTAD: Was there anything more to understand—except what's all too common in life? A calculating woman throws over a man the moment a better catch comes by.

15 MRS. LINDE: You think I'm so thoroughly calculating? You think I broke it off lightly?

KROGSTAD: Didn't you?

MRS. LINDE: Nils—is that what you really thought?

KROGSTAD: If you cared, then why did you write me the way you did?

MRS. LINDE: What else could I do? If I had to break off with you, then it was my job as well to root out everything you felt for me.

20 KROGSTAD (*wringing his hands*): So that was it. And this—all this, simply for money!

MRS. LINDE: Don't forget I had a helpless mother and two small brothers. We couldn't wait for you, Nils; you had such a long road ahead of you then.

KROGSTAD: That may be; but you still hadn't the right to abandon me for somebody else's sake.

MRS. LINDE: Yes—I don't know. So many, many times I've asked myself if I did have that right.

KROGSTAD (*more softly*): When I lost you, it was as if all the solid ground dissolved from under my feet. Look at me; I'm a half-drowned man now, hanging onto a wreck.

MRS. LINDE: Help may be near. 25

KROGSTAD: It was near—but then you came and blocked it off.

MRS. LINDE: Without my knowing it, Nils. Today for the first time I learned that it's you I'm replacing at the bank.

KROGSTAD: All right—I believe you. But now that you know, will you step aside?

MRS. LINDE: No, because that wouldn't benefit you in the slightest.

KROGSTAD: Not "benefit" me, hm! I'd step 30 aside anyway.

MRS. LINDE: I've learned to be realistic. Life and hard, bitter necessity have taught me that.

KROGSTAD: And life's taught me never to trust fine phrases.

MRS. LINDE: Then life's taught you a very sound thing. But you do have to trust in actions, don't you?

KROGSTAD: What does that mean?

MRS. LINDE: You said you were hanging 35 on like a half-drowned man to a wreck.

KROGSTAD: I've good reason to say that.

MRS. LINDE: I'm also like a half-drowned woman on a wreck. No one to suffer with; no one to care for.

KROGSTAD: You made your choice.

MRS. LINDE: There wasn't any choice then.

KROGSTAD: So—what of it? 40

MRS. LINDE: Nils, if only we two shipwrecked people could reach across to each other.

KROGSTAD: What are you saying?

MRS. LINDE: Two on one wreck are at least better off than each on his own.

KROGSTAD: Kristine!

MRS. LINDE: Why do you think I came 45 into town?

KROGSTAD: Did you really have some thought of me?

MRS. LINDE: I have to work to go on living. All my born days, as long as I can remember, I've worked, and it's been my best and my only joy. But now I'm completely alone in the world; it frightens me to be so empty and lost. To work for yourself—there's no joy in that. Nils, give me something—someone to work for.

KROGSTAD: I don't believe all this. It's just some hysterical feminine urge to go out and make a noble sacrifice.

MRS. LINDE: Have you ever found me to be hysterical?

50 KROGSTAD: Can you honestly mean this? Tell me—do you know everything about my past?

MRS. LINDE: Yes.

KROGSTAD: And you know what they think I'm worth around here.

MRS. LINDE: From what you were saying before, it would seem that with me you could have been another person.

KROGSTAD: I'm positive of that.

55 MRS. LINDE: Couldn't it happen still?

KROGSTAD: Kristine—you're saying this in all seriousness? Yes, you are! I can see it in you. And do you really have the courage, then—?

MRS. LINDE: I need to have someone to care for; and your children need a mother. We both need each other. Nils, I have faith that you're good at heart—I'll risk everything together with you.

KROGSTAD (gripping her hands):   Kristine, thank you, thank you—Now I know I can win back a place in their eyes. Yes—but I forgot—

MRS. LINDE (listening):   Shh! The tarantella. Go now! Go on!

60 KROGSTAD: Why? What is it?

MRS. LINDE: Hear the dance up there? When that's over, they'll be coming down.

KROGSTAD: Oh, then I'll go. But—it's all pointless. Of course, you don't know the move I made against the Helmers.

MRS. LINDE: Yes, Nils, I know.

KROGSTAD: And all the same, you have the courage to—?

MRS. LINDE: I know how far despair can 65 drive a man like you.

KROGSTAD: Oh, if I only could take it all back.

MRS. LINDE: You easily could—your letter's still lying in the mailbox.

KROGSTAD: Are you sure of that?

MRS. LINDE: Positive. But—

KROGSTAD (looks at her searchingly):   Is that 70 the meaning of it, then? You'll save your friend at any price. Tell me straight out. Is that it?

MRS. LINDE: Nils—anyone who's sold herself for somebody else once isn't going to do it again.

KROGSTAD: I'll demand my letter back.

MRS. LINDE: No, no.

KROGSTAD: Yes, of course. I'll stay here till Helmer comes down; I'll tell him to give me my letter again—that it only involves my dismissal—that he shouldn't read it—

MRS. LINDE: No, Nils, don't call the letter 75 back.

KROGSTAD: But wasn't that exactly why you wrote me to come here?

MRS. LINDE: Yes, in that first panic. But it's been a whole day and night since then, and in that time I've seen such incredible things in this house. Helmer's got to learn everything; this dreadful secret has to be aired; those two have to come to a full understanding; all these lies and evasions can't go on.

KROGSTAD: Well, then, if you want to chance it. But at least there's one thing I can do, and do right away—

MRS. LINDE (listening):   Go now, go quick! The dance is over. We're not safe another second.

80 KROGSTAD: I'll wait for you downstairs.

MRS. LINDE: Yes, please do; take me home.

KROGSTAD: I can't believe it; I've never been so happy. (*He leaves by way of the outer door; the door between the room and the hall stays open.*)

MRS. LINDE (*straightening up a bit and getting together her street clothes*):   How different now! How different! Someone to work for, to live for—a home to build. Well, it is worth the try! Oh, if they'd only come! (*Listening.*) Ah, there they are. Bundle up. (*She picks up her hat and coat.* NORA'S *and* HELMER'S *voices can be heard outside; a key turns in the lock, and* HELMER *brings* NORA *into the hall almost by force. She is wearing the Italian costume with a large black shawl about her; he has on evening dress, with a black domino open over it.*)

NORA (*struggling in the doorway*):   No, no, no, not inside! I'm going up again. I don't want to leave so soon.

85 HELMER: But Nora dear—

NORA: Oh, I beg you, please, Torvald. From the bottom of my heart, *please*— only an hour more!

HELMER: Not a single minute, Nora darling. You know our agreement. Come on, in we go; you'll catch cold out here. (*In spite of her resistance, he gently draws her into the room.*)

MRS. LINDE: Good evening.

NORA: Kristine!

90 HELMER: Why, Mrs. Linde—are you here so late?

MRS. LINDE: Yes, I'm sorry, but I did want to see Nora in costume.

NORA: Have you been sitting here, waiting for me?

MRS. LINDE: Yes. I didn't come early enough; you were all upstairs; and then I thought I really couldn't leave without seeing you.

HELMER (*removing* NORA'S *shawl*):   Yes, take a good look. She's worth looking at, I can tell you that, Mrs. Linde. Isn't she lovely?

MRS. LINDE: Yes, I should say—   95

HELMER: A dream of loveliness, isn't she? That's what everyone thought at the party, too. But she's horribly stubborn— this sweet little thing. What's to be done with her? Can you imagine, I almost had to use force to pry her away.

NORA: Oh, Torvald, you're going to regret you didn't indulge me, even for just a half hour more.

HELMER: There, you see. She danced her tarantella and got a tumultuous hand— which was well earned, although the performance may have been a bit too naturalistic—I mean it rather overstepped the proprieties of art. But never mind— what's important is, she made a success, an overwhelming success. You think I could let her stay on after that and spoil the effect? Oh no; I took my lovely little Capri girl—my capricious little Capri girl, I should say—took her under my arm; one quick tour of the ballroom, a curtsy to every side, and then—as they say in novels—the beautiful vision disappeared. An exit should always be effective, Mrs. Linde, but that's what I can't get Nora to grasp. Phew, it's hot in here. (*Flings the domino on a chair and opens the door to his room.*) Why's it dark in here? Oh yes, of course. Excuse me. (*He goes in and lights a couple of candles.*)

NORA (*in a sharp, breathless whisper*):   So?

MRS. LINDE (*quietly*):   I talked with him.   100

NORA: And—?

MRS. LINDE: Nora—you must tell your husband everything.

NORA (*dully*):   I knew it.

MRS. LINDE: You've got nothing to fear from Krogstad, but you have to speak out.

NORA: I won't tell.   105

MRS. LINDE: Then the letter will.

NORA: Thanks, Kristine. I know now what's to be done. Shh!

HELMER (*reentering*):   Well, then, Mrs. Linde—have you admired her?

MRS. LINDE: Yes, and now I'll say good night.

110 HELMER: Oh, come, so soon? Is this yours, this knitting?

MRS. LINDE: Yes, thanks. I nearly forgot it.

HELMER: Do you knit, then?

MRS. LINDE: Oh yes.

HELMER: You know what? You should embroider instead.

115 MRS. LINDE: Really? Why?

HELMER: Yes, because it's a lot prettier. See here, one holds the embroidery so, in the left hand, and then one guides the needle with the right—so—in an easy, sweeping curve—right?

MRS. LINDE: Yes, I guess that's—

HELMER: But, on the other hand, knitting—it can never be anything but ugly. Look, see here, the arms tucked in, the knitting needles going up and down—there's something Chinese about it. Ah, that was really a glorious champagne they served.

MRS. LINDE: Yes, good night, Nora, and don't be stubborn anymore.

120 HELMER: Well put, Mrs. Linde!

MRS. LINDE: Good night, Mr. Helmer.

HELMER (*accompanying her to the door*): Good night, good night. I hope you get home all right. I'd be very happy to—but you don't have far to go. Good night, good night. (*She leaves. He shuts the door after her and returns.*) There, now, at last we got her out the door. She's a deadly bore, that creature.

NORA: Aren't you pretty tired, Torvald?

HELMER: No, not a bit.

125 NORA: You're not sleepy?

HELMER: Not at all. On the contrary, I'm feeling quite exhilarated. But you? Yes, you really look tired and sleepy.

NORA: Yes, I'm very tired. Soon now I'll sleep.

HELMER: See! You see! I was right all along that we shouldn't stay longer.

NORA: Whatever you do is always right.

HELMER (*kissing her brow*):   Now my little   130 lark talks sense. Say, did you notice what a time Rank was having tonight?

NORA: Oh, was he? I didn't get to speak with him.

HELMER: I scarcely did either, but it's a long time since I've seen him in such high spirits. (*Gazes at her a moment, then comes nearer her.*) Hm—it's marvelous, though, to be back home again—to be completely alone with you. Oh, you bewitchingly lovely young woman!

NORA: Torvald, don't look at me like that!

HELMER: Can't I look at my richest treasure? At all that beauty that's mine, mine alone—completely and utterly.

NORA (*moving around to the other side of the*   135 *table*):   You mustn't talk to me that way tonight.

HELMER (*following her*):   The tarantella is still in your blood, I can see—and it makes you even more enticing. Listen. The guests are beginning to go. (*Dropping his voice.*) Nora—it'll soon be quiet through this whole house.

NORA: Yes, I hope so.

HELMER: You do, don't you, my love? Do you realize—when I'm out at a party like this with you—do you know why I talk to you so little, and keep such a distance away; just send you a stolen look now and then—you know why I do it? It's because I'm imagining then that you're my secret darling, my secret bride-to-be, and that no one suspects there's anything between us.

NORA: Yes, yes; oh, yes, I know you're always thinking of me.

HELMER: And then when we leave and I   140 place the shawl over those fine young rounded shoulders—over that wonderful curving neck—then I pretend that you're my young bride, that we're just coming from the wedding, that for the first time I'm bringing you into my house—that for the first time I'm alone with you—completely alone with you, your trembling young beauty! All this evening I've longed for nothing but you. When I saw you turn and sway in the tarantella—my blood was pounding till I couldn't stand it—that's why I brought you down here so early—

NORA: Go away, Torvald! Leave me alone. I don't want all this.

HELMER: What do you mean? Nora, you're teasing me. You will, won't you? Aren't I your husband—?

A knock at the outside door.

NORA (*startled*): What's that?

HELMER (*going toward the hall*): Who is it?

145 RANK (*outside*): It's me. May I come in a moment?

HELMER (*with quiet irritation*): Oh, what does he want now? (*Aloud.*) Hold on. (*Goes and opens the door.*) Oh, how nice that you didn't just pass us by!

RANK: I thought I heard your voice, and then I wanted so badly to have a look in. (*Lightly glancing about.*) Ah, me, these old familiar haunts. You have it snug and cozy in here, you two.

HELMER: You seemed to be having it pretty cozy upstairs, too.

RANK: Absolutely. Why shouldn't I? Why not take in everything in life? As much as you can, anyway, and as long as you can. The wine was superb—

150 HELMER: The champagne especially.

RANK: You noticed that too? It's amazing how much I could guzzle down.

NORA: Torvald also drank a lot of champagne this evening.

RANK: Oh?

NORA: Yes, and that always makes him so entertaining.

RANK: Well, why shouldn't one have 155 a pleasant evening after a well-spent day?

HELMER: Well spent? I'm afraid I can't claim that.

RANK (*slapping him on the back*): But I can, you see!

NORA: Dr. Rank, you must have done some scientific research today.

RANK: Quite so.

HELMER: Come now—little Nora talking 160 about scientific research!

NORA: And can I congratulate you on the results?

RANK: Indeed you may.

NORA: Then they were good?

RANK: The best possible for both doctor and patient—certainty.

NORA (*quickly and searchingly*): Certainty? 165

RANK: Complete certainty. So don't I owe myself a gay evening afterwards?

NORA: Yes, you're right, Dr. Rank.

HELMER: I'm with you—just so long as you don't have to suffer for it in the morning.

RANK: Well, one never gets something for nothing in life.

NORA: Dr. Rank—are you very fond of 170 masquerade parties?

RANK: Yes, if there's a good array of odd disguises—

NORA: Tell me, what should we two go as at the next masquerade?

HELMER: You little featherhead—already thinking of the next!

RANK: We two? I'll tell you what: you must go as Charmed Life—

HELMER: Yes, but find a costume for *that*! 175

RANK: Your wife can appear just as she looks every day.

HELMER: That was nicely put. But don't you know what you're going to be?

RANK: Yes, Helmer, I've made up my mind.

HELMER: Well?

180 RANK: At the next masquerade I'm going to be invisible.

HELMER: That's a funny idea.

RANK: They say there's a hat—black, huge—have you never heard of the hat that makes you invisible? You put it on, and then no one on earth can see you.

HELMER (*suppressing a smile*):   Ah, of course.

RANK: But I'm quite forgetting what I came for. Helmer, give me a cigar, one of the dark Havanas.

185 HELMER: With the greatest pleasure. (*Holds out his case.*)

RANK: Thanks. (*Takes one and cuts off the tip.*)

NORA (*striking a match*):   Let me give you a light.

RANK: Thank you. (*She holds the match for him; he lights the cigar.*) And now good-bye.

HELMER: Good-bye, good-bye, old friend.

190 NORA: Sleep well, Doctor.

RANK: Thanks for that wish.

NORA: Wish me the same.

RANK: You? All right, if you like—Sleep well. And thanks for the light. (*He nods to them both and leaves.*)

HELMER (*his voice subdued*):   He's been drinking heavily.

195 NORA (*absently*):   Could be. (HELMER *takes his keys from his pocket and goes out in the hall.*) Torvald—what are you after?

HELMER: Got to empty the mailbox; it's nearly full. There won't be room for the morning papers.

NORA: Are you working tonight?

HELMER: You know I'm not. Why—what's this? Someone's been at the lock.

NORA: At the lock—?

200 HELMER: Yes, I'm positive. What do you suppose—? I can't imagine one of the maids—? Here's a broken hairpin. Nora, it's yours—

NORA (*quickly*):   Then it must be the children—

HELMER: You'd better break them of that. Hm, hm—well, opened it after all. (*Takes the contents out and calls into the kitchen.*) Helene! Helene, would you put out the lamp in the hall. (*He returns to the room shutting the hall door, then displays the handful of mail.*) Look how it's piled up. (*Sorting through them.*) Now what's this?

NORA (*at the window*):   The letter! Oh, Torvald, no!

HELMER: Two calling cards—from Rank.

NORA: From Dr. Rank?   205

HELMER (*examining them*):   "Dr. Rank, Consulting Physician." They were on top. He must have dropped them in as he left.

NORA: Is there anything on them?

HELMER: There's a black cross over the name. See? That's a gruesome notion. He could almost be announcing his own death.

NORA: That's just what he's doing.

HELMER: What! You've heard something?   210 Something he's told you?

NORA: Yes. That when those cards came, he'd be taking his leave of us. He'll shut himself in now and die.

HELMER: Ah, my poor friend! Of course I knew he wouldn't be here much longer. But so soon—And then to hide himself away like a wounded animal.

NORA: If it has to happen, then it's best it happens in silence—don't you think so, Torvald?

HELMER (*pacing up and down*):   He'd grown right into our lives. I simply can't imagine him gone. He with his suffering and loneliness—like a dark cloud setting off our sunlit happiness. Well, maybe it's best this way. For him, at least. (*Standing still.*) And maybe for us too, Nora. Now we're thrown back on each other, completely. (*Embracing her.*) Oh you, my darling wife, how can I hold you close enough? You know what, Nora—time and again I've wished you were in some terrible danger, just so I could stake my life and soul and everything, for your sake.

215 NORA (*tearing herself away, her voice firm and decisive*):   Now you must read your mail, Torvald.

HELMER: No, no, not tonight. I want to stay with you, dearest.

NORA: With a dying friend on your mind?

HELMER: You're right. We've both had a shock. There's ugliness between us— these thoughts of death and corruption. We'll have to get free of them first. Until then—we'll stay apart.

NORA (*clinging about his neck*):   Torvald— good night! Good night!

220 HELMER (*kissing her on the cheek*):   Good night, little songbird. Sleep well, Nora. I'll be reading my mail now. (*He takes the letters into his room and shuts the door after him.*)

NORA (*with bewildered glances, groping about, seizing* HELMER'S *domino, throwing it around her, and speaking in short, hoarse, broken whispers*):   Never see him again. Never, never. (*Putting her shawl over her head.*) Never see the children either—them, too. Never, never. Oh, the freezing black water! The depths—down—Oh, I wish it were over—He has it now; he's reading it—now. Oh no, no, not yet. Torvald, good-bye, you and the children— (*She starts for the hall; as she does,* HELMER *throws open his door and stands with an open letter in his hand.*)

HELMER: Nora!

NORA (*screams*):   Oh—!

HELMER: What is this? You know what's in this letter?

225 NORA: Yes, I know. Let me go! Let me out!

HELMER (*holding her back*):   Where are you going?

NORA (*struggling to break loose*):   You can't save me, Torvald!

HELMER (*slumping back*):   True! Then it's true what he writes? How horrible! No, no, it's impossible—it can't be true.

NORA: It *is* true. I've loved you more than all this world.

HELMER: Ah, none of your slippery tricks.   230

NORA (*taking one step toward him*):   Torvald—!

HELMER: What *is* this you've blundered into!

NORA: Just let me loose. You're not going to suffer for my sake. You're not going to take on my guilt.

HELMER: No more play-acting. (*Locks the hall door.*) You stay right here and give me a reckoning. You understand what you've done? Answer! You understand?

NORA (*looking squarely at him, her face   235 hardening*):   Yes. I'm beginning to understand everything now.

HELMER (*striding about*):   Oh, what an awful awakening! In all these eight years—she who was my pride and joy—a hypocrite, a liar—worse, worse—a criminal! How infinitely disgusting it all is! The shame! (*NORA says nothing and goes on looking straight at him. He stops in front of her.*) I should have suspected something of the kind. I should have known. All your father's flimsy values—Be still! All your father's flimsy values have come out in you. No religion, no morals, no sense of duty—Oh, how I'm punished for letting him off! I did it for your sake, and you repay me like this.

NORA: Yes, like this.

HELMER: Now you've wrecked all my happiness—ruined my whole future. Oh, it's awful to think of. I'm in a cheap little grafter's hands; he can do anything he wants with me, ask for anything, play with me like a puppet—and I can't breathe a word. I'll be swept down miserably into the depths on account of a featherbrained woman.

NORA: When I'm gone from this world, you'll be free.

240 HELMER: Oh, quit posing. Your father had a mess of those speeches too. What good would that ever do me if you were gone from this world, as you say? Not the slightest. He can still make the whole thing known; and if he does, I could be falsely suspected as your accomplice. They might even think that I was behind it—that I put you up to it. And all that I can thank you for—you that I've coddled the whole of our marriage. Can you see now what you've done to me?

NORA (*icily calm*):   Yes.

HELMER: It's so incredible, I just can't grasp it. But we'll have to patch up whatever we can. Take off the shawl. I said, take if off! I've got to appease him somehow or other. The thing has to be hushed up at any cost. And as for you and me, it's got to seem like everything between us is just as it was—to the outside world, that is. You'll go right on living in this house, of course. But you can't be allowed to bring up the children; I don't dare trust you with them—Oh, to have to say this to someone I've loved so much! Well, that's done with. From now on happiness doesn't matter; all that matters is saving the bits and pieces, the appearance— (*The doorbell rings.* HELMER *starts.*) What's that? And so late. Maybe the worst—? You think he'd—? Hide, Nora! Say you're sick. (NORA *remains standing motionless.* HELMER *goes and opens the door.*)

MAID (*half dressed, in the hall*):   A letter for Mrs. Helmer.

HELMER: I'll take it. (*Snatches the letter and shuts the door.*) Yes, it's from him. You don't get it; I'm reading it myself.

245 NORA: Then read it.

HELMER (*by the lamp*):   I hardly dare. We may be ruined, you and I. But—I've got to know. (*Rips open the letter, skims through a few lines, glances at an enclosure, then cries out joyfully.*) Nora! (NORA *looks inquiringly at him.*) Nora! Wait—better check it again—Yes, yes, it's true. I'm saved. Nora, I'm saved!

NORA: And I?

HELMER: You too, of course. We're both saved, both of us. Look. He's sent back your note. He says he's sorry and ashamed—that a happy development in his life—oh, who cares what he says! Nora, we're saved! No one can hurt you. Oh, Nora, Nora—but first, this ugliness all has to go. Let me see— (*Takes a look at the note.*) No, I don't want to see it; I want the whole thing to fade like a dream. (*Tears the note and both letters to pieces, throws them into the stove and watches them burn.*) There—now there's nothing left— He wrote that since Christmas Eve you— Oh, they must have been three terrible days for you, Nora.

NORA: I fought a hard fight.

HELMER: And suffered pain and saw no   250 escape but—No, we're not going to dwell on anything unpleasant. We'll just be grateful and keep on repeating: it's over now, it's over! You hear me, Nora? You don't seem to realize—it's over. What's it mean—that frozen look? Oh, poor little Nora, I understand. You can't believe I've forgiven you. But I have, Nora; I swear I have. I know that what you did, you did out of love for me.

NORA: That's true.

HELMER: You loved me the way a wife ought to love her husband. It's simply the means that you couldn't judge. But you think I love you any the less for not knowing how to handle your affairs? No, no—just lean on me; I'll guide you and teach you. I wouldn't be a man if this feminine helplessness didn't make you twice as attractive to me. You mustn't mind those sharp words I said—that was all in the first confusion of thinking my world had collapsed. I've forgiven you, Nora; I swear I've forgiven you.

NORA: My thanks for your forgiveness. (*She goes out through the door, right.*)

HELMER: No, wait— (*Peers in.*) What are you doing in there?

255 NORA (*inside*): Getting out of my costume.

HELMER (*by the open door*): Yes, do that. Try to calm yourself and collect your thoughts again, my frightened little song-bird. You can rest easy now; I've got wide wings to shelter you with. (*Walking about close by the door.*) How snug and nice our home is, Nora. You're safe here; I'll keep you like a hunted dove I've rescued out of a hawk's claws. I'll bring peace to your poor, shuddering heart. Gradually it'll happen, Nora; you'll see. Tomorrow all this will look different to you; then every-thing will be as it was. I won't have to go on repeating I forgive you; you'll feel it for yourself. How can you imagine I'd ever conceivably want to disown you—or even blame you in any way? Ah, you don't know a man's heart, Nora. For a man there's something indescribably sweet and satisfying in knowing he's for-given his wife—and forgiven her out of a full and open heart. It's as if she belongs to him in two ways now: in a sense he's given her fresh into the world again, and she's become his wife and his child as well. From now on that's what you'll be to me—you little, bewildered, helpless thing. Don't be afraid of anything, Nora; just open your heart to me, and I'll be conscience and will to you both— (NORA *enters in her regular clothes.*) What's this? Not in bed? You've changed your dress?

NORA: Yes, Torvald, I've changed my dress.

HELMER: But why now, so late?

NORA: Tonight I'm not sleeping.

260 HELMER: But Nora dear—

NORA (*looking at her watch*): It's still not so very late. Sit down, Torvald; we have a lot to talk over. (*She sits at one side of the table.*)

HELMER: Nora—what is this? That hard expression—

NORA: Sit down. This'll take some time. I have a lot to say.

HELMER (*sitting at the table directly opposite her*): You worry me, Nora. And I don't understand you.

NORA: No, that's exactly it. You don't 265 understand me. And I've never under-stood you either—until tonight. No, don't interrupt. You can just listen to what I say. We're closing out accounts, Torvald.

HELMER: How do you mean that?

NORA (*after a short pause*): Doesn't anything strike you about our sitting here like this?

HELMER: What's that?

NORA: We've been married now eight years. Doesn't it occur to you that this is the first time we two, you and I, man and wife, have ever talked seriously together?

HELMER: What do you mean—seriously? 270

NORA: In eight whole years—longer even—right from our first acquaintance, we've never exchanged a serious word on any serious thing.

HELMER: You mean I should constantly go and involve you in problems you couldn't possibly help me with?

NORA: I'm not talking of problems. I'm saying that we've never sat down seriously together and tried to get to the bottom of anything.

HELMER: But dearest, what good would that ever do you?

NORA: That's the point right there; 275 you've never understood me. I've been wronged greatly, Torvald—first by Papa, and then by you.

HELMER: What! By us—the two people who've loved you more than anyone else?

NORA (*shaking her head*):   You never loved me. You've thought it fun to be in love with me, that's all.

HELMER: Nora, what a thing to say!

NORA: Yes, it's true now, Torvald. When I lived at home with Papa, he told me all his opinions, so I had the same ones too; or if they were different I hid them, since he wouldn't have cared for that. He used to call me his doll-child, and he played with me the way I played with my dolls. Then I came into your house—

280   HELMER: How can you speak of our marriage like that?

NORA (*unperturbed*):   I mean, then I went from Papa's hands into yours. You arranged everything to your own taste, and so I got the same taste as you—or I pretended to; I can't remember. I guess a little of both, first one, then the other. Now when I look back, it seems as if I'd lived here like a beggar—just from hand to mouth. I've lived by doing tricks for you, Torvald. But that's the way you wanted it. It's a great sin what you and Papa did to me. You're to blame that nothing's become of me.

HELMER: Nora, how unfair and ungrateful you are! Haven't you been happy here?

NORA: No, never. I thought so—but I never have.

HELMER: Not—not happy!

285   NORA: No, only lighthearted. And you've always been so kind to me. But our home's been nothing but a playpen. I've been your doll-wife here, just as at home I was Papa's doll-child. And in turn the children have been my dolls. I thought it was fun when you played with me, just as they thought it fun when I played with them. That's been our marriage, Torvald.

HELMER: There's some truth in what you're saying—under all the raving exaggeration. But it'll all be different after this. Playtime's over; now for the schooling.

NORA: Whose schooling—mine or the children's?

HELMER: Both yours and the children's, dearest.

NORA: Oh, Torvald, you're not the man to teach me to be a good wife to you.

HELMER: And you can say that?   290

NORA: And I—how am I equipped to bring up children?

HELMER: Nora!

NORA: Didn't you say a moment ago that that was no job to trust me with?

HELMER: In a flare of temper! Why fasten on that?

NORA: Yes, but you were so very right.   295
I'm not up to the job. There's another job I have to do first. I have to try to educate myself. You can't help me with that. I've got to do it alone. And that's why I'm leaving you now.

HELMER (*jumping up*):   What's that?

NORA: I have to stand completely alone, if I'm ever going to discover myself and the world out there. So I can't go on living with you.

HELMER: Nora, Nora!

NORA: I want to leave right away. Kristine should put me up for the night—

HELMER: You're insane! You've no right! I   300
forbid you!

NORA: From here on, there's no use forbidding me anything. I'll take with me whatever is mine. I don't want a thing from you, either now or later.

HELMER: What kind of madness is this!

NORA: Tomorrow I'm going home—
I mean, home where I came from.
It'll be easier up there to find something to do.

HELMER: Oh, you blind, incompetent child!

NORA: I must learn to be competent,   305
Torvald.

HELMER: Abandon your home, your husband, your children! And you're not even thinking what people will say.

NORA: I can't be concerned about that. I only know how essential this is.

HELMER: Oh, it's outrageous. So you'll run out like this on your most sacred vows.

NORA: What do you think are my most sacred vows?

310 HELMER: And I have to tell you that! Aren't they your duties to your husband and children?

NORA: I have other duties equally sacred.

HELMER: That isn't true. What duties are they?

NORA: Duties to myself.

HELMER: Before all else, you're a wife and mother.

315 NORA: I don't believe in that anymore. I believe that, before all else, I'm a human being, no less than you—or anyway, I ought to try to become one. I know the majority thinks you're right, Torvald, and plenty of books agree with you, too. But I can't go on believing what the majority says, or what's written in books. I have to think over these things myself and try to understand them.

HELMER: Why can't you understand your place in your own home? On a point like that, isn't there one everlasting guide you can turn to? Where's your religion?

NORA: Oh, Torvald, I'm really not sure what religion is.

HELMER: What—?

NORA: I only know what the minister said when I was confirmed. He told me religion was this thing and that. When I get clear and away by myself, I'll go into that problem too. I'll see if what the minister said was right, or, in any case, if it's right for me.

320 HELMER: A young woman your age shouldn't talk like that. If religion can't move you, I can try to rouse your conscience. You do have some moral feeling? Or, tell me—has that gone too?

NORA: It's not easy to answer that, Torvald. I simply don't know. I'm all confused about these things. I just know I see them so differently from you. I find out, for one thing, that the law's not at all what I'd thought—but I can't get it through my head that the law is fair. A woman hasn't a right to protect her dying father or save her husband's life! I can't believe that.

HELMER: You talk like a child. You don't know anything of the world you live in.

NORA: No, I don't. But now I'll begin to learn for myself. I'll try to discover who's right, the world or I.

HELMER: Nora, you're sick; you've got a fever. I almost think you're out of your head.

NORA: I've never felt more clearheaded and sure in my life. 325

HELMER: And—clearheaded and sure— you're leaving your husband and children?

NORA: Yes.

HELMER: Then there's only one possible reason.

NORA: What?

HELMER: You no longer love me. 330

NORA: No. That's exactly it.

HELMER: Nora! You can't be serious!

NORA: Oh, this is so hard, Torvald— you've been so kind to me always. But I can't help it. I don't love you anymore.

HELMER (*struggling for composure*): Are you also clearheaded and sure about that?

NORA: Yes, completely. That's why I can't 335 go on staying here.

HELMER: Can you tell me what I did to lose your love?

NORA: Yes, I can tell you. It was this evening when the miraculous thing didn't come—then I knew you weren't the man I'd imagined.

HELMER: Be more explicit; I don't follow you.

NORA: I've waited now so patiently eight long years—for, my Lord, I know miracles don't come every day. Then this crisis broke over me, and such a certainty filled me: *now* the miraculous event would occur. While Krogstad's letter was lying out there, I never for an instant dreamed that you could give in to his terms. I was so utterly sure you'd say to him: go on, tell your tale to the whole wide world. And when he'd done that—

340 HELMER: Yes, what then? When I'd delivered my own wife into shame and disgrace—

NORA: When he'd done that, I was so utterly sure that you'd step forward, take the blame on yourself and say: I am the guilty one.

HELMER: Nora—!

NORA: You're thinking I'd never accept such a sacrifice from you? No, of course not. But what good would my protests be against you? That was the miracle I was waiting for, in terror and hope. And to stave that off, I would have taken my life.

HELMER: I'd gladly work for you day and night, Nora—and take on pain and deprivation. But there's no one who gives up honor for love.

345 NORA: Millions of women have done just that.

HELMER: Oh, you think and talk like a silly child.

NORA: Perhaps. But you neither think nor talk like the man I could join myself to. When your big fright was over—and it wasn't from any threat against me, only for what might damage you—when all the danger was past, for you it was just as if nothing had happened. I was exactly the same, your little lark, your doll, that you'd have to handle with double care

now that I'd turned out so brittle and frail. (*Gets up.*) Torvald—in that instant it dawned on me that for eight years I've been living here with a stranger, and that I've even conceived three children—oh, I can't stand the thought of it! I could tear myself to bits.

HELMER (*heavily*): I see. There's a gulf that's opened between us—that's clear. Oh, but Nora, can't we bridge it somehow?

NORA: The way I am now, I'm no wife for you.

HELMER: I have the strength to make 350 myself over.

NORA: Maybe—if your doll gets taken away.

HELMER: But to part! To part from you! No, Nora no—I can't imagine it.

NORA (*going out, right*): All the more reason why it has to be. (*She reenters with her coat and a small overnight bag, which she puts on a chair by the table.*)

HELMER: Nora, Nora, not now! Wait till tomorrow.

NORA: I can't spend the night in a strange 355 man's room.

HELMER: But couldn't we live here like brother and sister—

NORA: You know very well how long that would last. (*Throws her shawl about her.*) Good-bye, Torvald. I won't look in on the children. I know they're in better hands than mine. The way I am now, I'm no use to them.

HELMER: But someday, Nora—someday—?

NORA: How can I tell? I haven't the least idea what'll become of me.

HELMER: But you're my wife, now and 360 wherever you go.

NORA: Listen, Torvald—I've heard that when a wife deserts her husband's house just as I'm doing, then the law frees him from all responsibility. In any case, I'm freeing you from being responsible. Don't feel yourself bound, any more than I will. There has to be absolute freedom for us both. Here, take your ring back. Give me mine.

HELMER: That too?

NORA: That too.

HELMER: There it is.

365   NORA: Good. Well, now it's all over. I'm putting the keys here. The maids know all about keeping up the house—better than I do. Tomorrow, after I've left town, Kristine will stop by to pack up everything that's mine from home. I'd like those things shipped up to me.

HELMER: Over! All over! Nora, won't you ever think about me?

NORA: I'm sure I'll think of you often, and about the children and the house here.

HELMER: May I write you?

NORA: No—never. You're not to do that.

370   HELMER: Oh, but let me send you—

NORA: Nothing. Nothing.

HELMER: Or help you if you need it.

NORA: No. I accept nothing from strangers.

HELMER: Nora—can I never be more than a stranger to you?

NORA (*picking up her overnight bag*):   Ah,   375
Torvald—it would take the greatest miracle of all—

HELMER: Tell me the greatest miracle!

NORA: You and I both would have to transform ourselves to the point that—Oh, Torvald, I've stopped believing in miracles.

HELMER: But I'll believe. Tell me! Transform ourselves to the point that—?

NORA: That our living together could be a true marriage. (*She goes out down the hall.*)

HELMER (*sinks down on a chair by the door,*   380
face buried in his hands):   Nora! Nora! (*Looking about and rising.*) Empty. She's gone. (*A sudden hope leaps in him.*) The greatest miracle—?

From below, the sound of a door slamming shut.

··●··●··➤ *Your* Turn
Talking and Writing about Lit

1. How does our view of Nora Helmer change during Act I of *A Doll's House*? How is she different at the beginning of Act II than she was at the beginning of Act I, and how is the transformation reflected in the stage setting and the character's actions?

2. Nora and Torvald Helmer have different perspectives on matters of truth and the law. How do these differences of understanding and perspective help depict their relationship and, at the same time, reveal some key themes in the play?

3. In Act I, Ibsen is carefully laying the groundwork for much that is to follow in Acts II and III. What signs are there in Nora's behavior in Act I that she may be capable of "rebellion" later on? One might also think of these as examples of foreshadowing.

4. Why is Nora "pale with terror" at the end of Act I?

5. Describe the importance of Kristine Linde to characterization and plot in the play.

6. Is there symbolic significance in the Christmas tree which appears at the end of Act I and the beginning of Act II? Is Nora's "wild dance" at the end of Act II also symbolic of larger themes and ideas?

7. Describe Ibsen's use of the motif of masks, costumes, disguises, and masquerade. How does this motif reveal some of the play's themes?

8. What is the importance of Dr. Rank to characterization, plot, and themes?

9. As Kristine Linde and Nils Krogstad move closer together in Act III, how does their relationship begin to serve as a foil to the Helmers' unraveling marriage? Are Kristine and Nils beginning their life together on different terms than the Helmers did? Do they have a greater chance for success as a result?

10. What is "the miracle" that Nora hopes for in Acts II and III? Has Torvald inadvertently encouraged her to hope for this earlier in the play?

11. What larger meaning resonates when Nora says, late in Act III, "Getting out of my costume," and "Yes, Torvald, I've changed my dress"?

12. Do you find it credible that Nora leaves at the end? Do you think the slamming of the door signals the permanent end of the marriage, or is there any chance for change in these two characters? Does the ending have final resolution, or is the play open ended?

13. Ibsen (like Chekhov) believed that the most important work of the artist is to pose the right questions, not to answer them. What important questions has Ibsen left us with at the end of *A Doll's House*?

14. **DIY** Write a scene of four pages or less, using dramatic form (that is, with characters' names, followed by their dialogue, and with stage directions in italics within parentheses). Your scene should have two characters who are experiencing some sort of conflict (for example, an employee and his or her boss, two people in a love relationship or dating relationship, or two coworkers who have a disagreement). Whether the scene has a positive or negative outcome—or an ambiguous outcome—is up to you. You are in control.

Talking Lit

The following selections offer some words from Ibsen's official biographer, a stage history of Noras across time, and general wisdom about characterization in drama.

Halvdan Koht, From "Women and Society:" *A Doll's House,* (1887–79)," Life of Ibsen

"We don't notice women," says Consul Bernick in one of the early drafts of *Pillars of Society*. Lona Hessel, the rebel of the play, is given the line in the final version, and the words are turned against the men: "You don't notice women." Now woman herself was rising in revolt against society and demanding her rights.

Women's rights had become a burning issue. John Stuart Mill's *The Subjection of Women* (1869), which raised the problem, was translated by Brandes into Danish in the same year. In 1871 Norwegian Mathilde Schjøtt published the anonymous pamphlet *A Conversation among Friends about the Subjection of Women* and her aunt, Aasta Hansteen, fought for "emancipation" in her own name. Camilla Collett's volumes, *Last Pages (Sidste Blade)*, published in 1872 and 1873, made a deep impression with their picture of the mental suffering endured by enslaved women and their analysis of how men become brutal and crude through contempt for women. The same theme had been basic in all of Mme. Collett's work since *The Governor's Daughters* in 1855. Now was the time to work for practical measures. Women began to organize clubs such as The Women's Reading Society of Oslo, founded in 1874, to expand their intellectual opportunities. They began to win places for themselves in the civil service and the school system. The issues were kept alive by Collett's *From the Camp of the Silent (Fra de Stummes Leir*, 1874), and by the sensational case of a Swedish noblewoman who came to Norway to announce in a series of lectures and in pamphlets that she had suffered a great injustice at the hands of a Norwegian student who had seduced her and then refused to marry her. Aasta Hansteen took up the cudgel on the noblewoman's behalf and the case was turned into a general debate on women's rights. Such "unfeminine" and uninhibited polemics antagonized all "good society," and by 1880 things had become so difficult for Aasta Hansteen, that she left for the greater freedom of America, not returning until 1889.

Aasta Hansteen was the model for Ibsen's Lona Hessel (at first named, even more suggestively, Lona Hassel). He had noticed the indignation her activities had aroused while he was in Norway in 1874, and he longed to put down her narrow-minded detractors. A robust and warm-hearted woman like this was just the kind of person he needed to break through the hypocritical family and social life of the Bernicks. Thus the first drafts of the play suggested it would be more on the woman's rights issue than it actually turned out to be. In the early drafts Ibsen ridiculed the "domesticity" of the old-fashioned housewives and contrasted them with the emancipated woman, bold in speech and even bolder in action. The new woman could win a victory for truth because she made use of that truly feminine gift of giving men "a glimpse of that non-logical, intuitive mode of thinking" that "has an inspiring and cleansing effect." Ibsen knew this gift from close observation of the "illogical" but strong-willed woman he had married. As long ago as 1870 he had described her consuming hatred of all convention.

The theme of his play was that man should not make it his goal in life to become a "pillar of society," but should rather become himself. The theme is basic to Ibsen's life as well as his writing. In everything it was a question of "realizing oneself" as a free agent. In the summer of 1879 he wrote to Bjørnson that his mission as a writer was "to inspire individuals, as many as possible, to freedom and independence." He reiterated his stand in reply to Bjørnson's request for support in his agitation for a "pure flag" (Norwegian red-white-and-blue without the foreign colors that marked the union with Sweden). "There are not in all Norway twenty-five free and independent souls. Let the mark of union stay; but erase the signs of monkhood from minds; take away the mark of prejudice and narrow-mindedness and subjection and baseless faith in authority, so that the individual can sail under his own flag. What they sail under now is neither pure nor their own."

This applied no less to women than to men. In *The Pretenders* a quiet, pathetic complaint sighs from the lips of the king's mother: "To love, to sacrifice all, and to be forgotten, that is a woman's story." In *Pillars of Society* the young Dina Dorf has the courage to defy society and refuse to bow to "all these intimidating considerations . . . all this killing respectability." In the first draft Ibsen shows her as willing to enter into an unconsecrated union with the man she loves; she would throw off all external bonds, even this hated thing of "betrothal," in order to be free, herself alone. She is a version of Svanhild in *Love's Comedy*, a new version that will not let "the world take her," but rather meets its challenge proudly. She is a woman of the same mettle as Hjørdis of *The Vikings at Helgeland*. Ibsen, it seems, believed that a woman could raise the standard of revolt against the conventions that trammeled the free mind more readily than man.

Ideas like this had been latent in him since youth; now they broke out in revolutionary form, particularly after his association with Camilla Collett in Dresden in 1871. At that time she had been amazed and angry with his old-fashioned attitudes toward women; when she came to Munich in the spring of 1877 and discussed marriage and the position of women with him again, she was still further provoked by the opinions he defended. He was probably in jest part of the time; he was completing *Pillars of Society* and contradicting Camilla was one way by which he could penetrate deeper into the thinking of this rebellious woman. The first impulse to write a play with emphasis on women may have come from these conversations; the idea for a new drama dealing precisely with woman's rebellion could have led him to eliminate from *Pillars of Society* a good deal of the material relating to women and their cause and to keep his attack concentrated on social morals, as the inclusiveness of the title indicates.

An old theme was about to take on new form. When *The League of Youth* appeared, Brandes had pointed out that the story of Selma, the youthful Mrs. Bratsberg, might well have been developed into a drama in its own right. This was the idea to which he now returned. Selma, "the fairytale princess," longing for the true fairytale, always kept on the outside and never permitted to make her contribution or to participate in the struggles of real life. She must always be protected from all that is ugly. Finally she cries out in anger: "You dressed me like a doll; you played with me, as one plays with a child. I would have rejoiced to bear a burden; I longed with all my heart for everything that storms, that lifts up, exalts." In *The*

League of Youth it was no more than an outburst, it was not drama. Now, a decade later, the outcry became rebellion. The theme had strong roots in his past thinking, and even in *Pillars of Society,* but he did not immediately discover the right form. *Pillars* came out in October, 1877; then an entire year passed before he made serious plans for the new play. He said that when he was through with a play he felt completely exhausted, emptied as though everything in his head had already been said.

In the meantime his hands were full of business matters. With the great success of his play in Germany, it became more important than ever to protect his rights to the income from his work. It was necessary that he appear as a German author, not simply a Norwegian or Danish one. Even in the Scandinavian countries he had to make contracts with the regular theatres and the traveling troupes and became involved in quarrels and lawsuits over various production problems. When the theatre in Bergen was reorganized in 1876, he personally drew up the contract he wanted with it. As the money came in, he had the added problem of investing it to secure his future. His publisher Hegel took care of the royalties from theatres in Denmark and Sweden; he handled the rest himself and began to invest in various Norwegian enterprises—the new streetcars in Oslo, a new bank in Bergen, a new steamship company in Kristiansand. He was not always lucky, but things generally went well and he accumulated a fortune that grew from year to year.

In August, 1878, he left Munich with the intention of returning to live in Rome; his son Sigurd had finished the Munich *gymnasium* and wished to study at the University of Rome. Ibsen himself longed for the warmth of the South. After a pleasant summer in Gossensass in the Alps, the town he had enjoyed so much in 1876, he arrived in Rome at the end of September.

Before he left Munich, he had gotten a letter from Victor Kieler, a teacher in Hillerød, Denmark, informing him briefly that he had been compelled to commit his wife to an insane asylum. The letter was to have a major effect on his thinking about the new play, and would in fact suggest its central conflict. In 1870 Kieler's wife, Laura, had sent Ibsen a "continuation" of *Brand,* which she called *Brand's Daughters.* She was Laura Petersen at that time, a twenty-year-old girl living in Trøndelag, and her book was a kind of edifying Christian tract, intended as an answer to the inhuman moral demands of Ibsen's play. Ibsen took an interest in the young girl and advised her to try her hand at writing *belles lettres.* When he met her the next year in Copenhagen, he was still more interested, for she was hardly what he had expected, but young, pretty, and vivacious. He invited her to Dresden and she came the following summer. For two months she was in the Ibsen home virtually every day; he liked her very much and gave her the name "the lark." Two or three years later she married in Denmark and began to write short stories. The young couple was poor, her husband's earnings as a teacher were low, and he fell ill as their financial troubles began to press down on him. According to their son, Kieler's temperament was "explosive," and he would fly into rages over household expenses. The doctor advised a long vacation in a warmer climate, and Laura secretly borrowed money in Norway to finance the trip. In 1876 they set off for

Switzerland and Italy, and on their way home stopped in Munich for a few days. Laura confided in Mrs. Ibsen and told her of her difficulties with the debt she owed for the trip, which she had not dared to tell her husband about. She had hoped to pay off the loan with money earned by her writing, but she had not been able to get anything published. In March, 1878, she sent Ibsen the manuscript of a book she wanted him to try to place with Gyldendal. Ibsen answered that the book was so hastily written that it was not in condition to be published—she herself had mentioned in her letter that she rushed the writing of the book. He sensed something behind this haste and wrote that "there must be something you are concealing in your letter." The only advice he could give her was to urge her to tell her husband about the debt so that he could help her. This was the last thing she dared to do, trying instead to get the debt postponed. When this failed, she wrote a forged note. The forgery was detected immediately, she got no money, and her husband learned of the whole thing. In a fury he demanded a divorce, and when she suffered a nervous breakdown she was committed to an asylum. In this catastrophe the marriage was dissolved.

As late as October 7, 1878, Ibsen was writing to Hegel for detailed information about the Kielers, and did not learn the full story for some time. The whole incident moved him deeply; he saw before him the vivacious young woman, secretly assuming burdens for the sake of her husband, even forging notes on his account, looking forward to the pride he would feel in her when the truth was known—and in the end driven to mental collapse and divorce. Ibsen knew well the power such frustration had to kill love; he had depicted it in *Brand*, when Agnes leaves Ejnar after discovering that he lacks the courage and strength to risk his life for another's salvation. He must have recalled what he had read in Kierkegaard's *Seducer's Diary*. The seducer describes the anticipation he has created in the young girl; she has something "eager, almost foolhardy in the way of expectation" in her eyes, "as if they demanded and were prepared to see the extraordinary every second." Kierkegaard called this "extraordinary" thing the "miracle" (*det "Vidunderlige"*), and he used the word again in *Repetition*, in referring to the love that reached "the threshold of the miracle." Did not every woman in fact live in expectation of the "miracle"? The problem for Ibsen was: what consequences when the "miracle" failed to happen? In placing the issue in the context of a violation of social customs and legal limitation he visualized the whole revolt that would follow upon the clash between a woman's unlimited demand and social regulations and accepted morality.

On October 19, 1878, three weeks after his return to Rome, he made the first "Notations for a modern tragedy." A point to be emphasized is that the gist of these "Notations" did not concern women's rights. When he wrote *Pillars of Society*, he was concerned with the falseness of society in general; now he wanted to dramatize the universal tragedy of the conflict between convention and truth, the conflict, as he said in his notes, between "natural feeling on one hand and faith in authority on the other." For him the true spokesman for the "natural" was woman, as he revealed in the chance remark in *Pillars of Society:* "Your society is a society of bachelor souls." He elaborated on this in "Notations" and wrote that modern society "is exclusively a male society, with laws written by men and with prosecutors and judges who judge female actions from a male point of view." Conflict was the inevitable result; for "there are two kinds of spiritual law, two kinds of conscience, one in man and a different one entirely in woman. They do not understand each other." A woman's natural point of view, her defense in every action, is the phrase: "But I did it for love." Laws that hinder acts of love or punish them are inconceivable to her. The result is that "the wife in the play finally does not know where to turn to find the right or the wrong." She loses her footing in society, and she must flee a husband who cannot free himself from social conventions and burst forth to what would be for her the "miracle."

This was the foundation for the drama that would be called *A Doll's House.* Ibsen had to reverse the tragedy of the Kieler household. There the husband wanted to leave; he would have it the other way around. At his own side was a woman who never bowed to conventions that offended common justice; he identified his own spirit of rebellion with hers.

It was a while before he could get down to steady work on the play. During the winter of 1878–79 the theme matured within him, but it took time for the moral dichotomy he pondered to take shape as recognizable human beings. Later, he told his wife that at first he saw the whole thing as in a world of mists, but out of this, little by little, human beings stood forth in stronger and stronger light. That winter he kept to himself, feeling the need to be alone: "Now and then, you know, one has to steal away even from one's own family," he once said. At the Scandinavian Society he would read newspapers from home, and sometimes fall into conversation or attend meetings and dinners, but it was evident that he was in a belligerent frame of mind. One evening after a meeting he stayed and drank Swedish punch, and then launched into an attack on several Danish theologians who were present, denouncing Christianity and all the superficial dogmas the clergy used to bulwark the old social order. He grew more and more fierce and when he went home in the early hours of the morning supported on each side by a young friend, he saw the world running completely downhill, with people growing more paltry by the minute, and their goals less and less worthy. Gunnar Heiberg, one of the young supports and eventually a distinguished Norwegian playwright, tried to comfort him by saying that at least he had written great and true things. But when he began to quote from the "Balloon Letter" Ibsen cried contemptuously, "Verse! Verse! Nothing but verse!"

Plans for the drama turned his thoughts more and more to the problems of women. There is a story that at this time he tried to persuade a Danish woman to start a magazine exclusively for women. In January, 1879, he proposed to the Scandinavian Society that a woman librarian be hired. As a second measure he recommended that women be given the right to vote in the society. This notion met with stronger opposition than he had anticipated, and at the decisive meeting on February 27 he had his comments for the debate carefully written out. He insisted that the present situation was a "humiliation" to women who, he insisted, possessed along with young people and the true artist, "the instinct of genius that unconsciously hits upon the truth." This view of women derives from the romantic tradition; it had given birth to such characters as Agnes in *Brand* and Solveig in *Peer Gynt*. What was different now was that the view became the basis for social demands on whose behalf Ibsen would take action. As he spoke before the society, he became so emotional that he abandoned his notes and spoke from his heart, fluent and powerful. Nonetheless, the cause was lost. He was furious and at his table in his usual haunt he would have none near him but those who had voted in favor of his proposal. He would not speak to any of his old friends who had voted against him; he would not even greet them in the street.

When he turned up at the society's spring banquet, in full regalia and with all his orders, everyone was delighted. He sat down somewhat apart, then suddenly he moved up to the table and began to speak, quietly at first, saying that he had recently wanted to introduce the society to new trends of the times, for no one could escape the force of great ideas, not even here. And how had they received his gift? As though he were a footpad, an assassin! Even women had conspired and agitated against him. By this time he was in such a furor of indignation that he could scarcely control his words. With flashing eyes and trembling lips, with his great mane of hair shaking, he upbraided the women with harsh, almost crude words. At last a Danish countess swooned and he quieted down, but he went on talking about the generally miserable state of most people, especially women, and their unnatural resistance to new ideas that would make them better, richer, more important. When he finished, he took his coat and walked out. He had had his release.

The account of this episode is derived from Gunnar Heiberg's recollections, written thirty years later and inevitably colored somewhat by his imagination. The effect must have been an impressive one, nevertheless, and the account gives an unquestionably accurate account of Ibsen's temperament in those days. His nerves were always keyed up while the creative process was going on.

By summer the play had taken shape enough for him to begin writing. Because of the city's heat he moved in the beginning of July to Amalfi, the old coastal town on the south side of the Sorrento peninsula. He did not live in the town proper, but in an old monastery that had been converted into a hotel, situated on a cliff that fell sharply into the sea. There was a view, the ocean for a refreshing swim, and the air was fresh.

He rewrote the play three times in the course of the summer, and each time the characters became more believable, the plot and speeches firmer and more natural. The first drafts spoke of the "woman problem," but this was forgotten as the play began to reflect life, not a theory. The young lady who would be the central character he called Nora. Many years later when he was asked why he had chosen this name, he answered quickly, "Well, you see, her name wasn't really Nora. She was christened 'Eleonora.' But at home they called her 'Nora' because she was such a little pet." Both names were taken from Ole Schulerud's sister, in fact, but the reply to the question indicates how thoroughly he had entered into the life of his heroine. One day while working on the play he said to his wife: "I've just seen Nora. She came right over to me and put her hand on my shoulder." "What was she wearing," his wife asked. "A simple blue woolen dress," Ibsen answered in all seriousness.

Ibsen used Laura Kieler for his model, at least in part. She herself was certain that Ibsen based Nora on her and maintained that he had first used the phrase "a doll's house" in referring to her home. There is no evidence, however, that Ibsen ever visited the Kielers in Hillerød, and Mrs. Kieler had a tendency to color facts with imagination. It was this very quality that made her so valuable to Ibsen. She had a warm heart and a desire to help all who suffered. And although she had an appreciation of the beautiful and a genuine sense of justice, she had no comprehension of the letter of the law and no consideration for simple facts. In copies of Ibsen's letters that she sent to the author of this book there appeared statements that did not correspond to the given dates. When he inquired about this, she answered in all innocence that she had simply exchanged something in one letter with a passage in another letter that she thought was better expressed. She did not understand that it could make any difference. Such an attitude easily explains how she could have begun telling little lies to her husband about the money she suddenly had in hand. The personality trait would be useful to Ibsen in creating his Nora. But Mrs. Kieler was not his model for Nora's decisive act of leaving her husband at the end of the play. For this he drew on his wife's character in part, and in greater degree from himself as well. A few of Nora's traits may have been taken from little Rikke Holst, who was so fond of pastries. In any case, his thoughts had gone back to Bergen, for he found there models for both Dr. Rank and lawyer Krogstad.

There was certainly no connection between Laura Kieler's husband and the Helmer of the play; the one evening they had spent together in 1876 was hardly enough to give Ibsen any knowledge about him. A more probable model was a Norwegian acquaintance in Munich, a pleasant, sociable person, who was said to rule his German-born wife with an iron hand. Helmer was first called "Stenbo," the same name first given to Stensgard in the drafts of *The League of Youth*. The name's obvious allusion to "stone" was considered too blatant a parody for the political whirligig of that play; here too the reference to the domineering husband was too obvious and the name gave way to the neutral middle-class Helmer, an echo from the Grimstad days. As happened with Consul Bernick, Helmer became less interesting the more Ibsen worked on him. In the first draft he was a man with a passion for science and art; a self-made man whose ignorance was an excuse for his coarse behavior. Ibsen gradually let him dwindle to an ordinary husband, neither better nor worse than most, except that he is an egotist of such dimensions that we can hardly take him seriously. There is an undeniable touch of caricature in having him say in the last act "Nora, I'm saved!" instead of the originally intended "Nora, you're saved!" The psychological gulf between Helmer and Nora is thus widened to a chasm.

The sharp outlines of the play's structure greatly add to its effectiveness. Every character has a function in terms of the main action, and every one helps to exert pressure on Nora until the final inescapable crisis which will either give her the "miracle" or else the death blow to her love. The action of the play is undeniably hurried. The wicked lawyer Krogstad is converted during one short conversation, and it takes little more than a day to transform Nora from a "lark" to an independent woman. But this is not psychologically implausible if one considers the long preparation for the change in her attitude. In the hands of a great actress the final conversation between Nora and her husband grows naturally out of the "lark" and her past; a greater challenge is to make the audience perceive that Nora is already beginning to throw off the "lark" disguise in Act One, that she is merely acting the part her husband requires. (Among the many actresses the author of this book has seen in the part, only Tore Segelcke was able to do this, when she played it at the National Theatre in Oslo in 1936.)

The play was finished toward the end of September, 1879, and published three weeks before Christmas in an 8,000 copy edition. A month later, and again three months later, new editions were required. A German translation entitled *Nora* appeared in Reclam's *Universal-Bibliothek* before the end of 1879 and sold in the thousands. Translations followed one upon the other: Finland 1880, England 1882, Poland 1882, Russia 1883, Italy 1884, etc. In a few years it had a world audience accorded to few books.

But this success was nothing in comparison with its triumphs in theatres around the world. Before Christmas 1879, the Royal Theatre in Copenhagen gave the première with Betty Hennings in the leading role. Next to stage it were the Dramatic Theatre in Stockholm, with Elise Hwasser, and Christiania Theatre in Oslo, with Johanne Juell, both in January, 1880. Various companies toured smaller Scandinavian towns. In February Ida Aalberg performed it in Finnish in Helsinki and it was given in German in Flensborg at the same time. Residenz-Theater in Munich was the first regular German theatre to stage the play on March 3, 1880, with Maria Ramlo; Ibsen himself was present to receive the tribute of the audience. Hedwig Niemann-Raabe played Nora in Hamburg, Dresden, Hannover, and Berlin soon after this. The next year it was given in Vienna and in Leningrad (in Polish); and in 1882 in Warsaw. Toward the end of the 1880's, the play became a standard feature in most theatre repertories and was played in every conceivable tongue in every conceivable location. Ibsen had become a world writer.

A Doll's House had an explosive impact on its time. The happy ending of *Pillars of Society* made it acceptable to all social circles and to people of divergent opinion. *A Doll's House* was relentless, carrying its moral conflict forward to an irreconcilable break with society's ordinary moral precepts, arousing opposition and dividing men's minds.

Never before the subject of so much controversy, Ibsen was the topic of debate in newspapers, periodicals, and books throughout Scandinavia and Germany. Ministers delivered sermons on the new play; people argued privately and publicly about it. The legal question of whether Nora could actually be condemned for forgery by the letter of the law was discussed at length. Some questioned the plausibility of Nora's sudden rejection of that almost-inherited and well-drilled morality and her rebirth as a rebel. This was, in fact, the most meaningful question, but it was overshadowed by the problem that concerned the play's contemporaries most: was it morally right for Nora to abandon her husband and children for the sake of her own intellectual freedom? She was being judged as an actual person, not as a character in a play. In one way this was Ibsen's greatest triumph. People did not ask whether Nora *had* to do what she did; they asked if she *ought* to have done it. Here was the crux of the problem, and it served to focus attention on the whole issue of women's rights. The play was interpreted as a plea for the emancipation of women, and Ibsen was hailed as the special poet of women, not simply as a rebel fighting for spiritual freedom in the abstract. He thus became the most dangerous enemy in the eyes of those who opposed rebellion, whether in society or in moral issues, and those who opposed women's rights.

He had, along with Bjørnson, so indoctrinated his Scandinavian readers that they had the courage to face the real issue he raised and reply affirmatively to his call for freedom. Ibsen had led the way in the movement which, by the end of the 1870's, saw a general victory in Norway for concepts of freedom and honesty, whether in history or natural science, in social or religious matters, in painting or in art. The voice of authority with which he now spoke lent strength to his work as a playwright.

Opposition to the play was much stronger outside Scandinavia. The German reaction was typical. Leading directors in Hamburg and Vienna told Ibsen that it would be impossible—or dangerous—to do the play with the original, unreconciled ending. When played this way at Munich, there was a clash between those who applauded and those who hissed their disapproval of the harsh, "immoral" outcome. The actress Frau Niemann-Raabe flatly refused to do the ending as written: "I would never leave my children," she explained. Ibsen was warned that some enterprising translator would rewrite the ending, and so he decided to do the "barbaric act of violence" himself. In the altered version, Helmer forces Nora to look in on her children in the bedroom; she cannot leave them and so agrees to stay with her husband. The true Ibsenian spirit was missing, and in 1880 when Frau Raabe played it, she could not capture the audience. In Berlin they laughed at the most moving passages, and Brandes, who saw the performance, shook his head: "Germany will never understand Ibsen." It soon became clear, however, that the original version would find its audience. Frau Ramlo's Munich performance was a triumph in spite of all opposition. Within a few years it was impossible to imagine the play in any other version than the original. When Frau Niemann-Raabe performed it this way, she secured the success that eluded her in 1880. Hedwig Wangel, a young German actress who played Nora in 1892 and then went on to a whole series of Ibsen roles, declared that *A Doll's House* had "opened the door to a whole new world for German women." In Germany, as elsewhere, the play fostered spiritual freedom.

The role of Nora was the first of a long series of parts that would prove so attractive to performers. After Nora came Mrs. Alving, Dr. Stockmann, Hjalmar Ekdal, Rebecca West, Hedda Gabler. . . . Frequently performers, particularly actresses, thought they would please Ibsen by thanking him for the magnificent parts he had written. He reacted with annoyance and cut them short: "I have never written parts; I have created human beings and human destinies." And it was precisely by creating true, three-dimensional human beings that he also created good acting parts. He cut away much that was mere theatricality, externals, and probed deep into the souls of his characters, exposing every secret yearning, and so he forced the actor to do the same, to exercise his talent to the utmost in order to reveal the full psychological truth in each character. The plays of Ibsen revitalized and renewed the integrity of the art of acting: they demanded greater empathy, greater honesty, a more complete giving of one's self than any dramatic art since Shakespeare.

One actress after another made the role of Nora her entry into success—from Johanne Juell in Norway to Miss Mori and Miss Mizutani in Japan. The Ibsen roles were moreover so rich that they kept pace with the emotional maturity of the performer. When Betty Hennings returned to the role of Nora after twelve years, she changed her interpretation completely; she was able to penetrate more deeply into the soul of the woman who was at once so childishly unaware of life and yet so brave before the unknown—weak and strong, rich and impoverished. The Nora of Johanne Dybwad changed in the same way. In 1890 at Christiania Theatre she was young herself, and her Nora was little more than a child, the happy "lark" girl who could not quite fathom the new reality; sixteen years later at the National Theatre she was a woman who hid a secret fear of life and whose sudden insight into terrors forced her thoughts into strange paths. New truths awoke in her almost compulsively, involuntarily. Dybwad's interpretation may have been influenced by Johanne Juell, her mother; she in turn passed the tradition on to Tore Segelcke, who was able to suggest an even deeper understanding of the change Nora undergoes.

The play itself seemed to change with time. More than once Ibsen said that he had not intended to write a play about women's rights, but only about human beings. And he never allowed the "women's rights ladies" to make him one of them, even though his moral indignation at subjugation never diminished. Twenty years later he told the Norwegian Society for Women's Rights that he actually did not know what women's rights were; he wanted to secure freedom for all mankind. Gradually both actors and spectators learned to see more of the humanity and less of the ideas of the play. In the beginning, Nora's lines in the last act were spoken as though part of a public debate; the great interpreters of the role made them a moment of private reckoning. Interpretation and audience reaction, however, did not always keep pace: the author of this book recalls an occasion when there was an obvious conflict between what was being played and what the audience wanted to hear. In 1908 the great Nazimova played the role in New York, with a passionate intensity that made Nora's transformation at the end completely an inner reality, conveyed in low-pitched emotion-laden words. The audience, on the other hand, applauded every line as though it were a political harangue, a collection of ideas that were still felt to be startling and revolutionary. Little by little the topical controversy died away; what remained was the work of art, with its demand for truth in every human relation. The artist could achieve no greater triumph.

Frederick J. Marker and Lise-Lone Marker "One Nora, Many Noras" from *Ibsen's Lively Art*, 1989

Although *The Pillars of Society* had caused its fair share of controversy when first produced in 1877, *A Doll's House* shook the very foundations of contemporary society and its supporting ethical structure. The world premiere of Ibsen's new play, staged at the Royal Theatre in Copenhagen on 21 December 1879, enjoyed what even the dramatist himself agreed was "unparalleled success," readily apparent in its exceptional run of twenty-one performances in repertory during the first season. Its popular appeal aside, however, the original production of *A Doll's House* ignited a firestorm of critical debate and dissent. This discussion is of special interest because it was, in this case, so obviously influenced by impressions drawn from the actual performance and in particular from the persuasive portrayal of Nora by Betty Hennings. Although the first edition of the text had been brought out by Gyldendal, Ibsen's Copenhagen publisher, some two weeks earlier, the theatre management had shrewdly persuaded most of the critics to save their principal review for the production. Perhaps as a result, the critical reaction to the play itself in performance did not, as one might suppose, focus on such abstract issues as the "problem" of women's rights or the moral validity of Nora's accusations in the famous discussion scene. Indeed, this scene, so prominent in Shaw's interpretation of the technical novelty in Ibsenism, provoked surprisingly little comment among the play's first theatrical reviewers. Instead, the real questions at issue became the dramatic motivation for Nora's behavior, the audience's reaction to what it perceived as an atmosphere of unrelieved pessimism, and, above all, the effect of Ibsen's disturbingly open ending—so unlike the more agreeably conventional resolution provided in *The Pillars of Society*, which had had its world premiere at this same theatre two years before. In fact, a number of commentators drew a direct parallel with the earlier play, comparing Nora's ethical dilemma to that of the selfish and fraudulent Karsten Bernick in *Pillars*. Among the more sympathetic critical voices, Vilhelm Topsøe maintained stoutly in *Dagbladet* (22 December 1879) that Nora remains "childishly innocent" in her guilt, by reason of the fact that her character is composed of a "strange mixture of right and wrong, of comprehension and lack of comprehension, of ignorance and flashes of realization." In a rather condescending review in *Fædrelandet* (22 December), poet and politician Carl Ploug was prepared to agree that, although she has broken the law, Nora never really loses the audience's sympathy. Nevertheless, Ploug found it impossible to condone or understand the fact that "when she realizes that by concealing the matter from her husband too long she has placed herself in the power of a person who will and can prostitute her and him, she still does not overcome her cowardice and find an opportunity to confide the trouble to her husband." The pugnacious critic and theatre manager M. W. Brun was more outspoken, vigorously denouncing as "psychologically false" the very idea that Nora does not confess to Helmer and obtain his forgiveness. Brun's harsh notice in *Folkets Avis* (24 December) set the tone of moral outrage which *A Doll's House* would continue to encounter during its first journey through the world. The play, this writer declared, "begins with small 'macaroon lies' which grow into 'white lies' and finally culminate in . . . a psycho-logical-dramatic lie," perpetrated by the playwright himself in his desire "to produce something which no one has ever seen or heard before." The psychological essence of this "falsification" was felt, by Brun and others, to consist in Nora's unnatural rejection of maternal love, seen in her "impossible" desertion of her three children. As a result, Brun insisted,

> we are left in the most painful mood, literally disgusted by a catastrophe which in the crudest manner departs from ordinary humanity in order to exalt the untrue, that which is equally outrageous in aesthetic, psychological and dramatic terms. I ask you directly: is there one mother among thousands of mothers, one wife among thousands of wives, who would behave as Nora behaves, who would desert husband, children and home merely in order to become a "human being"? I answer with conviction: no and again no!

Vilhelm Topsøe was among the few who disagreed: "With each line of dialogue exchanged between Nora and Helmer in the play's final scene, we feel the gulf between them widening more and more, and it creates a gripping effect to witness that bond being unravelled strand by strand." Although Topsøe's review in *Dagbladet* shared the opinion that Ibsen's rejection of maternal love constituted "the weak point" in his play, this critic asserted (rightly enough) that any reconciliation after such heightened suspense would have appeared "flat and foolish." If the critical response to Nora's final choice fluctuated, however, there was at least one dramaturgical point on which every reviewer of this production was in agreement: the "spiritual metamorphosis" which Nora undergoes in the third act was unanimously regarded as a glaring breach of dramatic logic. Conservative critic Erik Bøgh, who as the Royal Theatre's play reader coldly rejected *Ghosts* two years later, put it this way in *Dagens Nyheder* (22 December): "Nora has only shown herself as a little Nordic 'Frou-Frou' and as such she cannot be transformed in a flash to a Søren Kierkegaard in skirts." In one sense, this reaction to the improbable abruptness of Nora's transformation obviously reflects the specific performance given by Betty Hennings, whose characterization so profoundly influenced not only the reception but also the comprehension of Ibsen's play. In broader terms, meanwhile, the Danish critics had put their collective finger on the most crucial problem facing any actress or director undertaking this particular play.

To her contemporaries—including Ibsen—Betty Hennings *was* Nora, the veritable personification of the dramatist's literary creation. Even the surly Brun was obliged to concede that she presented "such an attractive, natural, and beautiful picture of the young, inexperienced, naive, and carefree wife and mother that one truly envied Helmer the treasure which he possessed." The novelist, actor, and critic Herman Bang writes that she transformed "even readers to spectators because, after we have but once seen her, she follows us from scene to scene, we see her and not Nora, even as we read." This happens, Bang continues in his exceptionally fine analysis of her acting style, "because we continually place the stress where Fru Hennings has placed it, because, influenced by her, we hesitate where she hesitates, we close our eyes where she closes them." At twenty-nine Hennings was the period's ideal of the charming, graceful ingenue, and as such her Nora was the embodiment of youthfulness, unconcerned gaiety, and childish caprice. Bang's impressionistic description captures perfectly the fundamental tone of childishness in her performance:

> Follow her in the first scene, as she flutters about with childish officiousness, childish helplessness, childish rashness. Watch her opening the packages to show what she has bought, she displays her purchases with childish wonder . . .

In her first scene with Mrs. Linde, speaking with childish haste, she

> whispers, looks around her, whispers again—all with the eagerness of a child talking behind her teacher's back. Something about this obliterates the significance of the secret, makes it—what it of course ought not to be—one of the important secrets of children, the inexhaustible content of school confidences created by the tedium of the lessons and of interest during recesses.

The same child-like quality was accentuated in her scene with her own children:

> One remembers her noise, her mobility, her extremely child-like manner of speaking, the rapidity of her gestures, the change in her diction, which takes on almost nervous speed during her long chatter with the children. For this monologue is chatter, and Fru Hennings' art, which once again has created an incomparable vignette out of this situation, gives speech to the children where the dramatist has left them silent.

Even in her first encounter with Krogstad she continued the same line of attack, moving from alarm to the childish defiance in which she seeks refuge with the declaration, "It was *I* who signed Papa's name."

This reading of Nora's initial character affected the ensuing development of the figure in several decisive ways. Looking back on Betty Hennings' performance in later essays, Edvard Brandes emphasized the total absence of eroticism in "this fine and chaste figure, who nonetheless is supposed to have had three children with Helmer in a rush of sensuality which at the end of the play she regrets." Although Hennings "struggled ably and successfully against the gulf which her temperament and personality placed between her and Ibsen's Nora," Brandes felt that, in particular, her technically skillful and vivacious tarantella lacked that "sensual abandon" which it requires as "the erotic high-point of the marriage." In this respect at least, the virginal, asexual child-wife delineated by Hennings had perhaps more in common with the idealized heroines of romantic fiction than with the passionate young woman who frees herself with difficulty from her physical relationship with her husband at the end of Ibsen's play.

Another, quite different consequence of this actress's approach was that it served to redirect the principal dramatic emphasis to the first two acts of the play—filled, remarked *Berlingske Tidende* (22 December), with a series of "charming pictures" in which "the sun-drenched comfort and happiness of the 'Dolls' House' are depicted, and in which the lark cavorts with her children, decorates the tree, and plays hide-and-seek." In reading the play, Vilhelm Topsøe observed, the "cheerless" third act is the focus of attention, but in performance one's interest centers instead on the development of dramatic crises throughout the second act, from the first moment when Nora is alone with the stripped Christmas tree to the closing seconds when, after her hectic tarantella, she shouts for champagne. As a former ballerina with exceptional pantomimic ability, Hennings was ideally suited to the visually expressive moments around which the Royal Theatre production was concentrated—the children's game interrupted by Krogstad's sudden appearance in the doorway (considered by many as the actress's best scene), the tree-trimming punctuated by Nora's mimic reactions to her husband's recital of Krogstad's unsavory background, the tarantella rehearsal. Each of these vignettes seemed, in the words of the reviewer for *Dags-Telegrafen* (23 December), "to stop in a tableau effect for an instant, imprinting its picture indelibly on the mind of the spectator and then moving on again in the inexorable progress towards the fateful consequences of the conclusion."

The transition to the subdued and chilling mood of the final act precipitated a jarring break with Nora's previous personality that most of the reviewers ascribed to the writing itself. "The cold and quiet clarity and seriousness which replace Nora's gay frivolity and spineless despair cannot come so quickly. They must be prepared for with many thoughts and considerations which the playwright has simply skipped over," Carl Ploug argued in *Fædrelandet*, contending that Ibsen is too easily tempted "to place dramatic effect above the truth which he has endeavored with great success to depict throughout the foregoing action." As for Betty Hennings, although Ploug found her voice too subdued to be audible in this section and Brandes criticized her lack of authority in her confrontation with Helmer, most commentators were unreserved in their praise for her handling of this undeniably difficult transition from songbird to new woman. She rose, Topsøe declared, from confusion and disappointment to become "what she must become, the greater of the two, completely superior to her husband." Years later, a cosmopolitan observer like Maurice Baring still marvelled at the coherence she achieved: "I have seen many Noras: Eleonora Duse and Réjane and Agnes Sorma in Berlin; but Fru Hennings played the part as if it had been written for her," the English novelist-diplomat recalled. "The irony was indeed harrowing, and the disenchantment complete; but irony, disillusion, weariness, disgust were all merged into a wonderful harmony, as the realities of life gradually dawned . . . She made the transformation, which whenever I had seen the play before seemed so difficult to believe in, of the Nora of the first act into the Nora of the last act seem the most natural thing in the world."

Yet the final emotional impression left by Nora's choice was, critics agreed, one of dissonance and confusion rather than triumph. The general feeling of disappointment and joylessness recorded by virtually every reviewer of the production was to a great extent the result of the fact that—as a spokesman for modernism like Edvard Brandes recognized—critics and audience alike harbored the views and sympathies of Torvald Helmer. As a consequence, his wife's decision to leave him seemed incomprehensible. As portrayed by Emil Poulsen he seemed, in the words of *Dags-Telegrafen*, "such a congenial, refined, professionally energetic and honest, domestically happy and likeable personality that his greatest offence seemed to be that he has chosen a frivolous little girl as his wife." His demands appeared, to this viewer and others, fully as reasonable as Nora's, whereas his faults were far less glaring. (Strindberg's famous attack on the play had, in other words, ample critical precedent.) In his review in *Ude og Hjemme* (4 January 1880), Edvard Brandes alone saw Helmer for what he is, "the intellectual aristocrat without intellect, arrogantly conservative partly by conviction and partly out of pragmatism, indifferent, but possessing all the opinions of good society."

Poulsen—a versatile actor whose Ibsen characterizations extended from his early Bishop Nikolas in *The Pretenders* (1871) to his restlessly grieving John Gabriel Borkman (1897)—was able, in Topsøe's view, to endow Helmer with "the right touch of vacillation, half educated, half amiable, a little arrogant, and cleverly ordinary." His finely detailed reading of the part was, Erik Bøgh observed, a remarkable filigree of contrasts and shadings that ranged from the "short-sighted, self-satisfied playfulness with his tormented wife" to the "exultant champagne mood that turns first to indignation and then at once to vapid jubilation" and on through "all the shifting moods of the closing scene, in which he must deliver the cues for Nora's divorce proceedings."

As to what Poulsen's characterization actually conveyed, however, opinions differed sharply. *Berlingske Tidende* saw him as the aesthete who shuns ugliness; beneath the aesthetic pleasure he takes in Nora lies deep and sincere love, manifested "in his sorrow when his lark is silenced in the last act and the sunlight seems to disappear from his home." By contrast, *Fædrelandet* was convinced that Poulsen conveyed the brutal, callous egoist behind the mask of the considerate and infatuated husband—sometimes too boldly underscored, as when "he staggers a little after returning from the ball: this makes the transition to seriousness and sorrow too intense." Herman Bang too saw Ibsen's Helmer as an egoist, but he considered Poulsen's interpretation "excessively coarse" and hence incognizant of what Bang regarded as this character's "totally aesthetic nature." "Poulsen has wished to prepare from the outset for the brutality which is one of the determining features in Helmer's character, and which breaks out as early as the second act where, despite Nora's pleas, he sends off the letter to Krogstad." The actor would, maintained Bang (unseconded by any other critic), "have achieved much more in terms of truth and power if he had played Helmer as nobler, finer, far more elegant than at present." Brandes disagreed, going so far as to assert that Emil Poulsen alone stood on a level with Ibsen's composition. However, Brandes' prediction that the shared philistine sympathy for Helmer and his ideas would cause the play to fail on the stage proved far from accurate.

Critical interpretations might conflict, but the artistic stature of the performances given by Betty Hennings and Emil Poulsen remained undisputed. Rather less effective were the characterizations of the other key figures in Nora's life-drama. As Mrs. Linde, Agnes Gjørling made little impression on the critics, while Sophus Petersen's melodramatic rendering of Krogstad convinced them that this shipwrecked sufferer was nothing more than a stock stage villain. The initial response to the presence of Doctor Rank in the play was utter bewilderment—ascribed by

Brandes to Peter Jerndorff's inability "to reveal the various and eternally changing movements of mind and spirit through his rather dry, flat voice. Passion, bitterness, envy, malice were totally foreign to him," making the actor incapable of portraying "Death's certain prey, the victim of melancholy, hopeless love's bitter cripple: Dr. Rank."

The first performance of a work that quite literally heralded the breakthrough of modernism in the European theatre was, perhaps inevitably, a hybrid, a transitional mixture of old and new methods. Throughout most of the nineteenth century, as we know, a director in the modern sense of the term was unknown. Hence, although the conservative and rather uninspired H. P. Holst was placed in charge of the "arrangement" of the Royal Theatre production of *A Doll's House*, one would search in vain for a director's script containing detailed instructions for movement, groupings, and line readings. Such matters of interpretation were still, to a far greater degree than now, the sovereign responsibility of the individual actor. Accordingly, actual rehearsals were few in number: only eleven were held, including the dress rehearsal, for this important premiere. Seen in this light, the practical significance of the carefully visualized, precisely coordinated *mise-en-scène* which Ibsen now began to write into each of his "modern" plays becomes readily apparent.

As for the setting itself, most of its elements were simply borrowed from the earlier production of *The Pillars of Society*, which was still in the repertory. In its attempt to establish a convincingly realistic environment of solid walls, lighted lamps, and doors that shut and banged with a familiar sound, the Royal Theatre relied for the most part on the explicit and implicit directions found in the text itself. Of particular interest, therefore, are those touches presumably added by Holst and his stage-manager in an effort to deepen the desired sense of a life-like milieu. The busy bank manager's offstage study, for example, was furnished in painstaking detail: "a desk with papers, boxes, writing materials, two candlesticks (which Helmer lights in Act III), match-holder, paperweight. Above the desk a painting and a photographic portrait. Chairs and a bookcase." The hallway landing, likewise only fleetingly glimpsed by the audience, was furnished with an authenticity that would, twenty years later, be hailed as an innovation in Stanislavski's productions of Ibsen and Chekhov. In the living-room itself, a well-stocked sewing-basket and a woodbox placed beside the stoneware oven gave the actors additional opportunities to create an atmosphere of living reality on the stage. Such items as flowering plants, floral bouquets, and chairs with flowered seat-covers conveyed an air of middle-class refinement in the Helmer household. Two provocative objects commented (whether intentionally or not) on Nora's two principal functions in the marriage; on the bookcase, among sets of books in expensive bindings, stood a bust of Venus, while a reproduction of Raphael's Madonna with Child hung conspicuously in the middle of the rear wall, above the piano.

From the outset, critics responded to Ibsen's poetic use of lighting values in *A Doll's House*. The gradual transition—literal as well as figurative—from initial brightness to encroaching darkness seemed a process "as unnoticed but as certain as the work of Nature itself, when day is transformed into night" (*Dags-Telegrafen*).

From the cheerful brightness of the first act, accentuated by the glittering decorations Nora hangs on the tree, the production modulated to the more somber mood of the second, underscored by such graphic details as the plundered Christmas tree, the torn and dishevelled masquerade costume, and the burnt-down candle stubs in the chandelier that hung over the middle of the room. During the intimate exchange between Nora and Doctor Rank at the very center of the play, the lights dimmed slowly until the crucial break-point in their scene ("And now you know you can confide in me as in no one else"); after it, Helene carried in the lamp at her mistress's bidding and the stage lights again brightened. In the final act, the return of the Helmers from the costume ball was illuminated only by the lights from the hallway and a small lamp on the round table (the battleground for the imminent confrontation). The atmosphere of bleakness and joylessness that affected many of the play's first reviewers in this final movement was intensified in theatrical terms by other elements as well: costume changes, as Nora lays aside her masquerade dress to reappear in "ordinary clothes with a small valise," and (live) sounds from beyond the room—music and distant voices from Consul Stenborg's party, steps heard softly on the stairs, and at last the punctuating slam of the street door below.

The actual physical staging of this influential premiere, closely tied as it was to Ibsen's own stage directions, typifies a pattern that varied little in the productions of *A Doll's House* that eventually followed elsewhere. (Even at the Royal Theatre, where the 1879 production stayed in the repertory for fully twenty-eight years, a well-acted modern revival directed by Gerda Ring in 1955 still relied to a surprising degree on the traditional "points" and groupings established by the original *mise-en-scène*.) On the other hand, this quality of sameness has inevitably been modified by the infinite variety inherent in the character of Nora herself, to which virtually every notable actress of each succeeding generation has sought to bring a fresh approach or a new tone.

A significant variation was thus introduced almost at once by Johanne Juell, whose performance at Christiania Theatre barely a month after the Copenhagen opening (20 January 1880) brought a new sense of genuine mental anguish to Nora's frantic scene with Mrs. Linde in the second act, just before the tarantella rehearsal ("If I should lose my mind—and that could well happen"). Edvard Brandes observed that, despite the slapdash character of this production as a whole, the young Norwegian actress "showed us how madness lurked in poor Nora's confused brain, as the terrible fear crushed her spirit. One's heart beat at that moment with the same feverish haste as Nora's own." Others were even more outspoken in preferring Johanne Juell to Betty Hennings, on the grounds that she seemed "the first to hold Nora's character together, so that the childish gaiety of the first act did not clash incomprehensibly and crudely with the mature seriousness that follows the catastrophe. The admired Nora of Fru Hennings thus fell into two parts, both equally striking in performance. But the gay little squirrel held not the slightest hint of that Nora whose terror later rouses her to seriousness." (The problem of the role's apparent bifurcation was, of course, by no means unique to Hennings' performance. When, for example, Beatrice Cameron undertook the part for the first time in New York exactly ten years later, the principal and persistent objection was that she "insist[ed] too strongly upon both extremes of her character," thereby causing it to seem inconceivable "that the weak and foolish creature of the first two acts . . . should be changed, in the twinkling of an eye, into a self-possessed and resolute woman, ready to fight her own way in the world rather than live in the same house with the husband in whom she has been disappointed.")

The great legendary Noras of this early period—Eleonora Duse, Gabrielle Réjane, Vera Kommisarjevskaya, Agnes Sorma and Janet Achurch—were all travelling stars who, in an age long before talking films and television, brought their highly individualistic approaches to the "problem" of Nora before mass audiences in every part of the civilized world. The best-known and probably the most controversial among them was Duse. Acting in a heavily cut Italian text, her restrained, quietly intense, and stubbornly anti-melodramatic interpretation of Nora seems to have caught most London critics by surprise and disappointed their expectations when she first appeared there in 1893. William Archer dismissed as "mere pedantry" her refusal "to give the slightest start" when Krogstad exposes her clumsy forgery, and he deplored the omission in her *Casa di Bambola* of such "touching" moments as Nora's scenes with Anne-Marie and with the children. Archer was satisfied, however, that at least the feverish tarantella, which he had always abhorred as an unnecessary concession to theatricality on Ibsen's part, was reduced by her to a quiet sequence in which she donned a crown of roses, seized the tambourine, danced a few tentative steps, and then sank down exhausted in a chair. Other critics were less tolerant of Duse's method. *Truth*, no champion of Ibsenism, objected (15 June 1893) that "she treats the play in perfectly straightforward fashion, not as a psychological study but as a domestic drama," while the *Times* (12 June) described her Nora as "a shallow, flighty, morbid, neuropathic creature upon whose course of conduct it is impossible to reckon . . . In ten minutes, when she has had time for a change of mood, nobody would be surprised to hear her returning cab-wheels outside." Yet this curt rejection of her final choice as mere caprice contradicts the evidence which Archer read in Duse's hollow-eyed, ashen face as she appeared at the beginning of the last act: "One felt that Helmer must indeed have drunk an incredible quantity of champagne not to see that the shadow of death lay over this woman."

What Archer saw, of course, was what Arthur Symons has described in a fine passage as a "kind of melancholy wisdom which remains in her face after the passions have swept over it." For Duse, in other words, the very expression of emotion became "all a restraint, the quieting down of a tumult until only the pained reflection of it glimmers out of her eyes, and trembles among the hollows of her cheeks." In the particular case of Nora, the underlying secret she seemed always to be holding back is best described by Gunnar Heiberg, a veteran Ibsen director who understood the challenge of his countryman's plays in a usefully practical way:

> Duse cut those scenes at the beginning of the play (the game under the table with the children, for example) which did not suit her purpose, and thus she obtained that consistency in the character which she was able to reveal. Behind the clouded

veil of infatuation which obscured husband and home and society for her, there waited, fully formed, the mature, wholly conscious woman, needing only an inducement to break through her veil. It became profound and simple. It was a symbol of the modern woman's passage from the home out into society. She concentrated first and foremost on the ruling idea upon which Ibsen, in her estimation, had built his play.

John Galsworthy Some Platitudes concerning Drama (1909) from *The Inn of Tranquility*, 1912

A drama must be shaped so as to have a spire of meaning. Every grouping of life and character has its inherent moral; and the business of the dramatist is so to pose the group as to bring that moral poignantly to the light of day. Such is the moral that exhales from plays like *Lear, Hamlet*, and *Macbeth*. But such is not the moral to be found in the great bulk of contemporary Drama. The moral of the average play is now, and probably has always been, the triumph at all costs of a supposed immediate ethical good over a supposed immediate ethical evil.

The vice of drawing these distorted morals has permeated the drama to its spine; discolored its art, humanity, and significance; infected its creators, actors, audience, critics; too often turned it from a picture into a caricature. A drama which lives under the shadow of the distorted moral forgets how to be free, fair, and fine—forgets so completely that it often prides itself on having forgotten.

Now, in writing plays, there are, in this matter of the moral, three courses open to the serious dramatist. The first is: To definitely set before the public that which it wishes to have set before it, the views and codes of life by which the public lives and in which it believes. This way is the most common, successful, and popular. It makes the dramatist's position sure, and not too obviously authoritative.

The second course is: To definitely set before the public those views and codes of life by which the dramatist himself lives, those theories in which he himself believes, the more effectively if they are the opposite of what the public wishes to have placed before it, presenting them so that the audience may swallow them like powder in a spoonful of jam.

There is a third course: To set before the public no cut-and-dried codes, but the phenomena of life and character, selected and combined, *but not distorted*, by the dramatist's outlook, set down without fear, favor, or prejudice, leaving the public to draw such poor moral as nature may afford. This third method requires a certain detachment; it requires a sympathy with, a love of, and a curiosity as to things for their own sake; it requires a far view, together with patient industry, for no immediately practical result.

It was once said of Shakespeare that he had never done any good to anyone, and never would. This, unfortunately, could not, in the sense in which the word "good" was then meant, be said of most modern dramatists. In truth, the good that Shakespeare did to humanity was of a remote, and, shall we say, eternal nature; something of the good that men get from having the sky and the sea to look at. And this partly because he was, in his greater plays at all events, free from the habit of drawing a distorted moral. Now, the playwright who supplies to the public the facts of life distorted by the moral which it expects, does so that he may do the public what he considers an immediate good, by fortifying its prejudices; and the dramatist who supplies to the public facts distorted by his own advanced morality, does so because he considers that he will at once benefit the public by substituting for its worn-out ethics, his own. In both cases the advantage the dramatist hopes to confer on the public is immediate and practical.

But matters change, and morals change; men remain—and to set men, and the facts about them, down faithfully, so that they draw for us the moral of their natural actions, may also possibly be of benefit to the community. It is, at all events, harder then to set men and facts down, as they ought, or ought not to be. This, however, is not to say that a dramatist should, or indeed can, keep himself and his temperamental philosophy out of his work. As a man lives and thinks, so will he write. But it is certain, that to the making of good drama, as to the practice of every other art, there must be brought an almost passionate love of discipline, a white heat of self-respect, a desire to make the truest, fairest, best thing in one's power; and that to these must be added an eye that does not flinch. Such qualities alone will bring to a drama the selfless character which soaks it with inevitability.

The word "pessimist" is frequently applied to the few dramatists who have been content to work in this way. It has been applied, among others, to Euripides, to Shakespeare, to Ibsen; it will be applied to many in the future. Nothing, however, is more dubious than the way in which these two words "pessimist" and "optimist" are used; for the optimist appears to be he who cannot bear the world as it is, and is forced by his nature to picture it as it ought to be, and the pessimist one who cannot only bear the world as it is, but loves it well enough to draw it faithfully. The true lover of the human race is surely he who can put up with it in all its forms, in vice as well as in virtue, in defeat no less than in victory; the true seer he who sees not only joy but sorrow, the true painter of human life one who blinks at nothing. It may be that he is also, incidentally, its true benefactor.

In the whole range of the social fabric there are only two impartial persons, the scientist and the artist, and under the latter heading such dramatists as desire to write not only for today, but for tomorrow, must strive to come.

But dramatists being as they are made—past remedy— it is perhaps more profitable to examine the various points at which their qualities and defects are shown.

The plot! A good plot is that sure edifice which slowly rises out of the interplay of circumstance on temperament, and temperament on circumstance, within the enclosing atmosphere of an idea. A human being is the best plot there is; it may be impossible to see why he is a good plot, because the idea within which he was brought forth cannot be fully grasped; but it is plain that *he is a good plot*. He is organic. And so it must be with a good play. Reason alone produces no good plots; they come by original sin, sure conception, and instinctive after-power of selecting what benefits the germ. A bad plot, on the other hand, is simply a row of stakes, with a character impaled on each—characters who would have liked to live, but came to untimely grief; who started bravely, but fell on these stakes, placed beforehand in a row, and were transfixed one by one, while their ghosts stride on, squeaking and gibbering, through the play. Whether these stakes are made of facts or of ideas, according to the nature of the dramatist who planted them, their effect on the unfortunate characters is the same; the creatures were begotten to be staked, and staked they are! The demand for a good plot, not unfrequently heard, commonly signifies: "Tickle my sensations by stuffing the play with arbitrary adventures, so that I need not be troubled to take the characters seriously. Set the persons of the play to action, regardless of time, sequence, atmosphere, and probability!"

Now, true dramatic action is what characters do, at once contrary, as it were, to expectation, and yet because they have already done other things. No dramatist should let his audience know what is coming; but neither should he suffer his characters to act without making his audience feel that those actions are in harmony with temperament, and arise from previous known actions, together with the temperaments and previous known actions of the other characters in the play. The dramatist who hangs his characters to his plot, instead of hanging his plot to his characters, is guilty of cardinal sin.

The dialogue! Good dialogue again is character, marshaled so as continually to stimulate interest or excitement. The reason good dialogue is seldom found in plays is merely that it is hard to write, for it requires not only a knowledge of what interests or excites, but such a feeling for character as brings misery to the dramatist's heart when his creations speak as they should not speak—ashes to his mouth when they say things for the sake of saying them—disgust when they are "smart."

The art of writing true dramatic dialogue is an austere art, denying itself all license, grudging every sentence devoted to the mere machinery of the play, suppressing all jokes and epigrams severed from character, relying for fun and pathos on the fun and tears of life. From start to finish good dialogue is handmade, like good lace; clear, of fine texture, furthering with each thread the harmony and strength of a design to which all must be subordinated.

But good dialogue is also spiritual action. In so far as the dramatist divorces his dialogue from spiritual action—that is to say, from progress of events, or toward events which are significant of character—he is stultifying $\tau\grave{o}$ $\delta\rho\alpha\mu\alpha$ the thing done; he may make pleasing disquisitions, he is not making drama. And in so far as he twists character to suit his moral or his plot, he is neglecting a first principle, that truth to Nature which alone invests art with handmade quality.

The dramatist's license, in fact, ends with his design. In conception alone he is free. He may take what character or group of characters he chooses, see them with what eyes, knit them with what idea, within the limits of his temperament; but once taken, seen, and knitted, he is bound to treat them like a gentleman, with the tenderest consideration of their mainsprings. Take care of character; action and dialogue will take care of themselves! The true dramatist gives full rein to his temperament in the scope and nature of his subject; having once selected subject and characters, he is just, gentle, restrained, neither gratifying his lust for praise at the expense of his offspring, nor using them as puppets to flout his audience. Being himself the nature that brought them forth, he guides them in the course predestined at their conception. So only have they a chance of defying Time, which is always lying in wait to destroy the false, topical, or fashionable, all—in a word—that is not based on the permanent elements of human nature. The perfect dramatist rounds up his characters and facts within the ring-fence of a dominant idea which fulfills the craving of his spirit; having got them there, he suffers them to live their own lives.

Plot, action, character, dialogue! But there is yet another subject for a platitude. Flavor! An impalpable quality, less easily captured than the scent of a flower, the peculiar and most essential attribute of any work of art! It is the thin, poignant spirit which hovers up out of a play, and is as much its differentiating essence as is caffeine of coffee. Flavor, in fine, is the spirit of the dramatist projected into his work in a state of volatility, so that no one can exactly lay hands on it, here, there, or anywhere. This distinctive essence of a play, marking its brand, is the one thing at which the dramatist cannot work, for it is outside his consciousness. A man may have many moods, he has but one spirit; and this spirit he communicates in some subtle, unconscious way to all his work. It waxes and wanes with the currents of his vitality, but no more alters than a chestnut changes into an oak.

For, in truth, dramas are very like unto trees, springing from seedlings, shaping themselves inevitably in accordance with the laws fast hidden within themselves, drinking sustenance from the earth and air, and in conflict with the natural forces round them. So they slowly come to full growth, until warped, stunted, or risen to fair and gracious height, they stand open to all the winds. And the trees that spring from each dramatist are of different race; he is the spirit of his own sacred grove, into which no stray tree can by any chance enter.

One more platitude. It is not unfashionable to pit one form of drama against another—holding up the naturalistic to the disadvantage of the epic; the epic to the belittlement of the fantastic; the fantastic to the detriment of the naturalistic. Little purpose is thus served. The essential meaning, truth, beauty, and irony of things may be revealed under all these forms. Vision over life and human nature can be as keen and just, the revelation as true, inspiring, delight-giving, and thought-provoking, whatever fashion be employed—it is simply a question of doing it well enough to uncover the kernel of the nut. Whether the violet come from Russia, from Parma, or from England, matters little. Close by the Greek temples at Paestum there are violets that seem redder, and sweeter, than any ever seen—as though they have sprung up out of the footprints of some old pagan goddess; but under the April sun, in a Devonshire lane, the little blue scentless violets capture every bit as much of the spring. And so it is with drama—no matter what its form—it need only be the "real thing," need only have caught some of the precious fluids, revelation, or delight, and imprisoned them within a chalice to which we may put our lips and continually drink.

And yet, starting from this last platitude, one may perhaps be suffered to speculate as to the particular forms that our renascent drama is likely to assume. For

POP CULTURE

Storming the Stage: Comics, Character, and Culture

The comic book took a long time to come into its own as a medium. Originally "pulp comics," the form dealt mainly with detective fiction, sci-fi, and horror themes. Featuring characters with names like the Shadow and Phantom, the stories focused on hard-boiled vigilantes and adventurer spies. Eventually one publisher, DC Comics, invented what we now consider the modern superhero character, Superman.

Marvel Comics, then known as Timely Comics, came up with a number of superhero characters as well, including Namor the Sub-Mariner, Human Torch, and Captain America. These characters were mainly dedicated to fighting Nazis and had little character development outside of their superheroic personas. Sometimes characters had alter egos, but they were mainly enhancers of their superpowers. For example, the person a Clark Kent was merely a part of Superman's ingenuity at concealing himself. Batman's Bruce Wayne alter ego made plausible the character's wealth and ability to make fantastic gadgets.

It wasn't until the advent of Spiderman that Marvel Comics experienced what fans now call its Golden Age. With the invention of the character Peter Parker, Marvel began focusing more of its storylines on the human side of its superheroes—the person behind the mask. Peter Parker had family problems, trouble with girls, and a hard time paying the rent. Comics began to combine their adolescent power fantasies with some very adult ideas. Superheroes now had bills. DC soon took the hint.

our drama is renascent, and nothing will stop its growth. It is not renascent because this or that man is writing, but because of a new spirit. A spirit that is no doubt in part the gradual outcome of the impact on our home-grown art, of Russian, French, and Scandinavian influences, but which in the main rises from an awakened humanity in the conscience of our time.

What, then, are to be the main channels down which the renascent English drama will float in the coming years? It is more than possible that these main channels will come to be two in number and situate far apart.

The one will be the broad and clear-cut channel of naturalism, down which will course a drama poignantly shaped, and inspired with high intention, but faithful to the seething and multiple life around us, drama such as some are inclined to term photographic, deceived by a seeming simplicity into forgetfulness

With these new elements of characterization and plausibility, Marvel was now able to tackle more real-life issues—a tradition that has carried into Marvel's recently successful film ventures. Spiderman's films still rely on the character of Peter Parker as much as on their stellar action sequences. The X-Men have maintained their metaphors for racism and civil rights. Female characters like Elektra (albeit scantily clad) show women in positions of great power.

Formatted with scripts similar to the medium of the stage, the process and effect of comics are not too distant. Compelling characters drive a great piece, whether it's performed in a theater or in thirty-two pages of a staple-bound comic book. With the rising popularity of deeper, more adult comics and graphic novels in the early 1990s owing to books like *Maus* and the work of Frank Miller, comics are becoming a more sophisticated, more adult art form.

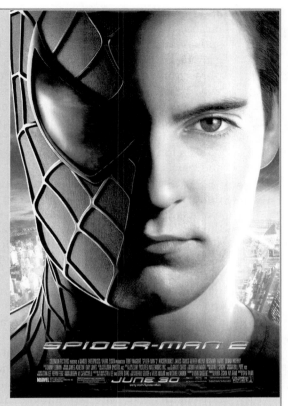

Tobey Maguire as Spiderman/Peter Parker, in Spiderman 2

of the old proverb, *"Ars est celare artem,"* and oblivious of the fact that, to be vital, to grip, such drama is in every respect as dependent on imagination, construction, selection, and elimination—the main laws of artistry—as ever was the romantic or rhapsodic play. The question of naturalistic technique will bear, indeed, much more study than has yet been given to it. The aim of the dramatist employing it is obviously to create such an illusion of actual life passing on the stage as to compel the spectator to pass through an experience of his own, to think, and talk, and move with the people he sees thinking, talking, and moving in front of him. A false phrase, a single word out of tune or time, will destroy that illusion and spoil the surface as surely as a stone heaved into a still pool shatters the image seen there. But this is only the beginning of the reason why the naturalistic is the most exacting and difficult of all techniques. It is easy enough to *reproduce* the exact conversation and movements of persons in a room; it is desperately hard to *produce* the perfectly natural conversation and movements of those persons, when each natural phrase spoken and each natural movement made has not only to contribute toward the growth and perfection of a drama's soul, but also to be a revelation, phrase by phrase, movement by movement, of essential traits of character. To put it another way, naturalistic art, when alive, indeed to be alive at all, is simply the art of manipulating a procession of most delicate symbols. Its service is the swaying and focusing of men's feelings and thought in the various departments of human life. It will be like a steady lamp, held up from time to time, in whose light things will be seen for a space clearly and in due proportion, freed from the mists of prejudice and partisanship.

And the other of these two main channels will, I think, be a twisting and delicious stream, which will bear on its breast new barques of poetry shaped, it may be, like prose, but a prose incarnating through its fantasy and symbolism all the deeper aspirations, yearning, doubts, and mysterious stirrings of the human spirit; a poetic prose drama, emotionalizing us by its diversity and purity of form and invention, and whose province will be to disclose the elemental soul of man and the forces of Nature, not perhaps as the old tragedies disclosed them, not necessarily in the epic mood, but always with beauty and in the spirit of discovery.

Such will, I think, be the two vital forms of our drama in the coming generation. And between these two forms there must be no crude unions; they are too far apart, the cross is too violent. For, where there is a seeming blend of lyricism and naturalism, it will on examination be found, I think, to exist only in plays whose subjects or settings—as in Synge's *Playboy of the Western World*, or in Mr. Masefield's *Nan*—are so removed from our ken that we cannot really tell, and therefore do not care, whether an absolute illusion is maintained. The poetry which may and should exist in naturalistic drama, can only be that of perfect rightness of proportion, rhythm, shape—the poetry, in fact, that lies in all vital things. It is the ill-making of forms that has killed a thousand plays. We want no more bastard drama; no more attempts to dress out the simple dignity of everyday life in the peacock's feathers of false lyricism; no more straw-stuffed heroes or heroines; no more rabbits and goldfish from the conjurer's pockets, nor any limelight. Let us have starlight, moonlight, sunlight, and the light of our own self-respects.

Student Essay

Student Jacqueline DeRosa takes a look at Nora Helmer's dilemma in light of the situation of nineteenth-century women.

Jacqueline DeRosa

English 102

Professor Barnard

A Lark Flies: Understanding Nora's Decision to Leave a Doll House

Henrik Ibsen's *A Doll's House* is, at first reading, seemingly melodramatic with a self-serving, arrogant heroine. Nora's turnaround at the end seemed out of character and unbelievable and her decision to leave her children, unconscionable. Indeed though many of society's constraints have been cast aside since the publication of the play, a mother abandoning her children is still taboo. Reading the play with the sensibilities of a 20th and 21st century mind is a handicap. It is not until after giving thought to the historical context of the play, as well as rereading the play itself, that this drama, with each and every sentence, reveals true insight into the life and mind of a 19th century woman. A slow realization dawns. Being a mother in modern times affords a woman the chance to leave her husband but take her children with her. Shelters are available, among other benefits society affords, and this makes it easy to forget a time where no such help could be found. Considering the actual lives of the Noras of that time, every bit of Nora's personality and ultimate decision becomes easier to understand. Henrik Ibsen's name should be synonymous with women's rights, although he protested this honor. Ibsen's biographer Halvdan Koht puts it this way:

> More than once Ibsen said that he had not intended to write a
> play about women's rights, but only about human beings. . . .
> Little by little the topical controversy died away; what remained

DeRosa 2

was the work of art, with its demand for truth in every human relation. The artist could achieve no greater triumph.

("Women and Society," paragraph 31)

Under this heading we find Nora, a 19th century housewife and mother who has been covertly paying a debt for some years now. Ibsen's stage directions made Nora seem, at first, arrogant (she tosses her head, she replies in disdain) as well as flighty (she is truly bird-like, flitting from spot to spot). Jane Fonda played Nora with a softness that made her seem more accessible but perhaps Ibsen uses these stage directions to contrast the more sedate yet determined Nora at play's end. Nora at first comes across as a combination of a conceited woman, "a girl with my ravishing appeal," "a godsend everything looks so well on me" and a braggart. She gives in to pride when she boasts to Kristine, a friend from her girlhood newly arrived in town, that she borrowed a large sum of money to finance a trip to Italy for her gravely ill husband. She also seems conniving when she reveals to Kristine that though she won't tell her husband of the debt now, she may save the revelation for a time when Torvald is no longer "enjoying my dancing and dressing up and reciting for him" and "Then it may be wise to have something in reserve." What first seems manipulative is later revealed to be clever as the reader realizes that a woman of that time had to find what little power she could. Nora's confession to Kristine that earning money "was almost like being a man" as well as her wish to swear in front of her husband illustrates her desire to assert herself. Her self-assurance later, after a visit from Krogstad who holds her note, that "I'm not so silly as all that" is comparable to her delusions of influence. When referring to Krogstad's

DeRosa 3

imminent job dismissal at the hands of her husband, Nora ventures "Oh, one does have a tiny bit of influence, I should hope. Just because I am a woman . . ." But only a moment later, when pushed by Krogstad to assert that influence she concedes she has "absolutely no influence."

Nora has another problem. She has a propensity for lying and her husband is aware of it. He cautions her, after comparing her to a spendthrift bird that "a songbird needs a clean beak to warble with. No false notes. That's the way it should be, isn't it?" He asks the question but doesn't give her the chance to answer. He answers himself, "Yes, I'm sure of it." He catches her in lie about macaroons when her kiss tastes sweet. Though the reader is struck by the irony that lies taste sweet to Torvald it is also noted that Nora cannot even have a treat without answering to her husband. A doll would just not be as pretty with rotted teeth. After Torvald discovers an "untruth" Nora tells about Krogstad being in their home she replies "you know I could never think of going against you." Although she has lied four times about the macaroons alone, to Nora, her lies are small and acceptable infractions. They are necessary for the ultimate loyalty she feels for her husband. She asks Kristine "Is it indiscreet to save your husband's life?" In fact, Nora has turned lying into an art form as she manipulates her husband by appealing to his vanity in an attempt to secure a bank position for Kristine. Nora cajoles him with "she's terribly eager to come under a capable man's supervision" and "she made the long trip down here to speak to you." But this very act will lead to her downfall as Kristine secures the job Krogstad is so determined to keep for his dignity and as a way to support his children.

DeRosa 4

Each character in the play is plagued by financial problems. Money and the lack of it is an overriding theme. Kristine had left Krogstad years before for a more secure marriage. Both Krogstad and Nora have forged documents to secure money. And Nora, when she finally leaves Torvald, will do so with a financial metaphor. "We're closing our accounts, Torvald." Nora's happiness for her husband's new bank position and the raise it provides prompts her to live up to her husband's condescending name for her, "spendthrift." Another patronizing nickname, squirrel, is ironic because unbeknownst to Torvald, Nora is foraging and nestling away, but it is money to pay off Torvald's life-saving debt she is after. Money means happiness to Nora; she revels in telling the delivery boy to keep the change, and when she speaks of the previous Christmas and her endeavors to earn money she tells Kristine the time "wasn't dull for me." Money also incites pride in Nora. When Kristine asks Nora if she won a lottery, Nora scoffs, "No art to that." She is proud of the debt she is paying as she tells Kristine, "I am capable of something too, hm?" But this sense of autonomy and accomplishment is diminished by Torvald, whose purse strings are the strings used to control her like a marionette. He tells her she is "like a woman!" when it comes to money and is not above comparing her to her father, who apparently did not prosper. Torvald's advice of "No debts! Never borrow!" comes too late. Nora has already borrowed and her cavalier dismissal of lenders—"Them? Who cares about them? They're strangers," and to Krogstad "You weren't any concern of mine"—will lead to her comeuppance. It is Torvald's insistence on treating Nora as a child with an allowance that influences everything she does, including the way she is raising her children.

DeRosa 5

Nora treats her children the way Torvald treats her. As she is Torvald's little doll, they are her little dolls, not real people with real thoughts and emotions. She is an unrealistic mother who assures her "doll babies" that no dogs could ever bite them. Like Torvald, she coddles and insulates. They are for showing off and then are dismissed to Anne-Marie, the nurse. Anne-Marie once gave up an illegitimate child and yet to Nora she seems to be a happy person. Does this subconsciously affect Nora, convincing her that a woman can leave her child behind and still be content? When Nora is led by Torvald to believe "a lying atmosphere infects the whole life of a home. Every breath the children take in is filled with the germs of something degenerate," she is so influenced by him she does not dismiss this but asks, "Are you sure?" At this point Torvald assures Nora that every child who has ever gone bad had a mother who was a chronic liar, and he unwittingly compares Nora to Krogstad who poisons his children year in and year out with lies. These statements shake Nora, and as the play progresses she entreats Anne-Marie to take more and more of a role in the children's lives. On Christmas Day she tells Anne-Marie, "I can't be with them as much as I was" and Anne-Marie's reply is that "Small children can get used to anything." When Anne-Marie tells Nora "the children are begging so hard to come in to Mama," Nora answers, "No, no, no, don't let them in to me! You stay with them Anne-Marie." It is interesting to note she does not say "in to the room" but rather "in to me." As Nora comes closer to being found out, she distances herself from her children and asks Anne-Marie whether children would "forget their mother if she was gone for good?" When Anne-Marie replies that her own daughter has not forgotten her, Nora takes the information in and then when asking

DeRosa 6

"how could you do it?" almost seems to be seeking instruction rather than explanation. At first when Kristine tells Nora she has no children or even a sense of loss to feed on, Nora is incredulous, but she then remarks on how free that must make one feel. All of these conversations come back to the reader when Nora makes her final decision.

There is another character besides Anne-Marie whose conversations with Nora seem to foreshadow Nora's situation. Dr. Rank is dying from a sickly spine that was compromised by his father's syphilis. His illness illustrates the belief of the time that a child pays for its parent's sin. Would Nora's children have to pay for her sin? At one point Dr. Rank tells Nora that "in every single family, in one way or another, this inevitable retribution of nature goes on." Then Dr. Rank remarks that "those who go away are soon forgotten" and that he will leave behind "no more than a vacant place that anyone can fill." When Nora asks Dr. Rank what he and she should wear to the next costume party, it is an allusion to the next stage of life that she knows she and Dr. Rank are about to embark on. She knows even then that they both have in common a doomed fate. Dr. Rank replies that he will be invisible and the reader knows this is because he will be dead. For all intents and purposes Nora will be invisible also; she will be dead to society. All of Dr. Rank's remarks about death parallel Nora's impending decision to leave her children. It is not by coincidence that Dr. Rank's death calling card is in the Helmers' mailbox at the same time as Krogstad's revealing letter. At this point the reader surmises that Nora's hopes for a "miracle" from Torvald are not to be.

DeRosa 7

On the surface, Torvald seems to be a character with a superior sense of morality. He forbids lying and debt and professes in
Act II, "[w]hen it really counts I have the strength and courage
enough as a man to take on the whole weight myself." Nora truly
believes in Torvald's love and character when she tells Dr. Rank
"how deeply, and how inexpressibly dearly Torvald loves me; he'd
never hesitate a second to give up his life for me." But Dr. Rank
notes prophetically that Torvald has a sharp distaste for anything
ugly. When Torvald says in Act III that he wishes Nora's life to be
in danger so he could heroically stake his life and soul for her
sake, Nora challenges that statement by telling him to read his
letter. And, of course, he does not rise to the occasion, ironically
calling Nora a hypocrite. He calls her a liar and tells her she will
never be trusted with her children again. It is at this point that he
demands she take off her shawl, part of a costume for a party
they had just been at. This costume comes to symbolize the
facade that Nora has been living behind. In fact, she has asked
Torvald to design it for her, to "take over and decide what I
should be," and though he had been too busy with bank affairs
he readily drops everything to do just that. When Anne-Marie
finds a box of masquerade clothing Nora says, "I'd love to rip
them in a million pieces!" This is a metaphor for the way she feels
about the "costume" she is forced to wear everyday. It is Torvald's
wish that she wear a costume of an Italian peasant and perform
a dance she learned in Capri. It is ironic that he places her in a
costume representative of the very place she put herself in debt
to bring him to. Though Torvald warns Nora of the dangers of
having to "wear a mask even with the nearest and dearest," he
dons a mask everyday. Torvald, who reveres only society's most

DeRosa 8

staid moral codes, is enticed by Nora's wild dancing in her costume. When Nora decides to leave Torvald she steps out of the costume both literally and figuratively.

And now, though Torvald decides to forgive her, Nora is enlightened. The fact that she has conceived three children with this stranger who would disown her so quickly makes her want to "tear myself to bits." This is just the way she felt about her debtor's note and the costume. She tells Torvald, "I am a human being no less than you—or anyway ought to try to become one." She realizes her most sacred vow is to herself. Suicide is no longer an option; she will return to her home town where it is "easier up there to find something to do." Already she feels that she can prove her worth somewhere else. Torvald has made her lose her confidence in her ability to mother, as she notes that the children "are in better hands than mine" and that the "way I am now, I'm no use to them." She tells him she is "not up to the job" and that she must educate herself. The woman who once cavalierly said "what do I care about dreary old society?" now fulfills that prophecy when Torvald speaks of "what people will say," and she replies "I can't be concerned about that." When Torvald calls her a "silly girl" and tells her "no one gives up honor for love," Nora reminds him that "millions of women have done just that." Not the least among them Nora, whose propensity for lying comes down to her declaration, "I did it out of love." And when Nora leaves, the reader is reminded of a statement Torvald made earlier to Kristine that will surely come back to haunt him, "An exit should always be effective . . . but that's what I can't get Nora to grasp."

DeRosa 9

Works Cited

Koht, Halvdan. "Women and Society: A Doll's House (1878–79)"
from *Life of Ibsen* by Halvdan Koht. New York: Benjamin Blom,
1971. 311–323.

Ibsen, Henrik. *A Doll's House. Access Literature.* Ed. Barbara Barnard
and David Winn. Boston: Wadsworth, 2005.

SETTING AND STAGING

Even street murals use setting and staging.

Urban murals often depict characters from history, literature, and everyday life in a particular physical or social setting, and they often contain elements of staging, as does a play presented on the stage or a film intended for the screen. Street murals also resemble tableaux (singular, a tableau) in which figures are "frozen in time" on a stage set. When historical or literary figures are involved, their depiction may also call to mind a narrative associated with the character's life (or characters' lives). This is also true of the representations of famous entertainers, political leaders, and other public figures whose "stories" are familiar to us.

In the large street mural you see reproduced here, scenes and figures from African American, African, and Afro-Caribbean history are vividly represented: Toussaint L'Ouverture (Haitian revolutionary leader whose followers drove the British and Spanish colonial forces from Haiti in 1798), Jesse Jackson, Ella Fitzgerald, and Malcolm X. Ordinary people are also depicted: a mother and baby, a grandmother with a child, a freed slave swinging his broken chain.

The top left mural, from a downtown Manhattan street, depicts everyday people, and the stage set is the neighborhood. The "props" that the characters are using—skateboard, saxophone—help characterize their lives and their neighborhood. The mural above depicts the history of the settlement and development of an Ozark mountain town, Eureka Springs, Arkansas. Different social groups and different settings in this mural represent different times and events in the history of the area, from the Native American community on the left to the pioneer wagon train behind them, the horse-drawn buggy and wagon in the middle, the family group and Model T Ford on the right. Two centuries (at least) of history are represented, and all on a "stage set" depicting interesting local cave and rock formations, hilly terrain, and a mix of pine and deciduous forest.

Physical Setting

As we saw while looking at the many settings depicted in the street murals on the previous pages, the discussion of **setting** may refer to many aspects of the work—physical, historical, and social. **Physical setting**, which also may be important, includes interior and exterior settings, landscape, climate, and weather conditions. In Arthur Miller's *Death of a Salesman*, we spend a great deal of time in the family home—in the **interior settings** of the kitchen and the sons' room. The backyard garden could almost be considered an interior setting as well. The **exterior setting** and the context in which this home sits are also of importance. The way the apartment buildings tower over the Lomans' little house shows visually that they have been left behind in the new economy. In the second paragraph of the opening stage directions "we see a solid vault of apartment houses around the small, fragile-seeming home." The Lomans are "hemmed in" by progress, in a sense. But it doesn't feel like progress to them; it dominates them and does not include them. Their small house is described as having "towering, angular shapes behind it, surrounding it on all sides."

Historical Setting

In addition to physical surroundings, **time** can be an important element of the work. This may involve **historical setting**, an important aspect of both *Othello* and *Fences*, for instance. Setting may also involve time in terms of the characters' personal **past, present, and future settings**. This aspect is extremely important in *Death of a Salesman* because the main character, Willy Loman, lives simultaneously in the past and the present and often mistakes memories or fantasies of the past for present reality.

Social Setting

In drama, as in fiction, the **social setting** (or social environment) may play a key role. Willy is an individual, but he also represents a typical experience within his historical time, as well as a universal human experience. Class differences are represented here too—for example, in the office scene between Willy and his boss, Howard, early in Act II. In the same scene, age differences (Willy is 63, Howard is 36) illuminate some of the social problems of aging in the workplace. Society's advances in technology are a factor (and are an aspect of both social and historical setting), since some members of society have access to them (Howard has a tape recorder—a new innovation at that time) and some do not (Willy fears the strange new device). The social setting is also the commercial environment of New York City and the northeastern United States, and it is also twentieth-century American society and the expectations and pressures of the so-called American dream (see Miller's essay "Tragedy and the Common Man" in the Talking Lit section).

Staging—Realistic and Fantastic

Although *Death of a Salesman* is an example of a modern play and modern social realism (as defined in Chapter 26), Miller has employed some **staging** techniques involving the use of fantasy and nonrealistic elements in order to depict his story. The use of both the real and the non-real helps Miller show vividly the confused interplay of past and present in Willy's mind. Some of the transitions to the past are complete, depicting how the character Willy in a sense "lives in the past." An example early in Act I (and a strategy which recurs again and again) is the transition from the present time (in Biff and Happy's bedroom) to the past (outside, with the younger Biff and Happy), accomplished with the following stage direction:

> (*Their light is out. Well before they have finished speaking, Willy's form is dimly seen below in the darkened kitchen. He opens the refrigerator, searches in there, and takes out a bottle of milk. The apartment houses are fading out, and the entire house and surroundings become covered with leaves. Music insinuates itself as the leaves appear.*)

At other times, the transition takes longer and past and present mingle for a time, as in the scene somewhat later in Act I in which Willy and Charley are playing cards in the present time, when Willy's brother Ben (a figure from the past whose characterization may also be part fantasy) enters.

> CHARLEY: Don't call me disgusting, Willy. (*Uncle Ben, carrying a valise and an umbrella, enters the forestage from around the right corner of the house. He is a stolid man, in his sixties, with a mustache and an authoritative air. He is utterly certain of his destiny, and there is an aura of far places about him. He enters exactly as Willy speaks.*)
> WILLY: I'm getting awfully tired, Ben. (*Ben's music is heard. Ben looks around at everything.*)

In this scene, the past and present mingle for several pages before we slip completely into the past. This staging strategy helps Miller show the extent of Willy's confusion of past and present, as he is talking aloud both to Charley (who is there with him) and to Ben (who is not there, and whom Charley cannot see). In a sense, through this technique, the inside of Willy's head is depicted on the stage. Sometimes, as with the characterization of Ben, the audience is uncertain of the line between reality and fantasy. This kind of uncertainty is introduced, in fact, in the second paragraph of the opening stage direction: "An air of the dream clings to the place, a dream rising out of reality."

Reading

Arthur Miller (1915–2005)

Arthur Miller

Arthur Miller was born in New York City to middle-class Jewish parents. His father, a clothing manufacturer, experienced a decline in his business, and the family had to move from Manhattan to a more modest home in Brooklyn. In 1938 Miller earned his B.A. from the University of Michigan, where he had begun writing plays and had won several prizes in drama. Six years later, he had his first Broadway production, *The Man Who Had All the Luck* (1947), although it closed after only a few performances. His second play on Broadway, *All My Sons* (1947), however, was both a critical and commercial success and launched his career. His next play, reprinted here, *Death of a Salesman* (1949), was awarded the Pulitzer Prize and confirmed Miller as an American playwright of international stature. Many other successful plays followed, including *The Crucible* (1953), a play about the Salem witch trials, which was also a response to the activities of the House Un-American Activities Committee during the McCarthy era. Miller was one of many writers, artists, and intellectuals who were questioned by Joseph McCarthy's committee about their association with Communists during the period known as the Red Scare. During this same period in his life, he was married (1956–61) to the actress Marilyn Monroe.

Death of a Salesman
Certain Private Conversations in Two Acts and a Requiem

CHARACTERS

WILLY LOMAN
LINDA, *his wife*

CHARLEY, *a neighbor*
BERNARD, *Charley's son*

BIFF ⎱ *his sons*
HAPPY ⎰

UNCLE BEN, *his older brother*

HOWARD WAGNER, *his employer*

THE WOMAN

JENNY, *Charley's secretary*

STANLEY, *a waiter*

MISS FORSYTHE ⎱ *young women*
LETTA ⎰

The action takes place in Willy Loman's house and yard and in various places he visits in the New York and Boston of today.

ACT 1

A melody is heard, played upon a flute. It is small and fine, telling of grass and trees and the horizon. The curtain rises.

Before us is the Salesman's house. We are aware of towering, angular shapes behind it, surrounding it on all sides. Only the blue light of the sky falls upon the house and forestage; the surrounding area shows an angry glow of orange. As more light appears, we see a solid vault of apartment houses around the small, fragile-seeming home. An air of the dream clings to the place, a dream rising out of reality. The kitchen at center seems actual enough, for there is a kitchen table with three chairs, and a refrigerator. But no other fixtures are seen. At the back of the kitchen there is a draped entrance, which leads to the living-room. To the right of the kitchen, on a level raised two feet, is a bedroom furnished only with a brass bedstead and a straight chair. On a shelf over the bed a silver athletic trophy stands. A window opens onto the apartment house at the side.

Behind the kitchen, on a level raised six and a half feet, is the boys' bedroom, at present barely visible. Two beds are dimly seen, and at the back of the room a dormer window. (This bedroom is above the unseen living-room.) At the left a stairway curves up to it from the kitchen.

The entire setting is wholly, or, in some places, partially transparent. The roofline of the house is one-dimensional; under and over it we see the apartment buildings. Before the house lies an apron, curving beyond the forestage into the orchestra. This forward area serves as the back yard as well as the locale of all WILLY'S

imaginings and of his city scenes. Whenever the action is in the present the actors observe the imaginary wall-lines, entering the house only through its door at the left. But in the scenes of the past these boundaries are broken, and characters enter or leave a room by stepping "through" a wall onto the forestage.

From the right, WILLY LOMAN, the Salesman, enters, carrying two large sample cases. The flute plays on. He hears but is not aware of it. He is past sixty years of age, dressed quietly. Even as he crosses the stage to the doorway of the house, his exhaustion is apparent. He unlocks the door, comes into the kitchen, and thankfully lets his burden down, feeling the soreness of his palms. A word-sigh escapes his lips—it might be "Oh, boy, oh, boy." He closes the door, then carries his cases out into the living-room, through the draped kitchen doorway.

LINDA, his wife, has stirred in her bed at the right. She gets out and puts on a robe, listening. Most often jovial, she has developed an iron repression of her exceptions to WILLY'S behavior—she more than loves him, she admires him, as though his mercurial nature, his temper, his massive dreams and little cruelties, served her only as sharp reminders of the turbulent longings within him, longings which she shares but lacks the temperament to utter and follow to their end.

LINDA (*hearing* WILLY *outside the bedroom, calls with some trepidation*). Willy!

WILLY.   It's all right. I came back.

LINDA.   Why? What happened? (*Slight pause.*) Did something happen, Willy?

WILLY.   No, nothing happened.

5 LINDA.   You didn't smash the car, did you?

WILLY (*with casual irritation*).   I said nothing happened. Didn't you hear me?

LINDA.   Don't you feel well?

WILLY.   I'm tired to the death. (*The flute has faded away. He sits on the bed beside her, a little numb.*) I couldn't make it. I just couldn't make it, Linda.

LINDA (*very carefully, delicately*).   Where were you all day? You look terrible.

10 WILLY.   I got as far as a little above Yonkers. I stopped for a cup of coffee. Maybe it was the coffee.

LINDA.   What?

WILLY (*after a pause*).   I suddenly couldn't drive any more. The car kept going off onto the shoulder, y'know?

LINDA (*helpfully*).   Oh. Maybe it was the steering again. I don't think Angelo knows the Studebaker.

WILLY.   No, it's me, it's me. Suddenly I realize I'm goin' sixty miles an hour and I don't remember the last five minutes. I'm—I can't seem to—keep my mind to it.

15 LINDA.   Maybe it's your glasses. You never went for your new glasses.

WILLY.   No, I see everything. I came back ten miles an hour. It took me nearly four hours from Yonkers.

LINDA (*resigned*).   Well, you'll just have to take a rest, Willy, you can't continue this way.

WILLY.   I just got back from Florida.

LINDA.   But you didn't rest your mind. Your mind is overactive, and the mind is what counts, dear.

20 WILLY.   I'll start out in the morning. Maybe I'll feel better in the morning. (*She is taking off his shoes.*) These goddam arch supports are killing me.

LINDA.   Take an aspirin. Should I get you an aspirin? It'll soothe you.

WILLY (*with wonder*).   I was driving along, you understand? And I was fine. I was even observing the scenery. You can imagine, me looking at scenery, on the road every week of my life. But it's so beautiful up there, Linda, the trees are so thick, and the sun is warm. I opened the windshield and just let the warm air bathe over me. And then all of a sudden I'm goin' off the road! I'm tellin' ya, I absolutely forgot I was driving. If I'd've gone the other way over the white line I might've killed somebody. So I went on again—and five minutes later I'm dreamin' again, and I nearly—(*He presses two fingers against his eyes.*) I have such thoughts, I have such strange thoughts.

LINDA.   Willy, dear. Talk to them again. There's no reason why you can't work in New York.

WILLY.   They don't need me in New York. I'm the New England man. I'm vital in New England.

LINDA.   But you're sixty years old. They   25 can't expect you to keep traveling every week.

WILLY.   I'll have to send a wire to Portland. I'm supposed to see Brown and Morrison tomorrow morning at ten o'clock to show the line. Goddammit, I could sell them! (*He starts putting on his jacket.*)

LINDA (*taking the jacket from him*).   Why don't you go down to the place tomorrow and tell Howard you've simply got to work in New York? You're too accommodating, dear.

WILLY.   If old man Wagner was alive I'd a been in charge of New York now! That man was a prince, he was a masterful man. But that boy of his, that Howard, he don't appreciate. When I went north the first time, the Wagner Company didn't know where New England was!

LINDA.   Why don't you tell those things to Howard, dear?

30 WILLY (*encouraged*).   I will, I definitely will.
     Is there any cheese?
 LINDA.   I'll make you a sandwich.
 WILLY.   No, go to sleep. I'll take some milk.
     I'll be up right away. The boys in?
 LINDA.   They're sleeping. Happy took Biff
     on a date tonight.
 WILLY (*interested*).   That so?
35 LINDA.   It was so nice to see them shaving
     together, one behind the other, in the
     bathroom. And going out together. You
     notice? The whole house smells of
     shaving lotion.
 WILLY.   Figure it out. Work a lifetime to
     pay off a house. You finally own it, and
     there's nobody to live in it.
 LINDA.   Well, dear, life is a casting off. It's
     always that way.
 WILLY.   No, no, some people—some
     people accomplish something. Did Biff
     say anything after I went this morning?
 LINDA.   You shouldn't have criticized him,
     Willy, especially after he just got off the
     train. You mustn't lose your temper with
     him.
40 WILLY.   When the hell did I lose my
     temper? I simply asked him if he was
     making any money. Is that a criticism?
 LINDA.   But, dear, how could he make any
     money?
 WILLY (*worried and angered*).   There's such
     an undercurrent in him. He became a
     moody man. Did he apologize when I left
     this morning?
 LINDA.   He was crestfallen, Willy. You
     know how he admires you. I think if he
     finds himself, then you'll both be happier
     and not fight any more.
 WILLY.   How can he find himself on a farm?
     Is that a life? A farmhand? In the
     beginning, when he was young, I thought,
     well, a young man, it's good for him to
     tramp around, take a lot of different jobs.
     But it's more than ten years now and he
     has yet to make thirty-five dollars a week!

 LINDA.   He's finding himself, Willy.   45
 WILLY.   Not finding yourself at the age of
     thirty-four is a disgrace!
 LINDA.   Shh!
 WILLY.   The trouble is he's lazy,
     goddammit!
 LINDA.   Willy, please!
 WILLY.   Biff is a lazy bum!   50
 LINDA.   They're sleeping. Get something to
     eat. Go on down.
 WILLY.   Why did he come home? I would
     like to know what brought him home.
 LINDA.   I don't know. I think he's still lost,
     Willy. I think he's very lost.
 WILLY.   Biff Loman is lost. In the greatest
     country in the world a young man with
     such—personal attractiveness, gets lost.
     And such a hard worker. There's one
     thing about Biff—he's not lazy.
 LINDA.   Never.   55
 WILLY (*with pity and resolve*).   I'll see him in
     the morning; I'll have a nice talk with
     him. I'll get him a job selling. He could
     be big in no time. My God! Remember
     how they used to follow him around in
     high school? When he smiled at one of
     them their faces lit up. When he walked
     down the street . . . (*He loses himself in
     reminiscences.*)
 LINDA (*trying to bring him out of it*).   Willy,
     dear, I got a new kind of American-type
     cheese today. It's whipped.
 WILLY.   Why do you get American when I
     like Swiss?
 LINDA.   I just thought you'd like a
     change—
 WILLY.   I don't want change! I want Swiss   60
     cheese. Why am I always being
     contradicted?
 LINDA (*with a covering laugh*).   I thought it
     would be a surprise.
 WILLY.   Why don't you open a window in
     here, for God's sake?
 LINDA (*with infinite patience*).   They're all
     open, dear.

WILLY. The way they boxed us in here. Bricks and windows, windows and bricks.

65 LINDA. We should've bought the land next door.

WILLY. The street is lined with cars. There's not a breath of fresh air in the neighborhood. The grass don't grow any more, you can't raise a carrot in the back yard. They should've had a law against apartment houses. Remember those two beautiful elm trees out there? When I and Biff hung the swing between them?

LINDA. Yeah, like being a million miles from the city.

WILLY. They should've arrested the builder for cutting those down. They massacred the neighborhood. (*Lost*) More and more I think of those days, Linda. This time of year it was lilac and wisteria. And then the peonies would come out, and the daffodils. What fragrance in this room!

LINDA. Well, after all, people had to move somewhere.

70 WILLY. No, there's more people now.

LINDA. I don't think there's more people. I think—

WILLY. There's more people! That's what's ruining this country! Population is getting out of control. The competition is maddening! Smell the stink from that apartment house! And another one on the other side . . . How can they whip cheese?

(*On* WILLY'S *last line,* BIFF *and* HAPPY *raise themselves up in their beds, listening.*)

LINDA. Go down, try it. And be quiet.

WILLY (*turning to* LINDA, *guiltily*). You're not worried about me, are you, sweetheart?

75 BIFF. What's the matter?

HAPPY. Listen!

LINDA. You've got too much on the ball to worry about.

WILLY. You're my foundation and my support, Linda.

LINDA. Just try to relax, dear. You make mountains out of molehills.

WILLY. I won't fight with him any more. If 80 he wants to go back to Texas, let him go.

LINDA. He'll find his way.

WILLY. Sure. Certain men just don't get started till later in life. Like Thomas Edison, I think. Or B. F. Goodrich. One of them was deaf. (*He starts for the bedroom doorway.*) I'll put my money on Biff.

LINDA. And Willy—if it's warm Sunday we'll drive in the country. And we'll open the windshield, and take lunch.

WILLY. No, the windshields don't open on the new cars.

LINDA. But you opened it today. 85

WILLY. Me? I didn't. (*He stops.*) Now isn't that peculiar! Isn't that a remarkable— (*He breaks off in amazement and fright as the flute is heard distantly.*)

LINDA. What, darling?

WILLY. That is the most remarkable thing.

LINDA. What, dear?

WILLY. I was thinking of the Chevvy. 90 (*Slight pause.*) Nineteen twenty-eight . . . when I had that red Chevvy—(*Breaks off.*) That's funny! I coulda sworn I was driving that Chevvy today.

LINDA. Well, that's nothing. Something must've reminded you.

WILLY. Remarkable. Ts. Remember those days? The way Biff used to simonize that car? The dealer refused to believe there was eighty thousand miles on it. (*He shakes his head.*) Heh! (*To* LINDA) Close your eyes, I'll be right up. (*He walks out of the bedroom.*)

HAPPY (*to* BIFF). Jesus, maybe he smashed up the car again!

LINDA (*calling after* WILLY). Be careful on the stairs, dear! The cheese is on the middle shelf! (*She turns, goes over to the bed, takes his jacket, and goes out of the bedroom.*)

(*Light has risen on the boys' room. Unseen,* WILLY *is heard talking to himself,* "Eighty thousand miles," *and a little laugh.* BIFF *gets out of bed, comes downstage a bit, and stands attentively.* BIFF *is two years older than his brother* HAPPY, *well built, but in these days bears a worn air and seems less self-assured. He has succeeded less, and his dreams are stronger and less acceptable than* HAPPY'S. HAPPY *is tall, powerfully made. Sexuality is like a visible color on him, or a scent that many women have discovered. He, like his brother, is lost, but in a different way, for he has never allowed himself to turn his face toward defeat and is thus more confused and hard-skinned, although seemingly more content.*)

95 HAPPY (*getting out of bed*).   He's going to get his license taken away if he keeps that up. I'm getting nervous about him, y'know, Biff?

BIFF.   His eyes are going.

HAPPY.   No, I've driven with him. He sees all right. He just doesn't keep his mind on it. I drove into the city with him last week. He stops at a green light and then it turns red and he goes. (*He laughs.*)

BIFF.   Maybe he's color-blind.

HAPPY.   Pop? Why he's got the finest eye for color in the business. You know that.

100 BIFF (*sitting down on his bed*).   I'm going to sleep.

HAPPY.   You're not still sour on Dad, are you, Biff?

BIFF.   He's all right, I guess.

WILLY (*underneath them, in the living-room*).   Yes, sir, eighty thousand miles—eighty-two thousand!

BIFF.   You smoking?

105 HAPPY (*holding out a pack of cigarettes*).   Want one?

BIFF (*taking a cigarette*).   I can never sleep when I smell it.

WILLY.   What a simonizing job, heh!

HAPPY (*with deep sentiment*).   Funny, Biff, y'know? Us sleeping in here again? The old beds. (*He pats his bed affectionately.*) All the talk that went across those two beds, huh? Our whole lives.

BIFF.   Yeah. Lotta dreams and plans.

HAPPY (*with a deep and masculine laugh*).   110 About five hundred women would like to know what was said in this room. (*They share a soft laugh.*)

BIFF.   Remember that big Betsy something—what the hell was her name—over on Bushwick Avenue?

HAPPY (*combing his hair*).   With the collie dog!

BIFF.   That's the one. I got you in there, remember?

HAPPY.   Yeah, that was my first time—I think. Boy, there was a pig! (*They laugh, almost crudely.*) You taught me everything I know about women. Don't forget that.

BIFF.   I bet you forgot how bashful you   115 used to be. Especially with girls.

HAPPY.   Oh, I still am, Biff.

BIFF.   Oh, go on.

HAPPY.   I just control it, that's all. I think I got less bashful and you got more so. What happened, Biff? Where's the old humor, the old confidence? (*He shakes* BIFF'S *knee.* BIFF *gets up and moves restlessly about the room.*) What's the matter?

BIFF.   Why does Dad mock me all the time?

HAPPY.   He's not mocking you, he—   120

BIFF.   Everything I say there's a twist of mockery on his face. I can't get near him.

HAPPY.   He just wants you to make good, that's all. I wanted to talk to you about Dad for a long time, Biff. Something's—happening to him. He—talks to himself.

BIFF.   I noticed that this morning. But he always mumbled.

HAPPY.   But not so noticeable. It got so embarrassing I sent him to Florida. And you know something? Most of the time he's talking to you.

125   BIFF.   What's he say about me?

HAPPY.   I can't make it out.

BIFF.   What's he say about me?

HAPPY.   I think the fact that you're not settled, that you're still kind of up in the air . . .

BIFF.   There's one or two other things depressing him, Happy.

130   HAPPY.   What do you mean?

BIFF.   Never mind. Just don't lay it all to me.

HAPPY.   But I think if you just got started—I mean—is there any future for you out there?

BIFF.   I'll tell ya, Hap, I don't know what the future is. I don't know—what I'm supposed to want.

HAPPY.   What do you mean?

135   BIFF.   Well, I spent six or seven years after high school trying to work myself up. Shipping clerk, salesman, business of one kind or another. And it's a measly manner of existence. To get on that subway on the hot mornings in summer. To devote your whole life to keeping stock, or making phone calls, or selling or buying. To suffer fifty weeks of the year for the sake of a two-week vacation, when all you really desire is to be outdoors, with your shirt off. And always to have to get ahead of the next fella. And still—that's how you build a future.

HAPPY.   Well, you really enjoy it on a farm? Are you content out there?

BIFF (*with rising agitation*).   Hap, I've had twenty or thirty different kinds of jobs since I left home before the war, and it always turns out the same. I just realized it lately. In Nebraska when I herded cattle, and the Dakotas, and Arizona, and now in Texas. It's why I came home now, I guess, because I realized it. This farm I work on, it's spring there now, see? And they've got about fifteen new colts. There's nothing more inspiring or—beautiful than the sight of a mare and a new colt. And it's cool there now, see? Texas is cool now, and it's spring. And whenever spring comes to where I am, I suddenly get the feeling, my God, I'm not gettin' anywhere! What the hell am I doing, playing around with horses, twenty-eight dollars a week! I'm thirty-four years old, I oughta be makin' my future. That's when I come running home. And now, I get here, and I don't know what to do with myself. (*After a pause.*) I've always made a point of not wasting my life, and everytime I come back here I know that all I've done is to waste my life.

HAPPY.   You're a poet, you know that, Biff? You're a—you're an idealist!

BIFF.   No, I'm mixed up very bad. Maybe I oughta get married. Maybe I oughta get stuck into something. Maybe that's my trouble. I'm like a boy. I'm not married, I'm not in business, I just—I'm like a boy. Are you content, Hap? You're a success, aren't you? Are you content?

HAPPY.   Hell, no!

140   BIFF.   Why? You're making money, aren't you?

HAPPY (*moving about with energy, expressiveness*).   All I can do now is wait for the merchandise manager to die. And suppose I get to be merchandise manager? He's a good friend of mine, and he just built a terrific estate on Long Island. And he lived there about two months and sold it, and now he's building another one. He can't enjoy it once it's finished. And I know that's just what I would do. I don't know what the hell I'm workin' for. Sometimes I sit in my apartment—all alone. And I think of the rent I'm paying. And it's crazy. But then, it's what I always wanted. My own apartment, a car, and plenty of women. And still, goddammit, I'm lonely.

BIFF (*with enthusiasm*).   Listen, why don't you come out West with me?

HAPPY.   You and I, heh?

145   BIFF.   Sure, maybe we could buy a ranch. Raise cattle, use our muscles. Men built like we are should be working out in the open.

HAPPY (*avidly*).   The Loman Brothers, heh?

BIFF (*with vast affection*).   Sure, we'd be known all over the counties!

HAPPY (*enthralled*).   That's what I dream about, Biff. Sometimes I want to just rip my clothes off in the middle of the store and outbox that goddam merchandise manager. I mean I can outbox him, outrun, and outlift anybody in that store, and I have to take orders from those common, petty sons-of-bitches till I can't stand it any more.

BIFF.   I'm tellin' you, kid, if you were with me I'd be happy out there.

150   HAPPY (*enthused*).   See, Biff, everybody around me is so false that I'm constantly lowering my ideals . . .

BIFF.   Baby, together we'd stand up for one another, we'd have someone to trust.

HAPPY.   If I were around you—

BIFF.   Hap, the trouble is we weren't brought up to grub for money. I don't know how to do it.

HAPPY.   Neither can I!

155   BIFF.   Then let's go!

HAPPY.   The only thing is—what can you make out there?

BIFF.   But look at your friend. Builds an estate and then hasn't the peace of mind to live in it.

HAPPY.   Yeah, but when he walks into the store the waves part in front of him. That's fifty-two thousand dollars a year coming through the revolving door, and I got more in my pinky finger than he's got in his head.

BIFF.   Yeah, but you just said—

HAPPY.   I gotta show some of those pompous, self-important executives over there that Hap Loman can make the grade. I want to walk into the store the way he walks in. Then I'll go with you, Biff. We'll be together yet, I swear. But take those two we had tonight. Now weren't they gorgeous creatures?   160

BIFF.   Yeah, yeah, most gorgeous I've had in years.

HAPPY.   I get that any time I want, Biff. Whenever I feel disgusted. The only trouble is, it gets like bowling or something. I just keep knockin' them over and it doesn't mean anything. You still run around a lot?

BIFF.   Naa. I'd like to find a girl—steady, somebody with substance.

HAPPY.   That's what I long for.

BIFF.   Go on! You'd never come home.   165

HAPPY.   I would! Somebody with character, with resistance! Like Mom, y'know? You're gonna call me a bastard when I tell you this. That girl Charlotte I was with tonight is engaged to be married in five weeks. (*He tries on his new hat.*)

BIFF.   No kiddin'!

HAPPY.   Sure, the guy's in line for the vice-presidency of the store. I don't know what gets into me, maybe I just have an overdeveloped sense of competition or something, but I went and ruined her, and furthermore I can't get rid of her. And he's the third executive I've done that to. Isn't that a crummy characteristic? And to top it all, I go to their weddings! (*Indignantly, but laughing*) Like I'm not supposed to take bribes. Manufacturers offer me a hundred-dollar bill now and then to throw an order their way. You know how honest I am, but it's like this girl, see. I hate myself for it. Because I don't want the girl, and, still, I take it and—I love it!

BIFF.   Let's go to sleep.

170 HAPPY.   I guess we didn't settle anything, heh?

BIFF.   I just got one idea that I think I'm going to try.

HAPPY.   What's that?

BIFF.   Remember Bill Oliver?

HAPPY.   Sure, Oliver is very big now. You want to work for him again?

175 BIFF.   No, but when I quit he said something to me. He put his arm on my shoulder, and he said, "Biff, if you ever need anything, come to me."

HAPPY.   I remember that. That sounds good.

BIFF.   I think I'll go to see him. If I could get ten thousand or even seven or eight thousand dollars I could buy a beautiful ranch.

HAPPY.   I bet he'd back you. 'Cause he thought highly of you, Biff. I mean, they all do. You're well liked, Biff. That's why I say to come back here, and we both have the apartment. And I'm tellin' you, Biff, any babe you want . . .

BIFF.   No, with a ranch I could do the work I like and still be something. I just wonder though. I wonder if Oliver still thinks I stole that carton of basketballs.

180 HAPPY.   Oh, he probably forgot that long ago. It's almost ten years. You're too sensitive. Anyway, he didn't really fire you.

BIFF.   Well, I think he was going to. I think that's why I quit. I was never sure whether he knew or not. I know he thought the world of me, though. I was the only one he'd let lock up the place.

WILLY (*below*).   You gonna wash the engine, Biff?

HAPPY.   Shh! (BIFF *looks at* HAPPY, *who is gazing down, listening.* WILLY *is mumbling in the parlor.*) You hear that? (*They listen.* WILLY *laughs warmly.*)

BIFF (*growing angry*).   Doesn't he know Mom can hear that?

185 WILLY.   Don't get your sweater dirty, Biff! (*A look of pain crosses* BIFF'S *face.*)

HAPPY.   Isn't that terrible? Don't leave again, will you? You'll find a job here. You gotta stick around. I don't know what to do about him, it's getting embarrassing.

WILLY.   What a simonizing job!

BIFF.   Mom's hearing that!

WILLY.   No kiddin', Biff, you got a date? Wonderful!

190 HAPPY.   Go on to sleep. But talk to him in the morning, will you?

BIFF (*reluctantly getting into bed*).   With her in the house. Brother!

HAPPY (*getting into bed*).   I wish you'd have a good talk with him. (*The light on their room begins to fade.*)

BIFF (*to himself in bed*).   That selfish, stupid . . .

HAPPY.   Sh . . . Sleep, Biff.

(*Their light is out. Well before they have finished speaking,* WILLY'S *form is dimly seen below in the darkened kitchen. He opens the refrigerator, searches in there, and takes out a bottle of milk. The apartment houses are fading out, and the entire house and surroundings become covered with leaves. Music insinuates itself as the leaves appear.*)

195 WILLY.   Just wanna be careful with those girls, Biff, that's all. Don't make any promises. No promises of any kind. Because a girl, y'know, they always believe what you tell 'em, and you're very young, Biff, you're too young to be talking seriously to girls. (*Light rises on the kitchen.* WILLY, *talking, shuts the refrigerator door and comes downstage to the kitchen table. He pours milk into a glass. He is totally immersed in himself, smiling faintly.*) Too young entirely, Biff. You want to watch your schooling first. Then when you're all set, there'll be plenty of girls for a boy like you. (*He smiles broadly at a kitchen chair.*) That so? The girls pay for you? (*He laughs.*) Boy, you must really be makin' a hit. (WILLY *is gradually*

*addressing—physically—a point offstage,
speaking through the wall of the kitchen, and
his voice has been rising in volume to that of
a normal conversation.*) I been wondering
why you polish the car so careful. Ha!
Don't leave the hubcaps, boys. Get the
chamois to the hubcaps. Happy, use
newspaper on the windows, it's the
easiest thing. Show him how to do it,
Biff! You see, Happy? Pad it up, use it
like a pad. That's it, that's it, good work.
You're doin' all right, Hap. (*He pauses,
then nods in approbation for a few seconds,
then looks upward.*) Biff, first thing we
gotta do when we get time is clip that big
branch over the house. Afraid it's gonna
fall in a storm and hit the roof. Tell you
what. We get a rope and sling her
around, and then we climb up there with
a couple of saws and take her down.
Soon as you finish the car, boys, I wanna
see ya. I got a surprise for you, boys.

BIFF (*offstage*).   Whatta ya got, Dad?

WILLY.   No, you finish first. Never leave a
job till you're finished—remember that.
(*Looking toward the "big trees"*) Biff, up in
Albany I saw a beautiful hammock. I
think I'll buy it next trip, and we'll hang
it right between those two elms.
Wouldn't that be something? Just
swingin' there under those branches. Boy,
that would be . . . (YOUNG BIFF *and* YOUNG
HAPPY *appear from the direction* WILLY *was
addressing.* HAPPY *carries rags and a pail of
water.* BIFF, *wearing a sweater with a block
"S," carries a football.*)

BIFF (*pointing in the direction of the car
offstage*).   How's that, Pop, professional?

WILLY.   Terrific. Terrific job, boys. Good
work, Biff.

200 HAPPY.   Where's the surprise, Pop?

WILLY.   In the back seat of the car.

HAPPY.   Boy! (*He runs off.*)

BIFF.   What is it, Dad? Tell me, what'd you
buy?

WILLY (*laughing, cuffs him*).   Never mind,
something I want you to have.

BIFF (*turns and starts off*).   What is it, Hap?   205

HAPPY (*offstage*).   It's a punching bag!

BIFF.   Oh, Pop!

WILLY.   It's got Gene Tunney's signature
on it! (HAPPY *runs onstage with a punching
bag.*)

BIFF.   Gee, how'd you know we wanted a
punching bag?

WILLY.   Well, it's the finest thing for the   210
timing.

HAPPY (*lies down on his back and pedals with his
feet*).   I'm losing weight, you notice, Pop?

WILLY (*to* HAPPY).   Jumping rope is good
too.

BIFF.   Did you see the new football I got?

WILLY (*examining the ball*).   Where'd you
get a new ball?

BIFF.   The coach told me to practice my   215
passing.

WILLY.   That so? And he gave you the ball,
heh?

BIFF.   Well, I borrowed it from the locker
room. (*He laughs confidentially.*)

WILLY (*laughing with him at the theft*).   I
want you to return that.

HAPPY.   I told you he wouldn't like it!

BIFF (*angrily*).   Well, I'm bringing it back!   220

WILLY (*stopping the incipient argument, to
HAPPY*).   Sure, he's gotta practice with a
regulation ball, doesn't he? (*To* BIFF)
Coach'll probably congratulate you on
your initiative!

BIFF.   Oh, he keeps congratulating my
initiative all the time, Pop.

WILLY.   That's because he likes you. If
somebody else took that ball there'd be
an uproar. So what's the report, boys,
what's the report?

BIFF.   Where'd you go this time, Dad? Gee,
we were lonesome for you.

WILLY (*pleased, puts an arm around each boy   225
and they come down to the apron*).
Lonesome, heh?

BIFF.   Missed you every minute.

WILLY.   Don't say? Tell you a secret, boys. Don't breathe it to a soul. Someday I'll have my own business, and I'll never have to leave home any more.

HAPPY.   Like Uncle Charley, heh?

WILLY.   Bigger than Uncle Charley! Because Charley is not—liked. He's liked, but he's not—well liked.

230 BIFF.   Where'd you go this time, Dad?

WILLY.   Well, I got on the road, and I went north to Providence. Met the Mayor.

BIFF.   The Mayor of Providence!

WILLY.   He was sitting in the hotel lobby.

BIFF.   What'd he say?

235 WILLY.   He said, "Morning!" And I said, "You got a fine city here, Mayor." And then he had coffee with me. And then I went to Waterbury. Waterbury is a fine city. Big clock city, the famous Waterbury clock. Sold a nice bill there. And then Boston—Boston is the cradle of the Revolution. A fine city. And a couple of other towns in Mass., and on to Portland and Bangor and straight home!

BIFF.   Gee, I'd love to go with you sometime, Dad.

WILLY.   Soon as summer comes.

HAPPY.   Promise?

WILLY.   You and Hap and I, and I'll show you all the towns. America is full of beautiful towns and fine, upstanding people. And they know me, boys, they know me up and down New England. The finest people. And when I bring you fellas up, there'll be open sesame for all of us, 'cause one thing, boys: I have friends. I can park my car in any street in New England, and the cops protect it like their own. This summer, heh?

240 BIFF *and* HAPPY (*together*).   Yeah! You bet!

WILLY.   We'll take our bathing suits.

HAPPY.   We'll carry your bags, Pop!

WILLY.   Oh, won't that be something! Me comin' into the Boston stores with you boys carryin' my bags. What a sensation! (BIFF *is prancing around, practicing passing the ball.*) You nervous, Biff, about the game?

BIFF.   Not if you're gonna be there.

WILLY.   What do they say about you in   245
school, now that they made you captain?

HAPPY.   There's a crowd of girls behind him everytime the classes change.

BIFF (*taking* WILLY'S *hand*).   This Saturday, Pop, this Saturday—just for you, I'm going to break through for a touchdown.

HAPPY.   You're supposed to pass.

BIFF.   I'm takin' one play for Pop. You watch me, Pop, and when I take off my helmet, that means I'm breakin' out. Then you watch me crash through that line!

WILLY (*kisses* BIFF).   Oh, wait'll I tell this in   250
Boston! (BERNARD *enters in knickers. He is younger than* BIFF, *earnest and loyal, a worried boy.*)

BERNARD.   Biff, where are you? You're supposed to study with me today.

WILLY.   Hey, looka Bernard. What're you lookin' so anemic about, Bernard?

BERNARD.   He's gotta study, Uncle Willy. He's got Regents[1] next week.

HAPPY (*tauntingly, spinning* BERNARD *around*).   Let's box, Bernard!

BERNARD.   Biff! (*He gets away from* HAPPY.)   255
Listen, Biff, I heard Mr. Birnbaum say that if you don't start studyin' math he's gonna flunk you, and you won't graduate. I heard him!

WILLY.   You better study with him, Biff. Go ahead now.

BERNARD.   I heard him!

BIFF.   Oh, Pop, you didn't see my sneakers! (*He holds up a foot for* WILLY *to look at.*)

WILLY.   Hey, that's a beautiful job of printing!

---

[1]**Regents:** a statewide proficiency examination administered in New York high schools.

260 BERNARD (*wiping his glasses*).   Just because he printed University of Virginia on his sneakers doesn't mean they've got to graduate him, Uncle Willy!

WILLY (*angrily*).   What're you talking about? With scholarships to three universities they're gonna flunk him?

BERNARD.   But I heard Mr. Birnbaum say—

WILLY.   Don't be a pest, Bernard! (*To his* BOYS) What an anemic!

BERNARD.   Okay, I'm waiting for you in my house, Biff. (BERNARD *goes off. The* LOMANS *laugh.*)

265 WILLY.   Bernard is not well liked, is he?

BIFF.   He's liked, but he's not well liked.

HAPPY.   That's right, Pop.

WILLY.   That's just what I mean. Bernard can get the best marks in school, y' understand, but when he gets out in the business world, y'understand, you are going to be five times ahead of him. That's why I thank Almighty God you're both built like Adonises. Because the man who makes an appearance in the business world, the man who creates personal interest, is the man who gets ahead. Be liked and you will never want. You take me, for instance. I never have to wait in line to see a buyer. "Willy Loman is here!" That's all they have to know, and I go right through.

BIFF.   Did you knock them dead, Pop?

270 WILLY.   Knocked 'em cold in Providence, slaughtered 'em in Boston.

HAPPY (*on his back, pedaling again*).   I'm losing weight, you notice, Pop? (LINDA *enters, as of old, a ribbon in her hair, carrying a basket of washing.*)

LINDA (*with youthful energy*).   Hello, dear!

WILLY.   Sweetheart!

LINDA.   How'd the Chevvy run?

275 WILLY.   Chevrolet, Linda, is the greatest car ever built. (*To the* BOYS) Since when do you let your mother carry wash up the stairs?

BIFF.   Grab hold there, boy!

HAPPY.   Where to, Mom?

LINDA.   Hang them up on the line. And you better go down to your friends, Biff. The cellar is full of boys. They don't know what to do with themselves.

BIFF.   Ah, when Pop comes home they can wait!

WILLY (*laughs appreciatively*).   You better go 280 down and tell them what to do, Biff.

BIFF.   I think I'll have them sweep out the furnace room.

WILLY.   Good work, Biff.

BIFF (*goes through wall-line of kitchen to doorway at back and calls down*).   Fellas! Everybody sweep out the furnace room! I'll be right down!

VOICES.   All right! Okay, Biff.

BIFF.   George and Sam and Frank, come 285 out back! We're hangin' up the wash! Come on, Hap, on the double! (*He and* HAPPY *carry out the basket.*)

LINDA.   The way they obey him!

WILLY.   Well, that's training, the training. I'm tellin' you, I was sellin' thousands and thousands, but I had to come home.

LINDA.   Oh, the whole block'll be at that game. Did you sell anything?

WILLY.   I did five hundred gross in Providence and seven hundred gross in Boston.

LINDA.   No! Wait a minute, I've got a 290 pencil. (*She pulls pencil and paper out of her apron pocket.*) That makes your commission . . . Two hundred—my God! Two hundred and twelve dollars!

WILLY.   Well, I didn't figure it yet, but . . .

LINDA.   How much did you do?

WILLY.   Well, I—I did—about a hundred and eighty gross in Providence. Well no—it came to—roughly two hundred gross on the whole trip.

LINDA (*without hesitation*).   Two hundred gross. That's . . . (*She figures.*)

295 WILLY.   The trouble was that three of the stores were half closed for inventory in Boston. Otherwise I woulda broke records.

LINDA.   Well, it makes seventy dollars and some pennies. That's very good.

WILLY.   What do we owe?

LINDA.   Well, on the first there's sixteen dollars on the refrigerator—

WILLY.   Why sixteen?

300 LINDA.   Well, the fan belt broke, so it was a dollar eighty.

WILLY.   But it's brand new.

LINDA.   Well, the man said that's the way it is. Till they work themselves in, y'know. (*They move through the wall-line into the kitchen.*)

WILLY.   I hope we didn't get stuck on that machine.

LINDA.   They got the biggest ads of any of them!

305 WILLY.   I know, it's a fine machine. What else?

LINDA.   Well, there's nine-sixty for the washing machine. And for the vacuum cleaner there's three and a half due on the fifteenth. Then the roof, you got twenty-one dollars remaining.

WILLY.   It doesn't leak, does it?

LINDA.   No, they did a wonderful job. Then you owe Frank for the carburetor.

WILLY.   I'm not going to pay that man! That goddam Chevrolet, they ought to prohibit the manufacture of that car!

310 LINDA.   Well, you owe him three and a half. And odds and ends, comes to around a hundred and twenty dollars by the fifteenth.

WILLY.   A hundred and twenty dollars! My God, if business don't pick up I don't know what I'm gonna do!

LINDA.   Well, next week you'll do better.

WILLY.   Oh, I'll knock 'em dead next week. I'll go to Hartford. I'm very well liked in Hartford. You know, the trouble is, Linda, people don't seem to take to me. (*They move onto the forestage.*)

LINDA.   Oh, don't be foolish.

WILLY.   I know it when I walk in. They seem to laugh at me.   315

LINDA.   Why? Why would they laugh at you? Don't talk that way, Willy. (WILLY *moves to the edge of the stage.* LINDA *goes into the kitchen and starts to darn stockings.*)

WILLY.   I don't know the reason for it, but they just pass me by. I'm not noticed.

LINDA.   But you're doing wonderful, dear. You're making seventy to a hundred dollars a week.

WILLY.   But I gotta be at it ten, twelve hours a day. Other men—I don't know—they do it easier. I don't know why—I can't stop myself—I talk too much. A man oughta come in with a few words. One thing about Charley. He's a man of few words, and they respect him.

LINDA.   You don't talk too much, you're just lively.   320

WILLY (*smiling*).   Well, I figure, what the hell, life is short, a couple of jokes. (*To himself*) I joke too much! (*The smile goes.*)

LINDA.   Why? You're—

WILLY.   I'm fat. I'm very—foolish to look at, Linda. I didn't tell you, but Christmas time I happened to be calling on F. H. Stewarts, and a salesman I know, as I was going in to see the buyer I heard him say something about—walrus. And I—I cracked him right across the face. I won't take that. I simply will not take that. But they do laugh at me. I know that.

LINDA.   Darling . . .

WILLY.   I gotta overcome it. I know I gotta   325
overcome it. I'm not dressing to advantage, maybe.

LINDA.   Willy, darling, you're the handsomest man in the world—

WILLY.   Oh, no, Linda.

LINDA.   To me you are. (*Slight pause.*) The handsomest. (*From the darkness is heard the laughter of a woman.* WILLY *doesn't turn to it, but it continues through* LINDA'S *lines.*) And the boys, Willy. Few men are idolized by their children the way you are. (*Music is heard as, behind a scrim to the left of the house,* THE WOMAN, *dimly seen, is dressing.*)

WILLY (*with great feeling*). You're the best there is, Linda, you're a pal, you know that? On the road—on the road I want to grab you sometimes and just kiss the life outa you.

(*The laughter is loud now, and he moves into a brightening area at the left, where* THE WOMAN *has come from behind the scrim and is standing, putting on her hat, looking into a "mirror" and laughing.*)

330 WILLY. 'Cause I get so lonely—especially when business is bad and there's nobody to talk to. I get the feeling that I'll never sell anything again, that I won't make a living for you, or a business, a business for the boys. (*He talks through* THE WOMAN'S *subsiding laughter;* THE WOMAN *primps at the "mirror."*) There's so much I want to make for—

THE WOMAN. Me? You didn't make me, Willy. I picked you.

WILLY (*pleased*). You picked me?

THE WOMAN (*who is quite proper-looking,* WILLY'S *age*). I did. I've been sitting at that desk watching all the salesmen go by, day in, day out. But you've got such a sense of humor, and we do have such a good time together, don't we?

WILLY. Sure, sure. (*He takes her in his arms.*) Why do you have to go now?

335 THE WOMAN. It's two o'clock . . .

WILLY. No, come on in! (*He pulls her.*)

THE WOMAN. . . . my sisters'll be scandalized. When'll you be back?

WILLY. Oh, two weeks about. Will you come up again?

THE WOMAN. Sure thing. You do make me laugh. It's good for me. (*She squeezes his arm, kisses him.*) And I think you're a wonderful man.

WILLY. You picked me, heh?   340

THE WOMAN. Sure. Because you're so sweet. And such a kidder.

WILLY. Well, I'll see you next time I'm in Boston.

THE WOMAN. I'll put you right through to the buyers.

WILLY (*slapping her bottom*). Right. Well, bottoms up!

THE WOMAN (*slaps him gently and laughs*).   345
You just kill me, Willy. (*He suddenly grabs her and kisses her roughly.*) You kill me. And thanks for the stockings. I love a lot of stockings. Well, good night.

WILLY. Good night. And keep your pores open!

THE WOMAN. Oh, Willy!

(THE WOMAN *bursts out laughing, and* LINDA'S *laughter blends in.* THE WOMAN *disappears into the dark. Now the area at the kitchen table brightens.* LINDA *is sitting where she was at the kitchen table, but now is mending a pair of her silk stockings.*)

LINDA. You are, Willy. The handsomest man. You've got no reason to feel that—

WILLY (*coming out of* THE WOMAN'S *dimming area and going over to* LINDA). I'll make it all up to you, Linda. I'll—

LINDA. There's nothing to make up, dear.   350
You're doing fine, better than—

WILLY (*noticing her mending*). What's that?

LINDA. Just mending my stockings. They're so expensive—

WILLY (*angrily, taking them from her*). I won't have you mending stockings in this house! Now throw them out! (LINDA *puts the stockings in her pocket.*)

BERNARD (*entering on the run*). Where is he? If he doesn't study!

WILLY (*moving to the forestage, with great   355
agitation*). You'll give him the answers!

BERNARD.   I do, but I can't on a Regents! That's a state exam! They're liable to arrest me!

WILLY.   Where is he? I'll whip him, I'll whip him!

LINDA.   And he'd better give back that football, Willy, it's not nice.

WILLY.   Biff! Where is he? Why is he taking everything?

360 LINDA.   He's too rough with the girls, Willy. All the mothers are afraid of him!

WILLY.   I'll whip him!

BERNARD.   He's driving the car without a license! (THE WOMAN'S *laugh is heard.*)

WILLY.   Shut up!

LINDA.   All the mothers—

365 WILLY.   Shut up!

BERNARD (*backing quietly away and out*).   Mr. Birnbaum says he's stuck up.

WILLY.   Get outa here!

BERNARD.   If he doesn't buckle down he'll flunk math! (*He goes off.*)

LINDA.   He's right, Willy, you've gotta—

370 WILLY (*exploding at her*).   There's nothing the matter with him! You want him to be a worm like Bernard? He's got spirit, personality . . . (*As he speaks,* LINDA, *almost in tears, exits into the living-room.* WILLY *is alone in the kitchen, wilting and staring. The leaves are gone, it is night again, and the apartment houses look down from behind.*) Loaded with it. Loaded! What is he stealing? He's giving it back, isn't he? Why is he stealing? What did I tell him? I never in my life told him anything but decent things. (HAPPY *in pajamas has come down the stairs;* WILLY *suddenly becomes aware of* HAPPY'S *presence.*)

HAPPY.   Let's go now, come on.

WILLY (*sitting down at the kitchen table*). Huh! Why did she have to wax the floors herself? Everytime she waxes the floors she keels over. She knows that!

HAPPY.   Shh! Take it easy. What brought you back tonight?

WILLY.   I got an awful scare. Nearly hit a kid in Yonkers. God! Why didn't I go to Alaska with my brother Ben that time! Ben! That man was a genius, that man was success incarnate! What a mistake! He begged me to go.

HAPPY.   Well, there's no use in—   375

WILLY.   You guys! There was a man started with the clothes on his back and ended up with diamond mines!

HAPPY.   Boy, someday I'd like to know how he did it.

WILLY.   What's the mystery? The man knew what he wanted and went out and got it! Walked into a jungle, and comes out, the age of twenty-one, and he's rich! The world is an oyster, but you don't crack it open on a mattress.

HAPPY.   Pop, I told you I'm gonna retire you for life.

WILLY.   You'll retire me for life on   380 seventy goddam dollars a week? And your women and your car and your apartment, and you'll retire me for life! Christ's sake, I couldn't get past Yonkers today! Where are you guys, where are you? The woods are burning! I can't drive a car! (CHARLEY *has appeared in the doorway. He is a large man, slow of speech, laconic, immovable. In all he says, despite what he says, there is pity, and, now, trepidation. He has a robe over pajamas, slippers on his feet. He enters the kitchen.*)

CHARLEY.   Everything all right?

HAPPY.   Yeah, Charley, everything's . . .

WILLY.   What's the matter?

CHARLEY.   I heard some noise. I thought something happened. Can't we do something about the walls? You sneeze in here, and in my house hats blow off.

HAPPY.   Let's go to bed, Dad. Come on.   385 (CHARLEY *signals to* HAPPY *to go.*)

WILLY.   You go ahead, I'm not tired at the moment.

HAPPY (*to* WILLY).   Take it easy, huh? (*He exits.*)

WILLY.   What're you doin' up?

CHARLEY (*sitting down at the kitchen table opposite* WILLY).   Couldn't sleep good. I had a heartburn.

390 WILLY.   Well, you don't know how to eat.

CHARLEY.   I eat with my mouth.

WILLY.   No, you're ignorant. You gotta know about vitamins and things like that.

CHARLEY.   Come on, let's shoot. Tire you out a little.

WILLY (*hesitantly*).   All right. You got cards?

395 CHARLEY (*taking a deck from his pocket*).   Yeah, I got them. Someplace. What is it with those vitamins?

WILLY (*dealing*).   They build up your bones. Chemistry.

CHARLEY.   Yeah, but there's no bones in a heartburn.

WILLY.   What are you talkin' about? Do you know the first thing about it?

CHARLEY.   Don't get insulted.

400 WILLY.   Don't talk about something you don't know anything about. (*They are playing. Pause.*)

CHARLEY.   What're you doin' home?

WILLY.   A little trouble with the car.

CHARLEY.   Oh. (*Pause.*) I'd like to take a trip to California.

WILLY.   Don't say.

405 CHARLEY.   You want a job?

WILLY.   I got a job, I told you that. (*After a slight pause*) What the hell are you offering me a job for?

CHARLEY.   Don't get insulted.

WILLY.   Don't insult me.

CHARLEY.   I don't see no sense in it. You don't have to go on this way.

410 WILLY.   I got a good job. (*Slight pause.*) What do you keep coming in here for?

CHARLEY.   You want me to go?

WILLY (*after a pause, withering*).   I can't understand it. He's going back to Texas again. What the hell is that?

CHARLEY.   Let him go.

WILLY.   I got nothin' to give him, Charley, I'm clean, I'm clean.

CHARLEY.   He won't starve. None a them   415 starve. Forget about him.

WILLY.   Then what have I got to remember?

CHARLEY.   You take it too hard. To hell with it. When a deposit bottle is broken you don't get your nickel back.

WILLY.   That's easy enough for you to say.

CHARLEY.   That ain't easy for me to say.

WILLY.   Did you see the ceiling I put up in   420 the living-room?

CHARLEY.   Yeah, that's a piece of work. To put up a ceiling is a mystery to me. How do you do it?

WILLY.   What's the difference?

CHARLEY.   Well, talk about it.

WILLY.   You gonna put up a ceiling?

CHARLEY.   How could I put up a ceiling?   425

WILLY.   Then what the hell are you bothering me for?

CHARLEY.   You're insulted again.

WILLY.   A man who can't handle tools is not a man. You're disgusting.

CHARLEY.   Don't call me disgusting, Willy. (UNCLE BEN, *carrying a valise and an umbrella, enters the forestage from around the right corner of the house. He is a stolid man, in his sixties, with a mustache and an authoritative air. He is utterly certain of his destiny, and there is an aura of far places about him. He enters exactly as* WILLY *speaks.*)

WILLY.   I'm getting awfully tired, Ben.   430 (BEN'S *music is heard.* BEN *looks around at everything.*)

CHARLEY.   Good, keep playing; you'll sleep better. Did you call me Ben? (BEN *looks at his watch.*)

WILLY.   That's funny. For a second there you reminded me of my brother Ben.

BEN.   I only have a few minutes. (*He strolls, inspecting the place.* WILLY *and* CHARLEY *continue playing.*)

CHARLEY.   You never heard from him again, heh? Since that time?

435 WILLY.   Didn't Linda tell you? Couple of weeks ago we got a letter from his wife in Africa. He died.

CHARLEY.   That so.

BEN (*chuckling*).   So this is Brooklyn, eh?

CHARLEY.   Maybe you're in for some of his money.

WILLY.   Naa, he had seven sons. There's just one opportunity I had with that man . . .

440 BEN.   I must make a train, William. There are several properties I'm looking at in Alaska.

WILLY.   Sure, sure! If I'd gone with him to Alaska that time, everything would've been totally different.

CHARLEY.   Go on, you'd froze to death up there.

WILLY.   What're you talking about?

BEN.   Opportunity is tremendous in Alaska, William. Surprised you're not up there.

445 WILLY.   Sure, tremendous.

CHARLEY.   Heh?

WILLY.   There was the only man I ever met who knew the answers.

CHARLEY.   Who?

BEN.   How are you all?

450 WILLY (*taking a pot, smiling*).   Fine, fine.

CHARLEY.   Pretty sharp tonight.

BEN.   Is Mother living with you?

WILLY.   No, she died a long time ago.

CHARLEY.   Who?

455 BEN.   That's too bad. Fine specimen of a lady, Mother.

WILLY (*to* CHARLEY).   Heh?

BEN.   I'd hoped to see the old girl.

CHARLEY.   Who died?

BEN.   Heard anything from Father, have you?

WILLY (*unnerved*).   What do you mean, 460 who died?

CHARLEY (*taking a pot*).   What're you talkin' about?

BEN (*looking at his watch*).   William, it's half-past eight!

WILLY (*as though to dispel his confusion he angrily stops* CHARLEY'S *hand*).   That's my build!

CHARLEY.   I put the ace—

WILLY.   If you don't know how to play the 465 game I'm not gonna throw my money away on you!

CHARLEY (*rising*).   It was my ace, for God's sake!

WILLY.   I'm through, I'm through!

BEN.   When did Mother die?

WILLY.   Long ago. Since the beginning you never knew how to play cards.

CHARLEY (*picks up the cards and goes to the 470 door*).   All right! Next time I'll bring a deck with five aces.

WILLY.   I don't play that kind of game!

CHARLEY (*turning to him*).   You ought to be ashamed of yourself!

WILLY.   Yeah?

CHARLEY.   Yeah! (*He goes out.*)

WILLY (*slamming the door after him*). 475 Ignoramus!

BEN (*as* WILLY *comes toward him through the wall-line of the kitchen*).   So you're William.

WILLY (*shaking* BEN'S *hand*).   Ben! I've been waiting for you so long! What's the answer? How did you do it?

BEN.   Oh, there's a story in that. (LINDA *enters the forestage, as of old, carrying the wash basket.*)

LINDA.   Is this Ben?

BEN (*gallantly*).   How do you do, my dear. 480

LINDA.   Where've you been all these years? Willy's always wondered why you—

WILLY (*pulling* BEN *away from her impatiently*).   Where is Dad? Didn't you follow him? How did you get started?

BEN.   Well, I don't know how much you remember.

WILLY.   Well, I was just a baby, of course, only three or four years old—

485 BEN.   Three years and eleven months.

WILLY.   What a memory, Ben!

BEN.   I have many enterprises, William, and I have never kept books.

WILLY.   I remember I was sitting under the wagon in—was it Nebraska?

BEN.   It was South Dakota, and I gave you a bunch of wild flowers.

490 WILLY.   I remember you walking away down some open road.

BEN (*laughing*).   I was going to find Father in Alaska.

WILLY.   Where is he?

BEN.   At that age I had a very faulty view of geography, William. I discovered after a few days that I was heading due south, so instead of Alaska, I ended up in Africa.

LINDA.   Africa!

495 WILLY.   The Gold Coast!

BEN.   Principally diamond mines.

LINDA.   Diamond mines!

BEN.   Yes, my dear. But I've only a few minutes—

WILLY.   No! Boys! Boys! (YOUNG BIFF *and* HAPPY *appear*.) Listen to this. This is your Uncle Ben, a great man! Tell my boys, Ben!

500 BEN.   Why, boys, when I was seventeen I walked into the jungle, and when I was twenty-one I walked out. (*He laughs.*) And by God I was rich.

WILLY (*to the* BOYS).   You see what I been talking about? The greatest things can happen!

BEN (*glancing at his watch*).   I have an appointment in Ketchikan Tuesday week.

WILLY.   No, Ben! Please tell about Dad. I want my boys to hear. I want them to know the kind of stock they spring from. All I remember is a man with a big beard, and I was in Mamma's lap, sitting around a fire, and some kind of high music.

BEN.   His flute. He played the flute.

505 WILLY.   Sure, the flute, that's right! (*New music is heard, a high, rollicking tune.*)

BEN.   Father was a very great and a very wild-hearted man. We would start in Boston, and he'd toss the whole family into the wagon, and then he'd drive the team right across the country; through Ohio and Indiana, Michigan, Illinois, and all the Western states. And we'd stop in the towns and sell the flutes that he'd made on the way. Great inventor, Father. With one gadget he made more in a week than a man like you could make in a lifetime.

WILLY.   That's just the way I'm bringing them up, Ben—rugged, well liked, all-around.

BEN.   Yeah? (*To* BIFF) Hit that, boy—hard as you can. (*He pounds his stomach.*)

BIFF.   Oh, no, sir!

510 BEN (*taking boxing stance*).   Come on, get to me! (*He laughs.*)

WILLY.   Go to it, Biff! Go ahead, show him!

BIFF.   Okay! (*He cocks his fists and starts in.*)

LINDA (*to* WILLY).   Why must he fight, dear?

BEN (*sparring with* BIFF).   Good boy! Good boy!

515 WILLY.   How's that, Ben, heh?

HAPPY.   Give him the left, Biff!

LINDA.   Why are you fighting?

BEN.   Good boy! (*Suddenly comes in, trips* BIFF, *and stands over him, the point of his umbrella poised over* BIFF'S *eye*.)

LINDA.   Look out, Biff!

520 BIFF.   Gee!

BEN (*patting* BIFF'S *knee*).   Never fight fair with a stranger, boy. You'll never get out of the jungle that way. (*Taking* LINDA'S *hand and bowing*) It was an honor and a pleasure to meet you, Linda.

LINDA (*withdrawing her hand coldly, frightened*).   Have a nice—trip.

BEN (*to* WILLY).   And good luck with your—what do you do?

WILLY.   Selling.

525 BEN.   Yes. Well . . . (*He raises his hand in farewell to all.*)

WILLY.   No, Ben, I don't want you to think . . . (*He takes* BEN'S *arm to show him.*) It's Brooklyn, I know, but we hunt too.

BEN.   Really, now.

WILLY.   Oh, sure, there's snakes and rabbits and—that's why I moved out here. Why, Biff can fell any one of these trees in no time! Boys! Go right over to where they're building the apartment house and get some sand. We're gonna rebuild the entire front stoop right now! Watch this, Ben!

BIFF.   Yes, sir! On the double, Hap!

530 HAPPY (*as he and* BIFF *run off*).   I lost weight, Pop, you notice? (CHARLEY *enters in knickers, even before the* BOYS *are gone.*)

CHARLEY.   Listen, if they steal any more from that building the watchman'll put the cops on them!

LINDA (*to* WILLY).   Don't let Biff . . . (BEN *laughs lustily.*)

WILLY.   You shoulda seen the lumber they brought home last week. At least a dozen six-by-tens worth all kinds a money.

CHARLEY.   Listen, if that watchman—

535 WILLY.   I gave them hell, understand. But I got a couple of fearless characters there.

CHARLEY.   Willy, the jails are full of fearless characters.

BEN (*clapping* WILLY *on the back, with a laugh at* CHARLEY).   And the stock exchange, friend!

WILLY (*joining in* BEN'S *laughter*).   Where are the rest of your pants?

CHARLEY.   My wife bought them.

540 WILLY.   Now all you need is a golf club and you can go upstairs and go to sleep. (*To* BEN) Great athlete! Between him and his son Bernard they can't hammer a nail!

BERNARD (*rushing in*).   The watchman's chasing Biff!

WILLY (*angrily*).   Shut up! He's not stealing anything!

LINDA (*alarmed, hurrying off left*).   Where is he? Biff, dear! (*She exits.*)

WILLY (*moving toward the left, away from* BEN).   There's nothing wrong. What's the matter with you?

BEN.   Nervy boy. Good!   545

WILLY (*laughing*).   Oh, nerves of iron, that Biff!

CHARLEY.   Don't know what it is. My New England man comes back and he's bleedin', they murdered him up there.

WILLY.   It's contacts, Charley, I got important contacts!

CHARLEY (*sarcastically*).   Glad to hear it, Willy. Come in later, we'll shoot a little casino. I'll take some of your Portland money. (*He laughs at* WILLY *and exits.*)

WILLY (*turning to* BEN).   Business is bad,   550
it's murderous. But not for me, of course.

BEN.   I'll stop by on my way back to Africa.

WILLY (*longingly*).   Can't you stay a few days? You're just what I need, Ben, because I—I have a fine position here, but I—well, Dad left when I was such a baby and I never had a chance to talk to him and I still feel—kind of temporary about myself.

BEN.   I'll be late for my train. (*They are at opposite ends of the stage.*)

WILLY.   Ben, my boys—can't we talk? They'd go into the jaws of hell for me, but I—

BEN.   William, you're being first-rate with   555
your boys. Outstanding, manly chaps!

WILLY (*hanging on to his words*).   Oh, Ben, that's good to hear! Because sometimes I'm afraid that I'm not teaching them the right kind of—Ben, how should I teach them?

BEN (*giving great weight to each word, and with a certain vicious audacity*).   William, when I walked into the jungle, I was seventeen. When I walked out I was twenty-one. And, by God, I was rich! (*He goes off into the darkness around the right corner of the house.*)

WILLY. . . . was rich! That's just the spirit I want to imbue them with! To walk into a jungle! I was right! (BEN *is gone, but* WILLY *is still speaking to him as* LINDA, *in night-gown and robe, enters the kitchen, glances around for* WILLY, *then goes to the door of the house, looks out and sees him. Comes down to his left. He looks at her.*)

LINDA.   Willy, dear? Willy?

560 WILLY.   I was right!

LINDA.   Did you have some cheese? (*He can't answer.*) It's very late, darling. Come to bed, heh?

WILLY (*looking straight up*).   Gotta break your neck to see a star in this yard.

LINDA.   You coming in?

WILLY.   Whatever happened to that diamond watch fob? Remember? When Ben came from Africa that time? Didn't he give me a watch fob with a diamond in it?

565 LINDA.   You pawned it, dear. Twelve, thirteen years ago. For Biff's radio correspondence course.

WILLY.   Gee, that was a beautiful thing. I'll take a walk.

LINDA.   But you're in your slippers.

WILLY (*starting to go around the house at the left*).   I was right! I was! (*Half to* LINDA, *as he goes, shaking his head*) What a man! There was a man worth talking to. I was right!

LINDA (*calling after* WILLY).   But in your slippers, Willy! (WILLY *is almost gone when* BIFF, *in his pajamas, comes down the stairs and enters the kitchen.*)

570 BIFF.   What is he doing out there?

LINDA.   Sh!

BIFF.   God Almighty, Mom, how long has he been doing this?

LINDA.   Don't, he'll hear you.

BIFF.   What the hell is the matter with him?

LINDA.   It'll pass by morning.   575

BIFF.   Shouldn't we do anything?

LINDA.   Oh, my dear, you should do a lot of things, but there's nothing to do, so go to sleep. (HAPPY *comes down the stairs and sits on the steps.*)

HAPPY.   I never heard him so loud, Mom.

LINDA.   Well, come around more often; you'll hear him. (*She sits down at the table and mends the lining of* WILLY'S *jacket.*)

BIFF.   Why didn't you ever write me about   580
this, Mom?

LINDA.   How would I write to you? For over three months you had no address.

BIFF.   I was on the move. But you know I thought of you all the time. You know that, don't you, pal?

LINDA.   I know, dear, I know. But he likes to have a letter. Just to know that there's still a possibility for better things.

BIFF.   He's not like this all the time, is he?

LINDA.   It's when you come home he's   585
always the worst.

BIFF.   When I come home?

LINDA.   When you write you're coming, he's all smiles, and talks about the future, and—he's just wonderful. And then the closer you seem to come, the more shaky he gets, and then, by the time you get here, he's arguing, and he seems angry at you. I think it's just that maybe he can't bring himself to—to open up to you. Why are you so hateful to each other? Why is that?

BIFF (*evasively*).   I'm not hateful, Mom.

LINDA.   But you no sooner come in the door than you're fighting!

BIFF.   I don't know why. I mean to change.   590
I'm tryin', Mom, you understand?

LINDA.   Are you home to stay now?

BIFF.   I don't know. I want to look around, see what's doin'.

LINDA. Biff, you can't look around all your life, can you?

BIFF. I just can't take hold, Mom. I can't take hold of some kind of a life.

595 LINDA. Biff, a man is not a bird to come and go with the springtime.

BIFF. Your hair . . . (*He touches her hair.*) Your hair got so gray.

LINDA. Oh, it's been gray since you were in high school. I just stopped dyeing it, that's all.

BIFF. Dye it again, will ya? I don't want my pal looking old. (*He smiles.*)

LINDA. You're such a boy! You think you can go away for a year and . . . You've got to get it into your head now that one day you'll knock on this door and there'll be strange people here—

600 BIFF. What are you talking about? You're not even sixty, Mom.

LINDA. But what about your father?

BIFF (*lamely*). Well, I meant him, too.

HAPPY. He admires Pop.

LINDA. Biff, dear, if you don't have any feeling for him, then you can't have any feeling for me.

605 BIFF. Sure I can, Mom.

LINDA. No. You can't just come to see me, because I love him. (*With a threat, but only a threat, of tears*) He's the dearest man in the world to me, and I won't have anyone making him feel unwanted and low and blue. You've got to make up your mind now, darling, there's no leeway any more. Either he's your father and you pay him that respect, or else you're not to come here. I know he's not easy to get along with—nobody knows that better than me—but . . .

WILLY (*from the left, with a laugh*). Hey, hey, Biffo!

BIFF (*starting to go out after* WILLY). What the hell is the matter with him? (HAPPY *stops him.*)

LINDA. Don't—don't go near him!

BIFF. Stop making excuses for him! He 610 always, always wiped the floor with you. Never had an ounce of respect for you.

HAPPY. He's always had respect for—

BIFF. What the hell do you know about it?

HAPPY (*surlily*). Just don't call him crazy!

BIFF. He's got no character—Charley wouldn't do this. Not in his own house— spewing out that vomit from his mind.

HAPPY. Charley never had to cope with 615 what he's got to.

BIFF. People are worse off than Willy Loman. Believe me, I've seen them.

LINDA. Then make Charley your father, Biff. You can't do that, can you? I don't say he's a great man. Willy Loman never made a lot of money. His name was never in the paper. He's not the finest character that ever lived. But he's a human being, and a terrible thing is happening to him. So attention must be paid. He's not to be allowed to fall into his grave like an old dog. Attention, attention must be finally paid to such a person. You called him crazy—

BIFF. I didn't mean—

LINDA. No, a lot of people think he's lost his—balance. But you don't have to be very smart to know what his trouble is. The man is exhausted.

HAPPY. Sure! 620

LINDA. A small man can be just as exhausted as a great man. He works for a company thirty-six years this March, opens up unheard-of territories to their trademark, and now in his old age they take his salary away.

HAPPY (*indignantly*). I didn't know that, Mom.

LINDA. You never asked, my dear! Now that you get your spending money someplace else you don't trouble your mind with him.

HAPPY. But I gave you money last—

625 LINDA.   Christmas time, fifty dollars! To fix
the hot water it cost ninety-seven fifty!
For five weeks he's been on straight
commission, like a beginner, an unknown!

BIFF.   Those ungrateful bastards!

LINDA.   Are they any worse than his sons?
When he brought them business, when
he was young, they were glad to see him.
But now his old friends, the old buyers
that loved him so and always found
some order to hand him in a pinch—
they're all dead, retired. He used to be
able to make six, seven calls a day in
Boston. Now he takes his valises out of
the car and puts them back and takes
them out again and he's exhausted.
Instead of walking he talks now. He
drives seven hundred miles, and when
he gets there no one knows him any
more, no one welcomes him. And what
goes through a man's mind, driving
seven hundred miles home without having earned a cent? Why shouldn't he talk
to himself? Why? When he has to go to
Charley and borrow fifty dollars a week
and pretend to me that it's his pay? How
long can that go on? How long? You see
what I'm sitting here and waiting for?
And you tell me he has no character? The
man who never worked a day but for
your benefit? When does he get the
medal for that? Is this his reward—to
turn around at the age of sixty-three and
find his sons, who he loved better than
his life, one a philandering bum—

HAPPY.   Mom!

LINDA.   That's all you are, my baby! (*To*
BIFF) And you! What happened to the
love you had for him? You were such
pals! How you used to talk to him on the
phone every night! How lonely he was
till he could come home to you!

630 BIFF.   All right, Mom, I'll live here in my
room, and I'll get a job. I'll keep away
from him, that's all.

LINDA.   No, Biff. You can't stay here and
fight all the time.

BIFF.   He threw me out of this house,
remember that.

LINDA.   Why did he do that? I never knew
why.

BIFF.   Because I know he's a fake and he
doesn't like anybody around who knows!

LINDA.   Why a fake? In what way? What   635
do you mean?

BIFF.   Just don't lay it all at my feet. It's
between me and him—that's all I have to
say. I'll chip in from now on. He'll settle
for half my pay check. He'll be all right.
I'm going to bed. (*He starts for the stairs.*)

LINDA.   He won't be all right.

BIFF (*turning on the stairs, furiously*).   I hate
this city and I'll stay here. Now what do
you want?

LINDA.   He's dying, Biff. (HAPPY *turns
quickly to her, shocked.*)

BIFF (*after a pause*).   Why is he dying?   640

LINDA.   He's been trying to kill himself.

BIFF (*with great horror*).   How?

LINDA.   I live from day to day.

BIFF.   What're you talking about?

LINDA.   Remember I wrote you that he   645
smashed up the car again? In February?

BIFF.   Well?

LINDA.   The insurance inspector came. He
said that they have evidence. That all
these accidents in the last year—
weren't—weren't—accidents.

HAPPY.   How can they tell that? That's a
lie.

LINDA.   It seems there's a woman . . . (*She
takes a breath as*)

⎰BIFF (*sharply but contained*).   What woman?   650
⎱LINDA (*simultaneously*). . . . and this
woman . . .

LINDA.   What?

BIFF.   Nothing. Go ahead.

LINDA.   What did you say?

BIFF.   Nothing, I just said what woman?   655

HAPPY.   What about her?

LINDA.   Well, it seems she was walking down the road and saw his car. She says that he wasn't driving fast at all, and that he didn't skid. She says he came to that little bridge, and then deliberately smashed into the railing, and it was only the shallowness of the water that saved him.

BIFF.   Oh, no, he probably just fell asleep again.

LINDA.   I don't think he fell asleep.

660 BIFF.   Why not?

LINDA.   Last month . . . (*With great difficulty*) Oh, boys, it's so hard to say a thing like this! He's just a big stupid man to you, but I tell you there's more good in him than in many other people. (*She chokes, wipes her eyes.*) I was looking for a fuse. The lights blew out, and I went down to the cellar. And behind the fuse box—it happened to fall out—was a length of rubber pipe—just short.

HAPPY.   No kidding?

LINDA.   There's a little attachment on the end of it. I knew it right away. And sure enough, on the bottom of the water heater there's a new little nipple on the gas pipe.

HAPPY (*angrily*).   That—jerk.

665 BIFF.   Did you have it taken off?

LINDA.   I'm—I'm ashamed to. How can I mention it to him? Every day I go down and take away that little rubber pipe. But, when he comes home, I put it back where it was. How can I insult him that way? I don't know what to do. I live from day to day, boys. I tell you, I know every thought in his mind. It sounds so old-fashioned and silly, but I tell you he put his whole life into you and you've turned your backs on him. (*She is bent over in the chair, weeping, her face in her hands.*) Biff, I swear to God! Biff, his life is in your hands!

HAPPY (*to* BIFF).   How do you like that damned fool!

BIFF (*kissing her*).   All right, pal, all right. It's all settled now. I've been remiss. I know that, Mom. But now I'll stay, and I swear to you, I'll apply myself. (*Kneeling in front of her, in a fever of self-reproach*) It's just—you see, Mom, I don't fit in business. Not that I won't try. I'll try, and I'll make good.

HAPPY.   Sure you will. The trouble with you in business was you never tried to please people.

BIFF.   I know, I—   670

HAPPY.   Like when you worked for Harrison's. Bob Harrison said you were tops, and then you go and do some damn fool thing like whistling whole songs in the elevator like a comedian.

BIFF (*against* HAPPY).   So what? I like to whistle sometimes.

HAPPY.   You don't raise a guy to a responsible job who whistles in the elevator!

LINDA.   Well, don't argue about it now.

HAPPY.   Like when you'd go off and swim   675 in the middle of the day instead of taking the line around.

BIFF (*his resentment rising*).   Well, don't you run off? You take off sometimes, don't you? On a nice summer day?

HAPPY.   Yeah, but I cover myself!

LINDA.   Boys!

HAPPY.   If I'm going to take a fade the boss can call any number where I'm supposed to be and they'll swear to him that I just left. I'll tell you something that I hate to say, Biff, but in the business world some of them think you're crazy.

BIFF (*angered*).   Screw the business world!   680

HAPPY.   All right, screw it! Great, but cover yourself!

LINDA.   Hap, Hap!

BIFF.   I don't care what they think! They've laughed at Dad for years, and you know why? Because we don't belong in this nuthouse of a city! We should be mixing cement on some open plain, or—or carpenters. A carpenter is allowed to whistle! (WILLY *walks in from the entrance of the house, at left.*)

WILLY.   Even your grandfather was better than a carpenter. (*Pause. They watch him.*) You never grew up. Bernard does not whistle in the elevator, I assure you.

685   BIFF (*as though to laugh* WILLY *out of it*). Yeah, but you do, Pop.

WILLY.   I never in my life whistled in an elevator! And who in the business world thinks I'm crazy?

BIFF.   I didn't mean it like that, Pop. Now don't make a whole thing out of it, will ya?

WILLY.   Go back to the West! Be a carpenter, a cowboy, enjoy yourself!

LINDA.   Willy, he was just saying—

690   WILLY.   I heard what he said!

HAPPY (*trying to quiet* WILLY).   Hey, Pop, come on now . . .

WILLY (*continuing over* HAPPY'S *line*).   They laugh at me, heh? Go to Filene's, go to the Hub, go to Slattery's, Boston. Call out the name Willy Loman and see what happens! Big shot!

BIFF.   All right, Pop.

WILLY.   Big!

695   BIFF.   All right!

WILLY.   Why do you always insult me?

BIFF.   I didn't say a word. (*To* LINDA) Did I say a word?

LINDA.   He didn't say anything, Willy.

WILLY (*going to the doorway of the living-room*).   All right, good night, good night.

700   LINDA.   Willy, dear, he just decided . . .

WILLY (*to* BIFF).   If you get tired hanging around tomorrow, paint the ceiling I put up in the living-room.

BIFF.   I'm leaving early tomorrow.

HAPPY.   He's going to see Bill Oliver, Pop.

WILLY (*interestedly*).   Oliver? For what?

705   BIFF (*with reserve, but trying, trying*).   He always said he'd stake me. I'd like to go into business, so maybe I can take him up on it.

LINDA.   Isn't that wonderful?

WILLY.   Don't interrupt. What's wonderful about it? There's fifty men in the City of New York who'd stake him. (*To* BIFF) Sporting goods?

BIFF.   I guess so. I know something about it and—

WILLY.   He knows something about it! You know sporting goods better than Spalding, for God's sake! How much is he giving you?

BIFF.   I don't know, I didn't even see him   710 yet, but—

WILLY.   Then what're you talkin' about?

BIFF (*getting angry*).   Well, all I said was I'm gonna see him, that's all!

WILLY (*turning away*).   Ah, you're counting your chickens again.

BIFF (*starting left for the stairs*).   Oh, Jesus, I'm going to sleep!

WILLY (*calling after him*).   Don't curse in   715 this house!

BIFF (*turning*).   Since when did you get so clean?

HAPPY (*trying to stop them*).   Wait a . . .

WILLY.   Don't use that language to me! I won't have it!

HAPPY (*grabbing* BIFF, *shouts*).   Wait a minute! I got an idea. I got a feasible idea. Come here, Biff, let's talk this over now, let's talk some sense here. When I was down in Florida last time, I thought of a great idea to sell sporting goods. It just came back to me. You and I, Biff—we have a line, the Loman Line. We train a couple of weeks, and put on a couple of exhibitions, see?

WILLY.   That's an idea!   720

HAPPY.   Wait! We form two basketball teams, see? Two water-polo teams. We play each other. It's a million dollars' worth of publicity. Two brothers, see? The Loman Brothers. Displays in the Royal Palms—all the hotels. And banners over the ring and the basketball court: "Loman Brothers." Baby, we could sell sporting goods!

WILLY.   That is a one-million-dollar idea!

LINDA.   Marvelous!

BIFF.   I'm in great shape as far as that's concerned.

725 HAPPY.   And the beauty of it is, Biff, it wouldn't be like a business. We'd be out playin' ball again . . .

BIFF (*enthused*).   Yeah, that's . . .

WILLY.   Million-dollar . . .

HAPPY.   And you wouldn't get fed up with it, Biff. It'd be the family again. There'd be the old honor, and comradeship, and if you wanted to go off for a swim or somethin'—well, you'd do it! Without some smart cooky gettin' up ahead of you!

WILLY.   Lick the world! You guys together could absolutely lick the civilized world.

730 BIFF.   I'll see Oliver tomorrow. Hap, if we could work that out . . .

LINDA.   Maybe things are beginning to—

WILLY (*wildly enthused, to* LINDA).   Stop interrupting! (*To* BIFF) But don't wear sport jacket and slacks when you see Oliver.

BIFF.   No, I'll—

WILLY.   A business suit, and talk as little as possible, and don't crack any jokes.

735 BIFF.   He did like me. Always liked me.

LINDA.   He loved you!

WILLY (*to* LINDA).   Will you stop! (*To* BIFF) Walk in very serious. You are not applying for a boy's job. Money is to pass. Be quiet, fine, and serious. Everybody likes a kidder, but nobody lends him money.

HAPPY.   I'll try to get some myself, Biff. I'm sure I can.

WILLY.   I see great things for you kids, I think your troubles are over. But remember, start big and you'll end big. Ask for fifteen. How much you gonna ask for?

740 BIFF.   Gee, I don't know—

WILLY.   And don't say, "Gee," "Gee" is a boy's word. A man walking in for fifteen thousand dollars does not say "Gee!"

BIFF.   Ten, I think, would be top though.

WILLY.   Don't be so modest. You always started too low. Walk in with a big laugh. Don't look worried. Start off with a couple of your good stories to lighten things up. It's not what you say, it's how you say it—because personality always wins the day.

LINDA.   Oliver always thought the highest of him—

WILLY.   Will you let me talk?

BIFF.   Don't yell at her, Pop, will ya?

WILLY (*angrily*).   I was talking, wasn't I?

BIFF.   I don't like you yelling at her all the 745 time, and I'm tellin' you, that's all.

WILLY.   What're you, takin' over this house?

LINDA.   Willy—

WILLY (*turning on her*).   Don't take his side all the time, goddammit!

BIFF (*furiously*).   Stop yelling at her! 750

WILLY (*suddenly pulling on his cheek, beaten down, guilt ridden*).   Give my best to Bill Oliver—he may remember me. (*He exits through the living-room doorway.*)

LINDA (*her voice subdued*).   What'd you have to start that for? (BIFF *turns away.*) You see how sweet he was as soon as you talked hopefully? (*She goes over to* BIFF.) Come up and say good night to him. Don't let him go to bed that way.

HAPPY.   Come on, Biff, let's buck him up.

LINDA.   Please, dear. Just say good night. It takes so little to make him happy. Come. (*She goes through the living-room doorway,* 755 *calling upstairs from within the living-room.*) Your pajamas are hanging in the bathroom, Willy!

HAPPY (*looking toward where* LINDA *went out*).   What a woman! They broke the mold when they made her. You know that, Biff?

BIFF.   He's off salary. My God, working on commission!

HAPPY.   Well, let's face it: he's no hot-shot selling man. Except that sometimes, you have to admit, he's a sweet personality.

BIFF (*decidedly*).   Lend me ten bucks, will ya? I want to buy some new ties.

HAPPY.   I'll take you to a place I know. Beautiful stuff. Wear one of my striped shirts tomorrow.

BIFF.   She got gray. Mom got awful old. Gee, I'm gonna go in to Oliver tomorrow and knock him for a—

HAPPY.   Come on up. Tell that to Dad. Let's give him a whirl. Come on.

BIFF (*steamed up*).   You know, with ten thousand bucks, boy!

HAPPY (*as they go into the living-room*). That's the talk, Biff, that's the first time I've heard the old confidence out of you! (*From within the living-room, fading off*) You're gonna live with me, kid, and any babe you want just say the word . . . (*The last lines are hardly heard. They are mounting the stairs to their parents' bedroom*).

LINDA (*entering her bedroom and addressing* WILLY, *who is in the bathroom. She is straightening the bed for him*).   Can you do anything about the shower? It drips.

WILLY (*from the bathroom*).   All of a sudden everything falls to pieces! Goddam plumbing, oughta be sued, those people. I hardly finished putting it in and the thing . . . (*His words rumble off.*)

LINDA.   I'm just wondering if Oliver will remember him. You think he might?

WILLY (*coming out of the bathroom in his pajamas*).   Remember him? What's the matter with you, you crazy? If he'd've stayed with Oliver he'd be on top by now! Wait'll Oliver gets a look at him. You don't know the average caliber any more. The average young man today—(*he is getting into bed*)—is got a caliber of zero. Greatest thing in the world for him was

to bum around. (BIFF *and* HAPPY *enter the bedroom. Slight pause.* WILLY *stops short, looking at* BIFF.) Glad to hear it, boy.

HAPPY.   He wanted to say good night to you, sport.

WILLY (*to* BIFF).   Yeah. Knock him dead, boy. What'd you want to tell me?

BIFF.   Just take it easy, Pop. Good night. (*He turns to go.*)

WILLY (*unable to resist*).   And if anything falls off the desk while you're talking to him—like a package or something—don't you pick it up. They have office boys for that.

LINDA.   I'll make a big breakfast—

WILLY.   Will you let me finish? (*To* BIFF) Tell him you were in the business in the West. Not farm work.

BIFF.   All right, Dad.

LINDA.   I think everything—

WILLY (*going right through her speech*).   And don't undersell yourself. No less than fifteen thousand dollars.

BIFF (*unable to bear him*).   Okay. Good night, Mom. (*He starts moving.*)

WILLY.   Because you got a greatness in you, Biff, remember that. You got all kinds of greatness . . . (*He lies back, exhausted.* BIFF *walks out.*)

LINDA (*calling after* BIFF).   Sleep well, darling!

HAPPY.   I'm going to get married, Mom. I wanted to tell you.

LINDA.   Go to sleep, dear.

HAPPY (*going*).   I just wanted to tell you.

WILLY.   Keep up the good work. (HAPPY *exits.*) God . . . remember that Ebbets Field game? The championship of the city?

LINDA.   Just rest. Should I sing to you?

WILLY.   Yeah. Sing to me. (LINDA *hums a soft lullaby.*) When that team came out— he was the tallest, remember?

LINDA.   Oh, yes. And in gold. (BIFF *enters the darkened kitchen, takes a cigarette, and leaves the house. He comes downstage into a golden pool of light. He smokes, staring at the night.*)

WILLY.   Like a young god. Hercules—something like that. And the sun, the sun all around him. Remember how he waved to me? Right up from the field, with the representatives of three colleges standing by? And the buyers I brought, and the cheers when he came out—Loman, Loman, Loman! God Almighty, he'll be great yet. A star like that, magnificent, can never really fade away! (*The light on* WILLY *is fading. The gas heater begins to glow through the kitchen wall, near the stairs, a blue flame beneath the red coils.*)

LINDA (*timidly*).   Willy dear, what has he got against you?

WILLY.   I'm so tired. Don't talk any more.

790   (BIFF *slowly returns to the kitchen. He stops, stares toward the heater.*)

LINDA.   Will you ask Howard to let you work in New York?

WILLY.   First thing in the morning. Everything'll be all right. (BIFF *reaches behind the heater and draws out a length of rubber tubing. He is horrified and turns his head toward* WILLY'S *room, still dimly lit, from which the strains of* LINDA'S *desperate but monotonous humming rise.* WILLY *stares through the window into the moonlight.*) Gee, look at the moon moving between the buildings! (BIFF *wraps the tubing around his hand and quickly goes up the stairs.*)

─────────(ACT 2)─────────

Music is heard, gay and bright. The curtain rises as the music fades away. WILLY, *in shirt sleeves, is sitting at the kitchen table, sipping coffee, his hat in his lap.* LINDA *is filling his cup when she can.*

WILLY.   Wonderful coffee. Meal in itself.

LINDA.   Can I make you some eggs?

WILLY.   No. Take a breath.

LINDA.   You look so rested, dear.

WILLY.   I slept like a dead one. First time in 5 months. Imagine, sleeping till ten on a Tuesday morning. Boys left nice and early, heh?

LINDA.   They were out of here by eight o'clock.

WILLY.   Good work!

LINDA.   It was so thrilling to see them leaving together. I can't get over the shaving lotion in this house!

WILLY (*smiling*).   Mmm—

LINDA.   Biff was very changed this morn- 10 ing. His whole attitude seemed to be hopeful. He couldn't wait to get downtown to see Oliver.

WILLY.   He's heading for a change. There's no question, there simply are certain men that take longer to get—solidified. How did he dress?

LINDA.   His blue suit. He's so handsome in that suit. He could be a—anything in that suit! (WILLY *gets up from the table.* LINDA *holds his jacket for him.*)

WILLY.   There's no question, no question at all. Gee, on the way home tonight I'd like to buy some seeds.

LINDA (*laughing*).   That'd be wonderful. But not enough sun gets back there. Nothing'll grow any more.

WILLY.   You wait, kid, before it's all over 15 we're gonna get a little place out in the country, and I'll raise some vegetables, a couple of chickens . . .

LINDA.   You'll do it yet, dear. (WILLY *walks out of his jacket.* LINDA *follows him.*)

WILLY.   And they'll get married, and come for a weekend. I'd build a little guest house. 'Cause I got so many fine tools, all I'd need would be a little lumber and some peace of mind.

LINDA. (*joyfully*).   I sewed the lining . . .

WILLY.   I would build two guest houses, so they'd both come. Did he decide how much he's going to ask Oliver for?

20 LINDA (*getting him into his jacket*).   He didn't mention it, but I imagine ten or fifteen thousand. You going to talk to Howard today?

WILLY.   Yeah. I'll put it to him straight and simple. He'll just have to take me off the road.

LINDA.   And, Willy, don't forget to ask for a little advance, because we've got the insurance premium. It's the grace period now.

WILLY.   That's hundred . . . ?

LINDA.   A hundred and eight, sixty-eight. Because we're a little short again.

25 WILLY.   Why are we short?

LINDA.   Well, you had the motor job on the car . . .

WILLY.   That goddam Studebaker!

LINDA.   And you got one more payment on the refrigerator . . .

WILLY.   But it just broke again!

30 LINDA.   Well, it's old, dear.

WILLY.   I told you we should've bought a well-advertised machine. Charley bought a General Electric and it's twenty years old and it's still good, that son-of-a-bitch.

LINDA.   But, Willy—

WILLY.   Whoever heard of a Hastings refrigerator? Once in my life I would like to own something outright before it's broken! I'm always in a race with the junkyard! I just finished paying for the car and it's on its last legs. The refrigerator consumes belts like a goddam maniac. They time those things. They time them so when you finally paid for them, they're used up.

LINDA (*buttoning up his jacket as he unbuttons it*).   All told, about two hundred dollars would carry us, dear. But that includes the last payment on the mortgage. After this payment, Willy, the house belongs to us.

35 WILLY.   It's twenty-five years!

LINDA.   Biff was nine years old when we bought it.

WILLY.   Well, that's a great thing. To weather a twenty-five year mortgage is—

LINDA.   It's an accomplishment.

WILLY.   All the cement, lumber, the reconstruction I put in this house! There ain't a crack to be found in it any more.

LINDA.   Well, it served its purpose.   40

WILLY.   What purpose? Some stranger'll come along, move in, and that's that. If only Biff would take this house, and raise a family . . . (*He starts to go.*) Good-by, I'm late.

LINDA (*suddenly remembering*).   Oh, I forgot! You're supposed to meet them for dinner.

WILLY.   Me?

LINDA.   At Frank's Chop House on Forty-eighth near Sixth Avenue.

WILLY.   Is that so! How about you?   45

LINDA.   No, just the three of you. They're gonna blow you to a big meal!

WILLY.   Don't say! Who thought of that?

LINDA.   Biff came to me this morning, Willy, and he said, "Tell Dad, we want to blow him to a big meal." Be there six o'clock. You and your two boys are going to have dinner.

WILLY.   Gee whiz! That's really somethin'. I'm gonna knock Howard for a loop, kid. I'll get an advance, and I'll come home with a New York job. Goddammit, now I'm gonna do it!

LINDA.   Oh, that's the spirit, Willy!   50

WILLY.   I will never get behind a wheel the rest of my life!

LINDA.   It's changing, Willy, I can feel it changing!

WILLY.   Beyond a question. G'by, I'm late. (*He starts to go again.*)

LINDA (*calling after him as she runs to the kitchen table for a handkerchief*).   You got your glasses?

WILLY (*feels for them, then comes back in*).   55 Yeah, yeah, got my glasses.

LINDA (*giving him the handkerchief*).   And a handkerchief.

WILLY.   Yeah, handkerchief.

LINDA.   And your saccharine?

WILLY.   Yeah, my saccharine.

60 LINDA.   Be careful on the subway stairs. (*She kisses him, and a silk stocking is seen hanging from her hand.* WILLY *notices it.*)

WILLY.   Will you stop mending stockings? At least while I'm in the house. It gets me nervous. I can't tell you. Please. (LINDA *hides the stocking in her hand as she follows* WILLY *across the forestage in front of the house.*)

LINDA.   Remember, Frank's Chop House.

WILLY (*passing the apron*).   Maybe beets would grow out there.

LINDA (*laughing*).   But you tried so many times.

65 WILLY.   Yeah. Well, don't work hard today. (*He disappears around the right corner of the house.*)

LINDA.   Be careful! (*As* WILLY *vanishes,* LINDA *waves to him. Suddenly the phone rings. She runs across the stage and into the kitchen and lifts it.*) Hello? Oh, Biff! I'm so glad you called, I just . . . Yes, sure, I just told him. Yes, he'll be there for dinner at six o'clock, I didn't forget. Listen, I was just dying to tell you. You know that little rubber pipe I told you about? That he connected to the gas heater? I finally decided to go down the cellar this morning and take it away and destroy it. But it's gone! Imagine? He took it away himself, it isn't there! (*She listens.*) When? Oh, then you took it. Oh—nothing, it's just that I'd hoped he'd taken it away himself. Oh, I'm not worried, darling, because this morning he left in such high spirits, it was like the old days! I'm not afraid any more. Did Mr. Oliver see you? . . . Well, you wait there then. And make a nice impression on him, darling. Just don't perspire too much before you

see him. And have a nice time with Dad. He may have big news too! . . . That's right, a New York job. And be sweet to him tonight, dear. Be loving to him. Because he's only a little boat looking for a harbor. (*She is trembling with sorrow and joy.*) Oh, that's wonderful, Biff, you'll save his life. Thanks, darling. Just put your arm around him when he comes into the restaurant. Give him a smile. That's the boy . . . Good-by, dear . . . You got your comb? . . . That's fine. Good-by, Biff dear.

(*In the middle of her speech,* HOWARD WAGNER, *thirty-six, wheels on a small type-writer table on which is a wire-recording machine and proceeds to plug it in. This is on the left forestage. Light slowly fades on* LINDA *as it rises on* HOWARD. HOWARD *is intent on threading the machine and only glances over his shoulder as* WILLY *appears.*)

WILLY.   Pst! Pst!

HOWARD.   Hello, Willy, come in.

WILLY.   Like to have a little talk with you, Howard.

HOWARD.   Sorry to keep you waiting. I'll   70 be with you in a minute.

WILLY.   What's that, Howard?

HOWARD.   Didn't you ever see one of these? Wire recorder.

WILLY.   Oh. Can we talk a minute?

HOWARD.   Records things. Just got delivery yesterday. Been driving me crazy, the most terrific machine I ever saw in my life. I was up all night with it.

WILLY.   What do you do with it?   75

HOWARD.   I bought it for dictation, but you can do anything with it. Listen to this. I had it home last night. Listen to what I picked up. The first one is my daughter. Get this. (*He flicks the switch and "Roll Out the Barrel" is heard being whistled.*) Listen to that kid whistle.

WILLY.   That is lifelike, isn't it?

HOWARD.   Seven years old. Get that tone.

WILLY. Ts, ts. Like to ask a little favor of you . . . (*The whistling breaks off, and the voice of* HOWARD's *daughter is heard.*)

80 HIS DAUGHTER. "Now you, Daddy."

HOWARD. She's crazy for me! (*Again the same song is whistled.*) That's me! Ha! (*He winks.*)

WILLY. You're very good! (*The whistling breaks off again. The machine runs silent for a moment.*)

HOWARD. Sh! Get this now, this is my son.

HIS SON. "The capital of Alabama is Montgomery; the capital of Arizona is Phoenix; the capital of Arkansas is Little Rock; the capital of California is Sacramento . . ." (*and on, and on*).

85 HOWARD (*holding up five fingers*). Five years old, Willy!

WILLY. He'll make an announcer some day!

HIS SON (*continuing*). "The capital . . ."

HOWARD. Get that—alphabetical order! (*The machine breaks off suddenly.*) Wait a minute. The maid kicked the plug out.

WILLY. It certainly is a—

90 HOWARD. Sh, for God's sake!

HIS SON. "It's nine o'clock, Bulova watch time. So I have to go to sleep."

WILLY. That really is—

HOWARD. Wait a minute! The next is my wife. (*They wait.*)

HOWARD's VOICE. "Go on, say something." (*Pause.*) "Well, you gonna talk?"

95 HIS WIFE. "I can't think of anything."

HOWARD's VOICE. "Well, talk—it's turning."

HIS WIFE (*shyly, beaten*). "Hello." (*Silence.*) "Oh, Howard, I can't talk into this . . ."

HOWARD (*snapping the machine off*). That was my wife.

WILLY. That is a wonderful machine. Can we—

100 HOWARD. I tell you, Willy, I'm gonna take my camera, and my band-saw, and all my hobbies, and out they go. This is the most fascinating relaxation I ever found.

WILLY. I think I'll get one myself.

HOWARD. Sure, they're only a hundred and a half. You can't do without it. Supposing you wanna hear Jack Benny, see? But you can't be at home at that hour. So you tell the maid to turn the radio on when Jack Benny comes on, and this automatically goes on with the radio . . .

WILLY. And when you come home you . . .

HOWARD. You can come home twelve o'clock, one o'clock, any time you like, and you get yourself a Coke and sit yourself down, throw the switch, and there's Jack Benny's program in the middle of the night!

WILLY. I'm definitely going to get one. Because lots of time I'm on the road, and I think to myself, what I must be missing on the radio!

105

HOWARD. Don't you have a radio in the car?

WILLY. Well, yeah, but who ever thinks of turning it on?

HOWARD. Say, aren't you supposed to be in Boston?

WILLY. That's what I want to talk to you about, Howard. You got a minute? (*He draws a chair in from the wing.*)

HOWARD. What happened? What're you doing here?

110

WILLY. Well . . .

HOWARD. You didn't crack up again, did you?

WILLY. Oh, no. No . . .

HOWARD. Geez, you had me worried there for a minute. What's the trouble?

WILLY. Well, tell you the truth, Howard, I've come to the decision that I'd rather not travel any more.

115

HOWARD. Not travel! Well, what'll you do?

WILLY. Remember, Christmas time, when you had the party here? You said you'd try to think of some spot for me here in town.

HOWARD.   With us?

WILLY.   Well, sure.

120 HOWARD.   Oh, yeah, yeah. I remember. Well, I couldn't think of anything for you, Willy.

WILLY.   I tell ya, Howard. The kids are all grown up, y'know. I don't need much any more. If I could take home—well, sixty-five dollars a week, I could swing it.

HOWARD.   Yeah, but Willy, see I—

WILLY.   I tell ya why, Howard. Speaking frankly and between the two of us, y'know—I'm just a little tired.

HOWARD.   Oh, I could understand that, Willy. But you're a road man, Willy, and we do a road business. We've only got a half-dozen salesmen on the floor here.

125 WILLY.   God knows, Howard, I never asked a favor of any man. But I was with the firm when your father used to carry you in here in his arms.

HOWARD.   I know that, Willy, but—

WILLY.   Your father came to me the day you were born and asked me what I thought of the name of Howard, may he rest in peace.

HOWARD.   I appreciate that, Willy, but there just is no spot here for you. If I had a spot I'd slam you right in, but I just don't have a single solitary spot. (*He looks for his lighter.* WILLY *has picked it up and gives it to him. Pause.*)

WILLY (*with increasing anger*).   Howard, all I need to set my table is fifty dollars a week.

130 HOWARD.   But where am I going to put you, kid?

WILLY.   Look, it isn't a question of whether I can sell merchandise, is it?

HOWARD.   No, but it's a business, kid, and everybody's gotta pull his own weight.

WILLY (*desperately*).   Just let me tell you a story, Howard—

HOWARD.   'Cause you gotta admit, business is business.

WILLY (*angrily*).   Business is definitely business, but just listen for a minute. You don't understand this. When I was a boy—eighteen, nineteen—I was already on the road. And there was a question in my mind as to whether selling had a future for me. Because in those days I had a yearning to go to Alaska. See, there were three gold strikes in one month in Alaska, and I felt like going out. Just for the ride, you might say.

HOWARD (*barely interested*).   Don't say.

WILLY.   Oh, yeah, my father lived many years in Alaska. He was an adventurous man. We've got quite a little streak of self-reliance in our family. I thought I'd go out with my older brother and try to locate him, and maybe settle in the North with the old man. And I was almost decided to go, when I met a salesman in the Parker House. His name was Dave Singleman. And he was eighty-four years old, and he'd drummed merchandise in thirty-one states. And old Dave, he'd go up to his room, y'understand, put on his green velvet slippers—I'll never forget—and pick up his phone and call the buyers, and without ever leaving his room, at the age of eighty-four, he made his living. And when I saw that, I realized that selling was the greatest career a man could want. 'Cause what could be more satisfying than to be able to go, at the age of eighty-four, into twenty or thirty different cities, and pick up a phone, and be remembered and loved and helped by so many different people? Do you know? When he died— and by the way he died the death of a salesman, in his green velvet slippers in the smoker of the New York, New Haven and Hartford, going into Boston—when he died, hundreds of salesmen and buyers were at his funeral. Things were sad on a lotta trains for months after that.

135

(*He stands up.* HOWARD *has not looked at him.*) In those days there was personality in it, Howard. There was respect, and comradeship, and gratitude in it. Today, it's all cut and dried, and there's no chance for bringing friendship to bear— or personality. You see what I mean? They don't know me any more.

HOWARD (*moving away, to the right*).   That's just the thing, Willy.

WILLY.   If I had forty dollars a week— that's all I'd need. Forty dollars, Howard.

140 HOWARD.   Kid, I can't take blood from a stone, I—

WILLY (*desperation is on him now*).   Howard, the year Al Smith[1] was nominated, your father came to me and—

HOWARD (*starting to go off*).   I've got to see some people, kid.

WILLY (*stopping him*).   I'm talking about your father! There were promises made across this desk! You mustn't tell me you've got people to see—I put thirty-four years into this firm, Howard, and now I can't pay my insurance! You can't eat the orange and throw the peel away—a man is not a piece of fruit! (*After a pause.*) Now pay attention. Your father—in 1928 I had a big year. I averaged a hundred and seventy dollars a week in commissions.

HOWARD (*impatiently*).   Now, Willy, you never averaged—

145 WILLY (*banging his hand on the desk*).   I averaged a hundred and seventy dollars a week in the year of 1928! And your father came to me—or rather, I was in the office here—it was right over this desk—and he put his hand on my shoulder—

HOWARD (*getting up*).   You'll have to excuse me, Willy, I gotta see some people.

Pull yourself together. (*Going out*) I'll be back in a little while. (*On* HOWARD'S *exit, the light on his chair grows very bright and strange.*)

WILLY.   Pull myself together! What the hell did I say to him? My God, I was yelling at him! How could I! (WILLY *breaks off, staring at the light, which occupies the chair, animating it. He approaches this chair, standing across the desk from it.*) Frank, Frank, don't you remember what you told me that time? How you put your hand on my shoulder, and Frank . . . (*He leans on the desk and as he speaks the dead man's name he accidentally switches on the recorder, and instantly*)

HOWARD'S SON.   ". . . of New York is Albany. The capital of Ohio is Cincinnati, the capital of Rhode Island is . . ." (*The recitation continues.*)

WILLY (*leaping away with fright, shouting*).   Ha! Howard! Howard! Howard!

HOWARD (*rushing in*).   What happened?   150

WILLY (*pointing at the machine, which continues nasally, childishly, with the capital cities*).   Shut it off! Shut it off!

HOWARD (*pulling the plug out*).   Look, Willy . . .

WILLY (*pressing his hands to his eyes*).   I gotta get myself some coffee. I'll get some coffee . . . (WILLY *starts to walk out.* HOWARD *stops him.*)

HOWARD (*rolling up the cord*).   Willy, look . . .

WILLY.   I'll go to Boston.   155

HOWARD.   Willy, you can't go to Boston for us.

WILLY.   Why can't I go?

HOWARD.   I don't want you to represent us. I've been meaning to tell you for a long time now.

WILLY.   Howard, are you firing me?

HOWARD.   I think you need a good long   160 rest, Willy.

WILLY.   Howard—

[1] **Al Smith:** Four-term governor of New York and the Democratic nominee for president in 1928 who lost to Herbert Hoover.

HOWARD.   And when you feel better, come back, and we'll see if we can work something out.

WILLY.   But I gotta earn money, Howard. I'm in no position to—

HOWARD.   Where are your sons? Why don't your sons give you a hand?

165 WILLY.   They're working on a very big deal.

HOWARD.   This is no time for false pride, Willy. You go to your sons and tell them that you're tired. You've got two great boys, haven't you?

WILLY.   Oh, no question, no question, but in the meantime . . .

HOWARD.   Then that's that, heh?

WILLY.   All right, I'll go to Boston tomorrow.

170 HOWARD.   No, no.

WILLY.   I can't throw myself on my sons. I'm not a cripple!

HOWARD.   Look, kid, I'm busy this morning.

WILLY (*grasping* HOWARD's *arm*).   Howard, you've got to let me go to Boston!

HOWARD (*hard, keeping himself under control*). I've got a line of people to see this morning. Sit down, take five minutes, and pull yourself together, and then go home, will ya? I need the office, Willy. (*He starts to go, turns, remembering the recorder, starts to push off the table holding the recorder.*) Oh, yeah. Whenever you can this week, stop by and drop off the samples. You'll feel better, Willy, and then come back and we'll talk. Pull yourself together, kid, there's people outside. (HOWARD *exits, pushing the table off left.* WILLY *stares into space, exhausted. Now the music is heard—* BEN's *music—first distantly, then closer, closer. As* WILLY *speaks,* BEN *enters from the right. He carries valise and umbrella.*)

175 WILLY.   Oh, Ben, how did you do it? What is the answer? Did you wind up the Alaska deal already?

BEN.   Doesn't take much time if you know what you're doing. Just a short business trip. Boarding ship in an hour. Wanted to say goody-by.

WILLY.   Ben, I've got to talk to you.

BEN (*glancing at his watch*).   Haven't the time, William.

WILLY (*crossing the apron to* BEN).   Ben, nothing's working out. I don't know what to do.

BEN.   Now look here, William. I've bought   180 timberland in Alaska and I need a man to look after things for me.

WILLY.   God, timberland! Me and my boys in those grand outdoors!

BEN.   You've a new continent at your doorstep, William. Get out of these cities, they're full of talk and time payments and courts of law. Screw on your fists and you can fight for a fortune up there.

WILLY.   Yes, yes! Linda, Linda! (LINDA *enters as of old, with the wash.*)

LINDA.   Oh, you're back?

BEN.   I haven't much time.   185

WILLY.   No, wait! Linda, he's got a proposition for me in Alaska.

LINDA.   But you've got—(*To* BEN) He's got a beautiful job here.

WILLY.   But in Alaska, kid, I could—

LINDA.   You're doing well enough, Willy!

BEN (*to* LINDA).   Enough for what, my   190 dear?

LINDA (*frightened of* BEN *and angry at him*). Don't say those things to him! Enough to be happy right here, right now. (*To* WILLY, *while* BEN *laughs*) Why must everybody conquer the world? You're well liked, and the boys love you, and someday—(*to* BEN)—why, old man Wagner told him just the other day that if he keeps it up he'll be a member of the firm, didn't he, Willy?

WILLY.   Sure, sure. I am building something with this firm, Ben, and if a man is building something he must be on the right track, mustn't he?

BEN.   What are you building? Lay your hand on it. Where is it?

WILLY (*hesitantly*).   That's true, Linda, there's nothing.

195 LINDA.   Why? (*To* BEN) There's a man eighty-four years old—

WILLY.   That's right, Ben, that's right. When I look at that man I say, what is there to worry about?

BEN.   Bah!

WILLY.   It's true, Ben. All he has to do is go into any city, pick up the phone, and he's making his living and you know why?

BEN (*picking up his valise*).   I've got to go.

200 WILLY (*holding* BEN *back*).   Look at this boy! (BIFF, *in his high-school sweater, enters carrying suitcase.* HAPPY *carries* BIFF'S *shoulder guards, gold helmet, and football pants.*) Without a penny to his name, three great universities are begging for him, and from there the sky's the limit, because it's not what you do, Ben. It's who you know and the smile on your face! It's contacts, Ben, contacts! The whole wealth of Alaska passes over the lunch table at the Commodore Hotel, and that's the wonder, the wonder of this country, that a man can end with diamonds here on the basis of being liked! (*He turns to* BIFF.) And that's why when you get out on that field today, it's important. Because thousands of people will be rooting for you and loving you. (*To* BEN, *who has again begun to leave*) And Ben! When he walks into a business office his name will sound out like a bell and all the doors will open to him! I've seen it, Ben, I've seen it a thousand times! You can't feel it with your hand like timber, but it's there!

BEN.   Good-by, William.

WILLY.   Ben, am I right? Don't you think I'm right? I value your advice.

BEN.   There's a new continent at your doorstep, William. You could walk out rich. Rich! (*He is gone.*)

WILLY.   We'll do it here, Ben! You hear me? We're gonna do it here! (YOUNG BERNARD *rushes in. The gay music of the* BOYS *is heard.*)

BERNARD.   Oh, gee, I was afraid you left   205 already!

WILLY.   Why? What time is it?

BERNARD.   It's half-past one!

WILLY.   Well, come on, everybody! Ebbets Field[2] next stop! Where's the pennants? (*He rushes through the wall-line of the kitchen and out into the living-room.*)

LINDA (*to* BIFF).   Did you pack fresh underwear?

BIFF (*who has been limbering up*).   I want to   210 go!

BERNARD.   Biff, I'm carrying your helmet, ain't I?

HAPPY.   No, I'm carrying the helmet.

BERNARD.   Oh, Biff, you promised me.

HAPPY.   I'm carrying the helmet.

BERNARD.   How am I going to get in the   215 locker room?

LINDA.   Let him carry the shoulder guards. (*She puts her coat and hat on in the kitchen.*)

BERNARD.   Can I, Biff? 'Cause I told everybody I'm going to be in the locker room.

HAPPY.   In Ebbets Field it's the clubhouse.

BERNARD.   I meant the clubhouse, Biff!   220

HAPPY.   Biff!

BIFF (*grandly, after a slight pause*).   Let him carry the shoulder guards.

HAPPY (*as he gives* BERNARD *the shoulder guards*).   Stay close to us now. (WILLY *rushes in with the pennants.*)

WILLY (*handing them out*).   Everybody wave when Biff comes out on the field. (HAPPY *and* BERNARD *run off.*) You set now, boy? (*The music has died away.*)

---

[2]**Ebbets Field:** A baseball stadium, the home of the Brooklyn Dodgers, torn down in 1960. Because it was used primarily for baseball, its locker rooms were called clubhouses.

BIFF.   Ready to go, Pop. Every muscle is ready.

225 WILLY (*at the edge of the apron*).   You realize what this means?

BIFF.   That's right, Pop.

WILLY (*feeling* BIFF'S *muscles*).   You're comin' home this afternoon captain of the All-Scholastic Championship Team of the City of New York.

BIFF.   I got it, Pop. And remember, pal, when I take off my helmet, that touch-down is for you.

WILLY.   Let's go! (*He is starting out, with his arms around* BIFF, *when* CHARLEY *enters, as of old, in knickers.*) I got no room for you, Charley.

230 CHARLEY.   Room? For what?

WILLY.   In the car.

CHARLEY.   You goin' for a ride? I wanted to shoot some casino.

WILLY (*furiously*).   Casino! (*Incredulously*) Don't you realize what today is?

LINDA.   Oh, he knows, Willy. He's just kid-ding you.

235 WILLY.   That's nothing to kid about!

CHARLEY.   No, Linda, what's goin' on?

LINDA.   He's playing in Ebbets Field.

CHARLEY.   Baseball in this weather?

WILLY.   Don't talk to him. Come on, come on! (*He is pushing them out.*)

240 CHARLEY.   Wait a minute, didn't you hear the news?

WILLY.   What?

CHARLEY.   Don't you listen to the radio? Ebbets Field just blew up.

WILLY.   You go to hell! (CHARLEY *laughs. Pushing them out*) Come on, come on! We're late.

CHARLEY (*as they go*).   Knock a homer, Biff, knock a homer!

245 WILLY (*the last to leave, turning to* CHARLEY).   This is the greatest day of his life.

CHARLEY.   Willy, when are you going to grow up?

WILLY.   Yeah, heh? When this game is over, Charley, you'll be laughing out the other

side of your face. They'll be calling him another Red Grange.[3] Twenty-five thousand a year.

CHARLEY (*kidding*).   Is that so?

WILLY.   Yeah, that's so.

CHARLEY.   Well, then, I'm sorry, Willy. But   250 tell me something.

WILLY.   What?

CHARLEY.   Who is Red Grange?

WILLY.   Put up your hands. Goddam you, put up your hands! (CHARLEY, *chuckling, shakes his head and walks away, around the left corner of the stage.* WILLY *follows him. The music rises to a mocking frenzy.*) Who the hell do you think you are, better than anybody else? You don't know every-thing, you big, ignorant, stupid . . . Put up your hands!

(*Light rises, on the right side of the forestage, on a small table in the reception room of* CHARLEY'S *office. Traffic sounds are heard.* BERNARD, *now mature, sits whistling to him-self. A pair of tennis rackets and an overnight bag are on the floor beside him.*)

WILLY (*offstage*).   What are you walking away for? Don't walk away! If you're going to say something say it to my face! I know you laugh at me behind my back. You'll laugh out of the other side of your goddam face after this game. Touchdown! Touchdown! Eighty thousand people! Touchdown! Right between the goal posts.

(BERNARD *is a quiet, earnest, but self-assured young man.* WILLY'S *voice is coming from right upstage now.* BERNARD *lowers his feet off the table and listens.* JENNY, *his father's secretary, enters.*)

JENNY (*distressed*).   Say, Bernard, will you   255 go out in the hall?

BERNARD.   What is that noise? Who is it?

JENNY.   Mr. Loman. He just got off the elevator.

---

[3]**Red Grange:** famous All-American running back at the University of Illinois (1923–1925).

BERNARD (*getting up*).   Who's he arguing with?

JENNY.   Nobody. There's nobody with him. I can't deal with him any more, and your father gets all upset everytime he comes. I've got a lot of typing to do, and your father's waiting to sign it. Will you see him?

260   WILLY (*entering*).   Touchdown! Touch—(*He sees* JENNY.) Jenny, Jenny, good to see you. How're ya? Workin'? Or still honest?

JENNY.   Fine. How've you been feeling?

WILLY.   Not much any more, Jenny. Ha, Ha! (*He is surprised to see the rackets.*)

BERNARD.   Hello, Uncle Willy.

WILLY (*almost shocked*).   Bernard! Well, look who's here! (*He comes quickly, guiltily, to* BERNARD *and warmly shakes his hand.*)

265   BERNARD.   How are you? Good to see you.

WILLY.   What are you doing here?

BERNARD.   Oh, just stopped by to see Pop. Get off my feet till my train leaves. I'm going to Washington in a few minutes.

WILLY.   Is he in?

BERNARD.   Yes, he's in his office with the accountant. Sit down.

270   WILLY (*sitting down*).   What're you going to do in Washington?

BERNARD.   Oh, just a case I've got there, Willy.

WILLY.   That so? (*Indicating the rackets*) You going to play tennis there?

BERNARD.   I'm staying with a friend who's got a court.

WILLY.   Don't say. His own tennis court. Must be fine people, I bet.

275   BERNARD.   They are, very nice. Dad tells me Biff's in town.

WILLY (*with a big smile*).   Yeah, Biff's in. Working on a very big deal, Bernard.

BERNARD.   What's Biff doing?

WILLY.   Well, he's been doing very big things in the West. But he decided to establish himself here. Very big. We're having dinner. Did I hear your wife had a boy?

BERNARD.   That's right. Our second.

WILLY.   Two boys! What do you know!   280

BERNARD.   What kind of deal has Biff got?

WILLY.   Well, Bill Oliver—very big sporting goods man—he wants Biff very badly. Called him in from the West. Long distance, carte blanche, special deliveries. Your friends have their own private tennis court?

BERNARD.   You still with the old firm, Willy?

WILLY (*after a pause*).   I'm—I'm overjoyed to see how you made the grade, Bernard, overjoyed. It's an encouraging thing to see a young man really—really—Looks very good for Biff—very—(*He breaks off, then*) Bernard—(*He is so full of emotion, he breaks off again.*)

BERNARD.   What is it, Willy?   285

WILLY (*small and alone*).   What—what's the secret?

BERNARD.   What secret?

WILLY.   How—how did you? Why didn't he ever catch on?

BERNARD.   I wouldn't know that, Willy.

WILLY (*confidentially, desperately*).   You were   290 his friend, his boyhood friend. There's something I don't understand about it. His life ended after that Ebbets Field game. From the age of seventeen nothing good ever happened to him.

BERNARD.   He never trained himself for anything.

WILLY.   But he did, he did. After high school he took so many correspondence courses. Radio mechanics; television; God knows what, and never made the slightest mark.

BERNARD (*taking off his glasses*).   Willy, do you want to talk candidly?

WILLY (*rising, faces* BERNARD).   I regard you as a very brilliant man, Bernard. I value your advice.

BERNARD.   Oh, the hell with the advice,   295 Willy. I couldn't advise you. There's just one thing I've always wanted to ask you.

When he was supposed to graduate, and the math teacher flunked him—

WILLY. Oh, that son-of-a-bitch ruined his life.

BERNARD. Yeah, but, Willy, all he had to do was go to summer school and make up that subject.

WILLY. That's right, that's right.

BERNARD. Did you tell him not to go to summer school?

300 WILLY. Me? I begged him to go. I ordered him to go!

BERNARD. Then why wouldn't he go?

WILLY. Why? Why! Bernard, that question has been trailing me like a ghost for the last fifteen years. He flunked the subject, and laid down and died like a hammer hit him!

BERNARD. Take it easy, kid.

WILLY. Let me talk to you—I got nobody to talk to. Bernard, Bernard, was it my fault? Y'see? It keeps going around in my mind, maybe I did something to him. I got nothing to give him.

305 BERNARD. Don't take it so hard.

WILLY. Why did he lay down? What is the story there? You were his friend!

BERNARD. Willy, I remember, it was June, and our grades came out. And he'd flunked math.

WILLY. That son-of-a-bitch!

BERNARD. No, it wasn't right then. Biff just got very angry, I remember, and he was ready to enroll in summer school.

310 WILLY (*surprised*). He was?

BERNARD. He wasn't beaten by it at all. But then, Willy, he disappeared from the block for almost a month. And I got the idea that he'd gone up to New England to see you. Did he have a talk with you then? (WILLY *stares in silence*.) Willy?

WILLY (*with a strong edge of resentment in his voice*). Yeah, he came to Boston. What about it?

BERNARD. Well, just that when he came back—I'll never forget this, it always mystifies me. Because I thought so well of Biff, even though he'd always taken advantage of me. I loved him. Willy, y'know? And he came back after that month and took his sneakers—remember those sneakers with "University of Virginia" printed on them? He was so proud of those, wore them every day. And he took them down in the cellar, and burned them up in the furnace. We had a fist fight. It lasted at least half an hour. Just the two of us, punching each other down the cellar, and crying right through it. I've often thought of how strange it was that I knew he'd given up his life. What happened in Boston, Willy? (WILLY *looks at him as at an intruder*.) I just bring it up because you asked me.

WILLY (*angrily*). Nothing. What do you mean, "What happened?" What's that got to do with anything?

315 BERNARD. Well, don't get sore.

WILLY. What are you trying to do, blame it on me? If a boy lays down is that my fault?

BERNARD. Now, Willy, don't get—

WILLY. Well, don't—don't talk to me that way! What does that mean, "What happened?" (CHARLEY *enters. He is in his vest, and he carries a bottle of bourbon*.)

CHARLEY. Hey, you're going to miss that train. (*He waves the bottle*.)

320 BERNARD. Yeah, I'm going. (*He takes the bottle*.) Thanks, Pop. (*He picks up his rackets and bag*.) Good-by, Willy, and don't worry about it. You know, "If at first you don't succeed . . ."

WILLY. Yes, I believe in that.

BERNARD. But sometimes, Willy, it's better for a man just to walk away.

WILLY. Walk away?

BERNARD. That's right.

325 WILLY. But if you can't walk away?

BERNARD (*after a slight pause*). I guess that's when it's tough. (*Extending his hand*) Good-by, Willy.

WILLY (*shaking* BERNARD'S *hand*). Good-by, boy.

CHARLEY (*an arm on* BERNARD'S *shoulder*). How do you like this kid? Gonna argue a case in front of the Supreme Court.

BERNARD (*protesting*). Pop!

330 WILLY (*genuinely shocked, pained, and happy*). No! The Supreme Court!

BERNARD. I gotta run. 'By Dad!

CHARLEY. Knock 'em dead, Bernard!
(BERNARD *goes off.*)

WILLY (*as* CHARLEY *takes out his wallet*). The Supreme Court! And he didn't even mention it!

CHARLEY (*counting out money on the desk*). He don't have to—he's gonna do it.

335 WILLY. And you never told him what to do, did you? You never took any interest in him.

CHARLEY. My salvation is that I never took any interest in anything. There's some money—fifty dollars. I got an accountant inside.

WILLY. Charley, look . . . (*With difficulty*) I got my insurance to pay. If you can manage it—I need a hundred and ten dollars. (CHARLEY *doesn't reply for a moment; merely stops moving.*) I'd draw it from my bank but Linda would know, and I . . .

CHARLEY. Sit down, Willy.

WILLY (*moving toward the chair*). I'm keeping an account of everything, remember. I'll pay every penny back. (*He sits.*)

340 CHARLEY. Now listen to me, Willy.

WILLY. I want you to know I appreciate . . .

CHARLEY (*sitting down on the table*). Willy, what're you doin'? What the hell is goin' on in your head?

WILLY. Why? I'm simply . . .

CHARLEY. I offered you a job. You can make fifty dollars a week. And I won't send you on the road.

WILLY. I've got a job.   345

CHARLEY. Without pay? What kind of a job is a job without pay? (*He rises.*) Now, look, kid, enough is enough. I'm no genius but I know when I'm being insulted.

WILLY. Insulted!

CHARLEY. Why don't you want to work for me?

WILLY. What's the matter with you? I've got a job.

CHARLEY. Then what're you walkin' in   350
here every week for?

WILLY (*getting up*). Well, if you don't want me to walk in here—

CHARLEY. I am offering you a job.

WILLY. I don't want your goddam job!

CHARLEY. When the hell are you going to grow up?

WILLY (*furiously*). You big ignoramus, if   355
you say that to me again I'll rap you one! I don't care how big you are! (*He's ready to fight. Pause.*)

CHARLEY (*kindly, going to him*). How much do you need, Willy?

WILLY. Charley, I'm strapped. I'm strapped. I don't know what to do. I was just fired.

CHARLEY. Howard fired you?

WILLY. That snotnose. Imagine that? I named him. I named him Howard.

CHARLEY. Willy, when're you gonna real-   360
ize that them things don't mean anything? You named him Howard, but you can't sell that. The only thing you got in this world is what you can sell. And the funny thing is that you're a salesman, and you don't know that.

WILLY. I've always tried to think otherwise, I guess. I always felt that if a man was impressive, and well liked, that nothing—

CHARLEY. Why must everybody like you? Who liked J. P. Morgan? Was he impressive? In a Turkish bath he'd look like a

butcher. But with his pockets on he was
very well liked. Now listen, Willy, I know
you don't like me, and nobody can say
I'm in love with you, but I'll give you a
job because—just for the hell of it, put it
that way. Now what do you say?

WILLY.   I—I just can't work for you,
Charley.

CHARLEY.   What're you, jealous of me?

365 WILLY.   I can't work for you, that's all,
don't ask me why.

CHARLEY (*angered, takes out more bills*).   You
been jealous of me all your life, you
damned fool! Here, pay your insurance.
(*He puts the money in* WILLY'S *hand.*)

WILLY.   I'm keeping strict accounts.

CHARLEY.   I've got some work to do. Take
care of yourself. And pay your insurance.

WILLY (*moving to the right*).   Funny,
y'know? After all the highways, and the
trains, and the appointments, and the
years, you end up worth more dead than
alive.

370 CHARLEY.   Willy, nobody's worth nothin'
dead. (*After a slight pause.*) Did you hear
what I said? (WILLY *stands still, dreaming.*)
Willy!

WILLY.   Apologize to Bernard for me when
you see him. I didn't mean to argue with
him. He's a fine boy. They're all fine
boys, and they'll end up big—all of them.
Someday they'll all play tennis together.
Wish me luck, Charley. He saw Bill
Oliver today.

CHARLEY.   Good luck.

WILLY (*on the verge of tears*).   Charley,
you're the only friend I got. Isn't that a
remarkable thing? (*He goes out.*)

CHARLEY.   Jesus!

(CHARLEY *stares after him a moment and follows. All light blacks out. Suddenly raucous
music is heard, and a red glow rises behind
the screen at right.* STANLEY, *a young waiter,
appears, carrying a table, followed by* HAPPY,
who is carrying two chairs.)

STANLEY (*putting the table down*).   That's all   375
right, Mr. Loman, I can handle it myself.
(*He turns and takes the chairs from* HAPPY
and places them at the table.)

HAPPY (*glancing around*).   Oh, this is better.

STANLEY.   Sure, in the front there you're in
the middle of all kinds a noise. Whenever
you got a party, Mr. Loman, you just tell
me and I'll put you back here. Y'know,
there's a lotta people they don't like it
private, because when they go out they
like to see a lotta action around them
because they're sick and tired to stay in
the house by theirself. But I know you,
you ain't from Hackensack. You know
what I mean?

HAPPY (*sitting down*).   So how's it coming,
Stanley?

STANLEY.   Ah, it's a dog's life. I only wish
during the war they'd a took me in the
Army. I coulda been dead by now.

HAPPY.   My brother's back, Stanley.   380

STANLEY.   Oh, he come back, heh? From
the Far West.

HAPPY.   Yeah, big cattle man, my brother,
so treat him right. And my father's coming too.

STANLEY.   Oh, your father too!

HAPPY.   You got a couple of nice lobsters?

STANLEY.   Hundred per cent, big.   385

HAPPY.   I want them with the claws.

STANLEY.   Don't worry, I don't give you no
mice. (HAPPY *laughs.*) How about some
wine? It'll put a head on the meal.

HAPPY.   No. You remember, Stanley, that
recipe I brought you from overseas? With
the champagne in it?

STANLEY.   Oh, yeah, sure. I still got it
tacked up yet in the kitchen. But that'll
have to cost a buck apiece anyways.

HAPPY.   That's all right.   390

STANLEY.   What'd you, hit a number or
somethin'?

HAPPY.   No, it's a little celebration. My
brother is—I think he pulled off a big

deal today. I think we're going into business together.

STANLEY. Great! That's the best for you. Because a family business, you know what I mean?—that's the best.

HAPPY. That's what I think.

395 STANLEY. 'Cause what's the difference? Somebody steals? It's in the family. Know what I mean? (*Sotto voce*) Like this bartender here. The boss is goin' crazy what kinda leak he's got in the cash register. You put it in but it don't come out.

HAPPY (*raising his head*). Sh!

STANLEY. What?

HAPPY. You notice I wasn't lookin' right or left, was I?

STANLEY. No.

400 HAPPY. And my eyes are closed.

STANLEY. So what's the—?

HAPPY. Strudel's comin'.

STANLEY (*catching on, looks around*). Ah, no, there's no—(*He breaks off as a furred, lavishly dressed girl enters and sits at the next table. Both follow her with their eyes.*) Geez, how'd ya know?

HAPPY. I got radar or something. (*Staring directly at her profile*) Oooooooo . . . Stanley.

405 STANLEY. I think that's for you, Mr. Loman.

HAPPY. Look at that mouth. Oh, God. And the binoculars.

STANLEY. Geez, you got a life, Mr. Loman.

HAPPY. Wait on her.

STANLEY (*going to the* GIRL'S *table*). Would you like a menu, ma'am?

410 GIRL. I'm expecting someone, but I'd like a—

HAPPY. Why don't you bring her—excuse me, miss, do you mind? I sell champagne, and I'd like you to try my brand. Bring her a champagne, Stanley.

GIRL. That's awfully nice of you.

HAPPY. Don't mention it. It's all company money. (*He laughs.*)

GIRL. That's a charming product to be selling, isn't it?

HAPPY. Oh, gets to be like everything else. 415 Selling is selling, y'know.

GIRL. I suppose.

HAPPY. You don't happen to sell, do you?

GIRL. No, I don't sell.

HAPPY. Would you object to a compliment from a stranger? You ought to be on a magazine cover.

GIRL (*looking at him a little archly*). I have 420 been. (STANLEY *comes in with a glass of champagne.*)

HAPPY. What'd I say before, Stanley? You see? She's a cover girl.

STANLEY. Oh, I could see, I could see.

HAPPY (*to the* GIRL). What magazine?

GIRL. Oh, a lot of them. (*She takes the drink.*) Thank you.

HAPPY. You know what they say in 425 France, don't you? "Champagne is the drink of the complexion"—Hya, Biff! (BIFF *has entered and sits with* HAPPY.)

BIFF. Hello, kid. Sorry I'm late.

HAPPY. I just got here. Uh, Miss—?

GIRL. Forsythe.

HAPPY. Miss Forsythe, this is my brother.

BIFF. Is Dad here? 430

HAPPY. His name is Biff. You might've heard of him. Great football player!

GIRL. Really? What team?

HAPPY. Are you familiar with football?

GIRL. No, I'm afraid I'm not.

HAPPY. Biff is quarterback with the New 435 York Giants.

GIRL. Well, that is nice, isn't it? (*She drinks.*)

HAPPY. Good health.

GIRL. I'm happy to meet you.

HAPPY. That's my name. Hap. It's really Harold, but at West Point they called me Happy.

GIRL (*now really impressed*). Oh, I see. How 440 do you do? (*She turns her profile.*)

BIFF. Isn't Dad coming?

HAPPY.   You want her?

BIFF.   Oh, I could never make that.

HAPPY.   I remember the time that idea would never come into your head. Where's the old confidence, Biff?

445 BIFF.   I just saw Oliver—

HAPPY.   Wait a minute. I've got to see that old confidence again. Do you want her? She's on call.

BIFF.   Oh, no. (*He turns to look at the* GIRL.)

HAPPY.   I'm telling you. Watch this. (*Turning to the* GIRL) Honey? (*She turns to him.*) Are you busy?

GIRL.   Well, I am . . . but I could make a phone call.

450 HAPPY.   Do that, will you, honey? And see if you can get a friend. We'll be here for a while. Biff is one of the greatest football players in the country.

GIRL (*standing up*).   Well, I'm certainly happy to meet you.

HAPPY.   Come back soon.

GIRL.   I'll try.

HAPPY.   Don't try, honey, try hard. (*The* GIRL *exits.* STANLEY *follows, shaking his head in bewildered admiration.*) Isn't that a shame now? A beautiful girl like that? That's why I can't get married. There's not a good woman in a thousand. New York is loaded with them, kid!

455 BIFF.   Hap, look—

HAPPY.   I told you she was on call!

BIFF (*strangely unnerved*).   Cut it out, will ya? I want to say something to you.

HAPPY.   Did you see Oliver?

BIFF.   I saw him all right. Now look, I want to tell Dad a couple of things and I want you to help me.

460 HAPPY.   What? Is he going to back you?

BIFF.   Are you crazy? You're out of your goddam head, you know that?

HAPPY.   Why? What happened?

BIFF (*breathlessly*).   I did a terrible thing today, Hap. It's been the strangest day I ever went through. I'm all numb, I swear.

HAPPY.   You mean he wouldn't see you?

BIFF.   Well, I waited for six hours for him,   465 see? All day. Kept sending my name in. Even tried to date his secretary so she'd get me to him, but no soap.

HAPPY.   Because you're not showin' the old confidence, Biff. He remembered you, didn't he?

BIFF (*stopping* HAPPY *with a gesture*). Finally, about five o'clock, he comes out. Didn't remember who I was or anything. I felt like such an idiot, Hap.

HAPPY.   Did you tell him my Florida idea?

BIFF.   He walked away. I saw him for one minute. I got so mad I could've torn the walls down! How the hell did I ever get the idea I was a salesman there? I even believed myself that I'd been a salesman for him! And then he gave me one look and—I realized what a ridiculous lie my whole life has been! We've been talking in a dream for fifteen years. I was a shipping clerk.

HAPPY.   What'd you do?   470

BIFF (*with great tension and wonder*).   Well, he left, see. And the secretary went out. I was all alone in the waiting-room. I don't know what came over me, Hap. The next thing I know I'm in his office—paneled walls, everything. I can't explain it. I— Hap, I took his fountain pen.

HAPPY.   Geez, did he catch you?

BIFF.   I ran out. I ran down all eleven flights. I ran and ran and ran.

HAPPY.   That was an awful dumb—what'd you do that for?

BIFF (*agonized*).   I don't know, I just—   475 wanted to take something, I don't know. You gotta help me, Hap, I'm gonna tell Pop.

HAPPY.   You crazy? What for?

BIFF.   Hap, he's got to understand that I'm not the man somebody lends that kind of money to. He thinks I've been spiting him all these years and it's eating him up.

HAPPY.   That's just it. You tell him something nice.

BIFF.   I can't.

480 HAPPY.   Say you got a lunch date with Oliver tomorrow.

BIFF.   So what do I do tomorrow?

HAPPY.   You leave the house tomorrow and come back at night and say Oliver is thinking it over. And he thinks it over for a couple of weeks, and gradually it fades away and nobody's the worse.

BIFF.   But it'll go on forever!

HAPPY.   Dad is never so happy as when he's looking forward to something! (WILLY *enters.*) Hello, scout!

485 WILLY.   Gee, I haven't been here in years! (STANLEY *has followed* WILLY *in and sets a chair for him.* STANLEY *starts off but* HAPPY *stops him.*)

HAPPY.   Stanley! (STANLEY *stands by, waiting for an order.*)

BIFF (*going to* WILLY *with guilt, as to an invalid*).   Sit down, Pop. You want a drink?

WILLY.   Sure, I don't mind.

BIFF.   Let's get a load on.

490 WILLY.   You look worried.

BIFF.   N-no. (*To* STANLEY) Scotch all around. Make it doubles.

STANLEY.   Doubles, right. (*He goes.*)

WILLY.   You had a couple already, didn't you?

BIFF.   Just a couple, yeah.

495 WILLY.   Well, what happened, boy? (*Nodding affirmatively, with a smile*) Everything go all right?

BIFF (*takes a breath, then reaches out and grasps* WILLY'S *hand*).   Pal . . . (*He is smiling bravely, and* WILLY *is smiling too.*) I had an experience today.

HAPPY.   Terrific, Pop.

WILLY.   That so? What happened?

BIFF (*high, slightly alcoholic, above the earth*). I'm going to tell you everything from first to last. It's been a strange day.

(*Silence. He looks around, composes himself as best he can, but his breath keeps breaking the rhythm of his voice.*) I had to wait quite a while for him, and—

WILLY.   Oliver?   500

BIFF.   Yeah, Oliver. All day, as a matter of cold fact. And a lot of—instances—facts, Pop, facts about my life came back to me. Who was it, Pop? Who ever said I was a salesman with Oliver?

WILLY.   Well, you were.

BIFF.   No, Dad, I was a shipping clerk.

WILLY.   But you were practically—

BIFF (*with determination*).   Dad, I don't   505 know who said it first, but I was never a salesman for Bill Oliver.

WILLY.   What're you talking about?

BIFF.   Let's hold on to the facts tonight, Pop. We're not going to get anywhere bullin' around. I was a shipping clerk.

WILLY (*angrily*).   All right, now listen to me—

BIFF.   Why don't you let me finish?

WILLY.   I'm not interested in stories about   510 the past or any crap of that kind because the woods are burning, boys, you understand? There's a big blaze going on all around. I was fired today.

BIFF (*shocked*).   How could you be?

WILLY.   I was fired, and I'm looking for a little good news to tell your mother, because the woman has waited and the woman has suffered. The gist of it is that I haven't got a story left in my head, Biff. So don't give me a lecture about facts and aspects. I am not interested. Now what've you got to say to me? (STANLEY *enters with three drinks. They wait until he leaves.*) Did you see Oliver?

BIFF.   Jesus, Dad!

WILLY.   You mean you didn't go up there?

HAPPY.   Sure he went up there.   515

BIFF.   I did. I—saw him. How could they fire you?

WILLY (*on the edge of his chair*).   What kind of a welcome did he give you?

BIFF.   He won't even let you work on commission?

WILLY.   I'm out! (*Driving*) So tell me, he gave you a warm welcome?

520 HAPPY.   Sure, Pop, sure!

BIFF (*driven*).   Well, it was kind of—

WILLY.   I was wondering if he'd remember you. (*To* HAPPY) Imagine, man doesn't see him for ten, twelve years and gives him that kind of a welcome!

HAPPY.   Damn right!

BIFF (*trying to return to the offensive*).   Pop look—

525 WILLY.   You know why he remembered you, don't you? Because you impressed him in those days.

BIFF.   Let's talk quietly and get this down to the facts, huh?

WILLY (*as though* BIFF *had been interrupting*).   Well, what happened? It's great news, Biff. Did he take you into his office or'd you talk in the waiting-room?

BIFF.   Well, he came in, see, and—

WILLY (*with a big smile*).   What'd he say? Betcha he threw his arm around you.

530 BIFF.   Well, he kinda—

WILLY.   He's a fine man. (*To* HAPPY) Very hard man to see, y'know.

HAPPY (*agreeing*).   Oh, I know.

WILLY (*to* BIFF).   Is that where you had the drinks?

BIFF.   Yeah, he gave me a couple of—no, no!

535 HAPPY (*cutting in*).   He told him my Florida idea.

WILLY.   Don't interrupt. (*To* BIFF) How'd he react to the Florida idea?

BIFF.   Dad, will you give me a minute to explain?

WILLY.   I've been waiting for you to explain since I sat down here! What happened? He took you into his office and what?

BIFF.   Well—I talked. And—and he listened, see.

WILLY.   Famous for the way he listens, y'know. What was his answer?   540

BIFF.   His answer was—(*He breaks off, suddenly angry.*) Dad, you're not letting me tell you what I want to tell you!

WILLY (*accusing, angered*).   You didn't see him, did you?

BIFF.   I did see him!

WILLY.   What'd you insult him or something? You insulted him, didn't you?

BIFF.   Listen, will you let me out of it, will   545 you just let me out of it!

HAPPY.   What the hell!

WILLY.   Tell me what happened!

BIFF (*to* HAPPY).   I can't talk to him!

(*A single trumpet note jars the ear. The light of green leaves stains the house, which holds the air of night and a dream.* YOUNG BERNARD *enters and knocks on the door of the house.*)

YOUNG BERNARD (*frantically*).   Mrs. Loman, Mrs. Loman!

HAPPY.   Tell him what happened!   550

BIFF (*to* HAPPY).   Shut up and leave me alone!

WILLY.   No, no! You had to go and flunk math!

BIFF.   What math? What're you talking about?

YOUNG BERNARD.   Mrs. Loman, Mrs. Loman! (LINDA *appears in the house, as of old.*)

WILLY (*wildly*).   Math, math, math!   555

BIFF.   Take it easy, Pop!

YOUNG BERNARD.   Mrs. Loman!

WILLY (*furiously*).   If you hadn't flunked you'd've been set by now!

BIFF.   Now, look, I'm gonna tell you what happened, and you're going to listen to me.

YOUNG BERNARD.   Mrs. Loman!   560

BIFF.   I waited six hours—

HAPPY.   What the hell are you saying?

BIFF.   I kept sending in my name but he wouldn't see me. So finally he . . . (*He continues unheard as light fades low on the restaurant.*)

YOUNG BERNARD.   Biff flunked math!

565   LINDA.   No!

YOUNG BERNARD.   Birnbaum flunked him! They won't graduate him!

LINDA.   But they have to. He's gotta go to the university. Where is he? Biff! Biff!

YOUNG BERNARD.   No, he left. He went to Grand Central.

LINDA.   Grand—You mean he went to Boston!

570   YOUNG BERNARD.   Is Uncle Willy in Boston?

LINDA.   Oh, maybe Willy can talk to the teacher. Oh, the poor, poor boy! (*Light on house area snaps out.*)

BIFF (*at the table, now audible, holding up a gold fountain pen*). . . . so I'm washed up with Oliver, you understand? Are you listening to me?

WILLY (*at a loss*).   Yeah, sure. If you hadn't flunked—

BIFF.   Flunked what? What're you talking about?

575   WILLY.   Don't blame everything on me! I didn't flunk math—you did! What pen?

HAPPY.   That was awful dumb, Biff, a pen like that is worth—

WILLY (*seeing the pen for the first time*).   You took Oliver's pen?

BIFF (*weakening*).   Dad, I just explained it to you.

WILLY.   You stole Bill Oliver's fountain pen!

580   BIFF.   I didn't exactly steal it! That's just what I've been explaining to you!

HAPPY.   He had it in his hand and just then Oliver walked in, so he got nervous and stuck it in his pocket!

WILLY.   My God, Biff!

BIFF.   I never intended to do it, Dad!

OPERATOR'S VOICE.   Standish Arms, good evening!

WILLY (*shouting*).   I'm not in my room!   585

BIFF (*frightened*).   Dad, what's the matter? (*He and* HAPPY *stand up.*)

OPERATOR.   Ringing Mr. Loman for you!

WILLY.   I'm not there, stop it!

BIFF (*horrified, gets down on one knee before* WILLY).   Dad, I'll make good, I'll make good. (WILLY *tries to get to his feet,* BIFF *holds him down.*) Sit down now.

WILLY.   No, you're no good, you're no   590
good for anything.

BIFF.   I am, Dad, I'll find something else, you understand? Now don't worry about anything. (*He holds up* WILLY'S *face.*) Talk to me, Dad.

OPERATOR.   Mr. Loman does not answer. Shall I page him?

WILLY (*attempting to stand, as though to rush and silence the* OPERATOR).   No, no, no!

HAPPY.   He'll strike something, Pop.

WILLY.   No, no . . .   595

BIFF (*desperately, standing over* WILLY).   Pop, listen! Listen to me! I'm telling you something good. Oliver talked to his partner about the Florida idea. You listening? He—he talked to his partner, and he came to me . . . I'm going to be all right, you hear? Dad, listen to me, he said it was just a question of the amount!

WILLY.   Then you . . . got it?

HAPPY.   He's gonna be terrific, Pop!

WILLY (*trying to stand*).   Then you got it, haven't you? You got it! You got it!

BIFF (*agonized, holds* WILLY *down*).   No, no.   600
Look, Pop. I'm supposed to have lunch with them tomorrow. I'm just telling you this so you'll know that I can still make an impression, Pop. And I'll make good somewhere, but I can't go tomorrow, see?

WILLY.   Why not? You simply—

BIFF.   But the pen, Pop!

WILLY.   You give it to him and tell him it was an oversight!

HAPPY.   Sure, have lunch tomorrow!

BIFF.   I can't say that—   605

WILLY.   You were doing a crossword puzzle and accidentally used his pen!

BIFF.   Listen, kid, I took those balls years ago, now I walk in with his fountain pen? That clinches it, don't you see? I can't face him like that! I'll try elsewhere.

PAGE'S VOICE.   Paging Mr. Loman!

WILLY.   Don't you want to be anything?

610 BIFF.   Pop, how can I go back?

WILLY.   You don't want to be anything, is that what's behind it?

BIFF (*now angry at* WILLY *for not crediting his sympathy*).   Don't take it that way! You think it was easy walking into that office after what I'd done to him? A team of horses couldn't have dragged me back to Bill Oliver!

WILLY.   Then why'd you go?

BIFF.   Why did I go? Why did I go! Look at you! Look at what's become of you! (*Off left,* THE WOMAN *laughs.*)

615 WILLY.   Biff, you're going to go to that lunch tomorrow, or—

BIFF.   I can't go. I've got no appointment!

HAPPY.   Biff, for . . .

WILLY.   Are you spiting me?

BIFF.   Don't take it that way! Goddammit!

620 WILLY (*strikes* BIFF *and falters away from the table*).   You rotten little louse! Are you spiting me?

THE WOMAN.   Someone's at the door, Willy!

BIFF.   I'm no good, can't you see what I am?

HAPPY (*separating them*).   Hey, you're in a restaurant! Now cut it out, both of you! (*The* GIRLS *enter.*) Hello, girls, sit down. (THE WOMAN *laughs, off left.*)

MISS FORSYTHE.   I guess we might as well. This is Letta.

625 THE WOMAN.   Willy, are you going to wake up?

BIFF (*ignoring* WILLY).   How're ya, miss, sit down. What do you drink?

MISS FORSYTHE.   Letta might not be able to stay long.

LETTA.   I gotta get up very early tomorrow. I got jury duty. I'm so excited! Were you fellows ever on a jury?

BIFF.   No, but I been in front of them! (*The* GIRLS *laugh.*) This is my father.

LETTA.   Isn't he cute? Sit down with us,   630
Pop.

HAPPY.   Sit him down, Biff!

BIFF (*going to him*).   Come on, slugger, drink us under the table. To hell with it! Come on, sit down, pal. (*On* BIFF'S *last insistence,* WILLY *is about to sit.*)

THE WOMAN (*now urgently*).   Willy, are you going to answer the door! (THE WOMAN'S *call puts* WILLY *back. He starts right, befuddled.*)

BIFF.   Hey, where are you going?

WILLY.   Open the door.   635

BIFF.   The door?

WILLY.   The washroom . . . the door . . . where's the door?

BIFF (*leading* WILLY *to the left*).   Just go straight down. (WILLY *moves left.*)

THE WOMAN.   Willy, Willy, are you going to get up, get up, get up, get up? (WILLY *exits left.*)

LETTA.   I think it's sweet you bring your   640
daddy along.

MISS FORSYTHE.   Oh, he isn't really your father!

BIFF (*at left, turning to her resentfully*).   Miss Forsythe, you've just seen a prince walk by. A fine, troubled prince. A hard-working, unappreciated prince. A pal, you understand? A good companion. Always for his boys.

LETTA.   That's so sweet.

HAPPY.   Well, girls, what's the program? We're wasting time. Come on, Biff. Gather round. Where would you like to go?

BIFF.   Why don't you do something for   645
him?

HAPPY.   Me!

BIFF.   Don't you give a damn for him, Hap?

HAPPY. What're you talking about? I'm the one who—

BIFF. I sense it, you don't give a good goddam about him. (*He takes the rolled-up hose from his pocket and puts it on the table in front of* HAPPY.) Look what I found in the cellar, for Christ's sake. How can you bear to let it go on?

650 HAPPY. Me? Who goes away? Who runs off and—

BIFF. Yeah, but he doesn't mean anything to you. You could help him—I can't! Don't you understand what I'm talking about? He's going to kill himself, don't you know that?

HAPPY. Don't I know it! Me!

BIFF. Hap, help him! Jesus . . . help him . . . Help me, help me, I can't bear to look at his face! (*Ready to weep, he hurries out, up right.*)

HAPPY (*starting after him*). Where are you going?

655 MISS FORSYTHE. What's he so mad about?

HAPPY. Come on, girls, we'll catch up with him.

MISS FORSYTHE (*as* HAPPY *pushes her out*). Say, I don't like that temper of his!

HAPPY. He's just a little overstrung, he'll be all right!

WILLY (*off left, as* THE WOMAN *laughs*). Don't answer! Don't answer!

660 LETTA. Don't you want to tell your father—

HAPPY. No, that's not my father. He's just a guy. Come on, we'll catch Biff, and, honey, we're going to paint this town! Stanley, where's the check! Hey, Stanley! (*They exit,* STANLEY *looks toward left.*)

STANLEY (*calling to* HAPPY *indignantly*). Mr. Loman! Mr. Loman! (STANLEY *picks up a chair and follows them off. Knocking is heard off left.* THE WOMAN *enters, laughing.* WILLY *follows her. She is in a black slip; he is buttoning his shirt. Raw, sensuous music accompanies their speech.*)

WILLY. Will you stop laughing? Will you stop?

THE WOMAN. Aren't you going to answer the door? He'll wake the whole hotel.

WILLY. I'm not expecting anybody.   665

THE WOMAN. Whyn't you have another drink, honey, and stop being so damn self-centered.

WILLY. I'm so lonely.

THE WOMAN. You know you ruined me, Willy? From now on, whenever you come to the office, I'll see that you go right through to the buyers. No waiting at my desk any more, Willy. You ruined me.

WILLY. That's nice of you to say that.

THE WOMAN. Gee, you are self-centered!   670 Why so sad? You are the saddest, self-centeredest soul I ever did see-saw. (*She laughs. He kisses her.*) Come on inside, drummer boy. It's silly to be dressing in the middle of the night. (*As knocking is heard*) Aren't you going to answer the door?

WILLY. They're knocking on the wrong door.

THE WOMAN. But I felt the knocking. And he heard us talking in here. Maybe the hotel's on fire!

WILLY (*his terror rising*). It's a mistake.

THE WOMAN. Then tell him to go away!

WILLY. There's nobody there.   675

THE WOMAN. It's getting on my nerves, Willy. There's somebody standing out there and it's getting on my nerves!

WILLY (*pushing her away from him*). All right, stay in the bathroom here, and don't come out. I think there's a law in Massachusetts about it, so don't come out. It may be the new room clerk. He looked very mean. So don't come out. It's a mistake, there's no fire. (*The knocking is heard again. He takes a few steps away from her, and she vanishes into the wing. The light follows him, and now he is facing* YOUNG

BIFF, *who carries a suitcase.* BIFF *steps toward him. The music is gone.*)

BIFF. Why didn't you answer?

WILLY. Biff! What are you doing in Boston?

680 BIFF. Why didn't you answer? I've been knocking for five minutes, I called you on the phone—

WILLY. I just heard you. I was in the bathroom and had the door shut. Did anything happen home?

BIFF. Dad—I let you down.

WILLY. What do you mean?

BIFF. Dad . . .

685 WILLY. Biffo, what's this about? (*Putting his arm around* BIFF) Come on, let's go downstairs and get you a malted.

BIFF. Dad, I flunked math.

WILLY. Not for the term?

BIFF. The term. I haven't got enough credits to graduate.

WILLY. You mean to say Bernard wouldn't give you the answers?

690 BIFF. He did, he tried, but I only got sixty-one.

WILLY. And they wouldn't give you four points.

BIFF. Birnbaum refused absolutely. I begged him, Pop, but he won't give me those points. You gotta talk to him before they close the school. Because if he saw the kind of man you are, and you just talked to him in your way, I'm sure he'd come through for me. The class came right before practice, see, and I didn't go enough. Would you talk to him? He'd like you, Pop. You know the way you could talk.

695 WILLY. You're on. We'll drive right back.

BIFF. Oh, Dad, good work! I'm sure he'll change it for you!

WILLY. Go downstairs and tell the clerk I'm checkin' out. Go right down.

BIFF. Yes, sir! See, the reason he hates me, Pop—one day he was late for class so I

got up at the blackboard and imitated him. I crossed my eyes and talked with a lithp.

WILLY (*laughing*). You did? The kids like it?

BIFF. They nearly died laughing!

WILLY. Yeah? What'd you do?

BIFF. The thquare root of thixty twee is . . . 700 (WILLY *bursts out laughing;* BIFF *joins him*). And in the middle of it he walked in! (WILLY *laughs and* THE WOMAN *joins in off-stage.*)

WILLY (*without hesitation*). Hurry downstairs and—

BIFF. Somebody in there?

WILLY. No, that was next door.

(THE WOMAN *laughs offstage.*)

BIFF. Somebody got in your bathroom!

WILLY. No, it's the next room, there's a 705 party.

THE WOMAN (*enters, laughing. She lisps this*). Can I come in? There's something in the bathtub, Willy, and it's moving! (WILLY *looks at* BIFF, *who is staring open-mouthed and horrified at* THE WOMAN.)

WILLY. Ah—you better go back to your room. They must be finished painting by now. They're painting her room so I let her take a shower here. Go back, go back . . . (*He pushes her.*)

THE WOMAN (*resisting*). But I've got to get dressed, Willy, I can't—

WILLY. Get out of here! Go back, go back . . . (*Suddenly striving for the ordinary*) This is Miss Francis, Biff, she's a buyer. They're painting her room. Go back, Miss Francis, go back . . .

THE WOMAN. But my clothes, I can't go 710 out naked in the hall!

WILLY (*pushing her offstage*). Get outa here! Go back, go back! (BIFF *slowly sits down on his suitcase as the argument continues offstage.*)

THE WOMAN. Where's my stockings? You promised me stockings, Willy!

WILLY.   I have no stockings here!

THE WOMAN.   You had two boxes of size nine sheers for me, and I want them!

715 WILLY.   Here, for God's sake, will you get outa here!

THE WOMAN (*enters holding a box of stockings*).   I just hope there's nobody in the hall. That's all I hope. (*To* BIFF) Are you football or baseball?

BIFF.   Football.

THE WOMAN (*angry, humiliated*).   That's me too. G'night. (*She snatches her clothes from* WILLY *and walks out.*)

WILLY (*after a pause*).   Well, better get going. I want to get to the school first thing in the morning. Get my suits out of the closet. I'll get my valise. (BIFF *doesn't move.*) What's the matter? (BIFF *remains motionless, tears falling.*) She's a buyer. Buys for J. H. Simmons. She lives down the hall—they're painting. You don't imagine—(*He breaks off. After a pause*) Now listen, pal, she's just a buyer. She sees merchandise in her room and they have to keep it looking just so . . . (*Pause. Assuming command*) All right, get my suits. (BIFF *doesn't move.*) Now stop crying and do as I say. I gave you an order. Biff, I gave you an order! Is that what you do when I give you an order? How dare you cry! (*Putting his arm around* BIFF) Now look, Biff, when you grow up you'll understand about these things. You mustn't—you mustn't overemphasize a thing like this. I'll see Birnbaum first thing in the morning.

720 BIFF.   Never mind.

WILLY (*getting down beside* BIFF).   Never mind! He's going to give you those points. I'll see to it.

BIFF.   He wouldn't listen to you.

WILLY.   He certainly will listen to me. You need those points for the U. of Virginia.

BIFF.   I'm not going there.

WILLY.   Heh? If I can't get him to change   725 that mark you'll make it up in summer school. You've got all summer to—

BIFF (*his weeping breaking from him*).   Dad . . .

WILLY (*infected by it*).   Oh, my boy . . .

BIFF.   Dad . . .

WILLY.   She's nothing to me, Biff. I was lonely, I was terribly lonely.

BIFF.   You—you gave her Mama's   730 stockings! (*His tears break through and he rises to go.*)

WILLY (*grabbing for* BIFF).   I gave you an order!

BIFF.   Don't touch me, you—liar!

WILLY.   Apologize for that!

BIFF.   You fake! You phony little fake! You fake! (*Overcome, he turns quickly and weeping fully goes out with his suitcase. WILLY is left on the floor on his knees.*)

WILLY.   I gave you an order! Biff, come   735 back here or I'll beat you! Come back here! I'll whip you! (STANLEY *comes quickly in from the right and stands in front of* WILLY, *who shouts at him.*) I gave you an order . . .

STANLEY.   Hey, let's pick it up, pick it up, Mr. Loman. (*He helps* WILLY *to his feet.*) Your boys left with the chippies. They said they'll see you home. (*A second waiter watches some distance away.*)

WILLY.   But we were supposed to have dinner together. (*Music is heard,* WILLY'S *theme.*)

STANLEY.   Can you make it?

WILLY.   I'll—sure. I can make it. (*Suddenly concerned about his clothes*) Do I—I look all right?

STANLEY.   Sure, you look all right. (*He flicks   740 a speck off* WILLY'S *lapel.*)

WILLY.   Here—here's a dollar.

STANLEY.   Oh, your son paid me. It's all right.

WILLY (*putting it in* STANLEY'S *hand*).   No, take it. You're a good boy.

STANLEY.   Oh, no, you don't have to . . .

745 WILLY.   Here's some more, I don't need it any more. (*After a slight pause.*) Tell me— is there a seed store in the neighborhood?

STANLEY.   Seeds? You mean like to plant? (*As* WILLY *turns,* STANLEY *slips the money back into his jacket pocket.*)

WILLY.   Yes. Carrots, peas . . .

STANLEY.   Well, there's hardware stores on Sixth Avenue, but it may be too late now.

WILLY (*anxiously*).   Oh, I'd better hurry. I've got to get some seeds. (*He starts off to the right.*) I've got to get some seeds, right away. Nothing's planted. I don't have a thing in the ground. (WILLY *hurries out as the light goes down.* STANLEY *moves over to the right after him, watches him off. The other waiter has been staring at* WILLY.)

750 STANLEY (*to the waiter*).   Well, whatta you looking at?

(*The waiter picks up the chairs and moves off right.* STANLEY *takes the table and follows him. The light fades on this area. There is a long pause, the sound of the flute coming over. The light gradually rises on the kitchen, which is empty.* HAPPY *appears at the door of the house, followed by* BIFF. HAPPY *is carrying a large bunch of long-stemmed roses. He enters the kitchen, looks around for* LINDA. *Not seeing her, he turns to* BIFF, *who is just outside the house door, and makes a gesture with his hands, indicating "Not here, I guess." He looks into the living-room and freezes. Inside,* LINDA, *unseen, is seated,* WILLY'S *coat on her lap. She rises ominously and quietly and moves toward* HAPPY, *who backs up into the kitchen, afraid.*)

HAPPY.   Hey, what're you doing? (LINDA *says nothing but moves toward him implacably.*) Where's Pop? (*He keeps backing to the right, and now* LINDA *is in full view of the doorway to the living-room.*) Is he sleeping?

LINDA.   Where were you?

HAPPY (*trying to laugh it off*).   We met two girls, Mom, very fine types. Here, we brought you some flowers. (*Offering them to her*) Put them in your room, Ma. (*She knocks them to the floor at* BIFF'S *feet. He has now come inside and closed the door behind him. She stares at* BIFF, *silent.*) Now what'd you do that for? Mom, I want you to have some flowers—

LINDA (*cutting* HAPPY *off, violently to* BIFF).   Don't you care whether he lives or dies?

HAPPY (*going to the stairs*).   Come upstairs, 755 Biff.

BIFF (*with a flare of disgust, to* HAPPY).   Go away from me! (*To* LINDA) What do you mean, lives or dies? Nobody's dying around here, pal.

LINDA.   Get out of my sight! Get out of here!

BIFF.   I wanna see the boss.

LINDA.   You're not to go near him!

BIFF.   Where is he? (*He moves into the* 760 *living-room and* LINDA *follows.*)

LINDA (*shouting after* BIFF).   You invite him to dinner. He looks forward to it all day—(BIFF *appears in his parents' bedroom, looks around, and exits*)—and then you desert him there. There's no stranger you'd do that to!

HAPPY.   Why? He had a swell time with us. Listen, when I—(LINDA *comes back into the kitchen*)—desert him I hope I don't outlive the day!

LINDA.   Get out of here!

HAPPY.   Now look, Mom . . .

LINDA.   Did you have to go to women 765 tonight? You and your lousy rotten whores! (BIFF *re-enters the kitchen.*)

HAPPY.   Mom, all we did was follow Biff around trying to cheer him up! (*To* BIFF) Boy, what a night you gave me!

LINDA.   Get out of here, both of you, and don't come back! I don't want you tormenting him any more. Go on now, get your things together! (*To* BIFF) You can sleep in his apartment. (*She starts to pick up the flowers and stops herself.*) Pick

up this stuff, I'm not your maid any
more. Pick it up, you bum, you! (HAPPY
turns his back to her in refusal. BIFF *slowly
moves over and gets down on his knees, picking up the flowers.*)

LINDA.   You're a pair of animals! Not one,
not another living soul would have had
the cruelty to walk out on that man in a
restaurant!

BIFF (*not looking at her*).   Is that what he
said?

770 LINDA.   He didn't have to say anything.
He was so humiliated he nearly limped
when he came in.

HAPPY.   But, Mom, he had a great time
with us—

BIFF (*cutting him off violently*).   Shut up!
(*Without another word,* HAPPY *goes
upstairs.*)

LINDA.   You! You didn't even go in to see if
he was all right!

BIFF (*still on the floor in front of* LINDA, *the
flowers in his hand; with self-loathing*).   No.
Didn't. Didn't do a damned thing. How
do you like that, heh? Left him babbling
in a toilet.

775 LINDA.   You louse. You . . .

BIFF.   Now you hit it on the nose! (*He gets
up, throws the flowers in the wastebasket.*)
The scum of the earth, and you're
looking at him!

LINDA.   Get out of here!

BIFF.   I gotta talk to the boss, Mom. Where
is he?

LINDA.   You're not going near him. Get out
of this house!

780 BIFF (*with absolute assurance, determination*).
No. We're gonna have an abrupt
conversation, him and me.

LINDA.   You're not talking to him!
(*Hammering is heard from outside the house,
off right.* BIFF *turns toward the noise.* LINDA
is suddenly pleading.) Will you please
leave him alone?

BIFF.   What's he doing out there?

LINDA.   He's planting a garden!

BIFF (*quietly*).   Now? Oh, my God! (BIFF
moves outside, LINDA *following. The light
dies down on them and comes up on the
center of the apron as* WILLY *walks into it. He
is carrying a flashlight, a hoe, and a handful
of seed packets. He raps the top of the hoe
sharply to fix it firmly, and then moves to the
left, measuring off the distance with his foot.
He holds the flashlight to look at the seed
packets, reading off the instructions. He is in
the blue of night.*)

WILLY.   Carrots . . . quarter-inch apart.   785
Rows . . . one-foot rows. (*He measures it
off.*) One foot. (*He puts down a package and
measures off.*) Beets. (*He puts down another
package and measures again.*) Lettuce. (*He
reads the package, puts it down.*) One foot—
(*He breaks off as* BEN *appears at the right and
moves slowly down to him.*) What a proposition, ts, ts. Terrific, terrific. 'Cause she
suffered, Ben, the woman has suffered.
You understand me? A man can't go out
the way he came in. Ben, a man has got
to add up to something. You can't, you
can't—(BEN *moves toward him as though to
interrupt.*) You gotta consider, now. Don't
answer so quick. Remember, it's a
guaranteed twenty-thousand-dollar
proposition. Now look, Ben, I want you
to go through the ins and outs of this
thing with me. I've got nobody to talk to,
Ben, and the woman has suffered, you
hear me?

BEN (*standing still, considering*).   What's the
proposition?

WILLY.   It's twenty-thousand dollars on the
barrelhead. Guaranteed, gilt-edged, you
understand?

BEN.   You don't want to make a fool of
yourself. They might not honor the policy.

WILLY.   How can they dare refuse? Didn't I
work like a coolie to meet every premium
on the nose? And now they don't pay
off? Impossible!

790 BEN. It's called a cowardly thing, William.

WILLY. Why? Does it take more guts to stand here the rest of my life ringing up a zero?

BEN (*yielding*). That's a point, William. (*He moves, thinking, turns.*) And twenty-thousand—that *is* something one can feel with the hand, it is there.

WILLY (*now assured, with rising power*). Oh, Ben, that's the whole beauty of it! I can see it like a diamond shining in the dark, hard and rough, that I can pick up and touch in my hand. Not like—like an appointment! This would not be another damned-fool appointment, Ben, and it changes all the aspects. Because he thinks I'm nothing, see, and so he spites me. But the funeral—(*Straightening up*) Ben, that funeral will be massive! They'll come from Maine, Massachusetts, Vermont, New Hampshire! All the old-timers with the strange license plates—that boy will be thunderstruck, Ben, because he never realized—I am known! Rhode Island, New York, New Jersey—I am known, Ben, and he'll see it with his eyes once and for all. He'll see what I am. He's in for a shock, that boy!

BEN (*coming down to the edge of the garden*). He'll call you a coward.

795 WILLY (*suddenly fearful*). No, that would be terrible.

BEN. Yes. And a damned fool.

WILLY. No, no, he mustn't, I won't have it! (*He is broken and desperate.*)

BEN. He'll hate you, William. (*The gay music of the* BOYS *is heard.*)

WILLY. Oh, Ben, how do we get back to all the great times? Used to be so full of light, and comradeship, the sleigh-riding in winter and the ruddiness of his cheeks. And always some kind of good news coming up, always something nice coming up ahead. And never let me carry the valises in the house, and simonizing,

simonizing that little red car! Why, why can't I give him something and not have him hate me?

BEN. Let me think about it. (*He glances at* 800 *his watch.*) I still have a little time. Remarkable proposition, but you've got to be sure you're not making a fool of yourself. (BEN *drifts off upstage and goes out of sight.* BIFF *comes down from the left.*)

WILLY (*suddenly conscious of* BIFF, *turns and looks up at him, then begins picking up the packages of seeds in confusion*). Where the hell is that seed? (*Indignantly*) You can't see nothing out here! They boxed in the whole goddam neighborhood!

BIFF. There are people all around here. Don't you realize that?

WILLY. I'm busy. Don't bother me.

BIFF (*taking the hoe from* WILLY). I'm saying good-by to you, Pop. (WILLY *looks at him, silent, unable to move.*) I'm not coming back any more.

WILLY. You're not going to see Oliver 805 tomorrow?

BIFF. I've got no appointment, Dad.

WILLY. He put his arms around you, and you've got no appointment?

BIFF. Pop, get this now, will you? Every time I've left it's been a fight that sent me out of here. Today I realized something about myself and I tried to explain it to you and I—I think I'm just not smart enough to make any sense out of it for you. To hell with whose fault it is or anything like that. (*He takes* WILLY'S *arm.*) Let's just wrap it up, heh? Come on in, we'll tell Mom. (*He gently tries to pull* WILLY *to left.*)

WILLY (*frozen, immobile, with guilt in his voice*). No, I don't want to see her.

BIFF. Come on! (*He pulls again, and* WILLY 810 *tries to pull away.*)

WILLY (*highly nervous*). No, no, I don't want to see her.

BIFF (*tries to look into* WILLY'S *face, as if to find the answer there*).   Why don't you want to see her?

WILLY (*more harshly now*).   Don't bother me, will you?

BIFF.   What do you mean, you don't want to see her? You don't want them calling you yellow do you? This isn't your fault; it's me, I'm a bum. Now come inside! (WILLY *strains to get away*.) Did you hear what I said to you? (WILLY *pulls away and quickly goes by himself into the house.* BIFF *follows*.)

815   LINDA (*to* WILLY).   Did you plant, dear?

BIFF (*at the door, to* LINDA).   All right, we had it out. I'm going and I'm not writing any more.

LINDA (*going to* WILLY *in the kitchen*).   I think that's the best way, dear. 'Cause there's no use drawing it out, you'll just never get along. (WILLY *does not respond*.)

BIFF.   People ask where I am and what I'm doing, you don't know, and you don't care. That way it'll be off your mind and you can start brightening up again. All right? That clears it, doesn't it? (WILLY *is silent, and* BIFF *goes to him*.) You gonna wish me luck, scout? (*He extends his hand*.) What do you say?

LINDA.   Shake his hand, Willy.

820   WILLY (*turning to her, seething with hurt*).   There's no necessity to mention the pen at all, y'know.

BIFF (*gently*).   I've got no appointment, Dad.

WILLY (*erupting fiercely*).   He put his arm around . . . ?

BIFF.   Dad, you're never going to see what I am, so what's the use of arguing? If I strike oil I'll send you a check. Meantime forget I'm alive.

WILLY (*to* LINDA).   Spite, see?

825   BIFF.   Shake hands, Dad.

WILLY.   Not my hand.

BIFF.   I was hoping not to go this way.

WILLY.   Well, this is the way you're going. Good-by. (BIFF *looks at him a moment, then turns sharply and goes to the stairs.* WILLY *stops him with*) May you rot in hell if you leave this house!

BIFF (*turning*).   Exactly what is it that you want from me?

WILLY.   I want you to know, on the train,   830 in the mountains, in the valleys, wherever you go, that you cut down your life for spite!

BIFF.   No, no.

WILLY.   Spite, spite, is the word of your undoing! And when you're down and out, remember what did it. When you're rotting somewhere beside the railroad tracks, remember, and don't you dare blame it on me!

BIFF.   I'm not blaming it on you!

WILLY.   I won't take the rap for this, you   835 hear? (HAPPY *comes down the stairs and stands on the bottom step, watching*.)

BIFF.   That's just what I'm telling you!

WILLY (*sinking into a chair at the table, with full accusation*).   You're trying to put a knife in me—don't think I don't know what you're doing!

BIFF.   All right, phony! Then let's lay it on the line. (*He whips the rubber tube out of his pocket and puts it on the table*.)

HAPPY.   You crazy—

LINDA.   Biff! (*She moves to grab the hose, but* BIFF *holds it down with his hand*.)

BIFF.   Leave it there! Don't move it!   840

WILLY (*not looking at it*).   What is that?

BIFF.   You know goddam well what that is.

WILLY (*caged, wanting to escape*).   I never saw that.

BIFF.   You saw it. The mice didn't bring it into the cellar! What is this supposed to do, make a hero out of you? This supposed to make me sorry for you?

WILLY.   Never heard of it.   845

BIFF.   There'll be no pity for you, you hear it? No pity!

WILLY (*to* LINDA).   You hear the spite!

BIFF.   No, you're going to hear the truth—what you are and what I am!

LINDA.   Stop it!

850 WILLY.   Spite!

HAPPY (*coming down toward* BIFF).   You cut it out now!

BIFF (*to* HAPPY).   The man don't know who we are! The man is gonna know! (*To* WILLY) We never told the truth for ten minutes in this house!

HAPPY.   We always told the truth!

BIFF (*turning on him*).   You big blow, are you the assistant buyer? You're one of two assistants to the assistant, aren't you?

855 HAPPY.   Well, I'm practically—

BIFF.   You're practically full of it! We all are! And I'm through with it. (*To* WILLY) Now hear this, Willy, this is me.

WILLY.   I know you!

BIFF.   You know why I had no address for three months? I stole a suit in Kansas City and I was in jail. (*To* LINDA, *who is sobbing*) Stop crying. I'm through with it. (LINDA *turns away from them, her hands covering her face.*)

WILLY.   I suppose that's my fault!

860 BIFF.   I stole myself out of every job since high school!

WILLY.   And whose fault is that?

BIFF.   And I never got anywhere because you blew me so full of hot air I could never stand taking orders from anybody! That's whose fault it is!

WILLY.   I hear that!

LINDA.   Don't, Biff!

865 BIFF.   It's goddam time you heard that! I had to be boss big shot in two weeks, and I'm through with it!

WILLY.   Then hang yourself! For spite, hang yourself!

BIFF.   No! Nobody's hanging himself, Willy! I ran down eleven flights with a pen in my hand today. And suddenly I stopped, you hear me? And in the middle of that office building, do you hear this?

I stopped in the middle of that building and I saw—the sky. I saw the things that I love in this world. The work and the food and time to sit and smoke. And I looked at the pen and said to myself, what the hell am I grabbing this for? Why am I trying to become what I don't want to be? What am I doing in an office, making a contemptuous, begging fool of myself, when all I want is out there, waiting for me the minute I say I know who I am! Why can't I say that, Willy? (*He tries to make* WILLY *face him, but* WILLY *pulls away and moves to the left.*)

WILLY (*with hatred, threateningly*).   The door of your life is wide open!

BIFF.   Pop! I'm a dime a dozen, and so are you!

WILLY (*turning on him now in an uncontrolled outburst*).   I am not a dime a dozen! I am Willy Loman, and you are Biff Loman! (BIFF *starts for* WILLY, *but is blocked by* HAPPY. *In his fury,* BIFF *seems on the verge of attacking his father.*) 870

BIFF.   I am not a leader of men, Willy, and neither are you. You were never anything but a hard-working drummer who landed in the ash can like all the rest of them! I'm one dollar an hour, Willy! I tried seven states and couldn't raise it. A buck an hour! Do you gather my meaning? I'm not bringing home any prizes any more, and you're going to stop waiting for me to bring them home!

WILLY (*directly to* BIFF).   You vengeful, spiteful mutt! (BIFF *breaks from* HAPPY. WILLY, *in fright, starts up the stairs.* BIFF *grabs him.*)

BIFF (*at the peak of his fury*).   Pop, I'm nothing! I'm nothing, Pop. Can't you understand that? There's no spite in it any more. I'm just what I am, that's all. (BIFF'S *fury has spent itself, and he breaks down, sobbing, holding on to* WILLY, *who dumbly fumbles for* BIFF'S *face.*)

WILLY (*astonished*).   What're you doing? What're you doing? (*To* LINDA) Why is he crying?

875 BIFF (*crying, broken*).   Will you let me go, for Christ's sake? Will you take that phony dream and burn it before something happens? (*Struggling to contain himself, he pulls away and moves to the stairs.*) I'll go in the morning. Put him—put him to bed. (*Exhausted,* BIFF *moves up the stairs to his room.*)

WILLY (*after a long pause, astonished, elevated*).   Isn't that—isn't that remarkable? Biff—he likes me!

LINDA.   He loves you, Willy!

HAPPY (*deeply moved*).   Always did, Pop.

WILLY.   Oh, Biff! (*Staring wildly*) He cried! Cried to me. (*He is choking with his love, and now cries out his promise.*) That boy— that boy is going to be magnificent! (BEN *appears in the light just outside the kitchen.*)

880 BEN.   Yes, outstanding, with twenty thousand behind him.

LINDA (*sensing the racing of his mind, fearfully, carefully*).   Now come to bed, Willy. It's all settled now.

WILLY (*finding it difficult not to rush out of the house*).   Yes, we'll sleep. Come on. Go to sleep, Hap.

BEN.   And it does take a great kind of man to crack the jungle. (*In accents of dread,* BEN'S *idyllic music starts up.*)

HAPPY (*his arm around* LINDA).   I'm getting married, Pop, don't forget it. I'm changing everything. I'm gonna run that department before the year is up. You'll see, Mom. (*He kisses her.*)

885 BEN.   The jungle is dark but full of diamonds, Willy. (WILLY *turns, moves, listening to* BEN.)

LINDA.   Be good. You're both good boys, just act that way, that's all.

HAPPY.   'Night, Pop. (*He goes upstairs.*)

LINDA (*to* WILLY).   Come, dear.

BEN (*with greater force*).   One must go in to fetch a diamond out.

WILLY (*to* LINDA, *as he moves slowly along the edge of the kitchen, toward the door*).   I just 890 want to get settled down, Linda. Let me sit alone for a little.

LINDA (*almost uttering her fear*).   I want you upstairs.

WILLY (*taking her in his arms*).   In a few minutes, Linda. I couldn't sleep right now. Go on, you look awful tired. (*He kisses her.*)

BEN.   Not like an appointment at all. A diamond is rough and hard to the touch.

WILLY.   Go on now. I'll be right up.

LINDA.   I think this is the only way, 895 Willy.

WILLY.   Sure, it's the best thing.

BEN.   Best thing!

WILLY.   The only way. Everything is gonna be—go on, kid, get to bed. You look so tired.

LINDA.   Come right up.

WILLY.   Two minutes. (LINDA *goes into the* 900 *living-room, then reappears in her bedroom.* WILLY *moves just outside the kitchen door.*) Loves me. (*Wonderingly*) Always loved me. Isn't that a remarkable thing? Ben, he'll worship me for it!

BEN (*with promise*).   It's dark there, but full of diamonds.

WILLY.   Can you imagine that magnificence with twenty thousand dollars in his pocket?

LINDA (*calling from her room*).   Willy! Come up!

WILLY (*calling into the kitchen*).   Yes, yes. Coming! It's very smart, you realize that, don't you, sweetheart? Even Ben sees it. I gotta go, baby. 'By! 'By! (*Going over to* BEN, *almost dancing*) Imagine? When the mail comes he'll be ahead of Bernard again!

BEN.   A perfect proposition all around.   905

WILLY.   Did you see how he cried to me? Oh, if I could kiss him, Ben!

BEN.   Time, William, time!

WILLY.   Oh, Ben, I always knew one way or another we were gonna make it, Biff and I!

BEN (*looking at his watch*).   The boat. We'll be late. (*He moves slowly off into the darkness.*)

910 WILLY (*elagiacally, turning to the house*).   Now when you kick off, boy, I want a seventy-yard boot, and get right down the field under the ball, and when you hit, hit low and hit hard, because it's important, boy. (*He swings around and faces the audience.*) There's all kinds of important people in the stands, and the first thing you know . . . (*Suddenly realizing he is alone*) Ben! Ben, where do I . . . ? (*He makes a sudden movement of search.*) Ben, how do I . . . ?

LINDA (*calling*).   Willy, you coming up?

WILLY (*uttering a gasp of fear, whirling about as if to quiet her*).   Sh! (*He turns as if to find his way; sounds, faces, voices, seem to be swarming in upon him and he flicks at them, crying*) Sh! Sh! (*Suddenly music, faint and high, stops him. It rises in intensity, almost to an unbearable scream. He goes up and down on his toes, and rushes off around the house.*) Shhh!

LINDA.   Willy? (*There is no answer.* LINDA *waits.* BIFF *gets up off his bed. He is still in his clothes.* HAPPY *sits up.* BIFF *stands there listening.* LINDA, *with real fear*) Willy, answer me! Willy! (*There is the sound of a car starting and moving away at full speed.*) No!

BIFF (*rushing down the stairs*).   Pop!

(*As the car speeds off, the music crashes down in a frenzy of sound, which becomes the soft pulsation of a single cello string.* BIFF *slowly returns to his bedroom. He and* HAPPY *gravely don their jackets.* LINDA *slowly walks out of her room. The music has developed into a dead march. The leaves of day are appearing over everything.* CHARLEY *and* BERNARD, *somberly dressed, appear and knock on the kitchen door.* BIFF *and* HAPPY *slowly descend the stairs to the kitchen as* CHARLEY *and* BERNARD *enter. All stop a moment when*

LINDA, *in clothes of mourning, bearing a little bunch of roses, comes through the draped doorway into the kitchen. She goes to* CHARLEY *and takes his arm. Now all move toward the audience, through the wall-line of the kitchen. At the limit of the apron,* LINDA *lays down the flowers, kneels, and sits back on her heels. All stare down at the grave.*)

REQUIEM

CHARLEY.   It's getting dark, Linda. (LINDA *doesn't react. She stares at the grave.*)   915

BIFF.   How about it, Mom? Better get some rest, heh? They'll be closing the gate soon. (LINDA *makes no move. Pause.*)

HAPPY (*deeply angered*).   He had no right to do that. There was no necessity for it. We would've helped him.

CHARLEY (*grunting*).   Hmmm.

BIFF.   Come along, Mom.

LINDA.   Why didn't anybody come?   920

CHARLEY.   It was a nice funeral.

LINDA.   But where are all the people he knew? Maybe they blame him.

CHARLEY.   Naa. It's a rough world, Linda. They wouldn't blame him.

LINDA.   I can't understand it. At this time especially. First time in thirty-five years we were just about free and clear. He only needed a little salary. He was even finished with the dentist.

CHARLEY.   No man only needs a little salary.   925

LINDA.   I can't understand it.

BIFF.   There were a lot of nice days. When he'd come home from a trip; or on Sundays, making the stoop; finishing the cellar; putting on the new porch; when he built the extra bathroom; and put up the garage. You know something, Charley, there's more of him in that front stoop than in all the sales he ever made.

CHARLEY.   Yeah. He was a happy man with a batch of cement.

LINDA.   He was so wonderful with his hands.

930 BIFF.   He had the wrong dreams. All, all, wrong.

HAPPY (*almost ready to fight* BIFF).   Don't say that!

BIFF.   He never knew who he was.

CHARLEY (*stopping* HAPPY'S *movement and reply. To* BIFF).   Nobody dast blame this man. You don't understand: Willy was a salesman. And for a salesman, there is no rock bottom to the life. He don't put a bolt to a nut, he don't tell you the law or give you medicine. He's a man way out there in the blue, riding on a smile and a shoeshine. And when they start not smiling back—that's an earthquake. And then you get yourself a couple of spots on your hat, and you're finished. Nobody dast blame this man. A salesman is got to dream, boy. It comes with the territory.

BIFF.   Charley, the man didn't know who he was.

935 HAPPY (*infuriated*).   Don't say that!

BIFF.   Why don't you come with me, Happy?

HAPPY.   I'm not licked that easily. I'm staying right in this city, and I'm gonna beat this racket! (*He looks at* BIFF, *his chin is set.*) The Loman Brothers!

BIFF.   I know who I am, kid.

HAPPY.   All right, boy. I'm gonna show you and everybody else that Willy Loman did not die in vain. He had a good dream. It's the only dream you can have—to come out number-one man. He fought it out here and this is where I'm gonna win it for him.

BIFF (*with a hopeless glance at* HAPPY, *bends   940 toward his mother*).   Let's go, Mom.

LINDA.   I'll be with you in a minute. Go on, Charley. (*He hesitates.*) I want to, just for a minute. I never had a chance to say good-by. (CHARLEY *moves away, followed by* HAPPY. BIFF *remains a slight distance up and left of* LINDA. *She sits there, summoning herself. The flute begins, not far away, playing behind her speech.*) Forgive me, dear. I can't cry. I don't know what it is, but I can't cry. I don't understand it. Why did you ever do that? Help me, Willy, I can't cry. It seems to me that you're just on another trip. I keep expecting you. Willy, dear, I can't cry. Why did you do it? I search and search and I search, and I can't understand it, Willy. I made the last payment on the house today. Today, dear. And there'll be nobody home. (*A sob rises in her throat.*) We're free and clear. (*Sobbing more fully, released*) We're free. (BIFF *comes slowly toward her.*) We're free . . . We're free . . .

(BIFF *lifts her to her feet and moves out up right with her in his arms.* LINDA *sobs quietly.* BERNARD *and* CHARLEY *come together and follow them, followed by* HAPPY. *Only the music of the flute is left on the darkening stage as over the house the hard towers of the apartment buildings rise into sharp focus, and the curtain falls.*)

·····▶ *Your* Turn
Talking and Writing About Lit

1. How does it serve Miller's thematic intentions in *Death of a Salesman* to have Willy Loman be a salesman? Why does the occupation of salesman help illuminate Miller's ideas about the American Dream better than, say, the occupation of transit worker?

2. What is the purpose of Ben in the play? How does his characterization suggest themes? How does he serve as a foil character for Willy?

3. Are some of the characters' names intended to be symbolic (Willy Loman, Biff, Happy)? If so, what do you think they represent?

4. Regarding plot, why does Miller have Biff and Happy both return home and stay in their old room? What purpose does this serve in terms of what Miller wants to show in the play?

5. What plot elements at and near the end of Act I lay the groundwork for what happens in Act II?

6. What is the significance of Willy's having the younger Biff and Happy "simonizing" his red Chevrolet? Does this symbolize the kinds of "work" he sends them into the world to do? How successful are they at the "work" for which he has prepared them?

7. Examine the various types of internal and external conflicts present in the play.

8. Which of his sons, Biff or Happy, is more like the salesman?

9. At the end of the play, is there any character who represents a hope for change?

10. How would you interpret Ben's often repeated, enigmatic statement, "The jungle is dark but full of diamonds"? How are we meant to interpret Ben's statement "Never fight fair with a stranger"?

11. What is the significance of flute music (as well as other types of music) in the play?

12. In this family, what has been passed on from one generation to the next? Can changes be made in this "legacy"?

13. Is Willy Loman solely responsible for his fate, or have others contributed to his downfall?

14. Discuss the uses of setting and staging by the author, citing specific examples from the play.

15. **DIY** Write a two- or three-page scene in which a character talks to someone from his (or her) past. In Miller's play, Willy Loman talks to his brother whom he admires and whose expectations he feels he cannot live up to. You may want to reverse the situation. What if your main character is talking to someone he feels he's wrongly dominated rather than someone he felt overshadowed by? Reverse the power roles in your scene! Your characters may be of any gender.

Talking Lit

In the essay that follows, Arthur Miller argues, "I believe that the common man is as apt a subject for tragedy in its highest sense as kings were."

Arthur Miller (1915–2005)

"Tragedy and the Common Man," 1949 from *Theater Essays of Arthur Miller*

In this age few tragedies are written. It has often been held that the lack is due to a paucity of heroes among us, or else that modern man has had the blood drawn out of his organs of belief by the skepticism of science, and the heroic attack on life cannot feed on an attitude of reserve and circumspection. For one reason or another, we are often held to be below tragedy—or tragedy above us. The inevitable conclusion is, of course, that the tragic mode is archaic, fit only for the very highly placed, the kings or the kingly, and where this admission is not made in so many words it is most often implied.

I believe that the common man is as apt a subject for tragedy in its highest sense as kings were. On the face of it this ought to be obvious in the light of modern psychiatry, which bases its analysis upon classic formulations, such as the Oedipus and Orestes complexes, for instance, which were enacted by royal beings, but which apply to everyone in similar emotional situations.

More simply, when the question of tragedy in art is not at issue, we never hesitate to attribute to the well-placed and the exalted the very same mental processes as the lowly. And finally, if the exaltation of tragic action were truly a property of the high-bred character alone, it is inconceivable that the mass of mankind should cherish tragedy above all other forms, let alone be capable of understanding it.

As a general rule, to which there may be exceptions unknown to me, I think the tragic feeling is evoked in us when we are in the presence of a character who is ready to lay down his life, if need be, to secure one thing—his sense of personal dignity. From Orestes to Hamlet, Medea to Macbeth, the underlying struggle is that of the individual attempting to gain his "rightful" position in his society.

Sometimes he is one who has been displaced from it, sometimes one who seeks to attain it for the first time, but the fateful wound from which the inevitable events spiral is the wound of indignity, and its dominant force is indignation. Tragedy, then, is the consequence of a man's total compulsion to evaluate himself justly.

In the sense of having been initiated by the hero himself, the tale always reveals what has been called his "tragic flaw," a failing that is not peculiar to grand or elevated characters. Nor is it necessarily a weakness. The flaw, or crack in the character, is really nothing—and need be nothing—but his inherent unwillingness to remain passive in the face of what he conceives to be a challenge to his dignity, his image of his rightful status. Only the passive, only those who accept their lot without active retaliation, are "flawless." Most of us are in that category.

But there are among us today, as there always have been, those who act against the scheme of things that degrades them, and in the process of action, everything we have accepted out of fear or insensitivity or ignorance is shaken before us and examined, and from this total onslaught by an individual against the seemingly stable

FROM PAGE TO SCREEN

Big Willy Meets the Thug Life

A Scene from the 1961 film adaptation of *West Side Story*

T he setting of an event is an integral part of that event. A conversation that takes place in a nightclub is not going to be the same conversation that takes place in a hospital room. While setting is certainly important in poetry or fiction, drama is a medium in which the author is presenting a physical stage setting to his or her audience. The details of what's on stage are essential to telling the story.

Some dramatists are very specific about what's on stage (for instance, Samuel Beckett—see Chapter 31). William Shakespeare, however, conveyed setting very sparsely in his stage directions. Partly because of this, a number of directors throughout the years have changed the time, setting, and costumes for Shakespeare's works in order to modernize them or highlight certain aspects of the characters and plot. Director/actor Kenneth Branaugh's

cosmos surrounding us—from this total examination of the "unchangeable" environment—comes the terror and the fear that is classically associated with tragedy.

More important, from this total questioning of what has been previously unquestioned, we learn. And such a process is not beyond the common man. In revolutions around the world, these past thirty years, he has demonstrated again and again this inner dynamic of all tragedy.

Insistence upon the rank of the tragic hero, or the so-called nobility of his character, is really but a clinging to the outward forms of tragedy. If rank or nobility of character was indispensable, then it would follow that the problems of those with rank were the particular problems of tragedy. But surely the right of one monarch to capture the domain from another no longer raises our passions, nor are our concepts of justice what they were to the mind of an Elizabethan king.

The quality in such plays that does shake us, however, derives from the underlying fear of being displaced, the disaster inherent in being torn away from our chosen image of what and who we are in this world. Among us today this fear is

From the 1996 film adaptation of *Romeo and Juliet* (starring Leonardo DiCaprio and Claire Danes)

Hamlet was set in the nineteenth century with flashy Victorian sets and costumes to highlight the wealth of the powerful burghers at that time. A recent film version of *Othello*, entitled simply *O*, is set in a high school to highlight the social back-biting central to the plot.

In the 1950s, the rise of young street gangs inspired the film *West Side Story*, a modernized adaptation of Shakespeare's *Romeo and Juliet* in which the language is updated, the Elizabethan costumes are traded for leather jackets, the swords become switchblades, and the warring families of Montague and Capulet become the Jets and the Sharks. This idea resurfaced again in a 1996 version of the play which kept the original language but set the story on Venice Beach, Florida, rather than in Venice, Italy.

One of the hallmarks of Shakespeare's work is that he deals forthrightly with basic human emotions like love and revenge and is less concerned with the specific trappings of the time or setting. These basic emotions and experiences lend themselves to any time and any setting, and any person can relate to them. Because of this, the conversion of swords to guns has not been the only change. In some cases, kingdoms have become corporations, as in a recent *Hamlet* starring Ethan Hawke. The science-fiction classic *Forbidden Planet* is another adaptation of Shakespeare's *The Tempest*, complete with laser guns and robots.

as strong, and perhaps stronger, than it ever was. In fact, it is the common man who knows this fear best.

Now, if it is true that tragedy is the consequence of a man's total compulsion to evaluate himself justly, his destruction in the attempt posits a wrong or an evil in his environment. And this is precisely the morality of tragedy and its lesson. The discovery of the moral law, which is what the enlightenment of tragedy consists of, is not the discovery of some abstract or metaphysical quantity.

The tragic right is a condition of life, a condition in which the human personality is able to flower and realize itself. The wrong is the condition which suppresses man, perverts the flowing out of his love and creative instinct. Tragedy enlightens—and it must, in that it points the heroic finger at the enemy of man's freedom. The thrust for freedom is the quality in tragedy which exalts. The revolutionary questioning of the stable environment is what terrifies. In no way is the common man debarred from such thoughts or such actions.

Seen in this light, our lack of tragedy may be partially accounted for by the turn which modern literature has taken toward the purely psychiatric view of life, or the purely sociological. If all our miseries, our indignities, are born and bred within our minds, then all action, let alone the heroic action, is obviously impossible.

And if society alone is responsible for the cramping of our lives, then the protagonist must needs be so pure and faultless as to force us to deny his validity as a character. From neither of these views can tragedy derive, simply because neither represents a balanced concept of life. Above all else, tragedy requires the finest appreciation by the writer of cause and effect.

No tragedy can therefore come about when its author fears to question absolutely everything, when he regards any institution, habit, or custom as being either everlasting, immutable, or inevitable. In the tragic view the need of man to wholly realize himself is the only fixed star, and whatever it is that hedges his nature and lowers it is ripe for attack and examination. Which is not to say that tragedy must preach revolution.

The Greeks could probe the very heavenly origin of their ways and return to confirm the rightness of laws. And Job could face God in anger, demanding his right, and end in submission. But for a moment everything is in suspension, nothing is accepted, and in this stretching and tearing apart of the cosmos, in the very action of so doing, the character gains "size," the tragic stature which is spuriously attached to the royal or the high born in our minds. The commonest of men may take on that stature to the extent of his willingness to throw all he has into the contest, the battle to secure his rightful place in his world.

There is a misconception of tragedy with which I have been struck in review after review, and in many conversations with writers and readers alike. It is the idea that tragedy is of necessity allied to pessimism. Even the dictionary says nothing more about the word than that it means a story with a sad or unhappy ending. This impression is so firmly fixed that I almost hesitate to claim that in truth tragedy implies more optimism in its author than does comedy, and that its final result ought to be the reinforcement of the onlooker's brightest opinions of the human animal.

For, if it is true to say that in essence the tragic hero is intent upon claiming his whole due as a personality, and if this struggle must be total and without reservation, then it automatically demonstrates the indestructible will of man to achieve his humanity.

The possibility of victory must be there in tragedy. Where pathos rules, where pathos is finally derived, a character has fought a battle he could not possibly have won. The pathetic is achieved when the protagonist is, by virtue of his witlessness, his insensitivity, or the very air he gives off, incapable of grappling with a much superior force.

Pathos truly is the mode for the pessimist. But tragedy requires a nicer balance between what is possible and what is impossible. And it is curious, although edifying, that the plays we revere, century after century, are the tragedies. In them, and in them alone, lies the belief—optimistic, if you will—in the perfectibility of man.

It is time, I think, that we who are without kings, took up this bright thread of our history and followed it to the only place it can possibly lead in our time— the heart and spirit of the average man.

Student Essay

Lisa Nappi explores the meanings and mysteries of Willy Loman's life and death.

Lisa Nappi
Professor Barnard
English 102

All the Wrong Dreams

Throughout our lives, we have dreams and ambitions that we want to achieve. People usually possess the desire to accomplish something worthwhile in life, to reassure themselves that they will forever be remembered. In the play *Death of a Salesman* by Arthur Miller, Willy Loman yearns to fulfill this dream and to better his life and the lives of his boys, Biff and Happy. Willy strives to achieve that "American Dream" so many desire.

Willy's sense of pride is a stumbling block in his life; he doesn't like people to give him advice or handouts, although he may need them. But the feeling of failure overwhelms him when he learns about the loss of his job. "But I got to be at it ten, twelve hours a day. Other men—I don't know—they do it easier. I don't know why—I can't stop myself—I talk too much." Willy, being a hard working man who tries his best, realizes that times have changed. His youthfulness has begun to fade. A man his age working ten to twelve hours a day is not sustainable. In Act II, Willy's boss Howard tells him, "I don't want you to represent us. I've been meaning to tell you for a long time now." When Willy first hears this, from a man so much younger than himself, he begins to cry. A man Willy's age working in a company that long doesn't deserve to be fired. It

Nappi 2

makes his life seem a waste, and makes him imagine himself as a failure. "I was fired and I am looking for a little good news to tell your mother, because the woman has waited and suffered," Willy tells his son. Willy is clueless about what is to come of his family, and he feels he has let everyone down. He failed to support his wife and sons. His life was basically devoted to impressing others, and the one job he had led him to failure.

Biff's character is one of a popular nature. When he was at school he was always popular, athletic and full of potential. All this changed, however, when he went to see his father in Boston. This is when Biff found out about Willy's affair. Finding this out crushed Biff and destroyed his image of his father. When he discovers that his father is a phony he says, "You fake! You phony little fake! You fake!" This shows how devastated Biff is when he finds out about his father's affair. Before Biff discovered his father's affair, he believed in the American dream. But when he discovered that his father, who relied so heavily on the American dream, had deceived him and his whole family, he realized that the American dream was as phony as his own father. This is when Biff rejects his father's dream, and his relationship with his father begins to deteriorate.

Guilt played a big role in Willy Loman's life. He lived many years feeling remorseful about cheating on his wife. "Now look Biff, when you grow up you'll understand about these things. You mustn't overemphasize a thing like this." Biff—Willy's principal source of pride—left him. Biff never trusted him again. Willy's guilt about lying to his loving son stays in his mind—also leaving Biff to hate his father. Whatever relationship they had before was shattered into millions of pieces that day in Boston. It killed Willy that his once loving son grew to hate him. Seeing his wife Linda mending stockings causes Willy to feel guilty, since he had routinely given stockings to the woman he had an affair with. "Will you stop mending stockings? At least while

Nappi 3

I'm in the house. It gets me nervous please!" He now realizes he should have given the new stockings to his loyal wife. These feelings of guilt along with the loss of his son Biff's trust leaves Willy with a great deal of pain and evidently causes his attempts at suicide.

As the play moves toward its tragic end, Willy's flashbacks become more frequent. His suicide attempts become more serious, and we see him more often descend into sadness and depression. Linda, suspecting that her husband wants to kill himself, finds a hidden rubber pipe connected to the gas line of the water heater. "I was looking for a fuse down in the cellar and behind the fuse box—it happened to fall out— a length of a rubber pipe—just short." Linda, scared, tried to take the pipe away every day but always found herself putting it back thinking she was betraying her husband. She began to confide in her sons about what she should do, but found them thinking the opposite.

Biff begins to find his father's lies and cover-ups unbearable. "Pop I'm nothing! I'm nothing Pop! Can't you understand that? There's no spite in it anymore. I'm just what I am that's all!" Willy had always relied on Biff to come home and surprise him with good news, but Biff tells Willy he can't do that any more because their lives are both shams. Biff begins to realize he and his father never were important and never will be. Biff cries to his father to make him understand. Biff's speech was the last meaningful thing that Willy heard, and he dies knowing his son did love him and never blamed him for his life. "The particulars concerning Willy's situation also have universal significance. Willy has lived passionately for values to which he is committed, and he comes to find that they are false and inadequate. He has loved his sons with a passion which wanted for them that which would destroy them."

For all of the feelings of guilt, sadness, and failure in Willy's life, at his requiem everyone (at least, the few who showed up) praised Willy for his good doings, forgetting his bad doings. "Nobody dast blame this man. A salesman is got to dream, boy. It comes with the territory." Charley, Willy's only close friend, explains how a salesman must dream to be successful. Willy may have had the wrong dreams, but he did what he was meant to do in life. "Willy is one vast contradiction, and this contradiction is his downfall. He is a nicer guy than Charley. He is so nice, as someone said once, he's got to end up poor. This makes Charley untroubled and a success, and Willy contradictory, neurotic, full of love and longing need for admiration and affection, full of a sense of worthlessness and inadequacy and dislocation and a failure" (Kazan 1).

The idea behind Miller's play is to reveal the numerous flaws in the American dream and to show that you must define success for yourself, or else it will define you. Willy believes sincerely that wealth is happiness and one's wealth is shown by the number of brand name goods you have. Willy then looks around and notices he has very few of those brand name goods, thus little money, and thus he is a failure. "Inevitably, no matter what material heights a man succeeds to, his life is brief and his comprehension finite, while the universe remains infinite and incomprehensible" (Gordon 1).

Willy also believes that failure cannot be tolerated in his family so he then lies to his family about how popular and successful he is. His lying influences his children to lie, thus spawning a continuing circle of lies. This is pointed out when Biff says, "We never told the truth for ten minutes in this house!" To this statement Happy responds. "We always told the truth!" This shows how that even when faced with the truth, the Loman family still can't accept it. Biff, however, refuses to lie any more, and he accepts the truth. He accepts that he was never anything big and that he "stole his way out of every job since high school." Willy, though, still wishes he could be a big success, and he wants it so much that he starts living in his own fantasy world. He lives in the past because then there was hope for him; whereas now there is no hope for him and he is doomed to failure.

Nappi 5

Willy's demise was one that could only have been avoided if he had changed his dream, and Willy was not going to do this. Willy stuck by his dream until the end, in the hopes that it would eventually pay off. Willy's sad ending left him to remain a salesman. He never made it to the top as he planned, nor ever got his son to trust him again. His death was basically a consequence of the ways of the world and of Willy's own wrongdoing. But what human being is perfect? Some get dealt good cards; others may not. What Willy should have done was follow his heart and not his material greed, and his life might not have ended as sadly as it did.

Works Cited

Gordon, Lois. "Death of a Salesman: An Appreciation." *The Forties: Fiction, Poetry, Drama*, Ed. Warren French. Deland, Florida: Everett/Edwards, Inc., 1969.

Kazan, Elia. "Excerpts from the notebook kept in preparation for directing *Death of a Salesman.*" *A Theater in Your Head.* Kenneth Thorpe Rowe. New York: Funk & Wagnalls, 1960.

Miller, Arthur. *Death of a Salesman. Access Literature.* Eds. Barbara Barnard and David Winn. Boston: Wadsworth, 2005.

MYTH AND DRAMA

Even tattoos use myth. For centuries,

the dragon has been a symbol of power and mystery. Depicted in countless legends, both Eastern and Western, the dragon has inspired in people both fear and worship. In medieval Europe, it was a blood-thirsty, fire-breathing figure, and its malevolence and ferociousness struck terror in all. In Asia, the mighty dragon is a mythical beast long celebrated for its benevolence, intelligence, and good will. The dragon has been a common symbol of identity for East Asian cultures. In fact, Chinese people all over the world are affectionately known as lung de chuan ren, or the "descendants of the dragon." Known in Chinese as lung, the Asian dragon was believed to have originated in China. Dragons in Japan are similar to their Chinese counterparts. Known as tatsu or ryu, Japanese dragons are also national symbols and the insignia of the royal family. According to Japanese lore, a single female dragon spawned nine young dragons—and like the Chinese, each of the nine became distinctive subtypes, reigning in heaven, the seas, and all points of the Earth. The mythical creature's presence in literary texts and on the bodies of people from all over the world is testament to its enduring significance.

The pictures of mythic elements in the body art shown on the previous pages illustrate that myths are present visually in the everyday world. Perhaps you or someone you know has a tattoo of a mythic character. Furthermore, these mythic patterns and elements seen in tattoos are present in many of the texts that we read—both in popular forms and classic literature. As we recognized in our discussions of Myth and Fiction (Chapter 9) and Myth and Poetry (Chapter 21), many mythic patterns (or archetypes) recur again and again and are common across many cultures. Several of these familiar patterns are found in Sophocles' *Oedipus the King*.

Hero Myths

Aristotle (384–322 B.C.E.) describes the tragic hero as one who "does not fall into misfortune through vice or depravity, but falls because of some mistake." Oedipus's mistakes are great but also unintentional, and he is the classic example of a tragic hero as defined by Aristotle. In addition, his heroic deeds recounted early in the play—outwitting the Sphinx, saving the city of Thebes, exercising strong and authoritative leadership in the community (which, in turn, worships him almost as a god)—remind us of other heroes of ancient mythology, such as Odysseus (Greek hero in Homer's *The Iliad* and *The Odyssey*), Theseus (Greek), Hercules (Greek), and Gilgamesh (Mesopotamian). These heroes, like Oedipus, often feel they have a duty to represent—and fight on behalf of—the entire community. Joseph Campbell, an influential scholar of world mythologies, wrote,

> [T]here is a certain typical hero sequence of actions which can be detected in stories from all over the world and from many periods of history. Essentially, it might even be said there is but one archetypal mythic hero whose life has been replicated in many lands by many, many people.
>
> (Joseph Campbell, *The Power of Myth* 166)

Campbell also refers to this archetypal hero as the "hero with a thousand faces." Among many other trials and tasks the hero often faces is the search for his father. Certainly, this is a key element in the Oedipus story; it is also an important element in the *Star Wars* films, in which hero Luke Skywalker searches for his father, eventually finding out the startling truth that his father is none other than Darth Vader.

Myths of Hidden and Revealed Identity

The myth is actually more cross-cultural than the above discussion might suggest. In his book *The World of Myth*, David Adams Leeming describes myths of many cultures which have a pattern similar to the Oedipus story: a child is hidden or exposed to die but is instead adopted and raised by others who don't know his origins; later the true identity is revealed.

[These details] are repeated in the stories of distantly separated heroes: Moses, who was hidden in a basket in the bulrushes and adopted by the pharaoh's daughter; the German Siegfried, who was left in a glass vessel in the river and adopted first by a doe and then by a blacksmith; the Polynesian demigod Maui, who was thrown into the sea and adopted by sea spirits; and the Greek Oedipus, who was left to die in the wilderness but was saved by a shepherd.

(Leeming, *The World of Myth* 226-227)

These stories of hidden and revealed identity are part of a larger body of story patterns having to do with the individual's quest for identity. Certainly, Luke Skywalker is a good example of this aspect of the hero pattern. Can you think of other characters from films, television series, or comic books who fit the archetypal hero patterns?

Reading

Sophocles (circa 496–406 B.C.E.**)**

The life of Sophocles spanned one of the most significant periods in the history of ancient Greece. Believed to have been born in 496 B.C.E., Sophocles saw Athenian culture reach significant heights between the Greek victories that ended the wars with the Persian Empire and the onset of the Peloponnesian wars in which Athens eventually lost to the military might of Sparta.

Sophocles

Until his death in 406 B.C.E., Sophocles played many roles in the life of the Athenian city-state: military leader, legislator, priest, and city official. But he is remembered above all for his plays. Although he is thought to have written over 120 works of drama, only a few have survived as complete and finished. *Oedipus the King, Oedipus at Colonus*, and *Antigone* constitute the trilogy in which he presents the life of Oedipus and his children. *Electra, Philoctetes, Ajax*, and *Maidens of Trachis* are the four other tragedies that have come down to us.

Prior to Sophocles, Greek drama presented the audience with no more than two characters on stage at one time. Sophocles, in a significant innovation, broke with tradition and allowed three characters to occupy the stage. Other playwrights, such as Euripides and Aeschylus, soon followed suit. He allowed individual actors to expand their roles and diminished somewhat the use of the chorus. As a result, his characters became more complex and were able to reveal greater psychological depth. Sophocles continued to rely on the chorus as an essential narrative device, however, and he added members to it as well, increasing the size of the chorus from twelve men to fifteen men. The fates of his central characters seem more driven by their own actions; the interplay of conflict and resolution between them as well as their own view of the world they inhabit attain a greater intricacy. These changes were substantial, and his plays successfully engaged Greek audiences and the Greek imagination for precisely those reasons. He was frequently awarded prizes at the festival competitions.

In *Oedipus the King*, one never loses sight of the hero as a man surrounded by and contending with forces far greater than himself. As king of Thebes, as head of a royal household, as a figure accustomed to success and power, Oedipus by any measure is a man favored by fortune, even in his present crisis. But Sophocles reveals him inevitably as overwhelmed by what is beyond his power to control or understand. He is assailed from within and from without by his pride, his doubts, and his fate.

Oedipus the King* (C. 430 B.C.)

Translated By Thomas Gould

CHARACTERS

OEDIPUS,[1] *the King of Thebes*
PRIEST OF ZEUS, *leader of the suppliants*
CREON, *Oedipus's brother-in-law*
CHORUS, *a group of Theban elders*
CHORAGOS, *spokesman of the Chorus*

TIRESIAS, *a blind seer or prophet*
JOCASTA, *the queen of Thebes*
MESSENGER, *from Corinth, once a shepherd*
HERDSMAN, *once a servant of Laius*
SECOND MESSENGER, *a servant of Oedipus*

MUTES

SUPPLIANTS, *Thebans seeking Oedipus's help*
ATTENDANTS, *for the Royal Family*
SERVANTS, *to lead Tiresias and Oedipus*
ANTIGONE, *daughter of Oedipus and Jocasta*
ISMENE, *daughter of Oedipus and Jocasta*

The action takes place during the day in front of the royal palace in Thebes. There are two altars (left and right) on the proscenium and several steps leading down to the orchestra. As the play opens, Thebans of various ages who have come to beg Oedipus for help are sitting on these steps and in part of the orchestra. These suppliants are holding branches of laurel or olive which have strips of wool[2] wrapped around them. Oedipus enters from the palace (the central door of the skene).

---

*Note that individual lines are numbered in the following play. When a line is shared by two or more characters, it is counted as one line.

[1]**Oedipus:** The name, meaning "swollen foot," refers to the mutilation of Oedipus's feet by his father, Laius, before the infant was sent to Mount Cithaeron to be put to death by exposure.

[2]**Wool:** Branches wrapped with wool are traditional symbols of prayer or supplication.

PROLOGUE[3]

OEDIPUS: My children, ancient Cadmus'[4] newest care,
why have you hurried to those seats, your boughs
5   wound with the emblems of the suppliant?
The city is weighed down with fragrant smoke,
with hymns to the Healer[5] and the cries of mourners.
10   I thought it wrong, my sons, to hear your words
through emissaries, and have come out myself,
I, Oedipus, a name that all men know.

15   *Oedipus addresses the Priest.*

Old man—for it is fitting that you speak
for all—what is your mood as you entreat me,
fear or trust? You may be confident
20   that I'll do anything. How hard of heart
if an appeal like this did not rouse my pity!
   PRIEST: You, Oedipus, who hold the power here,
you see our several ages, we who sit
25   before your altars—some not strong enough
to take long flight, some heavy in old age,
the priests, as I of Zeus,[6] and from our youths
30   a chosen band. The rest sit with their windings
in the markets, at the twin shrines of Pallas,[7]

and the prophetic embers of Ismēnos.[8]
Our city, as you see yourself, is tossed   35
too much, and can no longer lift its head
above the troughs of billows red with death.
It dies in the fruitful flowers of the soil,
it dies in its pastured herds, and in its   40
women's
barren pangs. And the fire-bearing god[9]
has swooped upon the city, hateful plague,
and he has left the house of Cadmus   45
empty.
Black Hades[10] is made rich with moans and weeping.
Not judging you an equal of the gods,
do I and the children sit here at your   50
hearth,
but as the first of men, in troubled times
and in encounters with divinities.
You came to Cadmus' city and unbound
the tax we had to pay to the harsh singer,[11]   55
did it without a helpful word from us,
with no instruction; with a god's assistance
you raised up our life, so we believe.

---

[3]**Prologue:** The portion of the play containing the exposition, or explanation, of what has gone before and what is now happening.
[4]**Cadmus:** Oedipus's great-great-grandfather (although Oedipus does not know this) and the founder of Thebes.
[5]**Healer:** Apollo, god of prophecy, light, healing, justice, purification, and destruction.
[6]**Zeus:** Father and king of the gods.
[7]**Pallas:** Athena, goddess of wisdom, arts, crafts, and war.

[8]**Ismēnos:** A reference to the temple of Apollo near the river Ismenos in Thebes. Prophecies were made here by "reading" the ashes of the altar fires.
[9]**fire-bearing god:** Contagious fever viewed as a god.
[10]**Black Hades:** Refers both to the underworld where the spirits of the dead go and to the god of the underworld.
[11]**harsh singer:** The Sphinx, a monster with a woman's head, a lion's body, and wings. The "tax" from which Oedipus freed Thebes was the destruction of all the young men who failed to solve the Sphinx's riddle and were subsequently devoured. The Sphinx always asked the same riddle: "What goes on four legs in the morning, two legs at noon, and three legs in the evening, and yet is weakest when supported by the largest number of feet?" Oedipus discovered the correct answer—man, who crawls in infancy, walks in his prime, and uses a stick in old age—and thus ended the Sphinx's reign of terror. The Sphinx destroyed herself when Oedipus answered the riddle. Oedipus's reward for freeing Thebes of the Sphinx was the throne and the hand of the recently widowed Jocasta.

Again now Oedipus, our greatest power,
60 we plead with you, as suppliants, all of us,
to find us strength, whether from a god's response,
or learned in some way from another man.
I know that the experienced among men
65 give counsels that will prosper best of all.
Noblest of men, lift up our land again!
Think also of yourself; since now the land
calls you its Savior for your zeal of old,
oh let us never look back at your rule
70 as men helped up only to fall again!
Do not stumble! Put our land on firm feet!
The bird of omen was auspicious then,
when you brought that luck; be that same man again!
75 The power is yours; if you will rule our country,
rule over men, not in an empty land.
A towered city or a ship is nothing
if desolate and no man lives within.
80 **OEDIPUS:**   Pitiable children, oh I know, I know
the yearnings that have brought you. Yes, I know
that you are sick. And yet, though you
85 are sick,
there is not one of you so sick as I.
For your affliction comes to each alone,
for him and no one else, but my soul mourns
90 for me and for you, too, and for the city.
You do not waken me as from a sleep,
for I have wept, bitterly and long,
tried many paths in the wanderings of thought,
95 and the single cure I found by careful search
I've acted on: I sent Menoeceus' son,
Creon, brother of my wife, to the Pythian
halls of Phoebus,[12] so that I might learn
100 what I must do or say to save this city.

Already, when I think what day this is,
I wonder anxiously what he is doing.
Too long, more than is right, he's been away.
But when he comes, then I shall be a traitor   105
if I do not do all that the god reveals.
PRIEST: Welcome words! But look, those men have signaled
that it is Creon who is now approaching!   110
OEDIPUS: Lord Apollo! May he bring Savior Luck,
a Luck as brilliant as his eyes are now!
PRIEST: His news is happy, it appears. He comes,   115
forehead crowned with thickly berried laurel.[13]
OEDIPUS: We'll know, for he is near enough to hear us.

Enter Creon along one of the parados.   120

Lord, brother in marriage, son of Menoeceus!
What is the god's pronouncement that you bring?   125
CREON: It's good. For even troubles, if they chance
to turn out well, I always count as lucky.
OEDIPUS: But what was the response? You   130
seem to say
I'm not to fear—but not to take heart either.
CREON: If you will hear me with these men present,   135
I'm ready to report—or go inside.

Creon moves up the steps toward the palace.

OEDIPUS: Speak out to all! The grief that burdens me   140
concerns these men more than it does my life.

---

[12]**Pythian halls** . . . **Phoebus:** The temple of Phoebus, Apollo's oracle or prophet at Delphi.

[13]**laurel.** Creon is wearing a garland of laurel leaves, sacred to Apollo.

CREON: Then I shall tell you what I heard from the god.

145 The task Lord Phoebus sets for us is clear: drive out pollution sheltered in our land, and do not shelter what is incurable.

OEDIPUS: What is our trouble? How shall we cleanse ourselves?

150 CREON: We must banish or murder to free ourselves
from a murder that blows storms through the city.

OEDIPUS: What man's bad luck does he
155 accuse in this?

CREON: My Lord, a king named Laius ruled our land
before you came to steer the city straight.

OEDIPUS: I know. So I was told—I never
160 saw him.

CREON: Since he was murdered, you must raise your hand
against the men who killed him with their hands.

165 OEDIPUS: Where are they now? And how can we ever find
the track of ancient guilt now hard to read?

CREON: In our own land, he said. What
170 we pursue,
that can be caught; but not what we neglect.

OEDIPUS: Was Laius home, or in the coun-tryside—
175 or was he murdered in some foreign land?

CREON: He left to see a sacred rite, he said;
He left, but never came home from his journey.

180 OEDIPUS: Did none of his party see it and report—
someone we might profitably question?

CREON: They were all killed but one, who fled in fear,
185 and he could tell us only one clear fact.

OEDIPUS: What fact? One thing could lead us on to more

if we could get a small start on our hope.

CREON: He said that bandits chanced on them and killed him—   190
with the force of many hands, not one alone.

OEDIPUS: How could a bandit dare so great an act—
unless this was a plot paid off from here!   195

CREON: We thought of that, but when Laius was killed,
we had no one to help us in our troubles.

OEDIPUS: It was your very kingship that was killed!   200
What kind of trouble blocked you from a search?

CREON: The subtle-singing Sphinx asked us to turn
from the obscure to what lay at our feet.   205

OEDIPUS: Then I shall begin again and make it plain.
It was quite worthy of Phoebus, and worthy of you,
to turn our thoughts back to the   210
murdered man,
and right that you should see me join the battle
for justice to our land and to the god.
Not on behalf of any distant kinships,   215
it's for myself I will dispel this stain.
Whoever murdered him may also wish
to punish me—and with the selfsame hand.
In helping him I also serve myself.   220
Now quickly, children: up from the altar steps,
and raise the branches of the suppliant!
Let someone go and summon Cadmus' people: 225
say I'll do anything.

Exit an Attendant along one of the parados.

Our luck will prosper
if the god is with us, or we have already fallen.   230

PRIEST: Rise, my children; that for which we came,
  he has himself proclaimed he will accomplish.
235 May Phoebus, who announced this, also come
  as Savior and reliever from the plague.

Exit Oedipus and Creon into the palace. The Priest and the Suppliants exit left and right
240 *along the parados. After a brief pause, the Chorus (including the Choragos) enters the orchestra from the parados.*

PARADOS[14]
STROPHE 1[15]

CHORUS: Voice from Zeus,[16] sweetly spoken, what are you
245 that have arrived from golden Pytho[17] to our shining
  Thebes? I am on the rack, terror shakes my soul.
  Delian Healer,[18] summoned by "ie!"
250 I await in holy dread what obligation, something new
  or something back once more with the revolving years,
  you'll bring about for me.
255 Oh tell me, child of golden Hope, deathless Response!

ANTISTROPHE 1

  I appeal to you first, daughter of Zeus, deathless Athena,
  and to your sister who protects this land,

Artemis,[19] whose famous throne is the   260
whole circle of the marketplace,
and Phoebus, who shoots from afar: iō!
Three-fold defenders against death, appear!
If ever in the past, to stop blind ruin   265
sent against the city,
you banished utterly the fires of suffering,
come now again!

STROPHE 2

Ah! Ah! Unnumbered are the miseries
I bear. The plague claims all   270
our comrades. Nor has thought
found yet a spear
by which a man shall be protected. What our glorious
earth gives birth to does not grow.   275
Without a birth
from cries of labor
do the women rise.
One person after another
you may see, like flying birds,   280
faster than indomitable fire, sped
to the shore of the god that is the sunset.[20]

ANTISTROPHE 2

And with their deaths unnumbered
dies the city.
Her children lie unpitied on the ground,   285
spreading death, unmourned.
Meanwhile young wives, and gray-
haired mothers with them,
on the shores of the altars, from this side and that,
suppliants from mournful trouble,   290
cry out their grief.
A hymn to the Healer shines,
the flute a mourner's voice.

---

[14]**Parados:** A song sung by the Chorus on first entering.
[15]**Strophe:** Probably refers to the direction in which the Chorus danced while reciting specific stanzas. *Strophe* may have indicated dance steps to stage left, *antistrophe* to stage right.
[16]**Voice from Zeus:** A reference to Apollo's prophecy. Zeus taught Apollo how to prophesy.
[17]**Pytho:** Delphi.
[18]**Delian Healer:** Apollo.

---

[19]**Artemis:** Goddess of virginity, childbirth, and hunting.
[20]**god . . . sunset:** Hades, god of the underworld.

295 Against which, golden goddess, daughter
of Zeus,
send lovely Strength.

STROPHE 3

Causing raging Ares[21]—who,
armed now with no shield of bronze,
300 burns me, coming on amid loud cries—
to turn his back and run from my land,
with a fair wind behind, to the great
hall of Amphitritē,[22]
or to the anchorage that welcomes no one,
305 Thrace's troubled sea!
If night lets something get away at last,
it comes by day.
Fire-bearing god . . .
you who dispense the might of lightning,
310 Zeus! Father! Destroy him with your
thunderbolt!

Enter Oedipus from the palace.

ANTISTROPHE 3

Lycēan Lord![23] From your looped
bowstring, twisted gold,
315 I wish indomitable missiles might be
scattered
and stand forward, our protectors; also
fire-bearing
radiance of Artemis, with which
320 she darts across the Lycian mountains.
I call the god whose head is bound in gold,
with whom this country shares its name,
Bacchus,[24] wine-flushed, summoned
by "euoi!,"
325 Maenads' comrade,
to approach ablaze
with gleaming . . .
pine, opposed to that god-hated god.

EPISODE 1[25]

OEDIPUS: I hear your prayer. Submit to
what I say   330
and to the labors that the plague
demands
and you'll get help and a relief from evils.
I'll make the proclamation, though a
stranger   335
to the report and to the deed. Alone,
had I no key, I would soon lose the track.
Since it was only later that I joined you,
to all the sons of Cadmus I say this:
whoever has clear knowledge of the man   340
who murdered Laius, son of Labdacus,
I command him to reveal it all to me—
nor fear if, to remove the charge, he must
accuse himself: his fate will not be cruel—
he will depart unstumbling into exile.   345
But if you know another, or a stranger,
to be the one whose hand is guilty, speak:
I shall reward you and remember you.
But if you keep your peace because of fear,
and shield yourself or kin from my   350
command,
hear you what I shall do in that event:
I charge all in this land where I have
throne
and power, shut out that man—no matter   355
who—
both from your shelter and all spoken
words,
nor in your prayers or sacrifices make
him partner, nor allot him lustral[26] water.   360
All men shall drive him from their
homes: for he
is the pollution that the god-sent Pythian
response has only now revealed to me.
In this way I ally myself in war   365
with the divinity and the deceased.[27]

21**Ares:** God of war and destruction.
22**Amphitritē:** The Atlantic Ocean.
23**Lycēan Lord:** Apollo.
24**Bacchus:** Dionysus, god of fertility and wine.

25**Episode:** The portion of ancient Greek plays that
appears between choric songs.
26**lustral:** Purifying.
27**the deceased:** Laius.

And this curse, too, against the one who
did it,
whether alone in secrecy, or with others:
370 may he wear out his life unblest and evil!
I pray this, too: if he is at my hearth
and in my home, and I have knowledge
of him,
may the curse pronounced on others
375 come to me.
All this I lay to you to execute,
for my sake, for the god's, and for
this land
now ruined, barren, abandoned
380 by the gods.
Even if no god had driven you to it,
you ought not to have left this stain
uncleansed,
the murdered man a nobleman, a king!
385 You should have looked! But now, since,
as it happens,
It's I who have the power that he had
once,
and have his bed, and a wife who shares
390 our seed,
and common bond had we had common
children
(had not his hope of offspring had bad
luck—
395 but as it happened, luck lunged at his
head);
because of this, as if for my own father,
I'll fight for him, I'll leave no means
untried,
400 to catch the one who did it with his hand,
for the son of Labdacus, of Polydōrus,
of Cadmus before him, and of Agēnor.[28]
This prayer against all those who
disobey:
405 the gods send out no harvest from
their soil,
nor children from their wives. Oh, let
them die

victims of this plague, or of something
worse. 410
Yet for the rest of us, people of Cadmus,
we the obedient, may Justice, our ally,
and all the gods, be always on our side!
CHORAGOS:[29] I speak because I feel the
grip of your curse: 415
the killer is not I. Nor can I point
to him. The one who set us to this
search,
Phoebus, should also name the guilty
man. 420
OEDIPUS: Quite right, but to compel
unwilling gods—
no man has ever had that kind of power.
CHORAGOS: May I suggest to you a second way? 425
OEDIPUS: A second or a third—pass over
nothing!
CHORAGOS: I know of no one who sees
more of what
Lord Phoebus sees than Lord Tiresias. 430
My Lord, one might learn brilliantly from
him.
OEDIPUS: Nor is this something I have
been slow to do.
At Creon's word I sent an escort—twice 435
now!
I am astonished that he has not come.
CHORAGOS: The old account is useless. It
told us nothing.
OEDIPUS: But tell it to me. I'll scrutinize 440
all stories.
CHORAGOS: He is said to have been killed
by travelers.
OEDIPUS: I have heard, but the one who
did it no one sees. 445
CHORAGOS: If there is any fear in him
at all,
he won't stay here once he has heard that
curse.

---

[28]**son . . . Agēnor:** Refers to Laius by citing his
genealogy.

[29]**Choragos:** Leader of the Chorus and principal commentator on the play's action.

450 OEDIPUS: He won't fear words: he had no fear when he did it.

Enter Tiresias from the right, led by a Servant and two of Oedipus's Attendants.

CHORAGOS: Look there! There is the man
455 who will convict him!
It's the god's prophet they are leading here,
one gifted with the truth as no one else.
OEDIPUS: Tiresias, master of all omens—
public and secret, in the sky and on
460 the earth—
your mind, if not your eyes, sees how
the city
lives with a plague, against which Thebes
can find
465 no Saviour or protector, Lord, but you.
For Phoebus, as the attendants surely
told you,
returned this answer to us: liberation
from the disease would never come
470 unless
we learned without a doubt who
murdered Laius—
put them to death, or sent them into exile.
Do not begrudge us what you may learn
475 from birds
or any other prophet's path you know!
Care for yourself, the city, care for me,
care for the whole pollution of the dead!
We're in your hands. To do all that he can
480 to help another is man's noblest labor.
TIRESIAS: How terrible to understand
and get
no profit from the knowledge! I knew this,
but I forgot, or I had never come.
485 OEDIPUS: What's this? You've come with
very little zeal.
TIRESIAS: Let me go home! If you will
listen to me,
You will endure your troubles better—
490 and I mine.
OEDIPUS: A strange request, not very kind
to the land

that cared for you—to hold back this
oracle!
TIRESIAS: I see your understanding comes 495
to you
inopportunely. So that won't happen to
me . . .
OEDIPUS: Oh, by the gods, if you
understand about this, 500
don't turn away! We're on our knees
to you.
TIRESIAS: None of you understands! I'll
never bring
my grief to light—I will not speak of 505
yours.
OEDIPUS: You know and won't declare it!
Is your purpose
to betray us and to destroy this land!
TIRESIAS: I will grieve neither of us. Stop 510
this futile
cross-examination. I'll tell you nothing!
OEDIPUS: Nothing? You vile traitor! You
could provoke
a stone to anger! You still refuse to tell? 515
Can nothing soften you, nothing
convince you?
TIRESIAS: You blamed anger in me—you
haven't seen.
The kind that lives with you, so you 520
blame me.
OEDIPUS: Who wouldn't fill with anger,
listening
to words like yours which now disgrace
this city? 525
TIRESIAS: It will come, even if my silence
hides it.
OEDIPUS: If it will come, then why won't
you declare it?
TIRESIAS: I'd rather say no more. Now if 530
you wish,
respond to that with all your fiercest
anger!
OEDIPUS: Now I am angry enough to
come right out 535
with this conjecture: you, I think,
helped plot

the deed; you did it—even if your hand,
cannot have struck the blow. If you

540 could see,
I should have said the deed was yours
alone.

TIRESIAS: Is that right! Then I charge you
to abide

545 by the decree you have announced: from
this day
say no word to either these or me,
for you are the vile polluter of this land!

OEDIPUS: Aren't you appalled to let a

550 charge like that
come bounding forth? How will you get
away?

TIRESIAS: You cannot catch me. I have the
strength of truth.

555 OEDIPUS: Who taught you this? Not your
prophetic craft!

TIRESIAS: You did. You made me say it. I
didn't want to.

OEDIPUS: Say what? Repeat it so I'll

560 understand.

TIRESIAS: I made no sense? Or are you
trying me?

OEDIPUS: No sense I understood. Say it
again!

565 TIRESIAS: I say you are the murderer you
seek.

OEDIPUS: Again that horror! You'll wish
you hadn't said that.

TIRESIAS: Shall I say more, and raise your

570 anger higher?

OEDIPUS: Anything you like! Your words
are powerless.

TIRESIAS: You live, unknowing, with those
nearest to you

575 in the greatest shame. You do not see the
evil.

OEDIPUS: You won't go on like that and
never pay!

TIRESIAS: I can if there is any strength in

580 truth.

OEDIPUS: In truth, but not in you! You
have no strength,

blind in your ears, your reason, and your
eyes.

TIRESIAS: Unhappy man! Those jeers you   585
hurl at me
before long all these men will hurl at you.

OEDIPUS: You are the child of endless
night; it's not
for me or anyone who sees to hurt you.   590

TIRESIAS: It's not my fate to be struck
down by you.
Apollo is enough. That's his concern.

OEDIPUS: Are these inventions Creon's or
your own?   595

TIRESIAS: No, your affliction is yourself,
not Creon.

OEDIPUS: Oh success!—in wealth,
kingship, artistry,
in any life that wins much admiration—   600
the envious ill will stored up for you!
to get at my command, a gift I did not
seek, which the city put into my hands,
my loyal Creon, colleague from the start,
longs to sneak up in secret and dethrone   605
me.
So he's suborned this fortuneteller—
schemer!
deceitful beggar-priest!—who has
good eyes   610
for gains alone, though in his craft he's
blind.
Where were your prophet's powers ever
proved?
Why, when the dog who chanted verse[30]   615
was here,
did you not speak and liberate this city?
Her riddle wasn't for a man chancing by
to interpret; prophetic art was needed,
but you had none, it seems—learned   620
from birds
or from a god. I came along, yes I,
Oedipus the ignorant, and stopped her—
by using thought, not angry from birds.
And it is I whom you now wish to banish,   625

---

[30]**dog . . . verse:** The Sphinx.

so you'll be close to the Creontian throne.
You—and the plot's concocter—will
drive out
pollution to your grief: you look quite old

630   or you would be the victim of that plot!
CHORAGOS: It seems to us that this man's
words were said
in anger, Oedipus, and yours as well.
Insight, not angry words, is what we need,

635   the best solution to the god's response.
TIRESIAS: You are the king, and yet I am
your equal
in my right to speak. In that I too am Lord.
for I belong to Loxias,[31] not you.

640   I am not Creon's man. He's nothing to me.
Hear this, since you have thrown my
blindness at me:
Your eyes can't see the evil to which
you've come,

645   nor where you live, nor who is in your
house.
Do you know your parents? Not
knowing, you are
their enemy, in the underworld and here.

650   A mother's and a father's double-lashing
terrible-footed curse will soon drive you
out.
Now you can see, then you will stare into
darkness.

655   What place will not be harbor to your cry,
or what Cithaeron[32] not reverberate
when you have heard the bride-song in
your palace
to which you sailed? Fair wind to evil

660   harbor!
Nor do you see how many other woes
will level you to yourself and to your
children.
So, at my message, and at Creon, too,

665   splatter muck! There will never be a man
ground into wretchedness as you will be.

OEDIPUS: Am I to listen to such things
from him!
May you be damned! Get out of here at
once!   670
Go! Leave my palace! Turn around
and go!

Tiresias begins to move away from Oedipus.

TIRESIAS: I wouldn't have come had you
not sent for me.   675
OEDIPUS: I did not know you'd talk
stupidity,
or I wouldn't have rushed to bring you to
my house.
TIRESIAS: Stupid I seem to you, yet to   680
your parents
who gave you natural birth I seemed
quite shrewd.
OEDIPUS: Who? Wait! Who is the one who
gave me birth?   685
TIRESIAS: This day will give you birth,[33]
and ruin too.
OEDIPUS: What murky, riddling things
you always say!
TIRESIAS: Don't you surpass us all at   690
finding out?
OEDIPUS: You sneer at what you'll find
has brought me greatness.
TIRESIAS: And that's the very luck that
ruined you.   695
OEDIPUS: I wouldn't care, just so I saved
the city.
TIRESIAS: In that case I shall go. Boy, lead
the way!
OEDIPUS: Yes, let him lead you off. Here,   700
underfoot,
you irk me. Gone, you'll cause no further
pain.
TIRESIAS: I'll go when I have said what I
was sent for.   705
Your face won't scare me. You can't
ruin me.

---

[31]**Loxias:** Apollo.
[32]**Cithaeron:** The mountain on which Oedipus was to
be exposed as an infant.

---

[33]**This day . . . birth:** On this day, you will learn who
your parents are.

I say to you, the man whom you have looked for

710 as you pronounced your curses, your decrees
on the bloody death of Laius—he is here!
A seeming stranger, he shall be shown to be

715 a Theban born, though he'll take no delight
in that solution. Blind, who once could see,
a beggar who was rich, through foreign lands

720 he'll go and point before him with a stick.
To his beloved children, he'll be shown
a father who is also brother; to the one
who bore him, son and husband; to his father,

725 his seed-fellow and killer. Go in
and think this out; and if you find I've lied,
say then I have no prophet's understanding!

Exit Tiresias, led by a Servant. Oedipus exits
730 *into the palace with his Attendants.*

STASIMON 1[34]
STROPHE 1

CHORUS: Who is the man of whom the inspired
rock of Delphi[35] said
he has committed the unspeakable

735 with blood-stained hands?
Time for him to ply a foot
mightier than those of the horses
of the storm in his escape;
upon him mounts and plunges the

740 weaponed
son of Zeus,[36] with fire and thunderbolts,
and in his train the dreaded goddesses
of Death, who never miss.

---

[34]**Stasimon:** Greek choral ode between episodes.
[35]**rock of Delphi:** Apollo's oracle at Delphi.
[36]**son of Zeus:** Apollo.

ANTISTROPHE 1

The message has just blazed,
gleaming from the snows   745
of Mount Parnassus: we must track
everywhere the unseen man.
He wanders, hidden by wild
forests, up through caves
and rocks, like a bull,   750
anxious, with an anxious foot, forlorn.
He puts away from him the mantic[37]
words come from earth's
navel,[38] at its center, yet these live
forever and still hover round him.   755

STROPHE 2

Terribly he troubles me,
the skilled interpreter of birds![39]
I can't assent, nor speak against him.
Both paths are closed to me.
I hover on the wings of doubt,   760
not seeing what is here nor what's
to come.
What quarrel started in the house of
Labdacus[40]
or in the house of Polybus,[41]   765
either ever in the past
or now, I never
heard, so that . . . with this fact for my
touchstone
I could attack the public   770
fame of Oedipus, by the side of the
Labdaceans
an ally, against the dark assassination.

ANTISTROPHE 2

No, Zeus and Apollo   775
understand and know things
mortal; but that another man

---

[37]**mantic:** prophetic.
[38]**earth's navel:** Delphi.
[39]**interpreter of birds:** Tiresias. The Chorus is troubled by his accusations.
[40]**house of Labdacus:** The line of Laius.
[41]**Polybus:** Oedipus's foster father.

can do more as a prophet than I can
for that there is no certain test,
780   though, skill to skill,
one man might overtake another.
No, never, not until
I see the charges proved,
when someone blames him shall I nod
785   assent.
For once, as we all saw, the winged
maiden[42] came
against him: he was seen then to be
skilled,
790   proved, by that touchstone, dear to the
people. So,
never will my mind convict him of
the evil.

EPISODE 2

Enter Creon from the right door of the skene
795 *and speaks to the Chorus.*

CREON: Citizens, I hear that a fearful
charge
is made against me by King Oedipus!
I had to come. If, in this crisis,
800   he thinks that he has suffered injury
from anything that I have said or done,
I have no appetite for a long life—
bearing a blame like that! It's no slight
blow
805   the punishment I'd take from what
he said:
it's the ultimate hurt to be called traitor
by the city, by you, by my own people!
CHORAGOS: The thing that forced that
810   accusation out
could have been anger, not the power of
thought.
CREON: But who persuaded him that
thoughts of mine
815   had led the prophet into telling lies?
CHORAGOS: I do not know the thought
behind his words.

---

[42]**winged maiden:** The Sphinx.

CREON: But did he look straight at you?
Was his mind right
when he said that I was guilty of this   820
charge?
CHORAGOS: I have no eyes to see what
rulers do.
But here he comes himself out of the
house.   825

Enter Oedipus from the palace.

OEDIPUS: What? You here? And can you
really have
the face and daring to approach my
house   830
when you're exposed as its master's
murderer
and caught, too, as the robber of my
kingship?
Did you see cowardice in me, by the   835
gods,
or foolishness, when you began this plot?
Did you suppose that I would not detect
your stealthy moves, or that I'd not fight
back?   840
It's your attempt that's folly, isn't it—
tracking without followers or
connections,
kingship which is caught with wealth
and numbers?   845
CREON: Now wait! Give me as long to
answer back!
Judge me for yourself when you have
heard me!
OEDIPUS: You're eloquent, but I'd be slow   850
to learn
from you, now that I've seen your malice
toward me.
CREON: That I deny. Hear what I have to
say.   855
OEDIPUS: Don't you deny it! You are the
traitor here!
CREON: If you consider mindless
willfulness
a prized possession, you are not thinking   860
sense.

OEDIPUS: If you think you can wrong a relative
and get off free, you are not thinking sense.

865 CREON: Perfectly just, I won't say no. And yet
what is this injury you say I did you?

OEDIPUS: Did you persuade me, yes or no, to send

870 someone to bring that solemn prophet here?

CREON: And I still hold to the advice I gave.

OEDIPUS: How many years ago did your

875 King Laius . . .

CREON: Laius! Do what? Now I don't understand.

OEDIPUS: Vanish—victim of a murderous violence?

880 CREON: That is a long count back into the past.

OEDIPUS: Well, was this seer then practicing his art?

CREON: Yes, skilled and honored just as

885 he is today.

OEDIPUS: Did he, back then, ever refer to me?

CREON: He did not do so in my presence ever.

890 OEDIPUS: You did inquire into the murder then.

CREON: We had to, surely, though we discovered nothing.

OEDIPUS: But the "skilled" one did not

895 say this then? Why not?

CREON: I never talk when I am ignorant.

OEDIPUS: But you're not ignorant of your own part.

CREON: What do you mean? I'll tell you if

900 I know.

OEDIPUS: Just this: if he had not conferred with you
he'd not have told about my murdering Laius.

905 CREON: If he said that, you are the one who knows.

But now it's fair that you should answer me.

OEDIPUS: Ask on! You won't convict me as the killer. 910

CREON: Well then, answer. My sister is your wife?

OEDIPUS: Now there's a statement that I can't deny.

CREON: You two have equal power in this 915 country?

OEDIPUS: She gets from me whatever she desires.

CREON: And I'm a third? The three of us are equals? 920

OEDIPUS: That's where you're treacherous to your kinsman!

CREON: But think about this rationally, as I do.
First look at this: do you think anyone 925
prefers the anxieties of being king
to untroubled sleep—if he has equal power?
I'm not the kind of man who falls in love
with kingship. I am content with a king's 930 power.
And so would any man who's wise and prudent.
I get all things from you, with no distress;
as king I would have onerous duties, too. 935
How could the kingship bring me more delight
than this untroubled power and influence?
I'm not misguided yet to such a point 940
that profitable honors aren't enough.
As it is, all wish me well and all salute;
those begging you for something have me summoned,
for their success depends on that alone. 945
Why should I lose all this to become king?
A prudent mind is never traitorous.
Treason's a thought I'm not enamored of;
nor could I join a man who acted so. 950
In proof of this, first go yourself to Pytho

and ask if I brought back the true response.
Then, if you find I plotted with that
955 portent
reader,[43] don't have me put to death by
your vote
only—I'll vote myself for my conviction.
Don't let an unsupported thought
960 convict me!
It's not right mindlessly to take the bad
for good or to suppose the good are
traitors.
Rejecting a relation who is loyal
965 is like rejecting life, our greatest love.
In time you'll know securely without
stumbling,
for time alone can prove a just man just,
though you can know a bad man in a
970 day.

CHORAGOS: Well said, to one who's anxious not to fall.
Swift thinkers, Lord, are never safe from
stumbling.

975 OEDIPUS: But when a swift and secret
plotter moves
against me, I must make swift
counterplot.
If I lie quiet and await his move,
980 he'll have achieved his aims and
I'll have missed.

CREON: You surely cannot mean you want
me exiled!

OEDIPUS: Not exiled, no. Your death is
985 what I want!

CREON: If you would first define what
envy is . . .

OEDIPUS: Are you still stubborn? Still
disobedient?

990 CREON: I see you cannot think?

OEDIPUS: For me I can.

CREON: You should for me as well!

OEDIPUS: But you're a traitor!

CREON: What if you're wrong?

OEDIPUS: Authority must be maintained. 995

CREON: Not if the ruler's evil.

OEDIPUS: Hear that, Thebes!

CREON: It is my city too, not yours alone!

CHORAGOS: Please don't, my Lords! Ah,
just in time, I see 1000
Jocasta there, coming from the palace.
With her help you must settle your
quarrel.

Enter Jocasta from the palace.

JOCASTA: Wretched men! What has 1005
provoked this ill-advised dispute? Have
you no sense of shame,
with Thebes so sick, to stir up private
troubles?
Now go inside! And Creon, you go home! 1010
Don't make a general anguish out of
nothing!

CREON: My sister, Oedipus your husband
here
sees fit to do one of two hideous things: 1015
to have me banished from the land—or
killed!

OEDIPUS: That's right: I caught him, Lady,
plotting harm
against my person—with a malignant 1020
science.

CREON: May my life fail, may I die
cursed, if I
did any of the things you said I did!

JOCASTA: Believe his words, for the god's 1025
sake, Oedipus,
in deference above all to his oath
to the gods. Also for me, and for these
men!

KOMMOS[44]

STROPHE 1

CHORUS: Consent, with will and mind, 1030
my king, I beg of you!

---

[43]**portent reader:** Apollo's oracle or prophet.

[44]**Kommos:** A dirge or lament sung by the Chorus and
one or more of the chief characters.

OEDIPUS: What do you wish me to
     surrender?
CHORUS: Show deference to him who was
1035   not feeble in time past
     and is now great in the power of his oath!
OEDIPUS: Do you know what you're
     asking?
CHORUS: Yes.
1040 OEDIPUS: Tell me then.
CHORUS: Never to cast into dishonored
     guilt, with an unproved
     assumption, a kinsman who has bound
     himself by curse.
1045 OEDIPUS: Now you must understand,
     when you ask this,
     you ask my death or banishment from
     the land.

STROPHE 2

CHORUS: No, by the god who is the
1050   foremost of all gods,
     the Sun! No! Godless,
     friendless, whatever death is worst of all,
     let that be my destruction, if this
     thought ever moved me!
1055   But my ill-fated soul
     this dying land
     wears out—the more if to these older
     troubles
     she adds new troubles from the two of
1060   you!
OEDIPUS: Then let him go, though it must
     mean my death,
     or else disgrace and exile from the land.
     My pity is moved by your words, not by
1065   his—
     he'll only have my hate, wherever he
     goes.
CREON: You're sullen as you yield; you'll
     be depressed
1070   when you've passed through this anger.
     Natures like yours
     are hardest on themselves. That's as it
     should be.
OEDIPUS: Then won't you go and let me be?

CREON: I'll go.   1075
     Though you're unreasonable, they know
     I'm righteous.

Exit Creon.

ANTISTROPHE 1

CHORUS: Why are you waiting, Lady?
     Conduct him back into the palace!   1080
JOCASTA: I will, when I have heard what
     chanced.
CHORUS: Conjectures—words alone, and
     nothing based on thought.
     But even an injustice can devour a man. 1085
JOCASTA: Did the words come from both
     sides?
CHORUS: Yes.
JOCASTA: What was said?
CHORUS: To me it seems enough! enough!   1090
     the land already troubled,
     that this should rest where it has
     stopped.
OEDIPUS: See what you've come to in
     your honest thought,   1095
     in seeking to relax and blunt my heart?

ANTISTROPHE 2

CHORUS: I have not said this only once,
     my Lord.
     That I had lost my sanity,
     without a path in thinking—   1100
     be sure this would be clear
     if I put you away
     who, when my cherished land
     wandered crazed
     with suffering, brought her back on course. 1105
     Now, too, be a lucky helmsman!
JOCASTA: Please, for the god's sake, Lord,
     explain to me
     the reason why you have conceived this
     wrath?   1110
OEDIPUS: I honor you, not them,[45]
     and I'll explain to you

---

[45]**them:** The Chorus.

how Creon has conspired
against me.

1115 JOCASTA: All right, if that will explain
how the quarrel started.

OEDIPUS: He says I am the murderer of
Laius!

JOCASTA: Did he claim knowledge or that
1120 someone told him?

OEDIPUS: Here's what he did: he sent that
vicious seer
so he could keep his own mouth innocent.

JOCASTA: Ah then, absolve yourself of
1125 what he charges!
Listen to this and you'll agree, no mortal
is ever given skill in prophecy.
I'll prove this quickly with one incident.
It was foretold to Laius—I shall not say
1130 by Phoebus himself, but by his ministers—
that when his fate arrived he would be
killed
by a son who would be born to him
and me.

1135 And yet, so it is told, foreign robbers
murdered him, at a place where three
roads meet.
As for the child I bore him, not three
days passed
1140 before he yoked the ball-joints of its feet,[46]
then cast it, by others' hands, on a track-
less mountain.
That time Apollo did not make our child
a patricide, or bring about what Laius
1145 feared, that he be killed by his own son.
That's how prophetic words determined
things!
Forget them. The things a god must track
he will himself painlessly reveal.

1150 OEDIPUS: Just now, as I was listening to
you, Lady,
what a profound distraction seized my
mind!

JOCASTA: What made you turn around so
1155 anxiously?

46**ball-joints of its feet:** The ankles.

OEDIPUS: I thought you said that Laius
was attacked
and butchered at a place where three
roads meet.

JOCASTA: That is the story, and it is told so 1160
still.

OEDIPUS: Where is the place where this
was done to him?

JOCASTA: The land's called Phocis, where
a two-forked road 1165
comes in from Delphi and from Daulia.

OEDIPUS: And how much time has passed
since these events?

JOCASTA: Just prior to your presentation
here 1170
as king this news was published to the
city.

OEDIPUS: Oh, Zeus, what have you willed
to do to me?

JOCASTA: Oedipus, what makes your heart 1175
so heavy?

OEDIPUS: No, tell me first of Laius'
appearance,
what peak of youthful vigor he had
reached. 1180

JOCASTA: A tall man, showing his first
growth of white.
He had a figure not unlike your own.

OEDIPUS: Alas! It seems that in my ignorance 1185
I laid those fearful curses on myself.

JOCASTA: What is it, Lord? I flinch to see
your face.

OEDIPUS: I'm dreadfully afraid the
prophet sees. 1190
But I'll know better with one more detail.

JOCASTA: I'm frightened too. But ask: I'll
answer you.

OEDIPUS: Was his retinue small, or did he
travel 1195
with a great troop, as would befit a
prince?

JOCASTA: There were just five in all, one a
herald.
There was a carriage, too, bearing Laius. 1200

OEDIPUS: Alas! Now I see it! But who was it,
Lady, who told you what you know about this?
1205 JOCASTA: A servant who alone was saved unharmed.
OEDIPUS: By chance, could he be now in the palace?
JOCASTA: No, he is not. When he returned
1210 and saw
you had the power of the murdered Laius,
he touched my hand and begged me formally
to send him to the fields and to the
1215 pastures,
so he'd be out of sight, far from the city.
I did. Although a slave, he well deserved
to win this favor, and indeed far more.
OEDIPUS: Let's have him called back in
1220 immediately.
JOCASTA: That can be done, but why do you desire it?
OEDIPUS: I fear, Lady, I have already said
too much. That's why I wish to see him
1225 now.
JOCASTA: Then he shall come; but it is right somehow
that I, too, Lord, should know what troubles you.
1230 OEDIPUS: I've gone so deep into the things I feared
I'll tell you everything. Who has a right
greater than yours, while I cross through this chance?
1235 Polybus of Corinth was my father,
my mother was the Dorian Meropē.
I was first citizen, until this chance
attacked me—striking enough, to be sure,
but not worth all the gravity I gave it.
1240 This: at a feast a man who'd drunk too much
denied, at the wine, I was my father's son.
I was depressed and all that day I barely
1245 held it in. Next day I put the question

to my mother and father. They were enraged
at the man who'd let this fiction fly at me.
I was much cheered by them. And yet it kept   1250
grinding into me. His words kept coming back.
Without my mother's or my father's knowledge
I went to Pytho. But Phoebus sent me away   1255
dishonoring my demand. Instead, other
wretched horrors he flashed forth in speech.
He said that I would be my mother's lover,   1260
show offspring to mankind they could not look at,
and be his murderer whose seed I am.[47]
When I heard this, and ever since, I gauged   1265
the way to Corinth by the stars alone,
running to a place where I would never see
the disgrace in the oracle's words come true.   1270
But I soon came to the exact location
where, as you tell of it, the king was killed.
Lady, here is the truth. As I went on,
when I was just approaching those three   1275
roads,
a herald and a man like him you spoke of
came on, riding a carriage drawn by colts.
Both the man out front and the old man himself[48]   1280
tried violently to force me off the road.
The driver, when he tried to push me off,
I struck in anger. The old man saw this, watched   1285
me approach, then leaned out and lunged down

---

[47]**be . . . am:** I would murder my father.
[48]**old man himself:** Laius.

with twin prongs[49] at the middle of my head!

1290 He got more than he gave. Abruptly—struck

once by the staff in this my hand—he tumbled

out, head first, from the middle of the

1295 carriage.

And then I killed them all. But if there is

a kinship between Laius and this stranger,

who is more wretched than the man you

1300 see?

Who was there born more hated by the gods?

For neither citizen nor foreigner

may take me in his home or speak to me.

1305 No, they must drive me off. And it is I

who have pronounced these curses on myself!

I stain the dead man's bed with these my hands,

1310 by which he died. Is not my nature vile?

Unclean?—If I am banished and even

In exile I may not see my own parents,

or set foot in my homeland, or else be yoked

1315 in marriage to my mother, and kill my father,

Polybus, who raised me and gave me birth!

If someone judged a cruel divinity

1320 did this to me, would he not speak the truth?

You pure and awful gods, may I not ever

see that day, may I be swept away

from men before I see so great and so

1325 calamitous a stain fixed on my person!

CHORAGOS: These things seem fearful to us, Lord, and yet,

until you hear it from the witness, keep hope!

OEDIPUS: That is the single hope that's left 1330
to me,

to wait for him, that herdsman—until he comes.

JOCASTA: When he appears, what are you eager for? 1335

OEDIPUS: Just this: if his account agrees with yours

then I shall have escaped this misery.

JOCASTA: But what was it that struck you in my story? 1340

OEDIPUS: You said he spoke of robbers as the ones

who killed him. Now: if he continues still

to speak of many, then I could not have killed him. 1345

One man and many men just do not jibe.

But if he says one belted man, the doubt

is gone. The balance tips toward me. I
did it. 1350

JOCASTA: No! He told it as I told you. Be certain.

He can't reject that and reverse himself.

The city heard these things, not I alone.

But even if he swerves from what 1355
he said,

he'll never show that Laius' murder, Lord,

occurred just as predicted. For Loxias

expressly said my son was doomed to 1360
kill him.

The boy—poor boy—he never had a chance

to cut him down, for he was cut down
first. 1365

Never again, just for some oracle

will I shoot frightened glances right and left.

OEDIPUS: That's full of sense. Nonetheless, send a man 1370

to bring that farm hand here. Will you do it?

JOCASTA: I'll send one right away. But let's go in.

---

[49]**lunged . . . prongs:** Laius strikes Oedipus with a two-pronged horse goad, or whip.

1375   Would I do anything against your wishes?

Exit Oedipus and Jocasta through the central door into the palace.

STASIMON 2
STROPHE 1

CHORUS: May there accompany me
  the fate to keep a reverential purity in
1380   what I say,
  in all I do, for which the laws have been set forth
  and walk on high, born to traverse the brightest,
1385   highest upper air; Olympus[50] only
  is their father, nor was it
  mortal nature
  that fathered them, and never will
  oblivion lull them into sleep;
1390   the god in them is great and never ages.

ANTISTROPHE 1

  The will to violate, seed of the tyrant,
  if it has drunk mindlessly of wealth and power,
  without a sense of time or true
1395   advantage,
  mounts to a peak, then
  plunges to an abrupt . . . destiny,
  where the useful foot
  is of no use. But the kind
1400   of struggling that is good for the city
  I ask the god never to abolish.
  The god is my protector: never will I give that up.

STROPHE 2

  But if a man proceeds disdainfully
1405   in deeds of hand or word
  and has no fear of Justice
  or reverence for shrines of the divinities
  (may a bad fate catch him

for his luckless wantonness!),
if he'll not gain what he gains with justice   1410
and deny himself what is unholy,
or if he clings, in foolishness, to the untouchable
(what man, finally, in such an action, will have strength   1415
enough to fend off passion's arrows from his soul!),
if, I say, this kind of
deed is held in honor—
why should I join the sacred dance?   1420

ANTISTROPHE 2

No longer shall I visit and revere
Earth's navel,[51] the untouchable,
nor visit Abae's[52] temple,
or Olympia,[53]
if the prophecies are not matched by events   1425
for all the world to point to.
No, you who hold the power, if you are rightly called
Zeus the king of all, let this matter not escape you   1430
and your ever-deathless rule,
for the prophecies to Laius fade . . .
and men already disregard them;
nor is Apollo anywhere   1435
glorified with honors.
Religion slips away.

EPISODE 3

Enter Jocasta from the palace carrying a branch wound with wool and a jar of incense. She is attended by two women.   1440

JOCASTA: Lords of the realm, the thought has come to me
  to visit shrines of the divinities

---

[50]**Olympus:** Mount Olympus, home of the gods, and treated as a god itself.

[51]**Earth's navel:** Delphi.
[52]**Abae's:** Abae was a town in Phocis where there was another oracle of Apollo.
[53]**Olympia:** Site of the oracle of Zeus.

1445 with suppliant's branch in hand and fragrant smoke.
For Oedipus excites his soul too much
with alarms of all kinds. He will not
judge
the present by the past, like a man of
1450 sense.
He's at the mercy of all terror-mongers.

Jocasta approaches the altar on the right and kneels.

Since I can do no good by counseling,
1455 Apollo the Lycean!—you are the closest—
I come a suppliant, with these my vows,
for a cleansing that will not pollute him.
For when we see him shaken we are all
afraid, like people looking at their helms-
1460 man.

Enter a Messenger along one of the parados. He sees Jocasta at the altar and then addresses the Chorus.

MESSENGER: I would be pleased if you
1465 would help me, stranger.
Where is the palace of King Oedipus?
Or tell me where he is himself, if you
know.
CHORUS: This is his house, stranger. He is
1470 within.
This is his wife and mother of his children.
MESSENGER: May she and her family find
prosperity,
if, as you say, her marriage is fulfilled.
1475 JOCASTA: You also, stranger, for you
deserve as much
for your gracious words. But tell me why
you've come.
What do you wish? Or what have you to
1480 tell us?
MESSENGER: Good news, my Lady, both
for your house and husband.
JOCASTA: What is your news? And who
has sent you to us?
1485 MESSENGER: I come from Corinth. When
you have heard my news

you will rejoice, I'm sure—and grieve
perhaps.
JOCASTA: What is it? How can it have this
double power? 1490
MESSENGER: They will establish him their
king, so say
the people of the land of Isthmia.[54]
JOCASTA: But is old Polybus not still in
power? 1495
MESSENGER: He's not, for death has
clasped him in the tomb.
JOCASTA: What's this? Has Oedipus'
father died?
MESSENGER: If I have lied then I deserve 1500
to die.
JOCASTA: Attendant! Go quickly to your
master,
and tell him this.

Exit an Attendant into the palace. 1505

Oracles of the gods!
Where are you now? The man whom
Oedipus
fled long ago, for fear that he should kill
him 1510
he's been destroyed by chance and not by
him!

Enter Oedipus from the palace.

OEDIPUS: Darling Jocasta, my beloved
wife, 1515
Why have you called me from the
palace?
JOCASTA: First hear what this man has to
say. Then see
what the god's grave oracle has come to 1520
now!
OEDIPUS: Where is he from? What is this
news he brings me?
JOCASTA: From Corinth. He brings news
about your father: 1525
that Polybus is no more! that he is dead!

---

[54]**land of Isthmia:** Corinth, Greek city-state situated on an isthmus.

OEDIPUS: What's this, old man? I want to
hear you say it.

MESSENGER: If this is what must first be
1530   clarified,
please be assured that he is dead and gone.

OEDIPUS: By treachery or by the touch of
sickness?

MESSENGER: Light pressures tip agéd
1535   frames into their sleep.

OEDIPUS: You mean the poor man died of
some disease.

MESSENGER: And of the length of years
that he had tallied.

1540 OEDIPUS: Aha! Then why should we look
to Pytho's vapors,[55]
or to the birds that scream above our
heads?[56]
If we could really take those things for
1545   guides,
I would have killed my father. But he's
dead!
He is beneath the earth, and here am I,
who never touched a spear. Unless he died
1550 of longing for me and I "killed" him that
way!
No, in this case, Polybus, by dying, took
the worthless oracle to Hades with him.

JOCASTA: And wasn't I telling you that
1555   just now?

OEDIPUS: You were indeed. I was misled
by fear.

JOCASTA: You should not care about this
anymore.

1560 OEDIPUS: I must care. I must stay clear of
my mother's bed.

JOCASTA: What's there for man to fear?
The realm of chance
prevails. True foresight isn't possible.
1565 His life is best who lives without a plan.
This marriage with your mother—don't
fear it.

How many times have men in dreams,
too, slept
with their own mothers! Those who   1570
believe such things
mean nothing endure their lives most
easily.

OEDIPUS: A fine, bold speech, and you are
right, perhaps,   1575
except that my mother is still living,
so I must fear her, however well you
argue.

JOCASTA: And yet your father's tomb is a
great eye.   1580

OEDIPUS: Illuminating, yes. But I still fear
the living.

MESSENGER: Who is the woman who
inspires this fear?

OEDIPUS: Meropē, Polybus' wife, old   1585
man.

MESSENGER: And what is there about her
that alarms you?

OEDIPUS: An oracle, god-sent and fearful,
stranger.   1590

MESSENGER: Is it permitted that another
know?

OEDIPUS: It is. Loxias once said to me
I must have intercourse with my own
mother   1595
and take my father's blood with these
my hands.
So I have long lived far away from
Corinth.
This has indeed brought much good luck, 1600
and yet,
to see one's parents' eyes is happiest.

MESSENGER: Was it for this that you have
lived in exile?

OEDIPUS: So I'd not be my father's killer, 1605
sir.

MESSENGER: Had I not better free you
from this fear,
my Lord! That's why I came—to do you
service.   1610

OEDIPUS: Indeed, what a reward you'd
get for that!

---

[55]**Pytho's vapors:** Prophecies of the oracle at Delphi.
[56]**birds . . . heads:** Prophecies derived from interpreting the flights of birds.

MESSENGER: Indeed, this is the main point of my trip,
1615   to be rewarded when you get back home.

OEDIPUS: I'll never rejoin the givers of my seed![57]

MESSENGER: My son, clearly you don't
1620   know what you're doing.

OEDIPUS: But how is that, old man? For the gods' sake, tell me!

MESSENGER: If it's because of them you won't go home.

1625   OEDIPUS: I fear that Phoebus will have told the truth.

MESSENGER: Pollution from the ones who gave you seed?

OEDIPUS: That is the thing, old man, I
1630   always fear.

MESSENGER: Your fear is groundless. Understand that.

OEDIPUS: Groundless? Not if I was born their son.

1635   MESSENGER: But Polybus is not related to you.

OEDIPUS: Do you mean Polybus was not my father?

MESSENGER: No more than I. We're both
1640   the same to you.

OEDIPUS: Same? One who begot me and one who didn't?

MESSENGER: He didn't beget you any more than I did.

1645   OEDIPUS: But then, why did he say I was his son?

MESSENGER: He got you as a gift from my own hands.

OEDIPUS: He loved me so, though from
1650   another's hands?

MESSENGER: His former childlessness persuaded him.

OEDIPUS: But had you bought me, or begotten me?

57**givers of my seed:** Meaning i.e., my parents. Oedipus still thinks Meropē and Polybus are his parents.

MESSENGER: Found you. In the forest   1655
hallows of Cithaeron.

OEDIPUS: What were you doing traveling in that region?

MESSENGER: I was in charge of flocks which grazed those   1660
mountains.

OEDIPUS: A wanderer who worked the flocks for hire?

MESSENGER: Ah, but that day I was your   1665
savior, son.

OEDIPUS: From what? What was my trouble when you took me?

MESSENGER: The ball-joints of your feet might testify.

OEDIPUS: What's that? What makes you   1670
name that ancient trouble?

MESSENGER: Your feet were pierced and I am your rescuer.

OEDIPUS: A fearful rebuke those tokens left for me!   1675

MESSENGER: That was the chance that names you who you are.

OEDIPUS: By the gods, did my mother or my father do this?

MESSENGER: That I don't know. He might   1680
who gave you to me.

OEDIPUS: From someone else? You didn't chance on me?

MESSENGER: Another shepherd handed you to me.   1685

OEDIPUS: Who was he? Do you know? Will you explain!

MESSENGER: They called him one of the men of—was it Laius?

OEDIPUS: The one who once was king   1690
here long ago?

MESSENGER: That is the one! The man was shepherd to him.

OEDIPUS: And is he still alive so I can see him?   1695

MESSENGER: But you who live here ought to know that best.

OEDIPUS: Does any one of you now present know

1700 about the shepherd whom this man has named?
Have you seen him in town or in the fields? Speak out!
The time has come for the discovery!

1705 CHORAGOS: The man he speaks of, I believe, is the same
as the field hand you have already asked to see.
But it's Jocasta who would know this best.

1710 OEDIPUS: Lady, do you remember the man we just
now sent for—is that the man he speaks of?

JOCASTA: What? The man he spoke of?
1715 Pay no attention!
His words are not worth thinking about. It's nothing.

OEDIPUS: With clues like this within my grasp, give up?
1720 Fail to solve the mystery of my birth?

JOCASTA: For the love of the gods, and if you love your life,
give up this search! My sickness is enough.

1725 OEDIPUS: Come! Though my mothers for three generations
were in slavery, you'd not be lowborn!

JOCASTA: No, listen to me! Please! Don't do this thing!

1730 OEDIPUS: I will not listen; I will search out the truth.

JOCASTA: My thinking is for you—it would be best.

OEDIPUS: This "best" of yours is starting
1735 to annoy me.

JOCASTA: Doomed man! Never find out who you are!

OEDIPUS: Will someone go and bring that shepherd here?
1740 Leave her to glory in her wealthy birth!

JOCASTA: Man of misery! No other name shall I address you by, ever again.

Exit Jocasta into the palace after a long pause.

CHORAGOS: Why has your lady left, Oedipus, 1745
hurled by a savage grief? I am afraid
disaster will come bursting from this silence.

OEDIPUS: Let it burst forth! However low this seed 1750
of mine may be, yet I desire to see it.
She, perhaps—she has a woman's pride—
is mortified by my base origins.
But I who count myself the child of Chance, 1755
the giver of good, shall never know dishonor.
She is my mother,[58] and the months my brothers
who first marked out my lowness, then 1760
my greatness.
I shall not prove untrue to such a nature
by giving up the search for my own birth.

STASIMON 3
STROPHE

CHORUS: If I have mantic power
and excellence in thought, 1765
by Olympus,
you shall not, Cithaeron, at tomorrow's full moon,
fail to hear us celebrate you as the countryman 1770
of Oedipus, his nurse and mother,
or fail to be the subject of our dance,
since you have given pleasure
to our king.
Phoebus, whom we summon by "ie!," 1775
may this be pleasing to you!

ANTISTROPHE

Who was your mother, son?
which of the long-lived nymphs
after lying with Pan,[59]

---

[58]**She . . . mother:** Chance is my mother.
[59]**Pan:** God of shepherds and woodlands, half man and half goat.

1780   the mountain roaming . . . Or was it a
       bride
       of Loxias?[60]
       For dear to him are all the upland
       pastures.
1785   Or was it Mount Cyllēnē's lord,[61]
       or the Bacchic god,[62]
       dweller of the mountain peaks,
       who received you as a joyous find
       from one of the nymphs of Helicon,
1790   the favorite sharers of his sport?

EPISODE 4

OEDIPUS: If someone like myself, who
       never met him,
       may calculate—elders, I think I see
       the very herdsman we've been waiting for.
1795   His many years would fit that man's age,
       and those who bring him on, if I am
       right,
       are my own men. And yet, in real
       knowledge,
1800   you can outstrip me, surely: you've seen
       him.

*Enter the old Herdsman escorted by two of
Oedipus's Attendants. At first, the Herdsman
will not look at Oedipus.*

1805   CHORAGOS: I know him, yes, a man of the
       house of Laius,
       a trusty herdsman if he ever had one.
       OEDIPUS: I ask you first, the stranger
       come from Corinth:
1810   is this the man you spoke of?
       MESSENGER: That's he you see.
       OEDIPUS: Then you, old man. First look at
       me! Now answer:
       did you belong to Laius' household once?
1815   HERDSMAN: I did. Not a purchased slave
       but raised in the palace.

---

[60]**Loxias:** Apollo.
[61]**Mount Cyllēnē's lord:** Hermes, messenger of the
gods.
[62]**Bacchic god:** Dionysus.

OEDIPUS: How have you spent your life?
       What is your work?
HERDSMAN: Most of my life now I have
       tended sheep.   1820
OEDIPUS: Where is the usual place you
       stay with them?
HERDSMAN: On Mount Cithaeron. Or in
       that district.
OEDIPUS: Do you recall observing this   1825
       man there?
HERDSMAN: Doing what? Which is the
       man you mean?
OEDIPUS: This man right here. Have you
       had dealings with him?   1830
HERDSMAN: I can't say right away. I don't
       remember.
MESSENGER: No wonder, master. I'll bring
       clear memory
       to his ignorance. I'm absolutely sure   1835
       he can recall it, the district was
       Cithaeron,
       he with a double flock, and I, with one,
       lived close to him, for three entire seasons,
       six months along, from spring right to   1840
       Arcturus.[63]
       Then for the winter I'd drive mine to my
       fold,
       and he'd drive his to Laius' pen again.
       Did any of the things I say take place?   1845
HERDSMAN: You speak the truth, though
       it's from long ago.
MESSENGER: Do you remember giving me,
       back then,
       a boy I was to care for as my own?   1850
HERDSMAN: What are you saying? Why
       do you ask me that?
MESSENGER: There, sir, is the man who
       was that boy!
HERDSMAN: Damn you! Shut your mouth!   1855
       Keep your silence!
OEDIPUS: Stop! Don't you rebuke his
       words.

---

[63]**Arcturus:** A star that is first seen in September in
the sky over Greece.

1860 Your words ask for rebuke far more than his.

HERDSMAN: But what have I done wrong, most royal master?

OEDIPUS: Not telling of the boy of whom he asked.

1865 HERDSMAN: He's ignorant and blundering toward ruin.

OEDIPUS: Tell it willingly—or under torture.

HERDSMAN: Oh god! Don't—I am old—
1870 don't torture me!

OEDIPUS: Here! Someone put his hands behind his back!

HERDSMAN: But why? What else would you find out, poor man?

1875 OEDIPUS: Did you give him the child he asks about?

HERDSMAN: I did. I wish that I had died that day!

OEDIPUS: You'll come to that if you don't
1880 speak the truth.

HERDSMAN: It's if I speak that I shall be destroyed.

OEDIPUS: I think this fellow struggles for delay.

1885 HERDSMAN: No, no! I said already that I gave him.

OEDIPUS: From your own home, or got from someone else?

HERDSMAN: Not from my own. I got him
1890 from another.

OEDIPUS: Which of these citizens? What sort of house?

HERDSMAN: Don't—by the gods!—don't, master, ask me more!

1895 OEDIPUS: It means your death if I must ask again.

HERDSMAN: One of the children of the house of Laius.

OEDIPUS: A slave—or born into the family?

1900 HERDSMAN: I have come to the dreaded thing, and I shall say it.

OEDIPUS: And I to hearing it, but hear I must.

HERDSMAN: He was reported to have
been—his son.   1905
Your lady in the house could tell you best.

OEDIPUS: Because she gave him to you?

HERDSMAN: Yes, my lord.

OEDIPUS: What was her purpose?

HERDSMAN: I was to kill the boy.   1910

OEDIPUS: The child she bore?

HERDSMAN: She dreaded prophecies.

OEDIPUS: What were they?

HERDSMAN: The word was that he'd kill
his parents.   1915

OEDIPUS: Then why did you give him up to this old man?

HERDSMAN: In pity, master—so he would take him home,
to another land. But what he did was   1920
save him
for this supreme disaster. If you are the one
he speaks of—know your evil birth and
fate!   1925

OEDIPUS: Ah! All of it was destined to be true!
Oh light, now may I look my last upon you,
shown monstrous in my birth, in   1930
marriage monstrous,
a murderer monstrous in those I killed.

Exit Oedipus, running into the palace.

STASIMON 4

STROPHE 1

CHORUS: Oh generations of mortal men,
while you are living, I will   1935
appraise your lives at zero!
What man
comes closer to seizing lasting blessedness
than merely to seize its semblance,
and after living in this semblance, to   1940
plunge?
With your example before us,
with your destiny, yours,

1945 suffering Oedipus, no mortal
can I judge fortunate.

ANTISTROPHE 1

For he,[64] outranging everybody,
shot his arrow[65] and became the lord
of wide prosperity and blessedness,
oh Zeus, after destroying
1950 the virgin with the crooked talons,[66]
singer of oracles; and against death,
in my land, he arose a tower of defense.
From which time you were called my king
and granted privileges supreme—in
1955 mighty
Thebes the ruling lord.

STROPHE 2

But now—whose story is more sorrowful
than yours?
Who is more intimate with fierce
1960 calamities,
with labors, now that your life is altered?
Alas, my Oedipus, whom all men know:
one great harbor[67]—
one alone sufficed for you,
1965 as son and father,
when you tumbled,[68] plowman[69] of the
woman's chamber.
How, how could your paternal
furrows, wretched man,
1970 endure you silently so long.

ANTISTROPHE 2

Time, all-seeing, surprised you living an
unwilled life

and sits from of old in judgment on the
marriage, not a marriage,
where the begetter is the begot as well.   1975
Ah, son of Laius . . . ,
would that—oh, would that
I had never seen you!
I wail, my scream climbing beyond itself
from my whole power of voice. To say it   1980
straight:
from you I got new breath—
but I also lulled my eye to sleep.[70]

EXODOS[71]

Enter the Second Messenger from the palace.

SECOND MESSENGER: You who are first   1985
among the citizens,
what deeds you are about to hear and see!
What grief you'll carry, if, true to your
birth,
you still respect the house of Labdacus!   1990
Neither the Ister nor the Phasis river
could purify this house, such suffering
does it conceal, or soon must bring to
light—
willed this time, not unwilled. Griefs hurt   1995
worst
which we perceive to be self-chosen ones.
CHORAGOS: They were sufficient, the
things we knew before,
to make us grieve. What can you add to   2000
those?
SECOND MESSENGER: The thing that's
quickest said and quickest heard:
our own, our royal one, Jocasta's dead.
CHORAGOS: Unhappy queen! What was   2005
responsible?
SECOND MESSENGER: Herself. The bitterest
of these events
is not for you, you were not there to see,
but yet, exactly as I can recall it,   2010

---

[64]**he:** Oedipus.
[65]**shot his arrow:** Took his chances; made a guess at the Sphinx's riddle.
[66]**virgin . . . talons:** The Sphinx.
[67]**one great harbor:** Metaphorical allusion to Jocasta's body.
[68]**tumbled:** Were born and had sex.
[69]**plowman:** Plowing is used here as a sexual metaphor.

---

[70]**I . . . sleep:** I failed to see the corruption you brought.
[71]**Exodos:** The final scene, containing the play's resolution.

you'll hear what happened to that
wretched lady.
She came in anger through the outer hall,
and then she ran straight to her marriage
2015 bed,
tearing her hair with the fingers of both
hands.
Then, slamming shut the doors when she
was in,
2020 she called to Laius, dead so many years,
remembering the ancient seed which
caused
his death, leaving the mother to the son
to breed again an ill-born progeny.
2025 She mourned the bed where she, alas,
bred double—
husband by husband, children by her
child.
From this point on I don't know how she
2030 died,
for Oedipus then burst in with a cry,
and did not let us watch her final evil.
Our eyes were fixed on him. Wildly
he ran
2035 to each of us, asking for his spear
and for his wife—no wife: where he
might find
the double mother-field, his and his
children's.
2040 He raved, and some divinity then
showed him—
for none of us did so who stood close by.
With a dreadful shout—as if some guide
were leading—
2045 he lunged through the double doors; he
bent the hollow
bolts from the sockets, burst into the room,
and there we saw her, hanging from
above,
2050 entangled in some twisted hanging
strands.
He saw, was stricken, and with a wild
roar
ripped down the dangling noose. When
2055 she, poor woman,

lay on the ground, there came a fearful
sight:
he snatched the pins of worked gold
from her dress,
with which her clothes were fastened: 2060
these he raised
and struck into the ball-joints of his eyes.[72]
He shouted that they would no longer see
the evils he had suffered or had done,
see in the dark those he should not have   2065
seen,
and know no more those he once sought
to know.
While chanting this, not once but many
times   2070
he raised his hand and struck into his
eyes.
Blood from his wounded eyes poured
down his chin,
not freed in moistening drops, but all at   2075
once
a stormy rain of black blood burst like hail.
These evils, coupling them, making them
one,
have broken loose upon both man and   2080
wife.
The old prosperity that they had once
was true prosperity, and yet today,
mourning, ruin, death, disgrace, and
every   2085
evil you could name—not one is absent.
CHORAGOS: Has he allowed himself some
peace from all this grief?
SECOND MESSENGER: He shouts that
someone slide the bolts and show   2090
to all the Cadmeians the patricide,
his mother's—I can't say it, it's unholy—
so he can cast himself out of the land,
not stay and curse his house by his own
curse.   2095
He lacks the strength, though, and he
needs a guide,

---

[72]**ball-joints of his eyes:** His eyeballs. Oedipus blinds
himself in both eyes at the same time.

for his is a sickness that's too great to bear.
Now you yourself will see: the bolts of
2100   the doors
are opening. You are about to see
a vision even one who hates must pity.

*Enter the blinded Oedipus from the palace, led
in by a household Servant.*

2105 CHORAGOS: Terrifying suffering for men
to see,
more terrifying than any I've ever
come upon. Oh man of pain
what madness reached you? Which god
2110   from far off,
surpassing in range his longest spring,
struck hard against your god-abandoned
fate?
Oh man of pain,
2115   I cannot look upon you—though there's
so much
I would ask you, so much to hear,
so much that holds my eyes—
such is the shudder you produce in me.
2120 OEDIPUS: Ah! Ah! I am a man of misery.
Where am I carried? Pity me! Where
is my voice scattered abroad on wings?
Divinity, where has your lunge transported me?
2125 CHORAGOS: To something horrible, not to
be heard or seen.

KOMMOS

STROPHE 1

OEDIPUS: Oh, my cloud
of darkness, abominable, unspeakable as
it attacks me,
2130   not to be turned away, brought by an evil
wind!
Alas!
Again alas! Both enter me at once:
the sting of the prongs,[73] the memory of
2135   evils!

---

[73]**prongs:** Refers both to the whip that Laius used and
to the two gold pins that Oedipus used to blind himself.

CHORUS: I do not marvel that in these
afflictions
you carry double griefs and double
evils.

ANTISTROPHE 1

OEDIPUS: Ah, friend,   2140
so you at least are there, resolute servant!
Still with a heart to care for me, the blind
man.
Oh! Oh!
I know that you are there. I recognize   2145
even inside my darkness, that voice of
yours.
CHORUS: Doer of horror, how did you
bear to quench
your vision? What divinity raised your   2150
hand?

STROPHE 2

OEDIPUS: It was Apollo there, Apollo,
friends,
who brought my sorrows, vile sorrows to
their perfection,   2155
these evils that were done to me.
But the one who struck them with his
hand,
that one was none but I, in wretchedness.
For why was I to see   2160
when nothing I could see would bring
me joy?
CHORUS: Yes, that is how it was.
OEDIPUS: What could I see, indeed,
or what enjoy—what greeting   2165
is there I could hear with pleasure, friends?
Conduct me out of the land
as quickly as you can!
Conduct me out, my friends,
the man utterly ruined,   2170
supremely cursed,
the man who is by gods
the most detested of all men!
CHORUS: Wretched in disaster and in
knowledge.   2175
oh, I could wish you'd never come to
know!

ANTISTROPHE 2

OEDIPUS: May he be destroyed, whoever
           freed the savage shackles
2180   from my feet when I'd been sent to the
           wild pasture,
           whoever rescued me from murder
           and became my savior—
           a bitter gift:
2185   if I had died then,
           I'd not have been such grief to self and kin.
CHORUS: I also would have had it so.
OEDIPUS: I'd not have returned to be my
           father's
2190   murderer; I'd not be called by men
           my mother's bridegroom.
           Now I'm without a god,
           child of a polluted parent,
           fellow progenitor with him
2195   who gave me birth in misery.
           If there's an evil that
           surpasses evils, that
           has fallen to the lot of Oedipus.
CHORAGOS: How can I say that you have
2200   counseled well?
           Better not to be than live a blind man.
OEDIPUS: That this was not the best thing
           I could do—
           don't tell me that, or advise me any more!
2205   Should I descend to Hades and endure
           to see my father with these eyes? Or see
           my poor unhappy mother? For I have
           done,
           to both of these, things too great for
2210   hanging.
           Or is the sight of children to be
           yearned for,
           to see new shoots that sprouted as
           these did?
2215   Never, never with these eyes of mine!
           Nor city, nor tower, nor holy images
           of the divinities! For I, all-wretched,
           most nobly raised—as no one else in
           Thebes—
2220   deprived myself of these when I
           ordained

that all expel the impious one—
god-shown
to be polluted, and the dead king's son![74]
Once I exposed this great stain upon me,   2225
could I have looked on these with steady
eyes?
No! No! And if there were a way to block
the source of hearing in my ears, I'd
gladly   2230
have locked up my pitiable body,
so I'd be blind and deaf. Evils shut out—
that way my mind could live in
sweetness.
Alas, Cithaeron, why did you receive me?   2235
Or when you had me, not killed me
instantly?
I'd not have had to show my birth to
mankind.
Polybus, Corinth, halls—ancestral,   2240
they told me—how beautiful was your
ward,
a scar that held back festering disease!
Evil my nature, evil my origin.
You, three roads, and you, secret ravine,   2245
you oak grove, narrow place of those
three paths
that drank my blood[75] from these hands,
from him
who fathered me, do you remember still   2250
the things I did to you? When I'd come
here,
what I then did once more? Oh
marriages! Marriages!
You gave us life and when you'd   2255
planted us
you sent the same seed up, and then
revealed
fathers, brothers, sons, and kinsman's
blood,   2260
and brides, and wives, and mothers, all
the most

---

[74]**I . . . son:** Oedipus refers to his own curse against
the murderer as well as his sins of patricide and
incest.
[75]**my blood:** i.e., "the blood of my father, Laius."

atrocious things that happen to mankind!
One should not name what never should
2265   have been.
Somewhere out there, then, quickly, by
the gods,
cover me up, or murder me, or throw me
to the ocean where you will never see me
2270   more!

*Oedipus moves toward the Chorus and they
back away from him.*

Come! Don't shrink to touch this
wretched man!
2275   Believe me, do not be frightened! I alone
of all mankind can carry these afflictions.

Enter Creon from the palace with Attendants.

CHORAGOS: Tell Creon what you wish for.
Just when we need him
2280   he's here. He can act, he can advise you.
He's now the land's sole guardian in
your place.
   OEDIPUS: Ah! Are there words that I can
speak to him?
2285   What ground for trust can I present? It's
proved
that I was false to him in everything.
   CREON: I have not come to mock you,
Oedipus,
2290   nor to reproach you for your former
falseness.
You men, if you have no respect for sons
of mortals, let your awe for the all-feeding
flames of lordy Hēlius[76] prevent
2295   your showing unconcealed so great a
stain,
abhorred by earth and sacred rain and
light.
Escort him quickly back into the house!
2300   If blood kin only see and hear their own
afflictions, we'll have no impious
defilement.

---

[76]**Hēlius.** The son.

OEDIPUS: By the gods, you've freed me
from one terrible fear,
so nobly meeting my unworthiness: 2305
grant me something—not for me; for you!
CREON: What do you want that you
should beg me so?
OEDIPUS: To drive me from the land at
once, to a place   2310
where there will be no man to speak
to me!
CREON: I would have done just that—had
I not wished
to ask first of the god what I should do.   2315
OEDIPUS: His answer was revealed in
full—that I,
the patricide, unholy, be destroyed.
CREON: He said that, but our need is so
extreme,   2320
it's best to have sure knowledge what
must be done.
OEDIPUS: You'll ask about a wretched
man like me?
CREON: Is it not time you put your trust   2325
in the god?
OEDIPUS: But I bid you as well, and shall
entreat you.
Give her who is within what burial
you will—you'll give your own her   2330
proper rites;
but me—do not condemn my fathers' land
to have me dwelling here while I'm alive,
but let me live on mountains—on
Cithaeron   2335
famed as mine, for my mother and my
father,
while they yet lived, made it my destined
tomb,
and I'll be killed by those who wished   2340
my ruin!
And yet I know: no sickness will destroy
me,
nothing will: I'd never have been saved
when left to die unless for some dread   2345
evil.
Then let my fate continue where it will!

As for my children, Creon, take no pains
for my sons—they're men and they will
2350   never lack
the means to live, wherever they may
be—
but my two wretched, pitiable girls,
who never ate but at my table, never
2355   were without me—everything that I
would touch, they'd always have a
share of it—
please care for them! Above all, let me
touch
2360   them with my hands and weep aloud my
woes!
Please, my Lord!
Please, noble heart! Touching with my
hands,
2365   I'd think I held them as when I could see.

*Enter Antigone and Ismene from the palace
with Attendants.*

What's this?
Oh gods! Do I hear, somewhere, my two
2370   dear ones
sobbing? Has Creon really pitied me
and sent to me my dearest ones, my
children?
Is that it?
2375 **CREON:**   Yes, I prepared this for you, for
I knew
you'd feel this joy, as you have always
done.
OEDIPUS: Good fortune, then, and, for
2380   your care, be guarded
far better by divinity than I was!
Where are you, children? Come to me!
Come here
to these my hands, hands of your brother,
2385   hands
of him who gave you seed, hands that
made
these once bright eyes to see now in this
fashion.

2390 *Oedipus embraces his daughters.*

He, children, seeing nothing, knowing
nothing,
he fathered you where his own seed was
plowed.
I weep for you as well, though I can't see   2395
you,
imagining your bitter life to come,
the life you will be forced by men to live.
What gatherings of townsmen will you
join,   2400
what festivals, without returning home
in tears instead of watching holy rites?
And when you've reached the time for
marrying,
where, children, is the man who'll run   2405
the risk
of taking on himself the infamy
that will wound you as it did my parents?
What evil is not here? Your father killed
his father, plowed the one who gave him   2410
birth,
and from the place where he was sown,
from there
he got you, from the place he too was
born.   2415
These are the wounds: then who will
marry you?
No man, my children. No, it's clear that
you
must wither in dry barrenness, unmarried.   2420

Oedipus addresses Creon.

Son of Menoeceus! You are the only
father
left to them—we two who gave them seed
are both destroyed: watch that they don't   2425
become
poor, wanderers, unmarried—they are
your kin.
Let not my ruin be their ruin, too!
No, pity them! You see how young   2430
they are,
bereft of everyone, except for you.
Consent, kind heart, and touch me with
your hand!

2435 *Creon grasps Oedipus's right hand.*

You, children, if you had reached an age
of sense,
I would have counseled much. Now,
pray you may live
2440 always where it's allowed, finding a life
better than his was, who gave you seed.

CREON: Stop this now. Quiet your weeping. Move away, into the house.

OEDIPUS: Bitter words, but I obey them.

2445 CREON: There's an end to all things.

OEDIPUS: I have first this request.

CREON: Tell me. I shall judge when I will
hear it.

OEDIPUS: Banish me from my homeland.

2450 CREON: You must ask that of the god.

OEDIPUS: But I am the gods' most hated
man!

CREON: Then you will soon get what you
want.

2455 OEDIPUS: Do you consent?

CREON: I never promise when, as now,
I'm ignorant.

OEDIPUS: Then lead me in.

CREON: Come. But let your hold fall from
2460   your children.

OEDIPUS: Do not take them from me, ever!

CREON: Do not wish to keep all of the
power.
You had power, but that power did not
follow you through life.   2465

*Oedipus's daughters are taken from him and led
into the palace by Attendants. Oedipus is led
into the palace by a Servant. Creon and the
other Attendants follow. Only the Chorus
remains.*   2470

CHORUS: People of Thebes, my country,
see: here is that Oedipus—
he who "knew" the famous riddle, and
attained the highest power,
whom all citizens admired, even envying 2475
his luck!
See the billows of wild troubles which he
has entered now!
Here is the truth of each man's life: we
must wait, and see his end,   2480
scrutinize his dying day, and refuse to
call him happy
till he has crossed the border of his life
without pain.

Exit the Chorus along each of the parados.   2485

········▶ *Your* **Turn**
Talking and Writing about Lit

1. Can Laius and Jocasta be said to be blameless in the unfolding of the play's
events? In seeking to escape the prophecies, can they be said to be equal victims of the fate suffered by Oedipus?

2. What are Oedipus's frailties and shortcomings? If it were in his power to
overcome them, how would that change his fate or the outcome of the play?

3. If irony can be defined as "a situation in which what appears to be true is
actually the opposite of the truth," then how does irony move the action of
the play forward?

4. Describe the relationship of the Chorus to the individual characters in the
play. Why is the Chorus necessary?

5. Is Oedipus a "hero" at the play's conclusion? If so, how does he correspond to the classical Greek notions of heroism? Do you think Oedipus is heroic? If not, why?

6. Can Tiresias and Creon be said to be antagonistic characters in relation to Oedipus? What are their respective purposes in the play, particularly where Oedipus is concerned?

7. The images of blindness and sight play powerful roles in the language of the play. Characterize the ways in which they provide insight into the characters and inform the thematic concerns of the play.

8. Are there significant class differences within the cast of characters? Is it crucial to the play's plot that the various Messengers seem to be divided between shepherd/slaves and titled aristocrats?

9. Is Oedipus essentially helpless before forces so much larger than he is, that he bears no responsibility for the outcome of the drama? If all Oedipus does or fails to do is predetermined by Apollo, what is his crime? Why must he suffer?

10. Is it possible to regard Oedipus as an action hero gone wrong? Throughout the play, his strength as a king and leader is extolled and yet much of what constitutes his qualities as a "strong man" leads to his destruction. Oedipus survives, minus his sight and his kingdom, but what does he take away from the outcome that might be described as triumphant? Is he merely pathetic?

11. **DIY** In Victorian England, productions of Shakespeare's *Romeo and Juliet* were rewritten so that endings were "happy" (nobody died, Romeo and Juliet got married, the Montagues and Capulets became good friends and amiable in-laws). Create a version of *Oedipus* in which everything turns out happily. How would you change things and what would it do to the play's meaning?

Talking Lit

According to Aristotle, "the plot must be so structured . . . that the one who is hearing the events unroll shudders with fear and feels pity at what happens: which is what one would experience on hearing the plot of the *Oedipus*."

Aristotle from *The Poetics* (c. 335 B.C.E.)

Translated by Gerald F. Else

The "parts" of tragedy which should be used as constituent elements were mentioned earlier; (. . .) but what one should aim at and what one should avoid in composing one's plots, and whence the effect of tragedy is to come, remains to be discussed now, following immediately upon what has just been said.

Since, then, the construction of the finest tragedy should be not simple but complex, and at the same time imitative of fearful and pitiable happenings (that being the special character of this kind of poetry), it is clear first of all that (1) neither should virtuous men appear undergoing a change from good to bad fortune, for that is not fearful, nor pitiable either, but morally repugnant; nor (2) the wicked from bad fortune to good—that is the most untragic form of all, it has none of the qualities that one wants: it is productive neither of ordinary sympathy nor of pity nor of fear—nor again (3) the really wicked man changing from good fortune to bad, for that kind of structure will excite sympathy but neither pity nor fear, since the one (pity) is directed towards the man who does not deserve his misfortune and the other (fear) towards the one who is like the rest of mankind—what is left is the man who falls between these extremes. Such is a man who is neither a paragon of virtue and justice nor undergoes the change to misfortune through any real badness or wickedness but because of some mistake; one of those who stand in great repute and prosperity, like Oedipus and Thyestes: conspicuous men from families of that kind.

So, then, the artistically made plot must necessarily be single rather than double, as some maintain, and involve a change not from bad fortune to good fortune but the other way round, from good fortune to bad, and not thanks to wickedness but because of some mistake of great weight and consequence, by a man such as we have described or else on the good rather than the bad side. An indication comes from what has been happening in tragedy: at the beginning the poets used to "tick off" whatever plots came their way, but nowadays the finest tragedies are composed about a few houses: they deal with Alcmeon, Oedipus, Orestes, Meleager, Thyestes, Telephus, and whichever others have had the misfortune to do or undergo fearful things.

Thus the technically finest tragedy is based on this structure. Hence those who bring charges against Euripides for doing this in his tragedies are making the same mistake. His practice is correct in the way that has been shown. There is a very significant indication: on our stages and in the competitions, plays of this structure are accepted as the most tragic, *if* they are handled successfully, and Euripides, though he may not make his other arrangements effectively, still is felt by the audience to be the most tragic, at least, of the poets.

Second comes the kind which is rated first by certain people, having its structure double like the *Odyssey* and with opposite endings for the good and bad. Its being put first is due to the weakness of the audiences; for the poets follow along, catering to their wishes. But this particular pleasure is not the one that springs from tragedy but is more characteristic of comedy.

Pity and Fear and the Tragic Act

Now it is possible for the fearful or pathetic effect to come from the actors' appearance, but it is also possible for it to arise from the very structure of the events, and this is closer to the mark and characteristic of a better poet. Namely, the plot must be so structured, even without benefit of any visual effect, that the one who is hearing the events unroll shudders with fear and feels pity at what happens: which is what one would experience on hearing the plot of the *Oedipus*. To set out to achieve this by means of the masks and costumes is less artistic, and requires technical support in the staging. As for those who do not set out to achieve the fearful through the masks and costumes, but only the monstrous, they have nothing to do with tragedy at all; for one should not seek any and every pleasure from tragedy, but the one that is appropriate to it.

Since it is the pleasure derived from pity and fear by means of imitation that the poet should seek to produce, it is clear that these qualities must be built into the constituent events. Let us determine, then, which kinds of happening are felt by the spectator to be fearful, and which pitiable. Now such acts are necessarily the work of persons who are near and dear (close blood kin) to one another, or enemies, or neither. But when an enemy attacks an enemy there is nothing pathetic about either the intention or the deed, except in the actual pain suffered by the victim; nor when the act is done by "neutrals"; but when the tragic acts come within the limits of close blood relationship, as when brother kills or intends to kill brother or do something else of that kind to him, or son to father or mother to son or son to mother—those are the situations one should look for.

Now although it is not admissible to break up the transmitted stories—I mean for instance that Clytemestra was killed by Orestes, or Eriphyle by Alcmeon—one should be artistic both in inventing stories and in managing the ones that have been handed down. But what we mean by "artistic" requires some explanation.

It is possible, then, (1) for the act to be performed as the older poets presented it, knowingly and wittingly; Euripides did it that way also, in Medea's murder of her children. It is possible (2) to refrain from performing the deed, with knowledge. Or it is possible (3) to perform the fearful act, but unwittingly, then recognize the blood relationship later, as Sophocles' Oedipus does; in that case the act is outside the play, but it can be in the tragedy itself, as with Astydamas' Alcmeon, or Telegonus in the *Wounding of Odysseus*. A further mode, in addition to these, is (4) while intending because of ignorance to perform some black crime, to discover the relationship before one does it. And there is no other mode besides these; for one must necessarily either do the deed or not, and with or without knowledge of what it is.

Of these modes, to know what one is doing but hold off and not perform the act (no. 2) is worst: it has the morally repulsive character and at the same time is not tragic; for there is no tragic act. Hence nobody composes that way, or only rarely, as for example, Haemon threatens Creon in the *Antigone*. Performing the act (with knowledge) (no. 1) is second (poorest). Better is to perform it in ignorance and recognize what one has done afterward (no. 3); for the repulsive quality does not attach to the act, and the recognition has a shattering emotional effect. But the best is the last (no. 4): I mean a case like the one in the *Cresphontes* where Merope is about to kill her son but does not do so because she recognizes him first; or in *Iphigenia in Tauris* the same happens with sister and brother; or in the *Helle* the son recognizes his mother just as he is about to hand her over to the enemy.

The reason for what was mentioned a while ago, namely that our tragedies have to do with only a few families, is this: It was because the poets, when they discovered how to produce this kind of effect in their plots, were conducting their search on the basis of chance, not art; hence they have been forced to focus upon those families which happen to have suffered tragic happenings of this kind.

The Tragic Characters

Enough, then, concerning the structure of events and what traits the tragic plots should have. As for the characters, there are four things to be aimed at. First and foremost, that they be good. The persons will have character if in the way previously stated their speech or their action reveals the moral quality of some choice, and good character if a good choice. Good character exists, moreover, in each category of persons; a woman can be good, or a slave, although one of these classes (*sc.* women) is inferior and the other, as a class, worthless. Second, that they be appropriate; for it is possible for a character to be brave, but inappropriately to a woman. Third is likeness to human nature in general; for this is different from making the character good and appropriate according to the criteria previously mentioned. And fourth is consistency. For even if the person being imitated is inconsistent, and that kind of character has been taken as the theme, he should be inconsistent in a consistent fashion.

An example of moral depravity that accomplishes no necessary purpose is the Menelaus in Euripides' *Orestes*; of an unsuitable and inappropriate character, the lamentation of Odysseus in the *Scylla* and the speech of Melanippe; and of the inconsistent, Iphigenia at Aulis, for the girl who pleads for her life is in no way like the later one.

In character portrayal also, as in plot construction, one should always strive for either the necessary or the probable, so that it is either necessary or probable for that kind of person to do or say that kind of thing, just as it is for one event to follow the other. It is evident, then, that the dénouements of plots also should come out of the character itself, and not from the "machine" as in the *Medea* or with the sailing of the fleet in the *Aulis*. Rather the machine should be used for things that lie outside the drama proper, either previous events that a human being cannot know, or subsequent events which require advance prophecy and exposition; for we grant the gods the ability to foresee everything. But let there be no illogicality in the web of events, or if there is, let it be outside the play like the one in Sophocles' *Oedipus*.

Since tragedy is an imitation of persons who are better than average, one should imitate the good portrait painters, for in fact, while rendering likenesses of their sitters by reproducing their individual appearance, they also make them better-looking; so the poet, in imitating men who are irascible or easygoing or have other traits of that kind, should make them, while still plausibly drawn, morally good, as Homer portrayed Achilles as good yet like other men.

Techniques of Recognition

What recognition is generically, was stated earlier; now as to its varieties: First comes the one that is least artistic and is most used, merely out of lack of imagination, that by means of tokens. Of these some are inherited, like "the lance that all the Earth-born wear," or "stars" such as Carcinus employs in his *Thyestes*; some are acquired, and of those some are on the body, such as scars, others are external, like the well-known amulets or the recognition in the *Tyro* by means of the little ark. There are better and poorer ways of using these; for example, Odysseus was recognized in different ways by means of his scar, once by the nurse and again by the swineherds. Those that are deliberately cited for the sake of establishing an

FROM PAGE TO SCREEN

Hollywood and the Evolving Cowboy Myth

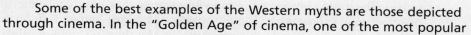

John Wayne

American culture has developed its own rich versions of mythic stories and patterns through fiction, poetry, drama, and film. One of the fascinations of American myth and folklore is the cowboy, a character popularized through heroic stories of stoic endurance, valiant championship of a long-suffering town or locale, feats of daring, and facing down all manner of evil forces. As is true in all mythologies, these heroes are sometimes based on real historical figures made larger than life. Many of the outlaws, lawmen, and popular figures from Western lore actually did exist, such as Billy the Kid, Davy Crockett, and Wild Bill Hickok.

Some of the best examples of the Western myths are those depicted through cinema. In the "Golden Age" of cinema, one of the most popular

identity, and all that kind, are less artistic, while those that develop naturally but unexpectedly, like the one in the foot-washing scene, are better.

Second poorest are those that are contrived by the poet and hence are inartistic; for example the way, in the *Iphigenia*, she recognizes that it is Orestes: *she* was recognized by means of the letter, but *he* goes out of his way to say what the poet, rather than the plot, wants him to say. Thus this mode is close kin to the error mentioned above: he might as well have actually worn some tokens. Similarly, in Sophocles' *Tereus*, the "voice of the shuttle."

Third poorest is that through recollection, by means of a certain awareness that follows on seeing or hearing something, like the one in the *Cypriotes* of Dicaeogenes where the hero bursts into tears on seeing the picture, and the one in Book 8 of the *Odyssey*: Odysseus weeps when he hears the lyre-player and is reminded of the War; in both cases the recognition follows.

Fourth in ascending order is the recognition based on reasoning; for example in the *Libation-Bearers*: "Somebody like me has come; nobody is like me but Orestes; therefore he has come." And the one suggested by the sophist Polyidus in

nt Eastwood
dit: Warner Bros./Kobal/The Picture Desk

actors of the time, John Wayne, was featured in such cowboy films as *Rio Bravo* (1959) and *True Grit* (1969). These films and others in the genre (perhaps most popularly *Shane* from 1953 starring Alan Ladd in the title roll) followed certain formulas. The good guys wore white hats, and the bad guys wore black (an unfortunate example of stereotyping by color). Gunfights were scheduled as noontime appointments. These legends were largely morality plays with clearly drawn lines between good and evil, in which justice triumphed in the end.

Later in the 1960s and 1970s, a new breed of cowboy films entered the picture: the "spaghetti Westerns" began coming out of Italy, most notably Sergio Leone's semitrilogy *The Man with No Name* starring Clint Eastwood. The protagonist of these films was far more morally ambiguous than earlier ones. He was often a mercenary, a gun hired by the highest bidder, with a shaky moral compass. These films shed light on a more gritty reality than the earlier Western films had. Interestingly enough, many of the story lines for these films were inspired by the samurai mythological stories of Japan, put on screen by Japanese director Akira Kurosawa. Leone's first in his popular series *Fistful of Dollars* (1964) is an adaptation Kurosawa's *Yojimbo* (1961), which follows a legendary samurai into a town where the hero pits two opposing gangs against one another.

speaking of the *Iphigenia*: it would have been natural, he said, for Orestes to draw the conclusion (aloud): "My sister was executed as a sacrifice, and now it is my turn." Also in the *Tydeus* of Theodectes: "I came expecting to find my son, and instead I am being destroyed myself." Or the one in the *Daughters of Phineus*: when they see the spot they reflect that it was indeed their fate to die here; for they had been exposed here as babies also. There is also one based on mistaken inference on the part of the audience, as in *Odysseus the False Messenger*. In that play, that he and no one else can string the bow is an assumption, a premise invented by the poet, and also his saying that he would recognize the bow when in fact he had not seen it; whereas the notion that he (the poet) has made his invention for the sake of the other person who would make the recognition, that is a mistaken inference.

The best recognition of all is the one that arises from the events themselves; the emotional shock of surprise is then based on probabilities, as in Sophocles' *Oedipus* and in the *Iphigenia*; for it was only natural that she should wish to send a letter. Such recognitions are the only ones that dispense with artificial inventions and visible tokens. And second-best are those based on reasoning.

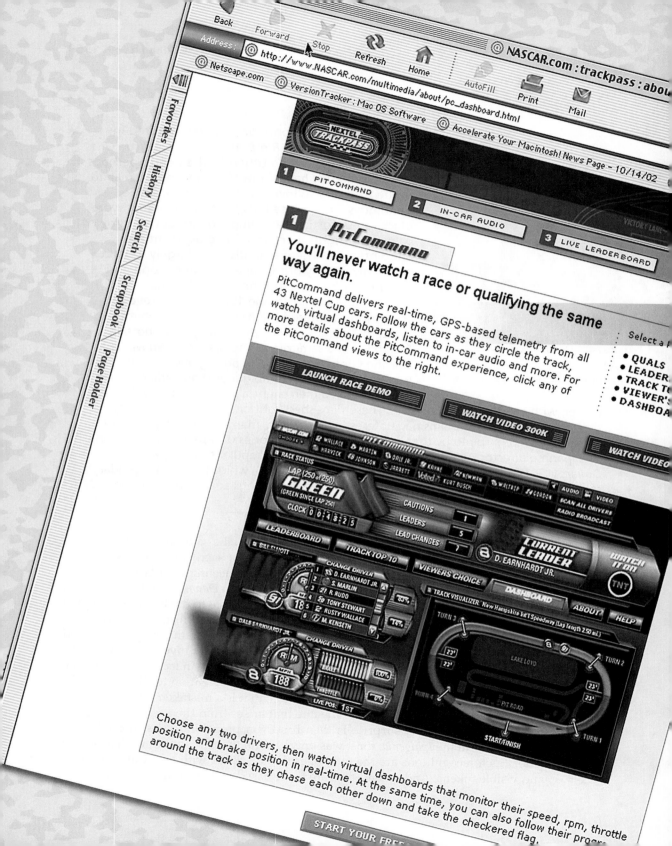

CUTTING EDGES:
Grassroots Theater

Even NASCAR uses audience participation.

NASCAR is the acronym for the National Association of Stock Car Auto Racing. NASCAR hosts a web-based simulation in which viewers experience a race as if they are in the driver's seat. The video and audio provide a realistic picture of what it's like to be behind the wheel in a NASCAR racecar. The virtual race is like grassroots theater in the sense that it uses audience participation to achieve its goal. As in theater, the actual value of NASCAR TrackPass PitCommand performance depends on this immediate connection between the audience and the performance on stage. Additionally, the "play" is nomadic. The entire street-level perform-ance, including set and players (who are virtual coun-terparts to real-life NASCAR racers), are brought to the audience through the Internet. The virtual play differs from more traditional grassroots theater in that here, the members of the audience are not in the same physical place—the audience members can be anywhere. Also, in virtual theater, an audience member can engage with the play at any time. The play doesn't start and stop at any set time. Nevertheless, NASCAR performance and other video games resemble grassroots theater in many ways, and nearly all uses audience participation for full effect.

Just as NASCAR.COM is open to the public, so grassroots theater is drama available to everyone. Luis Valdez, whose play *Los Vendidos* is one of the two plays featured in this chapter, did not come to the profession of playwriting or the world of the theatre as a student in a formal sense. He did not study drama or stagecraft as an undergraduate in a college or university. He was not introduced to the world of the theatre by attending performances of plays with his parents. Instead, Valdez grew up in Delano, California, the son of migrant workers who followed the harvests every year, north from the Coachella Valley on the eastern edge of the Mojave Desert to the Canadian border. His introduction to theatre came from his involvement with the United Farm Workers and the struggle of that union to organize farm laborers who then (and now) do the work of harvesting America's crops, often under difficult and hazardous conditions and for very little pay.

Valdez's plays come directly out of that experience and the larger experience of being a minority: a Latino who is part of a culture that is overwhelmingly Anglo. Naturally politics, an awareness of the large social issues of race and class, and a concern for how the powerless are treated by the powerful have become the focus of much that he has written and produced for the stage.

El Teatro Campesino

El Teatro Campesino (the Farmworkers' Theater) was formed as a company to produce "street theater" as part of a broader organizing effort on the part of the United Farm Workers, and it was in this struggle that Valdez found his subject and his voice. Plays were put on during organizing drives and as part of public demonstrations by the union and its membership to educate the public to the plight of the farmworkers as well as the larger issues of race, class, justice, and assimilation, on which Valdez focuses in the one-act play below. *Los Vendidos* is funny, moves quickly, and obviously has a number of points to make. This is worth saying, not to minimize the play's importance or significance, but to connect it to a tradition of grassroots theatre and street-level dramatic storytelling that hark back to the beginnings of drama itself.

The Long Tradition of Grassroots Theater

Quite often when the words "theater" and "play" are mentioned, one thinks, naturally enough, of Broadway and the productions of professional companies such as Steppenwolf in Chicago or the Orange Coast Repertory in California. Actors, directors, playwrights, and other professionals connected to the craft are often educated at the Julliard School, the Yale Drama School, the Pasadena Playhouse, or the Actors Studio, to name just a few. All of these places have produced nationally and internationally recognized "names" in theatre and film.

But long before drama and the theatre found a formal home in either academia or the commercial worlds of Broadway and Hollywood, the traditions of traveling companies of players and small groups of writers, performers, and craftspeople (costumers, set designers, stage managers, etc.) existed and thrived in cultures the world over. The traveling players who performed the "morality" plays of medieval Europe (such as *Everyman* and the Passion plays), for example, are in many ways the direct forebears of an organization like El Teatro Campesino. These were groups of actors whose performances spread "the word" from town to town, village to village, country to country. During the Middle Ages, of course, the plays were about Christian morality and how one should conduct oneself as a Christian. The moral reminders and often broad political points made in Valdez's play are very much the same as those of the early Christian companies whose intent was to involve and affect the thinking of the playgoer. Even after European culture became more secularized during the Renaissance, troupes of jongleurs—musicians, acrobats, clowns, and mountebanks medicine men—roamed much of Europe performing and adding to their repertoires, inventing, revising, and extending their work even as they traveled from place to place.

This is not to say that all grassroots theatrical experience was nomadic. The traditions of masques, commedia dell'arte, Punch-and-Judy shows, and street-level performance existed in the smallest villages and were often sustained and refreshed by the troubadour tradition which brought news and new material from different, even foreign, parts. Drama at this level established its unique place in literature by addressing whole communities and imaginatively engaging them in the storytelling process. *Everyman* (a morality play probably written around 1485 in England) is a drama with conflict, suspense, characterization, comedic performances, and a resolution of the sense that something is at stake—to be lost or gained—which the playgoer must wait for until the play's conclusion. It may seek to reinforce the values of the church, but it is not the same thing as a sermon. Because the visual and audible unfolding of the story takes place immediately in front of the audience, the play is different from the recitative or declaimed quality of poetry or storytelling.

Valdez and El Teatro Campesino are important here because they illustrate the capacity of drama to arise from the common experience of people whose voices aren't always heard amid the noise of the public discourse. As important as the "institution" of the theater is, his play and his company are reminders of drama's original function and versatility. Likewise, Judy Klass's play *The Locker Room*, featured in this chapter, depicts a satirical take on the everyday experiences of students.

Readings

Luis Valdez (b. 1940)

Luis Valdez was born in 1940 in Delano, California, to farmworkers. He was one of ten children. When he was eighteen, he attended San Jose State College. Although he began college as a math and physics major to please his parents, he eventually joined the theater and declared a major in English. He wrote and acted in plays at San Jose State, where his first full-length play, *The Shrunken Head of Pancho Villa* (1964), was produced. After college, Valdez wrote several plays in a form he called mito, or myth. One of them, *Bernabé* (1970), introduced a figure who wore a zoot suit and focused on historical issues concerning Chicanos. Another of his important plays. *Los Vendidos* (The Sellouts), was written in 1967 and continues to be performed.

Luis Valdez

In 1978 Valdez produced *Zoot Suit*, his first major success. He then wrote *Bandido!* (1982), which he calls "an antimelodrama," about a Mexican bandit named Tiburcio Vásquez, who was the last man publicly executed by law in San Jose, California, in 1875. In *I Don't Have to Show You No Stinking Badges!* (1986), about Buddy Villa and his wife, Connie, who have spent their working lives as extras in TV and films, Valdez uses videotaped inserts and music to make the play a multimedia experience.

In addition to writing plays, Valdez directs films and plays. He directed the film *Zoot Suit* (1981) and the film *La Bamba* (1987), the biography of Mexican American singer Richie Valens, who died in a plane crash with Buddy Holly in 1969. Valdez also wrote the script for that film. In 1987 he produced a television version of his 1983 play *Corridos! Tales of Passion and Revolution*. Performances of *Corridos!* filled a relatively large house in San Francisco for six months before moving to Los Angeles. Its subject is Mexican history.

Los Vendidos

SCENE: *Honest Sancho's Used Mexican Lot and Mexican Curio Shop. Three models are on display in Honest Sancho's shop: to the right, there is a* REVOLUCIONARIO, *complete with sombrero, car-rilleras,[1] and carabina 30–30. At center, on the floor, there is the* FARM WORKER, *under a broad straw sombrero. At stage left is,* JOHNNY, *the Pachuco[2] filero[3] in hand.*

CHARACTERS

HONEST SANCHO
SECRETARY
FARM WORKER
JOHNNY
REVOLUCIONARIO
MEXICAN-AMERICAN

---

[1]**Scene carrilleras** literally chin straps, but may refer to cartridge belts
[2]**Pachuco** Chicano slang for 1940s zoot suiter
[3]**filero** blade

HONEST SANCHO *is moving among his models, dusting them off and preparing for another day of business.*

SANCHO: Bueno, bueno, mis monos, vamos a ver a quien Vendemos ahora, ¿no? (*To audience.*) ¡Quihubo![4] I'm Honest Sancho and this is my shop. Antes fui contratista pero ahora logré tener mi negocito.[5] All I need now is a customer. (*A bell rings offstage.*) Ay, a customer!

SECRETARY: (*Entering.*)   Good morning, I'm Miss Jiménez from—

SANCHO: ¡Ah, una chicana! Welcome, welcome Señorita Jiménez.

SECRETARY: (*Anglo pronunciation.*)   JIM-enez.

5 SANCHO: ¿Qué?

SECRETARY: My name is Miss JIM-enez. Don't you speak English? What's wrong with you?

SANCHO: Oh, nothing, Señorita JIM-enez. I'm here to help you.

SECRETARY: That's better. As I was starting to say, I'm a secretary from Governor Reagan's office, and we're looking for a Mexican type for the administration.

SANCHO: Well, you come to the right place, lady. This is Honest Sancho's Used Mexican lot, and we got all types here. Any particular type you want?

10 SECRETARY: Yes, we were looking for some-body suave—

SANCHO: Suave.

SECRETARY: Debonair.

SANCHO: De buen aire.

SECRETARY: Dark.

15 SANCHO: Prieto.

SECRETARY: But of course not too dark.

SANCHO: No muy prieto.

SECRETARY: Perhaps, beige.

SANCHO: Beige, just the tone. Así como cafecito con leche,[6] ¿no?

SECRETARY: One more thing. He must be   20 hard-working.

SANCHO: That could only be one model. Step right over here to the center of the shop, lady. (*They cross to the* FARM WORKER.) This is our standard farm worker model. As you can see, in the words of our beloved Senator George Murphy, he is "built close to the ground." Also take special notice of his four-ply Goodyear huaraches, made from the rain tire. This wide-brimmed sombrero is an extra added feature—keeps off the sun, rain, and dust.

SECRETARY: Yes, it does look durable.

SANCHO: And our farm worker model is friendly. Muy amable.[7] Watch. (*Snaps his fingers.*)

FARM WORKER: (*Lifts up head*). Buenos días, señorita. (*His head drops.*)

SECRETARY: My, he's friendly.   25

SANCHO: Didn't I tell you? Loves his patrones! But his most attractive feature is that he's hard-working. Let me show you. (*Snaps fingers.* FARM WORKER *stands.*)

FARM WORKER: ¡El jale![8] (*He begins to work.*)

SANCHO: As you can see, he is cutting grapes.

SECRETARY: Oh, I wouldn't know.

SANCHO: He also picks cotton. (*Snap.* FARM   30 WORKER *begins to pick cotton.*)

SECRETARY: Versatile isn't he?

SANCHO: He also picks melons. (*Snap.* FARM WORKER *picks melons.*) That's his slow speed for late in the season. Here's his fast speed. (*Snap.* FARM WORKER *picks faster.*)

SECRETARY: ¡Chihuahua! . . . I mean, good-ness, he sure is a hard worker.

---

[4]**Bueno, bueno, . . . Quihubo** "Good, good, my cute ones, let's see who we can sell now, O.K.?"
[5]**Antes fui . . . negocito** "I used to be a contractor, but now I've succeeded in having my little business."

[6]**Así como . . . leche** like coffee with milk
[7]**Muy amable** very friendly
[8]**El jale** the job

SANCHO: (*Pulls the* FARM WORKER *to his feet.*) And that isn't the half of it. Do you see these little holes on his arms that appear to be pores? During those hot sluggish days in the field, when the vines or the branches get so entangled, it's almost impossible to move; these holes emit a certain grease that allow our model to slip and slide right through the crop with no trouble at all.

35 SECRETARY: Wonderful. But is he economical?

SANCHO: Economical? Señorita, you are looking at the Volkswagen of Mexicans. Pennies a day is all it takes. One plate of beans and tortillas will keep him going all day. That, and chile. Plenty of chile. Chile jalapenos, chile verde, chile colorado. But, of course, if you do give him chile (*Snap.* FARM WORKER *turns left face. Snap.* FARM WORKER *bends over.*) then you have to change his oil filter once a week.

SECRETARY: What about storage?

SANCHO: No problem. You know these new farm labor camps our Honorable Governor Reagan has built out by Parlier or Raisin City? They were designed with our model in mind. Five, six, seven, even ten in one of those shacks will give you no trouble at all. You can also put him in old barns, old cars, river banks. You can even leave him out in the field overnight with no worry!

SECRETARY: Remarkable.

40 SANCHO: And here's an added feature: Every year at the end of the season, this model goes back to Mexico and doesn't return, automatically, until next Spring.

SECRETARY: How about that. But tell me: does he speak English?

SANCHO: Another outstanding feature is that last year this model was programmed to go out on STRIKE! (*Snap.*)

FARM WORKER: ¡HUELGA! ¡HUELGA! Hermanos, sálganse de esos files.[9] (*Snap. He stops.*)

SECRETARY: No! Oh no, we can't strike in the State Capitol.

SANCHO: Well, he also scabs. (*Snap.*)   45

FARM WORKER: Me vendo barato, ¿y qué?[10] (*Snap.*)

SECRETARY: That's much better, but you didn't answer my question. Does he speak English?

SANCHO: Bueno . . . no pero[11] he has other—

SECRETARY: No.

SANCHO: Other features.   50

SECRETARY: NO! He just won't do!

SANCHO: Okay, okay pues. We have other models.

SECRETARY: I hope so. What we need is something a little more sophisticated.

SANCHO: Sophisti—¿qué?

SECRETARY: An urban model.   55

SANCHO: Ah, from the city! Step right back. Over here in this corner of the shop is exactly what you're looking for. Introducing our new 1969 JOHNNY PACHUCO model! This is our fast-back model. Streamlined. Built for speed, low-riding, city life. Take a look at some of these features. Mag shoes, dual exhausts, green chartreuse paint-job, dark-tint windshield, a little poof on top. Let me just turn him on. (*Snap.* JOHNNY *walks to stage center with a pachuco bounce.*)

SECRETARY: What was that?

SANCHO: That, señorita, was the Chicano shuffle.

SECRETARY: Okay, what does he do?

SANCHO: Anything and everything necessary for city life. For instance,   60

---

[9]**¡HUELGA! ¡HUELGA!** . . . **esos files** "Strike! Strike! Brothers, leave those rows."
[10]**Me vendo** . . . **qué** "I come cheap, so what?"
[11]**Bueno** . . . **no pero** "Well, no, but . . . "

survival: He knife fights. (*Snap.* JOHNNY *pulls out switch blade and swings at secretary.*)

(SECRETARY *streams.*)

SANCHO: He dances. (*Snap.*)

JOHNNY: (*Singing.*) "Angel Baby, my Angel Baby . . ." (*Snap.*)

SANCHO: And here's a feature no city model can be without. He gets arrested, but not without resisting, of course. (*Snap.*)

JOHNNY: ¡En la madre, la placa![12] I didn't do it! I didn't do it! (JOHNNY *turns and stands up against an imaginary wall, legs spread out, arms behind his back.*)

65 SECRETARY: Oh no, we can't have arrests! We must maintain law and order.

SANCHO: But he's bilingual!

SECRETARY: Bilingual?

SANCHO: Simón que yes.[13] He speaks English! Johnny, give us some English. (*Snap.*)

JOHNNY: (*Comes downstage.*) Fuck-you!

70 SECRETARY: (*Gasps.*) Oh! I've never been so insulted in my whole life!

SANCHO: Well, he learned it in your school.

SECRETARY: I don't care where he learned it.

SANCHO: But he's economical!

SECRETARY: Economical?

75 SANCHO: Nickels and dimes. You can keep JOHNNY running on hamburgers, Taco Bell tacos, Lucky Lager beer, Thunderbird wine, yesca—

SECRETARY: Yesca?

SANCHO: Mota.

SECRETARY: Mota?

SANCHO: Leños[14] . . . Marijuana. (*Snap.* JOHNNY *inhales on an imaginary joint.*)

80 SECRETARY: That's against the law!

JOHNNY: (*Big smile, holding his breath.*) Yeah.

SANCHO: He also sniffs glue. (*Snap.* JOHNNY *inhales glue, big smile.*)

JOHNNY: Tha's too much man, ése.

SECRETARY: No, Mr. Sancho, I don't think this—

SANCHO: Wait a minute, he has other qual- 85 ities I know you'll love. For example, an inferiority complex. (*Snap.*)

JOHNNY: (*To* SANCHO.) You think you're better than me, huh ése? (*Swings switch blade.*)

SANCHO: He can also be beaten and he bruises, cut him and he bleeds: kick him and he—(*He beats, bruises and kicks* PACHUCO.) would you like to try it?

SECRETARY: Oh, I couldn't.

SANCHO: Be my guest. He's a great scapegoat.

SECRETARY: No, really. 90

SANCHO: Please.

SECRETARY: Well, all right. Just once. (*She kicks* PACHUCO.) Oh, he's so soft.

SANCHO: Wasn't that good? Try again.

SECRETARY: (*Kicks* PACHUCO.) Oh, he's so wonderful! (*She kicks him again.*)

SANCHO: Okay, that's enough, lady. You 95 ruin the merchandise. Yes, our Johnny Pachuco model can give you many hours of pleasure. Why, the L.A.P.D. just bought twenty of these to train their rookie cops on. And talk about maintenance. Señorita, you are looking at an entirely self-supporting machine. You're never going to find our Johnny Pachuco model on the relief rolls. No, sir, this model knows how to liberate.

SECRETARY: Liberate?

SANCHO: He steals. (*Snap.* JOHNNY *rushes the* SECRETARY *and steals her purse.*)

JOHNNY: ¡Dame esa bolsa, vieja![15] (*He grabs the purse and runs. Snap by* SANCHO. *He stops.*)

---

[12]**En la . . . placa** "Wow, the police!"
[13]**Simón . . . yes** yeah, sure
[14]**Leños** "joints" of marijuana

---

[15]**Dame esa . . . , vieja** "Gimme that bag, old lady!"

(SECRETARY *runs after* JOHNNY *and grabs purse away from him, kicking him as she goes.*)

SECRETARY: No, no, no! We can't have any *more* thieves in the State Administration. Put him back.

100 SANCHO: Okay, we still got other models. Come on, Johnny, we'll sell you to some old lady. (SANCHO *takes* JOHNNY *back to his place.*)

SECRETARY: Mr. Sancho, I don't think you quite understand what we need. What we need is something that will attract the women voters. Something more traditional, more romantic.

SANCHO: Ah, a lover. (*He smiles meaningfully.*) Step right over here, señorita. Introducing our standard Revolucionario and/or Early California Bandit type. As you can see he is well-built, sturdy, durable. This is the International Harvester of Mexicans.

SECRETARY: What does he do?

SANCHO: You name it, he does it. He rides horses, stays in the mountains, crosses deserts, plains, rivers, leads revolutions, follows revolutions, kills, can be killed, serves as a martyr, hero, movie star—did I say movie star? Did you ever see *Viva Zapata? Viva Villa? Villa Rides? Pancho Villa Returns? Pancho Villa Goes Back? Pancho Villa Meets Abbot and Costello*—

105 SECRETARY: I've never seen any of those.

SANCHO: Well, he was in all of them. Listen to this. (*Snap.*)

REVOLUCIONARIO: (*Scream.*)   ¡VIVA VILLAAAAA!

SECRETARY: That's awfully loud.

SANCHO: He has a volume control. (*He adjusts volume. Snap.*)

110 REVOLUCIONARIO: (*Mousey voice.*)   ¡Viva Villa!

SECRETARY: That's better.

SANCHO: And even if you didn't see him in the movies, perhaps you saw him on TV. He makes commercials. (*Snap.*)

REVOLUCIONARIO: Is there a Frito Bandito in your house?

SECRETARY: Oh yes, I've seen that one!

SANCHO: Another feature about this one is 115
that he is economical. He runs on raw horsemeat and tequila!

SECRETARY: Isn't that rather savage?

SANCHO: Al contrario[16] it makes him a lover. (*Snap.*)

REVOLUCIONARIO: (*To* SECRETARY.)   ¡Ay, mamasota, cochota, ven pa'ca! (*He grabs* SECRETARY *and folds her back—Latin-lover style.*)

SANCHO: (*Snap.* REVOLUCIONARIO *goes back upright.*)   Now wasn't that nice?

SECRETARY: Well, it was rather nice. 120

SANCHO: And finally, there is one outstanding feature about this model I KNOW the ladies are going to love: He's a GENUINE antique! He was made in Mexico in 1910!

SECRETARY: Made in Mexico?

SANCHO: That's right. Once in Tijuana, twice in Guadalajara, three times in Cuernavaca.

SECRETARY: Mr. Sancho, I thought he was an American product.

SANCHO: No, but— 125

SECRETARY: No, I'm sorry. We can't buy anything but American-made products. He just won't do.

SANCHO: But he's an antique!

SECRETARY: I don't care. You still don't understand what we need. It's true we need Mexican models such as these, but it's more important that he be *American.*

SANCHO: American?

SECRETARY: That's right, and judging from 130
what you've shown me, I don't think you have what we want. Well, my lunch hour's almost over, I better—

SANCHO: Wait a minute! Mexican but American?

---

[16]**Al contrario** on the contrary

SECRETARY: That's correct.

SANCHO: Mexican but . . . (*A sudden flash.*) AMERICAN! Yeah, I think we've got exactly what you want. He just came in today! Give me a minute. (*He exits. Talks from backstage.*) Here he is in the shop. Let me just get some papers off. There. Introducing our new 1970 Mexican-American! Ta-ra-ra-ra-ra-ra-RA-RAAA!

(SANCHO *brings out the* MEXICAN-AMERICAN *model, a clean-shaven middle-class type in business suit, with glasses.*)

SECRETARY: (*Impressed.*) Where have you been hiding this one?

135 SANCHO: He just came in this morning. Ain't he a beauty? Feast your eyes on him! Sturdy US Steel frame, streamlined, modern. As a matter of fact, he is built exactly like our Anglo models except that he comes in a variety of darker Shades: naugahyde, leather, or leatherette.

SECRETARY: Naugahyde.

SANCHO: Well, we'll just write that down. Yes, señorita, this model represents the apex of American engineering! He is bilingual, college educated, ambitious! Say the word "acculturate" and he accelerates. He is intelligent, well-mannered, clean—did I say clean? (*Snap.* MEXICAN-AMERICAN *raises his arm.*) Smell.

SECRETARY: (*Smults.*) Old Sobaco, my favorite.

SANCHO: (*Snap.* MEXICAN-AMERICAN *turns toward* SANCHO.) Eric! (*To* SECRETARY.) We call him Eric Garcia. (*To* ERIC.) I Want you to meet Miss JIM-enez, Eric.

140 MEXICAN-AMERICAN: Miss JIM-enez, Lam delighted to make your acquaintance. (*He kisses her hand.*)

SECRETARY: Oh, my, how charming!

SANCHO: Did you feel the suction? He has seven especially engineered suction cups right behind his lips. He's a charmer all right!

SECRETARY: How about boards? Does he function on boards?

SANCHO: You name them, he is on them. Parole boards, draft boards, school boards, taco quality control boards, surf boards, two-by-fours.

SECRETARY: Does he function in politics? 145

SANCHO: Señorita, you are looking at a political MACHINE. Have you ever heard of the OEO, EOC, COD, WAR ON POVERTY? That's our model! Not only that, he makes political speeches.

SECRETARY: May I hear one?

SANCHO: With pleasure. (*Snap.*) Eric, give us a speech.

MEXICAN-AMERICAN: Mr. Congressman, Mr. Chairman, members of the board, honored guests, ladies and gentlemen. SANCHO *and* SECRETARY *appland.*) Please, please, I come before you as a Mexican-American to tell you about the problems of the Mexican. The problems of the Mexican stem from one thing and one thing alone: He's stupid. He's uneducated. He needs to stay in school. He needs to be ambitious, forward-looking, harder-working. He needs to think American, American, American, AMERICAN, AMERICAN, AMERICAN. GOD BLESS AMERICA! GOD BLESS AMERICA!! (*He goes out of control.*)

(SANCHO *snaps frantically and the* MEXICAN-AMERICAN *finally slumps forward, bending at the waist.*)

SECRETARY: Oh my, he's patriotic too! 150

SANCHO: Si, señorita, he loves his country. Let me just make a little adjustment here. (*Stands* MEXICAN-AMERICAN *up.*)

SECRETARY: What about upkeep? Is he economical?

SANCHO: Well, no, I won't lie to you. The Mexican-American costs a little bit more, but you get what you pay for. He's worth every extra cent. You can keep him running on dry martinis, Langendorf bread.

SECRETARY: Apple pie?

155 SANCHO: Only Mom's. Of course, he's also programmed to eat Mexican food on ceremonial functions, but I must warn you: an overdose of beans will plug up his exhaust.

SECRETARY: Fine! There's just one more question: How much do you want for him?

SANCHO: Well, I tell you what I'm gonna do. Today and today only, because you've been so sweet, I'm gonna let you steal this model from me! I'm gonna let you drive him off the lot for the simple price of—let's see taxes and license included— $15,000.

SECRETARY: Fifteen thousand DOLLARS? For a MEXICAN!

SANCHO: Mexican? What are you talking, lady? This is a Mexican-AMERICAN! We had to melt down two pachucos, a farm worker and three gabachos to make this model! You want quality, but you gotta pay for it! This is no cheap run-about. He's got class!

160 SECRETARY: Okay, I'll take him.

SANCHO: You will?

SECRETARY: Here's your money.

SANCHO: You mind if I count it?

SECRETARY: Go right ahead.

165 SANCHO: Well, you'll get your pink slip in the mail. Oh, do you want me to wrap him up for you? We have a box in the back.

SECRETARY: No, thank you. The Governor is having a luncheon this afternoon, and we need a brown face in the crowd. How do I drive him?

SANCHO: Just snap your fingers. He'll do anything you want.

(SECRETARY *snaps.* MEXICAN-AMERICAN *steps forward.*)

MEXICAN-AMERICAN: RAZA QUERIDA, ¡VAMOS LEVANTANDO ARMAS PARA LIBERARNOS DE ESTOS

DESGRACIADOS GABACHOS QUE NOS EXPLOTAN! VAMOS.[17]

SECRETARY: What did he say?

SANCHO: Something about lifting arms, 170 killing white people, etc.

SECRETARY: But he's not supposed to say that!

SANCHO: Look, lady, don't blame me for bugs from the factory. He's your Mexican-American; you bought him, now drive him off the lot!

SECRETARY: But he's broken!

SANCHO: Try snapping another finger.

(SECRETARY *snaps.* MEXICAN-AMERICAN *comes to life again.*)

MEXICAN-AMERICAN: ¡ESTA GRAN 175 HUMANIDAD HA DICHO BASTA! Y SE HA PUESTO EN MARCHA! ¡BASTA! ¡BASTA! ¡VIVA LA RAZA! ¡VIVA LA CAUSA! ¡VIVA LA HUELGA! ¡VIVAN LOS BROWN BERETS! ¡VIVAN LOS ESTUDIANTES! ¡CHICANO POWER![18]

(*The* MEXICAN-AMERICAN *turns toward the* SECRETARY, *who gasps and backs up. He keeps turning toward the* PACHUCO, FARM WORKER, *and* REVOLUCIONARIO, *snapping his fingers and turning each of them on, one by one.*)

PACHUCO: (*Snap. To* SECRETARY.)   I'm going to get you, baby! ¡Viva La Raza!

FARM WORKER: (*Snap. To* SECRETARY.)   ¡Viva la huelga! ¡Viva la Huelga! ¡VIVA LA HUELGA!

REVOLUCIONARIO: (*Snap. To* SECRETARY.)   ¡Viva la revolución! ¡VIVA LA REVOLUCIÓN!

REVOLUCIONARIO: (*Snap. To* SECRETARY.)   ¡Viva la revolución! ¡VIVA LA REVOLUCIÓN!

---

[17]**RAZA QUERIDA,** . . . **VAMOS** "Beloved Raza, let's pick up arms to liberate ourselves from those damned whites that exploit us! Let's go."

[18]**ESTA GRAN** . . . **CHICANO POWER** "This great mass of humanity has said enough! And it begins to march! Enough! Enough! Long live La Raza! Long live the Cause! Long live the strike! Long live the Brown Berets! Long live the students! Chicano Power!"

(*The three models join together and advance toward the* SECRETARY *who backs up and runs out of the shop screaming.* SANCHO *is at the other end of the shop holding his money in his hand. All freeze. After a few seconds of silence, the* PACHUCO *moves and stretches, shaking his arms and loosening up. The* FARM WORKER *and* REVOLUCIONARIO *do the same.* SANCHO *stays where he is, frozen to his spot.*)

180 JOHNNY: Man, that was a long one, ése.
    (*Others agree with him.*)
FARM WORKER: How did we do?
JOHNNY: Petty good, look all that lana, man! (*He goes over to* SANCHO *and removes the money from his hand.* SANCHO *stays where he is.*)
REVOLUCIONARIO: En la madre, look at all the money.
JOHNNY: We keep this up, we're going to be rich.
185 FARM WORKER: They think we're machines.
REVOLUCIONARIO: Burros.
JOHNNY: Puppets.
MEXICAN-AMERICAN: The only thing I don't like is—how come I always got to play the goddamn Mexican-American?

JOHNNY: That's what you get for finishing high school.
FARM WORKER: How about our wages, ése?   190
JOHNNY: Here it comes right now. $3,000 for you, $3,000 for you, $3,000 for you, and $3,000 for me. The rest we put back into the business.
MEXICAN-AMERICAN: Too much, man. Heh, where you vatos going tonight?
FARM WORKER: I'm going over to Concha's. There's a party.
JOHNNY: Wait a minute, vatos. What about our salesman? I think he needs an oil job.
REVOLUCIONARIO: Leave him to me.   195

(*The* PACHUCO, FARM WORKER, *and* MEXICAN-AMERICAN *exit, talking loudly about their plans for the night. The* REVOLUCIONARIO[19] *goes over to* SANCHO, *removes his derby hat and cigar, lifts him up and throws him over his shoulder.* SANCHO *hangs loose, lifeless.*)

───────────────

[19]**REVOLUCIONARIO:** (*To audience.*) He's the best model we got! ¡Ajúa! (*Exit.*)

····•▶ *Your* **Turn**
Talking and Writing about Lit

1. It's clear that Valdez relies on stereotypes in *Los Vendidos*. Why does he do this and how does this strategy contribute to making his point?

2. Is the character of Ms. Jimenez also a stereotype, and does she have a counterpart in one of the other characters? Why is the argument over the pronunciation of her name important?

3. Who are these strange people? The three "models" for sale in Honest Sancho's shop are very different: revolutionary, farm laborer, *pachuco*. Why has Valdez selected these three types, and how does he use them to advance the reader's awareness of the play's themes?

4. The play is funny and serious at the same time. How does it combine humor with serious social and cultural issues?

5. Is Valdez as aware of certain American stereotypes as well (such as the used car salesman)? What kind of character is Honest Sancho (to begin with, how honest is he really supposed to be) and who does he actually symbolize or represent?

6. Spanish terms and phrases are used frequently here. Why? Do they have a purpose other than establishing the background of the characters?

7. **DIY** Imagine the play restructured as a late-night television commercial. Could you write the "sales-pitch segments" as if they were commercial spots interrupting a movie? What would the movie be?

8. **DIY** Can you see the play being adapted for other groups who see themselves as marginalized, exploited, and repressed? What models would your "lot" feature for college students or workers in a mall or customers at a fast-food outlet?

Judy Klass (b. 1967)

Judy Klass was born and raised in New York City. Eighteen of Judy's one-act plays have been produced in New York and California, as well as in Vermont, Ohio, Kansas, Pennsylvania, New Jersey, and South Carolina. Some have had as many as nine productions. Her full-length plays *Transatlantic* and *Damage Control* have been produced in New York. Her short fiction, plays, and poems have appeared in *the Brooklyn Review*, *The Rockhurst Review*, *Asimov's Magazine*, *the Harpur Palate*, *The Brownstone Review*, *Suffusion*, *Tales of the Unanticipated*, *The Long Island Quarterly*, *The Princeton Arts Review*, *Pivot*, *Slant*, and *Wind Magazine*, among others. She cowrote the Showtime cable film adaptation of *In the Time of the Butterflies*. A screenplay of hers is under option at Paramount. She teaches English at Nassau Community College SUNY. In Judy's "Talking Lit" essay below, she discusses the origins of her play *The Locker Room* and the importance of grassroots community theater. Her country music CD "Brooklyn Cowgirl" is available at http://www.cdbaby.com/judyklass.

Judy Klass

The Locker Room

CHARACTERS

BILL: *A confident, competitive guy, who likes to think of himself as a ladies' man. A bully, when it comes to lesser men.*

RALPH: Equally cocky and confident. A friend to BILL, but he wouldn't mind bringing him down a peg or two.

DON: A bit of a yes man, to whomever seems to have the upper hand at any given moment.

EUGENE: An off-horse, an outsider. A sensitive idealist with odd ideas, less imposing than the others, deeply in love with SALLY.

SALLY: A girl torn between her love for BILL and the kind of fun they have together— and fear of losing her reputation.

Scene
A locker room.

Time
The present.

AT RISE: BILL, RALPH *and* DON *hang out together, changing, using deodorant, etc.* EUGENE *sits off by himself on another bench, ignored by the others, but listening to their conversation.*

BILL: Boy, what a work-out!

(*HE belches.* DON *nods*)

DON: I'll say.

BILL: It's funny, but these sessions really take a lot out of you. Kinda like girls, eh? (*HE laughs, smacks* DON *with the towel, as they both whoop.* RALPH *turns to* BILL, *leering, insinuating*)

RALPH: Speaking of which, Bill, how did your date with Sally go?

5 DON: Yeah, tell us. Was it *good* for you?

BILL: Well. (*Significant pause*) It was pretty intense. We started out just sitting on the couch, right? And we were discussing Socrates and *The Apology* and all, whatever. (*Getting excited*) And ten minutes later . . .

DON: God, you work fast!

BILL: Ten minutes later we were hot, and flushed, and deeply embroiled in a discussion of *Plato's Republic.*

(*There are whistles and cat-calls from* DON *and* RALPH. *They pump their fists in the air. But*

10 EUGENE *is obviously upset, angry. HE*

clenches his fists, wincing with pain at each revelation)

BILL (*CONT'D*):   And from there . . .

DON: Yes, yes?

BILL: From there I slid the discussion a little *wider* open. We were talking logical positivism, dialectical materialism . . .

DON: (*Impressed*) Wow! You got to second base.

BILL: (*Scornful*) We got beyond all that,   15 man. I mean, the sparks were starting to fly. I was giving her my opinion, she gave me hers . . .

RALPH: (*Sarcastic, fatherly tone*) Did you remember to use qualifiers?

BILL: Of course, dude, we qualified everything we said. I mean, I'm not stupid. It was a post–free speech discussion, all the way.

DON: (*Eager*) So, then what happened?

BILL: So, then we started comparing all different kinds of utopias—Sir Thomas More, Marx even . . . as I slowly, with the skill of a master, probed her views on class structure and the nature of leadership.

DON: You probed!   20

BILL: (*Illustrating with his hands, reliving the experience*) All while driving home my point of view. And then, get this, the conversation peaks with *both* of us damning complacency toward world problems— simultaneously, almost! We cried out that Voltaire was wrong! And we caressed the notion of building a new world, founded on ideals. (*HE looks around triumphantly at his two friends*) Well, I think that's pretty good for a second date.

DON: For a second date, man, that's amazing.

(*HE is sincere, almost in awe of* BILL. *But* RALPH *contemptuously turns away and begins chucking items into his own locker*)

RALPH: Good? you call that good? Wimp! You were out with Sally Summers. That girl spread her views on utopias wide for any guy who looks at her cross-eyed.

(EUGENE *has hidden his face in his hands. HE covers his ears, to try to block what they are saying*)

RALPH (*CONTD*):   She told you about Marx? She's the bimbo of Bolshevism! Utopias, Jesus. You could get that from sweating over a copy of *Philosophers Weekly*.

25 BILL: (*Incredulous*) Sally's talked about this stuff with other guys?

RALPH: (*Leering*) She's popular girl. She's got that great set (*Gesturing with hands*) of first edition Kierkegaard. They say she gives great Hegel.

DON: (*Giggles*) Yeah, I wouldn't mind taking her out for a Spinoza!

BILL: (*Glaring at* DON) Oh, you think that's funny, do you, Don?

DON: (*Scared, backing down*) Just kidding! Just kidding!

(EUGENE *is standing now. HE is steeling himself to say something. They are still oblivious to him.* BILL *is perplexed, not sure whether to believe* RALPH. *HE scratches himself*)

30 BILL: Hey, Ralph, no offense, guy, but this is a lot to take in.

RALPH: Hey, I'm just trying to do you a favor. This girl really likes the big, involved discussions, from what I've heard. She's into *French* theory. Know what I mean?

DON: Ooh la la!

(DON *moves away from* BILL *to escape possible retaliation.* RALPH *enunciates each syllable of each name with lascivious glee*)

RALPH: Lacan. Derrida. Baudrillard.
DON: *Zut alors!*
RALPH: Foucault—   35
BILL: Okay, enough!
RALPH: I ain't making it up.
(BILL *looks at him, sees HE is sincere*)
BILL: God, I had no idea she was so open-minded. She was such an ice princess last week when I talked to her about Descartes, and I asked her if she "was" because she "thought." And she slapped my face.

(DON *giggles, and covers his mouth to stifle it as* BILL *gives him another warning look*)

RALPH: I guarantee she'll really start putting out ideas if you go for broke.
BILL: Hmmm . . .   40

(EUGENE *can hold back no longer. Still, HE is timid. HE clears his throat*)

EUGENE: Excuse me.

(*They all turn; they are surprised to find that HE is even in the room, much less speaking to them*)

RALPH: Yeah, what?
EUGENE: I don't think that's very nice.

(*The others are entertained. They close in around him, goading him*)

BILL: What's not very nice?
DON: What? Huh?   45
RALPH: Tell us.
EUGENE: (*Sincere, slightly priggish*) Well, I don't think you should talk about girls that way. Get them to share their strongest convictions, their most intimate, personal views with you, when you're just using them.

(*The others snort and guffaw*)

RALPH: Oh, please, you lame little sissy.

DON: Blow it out your ear.

50 EUGENE: And not only that, but I read that girls don't respect boys who discuss and tell. They think it's very immature.

(*Again, the others exchange looks of disbelief, and dissolve in laughter.* RALPH *leans in close, terrifying* EUGENE)

RALPH: Listen, you clueless, dithering imbecile, where do you get off telling us what girls like? Who was the last person you had a philosophical discussion with? Your mother?

BILL: Face it, quiche-eater, we saw you in the seminar today.

DON: Yeah, we saw you!

RALPH: You couldn't argue your way out of a paper bag.

55 EUGENE: (*Trying to mask fear*) My spiritual and intellectual life is none of your business.

RALPH: Yeah, my ass it's not! (*Spits*) Tell us your views. Show us your technique. We're waiting.

EUGENE: (*Panicky*) Like what, what?

BILL: You're out with a girl. How do you ply her interest? How do you massage her id?

RALPH: How do you whet her appetite for debate? Huh? Huh?

60 EUGENE: Well—maybe I'd start off by asking her why she thinks we're here . . . (*Snorts and guffaws from the others*)

EUGENE (*CONT'D*):   And, and what she thinks the difference is between a good person and a bad person . . .

(*Roars, cat-calls from the others.* EUGENE *becomes desperate* . . .)

EUGENE (*CONT'D*):   And whether or not she believes in Santa Claus . . .

RALPH: Loooser!

BILL: This is really sad. Give this guy some Wheaties.

65 EUGENE: (*Gathering courage*) Well, look, there are other things you can do on a date besides all that. I mean, if I went out with a girl like Sally, I'd let her know I don't just want her for her mind!

BILL: (*Puzzled*) Well, what *do* you want her for?

EUGENE: For *her*, as a unique, *physical* person, with a body unlike that of anyone else . . . I like to touch girls, to engage in sexual foreplay, to experience sensual gratification with them. To have them touch *my* body.

(*As HE confesses all this, the others are disgusted, repelled, unnerved. They say things like "Ew" and "Ugh," and inch away from him*)

RALPH: Weirdo! Creep! Hey, it's "Mr. Tactile."

DON: Sicko! Get out of here.

70 BILL: They shouldn't allow you in guys' locker rooms, man.

(*They are exchanging uneasy looks, and* EUGENE *realizes HE may have revealed too much*)

EUGENE: I mean, I also like philosophy, don't get me wrong.

BILL: Yeah, yeah, I could just see this guy out on a date, with no one around, and a million things to discuss, and he wants to get all sensitive and concrete and "touch bodies."

RALPH: This is too depressing. Come on, guys, let's head over to the library.

DON: Library! Yes!

75 BILL: Hey guys, I'll meet you by the central computers, okay?

(RALPH *and* DON *go out pounding the lockers and walls, shouting "Library! Library!"* BILL *gathers up his books.* EUGENE, *very upset, looks off into the distance. This is a turning-point for him. HE is coming to some kind of decision)*

EUGENE: *I'll* show them I know philosophy. I'll show Sally I'm a man. I'll show them all!

(HE runs out. Through another door, SALLY *timidly pokes her head in)*

SALLY: Pssst! Bill!

BILL: *(Looks up, greatly surprised)* Sally! What are you doing here? I gotta go meet the guys at the reference desk . . .

SALLY: *(Enters the room, looks around)* Well, I've been worrying. You didn't tell the guys—you know—about . . . *(Whispering)* The "ideas" we discussed last night. Did you?

*(*BILL, *books in hand, walks out with his arm around her)*

BILL: Hey, baby, would I do that to you?   80 You can trust me . . .

(SHE is reassured. HE winks at the audience as they exit.)

LIGHTS DOWN

····▶ *Your* Turn
Talking and Writing about Lit

1. What aspects of a fairly common and familiar situation is Klass reversing here?

2. Why is this reversal of a normal and familiar situation funny?

3. Are the characters here still "stock" characters—stereotypes in other words?

4. In spite of the reversal of values, is the conflict between Bill and Eugene essentially any different than it would be in ordinary circumstances?

5. What are the larger issues Klass may be pointing to here? What is at stake here? What might be gained and lost by the characters?

6. Have the relationships between the characters changed at all as a result of the changes Klass has wrought?

7. **DIY**   Could you write a version in which Sally is discussing Bill with her friends in girl's locker room? What would she say, and what would her friends be saying? Would there be an equivalent of Eugene in your version?

8. **DIY**   What do you imagine Eugene does after he rushes out to the locker room? Try writing a scene from his point of view and in his voice.

Talking Lit

In this essay, written especially for *Access Literature*, Judy Klass, author of *The Locker Room* (above) discusses Off- and Off-Off-Broadway and Community Theater.

Judy Klass "Being Off or Off Off Broadway Could Mean Being Two Thousand Miles Away"

The Off and Off Off Broadway scene is a vital part of U.S. theater. Many Broadway shows are hugely elaborate musicals—often revivals of old shows, and nowadays often shows adapted from movies for the stage. Away from Broadway, there is room for quieter, or riskier, or more original and more serious work, as well as for great older plays that contain no songs or special effects to continue to have life. New playwrights can get their voices heard away from Broadway; there is more room for diverse casting, and for viewpoints audiences do not get exposed to in the bigger, more lavish productions. A lot of playwrights write short plays first—the dramatic equivalent of a short story—and see them go up in workshops and show-cases and one-act festivals. They learn their craft in this way, and first have the thrill of seeing directors and actors interpret their work, and then go on to write full-length plays. That's what I did.

My play THE LOCKER ROOM grew out of a comedy sketch (and short, funny one-acts are often not far removed from sketches) that was performed at Sarah Lawrence when I was a student there, at Oxford in England (with some lines re-written for Brits) and by a comedy troupe called Lost Cat in NYC. I played Sally in these student productions, and shot a film version of it on video. But when I expanded it into a play, I tried to layer it a little more, and I was not concerned with laughs only. It has more characters than most of my one-act plays, which are often two-people shows. My plays are usually a combination of humor and some seri-ous themes, as THE LOCKER ROOM is, though they tend to lean one way or the other. The Greeks would not have approved of mixing of comedy and drama; most playwrights from Shakespeare's era and on probably would.

It was interesting to see another director's interpretation of THE LOCKER ROOM when it went up in a short play festival at Theatre-Studio Incorporated in NYC. Even more interesting was a production in Chatham, New Jersey in the Jersey Voices Festival, by a director who slowed it way down and did not play it for laughs; he used music and furtive glances between characters, and turned physical love into a metaphor, somehow, for "the love that dare not speak its name." It was almost as if he had found a different play inside the one I had written! There are "Off Broadway" theaters all over the country. If you are interested in writing plays, try to get involved with your school's drama department, or see if there is a local theater company you can hook up with. Act, and/or work behind the scenes—Shakespeare

American Community Theater Is Alive and Well

Robert H. Leonard, associate professor of Theatre Arts at Virginia Tech and founding artistic director of the Road Company theater ensemble explains the importance of local theater:

Idiwanan An Chawe company of Zuni Pueblo, New Mexico, and Kentucky's Roadside Theate a 17-year cultural exchange, co-created and tou "Corn Mountain/Pine Mountain," a bilingual that explores differences and common ground their cultures.

> By its very nature, theater is a local event.
> Theater takes place with a specific group of people at a specific place and time.
> The moment of performance exists only with and for the group present at that time and place. The actual value of a theater performance depends on this immediate connection between the audience and the performance on stage.

did! Many students have never seen a play live; there is no substitute for that, if you want to write them. (I have had students write plays in which characters wander in and out of stores, shoplifting, and in and out of a mall movie theater, and then get on an escalator . . . And I have to ask them: "How would you stage this? How would you build the set?") Plays are very different from movies, and treading the boards or building the flats will help give you a feel for what they are about.

The Playwrights Noticeboard at stageplays.com, the msn.com group Absolutely Theatre, emerging, freewebspace.com/CompetitionChart.htm, and your own on-line searches will tell you about companies everywhere looking for ten or fifteen-minute plays or longer one-acts or full-length plays. When you write, keep the cast small, make every character count, avoid elaborate, expensive bits of business (no helicopters landing on stage as in the Broadway musical Miss Saigon!) and try to avoid a lot of scene changes. THE LOCKER ROOM breaks the small cast rule, but as in most of my one-act plays, there is only one location, and minimal set requirements. The best way to write a short one-act, (especially a serious play, as this one was not intended to be), is to put two very different characters in a room, arguing—and have each of them be a little bit in the right. You can peel away layers of the characters like layers of an onion, reveal more and more about

And Leonard credits the audience with a very potent level of participation in the performance:

> The successful theater performance blends the imaginations of those attending with those producing to create a union of images. This union of images can transport to tears or laughter, can shed welcome light on otherwise impenetrable mysteries, and can make delightfully mysterious the ordinary realities of our everyday lives.
>
> It is possible to get the impression that it is the theater artists who bring the imagery to the audience but, in fact, this is only half true. Whatever the performer brings to the stage, whatever the effects produced by the designers and artisans, the theater depends on the imagination, the life experience, the belief systems and the understanding of the world that the audience brings to the performance. The theater event actually happens in an imaginary space between the performance and the audience.
>
> (Robert H. Leonard, "Grassroots, Community-based Theater: A View of the Field and its Context," Community Arts Network, www.communityarts.net)

Across the country and around the world, local theater projects and ensembles help give voice to the experiences and opinions of ordinary people: the audience is the artist.

a relationship and show how it changes, and work into a scene as you never could on film, where producers don't like scenes to be more than three minutes long, and don't care too much if the characters are flat, and the dialogue is lame, or almost non-existent, so long as the visuals are snappy and fresh.

Film needs to be fast-paced, action-packed, and bounce from one striking location to another, often skimming along the surface of how the characters are affected. In contrast, you have the luxury, in a play, of developing contrasting characters through dialogue, and showing just how complicated and fascinating people and their relationships can be. If you have a shy side and an extroverted side, or if you are ambivalent about a controversial subject, and understand arguments on both sides—let the two characters, and the drama and conflict between them, come out of the two sides of you. Something electric can happen between two characters on a park bench, or in a living room or kitchen, if the actors are good and the audience believes in the struggle between them. In that sense, the "limitations" of theater as a form (where a lot of cutting around and special effects are not possible) are really a gift. Consider writing a play of your own. As you give life to fully-realized, three-dimensional characters we haven't seen before, and as the characters begin to tell you what they should say, instead of the other way round, you may find you really love it.

CHAPTER 3

A BOOKSHELF OF DRAMA

Samuel Beckett (1906–1989)

Krapp's Last Tape (1958)

A PLAY IN ONE ACT

SCENE: *A late evening in the future*

Krapp's den. Front center a small table, the two drawers of which open towards audience. Sitting at the table, facing front, i.e., across from the drawers, a wearish old man: Krapp.

Rusty black narrow trousers too short for him. Rusty black sleeveless waistcoat, four capacious pockets. Heavy silver watch and chain. Grimy white shirt open at neck, no collar. Surprising pair of dirty white boots, size ten at least, very narrow and pointed.

White face. Purple nose. Disordered gray hair. Unshaven.

Very near-sighted (but unspectacled). Hard of hearing.

Cracked voice. Distinctive intonation. Laborious walk.

On the table a tape-recorder with microphone and a number of cardboard boxes containing reels of recorded tapes.

Table and immediately adjacent area in strong white light. Rest of stage in darkness.

Krapp remains a moment motionless, heaves a great sigh, looks at his watch, fumbles in his pockets, takes out an envelope, puts it back, fumbles, takes out a small bunch of keys, raises it to his eyes, chooses a key, gets up and moves to front of table. He stoops, unlocks first drawer, peers into it, feels about inside it, takes out a reel of tape, peers at it, puts it back, locks drawer, unlocks second drawer, peers into it, feels about inside it, takes out a large banana, peers at it, locks drawer, puts keys back in his pocket. He turns, advances to edge of stage, halts, strokes banana, peels it, drops skin at his feet, puts end of banana in his mouth and remains motionless, staring vacuously before him. Finally he bites off the end, turns aside,

and begins pacing to and fro at edge of stage, in the light, i.e. not more than four or five paces either way, meditatively eating banana. He treads on skin, slips, nearly falls, recovers himself, stoops and peers at skin and finally pushes it, still stooping, with his foot over the edge of stage into pit. He resumes his pacing, finishes banana, returns to table, sits down, remains a moment motionless, heaves a great sigh, takes keys from his pockets, raises them to his eyes, chooses key, gets up and moves to front of table, unlocks second drawer, takes out a second large banana, peers at it, locks drawer, puts back keys in his pocket, turns, advances to edge of stage, halts, strokes banana, peels it, tosses skin into pit, puts end of banana in his mouth, and remains motionless, staring vacuously before him. Finally he has an idea, puts banana in his waistcoat pocket, the end emerging, and goes with all the speed he can muster backstage into darkness. Ten seconds. Loud pop of cork. Fifteen seconds. He comes back into light carrying an old ledger and sits down at table. He lays ledger on table, wipes his mouth, wipes his hands on the front of his waistcoat, brings them smartly together and rubs them.

KRAPP (*briskly*):   Ah! (*He bends over ledger, turns the pages, finds the entry he wants, reads.*) Box . . . thrree . . . spool . . . five. (*He raises his head and stares front. With relish.*) Spool! (*Pause.*) Spooool! (*Happy smile. Pause. He bends over table, starts peering and poking at the boxes.*) Box . . . thrree . . . thrree . . . four . . . two . . . (*with surprise*) nine! good God! . . . seven . . . ah! The little rascal! (*He takes up box, peers at it.*) Box thrree. (*He lays it on table, opens it, and peers at spools inside.*) Spool . . . (*he peers at ledger*) . . . five (*he peers at spools*) . . . five . . . five! . . . ah! the little scoundrel! 5

10

15   (*He takes out a spool, peers at it.*) Spool five.
(*He lays it on table, closes box three, puts it
back with the others, takes up the spool.*) Box
thrree, spool five. (*He bends over the
machine, looks up. With relish.*) Spooool!
20   (*Happy smile. He bends, loads spool on
machine, rubs his hands.*) Ah! (*He peers at
ledger, reads entry at foot of page.*) Mother at
rest at last . . . Hm . . . The black ball . . .
(*He raises his head, stares blankly front.
25   Puzzled.*) Black ball? . . . (*He peers again at
ledger, reads.*) The dark nurse . . . (*He raises
his head, broods, peers again at ledger, reads.*)
Slight improvement in bowel condition . . .
Hm . . . Memorable . . . what? (*He peers
30   closer.*) Equinox, memorable equinox. (*He
raises his head, stares blankly front. Puzzled.*)
Memorable equinox? . . . (*Pause. He
shrugs his shoulders, peers again at ledger,
reads.*) Farewell to—(*he turns the page*)—
35   love.

*He raises his head, broods, bends over machine,
switches on, and assumes listening posture; i.e.
leaning forward, elbows on table, hand cupping
ear towards machine, face front.*

40   TAPE (*strong voice, rather pompous, clearly
Krapp's at a much earlier time*):   Thirty-nine
today, sound as a—(*Settling himself more
comfortably he knocks one of the boxes off the
table, curses, switches off, sweeps boxes and
45   ledger violently to the ground, winds tape
back to beginning, switches on, resumes posture.*) Thirty-nine today, sound as a bell,
apart from my old weakness, and intellectually I have now every reason to sus-
50   pect at the . . . (*besitates*) . . . crest of the
wave—or thereabouts. Celebrated the
awful occasion, as in recent years, quietly
at the Winehouse. Not a soul. Sat before
the fire with closed eyes, separating the
55   grain from the husks. Jotted down a few
notes, on the back of an envelope. Good
to be back in my den, in my old rags.
Have just eaten I regret to say three

bananas and only with difficulty
refrained from a fourth. Fatal things for a   60
man with my condition. (*Vehemently.*) Cut
'em out! (*Pause.*) The new light above my
table is a great improvement. With all
this darkness round me I feel less alone.
(*Pause.*) In a way. (*Pause.*) I love to get up   65
and move about in it, then back here to . . .
(*hesitates*) . . . me. (*Pause.*) Krapp.

Pause.

The grain, now what I wonder do I mean
by that, I mean . . . (*hesitates*) . . . I sup-   70
pose I mean those things worth having
when all the dust has—when all *my* dust
has settled. I close my eyes and try and
imagine them.

Pause. Krapp closes his eyes briefly.   75

Extraordinary silence this evening, I strain
my ears and do not hear a sound. Old
Miss McGlome always sings at this hour.
But not tonight. Songs of her girlhood,
she says. Hard to think of her as a girl.   80
Wonderful woman though. Connaught, I
fancy. (*Pause.*) Shall I sing when I am her
age, if I ever am? No. (*Pause.*) Did I sing
as a boy? No (*Pause.*) Did I ever sing? No.

Pause.   85

Just been listening to an old year, passages at random. I did not check in the
book, but it must be at least ten or twelve
years ago. At that time I think I was still
living on and off with Bianca in Kedar   90
Street. Well out of that, Jesus yes!
Hopeless business. (*Pause.*) Not much
about her, apart from a tribute to her
eyes. Very warm. I suddenly saw them
again. (*Pause.*) Incomparable! (*Pause.*) Ah   95
well . . . (*Pause.*) These old P.M.s are
gruesome, but I often find them—(*Krapp
switches off, broods, switches on*)—a help
before embarking on a new . . . (*hesitates*)
. . . retrospect. Hard to believe I was ever   100

that young whelp. The voice! Jesus! And the aspirations! (*Brief laugh in which Krapp joins.*) And the resolutions! (*Brief laugh in which Krapp joins.*) To drink less, in particular. (*Brief laugh of Krapp alone.*)
105 Statistics. Seventeen hundred hours, out of the preceding eight thousand odd, consumed on licensed premises alone. More than 20%, say 40% of his waking life. (*Pause.*) Plans for a less . . .
110 (*hesitates*) . . . engrossing sexual life. Last illness of his father. Flagging pursuit of happiness. Unattainable laxation. Sneers at what he calls his youth and thanks to God that it's over. (*Pause.*) False ring
115 there. (*Pause.*) Shadows of the opus . . . magnum. Closing with a—(*brief laugh*)—yelp to Providence. (*Prolonged laugh in which Krapp joins.*) What remains of all that misery? A girl in a shabby green
120 coat, on a railway-station platform? No?

Pause.

When I look—

Krapp switches off, broods, looks at his watch, gets up, goes backstage into darkness. Ten sec-
125 *onds. Pop of cork. Ten seconds. Second cork. Ten seconds. Third cork. Ten seconds. Brief burst of quavering song.*

KRAPP (*sings*):   Now the day is over,
                          Night is drawing nigh-igh,
130   Shadows—[1]

Fit of coughing. He comes back into light, sits down, wipes his mouth, switches on, resumes his listening posture.

TAPE:—back on the year that is gone, with
135 what I hope is perhaps a glint of the old eye to come, there is of course the house on the canal where mother lay a-dying, in the late autumn, after her long viduity

(*Krapp gives a start*), and the—(*Krapp switches off, winds back tape a little, bends his ear closer to machine, switches on*)—a—dying, after her long viduity, and the—

Krapp switches off, raises his head, stares blankly before him. His lips move in the sylla-bles of "viduity"[2] No sound. He gets up, goes backstage into darkness, comes back with an enormous dictionary, lays it on table, sits down and looks up the word.

KRAPP (*reading from dictionary*):   State—or condition of being—or remaining—a widow—or widower. (*Looks up. Puzzled.*) Being—or remaining? . . . (*Pause. He peers again at dictionary. Reading.*) "Deep weeds of viduity" . . . Also of an animal, especially a bird . . . the vidua or weaver-bird . . . Black plumage of male . . . (*He looks up. With relish.*) The vidua-bird!

Pause. He closes dictionary, switches on, resumes listening posture.

TAPE:—bench by the weir from where I could see her window. There I sat, in the biting wind, wishing she were gone. (*Pause.*) Hardly a soul, just a few regu-lars, nursemaids, infants, old men, dogs. I got to know them quite well—oh by appearance of course I mean! One dark young beauty I recollect particularly, all white and starch, incomparable bosom, with a big black hooded perambulator, most funereal thing. Whenever I looked in her direction she had her eyes on me. And yet when I was bold enough to speak to her—not having been introduced—she threatened to call a policeman. As if I had designs on her virtue! (*Laugh Pause.*) The face she had! The eyes! Like . . . (*hesitates*) . . . chrysolite! (*Pause.*) Ah well . . . (*Pause.*) I was there when—(*Krapp*

140

145

150

155

160

165

170

175

---

[1]**Now . . . Shadows:** From the hymn "Now the Day Is Over" by Sabine Baring-Gould (1834–1924), author of "Onward, Christian Soldiers."

[2]**viduity:** Widowhood.

180 *switches off, broods, switches on again*)—the
blind went down, one of those dirty
brown roller affairs, throwing a ball for a
little white dog, as chance would have it.
I happened to look up and there it was.
185 All over and done with, at last. I sat on
for a few moments with the ball in my
hand and the dog yelping and pawing at
me. (*Pause.*) Moments. Her moments, my
moments. (*Pause.*) The dog's moments.
190 (*Pause.*) In the end I held it out to him
and he took it in his mouth, gently, gently. A small, old, black, hard, solid rubber
ball. (*Pause.*) I shall feel it, in my hand,
until my dying day. (*Pause.*) I might have
195 kept it. (*Pause.*) But I gave it to the dog.

Pause.

Ah well . . .

Pause.

Spiritually a year of profound gloom and
200 indigence until that memorable night in
March, at the end of the jetty, in the howling wind, never to be forgotten, when
suddenly I saw the whole thing. The
vision, at last. This I fancy is what I have
205 chiefly to record this evening, against the
day when my work will be done and perhaps no place left in my memory, warm
or cold, for the miracle that . . . (*hesitates*) . . .
for the fire that set it alight. What I sud-
210 denly saw then was this, that the belief I
had been going on all my life, namely—
(*Krapp switches off impatiently, winds tape
forward, switches on again*)—great granite
rocks the foam flying up in the light of
215 the lighthouse and the wind gauge spinning like a propellor, clear to me at last
that the dark I have always struggled to
keep under is in reality my most—(*Krapp
curses, switches off, winds tape forward,
220 switches on again*)—unshatterable association until my dissolution of storm and
night with the light of the understanding

and the fire—(*Krapp curses louder, switches
off, winds tape forward, switches on again*)—
my face in her breasts and my hand on 225
her. We lay there without moving. But
under us all moved, and moved us, gently, up and down, and from side to side.

Pause.

Past midnight. Never knew such silence. 230
The earth might be uninhabited.

Pause.

Here I end—

*Krapp switches off, winds tape back, switches
on again.* 235

—upper lake, with the punt, bathed off
the bank, then pushed out into the stream
and drifted. She lay stretched out on the
floorboards with her hands under her
head and her eyes closed. Sun blazing 240
down, bit of a breeze, water nice and
lively. I noticed a scratch on her thigh and
asked her how she came by it. Picking
gooseberries, she said. I said again I
thought it was hopeless and no good 245
going on, and she agreed, without opening her eyes. (*Pause.*) I asked her to look
at me and after a few moments—(*pause*)—
after a few moments she did, but the eyes
just slits, because of the glare. I bent over 250
her to get them in the shadow and they
opened. (*Pause. Low.*) Let me in. (*Pause.*)
We drifted in among the flags and stuck.
The way they went down, sighing, before
the stem! (*Pause.*) I lay down across her 255
with my face in her breasts and my hand
on her. We lay there without moving. But
under us all moved, and moved us, gently, up and down, and from side to side.

Pause. 260

Past midnight. Never knew—

*Krapp switches off, broods. Finally be fumbles
in his pockets, encounters the banana, takes it*

out, peers at it, puts it back, fumbles, brings out
265 *the envelope, fumbles, puts back envelope, looks*
at his watch, gets up and goes backstage into
darkness. Ten seconds. Sound of bottle against
glass, then brief siphon. Ten seconds. Bottle
against glass alone. Ten seconds. He comes back
270 *a little unsteadily into light, goes to front of*
table, takes out keys, raises them to his eyes,
chooses key, unlocks first drawer, peers into it,
feels about inside, takes out reel, peers at it,
locks drawer, puts keys back in his pocket, goes
275 *and sits down, takes reel off machine, lays it on*
dictionary, loads virgin reel on machine, takes
envelope from his pocket, consults back of it,
lays it on table, switches on, clears his throat,
and begins to record.

280 KRAPP: Just been listening to that stupid
bastard I took myself for thirty years ago,
hard to believe I was ever as bad as that.
Thank God that's all done with anyway.
(*Pause.*) The eyes she had! (*Broods, realizes*
285 *he is recording silence, switches off, broods.*
Finally.) Everything there, everything, all
the—(*Realizes this is not being recorded,*
switches on.) Everything there, everything
on this old muckball, all the light and
290 dark and famine and feasting of . . . (*hesi-*
tates) . . . the ages! (*In a shout.*) Yes!
(*Pause.*) Let that go! Jesus! Take his mind
off his homework! Jesus! (*Pause. Weary.*)
Ah well, maybe he was right. (*Pause.*)
295 Maybe he was right. (*Broods. Realizes.*
Switches off. Consults envelope.) Pah!
(*Crumples it and throws it away. Broods*
Switches on.) Nothing to say, not a
squeak. What's a year now? The sour cud
300 and the iron stool. (*Pause.*) Revelled in
the word spool. (*With relish.*) Spooool!
Happiest moment of the past half million. (*Pause.*) Seventeen copies sold, of
which eleven at trade price to free circu-
305 lating libraries beyond the seas. Getting
known. (*Pause.*) One pound six and
something, eight I have little doubt.

(*Pause.*) Crawled out once or twice,
before the summer was cold. Sat shivering in the park, drowned in dreams and   310
burning to be gone. Not a soul. (*Pause.*)
Last fancies. (*Vehemently.*) Keep 'em
under! (*Pause.*) Scalded the eyes out of
me reading *Effie* again, a page a day, with
tears again. Effie . . . (*Pause.*) Could have   315
been happy with her, up there on the
Baltic, and the pines, and the dunes.
(*Pause.*) Could I? (*Pause.*) And she?
(*Pause.*) Pah! (*Pause.*) Fanny came in a
couple of times. Bony old ghost of a   320
whore. Couldn't do much, but I suppose
better than a kick in the crutch. The last
time wasn't so bad. How do you manage
it, she said, at your age? I told her I'd
been saving up for her all my life (*Pause.*)   325
Went to Vespers once, like when I was in
short trousers. (*Pause. Sings.*)

Now the day is over,
Night is drawing nigh-igh,
Shadows—(*coughing, then almost*   330
inaudible)—of the evening
Steal across the sky.

(*Gasping.*) Went to sleep and fell off the
pew. (*Pause.*) Sometimes wondered in the
night if a last effort mightn't—(*Pause.*) Ah   335
finish your booze now and get to your
bed. Go on with this drivel in the morning. Or leave it at that. (*Pause.*) Leave it at
that. (*Pause.*) Lie propped up in the
dark—and wander. Be again in the dingle   340
on a Christmas Eve, gathering holly, the
red-berried. (*Pause.*) Be again on Croghan
on a Sunday morning, in the haze, with
the bitch, stop and listen to the bells.
(*Pause.*) And so on. (*Pause.*) Be again, be   345
again. (*Pause.*) All that old misery.
(*Pause.*) Once wasn't enough for you.
(*Pause.*) Lie down across her.

Long pause. He suddenly bends over machine,
switches off, wrenches off tape, throws it away,   350

puts on the other, winds it forward to the passage he wants, switches on, listens staring front.

TAPE:—gooseberries, she said. I said again I
355 thought it was hopeless and no good going on, and she agreed, without opening her eyes. (*Pause.*) I asked her to look at me and after a few moments— (*Pause.*)—after a few moments she did,
360 but the eyes just slits, because of the glare. I bent over her to get them in the shadow and they opened. (*Pause. Low.*) Let me in. (*Pause.*) We drifted in among the flags and stuck. The way they went
365 down, sighing, before the stem! (*Pause.*) I lay down across her with my face in her breasts and my hand on her. We lay there without moving. But under us all moved, and moved us, gently, up and down, and from side to side.   370

Pause. Krapp's lips move. No sound.

Past midnight. Never knew such silence. The earth might be uninhabited.

Pause.

Here I end this reel. Box—(*pause*)—three,   375
spool—(*pause*)—five. (*pause*) Perhaps my best years are gone. When there was a chance of happiness. But I wouldn't want them back. Not with the fire in me now. No, I wouldn't want them back.   380

Krapp motionless staring before him. The tape runs on in silence.

Curtain

SUSAN GLASPELL (1882–1948)

Trifles

CHARACTERS

SHERIFF	MRS. PETERS, *Sheriff's wife*
COUNTY ATTORNEY	MRS. HALE
HALE	

SCENE: *The kitchen in the now abandoned farmhouse of* JOHN WRIGHT, *a gloomy kitchen, and left without having been put in order—unwashed pans under the sink, a loaf of bread outside the bread-box, a dish-towel on the table—other signs of incompleted work. At the rear the outer door opens and the* SHERIFF *comes in followed by the* COUNTY ATTORNEY *and* HALE. *The* SHERIFF *and* HALE *are men in middle life, the* COUNTY ATTORNEY *is a young man; all are much bundled up and go at once to the stove. They are followed by the two women—the* SHERIFF'S *wife first; she is a slight wiry woman, a thin nervous face.* MRS. HALE *is larger and would ordinarily be called more comfortable looking, but she is disturbed now and looks fearfully about as she enters. The women have come in slowly, and stand close together near the door.*

COUNTY ATTORNEY: [*Rubbing his hands.*] This feels good. Come up to the fire, ladies.

MRS. PETERS: [*After taking a step forward.*] I'm not—cold.

SHERIFF: [*Unbuttoning his overcoat and stepping away from the stove as if to mark the beginning of official business.*]   Now, Mr. Hale, before we move things about, you explain to Mr. Henderson just what you saw when you came here yesterday morning.

COUNTRY ATTORNEY: By the way, has anything been moved? Are things just as you left them yesterday?

5 SHERIFF: [*Looking about.*] It's just the same. When it dropped below zero last night I thought I'd better send Frank out this morning to make a fire for us—no use getting pneumonia with a big case on, but I told him not to touch anything except the stove—and you know Frank.

COUNTRY ATTORNEY: Somebody should have been left here yesterday.

SHERIFF: Oh—yesterday. When I had to send Frank to Morris Center for that man who went crazy—I want you to know I had my hands full yesterday. I knew you could get back from Omaha by today and as long as I went over everything here myself—

COUNTRY ATTORNEY: Well, Mr. Hale, tell just what happened when you came here yesterday morning.

HALE: Harry and I had started to town with a load of potatoes. We came along the road from my place and as I got here I said, "I'm going to see if I can't get John Wright to go in with me on a party telephone." I spoke to Wright about it once before and he put me off, saying folks talked too much anyway, and all he asked was peace and quiet—I guess you know about how much he talked himself; but I thought maybe if I went to the house and talked about it before his wife, though I said to Harry that I didn't know as what his wife wanted made much difference to John—

10 COUNTRY ATTORNEY: Let's talk about that later, Mr. Hale. I do want to talk about that, but tell now just what happened when you got to the house.

HALE: I didn't hear or see anything; I knocked at the door, and still it was all quiet inside. I knew they must be up, it was past eight o'clock. So I knocked again, and I thought I heard somebody say, "Come in." I wasn't sure, I'm not sure yet, but I opened the door—this door [*Indicating the door by which the two women are still standing.*] and there in that rocker—[*Pointing to it.*] sat Mrs. Wright.

[*They all look at the rocker.*]

COUNTRY ATTORNEY: What—was she doing?

HALE: She was rockin' back and forth. She had her apron in her hand and was kind of—pleating it.

COUNTRY ATTORNEY: And how did she—look?

HALE: Well, she looked queer.   15

COUNTRY ATTORNEY: How do you mean—queer?

HALE: Well, as if she didn't know what she was going to do next. And kind of done up.

COUNTRY ATTORNEY: How did she seem to feel about your coming?

HALE: Why, I don't think she minded—one way or other. She didn't pay much attention. I said, "How do, Mrs. Wright, it's cold, ain't it?" And she said, "Is it?"—and went on kind of pleating at her apron. Well, I was surprised; she didn't ask me to come up to the stove, or to set down, but just sat there, not even looking at me, so I said, "I want to see John." And then she—laughed. I guess you would call it a laugh. I thought of Harry and the team outside, so I said a little sharp: "Can't I see John?" "No," she says, kind o' dull like. "Ain't he home?" says I. "Yes," says she, "he's home." "Then why can't I see him?" I asked her, out of patience. "'Cause he's dead," says she. "*Dead?*" says I. She just nodded her head, not getting a bit excited, but rockin' back and forth. "Why—where is he?" says I, not knowing what to say. She just pointed upstairs—like that. [*Himself pointing to the room above.*] I got up, with the idea of going up there. I walked from there to here—then I says, "Why, what did he die of?" "He died of a rope round his neck," says she, and just went on pleatin' at her apron. Well, I went out and called Harry. I thought I might— need help. We went upstairs and there he was lyin'—

20 COUNTRY ATTORNEY: I think I'd rather have you go into that upstairs, where you can point it all out. Just go on now with the rest of the story.

HALE: Well, my first thought was to get that rope off. It looked . . . [*Stops, his face twitches.*] . . . but Harry, he went up to him, and he said, "No, he's dead all right, and we'd better not touch anything." So we went back down stairs. She was still sitting that same way. "Has anybody been notified?" I asked. "No," says she unconcerned. "Who did this, Mrs. Wright?" said Harry. He said it businesslike—and she stopped pleatin' of her apron. "I don't know," she says. "You don't *know*?" says Harry. "No," says she. "Weren't you sleepin' in the bed with him?" says Harry. "Yes," says she, "but I was on the inside." "Somebody slipped a rope round his neck and strangled him and you didn't wake up?" says Harry. "I didn't wake up," she said after him. We must 'a looked as if we didn't see how that could be, for after a minute she said, "I sleep sound." Harry was going to ask her more questions but I said maybe we ought to let her tell her story first to the coroner, or the sheriff, so Harry went fast as he could to Rivers' place, where there's a telephone.

COUNTRY ATTORNEY: And what did Mrs. Wright do when she knew that you had gone for the coroner?

HALE: She moved from that chair to this one over here [*Pointing to a small chair in the corner.*] and just sat there with her hands held together and looking down. I got a feeling that I ought to make some conversation, so I said I had come in to see if John wanted to put in a telephone, and at that she started to laugh, and then she stopped and looked at me—scared. [*The* COUNTY ATTORNEY, *who has had his notebook out, makes a note.*] I dunno, maybe it wasn't scared. I wouldn't like to say it was. Soon Harry got back, and then Dr. Lloyd came, and you, Mr. Peters, and so I guess that's all I know that you don't.

COUNTRY ATTORNEY: [*Looking around.*] I guess we'll go upstairs first—and then out to the barn and around there. [*To the* SHERIFF.] You're convinced that there was nothing important here—nothing that would point to any motive?

SHERIFF: Nothing here but kitchen things. 25

[*The* COUNTY ATTORNEY, *after again looking around the kitchen, opens the door of a cupboard closer. He gets up on a chair and looks on a shelf. Pulls his hand away, sticky.*]

COUNTRY ATTORNEY: Here's a nice mess.

[*The women draw nearer.*]

MRS. PETERS: [*To the other woman.*] Oh, her fruit; it did freeze. [*To the* LAWYER.] She worried about that when it turned so cold. She said the fire'd go out and her jars would break.

SHERIFF: Well, can you beat the women! Held for murder and worryin' about her preserves.

COUNTRY ATTORNEY: I guess before we're through she may have something more serious than preserves to worry about.

HALE: Well, women are used to worrying 30 over trifles.

[*The two women move a little closer together.*]

COUNTRY ATTORNEY: [*With the gallantry of a young politician.*] And yet, for all their worries, what would we do without the ladies? [*The women do not unbend. He goes to the sink, takes a dipperful of water from the pail and pouring it into a basin, washes his hands. Starts to wipe them on the roller-towel, turns it for a cleaner place.*] Dirty towels! [*Kicks his foot against the pans under the sink.*] Not much of a house-keeper, would you say, ladies?

MRS. HALE: [*Stiffly.*] There's a great deal of work to be done on a farm.

COUNTRY ATTORNEY: To be sure. And yet [*With a little bow to her.*] I know there are some Dickson county farmhouses which do not have such roller towels. [*He gives it a pull to expose its length again.*]

MRS. HALE: Those towels get dirty awful quick. Men's hands aren't always as clean as they might be.

35 COUNTRY ATTORNEY: Ah, loyal to your sex, I see. But you and Mrs. Wright were neigh-bors. I suppose you were friends, too.

MRS. HALE: [*Shaking her head.*] I've not seen much of her of late years. I've not been in this house—it's more than a year.

COUNTRY ATTORNEY: And why was that? You didn't like her?

MRS. HALE: I liked her all well enough. Farmers' wives have their hands full, Mr. Henderson. And then—

COUNTRY ATTORNEY: Yes—?

40 MRS. HALE: [*Looking about.*] It never seemed a very cheerful place.

COUNTRY ATTORNEY: No—it's not cheerful. I shouldn't say she had the homemaking instinct.

MRS. HALE: Well, I don't know as Wright had, either.

COUNTRY ATTORNEY: You mean that they didn't get on very well?

MRS. HALE: No, I don't mean anything. But I don't think a place'd be any cheer-fuller for John Wright's being in it.

45 COUNTRY ATTORNEY: I'd like to talk more of that a little later. I want to get the lay of things upstairs now. [*He goes to the left, where three steps lead to a stair door.*]

SHERIFF: I suppose anything Mrs. Peters does'll be all right. She was to take in some clothes for her, you know, and a few little things. We left in such a hurry yesterday.

COUNTRY ATTORNEY: Yes, but I would like to see what you take, Mrs. Peters, and keep an eye out for anything that might be of use to us.

MRS. PETERS: Yes, Mr. Henderson. [*The women listen to the men's steps on the stairs, then look about the kitchen.*]

MRS. HALE: I'd hate to have men coming into my kitchen, snooping around and criticizing. [*She arranges the pans under sink which the LAWYER had shoved out of place.*]

MRS. PETERS: Of course it's no more than   50 their duty.

MRS. HALE: Duty's all right, but I guess that deputy sheriff that came out to make the fire might have got a little of this on. [*Gives the roller towel a pull.*] Wish I'd thought of that sooner. Seems mean to talk about her for not having things slicked up when she had to come away in such a hurry.

MRS. PETERS: [*Who has gone to a small table in the left rear corner of the room, and lifted one end of a towel that covers a pan.*] She had bread set. [*Stands still.*]

MRS. HALE: [*Eyes fixed on a loaf of bread beside the bread box, which is on a low shelf at the other side of the room. Moves slowly toward it.*] She was going to put this in there. [*Picks up loaf, then abruptly drops it. In a manner of returning to familiar things.*] It's a shame about her fruit. I wonder if it's all gone. [*Gets up on the chair and looks.*] I think there's some here that's all right, Mrs. Peters. Yes—here; [*Holding it toward the window.*] this is cherries, too. [*Looking again.*] I declare I believe that's the only one. [*Gets down, bottle in her hand. Goes to the sink and wipes it off on the outside.*] She'll feel awful bad after all her hard work in the hot weather. I remember the afternoon I put up my cherries last summer. [*She puts the bottle on the big kitchen table, center of the room. With a sigh, is about to sit down in the rocking-chair. Before she is seated realizes what chair it is; with a slow look at it, steps back. The chair, which she has touched, rocks back and forth.*]

MRS. PETERS: Well, I must get those things from the front room closet. [*She goes to the door at the right, but after looking into the other room, steps back.*] You coming with me, Mrs. Hale? You could help me carry them. [*They go in the other room; reappear,* MRS. PETERS *carrying a dress and skirt,* MRS. HALE *following with a pair of shoes.*] My, it's cold in there. [*She puts the clothes on the big table, and hurries to the stove.*]

55   MRS. HALE: [*Examining the skirt.*]   Wright was close. I think maybe that's why she kept so much to herself. She didn't even belong to the Ladies Aid. I suppose she felt she couldn't do her part, and then you don't enjoy things when you feel shabby. She used to wear pretty clothes and be lively, when she was Minnle Foster, one of the town girls singing in the choir. But that—oh, that was thirty years ago. This all you was to take in?

MRS. PETERS: She said she wanted an apron. Funny thing to want, for there isn't much to get you dirty in jail, goodness knows. But I suppose just to make her feel more natural. She said they was in the top drawer in this cupboard. Yes here. And then her little shawl that always hung behind the door. [*Opens stair door and looks.*] Yes, here it is. [*Quickly shuts door leading upstairs.*]

MRS. HALE: [*Abruptly moving toward her.*] Mrs. Peters?

MRS. PETERS: Yes, Mrs. Hale?

MRS. HALE: Do you think she did it?

60   MRS. PETERS: [*In a frightened voice.*]   Oh, I don't know.

MRS. HALE: Well, I don't think she did. Asking for an apron and her little shawl. Worrying about her fruit.

MRS. PETERS: [*Starts to speak, glances up, where footsteps are heard in the room above. In a low voice.*]   Mr. Peters says it looks bad for her. Mr. Henderson is awful sarcastic in a speech and he'll make fun of her sayin' she didn't wake up.

MRS. HALE: Well, I guess John Wright didn't wake when they was slipping that rope under his neck.

MRS. PETERS: No, it's strange. It must have been done awful crafty and still. They say it was such a—funny way to kill a man, rigging it all up like that.

MRS. HALE: That's just what Mr. Hale said. There was a gun in the house. He says that's what he can't understand.   65

MRS. PETERS: Mr. Henderson said coming out that what was needed for the case was a motive; something to show anger, or—sudden feeling.

MRS. HALE: [*Who is standing by the table.*] Well, I don't see any signs of anger around here. [*She puts her hand on the dish towel which lies on the table, stands looking down at table, one half of which is clean, the other half messy.*] It's wiped to here. [*Makes a move as if to finish work, then turns and looks at loaf of bread outside the bread box. Drops towel. In that voice of coming back to familiar things.*] Wonder how they are finding things upstairs. I hope she had it a little more redup[1] up there. You know, it seems kind of *sneaking.* Locking her up in town and then coming out here and trying to get her own house to turn against her!

MRS. PETERS: But Mrs. Hale, the law is the law.

MRS. HALE: I s'pose 'tis. [*Unbuttoning her coat.*] Better loosen up your things,

----

[1]redup: Tidied up.

Mrs. Peters. You won't feel them when you go out.

[Mrs. Peters *takes off her fur tippet, goes to hang it on hook at back of room, stands looking at the under part of the small corner table.*]

70 Mrs. Peters: She was piecing a quilt. [*She brings the large sewing basket and they look at the bright pieces.*]

Mrs. Hale: It's log cabin pattern. Pretty, isn't it? I wonder if she was goin' to quilt it or just knot it?

[*Footsteps have been heard coming down the stairs. The* Sheriff *enters followed by* Hale *and the* County Attorney.]

Sheriff: They wonder if she was going to quilt it or just knot it!

[*The men laugh, the women look abashed.*]

Country Attorney: [*Rubbing his hands over the stove.*]   Frank's fire didn't do much up there, did it? Well, let's go out to the barn and get that cleared up.

[*The men go outside.*]

Mrs. Hale: [*Resentfully.*]   I don't know as there's anything so strange, our takin' up our time with little things while we're waiting for them to get the evidence. [*She sits down at the big table smoothing out a block with decision.*] I don't see as it's anything to laugh about.

75 Mrs. Peters: [*Apologetically.*]   Of course they've got awful important things on their minds. [*Pulls up a chair and joins* Mrs. Hale *at the table.*]

Mrs. Hale: [*Examining another block.*]   Mrs. Peters, look at this one. Here, this is the one she was working on, and look at the sewing! All the rest of it has been so nice and even. And look at this! It's all over the place! Why, it looks as if she didn't know what she was about! [*After she has said this they look at each other, then start to*

glance back at the door. After an instant Mrs. Hale *has pulled at a knot and ripped the sewing.*]

Mrs. Peters: Oh, what are you doing, Mrs. Hale?

Mrs. Hale: [*Mildly.*]   Just pulling out a stitch or two that's not sewed very good. [*Threading the needle.*] Bad sewing always made me fidgety.

Mrs. Peters: [*Nervously.*]   I don't think we ought to touch things.

Mrs. Hale: I'll just finish up this end.   80 [*Suddenly stopping and leaning forward.*] Mrs. Peters?

Mrs. Peters: Yes, Mrs. Hale?

Mrs. Hale: What do you suppose she was so nervous about?

Mrs. Peters: Oh—I don't know. I don't know as she was nervous. I sometimes sew awful queer when I'm just tired. [Mrs. Hale *starts to say something, looks at* Mrs. Peters, *then goes on sewing.*] Well I must get these things wrapped up. They may be through sooner than we think. [*Putting apron and other things together.*] I wonder where I can find a piece of paper, and string.

Mrs. Hale: In that cupboard, maybe.

Mrs. Peters: [*Looking in cupboard.*]   Why,   85 here's a bird-cage. [*Holds it up.*] Did she have a bird, Mrs. Hale?

Mrs. Hale: Why, I don't know whether she did or not—I've not been here for so long. There was a man around last year selling canaries cheap, but I don't know as she took one; maybe she did. She used to sing real pretty herself.

Mrs. Peters: [*Glancing around.*]   Seems funny to think of a bird here. But she must have had one, or why would she have a cage? I wonder what happened to it.

Mrs. Hale: I s'pose maybe the cat got it.

Mrs. Peters: No, she didn't have a cat. She's got that feeling some people have about cats—being afraid of them. My cat got in her room and she was real upset and asked me to take it out.

90   MRS. HALE: My sister Bessie was like that. Queer, ain't it?

MRS. PETERS: [*Examining the cage.*]   Why, look at this door. It's broke. One hinge is pulled apart.

MRS. HALE: [*Looking too.*]   Looks as if someone must have been rough with it.

MRS. PETERS: Why, yes. [*She brings the cage forward and puts it on the table.*]

MRS. HALE: I wish if they're going to find any evidence they'd be about it. I don't like this place.

95   MRS. PETERS: But I'm awful glad you came with me, Mrs. Hale. It would be lonesome for me sitting here alone.

MRS. HALE: It would, wouldn't it? [*Dropping her sewing.*] But I tell you what I do wish, Mrs. Peters. I wish I had come over sometimes when *she* was here. I— [*Looking around the room.*]—wish I had.

MRS. PETERS: But of course you were awful busy, Mrs. Hale—your house and your children.

MRS. HALE: I could've come. I stayed away because it weren't cheerful—and that's why I ought to have come. I—I've never liked this place. Maybe because it's down in a hollow and you don't see the road. I dunno what it is, but it's a lonesome place and always was. I wish I had come over to see Minnie Foster sometimes. I can see now—[*Shakes her head.*]

MRS. PETERS: Well, you mustn't reproach yourself, Mrs. Hale. Somehow we just don't see how it is with other folks until—something comes up.

100   MRS. HALE: Not having children makes less work—but it makes a quiet house, and Wright out to work all day, and no company when he did come in. Did you know John Wright, Mrs. Peters?

MRS. PETERS: Not to know him; I've seen him in town. They say he was a good man.

MRS. HALE: Yes—good; he didn't drink, and kept his word as well as most, I guess, and paid his debts. But he was a hard man, Mrs. Peters. Just to pass the time of day with him—[*Shivers.*] Like a raw wind that gets to the bone. [*Pauses, her eye falling on the cage.*] I should think she would 'a wanted a bird. But what do you suppose went with it?

MRS. PETERS: I don't know, unless it got sick and died. [*She reaches over and swings the broken door, swings it again, both women watch it.*]

MRS. HALE: You weren't raised round here, were you? [MRS. PETERS *shakes her head.*] You didn't know—her?

MRS. PETERS: Not till they brought her   105 yesterday.

MRS. HALE: She—come to think of it, she was kind of like a bird herself—real sweet and pretty, but kind of timid and— fluttery. How—she—did—change. [*Silence; then as if struck by a happy thought and relieved to get back to everyday things.*] Tell you what, Mrs. Peters, why don't you take the quilt in with you? It might take up her mind.

MRS. PETERS: Why, I think that's a real nice idea, Mrs. Hale. There couldn't possibly be any objection to it, could there? Now, just what would I take? I wonder if her patches are in here—and her things. [*They look in the sewing basket.*]

MRS. HALE: Here's some red. I expect this has got sewing things in it. [*Brings out a fancy box.*] What a pretty box. Looks like something somebody would give you. Maybe her scissors are in here. [*Opens box. Suddenly puts her hand to her nose.*] Why—[MRS. PETERS *bends nearer, then turns her face away.*] There's something wrapped up in this piece of silk.

MRS. PETERS: Why, this isn't her scissors.

110   MRS. HALE: [*Lifting the silk.*]   Oh,
Mrs. Peters—it's—

[MRS. PETERS *bends closer.*]

MRS. PETERS: It's the bird.

MRS. HALE: [*Jumping up.*]   But, Mrs.
Peters—look at it! Its neck! Look at its
neck! It's all—other side *to.*

MRS. PETERS: Somebody—wrung—its—neck.

[*Their eyes meet. A look of growing comprehension, of horror. Steps are heard outside.*
MRS. HALE *slips box under quilt pieces, and sinks into her chair. Enter* SHERIFF *and* COUNTY ATTORNEY, MRS. PETERS *rises.*]

COUNTRY ATTORNEY: [*As one turning from serious things to little pleasantries.*]   Well ladies, have you decided whether she was going to quilt it or knot it?

115   MRS. PETERS: We think she was going to—knot it.

COUNTRY ATTORNEY: Well, that's interesting, I'm sure. [*Seeing the bird-cage.*] Has the bird flown?

MRS. HALE: [*Putting more quilt pieces over the box.*]   We think the—cat got it.

COUNTRY ATTORNEY: [*Preoccupied.*]   Is there a cat?

[MRS. HALE *glances in a quick covert way at* MRS. PETERS.]

MRS. PETERS: Well, not *now.* They're superstitious you know. They leave.

120   COUNTRY ATTORNEY: [*To* SHERIFF PETERS, *continuing an interrupted conversation.*]   No sign at all of anyone having come from the outside. Their own rope. Now let's go up again and go over it piece by piece. [*They start upstairs.*] It would have to have been someone who knew just the—

[MRS. PETERS *sits down. The two women sit there not looking at one another, but as if peering into something and at the same time holding back. When they talk now it is in the manner of feeling their way over strange ground, as if afraid of what they are saying, but as if they cannot help saying it.*]

MRS. HALE: She liked the bird. She was going to bury it in that pretty box.

MRS. PETERS: [*In a whisper.*]   When I was a girl—my kitten—there was a boy took a hatchet, and before my eyes—and before I could get there—[*Covers her face an instant.*] If they hadn't held me back I would have—[*Catches herself, looks upstairs where steps are heard, falters weakly.*]—hurt him.

MRS. HALE: [*With a slow look around her.*]   I wonder how it would seem never to have had any children around. [*Pause.*] No, Wright wouldn't like the bird—a thing that sang. She used to sing. He killed that, too.

MRS. PETERS: [*Moving uneasily.*]   We don't know who killed the bird.

MRS. HALE: I knew John Wright.   125

MRS. PETERS: It was an awful thing was done in this house that night, Mrs. Hale. Killing a man while he slept, slipping a rope around his neck that choked the life out of him.

MRS. HALE: His neck. Choked the life out of him. [*Her hand goes out and rests on the bird-cage.*]

MRS. PETERS: [*With rising voice.*]   We don't know who killed him. We don't *know.*

MRS. HALE: [*Her own feeling not interrupted.*]   If there's been years and years of nothing, then a bird to sing to you, it would be awful—still, after the bird was still.

MRS. PETERS: [*Something within her speaking.*]   130
I know what stillness is. When we homesteaded in Dakota, and my first baby died—after he was two years old, and me with no other then—

MRS. HALE: [*Moving.*]   How soon do you suppose they'll be through, looking for the evidence?

MRS. PETERS: I know what stillness is. [*Pulling herself back.*] The law has got to punish crime, Mrs. Hale.

MRS. HALE: [*Not as if answering that.*]   I wish you'd seen Minnie Foster when she wore a white dress with blue ribbons and stood up there in the choir and sang. [*A look around the room.*] Oh, I *wish* I'd come over here once in a while! That was a crime! That was a crime! Who's going to punish that?

MRS. PETERS: [*Looking upstairs.*]   We mustn't—take on.

135   MRS. HALE: I might have known she needed help! I know how things can be— for women. I tell you, it's queer, Mrs. Peters. We live close together and we live far apart. We all go through the same things—it's all just a different kind of the same thing. [*Brushes her eyes, noticing the bottle of fruit, reaches out for it.*] If I was you, I wouldn't tell her her fruit was gone. Tell her it *ain't*. Tell her it's all right. Take this in to prove it to her. She—she may never know whether it was broke or not.

MRS. PETERS: [*Takes the bottle, looks about for something to wrap it in; takes petticoat from the clothes brought from the other room, very nervously begins winding this around the bottle. In a false voice.*]   My, it's a good thing the men couldn't hear us. Wouldn't they just laugh! Getting all stirred up over a little thing like a—dead canary. As if that could have anything to do with— with—wouldn't they *laugh!*

[*The men are heard coming down stairs.*]

MRS. HALE: [*Under her breath.*]   Maybe they would—maybe they wouldn't.

COUNTRY ATTORNEY: No, Peters, it's all perfectly clear except a reason for doing it. But you know juries when it comes to women. If there was some definite thing. Something to show—something to make a story about—a thing that would

connect up with this strange way of doing it—

[*The women's eyes meet for an instant. Enter* HALE *from outer door.*]

HALE: Well, I've got the team around. Pretty cold out there.

COUNTRY ATTORNEY: I'm going to stay here   140 a while by myself. [*To the* SHERIFF.] You can send Frank out for me, can't you? I want to go over everything. I'm not satisfied that we can't do better.

SHERIFF: Do you want to see what Mrs. Peters is going to take in?

[*The* LAWYER *goes to the table, picks up the apron, laughs.*]

COUNTRY ATTORNEY: Oh, I guess they're not very dangerous things the ladies have picked out. [*Moves a few things about, disturbing the quilt pieces which cover the box. Steps back.*] No, Mrs. Peters doesn't need supervising. For that matter, a sheriff's wife is married to the law. Ever think of it that way, Mrs. Peters?

MRS. PETERS: Not—just that way.

SHERIFF: [*Chuckling.*]   Married to the law. [*Moves toward the other room.*] I just want you to come in here a minute, George. We ought to take a look at these windows.

COUNTRY ATTORNEY: [*Scoffingly.*]   Oh,   145 windows!

SHERIFF: We'll be right out, Mr. Hale.

[HALE *goes outside. The* SHERIFF *follows the* COUNTY ATTORNEY *into the other room. Then* MRS. HALE *rises, hands tight together, looking intensely at* MRS. PETERS, *whose eyes make a slow turn, finally meeting* MRS. HALE'S. *A moment* MRS. HALE *holds her, then her own eyes point the way to where the box is concealed. Suddenly* MRS. PETERS *throws back quilt pieces and tries to put the box in the bag she is wearing. It is too big. She opens box, starts to take bird out, cannot touch it, goes to pieces, stands there helpless. Sound of a knob turning in the other room.* MRS. HALE *snatches the box and puts it in the pocket of her big coat. Enter* COUNTY ATTORNEY *and* SHERIFF.]

COUNTRY ATTORNEY: [*Facetiously.*] Well, Henry, at least we found out that she was not going to quilt it. She was going to— what is it you call it, ladies?

MRS. HALE: [*Her hand against her pocket.*] We call it—knot it, Mr. Henderson.

Curtain

Milcha Sanchez-Scott (1955–)

The Cuban Swimmer (1984)

CHARACTERS:

MARGARITA SUÁREZ, *the swimmer*
EDUARDO SUÁREZ, *her father, the coach*
SIMÓN SUÁREZ, *her brother*
AÍDA SUÁREZ, *her mother*

ABUELA, *her grandmother*
VOICE OF MEL MUNSON
VOICE OF MARY BETH WHITE
VOICE OF RADIO OPERATOR

SETTING

The Pacific Ocean between San Pedro and Catalina Island.

TIME
Summer.

Live conga drums can be used to punctuate the action of the play.

SCENE 1

Pacific Ocean. Midday. On the horizon, in perspective, a small boat enters upstage left, crosses to upstage right, and exits. Pause. Lower on the horizon, the same boat, in larger perspective, enters upstage right, crosses and exits upstage left. Blackout.

SCENE 2

Pacific Ocean. Midday. The swimmer, Margarita Suárez, is swimming. On the boat following behind her are her father, Eduardo Suárez, holding a megaphone, and Simón, her brother, sitting on top of the cabin with his shirt off, punk sunglasses on, binoculars hanging on his chest.

EDUARDO: (*leaning forward, shouting in time to Margarita's swimming*) Uno, dos, uno, dos. Y uno, dos . . . keep your shoulders parallel to the water.

SIMÓN: I'm gonna take these glasses off and look straight into the sun.

EDUARDO: (*through megaphone*) Muy bien, muy bien . . . but punch those arms in, baby.

SIMÓN: (*looking directly at the sun through binoculars*) Come on, come on, zap me. Show me something. (*He looks behind at the shoreline and ahead at the sea.*) Stop! Stop, *Papi*! Stop!

Aída Suárez and Abuela, the swimmer's mother and grandmother, enter running from the back of the boat.

AÍDA and ABUELA: Qué? Qué es?   5

AÍDA: Es un shark?

EDUARDO: Eh?

ABUELA: Qué es un shark dicen?

Eduardo blows whistle. Margarita looks up at the boat.

SIMÓN: No, *Papi*, no shark, no shark. We've reached the halfway mark.

ABUELA: (*looking into the water*) A dónde está?   10

AÍDA: It's not in the water.

ABUELA: Oh, no? Oh, no?

AÍDA: No! *A poco* do you think they're gonna have signs in the water to say you are halfway to Santa Catalina? No. It's done very scientific. *A ver, hijo,* explain it to your grandma.

SIMÓN: Well, you see, Abuela—(*He points behind.*) There's San Pedro. (*He points ahead.*) And there's Santa Catalina. Looks halfway to me.

Abuela shakes her head and is looking back and forth, trying to make the decision, when suddenly the sound of a helicopter is heard.

15   ABUELA: (*looking up*)   *Virgencita de la Caridad del Cobre. Qué es eso?*

Sound of helicopter gets closer. Margarita looks up.

MARGARITA: *Papi, Papi!*

A small commotion on the boat, with Everybody pointing at the helicopter above. Shadows of the helicopter fall on the boat. Simón looks up at it through binoculars.

Papi—qué es? What is it?

EDUARDO: (*through megaphone*)   Uh . . . uh . . . uh, *un momentico . . . mi hija . . .* Your *papi's* got everything under control, understand?

Uh . . . you just keep stroking. And stay . . . uh . . . close to the boat.

SIMÓN: Wow, *Papi!* We're on TV, man! Holy Christ, we're all over the fucking U.S.A.! It's Mel Munson and Mary Beth White!

AÍDA: *Por Dios!* Simón, don't swear. And put on your shirt.

Aída fluffs her hair, puts on her sunglasses and waves to the helicopter. Simón leans over the side of the boat and yells to Margarita.

20   SIMÓN: Yo, Margo! You're on TV, man.

EDUARDO: Leave your sister alone. Turn on the radio.

MARGARITA: *Papi! Qué está pasando?*

ABUELA: *Que es la televisión dicen?* (*She shakes her head.*) *Porque como yo no puedo ver nada sin mis espejuelos?*

ABUELA *rummages through the boat, looking for her glasses. Voices of* MEL MUNSON *and* MARY BETH WHITE *are heard over the boat's radio.*

MEL'S VOICE: As we take a closer look at the gallant crew of *La Havana* . . . and there . . . yes, there she is . . . the little Cuban swimmer from Long Beach, California, nineteen-year-old Margarita Suárez. The unknown swimmer is our Cinderella entry . . . a bundle of tenacity, battling her way through the choppy, murky waters of the cold Pacific to reach the Island of Romance . . . Santa Catalina . . . where should she be the first to arrive, two thousand dollars and a gold cup will be waiting for her.

AÍDA: Doesn't even cover our expenses.   25

ABUELA: *Qué dice?*

EDUARDO: Shhhh!

MARY BETH'S VOICE: This is really a family effort, Mel, and—

MEL'S VOICE: Indeed it is. Her trainer, her coach, her mentor, is her father, Eduardo Suárez. Not a swimmer himself, it says here, Mr. Suárez is head usher of the Holy Name Society and the owner-operator of Suárez Treasures of the Sea and Salvage Yard. I guess it's one of those places—

MARY BETH'S VOICE: If I might interject a   30 fact here, Mel, assisting in this swim is Mrs. Suárez, who is a former Miss Cuba.

MEL'S VOICE: And a beautiful woman in her own right. Let's try and get a closer look.

Helicopter sound gets louder. MARGARITA, *frightened, looks up again.*

MARGARITA: *Papi!*

EDUARDO: (*through megaphone*)   *Mi hija,* don't get nervous . . . it's the press. I'm handling it.

AÍDA: I see how you're handling it.

35 EDUARDO: (*through megaphone*)   Do you hear? Everything is under control. Get back into your rhythm. Keep your elbows high and kick and kick and kick and kick . . .

ABUELA: (*finds her glasses and puts them on*) *Ay sí, es la televisión* . . . (*She points to helicopter.*) *Qué lindo mira* . . . (*She fluffs her hair, gives a big wave.*) *Aló América! Viva mi Margarita, viva todo los Cubanos en los Estados Unidos!*

AÍDA: *Ay por Dios*, Cecilia, the man didn't come all this way in his helicopter to look at you jumping up and down, making a fool of yourself.

ABUELA: I don't care. I'm proud.

AÍDA: He can't understand you anyway.

40 ABUELA: *Viva* . . . (*She stops.*) *Simón, comó se dice viva?*

SIMÓN: Hurray.

ABUELA: Hurray for *mi Margarita y* for all the Cubans living *en* the United States, *y un abrazo* . . . *Simón, abrazo* . . .

SIMÓN: A big hug.

ABUELA: *Sí*, a big hug to all my friends in Miami, Long Beach, Union City, except for my son Carlos, who lives in New York in sin! He lives . . . (*She crosses herself*) in Brooklyn with a Puerto Rican woman in sin! *No decente* . . .

45 SIMÓN: Decent.

ABUELA: Carlos, *no decente*. This family, *decente*.

AÍDA: Cecilia, *por Dios*.

MEL'S VOICE: Look at that enthusiasm. The whole family has turned out to cheer little Margarita on to victory! I hope they won't be too disappointed.

MARY BETH'S VOICE: She seems to be making good time, Mel.

50 MEL'S VOICE: Yes, it takes all kinds to make a race. And it's a testimonial to the all-encompassing fairness . . . the greatness of this, the Wrigley Invitational Women's Swim to Catalina, where

among all the professionals there is still room for the amateurs . . . like these, the simple people we see below us on the ragtag *La Havana*, taking their long-shot chance to victory. *Vaya con Dios!*

Helicopter sound fading as family, including MARGARITA, *watch silently. Static as* SIMÓN *turns radio off.* EDUARDO *walks to bow of boat, looks out on the horizon.*

EDUARDO: (*to himself*)   Amateurs.

AÍDA: Eduardo, that person insulted us. Did you hear, Eduardo? That he called us a simple people in a ragtag boat? Did you hear . . . ?

ABUELA: (*clenching her fist at departing helicopter*)   *Mal-Rayo los parta!*

SIMÓN: (*same gesture*)   Asshole!

AÍDA *follows* EDUARDO *as he goes to side of boat and stares at* MARGARITA.

AÍDA: This person comes in his helicopter   55 to insult your wife, your family, your daughter . . .

MARGARITA: (*pops her head out of the water*) *Papi?*

AÍDA: Do you hear me, Eduardo? I am not simple.

ABUELA: *Sí.*

AÍDA: I am complicated.

ABUELA: *Sí, demasiada complicada.*   60

AÍDA: Me and my family are not so simple.

SIMÓN: Mom, the guy's an asshole.

ABUELA: (*shaking her fist at helicopter*) Asshole!

AÍDA: It my daughter was simple, she would not be in that water swimming.

MARGARITA: Simple? *Papi* . . . ?   65

AÍDA: *Ahora*, Eduardo, this is what I want you to do. When we get to Santa Catalina, I want you to call the TV station and demand an apology.

EDUARDO: *Cállete mujer! Aquí mando yo.* I will decide what is to be done.

MARGARITA: *Papi*, tell me what's going on.

EDUARDO: Do you understand what I am saying to you, Aída?

70 SIMÓN: (*leaning over side of boat, to* MARGARITA)   Yo Margo! You know that Mel Munson guy on TV? He called you a simple amateur and said you didn't have a chance.

ABUELA: (*leaning directly behind Simón.*)   *Mi hija, insultó a la familia. Desgraciado!*

AÍDA: (*learning in behind* ABUELA)   He called us peasants! And your father is not doing anything about it. He just knows how to yell at me.

EDUARDO: (*through megaphone*)   Shut up! All of you! Do you want to break her concentration? Is that what you are after? Eh?

ABUELA, AÍDA, and SIMÓN shrink back.
EDUARDO paces before them.

Swimming is rhythm and concentration. You win a race *aquí.* (*Pointing to his head.*) Now . . . (*to* SIMÓN) you, take care of the boat, Aída *y Mama* . . . do something. Anything. Something practical.

Abuela and Aída get on knees and pray in Spanish.

Hija, give it everything, eh? . . . *por la familia. Uno . . . dos . . .* You must win.

SIMÓN *goes into cabin. The prayers continue as lights change to indicate bright sunlight, later in the afternoon.*

SCENE 3

Tableau for a couple of beats. EDUARDO *on bow with timer in one hand as he counts strokes per minute. Simón is in the cabin steering, wearing his sunglasses, baseball cap on backward.* ABUELA *and* AÍDA *are at the side of the boat, heads down, hands folded, still muttering prayers in Spanish.*

AÍDA **and** ABUELA: (*crossing themselves*)   *En el nombre del padre, del Hijo y del Espíritu Santo amén.*

EDUARDO: (*through megaphone*)   You're   75 stroking seventy-two!

SIMÓN: (*singing*)   Mama's stroking, Mama's stroking seventy-two. . . .

EDUARDO: (*through megaphone*)   You comfortable with it?

SIMÓN: (*singing*)   Seventy-two, seventy-two, seventy-two for you.

AÍDA: (*looking at the heavens*)   Ay, Eduardo, *ven acá,* we should be grateful that *Nuestro Señor* gave us such a beautiful day.

ABUELA: (*crosses herself*)   *Si, gracias a Dios.*   80

EDUARDO: She's stroking seventy-two, with no problem. (*He throws a kiss to the sky.*) It's a beautiful day to win.

AÍDA: *Qué hermoso!* So clear and bright. Not a cloud in the sky. *Mira! Mira!* Even rainbows on the water . . . a sign from God.

SIMÓN: (*singing*)   Rainbows on the water . . . you in my arms . . .

ABUELA **and** EDUARDO: (*Looking the wrong way.*)   *Dónde?*

AÍDA: (*pointing toward Margarita*)   There,   85 dancing in front of Margarita, leading her on . . .

EDUARDO: Rainbows on . . . *Ay coño!* It's an oil slick! You . . . you . . . (*To* SIMÓN.) Stop the boat. (*Runs to bow, yelling.*) Margarita! Margarita!

On the next stroke, MARGARITA *comes up all covered in black oil.*

MARGARITA: *Papi! Papi . . . !*

Everybody goes to the side and stares at MARGARITA, *who stares back.* EDUARDO *freezes.*

AÍDA: *Apúrate,* Eduardo, move . . . what's wrong with you . . . *no me oíste,* get my daughter out of the water.

EDUARDO: (*softly*)   We can't touch her. If we touch her, she's disqualified.

90 AÍDA: But I'm her mother.

EDUARDO: Not even by her own mother.
Especially by her own mother. . . . You
always want the rules to be different for
you, you always want to be the exception. (*To* SIMÓN.) And you . . . you didn't
see it, eh? You were playing again?

SIMÓN: *Papi*, I was watching . . .

AÍDA: (*interrupting*)   *Pues*, do something
Eduardo. You are the big coach, the
monitor.

SIMÓN: Mentor! Mentor!

95 EDUARDO: How can a person think around
you? (*He walks off to bow, puts head in
hands.*)

ABUELA: (*looking over side*)   *Mira como
todos los* little birds are dead. (*She crosses
herself.*)

AÍDA: Their little wings are glued to their
sides.

SIMÓN: Christ, this is like the La Brea
tar pits.

AÍDA: They can't move their little wings.

100 ABUELA: *Esa niña tiene que moverse.*

SIMÓN: Yeah, Margo, you gotta move,
man.

ABUELA *and* SIMÓN *gesture for* MARGARITA *to
move.* AÍDA *gestures for her to swim.*

ABUELA: *Anda niña, muévete.*

AÍDA: Swim, *hija*, swim or the *aceite* will
stick to your wings.

MARGARITA: *Papi?*

105 ABUELA: (*taking megaphone*)   Your *papi* say
"move it!"

MARGARITA *with difficulty starts moving.*

ABUELA, AÍDA and SIMÓN: (*laboriously counting*)   *uno, dos* . . . *uno, dos* . . .
anda . . . *uno, dos.*

EDUARDO: (*running to take megaphone from*
ABUELA)   *Uno, dos* . . .

SIMÓN *races into cabin and starts the engine.*
ABUELA, AÍDA *and* EDUARDO *count together.*

SIMÓN: (*looking ahead*)   *Papi*, it's over there!

EDUARDO: Eh?

SIMÓN: (*pointing ahead and to the right*)   It's   110
getting clearer over there.

EDUARDO: (*through megaphone*)   Now pay
attention to me. Go to the right.

SIMÓN, ABUELA, AÍDA *and* EDUARDO *all lean
over side. They point ahead and to the right,
except* ABUELA, *who points to the left.*

FAMILY: (*shouting together*)   *Para yá! Para yá!*

Lights go down on boat. A special light on
MARGARITA, *swimming through the oil, and on*
ABUELA, *watching her.*

ABUELA: *Sangre de mi sangre*, you will be
another to save us. En Bolondron, where
your great-grandmother Luz Suárez was
born, they say one day it rained blood.
All the people, they run into their houses.
They cry, they pray, *pero* your great-
grandmother Luz she had *cojones* like a
man. She run outside. She look straight at
the sky. She shake her fist. And she say to
the evil one, "*Mira* . . . (*beating her chest*)
coño, Diablo, aquí estoy si me quieres." And
she open her mouth, and she drunk the
blood.

Blackout

SCENE 4

Lights up on boat. AÍDA *and* EDUARDO *are on
deck watching* MARGARITA *swim. We hear the
gentle, rhythmic lap, lap, lap of the water, then
the sound of inhaling and exhaling as*
MARGARITA's *breathing becomes louder. Then*
MARGARITA's *heartbeat is heard, with the lapping
of the water and the breathing under it. These
sounds continue beneath the dialogue to the end
of the scene.*

AÍDA: *Dios mío.* Look how she moves
through the water . . .

EDUARDO: You see, it's very simple. It is a   115
matter of concentration.

AÍDA: The first time I put her in water she came to life, she grew before my eyes. She moved, she smiled, she loved it more than me. She didn't want my breast any longer. She wanted the water.

EDUARDO: And of course, the rhythm. The rhythm takes away the pain and helps the concentration.

Pause. AÍDA *and* EDUARDO *watch* MARGARITA.

AÍDA: Is that my child or a seal. . . .

EDUARDO: Ah, a seal, the reason for that is that she's keeping her arms very close to her body. She cups her hands, and then she reaches and digs, reaches and digs.

120   AÍDA: To think that a daughter of mine . . .

EDUARDO: It's the training, the hours in the water. I used to tie weights around her little wrists and ankles.

AÍDA: A spirit, an ocean spirit, must have entered my body when I was carrying her.

EDUARDO: (*to* MARGARITA)   Your stroke is slowing down.

Pause. We hear MARGARITA's *heartbeat with the breathing under, faster now.*

AÍDA: Eduardo, that night, the night on the boat . . .

125   EDUARDO: Ah, the night on the boat again . . . the moon was . . .

AÍDA: The moon was full. We were coming to America . . . *Qué romantico.*

Heartbeat and breathing continue.

EDUARDO: We were cold, afraid, with no money, and on top of everything, you were hysterical, yelling at me, tearing at me with your nails. (*Opens his shirt, points to the base of his neck.*) Look, I still hear the scars . . . telling me that I didn't know what I was doing . . . saying that we were going to die. . . .

AÍDA: You took me, you stole me from my home . . . you didn't give me a chance to prepare. You just said we have to go now, now! Now, you said. You didn't let me take anything. I left everything behind. . . . I left everything behind.

EDUARDO: Saying that I wasn't good enough, that your father didn't raise you so that I could drown you in the sea.

AÍDA: You didn't let me say even a good-   130 bye. You took me, you stole me, you tore me from my home.

EDUARDO: I took you so we could be married.

AÍDA: That was in Miami. But that night on the boat, Eduardo. . . .We were not married, that night on the boat.

EDUARDO: *No pasó nada!* Once and for all get it out of your head, it was cold, you hated me, and we were afraid. . . .

AÍDA: *Mentiroso!*

EDUARDO: A man can't do it when he is   135 afraid.

AÍDA: Liar! You did it very well.

EDUARDO: I did?

AÍDA: *Sí.* Gentle. You were so gentle and then strong . . . my passion for you so deep. Standing next to you . . . I would ache . . . looking at your hands I would forget to breathe, you were irresistible.

EDUARDO: I was?

AÍDA: You took me into your arms, you   140 touched my face with your fingertips . . . you kissed my eyes . . . *la esquina de la boca y* . . .

EDUARDO: *Sí, sí,* and then . . .

AÍDA: I look at your face on top of mine, and I see the lights of Havana in your eyes. That's when you seduced me.

EDUARDO: Shhh, they're gonna hear you.

Lights go down. Special on AÍDA.

AÍDA: That was the night. A woman doesn't forget those things . . . and later that night was the dream . . . the dream of a big country with fields of fertile land

and big, giant things growing. And there by a green, slimy pond I found a giant pea pod and when I opened it, it was full of little, tiny baby frogs.

AÍDA *crosses herself as she watches* MARGARITA. *We hear louder breathing and heartbeat.*

145 MARGARITA: Santa Teresa. Little Flower of God, pray for me. San Martin de Porres, pray for me. Santa Rosa de Lima, *Virgencita de la Caridad del Cobre,* pray for me. . . . Mother pray for me.

SCENE 5

Loud howling of wind is heard, as lights change to indicate unstable weather, fog and mist. Family on deck, braced and huddled against the wind. SIMÓN *is at the helm.*

AÍDA: *Ay Dios mío, qué viento.*

EDUARDO: (*through megaphone*)   Don't drift out . . . that wind is pushing you out. (*To* SIMÓN.) You! Slow down. Can't you see your sister is drifting out?

SIMÓN: It's the wind, *Papi.*

AÍDA: Baby, don't go so far. . . .

150 ABUELA: (*to heaven*)   *Ay Gran Poder de Dios, quita este maldito viento.*

SIMÓN: Margo! Margo! Stay close to the boat.

EDUARDO: Dig in Dig in hard. . . . Reach down from your guts and dig in.

ABUELA: (*to heaven*)   *Ay Virgen de la Caridad del Cobre, por lo más tú quieres a pararia.*

AÍDA: (*putting her hand out, reaching for* MARGARITA)   Baby, don't go far.

ABUELA *crosses herself. Action freezes. Lights get dimmer, special on* MARGARITA. *She keeps swimming, stops, starts again, stops, then, finally exhausted, stops altogether. The boat stops moving.*

155 EDUARDO: What's going on here? Why are we slopping?

SIMÓN: *Papi,* she's not moving! Yo Margo!

The family all run to the side.

EDUARDO: *Hija!* . . . *Hijita!* You're tired, eh?

AÍDA: *Por supuesto* she's tired. I like to see you get in the water, waving your arms and legs from San Pedro to Santa Catalina. A person isn't a machine, a person has to rest.

SIMÓN: Yo, Mama! Cool out, it ain't fucking brain surgery.

EDUARDO: (*to* SIMÓN)   Shut up, you. (*Louder to* MARGARITA.) I guess your mother's right for once, huh? . . . I guess you had to stop, eh? . . . Give your brother, the idiot . . . a chance to catch up with you.   160

SIMÓN: (*clowning like Mortimer Snerd*)   Dum dee dum dee dum ooops, ah shucks . . .

EDUARDO: I don't think he's Cuban.

SIMÓN: (*like Ricky Ricardo*)   *Oye,* Lucy! I'm home! Ba ba lu!

EDUARDO: (*joins in clowning, grabbing* SIMÓN *in a headlock*)   What am I gonna do with this idiot, eh? I don't understand this idiot. He's not like us, Margarita. (*Laughing.*) You think if we put him into your bathing suit with a cap on his head . . . (*He laughs hysterically.*) You think anyone would know . . . huh? Do you think anyone would know? (*Laughs.*)

SIMÓN: (*vamping*)   *Ay, mi amor.* Anybody looking for tits would know.   165

EDUARDO *slaps* SIMÓN *across the face, knocking him down.* AÍDA *runs to* SIMÓN's *aid.* ABUELA *holds* EDUARDO *back.*

MARGARITA: *Mía culpa! Mía culpa!*

ABUELA: *Qué dices hija?*

MARGARITA: *Papi,* it's my fault, it's all my fault. . . . I'm so cold, I can't move. . . . I put my face in the water . . . and I hear them whispering . . . laughing at me. . . .

AÍDA: Who is laughing at you?

170 MARGARITA: The fish are all biting me . . . they hate me . . . they whisper about me. She can't swim, they say. She can't glide. She has no grace. . . .Yellowtails, bonita, tuna, man-o'-war, snub-nose sharks, *los buracudas* . . . they all hate me . . . only the dolphins care . . . and sometimes I hear the whales crying . . . she is lost, she is dead. I'm so numb, I can't feel. *Papi! Papi!* Am I dead?

EDUARDO: *Vamos*, baby, punch those arms in. Come on . . . do you hear me?

MARGARITA: *Papi . . . Papi . . .* forgive me. . . .

All is silent on the boat. EDUARDO *drops his megaphone, his head bent down in dejection.* ABUELA, AÍDA, SIMÓN, *all leaning over the side of the boat.* SIMÓN *slowly walks away.*

AÍDA: *Mi hija, qué tienes?*

SIMÓN: Oh, Christ, don't make her say it. Please don't make her say it.

175 ABUELA: Say what? *Qué cosa?*

SIMÓN: She wants to quit, can't you see she's had enough?

ABUELA: *Mira, para eso. Esta niña* is turning blue.

AÍDA: *Oyeme, mi hija.* Do you want to come out of the water?

MARGARITA: *Papi?*

180 SIMÓN: (*to* EDUARDO) She won't come out until *you* tell her.

AÍDA: Eduardo . . . answer your daughter.

EDUARDO: *Le dije* to concentrate . . . concentrate on your rhythm. Then the rhythm would carry her . . . ay, it's a beautiful thing, Aída. It's like yoga, like meditation, the mind over matter . . . the mind controlling the body . . . that's how the great things in the world have been done. I wish you . . . I wish my wife could understand.

MARGARITA: *Papi?*

SIMÓN: (*to* MARGARITA) Forget him.

185 AÍDA: (*importing*) Eduardo, *por favor.*

EDUARDO: (*walking in circles*) Why didn't you let her concentrate? Don't you understand, the concentration, the rhythm is everything. But no, you wouldn't listen. (*Screaming to the ocean.*) Goddamn Cubans, why, God, why do you make us go everywhere with our families? (*He goes to back of boat.*)

AÍDA: (*opening her arms*) *Mi hija, ven,* come to *Mami.* (*Rocking.*) Your *mami* knows.

ABUELA *has taken the training bottle, puts it in a net. She and* SIMÓN *lower it to* MARGARITA.

SIMÓN: Take this. Drink it. (*As* MARGARITA *drinks,* ABUELA *crosses herself.*)

ABUELA: *Sangre de mi sangre.*

Music comes up softly. MARGARITA *drinks, gives the bottle back, stretches out her arms, as if on a cross. Floats on her back. She begins a graceful backstroke. Lights fade on boat as special lights come up on* MARGARITA. *She stops. Slowly turns over and starts to swim, gradually picking up speed. Suddenly as if in pain she stops, tries again, then stops in pain again. She becomes disoriented and falls to the bottom of the sea. Special on* MARGARITA *at the bottom of the sea.*

MARGARITA: *Ya no puedo* . . . I can't . . . 190 A person isn't a machine . . . *es mi culpa* . . . Father forgive me . . . *Papi! Papi!* One, two. *Uno, dos.* (*Pause.*) *Papi! A dónde estás?* (*Pause.*) One, two, one, two. *Papi! Ay, Papi!* Where are you . . . ? Don't leave me. . . .Why don't you answer me? (*Pause. She starts to swim, slowly.*) *Uno, dos, uno, dos.* Dig in, dig in. (*Stops swimming.*) *Par favor, Papi!* (*Starts to swim again.*) One, two, one, two. Kick from your hip, kick from your hip. (*Stops swimming. Starts to cry.*) Oh God, please . . . (*Pause.*) Hail Mary, full of grace . . . dig in, dig in . . . the Lord is with thee . . . (*She swims to the rhythm of her Hail Mary.*) Hail Mary, full of grace . . . dig in, dig in . . . the Lord is

with thee . . . dig in, dig in. . . .Blessed art
thou among women . . . *Mami*, it hurts.
You let go of my hand. I'm lost. . . . And
blessed is the fruit of thy womb, now and
at the hour of our death. Amen. I don't
want to die, I don't want to die.

MARGARITA *is still swimming. Blackout. She is
gone.*

SCENE 6

*Lights up on boat, we hear radio static. There is
a heavy mist. On deck we see only black outline
of* ABUELA *with shawl over her head. We hear
the voices of* EDUARDO, AÍDA, *and* RADIO
OPERATOR.

EDUARDO'S VOICE: *La Havana*! Coming
   from San Pedro. Over.
RADIO OPERATOR'S VOICE: Right, DT6-6,
   you say you've lost a swimmer.
AÍDA'S VOICE: Our child, our only
   daughter . . . listen to me. Her name is
   Margarita Inez Suárez, she is wearing a
   black one-piece bathing suit cut high in
   the legs with a white racing stripe down
   the sides, a white bathing cap with gog-
   gles and her whole body covered with
   a . . . with a . . .
EDUARDO'S VOICE: With lanolin and paraffin.
195 AÍDA'S VOICE: *Sí . . . con lanolin* and
   paraffin.
   More radio static. Special on SIMÓN, *on the
   edge of the boat.*
SIMÓN: Margo! Yo Margo! (*Pause.*) Man
   don't do this. (*Pause.*) Come on . . . Come
   on. . . . (*Pause.*) God, why does everything have to be so hard? (*Pause.*) Stupid.
   You know you're not supposed to die for
   this. Stupid. It's his dream and he can't
   even swim. (*Pause.*) Punch those arms in.
   Come home. Come home. I'm your little
   brother. Don't forget what Mama said.
   You're not supposed to leave me behind.
   Vamos, Margarita, take your little brother,

hold his hand tight when you cross the
street. He's so little. (*Pause.*) Oh, Christ,
give us a sign. . . .I know! I know! Margo,
I'll send you a message . . . like mental
telepathy. I'll hold my breath, close my
eyes, and I'll bring you home. (*He takes a
deep breath; a few beats.*) This time I'll
beep . . . I'll send out sonar signals like
a dolphin. (*He imitates dolphin sounds.*)

The sound of real dolphins takes over from
SIMÓN, *then fades into sound of* ABUELA *saying
the Hail Mary in Spanish, as full lights come
up slowly.*

SCENE 7

EDUARDO *coming out of cabin, sobbing,* AÍDA
holding him. SIMÓN *anxiously scanning the
horizon.* ABUELA *looking calmly ahead.*

EDUARDO: *Es mi culpa, sí, es mi culpa.* (*He
   hits his chest.*)
AÍDA: *Ya, ya viejo* . . . it was my sin . . . I
   left my home.
EDUARDO: Forgive me, forgive me. I've
   lost our daughter, our sister, our granddaughter, *mi carne, mi sangre, mis ilusiones.*
   (*To heaven.*) *Dios mío*, take me . . . take me,
   I say . . . Goddammit, take me!
SIMÓN: I'm going in.   200
AÍDA and EDUARDO: No!
EDUARDO: (*grabbing and holding* SIMÓN,
   speaking to heaven) God, take me, not my
   children. They are my dreams, my
   illusions . . . and not this one, this one is
   my mystery . . . he has my secret dreams.
   In him are the parts of me I cannot see.

EDUARDO *embraces* SIMÓN. *Radio static
becomes louder.*

AÍDA: I . . . I think I see her.
SIMÓN: No, it's just a seal.
ABUELA: (*looking out with binoculars*) *Mi*   205
   nietacita, dónde estás? (*She feels her heart.*)
   I don't feel the knife in my heart . . . my
   little fish is not lost.

Radio crackles with static. As lights dim on boat, Voices of MEL *and* MARY BETH *are heard over the radio.*

MEL'S VOICE: Tragedy has marred the face of the Wrigley Invitational Women's Race to Catalina. The Cuban swimmer, little Margarita Suárez, has reportedly been lost at sea. Coast Guard and divers are looking for her as we speak. Yet in spite of this tragedy the race must go on because . . .

MARY BETH'S VOICE: (*interrupting loudly*)   Mel!

MEL'S VOICE: (*startled*)   What!

MARY BETH'S VOICE: Ah . . . excuse me, Mel . . . we have a winner. We've just received word from Catalina that one of the swimmers is just fifty yards from the breakers . . . it's, oh, it's . . . Margarita Suárez!

Special on family in cabin listening to radio.

210   MEL'S VOICE: What? I thought she died!

Special on MARGARITA, *taking off bathing cap, trophy in hand, walking on the water.*

MARY BETH'S VOICE: Ahh . . . unless . . . unless this is a tragic . . . No . . . there she is, Mel. Margarita Suárez! The only one in the race wearing a black bathing suit cut high in the legs with a racing stripe down the side.

Family cheering, embracing.

SIMÓN: (*screaming*)   Way to go, Margo!

MEL'S VOICE: This is indeed a miracle! It's a resurrection! Margarita Suárez, with a flotilla of boats to meet her, is now walking on the waters, through the breakers . . . onto the beach, with crowds of people cheering her on. What a jubilation! This is a miracle!

Sound of crowds cheering. Lights and cheering sounds fade.

Blackout

PART 4

Getting Into Writing and Research

These last five lines from Saul Bellow's great novel are about the central character's relationships with the people he has encountered and gotten to know and the events he has lived through.

When he speaks of Columbus, he speaks of an ongoing exploration of a realm so vast that no one can possibly know everything about it. For Columbus, of course, it was the New World of the Western Hemisphere. For Augie it is the unknown territory (*terra incognita*) of his life, his times, and even himself.

He might well be speaking of the student of literature (and Augie is such a student). Reading and writing about what you have read is an on-going inquiry. You can always learn more about a poem, a short story, a novel, or a play in the same way that you can always learn more about your friends, your family, yourself.

Professors and critics who study literature know that they will never deliver the definitive word on Shakespeare, Zora Neale Hurston, Jane Austen, or August Wilson. Instead, their books and essays form an on-going inquiry into the nature of the works they study. Reading with an open mind and an attentive attitude, while being guided by clarity, concision, and good organization of one's sentence level language are essential to conveying your ideas about what you have read. This takes practice and persistence, the same discipline one applies to mastering a sport or musical instrument. Not every effort you make will be perfect the first time. But sticking to it and consistently exercising your abilities to read and write clearly will bring about fast and measurable improvement. It will also open up a world that will at once be familiar and new as you go about exploring it.

MICHELLE QUINONI

English 102-JE

What you are noticing here is Hawthorne's deliberate use of ambiguity.

The story of Young Goodman [...] had at a particular point of the story eve[...] statements that soon follow. Through[out th...] end, I came to the conclusion that the strange [...] town's people that Goodman knew were his wors[...]

Young Goodman Browns name seems to be [...] the chain of events that took place in the forest. The [...]

Goodman's name resemble strength, goodness, and possi[...]

A brief quotation could help illustrate your point here.

Goodman Brown leaves his wife Faith to go into the forest, [...] letting go, not only of his wife, but also of his own faith in Go[...] to do.

As he went into the forest, it seemed as though he knew [...] he knew of the evil that lay within this dark treacherous fore[...] strengthen or diminish his goodness as well as his faith in God. As he [...] surroundings, foreshadowing takes place when he suggests that the devil [...] very elbow. Immediately following that, the traveler on the road appears, ap[...]

Goodman, and begins to speak to him. Surprisingly, he is able to justify the fe[...]

Goodman Brown. It is clear that this stranger who is astonishingly all knowing, is [...] among the many who appear in the forest, as the one who is responsible for arrangin[...]

You are [...] a good s[...] here.

TALKING AND WRITING ABOUT LIT

s with

Brown

complex in that the understanding I

clash with the events or

hings seem contradictive. In the

vas in fact the devil and the

what he stands for in

d good in Young

well. As

ugh he is

ping there

This might be a more interesting title, and it could also be used to refer to "Wilderness," which the Puritans feared as a source of primal urges and potential chaos.

rory Contradictory

Possessive apostrophe

Yes — good, and what you mean here is that her name is symbolic.

Yes — good

"When we improve as readers, we improve as writers," according to poet and essayist Donald Hall. Indeed, the first step to thinking and writing productively about a work of literature is to read it carefully. See chapter 1, "Getting into Lit," for more advice about close reading and annotating of texts.

Read and Reread

After the work has been read through once for pleasure, it is a good idea to read a second time, this time more closely, making notes of questions and responses to the text. Each reader will respond somewhat differently to a given work of literature, and it is this variety of responses and opinions that makes literary discussion interesting. Each reader brings to the work a unique set of life experiences and background knowledge.

When rereading, make an effort to think critically about the story, poem, or play. Refer to the lists of study questions at the ends of chapters 2, 13, and 25: "Questions to Ask about Fiction," "Questions to Ask about Poetry," and "Questions to Ask about Drama." These questions can prompt exploration of additional aspects of the work and help you find openings to a deeper examination of the story, poem, or play.

Getting Started

If the reader is thinking critically—asking good questions of the text—then possible topics for an analytical essay will emerge naturally. For instance, when student Anita Shoup discovered similarities between two stories she had read for class, she had her first idea for the essay to follow. Thinking critically about the use of characterization and plot in the two works of fiction prompted her to develop an interesting and original approach to comparing them. In her essay "Fine Manners in the Face of Death: Shirley Jackson's 'The Lottery' and Flannery O'Connor's 'A Good Man Is Hard to Find,'" Shoup uses many quotations and concrete examples from the stories to show how the characters in both works fall back on conventional manners in the face of death. This is a unique interpretive approach, and Shoup pursues her thesis consistently and effectively throughout the paper, never losing the thread of her argument.

Many writers find **brainstorming** techniques like **freewriting** or **clustering** useful when that "bright idea" or new connection seems elusive. Freewriting loosens up the thought process for some writers because it introduces the element of "chaos" into their critical thinking. In other words, when freewriting to generate ideas, it is useful that those ideas being thrown around are not yet ordered or organized in a fixed way. This can help produce surprising results because it allows the mind to imagine new combinations and connections. The following is an example of freewriting about Shoup's topic:

> Something awful is happening—death, even death . . . and what are these characters doing? white gloves, hat, collar, cuffs in O'Connor—exchanging pleasantries on the village green in Jackson's story, worrying that the dishes are left in the sink. It's death and lace doilies here! Ceremony, something to fall back on in crisis? politeness adds to strangeness in both.

This is free association rather than organized argument, and it can lead the writer to some useful discoveries about connections between the stories. Many writers freewrite even more loosely, omitting punctuation and capitalization altogether and throwing grammatical caution to the wind. The point here is to get the ideas flowing; corrections can be made and organization imposed later in the process.

Clustering introduces further chaos and creativity into the thinking process by abandoning (temporarily) the need to think in a linear fashion or to compose ideas in sentences or even in lines of words. Instead, write words or phrases anywhere on a sheet of paper, connecting them with lines or encircling them together, imagining ideas, emotions, characters, and events in a new order as shown in the example below.

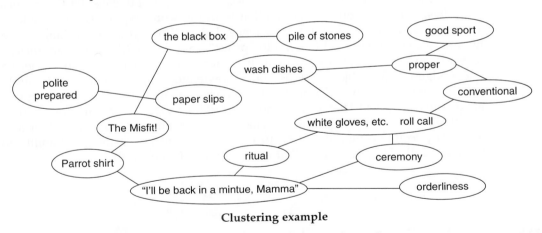

Clustering example

Developing the Thesis

The thesis (main idea, main point, or argument) of an essay is most captivating to the writer and most compelling to readers when it grows out of a genuine interest in the topic. During the brainstorming stage, a thesis should emerge and begin to shape itself. Whatever excites the writer or intrigues the writer—whether it be some aspect of a character, a political or social theme, a psychological connection between two unlikely characters, a pattern of imagery or symbolism in the setting—this is the stuff of which interesting thesis statements are made. Shoup's **thesis** grew out of her discovery that there was an interesting likeness in the two stories she had read and that that similarity or connection also illuminated something in both stories which shed light on human behavior. In her **introductory paragraph**, Shoup discusses the use of tradition and rituals in the face of death in both stories and then she writes, "In both stories, this behavior is adopted by all of the characters when they are placed in situations in which they are not sure how to behave. People often rely on manners when confronted with uncertain circumstances." This is her thesis, and she then proceeds to enumerate and develop examples in both stories to illustrate and support that thesis.

Shoup's subject area could be stated as "characters facing death in two stories," but the **thesis statement** in the above paragraph is a statement that goes beyond describing the subject area. The word "thesis," according to the *American Heritage Dictionary*, means "a proposition maintained by argument." It is a Latin word, derived from a Greek one, which means "a placing, a laying down, position, affirmation." The thesis states an opinion; it poses a position to be argued for and illustrated, and that is what makes it a thesis statement. As the above Latin and Greek derivation suggests, it also has a connotation of "staking out one's position" or of "taking a stand."

A note of caution is in order here, though. Your essay can be weakened or limited if you cling too tightly to that thesis. Often it's best to consider the thesis a **hypothesis** instead. You may be familiar with the word hypothesis from talking about the scientific method in your science classes. When you are working with a hypothesis, you are not yet looking to "prove" your theory (thesis or hypothesis); instead you are testing it, exploring its boundaries, its supports. You are gathering knowledge on the subject and, as your knowledge increases, your thesis might well change and evolve. If your thesis changes as you write and think, then you are on the right track! This flexible and creative approach—remaining open to new possibilities, even remaining open to changing your mind as you read and write—is the key to intellectual curiosity, to wisdom, and to increasing your ability to think critically. Hey, don't pass that up; get yourself some of that.

Rhetorical Modes/Analysis—Comparison and Contrast

The word "rhetoric" refers to the art of using language effectively. The best writing on literary topics takes place when the writer thinks creatively about what rhetorical strategies will serve the subject matter best. In developing an essay on a literary topic, various **rhetorical modes** are available to the writer. The sample student essays that appear in this chapter illustrate several rhetorical strategies for writing about works of literature. The first essay, by student Anita Shoup, is an essay of **comparison and contrast** of two works of short fiction. The writer finds both similarities and differences in the two works. She begins by discussing them both and stating her thesis. Then she spends several paragraphs analyzing aspects of Jackson's story in support of her thesis and follows with several paragraphs doing the same with O'Connor's story. Afterward, a block of analysis deals with both stories at once, in which she compares and contrasts her findings about the two works. Then Shoup concludes with a final paragraph, tying her discussion of the two stories together and relating the characters' behavior to the behavior of ordinary people in real life. A bare bones outline of her essay strategy would be as follows:

I. Introductory paragraph/statement of thesis

II. "The Lottery"—examples supporting the thesis

III. "A Good Man Is Hard to Find"—examples supporting the thesis

IV. Comparison and contrast of the two stories

V. Conclusion—tying it all together.

Comparison and contrast essays are also examples of an **analysis** of literary works. That is, they analyze the works in light of a particular element or elements of the works, usually examining a thematic link between the two, or an aspect of plot or characterization that they have in common.

Student Essay

Anita Shoup

Prof. Barnard

English 250.50

Fine Manners in the Face of Death:

Shirley Jackson's "The Lottery" and Flannery O'Connor's

"A Good Man Is Hard to Find"

In both of the stories, the characters confront death not as a battle to be waged with all of their capacity, but as an uncomfortable

Shoup 2

situation in which they suddenly do not know how to behave. The effects on the reader range from some feelings of discomfort at the very end of "The Lottery" to feelings of horror at the massacre of the family in "A Good Man Is Hard to Find."

Placed in improbable circumstances, "The Lottery'"s killers and victim never discuss why they have come there. Faced with the unspeakable, "A Good Man Is Hard to Find'"s victims do not admit to the killers or themselves that they know what is about to happen to them. Except for a hint from Bailey's wife, it is simply not spoken about.

In "The Lottery," all of the characters keep up neighborly appearances prior to the selection of the victim and later are paralyzed by traditions and rituals. In both stories, this behavior is adopted by all of the characters when they are placed in situations in which they are not sure how to behave. People often rely on manners when confronted with uncertain circumstances. The murderers in Jackson's story adhere to convention, because when the story begins, it is possible that any one of them may become the victim.

Snatches of conversation like Mrs. Hutchinson's "Wouldn't have me leave m'dishes in the sink, now, would you, Joe?" (paragraph 9) and Mr. Summers' "remember, take the slips and keep them folded until each person has taken one. Harry, you help little Dave." (paragraph 63) illustrate the group's dedication to a friendly, matter-of-fact approach to this event. They do not discuss the intent of their gathering. Only the children betray the mob's deadly true nature making "a great pile of stones" and stuffing their "pockets full of stones" (paragraph 2). Of course, unlike the adults, the children do not yet behave properly.

Shoup 3

As events move toward their appointed purpose, the victim, though abandoning polite conduct, still clings to the air of normalcy which gave her a place in the rational world. She does not once address what is going to happen to her. Instead, over and over again she protests that the contest "wasn't fair," adding that there wasn't "time enough" to choose (paragraph 45). The crowd maintains the polite facade, with Mrs. Delacroix urging her to "be a good sport, Tessie" (paragraph 46). We do not see their murderous nature until the final lines when "A stone hit her on the side of the head" (paragraph 77) ". . . and then they were upon her" (paragraph 79).

Though Mrs. Hutchinson makes herself an unsympathetic character by not dying well, and betraying her daughter's family in the process, we still feel an empathetic dread for any creature suddenly singled out by the crowd. Not only does Shirley Jackson reveal her characters' fears about acknowledging the situation that they are in, but she evokes in the reader our fear of becoming an outcast and a scapegoat.

O'Connor's characters in "A Good Man Is Hard to Find" have more than a fair dose of the qualities necessary to stand on cere-mony during a mass murder. Grandma wears "white gloves . . . collar and cuffs (of) white organdy trimmed with lace . . . (so that) in case of an accident, anyone seeing her dead on the highway would know at once that she was a lady" (paragraph 12). We will see that Bailey is a bit like his mother and the kids are a bit like their Mom. Bailey's mother adheres to the rules rigidly. When things turn ugly, Bailey plays the game too. Rather than admit what is happening, he tries to appeal to human understanding, of which there will be none. When confronted with the imminent death of his family and

Shoup 4

himself, he just tells the killers: "we're in a predicament!" (paragraph 81).

His wife is silent, but when she speaks during the massacre, she addresses the situation they are in honestly. She does not speak to the killers, but she's not pretending everything is okay when she screams "Where are they taking him?" (paragraph 102). She's no hero, but she doesn't kid herself either. Since the beginning of the story, the Mom has stayed away from Grandma's fantasyland. She's mature enough not to bother arguing with Grandma. She ignores her when Grandma says: "The children have been to Florida before, . . . You all ought to take them somewhere else for change . . . " (paragraph 2).

Her kids think Grandma's full of it too, and they're young enough to say so. They do not treat her as an adult, but instead, they constantly heckle her, as when June Star complains that "She has to go everywhere we go" (paragraph 7). And when Grandma tries to point out interesting sites in Georgia, John Wesley derides her and her interests by stating that "Tennessee is just a hillbilly dumping ground, and Georgia is a lousy state too" (paragraph 16).

While establishing these characters, O'Connor, aware of what she will subject us to later, goes out of her way to make them unlikable. These kids don't just insult Grandma; June Star even tells Red Sam's wife that she "wouldn't live in a broken-down place like this for a million bucks" (paragraph 31).

Maybe we're supposed to react to the Misfit's arrival by thinking: "Hey! Those kids don't talk so tough now, huh?" Certainly Bailey doesn't talk so tough. When invited to step into the woods, Bailey reemphasizes his "predicament" statement (paragraph 95).

Shoup 5

At this point, Bailey's similarities to his mother are increasingly apparent as they attempt to cope with the situation. Neither of them dares speak of the unspeakable. As desperation mounts, they both test the idea that if you just say something, it'll be true. He shouts: "I'll be back in a minute, Mamma, wait on me!" (paragraph 96). Grandma cries: "Come back this instant!" (paragraph 97), as if Bailey would have to obey and his playmates would just have to understand. Up until her death, Grandma switches back and forth between exclamations of pure pain—"Bailey Boy!"—and pure wishing—"I just know you're a good man." (paragraph 98).

The sound of pistol shots breaks Bailey's wife. When asked if she and her little girl "would . . . like to step off yonder with Bobby Lee and Hiram and join your husband?" she actually replies "Yes, thank you." June Star never loses her spirit, stating: "I don't want to hold hands with him (Bobby Lee), he reminds me of a pig." Mom's scream and the gunshots that follow just reinforce the idea of Bailey's fate in Grandma's mind, and she cries out to him like when he was growing up: "'Bailey boy, Bailey boy!' as if her heart would break" (paragraph 133).

O'Connor forces the characters and the reader to face horrible situations. The family is politely led off in groups to be executed. Her depictions of earthy characters, and her instinct for dialogue in the massacre are quite powerful. Granted, O'Connor attempts to make the characters unsympathetic. The kids are disrespectful, the father is intolerant, and Grandma is a racist. But when the horror starts, the kids are just kids, and that's how kids act. Dad's probably over-worked, and Mom's holding a baby! By the time they get around to Grandma, we even feel sorry for her. She's not too different than a lot of Grandmas, and she truly loves and mourns her son.

Shoup 6

Both O'Connor and Jackson hint at previous murders in a way that makes the story almost semi-horroresque. O'Connor is more straightforward, since we know that the Misfit is a murderer, but still it is chilling to read his comment "We buried our clothes that we had on . . . " "We borrowed these from some folks we met" (paragraph 99). After Bailey's murder the Misfit then puts on Bailey's shirt, which confirms (if anyone still had doubt) that Bailey is dead. The Misfit's discussion about his father also leaves us wondering whether he killed his father as the authorities say or whether his father died of the flu. Although the Misfit's behavior is absolutely unacceptable, during this part of the story, a feel of responsibility can emerge on the part of the reader, that perhaps in a way society is responsible for the making of a madman, and we remember all the real and innocent people who have been mistakenly accused or convicted, sent to jail, and receive a "training course" on how to be good criminal from the inmates. This can turn anyone who is not a solid, stable individual into a felon. Shirley Jackson doesn't directly address the previous murders, but the unnecessary focus on the Watson boy makes us wonder whether his father might have been the victim last year.

There is some interesting insight into the killers' psyches, but I don't care about them. I don't want to know the opinions of these monsters that will lead children into the bushes to be executed in front of helpless parents. There is no excuse for them. People use the excuse, "they made me do it" all too often. Nobody makes anyone commit a crime. All our actions are conscious decisions that we alone are responsible for, whatever the outcome. O'Connor's dialogue, especially that of the victims who remain in denial to the last, is poignant and rings true. This makes it all the more disturbing and the more difficult of the two stories to read.

Most of us are not heroes. The authors demonstrate that in extraordinary situations, people will cling to ordinary rituals in hopes that a world turned upside down may again right itself. A hero must be someone who recognizes what is happening, admits it to himself, and responds appropriately. The unifying element running through these stories is the self-deception of each of the characters, and how to varying degrees, they pay a price for their illusions. In both of the stories, the characters fall back on ordinary behavior to deal with aberrant circumstances. None of the characters will acknowledge that something awful is happening. This works well for brutes like the Misfit, who keeps up his polite chatter even as an innocent family is being wiped out at his behest. The authors seem to agree that when an individual or individuals are operating outside the bounds of reasonable behavior, most people will continue to play by the rules, and this will place them at a distinct disadvantage. Afraid to openly address the unthinkable, they cling to rational conversation, hoping that they can somehow endure until a world turned upside down rights itself again. Of course, that strategy doesn't pan out, but it gives the authors an unusual framework to hang their stories on.

Rhetorical Modes—Explication

The next student essay written as part of an in-class midterm exam—is very brief. Nevertheless, in "Poetic Techniques in Claribel Alegría's 'I Am Mirror' and Sylvia Plath's 'Mirror,'" student Annika Stachowski attempts to cover more than the analysis of a single aspect of the two works. This essay is an attempt at **explication** of the two poems. An explication differs from an analysis in as much as it examines all (or several) elements of a work, rather than singling out only one or two as a focus. In her essay, Stachowski chose to range over numerous aspects of the two poems, discussing sound, rhythm, line breaks and pacing, figures of speech, and themes. Although she does not discuss these elements as thoroughly in this exam essay as she would have been able to in a paper written outside of class, she has nevertheless covered a significant number of points in a compact discussion.

Student Essay

Annika Stachowski

Professor Barnard

English 220-07

Midterm Exam Essay

Poetic Techniques in Claribel Alegría's "I Am Mirror" and

Sylvia Plath's "Mirror"

Claribel Alegría makes use of various poetic techniques in her poem "I Am Mirror," as does Sylvia Plath in her poem "Mirror." Even though the similar titles of the poems suggest similar messages, the contents of and poetic techniques in the poems differ significantly.

"I Am Mirror" by Claribel Alegría is the more recent poem; she wrote it in 1978. The poem is a lyric that reflects social conditions during the civil war in El Salvador. Although the poem "I Am Mirror" lacks a regular rhyme scheme, short lines without any punctuation establish a certain rhythm. Some lines only consist of one word and make it hard for the reader to grasp the meaning of the sentence that it is a part of (13, 29, 36, 47). The rhythm of the poem reminds the reader of the sound of rattling rifles, which reinforces the poem's theme.

Stachowski 2

In addition, repetition emphasizes certain words such as "shouts" in lines 46 and 47, "hurt" and "hurts" in line 32 and 39 and the metaphor of the mirror in lines 10, 48 and 54. The metaphor of the mirror describes the speaker's attitude towards what he or she observes while he or she "wander[s] through the streets" which "are paved with pain" (20, 25). The speaker goes through different stages of pain. Sometimes she (or he) simply reflects the scenes of the streets like a mirror, and sometimes she cannot bear the emotions that the scenes create in her. The imagery of the speaker becoming a mirror in the end of the poem suggests that he or she has decided not to take the pain any longer.

Claribel Alegría makes use of enjambment throughout the poem. This technique serves to increase the pace, and at the same time to put the reader or listener off balance, as we are drawn down quickly from one short line to the next. In addition to the extended metaphor of the speaker as mirror, the poet also uses figurative language to stress the horror and violence of the described scenes. For example, line 15, "shouts like lightning bolts," is a simile, and line 25, "the streets are paved with pain," is a metaphor. The poignant lines "I hurt/therefore I exist" (32/33) are an allusion to Descartes' famous dictum "I think, therefore I am." These lines also serve to show that the speaker's experience is defined by the violence and pain that war has brought upon her society.

The poem "Mirror" by Sylvia Plath is not so much about an external conflict like a war but about the internal conflict of a woman aging. The mirror in the poem experiences the woman's despair and misery when she looks at herself. In terms of its form, "Mirror" is divided into two stanzas. There is no regular rhyme scheme, but a variety of rhetorical devices can be found in the poem. There are incidences of enjambment in lines 2, 7 and 17. And repetition helps to establish a rhythm: "I am silver and exact," "I am not cruel," "Now I am a lake," "I am important" (1, 4, 10, 15). Also, there is a drumbeat of rhythm in the repetitions within the first two lines: "I am," "I have," "I see," "I swallow."

Plath makes use of visual imagery of the opposite wall ("pink, with speckles"), of the woman ("tears and an agitation of hands"), and of the mirror itself ("four cornered") in order to make the poem more vivid. Despair and "darkness," however, dominate the tone in the poem, as in lines 9 ("Faces and darkness separate us over and over") and 16 ("Each morning it is her face that replaces the darkness"). The personification of the mirror, the candles and the moon (5, 8, 12, 13) helps to make the atmosphere in the poem mystical and spooky. The metaphor in line 5 is used to compare the mirror, the speaker of the lyric, to "The eye of a little god." This metaphor illustrates the power of the mirror, not only this particular mirror but the power of mirrors over human beings in general. Sylvia Plath uses a mythological allusion in line 10 to make the message of the poem clearer. The allusion refers to the myth of Narcissus, who was punished by the Greek gods for his vanity.

In the poem "Mirror," vanity has turned an aging woman into "a terrible fish," who cannot and does not want to accept the natural and inevitable process of aging (18). The metaphor in line 17/18 illustrates the woman's aging process. "In me she has drowned a young girl, and in me an old woman/Rises toward her day after day." As in "I Am Mirror," the poetic techniques in "Mirror" help to convey the poem's message in a way that the reader can *see*. These devices not only make it easier for the reader to understand the poems, they also make it a pleasure to read them.

Rhetorical Modes/Analysis—Argumentation

D. Scott Humphries's essay "More or Less a Moor: Racism in *Othello*" is an analysis of the characterization of William Shakespeare's main character Othello, as it relates to racism in Venetian (and Elizabethan English) society and to Iago's manipulation of what may be perceived as internalized racism within Othello himself. Humphries follows the characterization of Othello throughout the play, specifically in light of this issue. As he develops his **argument**, the writer uses many apt examples and quotations from the play to support his assertions. This essay is an example of a **persuasive essay**. In it, Humphries forcefully and thoroughly argues for the thesis presented in the opening paragraph; develops his argument in detail, offering a multitude of evidence from the play itself; and restates his thesis creatively in his concluding paragraph. Humphries's concluding sentence leaves no doubt that both the writer of the essay, and Shakespeare himself, are ultimately on Othello's side in terms of recognizing the harm that concealed racism can do to individuals and to a society: "Such a tragic result indicates that Shakespeare questions and criticizes, rather than supports, the values of his time and the idea of racism."

Student Essay

D. Scott Humphries

Professor Cristina León Alfar

Paper #2

More or Less a Moor: Racism in *Othello*

Racism existed during the Renaissance. According to *The Bedford Companion to Shakespeare*, "Shakespeare plays upon these anxieties in his depiction of such characters as Shylock the Jewish moneylender in *The Merchant of Venice*, Aaron the Moor in *Titus Andronicus*, and, most memorably, Othello" (McDonald 273). This paper will explore racism with specific reference to the issues it raises in Shakespeare's *Othello*. In *Othello*, the racism which Iago uses to launch his plan of revenge against Othello feeds off of racism already present in the culture, and off of Othello's insecurities as an assimilated outsider, so that Othello, with tragic consequences, falls prey to a well established set of assumptions about the inappropriateness of black men as statesmen, husbands, and fathers to Venetian citizens.

 Othello opens with a scene that immediately introduces the extreme racism present in society as well as Iago's ability to grasp the situation and use the issue of race to his advantage. Iago speaks of Othello (who has passed Iago over for promotion by choosing Cassio as his lieutenant and who has also secretly married Senator Brabantio's daughter Desdemona) without ever using his name. Iago refers to "his Moorship" (1.1.33), "the Moor" (1.1.39, 57), and so on throughout the scene. Roderigo, a past suitor of Desdemona, also refers to Othello with epitaphs such as "the thick-lips" (1.1.66), "a lascivious Moor" (1.1.124), and "an extravagant and wheeling stranger/Of here and everywhere" (1.1.134–35). But these two men do not curse Othello's character or his financial standing on their way to alert Brabantio. Their curses, noted above, are based solely on Othello's status as a visible outsider and are aimed directly at his race.

 As they reach Brabantio's house, Iago seems to have realized the power of these racial slurs as a weapon with which to raise Brabantio's anxieties to a fever pitch. Iago screams even uglier words up from the courtyard:

> Your heart is burst, you have lost half your soul.
> Even now, now, very now, an old black ram

Is tupping your white ewe. Arise, arise,

Awake the snorting citizens with the bell,

Or else the devil will make a grandsire of you. (1.1.87–91)

This passage reveals Iago's cunning as he plays on Brabantio's anxieties regarding race, racial purity and lineage. Before even mentioning what has happened or who is involved, Iago screams that Brabantio has "lost half your soul" (1.1.87). He implies that Brabantio has somehow become half of what he has been up until this point. He has insulted Brabantio directly and implied that something terrible has happened. And while he does not at first mention who or what he is talking about, he immediately alludes to Desdemona and Othello. He separates them into labels by using the colors black and white and relates these colors to barnyard animals as well, which adds an even baser connotation to the racial slurs he slings. As a third insult, he invokes the name of the devil. Iago has given Brabantio an image of Othello as an animal and devil and has linked these negative images to Othello's race by using the word "black." Iago also implies, in his slanderous reference to "snorting citizens," that the rest of society is or will be pulled down to the level of animals as a result of Othello and Desdemona's pairing. It is as if he is saying that if the citizens of Venice allow these "beasts" among them, they will, beginning with their daughters, be turned into animals as well. Iago proves, by using these racist words, that not only did anxieties regarding outsiders exist at the time, but that anxieties about racial purity and interracial marriage, in relation to visibly different outsiders, existed as well. By suggesting that Desdemona has become an animal by marrying Othello, Iago plays to Brabantio's anxieties about his heirs and his lineage.

Humphries 4

Iago further provokes Brabantio, who at first does not believe Iago, by continuing to play on Brabantio's already existing fears of the "other":

> IAGO. [. . .] you'll have your daughter covered with a Barbary horse, you'll have your nephews neigh to you, you'll have coursers for cousins and jennets for germans.
> BRABANTIO. What profane wretch are thou?
> IAGO. I am one, sir, that comes to tell you your daughter and the Moor are now making the beast with two backs.
> (1.1.110–15)

By suggesting that Brabantio's grandchildren will be animals, and knowing that this will produce a rage and fear in Brabantio, Iago demonstrates that the societal fears and anxieties surrounding the issues of race, racial purity, and lineage are deeply rooted and held as significant by even the most educated and important citizens, i.e., Senators, of Venice. In this passage Iago also continues his animal imagery in relation to Othello but has transformed Desdemona from a white ewe back into Brabantio's daughter. Perhaps Brabantio can emotionally distance himself from an "animal." But by reminding him that Desdemona is still his daughter, Iago forces him to confront, rather than distance himself, from his lineage with specific reference to his heirs. Desdemona has paired with an "animal," she is now "other," and her offspring (Brabantio's heirs) will also be "other." The animal imagery returns once again as the two lovers are portrayed as a single "beast with two backs" (1.1.115). This insulting image again plays on the fear that Venetian society, beginning with Desdemona, has been invaded and destroyed by someone or something that is less human than they are.

At first Brabantio calls Iago a "villain" (1.1.116). But he still listens to Iago's ongoing racial diatribe. Once unleashed, racism—and the deep-rooted fears that motivate it—is not easily turned off or moved away from. Brabantio's continued attention to Iago's venomous insults proves this. Roderigo aides Iago in stirring Brabantio's anxieties even further when he says:

> [. . .] that your fair daughter,
> At this odd-even and dull watch o'th' night,
> Transported with no worse nor better guard
> But with a knave of common hire, a gondolier
> To the gross clasps of a lascivious Moor—
> [...]
> Your daughter, if you have not given her leave,
> I say again hath made a gross revolt,
> Tying her duty, beauty, wit and fortunes
> In an extravagant and wheeling stranger
> Of here and everywhere. (1.1.120–35)

Even though Roderigo leaves out the animal references, he still depersonalizes the lovers by refusing to use their names. And racist thinking is evident in the adjectives Roderigo chooses to describe the daughter ("fair") and the Moor ("lascivious"). Roderigo has also, with his reference about the common gondolier, implied that the marriage of Othello and Desdemona is cheap or in some way tainted as other than noble and honorable. He has a point. Othello and Desdemona have kept their love and their union a secret. Racism is present in this decision. Why would a renowned and wealthy general steal away and secretly marry a senator's daughter unless he knows that he cannot, because of his race, directly ask her father for her hand without being denied? Surely Roderigo has guessed, as evidenced in the passage above ("if you know not this" 1.1.127), that Brabantio has not given his consent for this union. Roderigo, instigated by Iago, plays on this fear and suggests that Brabantio's daughter (i.e., his "property") has revolted resulting in her fortunes, and, thus, Brabantio's, being transferred to this other, this "extravagant and wheeling stranger/Of here and everywhere" (1.1.134–35), through the marriage. For Brabantio, it can only appear, as presented in this manner by Iago and Roderigo, that his home has been invaded and his property stolen by a foreign pirate, a dark alien. Brabantio is now convinced of that which he has secretly feared: his family's racial purity and his honor have been penetrated (literally and figuratively) by an outsider. Angry and upset, and significantly crying "O, treason of the blood!" (1.1.167), he heads first to the Inn, then to the Senate, to seek justice. Using underlying fears related to race, Iago has now deliberately enlisted Brabantio's aid in his plan of revenge against Othello.

The racism present in Venetian society continues to be evidenced as it combines itself with hypocrisy in Act One, scenes two and three. Othello and Iago meet Brabantio and his group on their way to the Senate. Othello's outward confidence in his position, his belief in his new marriage and assimilation into the Venetian culture, is clear when he agrees willingly to accompany Brabantio and face his accusations publicly. The Senate, although they agree to prosecute whoever has run off with Brabantio's property, i.e., Desdemona, in whatever way Brabantio wishes, renege as soon as it is Othello that stands accused. Not only has Othello served them well in the past, but also a new war with the

Humphries 7

Turks has broken out and they wish to dispatch Othello to Cyprus to serve them yet again. To the Duke and Senators Othello is more than just a Moor, he is "the valiant Moor" (1.3.47). He is also referred to by more than this label of Moor. The Duke calls him "Valiant Othello" (1.3.48). Calling him by name seems to signals that Othello is one of them, a well-respected and valuable citizen of Venice. They treat him seemingly as a respected citizen by allowing him to speak in his own defense, which he does eloquently. The Duke even concedes, after hearing Othello's speech describing his and Desdemona's courtship and secret passion, by saying "I think this tale would win my daughter, too" (1.3.170). Yet there is unspoken racism present in this scene. Othello is being used by the Senate and is only a good and useful citizen of Venice as long as he can go and win the Senate's war. If he were not of use, he would have been arrested and given to Brabantio for justice, as initially promised. The Duke's seemingly friendly and supportive comment about his own daughter possibly falling for Othello's tale is most certainly uttered as much in relief that it hasn't happened as in fear that it could have. This is racism combined with hypocrisy and again demonstrates the prevailing assumptions and fears of even the most educated citizens. Othello addresses these educated hypocrites as "Most potent, grave, and reverend signiors,/My very noble and approved good masters" (1.3.76–77). He does not call them racists. He never mentions their hypocrisy although he certainly must notice it. Rather than seethe with anger about the injustice of Venetian racism, Othello internalizes this racism. He falls prey to racism because he wants to fit in and fears he doesn't. If Iago hasn't yet found Othello's weak spot, he certainly must see it now as he watches Othello kowtow to these Senators.

Humphries 8

Brabantio shows his own hypocrisy and very much overtly demonstrates his racism when he reluctantly blesses the union of his daughter and Othello. Realizing that the Senate will not act against Othello, Brabantio attempts to save face by publicly blessing the marriage. He says to Othello that he gives him "that with all my heart/Which, but thou hast already, with all my heart/I would keep from thee" (1.3.192–94). This is an interesting choice of words. Why is he reluctant to bless the wedding of his daughter to a man who has both prestige and money, who is seemingly well respected in the community, and who has many times been a welcomed guest in Brabantio's home? According to Othello, Brabantio has, in the past, "loved me, oft invited me," (1.3.128) to spend time together with him. His hypocrisy and racism are evident in his reluctance to give his complete and happy acceptance to an otherwise seemingly perfect match. Othello is suitable as a dinner guest, but not as a son-in-law. The only reason he hesitates in welcoming Othello into his family as more than a guest must be due to Othello's race, his visibly different appearance as an outsider. Brabantio confirms this hypocrisy and racism and shows his real thoughts and anxieties regarding the racial purity of his family (and of all of Venice) when he closes the scene with "For if such actions may have passage free,/Bondslaves and pagans shall our statesmen be" (1.2.98–99). Although he has gone along with the Senate because of Othello's usefulness, he represents, with these words, the true underlying racial tension and prejudice present in Venetian society. These words reveal a well established set of assumptions about the inappropriateness of black men as statesmen, husbands, and fathers to Venetian citizens.

For all his confidence and his seemingly seamless assimilation, Othello is afraid that he will never really fit in, and it is this fear which Iago exploits. Iago's manipulation of Othello in this regard is a process that he rehearses with Roderigo in Act II, scene 1. Othello's most valuable proof of having made it as an assimilated Venetian, his marriage to Desdemona, is questioned by way of Desdemona's fidelity when Iago suggests to Othello that he "Look to your wife. Observe her well with Cassio" (3.3.198). This possible infidelity, Othello reasons with Iago's help and influence, is motivated by race. When Iago reminds Othello that Desdemona has deceived her father in order to marry him, Othello responds that he does "not think but Desdemona's honest" (3.3.226). Yet he shows his own doubt and internalized racism when he says "And yet how nature, erring from itself—" (3.3.228). It is clear in this line that he thinks Desdemona has somehow gone against her nature in choosing him. This is the very idea that Iago offered Roderigo earlier but here Othello has thought of it himself, thus indicating that he already has his own private worries about their interracial relationship. Iago capitalizes on this and increases Othello's doubt by adding:

> Ay, there's the point. As—to be bold with you—
> Not to affect many proposèd matches
> Of her own clime, complexion, and degree,
> Whereto we see in all things nature tends—
> Foh! One may smell in such a will most rank,
> Foul disproportion, thoughts unnatural.
> But pardon me. I do not in position
> Distinctly speak of her, though I may fear
> Her will, recoiling to her better judgement,
> May fall to match you with her country forms,
> And happily repent. (3.3.229–39)

Humphries 10

In this passage Iago says he is not talking directly about Desdemona when, in fact, he is. That he has planted enough doubt so far in Othello's mind is noted in how Othello allows him to use—and listens to—these somewhat ugly words. Othello also hears these words because Iago could be, as he claims, saying them about any white Renaissance woman. He is speaking about nature, about repenting to better judgment and following one's original nature about making an incorrect decision. He is speaking, indirectly, about the assumed nature of one's race. Nearly every line of Iago's speech is geared to play on the assumed nature of Desdemona in relation to her race and Othello's insecurities regarding their interracial union and its supposedly inherent differences. Although he knows Desdemona has chosen him, how can Othello believe their marriage will last when Iago whispers that Desdemona's will has gone against her very nature and that this errant will must someday return to that place from where it has strayed—"her own clime, complexion, and degree" (3.3.231)? Iago has cleverly played on Othello's racial insecurities so well that he reduces Othello from a strong, confident soldier into a quivering mass of suspicion. In fact, Iago has done this so perfectly that Othello is literally made sick with doubt and begins to have seizures as a result. Iago confirms that his plan is working when he says, as an aside to the audience:

> The Moor already changes with my poison.
> Dangerous conceits are in their natures poisons,
> Which at the first are scarce found to distaste,
> But, with a little, act upon the blood,
> Burn like the mines of sulphur. (3.3.326–330)

Iago shows here that he knows Othello's doubts regarding race can be easily manipulated and inflamed. But, after the first line, Iago could be speaking about people in general instead of merely about Othello. This generalization makes it evident that racial tensions and insecurities bubble below the surface in not only Othello but in everyone and are often just waiting to be fanned into a fire of fear and hate. Iago shows that he knows exactly how to manipulate these tensions in Othello and the speech itself offers yet more proof of the already existing racial tensions and insecurities present in Venetian society as well as in Othello.

In spite of his doubt, however, Othello still does not give in so easily to Iago's implied accusations about Desdemona. He charges Iago to provide "ocular proof" (3.3.361), which we know Iago deviously can. That this proof—Desdemona's stolen handkerchief—turns out to be a well manipulated lie also comes as no surprise. But the seeds of doubt are planted so effectively in Othello that the proof is merely an afterthought. These seeds can only grow because of Othello's own internalized racism. Othello reveals his internalized racism again when he says "Haply for I am black/and have not those soft parts of conversation/That chamberers have" (3.3.264–66). This is a very different Othello than the confident
man sure of his power and position who initially appears in the beginning of the play. The Othello first met by the audience was confident enough to know he could pull off an interracial marriage that would cement his place in Venetian society. This new Othello seems aware and insecure about his vulnerable position as an outsider. His remark regarding not being able to converse as well as "chamberers" also shows that he worries that he, by virtue of his race, is also not equal in class. Should his wife be false and his

Humphries 12

marriage, itself a calculated risk, dissolve, he will lose, he says, everything

> That make ambition virtue! O, farewell,
> Farewell the neighing steed and the shrill trump,
> The spirit-stirring drum, the ear-piercing fife,
> The royal banner, and all quality,
> Pride, pomp, and circumstance of glorious war!
> [. . .] Farewell! Othello's occupation's gone!
> (3.3.351–55, 358)

In the references here to army life and pageantry, Othello obviously means that he will lose his occupation and the status and power it allows him. But he will lose more than that and he knows it. When he says he will lose his "occupation," he also refers to his occupation in Venice as an assimilated outsider. Othello has worked too hard to give this up. Once he believes Iago's accusations, he feels he has no choice but to defend his honor and position by killing Desdemona. When the accusations are revealed, after her death, as untrue, he kills himself. He did not trust his faith. He did not trust his love or his wife. He trusted his internalized racism which Iago so willingly and expertly massaged and inflamed in order to exact his own revenge.

This paper shows that Shakespeare recognized the new and profound anxieties regarding race present in society during his adult life as England expanded into exploration and colonization, the result of such activities being an influx of previously unknown foreigners into its daily life. The examples offered here also illustrate Othello's descent into savagery, not because of his race, but because of his internalized racism. This adoption of Venetian (English) values leads to a loss of nobility in the otherwise proper Othello, who even

Humphries 13

Iago initially recognizes as a good husband and citizen, and leads him to murder the ever innocent Desdemona. Such a tragic result indicates that Shakespeare questions and criticizes, rather than supports, the values of his time and the idea of racism.

Works Cited

McDonald, Russ. *The Bedford Companion to Shakespeare*. Boston: Bedford/St. Martin's, 1996.

Shakespeare, William. *Othello, the Moor of Venice. Perrine's Literature.* 7th ed. Ed. Thomas R. Arp. Fort Worth: Harcourt Brace, 1998. 1130–1216.

Rhetorical Modes/Analysis—Fiction into Film

Randi Spinner's essay, "Bartleby: Not a Scrivener Anymore . . . " is an example of the comparison and contrast of a work of literature with a film adaptation based on the literary work—in this case, **fiction into film**. Spinner compares the short story "Bartleby the Scrivener," written by nineteenth-century author Herman Melville, with the film production *Bartleby*, directed by Anthony Friedman (1970). Her essay could also be called an analysis. Like most comparison and contrast essays, hers focuses on a particular element of the two works as a vehicle for her comparison. Spinner is particularly interested in the fact that Friedman changed the point-of-view character in the film version, thus changing the focus, the themes, and even the plot, as a result. Her essay presents a persuasive argument for her thesis, which is that a great deal was lost when Friedman shifted the narrative point of view from the lawyer (Melville's first-person narrator) to Bartleby himself. Spinner spends roughly half of her essay discussing Melville's lawyer as the point-of-view character in the short story (using many apt examples and quotations from the story itself). The second half of her essay is spent discussing how the shift in point of view in Friedman's adaptation results in plot changes and thematic disruption (here contrasting the two versions and offering examples from both).

Student Essay

Randi Spinner

Prof. Barnard

Term Paper

Bartleby: Not a Scrivener Anymore . . .

It is surprising that Anthony Friedman's film is entitled "Bartleby,"* since the presence of a character in the film named Bartleby is one of the very few features this film has in common with the short story it is based on, Herman Melville's "Bartleby the Scrivener." First, Friedman changes the setting of the story by recasting Melville's 19th century Wall Street scrivener as a 1970's London bookkeeper. In addition, he makes the lawyer an accountant, changes Turkey's name to Tucker, and substitutes or altogether omits various other characters from the original short story. More bothersome is the director's decision to change the story's primary focus from the lawyer's internal struggle over whether to help or fire Bartleby into Bartleby's own psychological problems. Friedman refocuses the story by changing the point of view character, which, in turn, alters the plot, and more importantly, the main theme of the original short story.

Point of view is perhaps the most crucial element in shaping the theme of "Bartleby the Scrivener." The plot is not complicated, yet it is the thoughts of the narrator which drive the plot to follow

---

Bartleby, directed by Anthony Friedman, distributed by The Video Catalog and White Star. 1970.

Spinner 2

the path it does. Melville's assignment of the lawyer as first person narrator is intentional. Bartleby is a static character who serves to ignite reactions from his dynamic boss, the lawyer, who swings back and forth like a pendulum between wanting to help and wanting to be rid of Bartleby. Certain text in the story reveals information that would not be available to the reader had the lawyer not been narrator, and clearly demonstrates that the lawyer's internal struggle is at the core of this story.

The lawyer constantly changes his mind about how to respond to Bartleby's "preference" not to fulfill the lawyer's requests. After the initial shock of hearing Bartleby's reply, "I would prefer not to" (paragraph 23), the lawyer admits that "with any other man [he] should have . . . thrust him ignominiously from [his] presence" (paragraph 37). However, instead the lawyer begins to reason with Bartleby because "in a wonderful manner [Bartleby] touched and disconcerted" (paragraph 37) him. Furthermore, the lawyer lets the readers know that his intention to befriend Bartleby lies in his desire to "cheaply purchase a delicious self- approval . . . [because Bartleby] will eventually prove a sweet morsel for [his] conscience" (paragraph 55). Even though the lawyer continues to get frustrated as time goes on, he still reasons to himself that Bartleby is "a valuable acquisition" (paragraph 86) and therefore should not be gotten rid of. In contrast, there are also times when the lawyer feels determined that he must fire Bartleby.

The lawyer spends much time pondering what to do about Bartleby. At one point the lawyer admits that although his "first emotions had been those of pure melancholy and sincerest pity . . . that same melancholy merge[d] into fear, that same pity into repulsion" (paragraph 95). This repulsion, combined with his realization that "it was [Bartleby's] soul that suffered, and his soul [the lawyer] could not reach" (paragraph 95), causes the lawyer to resolve to dismiss Bartleby. However, he is unable to follow through with his resolution because he "felt something superstitious knocking at [his] heart forbidding [him] to carry out [his] purpose" (paragraph 111). Another time, the lawyer makes the extreme statement that his "pre-destined purpose [in] life" and his "mission in this world" (paragraph 169) is to offer Bartleby office room for as long as he needs. His mind quickly changes when he is made aware that there are rumors about him circulating among his colleagues. He resolves to forever be rid of "this intolerable incubus" (paragraph 171), and consequently makes plans to change the location of his office.

As is demonstrated up to this point, the lawyer continues to vacillate with regard to what to do about Bartleby throughout the entire story. In fact, even after he changes offices, he goes back and asks Bartleby to come home with him so they can decide what to do with Bartleby at Bartleby's leisure. Such a kind-hearted measure seems to come about, not only because helping Bartleby may be self-serving, but because the lawyer feels the "bond of a common humanity . . . for both [he] and Bartleby were sons of Adam" (paragraph 91). In fact, the lawyer's sensitivity to commonalties has already been established in the story.

The lawyer's role as narrator allows him to foreshadow the way he is inclined to react to Bartleby based on previous incidents. For example, in the exposition of the story the lawyer describes his workers and their idiosyncrasics. He explains that Turkey works very well in the morning but is quite reckless with his blots in the afternoon. When the lawyer confronts him and asks him not to work in the afternoons, Turkey replies that "old age—even if it blot the page—is honorable . . .

with submission, sir, we *both* are getting old" (paragraph 9). The lawyer then admits to the readers that "this appeal to [his] fellow-feeling was hardly to be resisted" (paragraph 10). Furthermore, when the lawyer "saw that go he would not" (paragraph 10), he lets Turkey stay and do less important papers in the afternoon. This incident with Turkey, not included in the film, is demonstrative of the manner in which the lawyer will come to treat the situation with Bartleby.

Friedman directs "Bartleby" with the camera acting as a third person narrator whose focus is on Bartleby's psychological dilemmas. Therefore, the film only portrays the lawyer's, or the accountant's, internal struggle in a superficial manner. The accountant is seen being confused by and then frustrated by Bartleby's reply of "I prefer not to," oftentimes revised as "I'd rather not just now" and "I don't think I'd like to just at the moment." Also following the general story line, the accountant initially attempts to reason with Bartleby to try and get him to fulfill his requests. In the course of the film he is also seen discovering that Bartleby is living in the office, as is the case in the original story. The accountant follows the general plot line for most of the film, while his innermost thoughts are never fully revealed.

Friedman makes an attempt to shed light into the accountant's feelings by adding a scene where the accountant and a colleague discuss Bartleby over lunch. The accountant says that Bartleby "irritates" him and that he can not seem to just "sack," or fire, him. This added scene does not, however, successfully replace what would be revealed had the accountant been the focus of the film, like the lawyer is in the short story version, because no more is revealed through this scene than is accomplished by the various facial expressions, such as anger, which are already apparent on the accountant's face. The director of the film makes another attempt at

Spinner 5

expressing the accountant's frustration with Bartleby. There is a scene that shows the accountant making a phone call in order to change offices, and while he is dialing, the viewer sees for a duration of about four seconds, very fast paced clips of what the accountant is feeling at that time. These clips include the accountant strangling Bartleby and torturing him. While this scene reveals more than the previous one described, it still does not compare with the specific deeply felt emotions described in the written story.

One can make the case that it is more difficult to portray complex emotions on film than in written form. While this is sometimes true, in this case the accountant's feelings were not dealt with as thoroughly and specifically as possible because of the shift in point of view, not because of the difficulties involved in adapting a story into film. In the film *Bartleby*, the director not only rewords some lines, but adds scenes and dialogue in an effort to refocus the story.

Bartleby is a film about the psychological problems of Bartleby, which are not explored in the written story, rather than the struggle that takes place within the accountant. Instead of Melville's story's exposition wherein the lawyer describes his workers, the film begins with many added scenes about Bartleby, not the accountant. The film opens with sad music and the vision of Bartleby in a subway car looking out the window. In the next scene the viewers see Bartleby putting his bag into a locker in the station. Then, as the camera follows Bartleby as he walks along the crowded streets, the viewers hear Bartleby's voice as he makes a phone call inquiring about a job advertised in the paper. The voiceover continues as Bartleby recites the questions that appear on job applications. None of these scenes appear in the original short story. Added scenes that focus on Bartleby's solitude continue throughout the film.

     Although in the written story the lawyer comments that he has not "known him to be outside of [his] office" (paragraph 53), in the film version Bartleby goes outside quite a bit. On the weekends he is shown walking around town and also what seems to be a very crowded marketplace. In addition, he is often shown standing on a bridge looking down at the water. Another vision that Bartleby frequently has, according to the film, is that of a mass of birds or pigeons flying away as a group. Another added scene includes the time when Bartleby is alone in the office and he says out loud to himself: "I'm not afraid to talk to myself, everybody does . . . ," whereupon he then envisions a large group of loud birds flying somewhere. Clearly, the director of this film is primarily interested in establishing for the viewer a better sense of Bartleby's psychological state than is revealed in the written story.

     This new focus inevitably leads to plot changes. Other than the different setting in which this story takes place, the standard plot line shifts to accommodate the exploration of Bartleby's psyche. First, there were many added scenes involving Bartleby's experiences. These scenes stress Bartleby's immobility amidst the rushing world around him. He is always in deep inner concentration among a crowd of fast-paced people or fast-flying birds. Through use of these visual metaphors, the director implies an interpretation of Bartleby as feeling that the world is moving at too fast a pace for him, resulting in his feeling separated from the world and indifferent to it. This may explain why he progressively opts to do less and less. Second, instead of the lawyer asking Bartleby to come home with him, the accountant asks Bartleby if he wants to see a doctor. Then, instead of Bartleby being brought to a prison at the end of the story, he is taken to a mental hospital. This change in plot seems to be a natural progression of the new theme, Bartleby's deterioration and increased

Spinner 7

feeling of indifference and solitude. The voiceovers of Bartleby talking, along with added scenes about Bartleby's experiences, combine to suggest that this film has adopted a different point of view than the written story in order to explore the nature of Bartleby's static character rather than the nature of the lawyer's dynamic character.

Film directors do have the right to adapt a book or short story into a movie by altering some characteristics of the book or short story in an effort to better suit the film genre. However, in this case it would be misleading to call the film *Bartleby* an adaptation of the story "Bartleby the Scrivener." Rather, it is a revision of Melville's story. Clearly, there is no way to avoid dealing with the relationship between the lawyer and Bartleby (or the accountant and Bartleby.) However, in abandoning the lawyer as narrator, Friedman loses the true crux of the story, the lawyer's internal struggle. Simply, changing the point of view character must invariably change the focus of a story whose focus relies on the thoughts and feeling of the narrator himself.

Developing the Essay

Here, as in the brainstorming stage, it is good for individual writers to take different paths, if they wish, according to their different preferences. Some writers feel supported and guided by an outline and are reluctant to write without one. These writers should, by all means, proceed next to write that outline. Other writers, however, feel stifled and confined by an outline, and find it more productive to plunge into composing the first draft, building some momentum in developing its ideas, and then returning to reorganize and restructure the essay when the first draft is complete. Often restructuring is necessary on a major scale for writers who work this way. Others—blessed, perhaps, with second sight!—skip the outline, write the first draft, and think and write with such clarity that little revision is necessary. These writers are few, however, and most will need to revise whether they write with or without an outline. Some writers who use an outline find that a simple one can be of greater use than an elaborately complicated one. The simple outline is less rigid and allows the discussion of the topic to grow organically within the subheadings. Alternatively, some writers complete a first draft, then generate an outline to get a visual sense or "road map" of the draft. Outlining at this stage may help the writer visualize the essay's structure and recognize opportunities for revising and for reorganizing the argument more effectively.

Documenting Sources

Although an instructor may not require students to write a research paper or to study **secondary sources** (commentary, criticism, or other materials *about* the primary source), the writer still must document any quotations taken from the **primary source** (the work or works of fiction, poetry, or drama that you are analyzing). The sample student essay "More or Less a Moor: Racism in *Othello*," by Humphries, makes use of one secondary source (*The Bedford Companion to Shakespeare* by Russ McDonald) in addition to the primary source (*Othello* by William Shakespeare). Humphries followed MLA Documentation style, the style of source documentation recommended by the Modern Language Association. Most instructors in English courses will ask students to use this style of documentation, though some instructors in other disciplines might specify different guidelines to be followed (for instance, the APA guidelines, set forth by the American Psychological Association).

Writers of literary essays need to become familiar with two types of MLA documentation: in-text citations and the list of works cited. In Humphries's essay, the first **in-text citation** (in his first paragraph) is of his secondary source. Making a point about racism in the Renaissance, Humphries offers a supporting quotation from McDonald's *Bedford Companion to Shakespeare*. Because he is using a direct quotation of the author's exact words, the writer encloses the passage in quotation marks. He then cites in parentheses afterward the author's last name and the page number on which the quotation is found: "(McDonald 273)." Note that no comma is needed between the author's name and the page number.

In Humphries's second paragraph, he uses a different kind of in-text citation, noting act, scene, and line numbers for directly quoted words, phrases, or passages from Shakespeare's play: "'his Moorship' (1.1.33)." In this citation, the first numeral "1" refers to Act I, the second numeral "1" to Scene 1, and the last number, "21," to the line number. This makes clear to the reader the exact location of the quotation from the play. Note that when citing quotations from the primary work under discussion, there is no need to repeat the author's last name each time, as long as it is clear that the quotation is from the primary work. Note the format for a citation following a block quote (in Humphries's third and fourth paragraphs, and elsewhere). Longer quotations such as these need to be block quoted, but any quotation of four lines or less should be run in with the text of the paragraph. There is further information about in-text citations in the "MLA Documentation Guidelines" section in Chapter 33.

In addition to the in-text citations illustrated above, a **works cited list** appears at the end of Humphries's essay. Citations on this list appear in alphabetical order, by the last names of the authors. Consult the "MLA Documentation" section (chapter 33) for a guide to sample formats for different types of publications (a book by one author, an article in a scholarly journal, a literary work in an anthology, and so on). Many instructors who assign analytical essays and not a research paper will not ask for a Works Cited page, as long as students are using only the primary work or works as printed in the textbook. Students would, in this case, need a Works Cited page only if using a source other than those in the textbook. The "MLA Documentation" section also discusses paraphrasing and plagiarism and the correct use of quotations under various circumstances.

Revising and Editing the Essay

When the first draft has been completed, the revision process begins. Two problems often found in the first draft of a literary essay are (1) too much plot summary and (2) not enough evidence from the text. Examine the first draft essay to determine whether the focus on analysis is maintained. It is easy for beginning writers to fall into summarizing or "retelling the story" (or poem or play) instead of analyzing it. It is often useful to provide an anecdote or a summary of a scene to illustrate an analytical point (a brief description of a scene is one type of evidence the writer may offer to illustrate a point); however, when a brief piece of evidence turns into a full-blown retelling of the story, this is a problem. Assume that the reader (who is, in this case, the instructor) has already read the work or works in question. The student writer's main task, then, is to think critically about the literary works, not summarize them. In her essay "Bartleby: Not a Scrivener Anymore . . . ," Spinner frequently refers to scenes in the short story and the film, comparing and contrasting the way in which they are handled in Melville's original work and in Friedman's adaptation. The following, from the eighth paragraph of Spinner's essay, is an example of how to use a succinct reference to a scene, without falling into the temptation of excessive plot summary:

> Friedman makes an attempt to shed light into the accountant's feelings by adding a scene where the accountant and a colleague discuss Bartleby over lunch. The accountant says that Bartleby "irritates" him and that he cannot seem to just "sack," or fire, him. This added scene does not, however, successfully replace what would be revealed had the accountant been the focus of the film.

Here, Spinner refers to the scene briefly to remind the reader of its content. Then she immediately proceeds to analyze the scene and what it reveals about plot, focus, and narrative point of view. She does not make the mistake of retelling the entire scene, but instead assumes the reader is familiar with it and needs only to be reminded of its content. Thus she spends the bulk of her essay on analysis (specifically, using the rhetorical method of comparison and contrast).

Second, be sure that the essay offers evidence in support of its points. A common shortcoming in first drafts is the presence of unsupported generalizations about the literary work. If the writer makes a critical assertion about the work, it needs to be backed up with evidence. For example, in his second to last paragraph, Humphries wants to show how Othello's internalized racism contributes to his willingness to consider even flimsy and false "proofs" as confirmation of the innocent Desdemona's guilt. Humphries offers evidence from the text to support this assertion, using quotations and plot details from Act III, Scene 3 to illustrate his point. If he had left this idea unsupported by evidence, many readers might question its validity.

Is the essay logically organized, or does it need restructuring? Often it is useful to outline an essay after writing the first draft in order to assess whether the ideas flow logically and whether there are gaps in the argument. Are any points repeated unnecessarily? Are excessive examples used in illustrating a single point? Humphries shortened his essay by 25 percent from an earlier draft when he removed redundancies and eliminated excessive examples.

While revising, keep the thesis of the essay in mind. The thesis statement is the main (or controlling) idea, and everything in the essay (including every example and quotation) should contribute in some way to illustrating and supporting that main idea. Also review the thesis statement itself. Is the thesis stated clearly enough? Has the focus of the argument changed during the writing of the essay in such a way that the thesis (initially, really a hypothesis) needs to be refocused? Review the introductory and concluding paragraphs. It is sometimes good to revise these paragraphs last (after the body paragraphs). Occasionally the focus of an essay changes somewhat in revision (as a result of new discoveries or insights), and if it does, the thesis, introduction, and conclusion may need to be adjusted or modified to conform to the new focus.

Review the essay also for sentence-level errors and stylistic problems. Improve weak or confusing transitions between paragraphs and ideas. Does the essay move logically from point to point? Spinner employs effective transitions as "guideposts" within her well-organized and well-argued essay. For example, when she begins her fifth paragraph with the very useful transitional phrase, "As is demonstrated up to this point," what follows has indeed been demonstrated in the previous three body paragraphs.

Ensure sentence variety (vary the length and structure of the sentences to avoid monotony). Spinner's fifth paragraph illustrates this stylistic virtue as well. The sentences in that paragraph contain, respectively, 24 words, 30 words, 38 words, and 14 words, and the sentence structure varies, so that the construction and rhythm of sentences is not repetitious.

Avoid excessive use of the passive voice. Constructions such as "seems as if," "I think," and "I feel as though" should be kept to a minimum. Cultivate the active voice as a stronger vehicle for your ideas. For example, Spinner's fifth paragraph begins, "As is demonstrated up to this point" not "As it appears to be demonstrated." Her introductory paragraph begins, "It is surprising" not "I feel it is surprising" or "It may be surprising."

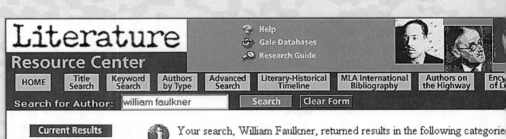

Literature
Resource Center

- 🐾 Help
- 🦫 Gale Databases
- 🔍 Research Guide

| HOME | Title Search | Keyword Search | Authors by Type | Advanced Search | Literary-Historical Timeline | MLA International Bibliography | Authors on the Highway | Ency of L |

Search for Author: william faulkner   [Search] [Clear Form]

Current Results

The Library of Congress

ℹ️ Your search, William Faulkner, returned results in the following categorie

| Biographies | Literary Criticism, Articles, & Work Overviews | Bibliographies | Additional Resources | Literary-Historical Timeline | In B |

William Faulkner
(1897-1962)

Variant(s): William (Cuthbert) Faulkner; William Cuthbert Faulkner; William Faulkner
Nationality: American
Genre(s): Essays; Film scripts; Letters (Correspondence); Novels; Poetry; Satires; Short
Literary Movement/Time Period: Modern American literature, Modernism (Literature), So

Page: 1

Below are items 1-8 of 8 found.

Update Mark List

 Add to Mark List

☐ Faulkner, William (Cuthbert)
"William (Cuthbert) Faulkner," in *Contemporary Authors*. (A profile of the author's life and works)

☐ Faulkner, William (Cuthbert)

C H A P T E R **33**

SOURCES FOR
RESEARCHING LIT

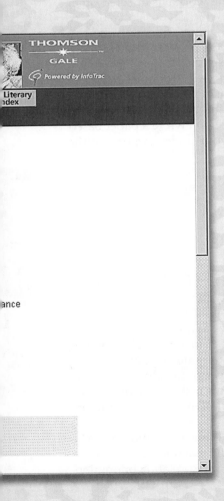

Writing The Literary Research Paper

A literary research paper requires the writer to make an argument about a particular text by discussing it in two ways. First, the writer examines one or more elements of the work; for example, by focusing on the role played by the setting in shaping a text, or on a moral or ethical question posed in the piece. The literary research paper also asks the writer to move beyond a close analysis of a text, however, and to consider not only what the writer thinks about the text, but also what other sources have to say about it. This kind of paper not only includes analysis of the text at hand, but also contextualizes the text by including information about what the author has said about his or her work, what critics have said, how the work has been used in other contexts, and even how the work has affected other people's lives, for example.

You might decide to write a literary research paper about William Faulkner's "Barn Burning." After you have read this short story, you could read the biography of Faulkner's life by Joseph Blotner, as well as his selected letters. You might also watch the 1980 video presentation based on the story (with Tommy Lee Jones). Finally, you might look through some electronic databases to find out what literary critics have said about it. After gathering all of this information, your opinion of Faulkner's work will probably be quite different than if you wrote a paper based solely on the short story. At the same time, however, your understanding of the work will have new depth.

Thinking Critically

Thinking critically is essential to writing a good literary research paper. As you examine your text and the evidence you have gathered, you will need to interpret what it means to you and to express that meaning in a clear and thoughtful way. Often, the best starting point to thinking critically is to be confident about thinking independently and to remind yourself that you are entitled to a particular point of view about the texts you are studying. This will help you immerse yourself in the work and arrive at some insightful conclusions. While you must always support your opinions with evidence, as you read and interpret a text, you shouldn't be afraid to be defensive, or even brash. Give yourself permission to have an opinion; this is the first step in successful critical thinking.

Thinking critically also requires patience, however. While it is important to be continually engaged as you consider evidence, it is equally essential to consider as much evidence as you can before arriving at a conclusive interpretation or opinion.

For example, you might assume that Grace Paley's "Samuel" is a story about how a young boy's reckless behavior results in death. With a little research, however, you will discover that the story's publication in the 1960s broadens its significance. Knowing that Paley first published this story in the *Atlantic Monthly* during a period of social unrest and, more specifically, a period of tensions between older and younger generations of Americans, adds a new and interesting layer to any discussion of the story. Having this information encourages you to ask a whole new series of questions. Why would Paley write this story? What was her political position during the 1960s?

In fact, asking questions is another way of encouraging yourself to think critically. As you gather materials, you should continually ask questions about "who," "what," "where," "when," and "why." Asking questions will encourage you to consider your sources from a variety of perspectives. It will also allow you to move continuously forward during the research and writing process.

Primary and Secondary Materials

As you begin the research process you'll want to identify the sources you consult as primary or secondary materials. The very nature of the literary research paper requires you to use a primary source. The text that is the focus of your study is your primary material because it is an original work. Many other sources are also considered primary materials. To return to the William Faulkner example, a primary material would be a letter written by Faulkner to one of his colleagues. Similarly, films, short stories, and novels can also be counted as primary materials. Primary materials include interviews, memos, manuscripts, memoirs, autobiographies, and records collected by a government agency. The benefit of consulting primary materials is that they allow you study and interpret an original idea. For example, if you want to understand why Amy Tan writes primarily autobiographical pieces, it would help to find an interview in which she answers that question.

A secondary material interprets, examines, or analyzes primary materials. Examples of secondary materials include reviews of films, novels, or essays; journal articles; dictionaries; encyclopedias; and newspaper articles. After you have reviewed several primary materials, you will want to consult secondary materials. These works can be particularly helpful if you are unfamiliar with the text you are analyzing. Most secondary materials include a review of the main arguments made about a particular text. For example, an analysis of Charlotte Perkins Gilman's "The Yellow Wallpaper" would explain that the piece is both a reflection on a personal experience and a political piece about the inhumanity of the treatment provided to women suffering from hysteria during the nineteenth century. While you are writing your literary research paper, it will be important to consider what other critics have said about the text you are examining. In this way, you can explain what is unique about your argument, as well as demonstrate to your audience that your argument is based on a thorough understanding of the most important discussions about the text you are examining. If you know whether the source you are reading is primary or secondary material, you will be able to understand, interpret, and use it effectively.

Using Sources Wisely

Print Sources—Books, Journals, Periodicals

When looking for print sources, you might begin by visiting your college, university, or local library. The library contains novels, magazines, newspapers, poetry, dictionaries, encyclopedias, films, music, and more. You can find most of the materials you are looking for by searching the library catalog. Today, most libraries have online catalogs which can be accessed from computer terminals. Some libraries even provide access through the Internet, which will allow you to search for materials from home if you have a computer and an online service. If your library does not have an online catalog, you can consult the physical card catalog. The catalogs are usually located in one large section.

Once you locate the library catalog you can begin searching for research materials. Most catalogs offer several search options. For example, you may want to look for print materials using the title or author of the piece. If you are not as familiar with the text you have chosen to analyze, you may want to conduct a more general search using a keyword or subject word. If you are having trouble identifying the subject or keyword your topic is associated with, try consulting the librarian on duty. You'll also want to note the call number assigned to the text you are searching for. All materials in the library are assigned a call number. Once you identify the materials you want to review, write down their call numbers and use a map of the library to locate them. Some useful print reference tools include

- *Bartlett's Familiar Quotations*
- *Cambridge History of English and American Literature*
- *Handbook of Rhetorical Devices*
- *Johnson's Dictionary of the English Language*
- *Oxford English Dictionary.*

Periodicals and journals that contain book reviews and literary criticism can also be found in the library. Book reviews are useful because they are good indicators of how the work was received by audiences upon its publication. Most reviews evaluate a work's plot and the quality of writing and give some information about the author. Although they do not contain the in-depth analysis of literary criticism, they can provide you with a brief overview of the text you are evaluating. When you look for a book review, you need to know the title of the book, the author's name, and the date of original publication. For more in-depth analysis, you will want to examine literary criticism written about a work. In most libraries, you can use a title search to look for a particular periodical or journal. Once you find the call number, you will know where all of the volumes of the periodicals and journals are located. Journal articles can also be found by using databases and indexes. Here is a list of some popular print indexes:

- *American Humanities Index*
- *British Humanities Index*
- *Columbia Granger's Index to Poetry in Anthologies and Columbia Granger's Index to Poetry in Collected and Selected Works*
- *Wellesley Index to Victorian Periodicals.*

Electronic Sources
Online Databases and Indexes

Most libraries contain a section in the online catalog that allows you to search through databases and indexes, too. While many of the databases provide full-text versions of the articles, others provide a citation only. If the database you are using does not provide you with the complete text of the article, you can use the information given to search the library catalog and find the print version. By typing the title of the journal into the online catalog, you should be able to locate it and the article. There are many excellent databases and indexes which contain information exclusively about literature:

- Academic Search Premier 1990–present (EBSCO)
- Arts & Humanities Citation Index 1975–present (ISI)
- Contemporary Authors Most current edition (Gale Group)
- Contemporary Literary Criticism Select (CLC Select) Most current edition (Gale Group)
- Dictionary of Literary Biography (DLB) Most current edition (Gale Group)
- Early English Books Online (EEBO) 1473–1700 (ProQuest)
- Eighteenth Century Collections Online (ECCO) 1701–1800 (Gale Group)
- English Poetry Database 600–1900 (Chadwyck-Healey)
- English Short Title Catalog 1473–1800 (Eureka)
- Expanded Academic ASAP 1980–present (Gale Group)
- FRANCIS (International Humanities and Social Sciences) 1984–present (Eureka)
- International Medieval Bibliography Online (IMB) 1967–present (Brepols Publishers)

- Inter-Play 19th century–present (Portland State University)
- Iter: Gateway to the Middle Ages and Renaissance 400–1700 (University of Toronto)
- Johnson's Dictionary of the English Language 1st (1755) and 4th (1773) eds. (CUP)
- Linguistics Abstracts Online 1981–present (Blackwell)
- Literature Online (LION) Dates of coverage vary (Chadwyck-Healey)
- Literature Resource Center Most current edition (Gale Group)
- LLBA (Linguistics and Language Behavior Abstracts) 1973–present (CSA)
- MLA Directory of Periodicals Most current edition (EBSCO)
- MLA International Bibliography 1963–present (EBSCO)
- Old English Corpus (University of Michigan Press)
- Oxford English Dictionary 2nd ed. 1989 (OUP)
- Oxford Reference Online Most current edition (OUP)
- PCI Full Text 1770–1995 (Chadwyck-Healey)
- Shakespeare Bibliography Online 1972–2001 (JHUP)
- Twentieth Century American Poetry 1901–present (Chadwyck-Healey)
- Twentieth Century English Poetry 1900–present (Chadwyck-Healey)
- What do I read next? Most current edition (Gale Group)
- World Shakespeare Bibliography Online 1972–2001 (JHUP)

Audiovisual Sources

Most libraries also contain audiovisual materials. You can often check out DVDs and VHS tapes or listen to CDs or tapes. These materials are usually located in a special section. In many cases, you can watch films or listen to music while you are in the library.

The Internet

The Internet can also be a good place to find sources. The easiest way to locate information online is to use one of the many available search engines. Popular and effective search engines include Yahoo!, Lycos, AltaVista, and Google. Like the library catalog, search engines contain a text entry box. You can enter any search term you like, but you will find researching more effective if you have very specific terms in mind. For example, if you wanted to find a list of Albert Camus's work using Google you might type in the words "Albert Camus bibliography." After you type in your terms and click on "Google Search" you will get a list of URLs. The URLs will range from personal home pages of Camus fans to a link to an animated cartoon inspired by the author. Because the Internet contains a wide range of information, some helpful, and some not, it is important that you narrow your search as much as possible. Google actually has a new version that allows you to search for scholarly information only: http://scholar.google.com. To find out more about what search engines are most effective, try going to Search Engine Watch.com <http://www.searchenginewatch.com/>. This website contains information about specific search engines and their benefits and limitations. Other websites aimed specifically at literature research include

- Atlantic Unbound <www.theatlantic.com>: an archive of *Atlantic Monthly* issues
- H-Net Reviews <www2.h-net.msu.edu/reviews/>: scholarly reviews in the humanities and social sciences
- The English Server <http://eserver.org>: contains primary works and critical analysis
- Humble Humanities Hub (http://www.humbul.ac.uk/): contains annotated links to scholarly web resources
- MIT Literature Guide <http://libraries.mit.edu/guides/subjects/literature/>: contains annotated links to scholarly literary websites
- Voice of the Shuttle <http://vos.ucsb.edu/> contains links to websites devoted to the humanities.

Evaluating Sources
Appropriateness

As you gather materials for your research paper, it is important that you continually evaluate them for appropriateness and reliability. In fact, if you apply critical thinking skills to the research process, you will find that you will spend your time more efficiently and effectively. One way to begin evaluating your sources is to consider their appropriateness to your research topic. If you decide to write a paper about Eudora Welty's "A Worn Path," you will find that the number of sources available to you is quite overwhelming. Consequently, it is important to remain extremely flexible. Don't be afraid to eliminate a source if the focus of your paper changes.

Other time-saving techniques include using a text's map to determine which parts will be most helpful to you. For example, before reading an entire book, peruse its table of contents or inspect the index and look for key words to identify the parts that will be most helpful to you. After finding a journal article, review the abstract and the section heads, or read the topic sentence of each paragraph to determine its relevancy to your topic. By examining the signs that an author provides to her or his work, you can save yourself time and identify the parts of a text that will be most helpful to you.

Reliability

Once you have determined that a source is appropriate for your research paper, you will want to evaluate its reliability. You might begin by assessing the author's credibility. A dependable author should follow all of the rules that we are expected to follow when writing our research papers. A credible author is respectful to the reader, uses evidence to support assertions, and addresses alternative opinions and points of view. Remember to examine an author's work closely for bias. An author who dismisses counterclaims to his or her argument, or one who uses a disparaging tone, is often biased.

If you are unfamiliar with an author's work, there are many ways to find out more about that writer's publication history. A book may contain a short biography of the writer on the jacket. Other authors list their credentials in the preface. The Internet can also be used to find out more about an author since many authors have their own web pages. Book reviews often list an author's credentials and previous work. Finally, credible authors clearly identify and cite any sources they have used.

Another way to determine a source's reliability is to examine the publication in which it appears. Works published by academic presses are generally more reliable than those published by commercial presses, which are more focused on profits. Academic journals, which publish only work that has been recommended by reviewers, are usually more credible than popular magazines. If you do want to use an article from a popular magazine, consider the magazine's reputation, the length of the article, and the credibility of the author to determine its reliability. Some well-respected magazines include the *Atlantic Monthly*, *Harper's Weekly*, and the *New Yorker*. Although you might assume that all newspapers are reliable, they too need to be evaluated. The *New York Times*, the *Washington Post*, and the *L.A. Times* are all well-respected newspapers. Still, you might find looking at local newspapers useful as well. If you want to find out how the residents of Ralph Ellison's hometown, Oklahoma City, responded to his short story "Flying Home," you might want to consult the local newspaper's reviews.

Websites are more difficult to evaluate, particularly because almost anyone who wants to post a website on the Internet can. As you review a website, make sure that you consider its content, timeliness, and the credibility of the author before you use it as a source in your paper. If the website includes citations in its content, this is a good indication that it is reliable. A website with active links is also usually reliable. Most websites indicate when they were last updated. Check this date to make sure that the site is being maintained and kept current. You can also use the techniques mentioned earlier to determine whether the site's author is credible. Finally, establish whether the website is a marketing tool by finding out who is sponsoring it. Many sites are actually commercial rather than informational and knowing who is paying to maintain the site will tell you whether this is the case.

MLA Documentation Guidelines

Citing Sources and Avoiding Plagiarism

It is essential that you **cite the source** when using quotations or ideas from the works of others. Today, with so many sources available online and the ease with which you can cut and paste information, it is easy to plagiarize, both intentionally and unintentionally. Plagiarism is a problem that extends beyond the classroom and into the real world. In 2003 *New York Times* reporter Jayson Blair resigned after it was discovered that he had been passing the work of other reporters off as his own. Blair faced severe career setbacks for his mistakes, but students also face serious consequences if they plagiarize. In many colleges and universities, plagiarism can end with anything from failing an assignment to expulsion. Perhaps if students understood how easy it is for professors and instructors to catch plagiarism, they would be more reluctant to try it. Most professors and instructors use Google to detect plagiarism, and other websites, including My DropBox.com and Turnitin.com, are specifically designed to catch students plagiarizing another author's work. By simply typing a sentence from a student's paper into the search text box, professors can usually locate the source a student is passing off as her or his own work. To avoid plagiarism, it is essential that you document your sources.

The rules of documentation described below are those recommended by the Modern Language Association (MLA), a professional association of English teachers, students, and professors. Use the MLA documentation style when writing essays on literary works (instructors in the social sciences may require the American Psychological Association, or APA, guidelines instead). The careful documentation of sources is essential in order to give credit to the original author of directly quoted words and passages, as well as original ideas or information from others, even if it is paraphrased rather than quoted directly. In addition to giving credit to other writers, documentation permits your reader to find the passage that you are quoting or referring to, if there is a need to look it up. The works cited page makes it possible to limit the amount of information provided in in-text citations, and it also provides the information your readers would need if they want to access the source you have used.

When documentation is lacking or inappropriately handled, the writer risks committing **plagiarism**, which is a theft of the intellectual property of others. Some writers may be guilty of this kind of theft because they are unaware of the need to document paraphrased material, or because they are careless in the way they summarize the ideas or words of others. For example, if Scott Humphries (sample student essay on *Othello*, printed in Chapter 32) had inappropriately paraphrased the idea he uses from McDonald's *Bedford Companion* in his first paragraph, it might look like this:

> ***Wrong:*** When depicting characters like Shylock the Jewish moneylender in *The Merchant of Venice*, Aaron the Moor in *Titus Andronicus* and Othello in *Othello*, Shakespeare is playing up cultural worries related to racism.

This way of representing McDonald's ideas as a paraphrase would be plagiarism because it simply restates the same idea, changing the order of the syntax and altering a word here and there. For instance, the use of "playing up" in place of "plays upon" is a thinly disguised theft of McDonald's words and ideas.

Humphries, of course, has no desire to trick the reader into thinking McDonald's ideas are his own. Instead, he uses a direct quotation and a page citation:

> *Right:* According to *The Bedford Companion to Shakespeare,* "Shakespeare plays upon these anxieties in his depiction of such characters as Shylock the Jewish money-lender in *The Merchant of Venice,* Aaron the Moor in *Titus Andronicus,* and, most memorably, *Othello*" (McDonald 273).

On the other hand, there is no need to document the first sentence of the essay ("Racism existed during the Renaissance.") since this is common knowledge. As long as no exact words or phrases from McDonald are used in that assertion, it does not need a citation.

In-Text Citations

Parenthetical references within the text of your essay will refer to the primary work or to the secondary sources listed on a works cited page. The most common type of reference is identification of a quotation or paraphrase that is run in with the text of your essay, as with the above example from Humphries. Note that the parenthetical reference comes before the period since it is part of the sentence, and also that there no comma is used between the author's last name and the page number: ". . . most memorably, Othello" (McDonald 273).

When it is clear in the text of the essay, the author's name is not needed in the citation. For instance, if Humphries's sentence began, "In his *Bedford Companion to Shakespeare,* author Russ McDonald writes," then his authorship would already be established and the citation could simply include the page number: ". . . most memorably, Othello" (273).

Additionally, in using quoted material run in with the text of the essay, writers should strive for **well-integrated quotations**. In the following passage from his second paragraph, Humphries illustrates the racist use of language by Iago and Roderigo by using well-integrated quotations:

> Iago refers to "his Moorship" (1.1.32), "the Moor" (1.1.39.57), and so on throughout the scene. Roderigo, a past suitor of Desdemona, also refers to Othello with epitaphs such as "the thick-lips" (1.1.66), "a lascivious Moor" (1.1.124), and "an extravagant and wheeling stranger / Of here and everywhere" (1.1.134–35).

Note the seamless grammar of both sentences above. The syntax should flow smoothly, with no breaks in the grammatical logic of the sentence. The last excerpt also serves as an example of the correct format for **poetry quotations** or quotations of verse from a dramatic work (as here) which are run in with the text of the essay. Use a slash (/) to indicate line breaks. Use a double slash (//) to indicate stanza breaks.

In addition to short quotations (four lines or less), which are run in with the text, one may need to use longer quotations (more than four lines), which are set off from the text, by using a **block quotation**. Humphries uses a block quotation in his fourth paragraph.

> IAGO. [. . .] you'll have your daughter covered with a Barbary horse, you'll have your nephews neigh to you, you'll have coursers for cousins and jennets for germans.
>
> BRABANTIO. What profane wretch are thou?
> IAGO. I am one, sir, that comes to tell you your daughter and the Moor are now making the beast with two backs. (1.1.110–15)

In the above example, note that the quotation marks are omitted; the blocked-in format already indicates that this is quoted material. Note also that the parenthetical citation appears outside the period (or other mark of end punctuation), and it is placed one space after the final punctuation. Within the parentheses, there is no need to cite the author because it is clear that this is a reference to the primary source under discussion, Shakespeare's *Othello*. If a reader needs to know which edition of the play is being cited, that information would be available on the works cited page. Citations of works of drama appear in the format used above. The numbers separated by periods represent the act, scene, and line numbers. Since the work being quoted is a play and includes an exchange of dialogue between characters, the identifying tags for the speakers are used (IAGO, BRABANTIO). These dramatic tags are usually represented in small capital letters.

Other Types of In-Text Citations and Examples

The above general material about parenthetical references is supplemented by the list below of sample references for various types of sources.

A work by two or three authors

Interesting questions have been asked about whether literature imitates life, or whether it should attempt to (Danziger and Johnson 161).

A work by more than three authors

An examination of literature in the modern period demonstrates the extent to which the old cultural order was called into question (Baym et al. 1674).

Note that no commas are needed above. The number 1674 refers to the page, not the year. Et al. is Latin for "and others."

A work in an anthology

In her essay "Notes to a Young(er) Writer," Sandra Cisneros writes about having attained the wisdom that she has much more to learn (Kanellos 52).

Cisneros's essay appears in an anthology edited by Kanellos. For more information on the book, the reader can go to the list of works cited, and the anthology will be listed under Kanellos.

A work with volume and page numbers

In their introduction to the Romantic Period, the authors cite the French Revolution as one influence on the development of literary trends (Abrams et al. 2:2).

The citation refers to Volume 2, page 2.

An indirect source

"The whole intricate question of method, in the craft of fiction," says Mr. Percy Lubbock, "I take to be governed by the question of the *point of view*—the question of the relation in which the narrator stands to the story" (qtd. in Forster 198).

Qtd. is an abbreviation of "quoted in."

The Works Cited Page

The list of works cited conventionally begins on a new page, following the last page of the essay. The centered title at the top of the page should be "Works Cited." The list should be arranged alphabetically, by the last name of the author. If the work has no author, alphabetize it by the first word of the title. The articles "a," "an," and "the" do not count as first words, so the title "An Introduction to Literary Criticism" would be alphabetized as "Introduction to Literary Criticism, An." Names of publishers may be abbreviated (such as "Wadsworth" for Wadsworth Publishers). The entire page is double-spaced, both between and within entries. Each entry begins its first line at the left margin, and subsequent lines of the entry are indented five spaces (or half an inch). Basically, each entry contains three types of information, separated by periods: author, title, and publishing details. The following are sample entries for different types of publications.

A book by a single author

Baxter, Charles. *Burning Down the House: Essays on Fiction*. Saint Paul: Graywolf Press, 1997.

A book by two or three authors

Danziger, Marlies K. and W. Stacy Johnson. *An Introduction to Literary Criticism*. Boston: Heath, 1961.

Note that only the first author's name is listed last name first. If there is a third name, separate the names with commas.

A book by more than three authors

Baym, Nina, et al., eds. *The Norton Anthology of American Literature*, 6th. ed. Shorter. New York: Norton, 2003.

Note that the abbreviation for editors is "eds." Use this to indicate that those named are editors rather than authors.

Two or more works by the same author

Erdrich, Louise. *The Antelope Wife*. New York: Harper Collins, 1998.
—*The Last Report on the Miracles at Little No Horse*. New York: Harper Collins, 2001.

An edited book

Kanellos, Nicolas, ed. *Hispanic-American Literature: A Brief Introduction and Anthology*. New York: Longman, 1995.

A book with a volume number

Abrams, M.H., et al., eds. *The Norton Anthology of English Literature*, Revised. Vol. 2. New York: Norton, 2003.

A short story in an anthology

Olsen, Tillie. "I Stand Here Ironing." *Literature: Reading, Reacting, Writing*, 5th ed. Ed. Laurie G. Kirszner and Stephen R. Mandell. Boston: Wadsworth, 2004. 203–09.

A poem in an anthology

Song, Cathy. "Leaving." *Modern Poems: A Norton Introduction*, 2nd ed. Eds. Richard Ellmann and Robert O'Clair. New York: Norton, 1989. 876–77.

A play in an anthology

Shaw, George Bernard. *Heartbreak House. Laurel British Drama: The Twentieth Century*. Ed. Robert W. Corrigan. New York: Dell, 1965. 42–134.

An article or essay in an anthology

Baldwin, James. "Many Thousands Gone." *Black Voices: An Anthology of Afro-American Literature*. Ed. Abraham Chapman. New York: NAL, 1968. 590–604.

More than one selection from the same anthology

Harjo, Joy. "She Had Some Horses." Vizenor. 281–82.
Ortiz, Simon. "My Father's Song." Vizenor. 260.
Vizenor, Gerald. *Native American Literature: A Brief Introduction and Anthology*. New York: Longman, 1997.

A translation

Gide, André. *Lafcadio's Adventures*. Trans. Dorothy Bussy. New York: Vintage/Random: 1925.

An article in a magazine

Menand, Louis. "The Seventies Show: What Did the Decade Mean?" *The New Yorker* 28 May 2001: 128–133.

If the article were not continuous—i.e., if it did not appear on consecutive pages—the page citation would read: 128+.

An article in a daily newspaper

Cotter, Holland. "Poetry Soaked in the Personal and Political." *New York Times* 30 May 2001, late ed.: E1+.

See note above about discontinuous pages.

An article in a reference book

"Aztec and Inca Civilizations." *The Columbia History of the World*. Eds. John A. Garraty and Peter Gay. New York: Harper, 1972.

A CD-ROM: Entry with a print version

Zurbach, Kate. "The Linguistic Roots of Three Terms." *Linguistic Quarterly* 37 (1994): 12–47. *Infotrac: Magazine Index Plus*. CD-ROM. Information Access. Jan. 1996.

A CD-ROM: Entry with no print version

"Bloomsbury Group." *Encarta 1996. CD-ROM. Redmond: Microsoft, 1996.*

An online source: Scholarly project

Pezzini, Hugo. "The Symposium." *Third Rail: An Online Creative Writing Community*. 2001. Hunter College, City University of New York. 30 May 2001<http://thirdrail.hunter.cuny.edu/pezzini.html>.

An online source: Personal or professional website

Atwood, Margaret. "Spotty-Handed Villainesses: Problems of Female Bad Behaviour in the Creation of Literature." *Margaret Atwood's home page*. 1994. 28 Oct. 1998 <http://www.web.net/owtoad/vlness. html>.

An online source: Article in a periodical with a print version

Barth, John. "Thinking Man's Minimalist: Honoring Barthelme." *The New York Times*. (September 3, 1989, Sunday, Late Edition, Section 7): 9. Online. Internet. 21 June 1998. 26 Nov. 2000 <http://www.nytimes.com/books/ 98/06/21/specials/barth-minimalist.html>.

An online source: Article in a periodical with no print version

Smith, Joan. "Salon Interview: Tobias Wolff." *Salon*. Dec. 1996. 1 Oct. 1999. <http://www.salonmagazine.com/dec96/interview96126.html>.

Student Research Paper

The following student research paper (written by the authors' son) models good practices in terms of using sources providing different perspectives. Best of all, Jake's essay is chock full of the kind of original thinking that we hope *you* will feel empowered to do. Go for it—think for yourself.

Jake Winn

English 220-22

Prof. M. A. Tata

"Everyday Use," Everyone's Issues

Alice Walker is far too intelligent a writer to take only one side of a cultural issue into account. More in touch with the complexity and depth of the human experience, she will take a rooted stance in the gray space in between two outlooks, usually leaning towards the more embattled camp, and make a critical examination of both. Her short story "Everyday Use" is a perfect example of her ability to look at the faults and merits of both sides of a cultural issue and look towards a third possibility that embraces both.

The two cultural standpoints examined in "Everyday Use" are those of the older generation (Black or Negro Americans) and the newly born standpoint of the "African-Americans," the sixties era black youth, who abandoned what they saw as a corrupt American

Winn 2

lineage in order to embrace their roots as African people. Because so
many aspects of Black American life had come from a history of
enslavement and oppression, many young black intellectuals
returned to Africa in order to rediscover the pre-slavery people they
had descended from. While some returned physically, flying back
and actually living with African families, many simply returned
spiritually, intellectually and socially to African traditions. They
adopted cultural African dress, such as the dashiki, and took African
names in order to distance themselves from a white culture which
had been imposed on them.

In an interview with Evelyn C. White (her biographer), Walker
counts herself as having been one of the youth involved in this new
movement. She herself went to Kenya and was given the same
name that the character Dee adopts in the story; Wangero. While
she loved and appreciated African culture, she was upset by the fact
that others in her generation were denying and belittling "the
ancestors that they knew . . . their parents and grand-parents . . .
and I often thought 'What do they think of us?'" Walker was also
critical of this new movement because often in the excitement of
adopting the lost traditions of African culture, things were mis-
adopted. "The kente cloth," Walker points out, "was only worn by
the kings. I'm not even sure if the queens were allowed to wear it"
(Walker, "Stitches").

Walker's criticism of the hypocrisies that came out of the
ideological return to Africa and her curiosity around the feelings of
those relatives who were having their efforts denied is what created the characters in "Everyday Use." Dee is clearly someone who
has embraced a cultural movement as a hip new idea, but not as

part of a truly personal philosophy. Mrs. Johnson represents an older generation that, for all its love and generosity, is still ashamed and ignorant below a hand of oppression. Because of this Dee "hated the house," (paragraph 10) "read to [Maggie and her mother] without pity" (paragraph 11) and looks down on their entire existence.

From the moment that Dee and Hakim-a-barber arrive on the farm, they hold an air of superiority about them. They take pictures of Mama Johnson and Maggie, making sure to include the worn out sharecropper house and the farm life behind it. Hakim-a-barber is quick to condescendingly grin and explain that "farming and raising cattle is not my style" (paragraph 44). He calls them mother and sister when he first arrives, but then calls their food unclean, not bothering to explain that this comes from his religious beliefs. He simply leaves it lying out on the dinner table as an insult. Dee runs about, snatching up anything that relates to her now-in-vogue impoverished roots in order to decorate her house.

The main artifacts of the story, the ones on which the turning point is hinged, are the quilts which are to go to Maggie. The artistic significance of the artifacts around the house, particularly the quilts, comes from a discovery and newfound respect of the artistic lives of Black American women who lived under sharecropping or slavery. One of the first works to promote this new idea of the artistic contributions of these oppressed women was Alice Walker's essay "In Search Of Our Mothers' Gardens" (the title essay of *In Search of Our Mothers' Gardens: Womanist Prose*) in which she makes the case for the artistry of household items made by black women under circumstances where art was prohibited.

Walker borrows from Virginia Wolff's book on women writers *A Room of One's Own* to ask how one creates if they do not even own themselves. When Wolff suggests numerous circumstances that have lost to us great writers (circumstances of class, time period, and expectations of women), Walker adds to that list the circumstances of slavery, abuse, and poverty (Walker, *In Search* 235). Walker suggests that the artistic mark left by her female ancestors, who were so actively discouraged from artistic expression, comes in the form of the household items that had to be made, rather than bought, because of poverty. These women "left [their] mark in the only materials [they] could afford, and in the only medium her position in society allowed her to use" (Walker, *In Search* 239)

It's very easy for us to see Dee and Hakim-a-barber as the villains of the story and Mama and Maggie as its heroes, but as Susan Farrell points out in her essay "Fight vs. Flight," Mama Johnson may be more appealing to us because of her humor and down-home ways, but she is hardly an ideal for future generations to strive for. When Mama Johnson compares herself to Dee she points out that she could never "[look] a strange white man in the eye," while Dee "would always look anyone in the eye. Hesitation was no part of her nature" (paragraph 6). Dee is clearly comfortable in her black skin and proud of her roots in a political sense. The fact that Dee has to read to Maggie and Mama Johnson also implies that they may be uneducated to the point of illiteracy. When Dee says "you ought to try to make something of yourself, too, Maggie" (paragraph 81), it's not out of malice, even though it's said in anger. Dee seems to genuinely want to make the world better.

What Dee is missing is an appreciation for the history of her recent ancestors, the history that Maggie knows so well. Aunt Dicie, Grandma Dee, Uncle Buddy and Henry James (Stash), are constantly present in the conversation that Dee Wangero is having with the other characters. While Dee only sees their artifacts through their hip artistic relevance, Maggic is the one who knows precisely where she comes from. Maggie can remember her whole family history and can appreciate it without those artifacts. In the end, that's what makes her most deserving of them.

The central artifacts of "Everyday Use" are the quilts which Dee tries to take for her artistic purposes as opposed to "backward . . . everyday use" (paragraph 66). Walker was one of the first writers to mention the significance of the quilt in African-American historical art. She holds this art form of intricately hand sewn quilting in high regard as an art form, but also brings light to its significance as a time for the women of the family to gather and communicate to each other. In this story, the quilt serves as a metaphor for the three women. Dee, Maggie and Mama Johnson are bound by blood even though they are vastly different. The quilts sewn by the women of Black American families were usually crafted by poor sharecroppers, and before that by slaves. Because these women artists had little material to work with, the quilts are usually a variety of different fabrics and prints stitched together (Walker, "Stitches"). The ones in this story are "all pieces of dresses Grandma used to wear" and have been handed down from the grandmother to Big Dee and Mama Johnson to finish (paragraph-61, 62).

Alice Walker was far too knowledgeable to simply write off any of these characters. Each one represents a segment of the sixties-era, female, African-American population. Mama Johnson is one of the true ancestors, one of those who had "spent the last two-hundred and fifty years trying to bring [blacks] to the point of revolt and revolution and claiming of the self," (Walker, "Stitches"). Dee is one of the revolutionary youth who, out of aberration of the indignities suffered by black Americans and because of her wisdom and education has "claimed a self that [her immediate ancestors don't] know much about" (Walker, "Stitches"). Both of these characters face Walker's criticism. Mama Johnson means well but, while it communicates the humor of the story, she is entirely ignorant to the changes going on in the world around her. Dee comes off as even less likeable. She is selfish, pretentious, and more of a trend follower than a person with true beliefs.

Works Cited

Farrell, Susan. "Fight vs. Flight: A re-evaluation of Dee in Alice Walker's 'Everyday Use.'" *Studies in Short Fiction*, Spring 1998 v35 i2 p179(9). Literature Resource Center. http://ezproxy.ncc.edu:2055/servlet/LitRC?vrsn=3&locID=sunynassau&srchtp=kywrd&c=3&stab=2048&ste=43&tbst=ksrch&tab=2&KA=Alice+Walker+Everyday+Use&n=10&docNum=A83585372&bConts=12849079.

Walker, Alice. "Everyday Use." *Access Literature*, Eds. Barbara Barnard and David Winn. (Boston: Wadsworth Publishers), 2005.

Walker, Alice. *In Search of Our Mothers' Gardens: Womanist Prose.*
New York: Harcourt Brace Jovanovich, 1983.
Walker, Alice. "Stitches in Time." Interview on DVD. By Evelyn C.
White. September 8, 2003. From *Everyday Use:* The Wadsworth
Original Film Series in Literature. Dir. Bruce R. Schwartz. Prod.
Thomson/Wadsworth, 2005.

CHAPTER 34

ACCESS TO LIT CRIT:
Pathways to
Interpretation

The analysis of literary works has been practiced at least since Aristotle theorized about the creation of meaning through dramatic works of tragedy in the fourth century B.C.E. in his *Poetics*. Today, there are various **schools of critical theory** which employ a variety of approaches to the analysis of works of literature. While some literary critics regard themselves as adherents of a particular theoretical strategy, most well-informed readers use these analytical approaches loosely and in combination with one another. Indeed, the critical approach employed in all of the chapter discussions in this textbook can be called **eclectic criticism** An eclectic approach leaves the reader free to make use of whatever analytical strategies are helpful in exploring a work of fiction, poetry, or drama.

Formalist Criticism

This school of literary criticism is also known as new criticism (though it has now been practiced for decades). Formalist critics believe that a work of literature must stand or fall on its own merits and must derive meaning only from what is within the boundaries of the work itself. Therefore, in analyzing a work, they consider only what is **intrinsic** (within the work itself) and nothing that is **extrinsic** (outside the work). Extrinsic considerations would include, for example, biographical information about the author or reference to the historical context in which the work was written.

An important contribution of formalist critics to the ongoing conversation that is literary discourse has been their interest in **close reading** of literary texts and in their exploration of how the elements of a literary work (such as symbolism, figurative language, rhythm, line breaks) may work together to achieve a unified effect. The idea of close reading to a formalist critic is similar to our definition of explication in Chapter 32, with the added notion of the unity of effect. The formalist critic is likely to find a work successful if it achieves this kind of unity; a work that seems at odds with itself, on the other hand, and fails to accomplish a unified effect or meaning (or bundle of meanings) might be considered to have failed or be flawed.

A formalist approach to Eudora Welty's short story "A Worn Path" (Chapter 5) might examine the figurative language used in the story, focusing specifically on the name of the main character. The story begins with a description. In the third sentence, Welty announces that the elderly African American woman making her way through the woods is named Phoenix Jackson. Phoenix carries a stick with her that makes "a grave and persistent noise in the still air, and [seems] meditative like the chirping of a solitary little bird." In the next paragraph, Welty describes Phoenix's complexion and writes that "a golden color ran underneath, and the two knobs of her cheeks were illumined by a yellow burning under the dark." Her hair is black, but also emits an "odor like copper."

The formalist critic might pay careful attention to the repeated references to birds, great age, and gold to argue that Phoenix is best understood as a human representative of the mythological bird, which symbolizes immortality and resurrection. In the Egyptian version of the story about the Phoenix, the sun-god flew home every 500 years to renew its strength. After arriving home, the bird burns itself in a fire, and from the ashes a new Phoenix arises. Similarly, Phoenix Jackson's journey to Natchez to obtain a medicine provides spiritual renewal for her and will physically renew her grandson.

Other examples from the story support this argument. Once she arrives at the charity ward, Phoenix sees "the document that had been stamped with the gold seal and framed in the gold frame, which matched the dream that was hung up in her head." In repeating the word *gold*, the author appeals to images of the mythological Phoenix, which was represented in this color by ancient Greeks and Egyptians. Once inside the ward, her appearance changes, and she stands with "a fixed and ceremonial stiffness over her body." In using words like fixed and ceremonial, the author equates Phoenix's demeanor with that of aristocracy, or a god, which also suggests that Phoenix is much like the immortal mythological bird. Finally, once she arrives at the office she refuses to speak until, "At last there came a flicker and then a flame of comprehension across her face, and she spoke." She then tells the nurse and attendant about her little grandson who swallowed lye. "He going to last," she says, "He wear a little patch quilt and peep out holding his mouth open like a little bird." Once she receives the medicine and the nurse offers her a nickel, Phoenix rises and holds out her hand. Much like the mythological bird, Phoenix has been burned by the harsh realities of life, but once she receives the medicine, she rises again with renewed strength, eager to return to her grandson.

Eudora Welty often used significant names to infuse meaning into her stories. Some examples include Mr. Petrie in "Petrified Man," Mrs. Rainy in "Shower of God," and Florabel in an early version of "The Burning." The formalist critic would not, however, find this information important. They would focus solely on the language used in the piece. Another aspect of the story that the formalists would not concern themselves with is the choice of an African American woman as the central figure in the story. Choosing to tell the story of an African American woman in 1941, before the end of segregation, was a political choice. In fact, Welty makes reference to the Civil War and America's long history of oppressing African Americans when she has Phoenix say that she "never did go to school" because she was "too old at the Surrender." The formalist would not find this information important to a discussion of the story.

Historical and New Historicist Criticism

Although there are significant differences between historical and new historicist criticism, both adherents would argue that knowing the cultural and historical context in which Welty's story was set are the keys to understanding it. Historical critics examine the social and intellectual milieu in which the author wrote. They consider the politics and social movements prevalent during the time period. The focus of historical criticism is on how literature is both a product and a shaper of society. In contrast, new historical critics take this position one step farther to argue that history is not a set of objective facts, but it is subject to interpretation and reinterpretation according to changes in society's power structures. Consequently, not only is it important to consider the historical circumstances under which a text was written, but also to note that each historical period is rife with conflicting versions of truth. New historicist critics, such as Michel Foucault, maintain that literary works contain evidence of these competing truths. Furthermore, because readers bring their contemporary set of social and cultural assumptions to a text, any interpretation of a literary work cannot help but be influenced by both the cultural and historical context in which the author wrote the work and the cultural and historical context of the reader. A new historicist critic would acknowledge how his or her contemporary assumptions might be influencing his or her reading of a literary work. Finally, new historicist critics point out the importance of acknowledging the literary work of previously ignored groups of people such as women and people of color. In many ways, new historicism is not only a literary theory, but also a political position. It encourages a more democratic approach to literature in as much as it encourages readers to embrace a variety of texts as worthy of literary analysis and study.

The historical critic might argue that Welty's story cannot be interpreted without first considering the social and historical context in which it was written. Even a cursory review of American history will show the craftsperson that racism pervaded American society during the 1940s. Although Welty does not give the reader a clear indication of the story's temporal context until near the end, when Phoenix explains that she was too old to attend school after the Civil War, it is clear that Phoenix lives in a time of racism. Phoenix's first encounter with a white person is a perfect example. After briefly conversing with Phoenix, who explains that she is going to town, the hunter dismisses her journey's importance by saying that he "knows . . . colored people" would never miss a chance to see Santa Claus. This condescending comment points to the hunter's racist view that all African Americans are the same. When the hunter drops a dime, Phoenix picks it up after distracting the hunter by challenging him to scare away a black dog. After the hunter chases the dog away, he returns and asks Phoenix if the gunshot scared her. He then points the gun directly at Phoenix and asks her if she is scared. She responds by saying that she is not scared because she has "seen plenty go off closer by" in her day "and for less than" what she has done. The hunter then explains that he would give her a dime if he had any money with him. Phoenix is given little respect by the hunter, and the reader might infer that he tells her to go home because he knows how dangerous it is for an African American woman to travel alone.

In contrast to the historical critic, the new historicist might focus on the same incident in the story but examine it from a cultural and historical perspective as well. Certainly, new historicists would acknowledge that the story is best understood as an example of how racism pervaded every aspect of life during the 1940s. They would point out that the story exemplifies the dominant white power structure of the period. Through social and political subjugation, white men and women often held the fate of African Americans in their hands. The hunter does not think twice about pointing a gun at Phoenix, and the nurse and attendant can decide the fate of Phoenix's grandson because Phoenix is so impoverished that she has to rely on charity for the medicine that he needs. The new historicist critic would, however, also make note of the ways in which Phoenix resists these power structures. By stealing the dime from the hunter and refusing to heed his advice to return home, by asking the nurse for more money, and even by asking another white person to tie her shoes, Phoenix challenges her assigned role in society. New historicist critics are quick to demonstrate the ways in which there is always room for resistance to the dominant social and cultural paradigms. In this way, they demonstrate the agency that people of color, for example, exercised to challenge those who assume that they are victims.

Archetypal and Mythological Criticism

At the core of archetypal and mythological criticism is the notion that texts point out the universality of the human experience and that we can use these stories to get at some objective truths about life. In this context, the word myth refers to stories beyond those about Greek, Roman, or Egyptian gods. Rather, myths are stories that reveal a culture's perception of itself, that show how human beings understand their own lives, and that attempt to explain a culture's origin, purpose, and future. Myths also show how many human experiences, such as life, death, and self-reflection, are universal. Most myths also contain archetypes, or characters, images, and themes, which symbolize meaningful experiences in human life. Some examples include death, rebirth, quests, descents to hell or ascents to heaven, the desire to know the future, and the desire to know one's origins.

Two of the most prominent proponents of this type of approach are Carl Jung and Joseph Campbell. It was Jung who developed a psychological theory of archetypes in his *Psychology of the Unconscious* (1916). Jung argued that there exists a collective unconscious that each human being is tapped into, and, therefore, there are certain symbols that everyone recognizes at a subconscious level. Joseph Campbell, best known for his 1985–1986 television series *The Power of Myth*, expanded on Jung's ideas. Campbell studied American Indian folklore and Arthurian romances. During his studies he found that similar themes appeared in the myths of these two vastly different cultures. One of the common themes is the idea of the hero's journey. In fact, Campbell inspired filmmaker George Lucas when he was writing the script for *Star Wars*. Campbell argued that because myths are similar across cultures, they must contain evidence of some fundamental truths about the human experience.

Archetypal/mythological critics would find much to say about Welty's "A Worn Path," but rather than focusing on Phoenix as an African American woman dealing with the racist living conditions of 1940s Mississippi, they would point out how Phoenix's story taps into the universal human experience of resurrection, or the hero's journey. Like formalist critics, archetypal/mythological critics would be quick to note the importance of the main character's name and the story of the Phoenix as a whole. They might also, however, discuss the universal theme of the hero's quest. Although her task, to obtain a bottle of medicine for her sick grandchild, is seemingly small, it is in fact filled with important meaning. As we find out, as soon as Phoenix reaches the doctor's office, her grandson's life hangs in the balance, which is why she is willing to risk her life, as the hunter points out to us when he tells her to return home. Like all heroes, Phoenix faces many challenges including thorns, the hot sun, a log across a creek, a dangerous dog, and a racist hunter. Much like Odysseus, Phoenix must be crafty as she negotiates her challenges. Her trickery of the hunter exemplifies this point and puts Phoenix in a long tradition of crafty heroes. And like all heroes, it takes the journey for her to remember her priorities. Although she initially forgets why she has traveled to town, once she remembers, she achieves a kind of rebirth and certainty. She rises from the ashes renewed and ready to journey home to her grandson.

Sociological Criticism

Unlike the archetypal/mythological critic, the sociological critic maintains that a literary work cannot be separated from the social and cultural context in which it was written. Rather than tapping into universal human truths and experiences, literature is a reflection of a particular society and its values. The sociological critic analyzes literature with the goal of explaining how a text exemplifies or reveals something about society's structure.

Feminist/Gender Criticism

Feminist/gender criticism was first defined as an approach to literary analysis in the late 1960s. Mary Ellman's *Thinking about Women* (1968), for example, points out that male authors often use stereotypes when portraying female characters. Kate Millet's *Sexual Politics* (1969) maintains that social power structures encourage men to dominate women. Although feminist critics often use a variety of theoretical perspectives to make their arguments, their primary agenda is to show how a literary work reflects or challenges a patriarchal (male dominated) view of society.

Feminists also point out that femaleness and maleness are socially constructed. Simone de Beauvoir, one of the most famous feminists, maintained that a person's gender identity is not determined by his or her sex, but by cultural conditioning. Furthermore, female is defined primarily as different from or "other" than male. The female is too often thought of as passive, emotional, and irrational as opposed to the male who is assertive, stoic, and rational.

The canon—those works deemed the best and most relevant—is often challenged by feminists. They maintain that most women authors are excluded from this group and therefore they work to include previously ignored texts by women. "A Worn Path" would be of special interest to feminist critics because it is written by a woman at a time when most of the literature defined as "great" was written by men.

Feminists might read "A Worn Path" as a story about a woman attempting to navigate patriarchal society. They might pay special attention to Phoenix's encounter with the hunter, her one direct interaction with a male in the story. Phoenix is impoverished, elderly, and single. Consequently, she is responsible for herself in a society in which she has very little power. A feminist critic might argue that Welty's story shows what a woman must do to survive in a culture in which she has little power. Phoenix takes advantage of the fact that the hunter views her as weak because she is a "Grandma." She craftily tricks the hunter so that she can get the dime he has dropped. Phoenix is also forced to maintain her dignity in the face of potential violence. When the hunter points his gun at her, she stands firm and defiant against it. A feminist critic might argue that Welty is demonstrating how difficult it is for women to survive given the sexism that pervades society.

Gay and Lesbian or Queer Theory

Gay and lesbian or queer theory maintains that all literary texts are representations of sexual identities. The gay and lesbian or queer theory critic looks for evidence of hidden sexual identities and tries to expose it. In this way, these critics work to push the meanings "out of the closet" or to help them come out. Often, a story's characters are studied using this paradigm. Critics look for the ways in which a character's identity is based on his or her sexuality.

A queer theory critic might focus on the absence of sexual identity in "A Worn Path." In choosing to make the main character a "grandma," Welty removes a discussion of sexuality from the story. This shapes her interactions with whites. While a young woman (of any race) traveling in the woods might have to fear for her sexual safety when encountering a male hunter, the elderly woman, although threatened, has less to fear in terms of being sexually molested by him. Furthermore, this fact provides the story with an inherent innocence. Phoenix and her grandson are both at ages when sex and all of the conflict associated with it, are, at least in most readers' minds, not an issue. The elderly and children are both viewed by conventional society as pure in this respect, and thus the conventional reader is more likely to sympathize with their plights and easily associate them with transcendence. Other readers, however, might find that these characteristics of the story are limitations that make it less relevant.

Marxist Criticism

The social and economic theories of Karl Marx form the basis of Marxist criticism. Marx and his colleague Frederich Engels argued that the capitalist middle class exploits the working class. Since the middle class is primarily responsible for producing the cultural products that people interact with, the subtext of these products supports the capitalist power structure. Engels and Marx both believed that eventually the working class will overthrow the middle class, but, until that time, society and its structures are inherently tainted by the values and agenda of the bourgeoisie (middle class).

The Marxist critic applies these theories to literary analysis by looking for the ways in which texts are a product of capitalist middle-class ideology, and a Marxist critic would have much to say about how "A Worn Path" is a reflection of those ideas. The Marxist critic would pay much attention to Phoenix's impoverishment and argue that the middle class degrades the working class through economic means. Phoenix is forced to pilfer a dime from the hunter because she knows that he would probably rather keep 10 cents than help a suffering, elderly woman. Similarly, Phoenix is concerned with her appearance in town because middle-class values maintain that appearance is the most important thing. She is too old to bend over and tie her shoes, but because she must look presentable, she goes out of her way to stop a woman carrying packages and asks for help. In addition, the fact that she must travel so far, and at such risk to herself, to acquire the life-sustaining medicine for her grandson makes evident that they do not have adequate access to health care.

Biographical Criticism

The biographical critic studies an author's life experiences to determine how they have shaped an author's work. Although it is tempting to assume that literary texts are actually memoirs in disguise, students should not assume that the experiences depicted in a work of literature are necessarily experiences of the writer. Often, the writer uses imaginary characters to illuminate some territory of the human experience, to depict the experiences of others—not necessarily his or her own.

The biographical critic would be quick to point out the similarities between her life and the events and characters in the short story "A Worn Path." Welty was born in 1909 in Jackson, Mississippi. Similarly, the story is set in Natchez, Mississippi. After attending high school and college, Welty returned home in 1931 after her father died. When her mother and brother fell ill, she became their caretaker and helped support the family financially through her writing. A biographical critic might also point out how Phoenix is the primary caretaker of her grandson. The biographical analysis might end at this point, however, and ignore some of the most interesting aspects of the story, including the fact that the author, Eudora Welty, is white and her main character, Phoenix Jackson, is African American.

Reader-Response Criticism

In direct contrast to formalism, reader-response criticism puts the reader at the center of the interpretation. A literary text, reader-response critics argue, is not separate and closed off. One might think of a literary text as a piece of chocolate cake. Everyone has a unique experience when they eat chocolate cake. We all bring different past experiences, different tastes, and different agendas when we come to the table. Similarly, each reader has a different understanding of a text, and many may be equally valid. Reader-response critics also stress that a reader may interpret a text differently the second or third time he or she reads it. This is called recursive-reading. For example, a newly married woman who read Alice Munro's "How I Met My Husband" in college might have a new and completely different perspective on the text than she did when she was a younger woman.

Reader-response criticism was first formulated by Norman Holland in *The Dynamics of Literary Response* (1968). German critic Wolfgang Iser followed Holland in 1974 arguing in his *The Implied Reader* that an effective reader must be familiar with the "codes" of writing. Consequently, reader-response criticism changes the purpose of the classroom. Rather than using it to teach students the correct interpretation of a text, the classroom is best used to instruct students in the methods and tools used by writers. Although there may not be one single interpretation of a text, one can learn the techniques available to writers. In 1980 Stanley Fish proposed that readers have similar responses to a text depending on their backgrounds. Readers with similar educational, socioeconomic, and political backgrounds will probably interpret a particular text in similar ways.

Eudora Welty's "A Worn Path" might be interpreted in a variety of ways depending on the experiences of the readers. A college student interested in the civil rights movement of the 1960s might focus on how the story is a commentary on rampant racism in the South. A middle-aged woman reading Welty's story for pleasure might respond by noting the loneliness and poverty that some elderly people are forced to confront. A male psychology major might attempt to determine whether Phoenix is mentally stable. Reader-response critics would argue that each of these responses is worthwhile.

Psychological or Psychoanalytical Criticism

Psychological or psychoanalytical criticism analyzes literature from the position that texts express the inner workings of the human mind. Much of this kind of criticism is drawn from the theories of Sigmund Freud (1846–1939), who is considered to be the founder of psychoanalysis. Freud argued that most humans are motivated by impulses of which they are unaware, that is, unconscious impulses. Society, he said, operates in such a way that we are forced to repress many of our natural instincts and desires. These instincts and desires do not simply disappear; they move to the unconscious part of our minds. To access the unconscious, Freud believed that we can examine our dreams or our culture. Literature, then, is a reflection of our unconscious.

Freud's division of the mind was actually more complicated than simply the conscious and the unconscious. He argued that the mind can be divided into the id, the ego, and the superego. The id is the irrational or emotional part of the mind. Some call it the primitive mind. The id contains all of our basic needs and emotions. It is also the source of libido sexual desire, and it operates according to the "pleasure principle." The id is what encourages us to seek instant gratification. The ego is a more rational part of the mind. It develops as we realize that living by the pleasure principle alone has grave consequences; therefore, it operates on the "reality principle." The ego actually works with the superego—which will be discussed shortly—and the id so that we maintain a balance between instant gratification and self-denial. The superego is what some might call the moral part of the mind. It tells us what our parents and, eventually, society values. It can also cause us a great deal of anxiety, however, since it tells us constantly to strive for perfection.

Two other concepts are important to familiarize yourself with before beginning a literary analysis using psychological or psychoanalytical criticism: the Oedipus complex and projection. Freud is perhaps best known for his theory called the Oedipus complex, named for the character in Sophocles' play. According to Freud, all young boys repress a desire to have sexual intercourse with their mothers and kill their fathers. As they grow into manhood, they repress this desire, and most resolve it before they reach puberty. Projection is a defense mechanism in which we identify in others impulses and flaws that are actually our own.

A psychoanalytic reading of "A Worn Path" might focus on whether Phoenix is mentally stable and point to the distinct possibility that she is repressing her grandson's death. Throughout the story, there are indications that she may not be in her right mind. As she walks along the path, Phoenix mistakes thorns for "a pretty little green bush." Phoenix continues on her way but sits down to rest and imagines that she sees a little boy bringing her a plate of marble-cake. She then asks a buzzard who it is watching. Later in the journey she mistakes a scarecrow for a ghost. Finally, once she reaches her destination, she forgets her purpose in coming.

The psychological critic might argue that once the reader finds out that Phoenix has traveled to get medicine for her dying grandson, it is clear that, in fact, her grandson has very likely already died. The nurse says that it is unusual for someone to suffer from this condition for so long, and she even asks her whether he has died. Phoenix responds that he has not died and that he is waiting for her to return. "We is the only two left in the world," she says. "He suffer and it don't seem to put him back at all." She continues and then says that she is not "going to forget him again, no, the whole enduring time." These words might be interpreted by the critic as an indication that the grandson has died. Perhaps Phoenix has difficulty remembering him because he passed away a long time ago. It seems odd that she would forget her purpose when she left him only half a day ago. Furthermore, her desire to believe he is alive is understandable given her age, her loneliness, and her poverty. It is clear that Phoenix's primary purpose in life is to take care of her sick grandchild. She has taken money not for herself, but to purchase a gift for him. Without this purpose, there is nothing left for her to do. Her words, "We is the only two left in the world," make this point particularly clear.

This interpretation by the psychological critic would, however, be quite at odds with the *writer's* intentions for the story. Eudora Welty has written an essay entitled "Is Phoenix Jackson's Grandson Really Dead?"* in which she makes clear that he is surely alive.

Cultural Criticism and Culture Studies

Cultural criticism is much like new historicism in that it emphasizes how literary texts are often windows into competing ideologies prevalent in a culture. One theory that was not discussed earlier, but is particularly relevant to cultural criticism is postcolonialism. The term postcolonialism was first coined by Edward Said in his book *Orientalism* (1978), in which Said argues that Europeans and Americans frequently use negative stereotypes to describe people of color. They often view themselves as good and moral and "other" people and cultures as inferior, lazy, deceitful, or irrational, for example. Consequently, postcolonialist criticism examines the ways in which negative stereotypes and assumptions shape how people of color are depicted in literary works. Furthermore, postcolonialists examine the position of the author who is writing a particular literary work. Like new historicist critics, postcolonialists point out that women and people of color have long been excluded from the canon. They also point out that people of color have rarely had the opportunity to tell their own stories.

---

*Found in *The Eye of the Story: Selected Essays and Reviews* by Eudora Welty (Random House, 1955), 159–162.

The postcolonial critic might point out, for example, that as a white woman, Welty is limited in her ability to tell the story of an African American woman. Although Welty may be able to empathize with an African American woman's plight, she can certainly never know what it was really like. They might point out that, sadly, there has often been an effort to prevent African Americans from telling their own stories. The new historicist critic would also, however, have to acknowledge his or her own cultural and historical perspective and that the values and power structures of the present inform his or her interpretation of the story.

Deconstructionist Criticism

Deconstruction was first introduced by the French philosopher Jacques Derrida. Derrida said that literary texts are actually representative of larger systems of discourse and so literary texts are representations of ideologies, or systems of belief. Derrida maintained that ideologies are defined not only by what they value, but what they do not value, and so it is essential that we identify opposites. For example, someone writing from a Christian perspective might "privilege" (or value more highly) the beliefs of a Christian character in contrast to those of a Buddhist. Consequently, the deconstructionist identifies opposition in a literary text as a means of uncovering the belief system that the text supports. Like formalists, deconstructionists play close attention to language and attempt to uncover the various meanings that it can contain.

A deconstructionist might point to the many potential readings of Phoenix's statements in the charity hospital. When answering the nurse's question about whether the grandson is dead, Phoenix is initially certain, but goes on to say more cryptically, "We is the only two left in the world . . . I remembers so plain now. I not going to forget him again, no, the whole enduring time. I could tell him from all the others in creation." Phoenix could be making some sweet and sentimental comments about her grandson, or she could be telling the reader that, in fact, her grandson is dead. Another possible interpretation is that she is indicating that she and her grandson are the only true human beings left given the racist climate in which they are living. Or, her initial confusion could simply be due to the fact that she is aged and his just taken a long journey. All of these potential interpretations would be accepted by the deconstructionist.

Eclectic Criticism

The best informed readers know how to think for themselves and employ an eclectic approach when analyzing literature. As you can see, many schools of thought actually overlap in some ways, so even the separate schools of criticism contain an element of eclecticism. A familiarity with each approach will help you read in more layered and interesting ways, but do not confine yourself to one way of thinking. Remember that to think critically means to approach a text with confidence and with questions. When you analyze a piece of literature, consider literary criticism as a tool rather than a set of rules you must follow.

GLOSSARY
of Literary Terms

absurd Ridiculous, meaningless, illogical; the novel, short story or play that presents a reality in which the authority of rationality and the straightforward evidence of common sense no longer hold sway. In Joseph Heller's novel, *Catch 22*, the central character, Yossarian, desperately wants to stop flying combat missions. He is told that only the insane are barred from flying, but anyone who wants to stop flying to avoid being killed must be sane; therefore, he must keep flying. That is Catch-22, the regulation that rules the lives of all the characters in the novel.

actions Depicting the actions of a character is one way the author or dramatist has of establishing characterization.

active reading The active reader, unlike the passive one, is experiencing the text more fully, with critical thinking skills engaged, alert to techniques and thematic nuances within the text at hand and to possible connections to other texts.

allegorical tale A work in which characters, events and objects on the literal level may also represent abstractions. In an allegory, elements that represent ideas beyond the literal level usually have a one-to-one correspondence with those ideas (in contrast to the use of symbolism, in which a single event, character or object may give rise to multiple meanings). The most commonly used example of allegory is John Bunyan's *Pilgrim's Progress*, in which the main character (Christian) journeys through adventures and hardships (such as the Slough of Despond) to reach his destination (the Celestial City). An animal allegory (or beast fable) is a tale featuring animal characters who exemplify human behavior.

alliteration The repetition of consonant sounds.

allusive/allusion An indirect reference to another text, or historical personage or event. Some types of allusion are: biblical, literary, historical and mythological.

ambiguity A text, character or event that has multiple possible meanings is ambiguous.

This effect is usually intentional on the part of the writer and adds thematic complexity to the work.

analysis/analyze In general terms, to analyze means to break the whole down into its parts, in order to better understand how it operates.

analysis vs. explication, of a poem When using these terms to describe rhetorical strategies, explication is usually understood to mean the examination of several aspects of a work; whereas analysis might focus on one element or aspect. An analysis of two poems might focus on the two poets' similar use of imagery; an explication might consider line breaks, meter, figurative language and sound, as well as imagery, in the two works.

anapestic A metrical foot consisting of two unstressed syllables followed by one stressed syllable.

antagonist The force that opposes the protagonist (the main character).

apostrophe In this use of figurative language, the speaker addresses an animal, object or absent human character.

archetype A cross-cultural story pattern. Basic types of stories, character types and concepts that recur in many different cultures. For example, peoples all over the earth tell stories of the creation of the world, of the hero's quest, of death and rebirth, of a supreme being or beings, of initiation (or coming-of-age), of apocalypse (end of the world) and afterlife. Flood stories (like the story of Noah in Judeo-Christian scriptures) are also common to almost all cultures.

argument, in a literary essay A literary discussion often presents a thesis and argues for that thesis by presenting evidence from the text (quotations and specific examples from the work).

assonance The repetition of vowel sounds.

avant-garde Literally, the "advance guard." We would call a work avant-garde if it uses new techniques (cutting-edge techniques) in the creation of an art form. These works are the most innovative, the most experimental—they play around with fictional, poetic or dramatic form, and they may use unorthodox content as well.

Avant-Pop This is a blending of two terms—avant-garde and pop culture. The concept of avant-pop has to do with the influence of media like television, comic books and movies and the borrowing of pop culture or common culture texts into the writing of fiction, poetry or drama. Avant-pop writers and artists resist the avant-garde attitude that ignores and abhors popular culture. Instead, their work embraces the intersection and interaction of present day commerce, advertising and technology with art and literature.

ballad A narrative poem which can be sung or recited.

ballad stanza A poem composed of quatrains in which the first and third lines are in iambic tetrameter and do not rhyme; the second and fourth lines are in iambic trimester and do rhyme.

behavior Revealing the behavior of a character is one way the author or dramatist has of establishing characterization.

block quotation A longer quotation, set off from the text by additional indentation.

brainstorming When generating ideas for developing an essay it is often helpful to brainstorm, making random associations and jotting down ideas informally.

caricature A character whose most pronounced and visible traits are overdrawn, exaggerated and distorted. For example, political cartoonists seize on one aspect of the appearance of national figures (Bill Clinton's nose, George W. Bush's ears) and build their caricatures around that feature by enlarging and embellishing it.

character A fictional person who is part of the narrative of a novel or short story. A "flat character" might be the waitress who brings the young couple their drinks at the café in Hemingway's short story "Hills Like White Elephants". She is simply there to perform a service that the reality of the scene requires. A "round character" would be Jig, the young woman who desperately wants to keep her child and whose short conversation with her lover reveals the impossibility of her situation and her growing realization of what kind of man her lover is. Characters are not always strictly "human" (Hal the murderous computer in *2001* or Smaug, the treasure hoarding dragon in J.R.R. Tolkien's *The Hobbit*), but these non-human characters always possess human traits (HAL's blind obedience to "the mission" and Smaug's greed) and they interact with other characters in much the same way that humans would.

characterization The development of a character; the depiction of a character in a work of literature.

chronologically In order by the calendar or by the clock; arranged in the order of occurrence.

cite the source Provide a parenthetical reference to the source in which a particular quotation or piece of information appears.

climax The point in a novel, story or play at which the most significant and meaningful action or event takes place.

close reading A close reading of a literary text is a detailed exploration of how the elements of a literary work (such as symbolism, figurative language, rhythm, line breaks) may work together to achieve a unified effect.

clustering See "brainstorming," above. When generating ideas for an essay, some writers also find it useful to scatter the words and phrases on a page in a deliberately disorderly fashion, in order to make new connections between ideas. Often writers may circle words or phrases and connect them to others with lines or arrows, to visualize relationships between concepts and topics.

coming-of-age stories A story which helps reveal the process of growth or increased awareness in the life of a young character. Also called an initiation story.

comparison and contrast A rhetorical mode which involves analyzing the similarities and differences between two works. Often the word "comparison" alone is also understood to mean a weighing of both likenesses and differences.

conflict In fiction or drama, the struggle or tension between the protagonist and the force that opposes the protagonist. Conflict may be external (character vs. character, character vs. environment) or internal (character vs. herself or himself).

connotative The connotative meaning of a word encompasses those associations that go beyond the dictionary (denotative) meaning.

contemporary sonnets Poems that incorporate variations on the traditional patterns. Some contemporary poets have made minor or more substantial alterations to the traditional sonnet form, and these poems are called contemporary sonnets. A contemporary sonnet may also make use of specific images taken from ordinary life; the use of assonance and slant rhyme or near rhyme is common. There is less emphasis on discovering a "sublime subject" and more on accommodating the form to the rhythms of everyday language.

contextual symbol A symbol that gathers a particular meaning within the context of a given literary work. A cultural or conventional symbol, on the other hand, is more widely recognized to have a broadly-understood meaning (the Christian cross or the Star of David are conventional symbols; the quilt and butter churn in Alice Walker's story "Everyday Use" are contextual symbols).

controlling metaphor A metaphor which is carried throughout all or part of a work. Also called extended metaphor.

conventional plot A plot containing the traditional structure of rising action, climax, falling action (denouement) and resolution.

conventional symbol A symbol with broadly understood meanings, as opposed to a "contextual symbol" (see above).

cosmic irony We recognize cosmic irony when there is a discrepancy between what characters desire or demand and what the universe (or fate, or God) provides.

couplet A pair of verse lines, often unified thematically and often rhyming.

dactylic A metrical foot consisting of one stressed syllable followed by two unstressed syllables.

denotative The denotative meaning of a word is its meaning according to the dictionary. See also "connotative."

dénouement Quite literally, "the untying of a knot," in French. This is the point at which the aftermath of the climax (in a short story or play) is presented to the reader, the concluding events leading to the end of the story, novel or play.

dialect Language usage peculiar to a specific region, urban area or cultural group.

dialogue Conversation between characters in a work; language spoken aloud; speech.

diction Language usage. The level of diction the writer chooses to use may be formal, informal, colloquial, or (most commonly), middle diction. "Dialect" (above) is also a term related to an author's or character's use of language.

dimeter A line of poetry that contains two metrical feet.

drama A work of literature written to be performed; a play.

dramatic irony Irony arises from the discrepancy between what the audience knows and what a character or characters know.

dynamic character A character who changes over the course of the work, as opposed to a static character.

eclectic An eclectic approach to analyzing and discussing literature leaves readers free to make use of whatever analytical strategies are helpful in exploring a work of fiction, poetry or drama. In other words, we are not limited to the methods of one critical approach but may see a work of literature from multiple perspectives and using various methods for analyzing the work.

editorializing omniscient narrator A narrative strategy in which the third person omniscient narrator may make judgments about the events or characters in the work, as opposed to a "neutral omniscient narrator," who does not make such judgments.

elements of drama Aspects of the dramatic genre, such as plot, characterization, setting and theme.

elements of fiction Aspects of the fictional genre, such as plot, characterization, setting and theme.

elements of literature Those terms that create a common critical vocabulary for the understanding, appreciation and discussion of literature. Meter, rhyme, image and scansion are all terms closely associated with poetry. Plot, character, setting and point-of-view are essential elements of both fiction and drama.

elements of poetry Aspects of the craft of poetry, such as speaker, line breaks, sound, rhythm and rhyme.

end rhyme The most common type of rhyme in poetry. Sounds at the ends of lines rhyme with one another.

end-stopped lines Lines of poetry which end with a full stop or significant pause, as opposed to "run-on lines."

English sonnet A poem of fourteen lines consisting of three quatrains and a concluding couplet and using the following rhyme scheme: *abab cdcd efef gg*. Also called a Shakespearean sonnet.

enjambment The use of a line of poetry in which the grammatical sense of the line runs down to the next line. A run-on line, as opposed to an "end-stopped line" (see above). The word enjambment is from the French and means "to straddle."

envoi (or **envoy**) A brief formal stanza concluding a poem.

epiphany An understanding, insight or revelation—often sudden—that shows the true nature of the situation to the character and the reader. This often occurs by means of a specific event: a passage of dialogue, a specific action or experience on the part of a character. Literally, a "showing forth."

eponymous A character who represents not just his or her individual experience but the experience of an entire people or an entire cultural group.

exact rhyme Rhyming words have identical sounds, as opposed to "near rhyme" or "slant rhyme" (below).

explication vs. analysis, of a poem See "analysis vs. explication, of a poem" (above).

exposition, in fiction The setting forth of information, often early in a work and often revealing the characters' situation.

extended metaphor See "controlling metaphor" (above).

exterior setting Physical setting involving outdoor (as opposed to indoor) setting; may involve climate, weather, season, terrain, urban or rural landscape.

external conflict See "conflict" (above).

extrinsic In the analysis of works of literature, extrinsic considerations would be those that are outside the boundaries of the story, poem or play itself. They would include, for example, biographical information about the author or reference to the historical context in which the work was written.

falling action In a conventional plot structure, the latter scenes of a work of fiction or drama, in which the characters' problems or conflicts are proceeding toward resolution. Also known as the dénouement (in French, "the untying of the knot").

fantasy A work or part of a work that is fantastic, or nonrealistic. Not taking place in the real world.

feet See foot.

fiction A literary work (usually of prose) relating events that did not actually happen but are invented by the author.

fiction into film A discussion of two art forms that examines and compares a work in fiction form and its treatment in cinematic form.

figurative language Language that is not meant literally but figuratively. See "figures of speech" (below).

figures of speech Literary devices such as metaphor, simile, personification and apostrophe, in which what is stated is not meant literally but is instead meant to provoke a fresh perception of the subject.

first person plural In fiction, a narrative point of view strategy employing the first person plural pronouns ("we," "us," "our") in order to tell the story from a collective first person view.

first person singular In fiction, a narrative point of view strategy employing the first person singular pronouns ("I," "me," "my") in order to tell the story from the first person point of view of a single character. This is the most common type of first person narration.

first person voice The term voice refers to all aspects of the narrative perspective. In addition to noting the first person point of view, it might also be used to discuss diction, style, level of usage, or dialect, if relevant.

fixed form Poetry written according to traditional fixed patterns (such as the sonnet, villanelle or haiku), as opposed to open form poetry.

flashbacks In fiction, scenes or passages that depict events from an earlier time, out of the chronological sequence of the story's present.

flat character In fiction or drama, a minor character that is not fully developed in the way that central characters need to be.

foil character A character whose behavior or attributes are in contrast to another, usually major character, thus serving to illuminate the different behavior of the more central character.

foot In poetry, a metrical term to describe a unit of measurement consisting of a combination of stressed and unstressed syllables. When a pattern of metrical feet emerges, the poem is said to have meter. The most common types of metrical feet in English are "iambic," "anapestic," "trochaic" and "dactylic" (see each).

foreshadowing In fiction or drama, clues or intimations regarding events yet to come in the narrative.

form In literary works, related to the structure or convention the piece adheres to. See also, "open form."

free verse See "open form."

freewriting In the writing process, "brainstorming" or free association in the generation of ideas for an essay or other piece of writing.

fully omniscient In fiction, a narrative strategy that employs the all-knowing third person narrator. The fully omniscient narrator may report past, present or future events and may also provide access to the internal thoughts and feelings of more than one character.

genres In literary discussion, types or kinds of literature (fiction, poetry and drama).

haiku A fixed form of poetry originating in Japanese literature. The haiku has seventeen syllables arranged in three lines of five, seven and five syllables. The three line endings are unrhymed.

heptameter A line of poetry that contains seven metrical feet.

hexameter A line of poetry that contains six metrical feet.

historical setting In fiction or drama, aspects of the setting which relate to the time period or cultural context in which the events of the story take place. For example, the historical setting of Ernest Hemingway's "Soldier's Home" is post World War I.

hyperbole A "figure of speech" (see above) that employs overstatement or exaggeration.

hypothesis A theory; a tentative explanation or statement that can be revised after further inquiry, research and study.

iambic foot A metrical "foot" (see above) consisting of one unstressed syllable followed by one stressed syllable.

imagery Language which appeals to the senses (sight, sound, touch, taste, smell).

imaginative writing Literature is imaginative writing because it is not restricted to conveying factual knowledge but involves invented characters and events as well.

initiation stories See "coming-of-age stories" (above).

in medias res From Latin, meaning "into the middle of things." In discussions of plot, this refers to a story or drama that begins in the middle of the events depicted in the work, rather than at the chronological beginning.

interior setting An indoor setting, in fiction or drama, as opposed to an "exterior setting" (see above).

internal conflict Conflict that takes place within a character, as opposed to "external conflict." Also see "conflict" (above).

internal rhyme In poetry, a rhyme scheme that makes use of some rhyming words appearing embedded within lines of poetry, rather than at the ends of lines. Etheridge Knight's "Watts Mother Mourns While Boiling Beans" employs a very precise scheme of internal rhyme.

intertextuality The technique of blending in images, references and sometimes whole passages from the media and pop culture into literary works. This can have startling and sometimes hilarious effects. The term intertextuality is also often used to refer to a text that incorporates snippets (or even whole chunks) of any other text.

in-text citation A source citation which appears within the essay rather than in the list of works cited at the end. See Chapter 33 "MLA Documentation Guidelines" for details.

intrinsic In the analysis of works of literature, intrinsic considerations would be those that are within the boundaries of the story, poem or play itself. They would include, for example, considerations related to form, technique and content of the work itself.

introductory paragraph A paragraph at the beginning of an essay in which the writer states the thesis and gives some sense of how the essay will seek to support or demonstrate that thesis.

irony The use of irony in literature (as in daily discourse) involves a contrast or discrepancy of some sort. "Situational irony" involves a discrepancy between appearance and reality, or a discrepancy between what the reader expects to happen and what actually does happen. "Verbal irony" (or sarcasm) involves a contrast between what is said and what is actually meant. "Dramatic irony" involves a discrepancy between what the reader knows and what a character or characters know. See "cosmic irony" also.

Italian sonnet A poem of fourteen lines that contains an octave (eight line stanza) and a sestet (six line stanza) and has the rhyme scheme *abbaabba cdecde* (or sometimes *cdccdc*). Also called a Petrarchan sonnet, after the fourteenth century Italian poet and practitioner of the form, Petrarch.

juxtaposition In poetry, the placing of two contrasting ideas or images side by side, in order to highlight or emphasize them, or to increase their emotional impact.

limited omniscient In narrative strategy, a third person point of view in which the narrator has access to the thoughts and feelings of only one character (or, rarely, two characters).

line breaks In poetry, refers to the way in which the poet has chosen to break the lines. A work may have short lines, for instance, creating a staccato effect. Or a poem may have long and flowing lines, as do many of the poems of Walt Whitman.

literary symbol A "contextual symbol" (see above) which is specific to a literary work or works but may not have the same meaning in the language generally. This is in contrast to a "conventional symbol" or cultural symbol that has a more broadly understood meaning.

lyric poem A poem that expresses the thoughts and feelings of a single speaker, in contrast to a "narrative poem" (see below).

magical realism In fiction, the use of mythical or fantastic details side by side with utterly realistic details. The best known practitioner of this technique is Gabriel García Márquez (see his story "A Very Old Man with Enormous Wings" in Chapter 9).

major character A character who is central to the action of a work of fiction or drama.

metafiction Fiction in which there is an awareness in the foreground of the story that a fiction is being created. Also called "self-reflexive narration" (see below). Tim O'Brien's story "How to Tell a True War Story" (Chapter 11) is an example of self-reflexive narration.

metaphor A "figure of speech" (see above) which employs a direct comparison of two dissimilar things. Claribel Alegría's poem, "I Am Mirror" (Chapter 15), for instance, the title itself contains the metaphorical statement that the speaker of the poem is a mirror.

meter In poetry, a pattern of stressed and unstressed syllables which can be measured in metrical feet (see "foot" above).

methods of characterization The various means by which an author of fiction or drama develops and reveals characters. Among these methods are: dialogue, exposition, behavior, physical appearance and thoughts.

metonymy A "figure of speech" (see above) in which an idea or thing is represented by something closely associated with it. For instance, the use of the phrase "silver screen" to represent the film industry is a metonymy.

mimesis In literary discourse, the word mimesis (from Greek) is used to refer to the way in which literary works are a reflection of (or imitation of) real life.

minimalism Minimalism in literature involves a spareness of style and an economy of form. For the minimalist, the emphasis is on imparting as little as possible in order to engage the reader's imaginative impulse to supply the missing details, action and meaning. The restraint and economy of many of Donald Barthelme's short stories would serve as a prime example of contemporary minimalism.

minimalist See minimalism.

minor character A character who is peripheral to the action of a work of fiction or drama and is therefore not as well-developed as the central characters.

mixed point of view A narrative point of view strategy that incorporates more than one of the traditional types of point of view. For example, Ralph Ellison's story "Flying Home" (Chapter 6) makes use of both first person and third person narration.

modern drama Dramatic works (plays) of the modern period, which is characterized by attention to realistic detail in sets and characterization, use of the vernacular in dialogue, a willingness to write about difficult social issues and an examination of the lives of ordinary characters, rather than the wealthy or well-born.

motivation Plausible grounds for a character's actions.

myth Myths are simply the stories we human beings have told ourselves to help explain our world—the social context as well as the natural world. Myths often grow out of oral "folk tale" traditions and help convey explanations of the world and the culture from one generation to the next. Some of these stories are also part of religious scriptures (from various of the worlds' religions), and some contain elements of magic, imagination, history, moral or cultural teachings. Some also contain profound spiritual, social or philosophical truths.

naïve or **unreliable narrator** A narrator whose version of events is (whether intentionally or unintentionally) not always accurate. This unreliability may be unintentional on the part of the character (in the case of the naïve narrator), but it is a device used intentionally by the author.

narrative poem A poem that tells a story (as opposed to a "lyric poem," which does not).

narrative voice The term voice refers to all aspects of the narrative perspective. In addition to narrative point of view, it might also be used to discuss diction, style, level of usage, or dialect, if relevant.

near rhyme Rhyming words have approximate (rather than identical) sounds, as opposed to "exact rhyme" (above). Also called "slant rhyme." In the second stanza of Theodore Roethke's poem "My Papa's Waltz," the rhyming endings "shelf" and "itself" are an example of exact rhyme; whereas, the endings "pans" and "countenance" are examples of near rhyme.

neutral omniscient narrator A narrative strategy in which the third person omniscient narrator does not make judgments about the events or characters in the work, as opposed to an "editorializing omniscient narrator," who does make such judgments.

nonrealistic A work or part of a work that makes use of magic, legend or myth. Fantastic; not taking place in the real world.

objective narrator A third person narrative strategy that does not provide internal access to any characters.

octameter A line of poetry containing eight metrical feet.

octave An eight-line stanza, especially the first eight lines of an "Italian sonnet" (see above).

omniscient In fiction, a narrative point of view that is all-knowing; that is, it can provide internal access to characters as well as information about past, present or future events.

onomatopoeia A "figure of speech" (see above) in which the word itself sounds like what is meant (for example, "hiss" or "fizzle").

open-ended A work in which there is no definite resolution or closure at the end. This is intentional on the part of the author, and it is often characteristic of works of the modern period, during which there has been a greater tendency to allow the reader to make up his or her own mind about how to interpret characters and events.

open form Poetry that is not written according to traditional fixed patterns (see "fixed forms"), but is instead more spontaneous and organic in its form. Also called "free verse."

pantoum A poem of at least 16 lines, comprised of quatrains. The second and fourth lines of each stanza are repeated as the first and third lines of the following stanza. See Clement Long's "Always the One Who Loves His Father Most" (Chapter 19).

parenthetical references Citations within parentheses to identify the source for a quotation, paraphrase, or piece of information.

parody An imitation of another work that makes fun of the peculiarities of the original work's style or conventions.

past, present and future settings A work of literature may be set in more than one time frame. This is true, for instance, of the story "Babylon Revisited" by F. Scott Fitzgerald (Chapter 5) and of the play "Death of a Salesman" by Arthur Miller (Chapter 24).

pentameter A line of poetry containing five metrical feet.

personification A "figure of speech" (see above) in which human attributes are assigned to an animal or thing. For example, personification of the fish is important in Elizabeth Bishop's "The Fish" (Chapter 16).

perspective of a major character Seeing events through the point of view of a character central to the action of a story or play.

perspective of a minor character Seeing events through the point of view of a character peripheral to the action of a story or play.

persuasive essay An essay that presents, develops and defends an argument.

Petrarchan sonnet See "Italian sonnet."

physical appearance One method of characterization in works of literature is description of the physical appearance of characters.

physical description See "physical appearance" above.

physical setting Relates to physical aspects of the setting of a work, such as furniture, machinery or other objects in a room (interior setting), or landscape, buildings, streets or roads (exterior setting).

place (setting) A setting in literature that is effectively depicted is often said to convey a strong sense of place. The author succeeds in creating with words the atmosphere of a neighborhood, town, region or a character's home or workplace.

plagiarism A theft of the intellectual property of others, often by representing someone else's words as one's own.

plot In fiction and drama, the author's deliberate selection and arrangement of incidents in the work. The order of events. A plot may be arranged "chronologically" or nonchronologically.

poetry A literary form composed in rhymed or unrhymed lines. The poet may use "fixed forms" or "open form" (see above).

poetry quotations Quotations from poetry or quotations of verse from a dramatic work. When these are run in with the text of the essay, use a slash (/) to indicate line breaks. Use a double slash (//) to indicate stanza breaks.

point of view Who tells the story and how. First person point of view employs the perspective of the "I" voice (or, more rarely, the first person plural, or "we" voice). The narrator may also be a character in the story (of either minor or major importance to the action) and may speak to the reader directly from his involvement in the story. Third person narrators stand at a greater remove and as a result their perspective is different. A third person narrator may be *omniscient*, in which case the narrator moves freely from character to character and knows all there is to know. Or, a third person narrator may be *limited* to the point-of-view of one character. An *objective* third person narrative provides no access at all to the internal thoughts and feelings of characters. Instead, the objective narrator is like a dispassionate and uninvolved "camera eye," showing the external action but not entering the minds of any characters.

pop culture Culture that arises from the "populace": literature, music, visual art, dance, etc., that is created most often by individuals or groups who are thought to be without any kind of 'formal training' or background in the arts. Rap and rock are popular forms, as are TV reality show and sitcoms, graffiti and comic books.

primary source The original work of literature under discussion (as opposed to a "secondary source" that comments on the primary work).

protagonist The central character in a work.

pyrrhic foot A metrical "foot" (see above) consisting of two unstressed syllables. This is not one of the four commonly used metrical feet.

quatrains In poetry, a stanza consisting of four lines. The lines may be rhymed or unrhymed, and they may or may not adhere to a metrical pattern.

realism In literature, characterized by an effort to reflect real life, particularly the lives of ordinary people, as opposed to the wealthy or well-born.

realistic Characterized by "realism" (see above).

reliability/unreliability In fiction, related to narrative strategy. The reliable narrator can generally be trusted to relate events and feelings accurately; whereas, the unreliable narrator is often not trustworthy. See also "naïve or unreliable narrator" (above).

repetition In literary works, especially fiction and poetry, words or phrases might be repeated deliberately in order to achieve certain effects. In poetry, repetition is sometimes used in open form poetry to establish a rhythm.

resolution In fiction and drama, it is said that a work has resolution if the reader or audience is able to feel relatively certain about the outcome for the characters (whether that outcome is favorable or unfavorable). If a work does not have resolution, then it is said to be "open-ended" (see above). Also see "conventional plot" (above).

reversal A change in fortune for a character, or a change of course in the plot of a work. Often refers to an ironic outcome at the end of a work of fiction or drama.

rhetorical modes Devices, methods or structures for organizing sentences or essays. At the essay level, some rhetorical modes are "analysis" (especially "comparison and contrast"), "explication" and "argument" (see above).

rhyme scheme The pattern of rhyme established in a poem. See also "end rhyme," "internal rhyme" and "near rhyme"

rhythm Especially related to sound in poetry. A pattern of stressed and unstressed sounds that results in the sense of a beat, as in music. In some works, rhythm is forcefully established; in others, it is of lesser importance.

rising action In fiction and drama, the passages earlier in a work, in which the characters' situation is being set forth and the problems and conflicts are being revealed to the reader or audience. See also "conventional plot."

role In drama, the part (or character) that an actor or actress portrays.

round character In fiction or drama, a character that is more fully developed, usually a major character in the work. Contrast to "flat character" (above).

run-on lines Lines of poetry in which the grammatical sense of the line runs down to the next line. Lines that do not end with a full stop or significant pause, as opposed to "end-stopped" lines (see above). Also called "enjambment" (see above).

satire The use of humor, irony and sarcasm to poke fun at human faults and foibles, or to make a critique of human nature and human societies. Human behavior depicted at its most extreme and made ridiculous as a result. Characters in Mel Brooks movies satirize the straightforward versions of those characters in their original forms: scientists and monsters in *Young Frankenstein* or cowboys, gunslingers and townsfolk of the American West in *Blazing Saddles*.

scansion Analysis of the metrical pattern of a poem. See Chapter 17.

scene A unit of action in drama that takes place all in one time frame. In fiction, a passage that is dramatized, often using dialogue and action, as opposed to a passage of exposition.

schools of critical theory Refers to the variety of approaches to analyzing works of litera- ture; different theories about how to interpret literature.

script (of a play or screenplay) The format that presents all of the scenes, action, dialogue and narrative for a play or movie.

secondary source A work that is a commentary upon the "primary source" or primary work under discussion. Secondary sources may include critical articles and essays of analysis, as well as interviews and other materials related to examining a primary work.

second person voice Relates to narrative strat- egy in fiction. Narration using the second person pronoun "you."

self-reflexive narration In fiction, a narrative strategy in which there is an awareness in the foreground of the story that a fiction is being created. Also called "metafiction" (see above). Rudolfo Anaya's story "B. Traven Is Alive and Well in Cuernavaca" (chapter 3) is an example of self-reflexive narration.

self-reflexive story See "self-reflexive narra- tion" (above).

sensory details In a literary work, details which help engage the reader's senses (sight, sound, taste, touch, smell).

sestet A six-line stanza, especially the last six lines of an "Italian sonnet" (see above).

sestina A "fixed form" poem (see) containing six six-line stanzas and a concluding three- line "envoy" stanza (see) . This form follows a very precise and complex pattern of repeated line endings. All lines are unrhymed.

setting In any work of literature, refers to the time and place which are evoked or in which the events take place. Setting may involve "interior setting," "exterior setting," or "his- torical setting" (see all above). In addition to the "physical setting" (above) of a work, the social environment may also be an important part of the context in which the characters find themselves.

Shakespearean sonnet See "English sonnet" (above).

show, don't tell Advice often given to and by fiction writers. A story is usually more effec- tively evoked when the fiction includes dramatized "scenes" (see above), rather than excessive telling, or indirect exposition.

showing In fiction, using directly rendered "scenes" (see above) including dialogue and action, as well as description.

simile A "figure of speech" (see above) that makes an indirect comparison of two dissimi- lar things, using comparative words such as "like" or "as." In Robert Burns's "Oh, My Love Is Like a Red, Red Rose," the title itself contains a simile comparing the sweetheart to a rose, using the word "like."

situational irony A type of irony in which what happens is not what we expect to happen, or there is a discrepancy between appearance and reality.

slant rhyme See "near rhyme" (above).

slice-of-life story A story which is not strongly plotted but instead appears to be simply a "snapshot" or "still portrait" of a moment in life. Anton Chekhov, a master of this type of brief story, is often credited with being its first practitioner.

social setting In fiction or drama, aspects of the setting that relate to the characters' social environment.

sonnet A type of "fixed form" poem (see above) containing fourteen lines. See specifically "English sonnet" and "Italian sonnet."

sound In poetry, refers to any of the devices of sound in a poem (for example, "alliteration," "assonance," "rhyme" and "rhythm") or their effects.

speaker In poetry, the voice that articulates the poem. Equivalent to the narrator or "narrative voice" of a work of fiction.

spondee (metrical foot) A metrical "foot" (see above) consisting of two stressed syllables. This is not one of the four commonly used metrical feet.

staging In drama, refers to aspects of the arrangement of stage set, positioning of char- acters on stage, and the manner in which the written drama is to be depicted in a live performance. Often the playwright provides such instructions in the stage directions. See Chapter 24.

stanzaic forms Poetry in which the lines are arranged into stanzas.

static character A character who does not change over the course of the work, as opposed to a "dynamic character."

style The manner in which a given author uses language in a given work. May relate to diction, voice, sentence structure, pacing, use of dialect (if relevant), or use of figurative language.

symbol In literature, an object, character or event in a work that represents something beyond the literal level of meaning. In Nathaniel Hawthorne's "The Birthmark" (Chapter 8), Georgiana's birthmark is first of all a literal birthmark; but it also represents her mortality, her heart, her humanity and her connection to the natural world.

synecdoche A figure of speech in which a part of something represents the whole. For example, "wagging tongues" might be used to represent gossiping neighbors.

syntax Sentence structure.

tanka A "fixed form" (see above) of poetry originating in the Japanese language. The tanka always has 31 syllables.

telling In fiction, the revealing of information through exposition rather than through directly rendered scenes. Contrast with "showing" (above).

tercet In poetry, a three-line stanza, often one in which the three lines rhyme and have some thematic unity.

tetrameter A line of poetry containing four metrical feet.

theme or **themes** The meaning or meanings that arise from a work of literature. A complex and successful work usually has multiple possible meanings and multiple viable interpretations.

thesis An assertion or argument that a writer makes in an essay or article.

thesis statement A statement (usually of one sentence or possibly two) that sets forth the argument to be made in an analytical essay.

third person voice Relates to narrative strategy in fiction. Narration using third person pronouns, "he," "she," "it." Third person perspectives include the "omniscient," "limited omniscient" and "objective" narrators (see each, above).

thoughts In fiction, internal thoughts and feelings of a character, usually represented through the "first person voice" or the "limited omniscient" or "omniscient" voices. This is also one method the writer has for developing characterization.

time (as aspect of setting) See "past, present and future settings" (above).

tone Aspects of a work that reveal the author's attitude toward the subject. For example, the images and line breaks in e.e. cummings' poem "in Just-" (Chapter 14) suggest a playful tone; whereas, the use of word choice and descriptive detail in T. Coraghessan Boyle's story "Carnal Knowledge" (Chapter 7) reveal the author's sarcastic and mocking tone toward the characters

trimeter A line of poetry containing three metrical feet.

trochaic A metrical "foot" (see above) consisting of one stressed syllable followed by one unstressed syllable.

understatement A "figure of speech" (see above) in which the speaker says less than is meant (the opposite of "hyperbole").

universal symbol A "conventional symbol" (or "cultural symbol") that has broadly understood meanings beyond the literary work in which it may appear. See also "symbol" and "conventional symbol" (above).

unreliability See **naïve or unreliable narrator**.

verbal irony Saying the opposite of what is actually meant; sarcasm.

verisimilitude Literally, "real-seemingness." Refers to the achievement in fiction or drama of the appearance of reality.

vernacular Relates to diction in a work. The vernacular is ordinary language spoken by ordinary people. Middle, informal or colloquial diction, as opposed to formal diction. See also "diction" (above).

villanelle A "fixed form" of poetry (see above) containing five "tercets" and a concluding "quatrain" (see). Only two rhyming endings are permitted throughout the entire poem, in a complex pattern of repeated lines and endings. See Chapter 18.

voice This term applies especially to fiction and poetry and relates to the full spectrum of aspects relating to a "narrative voice" or "speaker": "diction," "tone," "syntax," "style" and "dialect" (if relevant). See each above. The term may also relate to "sound" in poetry.

well-integrated quotations Using quotations embedded in text in such as way that the syntax flows smoothly, with no breaks in the grammatical logic of the sentences.

word choice Especially in poetry, but in fiction as well, the author chooses words carefully to convey the intended "tone," "imagery" (see both above) and, ultimately, meaning.

word order In poetry, the order in which words appear in a line or stanza.

works cited list A list of secondary and primary sources that appears at the end of an analytical essay, if outside sources are used. See "MLA Documentation Guidelines" in Chapter 33.

PHOTO CREDITS

p. 278 © 2003 Penquin Group Inc.

p. 279 Al Franken photo by © Jan Cobb Photography Ltd.; Reprinted by permission of HarperCollins Publishing

Chapter Seven

p. 280–1 top and center, DFO, Inc. as registered trademark owner

p. 280–1 bottom, IHOP Corporation

p. 286 AP Photo/Paul Hawthorne

p. 297 AP Photo/Jim McKnight

p. 306 Giulio Marcocchi/Getty Images

p. 320 Sophie Bassouis/Corbis Sygma

Chapter Eight

p. 333 Image Source Ltd/RF/Index Stock

p. 333 bottom (shopping cart icon), Chad Baker/Getty Images

p. 338 Photo by Harcourt Brace/Getty Images

p. 346 Bettmann/Corbis

p. 357 China Stock

p. 365 Erich Hartmann/Magnum Photos

Chapter Nine

p. 374 Peter Willi/Bridgeman Art Library

p. 375 Nike and the Swoosh Design logo are trademarks of Nike, Inc. and its affiliates. Used by permission

p. 380 Rene Burri/Magnum Photos

p. 385 Bettmann/Corbis

p. 394 Bettmann/Corbis

p. 402 (Detail) © Nancy Crampton

p. 403 Columbia/The Kobal Collection

Chapter Ten

p. 414 top left, Joseph Sohm/ChromoSohm Inc./Corbis

p. 414–5 center, Wesley Treat/www.wesleytreat.com

p. 414 bottom, Park Street/PhotoEdit

p. 419 AP Photo/Eric Miller

p. 426 Steve Liss/Time Life Pictures/Getty Images

p. 436 Bettmann/Corbis

p. 449 The Granger Collection, NY

Chapter Eleven

p. 460 *Triple Self Portrait* by Norman Rockwell. The Norman Rockwell Art Collection Trust/The Norman Rockwell Museum at Stockbridge, Massachusetts. Printed by permission of the Norman Rockwell Family Agency © 1960 the Norman Rockwell Family Entities

p. 465 Jerry Bauer

p. 474 Patrick Harbron/Landov

p. 476 Mary Randlett

p. 480 Sophie Bassouis/Corbis Sygma

p. 484 Christopher Felver/Corbis

p. 489 Jerry Bauer

p. 498 MGM/The Kobal Collection

p. 499 David Young-Wolff/PhotoEdit

Chapter Twelve

p. 500–1 Author photo

Chapter Thirteen

p. 554 AP Photo

p. 558 AP Photo

p. 559 top, George Eastman House. Photo by Nickolas Muray © Nickolas Muray Photo Archives

p. 559 bottom, Photo by Griffith J. Davis courtesy of Griffith J. Davis Family Collection

p. 562 Henri Cartier-Bresson/Magnum Photos

Chapter Fourteen

p. 586–7 www.whereareyou.com

p. 626 AP Photo

p. 627 Landov

Chapter Fifteen

p. 628–9 John Coletti

p. 664 Greenfield Review Press. Photo: Carol Bruchac

Chapter Sixteen

p. 694 AP Photo/Gino Domenico

Chapter Seventeen

p. 696 top, The Meow Mix Company

p. 696 left, The Advertising Archive

p. 696–7 center, The BURGER KING™ are used with permission from Burger King Brands, Inc.

p. 724 Ebet Roberts

p. 725 left, Paul Natkin/Photo Reserve Inc./TIPS

p. 725 right, Shooting Star Agency

Chapter Eighteen

p. 726 top, Hallmark Cards, Inc.

p. 726 left, Hallmark Cards, Inc.

p. 726 bottom, Hallmark Cards, Inc. Photo: Hulton Archives/Getty Images

p. 744 Library of Congress, Washington, DC/Bridgeman Art Library

Chapter Nineteen

p. 772   top left, Steve Lipofsky/Index Stock
p. 772–3 top right, Morton Beebe/Corbis
p. 772   bottom left, Peter Johansky/Index Stock
p. 772–3 bottom right, Chase Swift/Corbis
p. 802   Hulton Archive/Getty Images

Chapter Twenty

p. 804   top, © 2005 Authorized Mercedes-Benz Dealers. Photo by Steve Cooper/Fox Creative
p. 804–5 center, © 2005 Audi of America, Inc.
p. 804   bottom, Courtesy, Lexus of Manhattan
p. 851   AP Photo/Stefano Paltera

Chapter Twenty-One

p. 852–3 (goth girl) Jonathan Torgovnik/Corbis, (punk teens) Scott Houston/Corbis, (romantic dress) Maria Taglienti-Molinari/Botanica/Getty Images, (Jennifer Lopez) Frank Trapper/Corbis
p. 886   Musee Royaux des Beaux Arts de Belgique, Brussels, Belgium/Bridgeman Art Library Giaudon

Chapter Twenty-Two

p. 894–5 Stephanie Hanlon
p. 933   © Victor Bockris

Chapter Twenty-Three

p. 934–5 Author photo

Chapter Twenty-Four

p. 998   top, Hulton Archives/Getty Images
p. 998   center, © Nancy Crampton
p. 998   bottom, Patrick Harbron/Landov
p. 999   top, Bettmann/Corbis
p. 999   bottom, AP Photo
p. 1000   top, Barbara Barnard
p. 1000   bottom, Snark/Art Resource, NY
p. 1001   top, Bettmann/Corbis
p. 1001   center, Hulton Archive/Getty Images
p. 1001   center, AP Photo
p. 1001   bottom, © Nancy Crampton
p. 1002   top, AP Photo
p. 1002   bottom, Photographs and Prints Division, Schomburg Center for Research in Black Culture, The New York Public Library, Astor, Lenox and Tilden Foundations
p. 1003   top, AP Photo
p. 1003   center, Bettmann/Corbis
p. 1003   center, Photo by R.J. Runa

p. 1003   bottom, Hulton Archive/Getty Images
p. 2004   top, Time Life Pictures/Getty Images
p. 2004   bottom, Lisa Esposito
p. 2005   top, Time Life Pictures/Getty Images
p. 2005   center, The Granger Collection, NY
p. 2005   bottom, Time Life Pictures/Getty Images
p. 2006   top, AP Photo/Toby Talbot
p. 2006   bottom, Phillip Crutchfield
p. 2007   top, Photographs and Prints Division, Schomburg Center for Research in Black Culture, The New York Public Library, Astor, Lenox and Tilden Foundation
p. 2007   bottom, Christopher Felver/Corbis
p. 2008   top, Hulton Archive/Getty Images
p. 2008   center, The Granger Collection, NY
p. 2008   bottom, Hulton-Deutsch Collection/Corbis
p. 2009   top, Henri Cartier-Bresson/Magnum Photos
p. 2009   bottom, Michael Nicholson/Corbis
p. 2010   top, Photo by Time Life Pictures/Mansell/Getty Images
p. 2010   bottom, Courtesy, Amy King
p. 1011   top, Christopher Kelver/Corbis
p. 1011   center, Photograph from The Ward M. Canaday Center for Special Collections/The University of Toledo. By permission of the Etheridge Knight Estate
p. 1011   bottom, Bettmann/Corbis
p. 1012   top, Marina Ortiz
p. 1012   bottom, Christopher Felver/Corbis
p. 1013   top, photo by Frances Levine
p. 1013   bottom, Henri Cartier-Bresson/Magnum Photos
p. 1014   top, Courtesy Richard Newman
p. 1014   center, Christopher Felver/Corbis
p. 1014   bottom, North Wind Picture Archive
p. 1015   top, reprinted by permission of the Dudley Randall Estate
p. 1015   bottom, Doug Menuez/Corbis
p. 1016   top, Nancy R. Schiff/Hulton Archive/Getty Images
p. 1016   bottom, The Image Works
p. 1017   top, Bettman/Corbis
p. 1017   bottom, Mimmo Jodice/Corbis
p. 1018   top, Archivo Iconografico, S.A./Corbis
p. 1018   bottom (detail), © Nancy Crampton
p. 1019   top, Sylvia Salmi/Bettmann/Corbis
p. 1019   center, Christopher Felver/Corbis
p. 1019   bottom, Henry Guttmann/Getty Images
p. 1020   top, Hulton-Deutsch Collection/Corbis
p. 1020   center, Time Life Pictures/Mathew Brady Collection/National Archives/Getty Images
p. 1020   bottom, Lisa Larsen/Time Life Pictures/Getty Images

TEXT CREDITS

This page constitutes an extension of the copyright page. We have made every effort to trace the ownership of all copyrighted material and to secure permission from copyright holders. In the event of any question arising as to the use of any material, we will be pleased to make the necessary corrections in future printings. Thanks are due to the following authors, publishers, and agents for permission to use the material indicated.

Billy Collins "The City of Tomorrow" from *The Art of Drowning* by Billy Collins, © 1995. Reprinted by permission of the University of Pittsburgh Press.

Wendy Cope "Lonely Hearts" from *Making Cocoa for Kingsley* by Wendy Cope. Copyright © Wendy Cope 1986. Faber & Faber Ltd.

Gregory Corso "Marriage" from *The Happy Birthday of Death*, copyright © 1960 by New Directions Publishing Corp. Used by permission of New Directions Publishing Corp.

William Cowper "Epitaph on a Hare."

Hart Crane Excerpt from "The Bridge" from *The Complete Poems of Hart Crane* by Hart Crane, edited by Marc Simon. Copyright 1933, 1958, 1966 by Liveright Publishing Corporation. ©1986 by Marc Simon. Reprinted by permission of Liveright Publishing Corporation.

Stephen Crane "A Man Said to the Universe," published 1899.

Robert Creeley "To Define" from *The Collected Essays of Robert Creeley*. Copyright © 1989 by The Regents of the University of California. Reprinted by permission of the University of California Press.

Victor Hernandez Cruz "Mountains in the North: Hispanic Writing in the U.S.A" from *Red Beans*. Copyright © 1991 by Victor Hernandez Cruz. Reprinted with the permission of Coffee House Press, Minneapolis, Minnesota.

Victor Hernandez Cruz "Today Is a Day of Great Joy" from *Snaps* by Victor Hernandez Cruz. Copyright © 1969 by Victor Hernandez Cruz. Used by permission of the author.

Countee Cullen "Incident" and "Yet Do I Marvel" from *Color* by Countee Cullen. Copyright 1925 by Harper Brothers; renewed 1953 by Ida M. Cullen. Reprinted by permission of GRM Associates, Inc., Agents for the Estate of Ida M. Cullen.

e. e. cummings "O sweet spontaneous," "The Cambridge ladies who live in furnished souls," "next to of course god america i," "in Just-," "Buffalo Bill's," "1(a," and "since feeling is first". Copyright 1923,1951, © 1991 by the Trustees for the e. e. cummings Trust. Copyright © 1976 by George James Firmage, from *COMPLETE POEMS: 1904–1962* by e. e. cummings, edited by George J. Firmage. Used by permission of Liveright Publishing Corporation.

J.V. Cunningham "The Problem of Form." Read at the Library of Congress in October, 1962.

Don DeLillo "Videotape" from *Underworld* © 1997 by Don DeLillo. Reprinted with permission of Scribner, a division of Simon & Schuster, Inc.

Jacqueline DeRosa "Some Platitudes Concerning Drama."

Junot Diaz "Fiesta, 1980" from *DROWN*, copyright © 1996 by Junot Diaz. Used by permission of Riverhead Books, an imprint of Penguin Group (USA) Inc.

James Dickey "The Leap" from *The Whole Motion: New and Collected Poems, 1945–1992*, copyright © 1992 by James Dickey. Reprinted by permission of Wesleyan University Press.

Emily Dickinson "There's a certain Slant of light," "Because I could not stop for Death," "After Great Pain, a Formal Feeling Comes," "The Bustle in a House," "Some keep the Sabbath going to church," "Much Madness is divinest Sense," "I heard a fly buzz when I died," "A bird came down the walk," "A narrow fellow in the grass," "Tell all the Truth but tell it slant," "Apparently with no surprise," "I'm Nobody! Who are you?," "I dwell in possibility," "I felt a funeral in my brain," "Wild nights!, Wild nights!" Reprinted by permission of the publishers and the Trustees of Amherst College from *The Poems of Emily Dickinson*, Thomas H. Johnson, ed., Cambridge, Mass: The Belknap Press of Harvard University Press. Copyright © 1951, 1955, 1979, 1983 by the President and Fellows of Harvard College.

Annie Dillard *THE WRITING LIFE*, pp. 13–16. Copyright © 1989 by Annie Dillard. Reprinted by permission of HarperCollins Publishers, Inc.

Chitra Banerjee Divakaruni "Tiger Mask Ritual" and "Two Women Outside a Circus, Pushkar" from *Leaving Yuba City* by Chitra Banerjee Divakaruni, copyright © 1997 by Chitra Banerjee Divakaruni. Used by permission of Doubleday, a division of Random House, Inc.

Robert Herrick "Delight in Disorder" and "Upon Julia's Clothes" both published 1648.

Ernest Hemingway "Soldier's Home" from *The Short Stories of Ernest Hemingway*. Reprinted with permission of Scribner, an imprint of Simon & Schuster Adult Publishing Group. Copyright © 1925 by Charles Scribner's Sons. Copyright renewed © 1953 by Ernest Hemingway.

Conrad Hilberry "Tongue" from *The Moon Seen as a Slice of Pineapple* by Conrad Hilberry. Copyright © 1984 by the author. Reprinted by permission of the University of Georgia Press.

Linda Hogan "The Truth Is" from *Seeing through the Sun* by Linda Hogan (Amherst: University of Massachusetts Press, 1985). Copyright © 1985 by Linda Hogan.

John Hollander "A State of Nature" from *TYPES OF SHAPE* (1967); © 1967 and reprinted by permission of Yale University Press.

Gerard Manley Hopkins "The Windhover" from *Poems of Gerard Manley Hopkins*, 4th Edition by Hopkins, Gerard Manley. Edited by W.H. Gardner and N.H. MacKenzie. Used by permission of Oxford University Press.

Gerard Manley Hopkins "Pied Beauty," published 1918 and "God's Grandeur" (1844–1889).

Barbara Horn "Midnight Blue: Ray Charles and Roy Orbison Select Their Wardrobes" Used by permission of the author.

A.E. Houseman "Terrance, This Is Stupid Stuff," selections reprinted by permission of Henry Holt and Company and the Society of Authors as the literary representative of the Estate of A.E. Houseman.

A.E. Housman "To an Athlete Dying Young" from *A Shropshire Lad*.

David Huddle "Holes Commence Falling" from *Summer Lake: New and Selected Poems* by David Huddle. Copyright © 1999 by David Huddle. Reprinted by permission of Louisiana State University Press.

Langston Hughes "Lenox Avenue: Midnight," "Un-American Investigators," "Theme for English B," "Dream Boogie," "Harlem," "Evenin' Air Blues," "The Negro Speaks of Rivers," "Cross," "Negro," "Ballad of the Landlord," "I, Too," "Island," "Old Walt," "Democracy," "Mother to Son," "Same in Blues," "The Weary Blues," "Dream Variations," and "Subway Rush Hour" from *The Collected Poems of Langston Hughes* by Langston Hughes. Copyright © 1994 by The Estate of Langston Hughes. Used by permission of Alfred A. Knopf, a division of Random House, Inc.

Langston Hughes "Salvation" from *The Big Sea* by Langston Hughes. Copyright © 1940 by Langston Hughes. Copyright renewed 1968 by Arna Bontemps and George Huston Bass. Reprinted by permission of Hill and Wang, a division of Farrar, Straus and Giroux, LLC.

Langston Hughes "The Negro Artist and the Racial Mountain." Reprinted by permission of Harold Ober Associates Incorporated. First published in *The Nation*. Copyright © 1926 by Langston Hughes.

D. Scott Humphries "More or Less a Moor: Racism in Othello."

Henrik Ibsen "A Doll House" from *The Complete Major Prose Plays of Henrik Ibsen* by Henrik Ibsen, translated by Rolf Fjelde, copyright © 1965, 1970, 1978 by Rolf Fjelde. Used by permission of Dutton Signet, a division of Penguin Group (USA) Inc.

David Ives "Sure Thing," "The Philadelphia," and Preface to "All in the Timing" from *ALL IN THE TIMING* by David Ives, copyright © 1989, 1990, 1992 by David Ives. Used by permission of Vintage Books, a division of Random House, Inc.

David Ives "Some Origins" reprinted from the author's Preface to *Time Flies and Other Short Plays* by David Ives (Grove Press), pages vii–ix.

Shirley Jackson "Public Reception of 'The Lottery'" from *Come Along with Me* (1968), edited by her husband Stanley Edgar Hyman and published posthumously.

Shirley Jackson "The Lottery" from *The Lottery and Other Stories* by Shirley Jackson. Copyright © 1948, 1949 by Shirley Jackson. Copyright renewed 1976, 1977 by Laurence Hyman, Barry Hyman, Mrs. Sarah Webster and Mrs. Joanne Schnurer. Reprinted by permission of Farrar, Straus and Giroux, LLC.

INDEX
of First Lines of Poems

INDEX of Authors and Titles

INDEX of Literary Terms